HANDBOOK OF AUTISM AND
PERVASIVE DEVELOPMENTAL DISORDERS

Handbook of Autism and Pervasive Developmental Disorders

Third Edition

Volume 2: Assessment, Interventions, and Policy

Edited by

Fred R. Volkmar

Rhea Paul

Ami Klin

Donald Cohen

JOHN WILEY & SONS, INC.

Library of Congress Cataloging-in-Publication Data:

Handbook of autism and pervasive developmental disorders / edited by Fred R. Volkmar . . .
   [et al.].—3rd ed.
      p.   cm.
   Includes bibliographical references and index.
   Contents: V. 1. Diagnosis, development, neurobiology, and behavior—v. 2. Assessment, interventions, and policy.
   ISBN 0-471-71696-0 (cloth : v. 1)—ISBN 0-471-71697-9 (cloth : v. 2)—ISBN 0-471-71698-7 (set)
   1. Autism in children. 2. Developmental disabilities. 3. Autistic children—Services for. 4. Developmentally disabled children—Services for. I. Volkmar, Fred R.
   RJ506.A9H26   2005
   618.92′85882—dc22
                                                                    2004059091

To the Memory of Donald Cohen

At the time of his death, Donald Cohen was actively involved in the planning of this edition of the *Handbook*. His untimely passing made it impossible for him to see the final product. We are deeply grateful to him for his thoughtful counsel and mentorship as well as the truly impressive example he presented as a clinician-researcher. We hope that this *Handbook* is a testament to his vision and a fitting tribute to his memory.

Photo: Michael Marsland, Yale University

Contributors

M. Cherro Aguerre, MD
University of the Republic
School of Medicine
Cavia
Montevideo, Uruguay

George M. Anderson, PhD
Child Study Center
Yale University School of Medicine
New Haven, Connecticut

Joel R. Arick, PhD
Special Education
Portland State University
Portland, Oregon

Chris Ashwin, PhD
Autism Research Centre
University of Cambridge
Departments of Experimental Psychology
and Psychiatry
Cambridge, England

Grace T. Baranek, PhD, OTR/L
Division of Occupational Science
Department of Allied Health Sciences
University of North Carolina at Chapel Hill
Chapel Hill, North Carolina

Simon Baron-Cohen, PhD
Autism Research Centre
University of Cambridge
Departments of Experimental Psychology
and Psychiatry
Cambridge, England

Margaret L. Bauman, MD
Harvard Medical School
Massachusetts Hospital
Boston, Massachusetts

Jac Billington, BSc
Autism Research Centre
University of Cambridge
Cambridge, England

James W. Bodfish, PhD
Department of Psychiatry
University of North Carolina at Chapel Hill
Chapel Hill, North Carolina

Joel D. Bregman, MD
Center for Autism
North Shore Long Island Jewish Health
    System
Bethpage, New York

Courtney Burnette, MS
Department of Psychology
University of Miami
Coral Gables, Florida

Alice S. Carter, PhD
Department of Psychology
University of Massachusetts Boston
Boston, Massachusetts

Bhismadev Chakrabarti, BA, BSc
Autism Research Centre
University of Cambridge
Cambridge, England

KATARZYNA CHAWARSKA, PhD
Child Study Center
Yale University School of Medicine
New Haven, Connecticut

SOO CHURL CHO, MD
Division of Child and Adolescent Psychiatry
Seoul National University Hospital
Seoul, Korea

IAN COOK, MD
Department of Psychiatry and Behavioral
    Sciences
David Geffen School of Medicine at UCLA
Los Angeles, California

ELAINE E. COONROD, MS
Department of Psychology and Human
    Development
Vanderbilt University
Nashville, Tennessee

CHRISTINA CORSELLO, PhD
Autism and Communication Disorders Center
University of Michigan
Ann Arbor, Michigan

NAOMI ORNSTEIN DAVIS, MA
Boston University School of Medicine
Boston, Massachusetts

RUTH FALCO, PhD
Special Education
Portland State University
Portland, Oregon

PIERRE FERRARI, MD
Centre Hospitalier Public De Psychiatrie
    De L'Enfant Et De L'Adolescent
Foundation Vallee
Gentilly Cedex, France

PAULINE A. FILIPEK, MD
Department of Pediatrics and Neurology
University of California
Irvine College of Medicine
Orange, California

ERIC FOMBONNE, MD
McGill University
Department of Psychiatry at the Montreal
    Children's Hospital
Montreal, Quebec, Canada

JOAQUIN FUENTES, MD
GUATENA
San Sebastian, Spain

ANN FULLERTON, PhD
Special Education
Portland State University
Portland, Oregon

JOHN GERDTZ, PhD
Saint Mary's College of California
Moraga, California

PETER F. GERHARDT, EdD
Gerhardt Autism/Aspergers Consultation
    Group, LLC
Baltimore, Maryland

TEMPLE GRANDIN, PhD
Department of Animal Science
Colorado State University
Fort Collins, Colorado

RICHARD GRIFFIN, BA
Autism Research Centre
University of Cambridge
Cambridge, England

JAN S. HANDLEMAN, EdD
Douglas Developmental Disabilities Center
Rutgers, The State University of New Jersey
New Brunswick, New Jersey

FRANCESCA HAPPÉ, PhD (ALSO BA HONS
    OXFORD)
Social, Genetic and Developmental
    Psychiatry Centre
Institute of Psychiatry
King's College, London

SANDRA L. HARRIS, PhD
Douglas Developmental Disabilities Center
Rutgers, The State University of New Jersey
New Brunswick, New Jersey

PETER HOBSON, MD
The Tavistock Clinic
Adult Department
London, United Kingdom

DAVID L. HOLMES, EdD
Lifespan Services, LLC
Princeton, New Jersey

YOSHIHIKO HOSHINO, MD
Department of Neuropsychiatry
Hikarigaoka
Fukushima-shi, Japan

PATRICIA HOWLIN, MD
St. George's Hospital Medical School
Cranmer Terrace
London, United Kingdom

BROOKE INGERSOLL, PhD
Oregon Institute on Disability and
    Development Child Development and
    Rehabilitation
Center Oregon Health and Science University
Portland, Oregon

HEATHER K. JENNETT, MS
Douglas Developmental Disabilities Center
Rutgers, The State University of New Jersey
New Brunswick, New Jersey

WARREN JONES, BA
Child Study Center
Yale University School of Medicine
New Haven, Connecticut

AMI KLIN, PhD
Child Study Center
Yale University School of Medicine
New Haven, Connecticut

KATHY KOENIG , MSN
Child Study Center
Yale University School of Medicine
New Haven, Connecticut

JASON B. KONIDARIS
Norwalk, Connecticut

DAVID A. KRUG, PhD
Special Education
Portland State University
Portland, Oregon

LINDA J. KUNCE, PhD
Department of Psychology
Illinois Wesleyan University
Bloomington, Illinois

AMY LAURENT, OTR/L
Communication Crossroads
North Kingstown, Rhode Island

JOHN LAWSON, PhD
Autism Research Centre
University of Cambridge
Cambridge, England

GABRIEL LEVI, MD
Departimento di Scienze Neurologische e
Psichiatriche dell'eta Evolutina
Rome, Italy

JENNIFER A. LONCOLA, PhD
DePaul University
School of Education
Chicago, Illinois

LAUREN LOOS, MS
Autism Specialist
Oregon Department of Education
Salem, Oregon

CATHERINE LORD, PhD
UMACC
University of Michigan
Ann Arbor, Michigan

KATHERINE A. LOVELAND, PhD
University of Texas Health Sciences Center
    at Houston
Department of Psychiatry and Behavioral
    Sciences
Houston, Texas

MYRNA R. MANDLAWITZ, BA, MEd, JD
MRM Associates
Washington, DC

WENDY D. MARANS, MS, CCC/SLP
Child Study Center
Yale University School of Medicine
Private Practice
New Haven, Connecticut

LEE M. MARCUS, PhD
Division TEACCH
Department of Psychiatry
University of North Carolina School
    of Medicine
Chapel Hill, North Carolina

ANDREŚ MARTIN, MD
Child Study Center
Yale University School of Medicine
New Haven, Connecticut

MEGAN P. MARTINS, BA
Douglas Developmental Disabilities Center
Rutgers, The State University of New Jersey
New Brunswick, New Jersey

GAIL G. McGEE, PhD
Emory University School of Medicine
Department of Psychiatry and Behavioral
    Sciences
Atlanta, Georgia

JAMES McPARTLAND, MS
Child Study Center
Yale University School of Medicine
New Haven, Connecticut

ADRIENNE MERYL, BA
M.I.N.D. Institute
U.C. Davis Medical Center
Sacramento, California

GARY B. MESIBOV, PhD
Division TEACCH
University of North Carolina at Chapel Hill
Chapel Hill, North Carolina

RICHARD MILLS, CQSW, RMPA, MA, FRSA
NAS Southern Region Office
Church House, Church Road
Filton, United Kingdom

NANCY J. MINSHEW, MD
Western Psychiatric Institute and Clinic
Pittsburgh, Pennsylvania

MICHAEL J. MORRIER, MA
Emory University School of Medicine
Department of Psychiatry and Behavioral
    Sciences
Atlanta, Georgia

PETER MUNDY, PhD
Department of Psychology
University of Miami
Coral Gables, Florida

J. GREGORY OLLEY, PhD
Clinical Center for the Study of Development
    and Learning
University of North Carolina at Chapel Hill
Chapel Hill, North Carolina

SALLY OZONOFF, PhD
M.I.N.D. Institute
U.C. Davis Medical Center
Sacramento, California

VAYA PAPAGEORGIOU, MD
Medical Psychopedagogical Center of
    North Greece
Greece

L. DIANE PARHAM, PhD, OTR, FAOTA
Department of Occupational Science and
    Occupational Therapy
University of Southern California
Los Angeles, California

RHEA PAUL, PhD, CCC-SLP
Department of Communication Disorders
Southern Connecticut State University
New Haven, Connecticut

MICHAEL D. POWERS, MD
Center for Children with Special Needs
Glastonbury, Connecticut
and
Child Study Center
Yale University School of Medicine
New Haven, Connecticut

BARRY M. PRIZANT, PhD
Childhood Communication Services
Cranston, Rhode Island
and
Center for the Study of Human Development
Brown University
Providence, Rhode Island

SHERRI PROVENCAL, PhD
Department of Psychology
University of Utah
Salt Lake City, Utah

ISABELLE RAPIN
Albert Einstein College of Medicine
Bronx, New York

DIANA L. ROBINS, PhD
Department of Psychology
Georgia State University
Atlanta, Georgia

SALLY J. ROGERS, PhD
M.I.N.D. Institute
U.C. Davis Medical Center
Sacramento, California

EMILY RUBIN, MS, CCC/SLP
Communication Crossroads
Carmel, California

MICHAEL RUTTER, CBE, MD, FRCP,
    FRCPSYCH, FRS
Social, Genetic and Developmental
    Psychiatry Centre
Institute of Psychiatry
DeCrespigny Park
Denmark Hill
King's College, London

ANDERS RYDELIUS, MD, PhD
Karolinska Institute
Department of Woman and Child Health
Child and Adolescent Psychiatry Unit
St. Goran's Children's Hospital
Stockholm, Sweden

CELINE SAULNIER, PhD
Child Study Center
Yale University School of Medicine
New Haven, Connecticut

LAWRENCE SCAHILL, MSN, PhD
Child Study Center
Yale University School of Medicine
New Haven, Connecticut

MARTIN SCHMIDT, MD
Kinder Jundenpsychiatrische Klinik
Zentralinstitut fur Seelische Genundheit
Mannheim, Germany

ERIC SCHOPLER, PhD
Division TEACCH
Department of Psychiatry
University of North Carolina School
    of Medicine
Chapel Hill, North Carolina

LAURA SCHREIBMAN, PhD
Department of Psychology
University of California, San Diego
La Jolla, California

ROBERT T. SCHULTZ, PhD
Child Study Center
Yale University School of Medicine
New Haven, Connecticut

VICTORIA SHEA, PhD
Division TEACCH
The University of North Carolina at
    Chapel Hill
Chapel Hill, North Carolina

MIKLE SOUTH, MS
Department of Psychology
University of Utah
Salt Lake City, Utah

VIRGINIA WALKER SPERRY, MA
Child Study Center
Yale University School of Medicine
New Haven, Connecticut

MATTHEW STATE, MD, PhD
Child Study Center
Yale University School of Medicine
New Haven, Connecticut

WENDY L. STONE, PhD
Vanderbilt Children's Hospital
Nashville, Tennessee

RUTH CHRIST SULLIVAN, PhD
Autism Services Center
Huntington, West Virginia

DEAN SUTHERLAND, MS
Department of Speech Therapy
Canterbury University
Christchurch, New Zealand

JOHN A. SWEENEY, PhD
University of Pittsburgh
Western Psychiatric Institute and Clinic
Pittsburgh, Pennsylvania

PETER SZATMARI, MD
McMaster University
Department of Psychiatry
Faculty Health Sciences
Hamilton, Ontario, Canada

HELEN TAGER-FLUSBERG, PhD
Department of Anatomy and Neurobiology
Boston University School of Medicine
Boston, Massachusetts

KUO-TAI TAO, MD
Division of Nanging
Child Mental Health Research Center
Nanging, China

BRUCE TONGE, MD
Centre for Developmental Psychiatry
Monash Medical Center
Australia

KENNETH E. TOWBIN, MD
Mood and Anxiety Disorders Program
National Institute of Mental Health
Bethesda, Maryland

KATHERINE D. TSATSANIS, PhD
Child Study Center
Yale University School of Medicine
New Haven, Connecticut

BELGIN TUNALI-KOTOSKI, PhD
Center for Human Development Research
University of Texas Health Sciences Center
    at Houston
Houston, Texas

SAM TYANO
The Geha Psychiatric Hospital
The Beilinson Medical Center
Tel Aviv University Medical School
Tel Aviv, Israel

ERYN Y. VAN ACKER
College of Education
University of Illinois at Chicago
Chicago, Illinois

RICHARD VAN ACKER, PhD
College of Education
University of Illinois at Chicago
Chicago, Illinois

FRED R. VOLKMAR, MD
Child Study Center
Yale University
New Haven, Connecticut

HERMAN VAN ENGELAND, MD
Divisie Psychiatrie Kinder en
    Jeugdpsychiatrie
Utrecht, The Netherlands

SARA JANE WEBB, PhD
Center for Human Development and Disability
Autism Center Psychophysiology Laboratories
University of Washington
Seattle, Washington

AMY M. WETHERBY, PhD
Department of Communication Disorders
Executive Director, Center for Autism and
    Related Disorders
Florida State University
Tallahassee, Florida

SALLY WHEELWRIGHT, MA
Autism Research Centre
University of Cambridge
Cambridge, England

LORNA WING, MD
National Autistic Society Centre for Social
    and Communication Disorders
Bromley, Kent, United Kingdom

DIANNE ZAGER, PhD
Pace University
New York, New York

Editorial Board

Preface

A comprehensive *Handbook* devoted to *autism and pervasive developmental disorders* testifies to the volume of research, services, theory, and advocacy related to children and adults with the most severe disorders of development. Indeed, the third edition of this work is now literally two books. The expansion in size and sophistication reflects substantial advances in knowledge during the one decade that separates it from its predecessor published in 1997.

Autism has attracted remarkable interest and concern of clinicians and researchers from the time of its first scientific description over 60 years ago by Leon Kanner (1943). As a disorder that afflicts the core of socialization, it has posed scientific challenges to theories of developmental psychology and neurobiology as well as therapy and education. Virtually every type of theory relating to child development—cognitive, social, behavioral, affective, neurobiological—has been applied to understanding the enigmatic impairments and competencies of autistic individuals. And the results of empirical studies inspired by these diverse theoretical perspectives have enriched not only the field of autism but also the broad field of developmental psychopathology. Indeed, autism has served as a paradigmatic disorder for theory testing and research on the essential preconditions for normal social-cognitive maturation—expression and recognition of emotions, intersubjectivity, sharing a focus of interest with other people, the meaning and uses of language, forming first attachments and falling in love, empathy, the nuanced understanding of the minds of others—indeed, the whole set of competencies and motivations

that allow a child to become a family member and social being.

This *Handbook* is guided by a developmental psychopathological orientation (Cicchetti & Cohen, 1995). Within this framework, principles and findings about normal development are used to illuminate how development may become derailed and lead to pathological conditions, and, conversely, studies of disorders such as autism are used to cast light on normal developmental processes. Autism and other developmental disorders may serve as "experiments of nature." Their underlying biology and psychology, as well as the types of adaptations that individuals can use to compensate for their difficulties, may reveal mechanisms and processes that are otherwise concealed from awareness or scientific scrutiny.

As a serious, generally lifelong condition, autism has generated important challenges to the systems that relate to individuals with disabilities, including educational, vocational, medical, and psychiatric systems, as well as to social policy, legislation, and the legal system. Because of its multifaceted impact on development, autism also has focused the attention of all the professions concerned with children and adults with difficulties, including psychology, education, psychiatry, physical rehabilitation, recreational therapy, speech and language, nursing, pediatrics, neurology, occupational therapy, genetics, social work, law, neuroradiology, pharmacology—indeed, virtually every caring profession. By drawing these disciplines together in the clinic and laboratory, autism has helped forge the multidisciplinary approach to developmental disabilities. One goal of this *Handbook* is to provide an orientation of shared concepts and knowledge to facilitate the future collaboration among the disciplines and professionals who work with autistic individuals and their families.

Nothing strikes more at the core of a family's functioning than the birth of a child with a serious disability. Kanner recognized the central involvement of families in his first reports when he described the peculiarities of social relations in families who came for his consultation and care. In his first accounts, he misread the data presented to him and postulated an etiologic role of parental behavior in the pathogenesis of autism. This mistake haunted the field and pained families for many years; it still may arise in certain places, as ghosts tend to do. However, Kanner soon righted his theory and emphasized the central message of his initial report that autism is essentially a reflection of an inborn dysfunction underlying affective engagement. Because social interaction is a two-way street, parents and others who spend time with an autistic child will no doubt relate differently than with his or her socially engaged, ebullient, linguistically gifted siblings. Of interest, more recent genetic information about autism and Asperger syndrome, discussed in the *Handbook*, returns us to Kanner's observations about social variations and impairments running within families. New findings of aggregation of autism, cognitive problems, and social difficulties within families suggest that an underlying vulnerability may be transmitted from one generation to the next. If so, explicating the interaction between genetic and environmental factors in the course of these disorders will bring us back to questions not too far from where Kanner started his speculations.

The impact of autistic individuals on family life has changed with the creation of more adequate services. Burdens on families have been eased by early identification, initiation of educational and other treatments during the first years of life, suitable family guidance and support, high-quality educational and other programs, respite care, supportive living and other arrangements for adults with autism, effective pharmacological treatments, and knowledge that can guide lifetime planning. Yet, with perhaps rare exception, an autistic child in the family is experienced by parents, siblings, and extended family as profoundly painful. There can, of course, be consolations in dealing well with adversity; yet, however well a family and individual cope, a lifetime with autism brings with it more than a fair share of disappointment, sadness, and emotional scarring for all involved. Only with scientific advances that will prevent, greatly ameliorate, or even cure these conditions will this pain be fully eased. Clinicians and researchers have been drawn to autism in the hope of achieving this result, and their remarkable commitments are also reflected in this *Handbook* and in services throughout the world.

At times, however, therapeutic zeal has exceeded the knowledge available. The *Handbook* aims at providing authentic knowledge, broadly accepted by experts. Yet, we recognize that there are sometimes sharp differences of opinion and theoretical perspective and that today's wisdom may be tomorrow's delusion. Thus, it is important to foster diversity while encouraging everyone to pursue rigorous, empirical research that will improve future treatments. Scientific progress oddly leads to many divergent ideas and findings for a long time before a deeper level of clarity is achieved.

While we encourage tolerance of differing scientific views, we do not think that "anything goes." Virtually every month or two, parents and others who care for autistic children and adults are likely to hear announcements of new, miraculous treatments. They may be confused by the options and feel guilty for not making the sacrifices necessary to try still another approach. Today, within a stone's throw of our own university, parents are engaged in a medley of divergent treatments. As the recent review by the National Research Council (2001) has shown, a variety of treatments have now been shown to be effective for individuals with autism. The efficacy of a host of other treatments, commonly referred to as complementary or alternative treatments, remains to be scientifically well established. Often, such treatments compete with more traditional ones. Parents, and sometimes professionals, may feel at a loss in terms of evaluating such treatments and making sound, empirically based decisions about which treatment(s) should be pursued with respect to an individual child. Occasionally, differences between advocates and skeptics in relation to treatment ethics and efficacy arouse passions, including legal proceedings and splits between professionals or within the family. How are parents and professionals best able to make informed decisions?

Like other areas of science, the field of autism will advance when we adopt, whenever possible, the rigorous standards of scientific research. Indeed, our own work as clinician-researchers has led us to the conclusion that we should offer no less. Thus, in the *Handbook* we have attempted to provide a comprehensive account of current, scientific thinking and findings and to mark out speculation and theory for what these are. We also have eschewed accounts of ideas and treatments, however fascinating they might be, that are too far from the mainstream of scientific research and empirically guided practice. Such decisions are our responsibility and may leave some advocates feeling shortchanged or even angry; they retain their right to free speech and, who knows, may yet be vindicated.

In underlining the importance of data in guiding decisions about treatment, we also recognize that clinical care always occurs within a social context and is shaped by beliefs, values, and other historical and cultural values. Prevailing views about the rights of individuals with disabilities and their role in society have changed dramatically over the past decades. Embodied in legislation and judicial decision, the emergent viewpoints about rights to education, services, access, job opportunities—to basic human respect—have shaped services and improved the quality of the lives of individuals who would only decades ago have been subject to abuses of various types that limited freedom, stigmatized, or dehumanized. We have been delighted to see this view gaining increasingly wide acceptance around the world.

Parents and individuals with disabilities have been effective advocates. Communities and professionals have been sensitized to the subtle ways in which individuals with disabilities may be deprived of autonomy and are made to be more handicapped by lack of provision for their special needs. This trend has had a major impact on the care and treatment of individuals with autism, as well. Far more than most experts believed possible 20 or even 10 years ago, many individuals with autism have not only the right but also the capacities to participate within their communities—to study, work, live, recreate, and share in family life. The *Handbook* reflects this important educational and cultural evolution in which a philosophy of despair has given way to one of hope.

We also appreciate that there are enormous differences among individuals with autism and related conditions in their abilities and needs, among families in their strengths and resources, and among communities and nations in their own viewpoints and histories. These differences should be respected, and policy and discussion should recognize that "autistic people" do not form a homogeneous class. Clinicians and practitioners generally are able to keep the individual at the focus of concern, as we do when we think together with families about their unique child or with an adult with autism about his or her special life situation. At such times, broader issues of social policy recede into the background as the fullness of the individual's needs and interests are paramount. In shaping social policy and planning regional and national systems, however, there is a clear consensus for the approach to treatment and lifetime planning captured by the ideology of autonomy and community-based living and working. We hope that this orientation is conveyed by this *Handbook*. At the same time, there is no single, right formula for every child or adult with autism: A community and nation should strive to have available a spectrum of services to satisfy the varied and changing needs and values of individuals with autism and their families.

Clearly defined concepts are essential for communication among scientists, especially for interdisciplinary and international collaboration. In the field of autism and other behavioral disorders, there has been substantial progress in nosology and diagnosis. This progress has enhanced discussion, research, and cross-disciplinary exchange. It had the merit of underlining the concept of developmental disorder and the breadth of dysfunctions in social, cognitive, language, and other domains. Similarly, the introduction of multiaxial diagnosis underscored the need for patients to be seen from varied points of view and the need to supplement "categorical disorders" (e.g., autism) with knowledge about other aspects of functioning, including medical status and adaptive abilities. As we discuss in the first section of this *Handbook*, advances in classification have led new knowledge and increasingly focused and refined research. The consensus exemplified in *Diagnostic and Statistical Manual of Mental Disorders*, fourth edition (*DSM-IV*; American Psychiatric Association, 1994), and *International Classification of Diseases*, 10th edition, (*ICD-10*; World Health Organization, 1992), has stimulated a tremendous increase in research over the past decade. Today the two internationally recognized systems provide a consistent approach to the diagnosis of the most severe disorders of early onset. While there are still some regional or national diagnostic alternatives, the trend is, fortunately, toward consensus. At the same time, the universal acceptance of a standard meter and of Greenwich time does not ensure great science or lack of debate and much work remains to be done, but the current approach has helped provide a solid framework on which future refinements can sensibly be made.

The thousands of publications—scientific papers, monographs, chapters, books—about autism and pervasive developmental disorder are evidence of its intrinsic interest to researchers and clinicians and to the human importance of these disorders for those who suffer from them and their families. The growing body of books and resources specifically designed for parents and family members has been a noteworthy achievement of the past several years. At the same time, you could reasonably ask why a revision of the *Handbook* is needed now.

This third edition of the *Handbook of Autism and Pervasive Developmental Disorders* is the second revision of a book that first appeared in 1987. This edition quickly became established as an important scholarly resource. Within a decade much had changed, and the second edition of this volume appeared. The rapid pace of scientific progress was reflected in the second edition, which was expanded to increase coverage of new research and treatment methods. Preparations for this version of the *Handbook* began in 2000 with an expansion of the number of editors in light of the increasingly diverse and sophisticated body of research that was becoming available.

In this edition, we have retained the best features of the second edition with expanded coverage in selected areas. In many instances, authors have kindly revised earlier contributions in light of current research; in other cases, we have solicited new contributors and chapters. As a result of the expanded coverage, the book has expanded into two volumes with a total of nine sections. This more extensive coverage reflects the increasing depth and breadth of work within the field.

In creating this *Handbook*, we invited chapters from recognized scholars. The responses to the invitations were gratifying. Each completed chapter was reviewed by the editors and by two members of a distinguished editorial committee. The use of peer review is not typical for volumes such as this, and we are grateful that all authors of chapters welcomed this process. The reviewers wrote careful critiques, sometimes many pages in length; these reviews were provided to the authors for their consideration during revision. The interactive process of revising chapters has helped ensure that the contributions are as good as the field allows.

The past several years have seen a major increase in the funding of research on autism. While we are gratified by this increased support, we hope for even more because only through research will we be able to change incidence and alter the natural history of autistic and other pervasive disorders. The cost of caring for one autistic individual over a lifetime may be more than any single investigator will ever have to spend during a career of research. Many hundreds of millions of dollars are spent internationally on direct services; only a tiny percentage of this expenditure is devoted to any type of formal research. It is as if the United States committed all of its funding to building iron lungs and considered virology to be a secondary concern in relation to polio. To fully exploit the many new methods for studying brain development and brain-behavior relations and to attempt to translate biological and behavioral research findings into treatments will require substantial investment of research funds. The recent network of federal centers through the Collaborative Program of Excellence in Autism (CPEA) and the Studies to Advance Autism Research and Treatment (STAART) as well as through the Research Units on Psychopharmacology (RUPP) and the Centers for Disease Control (CDC) have already had major benefits. These benefits will eventually include not only a reduction in suffering and in costs for those with autism, but also important knowledge that will benefit a far larger group of children and adults with other serious neuropsychiatric and developmental disorders. We hope that one contribution of the *Handbook* will be to underscore the gains from systematic research and the importance of sustained support for multidisciplinary clinical research groups.

We wish to recognize the support that has been provided over the decades to our own clinical and research program by the National Institute of Child Health and Human Development, National Institute of Deafness and Communication Disorders, and the National Institute of Mental Health, as well as by the Korczak Foundation, the W. T. Grant Foundation, the Doris Duke Foundation, the Simon's Foundation, Cure Autism Now, the National Alliance for Autism Research, and private donors.

We thank the members of our editorial board for their excellent contributions to this process and Lori Kline, who helped us coordinate this effort, as well as the wonderful editorial staff at Wiley, who have consistently sought to help us deliver the best possible work. We have been very fortunate in being able to work within the scholarly environment provided by the Yale School of Medicine and the Child Study Center. The unique qualities of the Child Study Center reflect the contributions of generations of faculty who have committed themselves to clinical scholarship, teaching, and service. We particularly wish to acknowledge the guidance and support of senior mentors—Albert J. Solnit, Sally Provence, Sam Ritvo, Sara Sparrow, and Edward Zigler—as well as many colleagues and collaborators in this work, including Robert Schultz, Cheryl Klaiman, Larry Scahill, Matt State, Elenga Grigorenko, George Anderson, James Leckman, Kasia Chawarska, Katherine Tsatsanis, Wendy Marans, and Emily Rubin.

A *Handbook* portrays what is known and reveals what is poorly understood. Although many studies have been conducted and areas explored, there is no hard biological or behavioral finding that can serve as a reliable compass point to guide research; in spite of great efforts and decades of commitment by researchers and clinicians, the fate of most autistic individuals remains cloudy; and even with new knowledge, there are still too many areas of controversy. That investigators and clinicians, working alongside families and advocates, have learned so much, often with very tight resources, speaks to their commitment to understanding and caring for autistic children and adults. The goal of this *Handbook* is to document their achievements and inspire their future efforts.

FRED R. VOLKMAR, MD
AMI KLIN, PhD
RHEA PAUL, PhD

Yale Child Study Center
New Haven, Connecticut
November, 2004

REFERENCES

American Psychiatric Association. (1980). *Diagnostic and statistical manual of mental disorders* (3rd ed.). Washington, DC: Author.

American Psychiatric Association. (1994). *Diagnostic and statistical manual of mental disorders* (4th ed.). Washington, DC: Author.

Cohen, D. J., & Donnellan, A. M. (1987). *Handbook of Autism and Pervasive Developmental Disorders.* New York: Wiley.

Cicchetti D., & Cohen D. J. (1995). *Developmental Psychopathology.* (Vols. 1–2). New York: Wiley.

Kanner, L. (1943). Autistic disturbances of affective contact. *Nervous Child 2,* 217–250.

Volkmar, F., Klin, A., Siegel, B., et al. (1994). Field trial for autistic disorder in *DSM-IV. American Journal of Psychiatry, 151,* 1361–1367.

World Health Organization. (1977). *Manual of the international statistical classification of diseases, injuries and causes of death* (9th ed., Vol. 1). Geneva, Switzerland: Author.

World Health Organization. (1992). *The ICD-10 classification of mental and behavioral disorders. Clinical descriptions and diagnostic guidelines.* Geneva, Switzerland: Author.

World Health Organization. (1993). *The ICD-10 classification of mental and behavioral disorders. Diagnostic criteria for research.* Geneva, Switzerland: Author.

Contents

VOLUME 1: DIAGNOSIS, DEVELOPMENT, NEUROBIOLOGY, AND BEHAVIOR

SECTION I
DIAGNOSIS AND CLASSIFICATION

SECTION II
DEVELOPMENT AND BEHAVIOR

SECTION III
NEUROLOGICAL AND MEDICAL ISSUES

SECTION IV
THEORETICAL PERSPECTIVES

VOLUME 2: ASSESSMENT, INTERVENTIONS, AND POLICY

SECTION V
ASSESSMENT

SECTION VI
INTERVENTIONS

SECTION VII
PUBLIC POLICY PERSPECTIVES

SECTION VIII
INTERNATIONAL PERSPECTIVES

SECTION IX
PERSONAL PERSPECTIVES

SECTION V

ASSESSMENT

The assessment of individuals with autism and other pervasive developmental disorders calls on the expertise of various disciplines, including child and adolescent psychiatry, psychology, speech-language pathology, education, pediatrics, neurology, physical rehabilitation, and others. This section provides detailed discussion of methods available for rigorous assessment of the core symptom areas of impairment in individuals with autism and associated conditions, using a range of standardized, observational, and criterion-referenced measures of psychological functioning, communication, and behavior. These assessments are focused on the following purposes:

- Diagnostic evaluation that establishes eligibility for educational and clinical services and assigns an individual to a nosological category;
- To identify in each individual the unique profile of strengths and needs that characterize the form PDD takes in this particular person, in order to plan an individualized education and habilitation program;
- To document baseline functioning, against which postintervention status can be compared in each area of individual need;
- To help detail the range of phenotypic expression in the PDD population.

The Assessment section deals with issues relating to the development of screening methods, quantitative forms of diagnostic evaluation, and qualitative descriptions of behavior. These issues impact research on the pervasive developmental disorders as well-validated, reliable diagnostic instruments become increasingly necessary to ensure replicability across sites and studies, and to establish eligibility for intervention. Screening and diagnostic instruments with strong psychometric properties and high levels of consensus among experienced clinicians are crucial for ensuring progress and identifying cases for neurobiological, epidemiological, etiological, genetic, psychopharmacolocial, and behavioral studies. They are equally central to the clinical and educational treatment of PDDs, however, since the treatment of these children relies not only on appropriate diagnosis, but on the detailed description of strengths and needs for intervention.

Categorical diagnosis (as described in Section I of this *Handbook*) provides useful information that places an individual in a class. Such a classification has important implications for intervention, prognosis, and other areas, including legal rights; classification also may be critical for various approaches to etiological and other research. However, classification, by its nature, reduces individuality to achieve generality.

An important goal of assessment is to move beyond global descriptions to more refined, precise documentation of an individual's functioning in various domains (global intellectual level and specific verbal and performance abilities; social competence; receptive and expressive language skills and social use of language; self-care and other abilities of daily living, etc.). The assessment techniques outlined here provide valuable information about a particular individual that is both descriptive and often also prescriptive.

Assessment is also informative when it allows for placing the information about a particular individual within a broader, developmental or normative framework. In this approach, the child's functioning (and not only impairments) is placed in context. The child's scores and behavior are compared with what might be expected from normal children at that age or with that level of mental development. This developmental approach to assessment augments the usual, pathographic description of problems, symptoms, difficulties, or deficiencies that distinguish the person from the normal population.

When rigorous assessments are done with many children from the same diagnostic group, it is possible to integrate findings into a valid multidimensional description of the class. This process enriches categorical diagnoses; empirical findings from such assessment research are not simple restatements of the diagnostic criteria but expand the knowledge about the disorder. For example, studies on the neuropsychological functioning of individuals who are classified as Asperger's syndrome reveal patterns of psychological functioning that may underlie the clinical phenomenology and that are not simply predictable by the diagnostic criteria. Eventually, these findings may be useful in defining the class, along with or instead of the current diagnostic criteria. They can also be invaluable in the identification of subgroups within a larger diagnostic category. Subgroup identification has several important consequences. Carefully defined subgroups may be linkable to particular metabolic or genetic findings, for example. They may also be shown to be helpful in identifying particular intervention methods that work best for particular profiles.

Studies of large numbers of children from the same diagnostic group also allow for comparisons in specific dimensions (e.g., receptive language abilities) across groups. This can indicate the validity of drawing a specific diagnostic boundary between closely related diagnostic groups, for example, between Asperger's syndrome and high functioning autism.

To perform a formal behavioral or psychological assessment, the diagnostician must have expertise in the use of specific methods for acquiring the psychological and behavioral data, knowledge of the range of disorders, and clinical skills in forming relationships with individuals with disabilities, observing their approach and style of performance, as well as what they achieve, and understanding the meaning of findings that derive from the testing and observing. For the assessor to then use the data and create a formulation based on assessments, she or he must have an understanding of development and developmental psychopathology, the ways in which various domains or processes (language, cognition, social judgment, etc.) may relate to each other over the course of the individual's life and as revealed in current testing.

Finally, the results of assessments must be placed in the context of the opportunities that the individual with autism and associated disorders has had to develop, including the individual's opportunities for social relations, learning, recreation, and formal and informal learning about the world. We can anticipate that children who have had good, enriched programs, aimed at facilitating their competence, will appear quite different on assessments than those with less optimal or even restricted resources. Moreover, contextually based assessments can help to locate ways in which the environment might be engineered to ensure more frequent and appropriate opportunities for individuals to acquire and practice skills.

The results of careful and comprehensive assessment are a complex function of the individual's constitutional and neurobiological endowment, maturation, and personal history and experiences at home, in school, and in the community. Used appropriately, objective, rigorous assessment methodology can help guide and monitor effective intervention.

CHAPTER 27

Screening for Autism in Young Children

ELAINE E. COONROD AND WENDY L. STONE

Mounting evidence from early intervention research suggests that participation in specialized intervention programs at young ages is important for optimizing the long-term outcomes of children with autism. Despite evidence that autism can be identified as early as age 2, many children do not receive definitive diagnoses until they are considerably older, resulting in lost opportunities for specialized early intervention. Screening for autism in young children may promote earlier diagnosis and more widespread and systematic referrals to appropriate intervention programs. This chapter describes several issues related to the screening of young children for autism, including the early behavioral features of autism, the accuracy of early diagnosis, and the current state of the art of early screening measures for autism. Although the focus is on screening measures designed for young children with autism, measures used commonly with individuals of other age groups are also included.

EARLY IDENTIFICATION OF AUTISM

Autism is a developmental disorder that emerges early in life, with onset prior to 30 months in most cases (Short & Schopler, 1988; Volkmar, Stier, & Cohen, 1985). In fact, several studies have found that parents report the average age of symptom onset to be as young as 16 to 20 months (Short & Schopler, 1988; Spitzer & Siegel, 1990; Volkmar, Cohen, Hoshino, Rende, & Paul, 1988). The past decade has seen an increase in research focused on early diagnosis and early manifestations of autism symptomatology (Cox et al., 1999; Lord, 1995; Stone et al., 1999). This research has emphasized the importance of early social and communicative behaviors in differentiating young children with autism from developmentally matched comparison groups (Charman & Baird, 2002; Cox et al., 1999; Lord, 1995; Stone et al., 1999). Although sensory and motor difficulties may be evident for some young children with autism, these symptoms appear to be neither universal nor specific to the disorder (Baranek, 2002). A summary of recent findings on the early behavioral features and diagnosis of autism is presented; for a more in-depth discussion of this topic, see Rogers (2001).

At the preschool ages, the most consistently reported impairments—relative to developmentally matched controls—have been found for social-communicative behaviors in the areas of motor imitation (Dawson, Meltzoff, Osterling, & Rinaldi, 1998; Stone, Lemanek, Fishel, Fernandez, & Altemeier, 1990), functional play (Mundy, Sigman, Ungerer, & Sherman, 1986; Sigman & Ungerer, 1984), sharing and responding to affective information (Dissanayake & Crossley, 1996; Sigman, Kasari, Kwon, & Yirmiya, 1992; Snow, Hertzig, & Shapiro, 1987), and engaging in social referencing and joint attention (Dawson, Meltzoff, Osterling, Rinaldi, & Brown, 1998; Mundy et al., 1986; Phillips, Baron-Cohen, & Rutter, 1992; Wetherby, Yonclas, & Bryan, 1989). Although few observational studies have focused exclusively on children below the age of 4, deficits in joint attention and motor imitation have been documented in 2- and 3-year-old children with autism (Stone, Ousley, & Little-ford, 1997; Stone, Ousley, Yoder, Hogan, & Hepburn, 1997), as well as in 20-month-old children with autism (Charman et al., 1997). In addition, there is evidence that 20-month-old children with autism demonstrate a lack of re-sponsiveness to adult displays of distress (Charman et al., 1997).

Retrospective analyses of home videotapes have permitted the study of the behavioral manifestations of autism in infancy. Although this approach is limited by the lack of control over (and comparability of) situations in which children are filmed, results from this line of research suggest that some of the earli-est deficits in autism are in infants' early at-tempts to coordinate their attention and affect with others. Home videotapes of infants who receive a later diagnosis of autism have re-vealed social communicative deficits as early as 9 to 12 months in the areas of pointing to and showing objects, looking at others, smil-ing socially, orienting to visual stimuli, and orienting to their name (Adrien et al., 1993; Baranek, 1999; Osterling & Dawson, 1994; Osterling, Dawson, & Munson, 2002; Werner, Dawson, Osterling, & Dinno, 2000).

Increased understanding of the early be-havioral manifestations of autism has resulted in a corresponding improvement in our ability to provide early diagnoses. There is now evi-dence that the clinical diagnosis of autism can be made accurately at the age of 2. Early diag-noses of autism have been shown to be stable over a one-year period, with the large majority of children (88% to 100%) remaining on the autism spectrum (Cox et al., 1999; Lord, 1995; Stone et al., 1999). Interrater agreement for the differentiation between autism spectrum diagnoses and nonspectrum diagnoses is good (agreement = 87% and above, kappa = .59 and above), though the differentiation of diagnoses of autism versus pervasive developmental disorder-not otherwise specified (PDD-NOS) is more variable (agreement = 38% to 82%, kappa = below chance level to .58) and more dependent on the clinicians' level of experi-ence with very young children (Stone et al., 1999).

Unfortunately, there is a gap between re-search and clinical practice that results in many children failing to receive diagnoses of autism until older ages (Howlin & Asgharian,

1999; Siegel, Pliner, Eschler, & Elliot, 1988). The early diagnosis of autism is complicated by a number of factors, including the nature of the early deficits, the reluctance of profession-als to "label" or make a formal diagnosis for young children, and the scarcity of clinicians experienced in making early diagnoses (Rogers, 2001; Siegel et al., 1988). The most universal early symptoms, that is, those in the area of social-communicative skills, represent "negative symptoms," in that they involve the absence or reduced frequency of social and communicative behaviors that would be ex-pected for a child's developmental level (Fil-ipek et al., 1999). As such, they are more difficult to detect and evaluate than "positive symptoms" that involve the presence of un-usual sensory and motor behaviors. For exam-ple, it is much easier for an untrained observer to notice the presence of hand flapping than the absence of imitation, though the latter be-havior is likely to hold greater utility for early diagnosis of autism. Another factor complicat-ing early diagnosis is that our diagnostic meth-ods are not yet specialized for young children. Despite widespread recognition that the be-havioral symptoms of autism vary with age and development (Rutter, 1978; Siegel, Vu-kicevic, & Spitzer, 1990), few diagnostic methods for children under the age of 3 have been developed.

The clinical utility of providing an early autism diagnosis is supported by findings from the neurosciences as well as early intervention research. Studies of neural development have suggested that very young children have in-creased brain plasticity (Huttenlocher, 1994), which may result in greater opportunities for overcoming neurodevelopmental deficits within the early years. In addition, specialized early intervention programs have reported suc-cess in improving language functioning (Bondy & Frost, 1995), cognitive/developmen-tal skills (Harris, Handleman, Gordon, Kristoff, & Fuentes, 1991; McEachin, Smith, & Lovaas, 1993; Rogers & Lewis, 1989), and social behavior (Strain, Hoyson, & Jamieson, 1985) in young children with autism. There is also evidence that children who receive inter-vention at young ages have better outcomes than those who are older (Harris & Handle-man, 2000). Early intervention may be espe-cially critical in preventing a cascade of effects that result from early deficits and interfere with later functioning (Dawson, Ashman, & Carver, 2000; Happé, 1994; Mundy & Crowson, 1997; Mundy & Neal, 2001). Thus, the success of intervention may partly depend on the success with which we can identify infants and young children at risk for autism so that they can begin receiving intervention services as quickly as possible.

One way to improve on early identification is through screening for autism. The importance of early screening for autism has been emphasized by several practice parameters published by the American Academy of Neurology (Filipek et al., 2000), the American Academy of Pediatrics (American Academy of Pediatrics Committee on Children with Disabilities, 2001), and the National Academy of Sciences (Committee on Educational Interventions for Children with Autism, 2001). The availability of early screening measures for autism would serve a multitude of interests. First, it would help disseminate knowledge about the early features of autism from research settings to personnel in clinical community settings. For example, researchers examining the utility of one autism screening instrument note that health care workers value knowing which social and communication behaviors can be reliably examined and evaluated in young children (Charman et al., 2001). Second, by identifying children at younger ages, screening can prompt children's earlier referral to appropriate diagnostic and intervention services. Children who have been identified as having delays but for whom the specific diagnosis of autism has not yet been made may not receive the types of specialized intervention services found to be most effective with this population (Rogers, 2001). Finally, some screening measures may provide information about areas of specific social and communicative deficits and skills that could be used to inform intervention goals and treatment planning.

CHARACTERISTICS OF SCREENING MEASURES

The following section describes some general design and psychometric characteristics that should be considered in evaluating the utility of any screening measure.

General Characteristics

Screening has been defined as a brief assessment designed to identify children who are in need of a more comprehensive diagnostic evaluation due to risk of delay or disability (Meisels, 1985). As such, screening is the first of a multistep process that may also include rescreening, referral to a diagnostic center for further assessment, and referral to early intervention programs (Aylward, 1997). Screening measures differ from diagnostic measures in that they typically require less time, training, and experience to administer, and the results of screening measures indicate levels of risk for disability rather than provide a diagnosis.

Screening measures can vary according to the population for which they were designed or the level of the screening (Lord, Risi, & DiLavore, 1999; Siegel, 1996, 1998). Level 1 screening measures are designed to identify children at risk for disability from the general population, that is, those with typical development. Level 1 screening measures are often used in pediatric practices where they are administered to all children—whether there are concerns about developmental problems or not—during their well-child visits. Though there are a few Level 1 screening measures specifically designed to identify autism, most screening instruments at this level are designed to identify a broader range of developmental problems, such as motor, cognitive, and/or language delay. Level 2 screening measures for autism help differentiate children at risk for autism from those at risk for other developmental disorders, such as global developmental delay or language impairment. These screening measures are more often used in clinical settings such as child-find agencies, early intervention programs, or evaluation centers serving children with a variety of developmental problems.

The design of screening measures can differ across a variety of dimensions, including the format of administration (informant report, observational, or interactive), the length of time required for administration, the level of experience or training necessary, and degree of familiarity with the child required. For example, screening measures that require knowledge about multiple areas of the child's behavior across many situations and contexts generally need to be completed by a parent or caregiver. In contrast, measures employing a checklist of behaviors displayed in the immediate context can be completed by someone who has had substantially less prior experience with the child. The characteristics of a screening measure must be compatible with the purpose and settings for which it is intended. Because Level 1 screening measures are used to evaluate large numbers of children, most of whom do not have developmental problems, they need to be brief and easy to administer, and parent report questionnaires are often used. Level 2 screenings, however, require a more fine-grained analysis of developmental problems and, thus, may require more time or training to administer, score, and interpret than Level 1 screening measures.

Psychometric Characteristics

Psychometric characteristics most frequently considered when evaluating screening measures include sensitivity, specificity, positive predictive value, and negative predictive value. Professionals should have a clear understanding not only of the general meaning of these terms but also of how these values are affected by the specific setting in which the screening measure is used. A recent study indicates that some child mental health professionals do not understand how test psychometrics can be affected by the prevalence rates of a disorder (Clark & Harrington, 1999). Knowledge such as this is critical for informed autism screening because you would expect to find very different prevalence rates of the disorder, depending on the sample being screened, that is, a population-based sample or a clinic-based sample. Psychometric properties of screening measures and related issues are described next.

Sensitivity and Specificity

The accuracy of screening measures has traditionally been evaluated through sensitivity and specificity (Riegelman & Hirsch, 1989). *Sensitivity* refers to the proportion of children with developmental problems who are identified as being at risk by the screening measure, while *specificity* refers to the proportion of children without developmental problems who are identified as being not at risk (Aylward, 1997). The sensitivity and specificity of a screening mea-

sure are determined by comparing the results of the screen (i.e., risk or no risk) with the diagnostic "gold standard" for a disorder (Riegelman & Hirsch, 1989). Sensitivity and specificity can range in value from 0.0 to 1.0, with higher values indicating greater probability that those with and without the disorder will be correctly identified by the screening measure. In developing a screening measure, the goal is to identify a cutoff score in which both sensitivity and specificity are maximized.

General standards for adequate levels of sensitivity and specificity have been published. Sensitivity levels of .80 or higher are generally recommended (Glascoe, 1991; Squires, 2000), meaning that at least 80% of children who truly have developmental problems (as determined by a more comprehensive evaluation) should be identified by their scores on the screening measure. Recommended specificity levels range from .80 to over .90 (Glascoe, 1991; Squires, 2000), meaning that 80% to over 90% of children who have no developmental problems should be identified as being not at risk. Although these general guidelines can be helpful when evaluating a screening measure, they should not be the only considerations. The relative cost of incorrectly identifying a child as being at risk should be compared to the cost of failing to identify a child who is at risk for a disorder. Given the documented benefits of early intervention for children with autism, it may be more beneficial to overrefer children for further evaluation than to underrefer and potentially delay identification and treatment. In this case, a screening with higher sensitivity might be desirable.

Sensitivity and specificity are interrelated such that increasing one by changing the measure's cutoff score can affect the other, often detrimentally. For example, a measure's sensitivity can often be improved by lowering the cutoff score so that the likelihood of detecting those with disabilities is increased. However, at this lower threshold, it is also easier for those without disabilities to be misidentified as being at risk, resulting in a lower specificity (Aylward, 1997; Frankenburg, 1974). In the most extreme example, a screening measure's sensitivity can be raised to 100% by simply changing the cutoff to the lowest possible score, such that all scores would indicate risk for disability. However, the sensitivity would then be 0, and the screening measure, obviously, useless (Frankenburg, 1974).

Positive and Negative Predictive Value

Sensitivity and specificity indicate the proportion of children with and without the disability who are correctly identified by the screening measure. However, it is also important to know the proportion of children identified as being at risk (or not at risk) by the screening measure who actually have (or do not have) the disorder (Riegelman & Hirsch, 1989). This information is referred to as the positive and negative predictive values (also called positive and negative predictive power) of the screening measure. The *positive predictive value* (PPV) is the proportion of children identified as being at risk who have the disability; the *negative predictive value* (NPV) is the proportion of children identified as not being at risk who do not have the disability (Aylward, 1997). Like sensitivity and specificity, PPV and NPV are proportions with values ranging from 0.0 to 1.0, with higher values indicating greater probability that the screening result is correct.

PPV and NPV will vary according to the prevalence of the disorder; as the prevalence increases, PPV will increase and NPV will decrease. Conversely, as the prevalence of the disorder decreases, the PPV will decrease and the NPV will increase (Riegelman & Hirsch, 1989). For example, in a sample of 1,000 with a prevalence of 10%, a screening measure with a sensitivity of .80 and specificity of .80 will identify 260 individuals total as being at risk for the disorder (see Table 27.1). Because 80

of those individuals actually have the disorder, the resulting PPV is 80/260, or .31. The same measure will identify 740 individuals total as being not at risk. Because 720 of those individuals do not have the disorder, the resulting NPV is 720/740, or approximately .97. In a sample of 1,000 with a prevalence of 1%, the same measure will identify 206 individuals total as being at risk for the disorder (see Table 27.2). Because only 8 of those 206 individuals actually have the disorder, the resulting PPV is 8/206, or approximately .04. The same measure will identify 794 individuals total as being not at risk for the disorder. Because 792 of those 794 individuals do not have the disorder, the resulting NPV is 792/794, or approximately .99.

In practical terms, this means that a screening measure can be expected to have a higher PPV when it is used in a setting characterized by a higher prevalence of the disorder, such as a developmental clinic, compared to one characterized by a lower prevalence, such as a pediatrician's office. Of particular interest, Clark and Harrington (1999) note that for a screening measure with a sensitivity and specificity of .80, it takes a prevalence of about 25% to obtain a PPV above .50 and correctly identify children as being at risk for the disorder a little better than half of the time.

Summary

Screening measures can vary across a number of dimensions, including administration format and level of expertise required. Selection of an appropriate screening measure, therefore, requires consideration of the purpose and

TABLE 27.1   Positive and Negative Predictive Values for a Screening Measure with a Sensitivity and Specificity of .80 in a Population of 1,000 with a Disorder Prevalence Rate of 10%

	Diagnosed with Disorder		
	Yes	No	Total
Screen indicates risk	80	180	260
Screen indicates no risk	20	720	740
Total	100	900	1,000

Sensitivity = .80 (80/100); Specificity = .80 (720/900); Positive predictive value = .31 (80/260); Negative predictive value = .97 (720/740)

TABLE 27.2   Positive and Negative Predictive Values for a Screening Measure with a Sensitivity and Specificity of .80 in a Population of 1,000 with a Disorder Prevalence Rate of 1%

	Diagnosed with Disorder		
	Yes	No	Total
Screen indicates risk	8	198	206
Screen indicates no risk	2	792	794
Total	10	990	1,000

Sensitivity = .80 (8/10); Specificity = .80 (792/990); Positive predictive value = .04 (8/206); Negative predictive value = .99 (792/794)

context for which it is intended. Particular consideration should be given to a measure's sensitivity, specificity, and predictive values. Given the low prevalence of autism in the general population, you could expect that a Level 1 screening measure with acceptably high sensitivity would still have a low PPV. As a result, even the best Level 1 measure may mislabel more children as being at risk for an autism spectrum disorder than it correctly labels as at risk. This phenomenon highlights the critical need for further diagnostic assessment following screening. Moreover, because the prevalence of autism is often substantially higher in clinic-based populations, a Level 2 measure with similar sensitivity and specificity as a Level 1 measure will have a higher PPV than the Level 1 measure. Thus, it is difficult to directly compare the psychometric properties of Level 1 and Level 2 measures.

REVIEW OF SCREENING MEASURES

The following section contains a review of measures that can be used to screen for autism. Level 1 screenings are described first, with attention to both general developmental screenings and autism-specific screenings. A description of Level 2 screenings follows and includes both those designed specifically for very young children and those designed for a wider range of ages. Measures that are used exclusively for diagnostic purposes, such as the Autism Diagnostic Interview-Revised (ADI-R; Lord, Rutter, & Le Couteur, 1994) and the Autism Diagnostic Observation Schedule-Generic (ADOS-G; Lord et al., 2000) are beyond the scope of this chapter. Likewise, measures designed for the purpose of obtaining information about behaviors and levels of symptoms for research or clinical purposes but that do not provide risk cutoff scores, such as the Infant Behavior Summarized Evaluation (IBSE; Adrien et al., 1992) or the Parent Interview for Autism (PIA; Stone, Coonrod, Pozdol, & Turner, 2003; Stone & Hogan, 1993), are not described in this chapter.

Level 1 Screening Measures

There are two strategies for identifying young children at risk for autism within the general population. One approach is to select a screening measure designed to identify children at risk for a broad range of developmental problems (i.e., nonspecific screening), with the expectation that some children with autism will be identified because of their cognitive delays or language delays. The other approach is to use a screening that specifically targets the symptoms of autism (i.e., autism-specific screening). Examples of each are described in the following sections.

Nonspecific Screening Measures

Two types of nonspecific Level 1 screening measures are discussed: those that screen for deficits in many areas of development and those that focus exclusively on the areas of social-emotional and/or communication development. There are several existing measures designed to screen a broad array of developmental areas in general populations of children. The areas assessed by these measures typically include cognitive skills, communication and language, motor skills, social skills, self-help skills, and behavior. Because young children with autism often have cognitive or language delays, these measures will identify some children with autism, along with those who have other developmental disorders. Several nonspecific screening measures were endorsed in the Child Neurology Society and American Academy of Neurology practice parameters (Filipek et al., 1999); these measures include the Ages and Stages Questionnaire, Second Edition (ASQ; Bricker & Squires, 1999), the Child Development Inventories (CDIs; Ireton, 1992; Ireton & Glascoe, 1995), and the Parent's Evaluation of Developmental Status (PEDS; Glascoe, 1998). All are parent report measures with strong psychometric properties that were designed for use with very young children (i.e., under 36 months). The Brigance Screens (Brigance, 1986; Glascoe, 1996) are also recommended, but differ from the others in that they rely on clinician observation of elicited child behaviors. The commonly used Denver tests, the Denver-II, the Denver Developmental Screening Test-Revised, and the Revised Denver Pre-Screening Developmental Questionnaire (Frankenburg, 1986; Frankenburg, Dodds, Archer, Shapiro, & Bresnick, 1996), were not recommended in the practice parameters, as review of multiple studies found them to have unacceptable levels of sensitivity and specificity (Filipek et al., 1999). Although this approach has the intuitive appeal of casting a wide net and finding children with a broad array of developmental problems, data as to their sensitivity and specificity for the identification of autism are not available.

Given that social and communication deficits are strong early indicators of autism, screening for impairments in these areas can be another effective strategy for the early identification of children with autism. Several screening measures focusing on communication and/or social-emotional skills have been developed, though data supporting their utility for identifying children with autism are not yet available. One such measure is the Infant/Toddler Checklist from the Communication and Symbolic Behavior Scales Developmental Profile (CSBS DP; Wetherby & Prizant, 2002). The Checklist is a 24-item parent report questionnaire examining a range of early social and communication behaviors, some of which have specific relevance for young children with autism. The Checklist was designed to identify children from 6 to 24 months of age who have, or are at risk for developing, a communication impairment so that they can be referred for a developmental evaluation. It was designed for routine developmental screening in pediatricians' offices or early childhood programs serving infants and toddlers. The Checklist yields composite scores in three areas: social (e.g., use of communicative gestures), speech (e.g., use of sounds), and symbolic (e.g., use of objects), as well as a total score. It was normed on a sample of 2,000 children, and cutoff scores are available for composite and total scores. Other components of the CSBS DP, including a more extensive parent report questionnaire and a behavior sampling procedure, can be used to obtain more information about children identified as being at risk. The utility of this measure as a screener for autism is currently under investigation.

One social-emotional screening measure is the Temperament and Atypical Behavior Scale Screener (TABS Screener; Neisworth, Bagnato, Salvia, & Hunt, 1999). The TABS Screener is a 15-item parent report questionnaire that was designed for identifying atypical development of temperament or self-regulation in children between the ages of 11 and 71 months. Parents of children identified as being at risk by the TABS Screener can complete the TABS Assessment Tool, a 55-item questionnaire, to provide more information about their child's temperament and self-regulatory behavior. In addition to a total score, the TABS Assessment Tool provides four subscale scores for detached, hypersensitive/active, underreactive, and dysregulated behaviors. The authors state that behaviors evaluated by the Detached subscale are commonly associated with autism spectrum disorders, though information on the utility of this scale for identifying children with autism has not yet been provided.

Autism-Specific Screening Measures

Though the preceding measures demonstrate promise for use in early screening for autism, they were not designed specifically for children with autism, and their utility for this population has not been evaluated. Three autism-specific Level 1 screening measures are described next: the Checklist for Autism in Toddlers (CHAT; Baird et al., 2000; Baron-Cohen, Allen, & Gillberg, 1992; Baron-Cohen et al., 1996), the Modified Checklist for Autism in Toddlers (M-CHAT; Robins, Fein, Barton, & Green, 2001a), and the Pervasive Developmental Disorders Screening Test-Stage 1 (PDDST-Stage 1; Siegel, 1996, 1998; Siegel & Hayer, 1999). Psychometric and design properties of these measures are summarized in Table 27.3.

Checklist for Autism in Toddlers The CHAT (Baird et al., 2000; Baron-Cohen et al., 1992, 1996) is a general population screening measure designed for use during routine health care visits to identify 18-month-old infants at risk for autism. It consists of parent report and interactional items assessing pretend play, gaze monitoring, and protodeclarative pointing. To date, the CHAT has been the subject of more empirical work than any other Level 1 autism-specific screening.

In the first published study, the CHAT was administered to 50 randomly selected infants as part of their 18-month health care checkups. To ensure ease of administration, only those items passed by the largest proportion of infants were retained in the final version of the

TABLE 27.3   Screening Measures for Autism

| | Validity | | | | | | | | | | | |
| | Sensitivity | | | Specificity | | | PPV | | | NPV | | |
Level 1 Screening Measures	P	C	P/C	P	C	P/C	P	C	P/C	P	C	P/C
Checklist for Autism in Toddlers (CHAT)	.18–.38			.98–1.0			.05–.75			—		
		.65–.85				1.0						
Modified Checklist for Autism in Toddlers (M-CHAT)		.95–.97[a]			.95–.99[a]			.36–.79				.99[a]
Pervasive Developmental Disorders Screening Test-Stage 1 (PDDST-Stage 1)		.85			.71		—			—		
Level 2 Screening Measures												
Autism Behavior Checklist (ABC)	.38–.58 improved by lower cutoff			.76–.97			—			—		
Autism Screening Questionnaire/Social Communication Questionnaire (ASQ/SCQ)	.85–.96			.67–.80				.93			.55	
Childhood Autism Rating Scale (CARS)	.92–.98			—			—			—		
Gilliam Autism Rating Scale (GARS)		.48 improved by lower cutoff		—			—			—		
Pervasive Developmental Disorders Screening Test-Stage 2 (PDDST-Stage 2)	.69–.88			.25–.63			—			—		
Screening for Autism in 2-Year-Olds (STAT)		.92			.85			.86			.92	

Note: C = Clinic-based sample; P = Population-based sample; P/C = combined population and clinic-based samples; — = Not reported.

[a] These numbers represent estimates because follow-up with the no-risk group is not yet complete.

CHAT. This version was then administered at 18 months to a high-risk sample of 41 younger siblings of children with autism. The authors found that using the criteria of failure on two or more skill areas correctly identified the four infants diagnosed with autism at 30 months and did not misidentify any of the typically developing infants (Baron-Cohen et al., 1992).

To determine its utility as a general population screening, the CHAT was administered to more than 16,000 18-month-old infants by health care practitioners or, in a minority of cases, by the infant's primary caregiver (Baird et al., 2000; Baron-Cohen et al., 1996). In the most recent study, the number of passes and failures on three specific skill areas—pretend play, gaze monitoring, and protodeclarative pointing—was used to determine level of autism risk (high risk, medium risk, or no risk). In an effort to minimize false positives, any infant who was found to be at high risk from the 18-month screen was retested with the CHAT approximately one month later by a member of the research staff. Only about half of the medium-risk infants were retested due to resource constraints.

Extensive follow-up screening and surveillance procedures were used to identify all children with autism in the population-based sample. Procedures included rescreening the entire sample with different questionnaires at ages 3½ and 5½, reviewing medical and educational records at ages 7 to 8, and continuous monitoring of referrals for diagnostic assessments at regional clinics. Children either received comprehensive diagnostic evaluations from the research team or were classified diagnostically on the basis of review of their

Reliability			Design		
Interrater	Test-Retest	Internal Consistency	Ages	Format	Level of Expertise
—	—	—	18 months	Interview and interactive	Minimal
—	—	alpha = .83–.85	24 months	Parent Questionnaire	None
—	—	—	Under 6 years	Parent Questionnaire	None
K < .40 for most items; Agreement = < 70–95%	—	alpha = .38–.87	18 months and older	Behavioral Checklist	Minimal
—	—	.90	4 years and older	Parent Questionnaire	None
K = .75; Agreement = 90%	K = .64; r = .88	alpha = .73–.94	No specified[b]	Behavioral Checklist	Minimal
r =.55–.99	r = .81–.88	alpha = .88–.96	3–22 years	Behavioral Checklist	Minimal
—	—	—	Under 6 years	Parent Questionnaire	None
K =.88; Agreement = 94%	K = .88; r = .85	—	24–36 months	Interactive	Requires training

[b] Some data are available for children under 3 years old.

assessment records. Through all methods, 50 children with autism and 44 children with other PDDs were identified.

The sensitivity and PPV of the CHAT varied with risk level (i.e., high risk versus medium risk), screening procedure (i.e., initial CHAT score or CHAT retest score), and diagnosis (i.e., autism, PDD, or all autism spectrum disorders combined). Full details are provided by Baird and colleagues (2000). For identifying children with autism, sensitivity was maximized when a medium-risk level threshold was used with the initial CHAT score, resulting in 19 of 50 (38%) of children with autism being identified by the CHAT; however, PPV was only .05. Using the CHAT retest score with a high-risk threshold significantly increased PPV to .75 but resulted in a reduction in sensitivity to .18. Similarly, for identifying children with PDD, the medium-risk level threshold used with the initial CHAT score maximized sensitivity and correctly identified 14 of 44 (32%) children but resulted in a PPV of .03. Using the CHAT retest score with a medium-risk threshold increased PPV to .29, but there was a corresponding drop in sensitivity to .23. Overall, the high-risk threshold was better at identifying autism than PDD, while the medium-risk threshold identified both.

The specificity of the CHAT remained high (.98 or above) regardless of procedure. However, it is important to note that infants with severe developmental delay were excluded because of the health care practitioners' reluctance to have parents of infants with developmental problems complete additional assessments (Baird et al., 2000). Thus, the specificity of the CHAT within a population-based sample that does not exclude children with these developmental problems has not yet been examined.

The CHAT has also been evaluated in a clinical sample of previously diagnosed 2- and 3-year-old children (Scambler, Rogers, & Wehner, 2001). The medium-risk criteria defined by Baird et al. (2000) resulted in a sensitivity and specificity of .65 and 1.0, respectively. Scambler et al. developed their own scoring criteria based on the results, resulting in an increase of sensitivity to .85 without a decrease in specificity. Although these finding are encouraging, it is unclear how they will generalize to other clinical and population-based samples for several reasons. First, the observational portion of the CHAT was rated following approximately three hours of contact, which is a longer observation period than would be used in a typical screening context. Second, the fact that children had been diagnosed previously may have biased parental responses to questions about autism symptoms on the parent report portion of the CHAT. Finally, the new scoring criteria were developed post hoc and require replication on an independent sample. The need for future empirical work on the CHAT and the scoring system derived in this study has been acknowledged by the authors (Scambler et al., 2001).

Modified Checklist for Autism in Toddlers

The M-CHAT (Robins et al., 2001a) is an extended parent report version of the CHAT that was developed to serve as a Level 1 screening in pediatric settings. It comprises the nine CHAT parental report items, items to assess additional behaviors evaluated by the observational portion of the CHAT, and items to evaluate autism symptoms not assessed by the CHAT (e.g., repetitive behaviors). In the earlier stages of its development, the M-CHAT was administered to children as young as 18 months; however, the age of screening was raised to 24 months because of physicians' greater willingness to screen at that age and the possibility of developmental regression occurring between 18 and 24 months.

To evaluate the psychometric properties of the M-CHAT, a sample of 1,293 18- to 30-month-old children was recruited through pedi-atric well visits or through early intervention programs. Similar to the CHAT, a retest procedure was used in which the parents of any child deemed high risk (i.e., meeting M-CHAT cutoff criteria or otherwise determined to be at risk by physicians or early intervention workers) were telephoned by the researchers to confirm the child's M-CHAT score. Children meeting the cutoff criteria then received developmental evaluations. In total, 58 children received developmental evaluations, 74 received telephone follow-up but no evaluation, and 1,161 received no follow-up. Of the children receiving developmental evaluations, 39 received autism spectrum diagnoses and 19 received nonspectrum diagnoses. Follow-up of children who were determined to be not at risk by the M-CHAT was still underway at the time this study was published; as a result, it was not known at that time whether any children with autism spectrum disorders were missed by the M-CHAT. Therefore, as the authors note, the figures reported for sensitivity, specificity, and NPV can be considered only estimates. Two cutoff scores were examined: failure of any three items on the entire checklist or failure of 2 of 6 critical items identified by a discriminant function analysis. Internal consistency was high for both the entire checklist and the 6 critical items, with alpha coefficients of .85 and .83, respectively. Results varied depending on the cutoff score used and depending on whether children receiving retesting by telephone were considered false positives. Estimates of sensitivity ranged from .95 to .97, specificity from .95 to .99, PPV from .36 to .79, and the NPV was .99.

Since the initial report, 45% of the original sample has been rescreened and reevaluated. To date, 15 of 20 children with autism spectrum disorders and 3 of 6 children with nonspectrum disorders have retained their early diagnoses, and only one child previously missed by the M-CHAT has been identified. In addition, age 2 total M-CHAT scores were found to correlate with age 4 scores on the Childhood Autism Rating Scale (CARS; Robins et al., 2002).

Initial reports on the M-CHAT are promising, though continued research on its psychometric properties as a Level 1 population screening is necessary. In addition to obtaining follow-up diagnostic information for all children screened, it will be important to examine its properties in a purely population-based sample. The inclusion of children from a high-risk sample (i.e., those referred for early intervention services) is likely to have inflated the prevalence rate for autism and, therefore, the PPV. Robins, Fein, Barton, and Green (2001b) report that continued work on this measure is currently underway.

Pervasive Developmental Disorders Screening Test-Stage 1 The PDDST-Stage 1 (Siegel, 1996, 1998; Siegel & Hayer, 1999) is a parent report questionnaire designed to screen for autism spectrum disorders in children under 6 years of age. Items for the PDDST were based on areas of concern reported commonly by parents of young children later diagnosed with autism; questions focus on children's early behaviors in areas such as nonverbal communication, language, temperament, play, and social interaction. In addition to the full version of the PDDST, there are shorter versions designed for different levels of screening, each taking about 5 minutes to complete. It has not yet been published.

The PDDST-Stage 1 is intended for use in primary care settings to identify children who require further evaluation to rule out an autism spectrum disorder. To develop the cutoff score, a clinic-based sample of 197 very low birth-weight children was compared to 380 children diagnosed with autism, PDD-NOS, and other developmental disorders. Using the endorsement of three or more items as a cutoff, sensitivity and specificity are .85 and .71, respectively (Siegel & Hayer, 1999). However, the psychometric characteristics for the PDDST-Stage 1 have not yet been evaluated in a population-based sample.

Level 1 Summary

Several good general developmental screening measures are available for identifying children at risk for a broad range of disabilities from the general population, and measures of early communication skills and social-emotional characteristics may also have utility as early autism screening measures. However, these measures were not developed specifically to identify autism, and their ability to identify children at risk for autism has not yet been studied. Signif-

icantly fewer autism-specific Level 1 screening measures have been developed and, of those, only the CHAT has been studied in a population-based sample. However, the exclusion of children with severe disabilities from this sample complicates interpretation of the reported specificity. In addition, given its relatively low levels of sensitivity, the authors acknowledge that findings do not support its use for a total population screening for autism at a single time point (Charman & Baird, 2002). A population investigation of the M-CHAT is currently underway (Robins et al., 2001a), but until follow-ups are completed and data from clinic and population-based sample are considered separately, its utility as a Level 1 screening remains unclear. Similarly, the PDDST-Stage 1 has yet to be published or evaluated in a population-based sample. Additional research is needed before recommending universal screening for autism using any of the measures currently available.

Level 2 Screening Measures

The following sections describe autism-specific Level 2 screening measures, that is, measures that were designed to differentiate children at risk for autism from those at risk for other developmental disabilities. Measures designed exclusively for young children are described first, followed by measures that may be used with young children as well as older individuals.

Measures Designed for Young Children

Two Level 2 screening measures were designed specifically to identify young children at risk for autism spectrum disorders: the Pervasive Developmental Disorders Screening Test-Stage 2 (PDDST-Stage 2; Siegel, 1996, 1998; Siegel & Hayer, 1999) and the Screening Tool for Autism in Two-Year-Olds (STAT; Stone, Coonrod, & Ousley, 2000; Stone & Ousley, 1997). Psychometric and design properties of these measures are summarized in Table 27.3.

Pervasive Developmental Disorders Screening Test-Stage 2 The PDDST-Stage 2 (Siegel, 1996, 1998; Siegel & Hayer, 1999) is the Level 2 screening version for the PDDST described earlier. It is a parent report measure designed for children age 6 and under that evaluates early behaviors. The PDDST-Stage 2 was developed for use in developmental disorders clinics to differentiate children needing evaluations focusing on autism spectrum disorders from those needing more general developmental evaluations. Clinic-based samples of 260 children with autism/PDD-NOS and 120 children with other developmental disorders were used to develop the cutoff score. Depending on the cutoff scores used, reported sensitivity and specificity values range from .69 to .88 and .25 to .63, respectively (Siegel, 1996; Siegel & Hayer, 1999). Work with the PDDST is ongoing, and these preliminary findings are encouraging. Additional information about the development procedures, psychometric properties, and characteristics of the samples included is necessary to determine the utility of this measure.

Screening Tool for Autism in Two-Year-Olds

The STAT (Stone & Ousley, 1997; Stone et al., 2000) was designed as a Level 2 screening tool to differentiate children at risk for autism from those at risk for other developmental problems. The STAT is an interactive measure developed for children between the ages of 24 and 36 months, though investigation of its utility with both younger and older groups of children is currently underway. The STAT consists of 12 empirically derived items that are administered within a play-based context and are scored as pass or fail according to specific criteria. Items on the STAT assess play skills, communication skills, and imitation skills, and it takes approximately 20 minutes to administer. The initial STAT scoring system was developed and validated on a clinical sample of 19 children with autism and 54 children with nonautistic spectrum developmental problems obtained from consecutive referrals to a regional multidisciplinary diagnostic center. Using clinical diagnosis as the standard, a scoring system was derived that resulted in sensitivity and specificity rates of 1.00 and .91, respectively, for the development sample. When applied to the validation sample, sensitivity and specificity were .83 and .86, respectively, and positive and negative predictive values were .77 and .90, respectively. Because the children with autism had significantly lower mental ages than the children with nonautistic disorders, subgroups of children with and without autism were cre-

ated and matched on mental age. Similar psychometric properties were found for this matched sample (Stone et al., 2000).

In a subsequent study (Stone, Coonrod, Turner, & Pozdol, in press), signal detection was used to derive and validate a cutoff score for the STAT using developmentally matched groups of 26 children with autism and 26 children with nonspectrum disorders. Using clinical diagnosis as the diagnostic standard, a cutoff score was derived from the development sample, which was then independently tested on the validation sample. Applying this new cutoff score to the validation sample resulted in a sensitivity of .92, a specificity of .85, a PPV of .86, and an NPV of .92.

Concurrent validity of the STAT with the ADOS-G was assessed by comparing children's STAT risk category (i.e., autism risk versus no autism risk) with their ADOS-G diagnosis (i.e., autism versus no autism) for a larger sample of 50 children with autism, 17 children with PDD-NOS, and 39 children with nonspectrum disorders. For the purposes of this comparison, children who received an ADOS-G diagnosis of PDD-NOS were grouped with children receiving a nonspectrum diagnosis. Results revealed a Cohen's kappa of .77 and a percent agreement of 89% between the two measures.

The reliability of the STAT was also examined. Interrater agreement was assessed for a subset of 30 children by having two examiners score the STAT independently as it was administered. Cohen's kappa for risk category was .88, and average percent agreement across the 12 STAT items was 94%. Test-retest reliability for the STAT was examined for 18 children tested by two different examiners approximately 2 to 3 weeks apart. Cohen's kappa for risk category was .88, and the Pearson correlation between the total STAT scores was .85.

As a Level 2 screening, the STAT was designed for use in a number of settings, including clinics, child-find agencies, and early intervention centers. However, its psychometric properties have been evaluated only in a university-based developmental clinic, which may serve a higher proportion of children with autism than other community-based centers. In addition, because the STAT is an interactive measure, it requires training to ensure accurate administration and scoring. Future research examining the psychometric properties of the STAT in other community-based settings, as well as examining the ability of other community professionals to administer the STAT, is needed.

Non-Age-Specific Measures

Several Level 2 autism screening measures were not designed specifically for young children but may have utility for this age group. These measures and their psychometric properties are described next and summarized in Table 27.3.

Autism Behavior Checklist   The Autism Behavior Checklist (ABC; Krug, Arick, & Almond, 1980a, 1980b) is a 57-item behavior rating scale assessing behaviors and symptoms of autism in five areas including sensory behaviors (sensory), social relating (relating), repetitive behaviors (body and object use), language and communication skills (language), and social and adaptive skills (social and self-help). The content of the ABC was taken from behaviors described in other autism screening instruments available at the time of its development (e.g., Rimland's E-2 form), the final items and their wording being selected by the authors in consultation with other autism professionals. The ABC was developed on a large sample of individuals between the ages of 18 months and 35 years of age and was originally intended to measure levels of autism symptomatology in persons with severe disabilities for educational purposes. The ABC takes about 10 to 20 minutes to complete, and the authors recommend that the informant have at least 3 to 6 weeks or more experience with the individual being rated and that parents be consulted when possible to obtain more accurate information (Krug et al., 1980a).

In the development phase, the checklist was given to numerous professionals in the field who were asked to complete the form for an individual they knew. More than 1,000 completed questionnaires for children and adults with autism, mental retardation, visual and hearing impairments, emotional disturbance, and typical development were received and were used to determine the item score weights and cutoff scores, as well as to evaluate psychometric properties (Krug et al., 1980a, 1980b). Each item has a weighted score ranging from 1 to 4, and endorsed items are

summed to obtain subscale and total scores. Higher scores reflect greater impairments and higher levels of autism symptoms, with scores of 67 and above indicating a high probability of autism, scores of 53 and below indicating a low probability of autism, and scores between indicating that probability of autism is unclear and further assessment should be undertaken (Krug et al., 1980a). The authors report that in their development of the ABC, 90% of those who received a score of 68 or above had previous diagnoses of autism, and 95% of those who received a score below 53 had previous diagnoses of other nonautistic disorders.

Although the ABC has been used widely and possesses strengths in terms of its ease of administration and scoring, several concerns about its psychometric properties have been identified. For example, subscales were not empirically derived and were determined by grouping items based on face validity (Sturmey, Matson, & Sevin, 1992). Though the total score alpha was .87, alphas for the subscales ranged from .38 to .79, with inadequate alpha levels found for three of the five subscales (Sturmey et al., 1992). Moreover, examination of the factor structure of the ABC has failed to replicate the subscale groupings suggested by Krug et al. (Miranda-Linne & Melin, 2002; Wadden, Bryson, & Rodger, 1991).

In addition, although the initial study found that interrater reliability was high, with 95% agreement (Krug et al., 1980b), subsequent studies using more stringent measures of interrater reliability found that it was below 70% for most items, and kappas were below .40 (Volkmar, Cicchetti, et al., 1988). Studies have also found significant differences between parent and teacher reports, though it is not clear whether these findings indicate weaknesses specific to this instrument or reflect differences encountered commonly when using multiple informant reports (Szatmari, Archer, Fisman, & Streiner, 1994; Volkmar, Cicchetti, et al., 1988).

More important are questions concerning the sensitivity and specificity of the ABC. Although means for the subscale scores and total scores have been found to be significantly higher for individuals with autism than those with other disabilities (Krug et al., 1980b; Volkmar, Cicchetti, et al., 1988; Wadden et al., 1991), several studies have found that the proposed cutoff score of 67 results in a high number of false negatives (Nordin & Gillberg, 1996; Oswald & Volkmar, 1991; Sevin, Matson, Coe, & Fee, 1991; Volkmar, Cicchetti, et al., 1988; Wadden et al., 1991). In two separate studies, only 49% to 50% of children and adolescents who met *DSM-III-R* criteria for autism had ABC scores of 67 or above (Sevin et al., 1991; Wadden et al., 1991). Another study found that the cutoff score of 67 resulted in a sensitivity and specificity of .58 and .76, respectively, for a sample of children and adults with clinical diagnoses of autism or other developmental disorders (Oswald & Volkmar, 1991). Lowering the cutoff to 58 increased sensitivity to .75 but decreased specificity to .60. Similarly, a study involving Swedish children and adolescents with autism and other disabilities found a sensitivity of .38 and a specificity of .97 using the cutoff score of 67 (Nordin & Gillberg, 1996). A cutoff of 45 raised sensitivity to 1.00 and decreased specificity to .93. In addition, studies examining the convergent validity of the ABC with other measures of autism symptomatology have been equivocal; the ABC has been shown to correlate significantly with the Gilliam Autism Rating Scale (GARS; Gilliam, 1995), but correlations with the CARS have been variable (Eaves & Milner, 1993; Sevin et al., 1991).

Because its psychometric properties have not been examined in samples of young children, the utility of the ABC as an early screening for autism is unknown. Based on results with older participants, the cutoff scores may need to be revised. In addition, results of other studies suggest that the ABC could possibly be shortened to include only the most diagnostically sensitive items (Oswald & Volkmar, 1991; Wadden et al., 1991). Revision of items to increase their developmental relevance might be necessary prior to its use with young children. Ultimately, given that it was not originally designed to screen young children for autism, the ABC may have the most utility as a measure for older children and adults.

Childhood Autism Rating Scale The CARS (Schopler, Reichler, & Renner, 1988) is a 15-item behavioral rating scale developed to discriminate between children with autism and those with other developmental disorders. Several sources of information can be used to complete the CARS, including direct observation, parent report, and chart review. Minimal training is required, even for those professionals who have less experience with autism (Schopler et al., 1988). Each CARS item is scored on a 7-point continuum from 1 to 4 (including midpoints), with scores of 1 indicating that behavior is appropriate for the child's chronological age and scores of 4 indicating that behavior is severely abnormal for the child's chronological age. A total score is calculated by summing all item scores, and total scores of 30 or above are in the autism range. Scores of 30 to 36.5 suggest mild to moderate autism, while scores of 37 to 60 suggest severe autism.

The CARS was developed and refined on a sample of more than 1,500 children, more than half of whom were under the age of 5 (Schopler et al., 1988). It is widely used in both clinical and research contexts, and studies indicate that it demonstrates many strong psychometric properties. Though interrater reliability coefficients for individual items are somewhat variable, ranging from .10 to .93, most are above .50 (Schopler et al., 1988; Sevin et al., 1991). Reliability coefficients for the CARS total score have been strong, ranging from .68 to .80 and above (Garfin, McCallon, & Cox, 1988; Sevin et al., 1991). Even when ratings have been made using different sources of information, agreement has been relatively high. For example, total scores based on parent interview correlated at .82 with CARS total scores based on observations made during an assessment procedure; agreement for risk category (autism versus not autism) was 90% and kappa was .75 (Schopler et al., 1988). Over a 1-year period, the test-retest correlation for the CARS total score was .88, and agreement on diagnostic classification was 82%, with a kappa of .64 (Schopler et al., 1988).

Available information suggests that sensitivity of the CARS is high. Sevin and colleagues (1991) found that 92% of a sample of children and adults who met *DSM-III-R* (American Psychiatric Association, 1987) diagnostic criteria for autism also met the CARS cutoff. Similarly, Eaves and Milner (1993) found the CARS to be 98% sensitive in identifying children and adults diagnosed with autism, though diagnostic criteria for the participants in their study were not specified. However, the CARS has also been found to overidentify autism relative to the *DSM-III-R*

(Van Bourgondien, Marcus, & Schopler, 1992), which itself has been found to be more inclusive relative to clinical diagnosis (Lord, 1997; Volkmar & Marans, 1999). Nonetheless, over-inclusion does not present a significant problem for the CARS as a screening instrument (Lord, 1997; Volkmar & Marans, 1999). Overall, data on the sensitivity, specificity, and predictive values of the CARS for rigorously diagnosed samples are needed.

In her work on the early diagnosis of autism, Lord (1995, 1997) found that the CARS tended to overidentify autism in 2-year-old children with cognitive deficits. Age 3 CARS score was a more accurate predictor of diagnosis, even more so when the cutoff score was raised from 30 to 32. Stone and colleagues (1999) found good agreement between CARS classification and clinical diagnosis at age 2 (82% agreement, kappa = .64) and age 3 (84% agreement, kappa = .63) for children diagnosed with autism, PDD-NOS, or nonspectrum disorders. However, data were not examined to determine whether a different cutoff resulted in better agreement.

The CARS was designed to yield a single total score rather than multiple subscale scores. Studies examining the internal consistency of the CARS have found it to be strong, with alpha coefficients ranging from .73 to .94 (Garfin et al., 1988; Schopler, Reichler, DeVellis, & Daly, 1980; Sturmey et al., 1992). However, results of factor analytic studies with the CARS suggest that it may be multidimensional, with factors measuring social behavior, sensory behavior, emotional responses, and cognitive and behavioral consistency (DiLalla & Rogers, 1994; Stella, Mundy, & Tuchman, 1999). Factor-based scale scores may have several practical research and clinical applications in terms of their use in diagnosis, intervention planning and evaluation, and obtaining information about individual differences in symptom presentation (DiLalla & Rogers, 1994; Stella et al., 1999). For example, it may be that social factor scores, as opposed to total scores or other factor scores, have the most utility in the early diagnosis of young children with autism.

Gilliam Autism Rating Scale   The GARS (Gilliam, 1995) is a behavioral checklist designed to screen for autism, inform treatment goals, and measure response to intervention in 3- to 22-year-old individuals. It comprises 56 items grouped into four subtests evaluating early development, stereotyped behaviors, communication skills, and social interaction on a four-point frequency continuum. Items for the GARS were based on characteristics of autism described in the *DSM-IV* (American Psychiatric Association, 1994) and by the Autism Society of America (1994). The GARS requires little training and can be completed in approximately 5 to 10 minutes. The three primary GARS subtests can be completed by anyone familiar with the individual's behavior, including parents, caregivers, or teachers, though completion of the Developmental Disturbance subtest requires more detailed knowledge of the individual's early development.

During the development phase, the author contacted school personnel and parents and asked them to complete the GARS, resulting in a normative sample of more than 1,000 children, adolescents, and adults with autism. Raw scores for each subtest are used to derive subtest standard scores with means of 10 and standard deviations of 3, plus a composite standard score, the autism quotient, with a mean of 100 and a standard deviation of 10. Autism quotients of 90 and above indicate that it is likely that an individual has autism; quotients below 70 indicate it is unlikely that an individual has autism, and scores between indicate that the risk status is equivocal. The author reports that a comparison of GARS subscale and total scores for a sample of individuals with autism and individuals diagnosed with other disorders (such as mental retardation, emotional disturbance, and learning disabilities) revealed significantly higher scores for individuals with autism. In addition, results of a discriminant function analysis found that the autism quotient correctly classified 90% of this sample. However, interpretation of these findings is complicated by the fact that information about how these individuals were diagnosed was not provided, diagnoses were not confirmed, and the exact relation of these participants to the normative sample is unclear.

Internal consistency of the GARS subtests ranged from .88 to .93, with a coefficient of .96 for the autism quotient. Interrater reliability coefficients ranged from .83 to .99 for the autism quotient and from .55 to .99 for the subtest scores. Two-week test-retest coefficients ranged from .81 to .86 for the subtests, and the autism quotient was .88. The GARS autism quotient and the ABC total score were also found to be significantly correlated at .94.

The initial report on the GARS revealed strong psychometric properties. However, the GARS was designed for and normed on individuals age 3 and older, and its utility as a screening measure for younger children has not yet been examined. In addition, the only independent study evaluating the psychometric properties of the GARS indicates that its use as a screening measure for preschool and school-age children is questionable (South et al., 2002). The GARS was completed for 119 children who had been stringently diagnosed using the ADI-R, the ADOS-G, and *DSM-IV* criteria. Using an autism quotient of 90 as the cutoff, the GARS demonstrated a sensitivity of .48, failing to correctly classify over half of the sample. Lowering the cutoff to an autism quotient of 80 raised the sensitivity to .80. GARS scores were not correlated significantly with scores from the ADOS-G, and the correlations found between the ADI-R Social Interaction scale and GARS scores were small, ranging from .21 to .26. A revised version of the GARS, which may address some of the concerns raised by South et al., is reportedly in development.

Social Communication Questionnaire   The Social Communication Questionnaire (SCQ)—formerly known as the Autism Screening Questionnaire (ASQ; Berument, Rutter, Lord, Pickles, & Bailey, 1999)—is a 40-item parent report questionnaire designed to screen for PDDs in individuals age 4 and older. Items were taken from the ADI-R (Lord et al., 1994) algorithm and evaluate reciprocal social interaction, language and communication, and repetitive and stereotyped behaviors. Behaviors are rated as either present or absent. A unique feature of this screening is its developmental sensitivity; different versions of the questionnaire are used for children under 6 years and over 6 years, and total scores take into account whether the individual has language.

The SCQ demonstrates many strong psychometric properties (Berument et al., 1999). Parents and caregivers completed the SCQ for 160 individuals diagnosed with PDDs (including autism, atypical autism, Asperger syndrome, fragile X, and Rett syndrome) and 40 individuals diagnosed with non-PDD disorders (including conduct disorder, language delay, mental retardation, and other psychiatric diagnoses), ranging in age from 4 to 40 years. Either the ADI or ADI-R had been completed previously for these individuals through other research studies, and all ADI-R scores were translated into ADI scores to allow for comparison between the SCQ and the ADI. Results of correlation analyses between ADI and SCQ total scores and corresponding domain scores (including social interaction, language and communication, and repetitive and stereotyped behavior) were all significant, ranging from .55 to .71.

A cutoff score of 15 or above was derived empirically using receiver operating characteristic analyses. Comparing participants with PDDs to those with other diagnoses, the sensitivity of the SCQ was .85, specificity .75, PPV .93, and NPV .55. Comparing autism to other diagnoses excluding mental retardation, the sensitivity and specificity were .96 and .80, respectively; comparing autism to mental retardation, the sensitivity and specificity were .96 and .67, respectively. Thus far, test-retest and interrater reliability have not been evaluated for this instrument, but internal consistency using coefficient alpha was .90 for the total scale.

As noted earlier, the participants in this study had all been diagnosed previously, and parents had already completed either the ADI or ADI-R interview. Although the completion of these interviews and the SCQ was separated by a period of years, it is possible that previous experience with the interviews, as well as knowledge of their child's diagnosis, affected parents' responding on the SCQ and contributed to the high correlations between the SCQ and ADI. However, in a separate study, Bishop and Norbury (2002) found good agreement between SCQ and ADI-R diagnostic categories, even when the SCQ was completed prior to administration of the ADI-R. Nonetheless, because the SCQ items were taken from the ADI-R, one would expect relatively high agreement between the measures. The psychometric properties of the SCQ have not yet been examined fully in samples of young children, though work in this area has begun. A pilot study examining the utility of the SCQ in discriminating 2- to 4-year-old children with PDD from those with other developmental disorders suggests that the cutoff score may need to be modified to maintain adequate levels of sensitivity and that the specificity is lower when used with young children (Hanson, Sullivan, Thurm, Ware, & Lord, 2002). Additional empirical work is underway to determine the most appropriate cutoff scores for this age group.

Level 2 Summary

The STAT and PDDST-Stage 2 are the only two measures that were designed specifically for the early screening of autism in clinic-based populations. More data are available supporting the use of the STAT as a Level 2 screening measure; however, as an interactive measure, it requires more training and time to administer than the PDDST. As discussed in the previous section, preliminary information on the M-CHAT, as well as clinic-based research with the CHAT (Scambler et al., 2001), indicate that these measures hold promise as Level 2 screenings, though they are not designed for this purpose. Of the other autism screening tools that exist, only the psychometric properties of the CARS have been examined in children under the age of 3. Some evidence indicates that the CARS tends to overidentify autism in 2-year-old children with cognitive deficits, and revisions to the scoring system to make it more appropriate for young children have been suggested (Lord, 1995, 1997). Although diagnostic measures should be capable of differentiating very young children with autism from those with significant cognitive deficits, for screening purposes, it is often preferable to overrefer children for further evaluation than to underrefer; consequently, the potential utility of the CARS for young children should not be discounted. In general, the Level 2 screening measures not specifically designed for young children were developed prior to research indicating the primacy of early social-communicative behaviors; consequently, their overall item content may have less utility for early identification. In addition, concerns about the psychometric properties of the ABC and GARS should be

considered carefully by those wishing to examine their utility with younger populations.

CONCLUSION

In the past decade, empirical research has resulted in the identification of several social and communicative behaviors that have utility in the early diagnosis of autism, and it has demonstrated that the diagnosis of autism at age 2 can be reliable, valid, and stable. These advances have been accompanied by increased recognition of the importance of early diagnosis and increased interest in the development of autism screening measures for young children.

However, several empirical questions remain about the utility and psychometric properties of available Level 1 and Level 2 screening measures. Several Level 1 and Level 2 measures lack information about their predictive values and/or reliability. The utility of nonspecific Level 1 screening measures (e.g., the Infant/Toddler Checklist from the CSBS DP) in identifying young children with autism remains to be examined, as does the utility of Level 2 autism screening measures not specifically designed for young children. In addition, methodological issues concerning the development of existing Level 1 and Level 2 autism screening measures—such as the use of population-based versus clinic-based samples, the exclusionary criteria and diagnostic methods used, and whether children with PDD-NOS are included—complicate interpretation of psychometric findings for available measures.

Designed for 18-month-old infants, the CHAT screens for autism at a younger age than any other measure. As our knowledge about symptom expression in infants increases, future empirical work can explore the feasibility of screening for autism in even younger children. Revisions of existing measures may be necessary to capture differences in symptom presentation at these younger ages. Preliminary work on the STAT has begun for this purpose. A Level 1 screening measure for 14-month-old infants, the Early Screening for Autism (ESA; Dietz, Willemsen-Swinkels, Buitelaar, van Daalen, & van Engeland, 1999; Willemsen-Swinkels, Buitelaar, Dietz, van Daalen, & van Engeland, 1999), is currently being developed in the Netherlands, and psychometric studies are underway. Development and implementation of these types of measures may be complicated by the paucity of information concerning the stability of autism symptoms in infants, the reluctance of many professionals to screen (or label) children at younger ages, and the possibility of developmental regression occurring at older ages.

Many of the autism screening measures discussed in this chapter may tend to underidentify higher functioning children or children with milder variants of autism spectrum disorders (Filipek et al., 1999). For these children, despite parental concerns at young ages, diagnosis may occur much later, causing them to miss the opportunity to participate in specialized early intervention (Howlin & Asgharian, 1999). Revisions to existing instruments may be necessary to increase their sensitivity in identifying children functioning at higher verbal and/or cognitive levels. For example, when used as a measure of current symptom levels, the ABC failed to identify the majority of a group of higher functioning children and adolescents with autism (Yirmiya, Sigman, & Freeman, 1994). However, all were identified when parents completed the ABC for symptoms apparent at 3 to 5 years. Along similar lines, it has been suggested that the social factor score of the CARS, rather than the total score, may be more effective in identifying higher functioning children (Stella et al., 1999).

In addition, the growing awareness and interest in milder variants of autism among researchers and clinicians have spurred the development of new screening measures. Two measures at relatively more advanced stages of development are the Autism Spectrum Screening Questionnaire (ASSQ; Ehlers, Gillberg, & Wing, 1999) and the Childhood Asperger Syndrome Test (CAST; Scott, Baron-Cohen, Bolton, & Brayne, 2002). In contrast to the screening measures reviewed earlier in this chapter, these measures were designed to identify more subtle impairments demonstrated by school-age children with milder variants of the disorder. Because of their limited utility with young children with significant cognitive and language impairments, they have not been described here in detail. Although initial results are encouraging, both measures would benefit from further empirical examination.

Finally, although the ultimate goal of any screening program is to hasten referrals for appropriate early intervention, future research could examine several possible secondary benefits of screening for autism. For example, programs designed for early autism screening may serve to increase awareness and educate parents and professionals about the early features of the disorder. In addition, interactive screening measures may serve to identify specific areas of deficit that can be addressed through early intervention programming. In sum, the process of early screening should not be considered as an end in itself, but should be viewed as a means of increasing our understanding of autism and improving our ability to provide effective interventions that will optimize the outcomes of young children.

Cross-References

Issues of diagnosis and epidemiology of autism are discussed in Chapters 1 and 2, respectively, diagnostic measures are reviewed in Chapter 28. Chapters 29 through 33 focus on various aspects of assessment. The presentation of autism in infants and very young children is described in Chapter 8.

REFERENCES

Adrien, J. L., Barthelemy, C., Perrot, A., Roux, S., Lenoir, P., Hameury, L., et al. (1992). Validity and reliability of the Infant Behavioral Summarized Evaluation (IBSE): A rating scale for the assessment of young children with autism and developmental disorders. *Journal of Autism and Developmental Disorders, 22*, 375–394.

Adrien, J. L., Lenoir, P., Martineau, J., Perrot, A., Hameury, L., Larmande, C., et al. (1993). Blind ratings of early symptoms of autism based upon family home movies. *Journal of the American Academy of Child and Adolescent Psychiatry, 32*, 617–626.

American Academy of Pediatrics Committee on Children with Disabilities. (2001). The pediatrician's role in the diagnosis and management of autistic spectrum disorder in children. *Pediatrics, 107*, 1221–1226.

American Psychiatric Association. (1987). *Diagnostic and statistical manual of mental disorders* (3rd ed., rev.). Washington, DC: Author.

American Psychiatric Association. (1994). *Diagnostic and statistical manual of mental disorders* (4th ed.). Washington, DC: Author.

Autism Society of America. (1994). Definition of autism. *The Advocate: Newsletter of the Autism Society of America, 26,* 3.

Aylward, G. P. (1997). Conceptual issues in developmental screening and assessment. *Journal of Developmental and Behavioral Pediatrics, 18,* 340–349.

Baird, G., Charman, T., Baron-Cohen, S., Cox, A., Swettenham, J., Wheelwright, S., et al. (2000). A screening instrument for autism at 18 months of age: A 6-year follow-up study. *Journal of the American Academy of Child and Adolescent Psychiatry, 39,* 694–702.

Baranek, G. T. (1999). Autism during infancy: A retrospective video analysis of sensory-motor and social behaviors at 9–12 months of age. *Journal of Autism and Developmental Disorders, 29,* 213–224.

Baranek, G. T. (2002). Efficacy of sensory and motor interventions for children with autism. *Journal of Autism and Developmental Disorders, 32,* 397–422.

Baron-Cohen, S., Allen, J., & Gillberg, C. (1992). Can autism be detected at 18 months? The needle, the haystack, and the CHAT. *British Journal of Psychiatry, 161,* 839–843.

Baron-Cohen, S., Cox, A., Baird, G., Swettenham, J., Nightingale, N., Morgan, K., et al. (1996). Psychological markers in the detection of autism in infancy in a large population. *British Journal of Psychiatry, 168,* 158–163.

Berument, S. K., Rutter, M. L., Lord, C., Pickles, A., & Bailey, A. (1999). Autism screening questionnaire: Diagnostic validity. *British Journal of Psychiatry, 175,* 444–451.

Bishop, D. V. M., & Norbury, C. F. (2002). Exploring the borderlands of autistic disorder and specific language impairment: A study using standardised diagnostic instruments. *Journal of Child Psychology and Psychiatry, 43,* 1–13.

Bondy, A. S., & Frost, L. A. (1995). Educational approaches in preschool: Behavior techniques in a public school setting. In E. Schopler & G. B. Mesibov (Eds.), *Learning and cognition in autism* (pp. 311–333). New York: Plenum Press.

Bricker, D., & Squires, J. (1999). *Ages and Stages Questionnaires* (2nd ed.). Baltimore: Paul H. Brookes.

Brigance, A. (1986). *The Brigance screens.* North Billerica, MA: Curriculum Associates.

Charman, T., & Baird, G. (2002). Practitioner review: Diagnosis of autism spectrum disorder in 2- and 3-year-old children. *Journal of Child Psychology and Psychiatry, 43,* 289–305.

Charman, T., Baron-Cohen, S., Baird, G., Cox, A., Wheelwright, S., Swettenham, J., et al. (2001). Commentary: The Modified Checklist for Autism in Toddlers. *Journal of Autism and Developmental Disorders, 31,* 145–148.

Charman, T., Swettenham, J., Baron-Cohen, S., Cox, A., Baird, G., & Drew, A. (1997). Infants with autism: An investigation of empathy, pretend play, joint attention, and imitation. *Developmental Psychology, 33,* 781–789.

Clark, A., & Harrington, R. (1999). On diagnosing rare disorders rarely: Appropriate use of screening instruments. *Journal of Child Psychology and Psychiatry, 40,* 287–290.

Committee on Educational Interventions for Children with Autism. (2001). *Educating children with autism.* Washington, DC: National Academy Press.

Cox, A., Klein, K., Charman, T., Baird, G., Baron-Cohen, S., Swettenham, J., et al. (1999). Autism spectrum disorders at 20 and 42 months of age: Stability of clinical and ADI-R diagnosis. *Journal of Child Psychology and Psychiatry, 40,* 719–732.

Dawson, G., Ashman, S. B., & Carver, L. J. (2000). The role of early experience in shaping behavioral and brain development and its implications for social policy. *Development and Psychopathology, 12,* 695–712.

Dawson, G., Meltzoff, A. N., Osterling, J., & Rinaldi, J. (1998). Neuropsychological correlates of early symptoms of autism. *Child Development, 69,* 1276–1285.

Dawson, G., Meltzoff, A. N., Osterling, J., Rinaldi, J., & Brown, E. (1998). Children with autism fail to orient to naturally occurring social stimuli. *Journal of Autism and Developmental Disorders, 28,* 479–485.

Dietz, C., Willemsen-Swinkels, S. H. N., Buitelaar, J. K., van Daalen, E., & van Engeland, H. (1999, April). *Early detection of autism: Population screening.* Poster presented at the biennial meeting of the Society for Research in Child Development, Albuquerque, NM.

DiLalla, D. L., & Rogers, S. J. (1994). Domains of the Childhood Autism Rating Scale: Relevance for diagnosis and treatment. *Journal of Autism and Developmental Disorders, 24,* 115–128.

Dissanayake, C., & Crossley, S. A. (1996). Proximity and sociable behaviors in autism: Evidence for attachment. *Journal of Child Psychology and Psychiatry, 37,* 149–156.

Eaves, R. C., & Milner, B. (1993). The criterion-related validity of the Childhood Autism Rating Scale and the Autism Behavior Checklist. *Journal of Abnormal Child Psychology, 21,* 481–491.

Ehlers, S., Gillberg, C., & Wing, L. (1999). A screening questionnaire for Asperger syndrome and other high-functioning autism spectrum disorders in school age children. *Journal of*

Autism and Developmental Disorders, 29, 129–141.

Filipek, P. A., Accardo, P. J., Ashwal, S., Baranek, G. T., Cook, E. H., Jr., Dawson, G., et al. (2000). Practice parameter: Screening and diagnosis of autism: Report of the Quality Standards Subcommittee of the American Academy of Neurology and the Child Neurology Society. *Neurology, 55,* 468–479.

Filipek, P. A., Accardo, P. J., Baranek, G. T., Cook, E. H., Jr., Dawson, G., Gordon, B., et al. (1999). The screening and diagnosis of autistic spectrum disorders. *Journal of Autism and Developmental Disorders, 29,* 439–484.

Frankenburg, W. K. (1974). Selection of diseases and tests in pediatric screening. *Pediatrics, 54,* 612–616.

Frankenburg, W. K. (1986). *Revised Denver Pre-Screening Developmental Questionnaire.* Denver, CO: Denver Developmental Materials.

Frankenburg, W. K., Dodds, J., Archer, P., Shapiro, H., & Bresnick, B. (1996). The Denver II: A major revision and restandardization of the Denver Developmental Screening Test. *Pediatrics, 89,* 91–97.

Garfin, D. G., McCallon, D., & Cox, R. (1988). Validity and reliability of the Childhood Autism Rating Scale with autistic adolescents. *Journal of Autism and Developmental Disorders, 18,* 367–378.

Gilliam, J. E. (1995). *Gilliam Autism Rating Scale.* Austin, TX: ProEd.

Glascoe, F. P. (1991). Developmental screening: Rationale, methods, and application. *Infants and Young Children, 4,* 1–10.

Glascoe, F. P. (1996). *A validation study and the psychometric properties of the Brigance screens.* North Billerica, MA: Curriculum Associates.

Glascoe, F. P. (1998). *Collaborating with parents: Using Parents' Evaluation of Developmental Status to detect and address developmental and behavioral problems.* Nashville, TN: Ellsworth & Vandermeer.

Hanson, E., Sullivan, N., Thurm, A., Ware, J., & Lord, C. (2002, November). *Social Communication Questionnaire (SCQ).* Poster presented at the International Meeting for Autism Research, Orlando, FL.

Happé, F. G. E. (1994). Annotation: Current psychological theories of autism: The "Theory of Mind" account and rival theories. *Journal of Child Psychology and Psychiatry, 35,* 215–229.

Harris, S. L., & Handleman, J. S. (2000). Age and IQ at intake as predictors of placement for young children with autism: A four- to six-year follow-up. *Journal of Autism and Developmental Disorders, 30,* 137–142.

Harris, S. L., Handleman, J. S., Gordon, R., Kristoff, B., & Fuentes, F. (1991). Changes in cognitive and language functioning of preschool children with autism. *Journal of Autism and Developmental Disorders, 21,* 281–290.

Howlin, P., & Asgharian, A. (1999). The diagnosis of autism and Asperger syndrome: Findings from a survey of 770 families. *Developmental Medicine and Child Neurology, 41,* 834–839.

Huttenlocher, P. R. (1994). Synaptogenesis in human cerebral cortex. In G. Dawson & K. W. Fischer (Eds.), *Human behavior and the developing brain* (pp. 137–152). New York: Guilford Press.

Ireton, H. (1992). *Child development inventories.* Minneapolis, MN: Behavior Science Systems.

Ireton, H., & Glascoe, F. P. (1995). Assessing children's development using parents' reports: The Child Development Inventory. *Clinical Pediatrics, 34,* 248–255.

Krug, D. A., Arick, J. R., & Almond, P. J. (1980a). *Autism screening instrument for educational planning.* Austin, TX: ProEd.

Krug, D. A., Arick, J. R., & Almond, P. J. (1980b). Behavior checklist for identifying severely handicapped individuals with high levels of autistic behavior. *Journal of Child Psychology and Psychiatry and Allied Disciplines, 21,* 221–229.

Lord, C. (1995). Follow-up of two-year-olds referred for possible autism. *Journal of Child Psychology and Psychiatry, 36,* 1365–1382.

Lord, C. (1997). Diagnostic instruments in autism spectrum disorders. In D. J. Cohen & F. R. Volkmar (Eds.), *Handbook of autism and pervasive developmental disorders* (2nd ed., pp. 460–483). New York: Wiley.

Lord, C., Risi, S., & DiLavore, P. C. (1999, April). *From diagnosis to screening using longitudinal data in autism.* Poster presented at the biennial meeting of the Society for Research in Child Development, Albuquerque, NM.

Lord, C., Risi, S., Lambrecht, L., Cook, E. H., Jr., Leventhal, B. L., DiLavore, P. C., et al. (2000). The Autism Diagnostic Observation Schedule-Generic: A standard measure of social and communication deficits associated with the spectrum of autism. *Journal of Autism and Developmental Disorders, 30,* 205–223.

Lord, C., Rutter, M. L., & Le Couteur, A. (1994). Autism Diagnostic Interview-Revised: A revised version of a diagnostic interview for caregivers of individuals with possible pervasive developmental disorders. *Journal of Autism and Developmental Disorders, 24,* 659–685.

McEachin, J. J., Smith, T., & Lovaas, O. I. (1993). Long-term outcome for children with autism who received early intensive behavioral treatment. *American Journal on Mental Retardation, 97,* 359–372.

Meisels, S. J. (1985). *Developmental screening in early childhood* (Rev. ed.). Washington, DC: National Association for the Education of Young Children.

Miranda-Linne, F. M., & Melin, L. (2002). A factor analytic study of the Autism Behavior Checklist. *Journal of Autism and Developmental Disorders, 32,* 181–188.

Mundy, P., & Crowson, M. (1997). Joint attention and early social communication: Implications for research on intervention with autism. *Journal of Autism and Developmental Disorders, 27,* 653–676.

Mundy, P., & Neal, A. R. (2001). Neural plasticity, joint attention, and a transactional social-orienting model of autism. In L. M. Glidden (Ed.), *International review of research in mental retardation* (Vol. 23, pp. 139–168). San Diego, CA: Academic Press.

Mundy, P., Sigman, M., Ungerer, J., & Sherman, T. (1986). Defining the social deficits of autism: The contribution of non-verbal communication measures. *Journal of Child Psychology and Psychiatry, 27,* 657–669.

Neisworth, J. T., Bagnato, S. J., Salvia, J., & Hunt, F. M. (1999). *TABS manual for the Temperament and Atypical Behavior Scale.* Baltimore: Paul H. Brookes.

Nordin, V., & Gillberg, C. (1996). Autism spectrum disorders in children with physical or mental disability or both: II. Screening aspects. *Developmental Medicine and Child Neurology, 38,* 314–324.

Osterling, J. A., & Dawson, G. (1994). Early recognition of children with autism: A study of first birthday home videotapes. *Journal of Autism and Developmental Disorders, 24,* 247–257.

Osterling, J. A., Dawson, G., & Munson, J. A. (2002). Early recognition of 1-year-old infants with autism spectrum disorder versus mental retardation. *Development and Psychopathology, 14,* 239–251.

Oswald, D. P., & Volkmar, F. R. (1991). Signal detection analysis of items from the Autism Behavior Checklist. *Journal of Autism and Developmental Disorders, 21,* 543–549.

Phillips, W., Baron-Cohen, S., & Rutter, M. L. (1992). The role of eye-contact in goal detection: Evidence from normal infants and children with autism or mental handicap. *Development and Psychopathology, 4,* 375–384.

Riegelman, R. K., & Hirsch, R. P. (1989). *Studying a study and testing a test: How to read the medical literature* (2nd ed.). Boston: Little, Brown.

Robins, D. L., Fein, D., Barton, M. L., & Green, J. A. (2001a). The Modified Checklist for Autism in Toddlers: An initial study investigating the early detection of autism and pervasive developmental disorders. *Journal of Autism and Developmental Disorders, 31,* 131–144.

Robins, D. L., Fein, D., Barton, M. L., & Green, J. A. (2001b). Reply to Charman et al.'s commentary on the Modified Checklist for Autism in Toddlers. *Journal of Autism and Developmental Disorders, 31,* 149–151.

Robins, D. L., Fein, D., Barton, M. L., Green, J. A., Kleinman, J., & Dixon, P. (2002, July). *The M-CHAT: An American modification of the CHAT detects autism at age 2.* Paper presented at the World Association of Infant Mental Health, Amsterdam.

Rogers, S. J. (2001). Diagnosis of autism before the age of 3. In L. M. Glidden (Ed.), *International review of research in mental retardation* (Vol. 23, pp. 1–31). San Diego, CA: Academic Press.

Rogers, S. J., & Lewis, H. (1989). An effective day treatment model for young children with pervasive developmental disorders. *Journal of the American Academy of Child and Adolescent Psychiatry, 28,* 207–214.

Rutter, M. L. (1978). Diagnosis and definition of childhood autism. *Journal of Autism and Childhood Schizophrenia, 8,* 139–161.

Scambler, D., Rogers, S. J., & Wehner, E. A. (2001). Can the Checklist for Autism in Toddlers differentiate young children with autism from those with developmental delays? *Journal of the American Academy of Child and Adolescent Psychiatry, 40,* 1457–1463.

Schopler, E., Reichler, R. J., DeVellis, R. F., & Daly, K. (1980). Toward objective classification of childhood autism: Childhood Autism Rating Scale (CARS). *Journal of Autism and Developmental Disorders, 10,* 91–103.

Schopler, E., Reichler, R. J., & Renner, B. R. (1988). *The Childhood Autism Rating Scale (CARS).* Los Angeles: Western Psychological Services.

Scott, F. J., Baron-Cohen, S., Bolton, P., & Brayne, C. (2002). The CAST (Childhood Asperger Syndrome Test): Preliminary development of a UK screen for mainstream primary-school-age children. *Autism: International Journal of Research and Practice, 6,* 9–31.

Sevin, J. A., Matson, J. L., Coe, D. A., & Fee, V. E. (1991). A comparison and evaluation of three commonly used autism scales. *Journal of Autism and Developmental Disorders, 21,* 417–432.

Short, A. B., & Schopler, E. (1988). Factors relating to age of onset in autism. *Journal of Autism and Developmental Disorders, 18,* 207–216.

Siegel, B. (1996). *Pervasive Developmental Disorders Screening Test.* Unpublished manuscript, University of California at San Francisco.

Siegel, B. (1998, June). *Early screening and diagnosis in autistic spectrum disorders: The Pervasive Developmental Disorders Screening Test (PDDST).* Paper presented at the NIH State of the Science in Autism: Screening and Diagnosis Working Conference, Bethesda, MD.

Siegel, B., & Hayer, C. (1999, April). *Detection of autism in the 2nd and 3rd year: The Pervasive Developmental Disorders Screening Test (PDDST).* Poster presented at the biennial meeting for the Society for Research in Child Development, Albuquerque, NM.

Siegel, B., Pliner, C., Eschler, J., & Elliot, G. R. (1988). How children with autism are diagnosed: Difficulties in identification of children with multiple developmental delays. *Developmental and Behavioral Pediatrics, 9,* 199–204.

Siegel, B., Vukicevic, J., & Spitzer, R. L. (1990). Using signal detection methodology to revise *DSM-III-R:* Re-analysis of the *DSM-III-R* national field trials for autistic disorder. *Journal of Psychiatric Research, 24,* 293–311.

Sigman, M., Kasari, C., Kwon, J., & Yirmiya, N. (1992). Responses to the negative emotions of others by autistic, mentally retarded, and normal children. *Child Development, 63,* 796–807.

Sigman, M., & Ungerer, J. A. (1984). Cognitive and language skills in autistic, mentally retarded, and normal children. *Developmental Psychology, 20,* 293–302.

Snow, M. E., Hertzig, M. E., & Shapiro, T. (1987). Expressions of emotion in young autistic children. *Journal of the American Academy of Child and Adolescent Psychiatry, 26,* 836–838.

South, M., Williams, B. J., McMahon, W. M., Owely, T., Filipek, P. A., Shernoff, E., et al. (2002). Utility of the Gilliam Autism Rating Scale in research and clinical populations. *Journal of Autism and Developmental Disorders, 32,* 593–599.

Spitzer, R. L., & Siegel, B. (1990). The *DSM-III-R* field trial of pervasive developmental disorders. *Journal of the American Academy of Child and Adolescent Psychiatry, 29,* 855–862.

Squires, J. K. (2000). Identifying social/emotional and behavioral problems in infants and toddlers. *Infant-Toddler Intervention, 10,* 107–119.

Stella, J., Mundy, P., & Tuchman, R. (1999). Social and nonsocial factors in the Childhood Autism Rating Scale. *Journal of Autism and Developmental Disorders, 29,* 307–317.

Stone, W. L., Coonrod, E. E., & Ousley, O. Y. (2000). Screening Tool for Autism Two-Year-Olds (STAT): Development and preliminary data. *Journal of Autism and Developmental Disorders, 30,* 607–612.

Stone, W. L., Coonrod, E. E., Pozdol, S. L., & Turner, L. M. (2003). The Parent Interview for Autism-Clinical version (PIA-CV): A measure of behavioral change for young children with autism. *Autism: International Journal of Research and Practice, 7,* 9–30.

Stone, W. L., Coonrod, E. E., Turner, L. M., & Pozdol, S. L. (in press). *Psychometric properties of the STAT for early autism screening.* Journal of Autism and Developmental Disorders.

Stone, W. L., & Hogan, K. L. (1993). A structured parent interview for identifying young children with autism. *Journal of Autism and Developmental Disorders, 23,* 639–652.

Stone, W. L., Lee, E. B., Ashford, L., Brissie, J., Hepburn, S. L., Coonrod, E. E., et al. (1999). Can autism be diagnosed accurately in children under 3 years? *Journal of Child Psychology and Psychiatry, 40,* 219–226.

Stone, W. L., Lemanek, K. L., Fishel, P. T., Fernandez, M. C., & Altemeier, W. A. (1990). Play and imitation skills in the diagnosis of autism in young children. *Pediatrics, 86,* 267–272.

Stone, W. L., & Ousley, O. Y. (1997). *STAT Manual: Screening Tool for Autism in Two-Year-Olds.* Unpublished manuscript, Vanderbilt University, Nashville, TN.

Stone, W. L., Ousley, O. Y., & Littleford, C. D. (1997). Motor imitation in young children with autism: What's the object? *Journal of Abnormal Child Psychology, 25,* 475–485.

Stone, W. L., Ousley, O. Y., Yoder, P. J., Hogan, K. L., & Hepburn, S. L. (1997). Nonverbal communication in 2- and 3-year-old children with autism. *Journal of Autism and Developmental Disorders, 27,* 677–696.

Strain, P. S., Hoyson, M., & Jamieson, B. (1985, Spring). Normally developing preschoolers as intervention agents for autistic-like children: Effects on class deportment and social interaction. *Journal of the Division for Early Childhood,* 105–115.

Sturmey, P., Matson, J. L., & Sevin, J. A. (1992). Analysis of the internal consistency of three autism scales. *Journal of Autism and Developmental Disorders, 22,* 321–328.

Szatmari, P., Archer, L., Fisman, S., & Streiner, D. L. (1994). Parent and teacher agreement in the assessment of pervasive developmental disorders. *Journal of Autism and Developmental Disorders, 24,* 703–717.

Van Bourgondien, M. E., Marcus, L. M., & Schopler, E. (1992). Comparison of *DSM-III-R* and Childhood Autism Rating Scale diagnoses of autism. *Journal of Autism and Developmental Disorders, 22,* 493–506.

Volkmar, F. R., Cicchetti, D. V., Dykens, E., Sparrow, S. S., Leckman, J. F., & Cohen, D. J. (1988). An evaluation of the Autism Behavior Checklist. *Journal of Autism and Developmental Disorders, 18,* 81–97.

Volkmar, F. R., Cohen, D. J., Hoshino, Y., Rende, R. D., & Paul, R. (1988). Phenomenology and classification of the childhood psychoses. *Psychological Medicine, 18,* 191–201.

Volkmar, F. R., & Marans, W. D. (1999). Measures for assessing pervasive developmental and communication disorders. In D. Shaffer, C. P. Lucas & J. E. Ritchers (Eds.), *Diagnostic assessment in child and adolescent psychopathology* (pp. 167–205). New York: Guilford Press.

Volkmar, F. R., Stier, D. M., & Cohen, D. J. (1985). Age of recognition of pervasive developmental disorder. *American Journal of Psychiatry, 142,* 1450–1452.

Wadden, N. P. K., Bryson, S. E., & Rodger, R. S. (1991). A closer look at the Autism Behavior Checklist: Discriminant validity and factor structure. *Journal of Autism and Developmental Disorders, 21,* 529–541.

Werner, E., Dawson, G., Osterling, J., & Dinno, N. (2000). Recognition of autism spectrum disorder before one year of age: A retrospective study based on home videotapes. *Journal of Autism and Developmental Disorders, 30,* 157–162.

Wetherby, A. M., & Prizant, B. M. (2002). *Communication and Symbolic Behavior Scales Developmental Profile.* Baltimore: Paul H. Brookes.

Wetherby, A. M., Yonclas, D. G., & Bryan, A. A. (1989). Communicative profiles of preschool children with handicaps: Implications for early identification. *Journal of Speech and Hearing Disorders, 54,* 148–158.

Willemsen-Swinkels, S. H. N., Buitelaar, J. K., Dietz, C., van Daalen, E., & van Engeland, H. (1999, April). *Screening Instrument for the early detection of autism at 14 months.* Poster presented at the biennial meeting of the Society for Research in Child Development, Albuquerque, NM.

Yirmiya, N., Sigman, M., & Freeman, B. J. (1994). Comparison between diagnostic instruments for identifying high-functioning children with autism. *Journal of Autism and Developmental Disorders, 24,* 281–291.

CHAPTER 28

Diagnostic Instruments in Autistic Spectrum Disorders

CATHERINE LORD AND CHRISTINA CORSELLO

The development of diagnostic instruments in the past 30 years is an example of the interplay between clinical and research needs in the field of autism. When judged from field trials of diagnostic criteria (Volkmar et al., 1994), autism is one of the most reliably diagnosed disorders in child psychiatry. However, many diagnostic aspects of the disorder provide unique challenges, as well as raising issues shared with other childhood onset disorders. In this chapter, first general and then specific issues pertaining to designing and selecting instruments for diagnosis and measurement of core features of autistic spectrum disorders (ASDs) are considered. A brief historical review of some of the first standardized instruments used for diagnosis of autism is next, followed by short descriptions of some of the most common instruments used in diagnosis and measurement of the features that define ASD. The chapter concludes with information about the use of instruments for specific purposes, such as measuring change, ending with a general discussion. Because the emphasis of the chapter is on issues pertaining to the design and selection of measures, sections on individual instruments are not intended to be comprehensive. See review articles by Parks (1988) and Teal and Wiebe (1986), as well as original works cited in the text, for further information.

GENERAL ISSUES IN DIAGNOSIS OF AUTISTIC SPECTRUM DISORDERS

Autism and other pervasive developmental disorders (ASDs) are associated with a broad range of intellectual and language skills, particularly across time. This range affects the way that the disorder's defining symptoms are manifested. Because ASDs typically begin when children are infants or toddlers and continue into adulthood, precise identification of well-defined behaviors that are necessary and sufficient to diagnoses across developmental levels is a complex task (Lord, Pickles, DiLavore, & Shulman 1996; Volkmar et al., 1994). For example, although deficits in simple pretense and elicited imitation are typical of most children with autism at certain points in development, these deficits do not necessarily discriminate autism from other disorders at either very basic levels of development (i.e., age equivalents of under 12 months; Charman et al., 1998) or at much more sophisticated levels of development (i.e., very high-functioning verbal adults; Happé, 1995).

Appreciation is expressed to NICHD (U19HD35482) through the Collaborative Program for Excellence in Autism (CPEA) and NIMH (R01MH066496) that provided support to the authors during the preparation of this manuscript and to Colleen Hall, Kaite Gotham, Daniel Karstofsky, and Amanda Edgell, who helped in the preparation of this chapter.

The challenge presented by changes in development in autism is similar to issues that affect the measurement of general intellectual development in all children. In the case of general intelligence testing, however, years of investigation, access to large populations, and population samples of normative data have allowed the development of instruments such as the Wechsler tests (WISC-IV; Wechsler, 2003), WAIS-III (Wechsler, 1997), and WPPSI-III (Wechsler, 2002). These tests contain different tasks for children and adults at different levels. Standard scores are computed according to small gradations in age. In ASDs, with the exception of the revised Autism Diagnostic Observation Schedule (ADOS: Lord, Rutter, DiLavore, & Risi, 1999; Lord, Risi, et al., 2000), such grading has not yet been attempted, and may not be feasible, given the incidence and variability of the disorders.

In addition, while cognitive tests use chronological age and population demographics to define what is "average," identifying the "average" child with autism is much more complicated, particularly with small samples. Using large samples who have not been systematically assessed or recruited according to epidemiological standards may also lead to unrepresentative scores (see Ozonoff, South, & Miller, 2000). Eventually, pooled research samples that result in very large sample sizes and/or methods such as latent class analyses may be helpful in this endeavor (Mahoney et al., 1998). In the meantime, studies that explicitly compare distributions of different samples (e.g., Szatmari et al., 2002) provide important information about the consistency of diagnosis across populations.

In addition, as discussed in more detail later in this chapter, issues arise about how to best define comparison group to autism in order to generate appropriate norms. Providing normative data based on chronological age, as is done for most well-known general intellectual assessments, is not sufficient, because ASDs are often, but not always, associated with mental handicap. Thus, differences obtained between mentally handicapped children with autism and chronological-age matched nonautistic children who are not mentally handicapped may be attributed to autism, mental handicap, or both. On the other hand, the generation of norms based on all combinations of chronological age and level of mental handicap is not feasible without very large samples, and sometimes not even then (e.g., identifying infants with mild idiopathic mental retardation may be impossible).

A further factor is language delay. Even when level of mental handicap is addressed through a research design, children with autism-related disorders often (with some notable exceptions) show more severe language delays than other children of equivalent nonverbal level. Any diagnostic instrument that relies heavily on behaviors associated with receptive or expressive language competence must take this into account (Lord, Storoschuk, Rutter, & Pickles, 1993). However, exactly how to do so becomes a complex decision (Happé, 1995; Hobson, 1991). Trying to control for language delay may also "control for" autism itself. It may result in comparisons that are invalid for other reasons (e.g., comparing 2-year-olds with autism to nonhandicapped 8-month-olds of equivalent receptive language skill).

In addition, the relationship between autism and language impairment is complicated by the fact that the expressive language of individuals with no or very little spontaneous speech may not show as many abnormalities as the language of more verbally fluent persons with autism. This relationship affects attempts to quantify severity in any additive way. Thus, in the Autism Behavior Checklist (ABC; Krug, Arick, & Almond, 1980b) and in the Autism Diagnostic Interview-Revised (ADI-R; Rutter, Le Couteur, & Lord, 2003), both described later, an abnormality score is computed by adding the number of ways in which a child or adult's language is unusual (e.g., pronoun reversal, delayed echolalia, neologisms). This strategy results in individuals with more complex language scoring as more abnormal than individuals who cannot speak (Miranda-Linne, Fredrika, & Melin, 1997; Rutter et al., 2003). A recent factor analysis carried out on the ADI-R (Lord, Rutter, & Le Couteur, 1994; Tadevosyan-Leyfer et al., 2003) credited nonverbal children with maximum scores of severity on verbal items. This resulted in nonverbal children scoring as most severe on a hierarchy of language items, overlapping with children with the most sophisticated language and many abnormalities; not a result that is very meaningful or interpretable. The ADI-R attempts to avoid this problem by having separate domain scores for verbal and nonverbal communication; however, this strategy is not ideal for researchers who need a single overall severity score.

In general, classification systems and diagnostic instruments for ASDs have been most accurate in addressing autism in somewhat verbal, mildly to moderately mentally handicapped school age children. Classification systems and diagnostic instruments decrease in interpretability the farther one moves from this group (Lord & Bailey, 2002; Lord et al., 1996). Unfortunately, diagnostic instruments are most needed for children and adults who do not fall within this most easily recognized prototype. As discussed later, it is important that consumers who use diagnostic instruments take into account the biases that an instrument shows for populations who fall outside the most commonly studied group of children with autism, such as children with nonautism ASDs, such as Asperger's Disorder and Pervasive Developmental Disorders, Not Otherwise Specified (PDD-NOS). The difficulties are less relevant for Rett Syndrome and Fragile X, because these disorders have biological markers, however, questions remain when children with these disorders meet standard diagnostic criteria for autism.

Issues in Selecting the Appropriate Focus and Level of Analysis

An alternative to organizing a diagnostic instrument around very specific behaviors is to develop measures of broadly defined deficits, such as impairments in social reciprocity or circumscribed interests that are relevant to the behaviors of individuals across a range of chronological ages and developmental levels. However, answering questions about these broad conceptualizations may be difficult for naive observers, such as nonexpert clinicians (Volkmar et al., 1994) or parents (Schopler & Reichler, 1972). This seems especially true in diagnoses of young children (see Charman et al., 1998; DiLavore, Lord, & Rutter, 1995; Lord et al., 1993), for whom it may be difficult to disentangle well-coordinated social behaviors produced as part of familiar, physical routines from spontaneous, socially motivated

interactions. For example, in a study comparing parent report in a structured interview to direct observations, good agreement across the two methods for the occurrence of abnormalities emerged for only 3 of 16 items taken from *DSM-III-R:* abnormal social play, stereotyped body movements, and restricted range of interests (Stone & Lemanek, 1990). Differentiation for adults between deficits specific to autism and those associated with any severe, chronic psychiatric disorder that drastically limits social contact and everyday opportunities, also becomes more difficult (Rutter, Mawhood, & Howlin, 1992; Volkmar et al., 1994).

Parent and child reports are not interchangeable. This issue is most relevant to high-functioning older children, adolescents, and adults with autism and ASDs who can be asked to describe their own symptoms and concerns. For certain behaviors, parent report may be more valid and reliable over time (e.g., reports of friendships, development of play; Lord et al., 1989); for others, either direct observation (such as of very young children with autism; Lord, Cook, Leventhal, & Amaral, 2000) or self-reports, such as for mood and interest in the opposite sex (Howlin, Mawhood, & Rutter, 2000; Mawhood, Howlin, & Rutter, 2000), may be more accurate indicators. In other areas of developmental psychopathology, with a few notable exceptions (e.g., self-reports of anxiety or depressive feelings), informant accounts have often been better discriminators than alternative methods (Bird, Gould, & Staghezza, 1992).

Using multiple sources may address some of these issues by helping to place diagnostic information in developmental and social contexts. For example, if a child appeared fascinated by pencils during an observation, a parent's account of his fascination with stick-like materials at home would be important in evaluating whether this was a consistent focus or a brief interest. Information about a history of very limited social interaction beginning in early childhood can place reports of social isolation into context for an adult client. From the reverse perspective, observation of how a child responds when a parent is asked to call his name may be a helpful complement to a parent's description of the child's response to family members' attempts to get his attention at home. Ideally, diagnostic instruments would maximize use of direct observations and parents' and teachers' descriptions, while getting broader information directly from individuals with ASD without requiring them to draw inferences that they often do not have the knowledge to make (e.g., about the nature of autism and the applicability of that term to themselves). However, how to best combine information from multiple sources is not obvious (Kraemer, 1992; Offord et al., 1996). For example, one method of quantifying severity might be to consider information from different sources as separate repeated measures of a hypothetical construct, such as qualitative impairments in social interaction (Grinager, Cox, & Yairi, 1997).

Instruments also differ in the degree to which they emphasize the presence of observable abnormalities or the absence of normally developing features. Sometimes this distinction is arbitrary, as in descriptions of the use of gaze by children with autism as either "unusual eye contact" or "failure to use gaze to regulate social interaction in subtle ways." The former describes the presence of an abnormality and the latter describes the absence of a prosocial behavior. In young children with autism, the absence of behaviors such as eye contact, smiling, and social responses, may be more specific and more predictive of outcome than abnormalities (Lord, 1995; Venter, Lord, & Schopler, 1992). It is also more highly correlated with chronological and cognitive age (Tadevosyan-Leyfer et al., 2003). For other diagnostic features, the presence of clear abnormalities and the absence of normal development may be strongly related, but the two perspectives may not necessarily be the same. For example, developmental and behavioral intervention studies would suggest that the presence of unusual preoccupations and restricted interests is associated with the absence of early social play. If a child is taught developmentally appropriate play skills, he will show fewer stereotyped behaviors (Schopler, 1976); however, he may still have restricted interests. To our knowledge, this assumption has not been directly tested outside of evaluations of specific interventions.

Even though the two approaches (computing the presence of abnormalities and determining the number of absences of prosocial features) are clearly related, they have somewhat different implications for diagnostic instruments. Social-communicative features of autism tend to be described in terms of absences, while oddities in interests and behavior, as well as a few specific characteristics of language (e.g., stereotypic speech) tend to be described in terms of the presence of abnormalities. When they occur, odd behaviors, such as hand and finger mannerisms or repeated smelling of objects, may be more striking and obviously abnormal than the lack of typical development in a particular area. However, such obviously abnormal behaviors, even if a child or adult engages in them frequently at home or school, may not always occur during a relatively brief observation. For example, in one study, only 60% of verbal, mildly mentally handicapped adolescents with autism and 35% of very high-functioning, verbal adolescents with autism exhibited clearly observable repetitive behaviors during a half-hour structured observation, though all of these individuals were described by their parents as engaging in such behaviors at home on a regular basis (Lord et al., 1989). None of the language and chronological-age matched mentally handicapped and normally developing adolescents exhibited these behaviors during the observation. The *presence* of these behaviors during an observation was important diagnostically, but the *absence* during that one observation was not interpretable. As already noted, there is reason to believe that such abnormalities may be less directly related to clinical outcome than are social impairments and more broadly based aspects of communication (Cox et al., 1999; Venter et al., 1992). Nevertheless, brief descriptions of clearly abnormal behaviors, particularly sensory reactions to environmental stimuli, are more amenable to checklists and screening measures (Krug et al., 1980b; Rimland, 1971) than longerwinded descriptions of subtle differences in nonverbal social behaviors, though the abnormal behaviors may be less indicative of outcome and of diagnoses made by experienced clinicians than other measures.

It is important to remember that, in a diagnosis, the diagnosticians tend to find what they look for or ask about. That is, the content and the nature of the behaviors that are observed (or described) and the content and the nature of the ways in which they are reduced or "coded" affect the end product of diagnosis. Scales that employ linear approaches to scores (e.g., using a single total) with a single cut-off more easily quantify examples of dysfunction, but also are more likely affected by factors outside autism, most notably co-occurring mental retardation, than are instruments that require thresholds in different areas. Scales that require meeting of multiple thresholds are tied to specific classification systems and the theories that underlie them (e.g., *DSM IV* and *ICD-10*). Thus, they may underestimate cases because of requirements for distribution of scores or because the system is not quite correct (Cox et al., 1999; Hepburn, John, Lord, & Rogers, 2003; Lord, 1995; Pilowsky, Yirmiya, Shulman, & Dover, 1998).

For example, one study showed that both the Childhood Autism Rating Scale (CARS; Schopler, Reichler, & Renner, 1988) and the Autism Diagnostic Interview-Revised (Lord et al., 1994) were concordant with clinician's judgments of diagnosing autism in children at age 3 (Lord, 1995). Both were less accurate for children 2 years or younger, but for somewhat different reasons. The CARS consistently overdiagnosed nonautistic mentally handicapped children as having autism at age 2; CARS diagnoses of these children became more accurate by age 3, but were still less specific than has typically been reported for older children. The ADI-R was more accurate than the CARS with the nonautistic children at 2, but like the CARS it was over-inclusive for mentally handicapped and/or language delayed children. The ADI-R also failed to diagnose autism in about 10% of 2-year-olds who later met formal diagnostic criteria for the disorder because their parents did not report sufficient abnormal repetitive behaviors or abnormalities in language. Agreement between the ADI-R and CARS was in fact quite high; the difference was whether a simple total or thresholds across several domains (i.e., social reciprocity, communication, restricted, repetitive behaviors) were required for a diagnosis.

Similar results were found in another study comparing the ADI-R and CARS with older children (Pilowsky et al., 1998). The ADI-R resulted in good specificity, but poor sensitivity at detecting childhood autism at 20 months of age (Cox et al., 1999). Furthermore, the ADI-R was not sensitive to other Pervasive Developmental Disorders, such as Asperger's Disorder and PDD-NOS, when used with 20-month-old toddlers (Cox et al., 1999). Stone found that clinical diagnoses at age two identified children with later stable diagnoses of autism but not of PDD-NOS (Stone, Ousley, Yoder, Hogan, & Hepburn, 1997; Stone et al., 1999). As we discuss later, decisions of which approach is most appropriate may differ depending on the needs of the clinician or researcher and the developmental level of the child or adult who is assessed.

Implications of Information from Other Areas of Research for Diagnostic Instruments

Without a well-established biological marker, decisions about classification of autism and ASDs have often been based on the need to identify appropriate populations for services and research, rather than empirical bases (American Psychiatric Association, 1994; Volkmar et al., 1994; Wing & Gould, 1979). Though eventually, neurobiological factors may result in a re-sorting of diagnoses in autism/PDD, biological heterogeneity is expected within and among the spectrum disorders. Thus, we will be dependent on descriptions of social and other behaviors for some time. Yet, the behavioral boundaries between autism and other disorders in the spectrum, such as PDD-NOS and Asperger's Disorder, are not clearly defined, particularly when changes with development are taken into account (see Ghaziuddin, Tsai, & Ghaziuddin, 1992). Information, such as developmental trajectories and clustering of symptoms, that arises out of studies of diagnostic instruments may influence classification systems in the near future (Lord et al., 1996; Mahoney et al., 1998; Szatmari, Archer, Fisman, Streiner, & Wilson, 1995). The expectation is that diagnostic instruments may and should continue to change as more information is acquired.

Furthermore, priorities for the results of diagnoses may be different for clinical and research purposes. Clinical diagnoses offer families access to general information about their children, and is often the entry point to services. Service providers may use a diagnosis to allocate limited resources, whereas a priority for families and diagnosticians is to ensure that children or adults are not being excluded from appropriate services because of a particular label or classification (Wing & Attwood, 1987).

Researchers often prefer narrow diagnoses. Narrower formulations provide better cross-site reliability, eliminate outliers, and reduce overlap with control groups. Narrower diagnostic categories may reduce the likelihood of false positives. On the other hand, researchers seek populations of particular sizes and are interested in maximizing the number of participants who meet their criteria. All of these forces affect the goals addressed by diagnostic instruments and the ways in which they are used.

There is an urgent need for instruments to address diagnoses beyond autism, particularly ASDs, such as PDD-NOS and Asperger's Disorder. In part, the absence of replicable, reliable, and valid instruments in this area is related to the absence of clear diagnostic criteria for these disorders (Sponheim, 1996; Szatmari et al., 2002). A lack of empirical data affects the ability to discriminate these disorders both from autism and from disorders outside the autism spectrum (e.g., severe attention deficit; severe communication impairment), which in turn affects the development and the operationalization of these criteria.

There are numerous sets of diagnostic criteria for ASDs, especially for Asperger's Disorder, that suggest conceptualizations for them (Volkmar & Klin, 2001; Szatmari, 2000; Tantam, 2000), but that do not directly address the overlap with autism. In contrast, *DSM-IV* and *ICD-10* criteria define Asperger's Disorder purely in terms of its relationship with autism, but provide little conceptualization (*DSM-IV-TR*). Moreover, conceptualizations exist for disorders such as schizoid disorder and nonverbal learning disabilites; but without clear indications of their relationship with autism. As they are for Asperger's Disorder, *DSM-IV* criteria for PDD-NOS and *ICD-10* criteria for atypical autism are based solely on the basis of just missing autism criteria.

Developing standardized assessment instruments for Asperger's Disorder is particularly tricky because there is little consensus in how to define the disorder, little consistency in

the manner in which current criteria in the *DSM-IV* and the *ICD-10* should be applied, and little agreement as to whether the diagnosis is distinct from autism or is a subtype of autism (Klin, Pauls, Schultz, & Volkmar, in press). Several different definitions for Asperger's Disorder are currently used to make the diagnosis, including Gillberg's criteria, Szatmari's criteria, Tantum's criteria, and the criteria listed in *DSM-IV* and *ICD-10* (Leekam, Libby, Wing, Gould, & Gillberg, 2000). Some authors have reported that it is difficult, if not impossible, to diagnose Asperger's Disorder given the current diagnostic criteria, which requires that autism is excluded prior to making a diagnosis of Asperger's Disorder (Miller & Ozonoff, 1997; Szatmari et al., 1995).

There are also different opinions of what criteria to use to determine if Asperger's Disorder should be considered distinct from autism or not. Klin and his colleagues broach the need for a greater body of research on the validation of the syndrome (Klin, Sparrow, Marans, Carter, & Volkmar, 2000). Szatmari et al. (1995), on the other hand, argues that the decision should be based on clinical usefulness, taking into account course, response to treatment, and prognosis. Szatmari et al. indicates that the first priority should be to determine if there is a meaningful distinction between Asperger's Disorder and autism and a second priority should be to determine if there is a distinction between Asperger's Disorder and other related but also not well-defined groups (such as nonverbal learning disability). One of the difficulties is that different criteria for Asperger's Disorder change not only the individuals who receive that diagnosis, but also whom is then diagnosed with PDD-NOS and autism (Klin et al., in press).

At this point, there are very few instruments with extensive reliability and validity studies available to aide in the diagnosis of Asperger's Disorder. The few that are available are described in this chapter. Most researchers continue to modify instruments designed for diagnostic purposes for autism in research studies on Asperger's Disorder, particularly as there is still controversy as to whether it is a distinct syndrome.

Two Asperger's Disorder algorithms were developed for the DISCO (Leekam et al.,

2000), one of the algorithms was based on Gill-berg's criteria and the other on *ICD-10*. In the study by Leekam et al. (2000), 91 (45%) of the subjects met criteria for Asperger's Disorder using the algorithm based on Gillberg's crite-ria, while only 3 (1%) met criteria based on the *ICD-10*. In most cases, this was at least par-tially due to the *ICD-10* criteria requiring nor-mal language development prior to 3 years and age appropriate self-help or adaptive skills, or curiosity. This supports the difficulty in mak-ing the diagnosis based on current criteria as it is set forth in the diagnostic manuals. The au-thors of this article admit that they may have interpreted the *ICD-10* criteria more strictly than was intended. Also of importance was the finding that all 91 of the children who met algo-rithm cut-offs for Asperger's Disorder based on Gillberg's criteria also met *ICD-10* criteria for autism or atypical autism, again, highlight-ing the issue of the overlap between Asperger's Disorder and autism. Similar findings have been reported by numerous other researchers, including Ozonoff et al. (2000), Szatmari et al. (1995), and Klin, Volkmar, Sparrow, Cicchetti, and Rourke (1995).

Other instruments have tended to yield the same results. This is truly an unfortunate cycle: without reliable diagnostic criteria and measures, empirical findings are very difficult to interpret (Klin et al., in press; Sponheim, 1996). Without empirical data about the course and characteristics of nonautism pervasive de-velopmental disorders, attempts to differentiate between these disorders and autism will not be effective. Data from genetic and family stud-ies, as well as other neurobiological approaches, may make this task easier, but the results are also affected by instrumentation. Thus, re-searchers must arrive at working agreements that allow them to proceed in a reliable fashion.

In the face of these difficulties, autism as a field has the strength of its intense research history and the benefit of research teams from around the world investigating similar ques-tions. Descriptive and experimental research have offered solutions to some of these diffi-culties, such as identifying developmentally meaningful behaviors—joint attention, theory of mind, response to name—that discriminate autism from other disorders at various points in development. It offers the promise of other

knowledge, from new statistical techniques to neuroimaging to molecular genetics. As per-spectives on autism have shifted with new the-ories and empirical findings, strategies and content of instruments used for its diagnosis have also shifted in numerous ways. However, in the newer instruments, roots can almost always be traced to strategies begun in earlier work. Science offers clinicians the opportu-nity to learn from accumulated knowledge and empirical testing of hypotheses.

Psychometric Issues

The American Psychological Association (APA) has issued guidelines for the develop-ment of psychometric instruments in the United States. A number of factors affect the psychometric appropriateness of an instru-ment. These issues are raised as they apply to the question of diagnostic instruments for the autism spectrum in general, followed by more specific discussions of selected instruments. Selected standards from these guidelines are presented in Table 28.1 (reliability) and Table 28.2 (validity). Many diagnostic instruments in autism/PDD, as noted, have addressed some of these issues, but few or none have addressed all of them. In part, this lack of information is understandable because of difficulties in achieving sufficiently large well-documented samples; in part, it reflects the limited history of instrument development in autism.

Reliability

Reliability, which is the degree to which a score or decision is free from errors of mea-surement, requires assessment in a number of forms, including across raters, across time, and within an instrument. Often the term reli-ability is used to describe these separate as-pects of the stability of the results of an instrument as if they were interchangeable. However, this is not the case. For example, the degree to which different raters concur when using the same instrument cannot be deter-mined by measuring the internal characteris-tics of a test. The internal consistency (i.e., the degree to which different items on a scale measure the same concept) of an instrument can be quite high, even though its inter-rater

TABLE 28.1   Reliability and Errors of Measurement: Issues Related to Diagnosis of Autistic Spectrum Disorders

1. For each total score, subscore, or combination of scores that is reported, estimates of relevant reliabilities and standard errors of measurement should be provided in adequate detail to enable the test user to judge whether scores are sufficiently accurate for the intended use of the test.
2. The procedures that are used to obtain samples of individuals, groups or observations for the purpose of estimating reliabilities and standard errors of measurement, as well as the nature of the populations involved, should be described.
3. The conditions under which the reliability estimate was obtained and the situations to which it may be applicable should be explained clearly.
4. Coefficients based on internal analysis should not be interpreted as substitutes for alternate-form reliability or estimates of stability over time unless other evidence supports that interpretation in a particular context.
5. Where judgmental processes enter into the scoring of a test, evidence on the degree of agreement between independent scorings should be provided.
6. Where cut scores are specified for selection or classification, the standard errors of measurement should be reported for score levels at or near the cut score. For dichotomous decisions, estimates should be provided of the percentage of test takers who are classified in the same way on two occasions or on alternate forms of the test.

Selected and adapted from *Standards for Educational and Psychological Testing,* by AERA, APA, NCME, 1985, Washington, DC: American Psychological Association.

reliability is low. In a disorder such as autism that is defined by a pattern of difficulties across several areas (i.e., communication, social interaction, behavior), internal consistency in a scale is a worthwhile endeavor, but does not have the same meaning as in a scale that is not designed to describe a pattern of related, but different, deficits.

In the past, reliability estimates were often reported as correlations. A correlation measures whether the rankings of different individuals are similar across different raters. The difficulty with correlations is that the absolute scores of raters can be quite different, resulting in different diagnoses, even though they are highly correlated. That is, if one rater rated all participants relatively high and another rater rated the same participants relatively low and the raters had the same rankings of participants, the correlation of the two raters' scores would be high. If diagnosis is based on exceeding a certain threshold, the fact that the rankings of the raters agreed would not prevent the scores from resulting in different diagnoses for

TABLE 28.2   Validity: Issues Related to Diagnosis of Autistic Spectrum Disorders

1. Evidence of validity should be presented for the major types of inferences for which the use of a test is recommended.
2. If validity for some common interpretation has not been investigated, that fact should be made clear, and potential users should be cautioned about making such interpretations.
3. The composition of the validation sample should be described in as much detail as is practicable.
4. When criteria are composed of rater judgments, the relevant training, experience, and qualifications of the experts should be described.
5. When a test is proposed as a measure of a construct, that construct should be distinguished from other constructs. Evidence should be presented to show that a test does not depend heavily on extraneous constructs. If evidence indicates that a criterion measure is affected to a substantial degree by irrelevant factors, this evidence should be reported.
6. When criteria are composed of rater judgments, the degree of knowledge that raters have concerning ratee performance should be reported. The training and experience of the raters should be described.
7. If specific cut scores are recommended for decision making (for example, in differential diagnosis), the user's guide should caution that the rates of misclassification will vary depending on the percentage of individuals tested who actually belong in each category.

Selected and adapted from *Standards for Educational and Psychological Testing,* by AERA, APA, NCME, 1985, Washington, DC: American Psychological Association.

the same client. Thus, while correlations provide an important index of the relationship among scores, they are not sufficient to show agreement when cut-off scores are used to make categorical judgments about diagnoses.

In place of correlations, many investigators now employ measures of percent of agreement between pairs or larger groupings of raters. An agreement must be defined at a level commensurate with the aims of the instrument. It may be exact agreement or agreement within a certain number of points, depending how scores are to be used. Clinicians and researchers can then evaluate the frequency with which their coding agrees with that of another person for a given individual. There are no set standards for levels of agreement, but generally, in self-report and interview studies, researchers have been able to achieve 90% or greater agreement on individual categorical measures and at least 80% on individual observational codes, with greater agreement for pooled or summary scores.

Item-level inter-rater agreement is very important when an instrument is being developed because it allows for experimentation with which items yield the most valid scores. Many of the most well-known assessment instruments (i.e., the Wechsler tests, the Vineland Adaptive Behavior Scales) do not have this level of inter-rater reliability because the rely on total or domain scores and because the internal consistency of these domains or the total are well documented. In the field of ASD, because of gradually changing conceptualizations, recent instruments have actually aimed for the establishment of more specific reliability among raters in order to retain the flexibility to rework scoring systems as different diagnostic frameworks emerge.

The difficulty with using percent agreement as a metric is the role of chance. If there is a high frequency of extreme scores without much variation within different populations (e.g., almost all zeroes for nonautism or high scores for autism), correlations and percent agreement among raters can be quite high because of the likelihood of agreement based on using the extreme scores, without attention to individual differences. That is, having seen a child's performance on the first item of the test, a rater might predict that, because the child looked quite autistic on the first item, he will receive high scores on all further measures of abnormality. Having seen a typically developing child's behavior on the same first item, a rater might predict, based on the child's "normal" reaction to the first task, that she will receive "normal" scores on other items. If there is little variation across tasks and little overlap across populations, two raters might get better agreement using this strategy than by actually observing and coding the behaviors of the individual children. Specific statistics, called kappas (Cicchetti & Sparrow, 1981), allow some control of this phenomenon. However, no simple answer addresses all of these problems. Although kappas control for chance, they are sensitive to distributions and so, as with any statistic, must be interpreted in light of other information. Another strategy using reliability coefficients does not address the intersection between individual participants and individual raters, but allows quantification of the effects of each separately (Mundy, Sigman, Ungerer, & Sherman, 1986). This statistic tests whether scores are more affected by individual differences in children than by differences among raters. However, if there are large individual differences among children, finding that these differences exceed those among raters may not guarantee strong reliability.

These issues illustrate the importance of the nature of the samples on which psychometric analyses are conducted. Autism affects individuals across the lifespan who have a range of language and cognitive skills. If samples are not well matched and not relevant to the clinical or research contexts in which the instrument will be used, there will generally be little overlap in scores (e.g., if children with autism are compared to typical children). If instruments are developed only using very easily discriminable populations, documentation of reliable ratings will be difficult to achieve when statistics that take distributions into account are employed, although they may look good in terms of absolute agreement. When reliability estimates are presented only for totals, even when subscales are described and intended to be used, clinicians or researchers who want to base interpretations on specific items or subscales cannot do so. It is important that test users interpret their results within the context of the information that is available.

Sometimes the reverse is the case. Researchers may present detailed psychometric data for items, but not present reliability for the diagnostic categorization for which the scale is intended. This is particularly problematic for ASDs. It is not difficult to find an instrument that identifies more abnormal behaviors occurring in ASD than in typical development. However, seldom is this the goal of an instrument. To be useful diagnostically, instruments must discriminate children with autism or ASD from nonautistic severely mentally handicapped, language-impaired children. Because it is often difficult to set a threshold that includes children with mild autism identified as such and excludes nonautistic severely mentally handicapped children, consistency across raters and across time with which an individual falls in or out of the category of autism or ASD must be measured directly.

The issue of test-retest reliability in autism is complex. Changes in behavior due to development would be expected if administrations were separated by substantial amounts of time. Some learning may occur within the testing situation that affects a child's behavior if he or she is asked to carry out the same actions again. This is different than error in measurement, but still must be taken into account. In some cases, previous administration of an instrument (i.e., practice) may affect its scores or interpretation. For example, in the Autism Diagnostic Observation Schedule (ADOS, Module 1; Lord, Risi, et al., 2000), young children are taught a routine of bringing a balloon to the examiner if they do not do so spontaneously. If they are presented with the same task several weeks later, they may respond differently because of learning, not because of error in measurement. However, the examiner still needs to code the behavior he or she sees. Ideally, information about stability and expected changes across multiple administrations should be available for all instruments.

For diagnostic instruments, this information must be presented at the level of each individual's score and resulting diagnosis. Just because a task or instrument has been used in many studies, it cannot be assumed that it is reliable on an individual level at a standard appropriate for diagnostic work. Many experimental studies in psychology and psychiatry are primarily concerned with identifying group differences and so do not address issues at an individual level in much detail, if at all. For example, two studies reported substantial intra-individual variability across tasks and time in standard tasks used to assess theory of mind (see Chapters 41 and 42 in this book for a discussion of this concept) in autism (Holroyd & Baron-Cohen, 1993; Mayes & Zigler, 1992). While group effects on false belief tasks have had a major impact on the conceptualization of social-cognitive deficits in autism, and have been replicated across studies internationally, in neither of the recent studies were the results of the tasks sufficiently replicable within individuals to meet reasonable clinical standards for classification.

An important aspect of reliability is specification of exactly how and under what circumstances diagnostic instruments are to be used and how they are to be scored. Sometimes procedures reported in journal articles are described so briefly that it is difficult to determine what exactly was done and who did it. Differences in procedures, such as whether or not coding is carried out live or from videotape, whether interviews are done face to face or on the telephone, or how experienced in autism the raters are, may result in differences in scoring (Sanchez et al., 1995; Volkmar et al., 1994). It is helpful for users of instruments to know how, as "consumers," they might improve and evaluate their own reliability with an instrument.

In studies of reliability and validity, raters should be unaware of children's diagnostic categories or of scores on other diagnostic instruments, unless this information would typically be available prior to use of the instrument. If other information is assumed to be a critical part of the use of the instrument, this needs to be stated clearly as part of the procedures. For example, for the ADOS, general information about a participant's likely level of expressive language is crucial in selecting the appropriate module and so is considered part of the assessment. How this information is used is specified in the manual. In addition, description of the training required for a rater and the circumstances of the training and the administration are critical aspects of reliability.

Another factor to be considered in autism and ASDs is parents' awareness of their child's diagnosis. That is, in many research samples, parents of previously diagnosed autistic children are well versed in the characteristics of autism and how their children fit into the diagnostic scheme. Several recent studies have shown excellent agreement between questionnaires (i.e., the Social Communication Questionnaire [SCQ]; Rutter, Le Couteur, & Lord, 2003) and interview formats of similar items (i.e., the SCQ and ADI-R; Bishop & Norbury, 2002; Chakrabarti & Fombonne, 2001; Le Couteur, Lord, & Rutter, 2003; Lord et al., 1994; Vrancic et al., 2002 [Spanish SCQ by telephone]). However, if a parent report instrument is intended to be used in initial diagnoses, then it is appropriate that it is shown to be reliable and valid with caregivers who have not yet received formal diagnoses.

Validity

Validity is the most important aspect of a diagnostic instrument. Validation refers to the degree to which other evidence supports inferences drawn from the scores yielded by the diagnostic instrument. Thus, how validity is best measured is inherently related to the uses for which the instrument is intended.

Validity is often grouped into categories of content, construct, and criterion-related evidence. For the diagnosis of ASDs, questions of construct validity are related to those that underlie the diagnostic framework on which the instrument is based. For example, the ADI-R uses a concept of social reciprocity derived from theories of autism (see Lord & Bailey, 2002). It is operationalized in terms of specific questions to parents and caregivers about behaviors such as joint attention, shared enjoyment, comforting, and friendship. Data from studies of the ADI and ADI-R (Le Couteur et al., 1989; Lord et al., 1996) contributed to the understanding of this construct during preparation of *DSM-IV* and *ICD-10* criteria, along with results of observational studies and field trials, in showing that traditional measures of attachment were not strongly related to other measures of social reciprocity (Lord et al., 1993; Sigman & Ungerer, 1984; Volkmar et al., 1994). A further study suggested that

parental reports on the ADI, of autistic children's responses to separation and reunion (which were intended to be linked theoretically to conceptualizations of attachment) were more highly correlated with their children's communicative competence than the same children's observed responses to separation and reunion in a standardized setting (e.g., during administration of the Pre-Linguistic Autism Observation Schedule or PL-ADOS: DiLavore et al., 1995; Spencer, 1993).

Internal consistency for items within a diagnostic instrument can be used to support the assertion that a test measures a single construct. In ASD, this has meant support for the differentiation of ASDs from other developmental disorders or support for the three domains (social reciprocity; communication; restricted, repetitive behaviors) that define the syndrome. Measures of internal consistency for the most commonly used instruments in the diagnosis of autism (e.g., the ADI-R, the Autism Behavior Checklist or ABC, the ADOS, the Childhood Autism Rating Scale or CARS) have generally been high.

Content validity has to do with the degree to which a sample of items, tasks, or questions in an instrument are representative of a defined domain. In most cases, this domain is autism, either narrowly or broadly defined (i.e., ASD, PDD). For the purposes of this review, content validity is most often defined as the degree to which different instruments represent the diagnostic criteria for ASDs. Many of the instruments reviewed here predated the release of *DSM-IV* and *ICD-10* criteria for autism and so do not correspond to the three-domain approach specified in these diagnostic systems. The exceptions are the ADI-R and ADOS. These are special cases because interpretation of results from the original versions of these instruments, the ADI and ADOS/PL-ADOS, influenced strategies tested in the field trials and the *ICD-10* revisions.

Concurrent aspects of criterion-related validity of instruments have been most commonly addressed in the broad area of ASD by investigating the convergence between diagnostic categorizations yielded by another diagnostic instrument or with clinical judgment. As shown in Table 28.3, convergent validity for three of the most common diagnostic instruments (ADI, ADOS, CARS) available in English has been quite good. Convergence between the CARS and several other instruments (e.g., the Autism Behavior Checklist; Krug et al., 1993; the Real-Life Rating Scale or RLRS; Freeman, Ritvo, Yokota, & Ritvo, 1986) has been good. Also, as depicted in Table 28.3, all of the diagnostic instruments have been shown to be adequate in identifying clinically diagnosed children with autism, with relatively rare false negatives within a "prototypical" group of mildly to moderately mentally handicapped school age children with autism. There is more variability when instruments are used with younger (Lord, 1995; Lord et al., 1993) and older (CARS; Garfin, McCallon, & Cox, 1988; Piven, Harper, Palmers, & Arndt, 1996) populations, and with higher (Yirmiya, Sigman, & Freeman, 1994) and lower functioning groups (Fombonne, 1992; Lord et al., 1993). This pattern is not unique to the instruments, but reflects general difficulty in application of standard diagnostic criteria to various developmental levels. More detailed information about this issue is discussed next with descriptions of particular instruments.

An even more serious, though less widespread, issue is that of false positives. Instruments differ considerably in the number of studies that include comparison groups. They also differ in the degree to which the comparison groups represent typical populations for whom a diagnosis of autism or ASD might be considered and rejected. Often studies include a comparison group of nonautistic mentally handicapped or language impaired subjects, without sufficient information to determine the degree to which these subjects were comparable in ways other than the characteristics of autism to the autistic individuals. Autism is associated with particularly severe communication difficulties; and it is well established that the triad of deficits that define autism increases in frequency as level of mental retardation increases (Wing & Gould, 1979). Consequently, there is reason to be concerned that, without deliberate stratification, most comparison groups of nonautistic individuals will have markedly lower communication skills, adaptive

abilities, and perhaps even general intellectual skills than autistic participants. Thus, comparisons of such samples, even though they may be representative of the population at hand, could yield differences interpreted as specific to autism that may be more accurately linked to severity of mental handicap or communication impairment (Lord et al., 1993). This is another reason why data concerning the size, the characteristics, and the ascertainment of samples are especially important in evaluating instruments. In addition, more sophisticated statistical techniques, such as latent class analyses and logistic regression, may allow researchers to take into account both positive and negative predictive values within a single metric (though still dependent on adequate samples on which to make comparisons).

Little information concerning predictive validity of diagnostic instruments in autism exists except for a few studies using the ADI-R. Our own follow-up study of 2-year-olds who were referred to a pediatric clinic for an evaluation of possible autism, showed that both the ADI-R and the CARS tended to over-diagnose autism in mentally handicapped children at age 2. This was much less the case by age 3, and was less true for the ADI-R (in part, because of the requirement for a "triad" of deficits) than the CARS. On the other hand, Cox et al. (1999) found ADI-R diagnoses, when the threshold in repetitive behavior was not required, to be quite stable from 18 months to 3 years, for a select, higher-functioning group of children identified as having autism with a screening instrument called the CHAT (Baron-Cohen et al., 1992).

A follow-up study from early school age showed that retrospective ADI scores describing behavior at 4 to 5 years of age significantly predicted academic achievement and adaptive scores in adolescence and young adulthood in a group of mildly mentally handicapped to non-retarded autistic individuals (Venter et al., 1992). Social and communication deviance at age 5 made independent contributions, in addition to various measures of expressive and receptive language and nonverbal IQ, to current adaptive skill; whereas the severity of restricted and repetitive behaviors added to the predictive value of verbal and nonverbal predictors of academic achievement.

TABLE 28.3 Currently Available Diagnostic Instruments in Autism

Instrument	Reliability			Validity			General Information			
	Interrater	Test-Retest	Internal Consistency	Construct/Content	Convergent	Discriminant Matched Sample	Published Guidelines for Diagnostic Decision	Subscales	Most Appropriate For	Level of Expertise
Rimland's E-2 form (E-2)	Unpublished	Unpublished	Unpublished	Kanner (1943)	—	Poor	—	—	Screening	Parent checklist
Behavior Rating Instrument for Autistic and Atypical Children (BRIAAC)	S: good	—	S: variable	—	—	Limited	Yes	8	Current observation	Requires training
Real-Life Rating Scale (RLRS)	T: moderate I: marginal	—	T: good S: poor	ASA	CARS ABC	AUT/MR/TYP	—	5	Screening	Minimal
Social Responsiveness Scale (SRS)	T: high	T: high	T: high	DSM-IV	—	TYP/PSY/AUT/PDD/AS	No	3	Symptoms Severity Response to treatment	—
Pervasive Developmental Disorders Rating Scale (PDDRS)	T: high S: high	T: high S: high	T: good–high S: high	DSM-III-R	ABC	AUT/AD/LDD/MR/PDD-NOS/William's Syndrome	No	3	Preliminary stages	Minimal
Children's Social Behavior Questionnaire (CSBQ)	S: variable	T: high S: variable	S: variable	DSM-IV	CBCL ABC	PDD/ADHD/TYP/PSY/AUT	No	5	Current symptoms	Minimal
Childhood Autism Rating Scale (CARS)	T: high	—	T: high	DSM-III-R	ABC RLRS ADI	AUT/MR	Yes	4	Targeted screening[a]	Moderate/video available
Autism Behavior Checklist (ABC)	T: variable	—	T: good S: poor	—	CARS RLRS	—	Yes	2/5	Measuring maladaptive behavior	Minimal
Behavioral Summarized Evaluation-Revised (BSE-R)	T: high I: good	—	T: Adequate	—	Rimland E2	AUT/MR/MP	—	—	Symptoms for research	Requires training
Gilliam Autism Rating Scale (GARS)	T: high S: high	T: high S: high	T: high S: high	ASA; DSM-IV	ABC ADPR	AUT/MR/ED/LD (not matched)	Yes	4	Needs further evaluation	Parent checklist

Instrument	Reliability	Validity	Validity	Sample/Norms	Comparison instruments	Populations discriminated	Manual	(note)	Purpose	Training/format
Autism Diagnostic Interview-Revised (ADI-R)	S: high I: high	T: good	T: unpublished S: high	DSM-IV ICD-10	CARS ADOS	AUT/MR	Yes	3	Diagnostic clinics/research across developmental level	Experience, video, or requires training
Diagnostic Interview for Social and Communication Disorders (DISCO)	I: variable	—	—	ICD-10; Wing & Gould (1979); Gillberg, Gillberg, et al. (2001); DSM-IV, 1994	—	AUT/LD/LANG DIS	No	4	Educational planning	Requires training
Autism Diagnostic Observation Schedule (ADOS)	I: good T: high	T: Adequate	S: high	DSM-IV ICD-10	ADI-R CCC	MR/LANG DIS/PSY	Yes	3	Research and clinical diagnosis	Experience, video, or requires training
Psychoeducational Profile-Revised (PEP-R)	T: good	—	S: high	DSM-III-R	CARS	TYP	No	4	Intervention recommendations	Experience, video available
Adolescent and Adult Psychoeducational Profile (AAPEP)	S: variable T: high	—	—	—	—	—	No	6	Intervention recommendations	Experience,
Communication and Symbolic Behavior Scales (CSBS Behavior Sample)	T: high	T: high S: high	—	—	—	TYP/MR/ASD	No	5	Screening	Minimal, video available
Children's Communication Checklist (CCC)	T: high	—	T: high	—	—	AUT/AD/PDD-NOS/ADHD/LD/LANG DIS	—	5	Identifying pragmatic difficulties	Checklist
Asperger Syndrome (and high-functioning autism) Diagnostic Interview (ASDI)	I: high	I: high	—	Gillberg, Gillberg, et al. (2001); Szatmari (1995); ICD-10; DSM-IV	—	PSY/TYP	No	6	Still in preliminary stages	—
Australian Scale for Asperger's Syndrome (ASAS)	—	—	—	Behavior AS researchers define as AS	—	TYP/ASD/PSY	Yes	5	Screening	Questionnaire

[a] Most appropriate for school age children with mental retardation.

Note: All instruments are discussed in detail in text. AD = Asperger Disorder; ADHD = Attention Deficit Hyperactivity Disorder; AUT = Autistic; ED = Emotionally disturbed; I = Item; LANG DEL = Language delayed; LANG DIS = Language disorder; LD = Learning disabled; MP = Multiple handicap; MR = Mentally retarded; PDD-NOS = Pervasive Developmental Disorder-Not Otherwise Specified; PSY = Psychiatric disorder; S = Subscale; T = Total; TYP = Typical.

DIAGNOSTIC INSTRUMENTS FOR AUTISM

Next, instruments used in the diagnosis of autism and ASDs are discussed briefly following approximate chronological order according to when they were first introduced to the public and according to general categories of method. Descriptions are not meant to be comprehensive; some instruments will be described primarily as examples of kinds of measures or novel approaches. For more detailed information, the reader is referred to specific publications about each instrument or to a chapter by Parks (1988), for many of the older instruments. When several versions of the same or a similar scale have been disseminated, the focus is on the most recent version.

The First Empirically Developed Rating Scales and Questionnaires

The Rimland Diagnostic Form for Behavior-Disturbed Children (Form E-1) was the first widely used scale for the identification of autism (Rimland, 1968). It made an important contribution as a systematic diagnostic assessment that focused on a carefully selected range of symptoms rather than more abstract and inconsistently defined concepts, especially of emotional withdrawal. A revised form, Form E-2 is now scored without charge for parents by the Autism Research Institute in San Diego. Total scores are additive across all questions. The scale is based on the core symptoms defined by Kanner in 1943 and Kanner's belief (Kanner, 1962, as cited in Rimland, 1971) that only a relatively small percentage of children labeled as autistic have "pure" autism.

Many parents have found information from the Autism Research Institute to be helpful. Comparisons with other scales suggest that the diagnosis yielded by the E-2 form is different from those offered by most other instruments. In the original validation study of the Childhood Autism Rating Scale (CARS; Schopler, Reichler, DeVellis, & Daly, 1980; also see below), over 200 children who met autism criteria and another 200 children who did not were all rated on the E-2 form. Only 8 were considered autistic by Rimland using the E-2 form and of those 8, 3 were considered nonautistic on the CARS. In another study, diagnostic overlap with the Behavior Rating Instrument for Autistic and Atypical Children (BRIAAC; Ruttenberg, Dratman, Fraknoi, & Wenar, 1966) was poor (Cohen et al., 1978).

Basic psychometric data and scoring information for the E-2 have not been published in scientific journals (Masters & Miller, 1970). Several studies suggested differences between parent and staff reports using the scale (Davids, 1975; Prior & Bence, 1975) and limited differentiation between children with autism and children with other disorders. While current diagnostic frameworks such as *DSM-IV* and *ICD-10* continue to build on Kanner's original descriptions of autism (Kanner, 1943), the ways in which symptoms are operationalized and weighted have changed substantially. Thus, the E-2 form may serve as most useful to parents who are beginning to familiarize themselves with behaviors associated with autism, rather than as a measure of standard diagnoses of autism or related disorders.

The BRIAAC, is another scale that was created about the same time as Rimland's first diagnostic checklist (Ruttenberg, Kalish, Wenar, & Wolf, 1977; Ruttenberg et al., 1966). It consists of eight subscales that measure behavior in different areas, yielding a diagnosis of autism. A trained rater completes the scale after substantial observations. The BRIAAC was important historically because it used direct observations of behaviors, defined on the basis of descriptions in case notes (Parks, 1988). Psychometrics were computed on various samples, including at least one study of autistic, mentally handicapped, and normally developing children. Reliability estimates in the form of correlations have consistently been high, though the scoring criteria are complex. More sophisticated estimates of inter-rater or test-retest reliability are not yet published. Results from validity studies have not indicated that diagnostic classifications based on the BRIAAC correspond to those yielded by other instruments or clinical judgment (Cohen et al., 1978). Because it is based only on current observations, the BRIAAC has the potential to be used as a measure of therapeutic effectiveness (Wenar & Ruttenberg, 1976), if more up-to-date, rigorous standards for reliability can be met.

Another scale that has been influential in the field of ASDs has been the Handicaps, Behavior, and Skills schedule (HBS) (Wing & Gould, 1978). It was the first widely distributed semi-structured interview for parents and caregivers of children who were mentally retarded or autistic (referred to as "psychotic" at the time). It was used in the Camberwell epidemiological study and, as the source of data for that project, had a significant effect on the understanding of the "triad of impairments" seen in autism and related disorders (Wing & Gould, 1979). The HBS was not a diagnostic instrument, but a "framework for eliciting, systematically, clinical information to be used in conjunction with appropriate psychological tests for assessment and diagnosis" (Wing & Gould, 1978, p. 81). It provided standard questions and topics so that an interviewer could elicit enough information from a parent or caregiver to make an appropriate rating for each item. Formal scoring was mapped onto the Vineland Social Maturity Scale (Doll, 1965). The HBS took several hours to administer and consisted of 31 sections that included questions about both diagnostic and developmental issues. Psychometrics were based on 171 children between 2 and 15 years of age who comprised an epidemiological sample of children with IQs below 50 and/or who were receiving special services who lived in the London borough of Camberwell.

Reliability, judged on the basis of comparisons between pairs of ratings by parents, professional workers, and the authors, averaged from 77% to 81%. Summary ratings across informants and observations in the form of 3-point scales for each section showed near perfect agreement. Indices of association were stronger for the absence of skills than the presence, except for social development. Developmental variables were generally more reliable than ratings of behavioral abnormalities.

One unusual aspect of the reported research was comparisons among professional reports, parent reports, and the authors' direct observations of relevant behaviors. Parents tended to describe their children as more socially and emotionally responsive than did professionals, but to report more stereotyped movements and abnormal responses to sensory stimuli. The more severe the child's impairment, the better was the agreement. The mechanism for combining scores from differ-ent environments was unique and had the potential for usefulness in documenting changes in behavior. The HBS has now been substantially revised. This revision is discussed later as the Diagnostic Interview for Social and Communication Disorders (DISCO: Wing, Leekam, Libby, Gould, & Larcombe, 2002).

A final scale that was important in the first group of diagnostic instruments emerging in the 1970s was the Behavior Observation Scale (BOS; Freeman, Ritvo, Guthrie, Schroth, & Ball, 1978). It includes ratings of 24 behaviors, carried out in 10-second intervals of a video-taped free-play session. The BOS was the first scale that emphasized the importance of controlling the environment in which a child was observed, as well as standardizing what was observed. It used frequencies of behaviors to differentiate among diagnostic groups. The authors noted that this approach was not completely successful for several reasons. Frequencies of many behaviors were associated with developmental levels as much as diagnosis. In some cases, behaviors that occurred only rarely were very important, suggesting that frequency was a less critical variable than the quality of behavior.

The same authors then developed the Ritvo-Freeman Real Life Rating Scale (RLRS; Freeman et al., 1986) to assess behaviors that characterize autism more accurately, with an emphasis on unusual sensory behaviors. This scale can be used after observation of a 30-minute free-play period. Marginal to adequate reliability was found for individual items with adequate subscale and total inter-rater reliability using kappas (Freeman et al., 1986; Sevin, Matson, Coe, Fee, & Sevin, 1991) for relatively brief samples of behavior coded by raters with minimal training. For a sample of 24 children and adolescents with autism, 7 of 38 items did not occur at all and 4 others were very rare. Inter-rater reliability for another 9 items was not significant (Sevin et al., 1991). On the other hand, the correlation with the CARS total score was .77 for an autistic sample. Three of the five subscales (social relationships, sensory, and language) and the total had adequate to high internal consistency (Sturmey, Matson, & Sevin, 1992). No specific cut-offs for diagnosis are provided. Thus, the instrument is primarily useful as a general index of diagnostic features, and potentially a measure of change, rather than as an independent source of classification.

SCALES THAT MEASURE CORE DEFICITS IN AUTISM SPECTRUM DISORDERS

Social Responsiveness Scale

The Social Responsiveness Scale (SRS; Constantino, 2002), formerly the Social Responsivity Scale, is a questionnaire designed to be completed by an adult, such as a parent or teacher, who observes a child in social situations for the purpose of measuring difficulties in reciprocal social interactions on a continuum (Constantino, Przybeck, Friesen, & Todd, 2000). The questionnaire takes only 15 to 20 minutes to complete and consists of 65 items covering dimensions of communication (6 items), social interactions (35 items), and repetitive and stereotyped behaviors and interests (20 items) associated with ASDs. Each item rates the frequency, not the intensity of a behavior, on a scale from zero (not true) to three (almost always true). The item scores are totaled and result in a severity score along a continuum of difficulties in reciprocity in social interactions (Constantino & Todd, 2000).

Internal consistency of the measure was computed based on teacher completed questionnaires for 195 school children between the ages of 4 and 7 years, resulting in a Cronbach's alpha of .97. All 65 items were retained because reducing the number of items resulted in a reduced ability to distinguish subjects with PDD-NOS from clinical controls. In addition, factor loadings differed between groups of older and younger children. Test-retest reliability has been good with correlations reported between .83 and .88 (Constantino et al., 2004). Inter-rater reliability between parents and teachers ranged between correlations of .73 and .75 (Constantino & Todd, 2000; Constantino et al., 2004) and correlations between parents were also strong ($r = .91$). SRS scores were not related to IQ (Constantino et al., 2004) in one paper, but were in an earlier paper (Constantino, Przybeck, et al., 2000).

Scores on the SRS were significantly higher for children with diagnoses of autism, Asperger's Disorder, and PDD-NOS than for children in the epidemiological school sample or clinical sample, which was comprised of child psychiatry patients with and without Pervasive Developmental Disorders (PDD). The scores of children with diagnoses of PDDs were approximately 2 standard deviations above the mean of the children with non-PDD psychiatric diagnoses. Approximately 8% of the sample of school children had scores that exceeded the mean of the children with ASDs. While children with PDD-NOS had significantly higher scores than nonautistic children in the clinical sample, overlap occurred between the lower 20% of scores in the PDD-NOS group and the upper 20% of scores in the children with mood and anxiety disorders. Results of a latent class analysis and principle components analysis on the epidemiological sample of school children revealed differences in severity, but not in patterns of scores, suggesting a continuously distributed variable (Constantino et al., 2000).

Strong correlations have been reported between the ADI-R algorithm scores and SRS scores, both based on parent report (Constantino et al., 2004). Principal Component Analysis resulted in single factor explaining 35% of the variance (Constantino et al., 2004). At this point, the SRS is best used as a measure of severity of difficulties in social reciprocity, including odd behaviors. It has been used in genetic studies of ASDs (Constantino & Todd, 2000). The SRS does not take long to administer and demonstrates good reliability. Given that there is overlap between scores in ASD and non-ASD psychiatric populations, it's primary use is for measuring symptom severity and response to treatment.

Pervasive Developmental Disorders Rating Scale

The Pervasive Developmental Disorders Rating Scale (PDDRS) is a revision of an earlier scale developed (Eaves, 1990; Eaves & Hooper, 1987), and includes 51 items across three subscales (arousal, affect, and cognition), based on the *DSM-III-R*. Each behavior is rated on a 5-point Likert scale. The author suggests that both the total score and the arousal factor score meet the cutoff of one standard deviation below the mean (standard score > 85), to classify a child as PDD.

The internal consistency, test-retest reliability and inter-rater reliability of the measure were evaluated. Internal consistency was good, resulting in reliability coefficients between .79 and .90 for the scales and .92 on the total score. Test-retest and inter-rater reliability were strong when based on an initial sample in which rating pairs were collected over a mean of 8.33 months, with correlation coefficients between .87 and .91. In a second sample, inter-rater and test-retest reliability were evaluated based on ratings completed by two different respondents over 14 months. Reliability was lower in this situation ranging from .44 to .53 (Eaves, Campbell, & Chambers, 2000).

Convergent and discriminant validity of the instrument were measured by comparing scores on the PDDRS with scores on the ABC and evaluating the sensitivity and specificity of the instrument. Partial correlations, with chronological age as the control variable, were run on the ABC scales and the PDDRS factors. All correlations were significantly different from zero with the exception of PDDRS Cognition and ABC Relating and PDDRS Cognition and ABC Body and Object Use, for which correlations ranged from .32 to .81. The mean score on each scale was significantly higher in the autistic group than a nonautistic group that included nonautism ASDs as well as moderate to severe mental retardation and Williams Syndrome. Using the recommended cut-off score, sensitivity and specificity were 88%. The ABC and the PDDRS scores were consistent in classifying children with autism in 85% of the sample (Eaves et al., 2000). In the validity studies, no standard diagnostic procedure was used to define the sample. Thus, the authors suggest that the instruments be used for screening rather than for diagnostic purposes (Eaves et al., 2000). Because the control group included children with ASDs and there was not a standardized procedure for establishing diagnosis, it is possible that the instrument may miss some children with autism, given that it "screens out" children with related ASDs.

Children's Social Behavior Questionnaire

The Children's Social Behavior Questionnaire (CSBQ; Luteijn, Luteijn, Jackson, Volkmar, & Minderaa, 2000) covers areas associated with ASDs and was designed to be completed by parents or caregivers of children between the ages of 4 and 18 years. It includes 96 items, 66 of which fall into five factors: Acting-Out, Social Contact Problems, Social Insight Problems, Anxious/Rigid, and Stereotypical (Luteijn et al., 2000). Each item focuses on recent behavior (over the past 2 months) and is rated from zero ("does not describe the child") to two ("clearly applies to the child").

Internal consistency, inter-rater reliability and test-retest reliability were all evaluated for the questionnaire. Internal consistency was fair to excellent with Cronbach's alphas ranging from .76 on the Stereotypical scale to .92 on the Acting-Out scale. Inter-rater reliability between parents was good to excellent, with intra-class correlations ranging from .64 for the Anxious/Rigid scale to .85 for the Social Contacts scale. Test-retest reliability was also good to excellent for most scales, with intra-class correlations ranging from .62 on the Social Insight Problems scale to .90 on the Total, with the exception of the Stereotypical scale, which had a low intra-class correlation of .32 (Luteijn et al., 2000). Convergent and discriminant validity of the scales were measured by comparing scores on the CSBQ with scores on the Children's Behavior Checklist (CBCL; Achenbach, 1981) and the ABC (Krug et al., 1980a) and by comparing mean scores on the measure between diagnostic groups (Luteijn et al., 2000). The scales of the CSBQ were highly correlated with the scales of both the ABC and the CBCL. Three scales of the CSBQ were significantly correlated (.31 to .46) with scores from a checklist based on the *DSM-IV,* completed by a clinician. The exceptions were Acting-Out and Anxious/Rigid, indicating that these two scales were less specific to difficulties associated with an ASD. A discriminant function analysis revealed that 50% of children in the original five groups (PDD-NOS, high-functioning autistic children, attention deficit hyperactivity disorder, clinical control group, mentally retarded children, normal control group) could be correctly classified on the basis of the four discriminant functions: (1) General psychopathology, (2) Withdrawn behaviors, (3) Negative correlation with Social Insight Problems and a positive correlation with Anxious/Rigid, and (4) A strong relationship with

Stereotypical Behaviors and Anxious/Rigid Behaviors (Luteijn et al., 2000).

The authors suggest that the instrument may offer important contributions to research and clinical work, particularly because it revealed different patterns of scores in children with autism and children with PDD-NOS. Specifically, children with PDD-NOS scored higher on the Acting-Out scale than children with autism (Luteijn et al., 2000). One limitation is that the diagnostic groups were determined based on clinical diagnosis alone, rather than with standardized measures. In addition, the correlations of the CSBQ scales with the *DSM-IV* checklist were not high, although they were significant. At this point, the CSBQ remains in the early stages. Further investigation will be important in determining its research and clinical utility.

Achenbach System of Empirically Based Assessment

The Achenbach System of Empirically Based Assessment, Preschool Forms and Profiles (Achenbach & Rescorla, 2000) includes the CBCL for ages 1 year to 5 years, the Language Development Survey (LDS), and the Caregiver-Teacher report form (CTRF).

The CBCL is a questionnaire designed to be completed by parents or caregivers in a home setting, and only requires a fifth-grade reading level. The CBCL scores result in a Total Score, and Internalizing and Externalizing Scale, as well as Syndrome and *DSM* oriented Scales. The *DSM* Oriented Scales include a Pervasive Developmental Disorder Problems Scale that consists of 13 items. Each item is point rated on a 0 to 2 point scale based on behaviors over the past 2 months, with "0" indicating "not true," "1" indicating "sometimes true" or "somewhat true" and "2" indicating "very true" or "often true." Based on raw scores, T-scores can be calculated for each of the *DSM* Oriented Scales. There are cut points for the "borderline range" and the "clinical range." The C-TRF is a teacher rating form designed to be completed by daycare providers or teachers.

While the CBCL is not intended for diagnostic purposes, it is included in this chapter because it includes a Pervasive Developmental Disorders Scale as one of the *DSM* Oriented Scales. Achenbach and Rescorla (2000) specify that the *DSM* Oriented Scales are not equivalent to a diagnosis, because only behavior over the past 2 months is rated, the behaviors listed do not correspond exactly to diagnostic criteria, and the standard scores are based on age and gender comparisons and the *DSM-IV* is not. However, the scores could be used to identify children with behavior difficulties, and children who have elevated scores (borderline or clinical range) could be referred for further evaluation.

Test-retest reliability was quite high for the Pervasive Developmental Problems scale for both parents ($r = .86$) and teachers ($r = .83$) when the checklist was completed a second time 8 days after the initial rating. Inter-rater reliability on the Pervasive Developmental Problems Scale was moderate between parent to parent ratings ($r = .67$) and teacher to teacher ratings ($r = .67$).

Validity was assessed based on a "clinic referred sample" and a "non-referred sample." As a result, information is not available as to how valid the instrument is for screening specifically for ASD. While the CBCL and C-TRF should not be used as diagnostic instruments, they have potential value as screening tools or research measures of autistic behaviors.

CURRENTLY USED RATING SCALES

Childhood Autism Rating Scale

The Childhood Autism Rating Scale (CARS; Schopler, Reichler, & Renner, 1986) is the strongest, best-documented, and most widely used clinical rating scale for behaviors associated with autism. It has been used in studies all around the world and translated into many languages (Nordin, Gillberg, & Nyden, 1998; Pilowsky et al., 1998; Sponheim, 1996). It consists of 15 items on which children and adults are rated, generally after observation, on a 4-point scale. The scale requires minimal training. Training is available on videotape or in brief workshops. Points are added and a standard cut-off of 30 has been suggested and validated with various samples (Garfin et al., 1988; Schopler et al., 1980). Minor modifications have been suggested in which cut-offs are moved up a few points for very young children

(Lord, 1995) and down for high-functioning adolescents and adults (Mesibov, Schopler, Schaffer, & Michal, 1989).

Most of the information about the CARS is from studies of autistic children who function in the mild to moderate range of mental handicap. Studies of discriminant validity from carefully matched comparison groups are not yet available, though the CARS has been shown to discriminate autistic children from children without autism and some mental handicap (Schopler et al., 1988; Teal & Wiebe, 1986). Convergence between the CARS and the Autism Diagnostic Interview (ADI; Lord, 1995; Sevin et al., 1991; Venter et al., 1992) and correlations between CARS total scores and RLRS total scores (Sevin et al., 1991) were good for autistic children, but less good for young, nonautistic mentally handicapped children (Lord, 1995). Thus, the evidence that the CARS accurately identifies children with autism is stronger than the evidence that it discriminates between children with autism and mental-age matched children with other disorders.

The CARS was created before the introduction of *DSM-IV* and *ICD-10* diagnostic frameworks. It shows good agreement with clinicians' judgments using *DSM-III-R,* though it is somewhat over-inclusive compared to strict application of the criteria (Van Bourgondien, Marcus, & Schopler, 1992). Because, with the exception of the preceding reference, *DSM-III-R* was found to be more inclusive than clinicians' judgments of autism (Hertzig, Snow, New, & Shapiro, 1990; Volkmar, Cicchetti, Bregman, & Cohen, 1992), this finding suggests that the CARS identifies more children as having autism than the currently accepted three-domain diagnostic frameworks of *DSM-IV* (American Psychiatric Association, 1994) and *ICD-10* (World Health Organization, 1992). Children with minimal verbal skills and/or moderate to severe mental handicap may be more likely to fall into the range of autism, in part because items on the CARS rating language skill and mental handicap comprise part of the total score (Pilowsky et al., 1998). For the purposes of screening or determining services, over-inclusiveness of children with clear impairments is not as problematic as over-exclusion (Wing & Gould, 1979). However, implications may be different for research. The CARS cannot be used alone to make discriminations for complex diagnostic cases in which *DSM-IV* or *ICD-10* criteria are the standard; nevertheless, as discussed earlier, multiple sources are important in any diagnostic decision making and it may provide important information in addition to other sources (Nordin & Gillberg, 1996a, 1996b).

The CARS total score has held up to repeated, careful examinations, as internally consistent (Kurita, Kita, & Miyake, 1992; Sturmey et al., 1992) and reliable across raters (Garfin et al., 1988; Kurita et al., 1992; Sevin et al., 1991). Inter-rater reliability for individual items has been found to be more variable. Some of the scales (e.g., Relating to People, Imitation) have consistently shown high correlations between different raters' scores. Statistics such as kappas, which control for base rates, have not yet been employed (Garfin et al., 1988; Sevin et al., 1991). One of the important contributions of the CARS was the provision of specific anchorpoints for each item in a way that allows the rater to take into account developmental level. The difficulty with this strategy is that how anchorpoints are defined differs across items. Interpretation of scores on individual items, particularly given the inconsistent evidence of reliability at this level, must be carried out with care.

Besides direct observation by a clinician, for which the CARS was designed, it has also been used in chart review, scored directly by parents and teachers, and used as part of a parent interview (Schopler et al., 1988). On the whole, classifications and correlations between raters for total scores have been relatively high across different procedures. Several studies have suggested that clinicians tend to rate behaviors as more severe than do fathers or mothers (Bebko, Konstantareas, & Springer, 1987; Konstantareas & Homatidis, 1989), with other studies finding few differences (Freeman, Perry, & Factor, 1991; Schopler et al., 1988).

A factor analysis of the CARS of 90 children with clinical diagnoses of autism or PDD-NOS based on *DSM-III-R* criteria yielded five factors out of 15 items: Social Communication, Emotional Reactivity, Social Orienting, Cognitive and Behavioral Consistency, and Odd Sensory Exploration. Cognitive and Behavioral Consistency and Emotional Reactivity were significantly correlated with age;

Social Communication was significantly correlated with gender, IQ, and Vineland scores. Factor-based scales distinguished children with autism from those with PDD-NOS. It was suggested that use of these factor scores might increase the sensitivity of the CARS with younger and/or higher functioning individuals within the autistic spectrum (Stella, Mundy, & Tuchman, 1999).

Overall, the CARS is the most widely researched and employed rating scale of autism in the United States. Versions are available in numerous languages other than English. It is a reliable screening instrument for children with autism and mental retardation that can be used with minimal training across a range of situations. Its scores do not correspond to current formal diagnostic frameworks for autism, such as *DSM-IV* and *ICD-10,* and so for research purposes, it may identify a somewhat different population than suggested by those systems.

Autism Behavior Checklist

The Autism Behavior Checklist (ABC) is one component of the Autism Screening Instrument for Educational Planning (ASIEP; Krug et al., 1980b) and the only one that has been evaluated psychometrically. It builds on Rimland's Form E-2, the original Kanner criteria (1943), the Behavior Observation Schedule (Freeman et al., 1978), the BRIAAC (Ruttenberg et al., 1977), and several other sources. It contains 57 items in five areas: sensory, relating, body and object use, language and social interaction, and self-help. It was intended to be completed by teachers as an initial step in educational planning. No special training is required. It has also been used with parents on a retrospective basis for families of high-functioning children (Yirmiya et al., 1994) and on a current basis, yielding somewhat higher scores than with teachers (Volkmar et al., 1988). The rater completes dichotomous ratings, which are weighted according to the authors' data and yield a total score. Ranges, on the basis of a very large, but unspecified sample, are provided for a high probability of autism ($\geq$ 68), low probability of autism (under 53), and mixed. Several investigators have reported that the suggested cut-offs are too high, and result in a high proportion of false negatives (Miranda-Linne et al., 1997; Volkmar et al., 1988; Wadden, Bryson, & Rodger, 1991). More recently, Krug, Arick, and Almond (1993) recommended using a cut-off of greater than 53 for classifying a child as probably autistic. When using this lower cut-off, Eaves et al. (2000) found that overall classification accuracy was 80%, specificity (correct negatives) was 91% and sensitivity (correct positives) was 77%. Norms and standard profiles are provided for samples of autistic, typical, deaf, and blind students.

Initial estimates for inter-rater reliability were high, though based on small samples and not controlling for chance (Krug et al., 1980b). Later estimates have been less high (Volkmar et al., 1988). Discriminant validity has been variable, in part depending on whether investigators generated discriminant functions from data within their group or used the cut-offs suggested by the authors. In the latter case, there was considerable overlap between autistic and mentally handicapped populations (Volkmar et al., 1988). In the former case, diagnostic differentiation was, not surprisingly, better (Nordin & Gillberg, 1996b; Wadden et al., 1991). Current scores on the ABC did not meet criteria for most of a group of verbal adolescents with autism, but retrospective accounts did (Yirmiya et al., 1994). Differences in studies may also be related to the use of a somewhat broader definition of autism, in which case the ABC becomes more accurate in diagnosing autism, and inclusion of subjects with Down syndrome, which may decrease the false positive rate (Wadden et al., 1991).

Internal consistency for the total scale is good. Various investigations have yielded different results in terms of the internal consistency and intercorrelations of the five areas; both chronological and mental age may account for much of the variance. Subscales of relating and object/body use were the strongest in one study in terms of inter-item correlations and lack of rogue items (Sturmey et al., 1992). Several investigators have suggested that discriminant validity may be equally good using fewer items (Volkmar et al. 1994; Wadden et al., 1991).

Convergent validity between the ABC and other instruments has been measured for the CARS and the RLRS and found to be poor, suggesting that the ABC's usefulness as an independent diagnostic instrument may be limited, particularly since it was constructed before current theoretical frameworks for autism were proposed (Nordin & Gillberg, 1996b). For verbal autistic adolescents, retrospective parent ratings on the ABC about their children's behavior between 3 and 5 years, related to whether children were considered to have "residual" autism or not, but diagnosis did not correspond to the cut-offs suggested by the authors of the scale (Yirmiya et al., 1994).

The ABC emphasizes autistic symptomatology rather than prosocial behaviors and so is quite different than several of the other instruments, for example, the ADI-R. Because of its emphasis on observable features associated with, but not limited to autism, the ABC may be helpful in documenting change. This would be particularly true for changes in the presence of abnormal behaviors. Unlike several other autism scales that showed more consistent convergent validity with each other, the ABC is correlated with the American Association of Mental Deficiency (AAMD) Adaptive Behavior Scale-School Version (Sevin et al., 1991). The ABC alone cannot be considered a strong diagnostic instrument because of its limited relationship to current diagnostic frameworks. As it stands, it is of limited value as a screening instrument because of variable sensitivity. However, the ABC may be useful in documenting response to treatment and educational programming.

Revised Behavior Summarized Evaluation

The Revised Behavior Summarized Evaluation (BSE-R) is composed of items from two overlapping instruments, the Behavioral Summarized Evaluation scale (BSE) and the Infant Behavioral Summarized Evaluation scale (IBSE; Barthelemy et al., 1997) and is primarily designed to document behavioral symptoms associated with autism as they relate to neurophysiological measures. New items have been added concerning nonverbal communication, emotion, and perception, as well as intention and imitation. These scales are available in French and have been used in many basic research investigations of children with autism in France (for example, see Zakian, Malvy, Desombre, Roux, & Lenoir, 2000). There are

20 items in the BSE selected from 19 items from the autism factor in the IBSE, the form for children under 4 years of age (Adrien et al., 1992) and 20 in the original BSE (Barthelemy et al., 1990). Items are scored on a five-point scale administered by trained raters, on the basis of direct or videotaped observation, discussion of history, and access to information from multiple sources. With trained raters, most individual items have shown very good inter-rater reliability. Inter-rater reliability for total scores has been excellent, though ratings were not typically based on independently acquired information.

Factor analyses have shown loadings within one primary Interaction Disorder factor, accounting for 38% of the variance and a Modulation factor, accounting for 10%. Results from previous versions indicated adequate internal consistency (Adrien et al., 1992; Barthelemy et al., 1990). The Interaction factor was not correlated with age but was highly negatively correlated with IQ ($r = -.59$). Discriminant function analyses accurately grouped 80% to 85% of autistic and mentally handicapped children using the IBSE (Adrien et al., 1992). Interaction Disorder factor scores were correlated with expert ratings of severity of autism (Barthelemy et al., 1990, 1997). A cut-off score of 27 on the Interaction Disorder factor on the BSE-R yielded a sensitivity of .74 and a specificity of .71 (Barthelemy et al., 1997). Convergent validity with other measures except the Rimland E2 is not yet published. There is some suggestion that the BSE-R may be particularly helpful in measuring response to treatment (Boiron, Barthelemy, Adrien, Martineau, & Lelord, 1992) and in neurophysiological studies (Barthelemy et al., 1997).

The Gilliam Autism Rating Scale

The Gilliam Autism Rating Scale (GARS; Gilliam, 1995) is a parent-completed surveillance questionnaire, designed to indicate the probability that a child has autism. It is intended for individuals between 3 and 22 years of age. The questionnaire consists of 56 items across four subscales: Social Interaction, Communication, Stereotyped Behaviors, and Developmental Disturbances. The first three subscales listed are based on a child's current behavior, and the final scale is based on a child's developmental history. Each item is rated on a four-point scale, from "Never Observed" to "Frequently Observed." Item scores are totaled for each scale and correspond to a standard score with a mean of 10 and a standard deviation of 3. Typically, all scales of the GARS are completed. However, if a child is nonverbal and/or the parent does not have knowledge of the child's early history, the Communication or Developmental History scales may be omitted. A standard score or Autism Quotient can be based on 4, 3, or 2 scales of the GARS. An Autism Quotient is derived by summing relevant scale scores, yielding a standard score with a mean of 100 and a standard deviation of 15. The Autism Quotient is divided into seven ordinal categories, ranging from a "low probability" that a child has autism to a "high probability" that a child has autism.

Internal consistency of the items on the scale using Cronbach's alpha yielded coefficient alphas ranging from .88 to .96 (Gilliam, 1995). Correlations among individual GARS scales rating current behaviors are relatively high. The Developmental Disturbances scale was not significantly correlated with any of the other scales, although it was weakly, but significantly, correlated with the Autism Quotient, $r = .34$ (South et al., 2002). Test-retest reliability on a small sample of 11 children, using three of the scales (excluding Developmental History) revealed correlations between totals ranging from $r = .81$ (Communication) to $r = .88$ (Autism Quotient). Neither item agreement nor classification agreement across time or rater were reported. Finally, inter-rater reliability was evaluated for the various pairs of raters (parent-parent, teacher-teacher, and parent-teacher). Teacher-to-teacher and teacher-to-parent inter-rater reliability estimates were all strong, ranging from .85 to .99. Ratings were weakest for the Parent-to-Parent ratings with reliability ranging from .55 to .85 (Gilliam, 1995).

The initial reference sample for the GARS consisted of data collected for 1,092 children, adolescents, and adults (Gilliam, 1995). Although a parent or professional rater reported each individual's diagnosis, an independent professional did not verify it. Thus, there was no "gold standard" for diagnosis. Concurrent validity was evaluated by correlating standard scores on the GARS with scores on the ABC; all correlations were large and significant. Discriminant validity was evaluated by determining how well the measure discriminated between groups that were diagnosed with autism as compared to those who were not. Significant differences were found between the means of those diagnosed with autism versus those who were not. Using the Autism Quotient, 90% of the subjects were classified accurately.

A later independent study of the validity of the GARS was based on a sample of 119 individuals with autism, all of whom had extensive diagnostic evaluations, including the ADOS and the ADI-R, by experts in ASDs (South et al., 2002). The validity data from this study was disappointing, with the GARS receiving a sensitivity of .48 compared to "gold standard" diagnoses, indicating that 52% of children with autism (based on the ADI, ADOS, and clinical impression) were missed by this instrument (South et al., 2002). Convergent validity was also investigated by comparing the GARS scores to scores on the ADOS and the ADI-R (South et al., 2002). There were no significant correlations between any of the GARS scales and the ADOS. Small but significant correlations were reported between the ADI-R Social Interactions score and the GARS Social Interaction Scale ($r = .26$), Stereotyped Behaviors Scale ($r = .21$), and the Autism Quotient ($r = .23$).

Given the current information about its validity and the high rates of false negatives, the GARS cannot yet be used in isolation as a diagnostic tool. This is particularly concerning because, although most research projects have used the instrument in conjunction with other instruments (Asano et al., 2001; Owley et al., 2001), some studies have employed the GARS for diagnostic purposes (Schreck & Mulick, 2000). The use of this instrument may be even more problematic in clinical settings where the professionals know less about autism. In this context, many children with autism could be missed and not referred for appropriate services. The author intends to revise the instrument and has proposed using a lower cut-off score (South et al., 2002).

DIAGNOSTIC INTERVIEWS

Autism Diagnostic Interview-Revised

The Autism Diagnostic Interview-Revised (ADI-R) is a semi-structured, investigator-based interview for caregivers of children and adults for whom autism or pervasive developmental disorders is a possible diagnosis. Originally developed as a research diagnostic instrument (ADI; Le Couteur et al., 1989), the ADI-R has been modified to be appropriate for a broader age range of children than the original ADI (Lord et al., 1994). It is linked specifically to *ICD-10* and *DSM-IV* criteria. A revised shortened version is now available, consisting of about 93 items. The most recent version takes about 2 hours for an experienced interviewer to administer (Le Couteur, Lord, & Rutter, 2003). Researchers are required to participate in training workshops and to establish reliability with investigators from other centers. Clinicians are encouraged to use video training materials, and may use the instrument without intensive training within the ethical guidelines for test use in their professions. Nonetheless, administering the ADI-R requires general experience in both interviewing and working with individuals with autism to be effective. The ADI-R has been translated into 11 languages and the ADI and the ADI-R are cited as the "gold standard" for diagnosis in many countries.

Psychometric data for the ADI and ADI-R have been carefully acquired with attention to matching across samples and to maintaining as much "blindness" as possible for raters, but is based on very small samples (Rutter et al., 2003). This limitation is compensated for slightly by independent psychometric data published by other major research centers that have used the ADI or ADI-R as a diagnostic instrument (Constantino et al., 2004; Cuccaro, Shao, Grubber, et al., 2003; deBildt et al., 2004; Kolevzon et al., 2004; Saemundsen, Magnússon, Smári, & Sigurdardóttir, 2003). Inter-rater reliability has been good to excellent for individual items and excellent for domain scores, including those for each of the three subscales: social reciprocity, communication, and restricted, repetitive behaviors that correspond to the *DSM IV/ICD-10* do-

mains (see Chakrabarti & Fombonne, 2001; Rutter et al., 2003). Test-retest reliability, on a very small sample, was also good (Lord et al., 1994). Change over time is reflected in items that include whether the behavior "ever" occurred and items that focus on "current" manifestations. On the whole, however, the ADI-R is not intended to measure change. There has been a deliberate attempt to include items that will reflect autism of varying levels of severity and at varying points in development.

Internal consistency is excellent within the three domains. Differentiation between autistic and mentally handicapped children and adults is excellent, with the restriction that the instrument tends to be over-inclusive for individuals with mental ages of less than 18 months (Lord et al., 1993) and with severely to profoundly retarded individuals (Nordin & Gillberg, 1998). One study found that the ADI was slightly under-inclusive with very verbal children with autism or pervasive developmental disorders (Yirmiya et al., 1994); another study reported that it was over-inclusive (Mahoney et al., 1998). Convergent validity with the CARS was excellent after age 3 (Lord, 1995; Pilowsky et al., 1998); convergent validity with the Autism Diagnostic Observation Schedule (see below) has also been good for most samples (Hepburn et al., 2003; Lord, Risi, et al., 2000; Lord et al., 1989). The exception was a recent study of Bishop and Norbury (2002) in which children with language impairments, in some cases also with ASD, were given the ADI-R or SCQ, the ADOS, and the Communication Competence Checklist (CCC). ADI-R and SCQ classifications were comparable to school classifications but not with ADOS scores or scores on the CCC, which were similar to each other. It was not clear if this was related to specific difficulties using the ASD instruments in a relatively narrowly defined verbal sample, administration of a single module of the ADOS regardless of language level in some cases (all children were given Module 3) or differences in parent report and school classification systems and direct observations.

Because of the widespread use of the ADI-R in defining samples, there has been a recent surge of interest in how to use the ADI-R for a variety of other purposes beyond classification, including quantifying severity (Lord, Leventhal, & Cook, 2001; Spiker, Lotspeich, Dimiceli, Myers, & Risch, 2002; Szatmari et al., 2002; Volkmar & Lord, 1998), describing individual differences (Alarcón et al., 2002; Cuccaro, Shao, Bass, et al., 2003; Tanguay, Robertson, & Derrick, 1998) and creating more homogeneous subsets of participants for genetic analyses (Buxbaum et al., 2001; Freitag, 2002; Shao, Raiford, et al., 2002; Shao, Wolpert, et al., 2002; Tadevosyan-Leyfer et al., 2003). These studies have used a wide range of analytic techniques, sometimes related to different purposes, and have been carried out on a wide range of items (e.g., sometimes all ADI-R item scores are included; sometimes selected items, sometimes domain scores). Studies have varied considerably whether age, IQ or verbal level were controlled. It is clear that, depending on the ranges studied, all three of these features can affect ADI/ADI-R scores (Cox et al., 1999; Cuccaro, Shao, Bass, et al., 2003; Spiker et al., 1994).

Overall, no differences were found in domain scores for multiplex families compared to singletons (Cuccaro, Shao, Bass, et al., 2003). Factor analyses of domain scores and Vineland adaptive behavior scores (Sparrow, Balla, & Cicchetti, 1984) in two separate samples yielded a symptom number factor and a separate factor for level of functioning, determined by the Vineland adaptive behavior scores (Szatmari et al., 2002). Only the ADI-R domain of nonverbal communication showed any evidence of concordance within multiplex families (MacLean et al., 1999), a relationship also found by another research group (Freitag et al., 2002). In another sample, heritability was supported for a continuous severity gradient composed of ADI-R scores, verbal—nonverbal status and nonverbal IQ (Spiker et al., 2002). Several other studies that have measured concordance within twin pairs (Le Couteur et al., 1996) and families (Spiker et al., 1994) found contradictory results with little concordance on any dimension for monozygotic twins, but concordance for ADI-R repetitive scores found in families (Freitag et al., 2002; Spiker et al., 1994).

Several groups of genetics researchers have produced increased homogeneity and more significant results by subsetting groups by individual items within the ADI-R repetitive domain (Alarcón et al., 2002) or by the entire domain score (Silverman et al., 2002). Other studies have found that only particular combinations of items (e.g., insistence on sameness, compulsions) yielded similar results (Shao et al., 2003) for other genetic regions. Though potential genetic significance of repetitive behaviors emerges across papers, in most cases, studies have not replicated each other, nor have age, IQ, or verbal status been controlled consistently.

The other way in which the ADI-R has been used within genetic studies has been to produce subsets based on language delay (based on measures of age of first word or age of first phrase) or on current language level. Concordance for current verbal ability has been shown in some cases (Freitag et al., 2002; MacLean et al., 1999; Spiker et al., 2002), but on the whole, only delay in either first single words (Alarcón et al., 2002) or first phrases (Bradford et al., 2001; Buxbaum et al., 2001; Shao, Wolpert, et al., 2002) or delay accompanied by the presence of a language-delayed relative (Folstein & Mankoski, 2000) increased the significance of specific regions.

Several factor analyses and principal component analyses have been carried out, primarily with data from earlier versions of the ADI. In one study, factors emerged that reflected three aspects of social communication: Affective Reciprocity, Theory of Mind, and Joint Attention (Tanguay et al., 1998). In another study (Lord, 1990), social and communication items both loaded on two factors; in this case, the factors seemed to reflect initiations versus social responsiveness. In a recent study, six factors emerged, that together accounted for about 40% of the variance (Tadevosyan-Leyfer et al., 2003). These factors consisted of items scored for both current functioning and "ever"/most abnormal 4 to 5, that were present in both the early ADI and the ADI-R so they represent a particular subset of questions. Factors were validated in another sample using additional psychometric measures. Constantino and Todd (2003) recently reported a factor analysis of the ADI-R, with a different pattern.

It seems very likely that items within the ADI-R can be combined in more fruitful ways than the present algorithm domain scores. One consistent finding across these studies is the overlap between "communication" and "social" items, suggesting that they are not separate domains of skill (Lord, 1996; Tadevosyan-Leyfer et al., 2003; Tanguay et al., 1998). Several factors with different organizations of repetitive behaviors have also been proposed. To date, however, factors in this area and across other domains have differed considerably across investigations. The development of a more stable measure or measures of repetitive interests and behaviors will be an important contribution to better understanding of phenotypes in ASDs. Larger samples, including individuals without autism, will be necessary in order to control effects of age, verbal status and IQ. Replication across sites and samples will be crucial in determining the factors of greatest interest or usefulness.

ADI scores have also been shown to be related to ABC scores, given by history, for a group of high-functioning children (Yirmiya et al., 1994). Because of its clear link to *DSM-IV* and *ICD-10* and its mulitdimensional approach, the ADI-R offers the potential of providing empirical information and diagnostic guidance about other PDDs besides autism. However, cut-offs for nonautism pervasive developmental disorders are not yet available. Several investigations have proposed various cut offs, including one or two points below autism thresholds (over all the domains), but none have yet been empirically validated (Cox et al., 1999; Dawson et al., 2002).

The Diagnostic Interview for Social and Communication Disorders

The Diagnostic Interview for Social and Communication Disorders (DISCO: Wing et al., 2002) is a standardized, semi-structured interview, now in its ninth revision. It is based on the Handicaps, Behaviors and Skills schedule (HBS) (Wing & Gould, 1978, 1979). In 1990, a clinical need emerged for an instrument that extended beyond the school age years, into adulthood. At this time, the first version of the DISCO was developed to assess the pattern of development in individuals with ASDs and their individual needs (Wing et al., 2002). The primary purpose of the DISCO is not to provide a diagnostic classification. Rather, the instrument was designed to obtain information

on behaviors relevant to autism for the purpose of assisting clinicians in determining a child's development in different areas as well as his individual needs (Leekam, Libby, Wing, Gould, & Taylor, 2002). It is based on the concept of a spectrum of disorders rather than categorical diagnoses.

The DISCO is an investigator-based interview in which the interviewer asks questions designed to elicit descriptions of behavior and makes coding decisions based on the information provided. The coding of the items can be based on information obtained during the interview as well as through other information, such as direct observation. The DISCO includes items covering behavioral manifestations of the deficits associated with ASDs, including social interaction, communication, imagination, and repetitive activities. In addition, it includes items designed to assess developmental levels in a variety of domains. Many of these items are based on the Vineland Adaptive Behavior Scales (Sparrow et al., 1984). There is also a section on atypical behaviors that are not specific to autism. These include unusual responses to sensory stimuli, difficulties in attention and activity level, challenging behaviors, and other psychiatric disorders. Items relating to developmental delay are rated on a 3-point scale, as "delay," "minor delay," or "no problem." An actual age is coded for some of the developmental items. Atypical behaviors receive codes for "current" and "ever" and are rated as "severe," "minor," or "not present."

The reliability of the DISCO 9 was evaluated based on a sample of 82 children with diagnoses of ASDs, learning disability, or no diagnosis (typically developing) between the ages of 3 and 11 years of age (Wing et al., 2002). Inter-rater reliability was measured, comparing two interviewers/coders, using Kappa's alpha for items with two or three codes and by intraclass correlations (ICC) for items with four or more codes. Agreement was high (k or ICC > .75) for 85% of all ratings for both preschool age and school age children. Within the Developmental Skills area, the lowest agreements (.67 to .80) were for items that were not part of the diagnostic algorithm (e.g., reading, drawing). Of greater concern, was the low agreement (with kappas < .40) on some of the social interaction items and for many of the repetitive routine items, which are part of the diagnostic algorithm. Inter-rater reliability was higher for the "ever" items than for the "current" items. Based on this information, the authors plan to make some changes designed to improve reliability, which will be included in the DISCO 10.

While the DISCO was designed for clinical purposes, provisional algorithms have been written for research purposes. Recently, two diagnostic algorithms for the DISCO 9 were developed and investigated (Leekam et al., 2002). One of the algorithms was based on criteria for autistic disorder in the *ICD-10* (World Health Organization, 1992) and the other was based on the criteria for autistic spectrum disorder as defined by Wing and Gould (1979). When comparing clinical diagnosis to algorithm diagnoses for a sample of children with language disorders, learning disability, and autistic disorder, both algorithms were significantly related to a diagnosis of autistic disorder or nonautistic disorder. However, discrepancies were also found, primarily for the clinical nonautistic group using the *ICD-10* algorithm such that 10 children with clinical diagnoses of a language disorder or learning disability met *ICD-10* algorithm criteria for autistic disorder. Four children with a learning disability diagnosis met both *ICD-10* and Wing and Gould algorithm criteria for autistic disorder, while none with a language disorder met criteria using both algorithms. DISCO 9 algorithms were also generated for Gillberg's diagnostic criteria for Asperger's Disorder and *ICD-10* criteria for Asperger's Disorder. Of the 200 children included in the study, all of whom met *ICD-10* criteria for autism or atypical autism, only 3 (1%) met criteria for Asperger's Disorder based on the *DSM-IV* algorithm and 91 (45%) met criteria based on Gillberg's algorithm criteria (Leekam, Libby, et al., 2000).

The DISCO was primarily designed for clinical purposes, particularly for assisting in generating recommendations for individuals and adults with autistic spectrum disorders. The authors are revising the instrument to improve inter-rater reliability and to generate diagnostic algorithms that can be used for research purposes.

DIRECT OBSERVATION SCALES

Autism Diagnostic Observation Schedule

The Autism Diagnostic Observation Schedule (ADOS) is a standardized protocol for the observation of social and communicative behavior of children for whom a diagnosis of autism or ASDs is in question (Lord, Rutter, DiLavore, & Risi, 1999; Lord, Risi, et al., 2000). The original ADOS was developed in order to be used with children who had fluent phrase speech; the Pre-Linguistic Autism Diagnostic Observation Schedule (PL-ADOS) was intended for preschool children with little or no expressive language (DiLavore et al., 1995; Lord et al., 1989). Recently they have been combined and extended within a single instrument, the Autism Diagnostic Observation Schedule (Lord, Rutter, DiLavore, & Risi, 1999), formerly called the ADOS-G, with the PL-ADOS comprising most of Module 1, the original ADOS comprising most of Module 3, and the addition of new modules for children with some language but not fluent spontaneous speech (Module 2) and for high-functioning adolescents and adults (Module 4). The new ADOS thus provides the same information as the original ADOS and PL-ADOS for individuals ranging in age and development from nonverbal toddlers to verbally fluent adults of average or higher intelligence.

The ADOS and PL-ADOS were originally developed as companion instruments for the ADI. Their purpose is to provide a series of structured and semi-structured "presses" for social interaction, communication, and play that can be coded immediately following administration (although often videotapes are made as well). They are scored in the context of a diagnostic algorithm for autism. The rationale is that context can have very significant effects on social-communicative behaviors. Consequently, it is important to standardize contexts as well as judgments in any diagnostic observation of these behaviors. Both instruments can be administered by a trained examiner in about 30 to 45 minutes. Training and establishment of reliability with another center is required for research, but not for clinical use. A substantial amount of experience, skill, and practice in working with individuals with autism or PDD is necessary to use either instrument effectively.

Inter-rater reliability is very good for items and excellent for totals. Internal consistency within domains of social-communication and restricted-repetitive behaviors is excellent (Lord, Risi, et al., 2000); test-retest reliability is adequate. Discriminant validity is excellent for diagnostic algorithms using social-communication scores. In the normative data, within each module, social and communication scores were relatively independent of absolute expressive language level. However, recent studies have found relatively strong effects of level of verbal impairment (e.g., verbal IQ), communication scores, and for social domain scores, particularly with preschool children (Munson, Dawson, Lord, Rogers, & Sigman, in press).

The instruments were expanded into the four modules that comprise the ADOS because of varying problems of sensitivity and specificity by age and language level. Diagnostic algorithms for the PL-ADOS were under-inclusive for children with phrase speech with about 80% accuracy overall for autistic and/or nonautistic mentally handicapped 3- and 4-year-olds. For the original ADOS, the diagnostic algorithm was over-inclusive for children with mental handicap and difficult behaviors and was under-inclusive for very verbal adolescents, with about 87% accuracy comparing autistic to mentally handicapped and behavior-disordered, language impaired children. The design of four different modules has increased the diagnostic accuracy of the ADOS considerably, but nevertheless, it remains over-inclusive with very young (under 30 months), mentally retarded children (Hepburn et al., 2003), and under-inclusive with very mild, verbal adolescents and adults with autistic spectrum disorders (International Molecular Genetics Study of Autism Consortium, 1998; Lord, Risi, et al., 2000).

A recent factor analysis of the original ADOS yielded three factors that accounted for 72% of the variance (Robertson, Tanguay, L'Ecuyer, Sims, & Waltrip, 1999) in a sample of verbally fluent children with ASD. These factors, similar to those found in an analysis by the same authors of ADI data (Tanguay et al., 1998), were Joint Attention, Affective Reciprocity, and Theory of Mind. Theory of Mind scores on the two instruments were correlated

$r = .31$, but scores on the other factors were not. Together with findings from the related analysis of the ADI-R, these results highlight the importance of considering social development and communication together in the use of these diagnostic instruments.

Like the ADI, the ADOS was not originally intended to measure change, although it may be possible to use the standard behavior samples provided by the ADOS in conjunction with other coding systems as a measure of response to treatment (Owley et al., 2001). As is the case with the ADI, it is hoped that mulitdimensional scoring of the ADOS may allow for better quantification of nonautism pervasive developmental disorders, most notably PDD-NOS and Asperger's disorder. Clinically, the ADOS is particularly helpful in providing information concerning social and communicative functioning, which has been collected in a positive but standard context, to parents, therapists, and teachers.

The Psychoeducational Profile-Revised

The Psychoeducational Profile (PEP; Schopler & Reichler, 1979) is a developmental and diagnostic assessment instrument designed specifically for assessing children with ASDs. It was revised in 1990 (PEP-R; Schopler, Reichler, Bashford, Lansing, & Marcus, 1990), is currently under revision once again, and will soon be available as the Psychoeducational Profile-Third Edition (PEP-3). The instrument has been translated into several different languages. The PEP and PEP-R are most appropriate for use with children between the chronological ages of about 3 and 7 years. The normative sample included 420 children between 1 year and 7 years of age. Much of the available published information covers the PEP as well as the PEP-R. Because this is a chapter on diagnosis, only the pathology scales will be reviewed. The pathology scales of the PEP-R are designed to rate the severity of the characteristics of autism in the following areas: Response to Materials (8 items), Language (11 items), Affect & Development of Relationships (12 items), and Sensory Modalities (12 items). On these scales, pathology is rated as "absent," "mild" or "severe."

Both convergent and discriminant validity of the original PEP's pathology section have been evaluated. Schopler and Reichler (1979) reported a high correlation ($r = .80$) between pathology scores on the Childhood Autism Rating Scales (CARS) and pathology scores on the PEP. When comparing children with autism with children without autism, children with autism exhibited higher pathology scores on the PEP (Lam & Rao, 1993). Internal consistency of the diagnostic section of the PEP-R pathology subscales has been reported to be good, with Cronbach's alphas between .84 and .97 (Steerneman, Muris, Merckelbach, & Willems, 1997). Very little information is available on the inter-rater reliability of the pathology subscales of the PEP or the PEP-R. The one study that investigated inter-rater reliability reported a mean kappa score of .69 (Muris, Steerneman, & Ratering, 1997), which is considered adequate.

Much of the information available on the PEP is based on the original version of the measure. Many of the studies are small scale studies conducted on translations of the instrument. The developmental scores of the PEP-R have been used in outcome studies (Ozonoff & Cathcart, 1998; Panerai, Ferrante, & Caputo, 1997). In research, the pathology subscales are used much less frequently than the developmental subscales, which are most often administered to establish the developmental levels of lower functioning children with ASDs or to evaluate treatment outcomes. The PEP is frequently used in conjunction with the CARS in research studies measuring both diagnostic classification and developmental level.

The Adolescent and Adult Psychoeducational Profile

The Adolescent and Adult Psychoeducational Profile (AAPEP; Mesibov, Schopler, & Caison, 1989) is an extension of the PEP and was also developed by Division TEACCH. Like the PEP, the AAPEP is designed to assess individuals with ASDs for the purpose of developing individualized treatment goals and recommendations. The AAPEP is a criterion-referenced test and targets individuals over 12 years of age with moderate to severe mental retardation. As a result, the targeted areas focus on concerns that often appear as adulthood approaches and include matters such as semi-independent functioning and psychopathology in the community.

The AAPEP incorporates three separate scales: a direct observation scale and two interview sections (a home scale and school/work scale). Each scale includes six functioning areas: vocational skills, independent functioning, leisure skills, vocational behavior, functional communication, and interpersonal behavior. Little information is available on the validity and reliability of this instrument. Inter-rater reliability was evaluated by calculating the percent agreement between two independent raters and was determined to be sufficient (with the exception of Interpersonal Behaviors on the Direct Observation scale; $r = .68$), ranging from $r = .74$ to $r = .95$ (Mesibov, Schopler, & Caison, 1989; Mesibov, Schopler, Schaffer, & Landrus, 1988). There has been little research using the AAPEP; however, one study evaluated progress in adults with ASDs who were living in a group home setting (Persson, 2000).

There are few scales available for measuring functional behaviors and skills in adults with autism. The AAPEP is not intended for diagnostic purposes and focuses primarily on the assessment of skills required for independent living. The best application of the AAPEP is for identifying target areas for intervention or skill building.

RELATED DIAGNOSTIC AND BEHAVIORAL ASSESSMENT INSTRUMENTS

The Communication and Symbolic Behavior Scales, Developmental Profile

The Communication and Symbolic Behavior Scales, Developmental Profile (CSBS DP) is a standardized instrument designed for screening and evaluating communication and symbolic abilities in young children between the ages of 6 and 24 months (Wetherby & Prizant, 2002). The published version is based on an earlier version designed specifically for research purposes (Wetherby & Prizant, 1993). There are three separate parts of the CSBS DP, including a screening instrument (CSBS DP Infant and Toddler Checklist) and two follow up assessment tools: a parent questionnaire (CSBS DP Caregiver Questionnaire) and a direct observation section (CSBS DP Behavior Sample). The purposes of the CSBS DP are screening and identifying children at risk for language and developmental delays, not specifically autism, as well as assessment and identification of delays in social communication, expressive language, and symbolic abilities. The CSBS DP also provides an opportunity for documentation of progress over time. The CSBS DP consists of seven cluster areas (Emotion and Eye Gaze, Communication, Gestures, Sounds, Words, Understanding, Object Use) that are included in one of three composites (Social Communication, Expressive Speech & Language, and Symbolic Abilities).

Although the CSBS was not specifically designed to screen or evaluate young children with ASDs, there is evidence that information gathered from the Behavior Sample may have some value in screening for ASDs. Wetherby et al. (in press) compared children with ASDs, children with developmental delays, and children who were typically developing using the Systematic Observation of Red Flags (SORF) for Autism Spectrum Disorders in Young Children (Wetherby et al., in press), which is based on the Behavior Sample of the CSBS. The SORF includes 29 items from both the diagnostic criteria and research on ASDs in young children. It covers five composite areas and includes reciprocal social interaction, unconventional gestures, unconventional sounds and words, repetitive behaviors and restricted interests, and emotional regulation (Wetherby et al., in press). Inter-rater reliability for the SORF was high (89.7% to 100% agreement across children and 83% to 100% across items).

The SORF shows promise as a screening instrument, with sensitivity, specificity, positive and negative predictive values all over 80% (Wetherby et al., in press), based on the Behavior Sample. A discriminant function analysis indicated that when 15 red flags were considered, 100% of the children in the ASD group, 83% of the developmentally delayed group, and 100%

of the typical group were correctly predicted (Wetherby et al., in press). At this point, there are no cut-offs suggested, but children who demonstrate most of the 15 red flags should be referred for further evaluation. More investigation using the SORF and CSBS behavior sample with children with ASDs is warranted as it shows promise as a valuable screening tool.

The Children's Communication Checklist

The Children's Communication Checklist (CCC) was developed by Dorothy Bishop (1998) to assess pragmatic difficulties within the speech and language impaired population. Although there are several standardized tests available for assessing language form, such as syntax and phonology, adequate standardized assessment instruments for assessing pragmatic difficulties are very rare. The CCC is designed to be completed by a professional, such as a teacher or a speech and language therapist, who knows the child well (Bishop, 1998; Bishop & Baird, 2001). It consists of five scales assessing pragmatic aspects of speech: inappropriate initiation, coherence, stereotyped language, use of context, and rapport. In addition, it includes two item sets designed to assess other aspects of speech and language (speech production and syntactic complexity), as well as two item sets intended to assess nonlanguage features of autistic spectrum disorders (social relationships and interests). Each behavior is described, and the rater is asked to indicate if it "definitely applies," "applies somewhat," "does not apply," or if they are "unable to judge." Most of the data available on the CCC is based on children between the ages of 5 and 17 years.

There is debate in the literature as to whether there is a pure group of children with pragmatic difficulties and the extent to which they overlap with children with ASDs (Bishop, 1998; Botting & Conti-Ramsden, 1999). At least a subset of children with pragmatic language difficulties also meet criteria for an autistic spectrum disorder (Botting & Conti-Ramsden, 1999). This has led some individuals to hypothesize that Autistic Spectrum Disorders and Pragmatic Disorder may be related both in symptoms and etiology (Bishop, 1998). Although individuals with receptive-expressive language disorders generally tend to function better than adults with autism, when adults who were diagnosed with receptive-expressive impairments as children are assessed with the ADI-R and ADOS, there is considerable overlap in adult diagnosis. In one study, 60% of the developmental language disorder group was misclassified as autistic on at least one variable (social functioning, independence, or ritualistic/stereotyped behavior) and 33% of the autistic adults were misclassified as language impaired (Howlin et al., 2000). Other studies have found that when a score of less than 132 on the CCC (lower scores indicating greater pragmatic difficulties) is used as a cut-off, children with autism, semantic-pragmatic language impairments, or semantic-pragmatic language impairments plus autistic characteristics have lower scores than a speech language impaired group (Bishop, 1998). Another study found using this same cut-off, children with autism had lower scores than a learning disabilities group (Botting & Conti-Ramsden, 1999). The purpose of the CCC, however, is not to differentiate children with a language disorder from the general population, but rather to differentiate pragmatic difficulties from other aspects of language disorder within the language impaired population (Bishop, 1998; Bishop & Baird, 2001).

Validity of the instrument was evaluated by comparing scores on the CCC between three different diagnostic categories (Semantic-pragmatic pure—did not have autistic symptoms; Semantic-pragmatic plus—did have autistic symptoms or an autistic disorder, Other speech and language impairment—without pragmatic difficulties or autistic characteristics), based on school system classifications (Bishop, 1998). Based on this study, children with a composite score lower than 132 were more likely to be in the semantic-pragmatic pure or the semantic-pragmatic plus (pragmatic disorder plus some autistic characteristics) groups and those children with scores higher than 132 were more likely to be in the other speech and language impaired group (Bishop, 1998). Interestingly, parent ratings on the CCC relate more clearly to the child's diagnostic status than do ratings by teachers. The authors recommend combining parent and professional report to obtain the most accurate information.

INSTRUMENTS FOR ASPERGER'S DISORDER

The Asperger's Syndrome (and High-Functioning Autism) Diagnostic Interview

The Asperger's Syndrome (and High-Functioning Autism) Diagnostic Interview (ASDI) was developed as a diagnostic tool specifically tailored for verbally fluent autism and Asperger's Disorder (Gillberg, Gillberg, Rastam, & Wentz, 2001). The interview is based on Gillberg's diagnostic criteria for Asperger's Disorder, and includes 20 items that operationalize six criteria (Social, Interests, Routines, Verbal and Speech, Communication, and Motor). The ASDI is a structured interview that is administered to a person who knows the subject of the interview quite well, and has some knowledge of the subject's childhood. Each question is rated on a three-point scale. The interviewer is instructed to obtain details on actual behaviors to accurately code each item.

Initial reliability studies were conducted on a group of 20 individuals between 6 and 55 years of age. Inter-rater reliability was investigated and results indicated exact agreement for 96% of the ratings (383 out of 400 ratings), resulting in a kappa of .91. Test-retest reliability was also investigated, and complete agreement was achieved for 97% of the ratings (465 out of 480), resulting in a kappa of .92.

Validity was assessed by comparing algorithm item scores with a clinical diagnosis made by two independent neuropsychiatrists or neuropsychologists familiar with ASDs. All of the subjects who received a clinical diagnosis of Asperger's Disorder or Atypical Autism ($n = 13$) met five or six of the algorithm criteria for Asperger's Disorder on at least one of the ratings. Of the remaining 11 individuals who were not diagnosed with Asperger's Disorder, only one met five criteria. The authors acknowledge that many of the individuals who met algorithm criteria for Asperger's Disorder would also meet *DSM-IV* criteria for autism. This instrument is in the preliminary stages and further investigation is warranted prior to using it as a diagnostic instrument.

The Australian Scale for Asperger's Syndrome

The Australian Scale for Asperger's Syndrome (ASAS) was developed by Garnett and Attwood and published in Attwood's book, *Asperger's Syndrome: A guide for parents, professionals, people with Asperger's Syndrome and their partners* (Attwood, 1997), as well as on a web site (http://www.tonyattwood.co.uk). Although there are no peer reviewed published papers on this instrument, it is widely used by educational systems and parents, in large part because of the accessibility and popularity of the book and web site.

The ASAS covers five areas, which (as the developer of the instrument himself states) "loosely correspond to the five broad categories of behavior identified by other researchers to identify Asperger's Syndrome." These include social and emotional difficulties, cognitive skills deficits, communication skills deficits, specific interests, and motor clumsiness. The authors also indicate that there are at least two questions that are not based on current diagnostic criteria, because their clinical observations differed from what was reported in the literature. The instrument includes 19 items and is scored on a 7-point scale ranging from "rarely" (0) to "frequently" (6). Each item describes a behavior that the parent or teacher is asked to rate, followed by an example of that behavior.

A nonpeer reviewed study designed to evaluate the validity of the instrument in diagnosing Asperger's Disorder is available on Tony Attwood's web site. The study included children and adolescents between 3 and 19 years of age in three groups: a group of individuals referred to a clinic for Asperger's Disorder but not diagnosed with Asperger's Disorder, a group of individuals referred to a clinic and diagnosed with Asperger's Disorder, and a typical control group.

There are several concerns regarding the methods and design of this study. The ASAS was administered as an interview by a clinician, which is not the manner in which the instrument

is typically completed. It is intended to be completed as a questionnaire by a parent, teacher, or professional. Not only was it administered as an interview, but the interviewer was not blind to diagnosis. In addition, the clinical assessment consisted of "an unstructured clinical examination to decide whether they had AS." The assessment included a parent interview, an assessment with the child, a record review, and a diagnostic checklist. There were no standardized instruments used in the assessment. The relationship between the examiners in the Asperger's Clinic who made the diagnosis and the authors of the instrument was also unclear.

Based on a stepwise discriminant function analysis, accuracy for the predicted membership of the Asperger's Disorder group was 90%, and accuracy for the non-Asperger's group was 65%. Given its high sensitivity and low specificity, the authors recommend using this instrument as a screener, rather than as a diagnostic instrument at this time. They also caution against using the instrument clinically, given the lack of data on the reliability and validity of the instrument. Clearly, considering these results and the lack of carefully controlled studies, it is difficult to interpret results from the ASAS at this time.

Measuring Change in Core Behaviors

Investigators have often attempted to use diagnostic instruments in order to measure change in response to treatment. On the whole, this has not been very successful. This is partly due to the fact that most diagnostic instruments were designed to include a wide range of deficits associated with ASDs, and so they are not sufficiently sensitive to changes within an individual. In addition, expectations and contexts for behavior, especially for young children, frequently change with time (Lord et al., 2001; Volkmar & Lord, 1998). Although a child may be showing substantial improvement and acquiring specific behaviors, this improvement may not be measurable if the comparison is to the quality of interaction seen in typical children. On the other hand, for treatments that claim that they result in complete recovery, changes should be observable even in standard diagnostic instruments.

There are a number of well-known instruments that measure behaviors that are not specific to autism but that are frequently found in association with it. These measures have often been used in psychopharmacology research. The most prominent one is the Aberrant Behavior Checklist (ABC; Aman, 1994; Aman & Singh, 1986; Arnold et al., 2000). The Autism Behavior Checklist (also known as the ABC; Krug et al., 1980a), although less appropriate as a diagnostic instrument, has also been helpful in indicating the degree of overtly abnormal or impairing behaviors produced, particularly by those children who are both autistic and mentally handicapped. The Children's Global Assessment Scale (Shaffer et al., 1983) gives a general measure of impairment, which may be helpful for some investigators. In addition, the Maladaptive Behavior Scale from the Vineland Adaptive Behavior Scale (Perry & Factor, 1989) provides counts of particular maladaptive behaviors. The Real Life Rating Scale (Freeman et al., 1986) has also been used for this aim. On the whole, most of these scales were not designed for diagnosis or measuring change and do not have psychometric data to support this particular use. The exception is the Aberrant Behavior Checklist. Recently, several investigators have begun to use the ADOS either as a measure or as a context in which to measure treatment responsiveness. In our own research, we see more quantifiable changes if we re-administer identical items over extended time periods (several years) on the direct observation schedules (e.g., ADOS), even given the variability that this entails, than we do in parent reports, because of the very broad focus of the ADI. Time will tell if the ADOS has a sufficient range of presses and contexts to be useful in this way (Owley et al., 2001).

CONCLUSIONS

Overall, there is a wealth of information and options for the diagnosis of autism, but there is still much to be done to make our techniques stronger and broader in scope. There will always be trade-offs between acquiring the maximum amount of meaningful information and highest validity versus being able to reliably code and make decisions about information. Users of diagnostic instruments should be aware of the needs of their particular situation and population in order to make the most informed choice of instruments. In general, higher standards in terms of limiting the amount of information given to the user of an instrument tested (e.g., keeping examiners "blind" to diagnosis, attempting to use instruments with parents who have not yet received a diagnosis), and including measurements of test-retest reliability and appropriate analysis of reliability statistics, will aid in the interpretability of the instruments. Clear descriptions of exactly how instruments were used and are intended to be used, including cut-offs if categorical use is implied, are also critical.

It seems particularly important to recognize that there are a variety of needs having to do with formal diagnosis that may not be met by a single instrument. Screening of large populations for possible autism is most likely to occur with very young children and needs to be coordinated with developmental screening, because delays in language are inherently entwined with the recognition of autism in many children (see Stone, this volume). After a child has been identified as possibly having an ASD, procedures for early diagnosis may be rather different than screening methods. Diagnostic procedures will involve fewer children than screening and should have closer links to individual education and treatment plans, as well as outline possible mulitaxial diagnoses.

For research purposes, there is a need for lifetime diagnoses and standard procedures that presumably yield the same final interpretation (though not necessarily the same raw data) for the same individual at multiple points in his or her life. In contrast, there is also a need for measurement of change. It seems very unlikely that any one instrument will accomplish all of these objectives. However, for each of these needs, there are promising candidates. Ensuring that the relationship between various instruments and goals is well understood will also increase the usefulness of the endeavor. Recognizing that other factors, particularly level of development and language skill, have marked effects on most measurements in autism and pervasive developmental disorder is an important step in considering the meaning of any clinical or research result.

Finally, there is a great need for the extension of the current instruments to diagnosis of disorders other than autism in the autism spectrum. Part of the difficulty, as discussed in later chapters, is that the definitions and discriminations from autism of these disorders are not yet as clear as we would like. However, reliable ways of formally substantiating diagnoses such as PDD-NOS, Asperger's Disorders and atypical autism are needed so that researchers and clinicians can make informed decisions about the usefulness of these concepts. Various instruments have been proposed to study these disorders, but at this point, they have little relationship to each other and have not been found to be reliable. Consequently, they offer limited scientific usefulness. A priority for researchers is to work together to derive operationalized definitions and specific proposals for how their approaches add to or fit in with those of other researchers. In the meantime, clinicians must be careful to be informed about the kind of information a particular instrument provides and to consider the implications for the appropriateness of that information to their immediate clinical needs.

Cross-References

Issues in the diagnosis of autism and related conditions are discussed in Chapters 1 to 7. Other aspects of assessment are reviewed in Chapter 27 and in Chapters 29 to 33.

REFERENCES

Achenbach, T. M. (1981). *Childhood Behavior Checklist.* Burlington: University of Vermont, Department of Psychiatry.

Achenbach, T. M., & Rescorla, L. (2000). *Manual for the ASEBA forms and profiles.* Burlington: University of Vermont, Center for Children, Youth and Families.

Adrien, J. L., Perrot, A., Sauvage, D., Leddet, I., Larmande, C., Hameury, L., et al. (1992). Early symptoms in autism from family home movies: Evaluation and comparison between 1st and 2nd year of life using I.B.S.E. Scale. *Acta Paedopsychiatrica: International Journal of Child and Adolescent Psychiatry, 55*(2), 71–75.

Alarcón, M., Cantor, R. M., Liu, J., Gilliam, T. C., Geschwind, D. H., & Autism Genetic Research Exchange Consortium. (2002). Evidence for a language quantitative trait locus on chromosome 7q in multiplex autism families. *American Journal of Human Genetics, 70*(1), 60–71.

Aman, M. G. (1994). Instruments for assessing treatment effects in developmentally disabled populations. *Assessment in Rehabilitation and Exceptionality, 1,* 1–20.

Aman, M. G., & Singh, N. N. (1986). *Aberrant Behavior Checklist: Manual.* East Aurora, NY: Slosson Educational Publications.

American Psychiatric Association. (1994). *Diagnostic and statistical manual of mental disorders* (4th ed.). Washington, DC: Author.

Arnold, L. E., Aman, M. G., Martin, A., Collier-Crespin, A., Vitiello, B., Tierney, E., et al. (2000). Assessment in multisite randomized clinical trials of patients with autistic disorder: The Autism RUPP Network. *Journal of Autism and Developmental Disorders, 30*(2), 99–111.

Asano, E., Chugani, D. C., Muzik, O., Behen, M., Janisse, J., Rothermel, R., et al. (2001). Autism in tuberous sclerosis complex is related to both cortical and subcortical dysfunction. *Neurology, 57*(7), 1269–1277.

Attwood, T. (1997). *Asperger's syndrome: A guide for parents and professionals.* London: Jessica Kingsley.

Baron-Cohen, S., Allen, J., & Gillberg, C. (1992). Can autism be detected at 18 months? The needle, the haystack, and the CHAT. *British Journal of Psychiatry, 161*(1), 839–843.

Baron-Cohen, S., Cox, A., Baird, G., Swettenham, J., Nightingale, N., Morgan, K., et al. (1996). Psychological markers in the detection of autism in infancy in a large population. *British Journal of Psychiatry, 168*(2), 158–163.

Barthelemy, C., Adrien, J. L., Tanguay, P. E., Garreau, B., Fermanian, J., Roux, S., et al. (1990). The Behavioral Summarized Evaluation: Validity and reliability of a scale for the assessment of autistic behaviors. *Journal of Autism and Developmental Disorders, 20*(2), 189–204.

Barthelemy, C., Roux, S., Adrien, J. L., Hameury, L., Guerin, P., Garreau, B., et al. (1997). Validation of the Revised Behavior Summarized Evaluation Scale. *Journal of Autism and Developmental Disorders, 27*(2), 139–153.

Bebko, J. M., Konstantareas, M. M., & Springer, J. (1987). Parent and professional evaluations of family stress associated with characteristics of autism. *Journal of Autism and Developmental Disorders, 17*(4), 565–576.

Berument, S. K., Rutter, M., Lord, C., Pickles, A., & Bailey, A. (1999). Autism screening questionnaire: Diagnostic validity. *British Journal of Psychiatry, 175,* 444–451.

Bird, H. R., Gould, M. S., & Staghezza, B. (1992). Aggregating data from multiple informants in child psychiatry epidemiological research. *Journal of the American Academy of Child and Adolescent Psychiatry, 31*(1), 78–85.

Bishop, D. V. M. (1998). Development of the Children's Communication Checklist (CCC): A method for assessing qualitative aspects of communicative impairment in children. *Journal of Child Psychology and Psychiatry and Allied Disciplines, 39*(6), 879–891.

Bishop, D. V. M., & Baird, G. (2001). Parent and teacher report of pragmatic aspects of communication: Use of the Children's Communication Checklist in a clinical setting. *Developmental Medicine and Child Neurology, 43*(12), 809–818.

Bishop, D. V. M., & Norbury, C. F. (2002). Exploring the borderlands of autistic disorder and specific language impairment: A study using standardized diagnostic instruments. *Journal of Child Psychology and Psychiatry and Allied Disciplines, 43*(7), 917–929.

Boiron, M., Barthelemy, C., Adrien, J. L., Martineau, J., & Lelord, G. (1992). The assessment of psychophysiological dysfunction in children using the BSE scale before and during therapy. *Acta Paedopsychiatrica: International Journal of Child and Adolescent Psychiatry, 55*(4), 203–206.

Botting, N., & Conti-Ramsden, G. (1999). Pragmatic language impairment without autism: The children in question. *Autism, 3*(4), 371–396.

Bradford, Y., Haines, J., Hutcheson, H., Gardiner, M., Braun, T., Sheffield, V., et al. (2001). Incorporating language phenotypes strengthens evidence of linkage to autism. *American Journal of Medical Genetics, 105*(6), 539–547.

Buxbaum, J. D., Silverman, J. M., Smith, C. J., Kilifarski, M., Reichert, J., Hollander, E., et al. (2001). Evidence for a susceptibility gene for autism on chromosome 2 and for genetic heterogeneity. *American Journal of Human Genetics, 68*(6), 1514–1520.

Chakrabarti, S., & Fombonne, E. (2001). Pervasive developmental disorders in preschool children. *Journal of the American Medical Association [Special issue], 285*(24), 3093–3099.

Charman, T., Swettenham, J., Baron-Cohen, S., Cox, A., Baird, G., & Drew, A. (1998). An experimental investigation of social-cognitive abilities in infants with autism: Clinical implications. *Infant Mental Health Journal, 19*(2), 260–275.

Cicchetti, D. V., & Sparrow, S. S. (1981). Developing criteria for establishing inter-rater reliability of specific items: Applications to assessment of adaptive behavior. *American Journal of Mental Deficiency, 86*(2), 127–137.

Cohen, D. J., Caparulo, B. K., Gold, J. R., Waldo, M. C., Shaywitz, B. A., Ruttenberg, B. A., et al. (1978). Agreement in diagnosis: Clinical assessment and behavior rating scales for pervasively disturbed children. *Journal of the American Academy of Child Psychiatry, 17*(4), 589–603.

Constantino, J. N. (2002). *The Social Responsiveness Scale.* Los Angeles: Wester Psychological Services.

Constantino, J. N., Gruber, C. P., Davis, S., Hays, S., Passante, N., & Przybeck, T. (2004). The factor structure of autistic traits. *Journal of Child Psychology and Psychiatry, 45*(4), 719–726.

Constantino, J. N., Przybeck, T., Friesen, D., & Todd, R. D. (2000). Reciprocal social behavior in children with and without pervasive developmental disorders. *Journal of Developmental and Behavioral Pediatrics, 21*(1), 2–11.

Constantino, J. N., & Todd, R. D. (2000). Genetic structure of reciprocal social behavior. *American Journal of Psychiatry, 157*(12), 2043–2044.

Constantino, J. N., & Todd, R. D. (2003). Autistic traits in the general population: A twin study. *Archives of General Psychiatry, 60*(5), 524–530.

Cox, A., Klein, K., Charman, T., Baird, G., Baron-Cohen, S., Swettenham, J., et al. (1999). Autism spectrum disorders at 20 and 42 months of age: Stability of clinical and ADI-R diagnosis. *Journal of Child Psychology and Psychiatry and Allied Disciplines, 40*(5), 719–732.

Cuccaro, M. L., Shao, Y. J., Bass, M. P., Abramson, R. K., Ravan, S. A., Wright, H. H., et al. (2003). Behavioral comparisons in autistic individuals from multiplex and singleton families. *Journal of Autism and Developmental Disorders, 33*(1), 87–91.

Cuccaro, M. L., Shao, Y., Grubber, J., Slifer, M., Wolpert, C. M., Donnelly, S. L., et al. (2003). "Factor Analysis of Restricted and Repetitive Behaviors in Autism Using the Autism Diagnostic Interview-R." *Child Psychiatry and Human Development, 34*(1), 3–17.

Davids, A. (1975). Childhood psychosis: The problem of differential diagnosis. *Journal of Autism and Childhood Schizophrenia, 5*(2), 129–138.

Dawson, G., Webb, S., Schellenberg, G. D., Dager, S., Friedman, S., Aylward, E., et al. (2002). Defining the broader phenotype of autism: Genetic, brain, and behavioral perspectives. *Development and Psychopathology, 14*(3), 581–611.

de Bildt, A., Sytema, S., Ketelaars, C., Kraijer, D., Mulder, E., Volkmar, F., et al. (2004). Interrelationship between autism diagnostic observation schedule-generic (ADOS-G), autism diagnostic interview-revised (ADI-R), and the diagnostic and statistical manual of mental disorders (*DSM-IV-TR*) classification in children and adolescents with mental retardation. *Journal of Autism and Developmental Disorders 34*(2), 129–137.

DiLavore, P., Lord, C., & Rutter, M. (1995). Pre-Linguistic Autism Diagnostic Observation Schedule (PLADOS). *Journal of Autism and Developmental Disorders, 25*(4), 355–379.

Doll, E. A. (1965). *Vineland Social Maturity Scale.* Circle Pines, MN: American Guidance Service.

Eaves, R. C. (1990). *The factor structure of autistic behavior.* Paper presented at the annual Alabama Conference on Autism, Birmingham.

Eaves, R. C., Campbell, H. A., & Chambers, D. (2000). Criterion-related and construct validity of the Pervasive Developmental Disorders Rating Scale and the Autism Behavior Checklist. *Psychology in the Schools, 37*(4), 311–321.

Eaves, R. C., & Hooper, J. (1987). A factor analysis of psychotic behavior. *Journal of Special Education, 21*(4), 122–132.

Folstein, S. E., & Mankoski, R. E. (2000). Chromosome 7q: Where autism meets language disorder? *American Journal of Human Genetics, 67*(2), 278–281.

Fombonne, E. (1992). Diagnostic assessment in a sample of autistic and developmentally impaired adolescents. *Journal of Autism and Developmental Disorders, 22*(4), 563–581.

Freeman, N. L., Perry, A., & Factor, D. C. (1991). Child behavior as stressors: Replicating and extending the use of the CARS as a measure of stress: A research note. *Journal of Child Psychology and Psychiatry and Allied Disciplines, 32*(6), 1025–1030.

Freeman, B. J., Ritvo, E. R., Guthrie, D., Schroth, P., & Ball, J. (1978). The Behavior Observation Scale for Autism: Initial methodology, data analysis, and preliminary findings on 89 children. *Journal of the American Academy of Child Psychiatry, 17*(4), 576–588.

Freeman, B. J., Ritvo, E. R., Yokota, A., & Ritvo, A. (1986). A scale for rating symptoms of patients with the syndrome of autism in real life settings. *Journal of the American Academy of Child Psychiatry, 25*(1), 130–136.

Freitag, C. M. (2002). Phenotypic characteristics of siblings with autism and/or pervasive developmental disorder: Evidence for heterogeneity. *American Journal of Medical Genetics, 114*(7), 31.

Garfin, D. G., McCallon, D., & Cox, R. (1988). Validity and reliability of the Childhood Autism Rating Scale with autistic adolescents. *Journal of Autism and Developmental Disorders, 18*(3), 367–378.

Ghaziuddin, M., Tsai, L., & Ghaziuddin, N. (1992). Brief report: A comparison of the diagnostic criteria for Asperger's Syndrome. *Journal of Autism and Developmental Disorders, 22*(4), 643–649.

Gillberg, C., Gillberg, C., Rastam, M., & Wentz, E. (2001). The Asperger Syndrome (and high-functioning autism) Diagnostic Interview (ASDI): A preliminary study of a new structured clinical interview [Special issue]. *Autism, 5*(1), 57–66.

Gilliam, J. E. (1995). *Gilliam Autism Rating Scale.* Austin, TX: ProEd.

Grinager, A. N., Cox, N. J., & Yairi, E. (1997). The genetic basis of persistence and recovery in stuttering. *Journal of Speech and Hearing Research, 40*(3), 567–580.

Happé, F. G. E. (1995). The role of age and verbal ability in the theory of mind task performance of subjects with autism. *Child Development, 66*(3), 843–855.

Hepburn, S., John, A., Lord, C., & Rogers, S. (2003). *Sensitivity and specificity of the Autism Diagnostic Observation Schedule in young children.* Manuscript in preparation.

Hertzig, M. E., Snow, M. E., New, E., & Shapiro, T. (1990). *DSM-III* and *DSM-III-R* diagnosis of autism and pervasive developmental disorder in nursery school children. *Journal of the American Academy of Child and Adolescent Psychiatry, 29*(1), 195–199.

Hobson, R. P. (1991). Methodological issues for experiments on autistic individuals' perception and understanding of emotion. *Journal of the American Academy of Child and Adolescent Psychiatry, 32*(7), 1135–1158.

Holroyd, S., & Baron-Cohen, S. (1993). Brief report: How far can people with autism go in developing a theory of mind? *Journal of Autism and Developmental Disorders, 23*(2), 379–385.

Howlin, P., Mawhood, L., & Rutter, M. (2000). Autism and developmental receptive language disorder: A follow-up comparison in early adult life: Part II. Social, behavioural, and psychiatric outcomes. *Journal of Child Psychology and Psychiatry and Allied Disciplines, 41*(5), 561–578.

International Molecular Genetic Study of Autism Consortium. (1998). A full genome screen for autism with evidence for linkage to a region on chromosome 7q. *Human Molecular Genetics, 7*(3), 571–578.

Kanner, L. (1943). Autistic disturbances of affective contact. *Nervous Child, 2,* 217–250.

Klin, A., Pauls, D. L., Schultz, R., & Volkmar, F. R. (in press). Three diagnostic approaches to Asperger's syndrome: Implications for research. *Journal of Autism and Developmental Disorders.*

Klin, A., Sparrow, S. S., Marans, W. D., Carter, A., & Volkmar, F. R. (2000). Assessment issues in children and adolescents with Asperger syndrome. In A. Klin, F. R. Volkmar, & S. S. Sparrow (Eds.), *Asperger syndrome* (pp. 309–339). New York: Guilford Press.

Klin, A., Volkmar, F. R., Sparrow, S. S., Cicchetti, D. V., & Rourke, B. P. (1995). Validity and neuropsychological characterization of Asperger syndrome: Convergence with nonverbal learning disabilities syndrome. *Journal of Child Psychology and Psychiatry and Allied Disciplines, 36*(7), 1127–1140.

Kolevzon, A., Smith, C. J., Schmeidler, J., Buxbaum, J. D., & Silverman, J. M. (2004). Familial symptom domains in monzygotic siblings with autism. *American Journal of Medical Genetics Part B-Neuropsychiatric Genetics 129B,* 76–81.

Konstantareas, M. M., & Homatidis, S. (1989). Assessing child symptom severity and stress in parents of autistic children. *Journal of Child Psychology and Psychiatry and Allied Disciplines, 30*(3), 459–470.

Kraemer, H. C. (1992). Measurement of reliability for categorical data medical research. *Statistical Methods in Medical Research, 1*(2), 183–199.

Krug, D. A., Arick, J. R., & Almond, P. J. (1980a). *Autism screening instrument for educational planning.* Portland, OR: ASIEP Educational.

Krug, D. A., Arick, J. R., & Almond, P. J. (1980b). Behavior checklist for identifying severely handicapped individuals with high levels of autistic behavior. *Journal of Child Psychology and Psychiatry and Allied Disciplines, 21*(3), 221–229.

Krug, D. A., Arick, J. R., & Almond, P. J. (1993). *Autism screening instrument for educational planning* (2nd ed.). Austin, TX: ProEd.

Kurita, H., Kita, M., & Miyake, Y. (1992). A comparative study of development and symptoms among disintegrative psychosis and infantile autism with and without speech loss. *Journal of Autism and Developmental Disorders, 22*(2), 175–188.

Lam, M. K., & Rao, N. (1993). Developing a Chinese version of the Psychoeducational Profile (CPEP) to assess autistic children in Hong Kong. *Journal of Autism and Developmental Disorders, 23*(2), 273–279.

Le Couteur, A., Bailey, A., Goode, S., Pickles, A., Robertson, S., Gottesman, I., et al. (1996). A broader phenotype of autism: The clinical spectrum in twins. *Journal of Child Psychology and Psychiatry and Allied Disciplines, 37*(7), 785–801.

Le Couteur, A., Lord, C., & Rutter, M. (2003). *The Autism Diagnostic Interview: Revised* (ADI-R). Los Angeles: Western Psychological Services.

Le Couteur, A., Rutter, M., Lord, C., Rios, P., Robertson, S., Holdgrafer, M., et al. (1989). Autism Diagnostic Interview: A standardized investigator-based instrument. *Journal of Autism and Developmental Disorders, 19*(3), 363–387.

Leekam, S. R., Libby, S. J., Wing, L., Gould, J., & Gillberg, C. (2000). Comparison of *ICD-10* and Gillberg's criteria for Asperger syndrome [Special issue: Asperger syndrome]. *Autism, 4*(1), 11–28.

Leekam, S. R., Libby, S. J., Wing, L., Gould, J., & Taylor, C. (2002). The Diagnostic Interview for Social and Communication Disorders: Algorithms for *ICD-10* childhood autism and Wing and Gould autistic spectrum disorder. *Journal of Child Psychology and Psychiatry and Allied Disciplines, 43*(3), 327–342.

Lord, C. (1990). A cognitive-behavioral model for the treatment of social-communicative deficits in adolescents with autism. In R. J. McMahon & R. D. Peters (Eds.), *Behavior disorders of adolescence: Research, intervention and policy in clinical and school settings* (pp. 155–174). New York: Plenum Press.

Lord, C. (1995). Follow-up of two-year-olds referred for possible autism. *Journal of Child Psychology and Psychiatry, 36*(8), 1365–1382.

Lord, C. (1996). Treatment of a high-functioning adolescent with autism: A cognitive-behavioral approach. *Cognitive therapy with children and adolescents: A casebook for clinical practice* (pp. 394–404). New York: Guilford Press.

Lord, C., & Bailey, A. (2002). Autism spectrum disorders. In M. Rutter & E. Taylor (Eds.), *Child and adolescent psychiatry* (4th ed., pp. 636–663). Oxford, England: Blackwell.

Lord, C., Cook, E. H., Leventhal, B. L., & Amaral, D. G. (2000). Autism spectrum disorders. *Neuron, 28*(2), 355–363.

Lord, C., Leventhal, B. L., & Cook, E. H., Jr. (2001). Quantifying the phenotype in autism spectrum disorders. *American Journal of Medical Genetics, 105*(1), 36–38.

Lord, C., Pickles, A., DiLavore, P. C., & Shulman, C. (1996). *Longitudinal studies of young children referred for possible autism.* Paper presented at the biannual meeting of the International Society for Research in Child and Adolescent Psychopathology, Los Angeles.

Lord, C., Risi, S., Lambrecht, L., Cook, E. H., Jr., Leventhal, B. L., DiLavore, P. C., et al. (2000). The Autism Diagnostic Observation Schedule-Generic: A standard measure of social and communication deficits associated with the spectrum of autism. *Journal of Autism and Developmental Disorders, 30*(3), 205–223.

Lord, C., Rutter, M. L., DiLavore, P. C., & Risi, S. (1999). *Autism Diagnostic Observation Schedule—WPS* (WPS ed.). Los Angeles: Western Psychological Services.

Lord, C., Rutter, M. L., Goode, S., Heemsbergen, J., Jordan, H., Mawhood, L., et al. (1989). Autism Diagnostic Observation Schedule: A standardized observation of communicative and social behavior. *Journal of Autism and Developmental Disorders, 19*(2), 185–212.

Lord, C., Rutter, M. L., & Le Couteur, A. (1994). The Autism Diagnostic Interview—Revised: A revised version of a diagnostic interview for caregivers of individuals with possible pervasive developmental disorders. *Journal of Autism and Developmental Disorders, 24*(5), 659–685.

Lord, C., Storoschuk, S., Rutter, M., & Pickles, A. (1993). Using the ADI–R to diagnose autism in preschool children. *Infant Mental Health Journal, 14*(3), 1234–1252.

Luteijn, E., Luteijn, F., Jackson, S., Volkmar, F., & Minderaa, R. (2000). The Children's Social Behavior Questionnaire for milder variants of PDD problems: Evaluation of the psychometric characteristics. *Journal of Autism and Developmental Disorders, 30*(4), 317–330.

MacLean, J. E., Szatmari, P., Jones, M. B., Bryson, S. E., Mahoney, W. J., Bartolucci, G., et al. (1999). Familial factors influence level of functioning in pervasive developmental disorder. *Journal of the American Academy of Child and Adolescent Psychiatry, 38*(6), 746–753.

Mahoney, W. J., Szatmari, P., MacLean, J. E., Bryson, S. E., Bartolucci, G., Walter, S. D., et al. (1998). Reliability and accuracy of differentiating pervasive developmental disorder subtypes. *Journal of the American Academy of Child and Adolescent Psychiatry, 37*(3), 278–285.

Masters, J. C., & Miller, D. E. (1970). Early infantile autism: A methodological critique. *Journal of Abnormal Psychology, 75*(3), 342–343.

Mawhood, L., Howlin, P., & Rutter, M. L. (2000). Autism and developmental receptive language disorder—A comparitive follow-up in early adult life: Part I. Cognitive and language outcomes. *Journal of Child Psychology and Psychiatry and Allied Disciplines, 41*(5), 547–559.

Mayes, L. C., & Zigler, E. (1992). An observational study of the affective concomitants of mastery in infants. *Journal of Child Psychology and Psychiatry and Allied Disciplines, 33*(4), 659–667.

Mesibov, G. B., Schopler, E., & Caison, W. (1989). The Adolescent and Adult Psychoeducational Profile: Assessment of adolescents and adults with severe developmental handicaps. *Journal*

of Autism and Developmental Disorders, 19(1), 33–40.

Mesibov, G. B., Schopler, E., Schaffer, B., & Landrus, R. (1988). *Adolescent and Adult Psychoeducational Profile* (AAPEP): Volume IV. Austin, TX: ProEd.

Mesibov, G. B., Schopler, E., Schaffer, B., & Michal, N. (1989). Use of the Childhood Autism Rating Scale with autistic adolescents and adults. *Journal of the American Academy of Child and Adolescent Psychiatry, 28*(4), 538–541.

Miller, J. N., & Ozonoff, S. (1997). Did Asperger's cases have Asperger disorder? *Journal of Child Psychology and Psychiatry and Allied Disciplines, 38*(2), 247–251.

Minshew, N. J., & Goldstein, G. (1993). Is autism an amnesic disorder? Evidence from the California Verbal Learning Test. *Neuropsychology, 7*(2), 209–216.

Miranda-Linne, F. M., Fredrika, M., & Melin, L. (1997). A comparison of speaking and mute individuals with autism and autistic-like conditions on the Autism Behavior Checklist. *Journal of Autism and Developmental Disorders, 27*(3), 245–264.

Mundy, P., Sigman, M., Ungerer, J., & Sherman, T. (1986). Defining the social deficits of autism: The contribution of nonverbal communication measures. *Journal of Child Psychology and Psychiatry, 27*(5), 657–669.

Munson, J., Dawson, G., Lord, C., Rogers, S., & Sigman, M. (in press). *Cognitive profiles and adaptive functioning in preschool children with autism spectrum disorder versus developmental delay.*

Muris, P., Steerneman, P., & Ratering, E. (1997). Inter-rater reliability of the Psychoeducational Profile (PEP). *Journal of Autism and Developmental Disorders, 27*(5), 621–626.

Nordin, V., & Gillberg, C. (1996a). Autism spectrum disorders in children with physical or mental disability or both: Part I. Clinical and epidemiological aspects. *Developmental Medicine and Child Neurology, 38*(4), 297–313.

Nordin, V., & Gillberg, C. (1996b). Autism spectrum disorders in children with physical or mental disability or both: Part II. Screening aspects. *Journal of Child Psychology and Psychiatry, 38*(4), 314–324.

Nordin, V., & Gillberg, C. (1998). The long-term course of autistic disorders: Update on follow-up studies. *Acta Psychiatrica Scandinavica, 97*(2), 99–108.

Nordin, V., Gillberg, C., & Nyden, A. (1998). The Swedish version of the Childhood Autism

Rating Scale in a clinical setting. *Journal of Autism and Developmental Disorders, 28*(1), 69–75.

Offord, D. R., Boyle, M. H., Racine, Y., Szatmari, P., Fleming, J. E., Sanford, M., et al. (1996). Integrating assessment data from multiple informants. *Journal of the American Academy of Child and Adolescent Psychiatry, 35*(8), 1078–1085.

Owley, T., McMahon, W., Cook, E. H., Laulhere, T., South, M., Mays, L. Z., et al. (2001). Multisite, double-blind, placebo-controlled trial of porcine secretin in autism. *Journal of the American Academy of Child and Adolescent Psychiatry, 40*(11), 1293–1299.

Ozonoff, S., & Cathcart, K. (1998). Effectiveness of a home program intervention for young children with autism. *Journal of Autism and Developmental Disorders, 28*(1), 25–32.

Ozonoff, S., South, M., & Miller, J. N. (2000). *DSM-IV*-defined Asperger syndrome: Cognitive, behavioral and early history differentiation from high-functioning autism [Special issue: Asperger syndrome]. *Autism, 4*(1), 29–46.

Panerai, S., Ferrante, L., & Caputo, V. (1997). The TEACCH strategy in mentally retarded children with autism: A multidimensional assessment: Pilot study. *Journal of Autism and Developmental Disorders, 27*(3), 345–347.

Parks, S. L. (1988). Psychometric instruments available for the assessment of autistic children. In E. Schopler & G. Mesibov (Eds.), *Diagnosis and assessment in autism* (pp. 123–136). New York: Plenum Press.

Perry, A., & Factor, D. C. (1989). Psychometric validity and clinical usefulness of the Vineland Adaptive Behavior Scale and the AAMD Adaptive Behavior Scale for an autistic sample. *Journal of Autism and Developmental Disorders, 19*(1), 41–56.

Persson, B. (2000). Brief report: A longitudinal study of quality of life and independence among adult men with autism. *Journal of Autism and Developmental Disorders, 30*(1), 2061–2066.

Pilowsky, T., Yirmiya, N., Shulman, C., & Dover, R. (1998). The Autism Diagnostic Review–Revised and the childhood autism rating scale: Differences between diagnostic systems and comparison between genders. *Journal of Autism and Developmental Disorders, 28*(2), 143–151.

Piven, J., Harper, J., Palmer, P., & Arndt, S. (1996). Course of behavioral change in autism: A retrospective study of high-IQ adolescents and adults. *Journal of the American Academy of Child and Adolescent Psychiatry, 35*(4), 523–529.

Piven, J., Nehme, E., Simon, J., Barta, P., Pearl, G., & Folstein, S. E. (1992). Magnetic Resonance Imaging in autism: Measurement of the cerebellum, pons, and fourth ventricle. *Biological Psychiatry, 31*(5), 491–504.

Prior, M. R., & Bence, R. (1975). A note on the validity of the Rimland Diagnostic Checklist. *Journal of Clinical Psychology, 31*(3), 510–513.

Rimland, B. (1968). On the objective diagnosis of infantile autism. *Acta Paedopsychiatrica: International Journal of Child and Adolescent Psychiatry, 35*(4/8), 146–161.

Rimland, B. (1971). The differentiation of childhood psychoses: An analysis of checklists for 2,218 psychotic children. *Journal of Autism and Childhood Schizophrenia, 1*(2), 161–174.

Robertson, J. M., Tanguay, P. E., L'Ecuyer, S., Sims, A., & Waltrip, C. (1999). Domains of social communication handicap in autism spectrum disorder. *Journal of the American Academy of Child and Adolescent Psychiatry, 38*(6), 738–745.

Ruttenberg, B. A., Dratman, M. L., Fraknoi, J., & Wenar, C. (1966). An instrument for evaluating autistic children. *Journal of American Academy of Child Psychiatry, 5,* 453–478.

Ruttenberg, B. A., Kalish, B. I., Wenar, C., & Wolf, E. G. (1977). *Behavior rating instrument for autistic and other atypical children* (rev. ed.). Philadelphia: Developmental Center for Autistic Children.

Rutter, M., Le Couteur, A., & Lord, C. (2003). *Manual for the ADI–WPS version.* Los Angeles: Western Psychological Services.

Rutter, M., Mawhood, L., & Howlin, P. (1992). Language delay and social development. In P. Fletcher & D. Hall (Eds.), *Specific speech and language disorders in children: Correlates, characteristics, and outcomes* (pp. 63–78). London: Whurr.

Saemundsen, E., Magnússon, P., Smári, J., & Sigurdardóttir, S. (2003). Autism Diagnostic Interview-Revised and the Childhood Autism Rating Scale: Convergence and discrepancy in diagnosing autism. *Journal of Autism and Developmental Disorders 33*(3), 319–328.

Sanchez, L. E., Adams, P. B., Yusal, S., Hallin, A., Campbell, M., & Small, A. M. (1995). A comparison of live and videotape ratings: Comipramine and halperidol in autism. *Psychopharmacology Bulletin, 31*(2), 371–378.

Schopler, E. (1976). Towards reducing behavior problems in autistic children. In L. Wing (Ed.), *Early childhood autism* (pp. 221–246). London: Pergamon Press.

Schopler, E., & Reichler, R. J. (1972). How well do parents understand their own psychotic child?

Journal of Autism and Childhood Schizophrenia, 2(4), 387–400.

Schopler, E., & Reichler, R. J. (1979). *Individualized assessment and treatment for autistic and developmentally disabled children: Psychoeducational profile* (Vol. 1). Baltimore: University Park Press.

Schopler, E., Reichler, R. J., Bashford, A., Lansing, M. D., & Marcus, L. M. (1990). *Psychoeducational Profile–Revised.* Austin, TX: ProEd.

Schopler, E., Reichler, R. J., DeVellis, R., & Daly, K. (1980). Toward objective classification of childhood autism: Childhood Autism Rating Scale (CARS). *Journal of Autism and Developmental Disorders, 10*(1), 91–103.

Schopler, E., Reichler, R. J., & Renner, B. R. (1986). *The Childhood Autism Rating Scale (CARS) for diagnostic screening and classification of autism.* Irvington, NY: Irvington.

Schopler, E., Reichler, R. J., & Renner, B. R. (1988). *The Childhood Autism Rating Scale (CARS).* Los Angeles: Western Psychological Services.

Schreck, K. A., & Mulick, J. A. (2000). Parental report of sleep problems in children with autism. *Journal of Autism and Developmental Disorders, 30*(2), 127–135.

Sevin, J. A., Matson, J. L., Coe, D. A., Fee, V. E., & Sevin, B. M. (1991). A comparison and evaluation of three commonly used autism scales. *Journal of Autism and Developmental Disorders, 21*(4), 551–556.

Shaffer, D., Gould, M. S., Brasic, J., Ambrosini, P., Fisher, P., Bird, H., et al. (1983). A Children's Global Assessment Scale (CGAS). *Archives of General Psychiatry, 40,* 1228–1231.

Shao, Y. J., Cuccaro, M. L., Hauser, E. R., Raiford, K. L., Menold, M. M., Wolpert, C. M., et al. (2003). Fine mapping of Autistic disorder to chromosome 15q11-q13 by use of phenotypic subtypes. *American Journal of Human Genetics, 72*(3), 539–548.

Shao, Y. J., Raiford, K. L., Wolpert, C. M., Cope, H. A., Ravan, S. A., Ashley-Koch, A. A., et al. (2002). Phenotypic homogeneity provides increased support for linkage on chromosome 2 in autistic disorder. *American Journal of Human Genetics, 70*(4), 1058–1061.

Shao, Y. J., Wolpert, C. M., Raiford, K. L., Menold, M. M., Donnelly, S. L., Ravan, S. A., et al. (2002). Genomic screen and follow-up analysis for autistic disorder. *American Journal of Medical Genetics, 114,* 99–105.

Sigman, M., & Ungerer, J. (1984). Attachment behaviors in autistic children. *Journal of Autism and Developmental Disorders, 14*(3), 231–244.

Silverman, J. M., Smith, C. J., Schmeidler, J., Hollander, E., Lawlor, B. A., Fitzgerald, M., et al. (2002). Symptom domains in autism and related conditions: Evidence for familiality. *American Journal of Medical Genetics, 114*(1), 64–73.

Smalley, S. L., Tanguay, P. E., Smith, M., & Gutierrez, G. (1992). Autism and tuberous sclerosis. *Journal of Autism and Developmental Disorders, 22*(3), 339–355.

South, M., Williams, B. J., McMahon, W. M., Owley, T., Filipek, P. A., Shernoff, E., et al. (2002). Utility of the Gilliam Autism Rating Scale in research and clinical populations. *Journal of Autism and Developmental Disorders, 32*(6), 593–599.

Sparrow, S. S., Balla, D., & Cicchetti, D. (1984). *Vineland Adaptive Behavior Scales.* Circle Pines, MN: American Guidance Service.

Spencer, A. (1993). *Separation and reunion in autistic two year olds.* Unpublished doctoral dissertation, University of North Carolina, Chapel Hill.

Spiker, D., Lotspeich, L. J., Dimiceli, S., Myers, R. M., & Risch, N. (2002). Behavioral phenotypic variation in autism multiplex families: Evidence for a continuous severity gradient. *American Journal of Medical Genetics, 114*(2), 129–136.

Spiker, D., Lotspeich, L. J., Kraemer, H. C., Hallmayer, J., McMahon, W., Peterson, B., et al. (1994). Genetics of autism: Characteristics of affected and unaffected children from 37 multiplex families. *American Journal of Medical Genetics, 54*(1), 27–35.

Sponheim, E. (1996). Changing criteria of autistic disorders: A comparison of the *ICD-10* research criteria and *DSM-IV* with *DSM-III-R,* CARS, and ABC. *Journal of Autism and Developmental Disorders, 26*(5), 513–525.

Steerneman, P., Muris, P., Merckelbach, H., & Willems, H. (1997). Brief report: Assessment of development and abnormal behavior in children with pervasive developmental disorders: Evidence for the reliability and validity of the Revised Psychoeducational Profile. *Journal of Autism and Developmental Disorders, 27*(2), 177–185.

Stella, J., Mundy, P., & Tuchman, R. (1999). Social and nonsocial factors in the Childhood Autism Rating Scale. *Journal of Autism and Developmental Disorders, 29*(4), 307–317.

Stone, W. L., Lee, E. B., Ashford, L., Brissie, J., Hepburn, S. L., Coonrod, E. E., et al. (1999). Can autism be diagnosed accurately in children under 3 years? *Journal of Child Psychology and Psychiatry and Allied Disciplines, 40*(2), 219–226.

Stone, W. L., & Lemanek, K. L. (1990). Parental report of social behaviors in autistic preschoolers. *Journal of Autism and Developmental Disorders, 20*(4), 513–522.

Stone, W. L., Ousley, O. Y., Yoder, P., Hogan, K., & Hepburn, S. (1997). Nonverbal communication in 2- and 3-year-old children with autism. *Journal of Autism and Developmental Disorders, 27*(6), 677–696.

Sturmey, P., Matson, J. L., & Sevin, J. A. (1992). Brief report: Analysis of the internal consistency of three autism scales. *Journal of Autism and Developmental Disorders, 22*(2), 321–328.

Szatmari, P. (2000). Perspectives on the classification of Asperger Syndrome. In A. Klin (Ed.), *Asperger Syndrome* (pp. 403–407). New York, NY: Guilford Press.

Szatmari, P., Archer, L., Fisman, S., Streiner, D. L., & Wilson, F. (1995). Asperger's syndrome and autism: Differences in behavior, cognition, and adaptive functioning. *Journal of the American Academy of Child and Adolescent Psychiatry, 34*(12), 1662–1671.

Szatmari, P., Merette, C., Bryson, S. E., Thivierge, J., Roy, M. A., Cayer, M., et al. (2002). Quantifying dimensions in autism: A factor-analytic study. *Journal of the American Academy of Child and Adolescent Psychiatry, 41*(4), 467–474.

Tadevosyan-Leyfer, O., Dowd, M., Mankoski, R., Winklosky, B., Putnam, S., McGrath, L., et al. (2003). A principal components analysis of the Autism Diagnostic Interview-Revised. *Journal of the American Academy of Child and Adolescent Psychiatry, 42*(7), 864–872.

Tanguay, P. E., Robertson, J., & Derrick, A. (1998). A dimensional classification of autism spectrum disorder by social communication domains. *Journal of the American Academy of Child and Adolescent Psychiatry, 37*(3), 271–277.

Tantam, D. (2000). Psychological disorder in adolescents and adults with Asperger Syndrome. *Autism, 4*(1), 47–62.

Teal, M. B., & Wiebe, M. J. (1986). A validity analysis of selected instruments used to assess autism. *Journal of Autism and Developmental Disorders, 16*(4), 485–494.

Van Bourgondien, M. E., Marcus, L. M., & Schopler, E. (1992). Comparison of *DSM-III-R* and Childhood Autism Rating Scale diagnosis of autism. *Journal of Autism and Developmental Disorders, 22*(4), 493–505.

Venter, A., Lord, C., & Schopler, E. (1992). A follow-up study of high-functioning autistic children. *Journal of Child Psychology and Psychiatry and Allied Disciplines, 33*(3), 1489–1507.

Volkmar, F. R., Cicchetti, D. V., Bregman, J., & Cohen, D. J. (1992). Three diagnostic systems for autism: *DSM-III, DSM-III-R,* and *ICD-10* [Special issue: Classification and diagnosis]. *Journal of Autism and Developmental Disorders, 22*(4), 483–492.

Volkmar, F. R., Cicchetti, D. V., Dykens, E., Sparrow, S. S., Leckman, J. F., & Cohen, D. F. (1988). An evaluation of the Autism Behavior Checklist. *Journal of Autism and Developmental Disorders, 18*(1), 81–97.

Volkmar, F. R., & Klin, A. (2001). Asperger's disorder and higher functioning autism: Same or different? In L. M. Glidden (Ed.), *International review of research in mental retardation: Autism* (Vol. 23, pp. 83–110). San Diego, CA: Academic Press.

Volkmar, F. R., Klin, A., Siegal, B., Szatmari, P., Lord, C., Campbell, M., et al. (1994). Field trial for autistic disorder in *DSM-IV. American Journal of Psychiatry, 151*(9), 1361–1367.

Volkmar, F. R., & Lord, C. (1998). Diagnosis and definition of autism and other pervasive developmental disorders. In F. R. Volkmar (Ed.), *Autism and pervasive developmental disorders* (pp. 1–31). New York: Cambridge University Press.

Vrancic, D., Nanclares, V., Soares, D., Kulesz, A., Mordzinski, C., Plebst, C., et al. (2002). Sensitivity and specificity of the autism diagnostic inventory-telephone screening in Spanish. *Journal of Autism and Developmental Disorders, 32*(4), 313–320.

Wadden, N., Bryson, S. E., & Rodger, R. (1991). A closer look at the Autism Behavior Checklist: Discriminant validity and factor structure. *Journal of Autism and Developmental Disorders, 21*(4), 529–542.

Wechsler, D. (1991). *Manual for the Wechsler Intelligence Scale for Children–III.* San Antonio, TX: Psychological Corporation.

Wechsler, D. (1997) *Wechsler Adult Intelligence Scale, 3rd Edition.* San Antonio, TX: Psychological Corporation.

Wechsler, D. (2002). *Wechsler Preschool and Primary Scale of Intelligence–III.* San Antonio, TX: Psychological Corporation.

Wechsler, D. (2003). *Wechsler Intelligence Scale for Children (4th ed.).* San Antonio, TX:Psychological Corporation.

Wenar, C., & Ruttenberg, B. A. (1976). The use of BRIAAC for evaluating therapeutic effectiveness. *Journal of Autism and Childhood Schizophrenia, 6*(2), 175–191.

Wetherby, A., & Prizant, B. (1993). *Communication and Symbolic Behavior Scales* (Normed ed.). Baltimore: Paul H. Brookes.

Wetherby, A., & Prizant, B. (2002). *Communication and Symbolic Behavior Scales developmental profile* (First Normed Edition). Baltimore: Paul H. Brookes.

Wetherby, A., Woods, J., Allen, L., Cleary, J., Dickinson, H., & Lord, C. (in press). *Early indicators of autistic spectrum disorders in the second year of life.*

Wing, L., & Attwood, A. (1987). Syndromes of autism and atypical development. In D. J. Cohen & A. M. Donnellan (Eds.), *Handbook of autism and pervasive developmental disorders* (pp. 148–170). New York: Wiley.

Wing, L., & Gould, J. (1978). Systematic recording of behaviors and skills of retarded and psychotic children. *Journal of Autism and Childhood Schizophrenia, 8*(1), 79–97.

Wing, L., & Gould, J. (1979). Severe impairments of social interaction and associated abnormalities in children: Epidemiology and classification. *Journal of Autism and Developmental Disorders, 9*(1), 11–29.

Wing, L., Leekam, S. R., Libby, S. J., Gould, J., & Larcombe, M. (2002). The Diagnostic Interview for Social and Communication Disorders: Background, inter-rater reliability and clinical use. *Journal of Child Psychology and Psychiatry and Allied Disciplines, 43*(3), 307–325.

World Health Organization. (1992). *The ICD 10 Classification of Mental and Behavioral Disorders: Clinical descriptions and diagnostic guidelines.* Geneva, Switzerland: Author.

Yirmiya, N., Sigman, M., & Freeman, B. J. (1994). Comparison between diagnostic instruments for identifying high-functioning children with autism. *Journal of Autism and Developmental Disorders, 24*(3), 281–291.

Zakian, A., Malvy, J., Desombre, H., Roux, S., & Lenoir, P. (2000). Early signs of autism: A new study of family home movies. *Encephale-Revue De Psychiatrie Clinique Biologique Et Therapeutique, 26*(2), 38–44.

CHAPTER 29

Clinical Evaluation in Autism Spectrum Disorders: Psychological Assessment within a Transdisciplinary Framework

AMI KLIN, CELINE SAULNIER, KATHERINE TSATSANIS, AND FRED R. VOLKMAR

Autism is no longer considered a rare condition, and the number of children being referred for developmental disabilities assessments with a differential diagnosis of autism continues to increase every year. The increase in referrals creates the need for guidelines on best practices for assessment of individuals with autism spectrum disorders (ASDs; National Research Council [NRC], 2001), who are no longer seen primarily in academic centers specialized in those conditions, and whose disabilities and assets need to be assessed with no delay for service providers to generate individualized recommendations for treatment and interventions.

Children with autism and other pervasive developmental disorders (PDDs) present unique issues for clinical assessment. Examiners are confronted with great challenges resulting from profiles of development that cover the entire IQ and language spectrum. Additionally, in many cases, there are extreme variability and scatter across skills, and behavior problems need to be addressed to ensure validity and reliability of performance on standardized measures. Yet, developmentally based assessment of cognitive, social, communicative, and adaptive skills provides the essential bases on which decisions on diagnosis, eligibility for services, and program planning have to be made. Observations on the child's unique strengths and weaknesses have a major impact on the design of effective intervention programs.

This chapter provides a summary of overall approaches to clinical evaluation of children with ASDs, as well as a summary of psychological assessment within a transdisciplinary framework. This framework reflects the need for a cohesive clinical team benefiting from expertise in different disciplines (Klin et al., 1997), working together in a highly integrated manner while casting clinical phenomena within a developmental psychopathology perspective (Sparrow, Carter, Racusin, & Morris, 1995). Within transdisciplinary teams, the role of psychological assessment is to frame the understanding of clinical phenomena in terms of the child's developmental resources and challenges. Most symptoms in autism are mediated by levels and profiles of cognitive skills. We, therefore, single out this realm of assessment for a more detailed discussion in this chapter. Together with the assessment of communication (Chapter 30, this *Handbook,* this volume), qualitative and quantified observations of developmental abilities form the core on which clinical judgment is made about diagnostic formulations and programmatic intervention. It must be emphasized that the efforts of professionals from various other disciplines are often needed, such as physical and occupational therapy, pediatrics, genetics, and neurology. The emphasis on psychological skills in this chapter and communication skills in Chapter 30 reflects a commonly adopted priority, which, however, needs to be adjusted to the specific issues and concerns arising in individual cases presenting for evaluation. And while individualized developmental profiles typically form the basis for intervention programs, other areas can be critical for many children. Other chapters in the *Handbook* address issues not discussed in detail here, such as neurological problems (Chapter 18) and genetic vulnerabilities (Chapter 16). Other chapters also address in much greater detail some of the issues included in this chapter, such as diagnostic instrumentation (Chapters 27 and 28); behavioral approaches to promote learning and decrease maladaptive responses (Chapters 31, 34, and 35); sensory and motor problems in autism (Chapter 32); the development of communication, play, and imitation skills (Chapters 12 and 14); neuropsychological functioning and profiles (Chapter 13); and special considerations associated with different periods of children's life in school (Chapter 9). The focus of this chapter is on practical issues encountered by clinicians assessing children with ASDs. This work, however, cannot be done adequately without a thorough training in all of these developmental domains because the challenges of autism can be adequately characterized only against the backdrop of typical development. With these various chapters as background, therefore, we introduce the transdisciplinary approach to the clinical assessment of children with ASD and proceed with a more detailed discussion of psychological assessment methods, which require the combination of careful qualitative observations with the use of standardized and well-validated instruments.

A final word of introduction relates to the emphasis given in this chapter to the preschool and school-age periods of development. Most referrals to clinics are still within this age range, although the numbers of toddlers, on the one hand, and older and higher functioning children and adolescents, on the other hand, are increasing at a very fast pace. Readers interested in special issues involved in the assessment of toddlers and older and more cognitively able children and adolescents are referred to more detailed discussions of clinical evaluations of these two groups (e.g., Klin, Chawarska, Rubin, & Volkmar, 2004; Klin, Sparrow, Marans, Carter, & Volkmar, 2000).

A COMPREHENSIVE DEVELOPMENTAL APPROACH

Autism is the paradigmatic condition among a class of disorders marked by social and communication deficits and behavioral rigidities called the *pervasive developmental disorders* (American Psychiatric Association, 2000), also variably called the *autism spectrum disorders*. The term PDD was chosen because it implies disruptions in multiple areas of development, including not only social and communication disabilities but also atypical patterns in play and delays in cognitive development among many others. There is a need, therefore, to adopt a comprehensive developmental approach (Sparrow, Carter, et al., 1995), which emphasizes the assessment of multiple areas of functioning and the reciprocal impact of abilities and disabilities. As a substantial proportion of children with autism also present with mental retardation (Fombonne, 1999), it is important to cast both quantified and informal observations in terms of a developmental perspective. Hence the overall developmental or intellectual level establishes the frame within which we may interpret more meaningfully both the performance obtained and the behaviors observed during the assessment. By explicitly framing the assessment in terms of the normative course of development, it is possible to appreciate delays in the acquisition of skills that emerge systematically in typical children. This information allows the clinician to fully appreciate the departures from normal expectations that delineate autistic symptomatology. In toddlers, for example, the more obvious markers of autism may not be present (e.g., "mechanical voice," motor stereotypies). Therefore, it is often the absence of normative behaviors (e.g., reduced social orientation and rate of communicative approaches) rather than the display of aberrant behaviors that becomes the hallmark of risk for autism in this young age group (Wetherby, Prizant, & Schuler, 2000).

Multidisciplinary Teams

The need for assessment of multiple areas of functioning requires the involvement of professionals with different areas of expertise. To avoid multiple views of a child (which can be conflicted, thus confusing parents and service providers), there is an equal need for transdisciplinary cohesion in which a single coherent picture can emerge and be translated into a set of intervention recommendations. An interdisciplinary format also encourages discussion among the clinicians involved, with the beneficial effects of creating a more complex and accurate view of the child (e.g., due to variability of presentation across people, time, and setting), reconciling meaningful differences, and fully appraising the impact of findings in one area on other areas of functioning (e.g., language level and social presentation).

Multidisciplinary work can be associated not only with conflicted messages conveyed to parents but also with ineffectual reporting of findings. A plethora of individual reports is less helpful than a longer report that integrates input from all members of the evaluation team. Quantitative findings and their associated technical language (e.g., standard deviations and other psychometric terms) as well as discipline-specific concepts and terms should be explained to parents or avoided altogether if they do not contribute to any aspect of the child's evaluation or follow-up. A brief narrative summary, presenting succinctly the child's competencies and problems across domains and their implication for treatment and interventions, should be included in all clinical reports.

Variability across Settings

The settings in which the child is observed and tested can vary greatly in terms of familiarity, degree of structure and intrusion adopted by the adult interacting with the child, and complexity of the physical environment. If these factors are not fully considered, highly discrepant views of the child may emerge, leading to conflicted impressions or narrowly framed observations. Given that the child's presentation in different settings informs clinicians more comprehensively about areas of strengths and weaknesses and about optimal and less helpful educational environments, it is important to consider these factors explicitly and to deliberately alter them to obtain a more complete view of the child. Clinicians involved in

different sections of the assessment may adopt different approaches. Thus, the assessment of intellectual functioning may require a highly structured, adult-directed approach within a very bare testing environment to yield the child's "best" performance (e.g., maximizing attention and minimizing distractions). In contrast, the assessment of social presentation may require a much less intrusive approach to create opportunities to observe the extent to which the child spontaneously initiates social contact, requests desired objects, shares experiences with others, and seeks socially salient aspects of the environment. This more naturalistic approach is likely to create the greatest social interaction demands, given that in the absence of the typical adult scaffolding that takes place whenever a child interacts with an adult, the spontaneous social predispositions of the child and absence thereof are more likely to be observed (e.g., tendency for self-isolation, exploration of extraneous physical stimuli such as lights and shades rather than representational toys or people). It is also useful to explore the extent to which a child is able to profit from therapeutic interventions, intrusively interfering with what a child is doing and redirecting him or her to more socially engaged situations, while providing augmentative forms of communication such as pictures or modeled gestures. This approach can greatly inform the kinds of interventions that are likely to be of help in the child's daily treatment plan.

Children's presentation can vary greatly as a function of time of day and state (including level of fatigue, minor illness), among a host of other factors. The potential misleading effect of such conditions can be addressed by continuously seeking information from parents or caregivers as to how representative the child's behaviors are relative to what they are used to seeing in other settings. Equally informative is a systematic comparison of observations among the clinicians involved, who can outline discrepancies in observations as a function of the underlying factors creating the setting for each observation (e.g., early in the morning versus later in the day, first day versus second day, clinic-based versus school versus home-based observations). Differences in test results can also be examined with a view to variables such as familiarity with the task, inherent structure (forced choice versus generative), complexity, degree of novelty, mode of engagement (e.g., active versus passive), processing demands (e.g., verbal versus visual, unimodal versus multimodal), and external supports used (e.g., visual cues, verbal prompts).

Parents' Involvement

An understanding of findings related to specific skills measured in the assessment must be qualified in terms of the child's adjustment to everyday situations and real-life demands. This can be achieved only through the participation of parents in the assessment as a source of information. Although parents may not have the experience and objectivity to appreciate the extent to which their child conforms or not to normative expectations (e.g., this might be their first child; they might have developed a style of interaction in which the adult's approach masks the child's more marked social disabilities), the information they can provide has been shown to be both useful and sufficiently reliable to inform the diagnostic process (Lord, Rutter, & Le Couteur, 1994). This process includes historical data, observations of the child in naturalistic settings such as home and school program, and incidental observations such as a visit to the playground or a birthday party. By grounding the findings obtained during the assessment in·this contextual base of information, many advantages follow including a better sense of the child's developmental path, a validation of clinical observations, and the opportunity for comparisons across environments and situations.

Parental involvement is also advantageous from other perspectives. The clinician's intervention is likely to be much more effective if parents have the opportunity to directly observe what takes place in the evaluation and then to discuss specific behaviors (rather than more vague concepts or symptoms) with the clinicians afterwards. It is in the context of this understanding, as well as in the process of discussing a child's strengths and weaknesses and the required interventions emerging from this profile, that parents are optimally prepared to become advocates and coordinators of the child's intervention program.

Profile Scatter

As the profiles of children with ASDs typically involve great variability of skills across different domains (e.g., relative strengths on sensorimotor tasks contrasting with significant weaknesses in conceptual or language-mediated tasks), it is important to delineate a profile of assets and deficits rather than simply presenting an overall and often misleading summary score or measure because such global scores may represent the averaging of highly discrepant skills. Similarly, it is important not to generalize from an isolated performance (e.g., a "splinter" skill, peaks in performance on geometric puzzles, precocious reading decoding skills) to the overall impression of level of functioning because this, too, may be a gross misrepresentation of the child's capacities for learning and adaptation. The importance of sampling a range of abilities also lies in the fact that most psychological measures are not "pure" and do not assess one ability domain alone. Results are interpreted on the basis of multiple lines of converging evidence from different tests sharing common underlying factors.

Functional Adjustment

The understanding of findings related to specific skills measured in the assessment needs to take place in the context of the child's adjustment to everyday situations and adaptation to real-life demands. It entails several factors: First, a thorough assessment of the child's adaptive behaviors—that is, the child's ability to translate capacities into consistent, habitual behaviors fostering self-sufficiency in naturalistic settings—is essential. Second, there is a need to view assessment findings in terms of their impact on the child's ongoing adaptation, learning, and behavioral adjustment so that the interrelatedness of assessment and intervention is fully considered, with a view toward translating findings into directives for treatment and remedial approaches. Third, because the central and defining feature of autism and related disorders is a pervasive impairment of socialization, it is important to explore the interrelationships among social, communication, and emotional functioning and the other areas assessed to identify any contributors to social deficits and deviance (e.g., learning or language deficits), and, conversely, to consider the impact of the social disability on the child's behavior and performance in the various procedures comprising the assessment (e.g., difficulties with tasks requiring imitation or social cognition). Adequate consideration of these issues strengthens the interpretation of the assessment findings. Full consideration of functional adjustment aspects of testing procedures informs intervention strategies and strengthens the rationale for educational and other recommendations, transforming the evaluative process from a potentially anxiety-provoking situation overly focused on numerical results into a first step to a supportive and hope-building, as well as constructive and well-informed, intervention.

Delays and Deviance

Even though this distinction is implied in the developmental psychopathology approach outlined earlier, it is important to explicitly frame the assessment in terms of a distinction between normative course of development (i.e., the child's developmental resources) and deviant patterns of development and behavior (i.e., symptoms that are characteristic of the ASDs as well as comorbid symptomatology). The normative approach places the child's resources in the context of abilities and skills that emerge systematically (e.g., walking at around 11 to 13 months, joint attention skills at around 11 to 16 months, two-word combinations at around 18 to 24 months, understanding of beliefs and nonliteral speech at around 4 to 5 years) and describes advances or delays in the rate of acquisition of normative behaviors. In contrast, the deviance approach refers to behaviors that are not typically observed in normally developing children, representing deviations from normal expectations (e.g., pronounced body rocking or hand flapping). Normative behaviors are usually measured through well-normed instruments, allowing the examiner to place the child in a dimensional continuum available for the entire population of his or her age. In contrast, abnormal behaviors that have very low base rates and that do not follow systematic patterns across settings

and developmental level are more difficult to sample and to quantify, defying attempts to place the child in a dimensional continuum anchored by "normalcy" on one end and "extreme autism" on the other end. Therefore, normative capacities such as intellectual functioning or adaptive behavior can be measured using instruments built on age-based, population norms, whereas information on deviant behaviors needs to be obtained through diagnostic instrumentation that quantifies symptoms for relevant subgroups of people. However, although current diagnostic instruments are not population normed, they are nevertheless well standardized (see Chapter 28, this *Handbook,* this volume, on diagnostic instrumentation); that is, they set specific rules for sampling and eliciting behaviors and for coding and quantifying them.

Continuous Contact

The typical complexity of the child's clinical presentation may necessitate direct and continuous contact with the various professionals implementing the recommended interventions (e.g., teachers, speech pathologists, and occupational therapists). Such a team approach not only maximizes the efficacy of the interventions adopted but also establishes a partnership with all those involved in the child's care, clarifying objectives, aiding in specific problem solving, and monitoring the child's progress. It also reassures parents who have the complex task of processing a great amount of, often technical, information and of acquainting themselves with the various health, educational, and advocacy systems whose services are required for their child.

ESSENTIAL ELEMENTS OF CLINICAL EVALUATION IN AUTISM SPECTRUM DISORDERS

The comprehensive developmental approach outlined earlier calls for a highly integrated and, to some extent, necessarily overlapping, group of procedures aimed at obtaining information necessary for diagnostic determination and for outlining a comprehensive profile of assets and deficits needed to design and implement a program of treatment and intervention.

The essential elements in clinical assessment of children with ASDs include (1) a psychological evaluation including developmental or intellectual assessment and adaptive functioning, (2) a speech, language, and communication assessment, and (3) a diagnostic work-up, including a thorough health, behavioral, and educational and intervention history; aspects of autism as well as comorbid symptomatology as obtained through direct assessment and parental report; and familial vulnerabilities. In many cases, there is a need for additional assessment and consultation, including sensory, motor or neuropsychological functioning, neurological status, and clinical genetics. This section addresses each one of these areas of assessment.

Psychological Assessment

Developmental (for younger children) or intelligence (for older children) assessments capable of describing and measuring the child's current intellectual and other resources are critical in any clinical evaluation of individuals with developmental disabilities. These measures should frame subsequent observations in terms of the child's current potential to inform decisions about the kinds of intervention strategies from which the child is developmentally ready to profit. The overall goal of the psychological assessment is not only to establish a benchmark against which other measures and observations can be judged but also to characterize the child's specific style of learning and relative assets that need to be capitalized on in treatment.

In addition to framing the child's overall developmental level, the psychological assessment should more specifically describe patterns of both verbal and nonverbal functioning across several domains: (1) problem solving (e.g., can the child generate strategies and integrate information?), (2) concept formation (e.g., can the child abstract rules from specific instances or understand principles of categorization, order, time, number, and causation, and generalize knowledge from one context to another?), (3) reasoning (e.g., can the child transform information to solve visual-perceptual and verbal problems?), (4) style of learning (e.g., can the child learn from model-

ing, imitation, using visual cues, or verbal prompts?), and (5) memory skills (e.g., how many items of information can the child retain; is there a difference in the child's ability to recognize different kinds of stimuli such as objects, facts, or faces; are the child's memory skills in one modality better than in another such as visual versus verbal?). Other areas of psychological assessment include adaptive functioning (real-life independence skills), motor and visual-motor skills, play skills, and social cognition. Of these elements, the assessment of the child's demonstrated functional adjustment in day-to-day situations is probably the most critical. Universally, children with ASDs have adaptive skills that significantly lag behind their best performance in laboratory-based evaluations (Volkmar, Lord, Bailey, Schultz, & Klin, 2004). The discrepancy between intellectual potential and consistently displayed skills in naturalistic settings can be very pronounced in individuals with normative intelligence (e.g., Klin et al., in press), and it is typically already large even within the context of the reduced parameters of toddler development, with some children failing to achieve skills that are normatively acquired in the first few months of life (Klin, Volkmar, & Sparrow, 1992). Given that children with autism typically acquire many skills, spontaneously or as a result of structured intervention, but fail to use them in real life—indeed, difficulties in generalization are probably one of the most entrenched challenges in autism—it is crucial that detailed measures of adaptive behavior are obtained in a way that a plan for addressing disparities between potential and real-life capacities is fully outlined for service providers.

Speech, Language, and Communication Assessment

Particularly during the early childhood of individuals with ASD, but to some extent throughout life, communication patterns are inextricably tied to global social development. It is, therefore, not surprising that this area of development is invariably impaired in children with autism and represents a core aspect of assessment and possibly the most central area of intervention (Wetherby et al., 2000; Prizant,

Wetherby, & Rydell, 2000). Consequently, it is important that speech, language, and communication assessment is not limited in focus and measures to the more formal aspects of linguistic skills such as phonology, vocabulary, language comprehension and expression, or syntax. Thus, assessment in this domain should include qualitative observations and quantified measures (when possible) of skills such as prosody (i.e., communicative use of volume, pitch, rate, stress, and phrasing of speech), pragmatics (i.e., language use within the context of social interaction, turn taking, rules of presupposition—how much information to offer the conversational partner—and register—the style of communication to adopt given a particular social situation), metalinguistics (e.g., nonliteral speech such as metaphors, irony, sarcasm, and humor), the language of mental states (e.g., intentions, motivation, beliefs, thoughts, and feelings), and narrative skills. Observations and measurements in these areas should be presented within the context of the child's patterns of social interaction and relationships, as well as potential contributors to the understanding of a child's mood states (e.g., anxiety resulting from being perplexed by the complex communication demands of social life at school) and maladaptive behaviors (e.g., frustration-related aggression caused by limitations in language comprehension).

In younger children, a thorough assessment of preverbal communicative and social cognitive skills can be fundamental in establishing appropriate priorities for intervention. Thus, there is a need for qualitative and quantified information on skills such as communicative intent, joint attention, and symbolic behaviors, as well as the child's ability to self-regulate and learn (e.g., to calm down, explore a new situation, overcome a frustrating experience), making use of adults and of peers. It is particularly important to ensure that areas of known peak performance in children with ASD (e.g., single-word expressive vocabulary) are not considered to represent overall linguistic abilities (e.g., sentence comprehension, narrative skills) or communicative competence (e.g., the capacity for reciprocal social and communicative engagement).

Diagnostic Work-Up

The diagnostic process needs to integrate every aspect of the child revealed through the assessment (Lord & Risi, 2000). Cognitive level frames expectations as to social, communicative, and play skills. Speech and language levels qualify difficulties in social interaction, learning, and communication. Levels of adaptive functioning reveal discrepancies between demonstrated potential and real-life functional adjustment. They highlight challenges in spontaneous adjustment, particularly in the social domain, as well as areas for focal intervention when specific adaptive behaviors have not been mastered despite sufficient cognitive skills. This body of knowledge provides the necessary canvas for a careful delineation of departures from normalcy in terms of both developmental history and current presentation.

The diagnostic process is by necessity composed of two complementary strategies of data acquisition. First, parents need to provide a detailed view of their child's history and current representative behaviors. Second, direct observations are necessary to explore the parents' concerns and to obtain an independent sampling of the child's social, communication, and play behaviors, as well as other behavioral patterns related to exploration of the environment, self-regulation and self-stimulation, and reactions to environment stimuli.

The first part of the diagnostic process is thus to involve parents as a welcome and important source of information about the given child. Well before the visit to the clinic, parents should be requested to provide information about their child. This process primes them to think about developmental history, allows them to consult materials (e.g., videotapes, baby books) that can refresh their memory and to solicit the thoughts of other pertinent adults (e.g., grandparents, day care providers), promotes more detached observations of the child in naturalistic settings, and otherwise prepares them for the kind of interviews that they will complete during the evaluation. One efficient way to accomplish this goal is to provide parents with detailed forms that include developmental inventories (e.g., information on gestation, birth, developmental milestones, typical patterns of normative behaviors, lists of developmental concerns). Such inventories may also include screening instruments for the purpose of further preparing the clinicians to explore specific areas of concern. Additional areas to be covered include medical information, behaviors or symptoms of grave concern to parents, and family history (given the need to explore genetic liabilities).

From a diagnostic perspective, direct interview with parents is aimed at collecting a body of information on social, communication, play, and other forms of behavioral functioning that is of particular importance in diagnostic formulation. Although this can be achieved more informally, to ensure that major symptom areas are covered in conversation with parents, there are specific instruments that help structure these interviews in such a way that all relevant behavioral features are covered. Chief among these instruments is the Autism Diagnostic Interview-Revised (ADI-R; Rutter, Le Couteur, & Lord, 2003). This instrument was developed as a way of standardizing diagnostic procedures in multisite genetic research projects (Lord, 1997). It follows a semistructured format of interview with the parent or primary caregiver and includes an exhaustive list of items related to onset patterns, communication, social development and play, and restricted patterns of interests and behaviors, which are pertinent to the diagnosis of autism. Besides standardizing the obtainment of developmental history and current presentation, the ADI-R also provides a diagnostic algorithm that is keyed to the *Diagnostic and Statistical Manual of Mental Disorders,* fourth edition (*DSM-IV;* American Psychiatric Association, 1994), criteria for autism. Although the ADI-R offers these various advantages, some caution needs to be exercised to see it as part of the diagnostic process rather than synonymous with the final diagnostic formulation (see Chapter 28, this *Handbook,* this volume, for further details). For example, the ADI-R has some limitations in the case of young children with ASD relative to the gold standard of diagnosis by experienced clinicians (Lord, 1995). It tends to overdiagnose children with significant cognitive delays as having autism at age 2 but to underdiagnose a small proportion of

children who at age 2 do not show symptoms in the restricted patterns of interests and behaviors (thus failing to meet *DSM-IV* criteria for autism; Lord & Risi, 2000). Another area of limitation concerns the limited demonstrated contribution to the differential diagnosis of autism relative to other PDDs (e.g., Asperger syndrome), although this limitation is more a reflection of the nosologic status of the various PDDs rather than of a flaw in the instrument itself. In other words, while the PDDs can be fairly reliably separated from non-PDD conditions, distinctions among the PDDs are more problematic (see Chapters 1, 4, 6, and 21, this *Handbook,* Volume 1, for detailed reviews of nosologic difficulties associated with the classification of autism, Asperger syndrome, and PDD-not otherwise specified [NOS]). For example, one study found that interrater agreement for the diagnosis of autism versus a non-PDD condition is very high, but the rates are much lower for distinctions among the PDDs (e.g., between autism and Asperger syndrome or PDD-NOS; Klin, Lang, Cicchetti, & Volkmar, 2000). In many respects, some limitations of the ADI-R speak to the difficulties in using parental reports as sources of specific information relevant to a diagnosis of autism. What might not be obvious signs of abnormality in the way the child explores the environment or plays with toys to a parent may be seen very differently in direct observation by an experienced clinician. Hence it is important to both frame questions in a way that will make sense from the perspective of a parent's experience with his or her own child and supplement this information with direct observations.

The ADI-R probes cover primarily four areas of diagnostic information. The *early development domain* focuses on onset patterns including developmental milestones and age of recognition of specific concerns. The *communication domain* covers information on speech and language acquisition and typical autistic symptomatology (e.g., immediate echolalia, stereotyped utterances and delayed echolalia, social vocalization and reciprocal conversation, nonverbal communication, and attention to the human voice). The *social development and play domain* covers aspects of gaze behavior (e.g., eye contact, directing other people's attention through pointing), sensitivity to and appropriateness to social approaches, nature and range of facial expressions, prosocial behaviors (e.g., offering comfort), peer interaction, and play patterns (e.g., imitative play, pretend play by self and with others). The *restricted interests and behaviors domain* covers behaviors associated with circumscribed interests, unusual preoccupations, repetitive use of objects or interest in parts of objects, ritualistic behavior, unusual sensory interests, and motor mannerisms.

The second part of the diagnostic process involves direct observation of the child, and it should include observations of the child during more and less structured periods (e.g., unstructured spontaneous play sessions versus structured adult-guided cognitive testing), with different people (e.g., parents, siblings, or peers versus unfamiliar examiners), and in different situations (e.g., during conversation about the child's favorite topic versus conversations about the child's experiences at school or about social relationships). These various contrasts have the potential of creating a rich texture of observations for the characterization of both relative strengths and particularly challenging situations in the domains of social, communicative, play, and other behaviors. For example, a child who is overly focused and engaged when discussing a topic of circumscribed interest may become scattered, inattentive, "hyperactive," or maybe withdrawn and nonresponsive when asked to talk about experiences with friends. Social deficits and deviance are typically most apparent in unstructured times and when observations are focused on the child's own overtures and approaches. It is critical, therefore, that the child be given the opportunity to be left to his or her own devices for brief periods of time (e.g., exploring play materials). Whether the child becomes self-absorbed or attempts to involve the examiner, the nature of isolated activities (e.g., repetitive play or stereotypic exploration of toys), among a host of other important observations, can be made by means of these less intrusive approaches.

The sampling of spontaneous social, communication, and play skills is probably best done in the context of a diagnostic play and conversation session. This session should be set in as naturalistic a fashion as can be contrived in the context of a clinic environment. One standardized approach to creating such an environment is through the use of the Autism Diagnostic Observation Schedule (ADOS; Lord, Rutter, DiLavore, & Risi, 1999). Like the ADI-R, the ADOS was developed with a view to standardize diagnostic procedures in multisite genetic projects (Lord, 1997). The instruments are complementary in that one focuses on parents as sources of information (ADI-R) whereas the other focuses on direct observations (ADOS).

For younger children, the ADOS consists of a series of playlike "presses" in which a situation is created to generate observations of the spontaneous behaviors. It starts with a free play session that makes possible for the observer to sample the child's preferential patterns of attention (e.g., focusing on people vs. things) and play behaviors (e.g., focusing on cause-effect vs. representational play materials, solitary vs. socially engaged play). Opportunities for showing sensitivity to social cues (e.g., calling the child's name, trying to elicit a smile without touching the child), joint-attention behaviors (e.g., pointing to distant objects, creating highly attractive stimuli such as soap bubbles and waiting for the child to bring another person's attention to the bubbles), patterns of request and showing (e.g., showing attractive objects and then placing them out of the child's reach), imitative skills and familiarity with social routines (e.g., modeling actions on miniatures, creating a pretend birthday party), among others, are all created in a playful and seamless fashion. These observations are coded according to detailed criteria in the various clusters defining autism. For older individuals, the presses are created around conversations about daily events at school or other environments, about social difficulties, friendship experiences and relationships in general, chores and responsibilities in daily life, as well as through more directed activities eliciting spontaneous verbal and gestural communication, imitation, and shared pretend play or imaginative activity. As in the case of younger children, this body of observations is then coded according to detailed criteria in central areas of diagnostic consideration such as prosody and voice; echoing; idiosyncratic use of words and phrases; coordination of gaze, gesture, and verbal communication; facial expressions; empathy and insight into social relationships including an individual's own role in them; social and communicative reciprocity; and imagination and creativity, as well as the occurrence of narrow and interfering interests or stereotyped behaviors.

The ADOS provides a diagnostic algorithm that is keyed to *DSM-IV* (American Psychiatric Association, 1994). In contrast to the ADI-R, which makes possible a distinction only between autism and a non-PDD condition, the ADOS makes a distinction between autism and PDD-NOS on the basis of level of severity. For very young children, the ADOS appears to be more predictive of a subsequent diagnosis of autism than the parental reports obtained with the ADI-R (Lord & Risi, 2000; Lord et al., 1999). However, the more higher functioning toddlers (i.e., those with some language) may sometimes be misidentified as nonautistic. The ADOS has limitations when used with children below the developmental level of 18 months or so (Klin et al., 2003; also see Chapter 28, this *Handbook,* this volume). Data on older children also reinforce the notion that neither parent reports of history and current presentation or protocols based on direct observation can be viewed in isolation and that there are important gains to be made by combining these two complementary sources of diagnostic information.

Diagnostic Formulation and Differential Diagnosis

The diagnostic formulation should use and integrate qualitative and quantified data emerging from all of the other components of the assessment to better understand the child's developmental history and current presentation. Although one aspect of the diagnostic process is the diagnostic assignment of a syndrome label—for example, based on *DSM-IV-TR* (American Psychiatric Association, 2000) or *International Classification of Diseases,* 10th ed. (*ICD-10;* World Health Organization, 1992)—this is hardly its most important role. Given the heterogeneity of autism along all dimensions of abilities and symptomatology, a

diagnostic label, while necessary for communication among professionals and for deeming children eligible for special education services and other treatments, can hardly provide the basis for programmatic recommendations for intervention. Such recommendations are built on detailed, individualized profiles of relative strengths and significant deficits revealed through comprehensive assessments of the kind described here. Thus, in addition to a diagnostic label, the diagnostic formulation should provide some information about the nature and intensity of needed remediating services, as well as some indication of level of concern relative to eventual outcome.

The differential diagnosis of the ASDs includes primarily language and other specific developmental disorders and global developmental delays or mental retardation. In some cases, congenital sensory impairments such as deafness or reactive attachment disorder may have to be considered. Traditionally, children with language disorders have not been thought to exhibit the pattern of serious social deviance and deficits, impoverished pretend play and imagination, and stereotyped behaviors exhibited by children with autism. They may, in fact, exhibit relative strengths in gestural and other nonverbal forms of communication and are more likely to become more socially integrated to the extent that their means for communication are expanded. More recent follow-up studies of children with language disorders have blurred somewhat these clearcut lines of distinction (see Chapters 1 and 7, this *Handbook,* Volume 1), although the nature and pervasiveness of the social and communicative deficits in autism are still seen as of a much greater magnitude. In global delays or mental retardation, social and communicative skills are usually commensurate with the child's overall cognitive level, and deviant behaviors in all areas are much less common (with, maybe, the exception of severely to profoundly mentally retarded individuals, in relationship to which the differential diagnosis can be at times difficult). Congenitally deaf and congenitally blind children may exhibit some difficulties in social interaction and some repetitive activities (Hobson, 2002), although they are usually interested in social interaction and may make use of nonaffected modalities of expression (e.g., facial and bodily gestures in the case of deaf children) for the purpose of communication. Children with reactive attachment disorders have, by definition, experienced marked psychosocial deprivation that results in deficits in social interaction, most notably in attachment patterns (expressed as either withdrawal or indiscriminate friendliness). However, the quality of the social deficit is different from autism in that the disturbance tends to remit or diminish significantly after an appropriately responsive and nurturing psychosocial environment is provided.

In contrast to the relatively clear differential diagnosis of the PDDs relative to non-PDD conditions, diagnostic differentiation across the subcategories of the PDDs, and particularly between higher functioning autism (i.e., autism unaccompanied by mental retardation), Asperger syndrome, and PDD-NOS, is fraught with difficulty. The validity status of these differentiations is discussed in great detail in Chapters 1 to 7 of the *Handbook*. Although there are many reasons to consider the differentiation among these conditions, it is important to note and to convey to parents not only that the specific label is less important than the individualized diagnostic formulation as described earlier but also that there is consensual agreement among clinical researchers (Filipek et al., 1999; NRC, 2001; Volkmar et al., 1999) that, regardless of which of the PDDs is assigned to a given child, the nature and intensity of services to be provided should be the same as for a child with autism.

Other Areas of Assessment

Although the psychological and communication assessments and the diagnostic work-up form the core of every developmental disabilities evaluation of children with ASDs, a number of additional assessment considerations should be given on the basis of the specific challenges faced by individual children. Particularly, but not exclusively, in the case of younger children, assessment of reactions to sensory aspects of the environment, motor control and execution, self-regulation, and other domains of functioning typically covered by occupational and physical therapists

can be of great value in our effort to better understand the optimal levels of arousal for a given child, what distractions are making the child less available for learning, and which approach style is more likely to foster social engagement and reciprocal communication. Children with ASDs vary greatly in terms of their reactivity to the environment, self-regulation abilities in excitable situations, and need for either calming and soothing or animated and intrusive adult approaches in order to respond more meaningfully to others. Insights emerging from these observations can be critical in devising optimal classroom environments and teaching strategies. Conversely, the effectiveness of educational interventions can suffer greatly if enough consideration is not given to factors impacting on the child's attention to tasks, compliance, capacity for self-regulation, sensory-seeking behaviors, self-stimulatory behaviors, and other child-specific characteristics that are not necessarily part of the core features of the ASDs but that can be equally impairing. Thus, the goals of occupational and physical therapy assessments are to maximize the effectiveness of social, communicative, and cognitive activities by treating disruptive behaviors, optimizing the learning environment, and fostering more competence in the areas of self-awareness, motor planning, and visual-motor exploration of the environment. To accomplish these goals, occupational and physical therapists can join communication specialists and special educators within a common effort to create the best fit between environmental conditions and child-specific characteristics.

In the absence of medical concerns (see Chapter 20, this *Handbook,* Volume 1), exhaustive medical work-ups usually have limited clinical benefit (Klin et al., 1997). Therefore, in the absence of clinical indicators, brain and metabolic studies are unlikely to be of help. Nevertheless, a small number of medical exams should be considered. These include hearing assessments (this has to be done for any child with speech, language, and communication impairments), blood screening for fragile X syndrome (because a number of individuals with autism also exhibit fragile X syndrome), and a child neurology assessment if there is any concern about a possible seizure disorder because of periodic unresponsiveness (e.g., "absence spells" or staring in the distance for long periods, being unresponsive to calls and touch). When there is a family history of mental retardation or the cooccurrence of cognitive delays and dysmorphic features, a genetic evaluation and more extensive laboratory studies are required to rule out a possible genetic syndrome of mental retardation. Although additional medical procedures may be warranted in the case of individual children, the physician should consider their cost-benefit value (particularly in terms of the child's and family's discomfort) given the typically low yield of common medical exams in children with ASDs.

Summary of Clinical Assessment

The multifaceted nature of the clinical assessment of children with ASDs underscores the need for integration of the oftentimes voluminous information produced by the various clinicians. To prevent fragmentation, the contribution of each professional should not be confined to his or her own area of specialty (e.g., test scores); rather, the team should strive to pool clinical observations, despite the redundancy incurred, to obtain a more valid clinical picture of the child's presentation across different settings and persons and over time. And the quality of the clinical assessment should be judged on the basis of how individualized and detailed are the treatment and intervention recommendations emerging from this transdisciplinary procedure.

PSYCHOLOGICAL ASSESSMENT

The primary goal of the psychological assessment is to quantify the child's overall level of cognitive development, and it is important for several reasons:

1. It provides *a frame for the interpretation of all of the other qualitative and quantified observations* made as part of the evaluation. From a diagnostic standpoint, the diagnostic category of autism and other ASDs should be used only if a child's social disability exceeds what might be expected given his or her level of intellectual func-

tioning (Rutter, 1978). This is of particular importance in the case of individuals with mental retardation, who as a consequence of their cognitive limitations are likely to also exhibit social and language and communication difficulties but not in excess of what might be expected of same-age individuals at their cognitive and developmental level.

2. It provides *a frame for decisions on teaching strategies,* which may be entirely inappropriate if it targets an unrealistically higher or neglectfully lower capacity for learning. If the way the interventionist approaches the child implies unrealistically higher expectations, this discrepancy may cause a great deal of unnecessary frustration and maybe even maladaptive reactions such as withdrawal or aggression. If the discrepancy is in the other direction, the intervention may instill a great deal of underachievement in the program and maybe even boredom and lack of motivation in the child. Targeting the appropriate cognitive level allows the interventionist to increase difficulty at the right amount to create realistic challenges that can be successfully achieved.

3. The level of cognitive functioning has been shown to be possibly the most important factor mediating a wide range of clinical phenomena, such as severity of symptomatology in the social, language, and communication domains, as well as in terms of stereotypic behaviors and self-injury, and level of self-sufficiency (Volkmar et al., 1987), eventual outcome (see Chapter 7, this *Handbook,* Volume 1), and medical complications such as seizures (see Chapter 20, this *Handbook,* Volume 1).

4. In the United States, intellectual functioning below the normative range (i.e., IQ below 70) typically entitles individuals to additional services during the school years and lifelong benefits that may include additional personnel to help with respite care, access to residential care, assistive equipment, and others. In some states, individuals with ASD are not entitled to any services once they graduate from the school system unless they have been shown to have mental retardation. Critically, however, eligibility for these services typically

requires documentation (i.e., assessment using standardized measures of intellectual functioning) produced prior to the age of 18 years.

The careful assessment of overall cognitive functioning is, however, merely the first step of the psychological assessment. Almost by definition, individuals with ASDs have highly variable learning profiles and a great deal of scatter across multiple domains (see Chapter 13, this *Handbook,* Volume 1). Thus, overall cognitive scores may be the averaging of highly discrepant skills. Because appropriate interventions are meant to address needs and capitalize on strengths, this variability is of great importance for decisions on the type of teaching strategies to adopt, ways of compensating for significant deficits, and ways to use cognitive assets to make up for deficient development in other areas. For example, many individuals with ASDs profit from the use of visual strategies for learning, often to compensate for language deficits, but some may exhibit nonverbal learning disabilities and can make best use of verbal scripts rather than visual materials. Preconceptions about a child's learning style solely on the basis of the child's diagnostic label can lead to ineffectual, and sometimes even deleterious, teaching strategies. Quantification of variability and consistency across various areas of learning provide, therefore, a decisive contribution to the planning and implementation of educational and other interventions, where the main goal is to maximize the child's learning potential and to optimize the learning environment, which in turn makes it possible for the child to achieve a sense of mastery and self-control regardless of level of disability.

Besides the assessment of overall cognitive levels and detailed profiles of learning, the psychological assessment needs to cover one more critical area of development: the capacity for translating cognitive potential into real-life skills, typically referred to as the *assessment of adaptive behavior.* Almost by definition, individuals with ASD show a large discrepancy between cognitive potential as measured in the context of a standardized assessment of IQ and real-life skills as measured with standardized interviews using parents or

other caregivers as informants, favoring the former (Klin et al., in press). This discrepancy can reach magnitudes of 2 to 3 or even more standard deviations in the more cognitively able (or higher functioning) individuals, but it is also quite considerable even in severely mentally retarded individuals. Because real-life independency is ultimately one of the central goals for any individual with disabilities, the importance of the documentation of adaptive behavior deficits cannot be overly emphasized. In higher functioning individuals with ASD, the typical low scores in adaptive behavior help advocates to secure services and convey to others the importance of intervention for those individuals who otherwise might be considered too bright or too talented (in some isolated area) to require any help at all. In lower functioning individuals, quantified monitoring of adaptive behavior (i.e., periodic reassessment) helps the interventionists to ensure that the hierarchy of goals that they are pursuing in the individual's program is having the desired positive impact on the all-important, longer term goal of achieving the greatest degree of self-sufficiency.

For some individuals, there is a need to pursue a more detailed assessment of their learning profiles because they may exhibit areas of strength and deficit that cannot be adequately captured in general assessments of cognitive functioning such as IQ tests. These areas may involve difficulties with integrating fragments of information into coherent wholes (weak central coherence; see Chapter 24, this *Handbook,* Volume 1); difficulties in planning, organizing, and generating strategies to solve problems (i.e., executive dysfunction; see Chapter 22, this *Handbook,* Volume 1); difficulties in learning key concepts in social understanding such as mental states (i.e., theory of mind; see Chapter 23, this *Handbook,* Volume 1); and specific discrepancies in motor and visual motor, attention, and perception, as well as memory and learning skills (see Chapter 13, this *Handbook,* Volume 1). Some of these issues might require additional testing using standardized neuropsychological tests or qualitative observations obtained during less formal procedures such as a play session, a conversation sample, drawing activities, or additional interviews or inventories using parents or other caregivers as informants. However, in the context of a transdisciplinary evaluation, the addition of procedures needs to be weighed in terms of its potential yield for the overall insight into the child's profile and in ways that these contributions translate into practical recommendations for treatment and intervention. While most traditional elements of psychological assessment, from cognitive to personality assessments, may contribute something to this goal, there is a need to create a hierarchy of procedures on the basis of how necessary and central is the contribution to be achieved with a given procedure.

Issues in Psychological Assessment of Individuals with Autism Spectrum Disorder

Psychological assessments are analogous to single-subject experimental designs in which conditions are kept constant such that the child's abilities provide the only source of variance. The advantages of using standardized procedures lie in the fact that the evaluator can then compare the child's performance to the performance of same-age children using age-based norms. Even though the adherence to standardized procedures is of paramount importance for the valid and justified use of normative information, with some children with ASD, the rigid fulfillment of test instructions may sometimes not be possible. Although deviations from standard procedures should be avoided, it is sometimes necessary to make clinical modifications of procedures. Such adaptations are particularly critical to obtain a measure of the child's skills when doing otherwise would signify the obtainment of no measure at all. However, the examiner should be aware that as a consequence of such a break with standardized administration, results obtained should then be viewed with great caution, and the accompanying interpretation should make any deviations from standard administration explicit to the reader.

In testing sessions, it is always critical to consider the child's level of interest and engagement. Sometimes the usual verbal instructions and social reinforcements might not be effective to elicit the child's optimal cooperation and effort. In such situations, it is then necessary to empirically establish potential reinforcers for the particular child. For example, visual-spatial or hands-on tasks might have to be interspersed with verbally mediated measures to maintain an acceptable level of effort and engagement. Operant techniques may be particularly useful if an effective reinforcement can be identified, and, though not a primary choice, food reinforcers or even stereotypic interests and activities (e.g., winding up a music box, manipulation of a spin top) may be used to motivate the child.

A key component in appropriate psychological assessment is the choice of instruments to use with a given child. The examiner may have to adopt a hierarchy of procedures, choosing first those instruments that have been shown to best capture the concepts in question and that have the largest body of evidence and documentation in their favor. If such instruments are, however, not viable, then other, less optimal instruments might have to be chosen. In fact, in the case of children with ASD who have severe cognitive and/or language deficits, the examiner might need to have a thorough knowledge of psychological instruments not typically employed with the normative population. Several factors should be considered when choosing a test: (1) level of language skills required, (2) the complexity of the instructions and the tasks, (3) the level of social demands, (4) the utilization of timed tasks, and (5) number of shifts from one subtest or format to another. As an informal rule, instruments that require less language mediation and imitative skills (i.e., modeling), are more concrete and straightforward and more dependent on visual rather than auditory skills, require fewer attentional and cognitive shifts, and have fewer time constraints tend to be more appropriate for cognitive and language-delayed children with ASDs. An individual may obtain different results on tests tapping on the same psychological construct because of the different level of social or language demands included in the administration of each one on the tests, which is one of the reasons that profiles of psychological assessment results cannot be interpreted in isolation from the remainder of the procedures carried out in the transdisciplinary evaluation. For example, the interpretation of results on a neuropsychological battery in terms of the constructs purported to be examined in it (e.g., strengths and deficits in memory or executive functions) may not be fully warranted without consideration of the fact that the child may have a significant language comprehension deficit (as revealed in the communication assessment) and that the latter might be a more parsimonious explanation of the obtained profile. Similarly, a child with significant social and imitation deficits may score differently on a neuropsychological test of a given construct when it is computer-administered (thus avoiding the need for imitation of an examiner) relative to when the test is administered by the examiner (e.g., Ozonoff, 1995).

This consideration can be stated more generally in terms of the need for the professional carrying out the psychological assessment to be experienced not only in psychological testing but also in the work with children with ASDs and the peculiarities sometimes involved in their psychological profiles. Of these, one potentially great source of confusion relates to the children's areas of "peak performance," which can and often are dissociated from more general measures of overall cognitive functioning. Some young children may be able to read fluently (sometimes precociously) without, however, being able to understand what they read (i.e., hyperlexia; Grigorenko et al., 2003). Others may assemble sophisticated geometric puzzles extremely well, particularly if these can be solved by using parts-to-whole strategies (as in typical block design tests in which geometric designs need to be reproduced using colored blocks) but cannot perform basic verbally mediated tasks such as providing definitions of words or solving basic word puzzles. Knowledge of the typically extreme profiles of cognitive functioning and the oftentimes astonishing "islets of special ability" seen in some individuals with ASD is critical for any professional conducting psychological assessments. Lack of knowledge and experience in this respect may result in erroneous conclusions about and generalizations from the set of testing results.

Finally, It is important to consider that within each testing session a large amount of extremely important qualitative information is gathered. Nearly every aspect of the events taking place can be viewed as empirically derived information that may prove useful for the purpose of intervention. For example, the amount of structure imposed by the adult, the optimal pace for presentation of tasks, successful strategies to facilitate learning from modeling and demonstrations, and effective ways of containing off-task and maladaptive behaviors are all important observations that can be extremely useful for designing an appropriate intervention program. And within each test, there may be specific illustrations that create opportunities to convey to parents, in a more intuitive manner, the main themes emerging from results of the child's cognitive testing. For example, a particularly disjointed protocol of visual-motor testing involving copying of geometric designs can serve as a concrete illustration of the child's fragmented learning style, which in turn may have relevance to the understanding of the child's difficulties in social adaptation (e.g., focusing on isolated aspects of a social situation while missing the more holistic, and crucial, overall context or meaning).

Areas of Psychological Assessment

Traditional psychological evaluations comprise measures in the areas of intelligence (i.e., intellectual profile), adaptive behavior (i.e., level of self-sufficiency in real-life situations), achievement (i.e., proficiency in academic areas taught at school), additional neuropsychological functioning (i.e., higher cognitive or psychomotor processes), and personality (intrapersonal conflicts, emotional presentation, and style of social adaptation). With the exception of intelligence and adaptive behavior, which are essential components of any psychological evaluation, the other areas may or may not be included in the psychological assessment conducted within a transdisciplinary evaluation depending on the clinical priorities (e.g., referral questions), on direct observations made during the assessment (e.g., an important qualitative observation or quantified finding), and on other practical considerations (e.g., the amount of time allotted to the psychological assessment, the optimal length of time that the child's compliance and engagement can be maintained). The following discussion focuses on intellectual testing (and developmental testing for the younger child) and adaptive behavior. Achievement testing is typically conducted at schools rather than clinics, and if necessary to be included in the transdisciplinary evaluation, the instruments and procedures are not very different from the ways in which achievement assessment is carried out in less specialized settings. More traditional forms of personality assessment using projective techniques are typically of less importance than the assessment of social and communicative style and disabilities. Sometimes these forms of assessment are not possible because of a child's language limitations, extreme concreteness, and limitations in insight. When relevant and appropriate, however, such as in some cases of higher functioning individuals who may show fragmented or fragile thought processes or comorbid symptomatol-

ogy such as depression, projective measures can be administered using standardized methodology. The area of assessment that requires more serious consideration is neuropsychological testing, although a decision may have to be made in the course or as a result of more general cognitive testing in response to an important question emerging from observations or findings.

The most widely used instruments used in psychological assessments of individuals with ASD are provided in Table 29.1.

Intelligence

Although definitions of intelligence are almost as numerous as there are theorists who strive to define the concept (Sattler, 1988), there is a high degree of consensus among psychologists as to what specific, operationalized capacities should be measured to

TABLE 29.1   Recommended Instruments for Use In Psychological Assessment of Children with ASD

Area of Assessment	Instrument	Measurement	Age Range	Indication
Overall Cognitive Assessment	WPPSI-III	Full Scale IQ; Verbal & Performance IQ; Index Scores	2 years, 6 months to 7 years, 3 months	Standard IQ testing for young children
	WISC-IV	Full Scale IQ; Index Scores	6 years to 16 years 11 months	Standard IQ testing
	K-ABC-II	Mental Processing Index (Luria) or Fluid-Crystallized Index (CHC); Scale Index Scores	3 to 18 years	Mental processing and acquired knowledge
	DAS	General Conceptual Ability; Verbal, Nonverbal, & Spatial Cluster Scores	2 years, 6 months to 17 years, 11 months	Developmental abilities
	Leiter-R	Nonverbal Full IQ; Brief IQ; Reasoning Scores	2 years to 20 years, 11 months	For children with severe language limitations
Development Assessment	Mullen	Early Learning Composite; Domain Scores	Birth to 68 months	Nonverbal, language, & motor skills
Adaptive Behavior	Vineland	Adaptive functioning in communication, daily living, social, and motor domains	Birth to 18 years, 11 months	Required for the assessment of every child with ASD
Additional Neuropsychological Testing	NEPSY	Core Domain Scores; Scaled Scores	3 to 12 years	Neuropsychological development

obtain a useful indicator of a child's intellectual level (Snyderman & Rothman, 1987). These include verbal and nonverbal reasoning or abstract/conceptual thinking, problem solving, the capacity to acquire knowledge, linguistic competence, mathematical competence, memory, mental speed, and perceptual discrimination and organization. Most intelligence batteries currently in use include these areas in varying degrees. The various instruments differ, however, in terms of emphasis placed on linguistic skills, speed of performance (i.e., timed tasks), reliance on visual or auditory presentation, motor demands, and number of constructs tested.

As noted previously, individuals with ASDs cover the entire spectrum of intellectual functioning and formal language capacities. Nevertheless, a large number of children presenting for evaluation typically exhibit significant language delays, difficulties in social interaction, poor imitation skills, high levels of distractibility and off-task behaviors, and low tolerance for prolonged periods of testing. Accordingly, when necessary, testing procedures and instruments should be chosen to circumvent such difficulties while safeguarding validity and maximizing the sampling of skills.

Among the various intelligence batteries currently in use, the age-proven Wechsler scales—Wechsler Preschool and Primary Scale of Intelligence, third edition (WPPSI-III; Wechsler, 2002), and Wechsler Intelligence Scale for Children, fourth edition (WISC-IV; Wechsler, 2003)—provide the standards for the testing of intelligence in terms of psychometric properties, standardization procedures, and extent of research. Whenever possible, these batteries should be used because they provide valid measures across a large number of relevant constructs and yield profiles of functioning that can be readily translated into intervention objectives. The Wechsler scales' division of the various tasks into factor scores (Kaufman, 1994) can be particularly helpful in the interpretation of profiles of children with ASD given the typical performance scatter found in these children's protocols (McDonald, Mundy, Kasari, & Sigman, 1989). Whereas the WPPSI-III maintains the familiar verbal-performance IQ dichotomy, the WISC-IV yields a composite IQ score and four Index scores based on factors derived from the individual subtests:

1. *Verbal Comprehension,* an index of verbal knowledge and understanding obtained informally and through formal education.
2. *Perceptual Reasoning,* an index of problem-solving ability and reflection of the ability to interpret and integrate visually perceived material.
3. *Working Memory,* an index of the ability to attend to and retain information in memory, as well as perform mental operations.
4. *Processing Speed,* an index of speed of information processing, which requires focused execution and visual motor coordination.

Salient comparisons on both scales include the capacity for dealing with verbal versus visual content, as well as central and shared processes such as concept formation, reasoning ability, attention and concentration, and memory. For example, reasoning ability may be considered further in terms of abstraction abilities (conceptual versus concrete responses), associative versus analytic style, inductive versus deductive abilities, and use of verbal strategies to reason versus nonverbal (e.g., pattern recognition, visual analysis, perceptual organization). One of the core subtests not retained on this latest edition of the WISC is Picture Arrangement. The Picture Arrangement and Comprehension subtests were especially salient for this population because they are two measures thought to involve some social judgment. Whereas the Comprehension subtest requires the child to reason through questions that involve conventional knowledge of practical social situations, using verbal means, the Picture Arrangement subtest requires the child to arrange pictures in sequence to form a story about people and events. On the latter subtest, the information presented is visual, sequential, and contextual in nature. Often, performance discrepancies are observed on these two subtests and are strongly suggestive of a preference for one mode of processing versus another, with direct implications for treatment strategies. Related processing variables such as cognitive rigidity and distraction from internal or external sources during test performance should also be considered when interpreting test results for children with ASD.

The Wechsler scales are sometimes not viable for this population because of not only language requirements but also their reliance on timed tasks, knowledge of specific content, and number of tasks that are exclusively auditory in nature (and thus more susceptible to the disruptive effects of distractibility and poor rapport). Therefore, there is a need for alternative batteries that can provide measures of intellectual level with varying degrees of comprehensiveness. These batteries include, but are not limited to, the Kaufman-Assessment Battery for Children, second edition (K-ABC-II; Kaufman & Kaufman, 2004), and the Differential Abilities Scales (DAS; Elliot, 1990). The K-ABC-II is particularly useful because of its wide range (3 to 18 years), reduced emphasis on verbal abilities and acquired knowledge, attractiveness and straightforward nature of stimuli, close association with neuropsychological processes, and a provision included in the standardization procedure making possible for the examiner to teach and demonstrate initial items to the child. This latter provision allows for an opportunity to test the child's capacity for learning through demonstration and, at times, makes possible for the examiner to overcome the child's initial failure to understand instructions. Additionally, the K-ABC-II is expanded to provide a profile of learning style in terms of two different neuropsychological models: Luria and Cattell-Horn. The scales include Sequential Processing/Short-Term Memory (information is presented in serial order), Simultaneous Processing/Visual Processing (requires processing in an integrated, Gestalt manner), Learning Ability/Long-Term Storage and Retrieval, Planning Ability/Fluid Reasoning, and Crystallized Ability. Either approach provides information relevant to learning and teaching style. Although the K-ABC does not include a measure of understanding of social situations per se, it does contain a test of face recognition (or memory for faces) that has been shown to have diagnostic value (e.g., Klin et al., 1999).

The DAS is also a very useful measure of cognitive ability that is less verbally demanding, has few time constraints, and involves tasks that allow for hands-on performance through the use of manipulatives. Like the K-ABC-II, the DAS has a broad age range (from 2 years 6 months to 17 years 11 months) and allows for teaching items. The DAS also allows profile analysis including cluster score comparisons and subtest comparisons. The General Conceptual Ability (GCA) score is considered to be an excellent measure of general cognitive ability. Significant differences in cluster scores may represent differences in verbal ability, nonverbal reasoning ability, or spatial ability. Individual subtests can be compared for knowledge of word meanings (Word Definitions) versus forming abstract concepts (Similarities) or differences in spatial ability (Pattern Construction) and visual motor ability (Recall of Designs). Supplemental tests are provided to assess attention, memory, and achievement, and there is provision for a nonverbal composite score. The DAS is especially useful for the youngest age groups. A notable drawback is the variability in the test battery through the age levels covered by the instrument, limiting comparisons of test profiles and performance over time.

For children with no or very low levels of linguistic skills, the Leiter International Performance Scale-Revised (Leiter-R; Roid & Miller, 1997) is the test of choice if attempts to use the other batteries were unsuccessful or were considered a priori to be unlikely to provide useful sampling of the child's intellectual abilities (Tsatsanis et al., 2003). The instrument is expanded to include a Visualization and Reasoning (VR) battery and Attention and Memory (AM) battery, composed of 10 subtests each. The VR battery most closely resembles the original Leiter, and it measures traditional intelligence constructs such as nonverbal reasoning, visualization, and problem solving (Roid & Miller, 1997). The Leiter-R is normed for individuals between 2 years 0 months and 20 years 11 months of age with current normative data and good psychometric properties. Four subtests comprise a Brief IQ Screener for all ages, and two sets of six subtests (one set for children between 2 and 5 years and a second set for individuals 6 to 20 years) are used to obtain a full-scale IQ. Three composite scores are also yielded on the Leiter-R: *Fluid Reasoning*, which is available for all ages; *Fundamental Visualization*, obtained for children 2 to 5 years of age; and *Spatial Visualization,* available for the 11- to 20-year age. The provision of individual subtest and composite scores permits an analysis of profiles of performance including abilities related to visual scanning and visual discrimination, as well as pattern recognition, analogic reasoning, and visual parts to whole reasoning. The Leiter-R has minimal language demands in that both the administration and responses are nonverbal, and the basis of each subtest of the VR battery is visual matching. Despite its applicability for lower functioning and nonverbal individuals, the Leiter-R presents some limitations for very low-functioning individuals in that teaching trials are limited and that the materials quickly transition from manipulative foam shapes to stimulus cards. With the latter, individuals are required to either place the cards in an easel slot or point to the appropriate response stimulus, both of which require a degree of motoric ability that can be limited if not lacking in individuals with ASD.

When the Leiter-R proves to be too challenging to a given child, its older form, the Leiter International Performance Scale (Leiter, 1948) may offer an acceptable (though last resort) measure of nonverbal intelligence. The Leiter is based on a visual matching procedure that remains the same for the entire age range of the test (years 2 to 18). Items range from pairings of colors, shapes, and figures at early levels to items involving analogies and concepts at the later levels. Apart from its ability to attract and maintain the attention of more uncooperative autistic children, the Leiter has many advantages in this population (Shah & Holmes, 1985):

1. No speech is required from the examiner or the child (i.e., instructions are given in pantomime if needed).
2. The tasks are self-explanatory, and, for the initial items, unlimited demonstration is permitted.
3. The response format is uniform (placing blocks in a slot), and there is a consistent visual matching procedure.
4. With the exception of four items at higher levels, there are no timed tasks or time limits. This is a very useful attribute in the case of those children who do not under-

stand the need for speed, who have fleeting attention, or whose stereotypies interfere with their performance.
5. The Leiter requires only minimal record keeping, and the tasks can be introduced casually and in a playlike manner.

These are useful attributes when testing children with attentional and behavioral problems as well as high levels of activity. Unfortunately, these advantages are counterbalanced by several limitations including:

1. The scale measures primarily nonverbal skills and should not be seen as a measure of general intellectual ability.
2. There are too few items at each age level, which may lead to an inaccurate estimate of mental age.
3. Item difficulty level is not constant.
4. Many of the pictures used are outdated.
5. Unlike other psychological batteries, the Leiter uses a ratio IQ rather than standard scores.

When other batteries prove impractical, the combination of the Leiter with measures of listening vocabulary such as the Peabody Picture Vocabulary Test-Third Edition (PPVT-III; Dunn & Dunn, 1997) may provide an estimate of the child's overall intellectual level. However, both the Leiter and PPVT-III tend to provide somewhat inflated scores because these tests focus on domains of peak performance in the case of children with autism (see Shah & Holmes, 1985, and Tsai & Beisler, 1984, respectively).

Intellectual testing in very young children is achieved with the use of developmental scales. Although these scales provide an estimate of cognitive level, the concept of IQ is avoided in young children because of the close interdependence of cognitive functioning with other domains of development below the age of 3 or 4 years and because estimates of cognitive level within this age range may not be predictive of IQs obtained subsequently in school-age years. While some of the scales rely purely on parental report, others involve direct sampling of the child's skills across a number of relevant domains. Only the latter are discussed here, given that it is essential that direct assessment of developmental skills be performed. Scales based on parental report can be used to further contextualize and validate clinic-based data or if for any reason direct assessment cannot be conducted. Direct observation is necessary not only to obtain information about levels of performance (e.g., scores) but also to document styles of learning and a wide range of factors that impact on the child's learning potential. These observations are even more important in young children than in older individuals. Two developmental scales have been used most frequently in the assessment of young children with ASD: the Bayley Scales of Infants Development-II (Bayley; Bayley, 1993) and the Mullen Scales of Early Learning (Mullen, 1995). Although both scales allow for scoring some low frequency or difficult to elicit behaviors based on parental report, these are primarily performance-based scales assessing the child's development in several domains. This is done in the context of direct interaction with the child around goal-oriented activities.

The Bayley is the most widely used measure of developmental skills in both clinical and research settings. Its scales range from 1 to 42 months of age. The test consists of three main components: the Mental Development Index (MDI), Psychomotor Development Index (PDI), and Behavior Rating Scale (BRS). While the MDI provides information about the child's problem-solving and language skills, the PDI assesses the child's fine and gross motor skills. The BRS is a form designed to be used by the evaluators to rate the child's behavior during the testing, including attentional capacities, social engagement, affect and emotions, as well as the quality of movement and motor control. Although the Bayley provides a method for obtaining age-equivalent scores for four facets of development, namely Cognitive, Language, Social, and Motor, empirical support for the validity of these facet scores is limited (Bayley, 1993). The Bayley takes about 60 minutes to administer for children over 15 months. Despite its excellent statistical properties and its sensitivity to high-risk childhood conditions (Bayley, 1993), its value for the assessment of young children with autism can be limited, primarily because the summary scores are likely to be averages of

highly discrepant skills in the various domains, thus creating a great misrepresentation of the child's developmental skills. For example, the MDI summarizes scores in nonverbal problem solving, expressive and receptive language, as well as personal-social functioning. Children with autism typically present with a highly scattered profile of skills, with higher level nonverbal problem-solving skills (e.g., color matching, assembling puzzles), lower level expressive language skills (although this score may still be inflated due to the these children's higher single-word vocabulary relative to typically lower sentence construction skills), and lowest scores in receptive language (due to their difficulty in responding consistently to spoken language). Thus, any composite index score summarizing performance across a number of domains is likely to misrepresent the child's developmental profile. In many respects, the average of these scores will hardly convey the most important information to the special educators whose mission is to address the child's needs while capitalizing on the child's strengths. For this purpose, the profile, in all its variability and scatter, is more informative than overall scores. Similarly in the motor domain, a child may have relatively good gross motor skills but score poorly on fine motor tasks due to difficulties in motor imitation inherent to autism (see Chapter 14, this *Handbook,* Volume 1).

For these reasons, the popularity of the Mullen has increased dramatically in the past few years. The Mullen is a multidomain assessment scale that emphasizes the measurement of distinct abilities rather than developmental summaries. Its range is from birth to 68 months of age. It contains five domains: Visual Reception (primarily nonverbal visual discrimination, perceptual categorization, and memory), Receptive Language, Expressive Language, Fine Motor, and Gross Motor. The Mullen yields standard T scores in all five domains and an Early Learning Composite score based on the first four domains. The Mullen takes between 15 and 60 minutes to administer, depending on the child's age. Its separation of visual perceptual abilities from expressive and receptive language, as well as the separation of fine and gross motor skills, serves very well the assessment of young children with autism who, as noted, typically display highly scattered profiles.

Finally, very low functioning older individuals, who cannot reach a basal level of performance on any of the more traditional intellectual batteries, present a great challenge for clinical evaluations because there is a need for some estimate of their cognitive skills to establish the frame of reference for other observations, including the diagnostic work-up. These are individuals with mental age below the 2- to 3-year level. The use of developmental batteries is problematic because these tests involve materials that are more appropriate for infants and toddlers rather than adolescents or adults. Although there is no satisfactory solution, the examiner may choose to use selected tasks from a developmental battery that are less infant-specific such as puzzles and pegboards. Alternatively, the examiner may choose a developmental test that focuses on basic cognitive achievements such as object permanence and means-ends relationships that have implications for decision on intervention strategies intended to augment the individual's means of learning and communication. One example of such a test is the Uzgiris-Hunt Ordinal Scale of Infant Development (Uzgiris & Hunt, 1975), which focuses on Piagetian concepts rather than age-based norms. Such testing may be a little more appropriate to severely retarded adolescents and adults because profiles obtained with more traditional developmental batteries may carry very little relevance to the day-to-day real life of these individuals. It is unfortunate that a more appropriate test of intellectual functioning is not yet available for this group of very low-functioning, older individuals.

Despite the difficulties inherent in the intellectual testing of children with ASD, several studies have substantiated the validity and predictive usefulness of intelligence scores (Lord & Schopler, 1988). The clinician should be aware that the larger the sampling of cognitive skills (i.e., comprehensiveness of the test or combination of tasks), the higher the validity and accuracy of the estimate of intellectual functioning.

There are several measurement peculiarities in the assessment of autistic children. First, it should not be assumed that the correlations between different batteries reported in the test manuals are directly applicable to this group of children. This is a direct result of the atypical patterns of strengths and weaknesses observed among children with autism and related disorders. For example, measurements using one-word receptive or expressive picture vocabulary tests in typical populations are highly correlated with both overall measures of intelligence and language comprehension (Sattler, 1988). In children with ASD, however, correlations are much lower. Second, it is not unusual to observe a drop in standard scores over time. This phenomenon usually does not indicate a loss of acquired skills; rather, it suggests that the child's intellectual gains are not commensurate (i.e., they are at a slower rate) with gains in chronological age. Third, given autistic children's usual strengths in visual perceptual tasks and weaknesses in conceptual and reasoning tasks, it is not uncommon to observe a drop of standard scores at around school-entry level. This follows the typical developmental organization of test batteries that reduce the number of items dependent on perceptual discrimination and rote learning and increase the number of items requiring reasoning and concept formation during this transitional time.

Adaptive Behavior

Adaptive functioning refers to capacities for personal and social self-sufficiency in real-life situations. Its aim is to obtain a measure of the child's typical patterns of functioning in familiar and representative environments such as the home and the school, which may contrast markedly with the demonstrated level of performance and presentation in the clinic. It provides the clinician with an essential indicator of the extent to which the child is able to use his or her potential, as measured in the assessment, in the process of adaptation to environmental demands. The commonly found large discrepancy between intellectual level and adaptive level signifies that a priority should be made of instruction within the context of naturally occurring situations to foster and facilitate the use of skills to enhance quality of life. In addition, in most circumstances, a measure of adaptive level is required to establish a child's entitlement to services.

The most widespread measurement of adaptive behavior is provided by the Vineland Adaptive Behavior Scales (Sparrow, Balla, & Cicchetti, 1984b). The Vineland assesses capacities for self-sufficiency in various domains of functioning including Communication (receptive, expressive, and written language), Daily Living Skills (personal, domestic, and community skills), Socialization (interpersonal relationships, play and leisure time, and coping skills), and Motor Skills (gross and fine). These capacities are assessed on the basis of the individual's current daily functioning using a semistructured interview administered to a parent or other primary caregiver. The Vineland is available in three editions: (1) a survey form to be used primarily as a diagnostic and classification tool for normal to low-functioning children or adults (Sparrow et al., 1984b), (2) an expanded form for use in the development of individual education or rehabilitative planning (Sparrow, Balla, & Cicchetti, 1984a), and (3) a classroom edition to be used by teachers (Sparrow, Balla, & Cicchetti, 1985). Among the various editions, the expanded form is the most useful in the case of children with ASDs, whose level of adaptive functioning is usually much lower than their demonstrated intellectual level (Volkmar, Carter, Sparrow, & Cicchetti, 1993). Using the child's developmental level as a point of reference, this form makes it possible for the clinician to plan intervention on the basis of those skills that the child should have acquired given his or her intellectual level. Because the items of the Vineland were selected on the basis of their immediate relevance to real-life adaptation, the skills described therein can be readily incorporated into the child's intervention plan.

Several research studies (e.g., Volkmar et al., 1987) have helped delineate the usual profile obtained for autistic children. This typically consists of relative strengths in the areas of Daily Living and Motor Skills and significant deficits in the areas of Socialization and, to a lesser extent, Communication. Some studies (Klin et al., 1992; Volkmar et al., 1993) have demonstrated the utility of the Vineland for diagnostic purposes. Vineland supplementary norms for autistic individuals are now available (Carter et al., 1998). And, as noted, Vineland scores are very low even for higher functioning individuals with ASD (Klin et al., in press), whose adaptive scores can be viewed as a more accurate quantification of their disability relative to their cognitive potential.

A new and more comprehensive version of the Vineland is currently being standardized and will be available commercially in 2005. Among the various improvements, there has been a dramatic increase in the sampling of early emerging socialization skills. This improvement was introduced with the intent of increasing its utility in both clinical practice and research with individuals with autism and related disorders.

Additional Neuropsychological Assessment

In addition to intelligence batteries, additional neuropsychological testing may be used to complement a psychological assessment when there are indications of specific disabilities impacting on identifiable and discrete learning systems. These measures may include sensory-perceptual functions (tactile, visual, and auditory modalities); laterality and psychomotor functions related to speed and visual-motor integration; specific language learning and verbal and visual memory skills; concept formation; attention and executive functions including working memory, forward planning, categorization, and inferencing; strategy generation; and mental shifting. Such measures may also be indicated to explore the nature of a child's learning disability in greater detail. A commonly used neuropsychological battery for children ages 3 to 12 years is the NEPSY, which provides tasks in the domains of attention and executive functions, language, visual-spatial processing, sensorimotor functions, and memory and learning (Korkman, Kirk, & Kemp, 1998). Children with autism have been found to exhibit deficits in attention and executive functions and memory skills, particularly memory for faces, compared to normal controls (Korkman et al., 1998).

For possibly the majority of children with ASD presenting for evaluation at specialized clinics, extensive neuropsychological batteries may not offer a significant enough contribution to justify the cost, in time and effort, for their use. Nevertheless, the employment of selected tasks from these batteries (e.g., memory for faces on the NEPSY or K-ABC-II) may be justified for the purpose of hypothesis testing regarding observations emerging in general intellectual testing or in other areas of the evaluation. Also, given the centrality of executive functioning deficits in autism (see Chapter 22, this *Handbook,* Volume 1) and their deleterious impact on everyday functioning, the examiner may choose an inventory such as the Behavior Rating Inventory of Executive Functions (BRIEF; Isquith & Gioia, 2002) to document executive deficits with a view to target them for remediation.

Other brief tests exploring the child's visual-motor skills or motor functioning can be of value for some children whose learning and adaptation appear to be hindered by deficits in these skills. For example, the Beery Buktenica Developmental Test of Visual-Motor Integration (VMI; Beery & Buktenica, 1989) provides a quick assessment of the child's grapho-motor skills, perceptual accuracy, and hand-eye coordination. It may also reveal perseverative behaviors, laterality problems, and distortions, which may be indicative of neurological involvement (Stellern, Vasa, & Little, 1976). The Bruininks-Oseretsky Test of Motor Proficiency (Bruininks, 1978) provides useful measures of gross and fine motor skills and is indicated whenever the child appears to present with significant deficits in coordination. Some of these tests, however, are now typically employed by occupational and physical therapists at schools. Data on these domains may have a significant contribution to educational programming given the important role played by motor and coordination skills in learning processes, particularly for the young child. In this context, there is a need to integrate the various components of the educational program with a view to maximize learning opportunities in regard to those skills that are typically areas of weakness for children with ASD. For example, occupational therapy may include activities focused on the teaching of conceptual terms (e.g., quantity, position, size), problem solving, and awareness of self and others (e.g., body awareness, motor planning). This may be achieved with the use of large, three-dimensional objects or structures that can be moved, positioned, and played with the intent of teaching a concept via

multiple sensory modalities in a hands-on and exaggerated fashion.

Additional Social Emotional Assessment

As noted, traditional methods of personality assessment are typically not very useful in the evaluation of the majority of children with ASD because of limited linguistic and narrative skills and overconcreteness. Nevertheless, some studies (e.g., Dykens, Volkmar, & Glick, 1991) have demonstrated the usefulness of projective instruments such as the Rorschach Inkblot Test (Exner, 1990) in the diagnosis of disorganized thinking for a small group of higher functioning autistic individuals. More commonly, though, the use of simpler projective techniques such as drawings as well as play sessions may be more revealing with regard to social-cognitive skills, emotional presentation, and intrapsychic preoccupations that are typically not explored during other sections of the evaluation. However, these data can be appropriately interpreted only within the context of the child's overall developmental level and language skills.

Drawings may provide a wealth of information about cognitive level, interests, understanding of social life, primary attachments, and even diagnostic information. In the case of children with ASD, there are several specific guidelines that have to be kept in mind when requesting a child to produce a drawing and when interpreting this work. The child should have an opportunity to draw spontaneously before a specific request is made. The resultant work may be a perseverative interest, which may range from an oval stroke drawn repeatedly, to meaningful figures representing inanimate objects such as a clock or a piece of machinery. This work should be analyzed in terms of its perseverative quality, salience of social vis-à-vis inanimate elements, visual-perceptual coherence, and presence of unusual qualities given the child's age and developmental level. These unusual features may include a precocious sense of perspective and "realistic" representations such as visual occlusion (e.g., an object is partially superimposed on another with no overlapping lines as they might be perceived if someone was actually looking at them). Such features are important because normally developing children's drawings often reflect their symbolic or cognitive understanding of an object, for example, a person's body parts are drawn first and then clothed, resulting in overlapping strokes. In contrast, visual occlusion is thought to reflect the predominance of perceptual, rather than cognitive, determinants, in visual representation (Selfe, 1978) and is thought to be typical of at least some children with autism.

The child should then be requested to draw a person, himself or herself, and his or her family. This work can be analyzed in terms of traditional cognitive scoring systems (Harris, 1963) but also, and more importantly, in terms of the difference in quality between the inanimate and the social drawings. Particular attention should be paid to the sense of coherence of the human body and differentiation among people depicted in the drawing. It is also important to question the verbal child, to the extent possible, about the drawing because oftentimes what appears to be an indistinguishable stroke may represent the child's effort to comply with the request to draw a person.

Play offers innumerable opportunities to explore aspects of the child's development and behavior (see Chapter 14, this *Handbook*, Volume 1). These include cognitive quality, for example, functional/manipulative versus representative and imaginative, and the presence of role play (Fein, 1981), which provides an indication of the child's capacity for taking the perspective of others. This is an essential social-cognitive skill necessary for adequate interaction with others and development of self-understanding (Selman, Lavin, & Brion-Meisels, 1982). If opportunities to observe these phenomena are not available in the child's spontaneous play, the examiner may initiate play situations to directly explore the child's understanding of social-emotional phenomena. For example, a puppet setting can be used to elicit the child's responses to situations of joy and distress, as well as to explore the child's ability to impute mental states (e.g., beliefs, intentions) to others and predict their behavior accordingly (Baron-Cohen, 1988). These observations may help validate the measurements obtained with more standardized instruments to sample play skills such as the ADOS (see earlier Diagnostic Work-up section).

CONCLUSION

This chapter presents an overview of psychological assessment of children with ASD within the broader context of transdisciplinary evaluations. We advocate the use of a comprehensive developmental approach involving adherence to several core principles:

1. The adaptive and maladaptive functioning of individuals with autism must be interpreted in terms of the interrelationship between normative developmental expectations and the delays and typical deviant patterns of behavior associated with these conditions.
2. To fully capture an individual's psychological functioning, it is critical to assess, in an integrated fashion, multiple domains of functioning. The selection of relevant domains of functioning should be based on state-of-the-art knowledge of typical psychological profiles observed in individuals with ASD as well as the presenting problems of the specific individual. Tests should be chosen that are developmentally appropriate and that maximize the sampling of a wide range of skills.
3. In light of the variability in performance across time and settings typically observed in individuals with autism, it is essential that information be gathered from multiple sources, particularly those related to the individual's naturalistic settings (e.g., school, home).
4. In the administration and interpretation of specific tasks, attention should be paid to conditions that optimize or diminish performance (e.g., level of structure, social demands, task shifts).

REFERENCES

American Psychiatric Association. (1994). *Diagnostic and statistical manual of mental disorders* (4th ed.). Washington, DC: Author.

American Psychiatric Association. (2000). *Diagnostic and statistical manual of mental disorders* (4th ed., text rev.). Washington, DC: Author.

Baron-Cohen, S. (1988). Social and pragmatic deficits in autism: Cognitive or affective?

Journal of Autism and Developmental Disorders, 18, 379–402.

Bayley, N. (1993). *Bayley Scales of Infant Development* (2nd ed.). San Antonio, TX: Psychological Corporation.

Beery, K., & Buktenica, N. (1989). *The Beery-Buktenica developmental test of visual-motor integration* (3rd ed.). Cleveland, OH: Modern Curriculum Press.

Bruininks, R. H. (1978). *Bruininks-Oseretsky Test of Motor Proficiency.* Circle Pines, MN: American Guidance Service.

Carter, A., Volkmar, F. R., Sparrow, S. S., Wang, J.-J., Lord, C., Dawson, G., et al. (1998). The Vineland Adaptive Behavior Scales: Supplementary norms for individuals with autism. *Journal of Autism and Developmental Disorders, 28*(4), 287–302.

Dunn, L. M., & Dunn, L. M. (1997). *The Peabody Picture Vocabulary Test* (3rd ed.). Circle Pines, MN: American Guidance Service.

Dykens, E., Volkmar, F. R., & Glick, M. (1991). Thought disorder in high-functioning autistic adults. *Journal of Autism and Developmental Disorders, 21,* 291–321.

Elliott, C. D. (1990). *Differential Ability Scales: Introductory and technical handbook.* New York: Psychological Corporation.

Exner, J. E. (1990). *A Rorschach Workbook for the Comprehensive System* (3rd ed.). Asheville, NC: Author.

Fein, G. G. (1981). Pretend play in childhood: An integrative review. *Child Development, 52,* 1095.

Filipek, P., Accardo, P. J., Baranek, G. T., Cook, E. H., Jr., Dawson, G., Gordon, B., et al. (1999). The screening and diagnosis of autistic spectrum disorders. *Journal of Autism and Developmental Disorders, 29*(6), 439–484.

Fombonne, E. (1999). The epidemiology of autism: A review. *Psychological Medicine, 29*(4), 769–786.

Harris, D. B. (1963). *Children's drawings as measures of intellectual maturity: A revision and extension of the Goodenough Draw-a-Man Test.* New York: Harcourt, Brace & World.

Hobson, P. (2002). *The cradle of thought.* London: Macmillan.

Isquith, P. K., & Gioia, G. A. (2002). *Behavior Rating Inventory of Executive function: BRIEF.* Lutz, FL: PAR Psychological Assessment Resources.

Kaufman, A. S., & Kaufman, N. L. (2004). *Kaufman Assessment Battery for Children: Manual.* (2nd ed.). Circle Pines, MN: American Guidance Service.

Klin, A., Carter, A., Volkmar, F. R., Cohen, D. J., Marans, W. D., & Sparrow, S. S. (1997). Assessment issues in children with autism. In D. J. Cohen & F. R. Volkmar (Eds.), *Handbook of autism and pervasive developmental disorders* (2nd ed., pp. 411–418). New York: Wiley.

Klin, A., Chawarska, K., Rubin, E., & Volkmar, F. R. (2004). Clinical assessment of toddlers at risk of autism. In R. DelCarmen-Wiggins & A. Carter. *Handbook of infant and toddler mental health assessment* (pp. 311–336). Oxford, England: Oxford University Press.

Klin, A., Lang, J., Cicchetti, D. V., & Volkmar, F. R. (2000). Interrater reliability of clinical diagnosis and *DSM-IV* criteria for autistic disorder: Results of the *DSM-IV* autism field trial. *Journal of Autism and Developmental Disorders, 30*(2), 163–167.

Klin, A., Saulnier, C., Sparrow, S. S., Cicchetti, D. V., Lord, C., & Volkmar, F. R. (in press). Social and communication abilities and disabilities in higher functioning individuals with autism, Asperger syndrome, and PDD-NOS: The Vineland and the ADOS. *Journal of Autism and Developmental Disorders.*

Klin, A., Sparrow, S. S., de Bildt, A., Cicchetti, D. V., Cohen, D. J., & Volkmar, F. R. (1999). A normed study of face recognition in autism and related disorders. *Journal of Autism and Developmental Disorders, 29*(6), 497–507.

Klin, A., Sparrow, S. S., Marans, W. D., Carter, A., & Volkmar, F. R. (2000). Assessment issues in Asperger syndrome. In A. Klin, F. R. Volkmar, et al. (Eds.), *Asperger syndrome* (pp. 309–339). New York: Guilford Press.

Klin, A., Volkmar, F. R., & Sparrow, S. (1992). Autistic social dysfunction: Some limitations of the Theory of Mind Hypothesis. *Journal of Child Psychology and Psychiatry, 33*(5), 861–876.

Korkman, M., Kirk, U., & Kemp, S. (1998). NEPSY: *A Developmental Neuropsychological Assessment.* San Antonio, TX: Psychological Corporation.

Leiter, R. G. (1948). *Leiter international performance scale.* Chicago: Stoelting Company.

Lord, C. (1995). Follow up of two year olds referred for possible autism. *Journal of Child Psychology and Psychiatry, 36,* 1365–1382.

Lord, C. (1997). Diagnostic instruments in autism spectrum disorders. In D. J. Cohen & F. R. Volkmar (Eds.), *Handbook of autism and pervasive developmental disorders* (pp. 460–483). New York: Wiley.

Lord, C., & Risi, S. (2000). Diagnosis of autism spectrum disorders in young children. In A. M. Wetherby & B. M. Prizant (Eds.), *Autism spectrum disorders: A transactional de-*

velopmental perspective (pp. 11–30). Baltimore: Paul H. Brookes Publishing.

Lord, C., Rutter, M., DiLavore, P., & Risi, S. (1999). *Autism diagnostic observation schedule.* Los Angeles: Western Psychological Services.

Lord, C., Rutter, M., & Le Couteur, A. (1994). Autism Diagnostic Interview-Revised: A revised version of a diagnostic interview for caregivers of individuals with possible pervasive developmental disorders. *Journal of Autism and Developmental Disorders, 24*(5), 659–685.

Lord, C., & Schopler, E. (1988). Intellectual and developmental assessment of autistic children from preschool to school age: Clinical implications of two follow-up studies. In M. A. McDonald, P. Mundy, C. Kasari, & M. Sigman (1989). Psychometric scatter in retarded, autistic preschoolers as measured by the Cattell. *Journal of Child Psychology and Psychiatry, 30*(4), 599–604.

Mullen, E. M. (1995). *The Mullen Scales of Early Learning.* Circle Pines, MN: American Guidance Service.

National Research Council. (2001). *Educating children with autism. Committee on Educational Interventions for Children with Autism. (Division of Behavioral and Social Sciences and Education).* Washington, DC: National Academy Press.

Ozonoff, S. (1995). Reliability and validity of the Wisconsin Card Sorting Test in studies of autism. *Neuropsychology, 9*(4), 491–500.

Prizant, B. M., Wetherby, A. M., & Rydell, P. J. (2000). Communication intervention issues for young children with autism spectrum disorders. In A. M. Wetherby & B. M. Prizant (Eds.), *Autism spectrum disorders: A transactional developmental perspective* (pp. 193–224). Baltimore: Paul H. Brookes Publishing.

Roid, G. M., & Miller, L. J. (1997). *Leiter International Performance Scale-Revised: Examiner's Manual.* Wood Dale, IL: Stoelting.

Rutter, M. (1978). Diagnosis and definitions of childhood autism. *Journal of Autism and Childhood Schizophrenia, 8,* 139–161.

Rutter, M., Le Couteur, A., & Lord, C. (2003). *ADI-R Autism Diagnostic Interview-Revised.* Los Angeles: Western Psychological Services.

Sattler, J. M. (1988). *Assessment of Children* (3rd ed.). San Diego, CA: Author.

Selfe, L. (1978). *Nadia: A case of extraordinary drawing ability in an autistic child.* New York: Academic Press.

Selman, R. L., Lavin, D. R., & Brion-Meisels, S. (1982). Troubled children's use of self-reflection. In F. C. Serafica (Ed.), *Social-cognitive development in context.* New York: Guilford Press.

Shah, A., & Holmes, N. (1985). Brief report: The use of the Leiter International Performance Scale with children. *Journal of Autism and Developmental Disorders, 15,* 195–203.

Snyderman, M., & Rothman, S. (1987). Survey of expert opinion on intelligence and aptitude testing. *American Psychologists, 42,* 137–144.

Sparrow, S. S., Balla, D., & Cicchetti, D. (1984a). *Vineland Adaptive Behavior Scales, expanded edition.* Circle Pines, MN: American Guidance Service.

Sparrow, S. S., Balla, D., & Cicchetti, D. (1984b). *Vineland Adaptive Behavior Scales, survey edition.* Circle Pines, MN: American Guidance Service.

Sparrow, S. S., Balla, D., & Cicchetti, D. (1985). *Vineland Adaptive Behavior Scales, expanded edition.* Circle Pines, MN: American Guidance Service.

Sparrow, S. S., Carter, A. S., Racusi, G., & Morris, R. (1995). Comprehensive psychological assessment through the lifespan. In D. Cohen & D. Cicchetti (Eds.), *Manual of developmental psychopathology.* New York: John Wiley.

Stellern, J., Vasa, S. F., & Little, J. (1976). *Introduction to diagnostic-prescriptive teaching and programming.* Glen Ridge, NJ: Exceptional Press.

Tsai, L., & Beisler, J. M. (1984). Research in infantile autism: A methodological problem in using language comprehension as the basis for selecting matched controls. *Journal of the American Academy of Child Psychiatry, 23,* 700–703.

Tsatsanis, K. D., Dartnall, N., Cicchetti, D. V., Sparrow, S. S., Klin, A., & Volkmar, F. R. (2003). Concurrent validity and classification accuracy of the Leiter and Leiter-R in low-functioning children with autism. *Journal of Autism and Developmental Disorders, 33*(1), 23–30.

Uzgiris, I. C., & Hunt, J. McV. (1975). *Assessment in infancy: Ordinal scales of psychological development.* Urbana: University of Illinois Press.

Volkmar, F. R., Carter, A., Sparrow, S. S., & Cicchetti, D. V. (1993). Quantifying social development of autism. *Journal of Child and Adolescent Psychiatry, 32,* 627–632.

Volkmar, F., Cook, E. H., Jr., Pomeroy, J., Realmuto, G., & Tanguay, P. (1999). Practice parameters for the assessment and treatment of children, adolescents, and adults with autism and other pervasive developmental disorders.

Journal of the American Academy of Child and Adolescent Psychiatry, 38(12), 32S–54S.

Volkmar, F. R., Lord, C., Bailey, A., Schultz, R. T., & Klin, A. (2004). Autism and pervasive developmental disorders. *Journal of Child Psychology and Psychiatry, 45*(1), 1–36.

Volkmar, F. R., Sparrow, S. S., Goudreau, D., Cicchetti, D. V., Paul, R., & Cohen, D. J. (1987). Social deficits in autism: An operational approach using the Vineland Adaptive Behavior Scales. *Journal of the American Academy of Child and Adolescent Psychiatry, 26,* 156–161.

Wechsler, D. (2002). *Wechsler Preschool and Primary Scale of Intelligence* (3rd ed.). San Antonio, TX: Psychological Corporation.

Wechsler, D. (2003). *Wechsler Intelligence Scale for Children: Technical and Interpretive Manual.* (4th ed.). San Antonio, TX: Psychological Corporation.

Wetherby, A. M., Prizant, B. M., & Schuler, A. L. (2000). Understanding the nature of communication and language impairments. In A. M. Wetherby & B. M. Prizant (Eds.), *Autism spectrum disorders: A transactional developmental perspective* (pp. 109–142). Baltimore: Paul H. Brookes Publishing.

World Health Organization. (1992). *International classification of diseases* (10th ed.). Geneva, Switzerland: Author.

CHAPTER 30

Assessing Communication in Autism Spectrum Disorders

RHEA PAUL

Since disorders of communication are among the core symptoms of autism spectrum disorders (ASDs), the characterization of communication skills is one of the essential tasks in evaluating individuals with these syndromes. Communication includes not only the ability to speak and understand language, but also the capacity to send and receive messages through nonverbal channels, including gestures, gazes, facial expressions, and the paralinguistic signals, such as intonation, that accompany verbal communication. This chapter outlines the aspects of communication that are important to examine in individuals with ASDs at various stages of development, and presents methods of assessment that can be used with this population.

ASSESSING PRELINGUISTIC COMMUNICATION

ASDs are being diagnosed more often before the age of 3, as a result of research and treatment efforts focused on early identification and intervention. Although until recently, most children with autism were diagnosed during the preschool years (3 to 5), current practice is moving toward identifying children in the second and third year of life (See Chawarska, this *Handbook,* Volume 1; Stone, this *Handbook,* this volume), in order to afford children the benefit of early intervention, which has been shown to be especially effective in autism (McGee, Morrier, & Daly, 1999). One of the nearly universal features of

children with ASDs at this age level (with the exception of those with Asperger syndrome) is a significant delay in the acquisition of language. Yet a delay in language acquisition, in and of itself, is not diagnostic of autism. In fact, 10% to 15% of otherwise typical children show delays in language acquisition that are not associated with ASDs (Rescorla & Achenbach, 2002). Similarly, many children with mental retardation show delayed language without autistic symptoms (Cascella, 1999). Thus, the problem for clinicians working with toddlers with delayed language development becomes differentiating among these syndromes, which can all be associated with communicative difficulties.

There are, however, communicative behaviors that have been found to be more highly associated with ASDs than with other developmental disabilities, and these can assist in differential diagnosis. At the prelinguistic level of communication, these behaviors include:

- Depressed rate of preverbal communicative acts (Wetherby, Prizant, & Hutchinson, 1998)
- Delayed development of pointing gestures, both in terms of use and responsiveness (Dawson, Meltzoff, Osterling, Rinaldi, & Brown, 1998)
- Use of nonconventional means of communicating, such as pulling a person by the hand, instead of pointing or looking (Stone, Ousley, Yoder, Hogan, & Hepburn, 1997)

- Reduced responsiveness to speech and to hearing their name called (Osterling & Dawson, 1994)
- Restricted range of communicative behaviors, limited primarily to regulatory functions (getting people to do or not do things), with very limited use of communication for social interaction or to comment or establish joint attention (Mundy & Stella, 2000)
- Atypical preverbal vocalizations (Sheinkopf, Mundy, Kimbrough-Oller, & Steffens, 2000)
- Deficits in pretend and imaginative play (Rogers, this *Handbook,* Volume 1)
- Limited ability to imitate (Volkmar, Carter, Grossman, & Klin, 1997)

Since these behaviors appear to differentiate toddlers with ASDs from other children with developmental delays, the goal of communication assessment at this stage will be to focus the assessment on these areas. Standard early communication assessments can be used to substantiate the presence of a significant delay in communication development. Instruments like those listed in Table 30.1 can be used for this purpose.

Following the establishment of a significant delay, the communication evaluation of toddlers suspected of ASDs can focus on the areas known to be particularly impaired in these syndromes. These areas—including rate of communication (verbal or nonverbal), use of communicative gaze and gestures, quality of vocalization, responsiveness to speech and gestures, range of communicative functions expressed (whether restricted to regulatory functions or including social interaction and joint attentional functions), and use of play schemes—can be observed in naturalistic interactions that maximize the child's opportunity for demonstrating his or her most typical interaction style. Several instruments have been developed to structure play-like interactions that allow the sampling and assessment of these preverbal communicative behaviors. These instruments include:

- Communication and Symbolic Behavior Scale (CSBS; Wetherby & Prizant, 2002)
- Early Scale of Communication and Socialization (Mundy, Hogan, & Doehring, 1996; www.psy.miami.edu/faculty/pmundy)

TABLE 30.1   Communication Assessment Instruments for Toddlers

Assessment Instrument	Age Range	Area(s) Assessed	Assessment Method
Clinical Linguistic and Auditory Milestone Scale (Capute et al., 1986)	0–36 months	Expressive/receptive language	Observational scale
Communicative Development Inventory (Fenson et al., 1993)	8–36 months	Expressive/receptive vocabulary, gestures, play, early sentences	Parent report
Early Language Milestone Scale (Coplan et al., 1993)	0–36 months	Expressive/receptive language	Pass/fail screening
Initial Communication Processes Scale (Schery & Wilcoxen, 1982)	0–36 months	Preverbal and verbal communication	Observational scale
Language Development Survey (Rescorla, 1989)	12–36 months	Expressive vocabulary	Parent report
Preschool Language Scale (Zimmerman et al., 1992)	0–7 years	Expressive/receptive language	Standardized test
Receptive-Expressive Emergent Language Scale (Bzoch & League, 1991)	0–36 months	Expressive/receptive language	Parent report
Reynell Developmental Language Scale (Reynell & Huntley, 1987)	0–7 years	Expressive/receptive language	Standardized test
Rosetti Infant toddler Language Scale (Rosetti, 1995)	0–36 months	Preverbal and verbal communication	Criterion-referenced measure
Vineland Adaptive Behavior Scale (Sparrow, Balla, & Cicchetti, 1984)	0–18 years	Expressive/receptive/ written language	Caregiver report/ structured interview

- Communication Intention Inventory (Paul, 2001)
- Prelinguistic Communication Assessment (Stone et al., 1997)

These scales use a variety of techniques, such as communicative "temptations," to elicit the target behaviors, then compare the rate of production of these behaviors in children with suspected autism to the rates seen in similar elicitation conditions with typically developing children. An example can be seen in one item used in the CSBS:

The clinician offers the child an opaque bag and invites the child to pull a toy out of it. When the toy is revealed, the clinician notes whether or not the child attempts to show or share the toy with a parent or other adult in the room by extending the toy to the adult, looking at the adult then back to the toy, vocalizing, pointing, or producing a word approximation.

By observing the child in these structured play settings and noting the child's responses to the proffered activities, the appearance of communicative patterns that are typical of children with autism can be seen. This assessment can be summarized using a form similar to Table 30.2.

Communication Assessment in Older Nonverbal Children

Many individuals with ASDs do not develop speech as a form of communication. Current estimates suggest that 30% to 40% of people with autism remain mute throughout their lifetime (Tager-Flusberg, Paul, & Lord, this *Handbook*, Volume 1), although this figure is subject to change as more effective and earlier-instituted interventions are developed. For nonverbal individuals, communication assessment focuses not so much on differential diagnosis, as it does for very young children, but on assessing the individual's communicative strengths and needs. For many older nonverbal children, a form of Augmentative or Alternative Communication (AAC) will have to be established, to enable them to express their wants and needs in a way that has an effect on their environment and allows them to interact with others so as to have some control over their world. AAC systems are generally divided into two types: *unaided* systems, which involve only the communicator's own body as the means of communication (e.g., sign language or gesture systems); and *aided* systems, which make use of other tools, such as picture boards or computers.

According to Glennon (1997), evaluation for AAC begins with a needs assessment. That

TABLE 30.2   Summary of Communication Assessment for Toddlers Suspected of Autism

Means of Communication	Function of Communication							
	Request	Protest	Share Enjoyment	Comment/ Joint Attention	Pretend	Responds to Name	Responds to Speech	Identifies Objects by Name
Gaze to person								
3-point gaze*								
Conventional gesture								
Unconventional gesture								
Typical vocalization								
Unusual vocalization								
Echo								
Spontaneous speech								

*Child looks at object, at person, then back at object; or at person, at object, then back at person.

is, it is necessary to determine what the individual has to communicate, to whom, in what environments, and for what purposes. Needs assessment involves interviewing teachers and caregivers, as well as observing natural interactions between the client and important others including parents, teachers, siblings, and classmates. The checklist in Table 30.3 may be used to structure these observations. Needs assessment may also include data from a naturalistic interview that makes use of procedures like those in the CSBS and similar instruments, in which the clinician "tempts" the child to produce certain communicative behaviors and observes the results. In these observations, the clinician should take care to observe whether any maladaptive behaviors, such as head banging or rocking, are being used in situations in which the client has something to communicate (such as, "I want to stop this activity"), but does not have a more conventional means for communication and uses the maladaptive behavior to attempt to escape from frustration.

The communication needs assessment establishes the functions an individual is currently expressing and the means by which he or she attempts to do so. This information allows a clinician to begin an intervention program aimed at teaching the child more conventional means for getting across the ideas he or she already has in mind. In addition, the needs assessment focuses attention on the functions of communication the child is not yet using, or is expressing by maladaptive means, and suggests encouraging the expression of functions that are currently infrequent, as well as the use of more conventional forms of communication.

The choice of a means for communication is also a necessary part of the evaluation of a nonverbal child. Several factors need to be taken into consideration when evaluating a child for choice of an AAC modality. The first has to do with the cognitive requirements of the AAC system. Written forms of communication are the preferred AAC system whenever possible because they are the most flexible system with the greatest accessibility to typical communication partners. However, written forms require a relatively high level of cognitive development (typically at least a 5-year level), which may not be attained by all individuals with autism. Nonetheless, written forms should be considered even for clients with significant intellectual impairment, since reading and spelling have been shown to be areas of relative strength in children with ASDs (Lord & Paul, 1997). Work on literacy skills should be included as part of the intervention program for any child with ASD. Blischak and Schlosser (2003), Koppenhaver and Erikson (2003), and Mirenda (2003) provide suggestions for supporting literacy at various developmental levels in this population. If functional reading skills emerge, a written AAC system can be incorporated into the child's communication repertoire.

TABLE 30.3   Checklist for Communication Needs Assessment in Nonverbal Children with Autism

Communicative Function	Communicative Means						
	Word	Vocalization	Point	Other Gesture	Gaze Direction	Body Orientation	Maladaptive Means
Request objects							
Request actions							
Request information (question)							
Statement/comment							
Acknowledgement							
Response to yes/no Q							
Response to Wh-Q							
Other response							

A second aspect of AAC assessment is motor skill. The use of sign language, for example, requires relatively intact fine motor ability. Children who have significant deficits in motor skills may benefit from instruction in conventional gestures rather than the use of signs, at least as a first step. Fine motor assessment can be accomplished in collaboration with a physical or occupational therapist.

Another area of assessment for children requiring AAC systems concerns the ability to imitate, since the development of unaided systems such as signs will depend on the child's ability to imitate signs in order to learn to use them. Lack of imitation skill is one of the typical deficits seen in children with ASDs (Volkmar et al., 1997). Imitation skills should be examined, using informal procedures, inviting the child to imitate increasingly complex hand movements. If manual imitation is difficult to elicit, signs may have to be introduced through molding the child's hands.

Assessment for an AAC system also involves the determination of the child's level of symbolic development. Since aided AAC systems use symbols of some kind to represent concepts, it is necessary to determine the complexity of the symbols the child can use. The more symbolic and less iconic the child's symbol system is, the wider the range of meanings it can express. But, conversely, systems with low iconicity are more cognitively demanding. A hierarchy of complexity of symbols for AAC systems developed by Mirenda and Locke (1989) is shown in Table 30.4. Assessment for the selection of an AAC system should also include an assessment of the level of complexity/iconicity the child can manage. This can be accomplished through dynamic assessment methods, in which the child is shown, through demonstration and modeling, how to connect symbols to objects and activities. Assessment should begin at the lowest level of complexity. The child can be shown, for example, how to exchange a block for a box full of blocks that he can play with for a short time. If the child can successfully use this level of symbol, trials at the next higher level should be given (e.g., exchanging a color photo of the block for the box of blocks). This assessment can continue until the level at which the child can no longer make the connection between symbol and object is reached. At that point, the highest level of complexity at which the child was successful should be identified as the beginning level for his communication system. It will, however, be important to include ongoing assessment in the child's AAC program, so that he can gradually progress through higher levels of complexity of the symbol system. The ultimate goal for nonspeaking children would be to introduce a written system, since this is the most viable and flexible system available. Toward this end, the intervention program should contain instruction in preliteracy and literacy skills (letter matching and identification, word recognition,

TABLE 30.4   Hierarchy of Complexity of Symbols Used in AAC Systems

Symbol Type	Complexity/Iconicity
Objects	Least complex/most iconic
Color photos	
Black and white photos	
Miniature objects	
Detailed color drawings	
Black and white line drawings	
Writing	Most complex/least iconic

Adapted from "A Comparison of Symbol Transparency in Nonspeaking Persons with Intellectual Disability," by P. Mirenda and P. Locke, 1989, *Journal of Speech and Hearing Disorders, 54,* pp. 131–140.

phonological awareness, etc.) in addition to the direct instruction in the use of the AAC system (Koppenhaver & Erikson, 2003).

ASSESSING EARLY LINGUISTIC COMMUNICATION

Of the 60% of children with ASDs who acquire speech, most do so by the age of 6 (Paul & Cohen, 1985), although there have been case reports of nonspeaking children acquiring language in adolescence (Mirenda, 2003; Windsor, Doyle, & Siegel, 1994). In this section, assessment at the beginning of language acquisition, from the time at which the child begins using words as the primary form of communication to the point at which the child produces more or less complete sentences will be addressed. For the majority of children with ASDs, this period of development will occur during the preschool or early primary school age range (2 to 6 years), although some children may be chronologically older during this period of development.

Assessment of children in the early stages of language acquisition, again, should begin with a basic language evaluation, using standardized test procedures, so that the general level of receptive and expressive language can be identified. It is important to note that, in using standardized tests with individuals with ASDs, it may be necessary to modify the item presentation, in order to elicit responses. Marans (1997) suggests the following modifications:

- Providing reinforcement, such as edibles or stickers, for responding
- Changing order of presentation of items to keep the child's interest and reduce frustration
- Adding a gestural cue to "give me" when the child is asked to identify objects or pictures
- Providing additional demonstrations if child fails to attend or does not understand the task
- Repeating items or instructions

When these techniques are used, they should be noted in reporting the scores, but these accommodations are considered acceptable in order to overcome the social deficits

TABLE 30.5   Standardized Instruments for Assessing Early Language Development

Instrument	Areas Assessed
Peabody Picture Vocabulary Test/Expressive Vocabulary Test (Dunn & Dunn, 1997)	Receptive vocabulary/ expressive vocabulary
Preschool Language Scale-IV (Zimmerman et al., 2003)	Receptive/expressive syntax, semantics, morphology
Reynell Developmental Language Scales-III (Edwards et al., 1999)	Receptive language/ expressive language
Sequenced Inventory of Communicative Development (Hedrick et al., 1995)	Receptive language/ expressive language
Test of Early Language Development (Hresko et al, 1999)	Receptive/expressive semantics and syntax
Vineland Adaptive Behavior Scale (Sparrow et al., 1984)	Receptive/expressive/ written language

that interfere with test performance in this population.

It is especially important to assess both expressive and receptive language for children with ASDs. These children show more severe receptive language difficulties than are seen in other children with language disorders. A sampling of instruments that can be used at this level appears in Table 30.5.

Once standardized testing has established that a delay in language development is present, assessment should focus on detailing the communication profile of the child, with special attention to the kinds of communicative behaviors known to be typical in ASDs at this level. (See Tager-Flusberg et al., this *Handbook,* Volume 1, for detailed discussion.) These include:

- Reduced responsiveness to speech. Children with ASDs do not respond as reliably as other children to hearing their name called, or to the conversational obligation to answer when spoken to.
- Echolalia, including both immediate imitation of what is heard, and delayed imitation, or the repetition of strings of memorized language.
- Difficulty with pronouns. Individuals with ASDs often produce "you" instead of "me"

when referring to themselves. This is thought to reflect their tendency to echo what they hear others say.

- Unusual word use. People with ASDs sometimes attach idiosyncratic meanings to words.
- Difficulties with pragmatic or social uses of language.

The primary means for examining these aspects of language is to collect a sample of spontaneous speech during an interaction with the child. Since children with ASDs do not produce as high a rate of communication as children with other disabilities, it will be necessary to use elicitation procedures to get them to demonstrate their communicative abilities. A set of inviting toys can be used, and the examiner can use techniques like communication temptations to elicit speech from the child. Examples of the kinds of temptations that can be used in this setting include:

- Keeping toys to oneself, so the child needs to request them
- Eating a snack without offering any to the child, to elicit requests
- Offering the child the chance to pull objects out of opaque containers to elicit comments
- Engaging in a routine, such as rolling a ball back and forth, then suddenly switching, for example, to a truck
- Engaging in social routines, such as tickle games or finger plays, and interrupting the routine to get the child to request its continuation
- Offering the child an object or activity he or she does not like, to elicit a protest
- Offering parts of toys or puzzles, but withholding some, so the child needs to request them
- Pretending to misunderstand or not to hear a request or comment made by the child, in order to elicit a conversational repair
- Suddenly doing something silly or unexpected, such as putting on a funny hat or "Groucho" glasses, to elicit a comment

In addition, shared book reading opportunities provide another avenue for collecting language samples in this population. Language samples can be gathered on video or audiotape

for later transcription and analysis. In analyzing samples of language from children with ASDs at this level, the following areas should be examined:

- *Responsiveness to speech:* The number of times the child responds to his or her name can be examined as a proportion of the number of times the name was called. Similarly, the proportion of adult utterances to which the child responds with speech or meaningful gestures can also be calculated.
- *Mean utterance length:* This measure serves as a reference point of comparison for other language behaviors. Since syntax, which is indexed by utterance length (Brown, 1973), is a relative strength in ASDs, syntactic level can serve as a benchmark against which other areas of language can be measured.
- *Word use:* Vocabulary diversity can be assessed using either the number of different words in the sample or the Type-Token ratio (number of different words divided by total number of words spoken). Several of the computer assisted language analysis procedures currently available (e.g., Miller & Chapman's, 2000, *Systematic Analysis of Language Transcripts* [SALT]) automatically compute both these metrics from transcripts entered into their data systems (These compute MLU from tagged input, as well). The SALT also provides a reference database that allows for comparison of vocabulary diversity to a sample of typically developing children between the ages of 3 and 13. Note can also be taken of any idiosyncratic word uses observed in children with ASD.
- *Echololia:* The proportion of echoed to spontaneous utterances can be calculated. Echoed utterances can also be subdivided into immediate and delayed echolalia. The purposes of the echoed language should also be noted, so that more conventional forms can be taught for expressing these functions.
- *Pronoun use:* The number of inappropriate uses of pronouns can be calculated as a proportion of total pronoun use.
- *Pragmatics:* The social use of language is the area in which children with ASDs show the greatest range and severity of deficits. A variety of pragmatic coding schemes

have been developed for analyzing pragmatics in free speech (see Table 30.6).

Pragmatic skills can also be assessed by engaging the child in semi-structured conversational activities similar to those outlined above. When engaging in this kind of assessment, it is helpful to think of pragmatics as containing several domains, as outlined by Chapman (1981) and Grice (1975), each of which can be systematically probed. These include:

- *Communicative functions:* the purposes for which speech is used. Here, assessment would be aimed at enumerating the range of functions expressed, and particularly noting whether a range of communicative functions are used. The functions seen in typical children between ages 5 and 7 (Tough, 1977) include:
  —Directing others ("Put yours here.")
  —Self-directing ("I'm gonna cut the clay.")
  —Reporting on past and ongoing events ("We went to the beach.")
  —Reasoning ("The ice cream got soft cause we forgot to put it in the fridge.")
  —Predicting ("Mom'll get mad if I eat that.")
  —Empathizing ("She's crying cause you hurt her feelings.")

TABLE 30.6   Coding Schemes for Assessing Pragmatics in Conversation

Instrument	Description
Responsiveness/ Assertiveness Rating Scale (Girolametto, 1997)	Parent rating, using a five point scale (never to always) to answer 25 questions about child's behaviors in conversation
Pragmatic Protocol (Prutting & Kirchner, 1983)	Checklist based on direct observation; global ratings of conversational skills in eight areas
Discourse Skills Checklist (Bedrosian, 1995)	Frequency analysis of 40 discourse behaviors
Functional Communication Profile (Kleinman, 1994)	Qualitative rating of 16 social uses of language

—Imagining ("I'm the doctor; I'll fix your baby.")
—Negotiating ("If you be the baby, I'll share these cookies with you.")

- *Discourse management:* the organization of turns and topics in conversation. Assessment would focus on the ability of the client to:
  —Take a turn when the conversation warrants.
  —Give up the floor when appropriate.
  —Maintain others' topics appropriately.
  —Switch topics when cues are given.
  —Give cues when initiating a topic switch.
  —Follow the flow of topics throughout the conversation, without perseveration on favored topics

- *Register variation:* using language forms flexibly to match the interpersonal context. Assessment can investigate the client's ability to:
  —Use polite forms.
  —Talk differently to people of different ages and social status.
  —Ask in different ways, depending on whether asking for a favor (to borrow something) or a right (to have a borrowed object returned).
  —Use vocabulary appropriate to the topic, conversational partner, and situation.
  —Use informal, age-appropriate language with peers.

- *Presupposition:* knowing what it is reasonable to suppose the listener knows and needs to know. This ability to use conversational "mind-reading" allows speakers to give the right amount of information in conversation: not too much, which leads to sounding like a pedant or a "know-it-all;" and not too little, resulting in vague contributions and conversational breakdowns. This domain also includes the use of linguistic markers such as pronouns, ellipsis, and variations in word order to call listeners' attention to parts of the discourse the speaker wishes to highlight in order to relate statements to ideas introduced earlier in the conversation.

- *Conversational manner:* According to Grice (1975), contributions to conversation should be "clear, brief, and orderly." Assessment in this domain would involve noting the use of overly long, complex utterances on the one hand, or sparse conversational contributions that make the interaction feel like "pulling teeth" on the other. It would also take note of rambling, disorganized, tangential, or repetitive styles of speech.

Specific probes can be embedded in interactions to tap pragmatic behaviors in these domains that might not always emerge spontaneously. These probes could include:

- Asking the child to pretend to be the mommy or daddy to a doll or toy
- Having the child ask for an object, then telling him or her to ask nicer
- Providing an opportunity for the child to use contrastive stress, for example, by giving him or her a choice of two objects and presenting the wrong one
- Asking for clarification of something the child said
- Asking the child to describe a sequence, such as a set of pictures depicting a child dressing, and noting whether child:
  —Changes appropriately from noun at first mention (the boy) to pronoun (he) in later references
  —Changes appropriately from full sentence in the first description (The boy puts his sock on his foot) to elliptical sentence (He puts his shoe on [*his foot* is ellipted because it is redundant the second time])
  —Relates the sequence in a logical, organized manner

An example of a simple assessment form that might be used with this semi-structured assessment activity appears in Table 30.7.

ASSESSING COMMUNICATION IN CHILDREN WITH ADVANCED LANGUAGE

In high-functioning children with ASDs, including Asperger syndrome, advanced vocabulary and sentence structures are typically seen. For these children, verbal IQ may exceed nonverbal IQ and basic forms of language can be a relative strength. Yet, pragmatic and prosodic deficits usually persist and can cause serious problems in social interaction. These children may talk endlessly about their special interests, with little regard for the interest or attention of listeners. They may offend others with blunt comments or be overly, intrusively friendly in appropriate ways; they may pester people with incessant, repetitive questions, they may be unable to understand irony and humor in peer conversations; they may not know how to negotiate entry to into peer activities; they may use excessively flat or sing-song intonation patterns; they may talk "through the nose" or be unable to modulate their volume; they can have difficulty understanding content in literature and history courses because of their difficulties in understanding mental states and underlying feelings that motivate actions. These students can have a myriad of social communication problems that will result in a perception of oddity on the part of others, while showing age-appropriate or superior performance on basic tests of verbal skills and some areas of academic performance. This can often result in their having difficulty obtaining services for their communication difficulties, because these difficulties are hard to measure, using traditional assessment materials.

There are a few standard assessments that can sometimes demonstrate the pragmatic weaknesses of higher functioning individuals with ASDs. The *Comprehensive Assessment of Spoken Language* (Carrow-Woolfolk, 1999) has separate scales for both pragmatic judgment and supralinguistic forms (nonliteral uses of language, drawing inferences, and understanding of idiomatic language) that can be contrasted with lexical and syntactic skills. The *Test of Language Competence* (Wiig & Secord, 1989) examines understanding of multiple meanings, figurative usage and the ability to draw inferences and produce utterances appropriate for various social settings. Although these and other tests aimed at assessing pragmatic skills can sometimes demonstrate significant discrepancies between language form and function in students with ASDs at advanced language levels, even these measures occasionally fail to overcome the powerful cognitive strategies high-functioning individuals can marshal in the structured testing environment. For this reason, less formally structured, more naturalistic assessments are often necessary.

TABLE 30.7   Example Form for Assessing Pragmatics in Semi-Structured Conversation: Early Language Level

	Yes	No	No Opportunity
Communicative Functions			
Directing others	_____	_____	_____
Self-directing	_____	_____	_____
Reporting	_____	_____	_____
Reasoning	_____	_____	_____
Predicting	_____	_____	_____
Empathizing	_____	_____	_____
Imagining	_____	_____	_____
Negotiating	_____	_____	_____
Discourse Management			
Waits turn to speak	_____	_____	_____
Responds to speech w/ speech consistently	_____	_____	_____
Responds to speech w/ relevant remark	_____	_____	_____
Maintains other's topic for at least two turns	_____	_____	_____
Shifts topics appropriately	_____	_____	_____
Monitors interlocutor with gaze appropriately (looks at other when talking; looks at referents, then back at interlocutor)	_____	_____	_____
Register Variation			
Talks appropriately to unfamiliar adult (clinician)	_____	_____	_____
Demonstrates at least one register shift (e.g., in talk to baby doll or stuffed animal)	_____	_____	_____
Uses politeness conventions in requests (please)	_____	_____	_____
Can increase politeness when told to "ask nicer"	_____	_____	_____
Uses indirect requests spontaneously/appropriately	_____	_____	_____
Presupposition			
Uses pronouns appropriately	_____	_____	_____
Uses ellipsis appropriately	_____	_____	_____
Uses stress appropriately for emphasis and contrast	_____	_____	_____
Gives enough background information	_____	_____	_____
Can provide additional information when requested (A what?) for Conversational repair	_____	_____	_____
Manner of Communication			
Gives clear, relevant responses	_____	_____	_____
Talks appropriate amount	_____	_____	_____
Can relate sequence of actions clearly in organized fashion	_____	_____	_____

Landa et al. (1992) developed the Pragmatic Rating Scale (PRS) to be used to evaluate parents of individuals with autism to determine whether weaknesses in pragmatics were common across family members. This scale identifies 30 pragmatic behaviors that reflect abnormalities thought to be typical of autism, based on theoretical and clinical reports of major pragmatic behaviors in the literature. The rating is done by analyzing a 30-minute conversational interview sample. Topics to be included in this interview, which is based on the Autism Diagnostic Observation Scale (Lord et al., 2000) are:

1. Greeting and small talk.
2. Tell me about your school/job.
3. Tell me about your friends.
4. What makes you happy? Afraid? Angry? Annoyed? Proud?
5. Tell a story from a wordless picture book.
6. Describe action in a comic strip; place strip out of reach to encourage use of gestures.
7. What would you do if you won a million dollars?

Each behavior on the PRS is rated on a three point scale, where 0 = Normal; 1 = Moderately Inappropriate; 2 = Absent or Highly Inappropriate. The behaviors rated on the PRS appear in Table 30.8.

TABLE 30.8   Score Form

	0	1	2
Inappropriate or absent greeting	____	____	____
Strikingly candid	____	____	____
Overly direct or blunt	____	____	____
Inappropriately formal	____	____	____
Inappropriately informal	____	____	____
Overly talkative	____	____	____
Irrelevant or inappropriate detail	____	____	____
Content "out of sync" with interlocutor	____	____	____
Confusing accounts	____	____	____
Topic preoccupation/perseveration	____	____	____
Unresponsive to cues	____	____	____
Little reciprocal to-and-fro exchange	____	____	____
Terse	____	____	____
Odd humor	____	____	____
Insufficient background information	____	____	____
Failure to reference pronouns, or other terms	____	____	____
Inadequate clarification	____	____	____
Vague accounts	____	____	____
Scripted, stereotyped discourse	____	____	____
Awkward expression of ideas	____	____	____
Indistinct or mispronounced speech	____	____	____
Inappropriate rate of speech	____	____	____
Inappropriate intonation	____	____	____
Inappropriate volume	____	____	____
Excessive pauses, reformulations	____	____	____
Unusual rhythm, fluency	____	____	____
Inappropriate physical distance	____	____	____
Inappropriate gestures	____	____	____
Inappropriate facial expression	____	____	____
Inappropriate use of gaze	____	____	____
Subject's Total Score:	____		

0 = Normal; 1 = Moderately inappropriate; 2 = Absent or highly inappropriate. Total scores of 6 or above are typical of students with ASDs and are indicative of pragmatic disorders. From *Identifying Conversational Deficits in Autistic Spectrum Disorders Using the Yale Pragmatic Rating Scale*, by S. Miles, R. Paul, A. Klin, and F. R. Volkmar, in preparation.

Adapted from the Pragmatic Rating Scale, "Social Language Use in Parents of Autistic Individuals," by R. Landa et al., 1992, *Psychological Medicine, 22*, pp. 246–254.

Miles, Paul, Klin, and Volkmar (in preparation) analyzed data comparing PRS scores from adolescents with typical development to those of high-functioning teens with ASDs. Scores in the ASD group were consistently 6 and higher. Ninety percent scored higher than 8, with some subjects scoring above 20. Subjects in the typical group uniformly scored 5 or lower. These data suggest that scores above 6 on the PRS are likely to be indicative of a deficit in pragmatic ability.

Another method for assessing social communication skills in high-functioning students with ASDs is to use a semi-naturalistic probe task, sometimes called an in vivo (in a life-like setting) protocol. Paul, Chuba, Miles, Klin, and Volkmar (2003) developed the Yale in vivo Pragmatic Protocol (YiPP) to sample pragmatic abilities in this population (see Box 30.1).

A form for recording responses to this protocol appears in Table 30.9. This protocol can be used for informal observation of the ability of high-functioning students with ASDs to use a variety of forms of communication for which the context may not arise in an unstructured conversation. As such, it provides a somewhat broader look at the use of communication functions than may be obtained in a more natural interaction.

An additional aspect of social communication that can be assessed in higher functioning students with ASD is the ability to produce narratives. Norbury and Bishop (2003) reported on narratives from 8- to 10-year-old students with communication disorders, generated in response to a wordless picture book, *Frog, Where are You?* (Meyer, 1969). They showed that these children had difficulty referring appropriately to characters in the story using nouns and pronouns. In addition, they used less complex syntax and made more syntactic errors than typical peers, although there were few differences between children with autism and those with specific language impairments. These findings suggest that story generation tasks may be useful contexts for sampling higher levels of language production, and to contrast this performance to standardized measures, on which these students often appear to do well. Even though few diagnostic group differences were found in this study, narrative procedures like these can be used to identify individual children who provide very literal interpretations of pictures, fail to pull the story together with cohesive markers such as pronouns, do not provide temporal or causal links in their stories, or do not make clear how characters' feelings and states of mind motivate their actions. When these difficulties are present, they make apt targets for intervention in speech-language programs. Another advantage of narrative assessment is that since Norbury and Bishop have

---

BOX 30.1   Sequence of Actions for Yale in vivo Pragmatic Protocol

1. Examiner (E) brings subject (S) into testing room.
2. E pretends not to be able to work the video recorder (VCR is unplugged; no tape in player)—no cues given at first, then active solicitation of help.
3. E starts small talk conversation (vacation plans, job, school, etc.), then presents probes:
   - Decrease volume.
   - Muffle speech w/ paper/hand.
   - Use unknown acronyms ("There was an ASG where I stayed.")
   - Pause and wait for re-initiation of topic.
   - Look at watch/yawn/attempt to break into S's stream of speech.
   - Asks S to do E a favor; doesn't say what it is.
   - E says, "Well, we have some other things to get to." Note whether S observes termination of topic.
4. E knocks over cup of M&Ms, spilling them.
5. E gives S choice of magazines to read; provides one S did not choose.
6. Helper (H) knocks on door; comes in; E introduces H to S, waits for S to greet H; H gives E questionnaires for S to fill out; H leaves.
7. E asks S to fill out questionnaires; doesn't give pencil; gives Request for Clarification probes.
8. E says, "Well, I think I have to go to another meeting now." Waits for S to initiate closing.

TABLE 30.9   Recording form for Yale in vivo Pragmatic Protocol

Pragmatic Function	Probe Task Description	Subject Response A	B	NR	Comments/ Observations
Greet	During interview, a helper adult knocks on the door and comes in "to get something from room." Examiner introduces helper to subject, waits for subject to greet. If subject does not greet, helper greets and waits for a response.				
Request object	Examiner gives subject form to fill out, doesn't provide pencil				
Request clarification					
Low volume	Embed in both comments and questions.				
Distorted speech	Muffle speech with paper/hand.				
Unfamiliar information	Use bogus acronyms ("Do you use the MFPG?").				
Insufficient information	Give directions minus information necessary to complete. –"Fill out questions 1–5 on this form"—tell what to write in #s 1–3 only. –"Write the correct symbol next to each statement," give incomplete info on how to respond, for example, don't tell which symbol means true versus false. –"Do a favor for me" (fail to say what favor is).				
Express denial/ comment on object	Examiner gives subject a choice of magazines to read while examiner "writes some things down"; gives a different magazine from the one selected.				
Comment on action	Examiner gets up "to get something," and spills cup of M&Ms. An adult helper outside of room knocks on door (do with greeting activity).				
Manage topics					
Initiation	Examiner pauses during conversation and waits for subject to reinitiate.				
Maintenance	Observe ability to remain on topic (provide contingent comment/question).				
Response to cues to change topic	Examiner looks at watch, yawns, makes gestural / vocal attempts to "break in."				
Termination	Examiner stops talking and says, "Well, we have some other things to get to."				
Hypothesize	Examiner enlists subject's help to get VCR to work (VCR is unplugged, with no tape inside).				
Close interaction	Examiner says, "Well, I have another meeting to go to"; waits for subject to initiate closing when ending the interaction				

A = Appropriate response; I = Inappropriate response; NR = No response.

TABLE 30.10 Narrative Assessment Scoresheet

	Definition	Example	Potential Points	Normal range for 8–10 year olds with TD*	Points Earned
Global structure					
Initiating event	Problem that provides motivation for story	Boy wants to catch frog.	1 for mention of characters 1 for problem	1.7–1.9	
Attempts	Things characters do to solve the initial problem	Boy attempts to catch frog with net; catches his dog by mistake.	1 for each attempt reported	1.6–1.8	
Resolution	Satisfactory end to story that resolves initial problem	Frog follows boy home; he's happy when they're together.	1 for mention of intention of action 1 for feelings of character	1.2–1.4	
Local structure					
Length	Total number of sentences in child's story	The boy went to the pond.	One point for each sentence	25–48	
Syntax	1. Number of complex sentences in story	Subordinate clauses (*When the boy saw the frog, he ran toward it.*) Complement clauses (*The boy wished he could catch the frog.*) Verb complements (*The boy was trying to catch the frog.*) Full passive sentences (*The dog was caught by the net.*)	One point for each complex sentence	2.3–8.8	
	2. Number of tense marking errors	He look in the water.	One point for each error	0–1	
Semantics	Number of pieces of relevant information provided	1. Boy goes to pond. 2. Boy's dog goes along.	One point for each proposition	40–55	
Cohesion	Use of ambiguous pronouns	The boy and the frog looked at each other. *He* was mad.	One point for each ambiguous pronoun	0–3	
Mental state verbs	Use of verbs to describe thinking or talking	*Think, know remember, forget, say, tell.*	One point per mental verb	4.3–15.4	
Emotional terms	Use of words to describe emotions or internal states	The boy was sad.	One point per emotional term	0–3.6	

* TD = Typical development. These values are derived from the scores reported for typical control subjects. Adapted from "Narrative Skills of Children with Communication Impairments," by C. Norbury and D. V. M. Bishop, 2003, *International Journal of Language and Communication Disorders, 38*, pp. 287–314, using Mayer's (1968) *A Boy, a Dog, and a Frog.*

shown that students with ASD are not the only diagnostic group to experience these difficulties, narrative activities provide opportunities for group intervention that combines students with autism and those with more specific language disorders (SLI). Such groups can maximize clinician ability to address the needs of both kinds of students and to allow the children with SLI to provide more appropriate social models to students with ASD. Paul (2001) and Hughes, McGillivary, and Schmidek (1997) provide activities to address narrative difficulties in school-aged children that can be used in these contexts.

Several narrative assessment procedures are available to structure these assessments, including: the *Strong Narrative Assessment Procedure* (SNAP; Strong, 1998), the Story Structure Decision Tree (Westby, 1998), Lahey's (1988) Levels of Narrative Development, the adaptation of Applebee's (1978) system by Paul (2001), and the Narrative Rubrics (McFadden & Gillam, 1996). Table 30.10 on the previous page presents a worksheet based on Norbury and Bishop's (2003) research, as an example of a narrative assessment procedure.

Another area of significant disability in people with ASDs at advanced language levels is *prosody*. Prosody includes the musical aspects of speech; such as its rate, volume, melody, and rhythm patterns; which accompany the linguistic signal and modulate its meaning. Research suggests that the common prosodic problems seen in ASDs at the advanced language level include inappropriate use of stress, unusual intonation patterns, hypernasal speech, and decreased speech fluency (Shriberg et al., 2001). Anecdotal reports also suggest trouble with modulating volume in speech (Pronovost, Wakstein, & Wakstein, 1966).

The *Prosody Voice Screening Protocol* (PVSP; Shriberg, Kwiatkowski, & Rasmussen, 1990) is a measure that can be used to examine prosodic variables in free speech samples, in terms of stress, rate, phrasing (fluency), loudness, pitch, and voice quality. As a screening measure, the PVSP suggests a cutoff score of 80% for identifying a prosodic deficit. That is, if more than 80% of the subject's utterances are rated as inappropriate in one of the six areas above, according to the PVSP scoring procedures, the speech sample is considered to be demonstrating prosodic difficulties in that area. The PVSP has been used to study prosody in a variety of communication disorders, and has a database of typical speakers for comparison. It has undergone extensive interjudge agreement studies and demonstrates adequate reliability at the level of summative prosody-voice codes. However, the PVSP is highly labor intensive, requiring transcription and utterance-by-utterance judgments to be made for each

TABLE 30.11   Recording Form for Judging Prosodic Production in Spontaneous Speech

Clinical Judgement → Prosodic Parameter	Appropriate	Inappropriate	No Opportunity to Observe
Rate			
Stress in words			
Stress in sentences			
Fluency, use of repetition, revision			
Phrasing, use of pauses			
Overall pitch level, relative to age/gender			
Intonation (melody, patterns of speech)			
Voice quality			
Voice resonance (nasality)			

prosody/voice code. It also requires intensive training and practice before adequate skills levels can be obtained for raters.

Alternatively, speech samples gathered as part of the pragmatic assessment can also be evaluated informally for their prosodic characteristics. A clinician can pass a judgment (appropriate, inappropriate, no opportunity to observe) on each of the relevant domains of prosody, with special attention paid to stress, fluency, volume, intonation, and nasality. A recording sheet like the one in Table 30.11 on page 313 can be used to summarize this assessment. Although clinician judgment is often used to assess various aspects of communicative performance, prosody is an area in which few data exist to support the validity or reliability of these judgments. Clearly, the assessment of prosodic production is an area in which there is a great need for more research to establish boundaries of normality and develop more efficient methods of assessment.

CONCLUSION

The assessment of communication in ASDs requires more than standardized testing. Since the primary deficit in ASD centers on communication, rather than on language, assessment of individuals with these disorders requires both formal testing and careful observation of natural and semi-natural communicative activities. For children in prelinguistic phases of communication, assessment is aimed at establishing the communicative basis for a formal language system, and looking at the frequency, range, and means of expression of communicative acts. Older children at this level may require evaluation to determine the best alternative mode of communication if speech has not yet emerged. Children in the early stages of language use will need to be assessed not only in terms of their vocabulary and sentence structures, but with regard to the unusual communicative patterns that often accompany ASDs, such as echolalia, pronoun errors, and significant deficits in pragmatics and receptive language. For individuals at advanced language levels, assessment will focus on social uses of communication, particularly pragmatic, narrative, and prosodic skills. For people at all developmental levels and at all points along the autistic spectrum, a compre-hensive evaluation of strengths and needs in the area of communication by a clinician knowledgeable about the special issues germane to this population is essential to the development of an effective plan for improving communicative competence.

Cross-References

Development of communication is discussed in Chapter 12. Psychological assessment is discussed in Chapter 29; general issues in the assessment and treatment of communication in autism are discussed in Chapter 36; treatment of communication disorders in autism at early stages of development is discussed in Chapter 37; in later stages in Chapter 38; characteristics of children with autism are discussed in Chapters 8 and 9; social development as it relates to communication is discussed in Chapter 11; general methods for screening and diagnosis in autism are discussed in Chapters 27 and 28.

REFERENCES

Applebee, A. (1978). *A child's concept of story: Ages 2–17*. Chicago: University of Chicago Press.

Bedrosian, J. (1985). An approach to developing conversational competence. In D. Ripich & F. Spanelli (Eds.), *School discourse problems* (pp. 74–99). San Diego, CA: College-Hill Press.

Blischak, D., & Schlosser, R. (2003). Use of technology to support independent spelling by students with autism. *Topics in Language Disorders, 23*, 293–304.

Brown, R. (1973). *A first language: The early stages*. Cambridge, MA: Harvard University Press.

Bzoch, K., & League, R. (1991). *The Receptive Expressive Emergent Language Scale*. Gainesville, FL: Computer Management Corporation, Language Education Division.

Capute, A., Palmer, F., Shapiro, B., Wachtel, R., Schmidt, S., & Ross, A. (1986). Clinical Linguistic and Auditory Milestone Scale: Prediction of cognition in infancy. *Developmental Medicine and Child Neurology, 28*, 762–771.

Carrow-Woolfolk, E. (1999). *Comprehensive assessment of spoken language*. Circle Pines, MN: American Guidance Service.

Cascella, P. (1999). Communication disorders and children with mental retardation. *Child and Adolescent Psychiatric Clinics of North America, 8*, 61–76.

Chapman, R. (1981). Analyzing communicative intents. In J. Miller (Ed.), *Assessing language production in children: Experimental procedures* (pp. 111–138). Boston: Allyn & Bacon.

Coplan, J., Gleason, J. R., Ryan, R., Burke, M., & Williams, M. (1993). Validation of an early language milestone scale in a high-risk population. *Pediatrics, 70,* 677–683.

Dawson, G., Meltzoff, A., Osterling, J., Rinaldi, J., & Brown, E. (1998). Children with autism fail to orient to naturally occurring social stimuli. *Journal of Autism and Developmental Disorders, 28,* 479–485.

Dunn, L., & Dunn, L. (1997). *Peabody Picture Vocabulary Test-III.* Circle Pines, MN: American Guidance Service.

Edwards, S., Fletcher, P., Garman, M., Hughes, A., Letts, C., & Sinka, I. (1999). *Reynell Developmental Language Scales-III.* Windsor, England: NFER-Nelson.

Fenson, L., Dale, P., Reznick, S., Thal, D., Bates, E., Hartung, J., et al. (1993). *The Macarthur Communicative Developmental Inventories.* San Diego, CA: Singular Press.

Girolametto, L. (1997). Development of a parent report measure for profiling the conversational skills of preschool children. *American Journal of Speech-Language Pathology, 6,* 25–33.

Glennon, S., & DeCoste, D. (1997). *Handbook of Augmentative and Alternative Communication.* San Diego: Singular.

Grice, P. (1975). Logic and conversation. In P. Cole & J. Morgan (Eds.), *Syntax and semantics: Speech Acts* (Vol. 3, pp. 41–59). New York: Academic Press.

Hedrick, D., Prather, E., & Tobin, A. (1995). *Sequenced Inventory of Communication Development-Revised* (3rd ed.). Austin, TX: ProEd.

Hresko, W., Reid, K., & Hamill, D. (1999). *Test of early language development.* Austin, TX: ProEd.

Hughes, D., McGillivary, L., & Schmidek, M. (1997). *Guide to narrative language.* Eau Claire, WI: Thinking Publications.

Kleiman, K. (1994). *Functional Communication Scale.* East Moline, IL: Lingui Systems.

Koppenhaver, D., & Erikson, K. (2003). Natural emergent literacy supports for preschoolers with autism and severe communication impairments. *Topics in Language Disorders, 23,* 283–292.

Lahey, M. (1988). *Language disorders and language development.* New York: Wiley.

Landa, R., Piven, J., Wzorek, M., Gayle, J., Cloud, D., Chase, G., et al. (1992). Social language use in parents of autistic individuals. *Psychological Medicine, 22,* 246–254.

Lord, C., & Paul, R. (1997). Language and communication. In D. Cohen & F. R. Volkmar (Eds.), *Handbook of autism and pervasive developmental disorders* (2nd ed., pp. 195–225). New York: Wiley.

Lord, C., Risi, S., Lambrecht, L., Cook, E. H., Jr., Leventhal, B. L., DiLavore, P. C., et al. (2000). The Autism Diagnostic Observation Schedule Generic: A standard measure of social and communication deficits associated with the spectrum of autism. *Journal of Autism and Developmental Disorders, 30*(3), 205–223.

Marans, S. (1997). Assessment of communication. In D. Cohen & F. R. Volkmar (Eds.), *Handbook of autism and pervasive developmental disorders* (2nd ed., pp. 427–441). New York: Wiley.

Mayer, M. (1979). *A boy, a dog, and a frog.* New York: Penguin Books.

McFadden, T., & Gillam, R. (1996). An examination of the quality of narrative produced by children with language disorders. *Language, Speech and Hearing Services in Schools, 27,* 48–56.

McGee, G. G., Morrier, M. J., & Daly, T. (1999). An incidental teaching approach to early intervention for toddlers with autism. *Journal of the Association for Persons with Severe Handicaps, 24*(3), 133–146.

Meyer, M. (1969). *Frog, where are you?* New York: Dial Books.

Miles, S., Paul, R., Klin, A., & Volkmar, F. R. (in preparation). *Identifying conversational deficits in autistic spectrum disorders using the Yale Pragmatic Rating Scale.*

Miller, J., & Chapman, R. (2000). *Systematic analysis of language transcripts.* Madison: University of Wisconsin Press.

Mirenda, P. (2003). He's not really a reader: Perspectives on supporting literacy development in individuals with autism. *Topics in Language Disorders, 23,* 271–282.

Mirenda, P., & Locke, P. (1989). A comparison of symbol transparency in nonspeaking persons with intellectual disability. *Journal of Speech and Hearing Disorders, 54,* 131–140.

Mundy, P., Hogan, A., & Doehring, P. (1996). *Preliminary manual for the Abridged Early Social Communication Scales.* Available from www.psy.miami.edu/faculty/pmundy.

Mundy, P., & Stella, J. (2000). Joint attention, social orienting, and nonverbal communication in autism. In A. Wetherby & B. Prizant (Eds.), *Autism spectrum disorders: A transactional developmental perspective* (Communication and language intervention series, Vol. 9, pp. 55–77). Baltimore: Paul H. Brookes.

Norbury, C., & Bishop, D. V. M. (2003). Narrative skills of children with communication impairments. *International Journal of Language and Communication Disorders, 38,* 287–314.

Osterling, J., & Dawson, G. (1994). Early recognition of children with autism A study of first birthday home videos. *Journal of Autism and Developmental Disorders, 25,* 247–258.

Paul, R. (2001). *Language disorders from infancy through adolescence: Assessment and intervention.* St. Louis, MO: Mosby.

Paul, R., Chuba, H., Miles, S., Klin, A., & Volkmar, F. R. (2003). *Assessing pragmatic skills in individuals with autism and related disorders.* Paper presented at the National Convention of the American Speech-Language-Hearing Association, Chicago, IL.

Paul, R., & Cohen, D. (1985). Outcomes of severe disorders of language acquisition. *Journal of Autism and Developmental Disorders, 14,* 405–421.

Pronovost, W., Wakstein, M., & Wakstein, D. (1966). A longitudinal study of speech behavior and language comprehension in fourteen children diagnosed as atypical or autistic. *Exceptional Children, 33,* 19–26.

Prutting, C., & Kirchner, D. (1983). Applied pragmatics. In T. M. Gallagher & C. A. Prutting (Eds.), *Pragmatic assessment and intervention issues in language* (pp. 29–64). San Diego, CA: College-Hill Press.

Rescorla, L. (1989). The Language Development Survey: A screening tool for delayed language in toddlers. *Journal of Speech and Hearing Disorders, 54,* 587–599.

Rescorla, L., & Achenbach, T. M. (2002). Use of the Language Development Survey (LDS) in a national probability sample of children 18 to 35 months old. *Journal of Speech, Language, and Hearing Research, 45,* 733–743.

Reynell, J. K. & Huntley, M. (1987). *Reynell Development Language Scale* (3rd ed.). Windsor: NFER Nelson.

Rossetti, L. (1995). *The Rossetti Infant-Toddler Language Scales: A measure of communication and interaction.* East Moline, IL: Lingui Systems.

Schery, T., & Wilcoxen, A. (1982). *Initial Communication Processes Observational Scales.* Monterey, CA: CTB/McGraw-Hill.

Sheinkopf, S. J., Mundy, P., Kimbrough-Oller, D., & Steffens, M. (2000). Vocal atypicalities of preverbal autistic children. *Journal of Autism and Developmental Disorders, 30*(4), 345–354.

Shriberg, L. D., Kwiatkowski, J., & Rasmussen, C. (1990). *The Prosody-Voice Screening Profile.* Tucson, AZ: Communication Skill Builders.

Shriberg, L. D., Paul, R., McSweeney, J., Klin, A., Cohen, D., & Volkmar, F. R. (2001). Speech and prosody characteristics of adolescents and adults with high functioning autism and Asperger syndrome. *Journal of Speech, Language and Hearing Research, 44,* 1097–1115.

Sparrow, S., Balla, D., & Cicchetti, D. (1984). *Vineland Adaptive Behavioral Scales.* Circle Pines, MN: American Guidance Service.

Stone, W. L., Ousley, O. Y., Yoder, P. J., Hogan, K. L., & Hepburn, S. L. (1997). Nonverbal communication in 2- and 3-year-old children with autism. *Journal of Autism and Developmental Disorders, 27,* 677–696.

Strong, C. (1998). *Strong narrative assessment procedure* (SNAP). Eau Claire, WI: Thinking Publications.

Volkmar, F. R., Carter, A., Grossman, J., & Klin, A. (1997). Social development in autism. In D. J. Cohen & F. R. Volkmar (Eds.), *Handbook of autism and pervasive developmental disorders* (2nd ed., pp. 173–194). New York: Wiley.

Westby, C. (1998). Communication refinement in school-age and adolescence. In W. Haynes & B. Shulman (Eds.), *Communication development: Foundations, processes and clinical applications* (pp. 164–204). Baltimore: Williams & Wilkins.

Wetherby, A. M., Prizant, B. M., & Hutchinson, T. (1998). Communicative, social-affective, and symbolic profiles of young children with autism and pervasive developmental disorder. *American Journal of Speech-Language Pathology, 7,* 79–91.

Wetherby, A., & Prizant, B. M. (2002). *Communication and Symbolic Behavior Scale.* Baltimore: Paul H. Brookes.

Wiig, E., & Secord, W. (1989). *Test of language competence.* San Antonio, TX: Psychological Corporation.

Windsor, J., Doyle, S., & Siegel, G. (1994). Language acquisition after mutism: A longitudinal case study of autism. *Journal of Speech and Hearing Research, 37,* 96–105.

Zimmerman, I., Steiner, V., & Pond, R. (1992). *Preschool Language Scale-3.* San Antonio, TX: Psychological Corporation.

Zimmerman, I., Steiner, V., & Pond, R. (2003). *Preschool Language Scale-IV.* San Antonio, TX: Psychological Corporation.

CHAPTER 31

Behavioral Assessment of Individuals with Autism: A Functional Ecological Approach

MICHAEL D. POWERS

Behavioral assessment is an ongoing process designed to guide treatment planning by providing predictive, formative, and summative information about the behavior of an individual with autism. It is predictive in that data gathered prior to intervention are used to guide the development of individualized treatment plans. Over the course of treatment, ongoing progress is used in a formative manner to guide refinements and alterations to the treatment protocol. Behavioral assessment also provides a method for the formal summation of treatment effects by emphasizing the comparison of pre- and posttreatment performance or behavior rates. By emphasizing a multimethod approach for gathering information, behavioral assessment data can be comprehensive in scope. A reliance on objective and empirically valid methods of evaluation and analysis ensures both internal and external validity of assessment findings. Finally, the inclusion of developmental considerations into the assessment process ensures that factors, such as age expectations, developmental discontinuity, and the plasticity of behavior at various ages, will be considered in the treatment planning process.

In contrast to more traditional methods of assessment, behavioral assessment emphasizes description of stimulus (or antecedent) and consequent control over behavior. Thus, factors such as physical space configurations, heat and light, sensory acuity, fatigue and hunger, and the communicative intent of the behavior itself all are understood to affect behavior rates, as are reinforcers and punishers.

By emphasizing a hypothesis-testing process with decision-making grounded in objective, verifiable data, the role of inference is minimized. Finally, by appreciating both temporal and contextual bases of behavior, this approach permits more careful consideration of events that may inhibit or facilitate generalization and maintenance of behavior.

This chapter describes characteristics of contemporary behavioral assessment for individuals with autism from a functional ecological perspective. After providing a broad-band framework for assessment, domains of assessment are described. Finally, the relationship between assessment data and intervention planning is reviewed.

CHARACTERISTICS OF BEHAVIORAL ASSESSMENT: A FUNCTIONAL ECOLOGICAL APPROACH

Assessment of the behavior of an individual with autism involves four steps: (1) identification and description of the target behavior(s); (2) determination of setting events, and antecedent and consequent stimuli controlling the target behavior; (3) development and implementation of an intervention plan; and (4) evaluation of intervention effects (Powers & Handleman, 1984).

Earlier conceptualizations of behavioral assessment emphasized descriptions of behavior and consequences, with less attention to antecedent environmental, organismic, and interactional variables. Unfortunately, these conceptualizations often led to narrow treatment strategies, more limited generalization of effects, and less-than-optimal maintenance of treatment outcomes.

A functional ecological approach to assessment increases the likelihood that assessment methods (and the resultant data), intervention strategies, and outcomes are useful across the various environments that the individual with autism encounters. Through this process, four goals are addressed: (1) modification of the ecology of the target behavior, (2) manipulation of contingencies controlling the target behavior, (3) development of functionally equivalent response alternatives to replace the challenging behavior, and (4) development of new skill repertoires that are both functional and socially valid.

To integrate these goals within a functional ecological context, the assessment process should address the dimensions that are discussed next.

Developmental Sensitivity

Autism is characterized by developmental discontinuity. While behavioral assessment methods have traditionally been criticized for underemphasizing developmental factors in autism (Harris & Ferrari, 1983), more recent efforts at nomothetic assessment (e.g., Autism Diagnostic and Observation Scale; Lord, 1997; Childhood Autism Rating Scale; Schopler, Reichler, & Renner, 1986; Behavioral Development Questionnaire; Castelloe & Dawson, 1993) and idiographic assessment (e.g., Powers, 1988) have stressed the need to evaluate the child's behavior within a broader developmental context. Typical and atypical developmental sequelae within cognitive, social, communication, adaptive, and perceptual domains all must be considered to best describe the behavior of a *particular* individual within *specific* situations.

Emphasis on the Criterion of Ultimate Functioning

The criterion of ultimate functioning (L. Brown, Nietupski, & Hamre-Nietupski, 1976) emphasizes that assessment efforts and intervention objectives specifically target behavior that will be functional for the individual with a disability in real environments. In particular, the target behaviors identified to be increased should be those that will have longitudinal value, will replace problematic behavior with more adaptive response alternatives, and will facilitate integration into community settings with maximum independence.

Attention to Molar and Molecular Levels of Analysis

Behavioral assessment must integrate the specifics of a target behavior into environments within which the behavior occurs. At the molecular level, the clinician considers the behavior and its controlling variables by describing the behavior along six dimensions: (1) behavioral unity, (2) duration, (3) interresponse time, (4) latency, (5) intensity, and (6) topography. Behavioral unity describes the predictability of sequential target behavior onsets and offsets. Duration refers to the period of time covered by a response, while interresponse time refers to the amount of time separating one target behavior from another. Latency refers to the interval of time that elapses between the stimulus that occasions (or "triggers") a behavior and the occurrence of that behavior. Intensity refers to the magnitude of behavior. Assessment of intensity can be a rather subjective enterprise due to differences in perception and/or tolerance by observers. To objectify this situation, it is advisable to use permanent products or other verifiable indices whenever possible (e.g., number of tissue breaks caused by self-injury; the distance covered by the hand before striking an object or another person). Finally, a description of the topography of a behavior describes the physical actions undertaken when emitting that behavior. Often this entails a description of exactly what the individual does when performing the behavior. For example, one might describe the topograpy of aggression as the individual with autism picking up an object not intended for throwing, and throwing it at another person covering a distance greater than 12 inches. While this may appear to be reductionistic, recall that for behavioral assessment to better predict treatment outcomes, precision in the description of the behavior to be consequated must be emphasized.

Molar assessment evaluates the pervasiveness of a specific target behavior by understanding it within broader ecological contexts. These can include different environments such as home, school, or community, as well as the behavior within a normative developmental context in those environments. For example, the target behavior of hand-flapping may occur across multiple environments, but more frequently in different situations in each of those environments. At home, it may occur mostly frequently when the child's favorite television program is on, while at school it may occur during periods of heightened stress or unpredictability. While the behavior may look exactly alike in both situations, the cause of the behavior may be vastly different. Different treatment options may thus follow for the same behavior in these two situations because treatment must follow behavioral function, not behavior form.

Setting events that may exert control over the behavior are also identified (Halle & Spradlin, 1993). Setting events and the related construct of establishing operations (Michael, 1993) are conditions which occasion behavior, but do not themselves exert discriminative control over it. As such, setting events and establishing operations affect the momentary reinforcing and punishing value of a consequence, by their interaction with discriminative stimuli that are available. Physical conditions such as hunger, fatigue, and sensory acuity are organismic setting events. For example, when a child is fatigued or ill, the likelihood of more disruptive behavior in response to a difficult demand can be anticipated. The same degree of disruption may not be observed when the child is rested or healthy. In this case, the demand is the discriminative stimulus for disruptive behavior, and the disruptive behavior is presumably reinforced by escape from (or termination of) that demand. Illness changes the momentary reinforcing value of the behavior (when ill, the reinforcing value of escape from the demand will be particularly salient for the child), and the disruptive behavior may increase as a result. Illness functions as a setting event or establishing operation for disruptive behavior in this scenario.

Other types of setting events can be considered. Time of day, schedule changes, particular classrooms or staff configurations, and so on are environmental setting events. While these conditions may not exert contingent control over the target behavior, they "set the stage" for the behavior to occur by increasing the momentary value of the reinforcers available which maintain the challenging behavior. For example, face-slapping may be most likely to occur between 11:30 A.M. and 12:30 P.M. Monday through Friday. Functional analysis of this behavior (described in a later section of this chapter) identifies access to social attention as the maintaining variable. However, the high-probability setting (school, between 11:30 and 12:30) increases the likelihood for this behavior because the student:teacher ratio in the classroom decreases significantly because staff take their lunch breaks during this hour. Fewer staff means less attention for any one student, increasing the probability that the child's face-slapping will increase in order to access the social attention he or she seeks.

Emphasis on Multidimensional Assessment

A functional ecological assessment is multidimensional by design. In addition to conducting molecular and molar analyses of behavior, various contextual factors must be considered in order to address the functional analytic issues in assessment. These include an assessment of high and low probability times for behavior occurrence (Repp & Karsh, 1990); whether the behavior is part of a regular or predictable chain (Charlop & Trasowech, 1991); learning history for the target behavior (Powers & Handleman, 1984); the functional consequence of the behavior for the client and for others (Iwata, Pace, Kalsher, Cowdery, & Cataldo, 1990); the communicative intent of the behavior (K. A. Brown et al., 2000; Durand & Carr, 1991); and sensory or perceptual factors that may inhibit or occasion the behavior (J. E. Carr, Dozier, Patel, Adams, & Martin, 2002; Favell, McGimsey, & Schell, 1982). In addition, response covariation between motor, physiological, and verbal-cognitive processes cannot be assumed (Romanczyk & Matthews, 1998). Comprehensive behavioral assessment includes measures of each of these three do-mains, within the context of multimethod as-sessment. Evans (1986) provides a thoughtful discussion of this issue and its limitations. At-tention to these factors allows the clinician to address maintaining variables more efficiently and comprehensively, promoting generaliza-tion and maintenance.

Assessment across Multiple Systems of Interaction

Many variables contribute to the highly indi-vidualized behavioral, cognitive, and adaptive profile presented by an individual with autism. In recent years, increasing attention is being given to expanding the behavioral assessment and treatment process to include various sys-tems of interaction *beyond* the level of the in-dividual client with a particular target behavior (Powers, 1988). These include assess-ment of the family system (Harris, 1988, 1994); the family's readiness for change (Powers & Handleman, 1984); classroom cur-riculum (Dunlap, Kern-Dunlap, Clarke, & Robbins, 1991; Kern & Dunlap, 1998); the needs of siblings (Harris, 1994); peer reac-tions (McHale & Simeonsson, 1980); and the child's position within the family life cycle (Harris & Powers, 1984). Explicit considera-tion of child, family, environmental, and inter-actional variables facilitates an understanding of the reciprocal, bi-directional nature of be-havior. Treatment planning that accounts for this reciprocity can thereby be directed toward *both* the individual with autism and those per-sons or events in his or her environment im-pacting the behavior.

Emphasis on Strengths and Needs

Behavioral treatment that simply reduces or eliminates a problem behavior is inadequate to meet the life needs of the individual with autism. To facilitate long-term maintenance and generalization, the intervention must *also* teach new skills that are functionally equiva-lent response alternatives, skills that address and satisfy the motivators of the problem be-havior (Dunlap, 1993; Miltenberger, 1998). To accomplish this, the behavioral assessment process must identify functional strengths, skills, and preferences to be incorporated into the treatment plan. This will increase the like-lihood that prosocial behavior is taught *explic-itly* as a replacement for the problem behavior to be reduced. Where the targeted behavior is a skill deficit not currently in the child's reper-toire, attention to functional strengths and in-dividual preferences provides information that can be used to select new behaviors to teach, optimal teaching environments, to choose rein-forcers, and generally to effect a better "fit" between the skill to be taught and the learner's environment.

Use of Multiple Sources of Data

If individualized behavioral intervention pro-tocols are the objectives of assessment, then the behavioral assessment process must gener-ate as descriptive a data resource as possible. Molar and molecular analysis of behavior will generate a broad-band understanding of the target behavior in its relevant environment(s). However, other data sources may be consid-ered as well including information from psy-chological evaluations (Powers, 1988), family assessments (Harris, 1988), and diagnostic material (Volkmar & Cohen, 1988; Volkmar, Klin, & Cohen, 1997). Individual profiles of information processing/cognitive strengths and weaknesses derived from standardized psychological evaluations provide useful infor-mation about learning issues. Data from fam-ily assessments can offer information on family coping style, use of resources, and fam-ily adaptability and cohesion (Powers & Egel, 1989). Diagnostic information can also be of value. Powers (1984) described the advantages of incorporating syndromal diagnosis into the behavioral assessment process. The specificity and developmental sensitivity of the *DSM-IV* criteria for autism and related pervasive devel-opmental disorders provides a framework for understanding the breadth of symptoms pre-sented by a child that co-occur (and thus may be related functionally) with the target behav-ior. Other nomothetic measures such as the Autism Diagnostic and Observation Scale (Lord, 1997; Lord et al., 1989), the Childhood Autism Rating Scale (CARS; Schopler et al., 1986) and the Behavioral Development Ques-tionnaire (Castelloe & Dawson, 1993) also provide information useful to the assessment and treatment planning process.

Interdisciplinary Collaboration Is Essential

Behavioral assessment serves treatment planning. As noted earlier in this chapter, broad-based intervention increases the likelihood that the results of treatment will generalize and maintain. Recent advances in the understanding of the biological correlates of behavior and psychopharmacologic treatment (Crosland et al., 2003; McDougle, Price, & Volkmar, 1994), the complex relationship between severe behavior problems and communicative intent (E. G. Carr et al., 1994), the relationship between sensory preferences and learning rate (Dyer, 1987), the relationship between access to repetitive "neutralizing routines" and low rates of problematic behavior (Horner, Day, & Day, 1997) and the continuing development of effective instructional strategies (Snell, 1992) all highlight the need for integrating information from various disciplines in order to develop a more comprehensive treatment plan.

DOMAINS OF BEHAVIORAL ASSESSMENT

Completion of a comprehensive behavioral assessment involves four steps: (1) identification of the target behavior, (2) determination of variables controlling the target behavior, (3) development of a treatment plan, and (4) evaluation of the effectiveness of the treatment plan.

Identification of the Target Behavior

The precision implicit in behavioral treatment requires a clear, objective, verifiable, and operationalized definition of the target behavior. The behavior must be described with sufficient detail that independent observers would agree that the behavior had just been emitted (or had not) by the client. Where multiple behaviors are identified as targets they must be evaluated to determine whether they serve the same behavioral function. For example, the construct "aggressive and destructive behavior" may include aggression toward others as well as self-injurious behavior. Both of these

behaviors may function to gain escape (or avoidance) of demand situations. In contrast, aggression may function to gain escape while self-injury functions to provide reinforcing sensory feedback to the individual with autism. In this latter case, these two behaviors may be part of two different response classes and will require two different assessment and intervention protocols. By identifying the *form* the behavior takes (its topography, intensity, duration, and frequency), the clinician sets the stage for assessment of behavioral *function* in the next step.

The process of prioritizing target behavior includes description of several factors, including risk to the client and others, the resources available and necessary, and the social validity of the target behavior. Wolf (1978) proposes three broad areas for consideration when assessing social validity: (1) acceptability of treatment goals for target behavior selection, (2) acceptability of treatment procedures, and (3) acceptability of treatment outcomes. Assessment of the acceptability of goals, target behaviors, and procedures *prior* to implementation should increase the likelihood that consumers and families will support treatment efforts. Assessment of the social acceptability of intervention outcomes during and following treatment is more related to maintenance and generalization of those effects. J. E. Carr et al. (2002), Runco and Schreibman (1983, 1987) and Schreibman, Koegel, Mills, and Burke (1981) provide excellent examples of social validation with individuals with autism.

While social validity can be evaluated anecdotally and less formally, several methods for more systematic assessment have been proposed. Norm-based comparisons involve identification of competent models, and determination of criterion levels of performance on target behaviors of importance to the child with autism (Van Houten, 1979). Subjective evaluation (Kazdin, 1977) provides a global judgment as to whether observed behavior changes are seen as important to those individuals with whom the person with autism interacts.

Social validation is an important adjunct to the behavioral assessment process. Evaluation of social validity prior to beginning treatment provides a check-and-balance, increasing the likelihood that successful treatment will be both empirically and clinically meaningful to the person with autism and significant others in his or her life. When used with appropriate limitations (cf. Kazdin, 1977; Wolf, 1978), it provides synthetic validity (Anastasi, 1976) for objectively derived data, enhancing the value and generality of results obtained.

Beyond an operationalized description of the target behavior, assessment must identify alternative, prosocial behavior(s) to replace challenging behavior. Moreover, to be effective with respect to acquisition, generalization, and maintenance these response alternatives must be functionally equivalent to the target problem behavior.

As noted earlier in this chapter, a goal of behavioral intervention is to teach functionally equivalent alternative behavior(s) to replace the problematic target behavior. To accomplish this goal, the behavioral assessment process must first determine behavioral function, and then must identify one or more alternative behaviors that can be taught to the individual with autism, to take the place of the challenging behavior. The determination of functional equivalence in a proposed alternative behavior requires considerations of several dimensions, including the availability of the response, efficiency of the response, effort necessary to emit the response, and the functional equivalence of the response.

Availability refers to the actual presence of the alternative behavior in the repertoire of the individual with autism. *Efficiency* is achieved if the alternative behavior results in immediate and consistent reinforcing consequences. Alternative behaviors that require less response *effort* are more likely to be acquired and maintained. Finally, the alternative behavior must generate identical or superior reinforcing consequences as the problem behavior (E. G. Carr, 1988; O'Neill et al., 1997). Each of these domains should be assessed through indirect and direct methods, and ideally ultimately confirmed through functional analysis.

Determination of Variables Controlling the Target Behavior

This step involves an ecological assessment (investigating the physical environment, antecedent and consequent stimulus events, or-ganismic events, contingencies of reinforcement, the learning environment and learning history, and temporal analysis); indirect analysis using behavioral interviewing about the target behavior, with specific reference to its communicative value; reinforcer assessment with a special emphasis on sensory preferences; and functional analysis of the behavior, where the hypotheses generated with existing assessment data are tested empirically *prior* to proceeding with implementation of the treatment plan. Using indirect methods, descriptive analysis, and functional analysis (cf. Halle & Spradlin, 1993; Iwata, Vollmer, & Zarcone, 1990; Mace, Lalli, Pinter-Lalli, & Shea, 1993; O'Neill, Horner, Albin, Storey, & Sprague, 1990), this step provides a comprehensive basis for gathering information for treatment planning.

The physical, structural environment should be assessed to determine whether conditions such as noise, crowding, open versus small confined workspaces, and so on are related to the occurrence of the target behavior. For example, physical spaces that produce echoes (locker rooms, gyms, stairwells) may increase the probability of covering one's ears, of running away, motor stereotypies, and so on. To the extent that this hypothesis can be demonstrated functionally, a potential intervention might include altering the physical environment by using other space, or by masking or attenuating the (presumably aversive) auditory stimulus with headphones.

Conditions that immediately precede the occurrence of the target behavior (antecedent stimuli) and conditions that occur immediately following the target behavior (consequent stimuli) are considered. Antecedent stimuli can be classified as discriminative stimuli or as elicitors. Discriminative stimuli predict the expectation of a particular response for a person, because that person has learned that the stimulus provokes a response on their part that leads to a certain consequence by someone else. Elicitors, in contrast, evoke automatic emotional or physiological responses (e.g., tachycardia, sweating, and dilation of the pupils). These types of responses are important in the assessment of the individual with autism because target behavior maintained by sensory or "automatic" reinforcement (arousal reduction or induction) can be among the most difficult to treat. Identification of the automatic "triggers" that are elicited by environmental events may allow the clinician to intervene by removing the elicitor or by teaching the client to exert control over his own responding more purposefully (and less automatically).

Assessment of setting events and establishing operations contributes information on context that influences behavioral rate, impacting treatment planning opportunities. As discussed earlier, setting events are variables that influence an ongoing relationship between a stimulus and a response (Bijou & Baer, 1961). Establishing operations are variables that affect an individual by momentarily changing the reinforcing value of discriminative stimuli, and which also increase the frequency of behavior that has previously been reinforced (Michael, 1993). Both setting events and establishing operations emphasize attention to a range of antecedent conditions that alter response probability (e.g., illness, hunger, deprivation of social attention, unexpected schedule changes). While relevant distinctions between the two constructs exist (i.e., setting events can function as establishing operations, but *may not* under certain circumstances), for practical purposes both should be addressed in the assessment process because they help to identify antecedent events that are more distal to the target behavior, but which may also persist over time and affect that behavior (Miltenberger, 1998).

Consequent stimulus events are those imposed on the individual with autism after the target behavior has been emitted. These stimuli can be environmental or organismic. For example, the social attention, gentle touch and soothing talk provided a person immediately after a self-injurious episode may serve as reinforcing consequences of a more external nature, and may maintain the self-injury at unacceptable levels. In contrast, the self-injury may be reinforced by the sensory consequence it provides, quite independent from any external environmental event.

Organismic variables have been an area of increasing interest in the behavioral assessment of autism (see Kalachnik, Hanzerl, Sevenich, & Harder, 2003; Romanczyk & Matthews, 1998). Conditions that have a specific effect on the form and function of behavior (e.g., motor deficits associated

with Rett Syndrome, pharmacologic interventions, seizures, sensory impairments, gastroesophageal reflux) must be accounted for in the assessment process so that treatment planning can reflect the relationship between environmental factors and genetic, neurological, or biological factors that might exert control over the target behavior.

When assessing antecedent and consequent stimuli it is important to identify any behavior chains within which the target behavior may be embedded (Charlop & Trasowech, 1991). For antecedent stimuli, this is done by determining whether there is pattern of predictable behavior immediately preceding the target behavior. Thus, aggression that reliably occurs after the client has been frustrated in an attempt to obtain something, followed by his shouting, then menacing physical gestures, then physical aggression offers the clinician the option of intervening earlier in the chain (i.e., before the aggression occurs), in an attempt to preempt the response. When assessing for consequent stimulus behavior chains is useful to consider not only which consequence followed the target behavior, but also the *client's* response to that consequence. This allows assessment of ongoing clinician behavior that unwittingly may be reinforcing or punishing the behavior.

Contingencies of reinforcement refer to the particular conditions of reinforcement that influence the probability that a correct behavior or response will occur. Included here are schedules of reinforcement (Koegel, Schreibman, Britten, & Laitenen, 1979), reinforcer variation (Egel, 1981), task variation (Winterling, Dunlap, & O'Neill, 1987), and the use of sensory reinforcers (J. E. Carr et al., 2002; Durand & Carr, 1985; Dyer, 1987). By understanding the role and importance of reinforcement in learning the target behavior, the clinician may be able to intervene by altering reinforcement contingencies *prior* to the occurrence of the behavior.

Comprehensive assessment considers the teaching and learning environments the person with autism may participate in, as these situations may exert control over the target behavior as establishing operations or setting events (K. A. Brown et al., 2000; Horner, Sprague, & Flannery, 1993; Kern & Dunlap, 1998). Task ease or difficulty, boredom and fatigue, fast or slow pacing of presentation of instructional material, novelty of material, excessive auditory processing (versus visual processing) demands, a reliance on simultaneous processing (versus sequential processing), curricula that are poorly matched to learner ability, and so forth may increase the likelihood that the targeted behavior will occur. To the extent that one or more of these dimensions is implicated, intervention can be tailored to these concerns, again preempting the function of the target behavior by replacing it with a more appropriate response alternative.

Temporal analysis investigates the target behavior across time and within specific time periods. For example, the frequency of a behavior can be entered on a data sheet that is divided into 30-minute intervals for the entire day. Over the course of 1 or 2 weeks, patterns may be evident signaling high and low probability times for target behavior occurrence. These intervals can be keyed to specific events throughout the day or week, permitting additional assessment into those situations. Touchette, MacDonald, and Langer (1985) developed the scatterplot to organize temporal data. The scatterplot is a grid with time intervals on the ordinate that monitors individuals for rate or frequency of target behaviors throughout their day. These frequencies are then keyed to activities and activity changes. The visual display that results provides information on high- and low-frequency behavior times as these relate to environmental variables.

Indirect methods such as behavioral interviewing about the target behavior provides information on social and interpersonal factors that maintain or motivate behavioral performance and nonperformance across different situations. Information gathered in the behavioral assessment thus far has contributed to this understanding by providing convergent information on maintaining variables. More formal assessment of these variables can provide even more information, however. The Functional Analysis Screening Tool (FAST; Iwata & DeLeon, 1995) and the Motivation Assessment Scale (MAS; Durand & Crimmins, 1988) provide information on specific behavioral functions (e.g., positive reinforcement through social attention or by access to material reinforcers; negative reinforcement through es-

cape from demands or pain attenuation, automatic reinforcement). As adjuncts to direct observation of the target behavior, these screening tools provide useful information for treatment selection. If used to understand communicative function, treatment planning can also address the communicative intent of the target behavior, and be designed to teach alternative and more adaptive behavior serving the identical communicative function as the problem behavior (E. G. Carr & Durand, 1985). Other researchers (Anderson & Long, 2002; O'Neill et al., 1990) have advocated the value of structured descriptive formats for assessing antecedent and consequent events. All of these methods share common advantages. They are structured, relatively straightforward to administer, and provide broad-band information pertinent to treatment planning. While a common disadvantage is reliance on interview or reporting data (instead of direct observations), Anderson and Long (2002) report that structured descriptive assessment (SDA) generated similar hypotheses regarding behavioral function as did analogue functional analyses in most cases.

As behavioral assessment is intended ultimately to facilitate treatment planning, an assessment of reinforcer preferences must be an integral part of the process. Earlier, more simplistic reinforcer surveys identified materials and activities by form or type. For example, one might determine that a client preferred access to a particular toy, food, or television program. Researchers have broadened this process and have proposed that reinforcers be assessed by their stimulus preferences, including a wide range of *sensory conditions* for consideration (Dyer, 1987). The wisdom of this is evident if one recalls that autism is a disorder characterized by atypical responses to the sensory environment. Indeed, deviant responses to auditory, tactile, proprioceptive, vestibular, olfactory, and gustatory sensory events are not uncommon in the behavioral profiles of individuals within the autism spectrum. By conducting a functional assessment of stimulus (sensory) preferences, clinicians have access to a more specifically tailored set of material and sensory reinforcers, particularly those that have demonstrated value for the particular individual.

The final step in determining controlling variables involves conducting a functional analysis. Functional analysis is the systematic, objective, empirical manipulation and observation of variables presumed to exert influence over the target behavior in controlled settings. These variables are generated by the indirect and descriptive analysis methods described above, and permit the clinician to extend the assessment process *beyond* a description of factors *correlated* with the target behavior, to factors exerting functional *control* over the target behavior. Functional analysis involves creating controlled, analog conditions designed to "test" functions presumed to control behavior. For example, Iwata, Dorsey, Slifer, Bauman, and Richman (1982) evaluated four conditions presumed related to self-injurious behavior. These included social disapproval, task demand, unstructured play with materials, and sensory consequences. Each 15-minute condition was presented twice per day. Frequencies of self-injury were then calculated across the four conditions, and determinations made as to which condition exerted more stimulus control over the behavior. Advantages of controlled, analog analysis are related to the precision and specificity obtained. While some have argued that this step is always necessary (Iwata et al., 1990), others have noted that analog analysis may require more of a commitment of human and financial resources than is necessary (or available), and that concise and appropriate behavioral interventions can sometimes be inferred from observation and indirect methods (O'Neill et al., 1990).

DEVELOPMENT OF A TREATMENT PLAN

Behavioral assessment data provide the basis for intervention planning and evaluation. Thus, not only does assessment serve the predictive function noted in the beginning of this chapter, but it also provides the basis for ongoing (formative) and summative evaluation of intervention effectiveness. A functional ecological approach generates a wealth of information to be incorporated into the treatment plan. Interventions must address the controlling variables identified, and the contextual information related to behavior performance and nonperformance. Strategies to teach functional alternative communicative responses must be

incorporated. The use of differential reinforcement procedures to strengthen behaviors that are functionally equivalent and topographically incompatible is essential. Altering stimulus (antecedent) conditions formally addresses the ecological variables (setting events and establishing operations) identified. Finally, the incorporation of consequent procedures that are functionally compatible with desired outcomes and are socially valid (cf. Wolf, 1978) is necessary. These components are described in detail in Bregman & Gerdtz, Chapter 35.

Evaluation of the Effects of Treatment

Behavioral assessment begins with the identification of dependent measures that are objective, valid, and reliable. Once the target behavior is identified, defined operationally, and observed in a baseline or pretreatment setting, this baseline becomes the yardstick against which efficacy is measured. Behavioral assessment methods include anecdotal recording, direct observation of the target behavior in natural or analog settings, and analysis of permanent products (e.g., incident reports, nursing notes, number of skin breaks caused by biting).

While the use of direct observation procedures is considered a hallmark in behavioral assessment and treatment, certain issues must be considered. Reactivity to direct observation methods can influence both client (subject) and observer behavior. Client awareness of the observer or awareness of changes in the environment occasioned by the observer (e.g., the presence of a video camera with a red light that blinks while recording) can impact client behavior in ways atypical to the natural (unobserved) environment. Reactivity can also influence the observer and impact the reliability of data obtained.

Even though direct observation methods may be used, data obtained may not be accurate. Central to this issue is the concept of reliability, which describes the internal consistency of behavior observations or the interobserver agreement that the target behavior did in fact occur. Reliability of data is a core concept in behavioral assessment, as these data are used to predict and evaluate the efficacy of treatment. High rates of inter-observer agreement are indicative of higher quality observational data. Foster and Cone (1986) describe several factors that may influence reliability of observations. These include observer expectations that *their* performance will be evaluated; awareness of the identity of the rater; unsupervised collection on data; observer fatigue; setting variables in the observation environment; observer expectations; interactions between the observers, experimenters, and subjects of the observation; and demand characteristics of the experimental situation.

Various methods are used to calculate reliability for categorical data (i.e., data that are recorded as observed or not observed during established intervals). These include overall percentage agreement, percentage occurrence agreement, Kappa (K), and Phi (Φ). For data that are aggregated over an entire session, however, product-moment correlation's (*r*) or generalizablity analysis are often used (Foster & Cone, 1986).

Despite well defined target behaviors and careful training of observers, the accuracy of observations and inclusion or exclusion of ambiguous or borderline responses may shift subtly over time. Observer "drift" increases the systematic (and accidental) error of measured responses, and represents a threat to the quality of obtained data. A comprehensive review of factors affecting inter-observer reliability, and methods for assessment of observer drift, bias, and reactivity is beyond the scope of this chapter. Foster and Cone (1986) provide a detailed review and analysis of these issues. Finally, evaluation should occur in the context of an experimental or quasi-experimental design appropriate to the dependent measure (see Barlow & Hersen, 1984). Choice of method is determined by resources available, the risk associated with using a less precise method, and the degree of experimental control necessary to make valid outcome statements.

Related Issues for Comprehensive Assessment

In addition to determining the effect on the target behavior, a functional ecological approach suggests evaluation of procedural reliability, ecological validity, and generalization and maintenance. Procedural reliability represents the degree to which the intervention plan was carried out correctly by all intervenors (Billingsly, White, & Munson, 1980). The assessment of procedural reliability should be conducted while treatment is in progress in order to better inform ongoing decision making and interpretation of treatment effect.

Ecological validity refers to the extent to which the targets and settings addressed are functional in the individuals' everyday environment. The concept of ecobehavioral analysis (Rogers-Warren, 1984) or ecological assessment (Powers, 1997) provides strategies to increase the ecological validity of interventions. Specifically, behavioral assessment is conducted in the context of natural environments and situations the individual currently (or will in the near future) participate in. After first conducting an inventory of relevant environments (e.g., school) and subenvironments (e.g., small group instruction), the clinician proceeds to identify activities described in those subenvironments (e.g., completing an assignment independently and correctly) and defines the skills necessary to perform the activity (e.g., read the material, ask for assistance when needed). The client's *current* skill repertoire is then evaluated against this criterion, with treatment provided to develop the skills missing.

Finally, for target behavior to be functional in nontreatment settings, it must generalize and maintain over time. Unfortunately, attention to these important concepts is often given less emphasis by clinicians than the demonstration of initial changes in targeted behavior. As problems with generalization are endemic to individuals with autism, greater emphasis is warranted.

Generalization and maintenance go hand-in-hand. Simply put, skills taught that do not become fluent in nontraining environments, or those that do not last over time, are of limited value. Behavioral assessment of generalization and maintenance are not merely summative. That is, it is insufficient to become concerned about whether a skill transferred and maintained only *after* it was acquired. Stokes and Baer (1977) noted that the "train and hope" strategy could be supplanted by a technology of generalization designed to facilitate orderly transfer of skills. A more proactive (and predictive) strategy involves assessing three broad areas described by Stokes and Osnes (1988). These areas include an assessment of natural functional contingencies or reinforcement; assessment of diverse training opportunities; and an assessment of common stimuli that may serve as functional mediators of newly learned behavior.

An assessment of natural communities of reinforcement provides information on the type, frequency, and variety of reinforcers that are already available in the clients' environment. For example, if high rates of social approval are available (and low rates of material or food reinforcers are not widely used), the clinician may wish to exploit social approval as a reinforcer if it is functional to the client. Subsequent training would then provide social approval for the target behavior in both training and nontraining environments. Stokes and Osnes (1988) note that generalization is facilitated by training with sufficient exemplars. This implies programming explicitly with a diverse range of people, environments, settings, and materials. Prior identification of those training opportunities allows the clinician to vary systematically those stimulus dimensions that may otherwise control responding, so that rigid and artificial conditions of treatment are avoided.

Identifying stimuli that can serve as potential functional mediators to untrained settings is the third area described by Stokes and Osnes (1988). Functional mediators are stimuli that facilitate generalization, most likely because they serve as discriminative stimuli for targeted behavior. These can include objects or people in the physical environment present in both trained and untrained settings that help the client determine behavior that is expected (e.g., picture prompts, peer tutors). Once these objects or people are identified in the assessment, they can be incorporated into training protocols to promote generalization.

Expanding the scope of behavioral assessment to include procedural reliability, ecological validity, and generalization and maintenance move the assessment process beyond the molecular analysis of the target behavior and place it within the larger social and ecological context the client operates within.

This in turn facilitates more comprehensive understanding of treatment effectiveness and treatment failures.

Comprehensive, lasting change in the lives of individuals with autism should be the goal of intervention efforts. A functional ecological approach to behavioral assessment provides a framework for understanding behavioral excesses, deficits, and strengths from a broader systemic perspective, creating an educative base for intervention efforts. As interventions for behavioral challenges more precisely target and teach adaptive and functional response alternatives, the distinctions between behavioral treatment and effective education will fade.

Cross-References

Other aspects of assessments are addressed in this section (Chapters 27 through 32); behavioral intervention and behavior management are discussed in Chapters 34 and 35.

REFERENCES

Anastasi, A. (1976). *Psychological testing* (4th ed.). New York: Macmillan.

Anderson, C. M., & Long, E. S. (2002). Use of a structured descriptive assessment methodology to identify variables affecting problem behavior. *Journal of Applied Behavior Analysis, 35,* 137–154.

Barlow, D., & Hersen, M. (1984). *Single case experimental designs: Strategies for studying behavior change.* New York: Pergamon Press.

Bijou, S. J., & Baer, D. M. (1961). *Child development: A systematic and empirical theory.* Englewood Cliffs, NJ: Prentice-Hall.

Billingsly, F., White, O. R., & Munson, R. (1980). Procedural reliability: A rationale and an example. *Behavioral Assessment, 2,* 229–241.

Brown, K. A., Wacker, D. P., Derby, K. M., Peck, S. M., Richman, D. M., Sasso, G. M., et al. (2000). Evaluating the effects of functional communication training in the presence and absence of establishing operations. *Journal of Applied Behavior Analysis, 33,* 53–76.

Brown, L., Nietupski, J., & Hamre-Nietupski, S. (1976). Criterion of ultimate functioning and public school services for severely handicapped students. In M. A. Thomas (Ed.), *Hey, don't forget about me* (pp. 2–15). Reston, VA: Council for Exceptional Children.

Carr, E. G. (1988). Functional equivalence as a method of response generalization. In R. H. Horner, G. Dunlap, & R. L. Koegel (Eds), *Generalization and maintenance: Life-style changes in applied settings* (pp. 221–241). Baltimore: Paul H. Brookes.

Carr, E. G., & Durand, V. M. (1985). Reducing behavior problems through functional communication training. *Journal of Applied Behavior Analysis, 18,* 111–126.

Carr, E. G., Levin, L., McConnachie, G., Carlson, J. I., Kemp, D. C., & Smith, C. E. (1994). *Communication-based intervention for problem behavior.* Baltimore: Paul H. Brookes.

Carr, J. E., Dozier, C. L., Patel, M. R., Adams, A. N., & Martin, N. (2002). Treatment of automatically-reinforced object mouthing with noncontingent reinforcement and response blocking: Experimental analysis and social validation. *Research in Developmental Disabilities, 23,* 37–44.

Castelloe, P., & Dawson, G. (1993). Subclassification of children with autism and pervasive developmental disorder: A questionnaire based on Wing's subgrouping scheme. *Journal of Autism and Developmental Disorders, 23,* 229–241.

Charlop, M. H., & Trasowech, J. E. (1991). Increasing autistic children's daily spontaneous speech. *Journal of Applied Behavior Analysis, 24,* 747–761.

Crosland, K. A., Zarcone, J. R., Lindauer, S. E., Valdovinos, M. G., Zarcone, T. J., Hellings, J. A., et al. (2003). Use of functional analysis methodology in the evaluation of medication effects. *Journal of Autism and Developmental Disorders, 33,* 271–279.

Dunlap, G. (1993). Promoting generalization. In R. Van Houten & S. Axelrod (Eds.), *Behavior analysis and treatment* (pp. 269–296). New York: Plenum Press.

Dunlap, G., Kern-Dunlap, L., Clarke, S., & Robbins, F. R. (1991). Functional assessment, curricular revision, and severe behavior problems. *Journal of Applied Behavior Analysis, 24,* 387–397.

Durand, V. M., & Carr, E. G. (1985). Self-injurious behavior: Motivating conditions and guidelines for treatment. *School Psychology Review, 14,* 171–176.

Durand, V. M., & Carr, E. G. (1991). Functional communicaton training to reduce challenging behavior: Maintenance and application in new settings. *Journal of Applied Behavior Analysis, 24,* 251–264.

Durand, V. M., & Crimmins, D. B. (1988). Identifying the variables maintaining self-injurious behavior. *Journal of Autism and Developmental Disorders, 18,* 99–117.

Dyer, K. (1987). The competition of autistic stereotyped behavior with usual and specially assessed reinforcers. *Research in Developmental Disabilities, 8,* 607–626.

Egel, A. L. (1981). Reinforcer variation: Implications for motivating developmentally disabled children. *Journal of Applied Behavior Analysis, 14,* 345–350.

Evans, I. M. (1986). Response structure and the triple-response-mode concept. In R. D. Nelson & S. C. Hayes (Eds.), *Conceptual foundations of behavioral assessment* (pp. 131–155). New York: Guilford Press.

Favell, J. E., McGimsey, J., & Schell, R. (1982). Treatment of self-injury by providing alternative sensory activities. *Analysis and Intervention in Developmental Disabilities, 2,* 83–104.

Foster, S. L., & Cone, J. D. (1986). Design and use of direct observation procedures. In A. R. Ciminero, K. S. Calhoun, & H. E. Adams (Eds.), *Handbook of behavioral assessment* (2nd ed., pp. 253–324). New York: Wiley.

Halle, J. W., & Spradlin, J. E. (1993). Identifying stimulus control of challenging behavior. In J. Reichle & D. P. Wacker (Eds.), *Communicative approaches to challenging behavior* (pp. 83–109). Baltimore: Paul H. Brookes.

Harris, S. L. (1988). Family assessment in autism. In E. Schopler & G. B. Mesibov (Eds.), *Diagnosis and assessment in autism* (pp. 199–210). New York: Plenum Press.

Harris, S. L. (1994). *Siblings of children with autism.* Bethesda, MD: Woodbine.

Harris, S. L., & Ferrari, M. (1983). Developmental factors in child behavior therapy. *Behavior Therapy, 14,* 54–72.

Harris, S. L., & Powers, M. D. (1984). Behavior therapists look at the impact of the autistic child on the family system. In E. Schopler & G. B. Mesibov (Eds.), *The effects of autism on the family* (pp. 207–220). New York: Plenum Press.

Horner, R. H., Day, H. M., & Day, J. R. (1997). Using neutralizing routines to reduce problem behaviors. *Journal of Applied Behavior Analysis, 30,* 601–614.

Horner, R. H., Sprague, J. R., & Flannery, K. B. (1993). Building functional curricula for students with severe intellectual disabilities and severe problem behaviors. In R. VanHouten & S. Axelrod (Eds.), *Behavior analysis and treatment* (pp. 47–71). New York: Plenum Press.

Iwata, B. A., & DeLeon, I. G. (1995). The functional analysis screening tool (FAST). Talahassee: Florida Institute on Self Injury,

Department of Psychology, University of Florida.

Iwata, B. A., Dorsey, M. F., Slifer, K. J., Bauman, K. E., & Richman, G. S. (1982). Toward a functional analysis of self-injury. *Analysis and Intervention in Developmental Disabilities, 2,* 3–20.

Iwata, B. A., Pace, G. M., Kalsher, M. J., Cowdery, G. E., & Cataldo, M. F. (1990). Experimental analysis and extinction of self-injurious escape behavior. *Journal of Applied Behavior Analysis, 23,* 11–27.

Iwata, B. A., Vollmer, T. R., & Zarcone, J. R. (1990). The experimental (functional) analysis of behavior disorders: Methodology, applications, and limitations. In A. C. Repp & N. N. Singh (Eds.), *Perspectives on the use of non-aversive and aversive interventions for persons with developmental disabilities* (pp. 301–330). Sycamore, IL: Sycamore Publishing Co.

Kalacknik, J. E., Hanzerl, T. E., Sevenich, R., & Harder, S. R. (2003). Clonazepam behavioral side effects with an individual with mental retardation. *Journal of Autism and Developmental Disorders, 33,* 349–354.

Kazdin, A. E. (1977). Assessing the clinical or applied importance of behavior change through social validation. *Behavior Modification, 1,* 427–451.

Kern, L., & Dunlap, G. (1998). Curricular modifications to promote desirable classroom behavior. In J. K. Luiselli & M. J. Cameron (Eds.), *Antecedent control: Innovative approach to behavioral support* (pp. 289–307). Baltimore: Paul H. Brookes.

Koegel, R. L., Schreibman, L., Britten, K., & Laitenen, R. (1979). The effect of schedule of reinforcement on stimulus overselectivity in autistic children. *Journal of Autism and Developmental Disorders, 9,* 383–397.

Lord, C. (1997). Diagnostic instruments in autism spectrum disorders. In D. J. Cohen & F. R. Volkmar (Eds.), *Handbook of autism and pervasive developmental disorders* (2nd ed., pp. 460–483). New York: Wiley.

Lord, C., Rutter, M., Goode, S., Heemsbergen, J., Jordan, H., Mawhood, L., et al. (1989). The Autism Diagnostic Observation Schedule: A standardized observation of communicative and social behavior. *Journal of Autism and Pervasive Developmental Disorders, 19,* 185–212.

Mace, F. C., Lalli, J. S., Pinter-Lalli, E., & Shea, M. C. (1993). Functional analysis and treatment of aberrant behavior. In R. VanHouten & S. Axelrod (Eds.), *Behavior analysis and treatment* (pp. 75–99). New York: Plenum Press.

McDougle, C., Price, L. H., & Volkmar, F. R. (1994). Recent advances in the pharmacotherapy of autism and related disorders. *Child and Adolescent Psychiatric Clinics of North America, 3,* 71–89.

McHale, S. M., & Simeonsson, R. J. (1980). Effects of interaction on nonhandicapped children's attitudes toward autistic children. *American Journal of Mental Deficiency, 85,* 18–24.

Michael, J. (1993). Establishing operations. *The Behavior Analyst, 16,* 191–206.

Miltenberger, R. G. (1998). Methods of assessing antecedent influences on challenging behavior. In J. K. Luiselli & M. J. Cameron (Eds.), *Antecedent control: Innovative approaches to behavioral support* (pp. 47–65). Baltimore: Paul H. Brookes.

O'Neill, R. E., Horner, R. H., Albin, R. W., Sprague, J. R., Storey, K., & Newton, J. S. (1997). *Functional assessment and program development for problem behavior: A practical handbook.* Pacific Grove, CA: Brooks/Cole.

O'Neill, R. E., Horner, R. H., Albin, R. W., Storey, K., & Sprague, J. R. (1990). *Functional analysis of problem behavior: A practical assessment guide.* Sycamore, IL: Sycamore Publishing Co.

Powers, M. D. (1984). Syndromal diagnosis and the behavioral assessment of childhood disorders. *Child and Family Behavior Therapy, 6,* 1–15.

Powers, M. D. (1988). Behavioral assessment of autism. In E. Schopler & G. B. Mesibov (Eds.), *Diagnosis and assessment of autism* (pp. 139–165). New York: Plenum Press.

Powers, M. D. (1997). Behavioral assessment of autism. In D. J. Cohen & F. R. Volkmar (Eds.), *Handbook of autism and pervasive developmental disorders* (2nd ed., pp. 448–459). New York: Wiley.

Powers, M. D., & Egel, A. L. (1989). *Stress, coping and conflict in families of young autistic children.* Paper presented at the annual conference of the Association for Behavior Analysis, Philadelphia, PA.

Powers, M. D., & Handleman, J. S. (1984). *Behavioral assessment of severe developmental disabilities.* Rockville, MD: Aspen.

Repp, A. C., & Karsh, K. G. (1990). A taxonomic approach to the nonaversive treatment of maladaptive behavior of persons with developmental disabilities. In A. C. Repp & N. N. Singh (Eds.), *Perspectives on the use of non-aversive and aversive interventions for persons with developmental disabilities* (pp. 381–402). Sycamore, IL: Sycamore Publishing Co.

Rogers-Warren, A. K. (1984). Ecobehavioral analysis. *Education and Treatment of Children, 7,* 283–303.

Romanczyk, R. L., & Matthews, A. L. (1998). Physiological state as antecedent: Utilization of functional analysis. In J. K. Luiselli & M. J. Cameron (Eds.), *Antecedent control: Innovative approaches to behavioral support* (pp. 115–138). Baltimore: Paul H. Brookes.

Runco, M. A., & Schreibman, L. (1983). Parental judgments of behavior therapy efficacy with autistic children: A social validation. *Journal of Autism and Developmental Disorders, 13,* 237–248.

Runco, M. A., & Schreibman, L. (1987). Socially validating behavioral objectives in the treatment of autistic children. *Journal of Autism and Developmental Disorders, 17,* 141–147.

Schopler, E., Reichler, R. J., & Renner, B. R. (1986). *The Childhood Autism Rating Scale (CARS) for diagnostic screening and classification of autism.* New York: Irvington.

Schreibman, L., Koegel, R. L., Mills, J., & Burke, J. C. (1981). Social validation of behavior therapy with autistic children. *Behavior Therapy, 12,* 610–624.

Snell, M. (Ed.). (1992). *Instruction of students with severe dis-abilities* (4th ed.). New York: Macmillan.

Stokes, T. F., & Baer, D. M. (1977). An implicit technology of generalization. *Journal of Applied Behavior Analysis, 10,* 349–367.

Stokes, T. F., & Osnes, P. G. (1988). The developing applied technology of generalization and maintenance. In R. H. Horner, G. Dunlap, & R. L. Koegel (Eds.), *Generalization and maintenance* (pp. 5–19). Baltimore: Paul H. Brookes.

Touchette, P. E., MacDonald, R. F., & Langer, S. N. (1985). A scatterplot for identifying stimulus control of problem behavior. *Journal of Applied Behavior Analysis, 18,* 343–351.

Van Houten, R. (1979). Social validation: The evolution of standards of compentency for target behaviors. *Journal of Applied Behavior Analysis, 12,* 581–591.

Volkmar, F. R., & Cohen, D. J. (1988). Classification and diagnosis of childhood autism. In E. Schopler & G. B. Mesibov (Eds.), *Diagnosis and assessment in autism* (pp. 71–89). New York: Plenum Press.

Volkmar, F. R., Klin, A., & Cohen, D. J. (1997). Diagnosis and classification of autism and related conditions: Consensus and issues. In D. J. Cohen & F. R. Volkmar (Eds.), *Handbook of autism and pervasive developmental disorders* (2nd ed., pp. 5–40). New York: Wiley.

Winterling, V., Dunlap, G., & O'Neill, R. E. (1987). The influence of task variation on the aberrant behavior of autistic students. *Education and Treatment of Children, 10,* 105–119.

Wolf, M. M. (1978). Social validity: The case for subjective judgment or how applied behavior analysis is finding its heart. *Journal of Applied Behavior Analysis, 11,* 203–214.

CHAPTER 32

Sensory and Motor Features in Autism: Assessment and Intervention

GRACE T. BARANEK, L. DIANE PARHAM, AND JAMES W. BODFISH

Clinical practitioners often overlook assessment of sensory and motor features in autism, particularly during diagnostic evaluations that focus on the primary (i.e., social-communicative) features of the disorder. Sensory and motor characteristics, although not necessarily core features of autism, may contribute to differential diagnosis and have important implications for intervention planning. We use the general term *autism* in this chapter to convey disorders in the autistic spectrum, including Autistic Disorder, Asperger Disorder, and Pervasive Developmental Disorder, Not Otherwise Specified, however, references to individual categories within the autistic spectrum are specified where needed for clarification. The term *motor features* includes both voluntary and involuntary actions that are observable in daily life. *Sensory features* refer to behavioral manifestations of sensory processes (e.g., sensitization, habituation, discrimination, integration) that occur in the central nervous system.

Research on the nature of sensory and motor features in autism is still in its infancy, despite decades of phenomenological reports documenting these intriguing behaviors. In recent years, several new studies have emerged, providing rich descriptions of sensory or motor features; however, there is still a dearth of research on the processes underlying them. This chapter synthesizes the empirical literature characterizing sensory and motor phenomena, and where possible, discusses mechanisms thought to be responsible for these features. A discussion of state-of-the-art clinical assessment strategies and implications for interventions are also presented.

SENSORY-MOTOR DEVELOPMENT IN PERSONS WITH AUTISM

Sensory Features

Peculiar sensory features have been noted in persons with autism dating back to the earliest case studies on record. Kanner (1943) reported both sensory fascinations (e.g., watching light reflecting from mirrors) that provided seemingly endless joy, as well as heightened sensitivities (e.g., covering ears against noise) that caused distress in children with autism. Recent literature (Baranek, 2002; Cesaroni & Garber, 1991; O'Neill & Jones, 1997) provides myriad terms to describe these unusual features, including under- and overresponsiveness to various sensory stimuli, hypo- and hypersensitivities, preoccupations with sensory features of the environment, sensory-perceptual distortions, and paradoxical responses to sensory stimuli.

Depending on the level of specificity of the symptoms reported, prevalence rates of unusual

We wish to thank Drs. Jackson Roush and Margaret Creedon for their willingness to consult about aspects of vision and hearing in autism. We also thank Vesna Costello, Fabian David, and Allison Papovich for help in preparation of this manuscript.

sensory features vary from approximately 42% to 88% in samples of school-aged children with autism (Kientz & Dunn, 1997; Le Couteur et al., 1989; Ornitz, Guthrie, & Farley, 1977; Volkmar, Cohen, & Paul, 1986). Although these behaviors manifest across all sensory modalities (i.e., visual, auditory, gustatory, olfactory, tactile, proprioceptive, and vestibular), auditory sensitivities are most commonly noted (Bettison, 1996; Greenspan & Wieder, 1997; Talay-Ongan & Wood, 2000; Volkmar et al., 1986). Thus, sensory symptoms are relatively common, but perhaps not universal, in persons with autism.

Unusual sensory features also exist in the absence of known peripheral deficits; children with autism usually test within normal limits for visual or hearing acuity (Klin, 1993). Although individuals with autism are sometimes incorrectly diagnosed with peripheral hearing loss, conductive, sensorineural, or mixed hearing loss can cooccur with autism (Jure, Rapin, & Tuchman, 1991; Rosenhall, Nordin, Sandstrom, Ahlsen, & Gillberg, 1999). In a sample of 199 children with autism, Rosenhall and colleagues diagnosed mild to moderate sensorineural hearing loss in 7.9%, a profound sensorineural hearing loss in 3.5%, and conductive hearing loss associated with otitis media in 18.3%. The exact prevalence of specific visual impairments in persons with autism is unknown. Two studies (Kaplan, Rimland, & Edelson, 1999; Scharre & Creedon, 1992) indicated 18% to 50% of children with autism in their study had some difficulties with acuity (near and far), fixation, binocularity, and/or strabismus. However, these deficits do not seem sufficient to explain the unusual hypo- and hypersensitivities that exist in this population.

Earlier theories (e.g., Ornitz, 1989) proposed that autistic features were consequences of dysmodulation of sensory input, but these models were too general to explain all features of autism. Although newer neuropsychological theories (e.g., social cognition; executive function) better account for specific social-communicative deficits and restricted interests in autism, they do not adequately explain the unusual sensory features. Furthermore, empirical studies of mechanisms underlying these symptoms are lacking.

Some aspects of sensory processing, particularly visual-spatial perception, are often noted as strengths in this population (Happé, 1996). A piecemeal processing style (i.e., weak central coherence) may allow for excellence in certain visual skills, such as copying block designs, but does not rule out the possibility of coexistence of sensory modulation disruptions (e.g., hypo- or hyperresponsiveness to visual stimuli; Kientz & Dunn, 1997; Talay-Ongan & Wood, 2000) nor problems with intersensory integration (e.g., integration of visual with proprioceptive feedback) for motor responses (Kohen-Raz, Volkmar, & Cohen, 1992) documented in this population.

Although it is possible that individual sensory features have different etiologies, it is more likely that patterns of response across sensory modalities have similar physiological underpinnings. For example, *hypo*-responsiveness to sensory stimuli is associated with the lack of orienting in autism (Allen & Courchesne, 2001; Bryson, Landry, & Wainwright, 1997) and suggests deficits in attentional systems responding to information-laden stimuli (Courchesne et al., 1994; Dawson, Meltzoff, Osterling, Rinaldi, & Brown, 1998; Minshew, Sweeney, & Bauman, 1997), or perhaps in disengaging and rapidly shifting attention (e.g., Landry & Bryson, 2004). Although social orienting deficits are prominent, orienting to nonsocial sensory stimuli is also deficient in autism (Dawson et al., 1998; McGuire, Barnett, Baranek, & Suratt, 2001; Swettenham et al., 1998). In contrast, *hyper*-responsiveness is often equated with defensive (fight/flight) reactions, increased sympathetic activity or insufficient vagal tone, and hyperarousal (Porges, Doussard-Roosevelt, & Maiti, 1994).

Prevalence of various sensory responsiveness patterns has not been systematically investigated, but anecdotal reports exist. Greenspan and Wieder (1997) reported that 19% of preschool children with autism in their clinical samples displayed a predominantly hyperresponsive pattern, 39% displayed a hyporesponsive pattern, and 36% display a mixed pattern of sensory response. Phenomenological reports (Cesaroni & Garber, 1991; Grandin, 1992; D. Williams, 1994) provide corroborating evidence of fluctuating and coexisting sensory response patterns in some persons with autism. For example, an individual may show distress to certain sounds, textures, or sights, while ignoring others that may appear more intense in their stimulus properties.

Relation to Core Features

Sensory features are likely to cooccur with other behavioral manifestations of autism, suggesting different phenotypic subtypes (Eaves, Ho, & Eaves, 1994; Sevin et al., 1995). Wing and Gould (1979) characterized different sensory patterns in each of three social relatedness subtypes of autism. Baranek, Foster, and Berkson (1997b) noted that some sensory features (i.e., hyper-responsiveness to tactile stimuli) correlated more strongly with certain behavioral rigidities than with repetitive motor features in a group of children with autism and related developmental disorders. Although such studies have interesting etiological and prognostic implications, further research is needed to resolve whether or not different processes account for the various patterns of association.

Studies are increasingly employing controlled experiments to unravel the sensory issues that are often conflated with core features of autism. Nader, Oberlander, Chambers, and Craig (2004) found that although caregivers often perceived children with autism as being underresponsive to pain, detailed observational scales revealed that these children had heightened pain responses relative to typically developing children, as measured during routine venipuncture procedures. Physiological measures may be useful to further dissociate sensory-perceptual deficits from other issues, such as social disinhibition or emotion regulation difficulties. One study (Corona, Dissanayake, Arbelle, Wellington, & Sigman, 1998) found that heightened physiological arousal, often associated with sensory aversion, was not a sufficient explanation for social withdrawal in school-aged children with autism. Rather, these children failed to understand the meaning of social-communicative encounters, which may lead to withdrawal from peers.

Some researchers (e.g., Talay-Ongan & Wood, 2000) hypothesize that aberrant sensory features inhibit normal attachment and social learning processes, such as the construction of mental states. Stella (2001) found that early sensory features predicted later functional object play in young children with autism. Moreover, other studies (Baranek, 1999a; Dahlgren & Gillberg, 1989; Dawson, Osterling, Meltzoff, & Kuhl, 2000) suggest that in some cases, unusual sensory responses precede symptoms traditionally viewed as core features of autism. Basic orienting to sensory stimuli is an important prerequisite to joint attention and other aspects of social-communication that are deficient in autism.

Several theoretical models of autism (e.g., Loveland, 2001; Mundy & Neal, 2001; Waterhouse, Fein, & Modahl, 1996), posit that impairments in one developing system may have secondary consequences in later-developing systems, but it is difficult to sort out the nature of these transactional relationships. For example, although it is possible that altered sensory experiences (e.g., tactile defensiveness) may exacerbate social withdrawal, it is equally plausible that social-cognitive deficits (e.g., lack of social referencing or joint attention) interfere with interpretation of sensory experiences or perception of environmental affordances. Moreover, cooccurring deficits in social and nonsocial domains may reciprocally influence each other over time (E. Williams, Costall, & Reddy, 1999). More studies systematically investigating the developmental relationships of sensory features to core features of autism are needed.

Specificity of Deficits

Unusual sensory symptoms are associated with a variety of clinical diagnoses, including various types of developmental disabilities (Baranek et al., 2002; Ermer & Dunn, 1998; S. J. Rogers, Hepburn, & Wehner, 2003); thus, the uniqueness of sensory features to autism is questioned by some researchers (e.g., Stone & Hogan, 1993). This issue of specificity can be answered definitively only through studies utilizing appropriate developmental controls to sort out sensory characteristics uniquely associated with autism from those generally associated with mental retardation, which cooccurs in approximately 80% of this population.

Preliminary findings by Baranek and colleagues (Baranek, David, Poe, Stone, & Watson, 2004; McGuire, Barnett, Baranek, & Suratt, 2001), using both parent report and observational measures, have suggested that levels of hyperresponsiveness to sensory stimuli may be similar across developmentally delayed groups, whereas hyporesponsiveness may be more characteristic of autism. Two studies (Lord, 1995; S. J. Rogers, Hepburn, & Wehner, 2003) found that parents endorsed specific sensory symptoms at a significantly higher rate for preschoolers with autism than for those with nonspecific developmental delays. On the contrary, Stone and colleagues, using the *Parent Interview for Autism* (Stone & Hogan, 1993), did not find significant differences between autism and developmental delay with respect to sensory responses overall. Studies utilizing only typical comparisons (Kientz & Dunn, 1997; Ornitz, 1987; Talay-Ongan & Wood, 2000; Watling, Deitz, & White, 2001) overwhelmingly endorse higher rates of unusual sensory features across categories in preschool and school-aged children with autism.

Developmental Course

A developmental perspective is critical to understanding processes that underlie the various phenotypic expressions of autism (Bailey, Phillips, & Rutter, 1996). The developmental nature of sensory features are rarely studied in autism, however, and researchers disagree about the age at which unusual sensory features first appear (Baranek, 1999a; Stone & Hogan, 1993), and whether symptoms increase (Talay-Ongan & Wood, 2000) or decrease (Baranek et al., 2002; Baranek, Foster, & Berkson, 1997a) with age. Discrepant findings may reflect differences in age of samples and methods used.

Several studies (Dahlgren & Gillberg, 1989; Gillberg et al., 1990; Hoshino et al., 1982; Ohta, Nagai, Hara, & Sasaki, 1987; Ornitz et al., 1977) found that parents retrospectively report unusual sensory features in their children during their early development. Consistent with these reports, several observational studies using retrospective video analysis (Adrien et al., 1991, 1992; Baranek, 1999a) and one prospective case report (Dawson et al., 2000) provide preliminary evidence that subtle sensory symptoms of autism are present during infancy, even before parents become aware of developmental problems. Among the unusual sensory features noted in these studies were over/under-reactions

to sound, failure to orient to visual stimuli, self-stimulation, gaze aversion, and touch aversion.

Evidence from a few studies using observational methods suggests negative correlations between a person's developmental age and their levels of various sensory symptoms (Baranek & Berkson, 1994; Baranek et al., 2002). Caregiver report methods elicit somewhat mixed findings. For example, S. J. Rogers, Hepburn, and Wehner (2003) found no significant correlations between sensory reactivity and mental age in young children with various developmental disorders (including autism). In a cross-sectional study of children with autism from 4 to 14 years in age and those with typical development Talay-Ongan and Wood (2000) found that reports of sensory symptoms were higher in older children. In contrast, Baranek and colleagues (1997a) found that hyperresponsiveness to sound was more prominent in children than adult participants with developmental disorders including autism.

Studies based solely on parental perceptions of the child's sensory symptoms may pose a variety of confounding factors that need to be considered. For example, parents are less inclined to endorse items reflecting unusual behaviors before the child's diagnosis is confirmed (Stone & Hogan, 1993), and parents may underestimate the degree to which sensory problems affect their children (Nader et al., 2004; Parush, Doryon, & Katz, 1996). The likelihood of underestimating negative effects of sensory experiences appears greatest for young children, those who are less competent verbally, and those who have fewer cognitive resources to cope with stressful experiences.

Motor Features

Motor deficits appear to be present in at least a subgroup of children and adults with autistic disorders. Conceptually, motor symptoms in autism can be divided into voluntary and involuntary movement disorders. The existence of deficits in voluntary, goal-directed motor actions has been addressed from the standpoint of motor praxis, which involves the ability to conceptualize, plan, and execute voluntary, goal-directed actions. The existence of abnormal, involuntary movements has been addressed from the standpoint of movement disorders, which involve identification of seemingly involuntary, purposeless, or extraneous movements. Clearly, it is difficult to tell whether the motor actions of persons with autism are intentional, and a clear distinction between voluntary and involuntary actions may not always be possible. Furthermore, although conceptually distinct, voluntary and involuntary motor features in autism may share common etiologies and pathophysiologies. From a clinical standpoint, however, it is useful to distinguish these deficits to insure that both forms of motor deficit are addressed when present. For this reason, we have included a summary of the research findings and the assessment and treatment implications for both of these areas of motor deficit.

Voluntary Movements/Praxis

A variety of motoric challenges involve praxis, challenges such as learning how to handle tools, imitating novel movements of others, participating in sports, and exploring new environments. Praxis entails ideation (conceptualizing what to do), as well as motor planning (organizing a plan of action in time and space), and requires problem solving in order to move in a novel manner, as opposed to a familiar, previously practiced motor pattern (Ayres, 1985). Ideation has not been studied systematically in autism; however, clinical observations suggest that this is an area of difficulty (Trecker, 2001). Motor planning has been studied in more depth.

A commonly held, but not well substantiated, belief about individuals with autism is that their motor skills tend to be high, in contrast with low social and communication skills. Evidence for motor strengths comes primarily from studies employing simple, familiar tasks that are likely to have been practiced frequently, and thus may not place much, if any, demand on praxis (DeMyer, Barton, & Norton, 1972; Klin, Volkmar, & Sparrow, 1992; Stone, Ousley, Hepburn, Hogan, & Brown, 1999). For example, DeMyer and colleagues found that both low and high functioning children with autism had strengths in repetitive gross motor skills that are commonly encountered in everyday life (e.g., stair climbing). These researchers also reported strengths in visual-motor tasks (i.e., form-

boards), in contrast to relatively low skills in imitation of upper body movements and complex ball play. Interestingly, DeMyer and her colleagues were the first to suggest that autism involved a form of apraxia.

Several well designed studies document praxis deficits (i.e., problems with complex and novel motor tasks) in children with high functioning autism relative to typically developing controls. Specifically, difficulties are noted with performance on grooved pegboard tasks (Minshew, Goldstein, & Siegel, 1997; Smith & Bryson, 1998) as well as specific tests of apraxia, balance, gait, and repetitive thumb-finger opposition (Weimer, Schatz, Lincoln, Ballantyne, & Trauer, 2001). Parham, Mailloux, and Roley (2000) found that all performance on all praxis tests on the *Sensory Integration and Praxis Tests* (Ayres, 1989) was problematic for children with autism relative to matched controls, however, tasks involving imitation of nonsymbolic body positions and movement sequences (e.g., oral praxis) were exceptionally low relative to normative scores.

Researchers who utilized standardized motor tests that challenge praxis have detected problems in some persons with autism, relative to normative data. Manjiviona and Prior (1995), using the *Test of Motor Impairment* (Stott, Moyes, & Henderson, 1972), found that 50% of their sample of children with Asperger Disorder, and 67% of those with Autistic Disorder (high functioning), had clinically significant gross and fine motor impairments. Similarly, Ghaziuddin and Butler (1998) administered the *Bruininks-Oseretsky Test of Motor Performance* (Bruininks, 1978) to children with autism and found that they manifested significant coordination deficits as compared to the normative data. Those with a cognitive advantage (Asperger Disorder group) outperformed the other groups (Autistic Disorder; Pervasive Developmental Disorder, Not Otherwise Specified; PDDNOS); however, between-group differences disappeared when intelligence was statistically controlled.

Although studies of complex motor performance and imitation suggest that praxis is an area of difficulty for individuals with autism, they do not shed light on which of the many complex processes that contribute to praxis are specifically affected in autism. A few researchers have begun to examine specific aspects of motor performance, such as establishing a motor pattern with practice, changing a motor pattern in response to sensory cues, timing and sequencing a movement, inhibiting an action, or using sensory information to guide movement. Ozonoff and Strayer (1997) examined the ability to inhibit a previously useful motor response strategy when an auditory signal was given at unpredictable times. They found no differences between children with autism (without mental retardation) and typically developing controls matched for age and IQ. The study concluded that motor inhibition appears to be intact. Hughes (1996) utilized a "reach, grasp, and place" task to evaluate anticipation and adaptation of grasp patterns, concluding that high-functioning children with autism had a deficit in motor planning that may be the result of a problem in sequencing actions, a failure to predict the consequences of movement, or impaired visual control of movement. Rinehart, Bradshaw, Brereton, and Tonge (2001) showed that individuals with autism (high functioning) had deficits in preparing for action, but performed normally once execution of the movement began.

Imitation of actions and body positions is the most studied aspect of praxis in autism (Smith & Bryson, 1994). (See Chapter 14 on imitation and play in this *Handbook,* Volume 1.) Over the past decade, experimental research has provided convincing evidence that the imitation problems in autism are not the result of a fundamental difficulty with abstraction of meaning of actions (Hughes & Russell, 1993; S. J. Rogers, Bennetto, McEvoy, & Pennington, 1996; Stone, Ousley, & Littleford, 1997). Some researchers (DeMyer, Alpern, et al., 1972; Stone et al., 1997) have found that imitation of body movements is more impaired than object imitation skill in young children with autism. Thus, generating or using internal somatosensory representations of visually modeled actions is more difficult than reproducing actions that provide ongoing visual cues. Moreover, descriptive reports also suggest that oral praxis problems may be highly prevalent among individuals with autism (Adams, 1998; Page & Boucher, 1998; Parham et al., 2000). Such findings are consistent with speculations that a pro-

prioceptive deficit may be central to praxis difficulties (Weimer et al., 2001). In light of intriguing discoveries of cranial nerve and facial nucleus deficits in the brain stems of individuals with autism (Rodier, Ingram, Tisdale, Nelson, & Romano, 1996), these findings warrant further exploration.

Relationship to Core Features

Praxis issues are likely intertwined with the disturbances in social relatedness, communication, and stereotyped behavior that are the defining features of autism, but there is little research in this area. Currently, much attention is being given to the possibility that imitation deficits interfere with the early development of intersubjectivity, and lead to the emergence of communication disturbances in children with autism (Gopnik & Meltzoff, 1993; Hobson & Lee, 1999; S. J. Rogers & Pennington, 1991). Building on a growing body of developmental theory on intersubjectivity (Hatfield, Cacioppo, & Rapson, 1994; Stern, 1985), S. J. Rogers and Bennetto (2000) suggested that social relatedness involves interpersonal synchrony of bodies, voices, movements, facial expressions, and emotional states, and that the severe deficits in praxis and imitation experienced by individuals with autism could seriously undermine their emotional connectedness with others because of impaired physical synchronization during social exchanges.

In addition to social relatedness, other aspects of speech and language may be adversely affected by the praxis difficulties of individuals with autism. Although the reasons for the hypothesized linkage between praxis and language are not clear, some researchers have hypothesized a common underlying origin, such as a deficit in executive functions or in concept formation (Ayres, 1985). Two studies (Sigman & Ungerer, 1984; Stone et al., 1997) have reported a predictive relationship between early motor imitation and later language. Furthermore, S. J. Rogers and Bennetto (2000) suggested that underlying oral-motor dyspraxia (i.e., difficulty with sequencing and timing of oral movements) might account for the lack of expressive speech development in some children with autism. A study by Seal and Bonvillian (1997) found that sign vocabulary was significantly related to both fine motor and praxis test scores, suggesting motor planning ability is important in the acquisition of sign language by individuals with autism who use such augmentative systems.

Although it is plausible that deficits in ideational praxis contribute to the stereotyped patterns of behavior and limited play repertoire that are hallmarks of autism, few researchers have explored this notion. One study by Pierce and Courchesne (2001) demonstrated that children with autism in a novel environment demonstrated less exploration of novel objects and significantly more stereotyped/repetitive movement than typically developing children, although overall amount of physical activity (as in moving about the room) was similar between groups.

Specificity of Deficits

Difficulties with motor planning are often described in children with a variety of nonautistic developmental conditions, such as Developmental Coordination Disorder, Attention Deficit Hyperactivity Disorder, and nonspecific developmental delays. Therefore, questions arise as to whether some kinds of praxis problems are specific to autism (Pennington & Ozonoff, 1996).

Considerable evidence also points to a motor imitation deficit that is specific to autism, although the types of imitation tasks that discriminate autism from other disabilities differ across developmental age groups (S. J. Rogers & Bennetto, 2000; S. J. Rogers, Hepburn, Stackhouse, & Wehner, 2003; Smith & Bryson, 1994; Stone et al., 1997). Imitation skills related to oral-facial praxis appear particularly impaired in toddlers with autism, compared to controls with fragile X syndrome, other developmental disorders, and no disability; whereas praxis tasks that involve spontaneous object manipulations (without imitation) and standardized measures of fine and gross motor skills do not differentiate these same groups (S. J. Rogers, Hepburn, Stackhouse, et al., 2003). Rogers and her colleagues (S. J. Rogers et al., 1996) similarly identified deficits in imitation that could not be explained by visual recognition memory or motor execution problems Also, these deficits were specific to children with autism as compared to mental-age matched children with a variety of learning disabilities.

Beyond imitation, few researchers have examined complex, novel motor tasks as a potential area of impairment that is specific to autism. Limited evidence suggests that a basic deficit in ability to self-monitor simple actions is not specific to autism (Russell & Hill, 2001), but disturbances in anticipation and sequencing of movements could be unique to autism (Hughes, 1996).

Developmental Course

The possibility that motor imitation deficits may be an early indicator of autism is supported by several controlled studies. Stone and colleagues (1997) found that both body and object imitation skills improved from age 2 to 3 years, and that early imitation of body movements was predictive of later expressive language skills, while early object imitation was predictive of later play skills. Similarly, Charman and colleagues (1997) concluded from several cross-sectional investigations that children with autism improve between early childhood and school age on simple imitation tasks. However, research has not addressed whether or not children with autism ever "catch up" (i.e., perform comparably to typical peers).

With respect to more global aspects of voluntary movement development, some motor differences may be apparent in infants with autism. Using a well-controlled retrospective analysis of home videos, Baranek (1999a) found that the only prominent motor feature (of those she studied) in the autism group at 9 to 12 months of age was excessive mouthing of objects. Although other motor movements (e.g., repetitive arm, leg, or torso movements) and object manipulations (e.g., twiddling, banging) did not specifically differentiate the groups, both the infants with autism and those with developmental delays demonstrated unusual motor posturing that was negligible in the typical children. Several descriptive reports (e.g., Dawson et al., 2000; Ornitz et al., 1977; Teitelbaum, Teitelbaum, Nye, Fryman, & Maurer, 1998) also endorse unusual motor aspects during early infancy and note that symptoms worsen with time; however, longitudinal methods and systematic comparisons with other clinical groups are needed to provide more definitive conclusions. Future studies are also needed to investigate developmental trajectories of specific aspects of praxis (i.e., sequencing of goal-directed actions) within a variety of contexts.

Involuntary Movements

A variety of abnormal involuntary movements may occur in children and adults with autism (Leary & Hill, 1996; Wing, 1997). The presence of involuntary movements can contribute to the overall morbidity of autism; yet these features often go undetected in the routine clinical settings where autism is assessed and treated (Baron-Cohen, Scahill, Izaguirre, Hornsey, & Robertson, 1999; Leary & Hill, 1996; Lewis & Bodfish, 1998; Realmuto & Main, 1982; Wing, 1997). Abnormal involuntary movements are observable movements that are not under voluntary control and that occur in the context of a recognized neurological or psychiatric disease. There are many discrete types of abnormal involuntary movements; the discrete types can often cooccur; the resultant movements can occur in any effector system; and the occurrence of involuntary movements often follows a "waxing and waning" course of variable expression over time (Marsden, 1984). All these factors make clinical assessment and differential diagnosis difficult. These tasks are even more difficult in the context of autism as the variety of apparently voluntary motor behaviors or odd mannerisms that are part of the repetitive behavior domain of autism can further complicate the task of differential diagnosis of motor features (Lewis & Bodfish, 1998; Meiselas et al., 1989). A distinction can be made between spontaneous (idiopathic) involuntary movements (movements that arise as a natural part of the disease process) and medication-induced (iatrogenic) involuntary movements (movements that arise as a consequence of medication treatment and/or the withdrawal of medication treatment (Simpson & Angus, 1970). This distinction is important because medications that can produce involuntary movements are commonly used in the treatment of autism. In fact, the two most frequently used psychotropic medications for persons with autism are antipsychotics (dopamine-blocking agents) and serotonergic antidepressants (serotonin reuptake inhibitors). Both can produce involuntary movement disor-

ders in a significant minority of persons who receive these medications (Langworthy-Lam, Aman, & Van Bourgondien, 2002). It should be noted that relative to other primary and associated features of autism, movement disorders have received little empirical study to date.

Data from a combination of published case reports and empirical studies have demonstrated that a set of abnormal involuntary movements— tics, catatonia, dyskinesia, akathisia, bradykinesia, gait/posture abnormalities—appear with sufficient frequency in autism to warrant clinical attention. Several studies have reported the occurrence of motor and/or vocal tics in both children and adults with autism spectrum disorders, with a range in prevalence from 6% to 20% across studies (Baron-Cohen et al., 1999; Burd, Fisher, Kerbeshian, & Arnold, 1987; Comings & Comings, 1991; Realmuto & Main, 1982; Ringman & Jankovic, 2000). Obtained prevalence estimates for tic disorder appear related to the variety of assessment methods used across studies, because lower prevalence rates are reported when standardized tic assessment procedures are used and when strict diagnostic criteria for Tourette Syndrome are applied (i.e., cooccurrence of motor and vocal tics). For example, Baron-Cohen and colleagues (1999) assessed 447 children with autism and found that none had existing chart diagnoses of tic disorder, 151 (34%) had either motor or vocal tics based on clinical observation, and 32 (7%) met criteria for Tourette Syndrome (using clinical observation, results from the *Yale Global Tic Severity Scale,* Leckman et al., 1989, and *DSM-IV* criteria for Tourette Syndrome).

Several published reports (Damasio & Maurer, 1978; Realmuto & August, 1991; Wing, 1996; Wing & Shah, 2000) have documented the occurrence of catatonia or catatonia-like symptoms in children and adolescents with autism. Catatonia refers to a cluster of behavioral features (Joseph, 1992) including absence of speech (mutism), absence of movement (akinesia), and maintenance of imposed postures (catalepsy). Wing and Shah administered a conceptually derived semi-structured interview for catatonic features to the caregivers for a clinical population of 506 children with autistic spectrum disorders and found that 30 children (6%) met criteria for clinically significant catatonia.

Published reports (Bodfish, Symons, Parker, & Lewis, 2000; Campbell et al., 1990; Meiselas et al., 1989; Shay, Sanchez, Cueva, & Armenteros, 1993) have documented that both spontaneous dyskinesia and medication-induced dyskinesia can occur in a significant subgroup of children and adults with autism. In a study of the prevalence of spontaneous dyskinesia measured using a standardized movement disorder examination procedure, Bodfish and colleagues (2000) found that 10% of a sample of 32 adults with autism displayed clinically significant levels of dyskinesia. In a study of the prevalence of medication-induced dyskinesia, Campbell and colleagues found that 27% of a sample of 104 children with autism developed significant dyskinesia either during treatment with the traditional antipsychotic haloperidol (5%) or following withdrawal of haloperidol (22%). The significant increase in occurrence of dyskinesia following antipsychotic withdrawal mirrors that seen in other clinical groups and points to the potential for dyskinesias to be "masked" by antipsychotic treatment. Newer generation "atypical" antipsychotics that are associated with less drug-induced dyskinesia have been shown to be effective for treatment of behavioral disturbances in autism (McCracken et al., 2002). At this time, however, there are no data on the incidence of dyskinesia in autism following withdrawal of atypical antipsychotic agents.

Akathisia is a syndrome of involuntary motor fidgeting often accompanied by a subjective feeling of anxiety and restlessness (Sachdev, 1995). Brasic and colleagues (1994) reported the occurrence of akathisia in children with autism, and Bodfish and colleagues (2000) reported that 23% of a sample of adults with autism exhibited spontaneous akathisia on a formal exam. Bradykinesia generally refers to the slowing of movements as seen in Parkinson's disease, but is also refers to a delay in initiating, changing, or arresting movements. The occurrence of bradykinesia has been reported in case studies (DeMyer, 1976; Maurer & Damasio, 1982) and in kinematic studies of movement (Vilensky, Damasio, & Maurer, 1981) in children with autism. Gait and postural abnormalities similar to those seen in Parkinson's disease have also been reported (Gepner & Mestre, 2002; Hallett et al., 1993; Kohen-Raz et al.,

1992; Vilensky et al., 1981). Importantly, these studies of posture and gait used quantitative kinematic motion analysis techniques to identify movement disturbances in autism relative to clinical comparison groups. Such findings are more reliable than those from earlier studies, which typically used qualitative clinical observation techniques to characterize movement disorders.

Relation to Core Features

The association of the presence of involuntary movement disorders to core autistic symptomatology has not been rigorously studied using contemporary measures of the triad of core features (e.g., ADI-R domain scores). However, less formal evidence of linkage to primary features has been made within some of the discrete types of involuntary movement disorders seen in autism. Tics (Bodfish et al., 2000; Ringman & Jankovic, 2000; Wing & Shah, 2000), dyskinesia (Bodfish et al., 2000; Campbell et al., 1990), and akathisia (Bodfish et al., 2000) have each been shown to be positively related to restricted, repetitive behaviors in autism. In particular, the occurrence of these movement disorders is associated with an increased occurrence of lower-level repetitive behaviors such as stereotyped body and object movements, repetitive self-injurious behaviors, and compulsive behaviors. Overall severity of autism has not been found to be related to the severity of tics, catatonia, dyskinesia, or akathisia. By inference, then, it appears that involuntary movement disorders in autism are more related to repetitive behavior deficits than to social-communicative deficits (Lewis & Bodfish, 1998). Although a variety of voluntary motor deficits are associated with autism, no studies have examined the relation of involuntary movement disorders to deficits in voluntary movements (i.e., praxis) in this population.

Specificity of Deficits

Few studies have examined the specificity of the pattern of involuntary movement disorders seen in autism with respect to other neurodevelopmental disorders. Bodfish and colleagues (2000) compared samples of adults with autism and comorbid mental retardation to adults with nonspecific mental retardation (without autism) using standardized measures of tics, dyskinesia, and akathisia and found no differences between the samples on either the prevalence or the severity of these movement disorders. In line with these findings, other researchers have shown that the occurrence of dyskinesias (Campbell & colleagues, 1990), and the occurrence of gait abnormalities (Vilensky et al., 1981) is negatively related to IQ in children with autism, and the occurrence of catatonia is more likely among individuals with autism and comorbid mental retardation (Wing & Shah, 2000).

Developmental Course

Few studies have examined age-related differences in the expression of involuntary movement disorders in autism. None of the studies reviewed earlier found age to be significantly related to the expression of tics, dyskinesia, akathisia, or postural abnormalities. Vilensky and colleagues (1981) reported that gait disturbances improved with age in children with autism. In contrast, the occurrence of catatonia was found to be more likely in older (> 15 years) than younger (1 to 14 years) children with autism.

CLINICAL ASSESSMENT OF SENSORY AND MOTOR FEATURES

Inclusion of sensory and motor assessments may facilitate differential diagnosis, eligibility for services, or intervention planning for a given individual with autism. The assessment of sensory and motor features necessarily varies with the purpose for the evaluation, and specific assessment procedures depend to some extent on context (e.g., home, school, work environment, clinic). A variety of health and educational professionals (e.g., physicians, occupational therapists, physical therapists, psychologists, audiologists, speech and language pathologists, special educators) may take part in assessment of sensory and motor features in persons with autism. Initial assessment for diagnosis and/or intervention planning typically involves a mulitdisciplinary team, although specialists can also be called in for individual consultations as needs arise. A thorough understanding of the nature of autism, and experience with making test ac-

commodations for persons with a range of developmental functioning levels, are critical across disciplines.

Typically, physicians (e.g., neurologists or psychiatrists) perform neurodevelopmental examinations or assess specific neurological concerns, such as loss of motor functions, seizures, or psychopharmacological side effects. Ophthalmologists or optometrists conduct vision evaluations, whereas audiologists perform hearing evaluations—both are critical for differential diagnosis of unusual sensory and motor features and both have treatment implications. Psychologists may evaluate motor skills in the context of differential diagnosis through developmental or adaptive behavior scales, and in the context of functional analysis of stereotyped and repetitive behaviors. Occupational therapists and physical therapists are integral to a mulitdisciplinary evaluation team, especially when sensory or motor features interfere with a client's health or participation. Physical therapists assess motor skills, strength, gait, coordination, balance, and other components of posture and movement, as well as the need for physical accommodations in the community. Occupational therapists assess the impact of sensory features and motor difficulties in the context of meaningful daily life activities or occupations such as play, leisure, self-care, productive work, or socialization. A comprehensive occupational therapy assessment includes an evaluation of task and environmental features that interact with the client's intrinsic capabilities and may facilitate or inhibit participation. Speech-language pathologists have expertise to evaluate aspects of motor control (e.g., oral praxis; gesture use) that affect social communication. The following section specifically outlines a framework for assessment that guides intervention planning and summarizes state-of-the-art tools available for assessing various sensory and motor features of autism.

Assessment Framework Guiding Interventions

Existing research indicates that many individuals with autism are likely to experience difficulties with sensory and motor functions at some point in their lives. However, contemporary systems for studying disabilities, such as the International Classification of Functioning, Disability, and Health (ICF; World Health Organization [WHO], 2001), acknowledge that specific impairments that are intrinsic to the person, such as sensory or motor deficits, may not always have a direct correspondence with social participation and quality of life. Thus, a full assessment of an individual's health or disability status ideally addresses various dynamic components (i.e., body functions/structures, activities, participation, environmental factors, and personal factors). Although these components interact, a problem in one component does not necessarily imply a problem in another component. For example, one may have a body function impairment without having a limitation in participation (as when a person with a hearing impairment participates fully at her workplace); or one may experience difficulties in social participation without impairments or activity limitations (as when a person with a history of mental health problems faces social barriers due to stigma). Similarly, improvement in one component does not necessarily lead to improvement in another.

An assessment approach that dovetails well with this framework is the top-down model (Coster, 1998), in which evaluation begins with an inquiry into the most global level of assessment (i.e., social participation), then systematically addresses increasingly more specific aspects of engagement (i.e., activities and tasks), followed by evaluation of specific impairments (e.g., sensory or motor deficits). At each of these levels, the evaluator considers the influences of environmental opportunities and barriers (e.g., availability of programs in which the individual might participate), as well as personal background characteristics (e.g., cultural heritage). If we apply the top-down model to the sensory and motor assessment of individuals with autism, we begin with assessment of what matters most: the extent to which the person is able to participate in a lifestyle that meets individual needs and goals while simultaneously meeting societal expectations. This step includes identifying contextual obstacles and assets that are relevant to the person's lifestyle issues. The next step is to identify the tasks and activities that the individual is expected to do

and wants to do in his or her everyday environment, to evaluate how successfully the person is performing those activities, and to consider the general extent to which sensory and motor issues may be implicated. At this level, clinicians carefully assess contextual elements again. For example, they consider the environments in which the child is most and least successful in performing important tasks. They reflect on why the child may perform tasks with varying degrees of success across varying environmental contexts. Finally, assessment would turn to evaluation of specific sensory and motor abilities and impairments that are judged to have potential bearing on the task, activity, and participation difficulties that were previously identified.

Of course, most developed tests and evaluation procedures aim at this last layer of assessment—that is, specific impairments. Very few formal assessment tools focus on task/activity performance, participation, or context. In the future, test developers must devote more attention to these dimensions of functioning. Yet even without formal evaluation instruments, these dimensions should be important concerns in clinical assessment. Ultimately, considerations at the level of social participation should drive decision making with regard to priorities for both clinical assessment and intervention. We now turn our attention to assessments of specific sensory and motor functions.

Assessment of Sensory Features

Although most individuals with autism have adequate hearing and vision, qualified personnel should assess these functions. Any concerns should be resolved before evaluating other aspects of sensory processing. Vision and hearing evaluations depend upon the nature of the referral concerns, age, and level of cooperation of a client with autism (Filipek et al., 2000). Differential diagnosis of specific visual impairments in persons with autism can be difficult. Concerns about functional vision at any point in development should be referred for expert evaluation by a licensed optometrist or ophthalmologist, so that appropriate accommodations (e.g., prescription lenses) can be made. Vision evaluations may include tests for visual acuity, as well as ocular alignment, refractive error, stereopsis, and ocular diseases, if indicated. The Cardiff Acuity Test (Woodhouse, Adoh, & Oduwaiye, 1992), with vanishing optotypes, is an engaging screening tool designed for young children, but can also be used successfully with older nonverbal individuals, including those with autism (Adoh, Woodhouse, & Oduwaiye, 1992).

Hearing assessments conducted by licensed audiologists may be behavioral (e.g., behavioral observation audiometry, visual reinforcement audiometry, conditioned play audiometry) or electrophysiological (e.g., evoked otoacoustic emissions; auditory brainstem response). Because pediatric health care is moving toward universal newborn hearing screening, caregivers can identify and treat congenital hearing loss early. However, any concerns of hearing problems across the lifespan should alert professionals to the need for re-evaluation.

Assessments of sensory features are broadly defined as instruments or methods used to characterize unusual sensory symptoms or to evaluate aspects of sensory processing (e.g., modulation, discrimination, or integration functions) that are not the result of visual or hearing impairments per se. Assessing sensory features in the context of the person's everyday activities and in relation to their referral concerns/goals is ideal for intervention planning. This is best performed through multiple and direct observations of responses to various sensory experiences in the actual settings where such problems are reported and through documentation of the pattern with which these behavioral responses occur across time and situations. A comprehensive assessment begins with a systematic analysis of the person interacting with a specific task (e.g., eating a meal, playing with toys) in a natural environment (e.g., home, school, playground, or work) that involves caregivers and/or peers appropriate to the social context. This type of dynamic performance analysis produces a profile of the individual's strengths and weaknesses, as well as task and environmental features that support or hinder participation. Such an evaluation affords rich observations to inform intervention strategies. Currently, there are no standardized evaluations of this nature for any clinical population. For this reason, therapists depend heavily upon skilled clinical ob-

servations and analysis of sensory tasks (see Dunn, 2000). Preliminary attempts to design criterion-referenced checklists are in progress (e.g., School Assessment of Sensory Integration; Kuhaneck, Henry, & Glennon, 2003). Although such tools are not designed specifically for autism, they may be helpful to analyze sensory characteristics of tasks, both positive and negative, that impact on performance.

In many clinical and research situations, standardized norm-referenced assessments are preferred because they can be selected and interpreted on the basis of their psychometric characteristics, but few of these exist for measuring features in special populations such as autism. Likewise, standardized assessments that are conducted outside of the natural environment or that rely solely on contrived tasks may produce diagnostic findings, but their validity to real-life contexts may be limited. Assessments are sometimes conducted in clinical settings out of necessity (e.g., limited time, insurance coverage) or for purposes other than intervention planning (e.g., monitoring progress of specific functions, descriptive research). Thus, the balance of reliability and validity of the assessment may need to be reconciled on an individual basis. Supplementing standardized assessments with ecologically valid client and family interviews, reviewing videotapes of actual situations, or utilizing tasks that simulate natural conditions may increase the validity of the assessment process through convergence of sources and formats. Likewise, using observational measures in tandem with questionnaire data increases the reliability of findings. Various tools for evaluating sensory features are described later, grouped in categories reflecting two general formats (i.e., questionnaires and observational measures). It is important to note that although many of these assessments are designed to measure sensory functions, test items invariably require some type of behavioral or motoric response (e.g., pointing, looking, verbalizing), thus severe motor deficits may preclude accurate interpretation of test results.

Questionnaires and Structured Interviews

A comprehensive assessment of sensory features typically obtains an inventory of sensory experiences. The assessment may use either an interview or a checklist to document patterns of response across all sensory modalities (i.e., tactile, auditory, visual, olfactory, gustatory, proprioceptive and vestibular) that occur during routine activities (e.g., bathing/grooming, play, meals, school/work) and with temporal variation (e.g., morning, night). Usually, a caregiver (e.g., parent or teacher) serves as the informant for a child or for an adult with autism who is not able to respond for him- or herself. Some questionnaires can be modified as structured interviews if a caregiver cannot complete the form independently. Although there are numerous questionnaires available, many lack extensive psychometric development, and few were designed specifically for use with persons with autism. The following four caregiver report instruments (presented alphabetically) warrant more detailed description.

The *Evaluation of Sensory Processing* (ESP; Parham & Ecker, 2002) was developed for use with children ages 2 to 12 years that are suspected of having sensory processing difficulties, not specific to autism. It contains 76 items scored on a 5-point Likert scale indicating frequency of unusual responses across sensory modalities. The ESP has good internal consistency for 5 of its 6 sensory categories, acceptable interrater reliability, and evidence of validity with autism and other developmental disorders.

The *Sensory Experiences Questionnaire* (SEQ; Baranek, 1999b), formerly known as the *Sensory Supplement Questionnaire,* is a brief (35-item) assessment developed specifically for children with autism and other developmental disorders, ages 6 months through 6 years. The SEQ inquires about the frequency of unusual sensory experiences across modalities and parses out hypo- and hyperresponsive patterns to both social and nonsocial sensory stimuli. In addition, this scale also qualitatively documents intervening strategies used by caregivers that may be helpful for planning treatment. Preliminary studies (Baranek et al., 2004) indicate good internal consistency, test-retest reliability, and discriminant validity between autism and other developmental disorders.

The *Sensory Sensitivity Questionnaire-Revised* (Talay-Ongan & Wood, 2000) uses a yes/no format to inquire about hypo- and hypersensitivities across a variety of sensory

domains for a total of 54 items. Anecdotal comments made by parents are also recorded. The instrument was piloted with 30 children with autism and 30 typically developing peers, aged 4 to 14 years.

The *Sensory Profile* (Dunn, 1999), normed on a large sample of typically developing children aged 3 to 10 years, is a 125-item caregiver questionnaire that uses a 5-point Likert scale. It inquires about reactions to various sensory situations, as well as some behavioral and emotional consequences of sensory reactivity. Internal consistency ranged from .47 to .91, depending on the category. Psychometrics appear stronger for older age groups, since sample sizes were small for 3- to 5-year-olds. Infant/toddler and adolescent/adult versions, and a short form of the Sensory Profile are also available. Two studies (Kientz & Dunn, 1997; Watling et al., 2001) reported that the scales discriminated children with autism from typically developing children, and one study (S. J. Rogers, Hepburn, & Wehner, 2003) demonstrated discrimination between autism and nonspecific developmental delays.

Observational Assessments

Observations of sensory processing can be obtained formally or informally. Observations used for intervention planning should be comprehensive enough to provide a profile of strengths and weakness of the individual across a variety of sensory experiences that have direct application to daily life. Describing both quality (i.e., patterns of response) and stability (i.e., consistency) of performance is critical, because temporal fluctuations in response to sensory stimuli are common. Likewise, an analysis of sensory preferences or avoidances may be particularly useful for treatment planning. Assessment of sensory features for research purposes is often more focused in scope and relies heavily on systematic quantification of specific functions through standardized protocols. A variety of observational measures are available for testing specific sensory features or processes, but few were developed or field-tested for persons with autism. Adaptations, such as augmenting directions with visual cues or providing incentives for motivation, are often needed with this population to increase successful performance; however, it is critical to note that such adaptations to standardized procedures threaten the validity of the results and increase subjectivity in clinical interpretations. Likewise, none of these assessments are appropriate for children with significant motor impairments that limit manipulation of test items.

The *Sensory Integration and Praxis Tests* (SIPT; Ayres, 1989) have undergone more extensive standardization than other similar tests of sensory integration functions. However, they were designed to discriminate normal from dysfunctional sensory processes (e.g., kinesthesia, vestibular functions) in children ages 4.0 to 8.11 years with mild learning or behavioral concerns. They are less appropriate for children with autism who also have significant cognitive impairments. There is no provision for quantifying clinical observations of sensory modulation (i.e., hypo- or hyperresponsiveness). The cost and administration time for the full SIPT poses additional constraints in some clinical settings. Although widely available neuropsychological batteries (e.g., *Luria-Nebraska Neuropsychological Battery;* Golden, Purisch, & Hammeke, 1991) contain some tests tapping somatosensory functions, these may not be sensitive to the subtle problems experienced by persons with autism. *The Leiter International Performance Scale-Revised* (Roid & Miller, 1997), a nonverbal test of intelligence, includes a few sensory reactivity items in its social-emotional rating scales, which may be useful as a cursory screening. The *Miller Assessment for Preschoolers* (MAP; Miller, 1982), a standardized screening test (currently under revision) for children with mild developmental concerns, ages 2.9 through 5.8 years, includes a few relevant subtests tapping somatosensory functions (e.g., finger localization, stereognosis).

Two observational measures are currently under development for children with autism and related developmental disorders. The *Sensory Processing Assessment* (SPA; Baranek, 1999c) is a 20-minute behavioral test designed for ages 9 months through 6 years. It uses a semistructured play-based format to assess approach-avoidance patterns with sensory toys, orienting responses to social and nonsocial sensory stimuli, and habituation to repeated stimuli. The *Tactile Defensiveness and Discrimination Test-Revised* (TDDT-R; Baranek,

1998) assesses tactile processing in preschool and school-aged children. The five subtests are administered in a gamelike fashion to maximize engagement and to limit frustration.

A variety of well-standardized tests are available to assess specific sensory processes such as visual-spatial perception in the general population (e.g., *Beery-Buktenica Developmental Test of Visual Motor Integration,* fourth edition, Beery & Buktenica, 1997; the *Motor Free Visual Perception Test,* Colarusso & Hammill, 1996; and the *Test of Visual-Perceptual Skills [nonmotor] Revised,* Gardner, 1996). Although these are not developed specifically for persons with autism, they provide valid and reliable information in appropriate cases. In addition, behavioral assessments of central auditory processing (e.g., sound localization and lateralization, auditory discrimination, pattern recognition) are also widely available (Baran & Musiek, 1999), but not validated for use with persons with autism. Although such tests were designed for use with frank neurological impairments, they also have been used by audiologists and speech-language pathologists to test children with language and learning disabilities. The *Pediatric Speech Intelligibility Test* (Jerger & Jerger, 1984) and *the SCAN: A Screening Test for Auditory Processing Disorders* (Keith, 1986) are examples of assessment instruments for central auditory processing problems. Factors to be considered in test selection include the age of the client and linguistic and cognitive capabilities; however, the relatively high levels of cooperation and comprehension required by many of these behavioral tests preclude their use with persons with severe developmental disabilities such as autism. The auditory brainstem response (ABR) provides an electrophysiologic means of assessing brainstem-level auditory function, but objective assessment of higher levels in the auditory nervous system are more challenging. For example, clinical application of event-related potentials is complicated by uncertainties regarding their cerebral origin and role in cognitive processing (Baran & Musiek, 1999; Picton, 1992; Stapells, 2002).

Laboratory paradigms have been developed to measure sympathetic and parasympathetic reactions to sensory stimuli (McIntosh, Miller, Shyu, & Hagerman, 1999; Miller et al., 1999).

In this procedure, children enter a room decorated like a "pretend spaceship" and experience a series of olfactory, auditory, visual, tactile, and vestibular stimuli. Physiological measures (electrodermal reactivity and vagal tone) have discriminated patterns of typically developing children from those of children with sensory modulation disorders, including those with autism and fragile X syndrome. Although this protocol has limitations for clinical use, it may be useful to researchers interested in quantifying such patterns.

Motor Assessments

Assessment of the child's participation in daily life contexts usually begins with interview of parents or caregivers and teachers, and includes the perspective of the person with autism whenever possible. This assessment may be augmented by observation of the individual in the daily routines of home and school. Several formal assessment tools that may be used to augment this process are described next.

Motor Skills and Praxis

Adaptive behavior scales, such as the *Vineland Adaptive Behavior Scales* (VABS; Sparrow, Balla, & Cicchetti, 1984) may be helpful in screening for general areas of functioning that may be affected by motor difficulties. The VABS includes parent and teacher questionnaires that address functioning in socialization, communication, activities of daily living, and motor skills for individuals from birth through 18 years of age. The daily living and motor skills domains are particularly relevant to motor and praxis development. The VABS has strong psychometric properties and has been used in research with children with autism (Szatmari, Archer, Fisman, Streiner, & Wilson, 1995). However, scores obtained on the VABS may underestimate praxis ability, because items primarily address familiar, well-practiced motor skills rather than the ability to move effectively in novel or complex situations.

The *Pediatric Evaluation of Disability Inventory* (PEDI; Haley, Coster, Ludlow, Haltiwanger, & Andrellos, 1992) is a standardized, criterion-referenced parent interview that measures degree of disability within the context of naturally occurring activities at home and in the community. It is designed for young children aged 1 month through 7 years. Scores are obtained in domains of self-care, mobility, and social function, and take into consideration the amount of assistance the child needs. A shortcoming of this test is that it seems to be best suited for measuring disability in children with more severe motor limitations; therefore, it may not be sensitive to motor issues of higher functioning children with autism.

The *School Function Assessment* (SFA; Coster, Deeney, Haltiwanger, & Haley, 1998) is a reliable, validated tool that is designed to measure school functioning in children with disabilities, from kindergarten through sixth grade, by gathering information from school personnel who are familiar with the child's performance. It focuses on participation in school activity settings, such as playground or recess, bathroom and toileting, transportation to and from school, transitions to and from class, and mealtime or snack time. Summary scores can be compared to cut points that define the typical range of function in nondisabled children. This standardized instrument may be useful for identifying areas of difficulty in school participation that may warrant further evaluation of praxis functions and motor skills.

The *Revised Knox Preschool Play Scale* (PPS; Knox, 1997), a nonstandardized assessment of play development in children aged 6 months through 6 years, is scored by the examiner during observation of spontaneous play in familiar indoor and outdoor environments. A number of researchers have provided evidence of adequate reliability and validity (see Knox, 1997 for a review). Play ages are computed in four dimensions that address aspects of praxis and other motor functions: space management, materials management, pretense/symbolic, and social participation. Restall and McGill-Evans (1994) found that total PPS scores, and participation scores, differentiated between children with autism and matched nonautistic controls, aged 3 to 6 years, suggesting that the PPS may have clinical utility with this population.

Another play instrument, the *Test of Playfulness* (ToP; Bundy, 1997) addresses the positive affective as well as praxis and social interactive aspects of spontaneous play in familiar environments. This instrument was carefully developed to be a reliable and valid measure of playfulness, rather than skill or developmental level, in children aged 18 months to 10 years. It has not previously been used in research with children with autism, but its inclusion of items that reflect ideation may contribute a unique element to the assessment of these children.

If more specific assessment of praxis and motor skills is called for, a number of options are available. A great deal of information can be gleaned from systematic observation. Interdisciplinary play-based assessment for children with autism can be designed to probe for behaviors reflecting praxis and specific motor skills (Linder, 1993; Osterling, Brooks, Unis, & Watling, 2000). Although this approach does not yield standardized scores, it has the advantage of giving information about spontaneous behavior, which may be more representative of the child's functioning in everyday life. Furthermore, as Dawson and colleagues (2000) have pointed out, observations of free play may be more sensitive to autistic symptomatology than adult-administered tasks.

A number of motor tests are available that provide standardized scores. One such instrument, the *Toddler Infant Motor Evaluation* (TIME; Miller & Roid, 1994) covers domains of mobility, motor organization, postural stability, and functional performance for children from birth to 47 months. It is unique in that scores are based on ratings of spontaneous motor behavior, which may be more representative of the child's ability than scores on highly structured motor tests. However, scoring the TIME is complex and requires training.

More conventional motor development tests measure motor problems among children with a wide variety of developmental disabilities. Although norm-reference tests have the advantage of offering standardized scores, they usually require the child to cooperate with a lengthy period of highly structured task demands. This often is not feasible for children with autism, who may be unable or unwilling to perform motor tasks on command. Nevertheless, such tests may be useful for some, particularly the higher functioning children on the autism spectrum.

Two of the most widely used, standardized motor tests are *the Bruininks-Oseretsky Test of Motor Proficiency* (BOTMP; Bruininks, 1978) and the Peabody Developmental Motor Scales (PDMS; Folio & Fewell, 1983). The BOTMP is designed for a wide age span (ages $4\frac{1}{2}$ to $14\frac{1}{2}$ years), and provides norm-referenced scores for eight subtests (running speed and agility, balance, bilateral coordination, strength, upper-limb coordination, response speed, visual-motor control, and upper-limb speed and dexterity). Standard gross motor and fine motor composite scores can also be obtained. Ghaziuddin and Butler (1998) presented evidence that this test is sensitive to the motor problems of children with autism. The *Peabody Developmental Motor Scales* (PDMS; Folio & Fewell, 1983) provide norm-referenced scores on gross and fine motor scales for children from birth through 83 months of age. Osterling and colleagues (2000) described how they adapted this test as part of a comprehensive interdisciplinary assessment of a child with autism.

Several tests of sensory integration (e.g., *Miller Assessment for Preschoolers* [MAP]; *Sensory Integration and Praxis Tests* [SIPT]) mentioned previously in this chapter also provide measures of praxis abilities. For example, the MAP includes relatively quick subtests of rapid alternating movements (stamp), sequencing actions (block tapping), and manual abilities (maze). Individual items can be selected for administration, and percentile scores can be estimated separately, which is advantageous in situations where the child is cooperative with testing only for brief periods. The SIPT assesses imitation of nonsymbolic body positions and movements (Postural Praxis, Oral Praxis, Sequencing Praxis, Bilateral Motor Coordination), praxis on verbal command, and visual constructional praxis (Design Copying, Constructional Praxis). All of the praxis and motor tests have good reliability and validity, and are computer analyzed to provide standard scores. Parham and colleagues (2000) found that the SIPT praxis tests involving body imitation were sensitive to the types of difficulties experienced by high functioning children with autism. In addition, the *DeGangi-Berk Test of Sensory Integration* (DeGangi & Berk, 1983) is a criterion-referenced test for children ages 3 to 5 years old that focuses on postural and other aspects of motor control. Items on this test do not assess praxis ability per se, but may provide useful measures of some aspects of motor control.

Assessment of oral sensory-motor functioning is often overlooked, but probably should be included as part of an in-depth motor evaluation of children with autism, because this area may be problematic for many, if not most, children with autism (Adams, 1998; Page & Boucher, 1998; Parham et al., 2000; S. J. Rogers, Hepburn, Stackhouse, et al., 2003). Assessment of this area is indicated particularly for children with eating problems or limited food preferences. Few tests are available that assess oral praxis functions. One of the most reliable and valid tools is the Oral Praxis test of the SIPT, which requires the child to imitate nonsymbolic oral-facial movements (Parham et al., 2000). A briefer test of oral praxis for preschoolers, the Tongue Movements test of the MAP, provides a percentile score reflecting oral praxis ability. Reliability for this test alone is marginal as a result of the limited number of items, but the brevity and simplicity of this test makes it quite useful with young children who otherwise would be untestable on oral praxis. The *Behavioral Assessment Scale of Oral Functions in Feeding* (Stratton, 1981) is not a standardized test, but is a rating scale that provides a profile of oral-motor strengths and weaknesses through observations of eating in a natural or clinical environment. It is designed for use with children and young adults with disabilities from age 10 months to 21 years. Although psychometric data are limited for this scale, it offers the benefit of organizing observational data systematically, within a functional context.

Specific evaluation of visual-motor control is indicated for some children with autism, although this may be an area of strength for many high-functioning children. A number of very well developed visual-motor standardized tests are available to assess this domain, usually by asking the child to copy printed designs with paper and pencil. These include the *Developmental Test of Visual-Motor Integration* (VMI; Beery & Buktenica, 1997) for ages 2 to 15 years, the *Test of Visual-Motor Skills-Revised* (TVMS; Gardner, 1995) for ages 3 to 13 years 11 months, and the *Test of Visual-Motor Skills-Revised-Upper Limits* (Gardner, 1992), for ages 12 to 40 years. Psychometrically strong measures of visual-motor ability are also included in more comprehensive instruments, such as the BOTMP, MAP, and SIPT. A thorough assessment of visual-motor skill should include evaluation of motor-free visual perception, to ascertain whether visual-motor difficulties are due primarily to visual perception problems, motor coordination, or integration of visual and motor functions.

Parham (1987) presented guidelines for evaluating motor planning and ideation through observation when a child is not cooperative with standardized testing. To assess ideation, one observes the child in an unstructured situation, without prior adult instruction or modeling, within an environment furnished with objects, materials, or equipment that are not already familiar to the child. A paucity of exploratory behaviors, or repetition of the same habitual motor schemes (such as patting, banging, kicking, or stacking) with different objects, signals the possibility of ideation problems. Tomchek (2001) presents additional suggestions related to assessing motor skills through unstructured observations.

Involuntary Movements

Unlike the primary features of autism, which often are conspicuous to even casual or untrained observers, movement disorders in persons with autism frequently go undetected in routine clinical settings (Baron-Cohen et al., 2000; Lewis & Bodfish, 1998). This may be due to false attributions that the repetitive motor acts characteristic of movement disorders are part of the stereotyped, repetitive behavior domain that is characteristic of autism. Similarly, clinicians can believe that involuntary repetitive movements like tics or dyskinesias cannot be reliably distinguished from repetitive behaviors such as stereotypies (Meiselas et al., 1989). However, reliable differential diagnosis is possible in autism and related developmental disorders (Bodfish, Newell, Sprague, Harper, & Lewis, 1996, 1997; Bodfish et al., 2000; Brasic et al., 1994; Lewis & Bodfish, 1998). The key to differential diagnosis is the use of standardized and orthogonal movement disorder exams and rating scales.

At this time, there is no overall movement disorder exam and rating scale that sufficiently covers the variety of movement disorders seen in autism and has been applied to studies of movement disorders in autism. Although frequently thought of in this vein, the *Abnormal Involuntary Movements Scale* (AIMS), despite its name, is only a scale for measuring dyskinesia (Fann, Smith, Davis, & Domino, 1980). Two standardized instruments, the *Simpson-Angus Scale for Extrapyramidal Symptoms* (Simpson & Angus, 1970), and the *Modified Rogers Scale* (Lund, Mortimer, Rogers, & McKenna, 1991) both measure a wide range of abnormal involuntary movements and may be suitable for assessing persons with autism. Both scales involve standardized examination, observation, and scoring procedures, and both possess acceptable reliability and validity for both children and adults with developmental and psychiatric disorders (D. Rogers, 1992). Other options include the use of specific instruments developed for the assessment and measurement of discrete movement disorders. These include the *Yale Global Tic Severity Scale* for measuring tics (YGTSS; Leckman et al., 1989), the *Dyskinesia Identification System Condensed User Scale* for measuring dyskinesia (DISCUS; Kalachnik & Sprague, 1993), and the *Barnes Akathisia Scale* (Barnes, 1989) or the *Akathisia Ratings of Movement Scale* (ARMS; Bodfish et al., 1997). Each of these clinical rating scales has been demonstrated to have acceptable psychometric characteristics, and each has been used in previous studies of movement disorders in autism.

CONSIDERATIONS FOR INTERVENTION

Based on the assessment framework presented earlier, an individualized intervention approach ultimately should aim to maximize engagement in meaningful activities and social participation in the community. The combination of interventions selected should depend upon the goals of the client or family, the context within which the interventions are aimed, and the strength of the evidence (i.e., theoretical foundations and empirical studies) supporting these interventions. Specific intervention approaches may include developing skills or restoring functions, designing task modifications, teaching compensatory strategies, en-

hancing environmental affordances, or providing contextually relevant opportunities for generalization of skills.

Documenting a unique profile of strengths and weaknesses in sensory characteristics and motor performance can be useful for designing program elements that are most optimal for an individual with autism. Sensory-motor functions provide a means for learning important skills in other domains (e.g., social skills, leisure, vocational), thus, these features should be considered during intervention planning. However, it is by no means clear whether intervention specifically directed at remediation of a sensory or motor impairment will lead to improvement in the impaired capacity. Furthermore, it is not certain that improvement in a particular sensory or motor impairment will necessarily result in fuller social participation. The same argument can be made regarding other domains, such as speech or cognition. That is, successful remediation of a specific speech or cognitive impairment does not guarantee that the child will then be able to apply these skills to participate in daily life more fully, for example, in peer play groups that spontaneously form at recess. Although there are myriad treatments (e.g., sensory integration, vision therapy, auditory integration training) that aim to remediate the sensory symptoms or motor deficits in autism, few well-controlled empirical studies have tested their efficacy in this population. An extensive review of these treatments is beyond the scope of this chapter and is available elsewhere (Baranek, 2002).

Families of young children often desire developmental or remedial treatments, based on anecdotal information from therapists about their purported beneficial effects. These treatments can be expensive and time consuming, and need to be evaluated individually based on the best available evidence. Adaptive and compensatory techniques may be utilized by therapists when more immediate benefits or inclusion goals are stressed. Furthermore, skills that are not directly addressed in therapy, and practiced in naturalistic environments are least likely to improve, thus, it is unrealistic to expect improved participation (e.g., play with peers) from interventions that focus on improving sensorimotor capacities (e.g., fine motor grasp patterns). It is also critical to note that interventions focusing on personally meaningful activities are more likely to have positive outcomes and long-term health benefits as noted by studies with other populations (Bober, Humphry, Carswell, & Core, 2001; Clark et al., 1996).

Regardless of the specific intervention plan, it is unethical to provide a treatment without systematically monitoring its effects—both negative and positive. Given that autism is a heterogeneous disorder, presenting with different sensory and motor features across individuals, such heterogeneity is likely associated with differential treatment outcomes. Evaluation of a client's skills at three levels (sensory and motor function, performance in specific activities, and level of participation) is warranted. In particular, interventions that have not been tested rigorously should be subjected to close scrutiny, for example, by providing short-term intervention with systematic data collection. Single-subject research designs (e.g., multiple baseline designs) are optimal for this type of tracking.

CONCLUSION

There is a clear need for more carefully controlled research on the presence of sensory and motor features in autism and on the potential interactions of these symptoms with the core deficits of autism (e.g., social-cognitive deficits). For example, it is reasonable to expect reciprocal influences of praxis and social-communication skills as interchanges with other people generate many ideas for actions (Trecker, 2001), and meaningful physical actions provide opportunities for joint attention (E. Williams et al., 1999); however, these hypotheses need further study.

Research on the sensory and motor features of autism has largely proceeded independently, and future studies should jointly address these systems. For example, future research could investigate whether or not problems in sensory modulation may generate stress that interferes with the creation of ideas and motor plans for new activities, or whether or not proprioceptive difficulties are responsible for some of the motor control problems evident in autism.

It is likewise important for researchers to differentiate putative mechanisms from expressed features of sensory and motor behavior abnormalities. This should include both established mechanisms that appear to be operative in the production of the core deficits of autism, and potential sensory and motor processes that are known to be related to the expression of abnormal behaviors in other neurodevelopmental disorders. For example, frontostriatal circuits in the brain are thought to be involved in the expression of abnormal sensorimotor behaviors in Tourette syndrome; such behaviors may be phenomenologically similar to symptoms seen in autism.

Moreover, recent research has indicated that atypical sensory and motor features may occur very early in the course of autism and may precede identifiable social-communicative symptoms. Thus, clinical work on early identification and early intervention should include efforts to screen for potential sensory and motor features, and track developmental transactions and outcomes.

Autism is a heterogeneous disorder at the level of both etiology and expressed symptoms. Although limited at this point, the available research clearly indicates that the presence or absence of sensory and motor features can contribute to the heterogeneity of autism. When present, sensory and motor features can potentially impact the experiences and developmental trajectories of children with autism, and thus have clear implications for both clinical assessment and treatment. Practical, reliable, and valid screening instruments are available for clinicians to assess sensory and motor features. These may augment routine evaluation protocols for persons with autism.

Recent conceptualizations (Baranek et al., 2002; Humphry, 2002; Thelen & Smith, 1994) propose transactional effects among an individual's various intrinsic capacities (e.g., sensory and motor deficits), and other contextual factors that may either facilitate or inhibit performance. Thus, similar sensory and motor characteristics across persons with autism may result in varying patterns (strength or weakness) of performance in daily activities and differing levels of social participation for a given individual.

Implications of such recent classification systems for clinical practice include evaluating an individual with autism not only with respect to specific impairments in sensory and motor functions, but also with respect to the real-life activities and tasks the person is having difficulty with. Clinicians should also evaluate the degree to which a client's participation at home, in school, or at work, and in the community is full and satisfying to the individual him- or herself, and to his or her family. Through consideration of dynamic processes contributing to full social participation we can begin to formulate meaningful and successful interventions for persons with autism.

Cross-References

Attention and perceptual issues are discussed in Chapter 13; imitation and play are addressed in Chapter 14; neurobiological issues are addressed in Chapters 16 through 20; Chapter 51 provides a personal perspective on sensory issues in autism.

REFERENCES

Adams, L. (1998). Oral-motor and motor-speech characteristics of children with autism. *Focus on Autism and Other Developmental Disabilities, 13*(2), 108–112.

Adoh, T. O., Woodhouse, J. M., & Oduwaiye, K. A. (1992). The Cardiff Test: A new visual acuity test for toddlers and children with intellectual impairment. A preliminary report. *Optometry and Visual Science, 69*(6), 427–432.

Adrien, J. L., Barthelemy, C., Perrot, A., Roux, S., Lenoir, P., Hameury, L., et al. (1992). Validity and reliability of the Infant Behavioral Summarized Evaluation (IBSE): A rating scale for the assessment of young children with autism and developmental disorders. *Journal of Autism and Developmental Disorders, 22,* 375–394.

Adrien, J. L., Faure, M., Perrot, A., Hameury, L., Garreau, B., Barthelemy, C., et al. (1991). Autism and family home movies: Preliminary findings. *Journal of Autism and Developmental Disorders, 21*(1), 43–49.

Allen, G., & Courchesne, E. (2001). Attention function and dysfunction in autism. *Frontiers in Bioscience, 6,* D105–D119.

Ayres, A. J. (1985). *Developmental dyspraxia and adult onset apraxia.* Torrance, CA: Sensory Integration International.

Ayres, A. J. (1989). *Sensory Integration and Praxis Tests* (SIPT). Los Angeles: Western Psychological Services.

Bailey, A., Phillips, W., & Rutter, M. (1996). Autism: Towards an integration of clinical, genetic, neuropsychological, and neurobiological perspectives. *Journal of Child Psychology and Psychiatry, 37*(1), 89–126.

Baran, J. A., & Musiek, F. E. (1999). Behavioral assessment of the central auditory nervous system. In F. E. Musiek & W. F. Rintelmann (Eds.), *Contemporary perspectives in hearing assessment* (pp. 375–413). Boston: Allyn & Bacon.

Baranek, G. T. (1998). *Tactile Defensiveness and Discrimination Test: Revised.* Unpublished manuscript, University of North Carolina at Chapel Hill.

Baranek, G. T. (1999a). Autism during infancy: A retrospective video analysis of sensory-motor and social behaviors at 9–12 months of age. *Journal of Autism and Developmental Disorders, 29*(3), 213–224.

Baranek, G. T. (1999b). *Sensory Experiences Questionnaire* (SEQ). Unpublished manuscript, University of North Carolina at Chapel Hill.

Baranek, G. T. (1999c). *Sensory processing assessment for young children* (SPA). Unpublished manuscript, University of North Carolina at Chapel Hill.

Baranek, G. T. (2002). Efficacy of sensory and motor interventions for children with autism. *Journal of Autism and Developmental Disorders, 5*(32), 397–422.

Baranek, G. T., & Berkson, G. (1994). Tactile defensiveness in children with developmental disabilities: Responsiveness and habituation. *Journal of Autism and Developmental Disorders, 24,* 457–471.

Baranek, G. T., Chin, Y., Hess, L., Yankee, J., Hatton, D., & Hooper, S. (2002). Sensory processing correlates of occupational performance in children with fragile X syndrome: Preliminary findings. *American Journal of Occupational Therapy, 56*(5), 538–546.

Baranek, G. T., David, F. J., Poe, M. D., Stone, W., & Watson, L. R. (2004). *The Sensory Experiences Questionnaire: Discriminating response patterns in young children with autism, developmental delays, and typical development.* Manuscript submitted for publication.

Baranek, G. T., Foster, L. G., & Berkson, G. (1997a). Sensory defensiveness in persons with developmental disabilities. *Occupational Therapy Journal of Research, 17,* 173–185.

Baranek, G. T., Foster, L. G., & Berkson, G. (1997b). Tactile defensiveness and stereotyped behaviors. *American Journal of Occupational Therapy, 51*(2), 91–95.

Barnes, T. R. (1989). A rating scale for drug-induced akathisia. *British Journal of Psychiatry, 154,* 672–676.

Baron-Cohen, S., Scahill, V. L., Izaguirre, J., Hornsey, H., & Robertson, M. M. (1999). The prevalence of Gilles de la Tourette syndrome in children and adolescents with autism: A large scale study. *Psychological Medicine, 29,* 1151–1159.

Baron-Cohen, S., Wheelwright, S., Cox, A., Baird, G., Charman, T., Swettenham, J., et al. (2000). Early identification of autism by the CHecklist for Autism in Toddlers (CHAT). *Journal of the Royal Society of Medicine, 93*(10), 521–525.

Beery, K. E., & Buktenica, N. A. (1997). *Developmental Test of Visual-Motor Integration* (VMI). Parsippany, NJ: Modern Curriculum Press.

Bettison, S. (1996). The long-term effects of auditory training on children with autism. *Journal of Autism and Developmental Disorders, 26,* 361–374.

Bober, S. J., Humphry, R., Carswell, H. W., & Core, A. J. (2001). Toddlers' persistence in the emerging occupations of functional play and self-feeding. *American Journal of Occupational Therapy, 55*(4), 369–376.

Bodfish, J. W., Newell, K. M., Sprague, R. L., Harper, V. N., & Lewis, M. H. (1996). Co-occurrence of dyskinetic and stereotyped movement disorders among adults with mental retardation. *American Journal of Mental Retardation, 101,* 118–129.

Bodfish, J. W., Newell, K. M., Sprague, R. L., Harper, V. N., & Lewis, M. H. (1997). Akathisia in adults with mental retardation: Development of the Akathisia Ratings of Movement Scale (ARMS). *American Journal on Mental Retardation, 101,* 413–423.

Bodfish, J. W., Symons, F. J., Parker, D. E., & Lewis, M. H. (2000). Varieties of repetitive behavior in autism: Comparisons to mental retardation. *Journal of Autism and Developmental Disorders, 30,* 237–243.

Brasic, J. R., Barnett, J. Y., Kaplan, D., Sheitman, B. B., Aisemberg, P., Lafargu, R. T., et al. (1994). Clomipramine ameliorates adventitious movements and compulsions in prepubertal boys with autistic disorder and severe mental retardation. *Neurology, 44*(7), 1309–1312.

Bruininks, R. (1978). *Bruininks-Oseretsky Test of Motor Proficiency.* Circle Pines, MN: American Guidance Service.

Bryson, S. E., Landry, R., & Wainwright, J. (1997). A componential view of executive dysfunction in autism: Review of recent evidence. In J. A. Burack & J. T. Enns (Eds.), *Attention, development, and psychopathology* (pp. 232–259). New York: Guilford Press.

Bundy, A. C. (1997). *The test of playfulness.* Fort Collins: Colorado State University Press.

Burd, L., Fisher, W. W., Kerbeshian, J., & Arnold, M. E. (1987). Is development of Tourette disorder a market for improvement in patients with autism and other pervasive developmental disorders? *Journal of the American Academy of Child and Adolescent Psychiatry, 26,* 162–165.

Campbell, M., Locascio, J. J., Choroco, M. C., Spencer, E. K., Malone, R. P., Kafantaris, V., et al. (1990). Stereotypies and tardive dyskinesia: Abnormal movements in autistic children. *Psychopharmacology Bulletin, 26,* 260–266.

Cesaroni, L., & Garber, M. (1991). Exploring the experience of autism through firsthand accounts. *Journal of Autism and Developmental Disorders, 21*(3), 303–313.

Charman, T., Swettenham, J., Baron-Cohen, S., Cox, A., Baird, G., & Drew, A. (1997). Infants with autism: An investigation of empathy, pretend play, joint attention, and imitation. *Developmental Psychology, 33*(5), 781–789.

Clark, F., Azen, S. P., Zemke, R., Jackson, J., Carlson, M., Mandel, D., et al. (1996). Occupational therapy of independent-living older adults: A randomized controlled trial. *Journal of the American Medical Association, 278,* 1321–1326.

Colarusso, R. P., & Hammill, D. (1996). *Motor-Free Visual Perception Test: Revised.* Novato, CA: Academic Therapy.

Comings, D. E., & Comings, B. G. (1991). Clinical and genetic relationships between autism-pervasive developmental disorder and Tourette syndrome: A study of 19 cases. *American Journal of Medical Genetics, 39,* 180–191.

Corona, R., Dissanayake, C., Arbelle, S., Wellington, P., & Sigman, M. (1998). Is affect aversive to young children with autism? Behavioral and cardiac responses to experimenter distress. *Child Development, 69,* 1494–1502.

Coster, W. (1998). Occupation-centered assessment in children. *American Journal of Occupational Therapy, 52,* 337–343.

Coster, W., Deeney, T., Haltiwanger, J., & Haley, S. (1998). *School Function Assessment* (SFA). San Antonio, TX: Therapy Skill Builders.

Courchesne, E., Townsend, J. P., Akshoomoff, N. A., Yeung-Courchesne, R., Press, G. A., Murakami, J. W., et al. (1994). A new finding: Impairment in shifting attention in autistic and cerebellar patients. In S. H. Broman & J. Grafman (Eds.), *Atypical cognitive deficits in developmental disorders: Implications for brain function* (pp. 107–137). Hillsdale, NJ: Erlbaum.

Dahlgren, S. O., & Gillberg, C. (1989). Symptoms in the first two years of life. A preliminary population study of infantile autism. *European Archives of Psychiatry and Neurological Science, 238*(3), 169–174.

Damasio, A., & Maurer, R. (1978). A neurological model for childhood autism. *Archives of Neurology, 35,* 777–786.

Dawson, G., Meltzoff, A. N., Osterling, J., Rinaldi, J., & Brown, E. (1998). Children with autism fail to orient to naturally occurring social stimuli. *Journal of Autism and Developmental Disorders, 28*(6), 479–485.

Dawson, G., Osterling, J., Meltzoff, A. N., & Kuhl, P. (2000). Case Study of the development of an infant with autism from birth to two years of age. *Journal of Applied Developmental Psychology, 21,* 299–313.

DeGangi, G. A., & Berk, R. A. (1983). *DeGangi-Berk Test of Sensory Integration.* Los Angeles: Western Psychological Services.

DeMyer, M. K. (1976). Motor, perceptual-motor and intellectual disabilities of autistic children. In L. Wing (Ed.), *Early childhood autism* (2nd ed., pp. 169–196). Oxford, England: Pergamon Press.

DeMyer, M. K., Alpern, D. G., Barton, S., DeMyer, W. E., Churchill, D. W., Hingtgen, J. N., et al. (1972). Imitation in autistic, early schizophrenic, and nonpsychotic subnormal children. *Journal of Autism and Childhood Schizophrenia, 2,* 264–287.

DeMyer, M. K., Barton, S., & Norton, J. A. (1972). A comparison of adaptive, verbal, and motor profiles of psychotic and nonpsychotic subnormal children. *Journal of Autism and Childhood Schizophrenia, 2*(4), 359–377.

Dunn, W. (1999). *Sensory profile.* San Antonio, TX: Psychological Corporation.

Dunn, W. (2000). *Best practice occupational therapy. In community service with children and families.* Thorofare, NJ: Slack.

Eaves, L. C., Ho, H. H., & Eaves, D. M. (1994). Subtypes of autism by cluster analysis. *Journal of Autism and Developmental Disorders, 24*(1), 3–22.

Ermer, J., & Dunn, W. (1998). The sensory profile: A discriminant analysis of children with and without disabilities. *American Journal of Occupational Therapy, 52*(4), 283–290.

Fann, W. E., Smith, R. C., Davis, J. M., & Domino, E. F. (Eds.). (1980). *Tardive dyskinesia: Research and treatment.* Jamaica, NY: Spectrum.

Filipek, P. A., Accardo, P. J., Ashwal, S., Baranek, G. T., Cook, E. H., Jr., Dawson, G., et al. (2000). Practice parameter: Screening and diagnosis of autism: Report of the Quality Standards Subcommittee of the American Academy of Neurology and the Child Neurology Society. *Neurology, 55*(4), 468–479.

Folio, M. R., & Fewell, R. R. (1983). *Peabody Developmental Motor Scales and Activity Cards* (PDMS). Itasca, IL: Riverside.

Gardner, M. F. (1992). *Test of Visual-Motor Skills: Revised* (Upper Limits). Los Angeles: Western Psychological Services.

Gardner, M. F. (1995). *Test of Visual-Motor Skills: Revised* (TVMS). Los Angeles: Western Psychological Services.

Gardner, M. F. (1996). *Test of Visual Perceptual Skills: Revised* (Non-Motor; TVPS). Los Angeles: Western Psychological Services.

Gepner, B., & Mestre, D. R. (2002). Brief report: Postural reactivity to fast visual motion differentiates autistic from children with Asperger syndrome. *Journal of Autism and Developmental Disorders, 32*(3), 231–238.

Ghaziuddin, M., & Butler, E. (1998). Clumsiness in autism and Asperger syndrome: A further report. *Journal of Intellectual Disability Research, 42*(1), 43–48.

Gillberg, C., Ehlers, S., Schaumann, H., Jakobsson, G., Dahlgren, S. O., Lindblom, R., et al. (1990). Autism under age 3 years: A clinical study of 28 cases referred for autistic symptoms in infancy. *Journal of Child Psychology and Psychiatry, 31*(6), 921–934.

Golden, C. J., Purisch, A. D., & Hammeke, T. A. (1991). *Luria-Nebraska Neuropsychological Battery.* Los Angeles: Western Psychological Services.

Gopnik, A., & Meltzoff, A. (1993). Words and thoughts in infancy: The specificity hypothesis and the development of categorization and naming. *Advances in Infancy Research, 8,* 217–249.

Grandin, T. (1992). Calming effects of deep touch pressure in patients with autistic disorder, college students, and animals. *Journal of Child and Adolescent Psychopharmacology, 2*(1), 63–72.

Greenspan, S., & Wieder, S. (1997). Developmental patterns and outcomes in infants and children with disorders in relating and communicating: A chart review of 200 cases of children with autistic spectrum diagnoses. *Journal of Developmental and Learning Disorders, 1*(1), 87–141.

Haley, S. M., Coster, W. J., Ludlow, L. H., Haltiwanger, J. T., & Andrellos, P. J. (1992). *Pediatric Evaluation of Disability Inventory* (PEDI). San Antonio, TX: Therapy Skill Builders.

Hallett, M., Lebiedowska, M. K., Thomas, S. L., Stanhope, S. J., Denckla, M. B., & Rumsey, J. (1993). Locomotion of autistic adults. *Archives of Neurology, 50,* 1304–1308.

Happé, F. G. E. (1996). Studying weak central coherence at low levels: Children with autism do not succumb to visual illusions. A research note. *Journal of Child Psychology and Psychiatry, 37*(7), 873–876.

Hatfield, E., Cacioppo, J. T., & Rapson, R. L. (1994). *Emotional contagion.* New York: Cambridge University Press.

Hobson, R. P., & Lee, A. (1999). Imitation and identification in autism. *Journal of Child Psychology and Psychiatry, 40*(4), 649–659.

Hoshino, Y., Kumashiro, H., Yashima, Y., Tachibana, R., Watanabe, M., & Furukawa, H. (1982). Early symptoms of autistic children and its diagnostic significance. *Folia Psychiatrica Et Neurologica Japonica, 36*(4), 367–374.

Hughes, C. (1996). Brief report: Planning problems in autism at the level of motor control. *Journal of Autism and Developmental Disorders, 26,* 99–108.

Hughes, C., & Russell, J. (1993). Autistic children's difficulty with mental disengagement from an object: Its implications for theories of autism. *Developmental Psychology, 29,* 498–510.

Humphry, R. (2002). Young children's occupations: Explicating the dynamics of developmental processes. *American Journal of Occupational Therapy, 56*(2), 171–179.

Jerger, S., & Jerger, J. (1984). *The Pediatric Speech Intelligibility Test* (PSI). St. Louis, MO: Auditec.

Joseph, A. B. (1992). Catatonia. In A. B. Joseph & R. R. Young (Eds.), *Movement disorders in neurology and neuropsychiatry* (pp. 335–342). Oxford, England: Blackwell.

Jure, R., Rapin, I., & Tuchman, R. F. (1991). Hearing-impaired autistic children. *Developmental Medicine and Child Neurology, 33*(12), 1062–1072.

Kalachnik, J. E., & Sprague, R. L. (1993). The dyskinesia Identification System Condensed User Scale (DISCUS): Reliability, validity, and a total score cut-off for mentally ill and mentally retarded populations. *Journal of Clinical Psychology, 49*(2), 177–189.

Kanner, L. (1943). Autistic disturbances of affective contact. *Nervous Child, 2,* 217–250.

Kaplan, M., Rimland, B., & Edelson, S. M. (1999). Strabismus in autism spectrum disorder. *Focus on Autism and Other Developmental Disabilities, 14*(2), 101–105.

Keith, R. W. (1986). *SCAN: A screening test for auditory processing disorders.* San Antonio, TX: Psychological Corporation.

Kientz, M. A., & Dunn, W. (1997). A comparison of the performance of children with and without autism on the Sensory Profile. *American Journal of Occupational Therapy, 51*(7), 530–537.

Klin, A. (1993). Auditory brainstem responses in autism: Brainstem dysfunction or peripheral hearing loss? *Journal of Autism and Developmental Disorders, 23*(1), 15–35.

Klin, A., Volkmar, F. R., & Sparrow, S. S. (1992). Autistic social dysfunction: Some limitations of the theory of mind hypothesis. *Journal of Child Psychology and Psychiatry, 33,* 861–876.

Knox, S. H. (1997). Development and current use of the Knox Preschool Play Scale. In L. D. Parham & L. S. Fazio (Eds.), *Play in occupational therapy for children* (pp. 35–51). St. Louis, MO: Mosby.

Kohen-Raz, R., Volkmar, F. R., & Cohen, D. (1992). Postural control in children with autism. *Journal of Autism and Developmental Disorders, 22,* 419–432.

Kuhaneck, H. M., Henry, D., & Glennon, T. J. (2003). *The school assessment of sensory integration.* Paper presented at the 83rd annual conference and expo of the American Occupational Therapy Association, Washington, DC.

Landry, R., & Bryson, S. E. (2004). Impaired disengagement of attention in young children with autism. *Journal of Child Psychology and Psychiatry and Allied Disciplines, 45*(6), 1115–1122.

Langworthy-Lam, K., Aman, M., & Van Bourgondien, M. (2002). Prevalence and patterns of use of psychoactive medicines in individuals with autism in the autism society of North Carolina. *Journal of Child and Adolescent Psychopharmacology, 12*(4), 311–321.

Leary, M. R., & Hill, D. A. (1996). Moving on: Autism and movement disturbance. *Mental Retardation, 34,* 39–53.

Leckman, J. F., Riddle, M. A., Hardin, M. T., Ort, S. I., Swartz, K. L., Stevenson, J., et al. (1989). The Yale Global Tic Severity Scale: Initial testing of a clinician-rated scale of tic severity. *Journal of the American Academy of Child and Adolescent Psychiatry, 28*(4), 566–573.

Le Couteur, A., Rutter, M., Lord, C., Rios, P., Robertson, S., Holdgrafer, M., et al. (1989). Autism diagnostic interview: A standardized investigator-based instrument. *Journal of Autism and Developmental Disorders, 19*(3), 363–387.

Lewis, M. H., & Bodfish, J. W. (1998). Repetitive behavior disorders in autism. *Mental Retardation and Developmental Disabilities Research Reviews, 4,* 80–89.

Linder, T. W. (1993). *Transdisciplinary play-based assessment: A functional approach to working with young children.* Baltimore: Paul H. Brookes.

Lord, C. (1995). Follow-up of two-year-olds referred for possible autism. *Journal of Child Psychology and Psychiatry, 36*(8), 1365–1382.

Loveland, K. A. (2001). Toward an ecological theory of autism. In J. Burack, T. Charman, N. Yirmiya, & P. R. Zelazo (Eds), *The development of autism: Perspectives from theory and research* (pp. 17–37). Mahwah, NJ: Erlbaum.

Lund, C. E., Mortimer, A. M., Rogers, D., & McKenna, P. J. (1991). Motor, volitional and behavioural disorders in schizophrenia: 1.

Assessment using the Modified Rogers Scale. *British Journal of Psychiatry, 158,* 323–327.

Manjiviona, J., & Prior, M. R. (1995). Comparison of Asperger syndrome and high-functioning autistic children on a test of motor impairment. *Journal of Autism and Developmental Disorders, 25,* 23–29.

Marsden, D. D. (1984). Motor disorders in basal ganglia disease. *Human Neurobiology, 2,* 245–250.

Maurer, R. G., & Damasio, A. R. (1982). Childhood autism from the point of view of behavioral neurology. *Journal of Autism and Developmental Disorders, 12*(2), 195–205.

McCracken, J. T., McGough, J., Shah, B., Cronin, P., Hong, D., Aman, M. G., et al. (2002). Risperidone in children with autism and serious behavioral problems. *New England Journal of Medicine, 347*(5), 314–321.

McGuire, L., Barnett, C., Baranek, G. T., & Suratt, A. (2001). *Sensory Processing Assessment for Young Children (SPA): A pilot study.* 34th Annual Gatlinburg Conference on Research and Theory in Intellectual and Developmental Disabilities, Charleston, SC.

McIntosh, D. N., Miller, L. J., Shyu, V., & Hagerman, R. J. (1999). Sensory-modulation disruption, electrodermal responses, and functional behaviors. *Developmental Medicine and Child Neurology, 41,* 608–615.

Meiselas, K. D., Spencer, E. K., Oberfield, R., Peselow, E. D., Angrist, B., & Campbell, M. (1989). Differentiation of stereotypies from neuroleptic-related dyskinesias in autistic children. *Journal of Clinical Psychopharmacology, 9*(3), 207–209.

Miller, L. J. (1982). *Miller assessment for preschoolers* (MAP). San Antonio, TX: Therapy Skill Builder.

Miller, L. J., McIntosh, D. N., McGrath, J., Shyu, V., Lampe, M., Taylor, A. K., et al. (1999). Electrodermal response to sensory stimuli in individuals with fragile X syndrome: A preliminary report. *American Journal of Medical Genetics, 83,* 268–279.

Miller, L. J., & Roid, G. H. (1994). *The T.I.M.E: Toddler and infant motor evaluation.* San Antonio, TX: Therapy Skill Builder.

Minshew, N. J., Goldstein, G., & Siegel, D. J. (1997). Neuropsychologic functioning in autism: Profile of a complex information processing disorder. *Journal of the International Neuropsychological Society, 3*(4), 303–316.

Minshew, N. J., Sweeney, J. A., & Bauman, M. L. (1997). Neurological aspects of autism. In D. J. Cohen & F. R. Volkmar (Eds.), *Handbook of autism and pervasive developmental disorders* (2nd ed., pp. 344–369). New York: Wiley.

Mundy, P., & Neal, R. (2001). Neural plasticity, joint attention, and a transactional social-orienting model of autism. In L. M. Glidden (Ed.), *International review of research in mental retardation: Autism* (pp. 139–168). San Diego, CA: Academic Press.

Nader, R., Oberlander, T. F., Chambers, C. T., & Craig, K. D. (2004). Expression of pain in children with autism. *Clinical Journal of Pain, 20*(2), 88–97.

Ohta, M., Nagai, Y., Hara, H., & Sasaki, M. (1987). Parental perception of behavioral symptoms in Japanese autistic children. *Journal of Autism and Developmental Disorders, 17*(4), 549–563.

O'Neill, M., & Jones, R. S. (1997). Sensory-perceptual abnormalities in autism: A case for more research? *Journal of Autism and Developmental Disorders, 27*(3), 283–293.

Ornitz, E. M. (1987). Neurophysiology of infantile autism. In S. Chess & A. Thomas (Eds.), *Annual progress in child psychiatry and child development* (pp. 505–529). Philadelphia: Brunner/Mazel.

Ornitz, E. M. (1989). Autism at the interface between sensory and information processing. In G. Dawson (Ed.), *Autism: Nature, diagnosis, and treatment* (pp. 174–207). New York: Guilford Press.

Ornitz, E. M., Guthrie, D., & Farley, A. H. (1977). The early development of autistic children. *Journal of Autism and Childhood Schizophrenia, 7*(3), 207–229.

Osterling, J., Brooks, C., Unis, A., & Watling, R. (2000). A child with an autism spectrum disorder. In M. Guralnick (Ed.), *Interdisciplinary clinical assessment of young children with developmental disabilities* (pp. 281–306). Baltimore: Paul H. Brookes.

Ozonoff, S., & Strayer, D. L. (1997). Inhibitory function in nonretarded children with autism. *Journal of Autism and Developmental Disorders, 27,* 59–77.

Page, J., & Boucher, J. (1998). Motor impairments in children with autistic disorder. *Child Language Teaching and Therapy, 14,* 233–259.

Parham, L. D. (1987). Evaluation of praxis in preschoolers. *Occupational Therapy in Health Care, 4*(2), 23–36.

Parham, L. D., & Ecker, C. L. (2002). Evaluation of sensory processing. In A. Bundy, S. Lane, & E. Murray (Eds.), *Sensory integration: Theory and practice* (2 ed., pp. 194–196). Philadelphia: Davis.

Parham, L. D., Mailloux, Z., & Roley, S. (2000). *Sensory processing and praxis in high functioning children with autism.* Paper presented at the Research 2000 Conference of Pediatric Therapy Network, Redondo Beach, CA.

Parush, S., Doryon, Y. D., & Katz, N. (1996). A comparison of self-report and informant report of tactile defensiveness amongst children in Israel. *Occupational Therapy International, 3*(4), 274–283.

Pennington, B. F., & Ozonoff, S. (1996). Executive functions and developmental psychopathology. *Journal of Child Psychology and Psychiatry, 37*, 51–87.

Picton, T. W. (1992). The P300 wave of the human event-related potential. *Journal of Clinical Neurophysiology, 9*(4), 456–479.

Pierce, K., & Courchesne, E. (2001). Evidence for a cerebellar role in reduced exploration and stereotyped behavior in autism. *Biological Psychiatry, 49*, 655–664.

Porges, S. W., Doussard-Roosevelt, J. A., & Maiti, A. K. (1994). Vagal tone and the physiological regulation of emotion. *Monographs of the Society for Research in Child Development, 59*(2/3), 167–186.

Realmuto, G. M., & August, G. (1991). Catatonia in autistic disorder; a sign of comorbidity or variable expression? *Journal of Autism and Developmental Disorders, 21*, 517–528.

Realmuto, G. M., & Main, B. (1982). Coincidence of Tourette's disorder and infantile autism. *Journal of Autism and Developmental Disorders, 12*, 367–372.

Restall, G., & McGill-Evans, J. (1994). Play and preschool children with autism. *American Journal of Occupational Therapy, 48*(2), 113–120.

Rinehart, N. J., Bradshaw, J. L., Brereton, A. V., & Tonge, B. J. (2001). Movement preparation in high-functioning autism and Asperger disorder: A serial choice reaction time task involving motor reprogramming. *Journal of Autism and Developmental Disorders, 31*(1), 79–88.

Ringman, J. M., & Jankovic, J. (2000). Occurrence of tics in Asperger's syndrome and autistic disorder. *Journal of Child Neurology, 15*, 394–400.

Rodier, P. M., Ingram, J. L., Tisdale, B., Nelson, S., & Romano, J. (1996). Embryological origin for autism: Developmental anomalies of the cranial nerve motor nuclei. *Journal of Comparative Neurology, 36*, 351–356.

Rogers, D. (1992). *Motor disorders in psychiatry towards a neurological psychiatry.* Chichester, England: Wiley.

Rogers, S. J., & Bennetto, L. (2000). Intersubjectivity in autism: The roles of imitation and executive function. In A. Wetherby & B. Prizant (Eds.), *Autism spectrum disorders: A transactional developmental perspective* (Communication and language intervention series, pp. 79–107). Baltimore: Paul H. Brookes.

Rogers, S. J., Bennetto, L., McEvoy, R., & Pennington, B. F. (1996). Imitation and pantomime in high-functioning adolescents with autism spectrum disorders. *Child Development, 67*(5), 2060–2073.

Rogers, S. J., Hepburn, S. L., Stackhouse, T., & Wehner, E. (2003). Imitation performance in toddlers with autism and those with other developmental disorders. *Journal of Child Psychology and Psychiatry, 44*(5), 763–781.

Rogers, S. J., Hepburn, S., & Wehner, E. (2003). Parent reports of sensory symptoms in toddlers with autism and those with other developmental disorders. *Journal of Autism and Developmental Disorders, 33*(6), 631–642.

Rogers, S. J., & Pennington, B. F. (1991). A theoretical approach to deficits in infantile autism. *Development and Psychopathology, 3,* 137–162.

Roid, G. H., & Miller, L. J. (1997). *Leiter International Performance Scale: Revised.* Wood Dale, IL: Stoelting.

Rosenhall, U., Nordin, V., Sandstrom, M., Ahlsen, G., & Gillberg, C. (1999). Autism and hearing loss. *Journal of Autism and Developmental Disorders, 29*(5), 349–357.

Russell, J., & Hill, E. L. (2001). Action-monitoring and intention reporting in children with autism. *Journal of Child Psychology and Psychiatry, 42*, 317–328.

Sachdev, P. (1995). The development of the concept of akathisia: A historical overview. *Schizophrenia Research, 16*, 33–45.

Scharre, J., & Creedon, M. (1992). Assessment of visual function in autistic children. *Optometry and Vision Science, 69*, 433–439.

Seal, B. C., & Bonvillian, J. D. (1997). Sign language and motor functioning in students with autistic disorder. *Journal of Autism and Developmental Disorders, 27*, 437–466.

Sevin, J. A., Matson, J. L., Coe, D., Love, S. R., Matese, M. J., & Benavidez, D. A. (1995). Empirically derived subtypes of pervasive developmental disorders: A cluster analytic study. *Journal of Autism and Developmental Disorders, 25*(6), 561–578.

Shay, J., Sanchez, L., Cueva, J., & Armenteros, J. (1993). Neuroleptic-related dyskinesias and stereotypies in autistic children: Videotaped ratings. *Psychopharmacology-Bulletin, 29*(3), 359–363.

Sigman, M., & Ungerer, J. A. (1984). Cognitive and language skills in autistic, mentally retarded, and normal children. *Developmental Psychology, 20*, 293–302.

Simpson, G. M., & Angus, J. W. S. (1970). Drug-induced extrapyramidal disorders. *Acta Psychiatrica Scandinavica, 212*(Suppl.), 1–58.

Smith, I. M., & Bryson, S. E. (1994). Imitation and action in autism: A critical review. *Psychological Bulletin, 116*(2), 259–273.

Smith, I. M., & Bryson, S. E. (1998). Gesture imitation in autism: I. Nonsymbolic postures and sequences. *Cognitive Neuropsychology, 15,* 747–770.

Sparrow, S., Balla, D., & Cicchetti, D. (1984). *Vineland Adaptive Behavior Scales.* Circle Pines, MN: American Guidance Service.

Stapells, D. R. (2002). Cortical event-related potentials to auditory stimuli. In J. Katz (Ed.), *Handbook of clinical audiology* (5th ed., pp. 378–406). Baltimore: Williams & Wilkins.

Stella, J. (2001). *Social orienting in children with autism: Concurrent and predictive validity.* Poster presented at the Society for Research in Child Development Biennial Meeting. Minneapolis, MN.

Stern, D. N. (1985). *The interpersonal world of the infant: A view from psychoanalysis and developmental psychology.* New York: Basic Books.

Stone, W. L., & Hogan, K. L. (1993). A structured parent interview for identifying young children with autism. *Journal of Autism and Developmental Disorders, 23*(4), 639–652.

Stone, W. L., Ousley, O. Y., Hepburn, S. L., Hogan, K. L., & Brown, C. S. (1999). Patterns of adaptive behavior in very young children with autism. *American Journal of Mental Retardation, 104*(2), 187–199.

Stone, W. L., Ousley, O. Y., & Littleford, C. D. (1997). Motor imitation in young children with autism: What's the object? *Journal of Abnormal Child Psychology, 25*(6), 475–485.

Stott, D. H., Moyes, F. A., & Henderson, S. E. (1972). *Test of Motor Impairment* (TMI). Guelph, British Columbia, Canada: Brook Educational.

Stratton, M. (1981). Behavioral assessment scale of oral functions in feeding. *American Journal of Occupational Therapy, 35,* 719–721.

Swettenham, J., Baron-Cohen, S., Charman, T., Cox, A., Baird, G., Drew, A., et al. (1998). The frequency and distribution of spontaneous attention shifts between social and nonsocial stimuli in autistic, typically developing, and nonautistic developmentally delayed infants. *Journal of Child Psychology and Psychiatry, 39*(5), 747–753.

Szatmari, P., Archer, L., Fisman, S., Streiner, D. L., & Wilson, F. (1995). Asperger's syndrome and autism: Differences in behavior, cognition, and adaptive functioning. *Journal of the American Academy of Child and Adolescent Psychiatry, 34*(12), 1662–1670.

Talay-Ongan, A., & Wood, K. (2000). Unusual sensory sensitivities in autism: A possible crossroads. *International Journal of Disability, Development and Education, 47*(2), 201–212.

Teitelbaum, P., Teitelbaum, O., Nye, J., Fryman, J., & Maurer, R. (1998). Movement analysis in infancy may be useful for early diagnosis of autism. *Proceedings of the National Academy of Sciences, 95*(23), 13982–13987.

Thelen, E., & Smith, L. (1994). *A dynamic systems approach to the development of cognition and action.* Cambridge, MA: MIT Press.

Tomchek, S. (2001). Assessment of individuals with an autism spectrum disorder utilizing a sensorimotor approach. In R. Huebner (Ed.), *Autism: A sensorimotor approach to management* (pp. 103–138). Gaithersburg, MD: Aspen Press.

Trecker, A. (2001). Play and praxis in children with autism: Observations and intervention strategies. In H. Miller-Kuhaneck (Ed.), *Autism: A comprehensive occupational therapy approach* (pp. 133–151). Bethesda, MD: American Occupational Therapy Association.

Vilensky, J. A., Damasio, A. R., & Maurer, R. G. (1981). Gait disturbances in patients with autistic behavior. *Archives of Neurology, 38,* 646–649.

Volkmar, F. R., Cohen, D. J., & Paul, R. (1986). An evaluation of *DSM-III* criteria for infantile autism. *Journal of the American Academy of Child Psychiatry, 25*(2), 190–197.

Waterhouse, L., Fein, D., & Modahl, C. (1996). Neurofunctional mechanisms in autism. *Psychological Review, 103*(3), 457–489.

Watling, R. L., Deitz, J., & White, O. (2001). Comparison of Sensory Profile scores of young children with and without autism spectrum disorders. *American Journal of Occupational Therapy, 55*(4), 416–423.

Weimer, A. K., Schatz, A. M., Lincoln, A., Ballantyne, A. O., & Trauer, D. A. (2001). "Motor" impairment in Asperger syndrome: Evidence for a deficit in proprioception. *Developmental and Behavioral Pediatrics, 22,* 92–101.

Williams, D. (1994). *Somebody somewhere.* New York: Doubleday.

Williams, E., Costall, A., & Reddy, V. (1999). Children with autism experience problems with both objects and people. *Journal of Autism and Developmental Disorders, 29,* 367–378.

Wing, L. (1996). *The autistic spectrum: A guide for parents and professionals.* London: Constable.

Wing, L. (1997). The autistic spectrum. *Lancet, 350*(9093), 1761–1766.

Wing, L., & Gould, J. (1979). Severe impairments of social interaction and associated abnormalities in children: Epidemiology and classification. *Journal of Autism and Developmental Disorders, 9*(1), 11–29.

Wing, L., & Shah, A. (2000). Catatonia in autistic spectrum disorders. *British Journal of Psychiatry, 176,* 357–362.

Woodhouse, J. M., Adoh, T. O., & Oduwaiye, K. A. (1992). *Cardiff Acuity Test.* Windsor, England: Keeler.

World Health Organization. (2001). *ICF: International classification of functioning, disability, and health.* Geneva, Switzerland: Author.

SECTION VI

INTERVENTIONS

The driving force behind research on autism and pervasive developmental disorders is the search for increasingly effective and efficient forms of treatment. This is an extremely challenging goal. The impairments of individuals with autism begin in the first year or two of life; they are severe and broad based; they interfere with the unfolding of basic competencies in socialization and communication, they affect the most basic processes of attention and motivation that serve as a basis for all learning, they are often compounded by intellectual disability; they are of unknown origin and lifelong duration. As such, they present some of the most significant challenges to educators and clinicians, not to mention the families of afflicted individuals.

The planning of an intervention strategy must be carefully related to the assessment of a individual's current level of functioning, an understanding of the individual's strengths and difficulties, a theoretical and pragmatic model for planning and delivering long-term, stage-by-stage programming, and a vision of the individual's potential future. To be effective, an intervention strategy must be broad-gauged and relate to the full range of an individual's impairments. The interventions must recognize individual domains of difficulties (e.g., speech and language or motor skills) as well as the interaction among domains (e.g., the ways in which social and language development proceed). Because autism starts early and persists, the interventions must be thoughtfully adapted to the individual's chronological age and developmental phase. A program of education and socialization that is suitable for a

5-year-old would be incongruous with a young adult, even when developmental level in the two individuals is very similar.

The types and strategies for intervention are guided primarily by a pragmatic concern for what is useful in promoting development and adaptation. The primary locus for intervention is almost always educational, and the central professionals involved in intervention are educators. Through the application of scientific knowledge about learning and development, special educators aim at helping individuals with autism and other pervasive disorders to use their areas of competence, to expand their skills and capacities, and to develop approaches to circumventing areas of difficulty in order to move ahead in their personal and social adaptation. In this, special educators are equipped with theories about social, language, and other types of learning as well as models for teaching (curricula).

Approaches to intervention are guided by theories of developmental psychopathology that focus attention on particular domains. Thus, there is a general emphasis on the importance of social cognition and learning communicative and social skills, as well as on enhancing motivation to achieve and reduction of interfering and maladaptive behaviors. Intervention is also shaped by ideological considerations concerning the importance of preparing individuals to remain as fully a part of their communities as possible; to be able to take an active role in their families and broader social world; and to develop skills necessary for as independent and productive an adult life as possible.

Throughout the life of an individual with autism, families remain vital to the individual's welfare and development. A well-functioning strategy for intervention represents collaboration between family and professionals and reflects the values, style, and goals of the family. Only through such partnership can there be suitable and sensitive resolution of difficult issues that relate to methods for dealing with specific maladaptive behaviors, the accommodations needed for an individual to live within the family, the expression of sexual and other intimate behaviors, the types of work and exposure to risks that are acceptable, the role for medication, and the like.

Having a child or sibling with autism places particular burdens on families. When families are included in the program for intervention as full partners, their own special needs are also recognized and they are provided with suitable support and guidance. There is a delicate balance—different for different families and at various stages of an individual and family's life—between the model that emphasizes collaboration among professionals and families, and the model that recognizes and meets the needs of parents and siblings and sees them as requiring and deserving care in their own right. Encouraging parents to clearly define their views and wishes is an important step in resolving the tensions that can arise between the collaborative and clinical paradigms. The provision of fully informed consent is ethically central to all clinical and professional intervention with individuals with autism and their families. But intervention must go beyond consent alone. To be successful for the individual as well as for the family, families must feel ownership in the intervention program, through collaborating to develop its goals, structure, methods, and materials. This can sometimes involve making compromises about priorities in intervention, such as helping a child learn to say the family pet's name because this will allow him to interact more fully in family life, even though other language goals might appear more important to teachers and therapists; or giving a try to methods that the educational team might not feel comfortable with or be completely familiar with at first. As long as a compromise position can be reached, in which both educators and family agree on a course of

action and agree to monitor progress so changes can be made if a particular technique seems not to be achieving its goal, intervention can proceed on a collaborative basis.

In the United States and in most other nations in the world today, children with autism or other severe developmental problems live at home and participate in family life. Generally, they attend neighborhood schools and programs, sometimes spending all or part of their days with normal children who are close to them in age. In some nations, and for some children in the United States, programming takes place in specialized day settings. For younger children, these can consist of therapeutic nurseries and day programs; for older children, special classes or specialized schools for individuals with developmental disabilities. It is unusual in the United States, and in many other nations today, for children with autism and similar disorders to enter residential programs (such as hospitals, therapeutic treatment centers, or longer term facilities). However, occasional respite care and camps are useful for the family and for the individual child. And there some cases in which extremely severe behavioral difficulties require residential or hospital treatment, often for a limited time. Also, while home living may seem optimal, exceptions need to be respected: there are children without families, children whose families are unable to provide a suitable setting for them, children who themselves do better outside of the family, and individuals for whom foster care or other settings, including residential treatment, are clearly indicated. As individuals with autism mature and reach adulthood, and as their parents mature and reach old age, it is natural for them to have a transition from family life to another setting, such as a group home, supported apartment, or residential program.

Wherever an individual lives and is cared for, intervention strategies and the atmosphere of the program must respect the individual's humanity and personal value; programs must appreciate and enhance the individual's personal autonomy and individuality. For individuals with severe behavioral problems and intellectual disabilities, maintaining this attitude of concern, empathy, and respect has not been a simple matter in any setting—not in a school, hospital, or residential program. It requires constant attention, consciousness raising, self-assessment, monitoring, intensive staff support, and excellent administration. Without such vigilance, it is easy for humane standards to slip, as has been all too often the case in large institutions but also in nursing homes, special schools, group homes, independent living settings, and residential programs, and sometimes, tragically, in the context of a stressed family.

Care for the whole person with a developmental disability requires consideration, as well, of physical and general health needs. Individuals with autism, mental retardation, and other disabilities have a right to high-quality, comprehensive health care, including routine preventive health measures (such as immunizations and dental care) as well as special health evaluation and treatment (eye examinations, hearing, nutrition, orthopedic, etc.). Family practitioners may provide routine evaluation, monitoring, and treatment. In addition, individuals with developmental disabilities often require the special expertise of physicians with training and interest in autism and developmental disabilities. This is particularly important when there are complicated comorbid conditions—such as a seizure or metabolic disorder—or behavioral and psychiatric problems that require psychopharmacological treatment in combination with other behavioral approaches. It is important that medical management be closely integrated with other strategies for intervention, and that prescribing physicians work as members of the treatment team. Medication should be prescribed only in the context of an individual's full life—his or her experiences at home and in school, and the other, ongoing interventions that may be aimed at the same targets, for example, reduction of stereotypic, compulsive, or self-injurious behavior. Like any treatment, medication effects, both main effects and side effects, should be carefully monitored by relatively disinterested parties, such as educators, who should document

improvement for targeted symptoms. An advocate (a nurse, educator, physician, social worker, or other professional) working closely with parents can help coordinate the range of interventions, set up monitoring programs for medications and other interventions, and assure communication and collaboration among professionals and settings of care.

There is no cure for autism. Thus, clinicians must strive to ameliorate difficulties and help the individual with autism and the family cope as well as possible. Families and professionals need to be realistic about what can be achieved with current knowledge and methods while maintaining reasonable hope for future advances.

Where there is no cure, however, there are often countless treatments, especially when the clinical problems are urgent, as with autism. Autism can be a heart-breaking disorder. Professionals and others wish to be helpful, and in this field, as with other types of incurable medical disorders, hope and wish can breed belief in the benefits of an unproven therapy or even in a "miracle cure." It is not surprising that parents and professionals will hear about "breakthroughs" and "alternatives" that promise striking success but for which no rigorous studies or data are available.

Many treatments start with chance observation, and anecdotal reports may contain important truths. In the usual course of science, these hunches and observations become hypotheses that are rigorously tested, including studies of efficacy and safety. Only when the objective data about benefits and dangers are available should a potential treatment be undertaken outside of a careful research setting. One aspect of showing respect for individuals with autism and other disorders is to assure that interventions stand the test of rigorous investigation, publication of findings for peer review, and replication. The gradual improvement of interventions for individuals with autism and associated disorders, described in this section, is testimony to the value of this scientific approach.

CHAPTER 33

Curriculum and Classroom Structure

J. GREGORY OLLEY

Since the last edition of this book in 1997, there has been a remarkable increase in attention to the curriculum offered to students with autism. Many more formal curricula for students with autism spectrum disorder have been published for classroom use. Most of these curricula are focused primarily on higher functioning students with autism or Asperger syndrome. There has also been an increase in the number and quality of studies that examine the effect of curriculum or measure curricular outcomes. To help parents, teachers, and others find their way through this explosion of new information, several new publishers have emerged. In addition to the familiar newsletters and other publications associated with the Autism Society of America and the magazine, *Exceptional Parent, Autism-Asperger's Digest Magazine* (published by Future Horizons, Inc.) now offers a monthly summary of news, research, opinion, and resources. Further, curricula and a variety of education-related publications are being marketed to educators.

This chapter reviews new findings with an emphasis on materials that are readily available from publishers and on information that is supported by objective research. The reauthorized Elementary and Secondary Education Act, now known as the No Child Left Behind Act, requires that educators base their practices on "scientifically based research." In that spirit, this chapter emphasizes research-based practices, while recognizing that many of the commercially available curricula are based on the experiences of one or a few teachers. Table 33.1 provides a list of educational materials and resources, although this list is not intended to be

complete or to be an endorsement of any of these materials.

Much has changed since this topic appeared in the second edition of this book (Olley & Reeve, 1997). That chapter recognized the increasing emphasis on evidence-based practice by classifying information on curriculum, classroom structure, and related educational and therapeutic approaches in three categories. The chapter acknowledged that no curriculum was supported by a high standard of well-controlled and replicated research, but it did emphasize a group of approaches that had some research support based on conventional standards of science. The chapter referred to a second level of less stringent evidence as "conventional wisdom." These approaches were widely accepted but not supported by controlled research. The third group was made up of controversial approaches that were not widely supported and often had evidence indicating that they were not effective.

The current chapter again emphasizes approaches that have empirical support and wide acceptance in the field. However, the nature of research in autism makes it difficult to apply a consistent and stringent standard to judge scientific worth. Unlike studies of medical treatments, large numbers of participants, random assignment to treatments, or other hallmarks of traditional science seldom characterize autism research. Studies of curricular variables in autism are more likely to involve small numbers of children in multiple baseline or other single-subject designs. Rogers (1998) reviewed comprehensive treatment programs in autism using Lonigan, Elbert, and Johnson's (1998) criteria for empirically supported treatments.

TABLE 33.1   Publishers of Curricula for Students with Autism

Publisher	Address	Examples of Curricula
Academic Communication Associates, Inc.	P.O. Box 4279 Oceanside, CA 92052-4279 www.acadcom.com	Breakthroughs: How to Reach Students with Autism
Autism Society of North Carolina Bookstore (does not publish curricula but is a good source for many autism publications)	505 Oberlin Road, Suite 230, Raleigh, NC 27605-1345 www.autismsociety-nc.org	TEACCH structured teaching assessment; Visually Structured Tasks: Independent Activities for Students with Autism and Other Visual Learners
Future Horizons, Inc.	721 West Abram Street Arlington, TX 76013 www.futurehorizons-autism.com	Navigating the Social World
IEP Resources	P.O. Box 930160 Verona, WI 53593-0160 www.iepresources.com	One-on-One: Working with Low-Functioning Children with Autism
Institute for Child Development	Department of Psychology Binghamton University State University of New York Binghamton, NY 13902-6000 http://icd.binghamton.edu	IGS Curriculum
Jessica Kingsley Publishers	116 Pentonville Road London, N1 9JB. UK www.jkp.com	Relationship Development Intervention with Young Children: Social and Emotional Development Activities for Asperger Syndrome, Autism, PDD, and NLD
LinguiSystems	3100 Fourth Avenue East Moline, IL 61244 www.linguisystems.com	Autism and PDD Series (Play, Social Skills, Picture Stories, and Language Activities, Concept Development)
ProEd	8700 Shoal Creek Boulevard Austin, TX 78757-6897 www.proed.com	Higher Functioning Adolescents and Young Adults with Autism: A Teacher's Guide
Sopris West	4093 Specialty Place Longmont, CO 80504-5400 www.sopriswest.com	Teaching Kids and Adults with Autism: Building the Framework for Lifetime Learning
Team Asperger	304 West Schindler Place #208 Menasha, WI 54952 www.ccoder.com	Gaining Face: Educational Software to Teach Understanding of Facial Expressions

Rogers found only eight programs with sufficient data to merit review, and none of the studies met the standard for "well-established or probably efficacious treatments." Research on curriculum has the same limitations noted in Rogers's review. Thus, this chapter does not apply a strict standard to categorize the findings by their scientific merit.

This chapter addresses the evidence for curricular approaches in an effort to guide the reader through the confusion of claims and counterclaims that has been the hallmark of autism information for more than 50 years. The curricula and the research on curricular variables in this chapter focus primarily on research-based approaches to teaching educational goals. Leaf and McEachin (1999) have provided an overview of instruction to address noneducational goals that are common in autism (e.g., sleep and eating problems, toilet training).

Our knowledge of effective education practices continues to grow, but it is far from complete. Educators recognize that they are often required to make important decisions on topics that have inadequate foundation in research. Therefore, the field is guided by a great deal of common sense consensus, which I have referred to as "conventional wisdom." This information is important and often has support based on experience and anecdote over many years. Further, the "conventional wisdom" of autism curriculum is worthy of mention, because over time many of these commonly held beliefs can be subjected to scientific study. This chapter pays little attention to the third category, "controversial practices," a mix of promising new ideas with little or no evidence and approaches that promise dramatic results and avoid or resist objective evaluation of their effectiveness.

CURRICULUM, METHODS, AND OUTCOMES

Most research on education for children with autism and most comprehensive education programs emphasize teaching methods, but recent publications have called for an increase in attention to curriculum and the interaction of curriculum and methods of instruction (Browder, 2001; Dunlap, Kern, & Worcester, 2001). Research on curriculum for typically developing preschool children is also increasing, in part thanks to funding from the U.S. Department of Education's new Institute of Education Sciences.

Although curriculum is a basic term in education, its definition is not consistently agreed on. Dunlap et al. (2001) defined curriculum for students with autism broadly: "A student's curriculum comprises a range of practices and activities, including but not limited to the content of instruction, the manner in which instruction is delivered, the materials used to complete activities, and the scheduling of instruction" (p. 130). Wolery and Winterling (1997) also defined curriculum broadly to include "an organized description of a body of content, assessment procedures for selecting goals for instruction, and methods for teaching selected skills. Also, each of these elements should be based on a conceptually consistent foundation"

(p. 88). Most educators would agree that assessment, curriculum, and teaching methods are intertwined, but not all would agree with such a broad definition. Further, available curricula do not meet Wolery and Winterling's high standards. In fact, few published curricula include any data on student outcomes or "a conceptually consistent foundation."

Browder (2001) offered a more concise definition of curriculum as "a defined course of study." Despite the brevity of her definition, Browder's approach to curriculum includes detailed procedures for integrating assessment and individualized curriculum and measurement of student outcomes. Her extensive treatment of this subject is a useful guide for anyone who seeks to design education programs for students with autism or other disabilities. Her suggestions have also guided the standards for curricula that are expressed in this chapter. The interested reader should consult Browder's book for a complete guide, but for purposes of this chapter, the following points are important to note.

The available curricula for students with autism have not been evaluated as a package, but such research would be very difficult and probably not necessary. The published curricula should serve as guides to the content, sequence, and outcomes of instruction, but they must be modified for each student to reflect the student's learning characteristics and the culture of the family and community. Thus, an effective curriculum is one that provides a procedure for educators to individualize the content and sequence and to measure relevant student outcomes. Browder (2001) also stressed the quality assurance function of a curriculum. That is, a curriculum helps to keep educators focused on important life outcomes.

The process of individualizing curriculum is addressed throughout this chapter as it applies to students with autism, but Browder's recommendations are applicable to all students. She stressed the importance of socially valued outcomes, such as self-determination, and she described several variations of the person-centered planning process that can ensure that parents and significant others participate meaningfully in the development of curriculum and the individualized education program (IEP). Federal law gives parents a very strong role in this process, but many parents do not take full advantage of this opportunity. The curriculum-building process should ensure that students are working toward meaningful and valued adult outcomes.

Browder (2001) traced the shift in curricular emphasis that began in the 1980s. Prior to that time, curriculum emphasized almost exclusively skill building with the assumption that the specified skills were the key to adult success. The influence of the person-centered planning approach has shifted the emphasis to address the constraints that the environment places on learning. Browder suggested an approach to curriculum that includes both skill building and accommodations that address environmental obstacles to learning. Her approach is one of curriculum-based assessment that combines an ecological inventory approach to functional life skills and a more traditional academic curriculum.

Dunlap et al. (2001) also emphasized the importance of individualizing curriculum using curriculum-based assessment and reviewed the application of functional behavioral assessment to identifying curricular variables that are relevant for individual students with autism.

The chapters on curriculum and classroom structure in the earlier volumes of this book (Mirenda & Donnellan, 1987; Olley, 1987; Olley & Reeve, 1997) described the approaches that were popular at the time but emphasized that the differences among curricular approaches were rapidly disappearing. Today there are more autism programs than ever but more agreement on curriculum, particularly in the school-age years. This agreement is evident in the 2001 publication of a report from the Committee on Educational Interventions for Children with Autism (National Research Council, 2001). This panel of experts confirmed the view that education is the most valuable treatment available to children with autism and reviewed the available information. Several of the Committee's recommendations touched on curricular options and outcomes related to curriculum. In general, they concluded that the outcomes for students with autism should be "the same as for other children: personal independence and social responsibility. These goals imply progress in social and cognitive abilities, verbal and nonverbal communication skills, and adaptive

skills; reduction of behavioral difficulties; and generalization of abilities across multiple environments" (p. 5). The Committee further recommended that educators be accountable for outcomes and ". . . that ongoing measurement of treatment objectives and progress be documented frequently across a range of skill areas in order to determine whether a child is benefiting from a particular intervention and that the intervention be adjusted accordingly" (p. 5). The importance of curriculum is further evidenced in the recommendation for ". . . systematically planned, and developmentally appropriate educational activity toward identified objectives" (p. 6).

The Committee recommended specific curricular content. "The priorities of focus include functional spontaneous communication, social instruction delivered throughout the day in various settings, cognitive development and play skills, and proactive approaches to behavior problems" (p. 6). As to the issue of where education should take place, the Committee gave a cautious endorsement of inclusion when it stated the following. "To the extent that it leads to the acquisition of children's educational goals, young children with an autistic spectrum disorder should receive specialized instruction in a setting in which ongoing interactions occur with typically developing children" (p. 6).

The recommendations of this Committee represent the current consensus of experts. Thus, their recommendations for curricula can serve as useful categories to consider in this chapter. Further, these considerations should help teachers determine whether their curriculum is a "best practice" approach. Best practice should comprise the content areas noted by the Committee and individualized application of curricula that have research support. The category of conventional wisdom still has a place in the classroom, but as research continues to test these common assumptions, curricular decisions can be made up primarily of empirically supported practices.

CLASSROOM STRUCTURE

With few exceptions, current curricula continue to emphasize the conventional wisdom that children with autism learn more effectively and experience fewer signs of stress in well-structured learning environments. Structure is intended to make the learning environment clearer for learners who are easily confused or anxious in typical school settings. The curriculum and structure can help students with autism by making elements of the learning environment clearer and more predictable. For instance, the physical space, educational materials, sequence of activities, difficulty of the tasks, familiarity of the tasks, length of activities, and type of assistance available are common classroom considerations. Duker and Rasing (1989) found that removing distracting materials from the classroom reduced self-stimulation and increased on-task behavior. These variables have been studied in classrooms for many years and reviewed previously (Olley, 1999; Olley & Reeve, 1997).

In recent years, some additional aspects of structure have been examined in carefully controlled research and found to have proven benefits. For instance, several studies have shown that visual activity schedules can make many aspects of the curriculum clearer to students and provide many benefits in an efficient manner. This research and a detailed description of the use of activity schedules can be found in McClannahan and Krantz (1998). Activity schedules have become widely used in classrooms around the world to provide clear structure and thus ease the difficulty of transition from one environment to another, reduce problem behavior, and increase time engaged in learning.

Schreibman, Whalen, and Stahmer (2000) described another strategy for making future events more predictable in order to reduce disruption during transition. They showed three young children with autism videotapes of their individual transition problem settings. The videos traced the course of the transition from one location to another. To control for the effect of modeling, the videos did not include other people. Each of the children reduced disruptions dramatically in the settings shown in the videos, generalized this improvement to another setting, and maintained gains through a 1-month follow-up.

Division Treatment and Education of Autistic and Related Communication Handicapped CHildren (TEACCH) at the University of North Carolina has written teacher guides to providing visual structure (Faherty & Hearsey, 1996) and individualizing activity schedules (TEACCH, 1998).

WHERE TO TEACH

The consensus view on the best location for teaching children with autism has shifted over the past few decades. Before the Education for All Handicapped Children Act of 1975, children with autism were often excluded from public education. In the late 1970s, separate special education schools and separate autism classes within public schools grew. Since the mid-1970s, federal law has required education in the "least restrictive environment," but today many educators and parents speak of inclusion of students with autism with age-mates in all aspects of the education program. Some advocacy groups currently take the position that only full inclusion is acceptable for children with autism. As noted earlier, the Committee on Educational Interventions for Children with Autism (National Research Council, 2001) endorsed inclusion "to the extent that it leads to the acquisition of children's educational goals." The trend toward inclusion is clear, but many questions remain unanswered.

Commercial curricula are available for use in inclusion settings (e.g., Wagner, 1999). Several writers have addressed strategies to individualize curricula in inclusion classrooms. Browder and Wilson (2001) described an ecological assessment process for designing IEPs and individualized curricula. Myles and Simpson (1998) developed the autism inclusion collaboration model, which specifies the elements needed for successful inclusion: appropriately trained personnel; reduced class size; a collaborative problem-solving approach involving consultants, teachers, and parents; adequate teacher planning time; availability of paraprofessionals; and in-service training. Even with all of these elements present, Myles and Simpson acknowledged that full inclusion might not be the best plan for every student with autism.

The emphasis on inclusion can also conflict with the emphasis on education in community settings. For many years, educators have advocated for teaching community skills in community settings. Yet, if children with autism are removed from their inclusion classrooms to be taught in the community, they may miss key learning opportunities in the classroom and risk calling further attention to their "differentness." Browder and Cooper (2001) have given suggestions for individualizing curriculum to achieve a balance between community instruction and inclusion. They noted that some key goals for children with autism can be taught only in the community (e.g., dealing with unfamiliar people). A recent study by Taylor, Hughes, Richard, Hoch, and Coello (2004) provided a good example of the importance of teaching in natural community settings. These authors taught teenagers with autism to seek assistance when lost by prompting the students with a vibrating pager.

Most advocates for inclusion point out that problem behavior is often an obstacle to successful inclusion. Recent research on positive behavior support has emphasized applications in inclusion settings. Janney and Snell (2000) have provided a useful guide for educators to apply principles of behavior support and self-management to achieve successful inclusion.

Although many contend that inclusion will be the preferred education model of the future, a survey by Agran, Alper, and Wehmeyer (2002) found most teachers not to be in favor of inclusion for students with severe disabilities. Further, these teachers were typically not included in their schools' planning for inclusion. A study of the views of children with autism toward inclusion also provides important cautions. Ochs, Kremer-Sadlik, Solomon, and Sirota (2001) concluded that peers hold more influence over the success of inclusion than do teachers. The authors observed many successful and unsuccessful encounters between high-functioning students with autism and peers and concluded that peers who were aware of the autism diagnosis and had some understanding of the disorder were more accepting of differences and more likely to facilitate inclusion.

Although inclusion will, no doubt, remain a controversial topic, modifications to the curriculum are among the most practical, cost-effective strategies to implement inclusion. Reviews of curricular strategies for inclusion (Harrower, 1999; Wolery & Schuster, 1997) have noted the value of allowing students to choose activities and reinforcers, priming or practice in preparation for transition or a new

activity, smaller group size and opportunity for independent work, and other individualized curricular change.

SOCIAL SKILLS

In the last edition of this book, Olley and Reeve (1997) reviewed specialized curricula that addressed specific aspects of learning for students with autism (e.g., cognitive skills, communication, social skills) but acknowledged that curricular approaches were moving toward comprehensive and integrated models. Social interaction deficits are invariably intertwined with the language problems and narrowness of interest that make up current definitions of autism. This trend away from specialized curricula has continued in recent years, and distinctions among types of curricula are quickly fading. Although the contemporary emphasis is on comprehensive and individualized curriculum, many programs treat social skills as the core of their curricula. Thus, a review of curricula emphasizing social skills is still important.

Reduction of Problem Behavior

Simpson and Myles (1998) and Taylor (2001) have provided practical and readable overviews of the research-based approaches to teaching social skills. They noted the controversy between those who believe that problem behavior must be eliminated and basic classroom skills (e.g., sitting and listening, following spoken directions) taught first and those who believe that the curriculum must first motivate the child to learn.

Leaf and McEachin (1999) stated well the rationale for addressing disruptive behavior before progressing to teaching other skills. They noted that many teachers and parents choose not to change disruptive behavior, because their efforts are very likely to make the child upset and more disruptive in the short run. Nevertheless, these authors argued, disruptive behavior (tantrums, aggression, noncompliance, refusal to participate) interferes with learning language, social, and academic skills, and it is the factor most likely to prevent inclusion.

Fortunately, research using the curriculum as an independent variable has been useful in identifying effective and nonintrusive strategies to reduce problem behavior (reviewed by Kern & Dunlap, 1998; Wolery & Winterling, 1997). Research of this type typically uses a functional assessment of behavior to identify the antecedents and consequences that influence a target behavior. Based on these findings, researchers have manipulated the content of the activities, the materials used, and the form of student response to improve classroom performance. For instance, Kern and Dunlap pointed out that a common function of problem behavior in the classroom is negative reinforcement in the form of escape. If disruptive behavior leads to escape from a classroom activity, the teacher can change the activity's length, difficulty, familiarity, materials, setting of instruction, type of assistance available, visual cues, and so on to maintain the student's engagement.

This curricular approach to managing problem behavior is appealing, because it is preventive. The curriculum-based assessment approach advocated by Browder (2001) and Dunlap et al. (2001) should lead to an effective and individualized curriculum that includes a variety of functional activities to promote student engagement and learning. Such a curriculum should include a mix of new and somewhat challenging activities with familiar and motivating tasks. If these activities are presented to the student in the form of an activity schedule as described by McClannahan and Krantz (1998), the result is likely to be a student who is motivated to follow his or her schedule independently and learn new skills with minimal problem behavior.

Social Stories

Social stories is an approach that provides visual structure and sequencing to teach social skills and reduce problem behavior. The approach has grown in popularity over the past decade, and in recent years research has provided some objective support for its use with higher functioning students. Social stories are similar to an earlier procedure, "cognitive picture rehearsal" (Groden & LeVasseur, 1995), which emphasizes the use of reinforcing consequences in the stories and has been applied to lower functioning students. Both approaches present students with brief, individualized stories illustrated by line drawings. Hagiwara and Myles (1999) presented the sequence of

pictures using a computer. The stories guide the student through a social event that has previously led to problem behavior. Social stories are made up of four types of sentences (Gray, 1996, 1998). *Descriptive* sentences define the social setting and the behavior typical of that setting. *Directive* sentences instruct the student about appropriate responses. *Perspective* sentences indicate the perspective or reaction of others. *Control* sentences provide relevant cues in the specific social situation. Cognitive picture rehearsal puts more explicit emphasis on concluding the story with an outcome that is desirable or preferred for the individual in order to provide reinforcement.

C. Smith (2001) noted several potential advantages to social stories, including the likelihood that learned social skills would generalize to new settings. Several studies have reported that social stories can result in increases in social behavior and reductions in problem behavior. Lorimer, Simpson, Myles, and Ganz (2002) reviewed these studies and cautioned that they have confounded the effects of social stories with other social interventions. Lorimer et al. demonstrated that social stories reduced tantrums in a high-functioning 5-year-old boy using an ABAB design, but Smith's optimism about generalization was not confirmed. The frequency of tantrums increased when the social stories were not used.

Kuoch and Mirenda (2003) addressed the research design problems of earlier studies by presenting social stories as the independent variable not confounded by other factors. In this ABA design with three children 3 to 6 years old, social stories resulted in a reduction in problem behavior that continued when social stories were not presented. More recently, Barry and Burlew (2004) used social stories to teach new skills, rather than to reduce problem behavior. They taught two lower functioning children with autism (ages 7 and 8) to make choices and to engage in appropriate play. The study did not have a phase in which the social stories were removed, so no findings on generalization could be demonstrated.

The research on social stories is increasing, but most of the literature is still anecdotal. More information is needed on applications to lower functioning students and procedures to improve generalization. Nevertheless, social stories offer an appealingly nonintrusive way to teach social skills and reduce behavior problems.

Play and Leisure Curricula

The absence of age-appropriate play skills is a characteristic commonly used to diagnose autism in young children. Not surprisingly, most comprehensive curricula for young children include goals related to appropriate play and use of unstructured time (e.g., Handleman & Harris, 2001; Holmes, 1998; Leaf & McEachin, 1999). Many curricula aim to improve play competence in areas such as object play and symbolic play or to enhance children's "level of engagement in play and playfulness" (Baranek, Reinhartsen, & Wannamaker, 2001, p. 337). For young children, play is also the primary vehicle for teaching social skills and for many therapies. Activities carried out in play are often intended to improve motor or language or cognitive skills.

Play in Natural Settings

As the emphasis on inclusion has increased, research on curricular elements of play and related social skills has shifted to more natural settings. For example, Sigafoos and Littlewood (1999) extended their earlier classroom-based research on play to more spontaneous playground activities. They used the behavioral technique of behavior chain interruption to teach a 4-year-old boy with autism to request access to playground apparatus. The authors identified preferred play activities on the playground and interrupted them to require the child to say "play" in order to continue.

Shabani et al. (2002) examined free play between young children with autism and typically developing peers on the playground. They taught three boys with autism to make spoken initiations to play with peers by using a vibrating pager to prompt the initiations.

In addition to extending research on play to natural settings, studies have emphasized the importance of spontaneous, reciprocal play that is maintained by characteristics of the playmates and the setting, rather than reliant on continuing prompts, or instructions, or reinforcement by teachers. The leisure curriculum of Schleien and colleagues (Schleien, Meyer,

Heyne, & Brandt, 1995) is for individuals with a variety of disabilities. It emphasizes natural settings and leisure skills throughout a lifetime.

The most widely used strategy for teaching play and other social skills to children with autism in inclusion settings is to enlist the aid of a typically developing peer. DiSalvo and Oswald (2002) reviewed the research on these peer-mediated strategies and noted that they have been generally effective in increasing social initiations or social responses but not both. In a recent example, a study of a 4-year-old boy in an inclusion preschool found increases in initiations by peers and increases in responses by the target child (McGrath, Bosch, Sullivan, & Fuqua, 2003). Peer-mediated instruction of social skills has also been a key element of the Learning Experiences, an Alternative Program for Preschoolers and Their Parents (LEAP) preschool curriculum, which has shown impressive long-term benefits (Strain & Hoyson, 2000).

Modeling

Typically developing children learn most social skills by watching children and adults and imitating the social skills of others. The use of models has been a successful strategy for teaching social skills to many children, and it offers the promise of teaching spontaneous social interaction in natural settings. The success of inclusion and of instruction in settings with minimal structure relies, at least in part, on children's ability to learn by watching and imitating the behavior of others. Unfortunately, the benefits of just modeling or proximity to typical peers have been very limited for children with autism (reviewed by Taylor, 2001). Attending to the correct social stimulus is a deficit in virtually every child with autism, so successful curricula must rely on more than exposure to a model.

Jahr, Eldevik, and Eikeseth (2000) attempted to teach children with autism to engage in cooperative play using models but found that modeling alone was not effective. When the researchers also required the children with autism to give an oral description of the modeled activity, all six children learned to initiate and sustain episodes of cooperative play, vary their play, and transfer their skills to new play partners.

Structure Provided by Technology

Technology in the form of videotapes and computer-based presentations has also been successful in structuring the modeling strategy to teach social and cognitive skills. Video modeling has been used to teach complex play sequences to a preschooler (D'Ateno, Mangiapanello, & Taylor, 2003) and to teach perspective taking to three boys ages 6 to 9 (Charlop-Christy & Daneshvar, 2003). Another study of 7- to 11-year-old children found video modeling to be more effective than in vivo modeling to teach a variety of skills, including greetings, play, and self-help (Charlop-Christy, Le, & Freeman, 2000). A format in which the target child serves as the video model may be critical to making modeling effective for children with autism. Buggey, Toombs, Gardener, and Cervetti (1999) used video self-modeling to increase appropriate responses to questions in 7- to 12-year-olds. Wert and Neisworth (2003) presented four 4- and 5-year-old boys with videotapes of themselves making requests. The children showed increases in spontaneous requests.

Bernard-Opitz, Sriram, and Nakhoda-Sapuan (2001) used a computer program to present animated drawing and speech depicting common social problem situations to two groups of children with normal intelligence. One group had autism and one did not. Both groups learned a problem-solving skill that involved generating novel solutions to problems. The children with autism generated fewer novel solutions and were more variable than the typically developing group, but the children with autism did show modest evidence of generalization to new problems.

Technology has also been applied to instruction of a traditional academic skill: spelling. Kinney, Vedora, and Stromer (2003) taught generative spelling to an 8-year-old girl using a video model and video reinforcer presented on a notebook computer. These examples may be the beginning of many more studies to show the practical advantages of technology in presenting curriculum to students with autism in a clear and systematic form from which they can learn effectively. Technology may also provide important keys to individualized instruction in inclusion settings.

Scripts

A simple curricular strategy to teach play and other social skills is scripts. Although learning a script of a planned social interaction may seem contrary to teaching spontaneity, several studies have found scripted responses to generalize to spontaneous, original responses. Krantz and McClannahan (1993, 1998) and Sarokoff, Taylor, and Poulson (2001) taught scripted conversations, then faded the scripts and found that children with autism could initiate and maintain social exchanges without prompts from adults. In another study, nonreading students used audiotaped scripts and script fading to learn scripted interactions that generalized to nonscripted interactions (Stevenson, Krantz, & McClannahan, 2000).

Teaching Response Variability and Self-Management

Recent research has sought not only to reduce stereotyped responding but also to teach children with autism to vary the responses that they use to complete a task or solve a problem. "Insistence on sameness" was one of the characteristics of autism noted by Kanner (1943), and it continues to be regarded as a behavior pattern that interferes with both social and academic success. The ability to respond variably, rather than to perseverate on one response, can make students more effective problem solvers. Miller and Neuringer (2000) taught adolescents with autism to use both left and right buttons in a video game by reinforcing variable responding. The reinforcers were a smiley face on the video screen for a correct response and music and a piece of candy or 25 cents at the conclusion of a game.

Newman, Reinecke, and Meinberg (2000) extended the strategy of reinforcing variability by teaching young children with autism to self-reinforce following variable responding. Each of the three children had a different target behavior (play with a toy robot, response to questions, and drawing) for which variability was reinforced. The teacher simply instructed each child to respond in a different way (e.g., "How about a different color?") and provided a spoken prompt to take a penny each time that the child showed variation in the target behavior. The children later used the pennies to purchase treats of their choice. After fading out the prompts, the children continued to self-reinforce and to emit increased levels of variable behavior. These increases were maintained in a 1-month follow-up.

Self-management is also an important part of most behavioral curricula and pivotal response training, which are described later in this chapter.

Social Skills and Autism in Summary

Research continues to provide evidence for the value of many elements of curriculum for social skills. A comprehensive curriculum should include responding to the social overtures of other children and adults, initiating social behavior, minimizing stereotyped and perseverative behavior while using a flexible and varied repertoire of responses, and self-managing new and established skills. The social skills curriculum described by Taylor and Jasper (2001) is a good example of the application of all of these elements for children of different ages with autism.

Social Skills and Asperger Syndrome

The controversy about the validity of Asperger disorder continues (Freeman, Cronin, & Candela, 2002), but the controversy has not slowed the publication of curricula and related educational materials designed specifically for this population. Most of the emphasis in Asperger curricula has been on social skills, but these curricula have been different from those for children with autism. Asperger curricula have usually targeted higher level social behaviors that help the students to avoid standing out from their peers. Despite the growth in commercial curricula for students with Asperger syndrome, very little research evidence supports their use. Barnhill, Cook, Tebbenkamp, and Myles (2002) carried out an extensive 8-week instructional program for adolescents that focused on "paralanguage (deciphering varying tones of voice and rates of speech, understanding nonverbal sound patterns, and gaining meaning from others' marked emphases in speech) . . . identifying and responding to the facial expression of others" (p. 113). At the conclusion of the program, they found minimal changes. The authors surveyed parents and the participants in their study about skills that they thought were most important to teach. The respondents identified the following: how to talk on the phone, knowing your feelings, understanding the feelings of others, dealing with fear or anxiety, how to deal with bullies, how to resolve conflicts, how to talk to the opposite sex, accepting yourself, using self-control, how to ask for help, how to start and maintain conversations, and accepting criticism. The social validity of these curricular areas is important to note, but the research to date on teaching social skills to students with Asperger syndrome is meager.

As noted earlier, social skills curricula that are commercially available are often designed primarily for children with Asperger syndrome and contain activities that individual teachers or parents have found useful and practical (e.g., McAfee, 2002; Moyes, 2001). However, most elements of these curricula have not been subjected to careful research. Books by Simpson and Myles (1998; Simpson, Myles, Sasso, & Kamps, 1997) and reviews by Taylor (2001) and Weiss and Harris (2001) cover more of the autism spectrum and contain useful references to link their recommendations to a research base.

COGNITIVE SKILLS

Many researchers have pointed to the ways in which children and adults with autism understand or fail to understand emotions, facial expressions, symbolic or pretend play, and the perspective of others. Curricular approaches that emphasize these cognitive characteristics teach strategies and problem solving, rather than discrete skills (e.g., Butera & Haywood, 1995). Although the literature contains many studies that describe the cognitive differences that are common in children with autism, these characteristics have proven to be difficult to measure objectively and difficult to teach.

In recent years, the dominant research topic in the area of cognitive skills has been *theory of mind* (see Chapter 45, this volume). Several studies have described efforts to teach theory of mind to children with autism. Howlin,

Baron-Cohen, and Hadwin (1999) described a curriculum for teaching cognitive skills, including theory of mind (or *mind reading,* a term that has confused librarians attempting to catalogue this book). However, as a review by Charlop-Christy and Daneshvar (2003) indicated, attempts to teach theory of mind have been largely unsuccessful and have shown no evidence that the skill has generalized to new circumstances or to other cognitive or social behavior.

For instance, Chin and Bernard-Opitz (2000) taught conversation skills to three boys with autism ages 5 to 7 but found that their conversation skills did not generalize to improved theory of mind performance on a standard task. Charlop-Christy and Daneshvar (2003) preferred to use the term "perspective taking skills" to theory of mind but used the same basic paradigm to measure pre- and posttest performance. They used video modeling to teach perspective taking to three boys with autism ages 6 to 9. The combination of video modeling and teaching multiple exemplars also led to stimulus and response generalization, which had not been shown in any previous study.

The curricular topics of theory of mind (or perspective taking), emotional recognition, facial recognition, and problem solving are no longer of interest only to researchers and educators who espouse a cognitive approach. These skills are being taught in behavioral curricula and comprehensive curricula beginning in the preschool years (e.g., Weiss & Piccolo, 2001).

An example of a curriculum for infants and preschoolers that emphasizes cognitive and emotional development is Greenspan's (2000) "Floor Time" or Developmental, Individual-Difference, Relationship-Based (DIR) program. Although Greenspan has emphasized that his curriculum is comprehensive, descriptions of the program emphasize the development of relationships and affect. Proponents of DIR have disseminated information widely, but no controlled studies of the effectiveness of DIR have been published.

COMPREHENSIVE CURRICULA

As research progresses on curricular strategies that are most effective for students with

autism, the earlier curricular emphasis on single elements, such as social skills, communication, or particular cognitive styles is giving way to comprehensive curricula. The term *comprehensive* refers to curricula that include the knowledge and skills that all students need for success as well as specific curricular elements that can be individualized for students with autism. Most of the research and application using comprehensive curricula have been applied to preschool children.

Preschool Curricula

In recent years, research and program development have focused disproportionately on very young children. At least two factors are responsible for this emphasis. First, children with autism can now be reliably identified at much younger ages (see Chapters 22 and 23, this volume). Second, an often-cited study by Lovaas (1987) called attention to the possibility that children can make substantial gains if intensive treatment is provided at an early age. The past 15 years have generated many studies and the development of many models for preschool education in an effort to bolster or refute Lovaas's claim.

Handleman and Harris (2001) published a thorough description of 10 models for preschool services. Each description includes information on curriculum. The availability of this information is a striking change from earlier program descriptions that ignored curriculum as an important part of their models. Although the differences in educational approach are more striking in preschool programs than in school-age programs, the preschool curricula described by Handleman and Harris show a similarity of emphasis, indicating that experts are reaching consensus on this topic. Nearly all of the 10 programs include a combination of standard preacademic skills and preschool concepts with motor activities, self-help skills, and play. In addition, most of the models include emphasis on expressive language and social interaction. Each program has its special emphasis. For instance, the Princeton Child Development Institute (McClannahan & Krantz, 2001) implements its curriculum by teaching children to follow picture activity schedules and scripts for social interaction. The Walden Early Childhood

Programs (McGee, Morrier, & Daly, 2001) implement their curriculum in an incidental teaching format in which teachers follow the children's lead in determining the sequence of activities. Other behaviorally oriented programs (e.g., Rutgers Autism Program; Weiss & Piccolo, 2001) emphasize foundation skills, such as compliance with instructions, matching, imitation, and requesting.

Pivotal Response Training

Pivotal response training (PRT) emphasizes the teaching of core or pivotal skills that will make it easier for children with autism to learn all of the other components of a comprehensive curriculum. Robert Koegel and his colleagues have published extensively on this approach and its effectiveness (summarized in Koegel, Koegel, & McNerney, 2001). These pivotal skills reflect well-known characteristics of autism. The approach begins with "increasing the child's motivation to engage in social communicative interactions. This involves motivating the child to initiate social interactions, to self-regulate behavior, and to respond to complex interactions involving multiple cues" (p. 23). The strategies to increase motivation involve several curricular variables, such as offering choices of activities, materials, and topics; varying tasks by interspersing familiar (maintenance) tasks with unfamiliar tasks; and planning activities to individualize their length and difficulty and to ensure that naturally reinforcing consequences are available. Research on PRT has shown that these variables increase motivation as shown by improvements in language, social, and academic performance while also reducing disruptive behavior.

The ability to respond to multiple cues is considered pivotal because a narrowness of interest and attention is a common problem in autism. In the behavioral literature, this trait is referred to as *stimulus overselectivity*. To succeed in social or academic settings, children must be able to attend to relevant cues and ignore others. To use skills effectively, students must master another pivotal skill: self-management. PRT uses behavioral procedures, such as self-recording and self-reinforcement, to teach self-management and self-initiation.

These skills are "pivotal" because they generalize to new people and situations, and they lead to acquisition of other important skills that have not been directly taught. Koegel et al. (2001) reviewed many studies showing the efficiency of the approach and long-term improvements in disruptive behavior, language, social, and academic skills as well as attitude toward learning and enthusiasm.

Behavioral Curricula

Rogers's (1998) review of comprehensive treatment programs for children with autism found that all eight of the studies that met minimal scientific standards involved preschool children, and 7 of the 8 studies described behavioral programs. Thus, most of our knowledge of effective programs comes from work with young children using behavioral approaches. Earlier behavioral programs have been criticized for the narrowness of their curricula, but contemporary behavioral approaches offer comprehensive curricula that incorporate all or most of the elements discussed in this chapter.

The encouraging outcomes reported by Lovaas (1987) and subsequent criticism of Lovaas's research design (e.g., Gresham & MacMillan, 1997) have led to several replications (e.g., Eikeseth, Smith, Jahr, & Eldevik, 2002) and the growth of home programs for children with autism. Teachers and parents can now learn the Eden model on their home computer using a CD-ROM (Eden II Programs, 1999) and can learn the discrete trial teaching format and accompanying curriculum using a CD-ROM, PowerPoint slides, and manual (K. Smith, 2000).

Several behavioral programs have published rather detailed descriptions of their curricula (Leaf & McEachin, 1999; Lovaas, 2003; Romanczyk, 2002). They have some striking similarities to other curricula and some differences. The behavioral curricula are different in that they emphasize the importance of teaching prerequisite or foundation skills before teaching more conventional curricular content. These programs emphasize that the sequence of instruction is not absolutely rigid and must be individualized, but they do take into consideration typical developmental sequences, and they suggest an early emphasis on reduction of disruptive behavior (e.g., tantrums, self-stimulation). Leaf and McEachin also stressed the importance of addressing interfering problems, such as sleep disturbance, toilet accidents, and eating problems. Foundation skills include attending when multiple stimuli are present, which Lovaas addressed in part by curricular modifications and structure (breaking the lesson into small units, reducing distractions). Another prerequisite skill addressed by most behavioral programs is compliance. That is, young children are taught early in their programs to respond to adult instructions and to imitate the verbal and nonverbal cues of adults. Lovaas also placed great emphasis on discrimination learning early in the curriculum, because he has found it to be key to the acquisition of other academic, language, social, and emotional skills.

The other early skills in Lovaas's (2003) curriculum include sitting in a chair when instructed, completing a puzzle, dropping blocks into a bucket, and responding to the instruction, "Come here." After children master these early skills, comprehensive behavioral curricula resemble other curricula. They teach play and social skills, receptive and expressive language, independent work, motor skills, preschool concepts (color, shape, size, number, position, physical attributes), academic skills, leisure skills, choice making, self-help, and some skills that have been thought of previously as cognitive abilities (e.g., emotions, cause-effect, abstract reasoning, problem solving, and social awareness).

Comprehensive behavioral programs also draw on many of the curricular strategies reviewed in this chapter, such as scripts and script fading, activity schedules, and video modeling. However, many people continue to think of the discrete trial teaching method as the prime characteristic of Lovaas's (2003), Leaf and McEachin's (1999), and some other behavioral programs. This method includes the presentation of small units of information in the form of a direct instruction or a visual cue from the teacher to which the student is expected to respond. This format allows the opportunity for the adult to reinforce a correct response and move on to the next teaching trial. Discrete trial instruction is perhaps the best example of a teacher-directed approach. In contrast, some other behavioral approaches, such as incidental teaching (McGee et al., 2001) and PRT (Koegel et al., 2001), structure the learning environment to allow students

to take the initiative in an activity before providing reinforcement. These two contrasting methods of structuring the learning environment both stress learning through reinforcement, but the discrete trial approach controls the sequence and timing of learning opportunities much more, thus providing many more learning trials per hour. Lovaas (2003) emphasized the importance of "massed trials" to achieve faster and more efficient learning, whereas adherents of incidental teaching have emphasized the importance of reinforcing student initiative in more natural learning environments (Fenske, Krantz, & McClannahan, 2001; McGee et al., 2001).

TRANSITION TO ADULTHOOD

In the past decade, a larger percentage of children with autism have achieved the skills and been given the support to live their adult lives fully included in their communities. For those individuals who continue to require education and community services through adulthood, several writers have offered guides or formal curricula (DiLeo, 2000; Howlin, 1997). The adult curriculum of the Princeton Child Development Institute (McClannahan, MacDuff, & Krantz, 2002) is the most research-based of those currently available. It extends many of the same approaches offered for children while increasing the emphasis on home- and community-living skills. Adults learn self-care and social skills as well as more than 600 specific skills in areas such as money management, time, and recreation and leisure. Photographic or written activity schedules, which are widely used with young children, are also used effectively to structure the adult curriculum to encourage independent functioning.

The personal goals of many adults with disabilities focus on self-advocacy and self-determination, rather than the acquisition of new work or academic skills (Johnson, 1999). In recent years, the self-determination movement has included more individuals with autism who wish to have greater control over their finances and other major areas of decision. Little information is available on the outcomes of such efforts, although Fullerton and Coyne (1999) have described a self-determination program designed specifically for individuals with autism. It is likely that this emphasis will continue, and more data on adult outcomes in self-determination will be available soon.

SOCIAL VALIDITY

Several studies of curriculum reviewed in this chapter included measures of social validity as suggested by the Committee on Educational Interventions for Children with Autism (National Research Council, 2001). Most of the studies that included a measure of social validity asked parents if they thought that the intervention was acceptable and/or whether the changes in behavior were meaningful (e.g., Barnhill et al., 2002; Buggey et al., 1999; Chin & Bernard-Opitz, 2000; McGrath et al., 2003). This attention to social validity can be expected to increase in future research on all aspects of autism services.

CONCLUSION

The research findings on curricular strategies for students with autism that were reviewed in the previous editions of this book continue to be applied with success. In addition, the findings reviewed in this chapter reveal a satisfying trend toward continued research and innovation and the application of findings to comprehensive curricula.

Curricular approaches to instruction have sometimes been derived from principles of learning that are well established in basic research. They have sometimes originated with the informal observations of parents or teachers and the creative ideas that teachers apply to solving challenging problems. Regardless of their origins, many of these ideas are eventually subjected to scientific study, while others remain in the category of conventional wisdom. Some approaches, for whatever reasons, have not been subjected to controlled research, and others have been carefully studied and failed to show benefit.

Some approaches are poorly described and thus are difficult to test or replicate. Some approaches are vague or overly broad in stating their expected outcomes. This chapter is limited to treatment approaches that use curriculum or classroom structure to achieve clearly

stated educational outcomes. Therapies that promise broad improvements without stating clear educational outcomes have not been reviewed. Thus, some programs with distinct curricula remain in the category of controversial approaches, because they have either failed to carry out research on key parts of their curriculum (or other aspects of their method) or have resisted objective evaluation by others.

Fortunately, the curricular strategies that were supported by research in the last edition of this volume (Olley & Reeve, 1997) are still supported by research and practice. Some approaches that had little or no empirical support a few years ago have gained at least the promise of effectiveness through recent research (e.g., social stories, video modeling).

The research and program development of recent years have provided stronger support for conclusions about the effective components of curriculum. Although much research remains to be done, the following conclusions may be useful to developing programs and may encourage further research.

1. To some extent, more is better. More opportunities to learn, more exposure to peers who encourage social exchange, and more planned and structured instructional time are likely to promote learning. Although programs with many hours of teacher-directed activities (e.g., Lovaas, 2003) have been successful, there is also good evidence for pivotal response training and incidental teaching, which offer many hours of learning opportunities that are more child-directed.
2. Comprehensive curricula are available that incorporate all or most of the effective elements noted in this chapter. These elements include clear classroom structure in the form of:
   —Activity schedules
   —Individualized curricular modifications (e.g., student choice of length, difficulty, and familiarity of activities)
   —Clear physical boundaries with minimal distraction
   —Predictable routine
   —Individualized sequence of instruction based on developmental sequences where appropriate

—Maximum opportunity to generalize to new settings, tasks, and people

3. The content of comprehensive curricula include elements such as:
   —Assessment-based curricula
   —Traditional readiness skills for preschoolers and academic skills at all ages
   —Functional skills that prepare for adult responsibilities and independence
   —Strategies to reduce disruptive or maladaptive behavior
   —Cognitive skills, such as perspective taking
   —Social skills that include reciprocal interaction, initiation, and self-management
   —Functional communication

4. Curricula are now available for all ages, but the strong focus of research is on preschool or toddler-age children. Regardless of curricular orientation, programs stress early intervention and education, and parents increasingly expect such services.

5. Strategies for presenting learning opportunities have capitalized on the students' stronger visual learning skills. Examples include picture activity schedules, video modeling and self-modeling, picture scripts, and script fading. New applications of technology, such as vibrating pagers to prompt students, also offer promise.

6. Despite the growing consensus among experts and practitioners, serious disagreements continue to fuel debate among rival viewpoints. Although the concept of *evidence-based practice* is widely accepted, the presence (or absence) of published research support seems only slightly related to popularity of a curriculum. Supporters of behavioral approaches have been far more active in using scientific methods to evaluate their work. Scientific and anecdotal reports of their outcomes cannot be ignored, but not all children show dramatic gains, and children with lower intellectual functioning appear to benefit less. Behavioral researchers have also taken the lead in creating comprehensive curricula that borrow from ideas that were introduced by those from a cognitive or developmental orientation. Teachers and parents who wish to use this chapter to guide curricular decisions should focus on approaches that have published research support and individualize curricular decisions as suggested by Browder (2001).

These conclusions are congruent with those of the Committee on Educational Interventions for Children with Autism (National Research Council, 2001). The growing consensus on the components of effective education is, indeed, a hopeful sign for the future of students with autism.

Cross-References

Chapters 34 and 35 review behavioral interventions, Chapters 36 through 38 discuss issues in enhancing communication skills, and school-based programs are reviewed in Chapter 39. Issues in inclusion and model programs are addressed in Chapters 40 and 41. Collaborative work with families is described in Chapter 42, and issues in preparing personnel for work with children on the autism spectrum are discussed in Chapter 45.

REFERENCES

Agran, M., Alper, S., & Wehmeyer, M. (2002). Access to the general curriculum for students with significant disabilities: What it means to teachers. *Education and Training in Mental Retardation and Developmental Disabilities, 37,* 123–133.

Baranek, G. T., Reinhartsen, D. B., & Wannamaker, S. W. (2001). Play: Engaging young children with autism. In R. A. Huebner (Ed.), *Autism: A sensorimotor approach to management* (pp. 313–351). Gaithersburg, MD: Aspen Press.

Barnhill, G. P., Cook, K. T., Tebbenkamp, K., & Myles, B. S. (2002). The effectiveness of social skills intervention targeting nonverbal communication for adolescents with Asperger syndrome and related pervasive developmental delays. *Focus on Autism and Other Developmental Disabilities, 17,* 112–118.

Barry, L. M., & Burlew, S. B. (2004). Using social stories to teach choice and play skills to children with autism. *Focus on Autism and Other Developmental Disabilities, 19,* 45–51.

Bernard-Opitz, V., Sriram, N., & Nakhoda-Sapuan, S. (2001). Enhancing social problem solving in children with autism and normal children through computer-assisted instruction. *Journal* of Autism and Developmental Disorders, 31, 377–384.

Browder, D. M. (2001). Curriculum and assessment for students with moderate and severe disabilities. New York: Guilford Press.

Browder, D. M., & Cooper, K. J. (2001). Community and leisure skills. In D. M. Browder (Ed.), Curriculum and assessment for students with moderate and severe disabilities (pp. 244–276). New York: Guilford Press.

Browder, D. M., & Wilson, B. (2001). Using ecological assessment in planning for inclusion. In D. M. Browder (Ed.), Curriculum and assessment for students with moderate and severe disabilities (pp. 337–360). New York: Guilford Press.

Buggey, T., Toombs, K., Gardener, P., & Cervetti, M. (1999). Training responding behaviors in students with autism: Using videotaped self-modeling. Journal of Positive Behavior Interventions, 1, 205–214.

Butera, G., & Haywood, H. C. (1995). Cognitive education of young children with autism: An application of Bright Start. In E. Schopler & G. B. Mesibov (Eds.), Learning and cognition in autism (pp. 269–292). New York: Plenum Press.

Charlop-Christy, M. H., & Daneshvar, S. (2003). Using video modeling to teach perspective taking to children with autism. Journal of Positive Behavior Interventions, 5, 12–21.

Charlop-Christy, M. H., Le, L., & Freeman, K. A. (2000). A comparison of video modeling with in vivo modeling for teaching children with autism. Journal of Autism and Developmental Disorders, 30, 537–552.

Chin, H. Y., & Bernard-Opitz, V. (2000). Teaching conversational skills to children with autism: Effect on the development of a theory of mind. Journal of Autism and Developmental Disorders, 30, 569–583.

D'Ateno, P., Mangiapanello, K., & Taylor, B. A. (2003). Using video modeling to teach complex play sequences to a preschooler with autism. Journal of Positive Behavior Interventions, 5, 5–11.

DiLeo, D. (2000). Trainer's guide: Enhancing the lives of adults with disabilities (3rd ed.). St. Augustine, FL: Training Resources Network.

DiSalvo, C. A., & Oswald, D. P. (2002). Peer-mediated interventions to increase the social interaction of children with autism. Focus on Autism and Other Developmental Disabilities, 17, 198–207.

Duker, P. C., & Rasing, E. (1989). Effects of redesigning the physical environment on self-stimulation and on-task behavior in three autistic-type developmentally disabled individuals. Journal of Autism and Developmental Disorders, 19, 449–460.

Dunlap, G., Kern, L., & Worcester, J. (2001). ABA and academic instruction. Focus on Autism and Other Developmental Disabilities, 16, 129–136.

Eden II Programs. (1999). Autism Academy Course-Ware: Behavioral programming for children with autism [Computer software]. Massapequa, NY: Digital Vista.

Eikeseth, S., Smith, T., Jahr, E., & Eldevik, S. (2002). Intensive behavioral treatment at school for 4- to 7-year-old children with autism: A 1-year comparison controlled study. Behavior Modification, 26, 49–68.

Faherty, C., & Hearsey, K. (1996). Visually structured tasks: Independent activities for students with autism and other visual learners. Chapel Hill: University of North Carolina, Department of Psychiatry, Division TEACCH.

Fenske, E. C., Krantz, P. J., & McClannahan, L. E. (2001). Incidental teaching: A not-discrete-trial teaching procedure. In C. Maurice, G. Green, & R. M. Foxx (Eds.), Making a difference: Behavioral intervention for autism (pp. 75–82). Austin, TX: ProEd.

Freeman, B. J., Cronin, P., & Candela, P. (2002). Asperger syndrome or autistic disorder? The diagnostic dilemma. Focus on Autism and Other Developmental Disabilities, 17, 145–151.

Fullerton, A., & Coyne, P. (1999). Developing skills and concepts for self-determination in young adults with autism. Focus on Autism and Other Developmental Disabilities, 14, 42–52.

Gray, C. A. (1996). Social assistance. In A. Fullerton, J. Stratton, P. Coyne, & C. Gray (Eds.), Higher functioning adolescents and young adults with autism: A teacher's guide (pp. 71–90). Austin, TX: ProEd.

Gray, C. A. (1998). Social stories and comic strip conversations with students with Asperger syndrome and high-functioning autism. In E. Schopler, G. B. Mesibov, & L. J. Kunce (Eds.), Asperger syndrome or high-functioning autism? (pp. 167–198). New York: Plenum Press.

Greenspan, S. I. (2000). Children with autistic spectrum disorders: Individual differences, affect, interaction, and outcomes. Psychoanalytic Inquiry, 20, 675–703.

Gresham, F. M., & MacMillan, D. L. (1997). Autistic recovery? An analysis and critique of the empirical evidence on the Early Intervention Project. Behavioral Disorders, 22, 185–201.

Groden, J., & LeVasseur, P. (1995). Cognitive picture rehearsal: A system to teach self-control. In K. Quill (Ed.), *Teaching children with autism* (pp. 287–306). Albany, NY: Delmar.

Hagiwara, T., & Myles, B. S. (1999). A multimedia social story intervention: Teaching skills to children with autism. *Focus on Autism and Other Developmental Disabilities, 14,* 82–95.

Handleman, J. S., & Harris, S. L. (Eds.). (2001). *Preschool education programs for children with autism* (2nd ed.). Austin, TX: ProEd.

Harrower, J. K. (1999). Educational inclusion of children with severe disabilities. *Journal of Positive Behavior Interventions, 1,* 215–230.

Holmes, D. L. (1998). *Autism through the lifespan: The Eden model.* Bethesda, MD: Woodbine House.

Howlin, P. (1997). *Autism: Preparing for adulthood.* London: Routledge.

Howlin, P., Baron-Cohen, S., & Hadwin, J. (1999). *Teaching children with autism to mind-read: A practical guide for teachers and parents.* Chichester, England: Wiley.

Jahr, E., Eldevik, S., & Eikeseth, S. (2000). Teaching children with autism to initiate and sustain cooperative play. *Research in Developmental Disabilities, 21,* 151–169.

Janney, R., & Snell, M. E. (2000). *Behavioral support.* Baltimore: Paul H. Brookes.

Johnson, J. R. (1999). Leadership and self-determination. *Focus on Autism and Other Developmental Disabilities, 14,* 4–16.

Kanner, L. (1943). Autistic disturbances of affective contact. *Nervous Child, 2,* 217–250.

Kern, L., & Dunlap, G. (1998). Curriculum modifications to promote desirable classroom behavior. In J. K. Luiselli & M. J. Cameron (Eds.), *Antecedent control: Innovative approaches to behavioral support* (pp. 289–307). Baltimore: Paul H. Brookes.

Kinney, E. M., Vedora, J., & Stromer, R. (2003). Computer-presented video models to teach generative spelling to a child with an autism spectrum disorder. *Journal of Positive Behavior Interventions, 5,* 22–29.

Koegel, R. L., Koegel, L. K., & McNerney, E. K. (2001). Pivotal areas in intervention for autism. *Journal of Clinical Child Psychology, 30,* 19–32.

Krantz, P. J., & McClannahan, L. E. (1993). Teaching children with autism to initiate to peers: Effects of a script-fading procedure. *Journal of Applied Behavior Analysis, 26,* 121–132.

Krantz, P. J., & McClannahan, L. E. (1998). Social interaction skills for children with autism: A script fading procedure for beginning readers.

Journal of Applied Behavior Analysis, 31, 191–202.

Kuoch, H., & Mirenda, P. (2003). Social story interventions for young children with autism spectrum disorders. *Focus on Autism and Other Developmental Disabilities, 18,* 219–227.

Leaf, R., & McEachin, J. (Eds.). (1999). *A work in progress: Behavior management strategies and a curriculum for intensive behavioral treatment of autism.* New York: DRL.

Lonigan, C. J., Elbert, J. C., & Johnson, S. B. (1998). Empirically supported pychosocial interventions for children: An overview. *Journal of Clinical Child Psychology, 27,* 138–145.

Lorimer, P. A., Simpson, R. L., Myles, B. S., & Ganz, J. B. (2002). The use of social stories as a preventative behavioral intervention in a home setting with a child with autism. *Journal of Positive Behavior Interventions, 4,* 53–60.

Lovaas, O. I. (1987). Behavioral treatment and normal educational and intellectual functioning in young autistic children. *Journal of Consulting and Clinical Psychology, 55,* 3–9.

Lovaas, O. I. (Ed.). (2003). *Teaching individuals with developmental delays: Basic intervention techniques.* Austin, TX: ProEd.

McAfee, J. L. (2002). *Navigating the social world: A curriculum for individuals with Asperger's syndrome, high functioning autism and related disorders.* Arlington, TX: Future Horizons.

McClannahan, L. E., & Krantz, P. J. (1998). *Activity schedules for children with autism: Teaching independent behavior.* Bethesda, MD: Woodbine Press.

McClannahan, L. E., & Krantz, P. J. (2001). Behavior analysis and intervention for preschoolers at the Princeton Child Development Institute. In J. S. Handleman & S. L. Harris (Eds.), *Preschool education programs for children with autism* (2nd ed., pp. 191–213). Austin, TX: ProEd.

McClannahan, L. E., MacDuff, G. S., & Krantz, P. J. (2002). Behavior analysis and intervention for adults with autism. *Behavior Modification, 26,* 9–26.

McGee, G. G., Morrier, M. J., & Daly, T. (2001). The Walden Early Childhood Programs. In J. S. Handleman & S. L. Harris (Eds.), *Preschool education programs for children with autism* (2nd ed., pp. 157–190). Austin, TX: ProEd.

McGrath, A. M., Bosch, S., Sullivan, C. L., & Fuqua, R. W. (2003). Training reciprocal social interactions between preschoolers and a child with autism. *Journal of Positive Behavior Interventions, 5,* 47–54.

Miller, N., & Neuringer, A. (2000). Reinforcing variability in adolescents with autism. *Journal of Applied Behavior Analysis, 33,* 151–165.

Mirenda, P. L., & Donnellan, A. M. (1987). Issues in curriculum development. In D. J. Cohen & A. M. Donnellan (Eds.), *Handbook of autism and pervasive developmental disorders* (pp. 211–226). New York: Wiley.

Moyes, R. A. (2001). *Incorporating social goals in the classroom: A guide for teachers and parents of children with high-functioning autism and Asperger syndrome.* London: Jessica Kingsley.

Myles, B. S., & Simpson, R. L. (1998). Inclusion of students with autism in general education classrooms: The Autism Inclusion Collaboration Model. In R. L. Simpson & B. S. Myles (Eds.), *Educating children and youth with autism: Strategies for effective practice* (pp. 241–256). Austin, TX: ProEd.

National Research Council. (2001). *Educating children with autism* (Committee on Educational Interventions for Children with Autism, Division of Behavioral and Social Sciences and Education). Washington, DC: National Academy Press.

Newman, B., Reinecke, D. R., & Meinberg, D. L. (2000). Self-management of varied responding in three students with autism. *Behavioral Interventions, 15,* 145–151.

Ochs, E., Kremer-Sadlik, T., Solomon, O., & Sirota, K. G. (2001). Inclusion as social practice: Views of children with autism. *Social Development, 10,* 399–419.

Olley, J. G. (1987). Classroom structure and autism. In D. J. Cohen & A. M. Donnellan (Eds.), *Handbook of autism and pervasive developmental disorders* (pp. 411–417). New York: Wiley.

Olley, J. G. (1999). Curriculum for students with autism. *School Psychology Review, 28,* 595–607.

Olley, J. G., & Reeve, C. E. (1997). Issues of curriculum and classroom structure. In D. J. Cohen & F. Volkmar (Eds.), *Handbook of autism and pervasive developmental disorders* (2nd ed., pp. 484–508). New York: Wiley.

Rogers, S. J. (1998). Empirically supported comprehensive treatments for young children with autism. *Journal of Clinical Child Psychology, 27,* 168–179.

Romanczyk, R. G. (2002). *IGS curriculum.* Binghamton, NY: Binghamton University, Institute for Child Development.

Sarokoff, R. A., Taylor, B. A., & Poulson, C. L. (2001). Teaching children with autism to engage in conversational exchanges: Script fading with embedded textual stimuli. *Journal of Applied Behavior Analysis, 34,* 81–84.

Schleien, S. J., Meyer, L. H., Heyne, L. A., & Brandt, B. B. (1995). *Lifelong leisure skills and lifestyles for persons with developmental disabilities.* Baltimore: Paul H. Brookes.

Schreibman, L., Whalen, C., & Stahmer, A. C. (2000). The use of video priming to reduce disruptive transition behavior in children with autism. *Journal of Positive Behavior Interventions, 2,* 3–11.

Shabani, D. B., Katz, R. C., Wilder, D. A., Beauchamp, K., Taylor, C. R., & Fischer, K. J. (2002). Increasing social initiations in children with autism: Effects of a tactile prompt. *Journal of Applied Behavior Analysis, 35,* 79–83.

Sigafoos, J., & Littlewood, R. (1999). Communication intervention on the playground: A case study on teaching requesting to a young child with autism. *International Journal of Disability, Development and Education, 46,* 421–429.

Simpson, R. L., & Myles, B. S. (1998). *Educating children and youth with autism: Strategies for effective practice.* Austin, TX: ProEd.

Simpson, R. L., Myles, B. S., Sasso, G. M., & Kamps, D. M. (1997). *Social skills for students with autism* (2nd ed.). Reston, VA: Council for Exceptional Children.

Smith, C. (2001). Using social stories to enhance behaviour in children with autistic spectrum difficulties. *Educational Psychology in Practice, 17,* 337–345.

Smith, K. (2000). *The DT trainer administrator self paced training* [Computer software and manual]. Columbia, SC: Accelerations Educational Software.

Stevenson, C. L., Krantz, P. J., & McClannahan, L. E. (2000). Social interaction skills for children with autism: A script-fading procedure for nonreaders. *Behavioral Interventions, 15,* 1–20.

Strain, P. S., & Hoyson, M. (2000). The need for longitudinal, intensive social skills intervention: LEAP follow-up outcomes for children with autism. *Topics in Early Childhood Special Education, 20,* 116–122.

Taylor, B. A. (2001). Teaching peer social skills to children with autism. In C. Maurice, G. Green, & R. M. Foxx (Eds.), *Making a difference: Behavioral intervention for autism* (pp. 83–96). Austin, TX: ProEd.

Taylor, B. A., Hughes, C. E., Richard, E., Hoch, H., & Coello, A. R. (2004). Teaching teenagers with autism to seek assistance when lost. *Journal of Applied Behavior Analysis, 37,* 79–82.

Taylor, B. A., & Jasper, S. (2001). Teaching programs to increase peer interaction. In C. Maurice, G. Green, & R. M. Foxx (Eds.), *Making a difference: Behavioral intervention for autism* (pp. 97–162). Austin, TX: ProEd.

TEACCH. (1998). *TEACCH structured teaching assessment: Guides to individualizing the schedule and the work system.* Chapel Hill, NC: Author.

Wagner, S. (1999). *Inclusive programming for elementary students with autism.* Arlington, TX: Future Horizons.

Weiss, M. J., & Harris, S. L. (2001). Teaching social skills to people with autism. *Behavior Modification, 25,* 785–802.

Weiss, M. J., & Piccolo, E. (2001). The Rutgers Autism Program. In J. S. Handleman & S. L. Harris (Eds.), *Preschool education programs for children with autism* (2nd ed., pp. 13–27). Austin, TX: ProEd.

Wert, B. Y., & Neisworth, J. T. (2003). Effects of video self-modeling on spontaneous requesting in children with autism. *Journal of Positive Behavior Interventions, 5,* 30–34.

Wolery, M., & Schuster, J. W. (1997). Instructional methods with students who have significant disabilities. *Journal of Special Education, 31,* 61–79.

Wolery, M., & Winterling, V. (1997). Curricular approaches to controlling severe behavior problems. In N. N. Singh (Ed.), *Prevention and treatment of severe behavior problems: Models and methods in developmental disabilities* (pp. 87–120). Pacific Grove, CA: Brooks/Cole.

CHAPTER 34

Behavioral Interventions to Promote Learning in Individuals with Autism

LAURA SCHREIBMAN AND BROOKE INGERSOLL

The application of behavioral techniques to autism, like the diagnosis itself, has a relatively short history. However, the progress in the development and refinement of behavioral treatment has been swift and impressive. Prior to the mid-1960s, psychodynamic therapy was standard in the treatment of children with autism, reflecting the now-antiquated theory that the cause of autism was psychogenic. The monumental failure of the psychodynamic approach in the treatment of autism opened the door for the emerging field of applied behavior analysis. Applied behavior analysis grew out of the field of the experimental analysis of behavior, in which the general laws of learning derived from work with animal populations were applied to socially significant behaviors.

Behavioral procedures do not cure the disorder, but they have been shown to be extremely effective in substantially improving the lives of people with autism and those around them. This chapter describes current behavioral intervention techniques for the treatment of autism and discusses recent trends and continued challenges for the future of this intervention model.

BEHAVIORAL INTERVENTION STRATEGIES

Current behavioral interventions can trace their roots to studies conducted in the early 1960s. Prior to this time, it was commonly believed that children with autism could not learn. Ferster and DeMyer (1961, 1962) were among the first to demonstrate that children with autism could indeed learn and would do so if the systematic application of operant discrimination learning techniques was employed. They demonstrated that these children could learn new, albeit nonfunctional, behaviors under conditions where correct answers were followed by contingent applications of reinforcement. Later, other behavioral researchers demonstrated the utility of the systematic application of reinforcement, prompting, fading, chaining, and other behavioral procedures (see Schreibman, 1988, for a review). These early studies were mostly concerned with addressing isolated behaviors. Lovaas and his colleagues (e.g., Lovaas, 1977; Lovaas, Berberich, Perloff, & Schaeffer, 1966; Lovaas, Freitag, Gold, & Kassorla, 1965; Lovaas, Koegel, Simmons, & Long, 1973) were the first to develop a comprehensive, systematic package of behavioral interventions that addressed a wide range of behaviors in children with autism. Such interventions were associated with substantial decreases in inappropriate behaviors such as self-injury, self-stimulation, aggression, and tantrums as well as substantial increases in language, social, play, and academic skills. As the field of applied behavior analysis has evolved, so, too, have the intervention techniques designed for use with these children. Throughout this evolution, empirical validation and ongoing monitoring of progress through systematic data collection have remained central.

Structured Behavioral Interventions

Comprehensive structured behavioral interventions, also known as *discrete trial training,* are widely used in early intervention programs for children with autism. These procedures, described by Lovaas (1987), are very similar to the original operant techniques described in the 1960s. More recent elaborations have included increased focus on nonacademic skills such as play and peer interaction, decreased use of aversives, and more varied delivery of reinforcement. Programs using this procedure share the following basic components: (1) The learning environment is highly structured; (2) target behaviors are broken down into a series of discrete subskills and taught successively; (3) teaching episodes are initiated by the adult; (4) teaching materials are selected by the adult and rarely varied within a task; (5) the child's production of the target response is explicitly prompted; (6) reinforcers, albeit functional, are usually unrelated to the target response; and (7) the child receives reinforcement only for correct responding or successive approximations (Delprato, 2001). Discrete trial training has been credited with success in teaching children a variety of important behaviors (e.g., Baer, Peterson, & Sherman, 1967; Lovaas et al., 1966; Metz, 1965; Schroeder & Baer, 1972). In addition, this approach has been credited with impressive gains in children with otherwise poor prognoses (e.g., Lovaas, 1987) and in accelerated skill acquisition (Miranda-Linne & Melin, 1992). One oft-cited study found that 47% of preschool-age children with autism who had received intensive (40 hours per week), discrete trial intervention for 2 years achieved normal intellectual and educational functioning compared with 2% who received less intensive intervention (Lovaas, 1987). Although this study has been criticized for several methodological flaws (e.g., lack of random assignment, selecting only verbal subjects; Mesibov, 1993), it demonstrates the tremendous benefit of structured behavioral techniques in the instruction of children with autism.

Despite these impressive findings, the highly structured behavioral approach has been criticized on a number of grounds. First, the adult-directed nature of the instruction and the fact that the target behavior is brought under tight stimulus control have been shown to compromise the spontaneous use of the behavior (Carr, 1981). Second, the highly structured teaching environment (Lovaas, 1977) and use of artificial reinforcers (R. L. Koegel, O'Dell, & Koegel, 1987) have been shown to prevent generalization to the natural environment (e.g., Spradlin & Siegel, 1982). Finally, the highly structured teaching environment is not representative of natural adult-child interactions (Schreibman, Kaneko, & Koegel, 1991).

Naturalistic Behavioral Interventions

Structured operant teaching techniques have been modified over the years to address some of the shortcomings noted earlier. The resulting behavioral interventions are more naturalistic and child centered. The first naturalistic behavioral treatment was designed by Hart and Risley (1968) to teach the use of descriptive adjectives to disadvantaged preschoolers in a classroom setting. This study sought to increase generalization and spontaneous use of skills by teaching them in the context of ongoing classroom activities. Since their original conception, naturalistic behavioral intervention techniques have undergone a variety of procedural elaborations, yielding a variety of similar intervention techniques, including incidental teaching (Hart & Risley, 1968; McGee, Krantz, Mason, & McClannahan, 1983), mand-model (Rogers-Warren & Warren, 1980), time delay (Halle, Marshall, & Spradlin, 1979), milieu teaching (Alpert & Kaiser, 1992), interrupted behavior chains (Hunt & Goetz, 1988), and the natural language paradigm/pivotal response training (PRT; R. L. Koegel et al., 1987, 1989). Although the specific techniques were developed in different laboratories by researchers from different academic backgrounds, these approaches are similar in that they all share the following basic components: (1) The learning environment is loosely structured, (2) teaching occurs within ongoing interactions between the child and the adult, (3) the child initiates the teaching episode by indicating interest in an item or activity, (4) teaching materials are selected by the child and varied often, (5) the child's production of the target behavior is explicitly prompted, (6) a direct relationship exists between the child's response and the reinforcer, and (7) the child is reinforced for attempts to respond (Delprato, 2001; Kaiser, Yoder, & Keetz, 1992).

Despite their similarity, the techniques differ conceptually. Incidental teaching, mand-model, and time delay are all specific prompting procedures for increasing language that are implemented once the child has expressed interest in an item or activity (Mirenda & Iacono, 1988). In the incidental teaching approach, the adult waits for the child to initiate a request for a desired item or activity. The adult then prompts an elaborated response. The mand-model approach was developed for children who do not readily initiate (Rogers-Warren & Warren, 1980). In this procedure, the adult waits for the child to indicate interest in an item and then places an instruction for a particular behavior. If the child does not respond, the adult models the correct response for the child to imitate. The time delay procedure was designed to transfer the child's response from a verbal cue given by the adult to the environment (Halle et al., 1979). In this procedure, the adult waits for the child to indicate interest in an item and then approaches the child with an expectant look. If the child does not respond within 15 seconds, the adult uses a model or mand-model procedure. For all of these techniques, reinforcement is the delivery of the desired item or activity. Milieu teaching includes all three of these procedures as well as a direct model procedure in which the adult models language and the child is expected to imitate the adult's model to receive access to a desired item or activity (e.g., Kaiser, Ostrosky, & Alpert, 1993).

The interrupted behavior chain procedure uses naturally occurring routines as the context for requesting items or assistance. This procedure is typically used with children who have very limited initiations and are minimally motivated to communicate (Hunt & Goetz, 1988). The child is allowed to begin an activity, and then the adult prevents the child from completing the next step of the routine. The adult then uses mand-model or time delay to prompt the child to request the next step in the sequence. In this procedure, reinforcement is the ability to complete the next step in the behavior chain. This procedure differs from milieu teaching in that the instruction is

presented after the child begins the activity rather than before (Mirenda & Iacono, 1988).

PRT was designed based on a series of studies identifying important treatment components. It includes clear and appropriate prompts, child choice, turn taking, maintenance tasks, reinforcing attempts, responding to multiple cues, and a direct response-reinforcer relationship. PRT does not define the specific types of prompts to use; however, implementation of the procedure usually involves the same prompting strategies as those used in milieu teaching and interrupted behavior chains. In contrast to the other procedures that have focused almost exclusively on increasing verbal and nonverbal communication, PRT has been adapted to teach a variety of skills including symbolic (Stahmer, 1995) and sociodramatic play (Thorpe, Stahmer, & Schreibman, 1995) and joint attention (Whalen & Schreibman, 2003).

Empirical studies comparing naturalistic to the more structured techniques have validated the position that naturalistic strategies lead to more generalized and spontaneous use of skills (Charlop-Christy & Carpenter, 2000; Delprato, 2001; McGee, Krantz, & McClannahan, 1985; Miranda-Linne & Melin, 1992). In addition, studies have found that parents who have been trained to implement these techniques exhibit more positive affect while teaching their children (Schreibman et al., 1991), and both the parents and children exhibit more happiness and interest and less stress during family interactions (R. L. Koegel, Bimbela, & Schreibman, 1996) than families in which the parents have been trained to implement highly structured behavioral techniques. These findings suggest that the naturalistic approach is more enjoyable for parents and children and leads to a more positive family interaction style than the structured approach.

One question that has not yet been answered is whether intensive naturalistic interventions lead to similar or superior intellectual improvement as that which has been reported for intensive structured intervention (Lovaas, 1987). This comparison is difficult because intensive naturalistic intervention is typically conducted in classrooms, often inclusion based, and targets functional behaviors (e.g., McGee, Daly, & Jacobs, 1994), whereas intensive structured intervention is typically conducted in the home and often targets more cognitive behaviors, thus confounding any sort of direct comparison.

Augmentative and Alternative Communication Strategies

One area of common difficulty in the treatment of children with autism is teaching communication strategies to nonverbal children. Throughout the years, several types of augmentative/alternative communication strategies based on behavioral principles have been utilized with children with autism and other severe communication handicaps. These strategies include sign language (e.g., Carr, Binkoff, Kologinsky, & Eddy, 1978), picture boards and picture point systems (Mirenda & Santogrossi, 1985; Reichle & Brown, 1986), and picture exchange systems (Bondy & Frost, 1994).

Sign language has historically been the preferred method of treatment for nonverbal children. However, sign language is symbolic and requires the ability to imitate; therefore, many nonverbal children fail to acquire it. In addition, because the majority of the population is unfamiliar with signs, children using this system are often unable to communicate in the community.

Picture or iconic systems have been used to teach functional communication to children with autism who fail to acquire verbal or signed language. These systems (e.g., picture boards, picture exchange) seem to be easier to acquire than sign language (Anderson, 2002) and are readily recognizable to individuals who have not been trained in the system, thus increasing the number of people with whom the children can communicate successfully. The Picture Exchange Communication System (PECS) is the most widely used iconic system for nonverbal children (Bondy & Frost, 1994). This system requires that the child exchange a picture for a desired item or activity. Although the research on its effectiveness is limited, PECS has found wide acceptance in school-based intervention programs. Currently, more controlled research on this technique is being conducted, and findings suggest it is efficacious and that acquisition of PECS leads to increases in vocal speech (Charlop-Christy, Carpenter, Le, LeBlanc, & Kellet, 2002).

One important issue is which augmentative/alternative communication system is most effective for increasing communication skills in nonverbal children with autism. One study compared acquisition rates of modified signs and PECS pictures in nonverbal preschoolers with autism. Six children were trained to request desired items via each system. Results indicated that all six participants acquired pictures more rapidly and demonstrated better generalization to novel stimuli with PECS than with sign. However, the children had more spontaneous initiations and were more likely to pair verbalizations with sign (Anderson, 2002). In addition, this study found that children indicated a clear preference for one system over another, suggesting the importance of individualizing augmentative/alternative communication systems to the child's needs and preference.

Another important issue is whether teaching pictures or sign to nonverbal toddlers and preschoolers is superior to a language-only approach. Although there is little controversy over using augmentative/alternative communication systems with nonverbal, school-age children who have already shown the inability to acquire spoken language, there is less consensus as to whether to begin with an augmentative/alternative communication system for nonverbal toddler and preschool-age children who are just beginning intervention (i.e., Bondy & Frost, 1994; McGee, Morrier, & Daly, 1999). These results suggest a continued need for research to examine augmentative/alternative communication systems. We need to determine what child characteristics may be associated with success in verbal versus augmentative communication systems (e.g., PECS, sign). In addition, we need to examine which of these systems may promote vocal language in children with differing characteristics. There is much to do in this area of research.

Self-Management

Another struggle in the treatment of children with autism is independent learning. Although many behavioral treatment strategies are effective at teaching new skills, the presence of a treatment provider is usually necessary to maintain these behavioral gains. Techniques that encourage learning and maintenance of behavior without increased reliance on teacher or parent monitoring are thus highly desirable.

Self-management has been shown to reduce reliance on a therapist in normally functioning individuals (Kopp, 1988). These procedures include self-evaluation of performance, self-monitoring, and self-delivery of reinforcement. Self-management procedures have been adapted for use with individuals with autism and developmental delay. They typically involve teaching individuals to identify appropriate and inappropriate behavior, record their own behavior using stickers or other material, and reward themselves after exhibiting the appropriate behavior or refraining from the inappropriate behavior. The presence of the therapist is gradually faded so that the individual is able to continue to display appropriate behaviors in an unsupervised setting. Eventually, the self-management materials are also faded so that the individual is able to demonstrate self-control completely independently (R. L. Koegel, Koegel, & Parks, 1990).

Self-management procedures have been used to address a variety of behaviors in individuals with autism. They have been used to decrease inappropriate behavior such as self-stimulation (e.g., Mancina, Tankersley, Kamps, Kravits, & Parrett, 2000; R. L. Koegel & Koegel, 1990) and perseverative play (Newman, Reinecke, & Meinberg, 2000) as well as to increase appropriate behavior such as toy play (Stahmer & Schreibman, 1992), social initiations (L. K. Koegel, Koegel, Hurley, & Frea, 1992), and independent interactions with typical peers (Shearer, Kohler, Buchan, & McCullough, 1996).

While self-management has been shown to be successful with higher functioning individuals with well-established verbal language, lower functioning individuals with limited or no language are less likely to benefit from this approach. Accordingly, adaptations to the typical self-management procedure have been developed for use with these lower functioning individuals. Pictorial self-management uses photographs of individual steps of a task in a book format. This procedure involves teaching the child to complete the step associated with each picture, turn the page to view the next picture, and reinforce himself or herself after the task is complete. This strategy has been shown to increase lower functioning children's ability to perform self-help skills in the absence of adult supervision (Pierce & Schreibman, 1994).

Video Instruction

Interest in combining behavioral techniques with video for autistic individuals has recently emerged. Video technology has some intrinsic appeal as an instructional tool for this population. First, although not well documented in the literature, people have often suggested that children with autism are visual learners and typically excel in treatment modalities that rely on visual stimuli (e.g., Campbell, Lison, Borsook, Hoover, & Arnold, 1995; Charlop & Milstein, 1989; Pierce & Schreibman, 1994; Schreibman, Whalen, & Stahmer, 2000). Second, motivation may be enhanced because most children (including children with autism) typically enjoy watching videos. Third, videotapes can be replayed repeatedly without any variation, which might enhance learning in a population that benefits from predictability. Finally, the use of video does not typically require the direct intervention of an adult.

Video modeling has been the most well-researched form of video instruction for children with autism. Modeling research has shown that these children can learn new behaviors through the observation of predictable and repeated sequences (Charlop, Schreibman, & Tryon, 1983). Video modeling presents target behaviors in video format and has been shown to improve various skills in individuals with autism, including conversational speech (Charlop & Milstein, 1989; Sherer et al., 2001), verbal responding (Buggey, Tombs, Gardener, & Cervetti, 1999), helping behaviors (Reeve, 2001), purchasing skills (Haring, Kennedy, Adams, & Pitts-Conway, 1987), and daily living skills (Shipley-Benamou, Lutzker, & Taubman, 2002). This medium has also been shown to increase vocabulary, emotional understanding, attribute acquisition, number of play actions, duration of play, and play-related statements (Schwandt et al., 2002).

In addition to modeling, other forms of video technology have recently been used in combination with different behavioral techniques to promote appropriate behaviors. These include procedures such as priming (Schreibman et al., 2000), discrimination training (Matsuoka &

Kobayashi, 2000), and self-management (Thiemann & Goldstein, 2001).

Research examining the effect of the type of model used in video-based instruction has been equivocal. One study compared the effectiveness of using the target child as the videotaped model (self as a model) with a similar-age child model (other as model). This study found that although neither technique proved to be clearly superior, some individual children responded better to one or the other (Sherer et al., 2001). In contrast, a study comparing the use of video to in vivo instruction suggested that video modeling promotes faster acquisition and better generalization of new behaviors than in vivo modeling (Charlop-Christy, Le, & Freeman, 2000). In addition, these authors argued that video modeling is more cost effective because it does not require the use of a live model (Charlop-Christy et al., 2000). Although this is only a preliminary study, it offers some interesting considerations. Research examining alternative behavioral applications of video and fine-tuning current video instruction techniques is certainly warranted.

One cautionary note related to the use of video instruction (and other similar technologies) is that it not be used to the exclusion of in vivo behavioral interventions. Just because a child may learn certain skills better with one type of intervention does not mean that the intervention is better overall. One reason that children with autism may learn well from video is that video instruction can eliminate the social demands that in vivo instruction requires. However, like all children, children with autism are required to function in a social world and must be able to learn from their social environment. Therefore, it is suggested that the use of video instruction be balanced with the use of in vivo instruction, regardless of the efficacy of video instruction.

FUTURE DIRECTIONS AND CONTINUED CHALLENGES IN BEHAVIORAL TREATMENTS

The past 15 to 20 years have brought a tremendous broadening and sophistication of behavioral technology as it is applied to people with autism. The earlier work in the area has laid the foundation for the current state-of-the-art and for what will follow. The fact that we now view some of our early efforts as relatively "simplistic" and are now much more effective and efficient in providing treatment should in no way be considered as criticism of these earlier efforts. Quite the contrary, we are not moving away from our early efforts; rather, we are moving beyond them. We would not be where we are now if we had not been there first. Our future directions and challenges are represented in the current research of our field.

Generalization and Maintenance of Treatment Gains

One of the continued challenges in the treatment of children with autism is the generalization of treatment gains across environments and over time (e.g., Lovaas et al., 1973). The use of naturalistic behavioral teaching techniques and training family members to be intervention providers have been shown to improve generalization (McGee et al., 1985; R. L. Koegel, Schreibman, Britten, Burke, & O'Neill, 1982). Despite these efforts, generalization remains an obstacle in the treatment of many children with autism. Future studies that focus on improving the generalization and maintenance of skills in children with autism are needed.

Individualization of Treatment

The importance of individualization of treatment has long been recognized and is reflected in the creation of a child's individualized education plan (IEP). In this sense, the IEP is used to emphasize the need for individualized educational goals. However, the field is just beginning to recognize that there is no *one* treatment best suited to meet these goals. In fact, arguments relating to which behavioral treatment is superior are essentially meaningless because no treatment can boast substantial success in more than 50% to 70% of children. This variability in child response calls for the individualization of treatment strategies. Treatment variables and how they interact with child, family, and service provider characteristics are also crucial elements in the individualized treatment equation. The ultimate goal is to be in a position to determine a priori which treatment procedures will be most effective and efficient with a particular child and a particular family situation at a particular point in treatment.

Research on child characteristics that best predict treatment outcome for a particular intervention is just beginning (e.g., Anderson, 2002; Ingersoll, Schreibman, & Stahmer, 2001) but is hugely important. For example, one study has identified a behavioral profile of children who are likely to respond well to PRT and a separate profile of children who are likely to have a poor response to this treatment (Sherer & Schreibman, in press). These findings can help determine which children are appropriate candidates for PRT as well as provoke additional research to determine which alternative treatment options are most appropriate for children who meet the profile of a "nonresponder" to PRT (Schreibman, Stahmer, & Cestone, 2001). It is important that this subsequent study also found that the profile predicted outcome for PRT but not for another behavioral intervention, discrete trial training, thus suggesting the profile is indeed predictive of a specific treatment and not just response to treatment in general. As a field, it is important to continue to fine-tune this line of research, thus deriving the most benefit from early intervention.

In addition to child characteristics, it is important to consider the individual characteristics of the child's caregivers. The field is just beginning to examine how family variables interact with treatment effectiveness. Ethnicity, culture, marital status, parental attitudes, parental age, level of education, socioeconomic status, and other factors all may affect how treatment is best delivered and the ultimate effectiveness of the treatment. For example, research has shown that children of more responsive and educated parents are more likely to benefit from prelinguistic milieu teaching, while children of less responsive and educated mothers benefit more from responsive small group instruction (Yoder & Warren, 1998). Also, training in self-management may be more successfully implemented by parents for whom child independence is important (Schreibman & Koegel, 1996). However, certain cultures may not place a strong emphasis on child independence; thus, the parents may not choose to use self-management with their child or may use it ineffectively. Another example is the effect of stress. It

has been shown that parents of children with autism report being under high levels of stress (e.g., R. L. Koegel, Schreibman, Loos, & Dirlich-Wilhelm, 1992). Perhaps parents who are under a good deal of stress at a point in time would be poor candidates to implement training with their child; a clinician might then be the treatment provider of choice. At a later time, if the stress is reduced, these parents could perhaps very effectively implement the treatment.

It is also important to recognize teacher variables that predict the ability to learn and implement different intervention techniques. Given that the majority of intervention for children with autism is provided by teachers and paraprofessionals who may not have an extensive background in treatment techniques for this population, it is important to identify the best ways to teach them and discern which techniques they are likely to use. In response to increased attention on individualization of treatment, many researchers and service providers have come to recognize that multiple behavioral methodologies have a place within a comprehensive treatment program. Although there are still strong proponents of particular intervention philosophies, researchers and service providers must challenge themselves to explore multiple options for individual children. Most researchers and service providers have broadened their view of teaching methodology; however, despite the incorporation of multiple behavioral methodologies, change is still slow. Ideally, we would develop a set of formulas to allow us to evaluate a child and, based on research results, prescribe the best treatment for the child at that time. Continued assessment would then allow us to alter the child's treatment regimen in response to the child's changing needs. We are still in the initial stages of being able to match treatment procedures with specific children, but continued research in this area will no doubt be tremendously important in determining treatment decisions.

Integration of Disciplines

Although behavior modification provides a wealth of techniques to encourage learning and change behavior, the field has come to recognize that autism is a complex disorder, the cause of which cannot be explained by learning theory alone. To this end, the field has gravitated toward other disciplines to help in the development of more effective intervention targets and tools.

One such discipline is developmental psychology. Since their conception, naturalistic behavioral intervention strategies targeting communication have been heavily influenced by developmental research on language acquisition in typical children. More recently, some naturalistic behavioral interventions have added techniques traditionally limited to the developmental literature, such as indirect language stimulation and contingent imitation, to produce a combined approach, for example, enhanced milieu teaching (Hemmeter & Kaiser, 1994), prelinguistic milieu teaching (Warren, Yoder, Gazdag, & Kim, 1993), and reciprocal imitation training (Ingersoll, 2003).

Another recent trend has been the use of behavioral techniques to target deficits in autism identified in developmental literature but previously ignored in the behavioral literature. Many such autistic deficits, such as reciprocal imitation (Ingersoll & Schreibman, 2001, 2002), joint attention (Whalen & Schreibman, in press), symbolic play (Stahmer, 1995), and theory of mind (Garfinkle, 2000), which were originally identified by developmental psychologists, have been targeted using behavioral techniques in the past several years.

In addition, there has been an interest in whether targeting early social-communicative behaviors that are theoretically linked to later emerging behaviors in typical development leads to increased development of these later emerging behaviors in autism. For example, Whalen (2001) used a behavioral methodology to teach young children with autism to make joint attention initiations and found increases in language despite the fact that language was not directly targeted. Similarly, Ingersoll (2003) found increases in language, play, and joint attention after targeting reciprocal imitation. Behavioral research that is focused on targeting behaviors within a developmental framework is exciting and can only enhance the effectiveness of our interventions.

Future behavioral research will need to draw on the rapidly developing field of neuroscience. For example, more recent imaging techniques have confirmed the presence of attentional deficits (e.g., Courchesne et al., 1994), originally observed behaviorally (Lovaas, Schreibman, Koegel, & Rehm, 1971), which are likely involved in the development of a variety of autistic behaviors. In addition, recent work has suggested that face processing is impaired in autism and may lead to some of the abnormal social behavior observed in this population (Schultz et al., 2000). Newer behavioral research focused on targeting deficits identified by the field of neuroscience may lead to exciting new gains in child outcome. Additionally, imaging studies that examine functional changes in neurological systems that are a result of behavioral therapy will help to identify whether our treatment contributes to brain reorganization. Such studies are currently underway.

As a field, we should also collaborate with treatment approaches that are not considered behavioral but, nonetheless, share some common elements with behavioral interventions. For example, the Treatment and Education of Autistic and Related Communication-handicapped CHildren (TEACCH) model or structured teaching (Lord, Bristol, & Schopler, 1993) uses many forms of visual supports, such as picture schedules, to help individuals with autism navigate their world. Although the use of picture schedules is not inherently behavioral, many behavioral interventions have incorporated their use. For example, pictorial self-management combines the use of a picture schedule with self-reinforcement. Similarly, social stories (Gray & Garand, 1993), which provide a brief vignette of expected behavior in an upcoming social situation, are, in fact, a form of priming, which has been shown to be an effective behavioral strategy with children with autism (Schreibman et al., 2000; Zanolli, Daggett, & Adams, 1996).

Another intervention approach commonly used with children with autism is the developmental approach. This approach, which includes *floor time* (Greenspan & Wieder, 1998), is focused on building emotional reciprocity. One key component to floor time, following the child's lead, is also central to naturalistic behavioral strategies. Another central component, opening and closing circles of communication, shares many similarities with prompting and reinforcement strategies used in the naturalistic behavioral interventions.

Although proponents of the developmental approach do not consider it behavioral, in many ways, it is more similar to naturalistic behavioral interventions than naturalistic and structured behavioral interventions are to each other (Prizant, Wetherby, & Rydell, 2000). Similarly, sensory integrative therapy is also focused on following the child's lead and gradually increasing the level of demands to help the child increase his or her fine motor, play, language, and sensory processing skills (e.g., Ayres, 1972).

One very obvious difference between behavioral and nonbehavioral approaches is the focus on data collection and validation. Despite their common use and likely benefit, most nonbehavioral interventions have not been empirically validated, leading many behaviorists to doubt their efficacy. In recent years, the TEACCH model and social stories have undergone empirical study (e.g., Norris & Dattilo, 1999; Ozonoff & Cathcart, 1998) while developmental and sensory integrative interventions have lagged behind. Future research that examines the efficacy of these types of interventions and their overlap with behaviorally based interventions will undoubtedly improve both fields and result in better treatment options for children with autism.

A second difference between behavioral and nonbehavioral approaches is the use of fidelity of implementation. Traditionally, behaviorists rigorously define their procedures and monitor their correct implementation. These definitions create a common language among intervention providers and assist in the consistent implementation of the intervention. Other disciplines are beginning to recognize the importance of fidelity of implementation. As we progress in our collaboration, it is hoped that we continue to challenge ourselves to define fidelity of implementation and manualize our interventions to ensure consistency of treatment implementation.

One struggle in collaboration is the confusion between specific behavioral techniques and general principles of applied behavior analysis among professionals in other disciplines, as well as the public at large. In fact, some professionals have challenged the use of applied behavior analysis for children with autism because they are uncomfortable with the highly structured, adult-directed techniques used in discrete trial training, without recognizing that discrete trial training is only one of many behavioral techniques (e.g., Greenspan & Wieder, 1998). (The term *applied behavior analysis* actually refers to a specific research methodology—not a particular form of treatment.) As a field, we must clarify our principles to other disciplines in a clear manner that can highlight the similarities among disciplines and encourage collaboration.

Collaboration among Service Providers

Behavioral interventionists have become less focused on treatment provided exclusively by specialists in clinic settings, recognizing that children need to learn within the context of their daily lives (e.g., as provided by naturalistic teaching strategies). Treatment is being delivered by individuals with a wide range of experience in a variety of settings. Behavioral interventionists and researchers have also recognized the importance of family participation in treatment. Research has shown that parents can be trained to implement behavioral procedures with their children with autism and that this training leads to increases in a variety of skills (e.g., Alpert & Kaiser, 1992; Hemmeter & Kaiser, 1994). In addition, research has shown that parent training leads to more durable improvement than clinic-based treatment (R. L. Koegel et al., 1982).

There has also been an increase in the use of siblings (Celiberti & Harris, 1993) and peers as intervention agents (e.g., McGee, Almeida, Sulzer-Azaroff, & Feldman, 1992; Pierce & Schreibman, 1995, 1997). Research suggests that typical children as young as 2 years old can be trained to use behavioral strategies with peers with autism (Ingersoll & Stahmer, 2002). Sibling and peer-implemented behavioral interventions have been shown to increase social interaction (McGee et al., 1992), language (Pierce & Schreibman, 1997), and joint attention skills (Ingersoll & Stahmer, 2002; Pierce & Schreibman, 1997) of children with autism.

Given the variety of treatment providers and intervention settings in any one child's intervention program, collaboration is indispensable. Most children with autism receive intervention in multiple settings throughout their lifetime. Parents and teachers may not be using the same techniques, which in some cases can lead to a breakdown in behavior. For example, many nonverbal children use PECS in their classrooms; however, many of their families are not familiar with the system, do not have the materials in the home, or do not know which pictures their child can use. In this situation, the lack of collaboration between the home and the school may lead to missed opportunities to build communication. Interventionists need to plan for collaboration among all environments to ensure consistency in program implementation. Future research on ways to facilitate collaboration between settings is certainly warranted.

Continuum of Services

Much of the early behavioral research was conducted with older children, adolescents, and adults with autism and other severe disabilities. With the recognition of the importance of early intervention, there has been a tremendous increase in research devoted to treatments for young children with autism. This focus is necessary and exciting and has likely yielded better long-term outcomes for individuals with autism in general. However, despite better outcomes with the provision of early intervention services, the prognosis for adults with autism is still very poor. Therefore, it is necessary that research on treatment options for older individuals with autism grow in step with the research on these options for young children.

Dissemination

Another extremely important issue is how behavioral researchers can rapidly disseminate our findings so that they are widely applied. Like most scientific disciplines, behavioral interventions are developed and reported in professional journals. However, parents, teachers, and other frontline treatment providers are unlikely to be among the audience of the journals. We need to specifically target outlets that reach these personnel. Thus, publication of our work in media outlets and the popular press might be effective in making our treatments known.

Several behavioral methodologies have done this so far. Structured behavioral techniques have received widespread acceptance in both home-based and school programs, largely because they have been described in excellent detail in several commercially available manuals (e.g., Leaf & McEachin, 1999; Maurice, Green, & Luce, 1996). Similarly, PECS, which also has a comprehensive training manual (Frost & Bondy, 2000), has received wide acceptance in school programs across the country.

Discrete trial training has enjoyed a level of success and advocacy far beyond its objectively determined effectiveness (as mentioned earlier, no treatment is effective with all children with autism). This success is probably because of the Lovaas (1987) study reporting that 47% of very young children provided with 40 hours a week of this treatment achieved "normal" functioning. Despite cautions about the methodology of the study and the fact that the study participants might not be representative of the wide range of children with autism, parents understandably applauded the treatment as a potential "cure" and demanded the treatment for their children. (It is interesting, however, that few people seem to notice that 53% did *not* achieve normal functioning.) The Internet, autism organizations, and so on all provided a ready vehicle for the dissemination of this very hopeful information from the Lovaas study to parents so eager for an answer to their child's condition. This, in addition to widespread popular media coverage, proved to make intensive discrete trial training very popular indeed.

Conversely, some of the newer and more promising naturalistic behavioral interventions, self-management techniques, and the use of video technology have received less widespread acceptance and remain primarily within an academic setting. At least two possibilities for this difference in rate of dissemination arise. First, it is possible that there are less well-known, well-detailed manuals for these techniques. Second, it is possible that naturalistic techniques, self-management, and video technology are more complex and less user friendly for families and educators without a background in behavioral techniques. It is important for us to determine these barriers so that they can be overcome.

Another important goal of dissemination is to monitor the fidelity of implementation of behavioral treatments used in the community. Many of the teachers and therapists providing intervention to individuals with autism in the community do not have a firm background in behavioral principles. Given this reality, it is important to determine the quality of behavioral interventions being provided in the community as opposed to those provided in academic research settings and research training procedures to increase the effectiveness of intervention in the community.

CONCLUSION

As our knowledge of autism has increased, so, too, have the behavioral interventions designed to treat the disorder. One of the strengths of the field of behavior modification is the reliance on data collection to validate our procedures and monitor progress. As our own field has grown, we have become more open to differing treatment philosophies, more reliant on a variety of treatment providers, and more influenced by other fields. This expanding view of behavior analysis can only serve to improve interventions for individuals with autism. Behavioral intervention is arguably the most thoroughly studied treatment modality in the field. While we can cite some methodological shortcomings in some of the studies (e.g., small Ns, lack of random assignment), these are endemic not only to research on behavioral interventions but also to autism treatment in general. The necessity for continued research on effective treatments for this population is crucial, and, doubtless, behavioral interventions will be in the forefront of this research for some time to come.

Cross-References

Behavioral assessment is discussed in Chapter 31; management of challenging behaviors is addressed in Chapter 35.

REFERENCES

Alpert, C. L., & Kaiser, A. P. (1992). Training parents as milieu language teachers. *Journal of Early Intervention, 16,* 31–52.

Anderson, A. E. (2002). Augmentative communication and autism: A comparison of sign language and the picture exchange communication system (Doctoral dissertation, University of California, 2001). *Dissertation Abstracts International, 62,* 4269B.

Ayres, A. J. (1972). *Sensory integration and learning disorders.* Los Angeles: Western Psychological Services.

Baer, D. M., Peterson, R. F., & Sherman, J. A. (1967). The development of imitation by reinforcing behavioral similarity to a model. *Journal of the Experimental Analysis of Behavior, 10,* 405–416.

Bondy, A. S., & Frost, L. A. (1994). The Picture Exchange Communication System. *Focus on Autistic Behavior, 9,* 1–19.

Buggey, T., Toombs, K., Gardener, P., & Cervetti, M. (1999). Training responding behaviors in students with autism: Using videotaped self-modeling. *Journal of Positive Behavior Interventions, 1,* 205–214.

Campbell, J. O., Lison, C. A., Borsook, T. K., Hoover, J. A., & Arnold, P. H. (1995). Using computer and video technologies to develop interpersonal skills. *Computers in Human Behavior, 11,* 223–239.

Carr, E. G. (1981). Sign language. In O. I. Lovaas, A. Ackerman, D. Alexander, P. Firestone, M. Perkins, & A. L. Egel (Eds.), *The me book: Teaching manual for parents and teachers of developmentally disabled children* (pp. 153–161). Baltimore: University Park Press.

Carr, E. G., Binkoff, J. A., Kologinsky, E., & Eddy, M. (1978). Acquisition of sign language by autistic children: I. Expressive labelling. *Journal of Applied Behavior Analysis, 11,* 489–501.

Celiberti, D. A., & Harris, S. L. (1993). Behavioral intervention for siblings of children with autism: A focus on skills to enhance play. *Behavior Therapy, 24,* 573–599.

Charlop, M. H., & Milstein, J. P. (1989). Teaching autistic children conversational speech using video modeling. *Journal of Applied Behavior Analysis, 22,* 275–285.

Charlop, M. H., Schreibman, L., & Tryon, A. S. (1983). Learning through observation: The effects of peer modeling on acquisition and generalization in autistic children. *Journal of Abnormal Child Psychology, 11,* 355–366.

Charlop-Christy, M. H., & Carpenter, M. H. (2000). Modified incidental teaching sessions: A procedure for parents to increase spontaneous speech in their children with autism. *Journal of Positive Behavior Interventions, 2,* 98–112.

Charlop-Christy, M. H., Carpenter, M., Le, L., LeBlanc, L. A., & Kellet, K. (2002). Using the picture exchange communication system (PECS) with children with autism: Assessment of PECS acquisition, speech, social-communicative behavior, and problem behavior. *Journal of Applied Behavior Analysis, 35,* 213–231.

Charlop-Christy, M. H., Le, L., & Freeman, K. A. (2000). A comparison of video modeling with in vivo modeling for teaching children with autism. *Journal of Autism and Developmental Disorders, 30,* 537–552.

Courchesne, E., Townsend, J. P., Akshoomoff, N. A., Yeung-Courchesne, R., Press, G. A., Murakami, J., et al. (1994). A new finding: Impairment in shifting attention in autistic and cerebellar patients. In S. H. Broman & J. Grafman (Eds.), *Atypical cognitive deficits in developmental disorders: Implications for brain function* (pp. 101–137). Hillsdale, NJ: Erlbaum.

Delprato, D. J. (2001). Comparisons of discrete-trial and normalized behavioral intervention for young children with autism. *Journal of Autism and Developmental Disorders, 31,* 315–325.

Ferster, C. B., & Demyer, M. K. (1961). The development of performances in autistic children in an automatically controlled environment. *Journal of Chronic Diseases, 13,* 312–345.

Ferster, C. B., & Demyer, M. K. (1962). A method for the experimental analysis of the behavior of autistic children. *American Journal of Orthopsychiatry, 32,* 89–98.

Frost, L., & Bondy, A. (2000). *The Picture Exchange Communication System (PECS) training manual* (2nd ed.). Newark, DE: Pyramid Products.

Garfinkle, A. N. (2000). Using theory-of-mind to increase social competence in young children with autism: A model for praxis in early childhood special education (Doctoral dissertation, University of Washington, 2000). *Dissertational Abstracts International, 60,* 2444-A.

Gray, C. A., & Garand, J. D. (1993). Social stories: Improving responses of students with autism with accurate social information. *Focus on Autistic Behavior, 8,* 1–10.

Greenspan, S., & Wieder, S. (1998). *The child with special needs: Encouraging intellectual and emotional growth.* Reading, MA: Addison, Wesley Longman.

Halle, J. W., Marshall, A. M., & Spradlin, J. E. (1979). Time delay: A technique to increase language use and facilitate generalization in retarded children. *Journal of Applied Behavior Analysis, 12,* 431–439.

Haring, T. G., Kennedy, C. H., Adams, M. J., & Pitts-Conway, V. (1987). Teaching generalization of purchasing skills across community settings to autistic youth using videotape modeling. *Journal of Applied Behavior Analysis, 20,* 89–96.

Hart, B. M., & Risley, T. R. (1968). Establishing Use of Descriptive Adjectives in the Spontaneous Speech of Disadvantaged Preschool Children. *Journal of Applied Behavior Analysis, 1,* 109–120.

Hemmeter, M. L., & Kaiser, A. P. (1994). Enhanced milieu teaching: Effects of parent-implemented language intervention. *Journal of Early Intervention, 18,* 269–289.

Hunt, P., & Goetz, L. (1988). Teaching spontaneous communication in natural settings through interrupted behavior chains. *Topics in Language Disorders, 9,* 58–71.

Ingersoll, B. (2003). Teaching children with autism to imitate using a naturalistic treatment approach: Effects on imitation, language, play, and social behaviors (Doctoral dissertation, University of California, 2003). *Dissertation Abstracts International, 63,* 6120B.

Ingersoll, B., & Schreibman, L. (2001, November). *Training spontaneous imitation in children with autism using naturalistic teaching strategies.* Paper presented at the annual meeting of the International Meeting for Autism Research, San Diego, CA.

Ingersoll, B., & Schreibman, L. (2002, November). *The effect of reciprocal imitation training on imitative and spontaneous play in children with autism.* Poster presented at the annual meeting for the International Meeting for Autism Research, Orlando, FL.

Ingersoll, B., Schreibman, L., & Stahmer, A. (2001). Brief report: Differential treatment outcomes for children with autistic spectrum disorder based on level of peer social avoidance. *Journal of Autism and Developmental Disorders, 31,* 343–349.

Ingersoll, B., & Stahmer, A. (2002, May). *Teaching peer interaction skills in toddlers with autism: Effects of contingent imitation training.* Paper presented at the annual meeting of the Association for Behavior Analysis, Toronto, Canada.

Kaiser, A. P., Ostrosky, M. M., & Alpert, C. L. (1993). Training teachers to use environmental arrangement and milieu teaching with nonvocal preschool children. *Journal of the Association for Persons with Severe Handicaps, 18,* 188–199.

Kaiser, A. P., Yoder, P. J., & Keetz, A. (1992). Evaluating milieu teaching. In S. F. Warren & J. E. Reichle (Eds.), *Causes and effects in communication and language intervention* (pp. 9–47). Baltimore: Paul H. Brookes.

Koegel, L. K., Koegel, R. L., Hurley, C., & Frea, W. D. (1992). Improving social skills and disruptive behavior in children with autism through self-management. *Journal of Applied Behavior Analysis, 25,* 341–353.

Koegel, R. L., Bimbela, A., & Schreibman, L. (1996). Collateral effects of parent training on family interactions. *Journal of Autism and Developmental Disorders, 26,* 347–359.

Koegel, R. L., & Koegel, L. K. (1990). Extended reductions in stereotypic behavior of students with autism through a self-management treatment package. *Journal of Applied Behavior Analysis, 23,* 119–127.

Koegel, R. L., Koegel, L. K., & Parks, D. R. (1990). *How to teach self management skills to people with severe disabilities: A training manual.* Santa Barbara: University of California.

Koegel, R. L., O'Dell, M. C., & Koegel, L. K. (1987). A natural language teaching paradigm for nonverbal autistic children. *Journal of Autism and Developmental Disorders, 17,* 187–200.

Koegel, R. L., Schreibman, L., Britten, K. R., Burke, J. C., & O'Neill, R. E. (1982). A comparison of parent training to direct clinic treatment. In R. L. Koegel, A. Rincover, & A. L. Egel (Eds.), *Educating and understanding autistic children* (pp. 260–279). Houston, TX: College Hill Press.

Koegel, R. L., Schreibman, L., Good, A., Cerniglia, L., Murphy, C., & Koegel, L. (1989). *How to teach pivotal behaviors to children with autism: A training manual.* Santa Barbara: University of California.

Koegel, R. L., Schreibman, L., Loos, L. M., & Dirlich-Wilhelm, H. (1992). Consistent stress profiles in mothers of children with autism. *Journal of Autism and Developmental Disorders, 22,* 205–216.

Kopp, J. (1988). Self-monitoring: A literature review of research and practice. *Social Work Research and Abstracts, 24,* 8–20.

Leaf, R., & McEachin, J. (1999). *A work in progress: Behavior management strategies and a curriculum for intensive behavioral treatment of autism.* New York: DRL Books.

Lord, C., Bristol, M. M., & Schopler, E. (1993). Early intervention for children with autism and related developmental disorders. In E. Schopler, M. E. V. Bourgondien & M. M. Bristol (Eds.), *Preschool issues in autism* (pp. 199–221). New York: Plenum Press.

Lovaas, O. I. (1977). *The autistic child: Language development through behavior modification.* New York: Irvington.

Lovaas, O. I. (1987). Behavioral treatment and normal educational and intellectual functioning in young autistic children. *Journal of Consulting and Clinical Psychology, 55,* 3–9.

Lovaas, O. I., Berberich, J. P., Perloff, B. F., & Schaeffer, B. (1966). Acquisition of imitative speech by schizophrenic children. *Science, 151,* 705–707.

Lovaas, O. I., Freitag, G., Gold, V. J., & Kassorla, I. C. (1965). Experimental studies in childhood schizophrenia: Analysis of self-destructive behavior. *Journal of Experimental Child Psychology, 2,* 67–84.

Lovaas, O. I., Koegel, R., Simmons, J. Q., & Long, J. S. (1973). Some generalization and follow-up measures on autistic children in behavior therapy. *Journal of Applied Behavior Analysis, 6,* 131–166.

Lovaas, O. I., Schreibman, L., Koegel, R., & Rehm, R. (1971). Selective responding by autistic children to multiple sensory input. *Journal of Abnormal Psychology, 77,* 211–222.

Mancina, C., Tankersley, M., Kamps, D., Kravits, T., & Parrett, J. (2000). Reduction of inappropriate vocalizations for a child with autism using a self-management treatment program. *Journal of Autism and Developmental Disorders, 30,* 599–606.

Matsuoka, K., & Kobayashi, S. (2000). Understanding of other people's intentions in a child with autism: Environmental cues and generalizations using video discrimination training. *Japanese Journal of Special Education, 37,* 1–12.

Maurice, C., Green, G., & Luce, S. C. (Eds.). (1996). *Behavioral intervention for young children with autism: A manual for parents and professionals.* Austin, TX: ProEd.

McGee, G., Almeida, M. C., Sulzer-Azaroff, B., & Feldman, R. S. (1992). Promoting reciprocal interactions via peer incidental teaching. *Journal of Applied Behavior Analysis, 25,* 117–126.

McGee, G., Daly, T., & Jacobs, H. (1994). The Walden preschool. In S. Harris & J. Handleman (Eds.), *Preschool education programs for children with autism* (pp. 127–162). Austin, TX: ProEd.

McGee, G., Krantz, P. J., Mason, D., & McClannahan, L. E. (1983). A modified incidental-teaching procedure for autistic youth: Acquisition and generalization of receptive object labels. *Journal of Applied Behavior Analysis, 16,* 329–338.

McGee, G., Krantz, P. J., & McClannahan, L. E. (1985). The facilitative effects of incidental teaching on preposition use by autistic children. *Journal of Applied Behavior Analysis, 18,* 17–31.

McGee, G., Morrier, M. J., & Daly, T. (1999). An incidental teaching approach to early intervention for toddlers with autism. *Journal of the Association for Persons with Severe Handicaps, 24,* 133–146.

Mesibov, G. B. (1993). Treatment outcome is encouraging. *American Journal on Mental Retardation, 97,* 379–380.

Metz, J. R. (1965). Conditioning Generalized Imitation in Autistic Children. *Journal of Experimental Child Psychology, 4,* 389–399.

Miranda-Linne, F., & Melin, L. (1992). Acquisition, generalization, and spontaneous use of color adjectives: A comparison of incidental teaching and traditional discrete-trial procedures for children with autism. *Research in Developmental Disabilities, 13,* 191–210.

Mirenda, P., & Iacono, T. (1988). Strategies for promoting augmentative and alternative communication in natural contexts with students with autism. *Focus on Autistic Behavior, 3,* 1–16.

Mirenda, P., & Santogrossi, J. (1985). A prompt-free strategy to teach pictorial communication system use. *AAC: Augmentative & Alternative Communication; 1,* 143–150.

Newman, B., Reinecke, D. R., & Meinberg, D. L. (2000). Self-management of varied responding in three students with autism. *Behavioral Interventions, 15,* 145–151.

Norris, C., & Dattilo, J. (1999). Evaluating effects of a social story intervention on a young girl with autism. *Focus on Autism and Other Developmental Disabilities, 14,* 180–186.

Ozonoff, S., & Cathcart, K. (1998). Effectiveness of a home program intervention for young children with autism. *Journal of Autism and Developmental Disorders, 28,* 25–32.

Pierce, K., & Schreibman, L. (1994). Teaching daily living skills to children with autism in unsupervised settings through pictorial self-management. *Journal of Applied Behavior Analysis, 27,* 471–481.

Pierce, K., & Schreibman, L. (1995). Increasing complex social behaviors in children with autism: Effects of peer-implemented pivotal response training. *Journal of Applied Behavior Analysis, 28,* 285–295.

Pierce, K., & Schreibman, L. (1997). Multiple peer use of pivotal response training social behaviors of classmates with autism: Results from trained and untrained peers. *Journal of Applied Behavior Analysis, 30,* 157–160.

Prizant, B. M., Wetherby, A. M., & Rydell, P. J. (2000). Communication intervention issues for children with autism spectrum disorders. In A. M. Wetherby & B. M. Prizant (Eds.), *Autism spectrum disorders: A transactional developmental perspective* (pp. 193–224). Baltimore: Paul H. Brookes.

Reeve, S. A. (2001). Effects of modeling, video modeling, prompting, and reinforcement strategies on increasing helping behavior in children with autism (Doctoral dissertation, City University of New York, 2000). *Dissertation Abstracts International, 62,* 1561-B.

Reichle, J., & Brown, L. (1986). Teaching the use of a multipage direct selection communication board to an adult with autism. *Journal of the Association for Persons with Severe Handicaps, 11,* 68–73.

Rogers-Warren, A., & Warren, S. F. (1980). Mands for verbalization: Facilitating the display of newly trained language in children. *Behavior Modification, 4,* 361–382.

Schreibman, L. (1988). *Autism.* Thousand Oaks, CA: Sage.

Schreibman, L., Kaneko, W. M., & Koegel, R. L. (1991). Positive affect of parents of autistic children: A comparison across two teaching techniques. *Behavior Therapy, 22,* 479–490.

Schreibman, L., & Koegel, R. L. (1996). Fostering self-management: Parent-delivered pivotal response training for children with autistic disorder. In E. D. Hibbs & P. S. Jensen (Eds.), *Psychosocial treatments for child and adolescent disorders: Empirically based strategies for clinical practice* (pp. 525–552). Washington, DC: American Psychological Association.

Schreibman, L., Stahmer, A., & Cestone, V. (2001, November). *Turning treatment nonresponders into treatment responders: Development of individualized treatment protocols for children with autism.* Paper presented at the first annual meeting of the International Meeting for Autism Research, San Diego, CA.

Schreibman, L., Whalen, C., & Stahmer, A. C. (2000). The use of video priming to reduce disruptive transition behavior in children with autism. *Journal of Positive Behavior Interventions, 2,* 3–11.

Schroeder, G. L., & Baer, D. M. (1972). Effects of concurrent and serial training on generalized vocal imitation in retarded children. *Developmental Psychology, 6,* 293–301.

Schultz, R. T., Gauthier, I., Klin, A., Fulbright, R. K., Anderson, A. W., Volkmar, F., et al. (2000). Abnormal ventral temporal cortical activity during face discrimination among individuals with autism and Asperger syndrome. *Archives of General Psychiatry, 57,* 331–340.

Schwandt, W. L., Pieropan, K., Glesne, H., Lundahl, A., Foley, D., & Larsson, E. V. (2002, May). *Using video modeling to teach generalized toy play.* Paper presented at the annual meeting of the Association for Behavior Analysis, Toronto, Canada.

Shearer, D. D., Kohler, F. W., Buchan, K. A., & McCullough, K. M. (1996). Promoting independent interactions between preschoolers with autism and their nondisabled peers: An analysis of self-monitoring. *Early Education and Development, 7,* 205–220.

Sherer, M., Pierce, K. L., Paredes, S., Kisacky, K. L., Ingersoll, B., & Schreibman, L. (2001). Enhancing conversation skills in children with autism via video technology: Which is better, "Self" or "Other" as a model? *Behavior Modification, 25,* 140–158.

Sherer, M., & Schreibman, L. (in press). Individual behavioral profiles and predictors of treatment effectiveness for children with autism. *Journal of Consulting and Clinical Psychology.*

Shipley-Benamou, R., Lutzker, J. R., & Taubman, M. (2002). Teaching daily living skills to children with autism through instructional video modeling. *Journal of Positive Behavior Interventions, 4,* 165–175.

Spradlin, J. E., & Siegel, G. M. (1982). Language training in natural and clinical environments. *Journal of Speech and Hearing Disorders, 47,* 2–6.

Stahmer, A. C. (1995). Teaching symbolic play skills to children with autism using pivotal response training. *Journal of Autism and Developmental Disorders, 25,* 123–141.

Stahmer, A. C., & Schreibman, L. (1992). Teaching children with autism appropriate play in unsupervised environments using a self-management treatment package. *Journal of Applied Behavior Analysis, 25,* 447–459.

Thiemann, K. S., & Goldstein, H. (2001). Social stories, written text cues, and video feedback: Effects on social communication of children with autism. *Journal of Applied Behavior Analysis, 34,* 425–446.

Thorpe, D. M., Stahmer, A. C., & Schreibman, L. (1995). Effects of sociodramatic play training on children with autism. *Journal of Autism and Developmental Disorders, 25,* 265–281.

Warren, S. F., Yoder, P. J., Gazdag, G. E., & Kim, K. (1993). Facilitating prelinguistic communication skills in young children with developmental delay. *Journal of Speech and Hearing Research, 36,* 83–97.

Whalen, C. (2001). Joint attention training for children with autism and the collateral effects on language, play, imitation, and social behaviors (Doctoral dissertation, University of California, 2001). *Dissertation Abstracts International, 61,* 6122B.

Whalen, C., & Schreibman, L. (2003). Joint attention training for children with autism using behaviour modification procedures. *Journal of Child Psychology and Psychiatry, 44,* 456–468.

Yoder, P. J., & Warren, S. F. (1998). Maternal responsivity predicts the prelinguistic communication intervention that facilitates generalized intentional communication. *Journal of Speech, Language, and Hearing Research, 41,* 1207–1219.

Zanolli, K., Daggett, J., & Adams, T. (1996). Teaching preschool age autistic children to make spontaneous initiations to peers using priming. *Journal of Autism and Developmental Disorders, 26,* 407–422.

CHAPTER 35

Behavioral Interventions

JOEL D. BREGMAN, DIANNE ZAGER, AND JOHN GERDTZ

During the past three decades, behavioral interventions have become the predominant treatment approach for promoting the social, adaptive, and behavioral functioning of children and adults with autism. The sophistication of these strategies has increased substantially, reflecting advancements in technique and refinements in behavioral assessment. Behavioral approaches have been adopted increasingly for enhancing personal independence and responsible choice through skill development and habilitative training, increasing repertoires of prosocial behavior and leisure activities, and teaching methods of self-control and relaxation. In addition, behavioral interventions have been employed for reinforcing adaptive responses and suppressing maladaptive ones. The targets of treatment have included social, communicative, and behavioral responses. Of particular importance has been the development of improved methods of identifying environmental factors and events that precipitate and maintain maladaptive patterns of behavior.

During the past 10 years, there has been a trend favoring interventions that modify environmental precipitants of problem behaviors (e.g., antecedent or stimulus-based interventions), as well as those that teach competing, adaptive behavioral routines (e.g., instruction-based interventions such as functional communication, self-management, and visual schedules; Carr, Horner, et al., 1999). Another trend has been the inclusion of family members, teachers, and community supporters in the planning and implementation of behavioral interventions, thereby promoting the maintenance and generalization of treatment effects across individuals and naturalistic environments (Horner, Carr, Strain, Todd, & Reed, 2002). For this approach to be successful, family and community context must be considered in treatment planning, taking into account family schedules, responsibilities (caretaking, work, household), lifestyle, support, and styles of social interaction (Moes & Frea, 2000, 2002). In a recent study, contextualized behavioral support enhanced the value of functional assessment techniques and promoted the stability and durability of functional communication training in addressing the challenging behavior of several children with autism (Moes & Frea, 2002). Although problem behaviors may be successfully handled by parent-managed behavioral procedures, developmental progress may not be as robust as can be achieved by professionally directed program interventions (Bibby, Eikeseth, Martin, Mudford, & Reeves, 2002).

Persons with autism are at significant risk for the development of problem behaviors that tend to worsen if untreated and adversely affect educational, social, and community functioning (Horner et al., 2002). Optimal development depends on the successful identification and treatment of such problems, achieved through the strategies of functional assessment (Horner & Carr, 1997) and comprehensive intervention (Carr, Levin, et al., 1999b). By reducing maladaptive behavioral repertoires and replacing them with appropriate behaviors, behavioral interventions have been shown to improve the overall level of performance in individuals with autism (Kazdin, 1994; Zager, Shamow, & Schneider, 1999).

This chapter reviews recent literature on specific behavioral interventions developed to ameliorate the core features of autism and reduce the behavioral symptoms frequently associated with the syndrome. The maladaptive behaviors most often selected for treatment among those with developmental disorders (e.g., autism) include stereotypy, aggression, self-injury, property destruction, and disruptive behavior (Didden, Duker, & Korzilius, 1997). Discussions of learning theory, behavioral assessment, and educational interventions may be found in other chapters of this volume. Reference should be made to these chapters for discussions of the theoretical principles that underlie behavioral treatment, educational approaches for teaching adaptive skills, and methods of analyzing the functions of behavior in individual cases.

The success of a well-designed behavioral intervention program rests on the completion of a thorough functional analysis of behavior. Functional analysis serves as the blueprint for identifying the behavioral interventions that are most likely to influence the antecedent and consequent factors responsible for maintaining maladaptive patterns of behavior. By providing an assessment methodology that can often pinpoint the causes of problem behavior, functional analysis permits the design of a treatment plan that is specifically tailored to address maladaptive behavior (Pelios, Morren, & Tesch, 1999). Studies have shown that the more comprehensive and precise the functional assessment, the greater the likelihood that successful intervention strategies will be identified (Didden et al., 1997).

In reviewing the behavioral literature, it is important to consider methodological weaknesses that may influence the interpretation of reported findings. For example, in a recent review of behavioral intervention studies (which, itself, included several previous well-conducted reviews), reductions in problem behaviors on the order of 90% were reported across all behavioral classes and diagnostic categories (Horner et al., 2002). Although such dramatic improvement is clearly welcomed, methodological issues inherent in the studies may well have resulted in an inflation of the true benefits. For example, problem behaviors were identified and targeted for treatment without consideration of categorical diagnosis (e.g., autism) or neurobiological variables.

Although post hoc observations failed to uncover such relationships, it is unclear whether valid and reliable diagnostic and biological data were obtained prospectively. A number of other methodological issues have been present. Most behavioral treatment studies involve either single case designs or reports of very small sample size. The length of treatment follow-up is also generally limited, and intervening variables are not always analyzed. Treatment failures are rarely published, and few studies attempt to uncover demographic or clinical variables that are predictive of a favorable response. Therefore, although conclusions can be drawn about the efficacy of specific procedures in the individual cases presented, generalization to the broader population of persons with autism and maintenance of beneficial effects over time are difficult to assess. Nonetheless, as different research groups report successes for similar behavioral interventions, support for efficacy to the broader autism population accrues.

Articles were ascertained by a comprehensive computer search of several databases and a manual search of the relevant professional journals and texts published between 1984 and 2003. The following criteria were used to select sources for this review: (1) inclusion of subjects with a diagnosis of either autism or a related pervasive developmental disorder or the presence of "autistic-like behavior," (2) the use of at least one intervention type generally accepted as a valid behavioral procedure by professionals in the field of behavior modification or applied behavior analysis (studies employing several interventions needed to include at least one accepted procedure), (3) publication in refereed professional journals or professionally reviewed book chapters or presented at conferences following professional review, and (4) publication between 1984 and 2003. Although studies with methodological flaws (e.g., inadequate documentation of generalization and maintenance) were not excluded, these factors are noted in the paper.

The various behavioral strategies reviewed in this chapter are divided into the following general categories: antecedent interventions (those implemented before a target behavior is likely to occur in an effort to avert problems), consequence interventions (those implemented following the occurrence of a target behavior), and skill development interventions (behavioral programs designed to teach alternative, adaptive behaviors, thereby reducing the frequency and severity of maladaptive responses). Most of the recently published studies report on the efficacy of behavioral programs that include elements of all three major intervention types (antecedent, consequence, and skill development procedures). For purposes of this discussion, the interventions are classified according to the primary focus of the treatment package.

ANTECEDENT INTERVENTIONS

Increasingly, behavioral interventions have focused on preventing the occurrence of problem behaviors by identifying and appropriately modifying antecedent conditions rather than responding reactively by altering consequences (Reeve & Carr, 2000). Environmental engineering is becoming a preferred strategy for the prevention of problem behaviors (Horner et al., 2002). Antecedent interventions, as the name implies, involve procedures that are implemented before a target behavior occurs. The antecedent interventions (or stimulus-based procedures) can be further subdivided into those that are implemented relatively distant in time from the target behaviors and those implemented immediately before the target behaviors are expected to occur. The former procedures are sometimes known as *ecological* or *setting event interventions,* whereas the latter are often termed *immediate antecedents.*

There are a number of setting events, or remote antecedent interventions, that may be helpful in reducing problem behaviors exhibited by children and adults with autism. For example, Duker and Rasing (1989) reported that environmental changes designed to reduce visual distractions led to a decrease in self-stimulatory behavior and an increase in on-task behavior among three adolescents and adults with autism. In a review of studies on environmental modifications in the classroom, Mittenberger (1998) concluded that educational progress and adaptive behavior are enhanced by an identification and modification of environmental factors that precipitate and maintain problem behaviors. (See Gerhardt & Holmes, 1994, for an example of a comprehensive

behavioral evaluation program that includes an assessment of environmental factors.)

Early intervention services are antecedent interventions that are becoming increasingly important because of their potential for reducing the likelihood that problem behaviors will arise later in life (Anderson & Romanczyk, 1999). There is now much evidence that young children with autism who receive early intervention and educational services that focus on the development of functional communication, social skills, and personal independence may exhibit fewer behavioral problems as they grow older (Dunlap, Johnson, & Robbins, 1990; McGee, Daly, & Jacobs, 1994). These reports are encouraging. However, more research in this area is necessary to confirm the long-term preventative effects of early intervention and to determine which specific interventions of the treatment packages are responsible for a more favorable outcome. One potentially valuable remote antecedent intervention involves exposure to children who can serve as adaptive role models. For example, it has been reported that young children with autism who are in proximity to typically (i.e., normally) developing peers display significantly lower rates of aberrant behavior, such as stereotypy (Lanquetot, 1989; McGee, Paradis, & Feldman, 1993). Exposure to typical peers was definitely beneficial but was not sufficient to maintain clinically significant behavioral change without the addition of intensive behavioral treatment. Therefore, exposure to normal social role models may represent a useful antecedent procedure that enhances the success of an intensive and well-designed early intervention program.

In an effort to identify successful antecedent interventions, Touchette, MacDonald, and Langer (1985) developed a simple "scatter plot" data collection system to help identify possible situations and events in a daily schedule that may precipitate problem behaviors. The scatter plot data collection system can be used in a variety of clinical settings with relatively minor modifications. The authors provided case examples for using the scatter plot technique of data collection to identify antecedents for self-injurious and aggressive behaviors of three adolescents and adults with autism. Based on the information derived from the scatter plot, the authors modified several environmental factors, including staffing patterns and task assignments, resulting in a significant reduction in subjects' self-injury and aggression. Brown (1991) described another type of data collection method for identifying antecedents of problem behaviors exhibited by adults with developmental disabilities, including autism. The findings prompted modifications in the daily schedules of the subjects, which enhanced the success of a behavioral program in significantly decreasing problem behaviors. Based on a review of clinical research, Flannery and Horner (1994) concluded that adherence to a predictable daily schedule of events and activities can result in a reduction of disruptive behavior among persons with severe developmental disabilities.

There has been considerable interest in the role of antecedent exercise for improving the physical health and reducing the frequency and severity of behavioral problems of persons with autism and other developmental disabilities. There is evidence that antecedent exercise can reduce self-stimulatory behavior among children with autism (R. L. Koegel & Koegel, 1989) and aggressive behavior and stereotypy among adults with autism and mental retardation (Allison, Basile, & MacDonald, 1991; Elliott, Dobbin, Rose, & Soper, 1994). In the Allison et al. study, exercise was superior to the antianxiety medication lorazepam in reducing the frequency and severity of aggression manifested by an adult with autism and mental retardation. Unfortunately, due to staffing problems, the exercise program had to be abandoned, and the aggressive behaviors returned to previous levels (Hittner, 1994, pp. 125–126). There are indications that the exercise regime must be vigorous to be effective (Elliott et al., 1994). In a literature review of this topic, Gabler-Halle, Halle, and Chung (1993) found evidence to support the efficacy of antecedent exercise in reducing problem behaviors. However, the beneficial effects appear to be relatively short term. While physiological benefits may be short term, benefits over time may contribute to improved health and increased skill development from increased task engagement. In addition, many of the reported studies suffer from methodological design problems that limit the generalization of findings. Nonetheless, antecedent aerobic exercise has potential as a relatively

nonintrusive antecedent intervention for problem behavior, with the additional benefit of enhancing physical health and conditioning. Further research on this topic is warranted.

Immediate antecedent events and situations also have been identified in the literature as influencing the frequency and severity of behavioral problems. In a comprehensive review, Munk and Repp (1994) uncovered several factors in a teaching situation that influence the prevalence of behavioral difficulties. A number of these factors fall into the immediate antecedent category, including student choice of activities, variation in teaching lessons, task difficulty, and the dispersal of mastered tasks with novel tasks. Munk and Repp also outlined a useful framework for conducting functional analyses of problem behaviors in teaching environments and designing behavioral interventions to address these problems (see the chapter on behavioral assessment in this volume for a thorough discussion of functional analysis).

Studies involving children with autism have confirmed the influence of immediate antecedents in teaching situations. Robbins and Dunlap (1992) found that parents were able to teach young children with autism new tasks at home with appropriate professional support. However, problem behaviors increased significantly during the teaching process. These problems could be partially averted through the implementation of antecedent interventions, including the use of errorless learning techniques and the dispersal of mastered tasks with the new tasks being taught. However, Robbins and Dunlap argued that in some cases it might be preferable for parents to practice mastered skills that have already been taught to the children by professionals. Other investigators also have reported that systematic variation in the presentation of new tasks and mastered skills promotes learning and reduces behavioral problems among children and adults with autism (Dunlap, 1984; Weber & Thorpe, 1992; Winterling, Dunlap, & O'Neill, 1987). Other immediate antecedent interventions, such as the opportunity to express personal choice, appear to be effective in reducing the likelihood of disruptive behavior. For example, Dyer, Dunlap, and Winterling (1990) found that when students with autism and mental retardation were given the opportunity to choose the particular task to be taught, as well as the reinforcer to be earned for success, the frequency of problem behaviors decreased significantly.

The importance of conducting a proper functional analysis of antecedent variables and problem behaviors was highlighted by Taylor, Ekdahl, Romanczyk, and Miller (1994). In a study of four students with autism, the authors found that escape from the demands of teaching sessions was a common motivating factor for a variety of problem behaviors, including noncompliance, aggression, and the destruction of teaching materials. The object of the escape behavior was different among the students, however. Two of the students were motivated by escape from the task demands themselves, whereas the other two students were motivated by escape from social interaction with the teacher. These latter two students would perform the tasks if they were able to avoid social contact. Taylor et al. discussed possible antecedent interventions to address each type of escape behavior.

There are circumstances under which a specific setting event will precipitate behavioral problems for persons with autism. Kennedy and Itkonnen (1993) conducted functional analyses for two young adults with developmental disabilities (one with autism) to identify possible antecedent motivators of aggression and self-injury. For the subject with autism, the authors found that oversleeping in the morning set up a negative chain of events that often resulted in behavioral problems at school. With the implementation of a positive reinforcement program to reward the young adult for getting up at the correct time, the frequency and severity of problem behaviors later in the day decreased considerably. In a related study, Kennedy (1994) found that demands from staff to begin work or other tasks often resulted in problem behaviors (e.g., aggression, self-injury, noncompliance) for three subjects with mental retardation (two of whom also had autism). Social comments from staff generally did not elicit problem behaviors. Kennedy reduced the number of task demands and increased the number of social comments directed toward the subjects. Problem behaviors decreased significantly and remained at

relatively low levels, despite the gradual reintroduction of task demands.

Behavioral momentum, or high probability (high p) requests, constitutes another potentially powerful class of antecedent interventions, especially for the treatment of noncompliance. This type of procedure, which is relatively straightforward to implement, involves requesting the performance of a series of simple tasks ("say hi," "give me five," etc.) in a fairly rapid sequence. A low probability (low p) task (i.e., a task that has been previously resisted) is introduced into the sequence of requests. In many instances, the previously noncompliant individual will proceed to complete the low p task, which has been embedded in the series of high p tasks. In a review of research on the use of behavioral momentum procedures to treat noncompliant behavior among adults with mental retardation, Mace et al. (1988) found convincing support for the success of high p requests as antecedent interventions. Studies also document the success of behavioral momentum procedures among persons with autism. Davis, Brady, Williams, and Hamilton (1992) used high p requests with two preschool children with autism to promote appropriate responses to adult requests. The high p requests were effective and, in fact, generalized outside the treatment setting. Houlihan, Jacobson, and Brandon (1994) also reported the successful use of high p requests with preschool children with autism. The authors noted that a short interprompt interval (5 seconds) was more effective than a longer interval (20 seconds) in establishing the effectiveness of high p requests. However, there are situations in which high p requests may not be effective. For example, in their treatment program for noncompliance and self-injurious behavior motivated by escape, Zarcone, Iwata, Mazaleski, and Smith (1994) found that high p requests were not effective until an extinction component was added (i.e., prevention of physical escape from demands).

Appropriate antecedent interventions are particularly important in the behavioral treatment of rumination—the voluntary regurgitation, rechewing, and reswallowing of partially digested food. Rumination is relatively rare but can lead to serious health complications if left untreated (see Rast, 1992, for review).

Effective behavioral treatment of rumination begins with a functional analysis. Based on the specific findings, antecedent interventions can then be developed to target the identified factors, which typically include the amount of food consumed at mealtimes, the presence of distractions, the types of foods and liquids consumed, and the pace at which foods are presented (Luiselli, Medeiros, Jasinowski, Smith, & Cameron, 1994; McKeegan, Estill, & Campbell, 1987). In the treatment of rumination, antecedent interventions usually need to be supplemented with reinforcement programs delivered either alone (McKeegan et al., 1987) or in combination with extinction of escape through emesis (Luiselli et al., 1994). The combined treatment intervention was found to be effective in reducing high-frequency rumination to zero levels at 4 to 6 months' follow-up (Luiselli et al., 1994).

The usefulness of other antecedent interventions has been documented in the behavioral literature. For the treatment of rectal digging and sniffing exhibited by a woman with autism, M. D. Smith (1986) reported the efficacy of providing a variety of desirable odors (perfumes and soaps) on a fixed schedule while ignoring behavioral episodes. The target behaviors were maintained at near zero levels through 14 months of follow-up.

The manner in which skills are taught can serve as powerful antecedents for children and adults with autism. For example, Chen and Bernard-Opitz (1993) found that four elementary school children with autism exhibited significantly fewer behavioral problems (especially noncompliance) when task instructions were presented by a computer rather than by a teacher.

Stimulus Change Procedures

Stimulus change procedures usually involve the presentation of a novel or unfamiliar stimulus that is not directly antecedent or consequent to the specific problem behavior (for theoretical discussions of stimulus change procedures, see Carr, Robinson, & Palumbo, 1990; LaVigna & Donnellan, 1986). Relatively straightforward stimulus change procedures offer the behavioral clinician strategies that have the potential for rapidly reducing

the frequency and/or severity of problem behaviors. Carr et al. and LaVigna and Donnellan noted that stimulus change procedures may be particularly effective as crisis intervention techniques. Stimulus change techniques do not by themselves permanently alter behavior; however, they do offer a window of opportunity for the implementation of other interventions. For example, stimulus change can be used to interrupt a pattern of high-frequency problem behavior, thereby providing an opportunity to teach alternative skills or to reward alternative positive behaviors. Stimulus change techniques offer the potential for rapidly altering behavior and can be implemented in a variety of clinical settings with relative ease. Further research on this technique is, therefore, warranted. A variation of the stimulus change procedure was used by Van Houten (1993) in the treatment of severe self-injury (face slapping) exhibited by a child with autism. A functional analysis indicated that the high-frequency face slapping was motivated by the sensory reinforcement provided by the behavior. Van Houten placed small padded weights (1.5 pounds) on the child's wrists. This change in stimulus was sufficient to reduce face slaps to near zero levels for 5 months of follow-up.

CONSEQUENCE-BASED INTERVENTIONS

Consequence-based interventions are behavioral procedures that are implemented following the initiation or completion of a problem behavior. The most effective behavioral intervention package is likely to include a combination of antecedent and consequence-based interventions. The articles reviewed in this section are those that highlight consequence-based interventions as the primary treatment procedure.

Interruption and Redirection

Interventions involving interruption and redirection usually include physical prevention of the targeted behavior and redirection to another activity. Sensory extinction is one type of interruption that involves elimination of the sensory feedback obtained from certain repetitive aberrant behaviors. For example, if a person is reinforced by the vibrations and sounds of repetitively knocking on a table, it may be possible to reduce or eliminate the problem behavior by simply padding the table to eliminate the sensory feedback. The benefits and potential limitations of interruption and redirection were illustrated in the research of Maag, Wolchik, Rutherford, and Parks (1986). These authors studied the effects of a sensory extinction procedure on the self-stimulatory behavior of two boys with autism. Highly variable results were reported: Some self-stimulatory behaviors decreased, whereas others increased slightly.

Interruption procedures can be as direct as simply blocking the problem behavior. Mulick and Meinhold (1994) conducted a functional analysis of chronic hand mouthing manifested by a woman with autism and profound mental retardation. The behavior had resulted in serious medical problems. The functional analysis suggested that this behavior was primarily motivated by automatic, sensory reinforcement. The authors implemented a simple program to physically block attempts at hand mouthing. This procedure resulted in a significant decrease in hand mouthing, as well as an increase in academic engagement.

An interruption program was used by Bebko and Lennox (1988) to treat chronic bruxism (tooth grinding) in two young children with autism. The intervention consisted of a physical cue (i.e., a light touch of the chin) to prompt the child to open his mouth (a behavioral response that competes with bruxism). This intervention did not generalize until the cue was used in all environmental settings. As a result of this intervention, bruxism was reduced considerably, and a 2-year follow-up indicated that bruxism remained at low levels. Interruption and prompting were reported to be successful in reducing the stereotypic behavior and increasing the on-task behavior of five persons with developmental disabilities (Duker & Schaapveld, 1996).

Reinforcement-Based Interventions

A *reinforcer* can be defined as "a consequent stimulus that increases or maintains the future rate and/or probability of occurrence of a behavior" (Alberto & Troutman, 1999, p. 497). In general terms, a reinforcer is a situation or event that follows a particular behavior, resulting in an increased likelihood that the behavior will recur in the future. The goal of most behavioral interventions is to systematically reinforce desirable behaviors and reduce or eliminate reinforcers associated with undesirable behaviors. An increased usage of reinforcement-based procedures has been observed, beginning in the late 1980s (Pelios et al., 1999).

A reinforcer-based intervention will be successful only if the reinforcer(s) used are powerful enough to significantly motivate the individual to perform certain behaviors. Comprehensive guides to behavioral assessment are available, which include interview and observational techniques for identifying potential reinforcers (Mason, McGee, Farmer-Dougan, & Risley, 1989; O'Neill, Horner, Albin, Storey, & Sprague, 1990; Willis, LaVigna, & Donnellan, 1989). Mason et al. developed a rapid and effective observational method for identifying reinforcers for young children with autism. The authors then taught the children a number of specific tasks and used the reinforcers identified during the observations as rewards for task completion. The reinforcement program resulted in a significant increase in skill development and a corresponding decrease in behavioral problems exhibited during teaching sessions. Since the problem behaviors were not specifically targeted for intervention, it may be the implementation of structured teaching procedures and the use of reinforcers that serve to suppress problem behaviors during teaching sessions.

Durand, Crimmins, Caulfield, and Taylor (1989) suggested that the nature of problem behaviors themselves (e.g., self-stimulation, stereotypy) may provide important information for identifying potential reinforcers. This approach was followed by Charlop, Kurtz, and Casey (1990), who provided children with autism brief periods of time during which they could engage in stereotypy, echolalia, and perseveration as reinforcement for appropriate behavior at other times of the day. This brief access (5 seconds) served as a powerful reinforcer and resulted in a significant increase in appropriate behavior for all students. Behavioral problems did not increase, and there were no difficulties terminating access to the preferred behaviors at the end of 5 seconds. As Charlop et al. (1990) and Durand et al. have noted, serious behavior problems, such as aggression and self-injury, cannot be used as reinforcers. In such cases, appropriate reinforcers would need to be identified by a functional analysis.

There are a variety of reinforcement-based interventions known as *differential reinforcement* procedures. As the name implies, these procedures are designed to provide reinforcement in some situations, but not in others. The main categories of differential reinforcement procedures currently used include Differential Reinforcement of Other Behavior (DRO), Differential Reinforcement of Incompatible Behavior (DRI), Differential Reinforcement of Alternative Behavior (DRAlt or DRA), and Differential Reinforcement of Low Rates of Responding (DRL). Some behavioral intervention programs employ one type of differential reinforcement procedure, whereas others employ several, at times in conjunction with antecedent interventions, skill development procedures, and/or punishment. For the purposes of this discussion, the interventions are reviewed according to general type. Interventions with multiple elements are classified according to the main element of the behavioral program.

DRO is defined as "reinforcement for engaging in any response other than the target behavior for a set period of time" (LaVigna & Donnellan, 1986, p. 58). Of all the differential reinforcement interventions, DRO has received the most research attention and has been demonstrated to be effective for a variety of behavioral problems manifested by a diverse group of subject populations (LaVigna & Donnellan, 1986). Critical factors in the success of a DRO program include selection of appropriate reinforcers and use of proper reinforcement intervals that ensure motivation and avoid satiation. LaVigna and Donnellan and Repp, Felce, and Barton (1991) provide useful guidelines for the design of DRO programs, including methods for determining optimal reinforcer intervals. A number of studies utilizing DRO procedures have been reported for the treatment of children and adults with autism. Haring, Breen, Pitts-Conway, and Gaylord-Ross (1986) found that DRO procedures

implemented during teaching situations significantly reduced the frequency and severity of stereotypy exhibited by students with autism. Wong, Floyd, Innocent, and Woolsey (1992) reported that a treatment program that combined DRO with compliance training (i.e., systematic reinforcement for following directions) was effective in reducing the severe aggression, self-injury, and property damage of a hospitalized adult with autism. The benefits of this program were maintained at 1-year follow-up.

Ringdahl et al. (2002) studied the effectiveness of a DRO procedure to reduce the hand flapping of a child with autism. The hand flapping occurred in the absence of social consequences and when the child was alone. The DRO procedure involved presenting a preferred activity after an interval of time in which the child did not engage in flapping. In combination with verbal cues, the DRO procedure proved effective in reducing hand flapping.

Kennedy and Haring (1993) conducted functional analyses on three high school students with autism who exhibited behavioral problems at school, including aggression, disruptive vocalizations, and stereotypy. The analysis indicated that reinforcers for these behaviors included access to certain rewards, as well as escape from demands. The authors implemented a DRO program with a token economy, which enabled the students to earn tokens for refraining from disruptive behavior. The tokens could be exchanged for access to desired objects or for limited periods of escape from classroom demands. The DRO schedule was most effective when students had access to both types of reinforcement. The importance of a functional analysis (including assessment of environmental contexts) was supported by a study conducted by Haring and Kennedy (1990). Two students with severe disabilities (including autism) were studied in a classroom situation and in an after-school leisure program. In the classroom setting, DRO was effective in reducing disruptive behavior, whereas timeout was ineffective. However, in the after-school program, the reverse was true. M. D. Smith (1985) reported on the efficacy of a DRO program implemented in conjunction with a variety of antecedent interventions in the treatment of aggression and self-injury manifested by two group home residents with autism and mental retardation. The DRO program involved the delivery of reinforcers contingent on the absence of aggression and self-injury. The antecedent interventions included the scheduling of activities with the aid of pictures, food satiation, and the interspersal of preferred with unpreferred tasks. The treatment program succeeded in significantly reducing the frequency and severity of aggression and self-injury.

Although DRO is rather easy to understand on a conceptual level, it can be difficult to implement in some clinical settings. Paisey, Fox, Curran, Hooper, and Whitney (1991) used a DRO program, antecedent interventions (e.g., posted good behavior rules, relaxation procedures), and physical intervention techniques to treat the severe aggression of an 11-year-old boy with autism. The interventions were designed to be implemented at home by the parents. Although the interventions were conducted faithfully, they were not successful. An alternative program, which combined compliance training with extinction of escape from demands, was implemented by professional staff in the family home and proved to be successful. In view of these results, Paisey et al. recommended that caution be used in recommending that parents implement DRO programs for target behaviors such as severe aggression.

DRO programs can rapidly reduce the frequency and severity of problem behaviors in a variety of clinical settings. However, there are two major disadvantages in using DRO schedules of reinforcement. First, although DRO interventions focus on the problem or target behaviors, they do not teach alternative, adaptive behavioral responses. Second, DRO procedures result in the reinforcement of all behaviors (other than the target behaviors) that occur during reinforcement intervals. Problem behaviors that have not been directly targeted for intervention may, therefore, be inadvertently reinforced. Other differential reinforcement techniques have been developed to address the major problems related to the use of DRO. DRI interventions provide reinforcement for the *occurrence* of a behavior that is physically incompatible with the target behavior.

The theoretical assumption underlying DRI is that an individual cannot simultaneously engage in the target behavior and the incompatible behavior. Although conceptually straightforward, DRO procedures can be difficult to implement. Determination of the proper reinforcement interval can be critical to the success of the intervention. Furthermore, it may be extremely difficult to identify a behavior that is entirely incompatible with the target behavior. Finally, research support for the effectiveness of DRI is much less convincing than that for DRO (LaVigna & Donnellan, 1986).

Over the past 20 years, a number of studies involving the use of DRI with children and adults with autism have reported more encouraging findings. Azrin, Besalel, Janner, and Caputo (1988) studied a group of nine adolescents and adults with a variety of severe disabilities (including autism) who exhibited severe self-injurious behavior (SIB). The authors found that a behavioral intervention composed of response interruption (i.e., physical blocking of the SIB) combined with reinforcement of incompatible behaviors (DRI) was the most effective behavioral intervention for the treatment of the self-injury. Underwood, Figueroa, Thyer, and Nzeocha (1989) used the response interruption-DRI program described by Azrin et al. to treat SIB manifested by two adolescents diagnosed with autism and mental retardation. This intervention was effective for one subject, but not for the other. The nonresponder engaged in self-restraint behavior, and Underwood et al. hypothesized that self-injury accompanied by such self-restraint may represent a subtype of SIB that is relatively resistant to this intervention strategy.

McNally, Calamari, Hansen, and Keliher (1988) used a DRI schedule of reinforcement to treat polydipsia (excessive water consumption) in a woman with autism and mental retardation. The polydipsia was so severe that the woman was in danger of potentially fatal water intoxication. The authors provided edible reinforcers and a reduction in activity demands as rewards for the incompatible behavior of refusing offers of water. The woman's water consumption returned to normal levels. M. D. Smith (1987) successfully used a combined intervention of DRI plus DRA to treat the pica (consumption of nonfood items) of a man with autism and mental retardation. Reinforcers for this study included edibles, access to desired activities, and praise from staff. The subject received reinforcement for a "clean mouth" (DRI), plus reinforcers for remaining in his assigned work station, keeping his hands on work, and working quickly (DRA). Pica decreased and work productivity increased when the DRI/DRA programs were in effect. Pica increased when the reinforcement schedule was withdrawn and again diminished when the program was reinstated.

DRA is a version of DRI, in which the alternative, rewarded behavior is not completely incompatible with the target problem behavior. DRA can be used to reward a variety of positive alternative behaviors. Choosing an appropriate reinforcement interval is as important for DRA as it is for DRO and DRI. The obvious benefit of a DRA schedule is that the program can be used to teach the individual a variety of adaptive responses. However, DRA shares with DRI several drawbacks in comparison with DRO, including a slower rate of response and less empirical support. Dunlap, Koegel, Johnson, and O'Neill (1987) used a DRA program in combination with verbal reprimand to increase the on-task behavior of adults with autism participating in a vocational program. With the motivation provided by the DRA schedule (and reprimands delivered at home), the subjects remained on task for up to 8 hours, allowing staff members to gradually fade their supervision. Hittner (1994) used a combination of DRA, DRO, and medication (imipramine) to treat the severe aggression and self-injury of a man diagnosed with autism and mental retardation. The DRA schedule involved rewarding the subject every 30 minutes for remaining on task and following his schedule, while the DRO program provided reinforcers for the absence of aggression and self-injury during the same period. Both target behaviors decreased significantly and remained suppressed at 5 months' follow-up. It is difficult to separate the effect of the medication from the effects of the behavioral interventions in this study. However, significant suppression of problem behaviors did not begin until the DRA and DRO programs were added to the treatment plan.

The complexities of designing and combining behavioral treatment interventions were illustrated in the work of Vollmer, Marcus, and LeBlanc (1994). The authors conducted a functional analysis of the self-injurious behavior of three preschool children (one with "autistic-like" behaviors). The functional analyses were inconclusive as to the possible functions of the problem behaviors. Vollmer et al. then used reinforcer assessments to identify preferred items for each child. Self-injury decreased when the children were given access to the preferred items. For clinically significant reductions in the problem behaviors to occur, one child required a DRA schedule to reinforce appropriate toy play, whereas another required timeout as a consequence for his self-injurious behavior.

DRL is another differential reinforcement technique that rewards low rates of a target behavior. This intervention is appropriate only for behaviors that are essentially acceptable but that can be disruptive if they occur frequently or at high levels of intensity (e.g., asking frequent questions in class). When used appropriately, DRL is a potentially powerful technique that can result in a relatively rapid reduction in the rate of behavioral problems. Choosing the appropriate reinforcement interval is important, as it is for all the differential reinforcement techniques. Problems associated with the use of DRL include a limited foundation of research documenting efficacy as compared with DRO (LaVigna & Donnellan, 1986). Another problem with DRL is that this intervention does not, by itself, teach alternative positive behaviors. The published research on the DRL treatment of behavioral disturbances associated with autism is limited in comparison with that published for other differential reinforcement techniques.

Rotholz and Luce (1983) used tokens successfully to reward reductions in the self-stimulatory behavior of two boys with autism and mental retardation. Handen, Apolito, and Seltzer (1984) used a token program and DRL to systematically reduce the repetitive speech of an adolescent with autism. When the DRL program was withdrawn, the repetitive speech returned to baseline levels, and when the program was reinstated, the repetitive speech again decreased significantly and remained at low levels at 14 months' follow-up.

Differential reinforcement programs represent potentially powerful interventions that can often be implemented across clinical settings. Donnellan, LaVigna, Zambito, and Thvedt (1985) described an intensive behavioral intervention program designed to serve children and adults with different diagnoses (including autism) who exhibited a variety of serious problem behaviors. Behavioral interventions were administered in home and community settings. The program was generally effective in reducing or eliminating problem behaviors. A 2-year follow-up indicated that most of the clinical gains had been maintained. The programs included several different behavioral strategies including DRO, DRI, DRA, stimulus change, and relaxation procedures.

Extinction Procedures

Extinction as a behavioral procedure can be defined as "withholding reinforcement for a previously reinforced behavior to reduce the occurrence of that behavior" (Alberto & Troutman, 1999, p. 495). Extinction involves systematic cessation of previously reinforced behaviors (Simpson & Gagnon, 1999). Extinction procedures can be time consuming and difficult to implement in clinical settings and may result in a transient in behavioral problems before the problems are finally extinguished. Extinction does not teach alternative adaptive behaviors, unless it is used in combination with other interventions. However, these problems can be addressed through the graduated introduction of extinction procedures and the addition of differential reinforcement programs (Ducharme & Van Houten, 1994).

Several studies have reported benefits related to the use of extinction. Iwata, Pace, Cowdery, and Miltenberger (1994) discussed the use of extinction for the treatment of severe self-injury. A functional analysis often indicates that extinction of attention, extinction of escape from demands, or extinction of sensory reinforcement may be necessary for the effective treatment of many forms of severe self-injury. This use of the extinction procedure was illustrated in the article by Zarcone et al. (1994; previously discussed in the chapter). The authors found that behavioral momentum was not an effective treatment for escape-motivated self-injury until extinction from escape was added to the treatment program. The escape extinction involved physically preventing the

subject from escaping task demands through self-injury. Lalli, Casey, Goh, and Merlino (1994) found that antecedent activity schedules were not effective in controlling the aggression and property destruction of adolescents with mild mental retardation until escape-motivated behaviors were extinguished. Given the findings reported earlier, additional research on extinction procedures in clinical and community settings is warranted.

Noncontingent Reinforcement

Noncontingent reinforcement is rarely used, and few studies of this type of reinforcement have been conducted in the area of autism and other disabilities. Noncontingent reinforcement involves the provision of reinforcement on a fixed schedule or routine, despite the presence of problem behaviors. There are a number of obvious difficulties with this intervention. First, it may be difficult to motivate parents or clinical staff to provide ongoing reinforcement even when problem behaviors are occurring. The natural temptation is to stop the reinforcement and implement other interventions (usually punishment). Second, the intervention may accidentally reinforce untargeted problem behaviors that may require additional interventions at a later time. Third, this intervention does not, by itself, teach alternative positive behaviors. There are reasons to believe that this intervention may be useful in some circumstances. Noncontingent reinforcement is relatively easy to implement on a consistent basis and, when effective, results in rapid behavioral change. These factors improve the likelihood that parents and staff members will implement the program faithfully. Hagopian, Fisher, and Legacy (1994) described an interesting intervention using noncontingent reinforcement with 5-year-old quadruplets diagnosed with mental retardation and pervasive developmental disorder (PDD). The target behaviors were aggression and self-injury. A functional analysis indicated that these behaviors were primarily motivated by access to attention from adults. The investigators designed a program to provide the children with attention on a dense schedule of reinforcement (every 10 seconds). This schedule was gradually faded to noncontingent attention every 5 minutes.

The program was implemented in the family home, and problem behaviors decreased significantly. The parents also found that the program was relatively easy to implement. Behavioral improvement was maintained at 1 and 2 months' follow-up. Hagopian et al. recommended that if noncontingent reinforcement is used in a clinical setting, it should begin with a very dense schedule of reinforcement and gradually be faded to a leaner schedule as problem behaviors decrease.

Britton, Carr, Landaburu, and Romick (2002) studied the efficacy of noncontingent reinforcement as a treatment for automatically reinforced stereotypy. The experimenters identified preferred activities that they believed competed with certain sensory consequences of maladaptive actions, such as head rocking. The preferred activities were made available to three individuals with the hope that the individuals would select the preferred activities. For all three subjects, the repetitive sensory consequence activities remained at high levels despite the availability of preferred activities. These findings indicated that simple access to preferred activities is not sufficient to deter stereotypic sensory supported behaviors. In another study, differential-reinforcement-of-alternative-behavior schedules were successfully combined with noncontingent reinforcement to strengthen demands (Marcus & Vollmer, 1996).

Punishment Procedures

The use of punishment is one of the most controversial issues in the behavioral literature. Clinicians and ethicists have seriously questioned the use of these procedures. Some state that punishment should never be used, whereas others suggest that punishment may be indicated in the short-term treatment of serious behavioral disturbances, when used in conjunction with appropriate education, training, and reinforcement procedures. A more complete discussion of this issue follows at the end of this chapter. *Punishment* is defined in behavioral terms as "a consequent stimulus that decreases the future rate and/or probability of a behavior" (Alberto & Troutman, 1999, p. 497). As with other behavioral interventions, punishment is rarely implemented alone.

Rather, it is typically used together with reinforcement-based interventions, antecedent procedures, and skill development programs.

Similar to reinforcement, punishment (and what is experienced as punishing) can vary greatly from individual to individual. In an effort to identify punishers for the treatment of pica manifested by three young developmentally disabled children (two with PDDs), Fisher et al. (1994) conducted a systematic evaluation to identify both reinforcers and mild punishers for each child. A DRI schedule was implemented to provide reinforcement to the children for appropriate eating. Opportunities for pica were presented in a "baited environment," and children who engaged in pica received a punisher. Pica decreased rapidly with generalization of the benefits into the children's homes. Even though the program was successful, pica was not entirely eliminated, and safety precautions to prevent ingestion of inedible objects continued to be necessary at home and school.

Punishers seem to be more effective if they are systematically varied over time. Charlop, Burgio, Iwata, and Ivancic (1988) designed a program to reduce aggression and object throwing exhibited by three children with developmental disabilities (two of whom had autism). The authors identified a number of mild potential punishers (verbal reprimand, overcorrection, timeout) and compared the effects of using one punisher consistently with those of varying punishers over time. The use of varied punishers appeared to be more effective than the use of one type of punisher. The schedule used to deliver the punisher may also influence efficacy. Cipani, Brendlinger, McDowell, and Usher (1991) compared the effects of continuous and intermittent schedules of punishment on the self-injury of a 6-year-old with autism. Lemon juice squirted in the mouth contingent on self-injury immediately suppressed the behavior on both a continuous and an intermittent schedule. Manual guidance overcorrection as a punisher for self-injury was immediately effective if implemented continuously but took longer to become effective if implemented intermittently.

Punishment procedures can be effective even if implemented some time after the problem behavior has occurred. Van Houten and

Rolider (1988) treated three preschool children for biting and stomping on the feet of other children in the class. The punisher was movement suppression timeout in which the child had to face the wall for a specific period of time and not move or make a noise during that time. The child also received a verbal reprimand. If the aggressive behavior occurred at another time, the authors attempted to "recreate the scene" of the problem behavior as much as possible and then implement the timeout procedure. The frequency of the aggression was reduced to zero, and this was maintained at 1 and 4 months' follow-up. A previous study by Rolider and Van Houten (1985) found that movement suppression timeout was more effective than simple corner timeout in reducing the aggressive behavior of three children with severe disabilities. In addition to movement suppression timeout, the authors used a DRO schedule to reinforce the absence of aggressive behavior. Movement suppression timeout has also been used in treatment programs for adults. Matson and Keyes (1988) used this intervention in conjunction with highly structured activities, DRO, and choice making in a daily schedule to treat the severe aggression, self-injury, and property destruction of a man with autism and mental retardation. DRO and antecedent interventions were not effective in reducing the problem behavior. When a movement suppression timeout component involving contingent mechanical restraint was added, the behavioral problems decreased rapidly. The use of timeout was faded, and the positive benefits were maintained at 10 months' follow-up. Simple timeout may also be effective in treating some problem behaviors. For example, Mulick and Meinhold (1994) found that simple timeout eliminated the attention-motivated screaming and self-injury of a 30-month-old child diagnosed with PDD.

Chapman, Fisher, Piazza, and Kurtz (1993) used a combination of punishment and reinforcement-based interventions to treat the potentially life-threatening ingestion of drugs by an adolescent with mental retardation and autism. A functional analysis indicated that escape from task demands (especially work-related demands) was one of the primary motivators of this behavior. The subject was placed on a DRA schedule of reinforcement for completing work assignments, a DRI schedule for turning in any medication he found, and a punisher (performing his least favorite work activity) if he ingested medication. This intervention was effective in eliminating the ingestion of medication.

The efficacy of other punishment procedures has been studied. Rojahn, McGonigle, Curcio, and Dixon (1987) found that contingent water mist was more effective than aromatic ammonia in suppressing the pica of an adolescent with autism and severe mental retardation. The authors found that there was no increase in other problem behaviors with the use of water mist and that the problem behaviors remained suppressed at a 3-month follow-up. Jenson, Rovner, Cameron, Petersen, and Keskr (1985) found that contingent fine water mist, verbal reprimand, and praise for appropriate behavior delivered on a DRO schedule were effective in eliminating severe self-injury (self-biting) manifested by a young girl with autism. The reduction in self-injury generalized across staff members and settings and was maintained at a 6-month follow-up.

Punishers are sometimes used in combination with medication to reduce behavioral problems. Holttum, Lubetsky, and Eastman (1994) successfully used medication (clomipramine) plus contingent exercise to treat the severe trichotillomania (hair pulling) of a preschool girl with autism. When used alone, neither the medication nor the behavioral intervention was successful in reducing trichotillomania to acceptable levels. However, when used in combination, the interventions were effective in decreasing the behavior substantially.

The use of contingent electric shock as a punisher is occasionally reported in the behavioral literature. Williams, Kirkpatrick-Sanchez, and Crocker (1994) reported a treatment program for the severe self-injury of a young woman with autism and mental retardation. The program involved contingent electric shock, verbal reprimand, and contingent restraint for self-injurious behaviors. The procedure resulted in a significant reduction in self-injury, allowing for the discontinuation of the contingent shock following 30 months of treatment. Self-injury remained suppressed at follow-up 6 years later. However, another treatment program for severe self-injury using contingent electric shock, compliance training, DRO, and extinction of escape was not as successful (Williams, Kirkpatrick-Sanchez, & Iwata, 1993). The authors reported that after a period of initial success, the self-injurious behavior increased again at 6 months, despite the implementation of contingent shock.

Although the self-injury did not return to baseline levels, the use of contingent shock did not result in a clinically significant reduction in the target behaviors.

SKILL ACQUISITION

This type of intervention emphasizes the development of alternative positive behavioral skills to compete with, and ideally replace, problem behaviors. Skill acquisition is often used in conjunction with antecedent and consequence interventions, but, at times, the acquisition of new skills alone can reduce the frequency and severity of problem behaviors. An example of a skill acquisition program can be found in the work of Santarcangelo, Dyer, and Luce (1987). The investigators taught a group of young children with autism to play appropriately with toys. The teaching prompts were faded, and the children continued to be able to play in unsupervised settings. A reduction in disruptive behaviors also occurred, although these behaviors were not specifically targeted for intervention.

The skill acquisition programs reviewed in this chapter have been specifically designed to address various problem behaviors. General educational programs to teach new skills to persons with autism are reviewed in other chapters in this volume.

Skill acquisition programs generally fall into the following main categories: language and communication skills, self-management skills, and social skills. A comprehensive behavior management program may include interventions from all three categories. Studies are reviewed according to the major focus of the intervention package.

Language and Communication Skills

The development of functional language and communication skills to reduce the frequency and severity of problem behavior is one of the fastest growing areas in the field of behavioral intervention. The benefits of this type of intervention were illustrated in the report of McMorrow and Foxx (1986) on the treatment of echolalia exhibited by adults with autism. Using a systematic program of shaping, reinforcement, and extinction, the authors were able to significantly decrease echolalia and increase functional language (which generalized outside the immediate treatment setting).

Functional communication training (FCT) involves teaching a communicative response as an alternative to maladaptive behavior. Many problem behaviors, such as self-injury and aggression, serve a communicative function by expressing desires (e.g., for objects, activities, attention), representing a form of protest, or serving as a means of escaping task demands. FCT is not simply the replacement of a problem behavior; it is also an effective means of gaining access to reinforcers (Carr, 1988). Since many persons with autism and other severe disabilities do not have effective communication skills, an effective behavioral intervention will often require instruction in functional communication, as well as methods to deal with the problem behaviors (Doss & Reichle, 1989).

Carr and Durand (1985) conducted some of the early work in FCT. In one study, a functional analysis indicated that the disruptive behavior exhibited by four children with disabilities (one with autism) was motivated by escape from task demands and, in one case, a desire for attention from adults. The students were taught short phrases to request breaks from activities and attention, resulting in a decline in disruptive behavior. Carr and Durand emphasized the importance of conducting a functional analysis and teaching functionally equivalent communicative behavior (communication that is effective and efficient).

Durand and Crimmins (1987) taught a boy with autism and escape-motivated behaviors the phrase "help me." The use of this phrase resulted in being excused from task demands. As the child gained adaptive control in this manner, the frequency of the escape behaviors declined. Under some circumstances, stereotyped behaviors, such as body rocking and hand flapping, may respond to FCT. Durand and Carr (1987) found that the stereotyped behavior of children with autism increased during task demands and difficult requests and declined during easier tasks. A communication training program to enable the children to request assistance during difficult tasks resulted in a decline in the frequency of stereotypy.

FCT has been adapted for teaching nonverbal communication to supplement instruction in speech. For example, Carr and Kemp (1989) taught four preschool children with autism to point to a desired toy rather than engage in "autistic leading." Once a pointing response was established, the autistic leading of all four children declined significantly. Horner and Budd (1985) taught simple manual signs to an 11-year-old boy with autism who engaged in grabbing and yelling in school when he wanted particular items. Manual sign communication was taught most effectively in the actual school setting in which the signs were to be used. The authors found that once the student had mastered several simple signs, the frequency and severity of grabbing and yelling declined substantially.

FCT can be combined with a variety of antecedent, consequence, and other skill acquisition programs in the development of a comprehensive and effective behavioral intervention. Jayne, Schloss, Alper, and Menscher (1994) developed a comprehensive treatment program for elementary school students (several with autism or PDDs) who engaged in a variety of disruptive behaviors, such as screaming, hitting, and throwing objects. The program included systematic teaching procedures (system of least prompts), communication training to request help, and DRA reinforcement to reward appropriate communication. This program was successful in reducing the problem behaviors in the classroom. L. K. Koegel, Koegel, Hurley, and Frea (1992) used a combination of FCT, social skills training, self-management training, and differential reinforcement to improve the social skills of children with autism in community settings. As the children's communication and social skills improved, disruptive behaviors declined, even though these behaviors were not directly targeted for intervention. Carr and Carlson (1993) described an intensive behavioral treatment program for three adolescents with autism who exhibited aggression, property destruction, disruptive screaming, and

elopement behavior. The program, which was implemented in a community setting, involved a number of antecedent, consequence, and skill acquisition components including FCT, procedures for improving frustration tolerance, behavioral momentum, and other related interventions. Although this was a sophisticated behavioral program, the intervention was implemented by general group home staff in a community setting. The program resulted in an almost total elimination of problem behaviors and a corresponding increase in on-task performance and other adaptive behaviors.

The complexity of behavior problems that can result from communication deficits was illustrated in a report by Day, Horner, and O'Neill (1994). These investigators conducted a functional analysis of self-injury and aggression manifested by three persons with mental retardation (one of whom also had autism). The functional analysis indicated that the behaviors were motivated by access to food or objects in one setting and escape from demands in other settings. FCT was not effective until the subjects were taught communication skills sufficient to make requests for desired items and breaks from required tasks. This study, and the others discussed previously, emphasizes the importance of a functional analysis in designing effective behavioral interventions.

Sprague and Horner (1992) found that FCT was effective in reducing a number of problem behaviors (e.g., hitting self and others, screaming) exhibited by a child with autism. The authors of this study also found that attempts to eliminate one problem behavior resulted in an increase in other maladaptive behaviors of the same response class (i.e., behaviors that had similar effects in gaining reinforcement). Only FCT was effective in the overall suppression of the problem behaviors. Campbell and Lutzker (1993) found that FCT in combination with activities planning was effective in reducing the tantrums and property destruction of an 8-year-old boy with autism. This program was successfully implemented by a parent in the family home.

Durand and Carr (1991) demonstrated the potential long-term effectiveness of FCT in their study of three children with disabilities who engaged in disruptive behavior motivated by escape from demands and a desire for attention. The progress achieved in adaptive behavior and functional communication was maintained across settings at 18 and 24 months' follow-up.

Although FCT is beneficial in expanding the communicative repertoires of persons with disabilities and secondarily reducing a variety of behavioral problems, there are limitations to its effectiveness. Vollmer (1994) has suggested that FCT alone is not an appropriate treatment for maladaptive behaviors that are motivated by automatic or sensory reinforcement. Wacker et al. (1990) and Fisher et al. (1993) found that FCT was not effective without a punishment component for their subjects. However, when combined with other behavioral approaches, FCT and related interventions are effective in expanding communication skills and reducing maladaptive behavior across a variety of home and community settings. O'Neill and Sweetland-Baker (2001) found that both reinforcement and extinction procedures were needed to supplement FCT in order to achieve desired efficacy and that stimulus generalization occurs across some, but not all, untrained task situations.

Social Skills Training

A major impact in the behavioral functioning of children and adults with autism can be achieved by expanding their range of adaptive social skills. This seems logical given the fact that deficient social reciprocity represents one of the core features of the syndrome. In a review of social skills training in children with autism, Matson and Swiezy (1994) found that, although the field is in its infancy, the available research findings are promising. As investigators reach consensus on the definition and assessment of social skills, significant progress should be made. Presently, much of the current research on social skills in autism is focused on the preschool population. Several intriguing methods of training social skills among preschool children have been reported. Lefebre and Strain (1989) found that typically developing preschool children could be taught to initiate social interactions with their peers with autism. The general improvement in social behavior demonstrated by the children

with autism was maintained by group contingencies and teacher prompts. Oke and Schreibman (1990) reported that the disruptive behavior of a young boy with autism decreased after he was taught adaptive methods of initiating social contact with his peers.

Some social skills programs have been developed for adolescents and adults with autism. Agran, Salzberg, and Stowitschek (1987) used a combination of social skills training and self-management procedures to teach a group of adults with disabilities (one with autism) appropriate social behaviors on a work site. The behavioral gains were maintained at 3 to 4 months' follow-up. Dunlap et al. (1987) taught adolescents and adults with autism to respond appropriately to the social initiatives and task requests of untrained staff in community settings. The positive social behaviors were maintained in community settings by using infrequent and delayed contingency reinforcement programs.

One method of social skills training, pivotal response training (PRT), emphasizes responsiveness to multiple cues and improved motivation. PRT represents a potentially powerful approach to teaching social skills to persons with autism (R. L. Koegel et al., 1989). R. L. Koegel and Frea (1993) used PRT to teach basic social skills to two adolescents with autism. The training resulted in a significant improvement in social behavior and communication (e.g., reductions in verbal perseveration, inappropriate facial expressions), which generalized beyond the immediate treatment setting. Schreibman, Kaneko, and Koegel (1991) found that parents appeared happier and more relaxed when they used PRT methods with their children than when they used more structured teaching techniques.

Another social skill development strategy involves the use of social stories. Social stories describe social situations by studying social cues and social responses through individualized stories. Stories include descriptive information about reactions of other persons involved in particular situations and provide directive statements to guide individuals through situations with a behavior script (Gray & Gerard, 1993). In an ABAB trial, social stories were shown to be an effective strategy for reducing interrupting verbalizations and subsequent behavioral outbursts in a child with autism (Lorimer, Simpson, Myles, & Ganz, 2002).

Baker (2000) described a creative approach for improving social interactions between children with autism and their typically developing peers, namely, the thematic incorporation of ritualistic interests and behaviors into mutually enjoyable social activities. The investigator integrated the perseverative interests (e.g., movies) of several children with autism into typical games and invited classmates to join in. Appropriate social interactions and joint attention increased, and generalization to other games and children (including siblings) occurred.

There is some research evidence indicating long-term effectiveness of social skills training strategies. For example, Foxx and Faw (1992) reported that improvements in social skills were maintained 8 years following the completion of a social skills training program for adults with mental retardation.

Self-Management Procedures

Self-management procedures are behavioral strategies in which individuals take responsibility for monitoring their own behavior and administering contingent rewards and consequences. The major benefits of this type of intervention include increased independence, better generalization of treatment progress outside the immediate treatment setting, and greater success in addressing several problem behaviors simultaneously (R. L. Koegel, Frea, & Surratt, 1994; L. K. Koegel, Koegel, & Parks, 1992). These strategies are potentially beneficial for children and adults with autism. Self-management programs developed for persons with autism often make use of aids to assist in the self-monitoring process, such as pictorial or written schedules, task analyses, wrist-mounted counting devices, and so on. For example, MacDuff, Krantz, and McClannahan (1993) introduced photographic activity schedules to four boys with autism. With the aid of these schedules, the students learned to perform complex tasks, mastered a number of new behaviors, and experienced a decrease in disruptive behavior. In a follow-up study, Krantz, MacDuff, and McClannahan (1993)

trained the parents of three boys with autism to implement picture activity schedules within the home. The parents successfully taught their children to follow the schedules and, as a result, reported an increase in social engagement and a decrease in disruptive behavior (tantrums, aggression, and property destruction). Stahmer and Schreibman (1992) used self-management procedures to teach children with autism appropriate, independent toy play. The children learned to play appropriately in unsupervised settings and continued to do so at 1-month follow-up. Pierce and Schreibman (1994) used picture schedules and other self-management procedures to teach daily living skills to children with autism. As a result, the children began using the newly learned skills in a variety of unsupervised settings. In addition, their stereotypic behavior decreased.

Kamps, Kravits, and Parrett (2000) reported success in reducing repetitive vocalizations in a 12-year-old girl with autism by teaching her to monitor her own behavior. The child was taught to discriminate quiet from noisy behavior through modeling. Then she was taught to recognize her own noisy behavior. She was asked to record whether she was noisy or quiet during intervals and to reinforce herself for quiet intervals. As the child developed more skill in self-monitoring and reinforcing, the program was implemented in her public school classroom. Although the inappropriate vocalizations did decrease, the child continued to require adult prompts to remain engaged in the program.

RESPONDENT CONDITIONING PROCEDURES

Most of the behavioral interventions described in this chapter are based on the principles of operant conditioning. However, there are several behavioral strategies used in clinical practice that follow classical or respondent conditioning theory (see Alberto & Troutman, 1999, pp. 27–28, for a discussion).

Clinical behavioral interventions based on respondent conditioning tend to involve covert imagery or relaxation procedures. Although respondent conditioning procedures have been applied infrequently to persons with autism, several have proven to be useful. In some studies, behavioral programs incorporate interventions that reflect both respondent and operant principles.

Groden and Cautela (1988) used a covert conditioning program that involved imagining positive consequences for appropriate social behaviors to increase the verbal interactions of a group of three adolescents with autism. The program was successful in increasing appropriate social interactions with peers. In a case series, Groden, Cautela, Prince, and Berryman (1994) reported that social skills training and relaxation procedures decreased the disruptive behavior of subjects with autism and related handicaps. Lindsay, Fee, Michie, and Heap (1994) found that adults with severe mental retardation could learn simple relaxation techniques and apply them to reduce their level of disruptive behavior. Love, Matson, and West (1990) used a combination of operant strategies (modeling, reinforcement) and respondent conditioning (in vivo desensitization) to treat the phobias of two children with autism. The mothers of the children were taught to implement the procedures at home. The significant reduction in phobic anxiety that resulted was maintained at 1-year follow-up. In a more recent study, a child with autism successfully learned progressive relaxation skills, demonstrated a more relaxed demeanor when performing tasks, and exhibited a decrease in the duration of his disruptive behaviors following completion of progressive relaxation training (Mullins & Christian, 2001).

Procedures based on respondent conditioning offer a number of advantages over other behavioral interventions. First, these procedures can be used in a variety of clinical settings, resulting in improved maintenance and generalization of adaptive behavioral responses. Second, the personal independence of many people with autism can be enhanced by successful self-monitoring and the implementation of relaxation and covert conditioning responses.

DIFFERENTIAL EFFICACY OF BEHAVIORAL STRATEGIES

It is of particular importance for the treating clinician to have access to data outlining a hierarchy of behavioral strategies that are successful for treating specific behavioral problems. Unfortunately, there has been little research in this area. The literature is dominated by single-case designs and small case series that rarely include comparisons of different behavioral interventions or evaluate the influence of specific demographic and clinical variables on treatment outcome. However, several meta-analyses have been published that offer preliminary insight into these important issues among persons with developmental disorders (Gorman-Smith & Matson, 1985; Lennox, Miltenberger, Spengler, & Erfanian, 1988; Matson & Gorman-Smith, 1986). These studies suggest that the most responsive target behaviors include hyperactivity, stereotypy, and toileting problems, whereas the least responsive include self-injury and aggression (Lennox et al., 1988; Matson & Gorman-Smith, 1986). Specific intervention types may be most effective for particular problems. For example, differential reinforcement procedures, physical prompting, redirection, and skill training may be most efficacious for the treatment of anxiety, dysphoria, and inappropriate social behavior; extinction, social disapproval, and overcorrection for physiological problems (e.g., enuresis and encopresis); and more intensive punishment procedures (e.g., timeout and restraint) for destructive behavior (including self-injury and aggression; Lennox et al., 1988). There is a definite need for more studies to clarify the relationship between the types of behavior interventions and clinical variables (specific problem behaviors, demographics, etc.).

CURRENT AND FUTURE ISSUES IN BEHAVIORAL INTERVENTION

The research studies reviewed in this chapter demonstrate the utility and effectiveness of behavioral interventions in enhancing the adaptive behavior, productivity, and independence of children and adults with autism. The remainder of this chapter focuses on issues that are central to the field of behavioral intervention.

Maintenance and Generalization of Behavioral Interventions

Functional analysis assessment procedures are generally accepted as the basis for effective behavioral interventions. During recent years, the number of systematic studies pertaining to the use of functional analysis has been increasing

(Hile & Desrochers, 1993; Peterson & Martens, 1995). *Maintenance* refers to length of time following the end of initial treatment during which clinical benefits continue. *Generalization* refers to the degree to which positive behavioral change extends beyond the immediate treatment setting. Although it is theoretically and clinically possible for long-term maintenance to occur without generalization and generalization to occur without long-term maintenance, the optimal outcome is for both to follow the initial treatment phase.

Reviews of behavioral research in the field of developmental disabilities have indicated that the published research in this area does not clearly document the generalization and maintenance of positive behavior change (Scotti, Evans, Meyer, & Walker, 1991; Werry & Wollersheim, 1989). In their comprehensive review of behavioral interventions, Scotti et al. reported that less than one-half of the published studies in their review included documentation of maintenance and generalization of treatment effects. Furthermore, those studies that did include follow-up rarely reported data for more than 6 months. Scotti et al. recommended that future studies include more information about the subjects, a formal functional analysis, and objective measures of follow-up extended to a minimum of 6 to 12 months after initial treatment.

There is some support for the long-term effectiveness of behavioral interventions. For example, McEachin, Smith, and Lovaas (1993) published a 6-year follow-up of young children with autism who received intensive early behavioral treatment. A comparison group consisted of children who received less intensive intervention. The outcomes clearly favored the intensive treatment group, even after 6 years. However, there has been controversy about various aspects of the research design of the study (for commentary, see Baer, 1993; Foxx, 1993; Kazdin, 1993; Mesibov, 1993; Mundy, 1993).

Future behavioral research should focus on documenting the long-term maintenance and generalization of positive behavioral change. For the present, there is ample preliminary evidence indicating that behavioral procedures are the most effective treatment interventions for a variety of behavioral symptoms associated with autism.

Aversive and Nonaversive Interventions

During the past 10 years, a great deal of time and energy has been devoted to discussions and debate on the appropriateness of punishment procedures as behavioral treatment strategies (see Repp & Singh, 1990, for an overview). The major issues underlying this controversy are presented; however, a thorough review is beyond the scope of this chapter (for a more complete review, see Matson & Taras, 1989). Some professional organizations have advocated that punishment procedures never be used, and many states have adopted regulations that either ban or restrict their implementation. Currently, there is little justification for using aversive procedures as the sole treatment intervention, since they do not teach problem-solving strategies, communication skills, or adaptive ways of dealing with frustrations and stress. Even those who support a role for aversive interventions strongly support the development of effective nonaversive treatment approaches (e.g., T. Smith, 1990). Most would agree that, when used, aversive procedures should be reserved for serious behavioral problems (e.g., severe aggression, self-injury) and be part of a comprehensive program of alternative skill development and positive reinforcement. In addition, they should be implemented appropriately and reviewed regularly to ensure continuing efficacy and need. The controversy over punishment procedures has, in itself, stimulated some changes in the field. For example, it has encouraged the development of sophisticated, multielement, behavioral interventions for severe problem behaviors that can be implemented in community settings.

Guidelines for the use of behavior reduction procedures (including punishment) were presented by a panel of experts in the field of developmental disabilities who participated in a Consensus Development Conference on the Treatment of Destructive Behaviors in Persons with Developmental Disabilities, sponsored by the National Institutes of Health in 1989 (National Institutes of Health, 1991). Among their recommendations were the following:

1. Most successful approaches to treatment are likely to involve multiple elements of therapy (behavioral and psychopharmacological), environmental change, and education.

2. Treatment methods may require techniques for enhancing desired behaviors; for producing changes in social, physical, and educational environments; and for reducing or eliminating destructive behaviors.
3. Treatments should be based on an analysis of medical and psychiatric conditions, environmental situations, consequences, and skill deficits. In the application of any of these treatments, an essential step involves a functional analysis of existing behavioral patterns.
4. Behavior-reduction procedures should be selected for their rapid effectiveness *only* if the exigencies of the clinical situation require such restrictive interventions and *only* after appropriate review. These interventions should be used *only* in the context of a comprehensive treatment package.

The controversy over aversive interventions is likely to continue.

Social Validity

There is an increasing awareness that behavioral interventions should not only reduce the frequency and severity of problem behaviors but also be valued by those who receive the services, their families, and the larger community. Therefore, the outcome of behavioral interventions should document change in specific behaviors and, whenever possible, improve the support and options available to a child or adult with autism. As part of a comprehensive behavioral treatment program, these options should include opportunities throughout the day for a child or adult to make choices, learn new skills, and gain access to appropriate reinforcement. Meyer and Evans (1989) presented a useful discussion of methods for assessing, documenting, and implementing positive changes in a person's lifestyle. Schreibman (1994) also discussed several helpful methods for assessing the social validity of behavioral interventions and their outcomes.

Behavioral Interventions in the Community

A survey of families of children and adults with autism conducted by Dunlap, Robbins, and Darrow (1994) found that families frequently deal with problem behaviors. However, most of the families reported that they had little or no access to regular behavioral consultation. This is unfortunate since research indicates that behavioral consultation in community settings is effective for the treatment of many behavioral problems and can be delivered in an efficient manner (Derby et al., 1992; Harchik, Sherman, Sheldon, & Strouse, 1992; Northup et al., 1994).

When professional behavioral consultation is unavailable, families rely most heavily on teachers, other family members, and published materials for behavioral information. One of these resources, behavioral treatment manuals, constitutes an important source of information for families and behavioral clinicians (e.g., Carr et al., 1994; Dalrymple, 1991; Foxx, 1982a, 1982b; M. D. Smith, 1990). It has become increasingly important that behavioral analysts not only promote the development of user-friendly treatment manuals but also assist in the development of programs that make behavioral support more readily available to families and professionals in the community.

Computer Applications

Computers can be used to enhance the usefulness and efficiency of behavioral intervention programs. For example, computer programs can assist with data collection, the documentation of interventions, staff scheduling, and a variety of administrative tasks in programs for persons with developmental disabilities (Romanczyk, 1984). Some computer programs simplify the collection of direct observational data and provide an efficient method of data analysis (Repp & Karsh, 1990). In addition, sophisticated computer software systems have been developed to assist behavioral clinicians in locating and evaluating treatment programs (Hofmeister et al., 1994). In the future, advanced software programs play an increasingly important role in the development of behavioral interventions.

During recent years, behavioral treatment approaches for persons with autism have become more effective and more complex. It is likely that advances in behavioral treatment will continue into the future. However, the most important measure of success of such approaches will be the documented improvement they bring to the lives of children and adults with autism.

CONCLUSION

During recent years, an increasingly broad range of behavioral intervention strategies have been developed that expand prosocial behavioral repertoires and replace maladaptive responses with adaptive alternatives among children and adults with autism and related PDDs. Several recent trends are particularly noteworthy. These include the identification and modification of environmental and situational variables that influence the occurrence of both adaptive and maladaptive behavioral patterns, skill acquisition as a means of enhancing the effectiveness, competence, independence of those with PDD, and the active involvement of family members, teachers, and community supporters in the planning and implementation of behavioral interventions. These proactive approaches have increased the relevance and meaningfulness of behavioral changes and have enhanced the maintenance and generalization of treatment effects within and across natural social environments. Behavioral assessment approaches have become increasingly sophisticated, and have expanded to include consideration of the needs and priorities of families and communities, as well as internal physiological states that can influence behavioral outcomes.

Antecedent interventions (or stimulus-based procedures) have received increasing attention. These approaches focus on distant (or setting) events, as well as on more immediate behavioral precipitants. The former include optimal levels of environmental stimulation, predictable schedules and routines, antecedent physical exercise, favorable staffing patterns, and expansion of adaptive skills. The latter include the provision of personal choices, balanced task difficulty (adequate challenge without undue frustration), errorless learning techniques, behavioral momentum (embedding low probability tasks within a series of high probability tasks), and stimulus change procedures. Among the antecedent interventions, skill acquisition has been of particular interest, including functional communication training, social skills training, and self-management procedures.

Consequence-based interventions have emphasized reinforcement-based interventions (differential reinforcement programs) and de-emphasized interruption and redirection, extinction, and punishment.

Classical or respondent conditioning has focused increasingly on such strategies as covert imagery/relaxation and in vivo desensitization.

Cross-References

Issues of developmental and diagnostic assessment are discussed in Section VI (Chapters 27 through 32); other aspects of behavioral intervention are addressed in Chapter 34; speech-communication interventions are discussed in Chapters 36 through 38; issues related to school-based interventions are discussed in Chapter 33 and Chapters 39 through 41. Personnel preparation is discussed in Chapter 39.

REFERENCES

Agran, M., Salzberg, C. L., & Stowitschek, J. J. (1987). An analysis of the effects of a social skills training program using self-instructions on the acquisition and generalization of two social behaviors in a work setting. *Journal of the Association for Persons with Severe Handicaps, 12,* 131–139.

Alberto, P. A., & Troutman, A. C. (1999). *Applied behavior analysis for teachers* (3rd ed.). New York: Macmillan.

Allison, D. B., Basile, V. C., & MacDonald, R. B. (1991). Brief report: Comparative effects of antecedent exercise and lorazepam on the aggressive behavior of an autistic man. *Journal of Autism and Developmental Disorders, 21,* 89–94.

Anderson, S. R., & Romanczyk, R. G. (1999). Early intervention for young children with autism: Continuum-based behavioral models, *Journal of the Association for Persons with Severe Handicaps, 24,* 162–173.

Azrin, N. H., Besalel, V. A., Janner, J. P., & Caputo, J. N. (1988). Comparative study of behavioral methods of treating severe self-injury. *Behavioral Residential Treatment, 3,* 119–152.

Baer, D. M. (1993). Quasi-random assignment can be as convincing as random assignment. *American Journal on Mental Retardation, 97,* 373–375.

Baker, M. J. (2000). *Incorporating children with autism's thematic ritualistic behaviors into games to increase social play interactions with siblings.* Santa Barbara: University of California.

Bebko, J. M., & Lennox, C. (1988). Teaching the control of diurnal bruxism to two children with autism using a simple cueing procedure. *Behavior Therapy, 19,* 249–255.

Bibby, P., Eikeseth, S., Martin, N. T., Mudford, O. C., & Reeves, D. (2002). Progress and outcomes for children with autism receiving parent-managed intensive interventions. *Research in Developmental Disabilities, 23*(1), 81–104.

Britton, L. N., Carr, J. E., Landaburu, H. J., & Romick, K. S. (2002). The efficacy of noncontingent reinforcement as treatment for automatically reinforced stereotypy. *Behavioral Interventions, 17,* 93–103.

Brown, F. (1991). Creative daily scheduling: A nonintrusive approach to challenging behaviors in community residences. *Journal of the Association for Persons with Severe Handicaps, 16,* 75–84.

Campbell, R. V., & Lutzker, J. R. (1993). Using functional equivalence training to reduce severe challenging behavior: A case study. *Journal of Developmental and Physical Disabilities, 5,* 208–216.

Carr, E. G. (1988). Functional equivalence as a mechanism of response generalization. In R. H. Horner, G. Dunlap, & R. L. Koegel (Eds.), *Generalization and maintenance: Lifestyle changes in applied settings* (pp. 221–241). Baltimore: Paul H. Brookes.

Carr, E. G., & Carlson, J. I. (1993). Reduction of severe behavior problems in the community using a multicomponent treatment approach. *Journal of Applied Behavior Analysis, 26,* 157–172.

Carr, E. G., & Durand, V. M. (1985). Reducing behavior problems through functional communication training. *Journal of Applied Behavior Analysis, 18,* 111–126.

Carr, E. G., Horner, R. H., Turnbull, A. P., Marquis, J. G., Magito-McLaughlin, D., McAtee, M. L., et al. (1999). *Positive behavior support for people with developmental disabilities: A research synthesis* (Monograph series). Washington, DC: American Association on Mental Retardation.

Carr, E. G., & Kemp, D. C. (1989). Functional equivalence of autistic leading and communicative pointing: Analysis and treatment. *Journal of Autism and Developmental Disorders, 19,* 561–578.

Carr, E. G., Levin, L., McConnachie, G., Carlson, J. I., Kemp, D. C., & Smith, C. E. (1994). *Communication-based interventions for problem behavior. A user's guide for producing positive change.* Baltimore: Paul H. Brookes.

Carr, E. G., Levin, L., McConnachie, G., Carlson, J. I., Kemp, D. C., Smith, C. E., et al. (1999). Comprehensive multisituational intervention for problem behavior in the community: Long-term maintenance and social validation. *Journal of Positive Behavior Interventions, 1*(1), 5–25.

Carr, E. G., Robinson, S., & Palumbo, L. W. (1990). The wrong issue: Aversive versus nonaversive treatment. The right issue: Functional versus nonfunctional treatment. In A. C. Repp & N. N. Singh (Eds.), *Perspectives on the use of nonaversive and aversive interventions for persons with developmental disabilities* (pp. 361–379). Sycamore, IL: Sycamore Press.

Chapman, S., Fisher, W., Piazza, C. C., & Kurtz, P. F. (1993). Functional assessment and treatment of life-threatening drug ingestion in a dually diagnosed youth. *Journal of Applied Behavior Analysis, 26,* 255–256.

Charlop, M. H., Burgio, L. D., Iwata, B. A., & Ivancic, M. T. (1988). Stimulus variation as a means of enhancing punishment effects. *Journal of Applied Behavior Analysis, 21,* 89–95.

Charlop, M. H., Kurtz, P. F., & Casey, F. G. (1990). Using aberrant behaviors as reinforcers for autistic children. *Journal of Applied Behavior Analysis, 23,* 163–181.

Chen, S. H. A., & Bernard-Opitz, V. (1993). Comparison of personal and computer-assisted instruction for children with autism. *Mental Retardation, 31,* 368–376.

Cipani, E., Brendlinger, J., McDowell, L., & Usher, S. (1991). Continuous versus intermittent punishment: A case study. *Journal of Developmental and Physical Disabilities, 3,* 147–156.

Dalrymple, N. J. (1991). *Helping people with autism manage their behavior* (3rd ed.). Bloomington: Indiana Resource Center for Autism.

Davis, C. A., Brady, M. P., Williams, R. E., & Hamilton, R. (1992). Effects of high-probability requests on the acquisition and generalization of responses to requests in young children with behavior disorders. *Journal of Applied Behavior Analysis, 25,* 905–916.

Day, H. M., Horner, R. H., & O'Neill, R. E. (1994). Multiple functions of problem behaviors: Assessment and intervention. *Journal of Applied Behavior Analysis, 27,* 279–289.

Derby, K. M., Wacker, D. P., Sasso, G., Steege, M., Northup, J., Gigrand, K., et al. (1992). Brief functional assessment techniques to evaluate aberrant behavior in an outpatient setting: A summary of 79 cases. *Journal of Applied Behavior Analysis, 25,* 713–721.

Didden, R., Duker, P. C., & Korzilius, H. (1997). Meta-analytic study on treatment effectiveness for problem behaviors with individuals who have mental retardation. *American Journal on Mental Retardation, 101,* 387–399.

Donnellan, A. M., LaVigna, G. W., Zambito, J., & Thvedt, J. (1985). A time-limited intensive intervention program model to support community placement for persons with severe behavior problems. *Journal of the Association for Persons with Severe Handicaps, 10,* 123–131.

Doss, S., & Reichle, J. (1989). Establishing communicative alternatives to the emission of socially motivated excess behavior: A review. *Journal of the Association for Persons with Severe Handicaps, 14*(2), 101–112.

Ducharme, J. M., & Van Houten, R. (1994). Operant extinction in the treatment of severe maladaptive behavior. *Behavior Modification, 18,* 139–170.

Duker, P. C., & Rasing, E. (1989). Effects of redesigning the physical environment on self-stimulation and on-task behavior in three autistic-type developmentally disabled individuals. *Journal of Autism and Developmental Disorders, 19,* 449–460.

Duker, P. C., & Schaapveld, M. (1996). Increasing on-task behaviour through interruption-prompting. *Journal of Intellectual Disability Research, 40*(Pt 4), 291–297.

Dunlap, G. (1984). The influence of task variation and maintenance tasks on the learning and affect of autistic children. *Journal of Experimental Child Psychology, 37,* 41–64.

Dunlap, G., Johnson, L. F., & Robbins, F. R. (1990). Preventing serious behavior problems through skill development and early intervention. In A. C. Repp & N. N. Singh (Eds.), *Perspectives on the use of nonaversive and aversive interventions for persons with developmental disabilities* (pp. 273–286). Sycamore, IL: Sycamore Press.

Dunlap, G., Koegel, R. L., Johnson, J., & O'Neill, R. E. (1987). Maintaining performance of autistic clients in community settings with delayed contingencies. *Journal of Applied Behavior Analysis, 20,* 185–191.

Dunlap, G., Robbins, F. R., & Darrow, M. A. (1994). Parents' reports of their children's challenging behaviors: Results of a statewide survey. *Mental Retardation, 32,* 206–212.

Durand, V. M., & Carr, E. G. (1987). Social influences on "self-stimulatory" behavior: Analysis and treatment application. *Journal of Applied Behavior Analysis, 20,* 119–132.

Durand, V. M., & Carr, E. G. (1991). Functional communication training to reduce challenging behavior: Maintenance and application in new settings. *Journal of Applied Behavior Analysis, 24,* 251–264.

Durand, V. M., & Crimmins, D. B. (1987). Assessment and treatment of psychotic speech in an autistic child. *Journal of Autism and Developmental Disorders, 17,* 17–28.

Durand, V. M., Crimmins, D. B., Caulfield, M., & Taylor, J. (1989). Reinforcer assessment: 1. Using problem behavior to select reinforcers. *Journal of the Association for Persons with Severe Handicaps, 14,* 113–126.

Dyer, K., Dunlap, G., & Winterling, V. (1990). Effects of choice making on the serious problem behaviors of students with severe handicaps. *Journal of Applied Behavior Analysis, 23,* 515–524.

Elliott, R. O., Jr., Dobbin, A. R., Rose, G. D., & Soper, H. V. (1994). Vigorous, aerobic exercise versus general motor training activities: Effects on maladaptive and stereotypic behaviors of adults with both autism and mental retardation. *Journal of Autism and Developmental Disorders, 24,* 565–574.

Fisher, W. W., Piazza, C. C., Bowman, L. G., Kurtz, P. F., Sherer, M. R., & Lachman, S. R. (1994). A preliminary evaluation of empirically derived consequences for the treatment of pica. *Journal of Applied Behavior Analysis, 27,* 447–457.

Fisher, W. W., Piazza, C. C., Cataldo, M., Harrell, R., Jefferson, G., & Conner, R. (1993). Functional communication training with and without extinction and punishment. *Journal of Applied Behavior Analysis, 26,* 23–36.

Flannery, K. B., & Horner, R. H. (1994). The relationship between predictability and problem behavior for students with severe disabilities. *Journal of Behavioral Education, 4,* 157–176.

Foxx, R. M. (1982a). *Decreasing behaviors of persons with severe mental retardation and autism.* Champaign, IL: Research Press.

Foxx, R. M. (1982b). *Increasing behaviors of persons with severe mental retardation and autism.* Champaign, IL: Research Press.

Foxx, R. M. (1993). Sapid effects awaiting independent replication. *American Journal on Mental Retardation, 97,* 375–376.

Foxx, R. M., & Faw, G. D. (1992). An eight year follow-up of three social skills training studies. *Mental Retardation, 30*(2), 63–66.

Gabler-Halle, D., Halle, J., & Chung, Y. B. (1993). The effects of aerobic exercise on psychological and behavioral variables of individuals with developmental disabilities: A critical review. *Research in Developmental Disabilities, 14,* 359–386.

Gerhardt, P., & Holmes, D. L. (1994). The Eden Decision Model: A decision model with practical applications for the development of behavior decelerative strategies. In E. Schopler & G. B. Mesibov (Eds.), *Behavioral issues in autism* (pp. 247–276). New York: Plenum Press.

Gorman-Smith, D., & Matson, J. L. (1985). A review of treatment research for self-injurious and stereotyped responding. *Journal of Mental Deficiency Research, 29,* 295–308.

Gray, C., & Gerard, J. D. (1993). Social stories: Improving responses of students with autism with accurate social information. *Focus on Autistic Behavior, 8*(1), 1–10.

Groden, J., & Cautela, J. (1988). Procedures to increase social interaction among adolescents with autism: A multiple baseline analysis. *Journal of Behavior Therapy and Experimental Psychiatry, 19,* 87–93.

Groden, J., Cautela, J., Prince, S., & Berryman, J. (1994). The impact of stress and anxiety on individuals with autism and developmental disabilities. In E. Schopler & G. B. Mesibov (Eds.), *Behavioral issues in autism* (pp. 177–194). New York: Plenum Press.

Hagopian, L. P., Fisher, W. W., & Legacy, S. M. (1994). Schedule effects of noncontingent reinforcement on attention-maintained destructive behavior in identical quadruplets. *Journal of Applied Behavior Analysis, 27,* 317–325.

Handen, B. L., Apolito, P. M., & Seltzer, G. B. (1984). Use of differential reinforcement of low rates of behavior to decrease repetitive speech in an autistic adolescent. *Journal of Behavior Therapy and Experimental Psychiatry, 15,* 359–364.

Harchik, A. E., Sherman, J. A., Sheldon, J. B., & Strouse, M. C. (1992). Ongoing consultation as a method of improving performance of staff members in a group home. *Journal of Applied Behavior Analysis, 25,* 599–610.

Haring, T. G., Breen, C. G., Pitts-Conway, V., & Gaylord-Ross, R. (1986). Use of differential reinforcement of other behavior during dyadic instruction to reduce stereotyped behavior of autistic students. *American Journal of Mental Deficiency, 90,* 694–702.

Haring, T. G., & Kennedy, C. H. (1990). Contextual control of problem behavior in students with severe disabilities. *Journal of Applied Behavior Analysis, 23,* 235–243.

Hile, M. G., & Desrochers, M. N. (1993). The relationship between functional assessment and treatment selection for aggressive behaviors.

Research in Developmental Disabilities, 14, 265–274.

Hittner, J. B. (1994). Case study: The combined use of imipramine and behavior modification to reduce aggression in an adult male diagnosed as having autistic disorder. *Behavioral Interventions, 9,* 123–139.

Hofmeister, A. M., Althouse, R. B., Likins, M., Morgan, D. B., Ferrara, J. M., Jenson, W. R., et al. (1994). SMH.PAL: An expert system for identifying treatment procedures for students with severe disabilities. *Exceptional Children, 61,* 174–181.

Holttum, J. R., Lubetsky, M. J., & Eastman, L. E. (1994). Comprehensive management of trichotillomania in a young autistic girl. *Journal of the American Academy of Child and Adolescent Psychiatry, 33,* 577–581.

Horner, R. H., & Budd, C. M. (1985). Acquisition of manual sign use: Collateral reduction of maladaptive behavior, and factors limiting generalization. *Education and Training of the Mentally Retarded, 20,* 39–47.

Horner, R. H., & Carr, E. G. (1997). Behavioral support for students with severe disabilities: Functional assessment and comprehensive intervention. *Journal of Special Education, 31,* 84–104.

Horner, R. H., Carr, E. G., Strain, P. S., Todd, A. W., & Reed, H. K. (2002). Problem behavior interventions for young children with autism: A research synthesis. *Journal of Autism and Developmental Disorders, 32*(5), 423–446.

Houlihan, D., Jacobson, L., & Brandon, P. K. (1994). Replication of a high-probability request sequence with varied interprompt times in a preschool setting. *Journal of Applied Behavior Analysis, 27,* 737–738.

Iwata, B. A., Pace, G. M., Cowdery, G. E., & Miltenberger, R. G. (1994). What makes extinction work: An analysis of procedural form and function. *Journal of Applied Behavior Analysis, 27,* 131–144.

Jayne, D., Schloss, P. J., Alper, S., & Menscher, S. (1994). Reducing disruptive behaviors by training students to request assistance. *Behavior Modification, 18,* 320–338.

Jenson, W. R., Rovner, L., Cameron, S., Petersen, B. P., & Keskr, J. (1985). Reduction of self-injurious behavior in an autistic girl using a multifaceted treatment program. *Journal of Behavior Therapy and Experimental Psychiatry, 16,* 77–80.

Kamps, D., Kravits, T., & Parrett, J. (2000). Reduction of inappropriate vocalizations for a child with autism using a self-management treatment program. *Journal of Autism and Developmental Disorders, 30,* 599–606.

Kazdin, A. E. (1993). Replication and extension of behavioral treatment of autistic disorder. *American Journal on Mental Retardation, 97,* 377–379.

Kazdin, A. E. (1994). *Behavior modification in applied settings.* Belmont, CA: Brooks/Cole.

Kennedy, C. H. (1994). Manipulating antecedent conditions to alter the stimulus control of problem behavior. *Journal of Applied Behavior Analysis, 27,* 161–170.

Kennedy, C. H., & Haring, T. G. (1993). Combining reward and escape DRO to reduce the problem behavior of students with severe disabilities. *Journal of the Association for Persons with Severe Handicaps, 18,* 85–92.

Kennedy, C. H., & Itkonnen, T. (1993). Effects of setting events on the problem behavior of students with severe disabilities. *Journal of Applied Behavior Analysis, 26,* 321–327.

Koegel, L. K., Koegel, R. L., Hurley, C., & Frea, W. D. (1992). Improving social skills and disruptive behavior in children with autism through self-management. *Journal of Applied Behavior Analysis, 25,* 341–353.

Koegel, L. K., Koegel, R. L., & Parks, D. R. (1992). *How to teach self-management to people with severe disabilities: A training manual.* Santa Barbara: University of California, Graduate School of Education, Counseling/Clinical/School Psychology Program.

Koegel, R. L., & Frea, W. D. (1993). Treatment of social behavior in autism through modification of pivotal social skills. *Journal of Applied Behavior Analysis, 26,* 369–377.

Koegel, R. L., Frea, W. D., & Surratt, A. V. (1994). Self-management of problematic social behavior. In E. Schopler & G. B. Mesibov (Eds.), *Behavioral issues in autism* (pp. 81–97). New York: Plenum Press.

Koegel, R. L., & Koegel, L. K. (1989). Community-referenced research on self-stimulation. In E. Cipani (Ed.), *The treatment of severe behavior disorders: Behavior analysis approaches* (Monograph, 12, pp. 129–150). Washington, DC: American Association on Mental Retardation.

Koegel, R. L., Schreibman, L., Good, A., Cerniglia, L., Murphy, C., & Koegel, L. K. (1989). *How to teach pivotal behaviors to children with autism: A training manual.* Santa Barbara: University of California, Graduate School of Education, Counseling/Clinical/School Psychology Program.

Krantz, P. J., MacDuff, M. T., & McClannahan, L. E. (1993). Programming participation in family activities for children with autism: Parents' use of photographic activity schedules. *Journal of Applied Behavior Analysis, 26,* 137–138.

Lalli, J. S., Casey, S., Goh, H., & Merlino, J. (1994). Treatment of escape-maintained aberrant behavior with escape extinction and predictable routines. *Journal of Applied Behavior Analysis, 27,* 705–714.

Lanquetot, R. (1989). The effectiveness of peer modeling with autistic children. *Journal of the Multihandicapped Person, 2*(1), 25–34.

LaVigna, G. W., & Donnellan, A. M. (1986). *Alternatives to punishment: Solving behavior problems with non-aversive strategies.* New York: Irvington.

Lefebre, D., & Strain, P. (1989). Effects of a group contingency on the frequency of social interactions among autistic and nonhandicapped preschool children: Making LRE efficacious. *Journal of Early Intervention, 13,* 329–341.

Lennox, D. B., Miltenberger, R. G., Spengler, P., & Erfanian, N. (1988). Decelerative treatment practices with persons who have mental retardation: A review of five years of the literature. *American Journal on Mental Retardation, 92,* 492–501.

Lindsay, W. R., Fee, M., Michie, A., & Heap, I. (1994). The effects of cue control relaxation on adults with severe mental retardation. *Research in Developmental Disabilities, 15,* 425–437.

Lorimer, P. A., Simpson, R. L., Myles, B. S., & Ganz, J. B. (2002). The use of social stories as a preventative behavioral intervention in a home setting with a child with autism. *Journal of Positive Behavior Interventions, 4*(1), 53–60.

Love, S. R., Matson, J. L., & West, D. (1990). Mothers as effective therapists for autistic children's phobias. *Journal of Applied Behavior Analysis, 23,* 379–385.

Luiselli, J. K., Medeiros, J., Jasinowski, C., Smith, A., & Cameron, M. J. (1994). Behavioral medicine treatment of ruminative vomiting and associated weight loss in an adolescent with autism. *Journal of Autism and Developmental Disorders, 24,* 619–629.

Maag, J. W., Wolchik, S. A., Rutherford, J. B., Jr., & Parks, B. T. (1986). Response covariation on self-stimulatory behaviors during sensory extinction procedures. *Journal of Autism and Developmental Disorders, 16,* 145–154.

MacDuff, G. S., Krantz, P. J., & McClannahan, L. E. (1993). Teaching children with autism to use photographic activity schedules: Maintenance and generalization of complex response chains. *Journal of Applied Behavior Analysis, 26,* 89–97.

Mace, F. C., Hock, M. L., Lalli, J. S., West, B. J., Belfiore, P., Pinter, E., et al. (1988). Behavioral momentum in the treatment of noncompliance. *Journal of Applied Behavior Analysis, 21,* 123–141.

Marcus, B. A., & Vollmer, T. R. (1996). Combining noncontingent reinforcement and differential reinforcement schedules as treatment for aberrant behavior. *Journal of Applied Behavior Analysis, 29*(1), 43–51.

Mason, S. S., McGee, G. G., Farmer-Dougan, V., & Risley, T. R. (1989). A practical strategy for ongoing reinforcer assessment. *Journal of Applied Behavior Analysis, 22,* 171–179.

Matson, J. L., & Gorman-Smith, D. (1986). A review of treatment research for aggressive and disruptive behavior in the mentally retarded. *Applied Research in Mental Retardation, 7,* 95–103.

Matson, J. L., & Keyes, J. (1988). Contingent reinforcement and contingent restraint to treat severe aggression and self-injury in mentally retarded and autistic adults. *Journal of the Multihandicapped Person, 1,* 141–153.

Matson, J. L., & Swiezy, N. (1994). Social skills training with autistic children. In J. L. Matson (Ed.), *Autism in adults and children: Etiology, assessment and intervention* (pp. 241–260). Pacific Grove, CA: Brooks/Cole.

Matson, J. L., & Taras, M. E. (1989). A 20-year review of punishment and alternative methods to treat problem behaviors in developmentally delayed persons. *Research in Developmental Disabilities, 10,* 85–104.

McEachin, J. J., Smith, T., & Lovaas, O. I. (1993). Long-term outcome for children with autism who received early intensive behavioral treatment. *American Journal on Mental Retardation, 97,* 359–372.

McGee, G. G., Daly, T., & Jacobs, H. A. (1994). The Walden Preschool. In S. L. Harris & J. S. Handleman (Eds.), *Preschool education programs for children with autism* (pp. 127–162). Austin, TX: ProEd.

McGee, G. G., Paradis, T., & Feldman, R. S. (1993). Free effects of integration on levels of autistic behavior. *Topics in Early Childhood Special Education, 13*(1), 57–67.

McKeegan, G. F., Estill, K., & Campbell, B. (1987). Elimination of rumination by controlled eating and differential reinforcement. *Journal of Behavior Therapy and Experimental Psychiatry, 18,* 143–148.

McMorrow, M. J., & Foxx, R. M. (1986). Some direct and generalized effects of replacing an autistic man's echolalia with correct responses to questions. *Journal of Applied Behavior Analysis, 19,* 289–297.

McNally, R. J., Calamari, J. E., Hansen, P. M., & Keliher, C. (1988). Behavioral treatment of psychogenic polydipsia. *Journal of Behavior Therapy and Experimental Psychiatry, 19,* 57–61.

Mesibov, G. B. (1993). Treatment outcome is encouraging. *American Journal on Mental Retardation, 97,* 379–380.

Meyer, L. H., & Evans, I. M. (1989). *Nonaversive interventions for behavior problems: A manual for home and community.* Baltimore: Paul H. Brookes.

Mittenberger, R. G. (1998). Methods for Assessing antecedent influences on challenging behaviors. In J. K. Luiselli & M. J. Cameron (Eds.), *Antecedent control procedures for the behavioral support of persons with developmental disabilities* (pp. 47–66). Baltimore: Paul H. Brookes.

Moes, D. R., & Frea, W. D. (2000). Using family context to inform intervention planning for the treatment of a child with autism. *Journal of Positive Behavior Interventions, 2*(1), 40–46.

Moes, D. R., & Frea, W. D. (2002). Contextualized behavioral support in early intervention for children with autism and their families. *Journal of Autism and Developmental Disorders, 32*(6), 519–533.

Mulick, J. A., & Meinhold, P. M. (1994). Developmental disorders and broad effects of the environment on learning and treatment effectiveness. In E. Schopler & G. B. Mesibov (Eds.), *Behavioral issues in autism* (pp. 99–128). New York: Plenum Press.

Mullins, J. L., & Christian, L. (2001). The effects of progressive relaxation training on the disruptive behavior of a boy with autism. *Research in Developmental Disabilities, 22*(6), 449–462.

Mundy, P. (1993). Normal versus high-functioning status in children with autism. *American Journal on Mental Retardation, 97,* 381–384.

Munk, D. D., & Repp, A. C. (1994). The relationship between instructional variables and problem behavior: A review. *Exceptional Children, 60,* 390–401.

National Institutes of Health. (1991). *Treatment of destructive behaviors in persons with developmental abilities. NIH consensus development conference.* Washington, DC: U.S. Department of Health and Human Services.

Northup, J., Wacker, D. P., Berg, W. K., Kelly, L., Sasso, G., & DeRaad, A. (1994). The treatment of severe behavior problems in school settings using a technical assistance model. *Journal of Applied Behavior Analysis, 27,* 33–47.

Oke, N. J., & Schreibman, L. (1990). Training social initiations to a high-functioning autistic child: Assessment of collateral behavior change and generalization in a case study. *Journal of Autism and Developmental Disorders, 20,* 479–497.

O'Neill, R. E., Horner, R. H., Albin, R. W., Storey, K., & Sprague, J. R. (1990). *Functional analysis of problem behavior. A practical assessment guide.* Sycamore, IL: Sycamore Press.

O'Neill, R. E., & Sweetland-Baker, M. (2001). Brief report: An assessment of stimulus generalization and contingency effects in functional communication training with two students with autism. *Journal of Autism and Developmental Disorders, 31*(2), 235–240.

Paisey, T. J., Fox, S., Curran, C., Hooper, K., & Whitney, R. (1991). Reinforcement control of severe aggression exhibited by a child with autism in a family home. *Behavioral Residential Treatment, 6,* 289–302.

Pelios, L., Morren, J., & Tesch, D. (1999). The impact of functional analysis methodology on treatment choice for self-injurious and aggressive behavior. *Journal of Applied Behavior Analysis, 32,* 182–195.

Peterson, F. M., & Martens, B. K. (1995). A comparison of behavioral interventions in treatment studies for adults with developmental disabilities. *Research in Developmental Disabilities, 16,* 27–41.

Pierce, K. L., & Schreibman, L. (1994). Teaching daily living skills to children with autism in unsupervised settings through pictorial self-management. *Journal of Applied Behavior Analysis, 27,* 471–481.

Rast, J. (1992). Rumination. In E. A. Konarski, & J. E. Favell (Eds.), *Manual for the assessment and treatment of the behavior disorders of people with mental retardation* (pp. 1–9). Morganton, NC: Western Carolina Center Foundation.

Reeve, C. E., & Carr, E. G. (2000). Prevention of severe behavior problems in children with developmental disorders. *Journal of Positive Behavior Interventions, 2*(3), 144–160.

Repp, A. C., Felce, D., & Barton, L. E. (1991). The effect of initial interval size on the efficacy of DRO schedules of reinforcement. *Exceptional Children, 57,* 417–425.

Repp, A. C., & Karsh, K. G. (1990). A taxonomic approach to the nonaversive treatment of maladaptive behavior of persons with developmental disabilities. In A. C. Repp & N. N. Singh (Eds.), *Perspectives on the use of nonaversive and aversive interventions for persons with developmen-*

tal disabilities (pp. 331–347). Sycamore, IL: Sycamore Press.

Repp, A. C., & Singh, N. N. (1990). *Perspectives on the use of nonaversive and aversive interventions for persons with developmental disabilities.* Sycamore, IL: Sycamore Press.

Ringdahl, J. E., Andelman, A. S., Kitsukawa, K., Winborn, L. C., Barretto, A., & Wacher, D. P. (2002). Evaluation and treatment of covert stereotypy. *Behavioral Interventions, 17,* 43–49.

Robbins, F. R., & Dunlap, G. (1992). Effects of task difficulty on parent teaching skills and child behavior problems in young children with autism. *American Journal on Mental Retardation, 96,* 631–643.

Rojahn, J., McGonigle, J. J., Curcio, C., & Dixon, J. M. (1987). Suppression of pica by water mist and aromatic ammonia: A comparative analysis. *Behavior Modification, 11,* 65–74.

Rolider, A., & Van Houten, R. (1985). Movement suppression time-out for undesirable behavior in psychotic and severely developmentally delayed children. *Journal of Applied Behavior Analysis, 18,* 275–288.

Romanczyk, R. G. (1984). Micro-computers and behavior therapy: A powerful alliance. *Behavior Therapist, 7*(4), 59–64.

Rotholz, D. A., & Luce, S. C. (1983). Alternative reinforcement strategies for reduction of self-stimulatory behavior in an autistic youth. *Education and Treatment of Children, 6,* 363–377.

Santarcangelo, S., Dyer, K., & Luce, S. C. (1987). Generalized reduction of disruptive behavior in unsupervised settings through specific toy training. *Journal of the Association for Persons with Severe Handicaps, 12,* 38–44.

Schreibman, L. (1994). General principles of behavior management. In E. Schopler & G. B. Mesibov (Eds.), *Behavioral issues in autism* (pp. 11–38). New York: Plenum Press.

Schreibman, L., Kaneko, W. M., & Koegel, R. L. (1991). Positive affect of parents of autistic children: Comparison across two teaching techniques. *Behavior Therapy, 22,* 479–490.

Scotti, J. R., Evans, I. M., Meyer, L. H., & Walker, P. (1991). A meta-analysis of intervention research with problem behavior: Treatment validity and standards of practice. *American Journal on Mental Retardation, 96,* 233–256.

Simpson, R. L., & Gagnon, E. (1999). Structuring and management strategies for children and youth with autism. In D. B. Zager (Ed.), *Autism: Identification, education, and treatment* (2nd ed., p. 380). Mahwah, NJ: Erlbaum.

Smith, M. D. (1985). Managing the aggressive and self-injurious behavior of adults disabled by autism. *Journal of the Association for Persons with Severe Handicaps, 10,* 228–232.

Smith, M. D. (1986). Use of similar sensory stimuli in the community-based treatment of self-stimulatory behavior in an adult disabled by autism. *Journal of Behavior Therapy and Experimental Psychiatry, 17,* 121–125.

Smith, M. D. (1987). Treatment of pica in an adult disabled by autism by differential reinforcement of incompatible behavior. *Journal of Behavior Therapy and Experimental Psychiatry, 18,* 285–288.

Smith, M. D. (1990). *Autism and life in the community.* Baltimore: Paul H. Brookes.

Smith, T. (1990). When and when not to consider the use of aversive interventions in the behavioral treatment of autistic children. In A. C. Repp & N. N. Singh (Eds.), *Perspectives on the use of nonaversive and aversive interventions with persons with developmental disabilities* (pp. 287–297). Sycamore, IL: Sycamore Press.

Sprague, J. R., & Horner, R. H. (1992). Covariation within functional response classes: Implications for treatment of severe problem behavior. *Journal of Applied Behavior Analysis, 25,* 735–745.

Stahmer, A. C., & Schreibman, L. (1992). Teaching children with autism appropriate play in unsupervised environments using a self-management treatment package. *Journal of Applied Behavior Analysis, 25,* 447–459.

Taylor, J. C., Ekdahl, M. M., Romanczyk, R. G., & Miller, M. L. (1994). Escape behavior in task situations: Task versus social antecedents. *Journal of Autism and Developmental Disorders, 24,* 331–344.

Touchette, P. E., MacDonald, R. F., & Langer, S. N. (1985). A scatter plot for identifying stimulus control of problem behavior. *Journal of Applied Behavior Analysis, 18,* 343–351.

Underwood, L. A., Figueroa, R. G., Thyer, B. A., & Nzeocha, A. (1989). Interruption and DRI in the treatment of self-injurious behavior among mentally retarded and autistic self-restrainers. *Behavior Modification, 13,* 471–481.

Van Houten, R. (1993). The use of wrist weights to reduce self-injury maintained by sensory reinforcement. *Journal of Applied Behavior Analysis, 26,* 197–203.

Van Houten, R., & Rolider, A. (1988). Recreating the scene: An effective way to provide delayed punishment for inappropriate motor behavior. *Journal of Applied Behavior Analysis, 21,* 187–192.

Vollmer, T. R. (1994). The concept of Automatic Reinforcement: Implications for research in developmental disabilities. *Research in Developmental Disabilities, 15,* 187–207.

Vollmer, T. R., Marcus, B. A., & LeBlanc, L. (1994). Treatment of self-injury and hand mouthing following inconclusive functional analyses. *Journal of Applied Behavioral Analysis, 27,* 331–344.

Wacker, D. P., Steege, M. W., Northrup, J., Sasso, G., Berg, W., Reimers, T., et al. (1990). A component analysis of functional communication training across three typographies of severe behavior problems. *Journal of Applied Behavior Analysis, 23,* 417–429.

Weber, R. C., & Thorpe, J. (1992). Teaching children with autism through task variation in physical education. *Exceptional Children, 59,* 77–86.

Werry, J. S., & Wollersheim, J. P. (1989). Behavior therapy with children and adolescents: A twenty year overview. *Journal of the American Academy of Child and Adolescent Psychiatry, 28*(1), 1–18.

Williams, D. E., Kirkpatrick-Sanchez, S., & Crocker, W. T. (1994). A long-term follow-up of treatment for severe self-injury. *Research in Developmental Disabilities, 15,* 487–501.

Williams, D. E., Kirkpatrick-Sanchez, S., & Iwata, B. A. (1993). A comparison of shock intensity in the treatment of longstanding and severe self-injurious behavior. *Research in Developmental Disabilities, 14,* 207–209.

Willis, T. J., LaVigna, G. W., & Donnellan, A. M. (1989). *Behavior assessment guide.* Los Angeles: Institute for Applied Behavior Analysis.

Winterling, V., Dunlap, G., & O'Neill, R. E. (1987). The influence of task variation on the aberrant behaviors of autistic students. *Education and Treatment of Children, 10,* 105–119.

Wong, S. E., Floyd, J., Innocent, A. J., & Woolsey, J. E. (1992). Applying a DRO schedule and compliance training to reduce aggressive and self-injurious behavior in an autistic man: A case report. *Journal of Behavior Therapy and Experimental Psychiatry, 22,* 299–304.

Zager, D. B., Shamow, N. A., & Schneider, H. C. (1999). Teaching students with autism. In D. B. Zager (Ed.), *Autism: Identification, education, and treatment* (2nd ed., p. 380). Mahwah, NJ: Erlbaum.

Zarcone, J. R., Iwata, B. A., Mazaleski, J. L., & Smith, R. G. (1994). Momentum and extinction effects on self-injurious escape behavior and noncompliance. *Journal of Applied Behavior Analysis, 27,* 649–658.

CHAPTER 36

Critical Issues in Enhancing Communication Abilities for Persons with Autism Spectrum Disorders

BARRY M. PRIZANT AND AMY M. WETHERBY

In this chapter, we address critical issues in enhancing communication abilities of persons with Autism Spectrum Disorders (ASD). We begin with a consideration of the importance of a social and functional communication focus in educational and treatment efforts, followed by a comparison of general approaches to enhancing communication abilities. We then consider in detail specific dimensions that are crucial in planning appropriate educational and treatment efforts, with a focus on social communication goals. We discuss these dimensions in reference to widely disseminated education and treatment approaches discussed in the clinical and research literature. We also consider how a new model developed by the authors and their colleagues compares with available approaches relative to the critical issues presented.

First, we consider the overlapping concepts of social communication and functional communication. Social communication abilities entail the acquisition and use of conventional and socially appropriate verbal and nonverbal means to communicate for a variety of purposes across social contexts and partners. Communicative means may include gestures, sign language, pictures, picture symbols, words, and more complex language expressed through speech, visual systems, and voice output communication aides (VOCAs). Social communication also involves some degree of understanding of social events, in order to use social communicative skills appropriately. The term "functional communication abilities" refers to the degree to which

social communication abilities are relevant to an individual person's life experiences, including everyday activities and events. Functional communication abilities support greater participation and independence. These concepts clearly overlap, and abilities that are both social and functional are most desirable in communication enhancement efforts.

SOCIAL AND FUNCTIONAL COMMUNICATION ABILITIES ARE A PRIORITY IN EDUCATIONAL AND TREATMENT EFFORTS

For many years, researchers and clinicians have engaged in debates about the nature of the underlying deficits in ASD. Although diagnostic schemes have evolved and changed over the years since Leo Kanner's first description of "infantile autism" in 1943, two criteria for diagnosis have remained constant: ASD is virtually defined by difficulties in the (1) development of social communication abilities and (2) the development of social relationships (American Psychiatric Association, 1994). These essential criteria are relevant for all subcategories of autism spectrum disorders or pervasive developmental disorders. Furthermore, when research has examined the abilities that persons with autism most need to lead independent and productive lives, social communication abilities are inevitably at the top of the list. Communicative and language competence may primarily determine the extent to which individuals with ASD can develop relationships with others and participate in daily activities and routines at school, at home, and in the community. The level of communicative competence achieved by persons with ASD is closely related to the development of social behavior (Garfin & Lord, 1986) and measures of outcome (L. Koegel, Koegel, Shoshan, & McNerney, 1999; McEachin, Smith, & Lovaas, 1993). Moreover, gains in communication skills are directly related to the prevention and reduction of problem behavior (Carr & Durand, 1986; Reichle & Wacker, 1993). Furthermore, parents have identified lack of social communication abilities as among the most significant stresses they experience for children in the preschool and school years (Bristol & Schopler, 1984).

Providing effective programming to improve communication is challenging because it directly addresses the core developmental difficulties of individuals with ASD. Although there is a clear consensus of the importance of enhancing communication abilities for persons with ASD, intervention approaches vary greatly, and some approaches may even appear diametrically opposed in regard to specific priorities and procedures that are advocated to achieve these goals (Prizant & Wetherby, 1998). For example, some approaches focus primarily on linguistic forms or structural dimensions of speech and language, by building labeling vocabulary, phrases, and clauses through repetitive practice and rote training outside of natural events and social-communicative contexts. However, individuals with ASD are most challenged by a limited understanding of the conventions of reciprocal social communication and the use of conventional communicative means across social settings and partners (Prizant, Wetherby, Rubin, Laurent, & Rydell, 2003; Wetherby, Prizant, & Schuler, 1997), which may be manifest in a variety of challenges relative to developmental abilities and chronological age. In addition to limitations in the development of conventional gestures and spoken language, difficulties in the *social use* of nonverbal and verbal behavior have a major impact on communicative effectiveness (Prizant & Wetherby, 1987). Table 36.1 lists examples of challenges at preverbal, emerging language, and more advanced language stages. Because of these complex challenges and the importance of social communication

abilities for success in everyday activities, the development of spontaneous, functional communication abilities has been considered to be of the highest priority in efforts to improve communication (National Research Council [NRC], 2001; Prizant, 1982; Wetherby & Prizant, 1999).

SOCIAL COMMUNICATION LIMITATIONS ARE DIRECTLY RELATED TO PROBLEM BEHAVIOR

The close interrelationship between communicative deficiencies and development and maintenance of problem behavior has received considerable attention over the past 2 decades, which emphasizes the importance of improving social communication abilities (Reichle & Wacker, 1993). Problem behavior, including socially undesirable or unconventional behavior, and aggressive or disruptive behavior, may serve a number of communicative functions. Self-injury, tantrums, aggression, perseverative use of speech, and so forth may be the only means by which an individual with ASD can exert social control, not unlike patterns of problem behavior observed in younger children as they increasingly develop self-determination and a proactive sense of self. For persons with ASD, such behaviors serve functions such as protesting other's actions, terminating unpleasant situations, securing physical contact or attention, and initiating or regulating social interaction (for a more detailed discussion of these issues, see Carr et al., 1994; Prizant & Wetherby, 1987; Schuler & Prizant, 1985; Schuler, Wetherby, & Prizant, 1997). Furthermore, problem behaviors typically are related to more generalized states of high physiological arousal and emotional dysregulation. Therefore, efforts to support social communication abilities make up only one of a number of strategies to support emotional regulation (Prizant, Wetherby, Rubin, Laurent, & Rydell, in press).

The prevalence of undesirable communicative means, as related to emotional dysregulation, suggests that prosocial and appropriate communicative behavior may be improved if we can support emotional regulation by replacing such inappropriate means with more socially acceptable, conventional, and mutually satisfactory forms of communication for

TABLE 36.1   Examples of Challenges in Enhancing Social Communication Abilities at Various Developmental Levels

A. Challenges and issues at prelinguistic levels
  1. Establishing communicative intentionality.
  2. Uneven developmental profiles (developmental discontinuities).
  3. Problem behavior and communication limitations.
  4. Establishing nonspeech communication alternatives (gestures, picture communication, sign language).
  5. Establishing joint attention and reciprocal action.

B. Challenges and issues at emerging and early language levels
  1. The shift from presymbolic communication to language may be slow.
  2. Unconventional verbal behavior (UVB) may be produced for communicative as well as noncommunicative purposes.
  3. Generalization of early creative language and gestalt forms may be slow.
  4. Early language forms are typically used for a limited range of communicative functions or purposes.
  5. Although language may be used in a symbolic or quasi-symbolic manner, there is limited flexibility in the use of language forms.
  6. Early language use is influenced greatly by socioemotional factors, such as emotional regulation, and situational variables such as familiarity with activities.
  7. There may be considerable difficulties comprehending communicative partners' language and nonverbal signals.

C. Challenges and issues at more advanced language levels
  1. Language comprehension and social-cognitive limitations experienced by persons with ASD adversely affect conversational ability (e.g., perspective taking abilities).
  2. Verbal and nonverbal conventions of discourse, such as conventions for initiating, maintaining, and terminating conversations may be violated affecting the success of communicative exchanges.
  3. Learned verbal "scripts" may be applied too rigidly, with few, if any adjustments for different communicative or situational contexts.
  4. Ability to recognize and repair communication breakdowns may be limited.
  5. Unconventional verbal forms and idiosyncratic language used with clear intent may be difficult to "read," especially for unfamiliar partners.
  6. Language use in more socially complex and less familiar social situations may be especially challenging.

Adapted from "Enhancing Language and Communication: Language Approaches," pp. 572–605, by B. M. Prizant, A. L. Schuler, A. M. Wetherby, and P. Rydell, and "Enhancing Language and Communication: Prelanguage Approaches," pp. 539–571, by A. L. Schuler A. M. Wetherby, and B. M. Prizant, in *Handbook of Authism and Pervasive Developmental Disorders,* second edition, D. Cohen and F. R. Volkmar, eds., 1997, New York: Wiley.

social expression of intentions and social control (Prizant & Wetherby, 1987). This implies that supporting positive behavior and emotional regulation, and enhancing social communication abilities are interdependent and should be closely integrated in practice (Prizant, Wetherby, Rubin, & Laurent, 2003; Prizant et al., in press).

NRC Guidelines and Other Tenets of Practice

As noted, approaches to enhancing communicative abilities vary greatly. In an attempt to address the great diversity of approaches and differences of opinion regarding educational programming for children with ASD, the National Research Council of the National Academy of Sciences convened an expert committee of 12 professionals (including AW, coauthor of this chapter) representing a variety of disciplines and a range of philosophical orientations (e.g., behavioral and developmental orientations) toward educating students with ASD. The committee's charge was to review 20 years of educational and clinical research in order to draw conclusions and make recommendations regarding educational interventions for children with ASD from birth to 8 years of age. Their review of the research, conclusions, and recommendations were published in 2001 in a lengthy document, "Educating Children with Autism" (NRC, 2001).

The Committee (NRC, 2001) recommended that educational approaches should address the core deficits faced by children with ASD, and that meaningful outcome measures must address the following two areas:

1. Gains in initiation of spontaneous communication in functional activities.
2. Generalization of gains across activities, interactants (adults and peers), and environments.

The NRC Committee (NRC, 2001) also went on to identify six instructional priorities, all of which address social communicative and related abilities. These priorities are as follows:

Priority 1: Functional, spontaneous communication: Functional, spontaneous communication is defined by parameters of spontaneity and functionality across social settings and partners, in contrast to focusing on training vocabulary and grammatical forms outside of social contexts.

Priority 2: Social instruction in various settings: Different social settings offer different social communicative opportunities for children with ASD. Therefore, exposure to social learning opportunities in a variety of settings is a basic tenet of practice. It requires that activities be designed to enhance generalization of social communication skills and understanding of different social events.

Priority 3: Teaching of play skills focusing on appropriate use of toys and play with peers: The development of play skills at a level developmentally appropriate for a specific child is a high priority, which addresses communicative as well as social goals. Furthermore, social communication, by definition, occurs with a variety of partners. Therefore, play with peers is a necessary support for enhancing social communication abilities and relationships.

Priority 4: Instruction leading to generalization and maintenance of cognitive goals in natural contexts: With a focus on functional activities as primary contexts for learning, functional goals should be prioritized in a variety of developmental domains, including cognitive, social, and communicative, depending upon priorities set for an individual child. Therefore, the focus is on conceptually based understanding when teaching cognitive skills, whether such skills involve reading, number concepts, or more general problem-solving abilities.

Priority 5: Positive approaches to address problem behaviors: Problem behaviors are now considered within broader developmental parameters including social communication and emotional regulation. They are addressed in a preventive manner by prioritizing social communication skills that allow children to have social control through socially acceptable means (e.g., by teaching acceptable ways to protest, to make choices, or to request breaks from dysregulating circumstances). Contemporary approaches address problem behaviors relative to children's emotional state and physiological arousal, with the ultimate goal of developing a broad range of independent emotional regulatory capacities (i.e., self-regulatory capacities) as well as emotional regulatory capacities embedded in social transaction (mutual regulatory strategies; Prizant, Wetherby, Rubin, & Laurent, 2003).

Priority 6: Functional academic skills when appropriate: Once again, functionality and meaningfulness of activities and skills are priorities in contemporary practices, including language-related academic studies. In developing goals and activities to address those goals, service providers need to demonstrate that the activities and skills targeted in activities make significant differences in the lives of persons with ASD.

In summary, social communication and language abilities are now widely regarded as the most critical areas to address in supporting the development of persons with ASD. However, due to the diversity of approaches available, it is essential to analyze critically how approaches differ or are similar to one another.

UNDERSTANDING SIMILARITIES AND DIFFERENCES AMONG COMMUNICATION ENHANCEMENT APPROACHES: THE CATEGORICAL, THE BROAD DESCRIPTIVE, AND THE CONTINUUM ORIENTATION

The literature on communication enhancement for persons with ASD addresses similarities and differences among interventions in at least three distinct ways. We will use the terms *categorical, broad descriptive,* and *continuum* orientations to characterize different approaches. Information describing characteristics of educational approaches and programs used in this discussion derives, in part, from the NRC document "Educating Children with Autism" (2001), as well as from programmatic descriptions and critical reviews in recent published literature (e.g., Brown & Bambara, 1999; Heflin & Simpson, 1998; Prizant & Rubin, 1999; Prizant & Wetherby, 1998).

Categorical Orientation

A categorical orientation to describing communication interventions for children with ASD considers each program or approach to be a unique entity or package of elements. This orientation assumes that there is sufficient cohesiveness and homogeneity within a particular approach as to describe it as distinct and significantly different from other approaches. An additional assumption underlying a categorical orientation is that the elements or features descriptive of a particular approach do not overlap to any significant degree with other approaches. For example, the following is a partial list of approaches that have specified teaching practices, and in some cases, specific prescriptive curricula that are followed: speech-language training espoused by Lovaas (1981); the major component of the "Young Autism Project" also referred to as "Lovaas Therapy" (Leaf, 1998; McEachin et al., 1993); "Applied Verbal Behavior" based, in part, on the Assessment of Basic Language and Learning Skills (ABLLS) curriculum (Sundberg & Partington, 1998); "Pivotal Response Training" and the "Natural Language Paradigm" (L. Koegel, Koegel, Harrower, & Carter, 1999; R. Koegel, 1995); "The Picture Exchange Communication System" (Frost & Bondy, 1994); and the "Walden Preschool Model" (McGee, Morrier, & Daly, 1999). Clinics or schools may faithfully adopt practices of one approach as their major method for teaching social speech, language, and communication skills. Hypothetically, there should be a minimum level of fidelity in curriculum content and educational practice so that a particular categorical approach should be easily recognizable across different settings and practitioners.

A major shortcoming with a categorical orientation is that in practice there may be considerable variability in the implementation of an approach, as well as considerable overlap among different approaches when one analyzes the elements definitive of those approaches (NRC, 2001; Prizant & Wetherby, 1998). In fact, most research on efficacy of categorical approaches has been negligent in measuring fidelity of treatment practices (Prizant & Wetherby, 1998). Furthermore, as an approach evolves over time, specific teaching practices and the curriculum that is used may change significantly. In some cases, different practitioners may implement very different versions of an approach, even though the different versions are identified by the same name (Leaf, 1998).

We have argued previously (Prizant & Rubin, 1999; Prizant & Wetherby, 1998) that global claims about comparative efficacy of particular educational and communication training approaches are often weak and unfocused, as compared to others. There are two primary reasons. First, there is most often significant variability within the practice of a particular approach, and, second, there is a general lack of consideration of overlap between different "categories" of approaches. As a case in point, when ABA is discussed as one distinct category, as compared to other categories, significant differences within the practice of ABA may be obscured (Anderson & Romanczyk, 1999). For example, the predominant use of highly directive teaching strategies in ABA approaches that rely heavily on discrete-trial training as compared to more natural and child-centered teaching approaches (e.g., as observed in the contemporary ABA approaches such as the Natural Language Paradigm; R. Koegel & Koegel, 1995) may be "lumped together" when discussing ABA approaches even though both goals and teaching practices vary greatly (Cohen, 1999; Prizant & Wetherby, 1998).

In an analogous manner, important similarities among developmentally based approaches such as the DIR Model (Greenspan & Wieder, 1998, 1999), the RDI Model (Gutstein, 2000) and the SCERTS Model (Prizant et al., in press), and some contemporary ABA approaches such as the Natural Language Paradigm (Pivotal Response Training; R. Koegel & Koegel, 1995; L. Koegel, Koegel, Harrower, et al., 1999) and the Walden Preschool (McGee et al., 1999) may not even be considered when comparing approaches on a categorical basis. Examples of overlap among these approaches include a focus on child initiation and reciprocal turn taking, and play as an important context for learning. However, a categorical orientation still prevails in discussions of educational approaches and debates about treatment efficacy—an orientation that obscures the commonalities that exist across categories.

Broad Descriptive Orientation

Approaches to enhancing communication have also been characterized by descriptive practices based upon the primary goals or philosophical orientations of the approaches in more general and broad terms. Such characterizations address similarities across a number of approaches or programs allowing for a higher level categorization. Furthermore, this tack addresses common elements among a variety of practices. For example, Heflin and Simpson (1998) reviewed approaches falling into three general categories in considering treatment approaches for ASD: (1) interventions based on formation of interpersonal relationships (also referred to as "relationship-based" approaches), (2) "skill-based treatment programs," and (3) "physiologically oriented intervention programs." In their discussion, Heflin and Simpson acknowledged that a specific program or approach may have elements consistent with two or even three of the categories noted above. Other commonly used characterizations consistent with a broad descriptive orientation to categorizing educational programs include "behavioral versus developmental" or "structured" versus "semi-structured" versus "naturalistic."

Prizant and Wetherby (1998) have referred to broad descriptions of approaches for enhancing communication and related socioemotional abilities for children with ASD along a continuum based on the philosophical orientation and research literature from which such approaches were derived. Points on the continuum include "Traditional behavioral practices" at one end, versus "Social pragmatic, developmental approaches" on the other end, with "middle-ground approaches" or Hybrid Approaches occupying the middle (also see Warren, 1993). In this description, Prizant and Wetherby addressed the evolution of current educational and communication enhancement approaches from a historical perspective, with clear movement from primarily traditional behavioral approaches dominating in the 1970s and 1980s, with an increasing shift to developmental and hybrid approaches over the past 2 decades. They also noted that a number of specific dimensions may be identified that are more closely related to the actual implementation and practice within an approach, allowing for a more precise description of specific elements of programs. By doing so, Prizant and Wetherby introduced the notion of a continuum orientation, as an alternative to categorical and broad descriptive orientations, to more specifically characterize approaches to communication enhancement.

Continuum Orientation

In our effort to break down walls created by the predominance of categorical descriptions in the ASD literature, we noted (Prizant & Wetherby, 1998; Prizant, Wetherby, & Rydell, 2000) that multiple dimensions of approaches may be identified and viewed along a number of continua. Table 36.2 presents these dimensions as organized in four major categories: Teaching Practices, Learning Contexts, Child Characteristics, and Programmatic Goals. We saw the need to take this tack in describing approaches, because many contemporary educational programs increasingly integrate elements of different categorical approaches, resulting in greater flexibility and individualization of programming for children. For an individual child, the appropriateness of an approach may vary depending upon factors such as the child's social communication abilities, emotional regulatory capacities, developmental capacities in other areas, history of success with a particular approach, and parental preferences and priorities.

As compared to categorical and broad descriptive orientations, there are numerous advantages in considering approaches to communication enhancement along a number of distinct continua:

TABLE 36.2 Critical Dimensions to Consider in Communication Programming

A. Teaching practices
   1. Theoretical and research underpinnings
   2. Degree of prescription versus flexibility in teaching
   3. Use of directive versus facilitative interactional and teaching styles
   4. Approaches to problem behavior and emotional dysregulation
   5. Measurement of progress, including type and intensity of data collection
   6. Parent involvement and role of parents
   7. Use of visual supports and visually mediated activities

B. Learning contexts
   1. Naturalness of teaching activities or contexts
   2. Skill-based or activity-based learning opportunities
   3. Social complexity (e.g.,1 : 1, small group, large group)
   4. Role of typical or developmentally advanced peers

C. Child characteristics
   1. Individual differences in learning are addressed
   2. Child's Emotional Regulatory Profile is considered
   3. Age and developmental range covered

D. Programmatic goals for children
   1. Educational/treatment priorities in goal setting (i.e., domains of development)
   2. Augmentative—alternative communication goals and strategies
   3. Spontaneous, initiated communication is prioritized in goal setting
   4. Goals are based on developmental as well as functional criteria

1. Similarities as well as differences among different categorical approaches can be analyzed in a finer grained manner.
2. In specific reference to an individual student, elements that vary along each dimension may be systematically manipulated to best suit the needs and learning style of that student.
3. Teaching practices may be drawn from a variety of approaches as they are determined to best meet the needs of an individual student.
4. Movement toward greater independence for a student may be conceived as changes along various dimensions (e.g., greater flexibility

in teaching, use of a less directive interactive style in teaching; an increase in child-centered activities with increased opportunities for self-determination).

5. Future research may address specific elements and combinations of elements that may be most effective with students who demonstrate different developmental capacities and learning profiles, rather than focus on comparing different approaches at a more global categorical level. The NRC (2001) stated the need for future research to identify such critical elements, which it referred to as the "active ingredients" of intervention.

DIMENSIONS OF THE CONTINUUM

As noted above, a continuum orientation requires scrutiny of communication enhancement practices along a variety of dimensions: teaching practices, learning contexts, child characteristics, and programmatic goals for children (see Table 36.2). We will now discuss these dimensions with examples relative to different categorical approaches. It will be evident that these dimensions are not mutually exclusive.

Teaching Practices

1. *Theoretical/research underpinnings:* A broad continuum that has framed discussions about different approaches is whether an approach draws from developmental research and practice, behavioral research and practice, or both. All treatment and educational approaches have the potential to draw from the extensive literature on the development of children, with and without disabilities, and from the literature on developmentally appropriate practice in educational settings. However, on one end of the continuum, approaches may not draw from child development research, and may be predicated on primarily teaching children in formats of one child to one adult, with a focus on increasing or decreasing predetermined behaviors based upon a prescriptive program, or upon professionals' prior decisions about what a child needs to learn and how teaching is to occur. On the other end of the continuum, developmental research on children with and without disabilities provides a foundation for making decisions about goals, and teaching

strategies to achieve those goals, as well as appropriate contexts for learning. Approaches for working with children with ASD vary greatly in this dimension.

For example, traditional ABA approaches characterized by more adult-directed drills of targeted skills (e.g., Lovaas, 1981; Sundberg & Partington, 1998) draw primarily from operant models of learning in behavioral research and practice, whereas contemporary ABA approaches such as the Natural Language Paradigm and the Walden Preschool integrate practices from developmentally based early childhood practice, although they still rely on a learning theory framework to account for and document behavioral change in children (L. Koegel et al., 1999; McGee et al., 1999). However, contemporary ABA practices may not be guided by a well-articulated framework based upon the extensive research in child development (Prizant & Rubin, 1999). Nevertheless, information about developmental sequences and developmental support, based on child development research, has had a significant influence on these practices. For example, primary contexts of intervention now include play-based interaction with peers and natural activities and routines, with a focus on initiated communication and communicative reciprocity (L. Koegel et al., 1999; McGee et al., 1999).

When approaches draw most heavily from child development research and practice, they utilize developmental frameworks and developmental processes as the core foundation for determining goals, measuring progress, and selecting developmentally appropriate teaching practices. For example, the SCERTS (Social Communication, Emotional Regulation, Transactional Support) model (Prizant, Wetherby, Rubin, Laurent, & Rydell, 2003; Prizant et al., in press) is driven largely by developmental research in language, social communication, and socioemotional capacities such as emotional regulation. Specific priority goals in the SCERTS model are identified in the areas of social communication and emotional regulation, with the implementation of a range of transactional supports for children and families. The SCERTS model has a strong developmental focus, however, a child's functional needs and family priorities are factors that are considered along with goals guided by

research on child development. The DIR (Developmental, Individualized, Relationship-based) Model (Greenspan & Wieder, 1998, 1999) and RDI Model (Gutstein, 2000) are also grounded in developmental frameworks, but tend to focus less on specific social communication goals. Furthermore, developmentally-based teaching strategies addressing effective learning processes typically are infused into educational opportunities for children with ASD in the DIR and SCERTS Models.

Other major bodies of research and literature are relevant to underlying theoretical/research foundations. They include family systems theory and family-centered intervention. The SCERTS Model is heavily influenced by family systems theory and family-centered intervention practices (Dunst, Trivette, & Deal, 1988; Prizant & Bailey, 1992; Prizant & Meyer, 1993) as well as by research on positive behavioral supports in the contemporary ABA literature (Fox, Dunlap, & Buschbacher, 2000). Greenspan and Wieder's (1998) DIR Model is based upon Greenspan's model (Greenspan, 1992) of functional emotional development, with priority goals identified in socioemotional capacities and related abilities. The DIR model does not draw directly from research or literature on ABA practices.

2. *Degree of prescription versus flexibility in teaching:* Some approaches are highly prescriptive, in that teaching practices and goals are clearly specified and are to be followed faithfully. Prescriptive practices may specify how teaching materials are to be presented, how the teaching environment is to be structured or arranged, which types of child responses are considered acceptable or correct, and how adults should respond to acceptable as well as less acceptable responses. In highly prescriptive approaches, children's behavior may also be defined as "on task" or "off task," or as "compliant or non-compliant" (Lovaas, 1981). Such characterizations are in specific reference to how a child's behavior relates to a specified activity, or the teacher's agenda, regardless of its relevance to the social context or a child's focus of attention or intention. "Structured Teaching," the major instructional practice of the Division TEACCH approach (Schopler, Mesibov, & Hearsey, 1995) is another example of prescriptive teaching. Other

approaches may not follow a predetermined agenda or prescription for instruction. On this end of the continuum, there are greater possibilities for educators, clinicians, and parents to flexibly create learning opportunities, and to spontaneously capitalize on "teachable moments" based upon a child's focus of attention, interest, and how activities and events evolve. For this dimension, "Middle ground" approaches may have some degree of structure with specified goals that are predetermined; however, the child's partner is better able to depart from a prearranged agenda for either short periods, or for longer periods, depending upon the potential for creating and capitalizing on new and more effective learning opportunities, regardless of the original agenda. This is a common instructional practice of the SCERTS Model (Prizant, Wetherby, Rubin, Laurent, & Rydell, 2003; Prizant et al., in press) and the Walden Preschool (McGee et al., 1999). Some approaches such as Greenspan and Wieder's "floor-time," a major component of the DIR Model, has little predetermined structure and more general goals.

3. *Use of directive versus facilitative interactional and teaching styles:* This dimension is closely related to the issue of prescription versus flexibility in programming, as discussed above, but it focuses most specifically on adult interactional styles. A facilitative style, which currently is advocated by developmental and some contemporary behavioral literature, is characterized by:

1. Following a child's attentional focus
2. Offering choices and alternatives within activities
3. Responding to and acknowledging children's intent
4. Modeling a variety of communicative functions including commenting on a child's activities
5. Expanding and elaborating upon the topic of a child's verbal and nonverbal communication

An extreme facilitative style is captured by the phrase "follow the child's lead" with minimal direction provided on the part of the communicative partner. Use of a facilitative style is based on the assumption that a child's spontaneous and self-directed behavior is sufficiently organized and goal-directed to allow the partner to create productive learning opportunities with appropriate responses and guidance, but with minimal intrusion or redirection.

On the other end of the continuum is a "directive" style of interaction and teaching. As the term implies, the partner imposes greater demands on the child to communicate, respond, and behave in a particular manner. Directive styles are characterized by:

1. Frequent attempts to bring a child's attention to events or activities chosen by the partner.
2. A large proportion of questions designed to elicit specific answers, or directions designed to have children respond or perform in a particular manner.
3. More intrusive prompting strategies (physical or verbal) to support children to respond correctly.
4. Evaluative comments indicating whether a child's responses are appropriate or correct. The ultimate goal is for children to comply with the partner in order to achieve goals designated by the partner.

The "middle ground" on this continuum is selective use of directive or facilitative elements, depending upon the nature of the activity, the child's ability relative to the demands of the activity, as well as a child's emotional regulatory status. For example, in teaching a child self-help skills such as tying shoes, a more directive approach may be necessary, because learning this skill may initially require hand-over-hand direction due to the visual-motor and motor planning requirements. However, in fostering social-communication abilities for this same child, a less directive approach would be warranted because of the very different nature of learning to participate in social communicative interactions, and the importance of supporting communicative initiation.

More traditional ABA approaches have used more directive teaching practices and a predetermined sequence of goals (Lovaas, 1981; Sundberg & Partington, 1998), while more contemporary ABA practices have moved away from this orientation, with greater flexibility in teaching practices as well as greater individualization of goals (L. Koegel et al., 1999; McGee et al., 1999). The SCERTS and DIR models have a strong bias toward more facilitative styles for fostering social communication and emotional regulation. The justification is that research has demonstrated that the benefits of a more facilitative style include (1) providing a child with a sense of social control and communicative power, which has been found to result in increased initiations and more elaborate communicative attempts (Mirenda & Donnellan, 1986; Peck, 1985); (2) following a child's attentional focus and motivations reduces problems of compliance, supports self-determination, and may result in increased learning as a result of motivation and affective involvement; and (3) providing elaborated information and feedback appropriate to a child's level and attentional focus supports a child's communicative and language development through modeling of vocabulary and more varied language forms and functions.

For example, Mirenda and Donnellan (1986) found that, compared to a "directive" style, the use of a "facilitative" style for students with ASD resulted in higher rates of student-initiated interactions, question asking, and of conversational initiation. Rydell and Mirenda (1994) found that higher frequencies of generative utterances, initiations, and increased comprehension followed adult-facilitative utterances. Facilitative strategies have also been found to increase communicative initiation and social-affective signaling of children with ASD with limited or no language abilities (Dawson & Adams, 1984; Peck, 1985; Tiegerman & Primavera, 1984).

Appropriateness of style along the continuum of facilitativeness to directiveness is a child-specific issue, and can only be determined by observing the effect of partner style on interactions. Relative to a child's typical abilities, a good stylistic match should result in:

1. Increased regulation of attention (i.e., ability to maintain a mutual focus of attention with minimal prompting)
2. Active involvement in selecting and participating in activities
3. Frequent verbal and nonverbal communicative initiations

4. More elaborate communicative initiations
5. Positive affective involvement with the partner

A style may be thought to be more facilitative when these characteristics can be observed in children's behavior. For example, for a highly active and distractible child, a style that promotes a mutual attentional focus and more active involvement, even though it may have some directive qualities (e.g., physical prompting and limit setting), must be viewed as facilitative for that child. This same style, however, may have detrimental effects for a child with a lower activity level and greater attentional regulation. As Marfo (1990) has noted, the function of adult directiveness in supporting interactions is of overriding concern, not the presence or absence of features thought to be directive. In the SCERTS model, we advocate incorporating facilitative features in play and teaching interactions and gradually modifying style along the facilitativeness-directiveness continuum until an optimal match is found for a child.

4. *Approaches to problem behavior and emotional dysregulation:* Another important dimension of communication programming addresses the issue of how educational staff and others respond when a child is emotionally dysregulated or demonstrates problematic behavior. On one end of the continuum are more traditional behavior management approaches that focus on consequential or reactive procedures to stop a child from engaging in problem behavior when it occurs. Behavior reduction strategies have ranged from using aversive procedures or punishment (which are no longer considered acceptable practice), to ignoring "problem" behaviors when they occur. In the middle ground, Positive Behavioral Support (PBS) approaches (Fox et al., 2000) develop preventive and reactive strategies. They also address factors across social contexts related to patterns of behavior that are considered problematic, with the overriding goal of enhancing quality of life. In PBS, major tools are functional behavioral assessments derived from a behavior analytic framework (Repp & Horner, 1999). The SCERTS Model approach to emotional regulation utilizes a developmental focus with the long-term preventive goal of

developing a child's social communication and emotional regulatory capacities, along with reactive strategies to address problem behaviors related to emotional dysregulation (Prizant, Wetherby, Rubin, & Laurent, 2003).

There are a number of similarities between PBS and the SCERTS Model as they address problem behavior. Both share a common focus on positive and respectful approaches, manipulation of environmental variables, and the development of functional social communication. However, there also are clear distinctions. One distinction is that in the SCERTS model, a developmental, emotional regulatory framework, rather than a behavior analytic framework, analyzes and develops approaches to problem behavior. Due to the interdependence of emotional state and physiological arousal state, there must be careful monitoring and interpretation of behavioral indicators of physiological and emotional arousal, as well as knowledge of a child's self and mutual regulatory capacities.

The SCERTS Model also analyzes problem behavior relative to contextual and historical factors in order to determine the possible intentions or communicative functions underlying such behavior. The model also considers other factors, such as the child's health, arousal bias (hyper or hypoarousal), and emotional regulatory abilities, along with environmental stressors. Based upon scrutiny of these factors, a preventive plan is put into place, which may include some or all of the following strategies: significant modifications to a child's schedule or daily activities and experiences; modifications to interpersonal and learning supports; implementation of sensory processing and emotional regulatory supports; and when appropriate, biological or nutritional interventions to address factors shown to be related to problem behaviors (e.g., gastrointestinal problems, food allergies). The model also develops a plan to support a youngster's emotional regulation at the time when he or she is engaging in problem behavior. Finally, the SCERTS model recognizes that whether a behavior is considered problematic in the first place may vary greatly based upon individual differences across families, cultural groups, and even the gender of the parent. Thus, educators and clinicians must work closely with families and set priorities related to patterns of problem behavior.

5. *Measurement of progress, including types and intensity of data collection:* Measuring progress and accountability of services provided are now considered essential obligations for all service providers (NRC, 2001). However, different approaches may measure progress in different ways:

- *Qualitative versus quantitative approaches:* Qualitative approaches use descriptive and oftentimes informal and subjective means to measure progress. For example, professionals may keep descriptive notes based on observations of students, or may ask parents their impressions of progress. Descriptions may be very general or more specific, depending upon requirements of different agencies, skills of the professional, and nature of developmental progress being monitored. Such approaches may lack specificity and objectivity in monitoring progress; however, they may tap into the social (ecological) validity of progress that is measured (i.e., how do parents and others view progress, how do changes impact others across a variety of settings).

On the other end of the continuum, ongoing intensive quantitative data collection of a child's behavioral reactions and responses may occur in most if not all teaching interactions. This may include frequency counts of objectively defined behaviors (for communication, typically receptive and expressive language behaviors in structured drills) ideally resulting in sufficient data to document patterns of increases and decreases in behavioral responses, with a plan for multiple observations by different staff to assure reliability of observations. Possible shortcomings of ongoing intensive data collection include (1) the risk that such data collection approaches interfere with educators' and clinicians' ability to be highly responsive and spontaneous with children in reciprocal teaching interactions and (2) the possibility that frequency counts of behavior may address presence or absence of behavioral responses, but may not capture more meaningful developmental change (i.e., socially valid change) for a child.

- *Measuring generalization and carryover to natural environments:* Another continuum related to the distinction above is whether the emphasis is on measuring change in specific training contexts, or whether there is equal, if not greater concern for measuring progress across a variety of more natural contexts and social partners. It has been argued (NRC, 2001; Prizant & Wetherby, 1998) that traditional static measures of developmental progress such as changes in standardized test scores, or a sole reliance on frequency counts of behaviors, may not address the dynamic nature of social communication and emotional development, and may overlook core challenges faced by children with ASD.

One factor complicating the measurement of progress is that approaches with different underlying philosophies measure progress in a manner consistent with the philosophy of the approach. For example, behaviorally oriented educators focus on frequency counts of objectively defined behaviors as primary evidence of skill development (Anderson & Romanczyk, 1999). Developmentally oriented practitioners (e.g., Greenspan & Wieder, 1998; Gutstein, 2000) focus more on qualitative patterns of behavior indicative of developmental shifts rather than focusing primarily on frequency counts of correct or incorrect responses. Approaches such as the SCERTS Model (Prizant, Wetherby, Rubin, & Laurent, 2003), which address both skill development and changes in underlying developmental capacities, may use both frequency counts of behavior, as well as procedures to monitor developmental shifts, depending upon the areas addressed. For example, quantitative data collection may document acquisition of expressive vocabulary, while descriptive data collected across settings (e.g., home, school, community) and partners may address the nature and quality of communicative acts to document shifts from presymbolic to symbolic communication. Thus, the approach may use less intrusive data collection across contexts, in meaningful events and activities, as well as socially valid measures of progress completed by a range of caregivers.

6. *Parent involvement and role of parents:* Virtually all approaches value participation of parents because parent involvement is an important factor related to children's progress (NRC, 2001). However, the nature of such participation may vary greatly. On one end of the continuum, parents may be recruited as "teachers" to provide additional learning experiences as described by educators or consultants responsible for a child's program. In essence, parents are asked to provide and carry out similar training programs as those provided by the primary teachers or to hire additional personnel to implement teaching programs utilized in educational settings. This is most commonly observed in traditional ABA programs with prescribed curricula (Anderson & Romanczyk, 1999; Maurice, Green, & Luce, 1996). On the other end of the continuum, parent involvement and direct participation depend largely on priorities set by parents to achieve their social communication goals for the child across different activities and settings (Prizant, Wetherby, Rubin, & Laurent, 2003; Sussman, 1999).

Coming from a family-centered philosophy, the SCERTS Model considers family priorities as critical factors in goal setting and believes that family members' participation should be calibrated to their ability to support a child's development relative to different activities and contexts (Prizant, Wetherby, Rubin, & Laurent, 2003; Quinn, 2003; Wetherby et al., 1997). This is not seen as static, because family members may become increasingly involved or less involved in activities addressing goals designated by a child's team. We also believe there should be an emphasis on family members' involvement in supporting social communication skills in the context of everyday activities and routines, rather than primarily in separate teaching sessions. In our experience, this enables family members to take a more active role because such opportunities fit in better with the culture and lifestyle of the family.

7. *Use of visual supports and visually mediated activities:* Visual processing has been demonstrated to be a relative strength for many children with ASD (Schuler, 1995). It is now widely accepted that visual supports and visually mediated activities are effective, if not essential practices for the great majority of children with ASD (Quill, 1997; Wetherby

et al., 1997). Visual supports may be used in a variety of ways: as primary expressive communication systems (e.g., "low-tech": communication boards or as overlays on high-tech communication devices such as voice output communication aides; VOCAs; Mirenda & Erickson, 2000); or organizational supports (such as picture schedules or visual work systems). Nevertheless, approaches vary greatly as to the extent to which visual supports are considered an essential part of the approach. For example, approaches that rely heavily on visual supports include Structured Teaching (Schopler et al., 1995), the SCERTS model (Prizant, Wetherby, Rubin, Larent, & Rydell, 2003) and the Picture Exchange Communication System (Frost & Bondy, 1994). In contrast, other approaches such as the Natural Language Paradigm (L. Koegel et al., 1999), Lovaas Therapy (Lovaas, 1981), and Applied Verbal Behavior and the ABLLS Curriculum (Sundberg & Partington, 1998) may minimize use of visual supports, or see them only as alternatives for expressive communication when speech does not develop.

Learning Contexts

1. *Naturalness of teaching activities or contexts:* We define "naturalness" in reference to whether an activity or event designed for learning already occurs or can be scheduled to occur as a regular routine in a child's life experiences across a number of different contexts or environments. The quality of that event should be sufficiently similar to other events to make it most likely that a child will perceive the similarities, and therefore, "generalize" skills and understanding of events across different occurrences. As noted earlier, generalization of skills has been documented as a high priority in educational programming as well as in assessing meaningful change (NRC, 2001). Less natural, or "contrived" activities or contexts are those that are much less likely to occur in a child's daily experiences. Even if they can be arranged to occur, they may still bear little resemblance to more general activities of daily living. Based on a recent review of eight language intervention studies that compared primarily discrete trial activities, which are highly contrived and

bear little resemblance to everyday routines, to more natural normalized language activities (Delprato, 2001), normalized language training was found to be more effective than discrete-trial training. This was especially true for carryover of language skills to other settings. In comparing discrete trial intervention to more natural activities, Schreibman, Kaneko, and Koegel (1992) found a greater degree of child positive affect expressed by children and parents.

Traditional ABA approaches (e.g., Lovaas, 1981; Sundberg & Partington, 1998) tend to rely on more contrived contexts and adult-controlled teaching approaches, such as discrete trial teaching methodology in teaching receptive and expressive language skills. As noted, contemporary ABA approaches have moved to more natural activities as contexts for supporting social communication development (L. Koegel, Koegel, Harrower, et al., 1999; McGee et al., 1999; Strain & Kohler, 1998; Strain, McGee, & Kohler, 2001). We believe strongly that the ultimate goal in communication programming is for a child to be able to learn and practice and utilize social communication skills in naturalistic interactions across persons, settings, and circumstances. This is exemplified in an activity-based approach in the SCERTS Model (Prizant, Wetherby, Rubin, Laurent, & Rydell, 2003). Learning involves a child's increasing understanding and following of natural cues, conventions, and rules of interactions with peers in a variety of contexts. The focus becomes one of contingent interaction, reciprocal exchange, and interpersonal anticipatory behaviors between a child and his or her peers. Additionally, in teaching children skills necessary to participate successfully, there is an overriding concern for providing only the minimal support necessary (i.e., strategic support) so that children have opportunities to problem solve, develop, and apply skills as independently as possible.

2. *Skill-based or activity-based learning opportunities:* Closely related to the issue of naturalness of learning contexts is whether activities are designed to focus primarily on teaching skills outside the context of functional, goal-directed activities, or helping children to develop a sense of the meaning or purpose of activities by using logically structured and meaningful activities as the context

for learning. On one end of the continuum are traditional ABA approaches in which children may be taught skills in isolation, in a manner that is not linked to or embedded within a logical sequence of events that relates to an activity or event (Anderson & Romanczyk, 1999; Anderson, Taras, & O'Malley Cannon, 1996). On the other end of the continuum, children may be exposed to activities or events (with the hope that they will learn based upon exposure to those events), with too little attention (in our opinion) being given to targeting specific social communication skills that are required for a child to participate successfully.

We believe that attention must be given to acquisition of skills as well as to meaningfulness of activities and events (Prizant et al., in press; Wetherby et al., 1997). In the SCERTS Model, it is our bias primarily to use activities and events for learning in contrast to teaching skills in an isolated manner outside of the context of events or activities. We believe strongly that extensive practice of skills isolated from natural activities inhibits understanding and generalization of those skills to larger events and activities in a child's life. In addition, approaches that "train skills to mastery, and then generalize skills to other contexts" may actually contribute to situation-specific learning and lack of generalization (Prizant & Wetherby, 1998).

We feel that considerable attention should be given to providing children with multiple opportunities to practice social-communicative skills, a strategy we utilize in the SCERTS Model. However, teaching and learning should occur in activities and events that relate as closely as possible to more general life experiences in meaningful activities that already occur, or can be planned to occur outside of the specific teaching contents.

3. *Social complexity (e.g., 1:1, small group, large group):* To be as independent as possible, and to enjoy life's activities to their fullest, a child must be able to engage in interpersonal interactions with a variety of partners in different social contexts. In general, children with ASD have greater difficulty in larger, more complex social groupings, largely because of the differing social-communicative and emotional regulatory requirements of participating in groups with more people and more complex social rules (Prizant, Schuler, Wetherby, & Rydell, 1997). For enhancing communication, approaches vary greatly in reference to the extent to which children are exposed to groupings of different social complexity. On one end of the continuum are traditional ABA approaches in which children are educated primarily in a 1:1 (adult-child) learning context, especially in the first few years of educational programming, but in some cases, extending for many years. Underlying a primarily one-to-one approach, there is an often-stated belief that children with ASD cannot learn in more complex settings until they acquire particular "readiness" abilities such as attentional skills, compliance to directions, and imitation skills. However, there is no empirical support for this contention (Strain et al., 2001). On the other end of the continuum, children are primarily educated in group settings (small or large group) with few or no 1:1 learning opportunities.

In the SCERTS model, decisions regarding social groupings are individualized. Such decisions depend upon a child's social-communication and emotional regulatory capacities, and on the challenges posed by available educational settings. However, given that settings of different social complexity offer different types of social learning opportunities, most children will benefit from a program involving one-to-one, small-group, as well as larger-group activities appropriate to their chronological age and developmental capacities. For example, it obviously is not possible for a 4-year-old child to learn to play and learn with peers in a program that is primarily one to one (adult-child). On the other hand, placement in primarily large groups may not provide opportunities for a youngster to learn to attend to, and participate successfully in, small group communicative or conversational exchange. We believe that it is desirable for children to learn in social groupings of differing complexity, and that the proportion of time spent in different size groups must be tailored to the social communication goals that are set relative to different groupings, and to a youngster's ability to benefit from such learning opportunities.

4. *Role of typical or developmentally advanced peers:* For most educational approaches, a shared goal is to support children's success in

activities with other children as well as support the development of social relationships (NRC, 2001). However, different approaches place different priorities on activities with typical or developmentally advanced peers. On one end of the continuum, children may not be exposed to learning with peers until the children acquire certain readiness skills (Lovaas, 1981; Sundberg & Partington, 1998); this point is similar to the earlier discussion of complexity of social contexts. That is, it is believed that children must acquire certain readiness skills (e.g., imitation) before they can benefit from extensive learning opportunities with other children. On the other end of the continuum, opportunities for learning with peers are considered essential for the earliest stages of social communication programming, because initial goals may include the development of communication and play skills with other children (McGee et al., 1999; Strain et al., 2001). In the SCERTS model (Prizant, Wetherby, Rubin, & Laurent, 2003), learning with peers is a high priority, given the focus on social communication and play in everyday activities.

Child Characteristics

1. *Individual differences in learning are addressed:* A variety of children with ASD may experience similar challenges in social communication, emotional regulation, and learning. Significant individual differences across children, however, clearly may be observed and must be understood from a developmental perspective (Greenspan & Wieder, 1999, 2000; Wetherby et al., 1997). This is another dimension where different approaches may vary greatly. On one end of the continuum, most, if not all, children may be exposed to the same teaching curriculum with the same goals and teaching strategies, regardless of individual differences (Sundberg & Partington, 1998). On the other end of the continuum, approaches may be highly individualized depending upon a child's profile of strengths and needs.

For example, some language training approaches (Sundberg & Partington, 1998) do not address the issue of unconventional verbal behaviors, which include immediate and delayed echolalia, perseverative speech and in-

cessant questioning—common speech-language characteristics of children with ASD that are clearly related to their developmental learning style (Rydell & Prizant, 1995). Other approaches have advocated for the eradication of unconventional verbal behaviors (Lovaas, 1981). More individualized approaches, including developmentally based approaches such as the SCERTS Model, the DIR Model, and the Denver Model (Rogers, 2000), may set goals and determine teaching practices based on the children's individual strengths and needs, rather than following predetermined curricula and teaching strategies. In particular, the SCERTS Model addresses unconventional behavior from a learning-style perspective, and recognizes that approaches to unconventional behavior must be guided by the varied functions it may serve in social communication and emotional regulation. Furthermore, the SCERTS Model prioritizes mulitmodal social communication goals and visual strategies to a greater extent that these other developmentally based approaches, as they are closely related to learning style differences. We believe strongly that goals should be derived individually and guided by a child's individual learning style, functional needs, family priorities, and developmental frameworks in social communication.

2. *Emotional regulatory capacities are considered:* One area of challenge that has been documented for many years in literature on ASD (NRC, 2001; Reichle & Wacker, 1993) as well as by adults with ASD (Grandin, 1995) is emotional regulation. Emotional regulation is an essential and core underlying capacity that supports a child's "availability" for learning and for social engagement (Prizant et al., in press). Problems in emotional regulation are related to learning-style differences, difficulties in social understanding, as well as sensory sensitivities and sensory processing difficulties (Anzalone & Williamson, 2000). We consider the development of emotional regulatory capacities to be intimately related to language and communication development in children with and without disabilities (Prizant & Wetherby, 1990; Prizant, Wetherby, Rubin, & Laurent, 2003; Wetherby & Prizant, 1999). However, approaches vary greatly as to the emphasis with which they address these challenges.

In some approaches, behavior management goals are considered distinct from communication programming (Lovaas, 1981). As noted earlier, more contemporary ABA approaches have developed Positive Behavioral Supports that consider the relationship between communicative limitations and problem behaviors (Fox et al., 2000). In the SCERTS model, emotional regulation is a primary dimension of focus, and multiple factors related to emotional regulation and dysregulation are specifically identified and addressed (e.g., social-communicative difficulties are considered in specific reference to emotional regulation and arousal modulation). For children to be optimally available, they must have the emotional regulatory capacities and skills (1) to remain organized and well regulated in the face of potentially stressful circumstances (referred to as *self-regulation*), (2) to seek assistance and/or respond to others' attempts to provide support for emotional regulation when faced with stressful, overly stimulating or emotionally dysregulating circumstances (referred to as *mutual regulation*), and (3) to "recover" from being "pushed over the edge" or "under the carpet" into states of *extreme emotional dysregulation* or "*shutdown*," through self and/or mutual regulation strategies (referred to as *recovery from extreme dysregulation*).

Enhancing capacities for emotional regulation goes hand in hand with helping a child to more effectively maintain "*optimal arousal*," so that the child is not experiencing predominant patterns of being too "high" or too "low" with regard to the social and physical environment, or shifting too frequently between such extreme states of arousal. In the SCERTS Model, children's abilities and difficulties in emotional regulation are assessed systematically, and specific emotional regulatory strategies may include supporting children's ability to deal with daily challenges to maintaining well-regulated states.

3. Age and developmental range covered by an approach: A particular approach to enhancing social communication must be relevant for a child's chronological age and developmental capacities. For example, Picture Exchange Communication (PECs; Frost & Bondy, 1994) is most relevant for children from an early intentional communication stage to single and early multiword stages of communication. Lovaas therapy (Lovaas, 1981) is purported to be applicable to children, adolescents, and adults; however, the functionality of teaching procedures may be questionable. The developmental range covered in the Lovaas approach focuses on children at earlier cognitive and language skill levels. The DIR Model (Greenspan & Wieder, 1998) and the RDI Model (Gutstein, 2000) cover children with a range of developmental abilities from presymbolic levels to complex symbolic cognitive and communicative levels, although, as noted, there may not be a specific focus on social communication. The SCERTS model, in its current form, is applicable for children from earliest developmental stages to conversational stages, including the age range from birth up to 10 years of age, but the model may be relevant for older individuals as well (Prizant et al., in press).

Programmatic Goals for Children

1. *Educational/treatment priorities in goal setting (i.e., domains of development):* Children with ASD often present with multiple developmental needs, ranging from the acquisition of functional self-help skills, to the development of social communication and emotional regulatory capacities, to cognitive skills and academic learning. Different social communication approaches may vary greatly as to how they prioritize social communication goals relative to a child's overall program. Most approaches address a broad range of developmental needs; however, the focus of the program may be skewed toward particular areas of need. For example, approaches such as the SCERTS model, the RDI Model (Gutstein, 2000) and the DIR Model (Greenspan & Wieder, 1998) place a great deal of emphasis on social and emotional development, with the SCERTS model addressing social communication with great specificity. Social communication is also a focus of the Natural Language Paradigm (L. Koegel, Koegel, Harrower, et al., 1999), and learning with peers is a focus of the LEAP program and the Walden School models (Strain et al., 2001). Structured Teaching places greater emphasis on skills related to independent academic work and independent functional skills (Schopler et al., 1995).

Another related factor is whether the needs addressed are closely related to the core challenges experienced by children with ASD based upon research on ASD. On one end of the continuum, approaches may be based largely on teaching compliance, readiness skills, and language skills, with an emphasis on accumulation of information leading to correct responding in prescriptive teaching programs (Lovaas, 1981). On the other end of the continuum are approaches focused on enhancing abilities to directly address the core challenges in autism spectrum disorders. The SCERTS model is consistent with this latter focus, with priorities based on enhancing capacities in social communication and emotional regulation.

2. *Augmentative—alternative communication goals and strategies:* Different approaches place different degrees of emphasis on identification of AAC goals and strategies (Mirenda & Erickson, 2000). In general, approaches that place greater emphasis on social communication, rather than primarily on speech training, tend to value a wide range of AAC strategies as part of efforts to support communication development. However, other approaches that claim to focus on communication may not advocate or may minimize the use of AAC Communication (McGee et al., 1999) or support only a limited range of AAC options, such as sign language (e.g., Lovaas, 1981; Sundberg & Partington, 1998). This is despite the fact that research has demonstrated that a range of AAC options does not preclude, and likely supports, speech and language development (Mirenda & Erickson, 2000). Some approaches may begin with AAC approaches for nonspeaking children, but may quickly abandon their use when the children acquire any speech, while other approaches, including the SCERTS Model, use a multimodal strategy to develop a broad foundation of communication abilities into language stages in order to support communicative flexibility and adaptability across contexts and partners.

3. *Spontaneous, initiated communication is prioritized in goal setting:* For over 2 decades, we have advocated spontaneous, initiated communication as a priority (Prizant, 1982; Prizant & Wetherby, 1993; Wetherby et al., 1997). Recent research has demonstrated the importance of focusing on initiated, spontaneous communication (L. Koegel, Koegel, Shoshan, et al.,

1999), because a child's ability to initiate communication early in development has been found to be highly predictive of more positive social-communicative outcomes. Furthermore, as noted earlier, the report of the NRC (2001) guidelines highlights "functional spontaneous communication" as among the highest priorities in educational programming. Finally, clinical experience suggests that increased communicative initiation leads to greater participation in everyday activities and increased self-determination (Erwin & Brown, 2003). Communicative initiation also precludes "learned helplessness" and the development of behavioral difficulties due to increased competence in communicating needs more independently.

However, different approaches vary greatly as to the extent to which they emphasize initiated communication as a goal. For example, more traditional ABA approaches (Lovaas, 1981; Sundberg & Partington, 1998) place children primarily in a respondent role, especially when Discrete Trial Training is the instructional method of choice. Pivotal Response Training and the Natural Language Paradigm, contemporary ABA approaches (L. Koegel, Koegel, Harrower, et al., 1999), emphasize initiation. As noted earlier, the SCERTS Model (Prizant et al., in press) values initiated spontaneous communication across partners and contexts as a high priority goal in any child's program.

4. *Goals are based on developmental as well as functional criteria:* Approaches vary as to the basis on which goals are established. Some approaches utilize functional criteria. Goals are based on skills that are viewed as necessary to a child's needs, but specific goals set may not be based on a child's developmental capacities. For example, focusing on speech training for a presymbolic child, or teaching children at early stages of single word or early multiword communication to produce grammatical utterances and "say the whole sentence" would be viewed as functional, but in our opinion, developmentally inappropriate. Other approaches may be developmentally based, but goals may not specifically target functional needs in daily routines across settings (e.g., Greenspan & Wieder, 1998; Gutstein, 2000). In the SCERTS Model, the approach is functional as well as developmentally grounded because goals are

developed and are based on a child's developmental profile (Wetherby & Prizant, 1992; Wetherby, Prizant, & Hutchinson, 1998) as well as on parental priorities and actual communicative needs—especially when such needs pertain to everyday living routines and environments. Therefore, there is a clear and natural incentive to communicate. Stated differently, the perspective of the child and family is adopted so that goals are relevant to their daily experiences.

CONCLUSION

It is now recognized that there are many complex factors to be considered in developing appropriate educational programs for children with ASD. As noted, this is especially true for determining goals and teaching strategies to enhance social communication abilities, a clear priority for all persons with ASD. Given that there is no evidence that any one categorical approach is more effective than other approaches (Dawson & Osterling, 1997; NRC, 2001; Prizant & Wetherby, 1998), we have argued that considering different approaches from a categorical orientation provides little insight and offers less potential for individualized programming, which is now considered essential for best meeting the educational needs of individuals with ASD (NRC, 2001). However, there is evidence that the most effective approaches to enhancing communication abilities have the following characteristics: (1) efforts to enhance social communication abilities occur in social activities across a variety of natural contexts; (2) family members and peers are centrally involved in these activities and experiences; (3) functional, spontaneous, and initiated communication abilities are of the highest priority; and (4) approaches should be guided by current research and knowledge about the relationships among social communication abilities, problem behavior, and emotional regulation (NRC, 2001; Prizant, Wetherby, Rubin, & Laurent, 2003; Wetherby & Prizant, 1999).

As an alternative to categorical comparisons, we have also argued that it is potentially more fruitful to examine and scrutinize practices relative to a variety of dimensions,

including teaching practices, learning contexts, child characteristics, and programmatic goals. Therefore, we believe that it is incumbent upon professionals to be educated in a variety of approaches and teaching strategies to best support social communication as a priority. Furthermore, we believe that the next generation of educational approaches needs to incorporate social communication as a foundation for learning and for establishing meaningful relationships. These new approaches must be flexible enough to infuse evidence-based practices from a variety of perspectives.

REFERENCES

American Psychiatric Association. (1994). *Diagnostic and statistical manual of mental disorders* (4th ed.). Washington, DC: Author.

Anderson, S., & Romanczyk, R. (1999). Early intervention for young children with autism: Continuum-based behavioral models. *Journal of the Association of Persons with Severe Handicaps, 24,* 162–173.

Anderson, S., Taras, M., & O'Malley Cannon, B. (1996). Teaching new skills to young children with autism. In C. Maurice, G. Green, & S. Luce (Eds.), *Behavioral interventions for young children with autism* (pp. 181–194). Austin, TX: ProEd.

Anzalone, M. E., & Williamson, C. G. (2000). Sensory processing and motor performance in autism spectrum disorders. In A. Wetherby & B. Prizant (Eds.), *Autism spectrum disorders: A transactional developmental perspective* (Vol. 9, pp. 143–166). Baltimore: Paul H. Brookes.

Bristol, M., & Schopler, E. (1984). A developmental perspective on stress and coping in families of autistic children. In J. Blacher (Ed.), *Families of severely handicapped children.* New York: Academic Press.

Brown, F., & Bambara, L. (Eds.). (1999). Intervention for young children with autism. *Journal of the Association for Persons with Severe Handicaps, 24,* 3.

Carr, E. G., & Durand, V. (1986). The social-communicative basis of severe behavior problems in children. In S. Reiss & R. Bootzin (Eds.), *Theoretical issues in behavior therapy* (pp. 219–254). New York: Academic Press.

Carr, E. G., Levin, L., McConnachie, G., Carlson, J., Kemp, D., & Smith, C. (1994). *Communication-based intervention for problem behavior: A user's guide for producing positive change.* Baltimore: Paul H. Brookes.

Cohen, S. (1999). Zeroing in on autism in young children. *Journal of the Association of Persons with Severe Handicaps, 24,* 209–212.

Dawson, G., & Adams, A. (1984). Imitation and social responsiveness in autistic children. *Journal of Abnormal Child Psychology, 12,* 209–226.

Dawson, G., & Osterling, J. (1997). Early intervention in autism. In M. Guralnick (Ed.), *The effectiveness of early intervention* (pp. 307–326). Baltimore: Paul H. Brookes.

Delprato, D. (2001). Discrete trial and normalized language training for children with autism: A review. *Journal of Autism and Developmental Disorders, 31,* 315–325.

Dunst, C., Trivette, C., & Deal, A. (1988). *Enabling and empowering families: Principles and guidelines for practice.* Cambridge, MA: Brookline Books.

Erwin, E. J., & Brown, F. (2003). From theory to practice: A contextual framework for understanding self-determination in early childhood environments. *Infants and Young Children, 16,* 77–87.

Fox, L., Dunlap, G., & Buschbacher, P. (2000). Understanding and intervening with children's challenging behavior: A comprehensive approach. In A. Wetherby & B. Prizant (Eds.), *Autism spectrum disorders: A transactional developmental perspective* (Vol. 9, pp. 307–332). Baltimore: Paul H. Brookes.

Frost, L., & Bondy, A. (1994). *PECS: The picture exchange system training manual.* Cherry Hill, NJ: Pyramid Educational Consultants.

Garfin, D., & Lord, C. (1986). Communication as a social problem in autism. In E. Schopler & G. Mesibov (Eds.), *Social behavior in autism* (pp. 237–261). New York: Plenum Press.

Grandin, T. (1995). *Thinking in pictures.* New York: Bantam Books.

Greenspan, S. I. (1992). *Infancy and early childhood: The practice of clinical assessment and intervention with emotional and developmental challenges.* Madison, CT: International Universities Press.

Greenspan, S. I., & Wieder, S. (1998). *The child with special needs: Encouraging intellectual and emotional growth.* New York: Addison-Wesley.

Greenspan, S. I., & Wieder, S. (1999). A functional developmental approach to autism spectrum disorders. *Journal of the Association of Persons with Severe Handicaps, 24,* 147–161.

Greenspan, S. I., & Wieder, S. (2000). A developmental approach to difficulties in relating and communicating in autism spectrum disorders and related syndromes. In A. M. Wetherby & B. M. Prizant (Eds.), *Autism spectrum disorders: A developmental transactional perspective* (pp. 279–306). Baltimore: Paul H. Brookes.

Gutstein, S. (2000). *Autism/Asperger's: Solving the relationship puzzle.* Arlington, TX: Future Horizons.

Heflin, J., & Simpson, R. (1998). Interventions for children and youth with autism. *Focus on Autism and Other Developmental Disabilities, 13,* 194–221.

Kanner, L. (1943). Autistic disturbances of affective contact. *Nervous Child, 2,* 217–250.

Koegel, L. K., Koegel, R. L., Harrower, J., & Carter, C. (1999). Pivotal response intervention: Part I. Overview of approach. *Journal of the Association of Persons with Severe Handicaps, 24,* 174–185.

Koegel, L. K., Koegel, R. L., Shoshan, Y., & McNerney, E. (1999). Pivotal response intervention: Part II. Preliminary long-term outcome data. *Journal of the Association of Persons with Severe Handicaps, 24,* 186–198.

Koegel, R. L. (1995). Communication and language intervention. In R. Koegel & L. Koegel (Eds.), *Teaching children with autism* (pp. 17–32). Baltimore: Paul H. Brookes.

Koegel, R. L., & Koegel, L. K. (Eds.). (1995). *Teaching children with autism.* Baltimore: Paul H. Brookes.

Leaf, R. (1998, February). *Evolution of behavioral treatment.* Seminar presented at the Indiana Resource Center Symposium: Educational Choices for Young Children with Autism, Indianapolis, IN.

Lovaas, O. (1981). *Teaching developmentally disabled children: The "me" book.* Baltimore: University Park Press.

Marfo, K. (1990). Maternal directiveness in interactions with mentally handicapped children: An analytical commentary. *Journal of Child Psychology and Psychiatry, 31,* 531–549.

Maurice, C., Green, G., & Luce, S. C. (Eds.). (1996). *Behavioral intervention for young children with autism.* Austin, TX: ProEd.

McEachin, J. J., Smith, T., & Lovaas, O. (1993). Long-term outcome for children with autism who received early intensive behavioral treatment. *American Journal of Mental Retardation, 97,* 359–372.

McGee, G., Morrier, M., & Daly, T. (1999). An incidental teaching approach to early intervention for toddlers with autism. *Journal of the Association of Persons with Severe Handicaps, 24,* 133–146.

Mirenda, P., & Donnellan, A. (1986). Effects of adult interactional style on conversation behavior of students with severe communication problems. *Language, Speech and Hearing Services in Schools, 17,* 126–141.

Mirenda, P., & Erickson, K. (2000). Augmentative communication and literacy. In A. M. Wetherby & B. M. Prizant (Eds.), *Autism spectrum disorders: A developmental transactional perspective* (pp. 333–368). Baltimore: Paul H. Brookes.

National Research Council. (2001). *Educating children with autism* (Committee on Educational Interventions for Children with Autism, Division of Behavioral and Social Sciences and Education). Washington, DC: National Academy Press.

Peck, C. (1985). Increasing opportunities for social control by children with autism and severe handicaps: Effects on student behavior and perceived classroom climate. *Journal of the Association for Persons with Severe Handicaps, 4,* 183–193.

Prizant, B. M. (1982). Speech-language pathologists and autistic children: What is our role? Part I. Assessment and intervention considerations. *American Speech-Language Hearing Association Journal, 24,* 463–468.

Prizant, B. M., & Bailey, D. (1992). Facilitating the acquisition and use of communication skills. In D. Bailey & M. Wolery (Eds.), *Teaching infants and preschoolers with disabilities* (pp. 299–361). Columbus, OH: Merrill.

Prizant, B. M., & Meyer, E. C. (1993). Socioemotional aspects of communication disorders in young children and their families. *American Journal of Speech-Language Pathology, 2,* 56–71.

Prizant, B. M., & Rubin, E. (1999). Contemporary issues in interventions for autism spectrum disorders: A commentary. *Journal of the Association of Persons with Severe Handicaps, 24,* 199–217.

Prizant, B. M., Schuler, A. L., Wetherby, A. M., & Rydell, P. (1997). Enhancing language and communication: Language approaches. In D. Cohen & F. R. Volkmar (Eds.), *Handbook of autism and pervasive developmental disorders* (2nd ed., pp. 572–605). New York: Wiley.

Prizant, B. M., & Wetherby, A. M. (1987). Communicative intent: A framework for understanding social-communicative behavior in autism. *Journal of the American Academy of Child Psychiatry, 26,* 472–479.

Prizant, B. M., & Wetherby, A. M. (1990). Toward an integrated view of early language and communication development and socioemotional development. *Topics in Language Disorders, 10,* 1–16.

Prizant, B. M., & Wetherby, A. M. (1993). Communication in preschool autistic children. In E. Schopler, M. Van Bourgondien, & M. Bristol (Eds.), *Preschool issues in autism* (pp. 95–128). New York: Plenum Press.

Prizant, B. M., & Wetherby, A. M. (1998). Understanding the continuum of discrete-trial traditional behavioral to social-pragmatic developmental approaches in communication enhancement for young children with autism/PDD. *Seminars in Speech and Language, 19*(4), 329–353.

Prizant, B. M., Wetherby, A. M., Rubin, E., & Laurent, A. (2003). The SCERTS Model: A family-centered, transactional approach to enhancing communication and socioemotional abilities of young children with ASD. *Infants and Young Children, 16,* 296–316.

Prizant, B. M., Wetherby, A. M., Rubin, E., Laurent, A., & Rydell, P. (2003). The SCERTS Model: Enhancing communication and socioemotional abilities of young children with ASD. *Jenison Autism Journal, 14,* 2–19.

Prizant, B. M., Wetherby, A. M., Rubin, E., Laurent, A., & Rydell, P. (in press). *The SCERTS Model Manual: Enhancing communication and socioemotional abilities of young children with ASD.* Baltimore: Paul H. Brookes.

Prizant, B. M., Wetherby, A. M., & Rydell, P. (2000). Issues in enhancing communication and related abilities for young children with autism spectrum disorders: A developmental transactional perspective. In A. M. Wetherby & B. M. Prizant (Eds.), *Autism spectrum disorders: A transactional developmental perspective* (pp. 193–224). Baltimore: Paul H. Brookes.

Quill, K. (1997). Instructional considerations for young children with autism: The rationale for visually cued instruction. *Journal of Autism and Developmental Disorders, 27,* 697–714.

Quinn, J. (2003). The SCERTS Model: Our family's experience. *Jenison Autism Journal, 14,* 27–32.

Reichle, J., & Wacker, D. (Eds.). (1993). *Communicative approaches to challenging behavior.* Baltimore: Paul H. Brookes.

Repp, A. C., & Horner, R. H. (Eds.). (1999). *Functional analysis of problem behavior: From effective assessment to effective support.* Pacific Grove, CA: Brooks/Cole.

Rogers, S. (2000). The Denver model. In S. Harris & J. Handleman (Eds.), *Preschool education programs for children with autism* (2nd ed.). Austin, TX: ProEd.

Rydell, P. J., & Mirenda, P. (1994). Effects of high and low constraint utterances on the production of immediate and delayed echolalia in young children with autism. *Journal of the Autism and Developmental Disorders, 24,* 719–735.

Rydell, P. J., & Prizant, B. M. (1995). Educational and communicative approaches for children who use echolalia. In K. Quill (Ed.), *Teaching children with autism: Methods to increase communication and socialization* (pp. 105–132). Albany, NY: Delmar.

Schopler, E., Mesibov, G., & Hearsey, K. (1995). Structured teaching in the TEACCH curriculum. In E. Schopler & G. Mesibov (Eds.), *Learning and cognition in autism* (pp. 243–268). New York: Plenum Press.

Schreibman, L., Kaneko, W., & Koegel, R. (1992). Positive affect of parents of autistic children: A comparison across two teaching techniques. *Behavior Therapy, 22,* 479–490.

Schuler, A. L. (1995). Thinking in autism: Differences in learning and development. In K. Quill (Ed.), *Teaching children with autism: Strategies to enhance communication and socialization* (pp. 189–203). Hillsdale, NJ: Erlbaum.

Schuler, A. L., & Prizant, B. M. (1985). Echolalia in autism. In E. Schopler & G. Mesibov (Eds.), *Communication problems in autism.* New York: Plenum Press.

Schuler, A. L., Wetherby, A. M., & Prizant, B. M. (1997). Enhancing language and communication: Prelanguage approaches. In D. Cohen & F. R. Volkmar (Eds.), *Handbook of autism and pervasive developmental disorders* (2nd ed., pp. 539–571). New York: Wiley.

Strain, P., & Kohler, F. (1998). Peer mediated social intervention for children with autism. *Seminars in Speech and Language, 19,* 391–405.

Strain, P., McGee, G., & Kohler, F. (2001). Inclusion of children with autism in early intervention settings. In M. Guralnick (Ed.), *Early childhood inclusion: Focus on change.* Baltimore: Paul H. Brookes.

Sundberg, M. L., & Partington, J. W. (1998). *Teaching language to children with autism or other developmental disabilities.* Pleasant Hill, CA: Behavior Analysts.

Sussman, F. (1999). *More than words: Helping parents promote communication and social skills in children with autism spectrum disorder.* Toronto, Ontario, Canada: Hanen Centre.

Tiegerman, E., & Primavera, E. (1984). Imitating the autistic child: Facilitating communicative gaze behavior. *Journal of Autism and Developmental Disorders, 14,* 27–38.

Warren, S. (1993). Early communication and language intervention: Challenges for the 1990's and beyond. In A. Kaiser & D. Gray (Eds.), *Enhancing children's communication: Research foundations for intervention* (pp. 375–395). Baltimore: Paul H. Brookes.

Wetherby, A. M., & Prizant, B. M. (1992). Profiling young children's communicative competence. In S. Warren & J. Reichle (Eds.), *Causes and effects in communication and language intervention* (pp. 217–253). Baltimore: Paul H. Brookes.

Wetherby, A. M., & Prizant, B. M. (1999). Enhancing language and communication development in autism: Assessment and intervention guidelines. In D. Zager (Ed.), *Autism: Identification, education and treatment* (2nd ed., pp. 141–174). Mahwah, NJ: Erlbaum.

Wetherby, A. M., Prizant, B. M., & Hutchinson, T. (1998). Communicative, social/affective, and symbolic profiles of young children with autism and pervasive developmental disorders. *American Journal of Speech-Language Pathology, 7,* 79–91.

Wetherby, A. M., Prizant, B. M., & Schuler, A. L. (1997). Enhancing language and communication: Theoretical foundations. In D. Cohen & F. R. Volkmar (Eds.), *Handbook of autism and pervasive developmental disorders* (2nd ed., pp. 513–538). New York: Wiley.

CHAPTER 37

Enhancing Early Language in Children with Autism Spectrum Disorders

RHEA PAUL AND DEAN SUTHERLAND

Prizant and Wetherby (this *Handbook,* this volume) have outlined a range of issues to consider in developing programs to enhance communication in children with autistic spectrum disorders (ASDs). In this chapter, we present a set of basic communicative objectives that are appropriate for achieving this goal and consider a range of specific techniques that can be used in attaining these objectives. The focus in this chapter is on communication intervention for children in the prelinguistic and early language phases. Methods for children with advanced language are addressed by Marans, Rubin, and Laurent (this *Handbook,* this volume).

CORE COMMUNICATIVE DEFICITS AT THE PRELINGUISTIC STAGE

Prizant and Wetherby (this *Handbook,* this volume) and Marans et al. (this *Handbook,* this volume) have outlined the major challenges presented by children with autism at a range of language levels. These challenges are reiterated briefly here, as they pertain to children at early levels of communicative development.

As Chawarska (this *Handbook,* Volume 1) and Osterling and Dawson (1994) showed, *failure to attend to speech,* including failure to respond to name, is one of the earliest and strongest predictors of autism in young children. Unlike children with other developmental disabilities, children with autism are often even more impaired in their understanding of language than they are in their production

(Paul, Chawarska, Klin, & Volkmar, 2004). Thus, a central issue for intervention in the earliest phase of language development is to increase attention to and understanding of language.

A second core deficit that has been widely documented is the development of *joint attention skills* (Chawarska, this *Handbook,* Volume 1; Dawson, Hill, Spence, Galpert, & Watson, 1990; Kasari, Sigman, Mundy, & Yirmiya, 1990; Lord & McGee, 2001; Sigman & Ruskin, 1999; Wetherby, Prizant, & Hutchinson, 1998). These skills include coordinating attention between people and objects, drawing others' attention to objects or events for the purpose of sharing experiences, following the gaze and point gestures of others, shifting gaze between people and objects for the purpose of directing another's attention, and directing affects to others through gaze. Joint attention is thought to be an important foundation for language development (Bruner, 1974; Mundy, 2003) and has been shown to be a significant predictor of language outcome in children with ASDs (Mundy, Sigman, & Kasari, 1990).

In addition to showing deficits in the use of joint attention behaviors, children with autism also show overall *reduced rates of communication.* Although they do express some communicative intentions—usually those whose function is to get others to do or not do things for them (requests and protests)—even these acts are less frequent than the typical rates of communication seen in normally developing toddlers (Mundy & Stella, 2000; Wetherby et al., 1998). In addition, children with autism do not generally compensate for their lack of speech by using gestures or other forms of communication, particularly the more conventional forms, such as pointing or showing (Lord & McGee, 2001; Loveland & Landry, 1986; Wetherby et al., 1998). Therefore, the key areas to address in intervention for children at prelinguistic levels are increasing the rate, expanding the functions, and providing more conventional forms of communication.

One other core deficit area includes the deficits in other forms of *symbolic behavior,* apart from language, that are so typically seen in children with autism. Lack of pretend or imaginative play (Rogers, this *Handbook,* Volume 1; Stone, Ousley, Yoder, Hogan, & Hepburn, 1997; Wetherby & Prutting, 1984) and limited ability to imitate others (Charman et al., 2003) are the primary manifestations of this symbolic deficit at the prelinguistic level. As such, intervention programs aimed at improving communication skills need to incorporate these other forms of symbolic behavior.

INTERVENTION METHODS: AN OVERVIEW

Rogers (in press) and Goldstein (2002) have discussed interventions for communication in autism by describing three major approaches. The first they refer to as *didactic.* Didactic methods are based on behaviorist theory and take advantage of behavioral technologies such as massed trials, operant conditioning, shaping, prompting, and chaining. Reinforcement is used to increase the frequency of desired target behaviors. Teaching sessions using these approaches involve high levels of adult control, repetitive periods of drill and practice, precise antecedent and consequent sequences, and a passive responder role for the client. The adult directs and controls all aspects of the interaction. For this reason, we can refer to these methods as *teacher directed* (TD).

The second approach identified by Rogers (in press) and Goldstein (2002) is what they call *naturalistic.* These approaches attempt to incorporate behaviorist principles in more natural environments using functional, pragmatically appropriate social interactions,

instead of stimulus-response-reinforcement sequences. Naturalistic approaches focus on the use of *intrinsic,* rather than tangible or edible, reinforcers. Intrinsic reinforcers include the satisfaction of achieving a desired goal through communication (the client says, "I want juice" and gets juice), rather than more contrived, extrinsic reinforcers such as getting a token or being told "good talking." Finally, and perhaps most important, naturalistic approaches attempt to get clients to initiate communication, rather than casting them always in a responder role.

The final orientation in this classification scheme is called *developmental* or *pragmatic.* These approaches emphasize functional communication, rather than speech, as a goal. As such, they encourage the development of multiple aspects of communication, such as the use of gestures, gaze, affect, and vocalization, and hold these behaviors to be necessary precursors to speech production. Activities provide multiple opportunities and temptations to communicate; the adult responds to any child initiation by providing rewarding activities. Thus, the child directs the interaction and chooses the topics and materials from among a range that the adult provides. Teachers strive to create an affectively positive environment by following the child's lead and react supportively to any behavior that can be interpreted as communicative (even if it was not intended in that way).

In the following sections, we examine how these three approaches have been used in the literature to improve communication in children with autism at two communicative levels: prelinguistic and early language.

PRELINGUISTIC STAGE

During this stage of development children with autism spectrum disorders may show limited awareness of others as a source of comfort or enjoyment, and therefore as objects of communication. Others may demonstrate some ability to direct gestural and vocal messages to others, but these are usually limited primarily to requests for objects. They are often expressed in unconventional ways, such as by pulling a person toward an object, rather than by pointing at it.

Teacher-Directed Approaches

A large body of research has demonstrated that didactic approaches are an effective means of initially developing attention to and understanding of language, as well as initiating speech production in preverbal children with ASD. Discrete trial instruction (DTI), the most basic method within the TD approach, has been used extensively to teach receptive language. DTI entails dividing the chosen skill into components and training each component individually, using highly structured, drill-like procedures, until successfully accomplished. Intensive training utilizes shaping, prompting, prompt fading, and reinforcement strategies. A discrete trial is one cycle of a DTI teaching sequence. Each discrete trial involves the following four components:

1. Instructions or cues to which the child is expected to respond (Clinician displays a picture the child is to identify, demonstrates pointing to the picture in response to its name, e.g., "ball.")
2. Prompts to facilitate the child's response (Clinician uses a verbal and gestural model to demonstrate how the child is to point to the picture when it is named.)
3. Responses (Clinician names picture; child points to it.)
4. Appropriate reinforcement to motivate the child (Child is given a piece of cereal for the correct answer.)

These trials continue until the child produces the target response with minimal prompting; then the next step in the hierarchy of behaviors (e.g., correctly pointing to the named picture from among two pictures) is presented and trained.

Lovaas (1987) is generally credited with introducing the use of discrete trial techniques to the treatment of speech in autism during the 1970s and 1980s, although some work in this area had gone on earlier (Hewett, 1965; Wolf, Risley, & Mees, 1964). Original claims of "the Lovaas approach" methods to "cure" autism have been questioned, and outcomes appear to be limited to the elicitation of verbal production in the highest functioning individuals.

Nonetheless, a relatively large literature (based primarily on single case studies) has demonstrated the efficacy of TD approaches in eliciting vocal imitation (Ross & Greer, 2003) and speech from nonverbal children (Wolf et al., 1964; Yoder & Layton, 1988). Much controversy has focused on the intensity of intervention needed to achieve these goals. Lovaas had advocated for a minimum of 40 hours per week to obtain results similar to his. However, studies of preschool children with autism who were provided with 20 hours a week of intensive DTI have shown this level of intensity to be about equally effective (Sheinkopf & Siegel, 1998).

One recent example of a highly didactic approach to eliciting first words in children with autism is the *rapid motor imitation (RMI) response approach* presented by Tsiouri and Greer (2003). This method makes use of structured, operant instruction in producing rapid motor imitation sequences of actions the child can already do, involving large and small motor behaviors (e.g., clap, stamp, clap, tap table with finger, touch nose, tap) to get children in an "imitation mode." Once the child can reliably imitate these rapid sequences, a simple word is added to the end of the sequence by the teacher (clap, stamp, clap, tap table with finger, touch nose, tap, "bubble"). A word for a highly preferred object is chosen so that the reward for imitating the entire sequence is to get access to the object named at the end (the child gets to have bubbles blown after repeating the sequence). When this phase of training is mastered, the preferred item is shown to the child but no verbal model is presented. The child must produce a spontaneous request to gain the item. Following this request phase, a labeling phase of instruction is implemented. The procedure is the same, except that the item to be labeled is not highly preferred so that the child's goal in naming it is not to get it but simply to complete the imitation sequence. When the child labels the object (e.g., a sock), he or she is then given the opportunity to request the preferred object. (After imitating "sock" in response to being shown a sock, the child is shown the bubbles and the teacher waits until the child says "bubbles" to blow some.) Once this phase is mastered, the item to be labeled is shown at the end of the motor sequence, but no verbal model is presented. The child must label independently to get the opportunity to request the preferred item.

More broadly based behavioral approaches, generally known under the rubric of applied behavioral analysis (ABA) have also been employed with a wide range of autistic behaviors over the past 20 years. ABA frequently involves using the information acquired through functional analysis of antecedents and consequences to interpret the relationship between behavior and the circumstances in which it appears (Jensen & Sinclair, 2002). The primary emphasis in ABA is the use of intensive, direct instructional methods that alter particular behaviors in systematic and measurable ways (Anderson, Taras, & Cannon, 1996). While DTI is one method used within an ABA framework, it is not the only method included within this approach. Anderson and Romanczyk (1999) outline the methodological elements common to ABA approaches to instruction, including:

- *Functional analysis:* An objective assessment is made of the antecedents and consequences of behaviors to be elicited or eliminated. Behavioral theory assumes that behaviors are triggered by environmental events; its goal is to engineer the environment so that desirable behaviors are evoked and undesirable behaviors are extinguished. Antecedents for undesirable behaviors must be identified so that they can be removed from the child's experience and do not trigger the maladaptive behavior. Similarly, consequences that increase the frequency of desirable behaviors must be identified, so these can be provided to evoke new adaptive behaviors. The goal of functional analysis is to ascertain empirically the controlling variables that enhance or inhibit the expression of a behavior. This process involves not only observation but also testing of the hypotheses formed on the basis of these observations. If, for example, it appears that screaming is used to attempt to escape from a teaching situation, this hypothesis will be tested by first responding to the screaming by allowing the child to escape a task, then providing the child with a replacement

behavior, such as signing "Stop," that effectively accomplishes the same goal, and determining whether the child replaces the screaming with the sign. If so, more intensive training to fully replace the maladaptive with a more adaptive behavior is implemented.

- *Task analysis:* Goals targeted by functional analysis are broken down into their most fundamental steps. The first step is trained intensively until the child can produce it in response to the appropriate environmental stimulus with minimal prompting. The next step in the sequence is then "chained" to the first, so that the child must now produce both steps in the sequence to obtain reinforcement. "Backward chaining" is sometimes used in which the child is initially required to produce only the last step in a sequence; then earlier steps are systematically chained to the last, until the child can produce the entire sequence.

- *Selection and systematic implementation of effective reinforcers:* Children with autism often find unusual objects and activities rewarding. ABA approaches identify what serves as a reward for each individual, again by means of empirical observations, and then use these rewards according to systematically determined schedules to manage maladaptive behaviors and elicit more adaptive ones. Correct responses and behaviors are rewarded with positive reinforcement; incorrect responses and undesirable behaviors are disregarded to as great a degree as possible.

Like the more circumscribed DTI approaches, the efficacy of these more broadly defined ABA programs for eliciting new skills and reducing problematic behavior has been documented by numerous studies (e.g., Anderson & Romanczyk, 1999; Harris, Handleman, Gordon, Kristoff, & Fuentes, 1991; Smith, 2001; Smith, Groen, & Wynn, 2000; Yoder & Layton, 1988). It is particularly useful for children in the very early stages of communicative development for the purpose of increasing responsiveness to language, developing early receptive language concepts, increasing ability to imitate vocal behavior, eliciting first words and increasing expressive language complexity, increasing symbolic play, and decreasing behaviors that interfere with the child's ability to learn from instruction. Thus, both DTI and more comprehensive ABA approaches are legitimate aspects of early intervention programs for children with ASDs and are particularly useful for preverbal children in developing beginning speech and language comprehension, as well as the "learning to learn" skills that enable further growth, including sitting and attending to others, imitating, and tolerating the imposition of another's agenda on the child's activities.

Although, as we have seen, a variety of studies have documented the efficacy of TD approaches in eliciting initial language from previously nonspeaking children, these approaches rely heavily on teacher direction, prompted responses, and contrived forms of reinforcement. An inherent weakness in didactic approaches lies in the fact that they often lead to a passive style of communication, in which children respond to prompts to communicate but do not initiate communication or use the behaviors acquired in the TD setting spontaneously to interact with peers. Stokes and Baer (1977), for example, showed that lack of generalization outside the training context was a major weakness of TD approaches. These difficulties in generalizing and maintaining behaviors taught through didactic approaches, along with changes in theoretical views of language learning that emphasized the central role of social exchanges in the acquisition of language, led to the introduction of more naturalistic methods of intervention.

Naturalistic Methods

Hart and Risley (1968) were the first to attempt to apply operant principles to more functional communicative situations. Their major insight concerned the importance of providing the "instruction" *following,* rather than preceding, a child's initiation of communication. They then made access to the object of the child's interest contingent on the child's initiating some communicative exchange about it. Rogers (in press) cites McGee, Krantz, Mason, and McClannahan's (1983) list of key features of the naturalistic approach:

- Instructional episodes are initiated by the child's behavior toward objects the teacher "plants" in the environment;
- Instruction takes place in the context of natural activities, using objects of high interest to the child;
- The child selects the stimuli from a range provided by the teacher;
- The teacher delivers prompts based on the child's initiating behavior, rather than in a prescribed fashion.

Several examples of naturalistic methods designed for prelinguistic language levels are described next. All these methods share many aspects of TD approaches from which they are an outgrowth, and many ABA practitioners would consider these approaches to be well within the framework of contemporary ABA. These methods were developed to improve the generalization of gains made in more traditional behavioral intervention (Hart & Risley, 1975; McGee, Morrier, & Daly, 1999). They are moderately teacher directed, address goals specified by the adult, and rely on reinforcement, although the reinforcement is more intrinsic (the attainment of the child's desire or a social reinforcement) than the tangible rewards used in more traditional TD methods. The effectiveness of these methods has been amply documented in the literature, at least in single case studies, both for initiating speech in previously nonverbal children (R. L. Koegel, O'Dell, & Koegel, 1987) and for increasing the complexity of spoken language (Laski, Charlop, & Schreibman, 1988). Pragmatic aspects of language have also shown improvement using naturalistic teaching methods (Charlop & Trasowech, 1991).

Milieu Teaching

Milieu teaching is an umbrella term that describes language-teaching methods that are integrated into a child's natural environment (Goldstein, 2002). The early language skills of children with a range of developmental disorders, including autism, have been shown to be enhanced through milieu teaching methods (Kaiser, Yoder, & Keetz, 1992; McGee et al., 1999). Milieu teaching approaches include adaptations of TD methods wherein:

- Training is undertaken in everyday environments (e.g., home or classroom) rather than a "therapy room."
- Activities take place throughout the day, rather than only at "therapy time."
- Preferred toys and activities are included in the environment so that participation in activities is self-reinforcing.
- Adults encourage spontaneous communication by refraining from prompting and using "expectant waiting" (use of gaze, posture, and facial expression to indicate the adult expects the child to do something).
- The child initiates the teaching situation by gesturing or indicating interest in a desired object or activity.
- Teachers provide prompts and cues for expansion of the child's initiation.
- Expanded child responses are rewarded with access to a desired object or activity.

Examples of milieu teaching approaches appear in Table 37.1.

In general, milieu approaches like these have been shown to be associated with increased ability to initiate communication in children who did not show this ability previously (Matson, Sevin, Box, Francis, & Sevin, 1993). Nonverbal children have developed speech using these methods (e.g., R. L. Koegel, Koegel, & Surratt, 1992), and increases in the frequency, spontaneity, and elaboration of language have also been documented (Delprato, 2001; Goldstein, 2002; L. K. Koegel, 2000). Moreover, direct comparisons of TD and naturalistic approaches have shown some advantage for the more natural techniques, including maintenance and generalization of new behaviors (Delprato, 2001), although not all investigators accept this conclusion (e.g., Smith, 2001).

Prompts for Restructuring Oral Muscular Phonetic Targets (PROMPT)

Another naturalistic approach to initial speech production involves the use of the PROMPT system (Hayden-Chumpelik, 1984). This method was developed to address acquired speech disorders in adults. Its use in autism is based on the notion that a major limiting factor in speech development for children with ASD is *apraxia,* a deficit in the ability to

TABLE 37.1 Examples of Milieu Teaching Methods

Method	Source	Example Activity
Prompt-free	Mirenda & Santogrossi, 1985	Several pictures of toys or snacks are placed within a child's reach. When the child touches one of the pictures (whether clearly intentionally or not), the child is given the object pictured. This continues until the child uses the pictures intentionally and spontaneously to request desired objects.
Mand-Model approach	Rogers-Warren & Warren, 1980	Objects the child likes are placed in sight but out of reach around the classroom. The teacher observes the child and when interest in some object, even fleeting interest is noted, the teacher "mands" (requests) an utterance from the child with a stimulus such as "What's that?" If the child responds with the target word or gesture, he receives the toy to play with for a short time. It is later replaced so it can tempt him again.
Incidental teaching	Hart & Risley, 1975	Objects the child likes are placed in sight but out of reach around the classroom. The teacher waits for the child to indicate interest in an object by looking at it or pulling her toward it. When he does, she looks at him and uses expectant waiting, to allow him to initiate a request. If the child does not produce a conventional request, the teacher prompts with "What do you want?" If the child produces the target response (pointing to or naming the object), he receives the desired object to play with for a time. It is later replaced so it can tempt him again. If the child does not produce the target, the teacher provides a fuller prompt, such as request for direct imitation of the target ("You want the bear? Say, *bear.*") and receives the toy.

program voluntary sequences of motor movements for speech. The idea that apraxia is a major factor in failure to develop speech in ASD is controversial, but some investigators do adopt this position (e.g., Gernsbacher, 2002; Rogers, in press) although the prevalence of apraxic disorders in children with autism is by no means agreed on, even within this group. For those who see apraxia as a component of autistic communication disorders, an approach that attempts to address specific motor speech disorders becomes attractive.

The PROMPT method relies on structured tactile stimulation of the articulators to induce appropriate articulatory postures and movements for speech. Rogers (in press) has reported that although children with autism sometimes find the sensations of oral stimulation aversive at first, anecdotal observations suggest that they adjust to being touched, and some appear to go on to produce first words using this method. As of this writing, published studies of results of this intervention in autism have not appeared.

Another naturalistic method for initiating verbal production in autism is the minimal speech approach (MSA; Potter, & Whittaker, 2001). This method is similar in form to milieu teaching but contains the restriction that adults consistently reduce their speech to single- or two-word utterances supported by pictures or objects, using long (5- to 10-second) pauses at critical moments in interactions. These techniques are employed to make the child less dependent on adults for prompts to communicate. Questions are avoided in this approach for the same reason. If the child does not initiate communication when provided with an opportunity, the adult prompts nonverbally, then provides an appropriate single word only after the child has made a nonverbal response to the prompt. The MSA web site (http://trainland.tripod.com/carol.htm) provides the following example activity:

An adult holds two bottles of juice in front of the child and says nothing. If the child points to one, the adult gives him the bottle and may say, "drink." If the child does not respond, the adult, after a long pause, takes the child's finger and prompts him to point to one of the bottles, without speaking. Once the child produces a gesture to communicate a

choice, the adult gives the child his choice and may say, "drink."

Like milieu teaching, this approach attempts to provide multiple temptations to communicate throughout the child's day, makes use of expectant waiting, and avoids prompting before the child has initiated some form of communication. The premise unique to this approach is that children with autism "tune out" speech and voices, perhaps because language is too complex and overstimulating. The solution proposed by MSA is to provide only the most concrete, simple verbal input on a consistent basis *after* the child has made some nonverbal attempt to communicate. To provide maximal opportunities and temptations for communication, "proximal communication" strategies are used. These strategies involve a range of preferred, nonverbal interaction opportunities, such as rough-and-tumble play or imitating the child, which are initiated by the adult and then paused. The adult uses expectant waiting during these pauses to attempt to elicit some form of communication. The adult then provides a minimally verbal response that maps directly onto the child's communicative intent ("Tickle!") and reinitiates the preferred activity. Although Potter and Whittaker (2000) provide a rationale, description, and anecdotal support for this approach, empirical studies on its efficacy have not appeared in peer-reviewed journals.

Although some naturalistic approaches consist of a unitary set of techniques focused exclusively on the development of communication, others attempt to provide a more comprehensive approach to early intervention. The *natural language paradigm* (NLP) is an example of a more comprehensive form of milieu teaching that is intended to be the primary strategy used throughout the child's treatment program, rather than in individual activities (L. K. Koegel, Koegel, & Carter, 1998; R. L. Koegel et al., 1987). In programs that adopt this model, the child selects stimulus items, activities are changed regularly, and a wide variety of language is modeled for the child. Social reinforcement and opportunity to play with selected stimulus items are used as reinforcers, and all verbal attempts to communicate are reinforced. Skills the child has already acquired are targeted regularly between activities that target new skills; not only is child initiation of communication a focus of intervention but also back-and-forth turn taking is targeted. Parents of children with autism have been successfully trained to use NLP techniques to facilitate an increase in their children's expressive language (Laski et al., 1988).

A more recent example of a comprehensive naturalistic method is L. K. Koegel, Carter, and Koegel's (2003) pivotal response training (PRT). PRT is used to teach a small set of important skills that will lead to more general increases in communicative behavior. The key to this method lies in carefully selecting pivotal targets that, when changed, result in concomitant positive changes in related but untrained behaviors. Behaviors identified as pivotal for children at early communication stages appear in Table 37.2.

Training strategies employ milieu teaching and other naturalistically adapted ABA approaches provided within an inclusive setting in which more socially adept peers can serve as models and reinforcers. Koegel and colleagues have demonstrated that both the specific trained behaviors and more generalized increases in communication can be achieved by this approach (L. K. Koegel et al., 2003). Other comprehensive programs incorporate naturalistic approaches to enhancing communication, as well, including: the TEACCH method (Schopler, this *Handbook,* this volume; Schopler & Olley, 1982), the Douglass Developmental Disabilities Center (Harris, Handleman, Arnold, & Gordon, 2000), the Learning Experiences and Alternative Program (LEAP) preschool (Strain & Hoyson, 2000), the UCLA Young Autism Project (Smith, Donahue, & Davis, 2000), and the Walden approach (Strain, McGee, & Kohler, 2001). The Denver model (Rogers, Hall, Osaki, Reaven, & Herbison, 2000) also takes advantage of naturalistic methods within its generally child-centered orientation.

There is one significant problem with naturalistic teaching methods, however. Because of their reliance on allowing children to initiate, requiring interventionists to make more online decisions, they involve a significant level of training for interventionists and rely to some degree on clinician skill. Although it has been demonstrated that both parents and peers can

be taught to deliver naturalistic interventions successfully (Charlop & Trasowech, 1991; McGee, Krantz, Sulzer-Azaroff, & Feldman, 1992), these methods require more moment-to-moment decision making than didactic programs in which adult actions are clearly specified, unambiguous, and easily trained. Moreover, unlike didactic approaches, there are few materials available that outline comprehensive curricula; nor are there training opportunities that make it possible to master the approach from independent study of published manuals or through in-service training. Currently, then, it is difficult to disseminate these methods faithfully and efficiently to interventionists beyond those who created the approaches and their direct trainees.

Developmentally Based, Social-Pragmatic Strategies

The central tenets of this group of approaches include:

- Using the normal sequence of communicative development to provide the best guidelines for determining intervention goals.
- Providing intensified opportunities for children with ASD to engage in activities that are similar to those in which typically developing peers engage, in the belief that these are the most effective contexts for learning social and communication skills.
- Exploiting learning opportunities ("teachable moments") that naturally arise in the course of interactions, rather than relying on a predetermined curriculum.
- Facilitating interactions, including symbolic play, rather than addressing teacher-chosen goals, by:
  —Focusing on what a child is already interested in, acknowledging and responding to the child's intent, even if expressed unconventionally.
  —Modeling ways to communicate about activities the child chooses and is already engaged in.
  —Expanding on what the child produces spontaneously.
- Targeting *functional* goals for intervention, that is, targeting behaviors that are applicable to daily, meaningful activities in a

TABLE 37.2   Pivotal Behaviors

Pivotal Behavior	Rationale	Methods	Examples
Responding to multiple cues	To reduce stimulus over selectivity	*Within stimulus prompting:* Exaggerating the relevant components of a stimulus, then gradually fading these exaggerations. *Conditional discriminations:* Requires the child to discriminate on the basis of more than one feature.	When teaching the Sign for "more," the Sign is first demonstrated with large sweeping arm motions and exaggerated closing of the hands, which are gradually faded. When teaching colors, the child is asked to get a blue sock and is presented with a blue sock, a white sock, and a blue shirt, so that s/he must consider both the color and the item name in making a choice.
Increasing motivation	To increase responsiveness to social environment and enhance spontaneity and generalization	*Child choice:* Allow child to select preferred materials, topics, toys, and activities within teaching situations. *Natural reinforcers:* Rewards that are directly and functionally related to the task, so emitting target response naturally leads to obtaining reward. *Interspersing maintenance trials:* Provides practice of previously learned activities often to give child a sense of success and positive affect. *Reinforcing attempts:* Uses shaping to reward any goal directed behavior, even if it is not the direct target.	When teaching colors, child is allowed to choose colored candies. When teaching "cup," the child is given a cup with juice in it after s/he names the object. Teaching a new skill is preceded by several trials of a well-learned skill that has a high probability of being performed correctly. When teaching a pointing gesture as a request, a fist point is rewarded if it clearly indicates communication; then is shaped by gradually increasing requirement for index finger isolation.
Increasing self-regulation	Allows more active involvement in the intervention process; improves independence; provides more opportunities for social interaction without direct supervision	*Target behaviors are operationally defined:* Child has clear idea of what to monitor. *Reinforcers are identified:* Rewarding consequences are identified. *Self-monitoring device is selected and trained:* A simple method of tracking child's own behavior is provided. *Use of self-monitoring is validated.*	Through repeated modeling, child is taught to touch a teacher's arm whenever peer moves too close to him for comfort. Child is rewarded for alerting teacher rather than pushing peer by being allowed to play a favorite music box. Child gets a star and puts it on his hand each time he alerts teacher rather than pushing peer. Teacher checks child's hand after free-play period and provides praise for the number of stars he earned.
Increasing initiation of communication	Increase opportunities for spontaneous social learning and increased social competence	*Motivation to communicate is provided.* *Prompt/fade and shaping techniques are used to increase initiations.*	Preferred objects are placed in an opaque bag. Child is prompted to ask "What's that?" Child is allowed to play with toy after asking question. Prompts are gradually faded.

Source: Identified from "Pivotal Response Intervention," by L. K. Koegel, R. L. Koegel, J. Harrower, and C. A. Carter, 1999, *Journal of the Association for Persons with Severe Handicaps, 24,* pp. 174–186.

variety of contexts apart from the one in which they were originally learned.

- Assuming the "prerequisite" role of nonverbal communication, including gestures, gaze, vocalization, and other nonvocal means, in the development of language.

An assumption on which this approach is based is that children with autism develop language in the same way and following the same sequence as do typically speaking children. Thus, children who do not speak will first be encouraged to use other means of communicating to get ideas across, so they can discover the value of communication in the ability to regulate others' behavior and control interactions. Proponents of this approach, then, advocate the use of a variety of nonverbal forms of communication being used as a stepping stone to speech.

Augmentative and Alternative Communication Strategies

Originally developed to assist individuals with severe motoric impediments to speech production, augmentative and alternative communication (AAC) strategies provide a nonvocal option for communication. AAC methods are generally divided into two categories: *aided* and *unaided*. Unaided AAC systems include conventional gestures and body language, as well as use of manual signs. For children with ASD at early developmental levels, teaching conventional use of gestures such as pointing, showing, waving, and nodding is often a focus of intervention. It provides the child with some conventionally recognized actions that can be used to reliably affect the behavior of others. Use of gestures as a form of communication may be the first step in a developmental communication program for a nonspeaking child with ASDs.

Manual signs have also been used frequently as a communication modality for children with ASDs who do not talk. Seal and Bonvillian (1997) reported that the acquisition of signs is related to fine motor abilities, suggesting that children with low levels of fine motor development are less likely to benefit from this form of AAC. Goldstein (2002) reviewed a range of studies employing manual signs combined with speech (total communica-tion [TC] approaches) and concluded that TC can be effective for teaching early vocabulary both receptively and expressively. Lord and McGee (2001) argue that, while signs may support children in making a transition to first words, they are not generally an entry into a fully functional language system. Use of signs has not been found to preclude the production of speech, but at least one study (Yoder & Layton, 1988) suggests that teaching signs does not accelerate speech development, either.

Aided AAC systems range from relatively *lite-tech* methods to those that employ *high-tech* electronic devices, such as voice output communication aids (VOCAs), which allow a user to type a message or touch a picture that triggers a "spoken" output by a device with speech synthesis capacity. Lite-tech pictorial communication systems such as picture boards, on which a child indicates a choice or intention by pointing to a picture from an array, are frequently used as AAC devices for children at early communication levels with a variety of disabilities.

One pictorial method that has been used with children with autism is the Picture Exchange Communication System (PECS; Bondy & Frost, 1998). PECS integrates principles from both ABA and more "pragmatic" methods. A PECS program begins with teaching single word requests by means of exchanging a picture for an object, then moves on to building sentence structure. Like milieu teaching approaches, PECS incorporates child initiation of communicative acts by requiring the child to initiate an exchange by handing a picture to an adult to obtain the desired object. Direct verbal prompts such as "What do you want?" are avoided to help increase the spontaneity of requests. Once a powerful reinforcer is identified, the child is required to exchange a picture card with the trainer for the desired item. It is recommended that two trainers be used, with one guiding the child through the picture exchange when he or she reaches toward the reinforcer. Spontaneity and generalization of the picture exchanges are addressed by:

- Gradually increasing the distance between the child and the pictures
- Using the system in different environments
- Involving a variety of people
- Focusing on different reinforcers

The following example describes a PECS activity to develop requesting by using a desired toy as a reinforcer. A picture card of the toy is placed near the toy. When the child reaches for the toy, one trainer guides the child's hand toward the card to pick it up and hand it to the second trainer. When the second trainer receives the card, he or she immediately gives the child the toy. Once the child is able to reliably request the toy, the picture card is moved farther from the child so that the child must actively retrieve the card and then deliver it to the trainer to get the toy.

Training then focuses on the discrimination between symbols. This begins with a small number of items, usually two, which may be increased once the child can readily discriminate between the choices. Occasionally, children will not have sufficient symbolic ability to understand the relationship between a picture and the corresponding object. In that case, more concrete materials may have to be used initially. For example, parts of objects might initially be exchanged for the whole (an empty box of juice exchanged for a full one or a straw exchanged for a juice box with a straw). Gradually more abstract exchanges, moving from photographs to drawings, would then be introduced.

There are few well-controlled studies that assess the effectiveness of PECS on language development, with much of the support for the program provided by anecdotal reports. Charlop-Christy, Carpenter, LeBlanc, and Kellet (2002) conducted a study to examine the use of PECS with three preschool children with ASD and its effects on speech development. Results from this study indicated that all the children met the learning criteria for PECS and showed increases in use of speech. The effect of PECS on the spontaneous communication skills of a 6-year-old girl with autism was studied by Kravits, Kamps, Kemmerer, and Potucek (2002). Results indicated increased spontaneous expressive communication using a variety of modalities across all the environments in which PECS was trained. Its developers also argue for the efficacy of the PECS program by citing subjective reports on 66 children who used PECS for between 1 and 5 years (Bondy & Frost, 1998). These reports indicated that 59% ($n = 39$) developed functional speech and 30% ($n = 20$)

combined some functional speech with PECS. Still, these studies did not employ control groups or conditions; nor do they contrast the approach to those with more direct focus on speech. Therefore, it is not yet possible to know whether PECS is a more efficient method of eliciting first words than the didactic or naturalistic methods discussed earlier.

There is some limited evidence that nonspeaking individuals with autism can benefit from exposure to high-tech AAC devices, as well. Two youths with autism were among the participants in a study by Romski and Sevcik (1996), who showed increased expression using both spoken language and a computerized VOCA device over the course of a 2-year study, in which naturalistic teaching methods were employed to teach the use of the device. This approach also resulted in an increased use of communicative behaviors to request objects, respond to questions, and make comments among four children with autism in another study (Schepis, Reid, Behrmann, & Sutton, 1998). A case study of one child with autism by Light, Roberts, DiMarco, and Greiner (1998) also reported positive language outcomes when a VOCA was included as a component of a comprehensive communication system. Other components included gestures, natural speech, and a communication book. Finally, Bernard-Opitz, Sriran, and Sapuan (1999) used feedback from an IBM Speech Viewer to increase vocal imitation in children with autism. While these initial reports are promising, additional larger scale research is required to assess the efficacy of VOCAs in this population.

Unfortunately, high-technology devices are usually not sufficient to provide a fully functional language system to children with autism, since their core deficits are in communication, that is, having a motivation to send a message to another rather than in the vocal aspects of speech. Although, as we have seen, claims have been made for an apraxic basis for autism, there is little direct evidence to support the idea that it is the motor planning involved in speech that limits communication in this population. Rogers (in press), in discussing the role apraxia may play in the communicative deficits of children with ASDs, argues that it is general imitative ability, not speech motor deficits, that inhibits speech development for most nonverbal children with autism. She advocates addressing this issue with systematic didactic or naturalistic training of motor, facial, and vocal imitation. She suggests further that only a small minority of children with ASD, those who fail to benefit from this type of training, are the ones with a more fundamental verbal apraxia-like deficit. For these children, she suggests approaches such as PROMPT (Square-Storer & Hayden, 1989) or AAC. The implication of this recommendation is that apraxia-oriented approaches should be initiated only *after* an intensive attempt to develop vocal imitation and speech has been made and found unsuccessful.

There are few direct contrasts between AAC and straightforward speech instruction for children with autism. However, one study has compared the teaching of sign and speech to nonverbal children with ASD (Yoder & Layton, 1988). This study found no advantage in speech acquisition when signs were taught first. Although it does seem clear that the introduction of AAC systems to nonspeaking children with autism does not keep them from learning to talk, Rogers (in press) raises the important question as to whether AAC does anything to accelerate the development of speech. Although AAC is clearly useful for some children such as those with cerebral palsy who have motor deficits that inhibit the acquisition of intelligible speech, the vast majority of children with autism do not fall into this category. Thus, it is imperative to demonstrate that for children with the potential to talk, AAC approaches will lead to functional speech more quickly and efficiently than the well-documented TD and naturalistic approaches known to be effective at establishing verbal production in this population.

Comprehensive Developmental-Pragmatic Approaches

Like the didactic and naturalistic approaches discussed earlier, many programs that adopt a developmental orientation are designed to provide programming for children across their school day in areas that emphasize, but are not limited to, communication. Programs that adopt a developmental philosophy vary in the degree to which they moderate adult directiveness in their approach. At the most purely child-centered end of this continuum is the *Developmental, Individual-difference, Relationship-based* (DIR) or "Floor Time" approach of Greenspan and Weider (1999). This method is based on the theory that the root of autism lies in a deficit in attaching affect to developing motor and symbolic abilities. Features of the DIR include:

- *Following the child's lead; imitating the child's actions:* If a child is spinning the wheel on a toy car, the interventionist spins the wheel in the opposite direction in the hope of initiating a back-and-forth game.
- *Incorporating sensorimotor activities:* The adult attempts to focus on the child's attention on the partner as a source of pleasing activity by swinging the child or by applying firm pressure or joint compression—whatever the child appears to enjoy and increases attention to the adult.
- *Presenting problem-solving activities at appropriate developmental levels:* For example, the child may be confronted with a barrier to something he or she wants and encouraged to incorporate the adult in solving the problem.
- *Providing gestural circles of communication; playful obstruction of perseverative activities:* If the child continually bangs blocks together, the adult playfully inserts a hand between the blocks to attract the child's attention.
- *Requiring closure of communication circles:* When the child ignores an adult remark or action, the adult "plays dumb" and refuses to move on until the child closes the circle. For example, if the child wants to go outside and tries to open the door, the adult can close it and wait for the child to provide some communication about his or her desire before responding.
- *Ensuring that positive emotion is maintained throughout all therapeutic interactions.*

The only evaluation of this approach available is a review of case records by its originators (Greenspan & Weider, 1999), who report that more than 50% of children exposed to their intervention, in the context of an intensive, comprehensive educational program, "learn to be warm, emotionally expressive flexible children with a sense of humor, empathy, solid abstract thinking skills and age appropriate academic capacities" (p. 154). The authors caution that this group, however, was not a representative sample of children with ASD but rather "a subgroup capable of significant progress" (p. 154). These results have not been replicated or validated by other researchers as of this writing.

A similar philosophy is embodied in the comprehensive Son-Rise® program (Kaufman, 1994). This program advocates parent-administered home-based teaching for children with autism. Basic tenets of this program, provided on its web site (The Autism Treatment Center of America, 2003), include:

- Joining in a child's repetitive and ritualistic behaviors
- Utilizing a child's own motivation to advance learning and build the foundation for education and skill acquisition
- Teaching through interactive play
- Using energy, excitement, and enthusiasm to engage the child
- Employing a nonjudgmental and optimistic attitude
- Placing the parent as the child's most important and consistent teacher

This program makes strong claims not only for improving social communication but also for "curing" autism. While many testimonials are provided, no controlled research has been done to substantiate these claims.

Another child-centered program is found in Sussman's (1999) *More Than Words,* and its parent program, the Hanen approach (Girolametto, Greenberg, & Manolson, 1986). These are derived from approaches developed by The Hanen Centre® for training parents and teachers to facilitate language development by providing enriched, contingent, and stimulating input to children with a range of disabilities. The focus of More Than Words and the Hanen approach to autism in general is on training the parents and teachers of preschool children with ASD to promote communication and social skills within ordinary interactions throughout the child's day. Elements common to the activities found in More Than Words, as well as in child-centered, developmental intervention approaches generally, include:

- Following the child's lead by noticing what the child is doing, then joining in, even if the child attempts to refuse the adult's intrusion
- Treating any behavior as if it were communicative (e.g., if the child is playing with the parent's keys, treating it as a request to ride in the car and taking the child for a ride)
- Imitating child sounds and actions, rather than asking the child to imitate the adult
- Turning the child's preferred activities into games (e.g., if the child likes to roll cars back and forth, engaging in a car race game by intruding and imitating)
- Modeling and encouraging turn taking in a variety of sound and action games
- Using visual supports, such as picture cue cards, visual schedules, picture stories, computer games
- Using music to support attention to language by embedding simple language in short, slowly produced song formats with heavy stress placed on important words

More Than Words is not so much an intervention program as a guide to help parents and teachers provide joyful, naturalistic interactive episodes to enhance communication across the range of their child's experiences. Although there is a good deal of research to support the use of the Hanen approach in elaborating language for children with typical and delayed development (e.g., Clements-Baartman & Girolametto, 1995; Girolametto, 1988; Girolametto, Pearce, & Weitzman, 1996), there is very little empirical support for its use with children with ASDs (Coulter & Gallagher, 2001).

Another program of developmental-pragmatic activities can be found in Gutstein and Sheely (2002). Their relationship development intervention (RDI) focuses on activities that elicit interactive behaviors, with or without the use of language. Many are designed to help children focus on nonverbal aspects of communication, such as gaze direction or facial expression. The goal of these activities is to engage the child in a social relationship, rather than to achieve a specific behavioral objective. The theory on which this intervention is based is that once the child "discovers" the value of relationships through repeated joyous interpersonal activity, he or she will be more motivated to learn the skills necessary, such as language and interpretation of nonverbal behavior, to sustain these relationships. Principles of RDI include:

- Systematically building motivation by creating strong positive interactive experiences
- Evaluating readiness before teaching skills
- Using indirect prompts as invitations, rather than directions to interact
- Using face, intonation, and body language to highlight important information
- Using activities that can expand and evolve as the child develops
- Moving from work with one adult to a dyad to a group

An example of an RDI is the following: the adult holds a treat in one closed fist, displays both closed fists to the child, and then looks at the hand that holds the treat. The child is given repeated opportunities to "find" the treat in the hand the adult looks at. RDI activities are sequenced from those appropriate at the prelinguistic level up through those relevant to advanced language levels. No empirical studies of the effects of these methods have appeared in the literature.

The Social Communication Emotional Regulation Transactional Support (SCERTS) model, described in Chapter 30, and the Denver model (Rogers et al., 2000) are additional comprehensive approaches that make extensive use of developmental-pragmatic methods. These methods are more eclectic than the others discussed here and do allow the employment of more structured teaching techniques. In fact, many developmental approaches employ techniques such as organizing the environment and using expectant waiting that make them similar to naturalistic methods such as milieu teaching. Just as di-

dactic approaches can lean toward more naturalistic methods, so many developmentalists make use of semistructured naturalistic approaches, as well. Thus, it is best to think of the range of approaches available for enhancing communication along a continuum, rather than as a strict tripartite division (see Table 37.3).

Developmental-pragmatic approaches are widely used and advocated by many prominent communication specialists. One problem with these methods is that, to an even greater extent than naturalistic approaches, they require a high degree of sensitivity, creativity, and online decision making on the part of interventionists. Programs such as Hanen© have demonstrated that parents, teachers, paraprofessionals, and others can learn these methods, but they require extensive training, practice, and ongoing support. To some degree, then, the success of developmental-pragmatic programs hinges on the careful training, follow-up, support, and talent of those who deliver the intervention.

A second issue concerning developmental-pragmatic approaches is very little research that demonstrates their efficacy in eliciting first words from children with ASDs. Some research has shown them to be effective for children with other developmental delays (e.g., Fey & Proctor-Williams, 2000; Gillum, Camarata, Nelson, & Camarata, 2003; Girolametto et al., 1996). In addition, studies of child-centered methods have demonstrated their ability to increase imitation, gaze, turn taking, and joint attention (Buffington, Krantz, McClannahan, & Poulsen, 1998; Hwang & Hughes, 2000; Lewy & Dawson, 1992; Pierce & Schreibman, 1995) in preverbal children with autism. Little study, however, has been aimed at documenting the

TABLE 37.3   A Continuum of Methods for Enhancing Communication in Children with Autism Spectrum Disorders

Didactic	Naturalistic	Developmental-Pragmatic
Discrete Trial	Milieu Teaching	Child-Centered Approaches
RMI	PECS	RDI
Verbal Behavior	MSA	Hanen
PROMPT		DIR
Teach Me Language		
ABA		

capacity of these approaches to elicit first words from previously nonverbal children. One reason may be related to the tendency of developmental approaches to make use of AAC as an initial communication system in nonspeakers so that direct joint attention-to-speech development is not observed. In any case, despite the large literature explicating and advocating developmental approaches for preverbal children with ASD, very little empirical evidence has been presented to support their effectiveness in initiating spoken language with this population, although there are some data to support their efficacy in remediating other core communication deficits in prelinguistic children.

A related problem, highlighted by Rogers (in press), is that developmental approaches make the assumption that children with ASDs will use a typical style and developmental sequence in learning language and communication skills. The corollary of this assumption is that prelinguistic children with ASD benefit from the same kinds of supports that children with language delays do. Although there is a large literature on language acquisition in young children with autism (see Chapter 12), only one study to date has directly compared the developmental trajectory of language learning in autism to that in other developmentally delayed children. Tager-Flusberg et al. (1990) followed six children with autism and those with Down syndrome (DS) through the language development period and reported few differences between groups. Still, the specific speech difficulties related to oral motor dysmorphology and hypotonia in DS could have affected results. What we do know about the development of language in autism (Tager-Flusberg, Paul, & Lord, this *Handbook,* Volume 1) suggests that there are important differences in the scope, synchrony, and sequence of acquisition of language between children with ASDs and those with other developmental disorders. Paul et al. (2004), for example, reported that preverbal children with ASD have better phonological than semantic skills, whereas these skills are very closely related in both typical and delayed speech development (Paul & Jennings, 1992; Stoel-Gammon, 1991). Lord and Paul (1997) emphasized the dissociations between form

and function seen in autistic language development, which do not appear in the acquisition profile of other delayed groups. If there are fundamental differences in the language learning styles of children with ASD, then the use of methods that are effective with other language-delayed children cannot be assumed to work equally well with those who have ASD. Only controlled, direct comparisons of intervention methods will elucidate the efficacy of developmental-pragmatic approaches for the acquisition of spoken language in autism.

Conclusions: Prelinguistic Intervention

Programs to elicit initial communication behaviors and first words range from highly structured behavioral to open-ended, child-directed methods, with a range of naturalistic approaches between. Didactic and naturalistic methods are aimed specifically at eliciting speech from preverbal children with ASDs and have established efficacy for doing so in single case studies, although controlled experiments with random assignment to treatments, the gold standard of scientific evidence, have not been accomplished. Developmental-pragmatic approaches are aimed more broadly at the improvement of social communication and interaction and have a less well-established empirical track record for eliciting first words in children with ASDs, although they have been shown to increase preverbal behaviors such as imitation and joint attention. Developmental approaches that incorporate AAC methods such as signs and pictures have been shown to be compatible with the development of speech, although, again, their efficiency relative to straightforward speech treatment has not been established. Studies of developmental methods, too, fail to employ random assignment or case controls. Moreover, very few direct comparisons among intervention methods have been made. As a result, it is not possible to say that one is more effective than another. Importantly, too, little research exists on the relationship between child characteristics and intervention efficacy, so we do not know which approach will be the "best match" for a particular child. What does appear to be clear is that communicative deficits in preverbal children with autism are amenable to treatment and that a range of treatments have been shown useful in enhancing communicative behavior. Although older literature has suggested that only 50% of children with autism acquire functional speech (Lord & Paul, 1997), the introduction of early identification and intervention—as well as the development, assessment, and refinement of techniques to elicit speech in this population—will be likely to affect this statistic in the near future. L. K. Koegel (2000) has estimated that close to 90% of children with autism will be able to learn to talk as a result of these innovations. If this prediction turns out to be even partially accurate, it will represent a real triumph of special education and an extraordinary improvement in the quality of life for children with ASDs and their loved ones.

CORE COMMUNICATIVE DEFICITS AT THE EARLY LANGUAGE STAGE

Once children with autism begin using words, signs, or other conventional forms to express themselves, significant challenges to the development of communicative competence remain. One aspect of language development that is prominent in autism is the use of *echolalia,* that is, the imitation of what has been heard, either directly after it is spoken or as a delayed echo at a later time. Although echolalia is seen in typical development, in blind children, and in those with mental retardation, its use by children with autism is more extensive and prolonged than in other groups, and it is used for a wider range of functions (Prizant, Schuler, Wetherby, & Rydell, 1997). Although some echolalia appears to be noncommunicative and self-stimulatory (Prizant & Duchan, 1981), especially in young children, older children with autism often use echoes for a variety of communicative purposes. Research has shown that they tend to echo when they do not understand what has been said to them (Carr, Schreibman, & Lovaas, 1975), or when they do not have adequate language skills to construct a spontaneous response (Prizant & Duchan, 1981).

A related characteristic of early language in autism is *pronoun reversal,* primarily the tendency to use "you" instead of "I." Although this was at one time thought to reflect difficul-

ties in ego formation, it is now seen as another instance of echolalia, in which children refer to themselves as "you," as they have heard others refer to them (Fay, 1969). Again, this mistake is sometimes made by children with typical development or delays, but it appears more briefly and is used less extensively than by children with ASDs.

Another unusual feature of the early language of children with autism who speak is that, on standardized testing, *expressive language skills* tend to be *higher than receptive skills* (Charman et al., 2003). This is usually manifest in better naming ability than the ability to indicate pictures or objects named. Studies of preschool children with autism showed that development of language comprehension consistently lagged behind this development in children with specific language impairments, although the general sequence of development was similar (Paul & Cohen, 1984; Rutter, Mawhood, & Howlin, 1992). The early deficits in attention to language seen in children with autism seem a likely reason for these findings (Paul et al., 2004). It may be the case that young children with autism "know" the words they can say both receptively and expressively but do not respond consistently when they hear these words because language does not capture their attention. In any case, receptive language is an important focus for intervention in children with autism at early language stages, since it cannot be assumed that there is a strong foundation of receptive language on which expression can be built.

As Tager-Flusberg, Paul, and Lord (this *Handbook,* Volume 1) outline, children with autism do tend to show greater *delays in syntax* than could be accounted for by their nonverbal mental age; however, this is true for children with mental retardation, as well (Abbeduto, Furman, & Davies, 1989; Cascella, 1999). In general, acquisition of the formal aspects of language (phonology, syntax, morphology) follows the sequence of normal development, at a somewhat reduced rate, in children with autism who develop speech. The development of *word use is also a slowed-down version of normal* in many ways (Travis & Sigman, 2001). Children with autism tend to assign words to the same conceptual categories as others (recognizing things you sit on as chairs, for example; Boucher, 1988; Tager-Flusberg, 1985). In fact, some high-functioning individuals with autism take particular pleasure in words; they may read the dictionary as a hobby, for example, and may have large vocabularies for their age. However, *unusual and idiosyncratic word use,* such as inventing words, is frequently seen (Volden & Lord, 1991), and children with autism seem to have particular difficulty learning relational words, such as verbs, prepositions, and comparatives (Travis & Sigman, 2001). As children with autism learn words, they tend to construct rather rigid meanings and have difficulty understanding ambiguity and multiple-meaning words (Happé, 1995). Thus, work on vocabulary frequently needs to center on expanding the range of meanings and uses for words the child knows (see Marans et al., this *Handbook,* this volume).

Receptive language, as well as syntactic and phonological aspects of language development in autism, then, tend to be somewhat less advanced than developmental level would predict in children with autism. For those whose speech is just emerging and for whom echoed responses represent a large part of the output, these areas will require focused intervention in order to provide more functional and available forms for communication.

Another significant area of communicative challenge is the *prosody* or musical aspect of speech (Shriberg et al., 2001), including its rate, loudness, pitch, voice quality, and use of stress. Sheinkopf, Mundy, Oller, and Steffens (2000) and Dawson, Osterling, Meltzoff, and Kuhl (2002) showed that even prelinguistic vocalizations in young children with autism contained a significantly higher proportion of atypical vocal characteristics than did those of normal children. Paul, Shriberg, McSweeney, Klin, and Volkmar (in press) found that approximately half of high-functioning speakers with autism were rated as atypical in elements of prosodic production. When these differences are present, they tend to be persistent and to show little change over time, even when other aspects of language improve (DeMyer et al., 1973; Kanner, 1971; Rutter & Lockyer, 1967; Simmons & Baltaxe, 1975). Paul et al. showed that ratings of social and communicative competence were related to ratings of prosody in speakers with ASDs, suggesting

that difficulties in prosodic production affect listeners' attributions of competence to these individuals.

To date, there has been little research on the treatment of prosodic deficits in autism. Several commercially available programs have been developed for addressing prosodic difficulties in nonautistic speakers (e.g., Awad, Corliss, & Merson, 2003; Ray & Baker, 2000), but no research is available on their use with children with autism. Nonetheless, addressing prosodic deficits remains a largely unmet need in this population.

Pragmatics, or appropriate use of language in social situations, is the most prominent aspect of communicative deficit in this population (Tager-Flusberg, 1995). Children with autism are less likely than those with typical development to initiate communication, particularly with peers (McHale, Simeonsson, Marcus, & Olley, 1980). Overall rates of communication are very low, even in children who speak (Stone & Caro-Martinez, 1990). These children show reduced interest in language spoken to them; they are less likely to respond in a reciprocal fashion to the communicative bids of peers and more likely to produce self-directed, noncommunicative speech (Baltaxe, 1977). Chuba, Miles, Paul, Klin, and Volkmar (2003) reported that the following areas of pragmatics were most consistently impaired in speakers with autism:

- Use of gaze
- Production of irrelevant/inappropriate detail
- Conversational contributions not synchronized with ongoing conversation
- Topic preoccupation/perseveration
- Provision of insufficient background information
- Provision of vague, insufficiently informative responses
- Difficulty in taking the assertive role in reciprocal conversation

Most of these concern a difficulty in accurately judging what is appropriate to say in a given social context, a problem that may reflect, to some extent, the known difficulties in "theory of mind." In communication situations, this ability is manifest in knowing what is reasonable to expect others to already know (so they don't need to be told) or not know (so they need to be informed explicitly).

INTERVENTION METHODS AT THE EARLY LANGUAGE STAGE

Children with autism at the early language stage have begun using words and perhaps word combinations, but exhibit characteristic features of language in autism that can include pronoun reversals, immediate and delayed echolalia, abnormal prosody, and poor understanding of language relative to expressive ability. Their most prominent deficits are in using the language they have to interact effectively with others. Intervention programs that attempt to improve communication in these children need not only to improve the maturity of their language forms, but also enable more effective use of communication.

Didactic Approaches

ABA programs have been developed to address the expansion of early symbols into more elaborated forms of expression. One example is *Teach Me Language* (Freeman & Dake, 1997), a comprehensive language program that provides a step-by-step guide with in-depth detail on intervention activities targeting language areas such as grammar, syntax, concepts, and advanced narrative skills. Teach Me Language methodology is behavioral-based. Children are expected to follow a teacher's lead, and regular repetition of drills is a key feature in the program. The program was developed for children who have at least single word expressive language and some basic concept knowledge and was designed to help them make the transition from this emerging language stage to more fully developed forms of expression and functional communication. It also requires a visual learning style and the ability to sit at a table and attend to basic tasks. Methods used during Teach Me Language include:

- Table-based activities
- Visual and auditory instructions, examples and modeling of correct responses

- Multiple repetitions of activities with varying examples, until the child shows comprehension of the target concept
- Elicitation of a variety of responses from the child to avoid repetition of the same correct answer
- Cueing strategies that are gradually withdrawn as the child becomes competent in achieving targets

The program covers a range of language skills, including:

- *Social language:* Activities that focus on language use in social situations
- *General knowledge:* Aims to increase general knowledge to help build a solid base for future learning
- *Grammar and syntax:* Activities that target areas of language difficulty such as pronouns, questioning, and verbs
- *Advanced language development:* Complex language skills such as story and letter writing
- *Academic/language-based concepts:* Brainstorming, note taking, and verbal mediation

The *Verbal Behavior* program takes a Skinnerian approach to language learning, based on the research of Michael, Sundberg, and Partington (e.g., Sundberg, Michael, Partington, & Sundberg, 1995). The program, like Teach Me Language, provides a carefully sequenced curriculum for teaching language to children just emerging into symbolic communication, and it carries the curriculum through to those learning more advanced language forms. It uses a highly structured behavioral approach, incorporating techniques such as errorless teaching, specific quick-transfer (prompting and fading) procedures, and the use of discrete trial training during both intensive teaching sessions and in more naturalistic contexts. Language goals are structured in terms of Skinnerian categories of verbal behaviors, which include (hierarchically ordered):

- *Echoes:* Practice in imitating verbal behavior
- *Mands:* Verbal behaviors that produce an immediate benefit for the speaker (e.g., requests)

- *Tacts:* Labels
- *Reception by feature, function, and class (RFFC):* Responding to commonly used verbal stimuli (words)
- *Intraverbals:* Verbal, nonechoic responses to the verbal behavior of others; conversational responses

The program provides a complete sequence for teaching these verbal behavior skills, with levels of performance for each of the five verbal behavior categories. Table 37.4 briefly outlines these levels.

The Verbal Behavior program can be adapted for use not only with spoken language but also with alternative forms of communication for those children for whom they are appropriate. Carbone (2003) is one of the most active advocates of this method.

As in the didactic approaches for children at prelinguistic communication levels, these highly behavioral language teaching programs have the potential weakness of leading to passive styles of communication and limited levels of generalization. A search of reference databases found no reports of empirical evidence to support the specific use of the Teach Me Language program. However, Partington, Sundberg, and colleagues have published data indicating increases in verbal production using their method (e.g., Partington, Sundberg, Newhouse, & Spengler-Schelley, 1994; Sundberg & Michael, 2001; Sundberg et al., 1995). Still, little research is available on the functional effects of these programs on real-world communication or on their consequences for adaptive communication and independence. While they may result in the achievement of target behaviors within the behavioral framework, as most ABA programs do, there is little data on their general, long-term effects on the child's functioning.

At a slightly less traditionally behaviorist approach, the PECS program also provides a curriculum for children who have acquired basic symbolic communication skills. Once single word exchanges have been mastered, sentence structure is targeted. The aim is for the child to combine an "I want" picture with a picture of a desired item or activity. A "sentence strip" is used to attach the pictures and is passed to the communication partner. The sentences are further extended by the addition of other words such as adjectives, for example, "I want the *red* ball." Sentence strips are often color coded, so that, for example, there may be a green area for noun pictures that are framed in green, a blue area for verb pictures framed in blue, and a red area for adjective symbols framed in red, and so on. The next phase of the PECS moves from using the picture exchanges for requesting to encouraging commenting. This is done by introducing picture cards representing phrases such as, "I see," "I smell," and "I hear." Again, research on the efficacy of this stage of the program or its generalization to functional communication has not been reported.

These behaviorist programs that all take the normal sequence of language development as their framework do not specifically address the known deficits specific to ASDs. Few of these programs directly address echolalia and pronoun reversals, prosodic or pragmatic deficits, or even receptive language directly.

Naturalistic Approaches

Techniques that address deficits specific to autism have been discussed in the literature and generally employ a semistructured, naturalistic approach. For example, Manning and Katz (1991) suggested using echolalia to shape spontaneous language use by:

- Accepting echolalia as a legitimate form of communication
- Expanding the child's echolalic utterance to express its underlying communicative intent (A: Do you want a cookie? C: You want cookie. A: Oh, I understand. You can tell me, "I want a cookie.")
- Encouraging mitigated echolalia, then providing a model of a more appropriate response (A: See the puppies on this page? C: Puppies on page. A: Yes, you see them. You can tell me, "I see the puppies!")
- Providing opportunities to produce mitigated echolalia in familiar contexts, with visual cues, such as reading favorite books or reciting rhymes with picture cards (A: 1 little 2 little 3 little puppies. What can you count? Kitties? You do it. C: 1 little 2 little

TABLE 37.4   Sequence of Teaching "Verbal Behavior"

Mands	Echoes	Tacts	Receptive	Intraverbals
With single word	Imitate speech sounds	Names reinforcers	Follows instruction to do a reinforcing activity	Fill in words in songs
With reinforcer present	Imitates words	Names common objects	Follows instruction to look at a reinforcer	Fill in blanks in game activities
With reinforcer not present	Imitates phrases	Names people	Follows instruction to look at a common item	Say animal sounds
Without prompts	Imitates with prosody	Names pictures	Follows instruction to touch a reinforcer	Fill in words in common activities
Mands for action	Imitates with appropriate volume	Names ongoing actions	Follows instruction to touch a common item	Fill in items by feature, function, and class
Mands for missing items	Imitates with appropriate speed	Names with adjectives	Follows instruction to do something reinforcing out of context	Fill in words in stories
Mands with carrier phrases	Imitates novel words and phrases	Names with carrier phrases	Follows routine instructions	State examples of a category
Mands for information with wh-questions		Names body parts	Gives non-reinforcing item when asked	Give category, given members
Mands using adjectives		Names features of objects	Follow instruction to do motor action	Answer wh-questions
Mands using adverbs		Names one item out of an array with a carrier phrase	Selects reinforcing item from array	Name items previously seen
Mands using pronouns		Names item when told function	Selects one of two common items	Maintain conversation with reinforcement
		Names item when told feature	Selects common pictures when named	State activity when given description
		Names item when told category	Touches body parts when named	
		Names function of item	Touches pictures of body parts	
		Names category of item		

Adapted from *Promoting Speech Production Skills in Children with Autism,* by V. Carbone, 2003, Valley Cottage, NY: Carbone Clinic.

3 little kitties. A: Great! Now let's count fishies . . .)

Donnellan, Gossage, LaVigna, Schuler, and Traphagen (1976) suggested volume cueing, in which a whispered question is followed by a loud answer the child is meant to imitate (A: How are you? Say, **"I'm fine, thanks!"**). The student is encouraged to echo the loud portion, and the volume prompts are gradually faded. Carr et al. (1975) suggested teaching students to say "I don't know" rather than echoing to reduce the frequency of echolalia.

Paul (2001) and Fey, Long, and Finestack (2003) have suggested using focused stimulation as a naturalistic means of increasing receptive language skills in children with a variety of disabilities. Focused stimulation involves providing an interesting set of play materials and using simple, repetitive language to talk about the ongoing action in concrete, here-and-now terms, using many examples of forms the child needs to acquire. For example, if a child has difficulty with past tense, the teacher can engage the child in play with a set of toys and contrast present and past tense in the play action:

Barney is pushing the car. He's pushing. I see him pushing. Oh, look! He stopped! He pushed that car far! I watched while he pushed it! He pushed it a long way! Oh, he's pushing again . . . You tell me about it!

It is important to provide this stimulation not only for nouns (labels) but also for verbs (action words) and other kinds of words that talk about location (in, on), description (big, dirty), and greetings (hi, bye-bye). In these activities, the child is not required to imitate the clinician but to listen and interact as he or she gives examples of how to talk about activities. Focused stimulation has been demonstrated to improve language production and understanding in children with specific language disorders (Fey & Proctor-Williams, 2000) but has not been studied in children with autism.

Developmental-Pragmatic Approaches

There are fewer examples of detailed programs that take a more child-centered approach to teaching basic language to children with autism.

Prizant and Wetherby (this *Handbook,* this volume) advocate using the SCERTS model, a comprehensive program that allows the incorporation of an eclectic range of treatment methods and focuses on overarching goals that include improving social communication, encouraging behavioral self-regulation, and providing transactional supports to children with autism. This program has not yet been subjected to empirical study.

Quill (2000) has presented a comprehensive curriculum for developing social and communicative skills in young children with autism at various levels of functioning. The curriculum is also eclectic and advocates the full range of highly structured, naturalistic approaches and child-centered methods. It suggests focusing on the child's responsiveness to typical peers, rather than promoting initiations (p. 89). Intervention guidelines include organization of the environment to facilitate participation and cooperation, careful selection of materials, and activities structured to foster the target child's participation. Activities early in this sequence include:

- Closed-ended activities, such as putting features on a Mr. Potato Head
- A limited set of materials
- Separate materials for each player
- Activities that require no sharing, turn taking, or waiting (e.g., parallel play)

The target child is given coaching and practice in observing, responding to, and imitating the typical play partner in order to progress to activities that are more open-ended, use a wider variety of materials, and involve more interactive play. Coaching of typical peers to use strategies such as nonverbal cues to gain the target child's attention, to wait for a response, and to interpret unusual responses is also a part of this curriculum. Numerous examples of ways to embed these principles in typical preschool classroom activities are provided. As a synthetic, comprehensive curriculum, this program draws on methods from a variety of sources, but it does not provide any independent empirical validation of its efficacy.

Child-centered methods discussed at the prelinguistic level, including More Than Words (Sussman, 1999), "Floor Time" (Greenspan &

Weider, 1999), and RDI (Gutstein & Sheely, 2002), also contain components that can be used at higher language levels.

Increasing Social Communication

Apart from elaborating the form and increasing the frequency of language use, an additional important goal at the level of early language is to provide supports for children to engage in peer interactions, including pretend play, games, and conversations. During the preschool period, between 3 and 5 years of age, typical children develop a range of social interaction skills that are mediated in important ways by their language development. Garvey (1975) showed that children as young as 3 use language to negotiate play roles and activities (e.g., "I'll be the doctor and you can be the sick person"). Children with ASDs are less able to demonstrate these varied uses of language in the context of cooperative play and often show great difficulty in entering sociodramatic play situations without support, even when they do not show significant delays in the acquisition of the forms of language (Schuler & Wolfberg, 2002). For these reasons, social communication programs in the preschool period typically use play as the primary context. Schuler and Wolfberg argue that children with ASDs will require opportunities for *guided participation* in social play. There are two primary means of supplying this guidance: through coaching by adults and through mediation provided by trained peers. Reviews of literature on preschool social communication intervention reveal that children with ASDs do show increases in social play when appropriate supports are provided (Brown & Conroy, 2002; Lord & McGee, 2001; Rogers, 2000). Some of the interventions that have demonstrated effectiveness are reviewed next.

Adult-Mediated Interventions

Early studies in this area focused on teacher-directed interactions, using ABA procedures. Allen, Hart, Buell, Harris, and Wolf (1964) showed that restructuring teachers' reinforcements to socially isolated children, by ignoring their initiations to adults and reinforcing attention to peers, was enough to increase child-to-child interactions. Odom, Chandler,

Ostrosky, McConnell, and Reaney (1992) used teacher prompting without reinforcement to increase social interactions of young children with ASD. Individual coaching using teacher prompts and praise in the context of peer play was also found to increase rates of social initiation by target children, but these bids were responded to only half the time by typical peers (McConnell, Sisson, Cort, & Strain, 1991). Only when peer training was added did rates of successful interaction increase. Drasgow, Halle, Ostrosky, and Habers (1996) suggested that these procedures need to be practiced in all the environments in which generalization is to occur in order for the interactive behaviors to be maintained.

Goldstein, Wickstrom, Hoyson, Jamieson, and Odom (1988) used adults to teach sociodramatic scripts to two trios of preschool children (one target child with ASD and two peers with typical development) within an inclusionary preschool classroom environment. All children were taught each of three social roles (e.g., doctor, nurse, patient) using teacher instruction, which was systematically reduced over time. Results revealed that interaction and generalization improved during free play periods at preschool, but effects depended on the continuation of teacher prompts and did not lead to increases in other social exchanges during the rest of the class day.

Less operant, more developmental-pragmatic approaches to promoting social interaction have also been used. Wolfberg and Schuler (1999) provided an overview of an integrated play group model. Strategies include:

- Scaffolding interactions by acting as an interpreter for the target child and providing appropriate cues to interaction
- Guiding social communication by fostering invitations to play
- Enlisting reluctant peers
- Helping target children respond to peers' cues
- Maintaining and expanding interactions with narrative language
- Guiding play by incorporating the target child's unusual behaviors (e.g., lining up objects) into a meaningful play context (e.g., acting as clerk who neatens up shelves in a play store)

Wolfberg and Schuler (1999) present preliminary results of a case study that argue for the effectiveness of this approach.

Another naturalistic approach to social communicative intervention is referred to under the rubric of "friendship" activities (Brown & Conroy, 2002). These approaches typically rely on teachers' prompting children to compliment and show affection for each other within the naturally occurring routines of the preschool day (unlike the more operant approaches, which employ more structured training in out-of-class environments). McEvoy et al. (1988) report applying these techniques to preschool children with ASDs, with some positive results.

Krantz and McClannahan (1998) used script-fading procedures with preschoolers with minimal reading skills. The children were taught to use the written cues "Look" and "Watch me" to initiate conversation with adults who did not prompt but responded only to conversation directed to them. The scripts were faded by cutting away portions of the cue cards. Unscripted interactions were found to continue and generalize to new topics.

It is important to be aware that most of the studies reported earlier involved single subject or very small group designs and used general outcome measures, such as social initiations, without looking more specifically at the use of particular communication strategies (e.g., pointing, signing, talking). Thus, we have much to learn before we can identify the most efficient teacher-directed approaches for promoting verbal means of social interaction in young children with ASD.

Peer-Mediated Interventions

The drawbacks of adult-mediated play interventions appear to be that target children become dependent on adult input in order to continue interacting. Although some systematic fading procedures have attempted to address this problem (Odom et al., 1992), very highly trained adults are needed to implement them appropriately, and teachers often express reluctance to engage in them (McConnell, McEvoy, & Odom, 1992). Brown and Conroy (2002) point out that teacher-directed interventions may even serve to interrupt direct child-to-child interactions.

For these reasons, recent approaches to enhancing social interactions in this population have turned to peers as primary agents of intervention. Initially, it was hoped that merely placing children with disabilities in classrooms with typical peers would enhance social communication. However, empirical study suggests that this is not likely to be the case. Further, these studies employed children with a range of developmental disabilities and did not focus on the specific difficulties in socialization presented by children with ASDs.

The work of Strain and colleagues represents the most sustained effort to develop successful peer-mediated socialization strategies and provides the strongest empirical support (Odom & Brown, 1993; Odom & Strain, 1986; Odom et al., 1999; Strain, Shores, & Timm, 1977). In their approach, typical peers are taught to present and persevere in presenting "play organizers" to classmates with ASDs. Organizers consist of sharing, helping, giving affection, and praising. Peers are taught these skills in role-playing activities with adults and then are cued and reinforced by the adults in play sessions with target children. Reinforcements are carefully faded. Work by this group (Odom et al., 1999; Strain et al., 1977) as well as in replication studies (Brady, Shores, McEvoy, Ellis, & Fox, 1987; Sainato, Goldstein, & Strain, 1992) has demonstrated both generalization and maintenance. Strain, Kohler, Storey, and Danko (1994) have also shown that self-monitoring techniques can be used so that interactions are successfully maintained without adult reinforcement. The importance of delivering interventions within inclusive preschools rather than in laboratory settings for achieving generalization and maintenance has also been emphasized.

Despite the evidence supporting their success, these programs are difficult and labor-intensive to implement, requiring highly trained peers and precise adult control of the peer training. Although training manuals (Danko, Lawry, & Strain, 1998) and extensive discussions of the method in the research literature are available, teachers outside comprehensive, university- or hospital-based settings often object to implementing them (Odom, McConnell, & Chandler, 1994). Moreover, Strain and Hoyson (2000) have argued that a comprehensive inclusionary program implemented over a sustained period of time during the preschool period is necessary to achieve the levels of success reported in the literature. Thus, even if carefully implemented peer social communicative programs are instituted, they may not achieve maximum effectiveness without the other features offered by comprehensive programs.

As a consequence of these difficulties and limitations, some approaches have attempted to devise simpler forms of peer-mediated intervention. Goldstein and colleagues (English, Goldstein, Shafer, & Kaczmarek, 1997; Goldstein & Wickstrom, 1986) have extended their script-based methods to include peer mediation, for example. Their Buddy Skills Training Program teaches three simple strategies to peer "buddies":

1. STAY with your buddy: Maintain physical proximity to assigned partner.
2. PLAY with your buddy: Maintain proximity while continuing to play with your partner. (In programs specifically adapted for children with ASDs, partners are offered a choice of one activity each from a visual "choice board," then instructed to play with each partner's choice for half the "buddy period" session, usually 10 to 20 minutes.)
3. TALK with your buddy: Say your partner's name to establish joint attention, make suggestions for playing together, talk about the play, respond to what your partner says by repeating, saying more about it, or asking a question.

Research on this program demonstrated improvements in the frequency of social communication between buddies that persisted outside the specific "buddy time" sessions (English et al., 1997). English et al. noted that training the target children in buddy skills did not increase social interactions any further, suggesting that training typical peers is adequate to achieve the observed increases in reciprocity. This program was not developed specifically for children with ASDs, but recent extensions with specific modifications for children with ASDs, such as visual choice boards, have shown promise.

Another attempt at a simplified program is presented by Garfinkle and Schwartz (2002). Three children with ASD were taught to imitate peers during small group activities in an inclusionary preschool classroom. Results suggest that participants increased peer imitation be-

havior in the training setting and generalized them to free play settings, as well. Increases in other social behaviors, such as proximity to peers and number of peer interactions, were also reported to increase.

Conclusions: Early Language Intervention

The most elaborated curricula for developing language at this level are highly behavioral. Although these have some demonstrated efficacy, behavioral programs maintain weaknesses in terms of the development of passive communication styles and failures of generalization. Moreover, most programs aimed at early language development follow the typical developmental sequence and do not directly address the characteristic language difficulties associated with autism, such as echolalia. Developmental approaches for this stage of development have less fully elaborated curricula and limited empirical support.

Beyond acquiring more mature language, children with ASDs also require support for the development of social interactions as part of their communicative intervention program. Several social interaction programs have been presented in the literature, but studies involve very small samples and frequently require high levels of training and time investment. There have been few studies that compare different procedures for enhancing social interaction at this developmental level. Careful comparison studies among social communication training methods for children with ASDs are clearly needed.

CONCLUSION

Intervention for children with ASD at prelinguistic and early language stages has been shown to make a dramatic difference, at least in short-term outcome (Lord & McGee, 2001). Intervention methods that draw from a range of philosophies and make use of varying degrees of adult direction have been shown to be effective in increasing language and communicative behaviors, although direct comparisons among methods, controlled studies with random assignment to treatments, and long-term outcome studies are, as yet, lacking. Despite the gaps in our current knowledge, it is clear that children with autism benefit from intensive, early intervention that focuses on increasing the frequency, form, and function of communication. Available evidence shows that highly structured behavioral methods have important positive consequences for these children, particularly in eliciting first words. However, the limitation of these methods in maintenance and generalization of skills suggests that many children with autism will need to have these methods supplemented with less adult-directed activities to increase communicative initiation and to carry over learned skills to new settings and communication partners. A review of social skills training programs aimed at early communicative development points out the importance of providing opportunities for peer interactions with children who receive special training to include children with ASDs in their play. But the most important message to be taken from this review is that children with autism, whose core deficits involve a failure of communicative development, can learn to express their intentions, feelings, and interests, given appropriate and intensive instruction, practice, and mediated interactive opportunities. Although we may still argue about the most effective and efficient way to accomplish this goal, there can be no legitimate argument about the fact that the communication skills of children with autism can be improved significantly by intensive intervention using a range of methods.

Cross-References

For information on communication development, see Chapters 11 and 12; for additional information on communication intervention, see Chapters 36 and 38; for information on other aspects of development, see Chapters 13, 14, and 15; for information on intervention for other aspects of development, see Chapters 33, 34, and 35.

REFERENCES

Abbeduto, L., Furman, L., & Davies, B. (1989). Relation between receptive language and mental age of persons with mental retardation. *American Journal of Mental Retardation, 93,* 535–543.

Allen, K., Hart, B. M., Buell, J., Harris, F., & Wolf, M. (1964). Effects of social reinforcement on isolate behavior of a nursery school child. *Child Development, 35,* 511–518.

Anderson, S., & Romanczyk, R. G. (1999). Early intervention for young children with autism: Continuum-based behavioral models. *Journal of the Association for Persons with Severe Handicaps, 24,* 162–173.

Anderson, S., Taras, M., & Cannon, B. (1996). Teaching new skills to young children with autism. In C. Maurice (Ed.), *Behavioral intervention for young children with autism* (pp. 181–194). Austin, TX: ProEd.

Autism Treatment Center of America. (2003). *The Son-Rise Program.* Available from www.son-rise.org.

Awad, S., Corliss, M., & Merson, R. (2003). *Prosidy 2.0* [Computer program]. Vero Beach, FL: Speech Bin.

Baltaxe, C. (1977). Pragmatic deficits in the language of autistic adolescents. *Journal of Pediatric Psychology, 2,* 176–180.

Bernard-Opitz, V., Sriran, N., & Sapuan, S. (1999). Enhancing vocal imitations in children with autism using the IBM Speech Viewer. *Autism: International Journal of Research and Practice, 3,* 131–147.

Bondy, A., & Frost, L. (1998). The picture exchange communication system. *Seminars in Speech and Language, 19,* 373–389.

Boucher, J. (1988). Word fluency in high functioning autistic children. *Journal of Autism and Developmental Disorders, 18,* 637–654.

Brady, M., Shores, R., McEvoy, M. A., Ellis, D., & Fox, J. (1987). Increasing social interactions of severely handicapped autistic children. *Journal of Autism and Developmental Disorders, 17,* 375–390.

Brown, W., & Conroy, M. (2002). Promoting peer-related social communicative competence in pre-school children. In H. Goldstein, L. Kaczmarek, & K. English (Eds.), *Promoting social communication* (pp. 173–210). Baltimore: Paul H. Brookes.

Bruner, J. (1974). From communication to language: A psychological perspective. *Cognition, 3,* 255–287.

Buffington, D., Krantz, P., McClannahan, L., & Poulsen, C. (1998). Procedures for teaching appropriate gestural communication skills to children with autism. *Journal of Autism and Developmental Disorders, 26,* 165–167.

Carbone, V. (2003). *Promoting speech production skills in children with autism* [Workshop]. Valley Cottage, NY: Carbone Clinic.

Carr, E. G., Schreibman, L., & Lovaas, O. I. (1975). Control of echolalic speech in psychotic children. *Journal of Abnormal Child Psychology, 3,* 331–351.

Cascella, P. (1999). Communication disorders and children with mental retardation. *Child and Adolescent Psychiatry Clinics of North America, 8,* 61–76.

Charlop, M. H., & Trasowech, J. (1991). Increasing children's daily spontaneous speech. *Journal of Applied Behavior Analysis, 24,* 747–761.

Charlop-Christy, M. H., Carpenter, M., LeBlanc, L., & Kellet, K. (2002). Using the picture exchange communication system (PECS) with children with autism: Assessment of PECS acquisition, speech, social-communication behavior, and problem behavior. *Journal of Applied Behavior Analysis, 35,* 213–231.

Charman, T., Baron-Cohen, S., Swettenham, J., Baird, G., Drew, A., & Cox, A. (2003). Predicting language outcome in infants with autism and pervasive developmental disorder. *International Journal of Language and Communications Disorders, 38,* 265–285.

Charman, T., Drew, A., Baird, C., & Baird, G. (2003). Measuring early language development in preschool children with autism spectrum disorder using the MacArthur Communicative Development Inventory (Infant form). *Journal of Child Language, 30,* 213–236.

Chuba, H., Miles, S., Paul, R., Klin, A., & Volkmar, F. R. (2003). *Assessing pragmatic skills in individuals with autism and related disorders.* Poster presented at the National Convention of the American Speech-Language-Hearing Association, Chicago.

Clements-Baartman, & Girolametto, L. (1995). Facilitating the acquisition of two-word semantic relations by pre-schoolers with Down syndrome: Efficacy of interactive vs. didactic therapy. *Canadian Journal of Speech-Language Pathology, 19,* 103–111.

Coulter, L., & Gallagher, C. (2001). Evaluation of the Hanen Early Childhood Educators Programme. *International Journal of Language and Communication Disorders, 36,* 264–269.

Danko, C. D., Lawry, J., & Strain, P. S. (1998). *Social skills intervention manual packet.* Unpublished manuscript.

Dawson, G., Hill, D., Spence, A., Galpert, L., & Watson, L. (1990). Affective exchanges between young autistic children and their mothers. *Journal of Abnormal Child Psychology, 18,* 335–345.

Dawson, G., Osterling, J. A., Meltzoff, A. N., & Kuhl, P. (2002). Case study of the development of an infant with autism from birth to two years of age. *Journal of Applied Developmental Psychology, 21,* 299–313.

Delprato, D. (2001). Comparison of discrete trial and normalized behavioral language intervention for young children with autism. *Journal of*

Autism and Developmental Disorders, 31, 315–325.

DeMyer, B., Barton, S., DeMyer, W., Norton, J., Allen, J., & Steele, R. (1973). Prognosis in autism: A follow-up study. *Journal of Autism and Childhood Schizophrenia, 3,* 199–246.

Donnellan, A. M., Gossage, L., LaVigna, G. W., Schuler, A., & Traphagen, J. (1976). *Teaching makes a difference: A guide for developing successful classes for autism and other severely handicapped children.* Santa Barbara, CA: Santa Barbara Public Schools.

Drasgow, E., Halle, J., Ostrosky, M., & Habers, H. (1996). Using behavioral indication and functional communication training to establish an initial sign repertoire with a young child with severe disabilities. *Topics in Early Childhood Special Education, 16,* 500–521.

English, K., Goldstein, H., Shafer, K., & Kaczmarek, L. (1997). Promoting interactions among preschoolers with and without disabilities: Effects of a buddy system skills training program. *Exceptional Children, 63,* 229–243.

Fay, W. (1969). On the basis of autistic echolalia. *Journal of Communication Disorders, 2,* 38–47.

Fey, M., Long, S., & Finestack, L. (2003). Ten principles of grammar facilitation for children with specific language impairments. *American Journal of Speech-Language Pathology, 12,* 3–15.

Fey, M., & Proctor-Williams, K. (2000). Elicited imitation, modeling and recasting in grammar intervention for children with specific language impairments. In D. Bishop & L. Leonard (Eds.), *Specific speech and language disorders in children* (pp. 177–194). London: Psychology Press.

Freeman, S. K., & Dake, L. (1997). *Teach Me Language: A language manual for children with autism, Asperger's syndrome and related developmental disorders.* Langley, Canada: SKF Books.

Garfinkle, A. N., & Schwartz, I. S. (2002). Peer imitation: Increasing social interactions in children with autism and other developmental disabilities in inclusive preschool classrooms. *Topics in Early Childhood Special Education, 22,* 26–38.

Garvey, J. (1975). Requests and responses in children's speech. *Journal of Child Language, 2,* 41–63.

Gernsbacher, M. (2002, June). *A case study in autism and apraxia.* Paper presented at the Symposium for Research in Child Language Disorders, Madison, WI.

Gillum, H., Camarata, S., Nelson, K. E., & Camarata, M. N. (2003). A comparison of naturalistic and analog treatment effects in children with expressive language disorder and poor preintervention imitation skills. *Journal of Positive Behavior Interventions, 5,* 171–178.

Girolametto, L. (1988). Improving the social-conversation skills of developmentally delayed children: An intervention study. *Journal of Speech and Hearing Disorders, 53,* 156–167.

Girolametto, L., Greenberg, J., & Manolson, H. (1986). *Developing dialogue skills: The Hanen early language parent program.* New York: Thieme Medical.

Girolametto, L., Pearce, P., & Weitzman, E. (1996). The effects of focused stimulation for promoting vocabulary in young children with delays: A pilot study. *Journal of Children's Communication Development, 17*(2), 39–49.

Goldstein, H. (2002). Communication Intervention for children with autism: A review of treatment efficacy. *Journal of Autism and Developmental Disorders, 32,* 373–396.

Goldstein, H., & Wickstrom, S. (1986). Peer intervention effects on communicative interaction among handicapped and nonhandicapped preschoolers. *Journal of Applied Behavior Analysis, 19,* 209–214.

Goldstein, H., Wickstrom, S., Hoyson, M., Jamieson, B., & Odom, S. L. (1988). Effects of sociodramatic play training on social and communicative interaction. *Education and Treatment of Children, 11,* 97–117.

Greenspan, S., & Weider, S. (1999). A functional developmental approach to autism spectrum disorders. *Journal of the Association for Persons with Severe Handicaps, 24,* 147–161.

Gutstein, S., & Sheely, R. (2002). *Relationship development intervention with children, adolescents, and adults.* London: Jessica Kingsley.

Happé, F. G. E. (1995). Understanding minds and metaphors: Insights from the study of figurative language in autism. *Metaphor and Symbol, 10,* 275–295.

Harris, S. L., Handleman, J. S., Arnold, M., & Gordon, M. (2000). The Douglass Developmental Disabilities Center: Two models of service delivery. In J. Handleman & S. Harris (Eds.), *Preschool education programs for children with autism* (2nd ed., pp. 233–260). Austin, TX: ProEd.

Harris, S. L., Handleman, J. S., Gordon, R., Kristoff, B., & Fuentes, F. (1991). Changes in cognitive and language functioning of preschool children with autism. *Journal of Autism and Developmental Disabilities, 21,* 281–290.

Hart, B. M., & Risley, T. R. (1968). Establishing use of descriptive adjectives in the spontaneous speech of disadvantaged preschool children. *Journal of Applied Behavioral Analysis, 1,* 109–120.

Hart, B. M., & Risley, T. R. (1975). Incidental teaching of language in the preschool. *Journal of Applied Behavior Analysis, 8,* 411–420.

Hayden-Chumpelik, D. (1984). The PROMPT system of therapy: Theoretical framework and applications for developmental apraxia of speech. *Seminars in Speech and Language, 5,* 139–156.

Hewett, F. (1965). Teaching speech to an autistic child through operant conditioning. *American Journal of Orthophsychiatry, 35,* 927–936.

Hwang, B., & Hughes, C. (2000). The effects of social interactive training on early social communicative skills of children with autism. *Journal of Autism and Developmental Disorders, 30*(4), 331–343.

Jensen, V., & Sinclair, L. (2002). Treatment of autism in young children: Behavioral intervention and applied behavior analysis. *Infants and Young Children, 14,* 42–52.

Kaiser, A., Yoder, P. J., & Keetz, A. (1992). Evaluating milieu teaching. In S. Warren & J. Reichle (Eds.), *Causes and effects in communication and language intervention* (pp. 9–47). Baltimore: Paul H. Brookes.

Kanner, L. (1971). Follow-up study of eleven autistic children originally reported in 1943. *Journal of Autism and Childhood Schizophrenia, 1,* 119–145.

Kasari, A., Sigman, M., Mundy, P., & Yirmiya, N. (1990). Affective sharing in the context of joint attention. *Journal of Autism and Developmental Disorders, 20,* 87–100.

Kaufman, B. (1994). *Son-rise: The miracle continues.* Tiburon, CA: H. J. Kramer.

Koegel, L. K. (2000). Interventions to facilitate communication in autism. *Journal of Autism and Developmental Disorders, 30,* 383–391.

Koegel, L. K., Carter, C. M., & Koegel, R. L. (2003). Teaching children with autism self-initiations as a pivotal response. *Topics in Language Disorders, 23,* 134–145.

Koegel, L. K., Koegel, R. L., & Carter, C. M. (1998). Pivotal responses and the natural language teaching paradigm. *Seminars in Speech and Language, 19,* 355–371.

Koegel, L. K., Koegel, R. L., Harrower, J., & Carter, C. M. (1999). Pivotal response intervention: I. Overview of approach. *Journal of the Association for Persons with Severe Handicaps, 24,* 174–186.

Koegel, R. L., Koegel, L. K., & Surratt, A. (1992). Language intervention and disruptive behavior in preschool children with autism. *Journal of Autism and Developmental Disorders, 22,* 141–153.

Koegel, R. L., O'Dell, M., & Koegel, L. K. (1987). A natural language teaching paradigm for nonverbal autistic children. *Journal of Autism and Developmental Disorders, 17,* 187–200.

Krantz, P. J., & McClannahan, L. E. (1998). Social interaction skills for children with autism: A script-fading procedure for beginning readers. *Journal of Applied Behavior Analysis, 31,* 191–202.

Kravits, T., Kamps, D., Kemmerer, K., & Potucek, J. (2002). Brief report: Increasing communication skills for an elementary-aged student with autism using the Picture Exchange Communication System. *Journal of Autism and Developmental Disorders, 32,* 225–230.

Laski, K. E., Charlop, M. H., & Schreibman, L. (1988). Training parents to use the natural language paradigm to increase their autistic children's speech. *Journal of Applied Behavior Analysis, 21,* 391–400.

Lewy, A., & Dawson, G. (1992). Social stimulation and joint attention in young autistic children. *Journal of Abnormal Child Psychology, 20,* 555–566.

Light, J., Roberts, B., DiMarco, R., & Greiner, N. (1998). Augmentative and alternative communication to support receptive and expressive communication for people with autism. *Journal of Communication Disorders, 31,* 153–180.

Lord, C., & McGee, J. (2001). Social development. In C. Lord & J. McGee (Eds.), *Educating children with autism* (pp. 66–81). Washington, DC: National Academy of Sciences.

Lord, C., & Paul, R. (1997). Communication. In D. Cohen & F. Volkmar (Eds.), *Handbook of autism and pervasive developmental disorders* (2nd ed., pp. 195–225). New York: Wiley.

Lovaas, O. I. (1987). Behavioral treatment and normal educational and intellectual functioning in young autistic children. *Journal of Consulting and Clinical Psychology, 55,* 3–9.

Loveland, K. A., & Landry, S. H. (1986). Joint attention and language in autism and developmental language delay. *Journal of Autism and Developmental Disorders, 16,* 335–349.

Manning, A., & Katz, K. (1991). Facilitating functional communication with echolalic language users. *Focus on Autistic Behavior, 6,* 1–7.

Matson, J., Sevin, J., Box, M., Francis, K., & Sevin, B. (1993). An evaluation of two methods for increasing self-initiated verbalization in autistic children. *Journal of Applied Behavior Analysis, 26,* 389–398.

McConnell, S., McEvoy, M. A., & Odom, S. L. (1992). Implementation of social competence interventions in early childhood special education classes: Current practices and future directions. In S. Odom, S. McConnell, & M. McEvoy (Eds.), *Social competence of young children with disabilities: Issues and strategies for intervention* (pp. 277–306). Baltimore: Paul H. Brookes.

McConnell, S., Sisson, L., Cort, C., & Strain, P. S. (1991). Effects of social skills training and contingency management on reciprocal interaction of preschool children with behavioral handicaps. *Journal of Special Education, 24,* 473–495.

McEvoy, M. A., Nordquist, V., Twardosz, S., Heckaman, K., Wehby, J., & Denny, R. (1988). Promoting autistic children's peer interaction in an integrated early childhood setting using affection activities. *Journal of Applied Behavior Analysis, 21,* 193–200.

McGee, G. G., Krantz, P. J., Mason, D., & McClannahan, L. E. (1983). A modified incidental teaching procedure for autistic youth: Acquisition and generalization of receptive object labels. *Journal of Applied Behavior Analysis, 16,* 329–338.

McGee, G. G., Krantz, P. J., Sulzer-Azaroll, B., & Feldman, R. S. (1992). Promoting reciprocal interactions via peer incidental teaching. *Journal of Applied Behavior Analysis, 25,* 117–126.

McGee, G. G., Morrier, M. J., & Daly, T. (1999). An incidental teaching approach to early intervention for toddlers with autism. *Journal of the Association for Persons with Severe Handicaps, 24,* 133–146.

McHale, S. M., Simeonsson, R. J., Marcus, L., & Olley, G. (1980). The social and symbolic quality of autistic children's communication. *Journal of Autism and Developmental Disorders, 10,* 299–310.

Mirenda, P., & Santogrossi, J. (1985). A prompt-free strategy to teach pictorial communication system use. *Augmentative and Alternative Communication, 1,* 143–150.

Mundy, P. (2003). The neural basis of social impairments in autism: The role of the dorsal medial-frontal cortex and anterior cingulated system. *Journal of Psychology and Psychiatry, 47,* 793–809.

Mundy, P., Sigman, M., & Kasari, C. (1990). A longitudinal study of joint attention and language development in autistic children. *Journal of Autism and Developmental Disorders, 20,* 115–128.

Mundy, P., & Stella, J. (2000). Joint attention, social orienting, and nonverbal communications in autism. In B. Prizant & A. Wetherby (Eds.), *Autism spectrum disorders: A transactional developmental perspective* (pp. 55–78). Baltimore: Paul H. Brookes.

Odom, S. L., & Brown, W. (1993). Social interaction skills interventions for young children with disabilities in integrated settings. In C. Peck, S. Odom, & D. Bricker (Eds.), *Integrating young children with disabilities into community programs: Ecological perspectives on research and implementation* (pp. 39–64). Baltimore: Paul H. Brookes.

Odom, S. L., Chandler, L., Ostrosky, M., McConnell, S., & Reaney, S. (1992). Fading teacher prompts from peer-initiation interventions for young children with disabilities. *Journal of Applied Behavior Analysis, 25,* 307–317.

Odom, S. L., McConnell, S., & Chandler, L. (1994). Acceptability and feasibility of classroom-based social interaction interventions for young children with disabilities. *Exceptional Children, 60,* 226–236.

Odom, S. L., McConnell, S., McEvoy, M. A., Peterson, C., Ostrosky, M., Chandler, L., et al. (1999). Relative effects of interventions for supporting the social competence of young children with disabilities. *Topics in Early Childhood Special Education, 19,* 75–92.

Odom, S. L., & Strain, P. S. (1986). A comparison of peer initiation and teacher antecedent interventions for promoting reciprocal social interaction of autistic preschoolers. *Journal of Applied Behavior Analysis, 19,* 59–72.

Osterling, J. A., & Dawson, G. (1994). Early recognition of children with autism: A study of first birthday home videotapes. *Journal of Autism and Developmental Disorders, 24,* 247–257.

Partington, J., Sundberg, M., Newhouse, L., & Spengler-Schelley, M. (1994). Overcoming an autistic child's failure to acquire a tact repertoire. *Journal of Applied Behavior Analysis, 27,* 733–734.

Paul, R. (2001). *Language disorders from infancy through adolescence: Assessment and intervention* (2nd ed.). St. Louis, MO: Mosby.

Paul, R., Chawarska, K., Klin, A., & Volkmar, F. R. (2004). *Profiles of communication in toddlers with autism spectrum disorder.* Invited presentation at the American Psychological Association, Honolulu, HI.

Paul, R., & Cohen, D. J. (1984). Outcomes of severe disorders of language acquisition. *Journal of Autism and Developmental Disorders, 14,* 405–479.

Paul, R., & Jennings, P. (1992). Phonological behavior in toddlers with slow expressive language development. *Journal of Speech and Hearing Research, 35,* 99–107.

Paul, R., Shriberg, L., McSweeney, J. L., Klin, A., & Volkmar, F. R. (in press). Patterns of prosody and social communicative skills in high functioning autism and AS. *Journal of Autism and Developmental Disorders, 34.*

Pierce, K., & Schreibman, L. (1995). Increasing complex social behaviors in children with autism: Effects of peer-implemented pivotal response training. *Journal of Applied Behavior Analysis, 28,* 285–295.

Potter, C. A., & Whittaker, C. A. (2001). *Communication enabling environments for children with autism.* London: Jessica Kingsley.

Prizant, B. M., & Duchan, J. (1981). The functions of immediate echolalia in autistic children. *Journal of Speech and Hearing Disorders, 46,* 241–249.

Prizant, B. M., Schuler, A., Wetherby, A. M., & Rydell, P. J. (1997). Enhancing language and communication development: Language approaches. In D. Cohen & F. Volkmar (Eds.), *Handbook of autism and pervasive developmental disorders* (pp. 572–605). New York: Wiley.

Quill, K. (2000). *Do watch listen say: Social and communication intervention.* Baltimore: Paul H. Brookes.

Ray, B., & Baker, B. (2000). *Hypernasality modification program.* Austin, TX: ProEd.

Rogers, S. (2000). Interventions that facilitate socialization in children with autism. *Journal of Autism and Developmental Disorders, 30,* 399–409.

Rogers, S. (in press). Evidence-based intervention for language development in young children with autism. In T. Charman & W. Stone (Eds.), *Efficacy of intervention for autism.*

Rogers, S., Hall, T., Osaki, D., Reaven, J., & Herbison, J. (2000). A comprehensive integrated, educational approach to young children with autism and their families. In S. L. Harris & J. S. Handleman (Eds.), *Preschool education programs for children with autism* (2nd ed., pp. 203–234). Austin, TX: ProEd.

Rogers-Warren, A., & Warren, S. (1980). Mand for verbalization: Facilitating the generalization of newly trained language in children. *Behavior Modification, 4,* 230–245.

Romski, M., & Sevcik, R. (1996). *Breaking the speech barrier: Language development through augmented means.* Baltimore: Paul H. Brookes.

Ross, D., & Greer, R. (2003). Generalized imitation and the mand: Inducing first instance of speech in young children with autism. *Research in Developmental Disabilities, 24,* 58–74.

Rutter, M. L., & Lockyer, L. (1967). A five to fifteen year follow-up study of infantile psychosis: 1. Description of the sample. *British Journal of Psychiatry, 113,* 1169–1182.

Rutter, M. L., Mawhood, L. M., & Howlin, P. (1992). Language delay and social development. In P. Fletcher & D. Hall (Eds.), *Specific speech and language disorders in children: Correlates, characteristics and outcomes* (pp. 63–78). London: Whurr.

Sainato, D., Goldstein, H., & Strain, P. S. (1992). Effects of self-evaluation on preschool children's use of social interaction strategies with their classmates with autism. *Journal of Applied Behavior Analysis, 25,* 127–142.

Schepis, M., Reid, D., Behrmann, M., & Sutton, K. (1998). Increasing communicative interactions of young children with autism using a voice output communication aid and naturalistic teaching. *Journal of Applied Behaviour Analysis, 31,* 561–578.

Schopler, E., & Olley, G. (1982). Comprehensive educational services for autistic children. In C. Reynolds & T. Gutkin (Eds.), *Handbook of school psychology* (pp. 484–498). New York: Wiley.

Schuler, A., & Wolfberg, P. (2002). Promoting peer play and socialization. In A. Wetherby & B. Prizant (Eds.), *Autism spectrum disorders: A developmental perspective* (pp. 251–278). Baltimore: Paul H. Brookes.

Seal, B., & Bonvillian, J. (1997). Sign language and motor functioning in students with autistic disorder. *Journal of Autism and Developmental Disorders, 27,* 437–466.

Sheinkopf, S., Mundy, P., Oller, K., & Steffens, M. (2000). Vocal atypicalities of preverbal autistic children. *Journal of Autism and Developmental Disorders, 30,* 345–354.

Sheinkopf, S., & Siegel, B. (1998). Home-based behavioral treatment of young children with autism. *Journal of Autism and Developmental Disabilities, 28,* 15–23.

Shriberg, L., Paul, R., McSweeney, J. L., Klin, A., Cohen, D. J., & Volkmar, F. R. (2001). Speech and prosody characteristics of adolescents and adults with high functioning autism and Asperger syndrome. *Journal of Speech, Language and Hearing Research, 44,* 1097–1115.

Sigman, M., & Ruskin, E. (1999). Continuity and change in social competence of children with autism, Down syndrome and developmental delays. *Monographs of the Society for Research in Child Development, 64,* V-114.

Simmons, J., & Baltaxe, C. (1975). Language patterns in adolescent autistics. *Journal of Autism and Childhood Schizophrenia, 5,* 333–351.

Smith, T. (2001). Discrete trial training in the treatment of autism. *Focus on Autism and Other Developmental Disabilities, 16,* 86–92.

Smith, T., Donahue, P., & Davis, B. (2000). The UCLA Young Autism Project. In J. Handleman & S. Harris (Eds.), *Preschool education programs for children with autism* (2nd ed., pp. 29–48). Austin, TX: ProEd.

Smith, T., Groen, A., & Wynn, J. (2000). Randomized trial of intensive early intervention for children with pervasive developmental disorder. *American Journal of Mental Retardation, 105,* 269–285.

Square-Storer, P., & Hayden, D. (1989). PROMPT Treatment. In P. Square-Storer (Ed.), *Acquired apraxia of speech in aphasic adults: Theoretical and clinical issues* (pp. 190–219). Hillsdale, NJ: Erlbaum.

Stoel-Gammon, C. (1991). Normal and disordered phonology in two-year-olds. *Topics in Language Disorders, 141*(4), 21–32.

Stokes, R., & Baer, D. (1977). An implicit technology of generalization. *Journal of Applied Behavioral Analysis, 10,* 349–367.

Stone, W. L., & Caro-Martinez, L. (1990). Naturalistic observations of spontaneous communication in autistic children. *Journal of Autism and Developmental Disorders, 20,* 437–453.

Stone, W. L., Ousley, O. Y., Yoder, P. J., Hogan, K. L., & Hepburn, S. L. (1997). Nonverbal communication in 2- and 3-year-old children with autism. *Journal of Autism and Developmental Disorders, 27*(6), 677–696.

Strain, P., McGee, G., & Kohler, R. (2001). Inclusion of children with autism in early intervention environments. In M. Guralnick (Ed.), *Early childhood inclusion: Focus on change* (pp. 337–363). Baltimore: Paul H. Brookes.

Strain, P. S., & Hoyson, M. (2000). The need for longitudinal, intensive social skills intervention: LEAP follow-up outcomes for children with autism. *Topics in Early Childhood Special Education, 20,* 116–122.

Strain, P. S., Kohler, F. W., Storey, K., & Danko, C. D. (1994). Teaching preschoolers with autism to self-monitor their social interactions: An analysis of results in home and school settings. *Journal of Emotional and Behavioral Disorders, 2,* 78–88.

Strain, P. S., Shores, R., & Timm, M. (1977). Effects of peer social initiations on the behavior of withdrawn preschool children. *Journal of Applied Behavior Analysis, 10,* 289–298.

Sundberg, M., & Michael, J. (2001). The benefits of Skinner's analysis of verbal behavior for children with autism. *Behavior Modification, 25,* 698–724.

Sundberg, M., Michael, J., Partington, J., & Sundberg, C. (1995). The role of automatic reinforcement in early language acquisition. *Analysis of Verbal Behavior, 13,* 21–37.

Sussman, F. (1999). *More than words.* Toronto, Ontario, Canada: The Hanen Centre.

Tager-Flusberg, H. (1985). The conceptual basis for referential word meaning in children with autism. *Child Development, 56,* 1167–1178.

Tager-Flusberg, H. (1995). Dissociations in form and function in the language acquisition by children with autism. In H. Tager-Flusberg (Ed.), *Constraints on language acquisitions: Studies of atypical children* (pp. 175–194). Hillside, NJ: Erlbaum.

Tager-Flusberg, H., Calkins, S., Nolin, T., Baumberger, T., Anderson, M., & Chadwick-Dias, A. (1990). A longitudinal study of language acquisition in autistic and Down syndrome children. *Journal of Autism and Developmental Disorders, 20,* 1–21.

Travis, L., & Sigman, M. (2001). Communicative intentions and symbols in autism. In J. Burak, T. Charman, N. Yirmiya, & P. Zelazo (Eds.), *The development of autism.* Mahwah, NJ: Erlbaum.

Tsiouri, I., & Greer, R. D. (2003). Inducing vocal verbal behavior in children with severe language delays through rapid motor imitation responding. *Journal of Behavioral Education, 12,* 185–206.

Volden, J., & Lord, C. (1991). Neologisms and idiosyncratic language in autistic speakers. *Journal of Autism and Developmental Disorders, 21,* 109–130.

Wetherby, A. M., Prizant, B. M., & Hutchinson, T. (1998). Communicative, social-affective, and symbolic profiles of young children with autism and pervasive developmental disorder. *American Journal of Speech-Language Pathology, 7,* 79–91.

Wetherby, A. M., & Prutting, C. (1984). Profiles of communicative and cognitive-social abilities in autistic children. *Journal of Speech and Hearing Research, 27,* 364–377.

Wolf, M., Risley, T. R., & Mees, H. (1964). Application of operant conditioning procedures to the behaviour problems of an autistic child. *Behavior Research and Therapy, 1,* 305–312.

Wolfberg, P., & Schuler, A. (1999). Fostering peer interaction, imaginative play and spontaneous language in children with autism. *Child Language Teaching and Therapy, 15,* 41–52.

Yoder, P. J., & Layton, T. (1988). Speech following sign language training in autistic children with minimal verbal language. *Journal of Autism and Developmental Disorders, 18,* 217–229.

CHAPTER 38

Addressing Social Communication Skills in Individuals with High-Functioning Autism and Asperger Syndrome: Critical Priorities in Educational Programming

WENDY D. MARANS, EMILY RUBIN, AND AMY LAURENT

Social communication skills, or the lack thereof, play a major role in our success or inability to form social relationships that enable us to function happily and effectively in the communities and cultures within which we live. Our ability to engage reciprocally, to appreciate the communicative intent of others and to convey our own, to establish and maintain joint attention, and to appreciate another's perspective or point of view is essential to learning and to forming friendships. The capacity to appreciate nuances of mood, to empathize, and to understand the complexities of pretense, imagination, humor, sarcasm, irony, and other implicit messages contributes to the richness of our lives and of those around us with whom we have relationships.

For most of us, the underlying appreciation of social communicative behavior and use of skills permitting such complex interactions were never taught directly. Rather, our innate social interest in others and our ability to appreciate the complex verbal, nonverbal, and environmental cues that convey this social information permit us to form hypotheses, make inferences, adjust our impressions and actions accordingly, and reach a level of social sophistication that should not be underestimated (Nelson, 1985). It is only when we are faced with breakdowns in social behavior or with individuals for whom this social understanding does not come naturally that the complexities of social capacities and the difficulties of teaching them explicitly become apparent.

The pronounced social communication disability in individuals with high-functioning autism (HFA) and Asperger syndrome (AS) is often masked by relatively sophisticated linguistic abilities (i.e., the ability to produce novel and creative verbal utterances) and, in some cases, the presence of exceptional cognitive abilities such as a mechanical talent or a specialized knowledge about an academic subject area (Koenig, Rubin, Klin, & Volkmar, 2000). These areas of relative strength, however, stand in stark contrast to the inability to engage in mutually satisfying social interactions. Clearly, there is great heterogeneity among typically developing children, adolescents, and even adults with respect to their level of social competence in any given setting. For individuals with HFA and AS, however, learning style differences and developmental vulnerabilities remain significant challenges across all settings of their life and provide devastating barriers to achieving social communicative competence (Volkmar, Klin, Schultz, Rubin, & Bronen, 2000).

It is now well documented that positive long-term outcomes for individuals with HFA and AS are strongly correlated with the achievement of social communicative competence

(Garfin & Lord, 1986; Koegel, Koegel, Yoshen, & McNerney, 1999; National Research Council [NRC], 2001; Venter, Lord, & Schopler, 1992). Specific knowledge of the obstacles to achieving this long-term goal is essential, as individuals with these social disabilities will clearly benefit from opportunities to acquire strategies to engage in positive and successful experiences with a range of social partners and across a range of social settings. For example, we know that individuals who display a greater capacity to establish and follow the attentional and conversational focus of their communicative partners are more likely to initiate socially appropriate bids for interaction, follow turns and topics in conversation, use more sophisticated nonverbal gestures and symbolic language, and recognize and repair communicative breakdowns (Carpenter & Tomasello, 2000; Wetherby, Prizant, & Hutchinson, 1998). We also know that, by their very nature, social communication disabilities are transactional, and, thus, direct instruction with the individual does not necessarily ensure success across all social partners. Those who interact with the individual must learn to accommodate and modify their interactive style to facilitate success. As a result, to achieve positive long-term outcomes, effective programs must include learning supports and accommodations not only for the individual with the disability but also for all the social partners and settings within an individual's community (e.g., family members at home, peers and teachers at school, colleagues at work, and individuals within community settings; NRC, 2001; Prizant, Wetherby, Rubin, Laurent, in press).

Last, we know that challenges in social communication are part of a larger picture of developmental strengths and vulnerabilities (Prizant, Wetherby, & Rydell, 2000). In particular, we are concerned with an individual's ability to use language and information gained through social interactions for the purposes of self-monitoring his or her physiological arousal and emotional state. This capacity, otherwise referred to as *emotional regulation,* enables an individual to be organized and focused, to problem solve, to communicate, and to maintain social engagement (Bolick, 2001; Prizant, Wetherby, Rubin, & Laurent, 2001). Because individuals with HFA and AS are particularly challenged with interpreting the emotional states of others as well as appreciating and expressing their own, these factors further compromise their social communicative competence and can limit availability for learning and social engagement across contexts. Thus, this chapter provides an outline of: (1) our current understanding of the core challenges facing individuals with HFA and AS that compromise their social communicative competence, (2) the unique learning style differences often associated with HFA and AS, (3) implications for intervention and educational programming, and (4) critical priorities for developing a comprehensive intervention program designed to foster social communicative competence.

CORE CHALLENGES IN SOCIAL COMMUNICATION

Social communication is broadly defined as those competencies that contribute to an individual's ability to effectively communicate in social contexts. Although there is great heterogeneity in the social communicative profiles of individuals with HFA and AS, there is also a common pattern of impairments. Contemporary research has, in fact, identified that developmental vulnerabilities tend to fall into two primary areas: the capacity for joint attention and the capacity for symbol use (NRC, 2001; Prizant et al., 2000). The capacity for joint attention is central to the qualitative impairments in reciprocal social interaction, the most profound in its impact over time of the triad of diagnostic features used to define pervasive developmental disorders (PDDs) in the *DSM-IV* (American Psychiatric Association, 1994). Regardless of an individual's level of functioning or developmental stage, the capacity for joint attention allows an individual to orient and, likewise, attend to a social partner, to both read and share affective states, and to establish and follow another's attentional focus when sharing experiences in reciprocal conversation (Carpenter & Tomasello, 2000). An individual not only needs to acquire a range of grammatical forms, syntax, and vocabulary, but he or she also needs to develop a greater awareness of a social partner's perspective. For example, a child may have a great deal of language to communicate about a preferred topic, such as the makes and models of race cars, but may have difficulty determining whether the listener is paying attention to the conversation, interested in the topic, and/or has enough information to follow his or her ideas. These joint attention skills are essential for social problem solving and social judgment, which become areas of particular concern, especially during the preteen and adolescent years when the complexities of the social milieu are compounded by hormonal changes associated with puberty (Tantum, 2000). Table 38.1 lists those abilities that are compromised by having difficulties with joint attention (Prizant, Schuler, Wetherby, & Rydell, 1997; Prizant et al., in press; Volkmar et al., 2000).

The second diagnostic criterion in the *DSM-IV*, qualitative impairments in communication (American Psychiatric Association, 1994), otherwise referred to as the capacity for symbol use, also has a deleterious impact on an individual's drive toward social communicative competence. For individuals with HFA and AS, the relatively intact structural language skills and sometimes advanced vocabulary, reading decoding, or subject knowledge often masks the degree of difficulty experienced in semantics and higher level, nonliteral language use and connected discourse. Individuals with these social disabilities may fail to get "the gist" or "read between the lines." Thus, assimilating and accommodating new information, making connections to other knowledge, and integrating these in ways that provide them with a coherent sense of the world can be challenging (Landa, 2000). Additionally, the capacity for symbol use reflects an individual's ability to understand and adhere to the social "rules" of pragmatic discourse, which vary depending on the social context and the accepted standards of a social group, that is, "rules" that are, in a sense, symbolic expectations for conversational form. Through social experience and symbolic understanding, individuals typically learn to adapt their strategies for initiating, maintaining, and terminating conversation depending on the social setting (e.g., a friendly discussion at a picnic versus a formal debate in an academic course), the status of their social partner (e.g., a friend versus a teacher or a coworker versus an employer), or the purpose that they are trying to fulfill (e.g., persuade, humor, or impress). At more sophisticated levels, changes are also made in response to the cultural background of a social partner because conventions for conversational discourse vary greatly from one culture to the next (Carpenter & Tomasello, 2000) and because of other more subtle social parameters.

For individuals with HFA and AS, these variations in symbolic conventions across social partners and settings can be incomprehensible.

TABLE 38.1   Core Social Communication Challenges in HFA and AS

The Capacity for Joint Attention	The Capacity for Symbol Use
Understanding the communicative intentions and emotional state of a social partner	Acquiring higher-level linguistic rules, grammar and syntax, that clarify one's intent (e.g., subordinate clauses and conjunctions) across social partners and environments
Interpreting and using nonverbal communicative signals (e.g., facial expressions, prosody, body orientation and proximity, and gestures) as they relate to one's attentional focus, affective state, and intentions	Understanding and using verbal conventions for initiating, exchanging turns, and terminating interactions across different social partners and social situations (e.g., rules of politeness)
Considering appropriate topics of conversation, maintaining information, sharing across turns, and repairing communicative breakdowns based on the social context and a listener's perspective	Interpreting and using language in a flexible manner by responding to language that may contain: multiple meaning words, non-literal language, and irony
Modifying interpretation of more ambiguous language forms (e.g., sarcasm, humor, figurative expressions, etc.) depending upon the intentions or perspective of one's social partner	Using language as a tool for emotional regulation (e.g., preparing for changes in routine, preparing for the expectations of different social contexts, and using appropriate means to request assistance and comfort across social settings and social partners)

This pattern is largely due to concurrent vulnerabilities in the capacity for joint attention, as an individual needs to consider another's perspective to gauge the stigmatizing impact of unconventional social communicative behavior. As a result, it is not uncommon for an adherence to a more specific and unchanging set of "rules" of social discourse to develop over time (Klin & Volkmar, 1997). This extreme literalness or rigidity, as some would call it, is a common profile resulting from symbolic impairments in individuals with social learning disabilities. Table 32.1 presents those abilities typically impacted by challenges in the capacity for symbol use in individuals with HFA and AS (Attwood, 1998; Prizant et al., 1997, in press).

Specific deficits in the developmental capacities for joint attention and symbol use in individuals with HFA and AS do not remain stable throughout development. Rather, challenges in these capacities "may take different forms as a function of ongoing development" as well as a function of the negative impact that a social disability may have within that individual's social network (Schuler, 1995, p. 21). Since social interaction always involves others to some degree, secondary effects arise as a result of the atypical social communicative profile of the affected individuals. Potential social partners often perceive the unusual and/or lack of social overtures of individuals with HFA and AS as deviant or odd. Partners may avoid opportunities for interaction and/or react in a negative way (e.g., bullying and teasing). In some instances, these factors can hasten the development of social isolation (Schuler, 1995; Schuler & Wolfberg, 2000). Other children, adolescents, or adults may interpret limited initiations, responsiveness, or persistence as signs of a lack of interest or, worse, unfriendliness. They may see unusual and idiosyncratic communication styles and social bids as off-putting or "uncool," and they may react negatively to maladaptive behavioral outbursts, failing to appreciate their peers' inability to cope and express intentions or feelings in more socially appropriate ways. As a result, the very individuals who need the most practice with social interaction and communication often have fewer opportunities to do so (Lord, 1984). Thus, it is evident that individuals need to not only demonstrate developmental capacities in joint attention and symbol use to achieve social competence but also actively engage in social experiences across a range of social settings and social partners if they are to develop these skills. It is these social experiences as well as developmental capacities that facilitate an ability to interpret another's perspective and modify the individual's use and interpretation of language accordingly, taking into account the social context, critical factors in the achievement of social communicative competence.

CORE CHALLENGES IN EMOTIONAL REGULATION

Competencies in joint attention and symbol use are not the only prerequisites for the achievement of social communicative competence. Being able to attend to the most relevant information in a social setting, to problem solve, and to process information (both verbal and nonverbal) also rely on an individual's ability to maintain a state of active engagement, that is, an optimal state of arousal (Anzalone & Williamson, 2000; Degangi, 2000; Williams & Shellenberger, 1996). These abilities are reliant on an individual's capacity for emotional regulation, a developmental process that supports the attainment and maintenance of a steady internal state and facilitates adaptive functioning and active engagement across contexts (Wetherby, Prizant, & Schuler, 2000). Emotional regulation is believed to be critical for the development of socioemotional and communicative skills as well as for the development of relationships (Prizant & Meyer, 1993; Stern, 1985). This is due, in part, to the fact that emotions "emerge from and provide the foundation of human attachment and social communication" (NRC, 2000, p. 107). Emotional regulation is not synonymous with the suppression of emotion. Rather, it involves experiencing and utilizing all emotions effectively and fluidly in transactions with social partners while playing, while learning, and while in the pursuit of social goals with respect to situational demands (NRC, 2000). If an individual is able to regulate his or her emotions in an efficient manner, he or she is better able to interact with a variety of social partners in a variety of social contexts. In contrast, if individuals are not efficient in managing their emotions, they are prone to emotional overreaction, inattention, and avoidance of social interactions (Prizant et al., in press). Difficulty in regulating emotions can lead to an individual's experiencing a heightened emotional state, which can undermine the development and mastery of new skills as well as the application of previously mastered skills (Bolick, 2001; Prizant & Meyer, 1993). This is particularly true for the development of social communication because the capacity for joint attention and the capacity for symbol use are contingent on attention, memory, and executive functioning, all of which are widely regarded as products of efficient regulatory skills and the resulting ability to maintain a state of optimal arousal (Lyon, 1996; NRC, 2000).

Since individuals with HFA and AS find identifying and interpreting emotional states (both internal and external) particularly challenging, their ability to engage in emotional regulation across contexts is often vulnerable. These emotional regulatory challenges manifest themselves in a variety of ways, ranging from difficulties maintaining social engagement and sustaining focused attention, to challenges with recognizing and interpreting their own and others' physiological and emotional states (Attwood, 1998). The underlying factors contributing to these regulatory difficulties are varied and are the subject of ongoing debate in the literature. However, factors that are generally recognized include challenges

in social communication (i.e., difficulties with joint attention and understanding symbolic conventions; Wetherby et al., 2000), neurophysiological factors (e.g., sensory sensitivities, difficulty differentiating relevant stimuli in the environment from extraneous stimulation; Anzalone & Williamson, 2000; Asperger, 1944; Kientz & Dunn, 1997; Ornitz, 1989), and differences in the acquisition of motor skills (e.g., motor clumsiness and difficulties with visual-spatial perception; Anzalone & Williamson, 2000; Attwood, 1998).

Tronick (1989) differentiates emotional regulatory capacities into self-regulation skills and mutual regulation skills. Self-regulatory skills are regarded as strategies that are self-initiated and self-directed for the purpose of managing an individual's own arousal, emotions, behavior, and attention. Mutual regulatory skills are defined as strategies used to secure assistance from another as well as the ability to respond to assistance provided in an effort to maintain a well-regulated state. Both of these capacities are often significantly compromised in individuals with HFA and AS. Table 38.2 lists areas that are compromised because of difficulties with self- and mutual regulation.

As noted previously, these vulnerabilities are related, in part, to core challenges in communicating with and relating to others. Compromised abilities in the areas of joint attention (e.g., difficulty appreciating and sharing both emotional states and intentions) and symbol

TABLE 38.2   Core Emotional Regulation Challenges in HFA and AS

Mutual Regulation	Self Regulation
Understanding and interpreting the emotional state of self and others	Recognizing and interpreting one's own physiological and emotional state
Interpreting affective cues (e.g., facial expressions and gestures) as they relate to the intentions of social partners	Emotional reactivity and variable arousal state due to physiological factors (e.g., sensory sensitivity)
Expressing emotions in a socially conventional manner as a means to request assistance from others	Attending to relevant information in a social setting in order to problem solve, focus, and process information
Responding to assistance offered by others secondary to difficulties processing the verbal and/or nonverbal social cues of social partners	Grading reactions to coincide with the expectations of the current social situation
Maintaining social engagement and focused attention due to variability in arousal states	Ability to use effective behavioral strategies (e.g., sensory-motor regulatory strategies) that are deemed socially acceptable
	Ability to use cognitive strategies, such as "inner language" to anticipate and cope with potentially dysregulating events

use (e.g., difficulty understanding and expressing emotions in a socially conventional manner) impact the process of mutual regulation, making it difficult for an individual to solicit assistance from others and compromising the ability to utilize and interpret nonverbal communication (Volkmar et al., 2000). Often, these social communicative challenges, in conjunction with variable arousal states, interfere with the individual's ability to attend to social conventions and to benefit from inherent opportunities for learning within social interactions. In turn, these difficulties also negatively impact the ability to develop appropriate expressions of emotional states (Prizant et al., in press). Therefore, individuals with HFA and AS often lack both range and refinement of expression and typically exhibit an all-or-nothing reaction when displaying emotions (Attwood, 1998; McAfee, 2002).

Difficulties establishing shared attention with a social partner and communicating in a socially conventional manner further compromise the development of self-regulation and self-control in individuals with HFA and AS. These capacities are typically achieved through a process of socialization, in combination with biological predispositions. The emergence, and later mastery, of these skills is closely tied to adaptive functioning and social communicative competence (Degangi, 2000; NRC, 2000). Self-regulatory abilities that are typically evident in early development involve behavioral strategies (e.g., sensory-motor means) of regulating arousal level and emotions (e.g., seeking out comforting objects and modifying activity level) and are often elicited in response to state changes (e.g., hunger, fatigue, heightened emotions). As individuals continue to develop and their executive functioning capacities emerge, they begin to use their language and cognitive skills to assist with regulation of emotional and behavioral reactions, adding to those sensory-motor means previously acquired. Early capacities in this area include the ability to use "inner language" for self-regulation (Vygotsky, 1978), understanding of activity schedules, and the employment of avoidance strategies. This internal linguistic shift occurs with the developmental transition to symbolic communication, as inner language reflects an ability to represent events in memory and to problem solve through inner symbolic means. Inner language serves to organize social experience and behaviors, allowing the individual to think about and learn from past social events and plan for future social events. These abilities facilitate an individual's capacity to attend to social and environmental stimuli, plan a response, and anticipate social consequences. With limited ability to use inner language for these cognitive functions, it is less possible to plan for dysregulating events or to reflect on past experience in a manner that supports active engagement and emotional regulation across activities. These difficulties play a significant role in the presence of unpredictable reactions to daily social events often exhibited by individuals with HFA and AS.

Social communicative challenges also compromise the ability of individuals with HFA and AS to understand emotional concepts, particularly those that rely heavily on social norms or conventions (e.g., guilt, embarrassment, pride). An individual's ability to interact in a reciprocal manner with others is critical for developing the concept of emotional identification. It is through interactions with their social partners that individuals learn to "map" emotional words and concepts onto their own visceral states and experiences and, therefore, derive emotional meaning and affective concept development (NRC, 2000; Prizant & Meyer, 1993). For individuals with HFA and AS, difficulty attending to and deriving meaning from these interactions translates into difficulties understanding those emotions that reflect aspects of social relationships and complex interpersonal experiences. To understand "embarrassment," for example, an individual must develop a sense of self-consciousness by obtaining and using feedback in social contexts. Because individuals with HFA and AS have difficulty with these emotional concepts, their ability to anticipate and interpret the emotional reactions of others is compromised; thus, their acquisition of skills essential for the development of self-control and other sophisticated regulatory abilities is hindered (NRC, 2000). An individual may, for example, exhibit a limited ability to modify bids for communication to match the emotional states of communicative partners. When this concept of emotional reciprocity and viewing others' emotional states as different from, but related to, the individual's own is compromised, the individual often has difficulty with social interactions and tends to dominate conversations without regard for social partners' feelings, preferences, or opinions (Prizant et al., in press). These affective difficulties contribute, in part, to the ongoing challenges in forming peer relationships experienced by individuals with HFA and AS.

In addition to social communicative difficulties, neurophysiological factors complicate the process of maintaining a well-regulated state for individuals with HFA and AS. References to sensory sensitivity (e.g., hyperresponsivity to environmental stimulation) and resulting fluctuations in arousal level and physiological state are prevalent in the literature (Anzalone & Williamson, 2000; Attwood, 1998; Kientz & Dunn, 1997). Asperger (1944) himself described the individuals profiled in his initial works as having difficulty differentiating relevant from irrelevant stimuli in their environments. Additionally, developmental studies illustrate that individuals who present with hyperresponsive reactions to stimuli early on are at greater risk later in life for being socially withdrawn and anxious (Kagan, Reznick, & Snidman, 1987; Kagan & Snidman, 1991; Kagan, Snidman, & Arcus, 1998), characteristics often demonstrated in individuals with HFA and AS (Tantum, 2000). Variable physiological responses to environmental and internal stimuli often cause strong emotional reactions. If an individual is sensitive to tactile information (e.g., a peer inadvertently bumping into him or her while making the transition from one class to another), this stimulus may elicit an increase in arousal level as well as a strong fear response. In conjunction with the previously mentioned difficulties in interpreting intent, individuals with HFA and AS may have difficulties regulating their reaction and response to this innocuous event. Many factors contribute to arousal changes, including the social context, constitutional variables, repertoire of self- and mutual regulation strategies, and communicative partner style (Prizant et al., in press). Social interaction itself can have a dysregulating effect on the arousal level and emotions of an individual with HFA or AS. Interaction styles that are primarily verbal in

nature pose challenges to individuals with HFA because of their difficulties processing transient auditory information (Schuler, 1995). Similarly, individuals with AS are particularly challenged by nonverbal communication and dynamic visual information (Klin & Volkmar, 1997) and, thus, may respond with a heightened state of arousal when touched by a social partner, when a caregiver establishes close proximity, and/or when gestures are used without verbal language as a means of communicating an intent (see discussion of unique learning style differences later).

Challenges in maintaining an optimal state of arousal experienced by many individuals with HFA and ASDs often result in high levels of anxiety. An individual's attempt to cope with an overwhelming inability to modulate levels of arousal or anxiety may lead to a strong preference for routines and frequently to restricted areas of interest, as represented within the final diagnostic criteria identified in the *DSM-IV* for the disorders (American Psychiatric Association, 1994). Individuals with HFA and AS frequently engage in repetitive and restricted patterns of behavior, such as a preoccupation with a particular topic of conversation, academic subject area, or the completion of a manipulative task in a self-absorbed manner. These behaviors often reflect the individual's attempt to cope with an overwhelming inability to modulate levels of arousal or anxiety (Attwood, 1998). Attwood acknowledged that the greater level of stress an individual experiences, the greater is the likelihood that the intensity of a restricted area of interest will increase proportionately. Therefore, at times, behaviors that are often viewed by peers and caregivers as socially inappropriate and odd may actually serve an adaptive function, facilitating order, consistency, and relaxation (Attwood, 1998; Tantum, 2000).

THE IMPACT OF DIFFERENCES IN LEARNING STYLE ON INTERVENTION PLANNING

Notwithstanding the common pattern of impairments in social communication and emotional regulation across the different subtypes of PDD, there is increasing evidence to suggest that there are "different pathways to social learning disabilities" (Volkmar & Klin, 2002; Volkmar et al., 1994). Greater knowledge about the neuropsychological profile of strengths and needs in individuals with HFA and AS has led to useful gains in our understanding of what modalities, methods, and strategies are more effective in accommodating these distinct learning challenges within an individualized intervention program. The neuropsychological literature available provides suggestive evidence of several significant differences in learning style between individuals with HFA and individuals with AS (Volkmar & Klin, 2000, p. 52), a finding that has critical implications for our intervention planning. For example, results of the *DSM-IV* Autism/Pervasive Developmental Disorder Field Trial conducted by Volkmar et al. suggested that in some aspects of learning, individuals with AS performed better than individuals with HFA and, in other areas, the converse was the case. While individuals with AS demonstrate relatively preserved, if not precocious, verbal abilities, they often demonstrate significant vulnerabilities in nonverbal concept formulation, visual-spatial perception, and visual memory (Volkmar & Klin, 2000). For individuals with AS, vulnerabilities in these aspects of learning compromise their ability to attribute meaning to nonverbal social cues, process inflection and the emotional contours of voice, and integrate sequences of visual information to create a social and affective context. It is interesting that the presence of strong verbal skills in an individual with AS often provides an ideal modality for intervention because the individual can incorporate the use of verbal mediation throughout his or her day. This refers to the use of explicit, verbal instruction to facilitate awareness of the subtleties of social and emotional behavior that unaffected individuals typically learn incidentally through ongoing observations of nonverbal social cues in their environment during meaningful interactions (Attwood, 1998; Jahr, Eldevik, & Eikseth, 2000; Klin & Volkmar, 2000; Stewart, 2002). For individuals with AS, verbal language, in fact, often becomes a lifeline for learning about themselves and about the expectations of the social world.

Although developing an awareness of the subtleties of social and emotional behavior is also challenging for individuals with HFA,

differences in the contributing neuropsychological vulnerabilities are evident. Individuals with HFA demonstrate relative strengths in visual-spatial perception and visual memory while their verbal abilities (i.e., expressive language, comprehension, and verbal memory) are likely to be more impaired (Ozonoff & Griffith, 2000; Volkmar, Klin, & Cohen, 1997). Although difficulties with processing nonverbal social cues clearly exist in individuals with HFA, these challenges are more likely a result of a preference for static or nontransient visual information over fast-paced or transient visual cues, rather than a limited ability to process visual-spatial information (Schuler, 1995). Additionally, individuals with HFA, unlike individuals with AS, often present with a gestalt, as opposed to an analytic learning style (Prizant, 1983), which further compromises their abilities to break down larger units of information into smaller units of meaning (e.g., individual words within a verbal utterance, subtle social cues such as a change in facial expression, and variations in intonation), particularly when that information is transient in nature (e.g., fast-paced social cues and verbal language). Therefore, the provision of static visual cues is an appropriate accommodation when supporting individuals with HFA in their awareness of social conventions (Groden & LeVasseur, 1995; Hodgdon, 1995). Verbal mediation strategies, although often helpful with individuals with AS, may prove to be less effective for individuals with HFA given that this modality is transient and requires analytic processing, two identified areas of relative weakness in HFA (Klin & Volkmar, 2000; Prizant & Schuler, 1987).

Despite these significant differences in learning style, the commonalities that individuals with HFA and AS demonstrate with respect to impairments in social communication and emotional regulation speak to their need for similar accommodations within an educational program. Difficulties understanding the communicative intentions and emotional states of a social partner, compounded by difficulties recognizing social conventions across contexts, contribute to a common preference for learning within predictable routines, for very explicit instruction, and for explanation about implicit social messages (Schuler, 1995). It is these common learning preferences in individuals with both HFA and AS that require differentiation of the salient from nonsalient features of social interactions and an increase in recognition that when a person is anxious or overwhelmed, as is often the case within more novel or unstructured social contexts, learning is unlikely to take place. Thus, individuals with HFA and AS, as well as individuals with other types of social learning disabilities, will benefit from programs that incorporate: (1) accommodations that foster an individual's ability to remain well regulated and, therefore, less anxious as he or she traverses through the constant flow of social interactions within each day, (2) accommodations that support an awareness of the intentions and affective states of the individual's social partners, and (3) accommodations that facilitate an awareness of the predictable aspects of more novel social events (e.g., the temporal flow, the social conventions, and communicative intentions of those involved).

Additionally, it is appropriate to consider the common modalities that appear to be effective methods of supporting social communicative competence in individuals with both HFA and AS. Although visual-spatial perception can be challenging for individuals with AS, we know that reading, that is, the written word, is often a relative strength secondary to their strengths in word recognition and verbal language (Rourke & Tsatsanis, 2000). Individuals with HFA also share this relative strength in reading because the written word in contrast to oral language is nontransient and visual by nature, and their ability to process the written modality often far exceeds their ability to process oral language (Wetherby et al., 2000). Regardless of the origins of this learning strength, it has led to a number of universal strategies for intervention including the provision of visual supports incorporating the written word for: (1) increasing an individual's preparedness for and independence when making transitions across activities, (2) progressing through steps within tasks, (3) making choices, and (4) accepting changes in routine (Dalrymple, 1995; Myles & Simpson, 1998). Written cues have also been helpful, in some cases, for supporting social conversational skills within classroom settings (Freeman & Dake, 1997; Krantz & McClannahan, 1998) as well as for enhancing an awareness of social conventions and perspective taking (Gray, 1995; Gray & Garand, 1993; Hagiwara & Myles, 2001). Although the effectiveness of each of these individual strategies may vary from one individual to the next, an understanding of an individual's learning strengths and preferences should clearly form the basis of an appropriate intervention plan (NRC, 2001). Table 38.3 provides a summary of the impact of distinct neuropsychological learning differences between individuals with HFA and AS and our understanding of what modalities, methods, and strategies are more effective within an individualized intervention program.

In addition to these unique neuropsychological patterns, the impact that challenges in

TABLE 38.3   The Impact of Learning Style Differences in HFA and AS on Modalities of Intervention

High Functioning Autism (HFA)	Asperger Syndrome (AS)
• Strengths in visual-spatial perception and visual memory • Preference for nontransient or static information • Weaknesses in expressive and receptive language and verbal memory	• Weaknesses in visual-spatial perception and visual memory • Strengths in expressive and receptive language and verbal memory
Implications The provision of static visual cues is an appropriate accommodation when supporting individuals with HFA in their awareness of social conventions. Verbal mediation strategies, although often helpful with individuals with AS, may prove to be less effective for individuals with HFA secondary to the transient and language-based nature of this modality of learning.	*Implications* The strong verbal abilities skills characteristic of AS often provide an ideal modality for intervention, as the use of verbal mediation can be incorporated throughout his or her day. This refers to the use of explicit, verbal instruction to facilitate awareness of the subtleties of social and emotional behavior that unaffected individuals typically learn incidentally through ongoing observations of nonverbal social cues in their environment.

emotional regulation may have on learning style (e.g., attention, social engagement, problem solving, executive functioning) has critical implications for developing an individualized intervention plan. Therefore, when designing an educational program designed to support social communicative competence, it is essential to address the core emotional regulatory challenges faced by individuals with HFA and AS throughout their daily routines (Myles & Simpson, 1998; Prizant et al., in press). Addressing these problems will enhance the efficacy of programming, promote social acceptability among a network of peers and, thereby, increase the capacity to engage in positive social experiences across settings and partners. The development of both the capacity for self-regulation and the capacity for mutual regulation ensures that the individual with a social disability and his or her social partners develop an ability to engage in reciprocal interactions where both partners are actively engaged, provide clear expressions of emotional state, and utilize effective and socially appropriate coping mechanisms that reduce anxiety and variations in arousal and emotional state.

Fostering emotional regulation may require social partners to modify both their interaction styles and the environment so that an individual can remain actively engaged in a particular social setting (see later discussion on transactional supports). However, the goal is for the individual to manage independently in these areas, thereby decreasing the need for environmental modifications. Appropriate goals to be addressed may include, but are not limited to, the following: (1) increasing the individual's ability to acquire and use socially acceptable behavioral strategies to support engagement and attention in daily activities and to cope with unexpected schedule changes and transitions, (2) increasing the individual's ability to use socially acceptable nonverbal and verbal expressions for social control and expressing his or her emotional state, and (3) increasing the individual's ability to acquire and utilize cognitive-linguistic strategies to support his or her attention to activities and daily routines (e.g., through the use of rehearsal and self-regulatory language, by reference to visual supports; Prizant et al., in press).

For individuals with HFA and AS, it is also critical to foster abilities in the areas of emotional identification and emotional understanding so that they are more able to grade their emotional reactions to specific events or incidents and to display their emotions in more conventional ways. Therefore, the following goals are viewed as critical for fostering increased social communicative and emotional regulatory competence:

1. Increasing the individual's acquisition of conventional verbal and nonverbal communication forms for requesting assistance and/or organizing supports.
2. Increasing the individual's ability to use specific vocabulary or conversational devices to express emotional state and arousal level.
3. Increasing the ability to identify and express emotional state and arousal level as well as using regulating strategies, with and without the use of visual supports.
4. Increasing social understanding and social expectations through language-based strategies (see later discussion on transactional supports).

Because expression of emotional state and coping strategies are person and context specific, these goals and supports should be implemented throughout an individual's day across a variety of social partners and social settings.

EDUCATIONAL PROGRAMMING FOR INDIVIDUALS WITH HIGH-FUNCTIONING AUTISM AND ASPERGER SYNDROME

To make informed decisions about the curriculum and methodology of an educational program designed to foster social communicative competence in individuals with HFA and AS, you must maintain an awareness of the state of the science in the field, particularly in relation to empirical studies demonstrating the efficacy of specific approaches, curricula, or methodologies. This is especially critical when working with this population, as a number of specific, programmatic approaches are available reflecting different philosophical views, and, in some cases, proponents of these programs have made claims that their approach is superior to other approaches (Green, 1996; Smith, 1996). Although there remains great controversy in the field as to which intervention approach is the most appropriate, it is premature to claim that "any one approach is more effective than other approaches" (Prizant & Rubin, 1999, p. 199). Empirical research has, in fact, demonstrated the effectiveness of a range of approaches that vary in their curriculum and methodology (Dawson & Osterling, 1997; Rogers, 1996); and, perhaps more importantly, a number of studies suggest that "no one approach is equally effective for all children" (Prizant & Rubin, 1999, p. 199). Thus, it is critical to create an educational program that fosters success with a specific individual, his or her family, and that individual's social network. The Committee on Educational Interventions for Children with Autism was a panel formed by the NRC (2001) to review empirical research in the field, literature from model programs, and literature from general education and child development. Their charge allowed the committee to formulate specific recommendations for educational programming, provide guidelines to direct public policy, and indicate the need for more ecologically valid outcome measures (described further later). The findings of the committee support the notion that "effective services will and should vary considerably across individual children, depending on a child's age, cognitive and language levels, behavioral needs, and family priorities" (NRC, 2001, p. 220).

Educational Guidelines

When developing an appropriate educational program for an individual with HFA or AS, individualization of curriculum, learning accommodations, and settings are of paramount importance. Social skills do not exist in a vacuum, and to teach them effectively, the individual must be considered as a whole from a developmental perspective. His or her strengths and needs, learning style, specific interests, preferences, and regulatory capacities and vulnerabilities should be understood and planned for when organizing the program. Likewise, the Committee on Educational Interventions for Children with Autism provided a number of

recommendations for programming and outcome measures to guide our work. These include, but are not limited to: (1) addressing functional and spontaneous communication, (2) implementing supports for social communicative competence across a range of social settings, and (3) providing opportunities for guided instruction within natural contexts (e.g., peer interactions, inclusion opportunities). Additionally, consideration of the range of factors that may be contributing to problem behaviors is considered critical as a means of supporting each individual's personal responsibility for his or her social behavior (NRC, 2000, 2001, p. 221). Last, the committee strongly recommended that meaningful outcome measures be incorporated on an ongoing basis (i.e., 3-month intervals; NRC, 2001, p. 220), as part of each individual's educational program, as a way of assessing generalization of gains across social partners, social settings, and activities (NRC, 2001, p. 228). Thus, social competence cannot be measured without attention to an individual's adaptation and success within day-to-day activities in natural contexts.

Despite this recommendation and our clinical awareness of what we want to achieve, it is not uncommon in programming for social communication skills that different target goals and objectives are treated as discrete entities and/or that provision of designated social opportunities at specific times of the day (e.g., Circle of Friends, Lunch Bunch, or social skills groups) is considered to encompass and to address the social needs of an individual. While many of the specific goals or activities are appropriate and beneficial components of an educational program, fostering social communication must be understood as integral across an individual's day (e.g., each class at school, lunch, recess, transition times), across contexts (e.g., school, home, and community), and across social partners (e.g., peers, teachers, siblings and parents, coworkers, and members of shared groups). Facilitating social skill development does not rest solely with the speech-language pathologist, occupational therapist, social worker, psychologist, counselor or paraprofessional, nor does it rest only with the parents. Rather it is shared among all those coming into contact with the individual, including peers, coworkers, and members of the community. Although certain team members will have more responsibility for developing and implementing aspects of the social programming than others, a critical piece in the program planning is to integrate and make the connections among what is being taught; why the skills are needed; how, when, and where to use them; and, most importantly, with whom. This cohesive and comprehensive approach should be at the core of facilitating social communicative competence, since the ability to integrate and apply learned skills and the capacity to generalize them forms the essence of social understanding that is so challenging for individuals with HFA and AS. Skills being taught should, therefore, not be considered the end product but need to be worked on with attention to: (1) the contexts in which they occur naturally, (2) the reciprocal adaptations demanded by social partners, and (3) the ability to then generalize the skills to other contexts and individuals. The complexity of planning an educational program that integrates social skills across settings is not to be underestimated. Nevertheless, the outcomes are more likely to have ecological validity and real life payoff. For any given individual, the planning of a social skills educational program must be individualized and take into account the lifestyle and demands that will dictate priority needs, supports to be developed within the community, choices of materials and activities, and individuals to be included.

The success of any educational program should include measures of its relevance and functional impact on an individual's day-to-day life, that is, meaningful outcome measures. Schwartz (2000) discusses the notion of using "membership" as an important measure of whether an educational program designed to support social communicative competence has been successful. Schwartz pointed out that social skills are not a goal in and of themselves; rather, the objective is to support the learning of social behaviors, including social communication, that permit and promote the development of meaningful relationships that are culturally relevant. Based on a 5-year multisite project using natural settings to support children's social relationships conducted by Meyer, Grenot-Scheyer, Schwartz, and Harry (1998), the following guidelines for socially and ecologically valid interventions were suggested. Interventions should be:

1. Consistent with the social expectations of a given context;
2. Feasible with respect to available resources—personnel, expertise, and materials;
3. Sustainable over time;
4. Owned and operated by the constituency or community within which they occur (teachers, parents, and students);
5. Culturally inclusive; and
6. Intuitively appealing.

Primary Dimensions of Intervention

In the case of social learning disabilities, we must remember that the social impairment is not solely due to the developmental vulnerabilities and learning style differences of the individual with HFA and AS; rather, the "social impairment is shared" with all of those attempting to engage or, for that matter, disengage with the individual (Gray, 2001). As noted earlier, social isolation can be hastened by the negative perceptions that idiosyncratic styles of communication often create among a larger peer network (Lord, 1984; Schuler, 1995). Additionally, the success of any given social exchange relies not only on an individual's ability to adhere to social conventions, remain actively engaged, and accurately consider another's intents but also on the social partner's ability to adapt his or her interpersonal style and the environment to match the needs of the individual with the social disability. As Gray indicated, we, as social partners, "are part of the problem" and, thus, should be "part of the solution" as well. An additional factor is the impact of a social disability on that individual's family, with respect to not only their interpersonal style and the home environment but also their emotional well-being or adjustment. Recent studies have shown that more positive outcomes are associated with the provision of family support and mechanisms for coping with the stress of raising and living with an individual with a social disability (NRC, 2001). The Social Communication Emotional Regulation Transactional Supports (SCERTS) model provides a comprehensive framework to follow when designing an educational program to foster social communicative competence in individuals with social communication disabilities (Prizant et al., in press). This framework includes the following dimensions designed to foster social communicative competence in individuals with HFA and AS: (1) interpersonal supports across social partners (e.g., communicative style adjustments with peers, teachers, family members, and members of the community); (2) learning and educational supports (e.g., visual/written supports and environment arrangement/modifications); and (3) family supports (e.g., educational support as well as ongoing emotional support).

Specific accommodations and learning strategies are discussed next as they relate to these primary dimensions. Table 38.4 summarizes these accommodations.

Interpersonal Supports

To foster success within social interactions between the individual with HFA and AS and his or her social partners, the emphasis should not solely be on the individual with a social learning disability. Rather, a critical emphasis needs to be placed on supporting a partner's ability to make communicative style adjustments to support the interaction. Communicative style adjustments relate to the specific

TABLE 38.4   Transactional Supports for Individuals with HFA and AS

I. Interpersonal supports
   a. Identify the qualities of a social partner's use of verbal and nonverbal forms of communication that are either facilitative or provide barriers to an individual's attempts to engage in reciprocal social communicative exchanges and maintain active engagement.
   b. Implement communicative style adjustments to adapt to the unique learning style differences of an individual with HFA and AS. For example, the use of explicit and clear expressions of one's intentions and emotional states, devoid of idioms and sarcasm, often supports the processing abilities of an individual with HFA or AS. In contrast, the use of a high rate of nonverbal social cues (e.g., raising one's eyebrows to indicate distaste) when interacting with individuals with AS or the use of verbal language in the absence of static visual cues (e.g., concrete gestures) with an individual with HFA may actually provide barriers to achieving successful communicative exchange. Consideration should also be given to factors such as vocal volume, rate of speech, prosody, proximity, and physical contact.
   c. Coordinate communicative style adjustments across all of the individual's social partners (e.g., peers, teachers and professionals, family members, and members of the community).

II. Learning and educational supports
   a. Design visual and organizational supports to foster social communication and emotional regulation across social partners and social contexts (e.g., understanding the communicative intentions and emotional state of another, understanding of time and activity structure as a means of preparing for potentially dysregulating events, and identifying one's emotional state and socially acceptable coping strategies).
   b. Arrange and modify the physical environment to support social communication and emotional regulation. For example, accommodations such as clear physical boundaries for activities, clear temporal structure, reducing levels of auditory and visual stimulation, if appropriate, and providing opportunities to engage in social interactions in small group contexts. Consideration should also be given to the demands of a given environment, as expectations should be appropriately matched to an individual's unique challenges and learning style (e.g., curriculum modifications, reduced expectations for homework).

III. Family support
   a. Specific accommodations should be developed across all family members who interact with the individual with HFA and AS. A particular emphasis should be placed on fostering an understanding of the nature of the disability and the communicative style adjustments, learning supports, and environmental arrangements that can be implemented in order to facilitate more positive social exchanges and development in the areas of social communication and emotional regulation.
   b. Emotional support should also be provided in both one-to-one and group contexts by supporting each family member's ability to cope with the stress and challenges of raising or interacting with an individual with HFA or AS. A particular emphasis should be placed on supporting an ability to identify priorities and develop appropriate expectations and realistic, achievable goals for the family as a whole as well as the individual's ongoing development and drive toward social communicative competence.

modifications that a social partner might make with respect to interpersonal style, use of expressive language, and use of nonverbal forms of communication (e.g., gestures, facial expressions, and intonation) to match the unique needs of the individual with HFA or AS (Prizant et al., in press; Quill, 1995). Identifying those aspects of interactions that either support or interfere with an individual's ability to engage in successful, self-initiated, and reciprocal interactions allows for greater attunement when facilitating interactions across social partners and settings. These interpersonal supports should be targeted across parents, peers, teachers, professionals, and other members of the community, and may vary depending on the partner's role in enabling the development of each individual's social competence throughout his or her daily routine. Because the impact of a social disability on family members is unique to that of other social partners, providing family support is discussed in greater detail.

Interpersonal Support for Peers

Individuals with HFA and AS often demonstrate an interest in peers, and, particularly as they mature, they yearn for friendships and social acceptance. The nature of their social impairment, however, compromises their understanding of the social conventions necessary for entering into play-based interactions, joining in social conversations, and/or engaging in the repartee that comes so naturally to their peers (Schuler & Wolfberg, 2000). These challenges reinforce a tendency that already exists for those with HFA and AS to become adult-directed and to turn toward their teachers, caregivers, or employers rather than their peers as partners in interactions. Because children learn through observation, imitation, and collaboration with peers, more typical learning strategies are less common in HFA and AS. Consequently, there is a dual risk of social isolation, that is, limited opportunities for learning within social interactions with peers and learned helplessness—an overreliance on adults for prompting or cueing of behaviors.

In a school setting, simply being alongside peers in an integrated classroom will not allow students with HFA and AS to develop social skills and engage in interactions or form friendships (Kohler, Strain, & Shearer, 1996). The individualized educational plan with its social goals and objectives should, therefore, be designed to develop the individual's capacity for joint attention and understanding of symbolic conventions (see Table 32.1) to maximize the likelihood that the individual is equipped to use opportunities, both created and naturally occurring, for practicing and engaging in positive bids for social interaction. The other essential part of the equation is to provide the peer group with specific strategies and support. Peer training and support is required to foster a level of understanding as well as communicative style adjustments for supporting and engaging the individual with a social disability in ways that are sensitive, pleasurable, and appropriate for the context. When thoughtful approaches to peer-mediated intervention are implemented, as in the use of peer-implemented pivotal response training, integrated play groups, play organizers, and buddy skills training programs (discussed in greater detail later), research shows that the interactions between individuals with HFA and AS and their typical peers tend to increase across contexts and that, on occasion, those interactions extend to other students as well (English, Goldstein, Shafer, & Kaczmarek, 1997; Goldstein & Wickstrom, 1986; Oke & Schreibman, 1990; Pierce & Schreibman, 1995; Strain, Kohler, Storey, & Danko, 1994; Wolfberg, 1988). This results in an enlarged social network and expands the frequency with which the affected individual will have the opportunity to practice and experience social success through his or her day and over time.

Failure to include the individual's peer network in a support program may contribute to peers' misinterpretation or anxiety about unexpected behaviors and responses or, for those affected individuals whose style is more passive, to peers' decreased expectations and attempts to engage them socially, thereby reducing the very opportunities for interaction that they need. Likewise, you must observe and seek the input of typical peers to ensure that the social conventions being fostered are relevant and age appropriate because acceptance into a given network or community of social partners requires expertise in the particular interpersonal styles used within a given context and peer group. Particularly during the adolescent years, these conventions (e.g., the language used, the style of dress, and preferred topics of conversation) may vary from group to group or time to time. Failure to attend to these important nonverbal and verbal features may jeopardize successful attempts to engage. It is important to deemphasize the role of teacher as instructor and increase the peers' responsibility for the successful social interaction (Brown & Conroy, 2002). In many instances, it appears that not only can peer-mediated interventions be as effective as teacher-based instruction but also, more importantly, there may be some generalization of spontaneous social bids across peers and settings, as the students begin to recognize each other as potential partners independent of the adults around them (Oke & Schreibman, 1990; Pierce & Schreibman, 1995; Strain et al., 1994). It is important to keep in mind that while peers become more active as facilitators, they continue to require support and supervision from the adults who develop the students' skills and understanding of how best to promote interactions. In addition, staff must try to ensure that the individuals with HFA or AS do not become passive or reliant on their peer supports and that they are seen as partners with responsibilities within the interactions.

The involvement of a peer network depends, in part, on the developmental level and the settings in which the students are engaged. Younger peers, for example, may simply need reassurance regarding the reasons for a given individual's difficulties with emotional regulation, how to reinforce more positive and adaptive responses, and how to simply redirect to desirable or regulating activities. Likewise, these peers would benefit from explicit training and support in how to modify their use and interpretation of language and nonverbal forms of communication when engaged in communicative exchanges with the individual with HFA or AS. Social skills programs and play-based groups that incorporate simple cues for peers, such as the integrated play group model presented by Wolfberg (2003), play organizers offered by Odom et al. (1999), the buddy skills training program presented by English et al. (1997), and pivotal response training presented by Pierce and Schreibman (1995, 1997), foster social partners' ability to modify their communicative style by acting more responsively; providing social overtures such as prompting, choices, and praise; and using natural reinforcement appropriate to the given social context.

Older peers may receive more explicit information about the nature of HFA and AS within a broader context of appreciating differences and increasing tolerance for these within the school community as a whole. Approaches such as the Circle of Friends and peer networks capitalize on the sensitivity of typical peers, as their curricula are designed to foster awareness of learning style differences across individuals and to teach the critical communicative style adjustments that can allow for more positive social exchanges both within social group settings and outside the school environment (Haring & Breen, 1992; Kamps, Potucek, Lopez, Kravits, & Kemmerer, 1997; Whitaker, Barratt, Joy, Potter, & Thomas, 1998).

Some peer group programs targeting academic, as opposed to social skills and play, have led to secondary gains in social interaction between participating students. In studies using classwide peer tutoring (Kamps, Barbetta, Leonard, & Delquadri, 1994) and cooperative learning groups (Kamps, Leonard, Potucek, & Garrison, 1995), students with HFA and their typical classroom peers worked cooperatively to improve reading skills (fluency and comprehension), understanding of vocabulary, and question comprehension by participating in academic-based games for practice of skills. An important part of the process was role reversal—each student took the role of trainer and trainee at different points, providing an opportunity for equal status and for perspective taking. Outcomes included gains in the targeted academic areas, but perhaps more importantly, greater engagement in the academic process, more peer interaction and integration, and greater duration of engagement in social interaction. Results indicated that use of peers proved as effective an outcome as teacher-delivered intervention, and it was felt that the inherent structure of the tasks promoted the communicative style adjustments that were needed to foster successful engagement across the individuals with HFA and their peers.

Last, a number of peer support programs and curricula have been developed to foster success within groups of children working on common social learning objectives and goals, strategies which are also applicable within integrated settings. The I LAUGH model presented by Winner (2002) and Navigating the Social World presented by McAfee (2002), for example, provide a framework for addressing vulnerabilities in social communication by incorporating learning style accommodations and communicative style adjustments across the day as well as within group learning contexts with peers with difficulties with social cognition. Relationship development intervention (RDI; Gutstein, 2000) is another curricular model that approaches the building of capacities for social relationships from a developmental perspective by placing an emphasis on fostering genuine pleasure from social interactions with others, replicating the progression in affective-emotional development of typical infants and children. In the RDI approach, children are often paired with other children with similar social communication challenges, at least initially. The rationale for this accommodation is due, in part, to the notion that typical peers are so adept at social interactions that they simply take too much responsibility, potentially increasing learned helplessness within the children with HFA and AS. Within the structure of the sessions, "experience-sharing" activities and games are designed to promote awareness of and attunement to the other children, in contexts where they are actively enjoying themselves, while also developing their sense of self- and mutual regulation. This approach aims to promote the underpinnings for social relationship building that will increase the individual's desire to initiate, maintain, and extend interactions with others. Key elements of these curricula and intervention models are their appreciation of the transactional nature of social communication, as support is provided both to the individual with the disability as well as his or her peers, partners, and larger social network.

Interpersonal Supports for Teachers and Professionals

Within a comprehensive educational program designed to foster social communicative competence, it would be appropriate for interpersonal supports to be developed across all teachers, professionals, and paraprofessionals who will be working directly with the individual with HFA or AS as well as those who come into regular, albeit less frequent, contact. In a manner similar to peer-mediated interventions, a critical first step will be to identify the qualities of a specific teacher's or professional's use of verbal and nonverbal forms of communication that are either facilitative or provide barriers to attempts to engage in reciprocal social communicative exchanges and maintain active engagement. Communicative style adjustments should then be developed to adapt to the unique learning style differences of an individual with HFA and AS. For example, the use of explicit and clear expressions of an individual's intentions and emotional states, devoid of idioms and sarcasm, often supports the processing abilities of an individual with HFA or AS. In contrast, the use of a high rate of nonverbal social cues (e.g., raising the eyebrows to indicate distaste) when interacting with individuals with AS or the use of verbal language in the absence of static visual cues (e.g., concrete gestures or written language) with an individual with HFA may impede the achievement of successful communicative exchanges. Consideration should also be given to factors such as vocal volume, rate of speech, pause time for processing and formulation of a response, prosodic variations, proximity, and physical contact.

In middle school and high school settings, this assessment process can be complicated because the number of teachers and professionals that a student will likely come in regular contact with increases significantly from elementary school settings. Consequently, careful consideration should be given to the composition of a student's educational team because the unique learning style differences of individuals with HFA and individuals with AS require a significant commitment on the part of the educational staff to provide accommodations such as modifying the use of nonverbal versus verbal discourse for a particular individual. As with any other job or occupation, there are individuals whose natural temperaments and interests make them the ideal candidates for working with individuals with HFA and AS, and there are others who, through no fault of their own, may be less suited to this work. It is important for both staff and recipients of training to be honest about their strengths and what they find more challenging in the task of teaching this population. Characteristics that may increase the likelihood of becoming a positive facilitator for an individual with HFA or AS include, but are not limited to, curiosity about learning style differences, a capacity for organization and temporal structure, and flexibility with respect to the interactive style adopted with individual students. Additionally, those teachers and professionals who present with more than usually well-developed social skills, affective attunement, and unlimited patience when faced with unconventional social behavior are often the most adept at reflecting, analyzing, and putting into place effective interventions. These interventions can help in preventing a high frequency of social communicative breakdowns and social and environmental antecedents that lead to states of emotional dysregulation for individuals with HFA and AS. It is also important to be able to share some of the responsibilities, to have a capacity to supervise, and to appreciate the experience of parents, welcoming them as part of the team.

Training of educators should be paramount and should include all members of the school community. The degree of training may vary, however, depending on the level of responsibility for the implementation of the individualized educational programming. Those with direct responsibility such as special education teachers and therapeutic personnel (e.g., school psychologists, speech-language pathologists, occupational therapists), for example, should have specific expertise in HFA and AS and would benefit from knowledge of the core challenges that compromise the development of social communicative competence in these social disabilities (e.g., core challenges in social communication and emotional regulation). These staff members should also be familiar with the specific modalities, methods, and strategies that are the most effective in accommodating the distinct learning challenges associated with these social disabilities within an individualized educational program. Other personnel such as paraprofessionals, regular education teachers, and administrators should receive in-service training on the unique learning styles and developmental

profiles of students with social learning disabilities in order to foster greater awareness of how to teach to their strengths, how to understand and read their reactions, and how to support their academic and social growth in the mainstream or nonacademic arenas in which they will be placed. Those personnel who may be less visible, but are frequently in charge during the more challenging parts of the day (e.g., bus drivers, crossing guards, cafeteria workers, and recess monitors), also need to be familiar with the specific communicative style adjustments that facilitate positive social communicative interactions and those that may result in communicative breakdowns and frustration on the part of students with HFA and AS. These staff members are, in fact, critical because students with HFA and AS are vulnerable during times of transition (e.g., riding a bus or walking to school), when their time is unstructured as it often is during recess, and when the social demands are particularly high such as in a cafeteria setting. For this group of staff, there will likely be very specific routines/demands that occur during their time with the student (e.g., lunch routines, traveling on the bus). An analysis of what happens and how a student manages these routines will allow for planning and staff support so that action plans, visual supports, environmental modifications, and practice of the events can occur. Should difficulties arise, an understanding of the elements that may be interfering can lead to changes and modifications that allow for greater success. For example, where a student sits on a bus, who sits next to him or her, having the student meet the driver, and ensuring that he or she knows the routine for getting to and from the bus will likely alleviate anxiety and promote a smooth transition. Some students may benefit from having something that they can do on the bus—listening to music, looking at a favorite book, or having a preferred toy to play with—allowing them to cope with the trip more comfortably.

Interpersonal Supports for Members of the Community

Although the family and those close to the individual with HFA and AS form their community at an early age, the range of opportunities that are age appropriate and culturally typical greatly expand as an individual matures. These unique social experiences coupled with developmental capacities in social communication and emotional regulation set the stage for social awareness and growth. Such opportunities can facilitate an ability to interpret another's perspective as well as an ability to modify the use and interpretation of language based on the perspectives of those involved and/or the social context. These opportunities for active engagement across a range of social partners and social settings are, indeed, a critical factor in the achievement of social communicative competence and may form the basis for important leisure time activities and group membership. Selection of community-based activities, however, should be based on the preferences and unique learning style strengths of an individual with HFA and AS, as well as a consideration of the social demands related to the activity. Since communicative style adjustments should be embedded within these community settings and across the social partners within them, it is essential to predetermine who will be running, teaching, or organizing programs and whether they will be open and willing to adjust their use of nonverbal and verbal forms of communication when interacting with the individual with HFA or AS to facilitate successful social exchanges and maintain emotional regulation. Parents may find that their role as assistant coach, volunteer parent, or administrative assistant allows for the additional interpersonal support necessary for successful inclusion in clubs, sports, and/or extracurricular activities.

For many, though not all individuals with HFA and AS, team sports are particularly challenging because they require both motor skills and social awareness for team playing. In particular, team experiences at the school-age, middle school, and high school levels are clearly challenging because the player needs to cooperate, integrate temporal motor movements with visual tracking, and simultaneously attend to verbal and nonverbal cues during fast-paced (i.e., transient) social interactions. The competitive nature of these events also diminishes the likelihood that peers will be tolerant of "someone learning on the job." Interpersonal supports such as having a social partner modify his or her use of nonverbal or verbal discourse are not likely

to occur in these fast-paced and competitive contexts. Sports such as swimming, martial arts, skiing, and horseback riding are more individualized, yet occur within social group settings. Since interactions with peers are less fast-paced in these contexts, they may allow for communicative style adjustments and time to foster positive social communicative exchanges. These activities may, as a result, build self-esteem and confidence and can be lifelong pastimes that allow for shared experiences. Likewise, Special Olympics, bowling leagues, chess clubs, and music/drama groups provide many teens and young adults with typical social and physical opportunities that are structured and offer genuine pleasure and a sense of achievement. The experience of being competent and adept provides a more balanced base from which to interact and may, therefore, allow for somewhat different and more "typical" social opportunities. Social coaching for both partners in the interaction may facilitate further development of social relationships that are mutually satisfying.

The need for interpersonal supports will continue to be essential as the individual with HFA and AS matures and transitions from high school into postsecondary educational settings, supported living arrangements, and/or group homes (if appropriate). Once again, knowing what the social and communicative demands are in a given situation can allow for tailoring of specific skills to help the individuals to fit in and feel capable of meeting the expectations of the new situation. Additionally, educational opportunities for the broader community (e.g., law enforcement agencies, religious institutions, and vocational settings) can be beneficial when ensuring the long-term goal of providing interpersonal supports that foster social communicative competence for an individual with HFA and AS. For example, education programs designed to foster awareness among law enforcement agencies provide a critical aspect of community teaching, since individuals with ASDs are not immune from situations in which they may be involved with the legal system. The stress involved in situations such as minor car accidents, misunderstandings, or having been led unwittingly into a situation involving some illegal activity places tremendous burdens on self-regulatory capacities, interpersonal skills, and the ability to communicate and advocate effectively for oneself. Having a police department with staff who are informed about social disabilities and psychiatric disorders is essential if the situation is to be understood and resolved in an informed, accurate, and fair manner. It is also critical to have advocates and lawyers who can be available to ensure that individuals are aware of their rights, to provide an accurate account of their role, and to ensure that their intents as well as their actions are both assessed and understood.

As adults, individuals with these social disabilities will still greatly benefit from the support of professionals and mentors with specific training who can ensure that communicative style adjustments are implemented across all social partners and across daily routines and settings (e.g., academic settings, living arrangements, and places of employment).

Learning and Educational Supports

As discussed previously, there are significant differences as well as commonalities in learning styles between individuals with HFA and AS. Designing appropriate learning and educational supports to facilitate social communicative competence requires a careful consideration of the individual's unique profile of strengths and needs, the expectations of a given social context, as well as the priorities of the family (NRC, 2001). With respect to the commonalities in core challenges in social communication and emotional regulation among individuals with HFA and AS, they will need a similar range of learning accommodations. These supports tend to fall within two primary categories: visual and organizational supports and environmental modifications (Prizant et al., in press).

Visual and Organizational Supports

Visual and organizational supports should be designed to foster an individual's capacities for social communication and emotional regulation across social partners and social contexts based on core challenges in these domains (e.g., understanding the communicative intentions and emotional state of another, understanding of time and activity structure as a means of preparing for potentially dys-

regulating events, and identifying an individual's emotional state and socially acceptable coping strategies). Although individuals with HFA and AS can be different with respect to their abilities to process verbal language and visual-spatial information (as discussed previously), they share a common area of relative strength in processing the written word (Rourke & Tsatsanis, 2000; Wetherby et al., 2000). This common modality has led to the development of a number of effective visual and organizational supports for individuals with HFA and AS.

The implementation of visual and organizational supports will depend, in part, on the current goals of the educational plan for an individual with HFA and AS. When fostering the understanding and use of verbal conventions for initiating, exchanging turns, and terminating interactions across different social settings, supports such as dialogue scripts (Krantz & McClannahan, 1998) capitalize on the common modality of the written word as a learning strength and foster an individual's ability to engage in basic social conversations as well as conversational discourse within unique social contexts (e.g., dating and attending family celebrations). Modifications to these dialogue scripts, however, are often appropriate to ensure that an individual attends not only to his or her verbal discourse but also to the verbal discourse of his or her social partner. Thus, learning supports that involve a review of the content exchanged within these social conversations clearly serve to augment these social communicative exchanges. These include, but are not limited to, the use of comic strip conversations (Gray, 1994), video replay (i.e., videotaping and reviewing actual social exchanges with peers and social partners), and video modeling (i.e., the use of videos to model appropriate conversational skills and social conventions). Research has, in fact, documented the effectiveness of the use of video within educational programs designed to foster social communication skills (Charlop & Milstein, 1989). This support fostered an improved rate of skill acquisition, generalization of skills, and maintenance of skills for as long as 15 months. Thus, both dialogue scripts and video-based instruction provide appropriate visual and organizational supports for enhancing conversational conventions.

When fostering an individual's ability to acquire and use cognitive-linguistic strategies to support attention and active engagement throughout daily routines, visual and organizational supports can be implemented to develop an awareness of the temporal structure and social communicative expectations of specific events. As noted earlier, the use of the written modality allows otherwise transient auditory information to be presented in a way that is static and present long enough to be understood. It also allows for the salient and most necessary information to be presented, while decreasing extraneous stimuli that may distract or confuse. The use of a written schedule, for example, provides a clear sequence that can map the actual unfolding of an event that is far easier to appreciate than the rapidly fading, temporal equivalent of nonverbal social cues and the verbal modality. It, thereby, reduces the load on short-term working memory and allows for reflection on cause and effect. In addition, with this more permanent way of representing event sequences, it is possible to reduce unpredictability and accompanying anxiety, fostering better emotional regulation, which increases availability for social engagement and reduces maladaptive social behavior (Dalrymple, 1995; Myles & Simpson, 1998).

Visual and organizational supports can also be used to foster an awareness of another's intentions, emotional states, and perspectives. This developmental goal leads to improved social communicative reciprocity as well as increased emotional regulatory capacities, as the individual's ability to accurately read another's intents contributes to sustaining a more reciprocal interaction (Prizant et al., in press). Gray and Garand (1993) discussed the use of social stories as a visual modality for enhancing an individual's awareness of a social partner's perspective and the impact of this social information on his or her own perspective and social communicative behaviors. This learning support involves consideration of the following critical elements:

1. The perspective of the affected individual, a frequently overlooked variable, although often central to correctly understanding the potential causes of social difficulties as well as effective interventions;

2. The use of simple visual cues (e.g., simple pictures, cartoons, written text, and rule-based color coding);

3. Careful attention to the social context to determine what social conventions are appropriate;

4. Extraction of those salient features in a social situation that are the most relevant;

5. Explicit directions as to what behaviors/responses might be appropriate;

6. Inclusion of possible emotional reactions, that is, the social partner's perspective;

7. Explanation as to why a particular choice of positive behaviors will provide a positive consequence with respect to the perspectives of self as well as others; and

8. An attempt to unravel the complexities of later social relationships and to make positive social choices and decisions.

By implementing tools such as social stories prior to an anticipated social event, you can provide an individual with HFA and AS with a cognitive-linguistic strategy to prepare and rehearse socially appropriate conversational discourse and emotional regulatory strategies (Hagiwara & Myles, 2001). As an instructional strategy, social stories were designed with a specific directive to be implemented in a positive rather than a negative manner so that the individual is encouraged to develop more adaptive behaviors, rather than being reminded of those to be extinguished. Perhaps most importantly, these supports should be designed with respect to the specific contexts in which social events are occurring so that the final intervention is personalized and functional for the individual with HFA and AS.

Additional strategies using visual/written means to facilitate social problem solving have been developed as part of the I LAUGH model (Winner, 2002), the Teach Me Language program (Freeman & Dake, 1997), and by Roosa (1997), whose Situations Options Choices Strategies and Stimulation (SOCCSS) program provides a sequence to facilitate an individual's understanding of a social problem, an appreciation of having more than one option for a response, and an awareness that each choice will also have its own consequence. Again, these approaches foster more flexible thinking, provide more than one perspective, and encourage active participation on the part of the individual so that he or she is empowered to develop social decision making and social cognition.

Environmental Modifications

A preference for learning within predictable routines and for very explicit instruction of implicit social messages is a common pattern noted across individuals with HFA and AS (Schuler, 1995). This preference is secondary, in part, to persistent difficulties with understanding the communicative intentions and emotional states of social partners and difficulties with maintaining a steady emotional and physiological state of arousal, that is, active engagement in a given social environment. These patterns speak to the need to modify each of the social settings that an individual engages in within daily routines. Special events (e.g., family celebrations or vacations) that fall outside the usual routine will require even more careful consideration. Environments should be arranged or modified to support an individual's capacities for social communication and emotional regulation. For example, accommodations might include clear physical boundaries for activities, clear temporal structure, reducing levels of auditory and visual stimulation, if appropriate, and offering opportunities to engage in social interactions in small group contexts (Dalrymple, 1995). Consideration should also be given to the demands of a given environment, as expectations should be appropriately matched to an individual's unique challenges and learning style (e.g., curriculum modifications, reduced expectations for homework). For some children, haircuts, dental appointments, and other necessary life events cause dysregulation because the unusual setting, need for intrusion on the part of novel adults, and, at times, unpleasant physiological response all contribute to high levels of tension and behavioral disruption. Families can be helped by finding professionals in the community who have dealt with children on the spectrum before and whose reputations for patience and understanding precede them. Children can accompany other family members when they have appointments so that the setting, required seating, noises, and smells become somewhat familiar.

During these "practice" visits, it might be helpful to have the child sit in the chair, press a button, or turn on the water as real-life opportunities for experiencing cause and effect, experiencing control over some aspect of the environment, which may help to decrease anxiety and give a sense of mastery. Using a social story or simple photo series that explains the sequence of events for the appointment may then allow for a successful first time of the child's own, one which he or she can then share with extended family and friends.

Family Supports

An individual initially develops his or her self-confidence as a social communicative partner through positive social interactions and successful communicative exchanges within the context of interactions with family members (e.g., parents, siblings, and grandparents) and eventually during social experiences across settings and partners. The family and home contexts, in fact, follow an individual throughout his or her life, while specific educational contexts and professionals "come and go" (Domingue, Cutler, & McTarnaghan, 2000, p. 380). Likewise, the experiences of a family unit contribute greatly to an individual's social communicative competence, as daily family routines (e.g., shopping and going to dinner) and family celebrations (e.g., weddings, birthday parties) provide the context for social and cultural learning (i.e., understanding symbolic conventions). Thus, the individual's home and family settings are clearly critical contexts for addressing his or her drive toward achieving social communicative competence. Interpersonal supports (e.g., communicative style adjustments) and learning supports (e.g., visual tools and environmental arrangement) for use within the home and family contexts must be part of a comprehensive educational program (Prizant et al., in press). This accommodation, which has been supported by the NRC, requires the provision of therapeutic and educational support to family members with a particular focus on: (1) supporting an understanding of the nature of the social disability consistent with HFA or AS, as appropriate to the individual family and (2) developing specific modifications that

can be embedded across the day to foster social communication and emotional regulation
(NRC, 2001, p. 219).

All too often, a pattern of interactive
breakdown develops, whereby an individual is
not able to effectively communicate his or her
intent to a family member and/or a family
member is ineffective at reciprocating the
exchange. This pattern often leads to the perception and often the real experience that interactions with the individual with HFA and
AS are stressful and, in some cases, the interactions produce anxiety and frustration for
both the individual and his or her family members. When appropriate supports are established, family members will be more likely to
experience a sense of competence as effective
communicative and social partners with respect to their children or siblings with HFA or
AS (Dawson & Osterling, 1997).

The role of family support when implementing strategies designed to enhance social
communicative competence for an individual
with HFA and AS, however, is not limited to
the provision of specific training and educational input. Rather, long-term positive outcomes for individuals with social disabilities
require sustained efforts to reduce the emotional stress associated with raising or living
with an individual with a disability by providing individualized and family-centered emotional support (Dawson & Osterling, 1997;
NRC, 2001). "Adaptation to having a child
with a disability is a lifelong process that occurs in a vastly different manner from family
to family and even among family members
within the same family" (Domingue et al.,
2000, p. 373). Therefore, the provision of contexts for one-on-one emotional support and
counseling to foster appropriate expectations
and achievable goals for family life is another
critical component of an educational program
for an individual with HFA and AS.

CONCLUSION

Although there is great heterogeneity across
individuals with HFA and AS with respect to
personal circumstances (e.g., social settings,
family life, and culture) and learning style,
there is a common pattern of impairments in
social communication (i.e., the capacity for

joint attention and understanding of symbolic
conventions) and emotional regulation (i.e.,
the ability to maintain a state of active engagement across social contexts) that compromises
the ability to achieve social communicative
competence. These learning style differences
and developmental vulnerabilities remain a significant challenge across all settings throughout an individual's life and provide potential
barriers to achieving social communicative
competence that can be, in many cases, devastating to the individual (Volkmar et al., 2000).
While the social impairment is attributable
largely to the developmental vulnerabilities
and learning style differences of the individual
with HFA and AS, the "social impairment is
shared" across all of those who have social
contact, positive or negative, with the individual (Gray, 2001). Therefore, the success of any
given social exchange relies not only on an individual's ability to adhere to social conventions, remain actively engaged, and accurately
consider another's intents, but also on a social
partner's ability to adapt his or her interpersonal style and the environment to match the
needs of the individual with the social disability. Thus, comprehensive programming designed to foster social communicative competence must be understood as integral across an
individual's day (e.g., each class at school),
across contexts (e.g., school, home, and community), and across social partners. Additionally, it is critical to consider the following
sources of information when designing an individualized educational program: (1) our current understanding of the core challenges that
compromise social communicative competence
that are faced by individuals with HFA and AS,
(2) the unique learning style differences often
associated with HFA and AS, and (3) our
awareness of the critical priorities for developing a comprehensive intervention program
designed to foster social communicative competence (e.g., establishing interpersonal supports, learning and educational supports, and
the provision of family-centered supports). To
develop social communicative competence
within functional and natural settings, you
must keep in mind the importance of supporting an individual's capacity for emotional regulation. The latter fosters active engagement
across a range of social contexts, the capacity

to appreciate the various social conventions of these contexts, and the capacity to consider the emotional state, intents, and needs of various social partners.

Cross-References

For information on communication development, see Chapters 11 and 12; for additional information on communication intervention, see Chapters 36 and 37; for information on other aspects of development, see Chapters 13, 14, and 15. For information on intervention for other aspects of development, see Chapters 33, 34, and 35.

REFERENCES

American Psychiatric Association. (1994). *Diagnostic and statistical manual of mental disorders* (4th ed.). Washington, DC: Author.

Anzalone, M., & Williamson, G. (2000). Sensory processing and motor performance in autism spectrum disorders. In A. M. Wetherby & B. M. Prizant (Eds.), *Autism spectrum disorders; A transactional developmental perspective* (pp. 143–166). Baltimore: Paul H. Brookes.

Asperger, H. (1944). Die "Autistischen psychopathen" im kindersalter ["Autistic psychopathy" in childhood]. *Archive fur Psychiatrie und Nervenkrankheiten, 117,* 76–136.

Attwood, T. (1998). *Asperger's syndrome: A guide for parents and professionals.* London: Jessica Kingsley.

Bolick, T. (2001). *Asperger syndrome and adolescence: Helping preteens and teens get ready for the world.* Gloucester, MA: Fair Winds Press.

Brown, W. H., & Conroy, M. A. (2002). Promoting peer-related social-communicative competence in preschool children. In H. Goldstein, L. A. Kaczmarek, & K. M. English (Eds.), *Promoting social communication: Children with developmental disabilities from birth to adolescence* (pp. 173–210). Baltimore: Paul H. Brookes.

Carpenter, M., & Tomasello, M. (2000). Joint attention, cultural learning, and language acquisition. In A. M. Wetherby & B. M. Prizant (Eds.), *Autism spectrum disorders: A transactional, developmental perspective* (pp. 31–54). Baltimore: Paul H. Brookes.

Charlop, M. H., & Milstein, J. P. (1989). Teaching autistic children conversational speech using video modeling. *Journal of Applied Behavior Analysis, 22,* 275–285.

Dalrymple, N. J. (1995). Environmental supports to develop flexibility and independence. In K. Quill (Ed.), *Teaching children with autism: Strategies to enhance communication and socialization* (pp. 243–264). Albany, NY: Delmar.

Dawson, G., & Osterling, J. A. (1997). Early Intervention in autism. In M. J. Guralnick (Ed.), *The effectiveness of early intervention* (pp. 307–326). Baltimore: Paul H. Brookes.

Degangi, G. A. (2000). *Pediatric disorders of regulation in affect and behavior: A therapist's guide to assessment and treatment.* San Diego, CA: Academic Press.

Domingue, B., Cutler, B., & McTarnaghan, J. (2000). The experience of autism in the lives of families. In A. Wetherby & B. Prizant (Eds.), *Autism spectrum disorders; a transaction developmental perspective* (pp. 369–393). Baltimore: Paul H. Brookes.

English, K., Goldstein, H., Shafer, K., & Kaczmarek, L. (1997). Promoting interactions among preschoolers with and without disabilities: Effects of a buddy skills training program. *Exceptional Children, 63,* 229–243.

Freeman, S. K., & Dake, L. (1996). *Teach Me Language: A language manual for children with autism, Asperger's syndrome and related developmental disorders.* Langley, Canada: SKF Books.

Garfin, D., & Lord, C. (1986). Communication as a social problem in autism. In E. Schopler & G. Mesibov (Eds.), *Social behavior in autism* (pp. 237–261). New York: Plenum Press.

Goldstein, H., & Wickstrom, S. (1986). Peer intervention effects on communicative interaction among handicapped and nonhandicapped preschoolers. *Journal of Applied Behavior Analysis, 19,* 209–214.

Gray, C. (1994). *Comic strip conversations and social stories.* Arlington, TX: Future Horizons.

Gray, C. (1995). Teaching children with autism to "read" social situations. In K. Quill (Ed.), *Teaching children with autism: Strategies to enhance communication and socialization* (pp. 219–242). Albany, NY: Delmar.

Gray, C. (2001, March). *Correct, confront, concede or teach? How traditional teaching responses model inappropriate social behavior.* Paper presented at the 6th Annual Autism Spectrum Disorder Symposium, Providence, RI.

Gray, C., & Garand, J. (1993). Social Stories: Improving responses of students with autism with accurate social information. *Focus on Autistic Behavior, 8,* 1–10.

Green, G. (1996). Early behavioral intervention for children with autism. In C. Maurice, G. Luce, & S. Luce (Eds.), *Behavioral interventions for young children with autism* (pp. 29–44). Austin, TX: ProEd.

Groden, J., & LeVasseur, P. (1995). Cognitive picture rehearsal: A system to teach self-control. In K. Quill (Ed.), *Teaching children with autism: Strategies to enhance communication and socialization* (pp. 287–306). Albany, NY: Delmar.

Gutstein, S. (2000). *Autism Asperger: Solving the relationship puzzle.* Arlington, TX: Future Horizons.

Hagiwara, R., & Myles, B. S. (2001). A multimedia social story intervention: Teaching skills to children with autism. *Focus on Autism and Other Developmental Disabilities, 2*(14), 82–95.

Haring, T. G., & Breen, C. G. (1992). A peer-mediated social network intervention to enhance the social integration of persons with moderate and severe disabilities. *Journal of Applied Behavior Analysis, 25,* 319–333.

Hodgdon, L. (1995). Solving social behavioral problems through the use of visually supported communication. In K. Quill (Ed.), *Teaching children with autism: Strategies to enhance communication and socialization* (pp. 265–286). Albany, NY: Delmar.

Jahr, E., Eldevik, S., & Eikseth, S. (2000). Teaching children with autism to initiate and sustain cooperative play. *Research in Developmental Disabilities, 21,* 151–169.

Kagan, J., Reznick, J. S., & Snidman, N. (1987). The physiology and psychology of behavioral inhibition in children. *Child Development, 58,* 1459–1473.

Kagan, J., & Snidman, N. (1991). Infant predictors of inhibited and uninhibited profiles. *Psychological Science, 2,* 40–44.

Kagan, J., Snidman, N., & Arcus, D. (1998). Childhood derivatives of high and low reactivity in infancy. *Child Development, 69,* 1483–1493.

Kamps, D. M., Barbetta, P., Leonard, B., & Delquadri, J. (1994). Classwide peer tutoring: An integration strategy to improve reading skills and promote peer interactions among students with autism and general education peers. *Journal of Applied Behavioral Analysis, 27*(1), 49–61.

Kamps, D. M., Leonard, B., Potucek, J., & Garrison, H., L. (1995). Cooperative Learning Groups in Reading: An integration strategy for students with autism and general classroom peers. *Behavioral Disorders, 21*(1), 89–109.

Kamps, D. M., Potucek, J., Lopez, A. G., Kravits, T., & Kemmerer, K. (1997). The use of peer networks across multiple settings to improve social interaction for students with autism. *Journal of Behavioral Education, 7*(3), 335–357.

Kientz, M., & Dunn, W. (1997). A comparison of the performance of children with and without autism on the sensory profile. *American Journal of Occupational Therapy, 51,* 530–537.

Klin, A., & Volkmar, F. R. (1997). Asperger's syndrome. In D. Cohen & F. R. Volkmar (Eds.), *Handbook of autism and pervasive developmental disorders* (2nd ed., pp. 94–122). New York: Wiley.

Klin, A., & Volkmar, F. R. (2000). Treatment and intervention guidelines for individuals with Asperger Syndrome. In A. Klin, F. R. Volkmar, & S. S. Sparrow (Eds.), *Asperger syndrome* (pp. 340–366). New York: Guilford Press.

Koegel, L. K., Koegel, R. L., Yoshen, Y., & McNerney, E. (1999). Pivotal response intervention II: Preliminary long-term outcome data. *Journal of the Association for Persons with Severe Handicaps, 24,* 186–198.

Koenig, K., Rubin, E., Klin, A., & Volkmar, F. R. (2000). Autism and the pervasive developmental disorders. In C. Zeanah (Ed.), *Handbook of infant mental health* (2nd ed., pp. 298–310). New York: Guilford Press.

Kohler, F. W., Strain, P. S., & Shearer, D. D. (1996). Examining levels of social inclusion within an integrated preschool for children with autism. In L. K. Koegel, R. L. Koegel, & G. Dunlap (Eds.), *Positive behavioral support: Including people with difficult behavior in the community* (pp. 305–332). Baltimore: Paul H. Brookes.

Krantz, P. J., & McClannahan, L. E. (1998). Social interaction skills for children with autism: A script fading procedure for beginning readers. *Journal of Applied Behavior Analysis, 31,* 191–202.

Landa, R. (2000). Social language use in Asperger syndrome and high-functioning autism. In A. Klin, F. R. Volkmar, & S. S. Sparrow (Eds.), *Asperger syndrome* (pp. 125–155). New York: Guilford Press.

Lord, C. (1984). The development of peer relations in children with autism. In F. Morrison, C. Lord, & D. Keating (Eds.), *Applied developmental psychology* (pp. 165–229). San Diego, CA: Academic Press.

Lyon, G. R. (1996). The need for conceptual and theoretical clarity in the study of attention, memory, and executive function. In G. R. Lyon & N. Karsnegor (Eds.), *Attention, memory and executive function* (pp. 3–9). Baltimore: Paul H. Brookes.

McAfee, J. (2002). *Navigating the social world: A curriculum for individuals with Asperger's syndrome, high functioning autism, and related disorders.* Arlington, TX: Future Horizons.

Meyer, L., Grenot-Scheyer, M., Schwartz, I., & Harry, B. (1998). Participatory research approaches for the study of social relationships of children and youth. In L. Meyer, H. Park, M. Grenot-Scheyer, I. Schwartz, & B. Harry (Eds.), *Making friends: The influences of culture and development* (pp. 3–29). Baltimore: Paul H. Brookes.

Myles, B. S., & Simpson, R. (1998). *Asperger syndrome: A guide for educators and parents.* Austin, Texas: ProEd.

National Research Council. (2000). *From neurons to neighborhoods* (Committee on Integrating the Science of Early Childhood Development. Institute of Medicine). Washington, DC: National Academy Press.

National Research Council. (2001). *Educating children with autism* (Committee on Educational Interventions for Children with Autism, Commission on Behavioral and Social Sciences and Education). Washington, DC: National Academy Press.

Nelson, K. (1985). *Making sense: The acquisition of shared meaning.* San Diego, CA: Academic Press.

Odom, S. L., McConnell, S. R., McEnvoy, M. A., Peterson, C., Ostrosky, M., Chandler, L. K., et al. (1999). Relative effects of interventions for supporting the social competence of young children with disabilities. *Topics in Early Childhood Special Education, 19,* 75–92.

Oke, N. J., & Schreibman, L. (1990). Training social initiations to a high functioning autistic child: Assessment of collateral behavior change and generalization in a case study. *Journal of Autism and Developmental Disabilities, 20,* 479–497.

Ornitz, E. (1989). Autism at the interface between sensory processing and information processing. In G. Dawson (Ed.), *Autism: Nature, diagnosis and treatment* (pp. 174–207). New York: Guilford Press.

Ozonoff, S., & Griffith, E. (2000). Neuropsychological function and the external validity of Asperger syndrome. In A. Klin, F. R. Volkmar, & S. S. Sparrow (Eds.), *Asperger syndrome* (pp. 72–96). New York: Guilford Press.

Pierce, K., & Schreibman, L. (1995). Increasing complex social behaviors in children with autism: Effects of peer-implemented pivotal response training. *Journal of Applied Behavior Analysis, 28,* 285–295.

Pierce, K., & Schreibman, L. (1997). Multiple peer use of pivotal response training to increase social behaviors of classmates with autism: Results from trained and untrained peers. *Journal of Applied Behavior Analysis, 30,* 157–160.

Prizant, B. M. (1983). Language and communication in autism: Toward an understanding of the "whole" of it. *Journal of Speech and Hearing Disorders, 48,* 296–307.

Prizant, B. M., & Meyer, E. C. (1993). Socioemotional aspects of communication disorders in young children and their families. *American Journal of Speech-Language Pathology, 2,* 56–71.

Prizant, B. M., & Rubin, E. (1999). Contemporary issues in interventions for autism spectrum disorders: A commentary. *Journal of the Association for Persons with Severe Handicaps, 24*(3), 199–208.

Prizant, B. M., Schuler, A. L., Wetherby, A. M., & Rydell, P. J. (1997). Enhancing language and communication: Language approaches. In D. Cohen & F. R. Volkmar (Eds.), *Handbook of autism and pervasive developmental disorders* (2nd ed., pp. 572–605). New York: Wiley.

Prizant, B. M., Wetherby, A. M., Rubin, E., & Laurent, A. (2001, November). *SCERTS: A Transactional-Developmental Intervention Model for Autism Spectrum disorders.* Paper presented at the American Speech-Language-Hearing Association National Conference, New Orleans, LA.

Prizant, B. M., Wetherby, A. M., Rubin, E., & Laurent, A. (in press). The SCERTS Model: A family-centered, transactional approach to enhancing communication and socioemotional abilities of young children with ASD. *Infants and Young Children.*

Prizant, B. M., Wetherby, A. M., & Rydell, P. J. (2000). Communication intervention issues for children with autism spectrum disorders. In A. M. Wetherby & B. M. Prizant (Eds.), *Autism spectrum disorders: A transactional developmental perspective* (pp. 193–224). Baltimore: Paul H. Brookes.

Quill, K. A. (1995). Enhancing children's social-communicative interactions. In K. A. Quill (Ed.), *Teaching children with autism: Strategies to enhance communication and socialization* (pp. 163–189). Albany, NY: Delmar.

Rogers, S. (1996). Brief report: Early intervention in autism. *Journal of Autism and Developmental Disorders, 26,* 243–246.

Roosa, J. (1997). SOCCSS: Situations Options Consequences Choices Strategies Simulation. In B. S. Myles & R. Simpson (Eds.), *Asperger syndrome: A guide for educators and parents* (pp. 79–82). Austin, TX: ProEd.

Rourke, B. P., & Tsatsanis, K. D. (2000). Nonverbal learning disabilities and Asperger syndrome. In A. Klin, F. R. Volkmar, & S. S. Sparrow (Eds.), *Asperger syndrome* (pp. 231–253). New York: Guilford Press.

Schuler, A. L. (1995). Thinking in autism: Differences in learning and development. In K. Quill (Ed.), *Teaching children with autism: Strategies to enhance communication and socialization* (pp. 11–31). Albany, NY: Delmar.

Schuler, A. L., & Wolfberg, P. J. (2000). Promoting peer play and socialization: The art of scaffolding. In A. M. Wetherby & B. M. Prizant (Eds.), *Autism spectrum disorders: A transactional perspective* (pp. 251–277). Baltimore: Paul H. Brookes.

Schwartz, I. (2000). Standing on the shoulders of giants: Looking ahead to facilitating membership and relationships for children with disabilities. *Topics in Early Childhood Special Education, 20*(2), 123–128.

Smith, T. (1996). Are other treatments effective? In C. Maurice, G. Green, & S. Luce (Eds.), *Behavioral interventions for young children with autism* (pp. 45–59). Austin, TX: ProEd.

Stern, D. (1985). *The interpersonal world of the infant.* New York: Basic Books.

Stewart, K. (2002). *Helping a child with nonverbal learning disorder or Asperger's syndrome: A parent's guide.* Oakland, CA: New Harbinger.

Strain, P. S., Kohler, F. W., Storey, K., & Danko, C. D. (1994). Teaching preschoolers with autism to self-monitor their social interactions: An analysis of results in home and school settings. *Journal of Emotional and Behavioral Disorders, 2*(2), 78–88.

Tantum, D. (2000). Adolescence and adulthood of individuals with Asperger syndrome. In A. Klin, F. R. Volkmar, & S. S. Sparrow (Eds.), *Asperger syndrome* (pp. 367–399). New York: Guilford Press.

Tronick. (1989). Emotions and emotional communication in infancy. *American Psychologist, 44,* 112–149.

Venter, A., Lord, C., & Schopler, E. (1992). A follow-up study of high-functioning autistic children. *Journal of Child Psychology and Psychiatry, 33,* 489–507.

Volkmar, F. R., & Klin, A. (2000). Diagnostic issues in Asperger syndrome. In A. Klin, F. R. Volkmar, & S. S. Sparrow (Eds.), *Asperger syndrome* (pp. 25–71). New York: Guilford Press.

Volkmar, F. R., Klin, A., & Cohen, D. J. (1997). Diagnosis and classification of autism and related conditions: Consensus and issues. In D. J. Cohen & F. R. Volkmar (Eds.), *Handbook of autism and pervasive developmental disorders* (2nd ed., pp. 5–40). New York: Wiley.

Volkmar, F. R., Klin, A., Schultz, R., Rubin, E., & Bronen, R. (2000, February). Clinical case conference: Asperger's disorder. *American Journal of Psychiatry, 2*(157), 262–267.

Volkmar, F. R., Klin, A., Siegel, B., Szatmari, P., Lord, C., Campbell, M., et al. (1994). Field Trial for Autistic Disorder in *DSM-IV*. *American Journal of Psychiatry, 151,* 1361–1367.

Vygotsky, L. (1978). *Mind in society: The development of higher psychological processes.* Cambridge, MA: Harvard University Press.

Wetherby, A. M., Prizant, B. M., & Hutchinson, T. (1998). Communicative, social-affective, and symbolic profiles of young children with autism and pervasive developmental disorders. *American Journal of Speech-Language Pathology, 7,* 79–91.

Wetherby, A. M., Prizant, B. M., & Schuler, A. L. (2000). Understanding the nature of communication and language impairments. In A. M. Wetherby & B. M. Prizant (Eds.), *Autism spectrum disorders: A transactional developmental perspective* (pp. 109–141). Baltimore: Paul H. Brookes.

Whitaker, P., Barratt, P., Joy, H., Potter, M., & Thomas, G. (1998). Children with autism and peer group support: Using circles of friends. *British Journal of Special Education, 2*(25), 60–64.

Williams, M. S., & Shellenberger, S. (1996). *How does your engine run? A reader's guide to the alert program for self-regulation.* Albuquerque, NM: Therapy Works.

Winner, M. (2002). *Thinking about you thinking about me.* San Jose, CA: Author.

Wolfberg, P. (1988). *Integrated play groups for children with autism and related disorders.* Unpublished master's thesis, San Francisco State University.

Wolfberg, P. (2003). *Peer play and the autism spectrum: The art of guiding children's socialization and imagination: Integrated Play Groups field manual.* Shawnee Mission, KS: Autism Asperger.

CHAPTER 39

School-Based Programs

JOEL R. ARICK, DAVID A. KRUG, ANN FULLERTON, LAUREN LOOS, AND RUTH FALCO

No area of special education has sparked more controversy, in recent years, than the provision of early intervention for young children with autism. Although families, their advocates, and professionals have engaged in extensive debates, over the last decade, about the efficacy of various treatments and educational strategies, documentation has emerged indicating that intensive early intervention can have significant, positive outcomes for young children with autism. These positive effects include acceleration of developmental rates, significant language gains, and improved social behavior, with a decrease in the symptoms of autism (S. J. Rogers, 2000). Effective intervention for children with autism, within a cost-effective, public program is of importance to school districts throughout the nation.

Several promising programs have been documented (Dawson & Osterling, 1997; Fox, Dunlap, & Philbrick, 1997; Green, 1996; Greenspan & Wieder, 1997; Harris & Handleman, 1994; Olley, Robbins, & Morrelli-Robbins, 1993; S. J. Rogers, 2000). However, The Young Autism Project (Lovaas, 1987, 1996), set a standard for such programs, when it reported that 9 (47%) of 19 children, who received intensive early intervention, successfully completed first grade and obtained average or above average IQ scores. This program uses principles of applied behavior analysis and emphasizes discrete trial teaching methods. Proponents recommend 40 hours per week of one-to-one intervention for up to 2 years, with an emphasis on remediation of speech and language deficits. These services are provided, at least initially, in the

child's home. Advocates for the Lovaas program have promised that children's long-term functioning will improve substantially if parents will obtain this very intensive behavioral intervention for their children (Maurice, Green, & Luce, 1996). Parents have embraced these promises with great fervor and hope.

Many of the early-intervention and early-childhood special education programs were operated by public education early-intervention agencies during the 1990s. They provided children with autism services similar to those provided for other children with developmental delay and disabilities. In addition, early-childhood special education programs had emphasized the philosophy of developmentally appropriate practices, and the inclusionary philosophy of special education (Fox, Hanline, Vail, & Galant, 1994). These trends resulted in a decreased emphasis on specific, teacher-directed instruction for children with special needs and an increased emphasis upon child-directed learning (Bricker, 1998).

Within this context, it is not surprising that there has been a disparity between the expectations of parents of young children with autism and those of public school professionals responsible for early-childhood special education. This disparity has led to numerous due process hearings and court cases that have resulted in orders for intensive early-intervention programs for children with autism, including orders for school districts to fund programs offering 40 hours per week of home-based, one-to-one intervention, often implemented by private service providers (Levin & Weatherly,

1997; LRP Publications, 1997; Mandalawitz, 1996). This process of litigating services for children with autism has raised costs for education agencies, resulted in highly stressful relations between service providers and parents, and led to inequitable provision of services. Within this context, it is critically important for all school programs to demonstrate a replicable model for serving all young children with autism, using research-based approaches. School-based programs can be designed to assist teachers to provide appropriate, behaviorally based instruction to young children with autism. For the past several years, the authors have been assisting public school early-childhood and school-age programs to successfully implement an applied behavioral program with an integrated curriculum (Arick et al., 2003).

The controversy surrounding the demands for intensive early-intervention models has often overshadowed the promising results found in the recent literature. Dawson and Osterling (1997) reviewed eight promising programs and identified six common, essential elements they believe parents should expect a school district to provide for their child. Several models of intervention have published credible results of program evaluation, while implementing these elements in very different ways (S. J. Rogers, 2000). In addition, research has documented a variety of specific, effective strategies that contribute to positive outcomes for children with autism (e.g., Arick, & Falco, 1989; Fox et al., 1997; Goldstein & Strain, 1988; Handleman, Harris, Kristoff, Fuentes, & Alessandri, 1991; R. L. Koegel, O'Dell, & Koegel, 1987; Krantz, McDuff, & McClannahan, 1993; McGee, Daley, & Jacobs, 1994; Pierce & Schreibman, 1995; Stahmer, 1995). School curricula for children with autism should build on the work of researchers and provide a systematic method to implement a school or home-based program for young children with autism.

STRATEGIES FOR TEACHING BASED ON AUTISM RESEARCH

Research-based methods demonstrated to be effective for teaching young children with autism include Discrete Trial Training, Pivotal Response Training, and Teaching Functional Routines (see Table 39.1). An integrated approach can capitalize on the strengths of these techniques by using them in a specific combination. Although these three strategies are the basis for teaching many skills, their implementation will vary according to a child's needs and the setting. For example, a child receiving an intensive behavioral program at the initial-level of communication development will re-

TABLE 39.1   Instructional Strategies Used in the STAR Program (Definitions)

Discrete Trial Training (DT): Skills are taught in a logical sequence building on previously learned skills. Concepts to be taught are identified and then broken down into specific program elements for instruction. Each instructional session consists of a series of discrete trials. A discrete trial consists of a four-step sequence: (1) instructional cue, (2) child response, (3) consequence (generally a positive reinforcer) and, (4) pause. Data is collected to monitor the child's progress and to help determine when a pre-set criteria has been reached. DRT is used to teach receptive language concepts, pre-academic concepts and some mid- and advanced-level expressive language concepts. (Krug et al., 1979, 1981; Leaf & McEachin, 1999; Lovaas, 1981, 1987; Smith, 2001)

Pivotal Response Training (PRT): This training is also based on the four-step sequence: cue, child response, consequence, and pause. However, trials within PRT are incorporated into the environment in a functional context. During PRT, the child chooses the activity or object and the reinforcer is a natural consequence to the behavior being rewarded. The nature of this strategy makes it possible to engage the child throughout all activities and locations throughout the day. (R. L. Koegel et al., 1987, 1989; Laski et al., 1988; Pierce & Schreibman, 1995; Schreibman & Koegel, 1996)

Teaching Functional Routines (FR): Functional routines are predictable events that involve a chain of behaviors. Routines are generally associated with a functional outcome for the child. Some common example routines that all children engage in are: the restroom routine, arrival routine, and snack routine. The functional outcome of a routine usually serves as the reinforcer for typically developing children. (Brown et al., 1987; Cooper et al., 1987; Falco et al., 1990; Marcus et al., 2000; McClannahan & Krantz, 1999)

quire that many of his or her skills be initially taught in a one-to-one setting. As children progress and move into more inclusive environments, the same strategies will be used in slightly different ways in both one-to-one and group instruction. To ensure consistency, these techniques should also be extended to peer tutoring and parent education.

The curriculum needs of children with autism are extensively documented in the literature and summarized in the 2001 National Research Council report (Educating Children with Autism). The report suggests that effective school-based programs should address the critical curriculum needs identified for young children with autism. Typically, curriculum needs are identified as falling within the following six areas: expressive language, receptive language, spontaneous language, preacademic concepts, functional routines, and play and social interaction. In addition to choosing the appropriate curriculum content, the research suggests that instructional strategy is also important to consider. The instructional strategies of Discrete Trial, Pivotal Response Training, and Functional Routines have been identified by the literature to be effective with children with autism (Arick, Loos, Falco, & Krug, 2004; Green, 2001; Koegel, Koegel, Harrower, & Carter, 1999; Krug, Rosenblum, Almond, & Arick, 1981; Lovaas, 1981, 1987; Marcus, Schopler, & Lord, 2000; National Research Council [NRC], 2001).

We suggest using applied behavioral analysis (ABA) methodology as the instructional base for teaching children with autism. A major contribution of ABA has been the large number of interventions derived from its procedures over the past 50 years. The foundation of behavioral principles established by the ABA model include an attention to motivation; systematic task analyses; generalized techniques for building new skills through prompting, shaping, chaining, fading; as well as strategies of self-management (Green, 2001; Schreibman, 2000). Important instructional systems based on these principles of ABA include the three primary instructional techniques of Discrete Trial Training, Pivotal Response Training, and Teaching Functional Routines.

These three behavioral instructional strategies, identified from recent research

literature, can be used in combination with specific appropriately matched curriculum content areas. Prizant and Rubin (1999) suggest that this type of individualized curriculum approach should address the needs of many children with autism.

Described in this section is a curriculum approach developed by the authors through their work with children with autism since 1972. The book *Autistic and Severely Handicapped in the Classroom* (1981) by Krug and colleagues documented some of the author's early work. Arick, Loos, and Falco, began working together in 1997, to provide consultation services to many programs for children with autism in the Pacific Northwest. They developed a comprehensive curriculum appropriate for young children with autism, called Strategies for Teaching based on Autism Research: STAR (Arick, Loos, et al., 2004). Many of the instructional procedures described in this chapter have been successfully used with over 100 children in Oregon under the direction of the authors. In a report completed by one of the countywide agencies in Oregon, the STAR curriculum methods and instructional strategies of this early-childhood/elementary school-based program were evaluated. The report monitored the progress of 25 children with autism from five different classroom settings in which the authors provided consultation services. Using the assessment methods described in an article by Arick and colleagues (2003), the report documents the progress made by these children over the 2001/2002 school year. Children engaged in this curriculum, on average, gained more than a month of language age for every month of instruction. In addition, their functional communication and social skills increased.

A more widespread study of the use of the STAR program was conducted as part of the Autism Outcome Study in the state of Oregon. Arick and colleagues (2003) describe how teachers throughout the state of Oregon were provided training in the use of the STAR curriculum. The progress of 67 children with autism was monitored. That study showed that the majority of the children made significant progress in social interaction, expressive speech, and use of language concepts. In addition, they displayed significant decreases in behaviors associated with autism spectrum disorders.

The development of the STAR program has been guided by the national research on effective practices identified in the literature. The curriculum content and the instructional methods used in this integrated curriculum are often described in the literature as effective with children with autism.

Early-childhood and school-age programs need to monitor the educational progress of children with autism. Several assessment instruments have been developed and standardized to assist in the diagnosis and educational progress monitoring. The Autism Screening Instrument for Educational Planning (ASIEP-2) is one of these instruments (Krug, Arick, & Almond, 1993). The ASIEP-2 helps with diagnosis, and several subtests of the ASIEP-2 can help to monitor the progress of young children with autism over time (Frye & Walker, 1998). According to the *Mental Measurement Yearbook* (Turton, 1986), the ASIEP-2 subtests have been shown to have reliability and validity with this population of children. An autism spectrum disorder outcome study conducted in Oregon (Arick et al., 2003) is a good example of progress monitoring using the ASIEP-2. Students with autism were followed intensely for over 3 years.

Ongoing and future research will indicate more about the effectiveness of a variety of interventions, but the work of numerous practitioners and researchers over the past 50 years has demonstrated that ABA provides an effective set of principles for teaching students who have autism spectrum disorder (Koegel et al., 1999; Lovaas, 1987; Schreibman, 2000). However, the technology of ABA provides instructional techniques, not a curriculum for working with children with autism. The STAR program provides a comprehensive curriculum for teachers to effectively implement ABA instructional strategies.

Applied Behavior Analysis Related to Instruction

Applied behavior analysis refers to the basic theories of behavior developed by Watson (1913), Thorndike (1921), Skinner (1938), and others, and subsequently refined into a general method of instruction for individuals with autism (Baer, Wolf, & Risley, 1968) in the 1960s. Teaching methods based on ABA, include the research-based instructional strategies used with Discrete Trial Training, Pivotal Response Training, and Teaching Functional Routines.

The ABA process includes conducting a baseline assessment; implementing a behavioral intervention (such as Discrete Trial or Pivotal Response Training); collecting ongoing data during intervention, making intervention changes based on data collected; reassessing the effect on the target behavior; generalizing the application of the target behavior; and repeating the process as necessary (Baer et al., 1968; Green, 2001).

When used in combination with an appropriate curriculum sequence, these ABA instructional strategies can provide a powerful tool for enabling children with autism to meet important educational goals. Often, an important missing link in the field of special education is a comprehensive, researched-based curriculum that uses the full range of instructional and behavioral techniques available to the educator. The STAR integrated curriculum provides this approach.

In the behavioral view, autism is a syndrome of behavioral deficits and excesses that have a biological basis, but can be changed through structured interactions with the environment. A combination of ABA intervention techniques can provide multiple planned opportunities for the learner to develop and practice skills, so learning can occur and be generalized to a variety of environments. These ABA procedures need to be used not only to teach skills in isolation, but also to teach students to use skills learned in their daily routines. The ABA provides a powerful technology of instruction. High levels of precision in the instructional process and intervention procedures are required to meet the challenge of effectively teaching children with autism. The school-based integrated curriculum we propose uses a planned combination of ABA instructional techniques and appropriate curriculum content to provide young children with autism an individualized educational program. The program we propose is also designed to teach the use of skills within daily routines. The effectiveness of the program should be continuously monitored using daily data and standardized measures. Data from these measures should be used to make ongoing programming decisions. Reviewing a few learning characteristics of children with autism can show the need for this type of program.

Learning Characteristics of Children with Autism Related to Curriculum Needs

Research studies conducted over the past 40 years have repeatedly demonstrated that children with autism present several learning characteristics that require specific instructional skills (Arick, Loos, et al., 2004). A particularly challenging learning characteristic of children with autism is the *failure to make critical discriminations* when exposed to new learning. For instance, problems with auditory discrimination can result in having difficulty connecting words to objects and people. This difficulty is sometimes present when performing very simple auditory or visual discriminations. As a result of this learning characteristic, most behavior analytic curricula developed since the 1960s have included techniques for teaching learners with autism to discriminate among various types of stimuli. These techniques include a variety of discrimination-teaching methods including match-to-sample trials, use of a distracting stimulus, extrastimulus prompting, and within-stimulus prompting (Arick & Krug, 1978; Green, 2001; Schreibman, 1975). Discrimination-teaching procedures are a basic requirement to effectively teach learners with autism to discriminate both visual and auditory stimuli. Discrete Trial programs are specifically designed to teach the child to associate words with objects, people, actions, and events.

Although various ABA paradigms are used to deliver antecedents and consequence, most also have discrimination learning as an element of their methodology; it is primarily Discrete Trial Training that focuses on this aspect of learning. An effective school-based curriculum should prioritize discrimination issues by using Discrete Trial Training strategies that (1) carefully present stimuli in a systematic manner and with planned repetition; (2) provide a planned process for teaching the relationship of words to functional objects, people, and other important concepts; and (3) use systematic visual stimulus to teach important functional auditory discriminations. An effective program will also provide the student with opportunities to use newly learned skills within their daily routines in order to generalize the use of the skills in context.

A second and fundamental core learning deficit exhibited by children with autism that specifically impedes language development is *joint attention deficit* (Mundy, Sigman, & Kasari, 1990; Stone, Ousley, Yoder, Hogan, & Hepburn, 1997; Wetherby, Prizant, & Hutchinson, 1998). Joint attention is the ability to coordinate attention between people and objects and involves advanced gesturing such as showing, waving, and pointing. Autistic children with deficits in joint attention have difficulty coordinating attention between people and objects, orienting and attending, and following the gaze and pointing of another person. Failure to acquire gestural joint attention appears to be a critical developmental milestone in early normal language development and has been found in several studies to be a common deficit in preschool children with autism (Mundy et al., 1990). A school-based curriculum can address these issues by using Pivotal Response Training and Functional Routine strategies to teach the child to use language in naturalistic settings and to teach joint play activities. Using these strategies, teachers can show children how to understand the relationship between people and objects and how to interact with others.

Another learning characteristic that is apparent in children with autism is their difficulty in generalizing newly learned skills. Discrete Trial Training has been used to teach new skills, often called acquisition learning. In many cases when a new skill is learned in Discrete Trial, such as to match colors, the skill may not be used functionally by the child without planning for generalization and teaching the child to use this skill within a variety of contexts. Generalization of skills has been identified as an important aspect to consider in designing any instruction for children with autism (Prizant & Wetherby, 1998; Smith, 2001). Smith indicates that incidental teaching and other instructional approaches may be more effective than Discrete Trial Training for helping children transfer skills to new settings. He goes on to say that the incidental teaching approaches and Discrete Trial Training often complement each other. There are several methods that can be used to teach the generalization of skills. First, the Discrete Trial programs themselves are meant to teach functional skills that can be used in multiple settings. Second, each new skill learned should be practiced in a more student-directed setting, using Pivotal Response Training. Third, newly learned skills are to be taught during the students' normal activities by embedding the skills into Functional Routine programs.

Prizant and Rubin (1999) wrote:

1. Research has supported the effectiveness of a range of approaches that differ in both underlying philosophy and practice (Dawson & Osterling, 1997; S. J. Rogers, 2000).

2. No evidence exists that any one approach is more effective than others (Dawson & Osterling, 1997; Sheinkopf & Siegel, 1998).

3. No one approach is equally effective for all children. Not all children in outcome studies have benefited to the same degree from a specific approach (Dawson & Osterling, 1997; S. J. Rogers, 2000).

INSTRUCTIONAL TECHNIQUES FOR CHILDREN WITH AUTISM

Discrete Trial Training

Discrete Trial Training is one of a variety of approaches in the STAR program that use principles of ABA. Discrete Trial Training begins with a comprehensive assessment of each learner's current skills and needs, typically by observing the learner directly in a variety of situations. Every skill that is selected for instruction is defined in clear, observable terms and then broken down into its component parts (Arick, Loos, et al., 2004; Krug et al., 1981). Each component response is taught by presenting a specifically defined antecedent (cue or prompt). When a target response occurs, it is followed immediately by a consequence that has been found to be reinforcing to the learner. Responses other than the target response are ignored. Each antecedent-response-consequence cycle is a learning trial. These trials are repeated many times until the learner performs the response correctly and fluently (Green, 2001). The student responses are recorded, based on defined, specific objective criteria. Usually, the data is then summarized to show the learner's progress.

The Discrete Trial system reported by Donnellan-Walsh (1976) enabled the controlled presentation of stimulus and consequence for a precise, continuous evaluation of performance and provided the ability to make immediate adjustment in teaching strategy. The Discrete Trial Training strategy generally employs a teaching staff to student ratio of one-to-one to ensure the accuracy of programs and to maximize student attention.

Current implementation of ABA in the treatment of autism often involves the exclusive use of Discrete Trial methodology. This technique breaks tasks down to their simplest teachable components. Components are taught by presenting a specific cue to the child. If the child gives a specific correct response, a reward is given. A short pause precedes presentation of the next cue. If the child responds incorrectly, the cue should be represented and the child should be given a prompt to ensure that the child does not make another error. Children who participate in Discrete Trial programs are typically taught tasks from a standard curriculum (Lovaas, 1981; Maurice et al., 1996). The curriculum consists of a hierarchy of skills starting with attending (e.g., "look at me" and "hands down") and imitation. Skills advance through varying levels of social, language, academic, and play drills.

The individualized Discrete Trial Training procedures developed, and refined over the years have proven extremely effective with students with autism. Prizant and Wetherby (1998) indicate that various researchers suggest, based on the Lovaas study of 1987, that the instructional procedures of Discrete Trial Training should be the primary instructional method for teaching many new forms of behavior and new discriminations to children with autism. However, researchers have recently suggested that these children also require incidental teaching and other instructional approaches to generalize these skills to new situations. For generalization to occur, the skills need to be practiced and reinforced in many different settings and with different people (Prizant & Wetherby, 1998; Smith, 2001).

Discrete Trial Training is effective for teaching many skills and is probably the best current method for teaching academic and receptive language skills. However, even when correctly and consistently implemented, exclusive use of the Discrete Trial method can result in lack of generalization of acquired skills. Children can become dependent on the teacher and on cues that appear in teaching sessions. Even when skills are learned, it is often difficult for children to use them in the appropriate contexts without direct cues.

Initially, Discrete Trial Training is the primary method for teaching a child with autism preacademic skills, most receptive language concepts/skills and some more complex expressive language discriminations. These areas of the curriculum most closely align with the Discrete Trial procedures. In normal communication situations, a verbal cue is typically provided to elicit a receptive language response from another person, and in general a verbal cue is typically given to teach a preacademic concept to a child. The primary method used to teach expressive language, play, and social interaction skills, in a more natural and contextually appropriate way, is Pivotal Response Training (PRT; R. L. Koegel et al., 1989). Daily routines and self-care skills are taught using a strategy called Functional Routines instruction (FR; Arick & Falco, 1989; Krantz et al., 1993). Skills taught with DT training and PRT are then integrated into the children's day by teaching them in context, using Functional Routine instruction.

Pivotal Response Training

Pivotal Response Training is a behavioral-based method used in the STAR program and addresses the need for the child to learn to respond in a more natural child-centered way, than traditional Discrete Trial Training uses. Pivotal Responses are those that affect wide areas of a child's functioning. The specific pivotal responses targeted are motivation and responsiveness to multiple cues. Some researchers suggest that this technique can be more effective than Discrete Trial Training in increasing spontaneous use of expressive language and increased generalization and

maintenance of those behavioral changes (R. L. Koegel et al., 1987; Laski, Charlop, & Schreibman, 1988).

In the school-based model presented here, Pivotal Response Training is used to target expressive language and play skills. Although it uses a Discrete Trial paradigm, the major components make it significantly different. In Pivotal Response Training, trials are child-directed, and teachers work within the student's preferred activities. Elicited responses are appropriate to the activity (e.g., if the child has chosen to work with bubbles, elicited language might be "bubbles"; "I want bubbles"; "blow") and the student is reinforced for good attempts along with correct responses. Spontaneous actions are encouraged. These actions are facilitated by the teacher's controlling access to a desired item and waiting until the student responds appropriately (e.g., The student sees the bubbles on the table and says "I want" while gesturing toward bubbles).

Pivotal Response Training has also been shown to be an effective method for teaching functional and symbolic play skills (Stahmer, 1995), and sociodramatic play (Thorp, Stahmer, & Schreibman, 1995). Teaching play through the use of Pivotal Response Training will be facilitated by using the same principles as those used to teach language, except that the targeted behaviors will be functional levels of play.

Teaching within Functional Routines

Even when skills are learned, whether by Discrete Trial or Pivotal Response Training, it is frequently difficult for children to use them in the appropriate contexts without direct cues (Arick, Loos, et al., 2004). A way to effectively address this is to teach skills within a functional routine. In this context, behaviors can more easily come under the control of natural cues in the environment (Cooper, Heron, & Heward, 1987).

Functional routines can be interspersed throughout the day for each child at all levels. Routines might include arrival, transition, mealtime, toileting, and recreational routines such as playground or walks. Each routine should be broken down into simple steps, which can be taught using the most appropriate behavioral method. For example, a transition routine may consist of a cue for transition, checking a schedule, pulling a line-drawing card from the schedule to indicate the next activity, taking the card to the next designated location of the new activity, putting the card into a pocket by a match-to-sample technique, and beginning the new activity. Each one of these components will be taught within the context of performing the routine, enabling children to eventually rely on natural cues and reinforcers to maintain their behavior. When the child has learned some appropriate receptive or expressive language skills in its Discrete Trial or Pivotal Response Training sessions, these skills can then be added to the STAR Functional Routine Program Data Worksheet. The skill is then integrated into the routine at appropriate intervals. An example of this would be to integrate the receptive language skill of being able to respond to the cue "get coat." This skill can be integrated into the departure routine.

APPROPRIATE CURRICULUM CONTENT

The integrated school-based curriculum approach used in the STAR program was developed to provide instruction to children with autism in several interrelated areas and provide a comprehensive individualized educational program. The curriculum areas correspond directly to the needs of children with autism, as documented in the literature.

The following sections describe the rationale for focusing a school-based curriculum in these areas.

Communication Skills (Expressive/ Receptive Language and Spontaneous Language)

Children with autism often have delay or impairment in the area of communication. Many young children with autism do not use appropriate communication to make requests. Other children with autism are able to communicate requests, but are not able to describe the activities of the world around them. Chapter 37 in this volume covers the area of communication and skill development in detail.

Daily Routines

Skills for daily routines are usually taught through a process that begins with a task analysis, a process for breaking down a skill into its component parts (Haring, 1988). Instruction then proceeds through a process of teaching each component skill in small steps and ultimately chaining the sequence of behaviors together. Studies have shown that individuals with autism can be taught purchasing skills and other community living skills, such as using vending machines (McClannahan & Krantz, 1999). In addition, teaching routines such as clothing selection, pedestrian safety, bus riding, and independent walking can substantially enhance community access for individuals with autism (Gruber, Reeser, & Reid, 1979; Sprague & Horner, 1984).

Preacademic Skills

Autistic spectrum disorders (ASDs) are a constellation of disorders that affect many aspects of thinking and learning. Thus, educational interventions cannot assume a typical sequence of learning; interventions must be individualized. Some children with autism can learn academic skills quickly and effectively. Other children with autism struggle to discriminate simple aspects of academic instruction such as colors or shapes. In the years since Kanner's work, it has become apparent that although some areas of intellectual development are often relatively strong, many other areas are significantly developmentally delayed. Children with ASD have unique patterns of development, both as a group and as individuals. Many children with ASD have relative strengths that can be used to buttress their learning. For example, a child with strong visual-spatial skills may learn to read words to cue social behavior, and a child with good auditory memory may develop a repertoire of socially appropriate phrases for specific situations (National Research Council, 2001). It is possible to use the strengths of individual children to assist them to learn language and their world around them. The instruction of academic skills can teach the child how to perform academic skills and provide a bridge to learn language and social skills.

Play Skills

By definition, children with autism demonstrate impairments in relationships to peers and the use of symbolic or dramatic play. Peer interactions are characterized by low rates of initiation and response (Corona, Dissanayake, Arbelle, Wellington, & Sigman, 1998). Children with autism appear to pay less attention to other people's emotional displays than do comparison groups and demonstrate less imitation of other people's actions, movements, and vocalizations (DeMyer et al., 1972; Stone et al., 1997). Among toddlers with autism, Charman (1997) reported that the production of symbolic play acts was markedly deficient. In addition, other studies have found more repetitive and immature play in children with autism (Libby, Powell, Messer, & Jordan, 1998). Several investigators have found that interventions for stimulating symbolic play development in preschoolers with autism have been successful (Goldstein & Strain, 1988; Stahmer, 1995; Thorp et al., 1995).

Social Interaction Skills

Difficulties with social interactions have been one of the consistent hallmarks of autism from its first description (Kanner, 1943). The behavioral approach to treating social interaction difficulties of autism has been in use since the 1960s. Numerous interventions, based on behavioral approaches, have successfully taught social behaviors to children with autism. Odom and Strain (1986) reviewed the literature and found that direct teaching children with autism to interact with peers has been successful, teaching typical peers to interact with children who have autism has also been successful, and a combination of these approaches has been most effective. Typically developing peers have successfully learned to use incidental teaching (McGee, Almeida, Sulzer-Azaroff, & Feldman, 1991) and Pivotal Response Training (Pierce & Schreibman, 1995) to increase reciprocal interaction with their peers who have autism.

TEACHING AREAS AND GENERAL STRATEGIES

For conceptual and organizational purposes, curriculum can be divided into major teaching areas. The six areas we recommend are expressive language, receptive language, spontaneous language, preacademic concepts, play skills, social interaction skills, and functional routines. Table 39.2 shows the interaction between each instructional strategy and the curriculum areas for which it is primarily used. Table 39.2 also shows the ways in which multiple strategies can address some curriculum areas.

Using different strategies within the same curriculum area facilitates generalization and maintenance of acquired skills. For example, expressive language taught primarily using Pivotal Response Training, is also incorporated into Discrete Trial and Functional Routines. This helps to prevent dependence on situational cues for language use.

Because of the instructional precision required to effectively teach children with autism, it is important that teachers utilize systematic, carefully considered approaches. One of the best ways to accomplish this is to have a carefully developed program with a detailed overall program scope and sequence. The program's scope and sequence should be organized developmentally.

A program plan is a detailed lesson plan that can be used by an instructional assistant, teacher, parent, or tutor to teach a specific skill or routine. Program plans are written in a format to ensure that appropriate Discrete Trial, Pivotal Response Training and/or Functional Routines strategies are followed. To promote generalization, many skills are taught by more than one instructional strategy.

To be effective, an integrated school-based curriculum is required and should be designed to provide a comprehensive educational program for children with autism. It can be effectively organized by learning level and by teaching strategy.

Curriculum materials and record forms can become extensive, so it is important for teachers to maintain a well-organized system. We have found that a folder system works well. Each folder contains an instructional program plan for teaching a specific concept and data sheets for recording learning. Each instructional program provides the needed instructions for teaching the concept being addressed and can be readily used by

TABLE 39.2   Interaction of Instructional Strategies and Curriculum Areas

Curriculum Areas Used in STAR Program	Instructional Strategies Used in STAR Program		
	Pivotal Response Training	Discrete Trial Training	Teaching Functional Routines
Expressive language	All expressive language programs	Specific imitative sounds/words Specific labels Most mid-level and advance programs	Develop generalization of expressive language
Receptive language	Taught incidentally within context of other Pivotal Response Training programs	All receptive language programs	Generalize use of receptive language within routines
Spontaneous language	All spontaneous language instruction programs	Reinforce spontaneous language when it occurs	Set up situations in which the student needs to use spontaneous language
Functional routines	Expand expressive language using Pivotal Response Training strategies within routine	Expand receptive language using Discrete Trial within routine	All activities comprised of a predictable chain of behaviors
Preacademic skills	Expand and generalize use of preacademic skills	All preacademic programs	Generalize use of preacademic skills within routines
Play skills and social interaction skills	Play skills are taught with Pivotal Response Training-play programs, and incidentally during Pivotal Response Training-language	Social interaction and play is taught incidentally during 1:1 Discrete Trial sessions	Develop appropriate play and social interaction during all appropriate routines (e.g., Play a game with a peer; recess routine with a peer buddy)

instructional assistants. Data sheets are used to monitor student progress.

A complete set of program plans is needed to assist other staff to implement a behaviorally based program for children with autism in the public schools. The STAR program provides a complete and comprehensive set of program plans and materials needed to implement a behaviorally based program for young children with autism in the public schools (Arick, Loos, et. al., 2004).

Research shows that intensive early intervention for children with autism can make a difference in their rate of progress (Lovaas, 1987; Smith, 2001). The National Research Council (2001) recommended that educational services begin as soon as a child is suspected of having an ASD and that those services should use systematically planned instruction.

Early stages of learning for many children with autism requires one-to-one instructional sessions for at least part of the day in order to achieve learning success. Some programs can be taught in a quiet setting within a classroom, while other programs can be taught throughout the school environment. The environment should be organized so that the child has an opportunity to practice the transition routine several times during the day. Transition routines can involve the use of a visual schedule to help children be independent during their transitions between activities.

One common process for implementing individual one-to-one instruction is to organize the child's day into a combination of instructional one-to-one rotations, small group instruction, and other types of instructional settings (depending on the needs of the child, e.g., inclusion in regular education). The Discrete Trial and Pivotal Response Training sessions would be carried out during the one-to-one rotations. The number of rotations will vary based on each child's individual needs. Our own work suggests that one-to-one instruction should occur four to five times per week. The length of each Discrete Trial rotation will vary between 5 to 30 minutes depending on the child. Another factor to consider is the child's age.

If the child is between 2 to 5 years of age, the program should include a combination of one-to-one, small group, and preschool activities. It is more consistent for the child's program if all of these services can be done by a core group of staff members. It is often helpful if the staff member who is teaching the child during the one-to-one sessions is familiar with the skills the child needs to generalize into the small-group and preschool activities. However, it is a good idea to have a variety of staff work with the child over time so that the child learns to respond to a variety of people. This may mean that a staff member is assigned to the child for 2 to 3 weeks and then switches to another child after that time period. If this is not possible, the staff person who provides one-on-one services needs to inform the next staff member about the skills the child has learned in the Discrete Trial or Pivotal Response Training session during a staff meeting or through conversation prior to the time the child goes to small group or preschool.

In our experience, the best preschool environment for the child at the beginning level of instruction is a very structured environment. It is very important for the preschool activities to be scheduled and supervised in a systematic way that allows children with autism to respond using skills they have been learning in their one-on-one sessions. The preschool environment needs to provide a consistent classroom schedule of activities and allow for the child with autism to have an individualized adapted schedule if needed. It is usually better if the amount of free play time is at a minimum and if the preschool activities are fairly structured, adult-directed activities with enough adults to assist peers to interact with the child with autism. Sometimes, this environment is available in an integrated preschool (i.e., a combination of typical peers and children with

autism). In rare cases, this environment may also be available in a typical preschool.

School-age children with autism should be doing many of the typical school routines performed by all students. This will involve practicing routines such as eating lunch, arriving at school, recess, and others that are appropriate to the child's age. By participating in these routines, the child will become more familiar with the school environment, and the child's independence level at school should improve.

INSTRUCTING MIDDLE SCHOOL AND HIGH SCHOOL STUDENTS WITH AUTISM

In this section, the strengths and challenges for adolescents with ASD in the areas of sensory differences and anxiety, academic achievement, and social functioning are summarized. Ways that parents, teachers, and peers can support youth with ASD in each of these areas in school are described. In addition, needs and accommodations related to identity formation and the transition to adulthood, which are critical tasks in adolescence and young adulthood, are addressed. Self-reports from individuals with ASD, research findings, and best practices among teachers and autism specialists are included.

Personal accounts from adolescents with ASD of their perceptions and experiences during middle and high school (Carrington & Graham, 2001; Ward & Alar, 2000) are useful in understanding why certain supports are needed.

Sensory Differences and Anxiety

Researchers, parents, and persons with autism have all reported that individuals with ASD have different responses to sensory stimuli. One learns about the world through one's senses. Thus, a different sensory system can be associated with developing a different understanding of environmental events and human behaviors.

More than one sense may be affected and both hyper- and hyposensitivities may be experienced at the same time. Some persons with ASD report that when there is too much sensory stimulation, they experience sensory overload (Grandin, 1992) and a temporary shutdown of, for example, vision or hearing (D. Williams, 1994). Another experience that is described is an inability to focus on a specific sensory input if there is too much sensory background present (e.g., using the phone in an airport; Grandin & Scariano, 1986). A related experience of some persons with ASD is being unable to shift one's attention from one sensory modality to another (e.g., from visual to auditory input; Grandin, 1992; D. Williams, 1994). Studies have shown that some persons with ASD have difficulty shifting between different cues in one sensory modality (Wainwright-Sharp & Bryson, 1993), and with shifting attention between sensory modalities (Courchesne, Akshoomoff, & Ciesielski, 1990). Studies suggest that portions of the brain that regulate sensory input may be different in persons with ASD (Bauman & Kemper, 1994).

Differences in various sensory systems, including auditory, olfactory, gustatory, vestibular, and visual systems have been reported. A survey of over 12,000 parents of ASD children indicated that approximately 40% of their children exhibit some form of painful hearing (Rimland, 1990). Adolescents with ASD with hypersensitive olfactory sense report that they can tell what their teachers had for dinner the night before by smelling their breath from the middle of the classroom (Fullerton, personal communication, 1995). Others cannot tolerate certain food textures or tastes. Individuals with autism report difficulty with eye contact, overreliance on peripheral vision, sensitivity to light and color, tunnel vision, and differences in how temporal-spatial relationships are visually perceived (Rimland, 1964; Slavik, 1983; Volkmar & Mayes, 1990; Wulf, 1994). D. Williams (1994) reports that her visual perception fragments scenes and objects, and she cannot distinguish between the foreground and background. She was not aware that she saw things differently until she tried corrective lenses. According to her, the lenses allowed her to look directly at an object, scene, or person and see the parts and whole as one, integrated perception.

Some, but by no means all, persons with autism have had these experiences. Some individuals with ASD report that their sensory sensitivities decreased with age. They suspect that this occurred because they learned to adapt to or cope with the sensitivity. For example, vision or hearing others, no change occurred with age; and as adults they have made lifestyle choices in order to reduce, for example, the level of auditory stimulation in their home (A. Fullerton, personal communication, 1992–1993). It is critical that teachers and peers of adolescents with ASD acknowledge that a middle or high school student with ASD may be experiencing different and stressful sensory experiences from other students and provide needed understanding and accommodation.

Emotions, Stress, Anxiety during Adolescence

The emotional upheavals of adolescence can be very difficult for the young person with ASD. They may have to cope with the changes adolescence brings without as many opportunities for peer group discussion and support enjoyed by others at this life stage (Dewey & Everard, 1974). Youth with autism and ASD exhibit a greater rate of anxiety and depression, with a significant impact on overall adaptation (Kim, Szatmari, Bryson, Streiner, & Wilson, 2000).

With increased awareness of differences in social situations, repeated lack of success in forming friendships, and the increased demands for more abstract and complex academic assignments, adolescents with autism and ASD are vulnerable to depression (K. Williams, 2001; Wing, 1981, 1992). Depression may manifest itself in ways that are hard to detect, such as a decreased desire for social contact, and increased adherence to certain routines and solitary interests (Wing, 1981, 1992) or greater levels of disorganization, inattentiveness, and isolation (Williams, 2001).

Many persons with ASD report social situations are often very stressful and confusing. Because of their intellectual strengths, more is expected of higher functioning persons with autism than from persons with more obvious challenges (Wing, 1992). The effort to avoid doing the wrong thing in social situations, particularly when unsure what the wrong thing would be, can be highly stressful. For example, one young man explained that "as a general rule, the more 'normal' [my] behavior appears, the more guarded and anxious [I am]" (Cesaroni & Garber, 1991, p. 309).

In addition to such situational anxiety, some persons with ASD experience a physiologically based, constant, exhausting anxiety (Bemporad, 1979; Grandin, 1992; Rumsey et al., 1985). Grandin experienced this with the onset of puberty. Temple said it "was like a constant feeling of stage fright. . . . Just imagine how you felt when you did something really anxiety provoking, such as your first public speaking engagement. Now just imagine if you felt that way most of the time for no reason. . . . It was like my brain was running at 200 miles an hour, instead of 60 miles an hour." (p. 111). Parents have observed that one of the reasons it is so hard for individuals with autism to adjust to a sudden change is that they stay in a state of hyperarousal much longer than others (McDonnell, 2000).

Supports for Sensory Differences, Anxiety, and Emotional Vulnerability

A variety of supports have been used to prevent or reduce anxiety and stress for youth with ASD and to provide emotional safety. One of the most important components in reducing stress- and anxiety-related behaviors is to prevent them by providing instructions and information in ways that the adolescent with autism can understand. For many individuals with ASD, this often involves providing information visually. A second vital component for preventing stress-related outbursts is to prepare and inform the adolescent with autism ahead of time about changes in routine and about what will happen during a new activity. Examples of methods to provide information visually are offered later in this section.

Another way to reduce stress and anxiety, and divert an emotional outburst or a shutdown in sensory and cognitive processing is to have a preplanned process in which the student can take a break from an activity or class. The noise, activity level, academic stressors, peer relationships, and unforeseen events are all challenging for the adolescent in middle or high school. Usually, a procedure is worked out among the student, teacher, and other staff in the school. The teacher makes an effort to know what behaviors indicate the student is reaching his or her limit and becoming agitated. The student and teacher may also work out a visual sign or other method by which the student can request a break. The break may involve stepping out into the hall next to the classroom and, if

more time is needed, going to a predetermined supervised office area or other classroom in the school. The student returns to class as soon as he feels calm and able to focus on schoolwork. The student meets with the teacher to make up work missed (Safran, 2002).

Establishing a predetermined plan for escape and taking a break provide the student with autism a much-needed safety valve for making it through the school day. Adolescents with ASD report that after each stressful school day, they spend an hour or more at home minimizing sensory stimulation and regaining their composure before they engage in other activities (Fullerton, personal communication, 1995).

It is important to provide a safety net for the student with ASD by having an identified support person in the school (e.g., guidance counselor, special education teacher) to meet with briefly every day. This staff member (who knows the student well) can assess how well she is coping and also gather observations from other teachers if needed. Because students with ASD have such difficulty recognizing and expressing their fears or anxieties, the daily check-in can prevent anxieties from escalating into a meltdown (K. Williams, 2001).

For some students, exercise is an excellent way to reduce stress. Grandin (1992) found strenuous exercise helped her reduce stress and anxiety during her teen years. One high school student knew that if she could run for a half-hour in the middle of the day, she could focus on her studies in the afternoon. She didn't know however, how to advocate for herself and frame this request as an accommodation. School personnel refused to change her schedule so that she could have PE at the needed time (Fullerton, personal communication, 1995). While remembering that communication is difficult for students with ASD, we need to find ways to listen to what they think might help them be successful in school.

Medication is often beneficial in reducing anxiety. However, persons with autism can be extremely sensitive to the effects of medication, and it is critical that a physician knowledgeable about autism help determine the proper medication and dosage level (Grandin, 1992; McDonnell, 2000).

Occupational therapy can offer prescribed sensory activities to improve sensory integration and reduce sensitivity (Myles, Cook,

Miller, Rinner, & Robbins, 2000). Grandin's (1992) anxiety led her to invent a "squeeze machine" at age 18. The machine allows a person to control the amount of pressure he applies to the sides of his body by pulling on a lever. The deep pressure provided by the squeeze machine can be very calming.

Another useful strategy is to learn relaxation techniques. Grodin and her associates (Cautela & Grodin, 1978; Harrington, Samdperil, Groden, & Groden, 1991) have developed relaxation and imagery programs for persons with autism to reduce stress. Many autism specialists agree that learning to use relaxation techniques and to recognize when one needs them is very important. Relaxation techniques reduce outbursts and disruptive actions (Mullins & Christian, 2001). Autism consultants have developed visually supported routines to help adolescents recognize when they are anxious, so they can self-direct a process to calm down, refocus, and then rejoin an activity (Buron & Curtis, 2004).

It is important that youth with ASD who have sensory and anxiety issues be taught a way to recognize when they are stressed and then a procedure for taking a break, calming down, and regaining their physical and emotional equilibrium. It is equally important that staff in schools, recreation programs, and other programs take seriously the youth with autism's need to be supported in modulating the level of sensory input and social and cognitive demands they experience so that they can function optimally.

Cognitive Strengths and Challenges

The cognitive style of individuals with autism is described as one in which information is taken in with little analysis or integration (Frith, 1989; Janzen, 1993; Prizant, 1983). All of the aspects of an experience are taken in and may be remembered with equal significance. The person with autism has difficulty extracting from the situation what others would see as the most relevant, functional, or meaningful features. The cognitive style described by Janzen (1996) and Frith (1989) is reflected in how persons with autism attend, learn, remember, and solve problems.

Sometimes, not seeing the overall context can be useful. Some children with autism can memorize a meaningful sentence and a random list of words equally well. Children *without* autism, however, find it harder to remember a random list of words than meaningful sentences. These findings suggest that the child with ASD may not perceive or use the overall meaning to be found in a problem in order to solve the problem (Frith, 1989).

Some individuals with autism are able to focus and sustain their attention (Rumsey & Hamburger, 1988), while others experience Attention Deficit Hyperactive Disorder (ADHD). For some individuals, it is difficult to activate their attention, to stay focused, or to flexibly shift their attention when it is adaptive to do so. For example, some individuals with autism find it difficult to rapidly scan stimulus materials and make a quick response, or to shift their attention midstream during a cognitive task (Rumsey, 1992).

Many persons with ASD have excellent long-term memories and can recall in minute detail events that occurred years before. This has been considered to be a form of idetic memory where all aspects of an event are stored and can later be fully retrieved. Often, higher functioning persons with autism have excellent rote memories and learn new factual, concrete information accurately after a single presentation. However, they may not attach meaning to the information (Janzen, 1996). Studies suggest that individuals with autism encode words at a literal level whereas persons without autism use associative or semantic features in order to remember. Thus, "rote memory, unaltered by active encoding or deeper levels of processing may be characteristic of autism . . ." (Rumsey, 1992, p. 47).

Problem Solving

Some higher functioning persons with ASD have difficulty with a wide range of problem-solving tasks. They may understand the language involved in the problem and have excellent visioperceptual skills but run into difficulty because they do not integrate information to draw inferences (Rumsey & Hamburger, 1988). On other problem-solving tasks, they may repeat the same errors and have difficulty learning from experience (Hoffman & Prior, 1982). These challenges with problem-solving tasks are less evident in persons with Asperger's Syndrome (Rumsey,

1992). However, adolescents with ASD have difficulty learning and integrating social information into their problem solving. When presented with novel problem-solving tasks via videotaped scenarios in real-life social contexts, adolescents with ASD were impaired in recounting the pertinent facts, generating possible high-quality problem solutions, and selecting optimal and preferred solutions. They differed the most from the typically developing youth in the social appropriateness of their solutions (Channon, Charman, Heap, Crawford, & Rios, 2001).

Visual Thinker

Some persons with autism describe themselves and are observed to be strong visual thinkers. They have excellent ability to remember and retrieve visual images. Grandin (1992) states that "all my thinking is visual." Dr. Grandin is a professor in animal husbandry and has built an international consulting business designing livestock processing plants. She notes, "visual thinking is an asset for an equipment designer. I am able to 'see' how all the parts of a project will fit together and see potential problems . . ." (Grandin, 1992, p. 116). "I am able to visualize a motion picture of the finished facility in my imagination . . ." (p. 117).

Some young adults with autism report that they cannot remember long strings of auditory information. When too much and too long a string of verbal information comes their way they shut down, but when the same information is presented visually in pictures and words, they know what to do. These individuals ask others to write down the steps in a task for them so that they can learn the task (Grandin, 1992; D. Williams, 1992). Janzen (1993) suggests that persons with autism have difficulty "organizing information for themselves but if it is organized visually to highlight the meaning, relationships, and sequences, they learn remarkably fast. . . ."

Individuals with autism suggest that there is a link between their tendency to take things literally and their use of visualization to think about and organize information (Lissner, 1992). Because they are translating the words spoken to them into visual images for those words, they are more likely to interpret the meaning and intention of the speaker's

question differently than intended. They suggest that they "think in pictures" rather than in words that are laden with socially based symbolic meanings (Grandin, 1992; Lissner, 1992).

Changing Academic Demands in Middle and High School

As a youth reaches middle and high school, the academic curriculum demands more abstract thinking and more open-ended problem solving. Students must be able to multitask and study, and complete homework and assignments from many different classes each week. A middle school student is expected to learn to self-organize school work and independently monitor and manage time to complete multiple assignments by their respective due dates. The physical environment of the middle school and high school is usually larger and more complex than in elementary schools. Students are expected to independently and quickly find their way between classes. These new academic requirements for more complex and abstract thinking and self-organization can be difficult and stressful for the student with ASD. Moreover, much of the information needed to operate in the school environment and presented in class is spoken. Auditory information, on its own, can be unreliable, misinterpreted, or simply not comprehended by students with autism.

As the youth with autism struggles to meet and understand these new expectations, they may do things that others view as inappropriate. Often, teachers, youth leaders, and peers misinterpret the behavior of middle and high school students with autism. The inappropriate behavior of a student with autism may, at first glance, resemble some of the typical acting out behaviors of adolescents, but in reality it is motivated by an entirely different set of needs associated with the characteristics of autism. When a student is inattentive, a teacher often thinks he is daydreaming when the student with autism may not understand what to do or where to start. If a student keeps asking the same question over and over, a classroom teacher is likely to interpret this as attention seeking. But the student with ASD may simply be confused and may be having difficulty understanding (Stratton, 1996).

Academic Supports

Adolescent students with ASD may need a variety of supports to learn, participate, and complete assignments in the secondary classroom. Many students with autism have great difficulty learning and remembering information they hear. Often, visual supports are needed to provide a clear meaningful picture to the student.

Academic supports begin with assessment of skills and learning style. The use of visuals is an effective support for understanding and participation in the more complex curriculum for many students. Assignments, homework, tests, and grading procedures may need modification so that the student with autism can understand and meet expectations. In class, students need supports for appropriate social behavior. Last, students need explicit instruction and help in organization and time management to handle their schoolwork.

Academic Assessment

Formal and informal assessment can be useful in determining a student's strengths and weaknesses in academic skills and learning style. Hagiwara (2001) and Griswold, Barnhill, Myles, Hagiwara, and Simpson (2002) discuss the use of standardized achievement and problem-solving tests with students with ASD. Subtest performance can reveal relative perceptual and verbal strengths and facets of the students' approach to problem solving.

Stratton (1996) has developed a series of assessment questions to be answered through informal assessment and observation to reveal a student with autism's learning style and approach to tasks. Hagiwara (2001) offers an informal assessment process to examine reading, math, writing, and oral language skills in a diagnostic sequence and to examine student learning traits such as learning style, behavioral patterns, strategies, and environmental predictability.

Supports for Learning Concepts and Language Comprehension

Students with ASD may learn facts using their rote memory skills but have difficulty understanding and using conceptual knowledge in academic problem solving. Using visual

supports enhances conceptual learning and language comprehension. For example, students can benefit from seeing a semantic organizer that visually depicts the main topics/concepts in a lesson as the teacher lectures or leads a discussion. These can be prepared ahead of time but can be especially effective if the semantic organizer is drawn as the material is presented (Pefiesson & Desser, 1989). When teaching a student a new concept, start with the student's own experience or information about the concept and then add new information, relating it to what the student already knows. As the lesson unfolds, create a semantic organizer that shows the relationships between the concepts (Stratton, 1996).

Providing Instruction/Directions for Assignments and Tasks

Many students with ASD will follow written or pictorial directions literally and precisely, but not read between the lines if important steps or considerations are missing. Thus, teachers cannot assume the student will infer from prior knowledge what to do if instructions are incomplete. At the same time, a student with ASD's ability to follow written/pictorial directions is an important strength, because it means that with the proper supports, the student need not be under the constant verbal direction of teachers, but can perform more independently.

Directions need to be explicit and concrete, with clear parameters for the scope of the work and what the finished product will look like. To avoid frustration, it is important to estimate how long the project will take the student given the student's learning style, and to provide sufficient time. When developing visual instructions, teachers need to inform the student how much work they are to do, where to begin, what to do, and in what order. Then, when it is finished, where to turn the assignment in and what to do next (Stratton, 1996).

Instructions for essays and other writing assignments need to be carefully reviewed in light of the student's level of language comprehension. Instead of open-ended choices, the teacher may need to provide a specific topic, state exactly how much to write, what to write, how to write the paper, and how students will know when they are finished. For example, instructions for an essay might be: "Tell me three things about _____ ." Then, check in with the student shortly thereafter to make sure they are not confused, are able to get started, and on the right track (Stratton, 1996).

Modifying Assignments and Homework

The learning strengths and challenges of students with ASD need to be considered in designing assignments and homework. Students with ASD may need fewer repetitions and practice problems to learn a new skill, but may take longer to complete each problem. Thus, assigning fewer problems may be appropriate. To support a student's cognitive learning, homework in which the student previews the concepts and vocabulary for the next day's lesson may be more important than review of past material (Stratton, 1996).

Modifying Tests and Grading

For many students with ASD, test taking can be highly stressful because of anxiety over being incorrect, not understanding the words or task, or needing more time to process information. Taking the test in a quiet location, without time limits, in several shorter sessions, or in a different format (oral, written, pictorial) may be helpful. During the test, students may not ask for clarification when they need to. A cue card with reminders such as "Remember to ask for help if you are not sure about a word" and "Remember to relax" can prompt the student. Teachers can also check a student's understanding of a test question. The student may know the answer but need help with the meaning of one word in the context used in order to understand the test question.

Students with ASD can have difficulty understanding the concept of grading and how grades are related to their incremental performance in a class as well as to life goals. A lack of understanding about grades can eliminate grades as a motivator. For others, anxiety about grades can affect overall behavior. The teacher may need to develop with the student a written/pictorial agreement that specifies in concrete ways, what work and amount of work are tied to certain grades. In order to give a student feedback, toward the end of a class the teacher may give them a copy of a grade report with the grade earned thus far. If the student would like to improve the grade, then a specific plan with tasks, timelines, and checkpoints can be developed with the teacher.

Group Work and Class Discussions

During small-group work, the students with ASD may need written instructions of what to do and a description of the process, the roles of group members, and the end product. Instructions should also include cues and information that will support appropriate social behavior in the group (see Stratton, 1996, for examples).

During class discussions, a student with ASD may not understand the topic or purpose of a discussion. As a result, she may say or do things that their classmates find humorous or odd. If the teacher shows respect and care for the student, classmates will often model the teacher's behavior toward the student. When the student with ASD makes an off-topic comment, the teacher should attempt to link it to the discussion and then redirect the student to the topic with "Thank you, now tell me one thing about _____ ." As with cooperative learning groups, the student with ASD can make more meaningful contributions if he is introduced to the concepts and vocabulary beforehand and has visual cues/reminders available to him during the discussion (Stratton, 1996).

Organization and Time Management

Young people with autism process information in ways that significantly affect their ability to organize materials or information and to manage time. Because they do not know how to organize a task, they often become immobilized or unable to begin. Teachers may misinterpret this as meaning the individual cannot do the task or is being noncompliant. As a result, their difficulties with organization can interfere with using their other capabilities (Coyne, 1996).

Organization is very conceptual. One must be able to see the whole picture and the components, and apply an organizing principle. The individual with ASD has difficulty sorting out important from unimportant information and seeing how materials or information can be rearranged in an organized structure. Time management requires the assignment of relative importance or priority to activities, and an understanding of time concepts, the duration of different activities, and temporal sequencing. These are difficult skills for many individuals with autism. They are not able to predict how long is needed to do a task and what task needs to be first, second, and so on.

Some youth with autism compensate for their disorganization by developing rigid routines and rituals to make life more ordered. These young people often insist on sameness and become upset if others rearrange the order they have created. Others may need to rigidly follow a particular sequence of steps in order to carry out a daily routine. These routines and rituals are difficult to change (Coyne, 1996).

Adolescents with ASD require specific training in organization and time management, which is adapted to their cognitive style and utilizes their strengths as visual learners.

Organization and time management systems need to utilize visual aids and structure that clearly indicate where to keep materials, the sequence of steps in a task, and the sequence of activities over time. The student needs to be actively involved in choosing elements (colors, labels) for the system and physically constructing the system. Useful tools to be developed include an organized study area, assignment folders for classes, calendar systems, and planning charts for completing assignments (Coyne, 1996).

Social Supports

Changing Peer Relationships in Adolescence

As adolescents, individuals develop greater capacity for abstract thinking and perspective taking, their social interactions becomes more complex. In late childhood, the format and context for social interaction is fairly clear and concrete. Children play games, engage in activities, and do stuff together. But in adolescence, social interaction becomes much more abstract, and the social rules and cues are more vague. Teens spend more time hanging out or talking endlessly about other peers and what's happening. Adolescents increasingly realize that others have thoughts and feelings different from their own. These developmental changes impact friendship and peer relationships.

The teen with autism may have a difficult time knowing that the rules have changed and understanding the new, more complex and subtle social rules. Miscommunications with peers or teasing may occur right at the time when the teen with autism, just like her peers, has become keenly interested in new kinds of social relationships. As a result, such miscommunications are especially painful. In this manner, the social gap between students with autism and their peers can widen during adolescence.

Developing Social Interventions

The extreme difficulty adolescents with ASD have in understanding social situations and reading social cues has been documented in a number of studies (Bauminger & Kasari, 2000; Sigman & Ruskin, 1999).

Because youth with autism have difficulty internalizing social rules, it is challenging to develop an effective social skills training program. For example, adolescents with ASD who participated in a class to learn how to decipher paralanguage cues and facial expressions did not show significant gains in 8 weeks as measured by a standardized prepost assessment. Some of the youth, however, were better able to interpret such social cues in natural settings after the training (Barnhill, Cook, Tebbenkamp, & Myles, 2002).

Gustein and Whitney (2002) discuss the importance of being able to meaningfully share experiences with other people in the overall development of social competence. They offer guidelines for developing interventions for individuals with ASD. They note that one of the challenges in designing such interventions is the fact that because individuals with ASD have difficulties understanding social relationships and situations, their opportunities to experience the benefits of social relationships have been seriously limited. By the time children with ASD reach adolescence, they have missed many opportunities to experience the intrinsic rewards of experience sharing with others and instead have much more often experienced rewards from other activities.

In assisting the adolescent or young adult, one must provide guideposts that are concrete and descriptive, while making it clear that these guidelines will not always apply and that they are likely to change. Providing working social rules is better than providing no information at all. But simplistic advice and directives that is not based on an understanding of autism is not helpful (Dewey, 1980). In designing social interventions, it is critical to understand how an individual with autism is viewing a social situation (Gray, 1996).

Provide Social Information and Support

Information about social situations, enhanced with visual supports, makes communication and social information easier for people with autism to understand (Gray, 1993; Odor & Watts, 1991; Quill, 1991, 1992). Gray has developed two social intervention strategies for children and adolescents with autism: *comic strip conversations* (Gray, 1994) and *social stories* (Gray, 1993). The intent of these interventions is to provide social assistance to individuals with autism so that they can better understand a social situation and choose to change their own behavior rather than any attempt to control their behavior. The purpose is to reveal the youth's understanding of a social situation, provide information that will help better predict and interpret social situations, and provide alternative and more effective social responses in special situations.

Comic strip conversations are a process of drawing out what people do, say, and may be thinking during a social interaction. Stick figures, talking and thought bubbles, symbols, and colors for different feelings are used to visually illustrate a conversation, explore problem situations, and visually identify new solutions. Youth with autism and adults draw as they talk about a situation. The adult can illustrate important social concepts, and the adolescent can share her perspective on the situation (Gray, 1996).

Social stories are written for a specific individual and a specific situation in order to share accurate social information and identify expected responses in the situation. A specific text structure is used in writing social stories that reflects the learning style of individuals with autism and ensures that the story offers perspective and description so that the reader gains understanding. Social stories with adolescents are less effective if they are too directive, telling the individual what to do. Instead, a well-written story can offer a youth the un-

derstanding of a situation he needs to be motivated to respond differently or be less anxious and confused (Gray, 1996).

Anecdotal reports and case studies attest to the effectiveness of providing social information, social stories, and social cartooning to help students with autism understand a wide range of situations in school and then choose to change their own behavior in those situations (Fullerton, personal communication, 2001). Teachers have used social stories and social cartooning to help adolescents with Asperger's Disorder to respond appropriately in social situations with peers and to get to class on time (M. F. Rogers & Myles, 2001). Social stories can be used for interventions for social understanding, support for social problem solving, and preparation for social situations.

Marks and colleagues (1999) describe several strategies to support adolescents with ASD in schools. These strategies are built upon the student's cognitive style including social supports, providing social opportunities, providing safety, and teaching coping strategies. Myles and Simpson (2001) offer various strategies for helping youth with ASD learn the hidden curriculum of social rules and roles in school. Strategies include using social stories, acting lessons, self-esteem-building activities, cartooning, social autopsies, and social learning strategies. A social learning strategy involves describing the different options and their respective consequences available in a social situation and then choosing an option that is then role-played and rehearsed. Another social behavior learning strategy uses the mnemonic SODA (Stop, Observe, Deliberate, and Act) to help students with ASD to initiate and practice social interaction skills (Mock, 2001). Adolescents with autism showed improvements in social cognition/social problem solving, emotion understanding, and social interactions after participation in a curriculum in social problem solving and recognizing emotions for 7 months (Bauminger, 2002).

Supports to Cope with Teasing

Children and youth with ASD can be especially vulnerable to teasing and bullying from peers for several reasons. First, individuals with ASD may not read the social cues and contexts involved and not realize at first that peers are making fun of them. Second, the individual with ASD's tendency to understand language literally and social naivete can result in being duped by peers into doing things they don't realize are inappropriate. Third, once individuals with ASD realize that they are being targeted by peers, they don't know how to ignore it, deflect it, or enlist the support of adult allies. Left with no appropriate defenses, individuals with ASD can go to extremes of avoidance or reaction as the only alternatives they see available to them. A young man with ASD offers a description of these problems during his middle school experiences (Ward & Alar, 2000).

Gray (2004) identifies two type of bullying experienced by youth with ASD; *Backhanded Bullying* involves the use of kind gestures or statements with the intent to mislead. *Absurd Information and Requests* involves the use of directives to engage in out-of-context, silly, or inappropriate activities, gestures, or tasks. Both forms capitalize on the youth with ASD's limited friendships and tendency to interpret information literally. Gray (2004) has developed a curriculum to help youth with ASD know what to do when teased or bullied and to help adults be problem solvers and allies. The curriculum uses visual teaching methods and social information to help youth recognize teasing, clear steps for responding, and role-play scenarios for practicing appropriate responses. Although infrequent, should an individual with ASD become aggressive in response to negative peer interactions, providing social information through the use of visuals can be effective (Simpson & Myles, 1998).

Identity Development and Self-Knowledge

Like their peers, adolescents with autism grapple with forming an adult worldview and self-identity. Their cognitive capacity to think about more complex information is also increasing albeit in directions shaped by their cognitive style and strengths. If the young person has difficulty with time and social concepts, she can be confused about what becoming an adult means. For example, one high school student became increasingly concerned with the implications of the expression "when you graduate, you'll be an adult and you will have to . . ." that was used by his teachers. He took this statement literally and couldn't understand how graduation would make him an adult when he

had never had a date, didn't have his driver's license yet, and so on. In his mind he wondered, "How can I be an adult when these things haven't happened yet?" In time, his teachers realized the source of his confusion (Fullerton, personal communication, 1994).

A young adult may seek a concrete or quantifiable definition of an abstract social concept that he wants to understand. When it is explained that the concept cannot be defined in this way, the young adult may respond by asking the question differently but with the same aim; to attain a concrete definition. The young adult attempts to find the right line of questioning that will draw forth an explanation he can understand.

Young adults with autism state that since childhood they have known they were different from others, but it was in adolescence that it became important to them to have a reason for why they were different (McDonnell, personal communication, 1993; D. Williams, 1992). For these young adults, it followed that if the reason could be found, then it could be changed. The young adult can be highly motivated toward increased self-knowledge. But like all of us, they seek reasons that make sense to them.

Emerging self-awareness can also take the form of realizing that others know something that I don't know. The person's goal may then become to ask others questions that will elicit from an answer in concrete or quantifiable terms that they can then put into practice (McDonnell, personal communication, 1993). D. Williams (1994) recalls how much she wanted others to give her rules that would work in any situation, rules without exceptions for how to be in the world. For instance, Sinclair (1992) requested a manual for how to deal with extraterrestrials. Adolescents with autism can benefit from experiences in which they can meet with peers with autism, learn about autism, and share their experiences (Fullerton & Coyne, 1999). Students with ASD are able to develop greater understanding of their challenges and develop coping strategies for social interactions, organization, and community living.

Transition to Adulthood

An important component of secondary education is preparing for the transition to adulthood.

In special education, extensive curricula in transition and self-determination are available; all students participate in transition planning; they identify their goals and plan learning activities during high school that will lead toward those goals. Students with autism can have difficulty with the concepts of goals and life planning, due to their challenges in self-organizing, sequencing, and time concepts. Visual and social supports as well as assistance in organizing and sequencing information can help students with autism participate in a transition program (Fullerton & Coyne, 1999).

Life Skills and Recreation

An assessment of daily living skills may be conducted for educational planning as well as determining long-term support needs. The Home Life Checklist is a comprehensive assessment developed by an autism specialists (Dalrymple, 1987). An example of a program that includes both an assessment and curriculum component for teaching life skills is the Functional Assessment and Curriculum for Teaching Everyday Routines (FACTER; Arick, Nave, Hoffman, & Krug, 2004). Visual supports and systems can help individuals learn daily living tasks (Bergstrom, Pattavina, Martella, & Marchand-Martella, 1995). Extended school-year programs can provide an excellent opportunity to learn to use public transportation and how to participate in community recreation (Coyne & Fullerton, 2004). The development of leisure outlets and skills is important in the overall quality of life, can reduce isolation, and let an individual develop relationship with others who share her interests (Coyne & Fullerton, 2004).

Cross-References

Developmental aspects of autism and related disorders are reviewed in Chapters 8 to 10; Chapters 27 to 33 discuss issues in assessment, working with families is addressed in Chapter 42; vocational supports are described in Chapter 43.

REFERENCES

Arick, J., & Falco, R. (1989). *Project QUEST: Final report.* Portland, OR: Portland State University.

Arick, J. R., & Krug, D. A. (1978, September). Autistic children: A study of learning characteristics and programming needs. *American Journal of Mental Deficiency, 83*(2), 200–202.

Arick, J. R., Loos, L., Falco, R., & Krug, D. A. (2004). *Strategies for teaching based on autism research: STAR.* Austin, TX: ProEd.

Arick, J. R., Nave, G., Hoffman, T., & Krug, D. A. (2004). *Functional assessment and curriculum for teaching everyday routines.* Austin, TX: ProEd.

Arick, J. R., Young, H., Falco, R., Loos, L., Gense, M., & Johnson, S. (2003). Designing an outcome study to monitor the progress of students with autism spectrum disorder. *Focus on Autism and Other Developmental Disabilities 18*(2), 75–87.

Baer, D. M., Wolf, M. M., & Risley, T. R. (1968). Some current dimensions of applied behavior analysis. *Journal of Applied Behavior Analysis, 1*, 91–97.

Barnhill, G. P., Cook, K. T., Tebbenkamp, K., & Myles, B. S. (2002). The effectiveness of social skills intervention targeting nonverbal communication for adolescents with Asperger syndrome and related pervasive developmental delays. *Focus on Autism and Other Developmental Disabilities, 17*(2), 112–118.

Bauman, M. L., & Kemper, T. L. (1994). Neuroanatomic observations of the brain in autism. In M. L. Bauman & T. L. Kemper (Eds.), *The neurobiology in autism* (pp. 119–145). Baltimore: Johns Hopkins University Press.

Bauminger, N. (2002). The facilitation of social-emotional understanding and social interaction in high-functioning children with autism: Intervention outcomes. *Journal of Autism and Developmental Disorders, 32*(4), 283–298.

Bauminger, N., & Kasari, C. (2000). Loneliness and friendship in high-functioning children with autism. *Child Development, 2*, 447–456.

Bemporad, J. R. (1979). Adult recollections of a formerly autistic child. *Journal of Autism and Developmental Disorders, 9*, 179–197.

Bergstrom, T., Bergstrom, T., Pattavina, S., Martella, R. C., & Marchand-Martella, N. (1995). Microwave fun: User-friendly recipe cards. *Teaching Exceptional Children, 28*(1), 61–63.

Bricker, D. (1998). *An activity-based approach to early intervention* (2nd ed.). Baltimore: Paul H. Brookes.

Brown, F., Evans, I. M., Weed, K. A., & Owen, V. (1987). Delineating functional competencies: A component model. *Journal of the Association for Persons with Severe Handicaps, 12*, 117–124.

Buron, K. D., & Curtis, M. (2004). *Incredible 5-Point Scale: Assisting students with Autism*

Spectrum disorders in understanding social interactions and controlling their emotional responses. Shawnee Mission, KS: Autism Asperger Publishing.

Carrington, S., & Graham, L. (2001). Perceptions of school by two teenage boys with Asperger Syndrome and their mothers: A qualitative study. *International Journal of Research and Practice, 5*(1), 37–48.

Cautela, J., & Groden, J. (1978). *Relaxation: A comprehensive manual for adults, children and children with special needs.* Champaign, IL: Research Press.

Cesaroni, L., & Garber, M. (1991). Exploring the experience of autism through firsthand accounts. *Journal of Autism and Developmental Disorders, 21*(3), 303–313.

Channon, S., Charman, T., Heap, J., Crawford, S., & Rios, P. (2001). Real-life-type problem-solving in Asperger's syndrome. *Journal of Autism and Developmental Disorders, 31*(5), 461–469.

Charman, T. (1997). Brief report: Prompted pretend play in autism. *Journal of Autism and Developmental Disorders, 27,* 325–352.

Cooper, J. O., Heron, T. E., & Heward, W. L. (1987). *Applied behavior analysis.* Columbus, OH: Merrill.

Corona, R., Dissanayake, M., Arbelle, S., Wellington, P., & Sigman, M. (1998). Is affect aversive to young children with autism? Behavioral and cardiac responses to experimenter distress. *Child Development, 69,* 1494–1502.

Courchesne, E., Akshoomoff, N. A., & Ciesielski, K. T. (1990). *Shifting attention abnormalities in autism: ERP and performance evidence.* Poster presented at the meeting of the International Neuropsychological Society, Orlando, FL.

Coyne, P. (1996). Organization and time management strategies. In A. Fullerton, J. Stratton, P. Coyne, & C. Gray (Eds.), *Higher functioning adolescents and young adults with autism: A teachers guide* (pp. 79–103). Austin, TX: ProEd.

Coyne, P., & Fullerton, A. (2004). *Supporting individuals with autism in recreation.* Champaign, IL: Sagamore.

Dalrymple, N. (1987). *Home Life Checklist: Adolescents and young adults.* Bloomington: Indiana Center on Autism.

Dawson, G., & Osterling, J. (1997). Early intervention in autism: Effectiveness and common elements of current approaches. In M. J. Guralnick (Ed.), *The effectiveness of early intervention: Second generation research* (pp. 307–326). Baltimore: Paul H. Brookes.

DeMyer, M. K., Alpern, G. D., Barton, S., DeMyer, W. E., Churchill, D. W., Hingtgen, J. N., et al.

(1972). Imitation in autistic, early schizophrenic, and nonpsychotic subnormal children. *Journal of Autism and Childhood Schizophrenia, 2,* 264–287.

Dewey, M. A. (1980, September). *The socially aware autistic adult and child.* Presentation given at Warwick Conference, Warwick, England.

Dewey, M., & Everard, M. (1974). The near normal autistic adolescent. *Journal of Autism and Childhood Schizophrenia, 4,* 348–356.

Donnellan-Walsh, A. (1976). *Teaching makes a difference.* Santa Barbara, CA: Santa Barbara County Schools, Autism Dissemination Project.

Falco, R., Janzen, J., Arick, J. R., & DeBoer, M. (1990). *Project QUEST inservice manual.* Unpublished manuscript, Portland State University, Portland, Oregon.

Fox, L., Dunlap, G., & Philbrick, L. (1997). Providing individual supports to young children with autism and their families. *Journal of Early Intervention, 21,* 1–14.

Fox, L., Hanline, M., Vail, C., & Galant, K. (1994). Developmentally appropriate practice: Applications for young children with disabilities. *Journal of Early Intervention, 18,* 243–257.

Frith, U. (1989). *Autism: Explaining the enigma.* Oxford, England: Blackwell Press.

Frye, V., & Walker, K. (1998). Review of the Autism Screening Instrument for Educational Planning, *Journal of Psychological Assessment, 16,* 280–285.

Fullerton, A., & Coyne, P. (1999). Developing skills and concepts for self-determination in young adults with autism. *Focus on Autism and Other Developmental Disabilities, 14*(1), 42–52, 63.

Goldstein, H., & Strain, P. (1988). Peers as communication intervention agents: Some new strategies and research findings. *Topics in Language Disorders, 9,* 44–57.

Grandin, T. (1992). An inside view of autism. In E. Schopler & G. B. Mesibov (Eds.), *High functioning individuals with autism* (pp. 105–126). New York: Plenum Press.

Grandin, T., & Scariano, M. M. (1986). *Emergence labeled autistic.* Novato, CA: Arena Press.

Gray, C. (1993). *The social story book.* Jenison, MI: Jenison Public Schools.

Gray, C. (1994). *Comic strip conversations.* Jenison, MI: Jenison Public Schools.

Gray, C. (1996). Social assistance. In A. Fullerton, J. Stratton, P. Coyne, & C. Gray (Eds.), *Higher functioning adolescents and young adults with autism: A teachers guide* (pp. 71–90). Austin, TX: ProEd.

Gray, C. (2004). Gray's guide to bullying. *Jenison Autism Journal: Creative Ideas in Practice,*

16(1), 1–60. (Available from Jenison Public Schools, Jenison, MI)

Green, G. (1996). Early behavioral intervention for autism: What does the research tell us. In C. Maurice, G. Green, & S. C. Luce (Eds.), *Behavioral intervention for young children with autism: A manual for parents and professionals* (pp. 15–27). Austin, TX: ProEd.

Green, G. (2001). Behavior analytic instruction for learners with autism: Advances in stimulus control technology. *Focus on Autism and Other Developmental Disabilities, 16,* 72–85.

Greenspan, S. J., & Wieder, S. (1997). Developmental patterns and outcomes in infants and children with disorders in relating and communication: A chart review of 200 cases of children with autism spectrum diagnosis. *Journal of Developmental and Learning Disorders, 1,* 87–141.

Griswold, D. E., Barnhill, G. P., Myles, B. S., Hagiwara, T., & Simpson, R. (2002). Asperger syndrome and academic achievement. *Focus on Autism and Other Developmental Disabilities, 17*(2), 94–109.

Gruber, B., Reeser, R., & Reid, D. H. (1979). Providing a less restrictive environment for profoundly retarded persons by teaching independent walking skills. *Journal of Applied Behavior Analysis, 12,* 285–297.

Gustein, S. E., & Whitney, T. (2002). Asperger syndrome and the development of social competence. *Focus on Autism and Other Developmental Disabilities, 17*(3), 161–171.

Hagiwara, T. (2001). Academic assessment of children and youth with Asperger syndrome, pervasive developmental disorders-not otherwise specified, and high-functioning autism. *Assessment for Effective Intervention, 27*(1/2), 89–100.

Handleman, J. S., Harris, S. L., Kristoff, B., Fuentes, F., & Alessandri, M. (1991). A specialized program for preschool children with autism. *Language, Speech, and Hearing Services in School, 22,* 107–110.

Haring, N. G. (1988). *Generalization for students with severe handicaps: Strategies and solutions.* Seattle: University of Washington Press.

Harrington, B., Samdperil, D. L. (Producers), Groden, G., Groden, J. (Directors). (1991). *Breaking the barriers II* [Videotape]. Providence, RI: Groden Center.

Harris, L. L., & Handleman, J. S. (Eds.). (1994). *Preschool education programs for children with autism.* Austin, TX: ProEd.

Hoffmann, W. L., & Prior, M. R. (1982). Neuropsychological dimensions of autism in children: A test of the hemispheric dysfunction hypothesis. *Journal of Clinical Neuropsychology, 4,* 27–41.

Janzen, J. E. (1993). *Understanding autism in the young child: Practical intervention strategies* (Rapsource Access Project). (Available from School of Extended Studies, Portland State University, P. O., Box 1491, Portland, OR)

Janzen, J. E. (1996). *Understanding the nature of autism.* San Antonio, TX: Therapy Skill Builders.

Kanner, L. (1943). Autistic disturbances of affective contact. *Nervous Child, 2,* 217–250.

Kim, J. A., Szatmari, P., Bryson, S. E., Streiner, D. L., & Wilson, F. J. (2000). The prevalence of anxiety and mood problems among children with Autism and Asperger Syndrome. *International Journal of Research and Practice, 4*(2), 117–132.

Koegel, L. (1995). Communication and language intervention. In R. Koegel & L. Koegel (Eds.), *Teaching children with autism* (pp. 17–32). Baltimore: Brookes.

Koegel, L. K., Koegel, R. L., Harrower, J. K., & Carter, C. M. (1999). Pivotal response intervention: I. Overview of approach. *Journal of the Association for Persons with Severe Handicaps, 24,* 174–185.

Koegel, R. L., O'Dell, M. C., & Koegel, L. K. (1987). A natural language paradigm for teaching nonverbal autistic children. *Journal of Autism and Developmental Disorders, 17,* 187–199.

Koegel, R. L., Schreibman, L., Good, A., Cerniglia, L., Murphy, C., & Koegel, L. K. (1989). *How to teach pivotal behaviors to children with autism: A training manual.* Santa Barbara: University of California.

Krantz, P. J., McDuff, M. T., & McClannahan, L. E. (1993). Programming participation in family activities for children with autism: Parents use of photographic activity schedules. *Journal of Applied Behavior Analysis, 26,* 137–138.

Krug, D. A., Arick, J. R., & Almond, P. J. (1993). *Autism screening instrument for educational planning* (2nd ed.). Austin, TX: ProEd.

Krug, D. A., Arick, J. R., Almond, P. J., Rosenblum, J. F., Scanlon, C., & Border, M. (1979). Evaluation of a program of systematic instructional procedures for preverbal autistic children. *Improving Human Performance, 8,* 29–41.

Krug, D. A., Rosenblum, J. F., Almond, P. J., & Arick, J. R. (1981). *Autistic and severely handicapped in the classroom: Assessment, behavior management, and communication training.* Portland, OR: ASIEP.

Laski, K. E., Charlop, M. H., & Schreibman, L. (1988). Training parents to use the natural language paradigm to increase their autistic children's speech. *Journal of Applied Behavior Analysis, 21,* 391–400.

Leaf, R., & McEachin, J. (1999). *A work in progress: Behavior management strategies and a curriculum for intensive behavioral treatment of autism.* Austin, TX: ProEd.

Levin, C. G., & Weatherly, J. J. (1997). *Point-counterpoint: The Lovaas controversy.* Paper presented at Special Education and the Law Conference, Portland, Oregon.

Libby, S., Powell, S., Messer, D., & Jordan, R. (1998). Spontaneous play in children with autism: A reappraisal. *Journal of Autism and Developmental Disorders, 28,* 487–497.

Lissner, K. (1992). Insider's point of view. In E. Schopler & G. B. Mesibov (Eds.), *High-functioning individuals with autism* (pp. 303–306). New York: Plenum Press.

Lovaas, O. I. (1981). *Teaching developmentally disabled children: The me book.* Austin, TX: ProEd.

Lovaas, O. I. (1987). Behavioral treatment and normal educational and intellectual functioning of young autistic children. *Journal of Consulting and Clinical Psychology, 55,* 3–9.

Lovaas, O. I. (1996). The UCLA young autism model of service delivery. In C. Maurice, G. Green, & S. C. Luce (Eds.), *Behavioral intervention for young children with autism: A manual for parents and professionals* (pp. 241–249). Austin, TX: ProEd.

LRP Publications. (1997, February, 4–5). *Formal Lovaas critique written to aid districts in legal cases.* Early Child Report, 4–5.

Mandalawitz, M. (1996). *Lovaas, TEACCH, and the public system: The court as referee.* Paper presented at the 17th National Institute, National Association of Directors of Special Education, Alexandria, VA.

Marcus, L., Schopler, E., & Lord, C. (2000). TEACCH services for preschool children. In J. S. Handleman & S. L. Harris (Eds.), *Preschool education programs for children with autism* (57–67). Austin, TX: ProEd.

Marks, S. U., Shrader, C., Levine, M., Hagie, C., Longaker, T., Morales, M., et al. (1999). Social skills for social ills: Supporting the social skills development of adolescents with Asperger's Syndrome. *Teaching Exceptional Children, 32*(2), 56–61.

Maurice, C., Green, G., & Luce, S. C. (1996). *Behavioral intervention for young children with autism: A manual for parents and professionals.* Austin, TX: ProEd.

McClannahan, L. E., & Krantz, P. J. (1999). *Activity schedules for children with autism: Teaching in-*

dependent behavior. Bethesda, MD: Woodbine House.

McDonnell, J. T. (2000). When things are too exciting: Autism and intensity. *Focus on Autism and Other Developmental Disabilities, 15*(4), 211–213.

McGee, G. G., Almeida, M. C., Sulzer-Azaroff, B., & Feldman, R. S. (1991). Promoting reciprocal interactions via peer incidental teaching. *Journal of Applied Behavior Analysis, 25,* 117–126.

McGee, G. G., Daley, T., & Jacobs, H. A. (1994). The Walden preschool. In S. Harris & J. S. Handleman (Eds.), *Preschool education programs for children with autism* (pp. 127–162). Austin, TX: ProEd.

Mock, M. A. (2001). SODA strategy: Enhancing and social interaction skills of youngsters with Asperger's syndrome. *Intervention in School and Clinic, 36*(5), 272–278.

Mullins, J. L., & Christian, L. (2001). The effects of progressive relaxation on the disruptive behavior of a boy with autism. *Research in Developmental Disabilities, 22*(6), 449–462.

Mundy, P., Sigman, M., & Kasari, C. (1990). A longitudinal study of joint attention and language development in autistic children. *Journal of Autism and Developmental Disorders, 20,* 115–128.

Myles, B. S., Cook, K. T., Miller, N. E., Rinner, L., & Robbins, L. A. (2000). *Asperger syndrome and sensory issues: Practical solutions for making sense of the world.* Shawnee Mission, KS: Autism Asperger.

Myles, B. S., & Simpson, R. L. (2001). Understanding the hidden curriculum: An essential social skill for children and youth with Asperger syndrome. *Intervention in School and Clinic, 36*(5), 279–286.

National Research Council. (2001). *Educating children with autism* (Committee on Educational interventions for children with autism, Division of Behavioral and Social Sciences and Education). Washington, DC: National Academy Press.

Odom, S. L., & Strain, P. S. (1986). A comparison of peer-initiation and teacher-antecedent interventions for promoting reciprocal social interaction of autistic preschoolers. *Journal of Applied Behavior Analysis, 19,* 59–71.

Odor, S., & Watts, E. (1991). Reducing teacher prompts in peer-mediated interventions for young children with autism. *Journal of Special Education, 25,* 26–43.

Olley, J. G., Robbins, F. R., & Morrelli-Robbins, M. (1993). Current practices in early intervention for children with autism. In E. Schopler, M. E. Van Bourgondien, & M. M. Bristol (Eds.),

Preschool issues in autism (pp. 223–245). New York: Plenum Press.

Pefiesson, R. S., & Desser, P. R. (1989). *Semantic organizers.* Rockville, MD: Aspen Press.

Pierce, K., & Schriebman, L. (1995). Increasing complex social behaviors in children with autism: Effects of peer-implemented pivotal response training. *Journal of Applied Behavior Analysis, 28,* 285–295.

Prizant, B. M. (1983). Language acquisition and communicative behavior in autism: Toward an understanding of the "whole" of it. *Journal of Speech and Hearing Disorders.* 48, 296–307.

Prizant, B. M., & Rubin, E. (1999). Contemporary issues in interventions for autism spectrum disorders: A commentary. *Journal of the Association for Persons with Severe Handicaps, 24,* 199–208.

Prizant, B. M., & Wetherley, A. (1998). Understanding the continuum of discrete-trial traditional behavioral to social-pragmatic developmental approaches in communication enhancement for young children with autism/PDD. *Seminars in Speech and Language, 19,* 329–353.

Quill, K. (1991). *Teaching children with autism and pervasive developmental disorders using visual aids* [Videotape]. Manchester, MA: The Autism Institute.

Quill, K. (1992). Enhancing pragmatic development in verbal students with autism: Principles of adult student interaction (Presentation at the 1992 annual conference of the Autism Society of America). *Autism Society of America Conference Proceedings,* 89–90.

Rimland, B. (1964). *Infantile autism.* New York: Appleton-Century-Crofts.

Rimland, B. (1990). Sound sensitivity in autism. *Autism Research Review International, 4,* 3, 6.

Rogers, M. F., & Myles, B. S. (2001). Using social stories and comic strip conversations to interpret social situations for an adolescent with Asperger Syndrome. *Intervention in School and Clinic, 36*(5), 310–313.

Rogers, S. J. (2000). Interventions that facilitate socialization in children with autism. *Journal of Autism and Developmental Disorders, 30,* 399–409.

Rumsey, J. M. (1992). Neuropsychological studies of high-level autism. In E. Schopler & G. B. Mesibov (Eds.), *High-functioning individuals with autism* (pp. 41–64). New York: Plenum Press.

Rumsey, J. M., Duara, R., Grady, C., Rapoport, J. L., Margolin, R. A., Rapoport, S. L., et al. (1985). Brain metabolism in autism. *Archives of General Psychiatry, 42,* 448–455.

Rumsey, J. M., & Hamburger, S. D. (1988). Neuropsychological findings in high-functioning men with infantile autism, residual state. *Journal of Clinical and Experimental Neuropsychology, 10,* 201–221.

Safran, J. S. (2002). Supporting students with Asperger's Syndrome in general education. *Teaching Exceptional Children, 34*(5), 60–66.

Schreibman, L. (1975). Effects of within-stimulus and extra-stimulus prompting on discrimination learning in autistic children. *Journal of Applied Behavior Analysis, 8,* 91–112.

Schreibman, L. (2000). Intensive behavioral/psychoeducational treatments for autism: Research needs and future directions. *Journal of Autism and Developmental Disorders, 30,* 373–378.

Schreibman, L., & Koegel, R. L. (1996). Fostering self-management: Parent-delivered pivotal response training for children with autistic disorder. In E. D. Hibbs & P. S. Jensen (Eds.), *Psychosocial treatment for children and adolescent disorders: Empirically based strategies for clinical practices* (pp. 525–552). Washington, DC: American Psychological Association.

Sheinkopf, S. J., & Siegel, B. (1998). Home-based behavioral treatment of young children with autism. *Journal of Autism and Developmental Disorders, 28,* 15–23.

Sigman, M., & Ruskin, E. (1999). Continuity and change in the social competence of children with autism, Downs syndrome, and developmental delays. *Monographs of the Society for Research in Child Development, 64*(1, Serial No. 256).

Simpson, R. L., & Myles, B. S. (1998). Aggression among children and youth who have Asperger's syndrome: A different population requiring different strategies. *Preventing School Failure, 42*(4), 149–153.

Sinclair, J. (1992). Bridging the gaps: An inside-out view of autism (or, do you know what I don't know?). In E. Schopler & G. B. Mesibov (Eds.), *High functioning individuals with autism* (pp. 294–302). New York: Plenum Press.

Skinner, B. F. (1938). *The behavior of organisms: An experimental analysis.* New York: Appleton-Century.

Slavik, B. A. (1983). Vestibular stimulation and eye contact in autistic children. *American Journal of Occupational Therapy, 37,* 17.

Smith, T. (2001). Discrete Trial Training in the treatment of autism. *Focus on Autism and Other Developmental Disabilities, 16,* 86–92.

Sprague, J. R., & Horner, R. H. (1984). The effects of single instance, multiple instance, and general case training on generalized vending machine use by moderately and severely handicapped students. *Journal of Applied Behavior Analysis, 17,* 273–278.

Stahmer, A. C. (1995). Teaching symbolic play skills to children with autism using pivotal response training. *Journal of Autism and Developmental Disorders, 25,* 123–141.

Stone, W. L., Ousley, O. Y., Yoder, P., Hogan, K., & Hepburn, S. (1997). Nonverbal communication in 2- and 3-year old children with autism. *Journal of Autism and Developmental Disorders, 27*(6), 677–696.

Stratton, J. (1996). Adapting instructional materials and strategies. In A. Fullerton, J. Stratton, P. Coyne, & C. Gray (Eds.), *Higher functioning adolescents and young adults with autism: A teachers guide* (pp. 51–77). Austin, TX: ProEd.

Thorndike, E. L. (1921). *The psychology of learning.* New York: Columbia University, Teachers College.

Thorpe, D. M., Stahmer, A. C., & Schriebman, L. (1995). Effects of sociodramatic play training on children with autism. *Journal of Autism and Developmental Disorders, 25,* 265–282.

Turton, L. (1986). Independent review of the Autism Screening Instrument for Educational Planning. *Mental measurement yearbook* (pp. 120–122). Highland Park, NJ: Gryphon Press.

Volkmar, F. R., & Mayes, L. C. (1990). Gaze behavior in autism. *Development and Psychopathology, 2,* 61–69.

Wainwright-Sharp, J. A., & Bryson, S. E. (1993). Visual orienting deficits in high-functioning people with autism. *Journal of Autism and Developmental Disorders, 23*(1), 1–13.

Ward, M., & Alar, N. (2000). Being autistic is part of who I am. *Focus on Autism and Other Developmental Disabilities, 15*(4), 232–235.

Watson, J. B. (1913). Psychology as a behaviorist views it. *Psychological Review, 20,* 158–177.

Wetherby, A., Prizant, B., & Hutchinson, T. (1998). Communicative, social-affective, and symbolic profiles of young children with autism and pervasive developmental disorder. *American Journal of Speech-Language Pathology, 7,* 79–91.

Williams, D. (1992). *Nobody nowhere: The extraordinary autobiography of an autistic.* New York: Avon Books.

Williams, D. (1994). *Somebody somewhere: Breaking free from the world of autism.* New York: Times Books.

Williams, K. (2001). Understanding the student with Asperger syndrome: Guidelines for teachers. *Intervention in School and Clinic, 36*(5), 287–292.

Wing, L. (1981). Asperger's syndrome: A clinical account. *Psychological Medicine, 11,* 115–129.

Wing, L. (1992). Manifestations of social problems in high-functioning autistic people. In E. Schopler & G. B. Mesibov (Eds.), *High-functioning individuals with autism* (pp. 129–142). New York: Plenum Press.

Wulf, G. (1994). Sustained eye contact: One woman's victory. *Autism Network International Newsletter, 1*(3), 7.

CHAPTER 40

Helping Children with Autism Enter the Mainstream

JAN S. HANDLEMAN, SANDRA L. HARRIS, AND MEGAN P. MARTINS

Educators and psychologists are becoming increasingly adept at preparing children with autism to enter mainstream educational settings. Developments in applied behavior analysis enable some very young children to be fully included with their normally developing peers when they reach kindergarten or first grade (e.g., Fenske, Zalenski, Krantz, & McClannahan, 1985; Handleman & Harris, 2001; Lovaas, 1987). Other children, although not making such dramatic changes, can nonetheless function at least in part within the same classes as their peers. Inclusive programs have increasingly become available for these children as a result of the legal mandate that children receive educational services in the least restrictive environment and the cultural imperative to include children with various disabilities in mainstream settings. However, descriptions of effective programs and strategies to promote successful inclusion are not broadly available to educators. This chapter reviews current empirically based technology for including children with autism in the mainstream, and describes several models for this process.

DEFINITION

The terms *mainstream, inclusion,* and *integration* are used in varying ways throughout the educational literature. No single set of terminology has yet emerged. In an early article, Odom and Speltz (1983) recommended that a class be called an integrated special education class when it predominantly includes children with a disability, along with some normally developing peers. A class in the regular education system that has one or more children with special needs would be called a mainstreamed special education class. Mainstreamed classes are built around the regular education model, while integrated classes are developed within an individualized special education model. We use that vocabulary in the present chapter. We also use the term *inclusion* to refer to any situation that brings children with autism together with their peers for specific educational purposes. We review the literature on the development of social skills in children with autism, suggestions for social inclusion, and models of inclusion. These issues are at the heart of effectively involving children with autism in regular educational settings.

SOCIAL SKILLS

Competent social skills are essential for effective inclusion of children with autism in mainstreamed classes. Children with Autistic Disorder or Asperger's Disorder, even when they possess normal intellectual ability, have grave problems understanding the social transactions of childhood. These limitations make them stand out among their peers and can lead to rejection by other children.

Mastering social skills appears daunting. Not only must the child learn a full range of skills that should be generalized to a bewildering variety of settings and people, but these skills should also extend beyond the memorizing of rote responses, to spontaneous behavior in novel contexts. Among the social skills documented to be useful for children with autism are playing games (Coe, Matson,

Fee, Manikam, & Linarello, 1990), being affectionate (McEvoy et al., 1988), responding to greetings (Nientimp & Cole, 1992), being assertive in conversation and play (McGee, Krantz, & McClannahan, 1984; Weiss & Harris, 2001), perspective taking (Travis, Sigman, & Ruskin, 2001), recognizing other people's needs (Harris, Handleman, & Alessandri, 1990), and asking for help and requesting things from peers (Gonzalez-Lopez & Kamps, 1997).

An important decision in teaching social skills is the extent to which the teacher, peer, or child with autism is the primary locus of instruction. For example, early strategies for teaching social behaviors to children who were deficient in these skills relied heavily on adult mediation to reinforce appropriate behavior (e.g., Strain, Shores, & Kerr, 1976; Strain & Timm, 1974). This strategy had limited durability because the interactions were dependent on adult reinforcement, and when the adult was not present, the social behavior of the child with autism declined (e.g., Odom, Hoyson, Jamieson, & Strain, 1985).

Another approach to teaching social skills focuses on teaching normally developing peers to initiate interactions with children with autism (e.g., Odom & Strain, 1986; Strain, 1983; Strain, Kerr, & Ragland, 1979). Early studies of these interventions were often limited by the willingness of the peer to initiate, and did not result in increased initiations by the child with autism. From these early studies it was clear that the child with autism must become an initiator of interactions, rather than a passive respondent.

Educationally, there is no good reason to separate the domains of teacher, peer or child-focused intervention. Although we review each area of research separately, an optimal setting would combine adult mediation, responsive peers, and a well-prepared child with autism. In our experience, the well-prepared child with autism has an interest in other children, can learn in a small group, and does not engage in a great many intrusive or disruptive behaviors that might frighten peer children.

Peers' Initiation

Normally developing peers are valuable for modeling social skills and language for children with autism. Much of this research has been with preschool-aged children (e.g., Odom & Strain, 1986; Odom et al., 1985), some with older, elementary-school-aged children (e.g., Blew, Schwartz, & Luce, 1985; Lord & Hopkins, 1986; Sasso & Rude, 1987), or with children who have mild disabilities serving as models for more impaired youngsters (e.g., Shafer, Egel, & Neef, 1984).

Physical proximity alone is not sufficient to allow children with autism to benefit from the modeling of their peers; special training helps peers be effective models (Pierce & Schreibman, 1997). For example, Carr and Darcy (1990) used peer modeling and prompting to teach children with autism to play "Follow the Leader." Having the peer ask the child with autism to watch him or her was not sufficient to teach the new skill; the peer had to model and physically prompt the child with autism. McGee, Almeida, Sulzer-Azaroff, and Feldman (1992) taught normally developing preschoolers to use incidental teaching strategies when interacting with classmates who had autism. The peers learned to request responses and praise the child with autism for appropriate behaviors during free play. Adult supervision helped establish the skills, but was then faded. Although peers were effective in the play setting, they did not show spontaneous generalization of initiations to the lunch table. McGee and her colleagues (1992) found that being a peer tutor did not have a negative impact on a child's popularity with other classmates. Furthermore, Kamps and colleagues (2002) compared the amount of time children with autism spent engaged with peers who had participated in a social skills training program, with familiar peers, and with unfamiliar peers. The researchers found that the target children spent more time socially engaged with the trained peers.

In a study by Goldstein, Kaczmarek, Pennington, and Shafer (1992), peers learned to make comments that did not demand a response from the child with autism, at least not to the extent that a question or request might do. Increases in nondemanding social initiations by the peers led to a substantial increase in the social behaviors of the children with autism. This study broadened the potential repertoire of helpful peer behaviors to include comments and acknowledgments, along with the initiations of play and other requests used in previous studies. Garfinkle and Schwartz (2002) taught children with autism in an integrated preschool to follow the lead of a peer using prompting and verbal praise. Although the results varied among the participants and the overall levels of peer imitation and social interaction were low, all of the children displayed increases in their levels of imitation and interaction, both in the training and generalization settings. On a social validity questionnaire, the adult participants reported that the intervention was easy to implement, and they believed it was valuable for the children.

Interventions with older children, to teach more advanced social skills, require different methods from those used to teach preschoolers how to play. Haring and Breen (1992) recruited normally developing junior high school students to create a school-based social network for youngsters with autism. These adolescents and an adult facilitator discussed strategies for promoting greater social interaction and then self-monitored their activities with their classmates who had disabilities. The study found an increase in the frequency and appropriateness of interactions in natural settings, using the social network. When the project was completed, many peers described their classmate with a disability as a friend and were likely to initiate interactions that were not assigned by the adult facilitator. Garrison-Harrell, Kamps, and Kravitz (1997) have reported similar findings, which support peer network strategies to create positive social environments for students with autism.

Other studies have demonstrated the benefits of peer self-monitoring. For example, Morrison, Kamps, Garcia, and Parker (2001) demonstrated that peers aged 10 to 13 years were able to self-monitor skills such as requesting, commenting, and sharing with children with autism. The results indicated that the peers were also effective at increasing the social initiations and time spent in interaction by children with autism. Self-monitoring of social initiations can be effective for preschoolers as well as older peers. Sainato, Goldstein, and Strain (1992) taught young peers how to get the attention of a child with autism, initiate a play activity, and respond to the child with autism. After the peers mastered these skills, they learned to evaluate their own performance.

These self-evaluation strategies improved the peers' social interaction skills. Although teacher prompts are important for helping preschool peers initiate a social skills intervention, after the children have started to interact effectively, the prompts should be faded systematically (Odom, Chandler, Ostrosky, McConnell, & Reaney, 1992; Odom & Watts, 1991). McGee and her colleagues (1992) found that adult prompts risk being intrusive if continued after the peers master the requisite skills. Adult attention may adversely influence the richness of the child-to-child exchange (Kliewer, 1995).

Peers have also been effective at using components of naturalistic teaching strategies to increase social behaviors in children with autism. In a study by Pierce and Schreibman (1997), 7- to 8-year-old peers were trained in a modified version of the naturalistic strategy, termed Pivotal Response Training (PRT), that includes components such as incorporating choice, using varying stimuli, modeling social behaviors, reinforcing attempts, and encouraging conversation. During interactions with the trained peers, children with autism demonstrated more use of language and varied play with toys; and these increases generalized across settings, stimuli, and peers.

Younger peers need more adult support than older ones (Odom & Watts, 1991). Lord and Hopkins (1986) reported that children ages 10 to 12 years were more effective than children 5 to 6 years of age in adapting their behavior to the needs of a developmentally disabled partner. Meyer and her colleagues (1987) similarly found that for elementary-school-aged children, adult supervision was not essential. With older children, it may be important to use high social-status peers as models. Sasso and Rude (1987) reported that higher status peers made more initiations to the children with autism than did lower status peers in an elementary school. Additionally, when children with more severe communication and social disabilities are integrated into a classroom, more peer training may be beneficial. To increase social interactions between peers and children with autism, Gonzalez-Lopez and Kamps (1997) found it useful to train peers in their program to give easy instructions, demonstrate skills, give praise and support, and ignore inappropriate behaviors. Although the peers differed widely in their use of the added skills, the authors noted that all the trained peers increased the use of at least some of the skills.

Classwide Intervention

Interventions designed to help children with autism may also be beneficial to their normally developing peers. In the academic realm, Harris, Handleman, Gordon, Kristoff, and Fuentes (1991) reported that peers, as well as children with autism, showed significant developmental gains in language after being together in an integrated class. The children with autism, but not the peers, also showed an increase in IQ after one school year.

Working with school-aged children, Kamps, Barbetta, Leonard, and Delquadri (1994) designed a peer tutoring program in which tutor-learner pairs worked together on reading skills. This was a classwide intervention that included three high functioning children with autism. The intervention, valued by students and teacher alike, improved reading fluency for both children with autism and typical peers. Similarly, in a study of fourth grade cooperative learning groups, both children with autism and their peers showed increased mastery of information, and increased frequency of interaction in a small-group context (Dugan et al., 1995). A peer buddy system has also been used in integrated classrooms to increase the social interaction between children. In a study by Laushey and Heflin (2000), all the children in an integrated kindergarten classroom had a daily buddy. The children were taught to play with, stay with, and talk to their buddy during certain portions of the school day. The authors demonstrated that the intervention was effective in increasing the number of non-adult-directed appropriate social skills for both participants. These studies were creative demonstrations of the possibility of enhancing overall classroom functioning while mainstreaming children with autism among their peers.

In another study, Kamps and her colleagues (1992) used social skills groups to teach first grade children with autism and their peers to increase their interactions. All the children learned to initiate, respond, and sustain interactions. They also learned to greet others and discuss a variety of subjects. The children also practiced social skills such as giving and receiving compliments, turn taking, and offering and requesting assistance. As a result of training, the children with autism increased their social initiations and responses to their peers, and the peers in turn increased their responsiveness to the children with autism.

Social scripts are another tool for increasing independent, generalized social interactions among children with autism and normally developing preschoolers. Goldstein and Cisar (1992) taught children with autism and their peers verbal and nonverbal scripts for pretend play. After the children mastered the scripts, they showed improved social interaction and communication. The use of scripts may be valuable for teaching fantasy play, a skill that is especially challenging for many children with autism.

Initiations by the Child with Autism

Because trained peers are not always part of the real world, it is helpful when children with autism can initiate interactions, as well as respond to the initiations of others. The role of self-initiation was shown by Oke and Schreibman (1990), who initially taught nonhandicapped peers to initiate interactions with a child with autism. Although level of social interaction by both the peers and the child with autism immediately increased, there was a subsequent decline in responding by the child with autism when the peers, who were no longer reinforced for initiating interactions, decreased their initiations. In the next phase of the study, when the child with autism learned to make initiations, his level of responding rose again, and this time was accompanied by a decline in his disruptive behavior. An interesting aspect of this research was the use of videotape feedback to help the child with autism learn appropriate play skills. Similar benefits from videotaped feedback were found by Kern-Dunlap and colleagues (1992) with children having severe emotional and behavioral problems.

Belchic and Harris (1994) taught children with autism to initiate and sustain an interaction with a normally developing peer in an integrated preschool by first teaching the child to initiate play with the adult trainer, and then transferring this skill to other children. The children with autism generalized social initiations, from the classroom to the playground, to an untrained child with autism, and to their brother or sister at home.

Teaching self-management of social skills can be effective for older children, as well as for preschoolers. Koegel, Koegel, Hurley, and Frea (1992) taught school-aged children with autism who had severe social deficits how to increase appropriate social behavior in the community. The children learned to monitor their own social responses and showed a collateral decrease in inappropriate behavior. In a study by Thiemann and Goldstein (2001), school-aged children with autism watched videotapes of time spent in social interaction with a peer. The children were taught to record instances of appropriate social-communicative behaviors and to exchange the instances for tangible reinforcement. The findings indicated that this video feedback intervention was effective in increasing target social behaviors. Like the work of Belchic and Harris (1994) with preschool children, these techniques put the locus of control for social initiation in the hands of the child with autism, not the peers. They therefore have the potential to be valuable in settings where naive peers do not initiate contact.

Suggestions for Social Inclusion

Based on her clinical experience, Lord (1995) makes a series of suggestions for social inclusion of children with autism. These guidelines concern the context, the role of the peers, the role of the adult, and the needs of the child with autism. In terms of the context, one recommendation is to ensure that the activities are interesting and attractive (Carr & Darcy, 1990). These should be things that all of the children might enjoy and should not demand responses too complex for the children with autism. Carr and Darcy point to the importance of using multiple training objects, such as a toy truck and bubbles, to encourage the child to attend to peers in addition to objects used in training. Lord (1995) reports that having a theme for the group activity (e.g., holidays, community helpers) can provide an

organizing format for the session. The physical environment should be arranged to increase proximity among the children, and the activities should be ones that require cooperation or interaction (Demchak & Drinkwater, 1992). Furthermore, Harrower and Dunlap (2001) suggest that picture activity schedules can be easily incorporated into a general education classroom. Picture activity schedules reduce the number of prompts a classroom aide must provide and can inform students with autism about upcoming activities or changes in schedule. Group activities should be relatively brief, with very young children having 5 or 10 minute sessions, and older children going as long as a half hour. Lord (1995) suggests that in her experience frequent meetings increase a sense of group identity, as does having group rituals that are part of every meeting.

In effective inclusion, peers receive general instructions such as persisting in their effort to engage the child with autism, joining that child's activities, using simple language, praising efforts to interact, and calling an adult if there are problems. Lord (1995) suggests that children with autism comprise less than half the group.

Among the essentials for effective inclusion is preparation of the classroom teacher (Hundert & Hopkins, 1992). Demchak and Drinkwater (1992) urge that teachers learn inclusion techniques and behavior management skills before bringing children with disabilities into the regular classroom. Furthermore, even brief training programs for support staff may increase the benefit that children with disabilities gain from inclusive environments (Schepis, Ownby, Parsons, & Reid, 2000). Lord (1995) describes the adult's role as one of a mediator rather than an active participant in the interaction. She suggests that the adult respond to the child with autism primarily through the peers or through the arrangement of the environment rather than by direct intervention.

**TEACHERS' AND
PARENTS' PERSPECTIVES**

The attitudes of special education and regular education teachers can stall or facilitate inclusion (Odom & McEvoy, 1990), and these two groups of educators may differ on the criteria for this goal. For example, the competencies for entering a mainstreamed class are viewed differently by regular and special education teachers, and vary by the child's age. In setting criteria for inclusion in second or third grade classes, regular education teachers, in contrast to special education teachers, give higher priority to the ability to read and write, and to the absence of behavior problems (Hanrahan, Goodman, & Rapagna, 1990). By contrast, when asked about the criteria for mainstreaming the kindergarten child, regular education teachers rate academic preparation as less important than do the special education teachers (Hanrahan, Goodman, & Rapagna, 1985). Kindergarten teachers may be more concerned about the social adjustment of their students, while second and third grade teachers recognize that academic competence is important to a child's effective classroom functioning (Hanrahan et al., 1990).

Kasari, Freeman, Bauminger, and Alkin (1999) surveyed parents of children with autism and parents of children with Down's syndrome regarding their opinions about inclusion, their child's educational placement, and their desire to change their current educational placement. These authors found that parents of children with autism were more likely to endorse a mainstreamed educational environment for their children than full inclusion, while parents of children with Down's syndrome preferred inclusion for their child and were less likely to accept mainstreaming as an option for their child. Over half of the parents of children with autism said they believed their child's needs could not be met in an inclusive classroom, indicating that these parents were likely more concerned with obtaining appropriate services for their children than with being in an included environment. In another study, Palmer, Fuller, Arora, and Nelson (2001) also indicated that parents who do not support an inclusive environment do so because they believe that their child's disability reduces the advantages of an inclusive environment.

Parents may be ambivalent about where their child belongs on the spectrum of inclusion. That perspective is an important consideration in the placement process. Guralnick, Connor, and Hammond (1995) interviewed parents of preschool-aged children with disabilities. They found that mothers of children in inclusive programs and those in specialized programs viewed their child's educational setting as valuable in helping the child establish peer relationships and friendships. Mothers of children in the inclusive settings reported that their child played better and was more social because of the peer children. However, both groups of mothers were concerned about their child's social rejection. Guralnick and colleagues (1995) point out that while parents want their children exposed to the "real world," they fear their youngsters will suffer painful rejection in that setting. These fears are not without foundation. For example, Guralnick and Groom (1987) found that children with mild disabilities are less accepted and more rejected than their peers in a play group. Rejection and social isolation may occur in any setting. It is therefore critical that administrators and staff be sensitive to the needs of every person who is part of a social setting. For many families, the primary concern may not be the location of services, but the excellence of services, regardless of setting.

OUTCOMES OF INCLUSION

Data on the benefits of inclusion for the language, general development, and social development of children with disabilities are limited, and only a few of these studies involve children with autism. Durbach and Pence (1991) found that young children with various disabilities used more language in a segregated setting than in an inclusive one; they also noted that an adult mediator was important in supporting language in either setting. Harris, Handleman, Kristoff, Bass, and Gordon (1990) reported that children with autism made equivalent language gains over one school year, regardless of whether they were in an integrated or segregated setting. Changes in general developmental level in children with a variety of disabilities show a similar pattern, with no clear benefits for inclusive settings (Buysse & Bailey, 1993; Fisher & Meyer, 2002).

Social behavior appears to be the domain with the greatest potential to benefit from inclusion in the preschool years. Fisher and Meyer (2002) assessed developmental and social gains made by students with a variety of disabilities in both inclusive and segregated settings. They noted that children in inclusive educational environments made greater gains in social competence. Buysse and Bailey (1993) have also reported that for preschool children with a variety of disabilities, growth in social behavior and play skills is greater in inclusive than segregated settings. These authors caution that research has not shown the extent to which increased social exchanges enable children to establish true friendships and enduring social inclusion. This is of special concern for children with autism.

MODELS OF INCLUSION

The striking benefits from early, intensive intervention have enabled an increasing number of programs to focus on including these youngsters with typically developing peers (Lovaas, 1987; Strain, 1983). Many of these programs are contributing to our understanding of key variables for success in inclusion. For example, most discussions of methods of inclusion typically recognize a continuum of options ranging, from part-time community experiences to full inclusion in regular classes (Handleman & Harris, 2001; Harris & Handleman, 1994). This sensitivity to the highly individual nature of the inclusion process promotes the careful planning and monitoring that are central to the education of students with autism (Handleman & Harris, 1986).

The educational programs discussed in this chapter emphasize different features and strategies. Although they are located in a variety of settings, including public schools, private special education facilities, and universities, each program maintains a strong commitment to supportive, inclusive programming, and they all have a proven track record of effectiveness. Although we have highlighted special features of each program for didactic purposes, there is considerable overlap in methods from one program to the next, and components linked with one program are likely to be found in others as well.

Individualized, Comprehensive Programming

Two decades of research and clinical experience confirm the value of comprehensive behavioral programming for children with autism (Handleman & Harris, 2001; Harris &

Handleman, 1994). This is illustrated in programs operated by the Princeton Child Development Institute (McClannahan & Krantz, 2001) and the Children's Unit for Treatment and Evaluation (Romanczyk, Lockshin, & Matey, 2001), which emphasize individualized planning for effective community education. These programs view inclusive education as a function of a child's needs, and such programs should be assessed and provided solely on an individual basis.

These programs both emphasize the building of skills that promote participation in community life. For example, being able to follow instructions, to generalize concepts, and to delay reinforcement are viewed as important prerequisites to responding to the multitude of experiences in a typical school or social setting. Both preschool programs follow a detailed curriculum designed to promote systematic developmental and behavioral progress.

Transition activities by the Princeton Child Development Institute and the Children's Unit reflect a continuum of options and typically includes initial involvement in local day camps, religious schools, or other neighborhood activities. Like many of the other preschool models, decisions about inclusive education are based on systematic assessment, planning, and implementation. A carefully monitored transition plan guides movement to alternate programs.

Early Inclusion

Classes operated by the Walden Preschool (McGee, Morrier, & Daly, 2001) and the LEAP preschool (Strain & Cordisco, 1994) support the commitment to inclusive education by enrolling students with a range of developmental needs in the same class from the very start. The approach of these programs reflects the philosophy that typical children are very good intervention agents for children with autism and that inclusive settings offer these students the benefits of enriched experiences.

Both the Walden and LEAP programs have a curriculum that includes careful planning and scheduling of activities to promote social inclusion. Emphasizing, for example, the importance of developmentally appropriate goals and strategies, experiences at the LEAP preschool include early childhood activities and behavioral programming. Intervention at

Walden involves the systematic use of incidental teaching procedures (McGee, Morrier, & Daly, 2001). Both programs promote the continuum of inclusive opportunities by developing and implementing systematic transitional plans to community placements.

A hallmark of the Walden and LEAP programs, as well as most other exemplary programs, is a commitment to staff training. Careful planning and preparation of educational experiences are critical variables for program effectiveness. For example, maintaining enthusiasm, making complex teaching judgments, and accurately tracking student progress are some of the very important teacher competencies that are encouraged by these programs.

Steps to Inclusion

The May Center for Early Childhood Education (Anderson, Campbell, & O'Malley Cannon, 1994) and the Douglass Developmental Disabilities Center (Harris, Handleman, Arnold, & Gordon, 2001) are examples of programs that provide a progression of experiences for preschoolers from segregated to inclusive programming. The approach to inclusion by these programs reflects the philosophy that for some children initial segregated intervention may increase their ability to benefit from subsequent inclusive opportunities. Instruction is initially designed to include fundamental skills that will eventually enhance responsiveness to community-based applications. Placement along a continuum of classroom settings is then based on a child's readiness for a curriculum that includes systematically guided inclusion experiences.

Both programs provide sequential movement from individual, to small group, to inclusive programming. For example, classes at the Douglass Developmental Disabilities Center include a prep class that offers exclusive one-to-one teaching, a small group preschool that provides instruction in groups of increasing size, and the Small Wonders program where students with autism attend school with typically developing peers. The May Center operates very similar classes. In both programs, as children move along the continuum, the complexity of the curriculum systematically increases with the goal of approximating community-based experiences.

Both the May and Douglass programs carefully manage the transition to mainstream settings. A highly systematic process includes initial assessment visits by the teacher to public and private settings, and then the development of a comprehensive transition plan. There are many variables to consider, such as staff-student ratio, classroom structure, and school-life activities. After a complete assessment of the skills needed in the identified setting, the child's requisite skills are evaluated, and the curriculum modified accordingly. The transition process is further enhanced by having the student attend the new school for increasing periods of time prior to enrollment, and both programs provide formal follow-up support services. The success of this inclusion effort, however, often relies on advocacy efforts and educational support services, as well as the preparation of the child.

Statewide Services

The Delaware Autistic Program (Bondy & Frost, 1994) and Treatment and Education of Autistic and Related Communication-Handicapped Children (TEACCH) in North Carolina (Marcus, Schopler, & Lord, 2001) are models of statewide service delivery for students with autism. Both programs, which are responsible for providing educational services for students throughout their respective states, share the common philosophy that a continuum of services should be available, from complete inclusion to highly specialized programming. This full range of resources is believed to enable both states to meet the federal mandate for a free and appropriate education within the least restrictive environment on an individual basis.

Providing statewide programs presents the challenges of matching the needs of students with the resources of the local community. Consideration for variables such as population, distance, and services for typical children increases the complexity of these statewide systems. For example, one town may share the same elementary school, or another, provide resources on a regional basis. Developing a statewide continuum of program options often reflects these and other demographic and logistical concerns.

Both the Delaware and North Carolina models support the commitment to providing inclusive options for students with autism through a continuum of services and placements. Local mainstreaming experiences in day care centers or preschools supplement specialized categorical programs, and some communities provide full inclusive experiences. In addition, some students may receive home intervention services either on an exclusive or part-time basis.

Planning Inclusion Activities

As reflected by the variety of models, meeting the challenges of inclusive education depends on many issues that determine the ultimate complexion of the preschool program. For example, one feature that is highlighted by the Montgomery County Public School System Preschool for Children with Autism (Egel, 1994) is the comprehensive system of inclusive activities. Classroom events in this preschool program are conducted in the context of naturally occurring situations such as free play, lunch, story time, and recess. When designing educational experiences for the children, the staff of the Montgomery program considers variables such as the student-teacher ratio, rate of attention, and the type of materials used in the integrated setting. The program then assesses this information, in order to modify the child's program activities and approximate those conducted in the community Headstart class. Children then attend Headstart as early as possible according to an integration plan that specifies time, activities, and staffing.

The Role of Peers

All of the programs described in the present chapter value the importance of the typical peer as a model. This issue is particularly exemplified by the Berkshire Hills Learning Center (Powers, 1994). Program development efforts for this inclusive preschool class consider peer-specific variables such as age, developmental level, social comfort, and effective modeling skills. Peer-training activities are then matched to educational need and targeted for instruction. The curriculum that

emerges provides rich educational experiences, both for the children with autism and their peers.

Follow-up services are also a critical feature of inclusive programming in the Berkshire Hills program. For example, providing in-class supports and consultation services are some of the follow-up resources that are available to families and agencies after graduation. The ultimate success of the transition process depends on the ongoing review and monitoring of student progress.

The various programs just described produce a wide range of student outcomes. Many schools report a number of students each year who are able to be fully included with varying levels of support. Also, most agencies describe part-time mainstreaming experiences. Each of the programs also identifies children who continue to require specialized programming beyond the preschool years. All of these findings support the view that successful inclusive education for the young child with autism is a function of individual need and response to intervention.

The range of program options offered by these distinguished service providers reflect current thinking regarding integrated education for the preschooler with autism. Whether provided on a local or statewide basis, or in the private school or university, variables such as segregated programming, peer modeling, and the exclusivity of the included experience become common concerns of this intricate issue. The continued evolution of the continuum of program options should provide the clarification that is needed to answer the many questions regarding integrated education.

Early Education and Beyond

Giving students with autism broadened educational experiences, including integrated opportunities is becoming a standard for many programs. Whether participating in community experiences where children can engage in parallel play with typical children on the playground or attending classes with same age peers, children with autism are increasingly entering the mainstream. Although there are numerous reports of successful inclusion programs at the preschool and elementary levels, the field is now faced with the challenge of developing effective supports at the middle school and beyond.

As the differences between early, middle, and secondary school education are considered, preschool and elementary-age programs seem to offer a structure that is especially favorable for including the student with autism. For example, developmentally based curricula provide specific skill sequences to be taught, and the predictability of classroom routines and structures can help to guide social skills programming. On the other hand, it is the unpredictability of social experiences in the middle and secondary school programs, combined with the variability in course content and limited self-contained and specialized settings that hinder the development of specific strategies and experiences to promote the successful inclusion of children with autism. Early reports describe the highly individualized nature of these efforts to include students with autism in middle and secondary school programs, with the minimum components of administrative ownership, professional consultation, and staff training. As the children with autism who did well socially in the early school years now reach middle and high school programs, there is an increasing demand for sophisticated programming for these older students.

CONCLUSION

Including children with autism in classes with their normally developing peers is helpful in improving their social skills. A significant body of research exists to guide the educator in facilitating social interactions among children with disabilities and their classmates. Table 40.1 summarizes several of these empirically supported interventions that promote social interaction and successful inclusion. Benefits in the domains of language and general development are not as well documented. An important focus of social skills training appears to be teaching the child with autism to initiate interactions and respond to the efforts of his or her peers. Adult support for both the peers and the children with autism, especially in the early stages of learning is important. It is also important to have receptive peers who

TABLE 40.1   Empirically Supported Interventions

Peer modeling

Peer self-monitoring of initiations to child with autism

Social skills groups

Peer buddy system for all students

Picture activity schedules for classroom

Social scripts and script fading

Focus on initiation skills

Self-management of initiation, on-task, and social skills

Inclusion techniques (i.e., teacher respond to child through peers or arrangement of environment rather than direct intervention)

Behavior management skills

will be patient with the awkward initial efforts of the child with autism. Although shown to be effective for some children, especially those who are very young, the benefits of inclusion have not yet been fully evaluated. For example, we do not know the optimal blend or sequencing of special and regular educational experience for the child with autism. A variety of models have been developed, with little comparative data among them. Thus, much of the research to evaluate inclusion remains to be done (Buysse & Bailey, 1993).

In the absence of definitive data, we believe the extent of inclusion should be adjusted to fit each child and may vary at different points in the child's education. Very young children with autism require an initial intensity of instruction that may best be done one to one (e.g., Harris & Handleman, 1994; Lovaas, 1987). After that, the appropriate setting will be dictated by the child's skills and the best available resources. Higher functioning children with autism who have good cognitive abilities, few disruptive behaviors, and some awareness of other people, might profitably spend the full school day with their peers in a regular class. These children will need some special support in the classroom, especially for their social development, but can often benefit from the full academic curriculum. Other children with autism might share some classes with normally developing peers and return to a specialized setting for other experiences. The most impaired children might share cafeteria and recreational services with their peers, but do other work in a segregated class. In order to promote successful experiences, the child's age, cognitive abilities, behavior problems, and social awareness should all be considered in making these plans, along with the necessary resources.

Cross-References

Assessment issues are discussed in Chapters 27 through 32, Curriculum Development in Chapter 33, and working with families in Chapter 42. Personnel Preparation is addressed in Chapter 45.

REFERENCES

Anderson, S. R., Campbell, S., & O'Malley Cannon, B. (1994). The May Center for Early Childhood Education. In S. L. Harris & J. S. Handleman (Eds.), *Preschool education programs for children with autism* (pp. 15–36). Austin, TX: ProEd.

Belchic, J. K., & Harris, S. L. (1994). The use of multiple peer exemplars to enhance the generalization of play skills to the siblings of children with autism. *Child and Family Behavior Therapy, 16,* 1–25.

Blew, P., Schwartz, I. S., & Luce, S. (1985). Teaching functional community skills to autistic children using nonhandicapped peer tutors. *Journal of Applied Behavior Analysis, 18,* 337–342.

Bondy, A. S., & Frost, L. A. (1994). The Delaware autistic program. In S. L. Harris & J. S. Handleman (Eds.), *Preschool education programs for children with autism* (pp. 37–54). Austin, TX: ProEd.

Buysse, V., & Bailey, D. B. (1993). Behavioral and developmental outcomes in young children with disabilities in integrated and segregated settings: A review of comparative studies. *Journal of Special Education, 26,* 434–461.

Carr, E. G., & Darcy, M. (1990). Setting generality of peer modeling in children with autism. *Journal of Autism and Developmental Disorders, 20,* 45–59.

Coe, D., Matson, J., Fee, V., Manikam, R., & Linarello, C. (1990). Training nonverbal and verbal play skills to mentally retarded and autistic children. *Journal of Autism and Developmental Disorders, 20,* 177–187.

Demchak, M., & Drinkwater, S. (1992). Preschoolers with severe disabilities: The case against segregation. *Topics in Early Childhood Education, 11*(4), 70–83.

Dugan, E., Kamps, D., Leonard, B., Watkins, N., Rheinberger, A., & Stackhaus, J. (1995). Effects of cooperative learning groups during social studies for students with autism and their fourth-grade peers. *Journal of Applied Behavior Analysis, 28,* 175–188.

Durbach, M., & Pence, A. R. (1991). A comparison of language production skills of preschoolers with special needs in segregated and integrated settings. *Early Child Development and Care, 68,* 49–69.

Egel, A. L. (1994). The Montgomery County Public School System preschool for children with autism. In S. L. Harris & J. S. Handleman (Eds.), *Preschool education programs for children with autism* (pp. 55–70). Austin, TX: ProEd.

Fenske, E. C., Zalenski, S., Krantz, P. J., & McClannahan, L. E. (1985). Age at intervention and treatment outcome for autistic children in a comprehensive intervention program. *Analysis and Intervention in Developmental Disabilities, 5,* 49–58.

Fisher, M., & Meyer, L. H. (2002). Development and social competence after two years for students enrolled in inclusive and self-contained educational programs. *Research and Practice for Persons with Severe Disabilities, 27,* 165–174.

Garfinkle, A. N., & Schwartz, I. S. (2002). Peer imitation: Increasing social interactions in children with autism and other developmental disabilities in inclusive preschool classrooms. *Topics in Early Childhood Special Education, 22,* 26–38.

Garrison-Harrell, L., Kamps, D., & Kravitz, T. (1997). The effects of peer networks on social-communicative behaviors for students with autism. *Focus on Autism and Other Developmental Disabilities, 12,* 241–254.

Goldstein, H., & Cisar, C. L. (1992). Promoting interaction during sociodramatic play: Teaching scripts to typical preschoolers and classmates with disabilities. *Journal of Applied Behavior Analysis, 25,* 265–280.

Goldstein, H., Kaczmarek, L., Pennington, R., & Shafer, K. (1992). Peer-mediated intervention: Attending to, commenting on, and acknowledging the behavior of preschoolers with autism. *Journal of Applied Behavior Analysis, 25,* 289–305.

Gonzalez-Lopez, A., & Kamps, D. M. (1997). Social skills training to increase social interactions between children with autism and their typical peers. *Focus on Autism and Other Developmental Disabilities, 12,* 2–14.

Guralnick, M. J., Connor, R. T., & Hammond, M. (1995). Parent perspectives of peer relationships and friendships in integrated and specialized programs. *American Journal on Mental Retardation, 99,* 457–476.

Guralnick, M. J., & Groom, J. M. (1987). The peer relations of mildly delayed and nonhandicapped children in mainstreamed play groups. *Child Development, 58,* 1556–1575.

Handleman, J. S., & Harris, S. L. (1986). *Educating the developmentally disabled: Meeting the needs of children and families.* San Diego, CA: College Hill.

Handleman, J. S., & Harris, S. L. (Eds.). (2001). *Preschool education programs for children with autism* (2nd ed.). Austin, TX: ProEd.

Hanrahan, J., Goodman, W., & Rapagna, S. (1985). Instructional priorities for the integration of mentally handicapped children as judged by special class teachers and regular class teachers. *Canadian Journal of Special Education, 1,* 101–108.

Hanrahan, J., Goodman, W., & Rapagna, S. (1990). Preparing mentally retarded students for mainstreaming: Priorities of regular and special school teachers. *American Association on Mental Retardation, 94,* 470–474.

Haring, T. G., & Breen, C. G. (1992). A peer-mediated social network intervention to enhance the social integration of persons with moderate and severe disabilities. *Journal of Applied Behavior Analysis, 25,* 319–333.

Harris, S. L., & Handleman, J. S. (Eds.). (1994). *Preschool education programs for children with autism.* Austin, TX: ProEd.

Harris, S. L., Handleman, J. S., & Alessandri, M. (1990). Teaching youths with autism to offer assistance. *Journal of Applied Behavior Analysis, 23,* 297–305.

Harris, S. L., Handleman, J. S., Arnold, M. S., & Gordon, R. F. (2001). The Douglas Developmental Disabilities Center: Two models of service delivery. In J. S. Handleman & S. L. Harris (Eds.), *Preschool education programs for children with autism* (2nd ed., pp. 233–260). Austin, TX: ProEd.

Harris, S. L., Handleman, J. S., Gordon, R., Kristoff, B., & Fuentes, F. (1991). Changes in cognitive and language functioning of preschool children with autism. *Journal of Autism and Developmental Disorders, 21,* 281–290.

Harris, S. L., Handleman, J. S., Kristoff, B., Bass, L., & Gordon, R. (1990). Changes in language development among autistic and peer children in segregated and integrated preschool settings. *Journal of Autism and Developmental Disorders, 20,* 23–31.

Harrower, J. K., & Dunlap, G. (2001). Including children with autism in general education classrooms: A review of effective strategies. *Behavior Modification, 25,* 762–784.

Hundert, J., & Hopkins, B. (1992). Training supervisors in a collaborative team approach to promote peer interactions of children with disabilities in integrated preschools. *Journal of Applied Behavior Analysis, 25,* 385–400.

Kamps, D. M., Barbetta, P. M., Leonard, B. R., & Delquadri, J. (1994). Classwide peer tutoring: An integration strategy to improve reading skills and promote peer interactions among students with autism and general education peers. *Journal of Applied Behavior Analysis, 27,* 49–61.

Kamps, D. M., Leonard, B. R., Vernon, S., Dugan, E. P., Delquadri, J. C., Gershon, B., et al. (1992). Teaching social skills to students with autism to increase peer interactions in an integrated first-grade classroom. *Journal of Applied Behavior Analysis, 25,* 281–288.

Kamps, D. M., Royer, J., Dugan, E., Kravitz, T., Gonzalez-Lopez, A., Garcia, J., et al. (2002). Peer training to facilitate social interaction for elementary students with autism and their peers. *Exceptional Children, 68,* 173–187.

Kasari, C., Freeman, S. F. N., Bauminger, N., & Alkin, M. C. (1999). Parental perspective in inclusion: Effects of autism and Down syndrome. *Journal of Autism and Developmental Disabilities, 29,* 297–305.

Kern-Dunlap, L., Dunlap, G., Clarke, S., Childs, K. E., White, R. L., & Stewart, M. P. (1992). Effects of a videotape feedback package on the peer interactions of children with serious behavioral and emotional challenges. *Journal of Applied Behavior Analysis, 25,* 355–364.

Kliewer, C. (1995). Young children's communication and literacy: A qualitative study of language in the inclusive preschool. *Mental Retardation, 33,* 143–152.

Koegel, L. K., Koegel, R. L., Hurley, C., & Frea, W. D. (1992). Improving social skills and disruptive behavior in children with autism through self-management. *Journal of Applied Behavior Analysis, 25,* 341–353.

Laushey, K. M., & Heflin, L. J. (2000). Enhancing social skills of kindergarten children with autism through the training of multiple peers as tutors. *Journal of Autism and Developmental Disorders, 30,* 183–193.

Lord, C. (1995). Facilitating social inclusion. In E. Schopler & G. B. Mesibov (Eds.), *Learning and cognition in autism* (pp. 221–240). New York: Plenum Press.

Lord, C., & Hopkins, J. M. (1986). The social behavior of autistic children with younger and same-age nonhandicapped peers. *Journal of Autism and Developmental Disorders, 16,* 249–262.

Lovaas, O. I. (1987). Behavioral treatment and normal educational and intellectual functioning in young autistic children. *Journal of Consulting and Clinical Psychology, 55,* 3–9.

Marcus, L., Schopler, E., & Lord, C. (2001). TEACCH services for preschool children. In J. S. Handleman & S. L. Harris (Eds.), *Preschool education programs for children with autism* (2nd ed., pp. 215–232). Austin, TX: ProEd.

McClannahan, L. E., & Krantz, P. J. (2001). Behavior analysis and intervention for preschoolers at the Princeton Child Development Institute. In J. S. Handleman & S. L. Harris (Eds.), *Preschool education programs for children with autism* (2nd ed., pp. 191–213). Austin, TX: ProEd.

McEvoy, M. A., Nordquist, V. M., Twardosz, S., Heckaman, K. A., Wehby, J. H., & Denny, R. K. (1988). Promoting autistic children's peer interactions in an integrated early childhood setting using affection activities. *Journal of Applied Behavior Analysis, 21,* 193–200.

McGee, G. G., Almeida, M. C., Sulzer-Azaroff, B., & Feldman, R. S. (1992). Prompting reciprocal interactions via peer incidental teaching. *Journal of Applied Behavior Analysis, 25,* 117–126.

McGee, G. G., Krantz, P. J., & McClannahan, L. E. (1984). Conversational skills for autistic adolescents: Teaching assertiveness in naturalistic game settings. *Journal of Autism and Developmental Disorders, 14,* 319–330.

McGee, G. G., Krantz, P. J., & McClannahan, L. E. (1986). An extension of incidental teaching procedures to reading instruction for autistic children. *Journal of Applied Behavior Analysis, 19,* 147–157.

McGee, G. G., Morrier, M. J., & Daly, T. (2001). The Walden Early Education Programs. In J. S. Handleman & S. L. Harris (Eds.), *Preschool education programs for children with autism* (2nd ed., pp. 157–190). Austin, TX: ProEd.

Meyer, L. H., Fox, A., Schermer, A., Ketelsen, D., Montan, N., Maley, K., et al. (1987). The effects of teacher intrusion on social play interactions between children with autism and their nonhandicapped peers. *Journal of Autism and Developmental Disorders, 17,* 315–332.

Morrison, L., Kamps, D., Garcia, J., & Parker, D. (2001). Peer mediation and monitoring strategies to improve initiations and social skills for students with autism. *Journal of Positive Behavior Interventions, 3,* 237–250.

Nientimp, E. G., & Cole, C. L. (1992). Teaching socially valid social interaction responses to students with severe disabilities in an integrated school setting. *Journal of School Psychology, 30,* 343–354.

Odom, S. L., & McEvoy, M. A. (1990). Mainstreaming at the preschool level: Potential barriers and tasks for the field. *Topics in Early Childhood Special Education, 10*(2), 48–61.

Odom, S. L., & Speltz, M. L. (1983). Program variations in preschools for handicapped and nonhandicapped children: Mainstreamed vs. integrated special education. *Analysis and Intervention in Developmental Disabilities, 3,* 89–103.

Odom, S. L., & Strain, P. S. (1986). A comparison of peer-initiation and teacher-antecedent intervention for promoting reciprocal social interactions of autistic preschoolers. *Journal of Applied Behavior Analysis, 19,* 59–71.

Odom, S. L., & Watts, E. (1991). Reducing teacher prompts in peer-mediated interventions for young children with autism. *Journal of Special Education, 25,* 26–43.

Odom, S. L., Chandler, L. K., Ostrosky, M., McConnell, S. R., & Reaney, S. (1992). Fading teacher prompts from peer-initiation interactions for children with disabilities. *Journal of Applied Behavior Analysis, 25,* 307–317.

Odom, S. L., Hoyson, M., Jamieson, B., & Strain, P. S. (1985). Increasing handicapped preschoolers' peer social interactions: Cross-setting and component analysis. *Journal of Applied Behavior Analysis, 18,* 3–16.

Oke, N. J., & Schreibman, L. (1990). Training social initiations to a high-functioning autistic child: Assessment of collateral behavior change and generalization in a case study. *Journal of Autism and Developmental Disorders, 20,* 479–497.

Palmer, D. S., Fuller, K., Arora, T., & Nelson, M. (2001). Taking sides: Parent views on inclusion for their children with severe disabilities. *Exceptional Children, 67,* 467–484.

Pierce, K., & Schreibman, L. (1997). Using peer trainers to promote social behavior in autism: Are they effective at enhancing multiple social modalities? *Focus on Autism and Other Developmental Disabilities, 12,* 207–218.

Powers, M. D. (1994). The Berkshire Hills Learning Center. In S. L. Harris & J. S. Handleman (Eds.), *Preschool education programs for children with autism* (pp. 163–180). Austin, TX: ProEd.

Romanczyk, R. G., Lockshin, S. B., & Matey, L. (2001). The children's unit for treatment and evaluation. In J. S. Handleman & S. L. Harris

(Eds.), *Preschool education programs for children with autism* (2nd ed., pp. 49–94). Austin, TX: ProEd.

Sainato, D. M., Goldstein, H., & Strain, P. S. (1992). Effects of self-evaluation on preschool children's use of social interaction strategies with their classmates with autism. *Journal of Applied Behavior Analysis, 25,* 127–141.

Sasso, G. M., & Rude, H. A. (1987). Unprogrammed effects of training high-status peers to interact with severely handicapped children. *Journal of Applied Behavior Analysis, 20,* 35–44.

Schepis, M. M., Ownby, J. B., Parsons, M. B., & Reid, D. H. (2000). Training support staff for teaching young children with disabilities in an inclusive preschool. *Journal of Positive Behavior Interventions, 2,* 170–178.

Shafer, M. S., Egel, A. L., & Neef, N. A. (1984). Training mildly handicapped peers to facilitate changes in the social interaction skills of autistic children. *Journal of Applied Behavior Analysis, 17,* 461–476.

Strain, P. S. (1983). Generalization of autistic children's social behavior change: Effects of developmentally integrated and segregated settings. *Analysis and Intervention in Developmental Disabilities, 3,* 23–34.

Strain, P. S., & Cordisco, L. K. (1994). LEAP Preschool. In S. L. Harris & J. S. Handleman (Eds.), *Preschool education programs for children with autism* (pp. 225–244). Austin, TX: ProEd.

Strain, P. S., Kerr, M. M., & Ragland, E. U. (1979). Effects of peer-mediated social initiations and prompting/reinforcement procedures on the social behavior of autistic children. *Journal of Autism and Developmental Disorders, 9,* 41–54.

Strain, P. S., Shores, R. E., & Kerr, M. M. (1976). An experimental analysis of "spill over" effects on the social interaction of behaviorally handicapped preschool children. *Journal of Applied Behavior Analysis, 9,* 31–40.

Strain, P. S., & Timm, M. A. (1974). An experimental analysis of social interaction between a behaviorally disordered preschool child and her classroom peers. *Journal of Applied Behavior Analysis, 7,* 583–590.

Thiemann, K. S., & Goldstein, H. (2001). Social stories, written text cues, and video feedback: Effects on social communication of children with autism. *Journal of Applied Behavior Analysis, 34,* 425–446.

Travis, L., Sigman, M., & Ruskin, E. (2001). Links between social understanding and social behavior in verbally able children with autism. *Journal of Autism and Developmental Disorders, 31,* 119–130.

Weiss, M. J., & Harris, S. L. (2001). *Reaching out, joining in: Teaching social skills to young children with autism.* Bethesda, MD: Woodbine House.

CHAPTER 41

Models of Educational Intervention for Students with Autism: Home, Center, and School-Based Programming

SANDRA L. HARRIS, JAN S. HANDLEMAN, AND HEATHER K. JENNETT

Following the demonstration that early intensive behavioral intervention can have a measurable impact on the developmental trajectory of some young children with autism (Lovaas, 1987), there has been a proliferation of treatment programs for these youngsters. Our goal in this chapter is to look at three basic approaches to the treatment of autism—the home-based, center-based, and school-based models—and consider their strengths and weaknesses. Most of the programs we review here are based on the principles of applied behavior analysis (ABA), but other highly regarded programs derived from structured teaching as embodied by the TEACCH program (e.g., Schopler, Mesibov, & Hearsey, 1995) and from a developmental perspective as reflected in the work of Rogers and her colleagues (e.g., Rogers, Hall, Osaki, Reaven, & Herbison, 2001) are also discussed. Although each program included here reflects the theoretical commitment and personal values of the people who direct it, common threads tie together these highly regarded programs. These commonalities are as interesting as the differences. We consider the similarities and differences, strengths, and weaknesses that are associated with each model. Where there is research examining the impact of a particular program on the development of children with autism, we summarize those findings.

The term *home-based* refers to programs where the majority of the child's initial instructional hours are delivered in the home, usually by a team of service providers who may be hired by the family or by the supervising professional. This definition differentiates home-based programs from other services that are delivered to families who have their child in a center-based or school-based program and for whom the home-based hours do not constitute the majority of the child's instructional time. Children served within a home-based model typically transition to a school setting at some point in their treatment with a goal toward integrating them into a normalized setting. This model is best known through the research of Lovaas (1987), although it has been adopted by a variety of service providers and families.

Center-based services are delivered in a specialized setting devoted to meeting the needs of children on the autism spectrum. Some of the university-based research programs, including our own at Rutgers and that of Romanczyk (e.g., Romanczyk, Lockshin, & Matey, 2001) at Binghamton University, fall into this category. In this approach, the children spend their instructional day in a specialized setting. Families are typically trained in the treatment methods and are expected to provide instructional support at home, often in the form of generalization of new skills, and to work on skills that are part of the child's natural home environment such as bath time, bed time, and family meals. In most center-based programs, children are eventually integrated into classes with typical children either in a class within the center or a school-based setting.

Children in *school-based* settings may be in a special class for children with autism in a public school, or they may be included in a typical education classroom. Parents of these children, like those families who have their children in center-based programs, are usually expected to support the educational program of their child through their own efforts at home. The best-known example of a school-based model is the TEACCH program in which individual specialized classrooms are operated within regular schools throughout North Carolina. Alternatively, in Rogers's Denver model, experts consult to schools where one or more children may be included in a regular class.

CENTER-BASED PROGRAMS

In 1970, Lovaas and his colleagues began to provide comprehensive clinical services to children with autism and their families in the home and community, as opposed to psychiatric hospitals (Smith, Donahoe, & Davis, 2001). Based on the effectiveness of this home-based model of intervention, the early 1970s witnessed the introduction of the center-based approach to educating the child with autism (e.g., the Douglass Developmental Disabilities Center; Harris, Handleman, Arnold, & Gordon, 2001; the Princeton Child Developmental Institute; McClannahan, & Krantz, 2001). Center-based programs continued to grow for the next 3 decades and became a common and preferred setting to provide specialized educational supports and services to students with autism and their families. The often segregated and self-contained nature of center-based programs promoted a concentration of services that could be systematically monitored and a consistency of intervention that was not possible in other environments. One major benefit from these programs has been a plethora of research on ABA teaching technology.

The National Research Council of the National Academy of Sciences (2001) proposed the following program quality indicators for programs serving children with autism: (1) specific curricula, (2) highly supportive instructional environments, (3) maintenance and generalization strategies, (4) predictable routines, (5) functional behavior management procedures, (6) systematic transitional planning, (7) collaborative family involvement, (8) family supports, (9) low student-to-staff ratios, (10) highly trained staff, (11) comprehensive professional resources, and (12) staff supervision and program review mechanisms. Most center-based ABA programs feature these components and can often make them readily available to students. While these quality indicators are the hallmarks of many center-based programs, some programs may feature a particular element more than the others. The following center-based programs, well known for being quality programs, each offer a distinctive contribution.

Children's Unit for Treatment and Evaluation (Children's Unit)

The Children's Unit is one of three service divisions of the Institute for Child Development at the State University of New York at the Binghamton Campus (Romanczyk et al., 2001). The Children's Unit was established in 1975 and serves children 12 months though 12 years of age with autistic spectrum disorders as well as children with emotional and developmental disorders. The preschool and school-age programs are similar in structure and differ primarily by age. The Children's Unit operates 5 hours a day, 5 days a week, 12 months a year; and funding for the program comes from various state and county agencies. The philosophy of the program is highlighted in the following first line from the program brochure: "Our guiding philosophy is to employ intensive, child-centered, empirically validated educational and clinical procedures."

Alpine Learning Group (Alpine)

Alpine, founded in 1989, serves students diagnosed with autism and pervasive developmental disorders, ages 3 years to 21 years (Meyer, Taylor, Levin, & Fisher, 2001). Students are admitted to a full-day, year-round day program and receive related outreach services in the home. Preschool and school-age programming at Alpine is committed to the principles of ABA and supported by comprehensive and ongoing staff training. Coordinated school and home teaching and systematic transitional programming to less specialized settings are hallmarks of the Alpine program.

Walden Early Childhood Programs (Walden)

Walden was established on the campus of the University of Massachusetts at Amherst in 1985 and relocated to Emory University School of Medicine in Atlanta, Georgia, in 1991, where it is a component of the Emory Autism Resource Center (McGee, Morrier, & Daly, 2001). Walden provides a continuum of early education to toddlers, preschoolers, and prekindergarten-age children with autism and their typical peers. The curriculum is guided by the assumption that early childhood education should emphasize social and language development and that incidental teaching can support successful inclusion. Active parent and professional collaboration is a feature of the Walden program.

Princeton Child Development Institute (PCDI)

The PCDI was founded in 1970 as a private nonprofit agency serving children with autism (McClannahan & Krantz, 2001). PCDI has grown to include an early intervention program for children younger than 3 years of age, preschool and school-age educational programs, two community-based family-style group homes, and career development and supported employment programs for adults. ABA methodology guides all programming at PCDI, including a highly systematic competency-based staff training and supervision process. A feature of the PCDI programs is the highly precise use of activity schedules to structure learning experiences for the children and adults who are enrolled.

Douglass Developmental Disabilities Center (DDDC)

The DDDC was established in 1972 at Rutgers, The State University of New Jersey (Harris et al., 2001). Over the past 30 years, the DDDC has grown to include the original Douglass School, Douglass Outreach, the Division of Adult and Transition Services, and the Division of Research and Training. Educational services at the DDDC are blended with ongoing research and comprehensive training that ensures the implementation of state-of-the-art ABA programming and innovations in clinical intervention. A distinctive feature of the DDDC is a staged preschool program that systematically moves children from intensive teaching experiences to small group and integrated instruction in preparation for transition to community-based programs.

Learning Experiences, an Alternative Program for Preschoolers and Their Parents (LEAP)

The LEAP preschool opened in 1982 as part of the Early Childhood Intervention Program at Western Psychiatric Institute and Clinic, University of Pittsburgh (Strain & Cordisco, 1994). The program currently operates additional classrooms in the Denver Public School System and is now administered at the University of Colorado School of Education. LEAP includes preschool classes, parent training activities, and outreach services, and was the first program in the United States to integrate children with autism with typical peers. The curriculum blends the ABA approach with developmentally appropriate practices and features peer-mediated social skills interventions.

Differences and Similarities among Programs

While the six center-based programs described in this chapter include state-of-the-art and innovative interventions and supports, as models in the field, each offers a unique focus that has contributed to ABA practices. For example, the program at the DDDC presents a unique structure for organizing preschool classes for children with autism (Harris et al., 2001). The DDDC offers a continuum of services, which initially begins with enrollment in the Prep class featuring primarily one-to-one ABA instruction. As the students progress, they may enter the Small Group Preschool class where paired and small group educational experiences are offered with a range of behavioral strategies to prepare the children for possible admission to the Small Wonders Preschool class. In the Small Wonders program, children with autism attend school with typical children and are exposed to a developmentally based and behaviorally supported preschool curriculum. This staged progression often culminates with the design of a transitional plan that systematically introduces the child to public school education. To complete the continuum of program options at the DDDC, the outreach division offers comprehensive school- and home-based services.

Many center-based programs for children with autism have benefited from the work of Romanczyk and his colleagues (Romanczyk et al., 2001) in developing the individualized goal setting (IGS) curriculum. The IGS, developed at the Children's Unit, provides a guide to development in 19 areas, each with specific levels of development that are composed of stages with specific behaviorally referenced tasks (Romanczyk & Lockshin, 1982). The tasks serve as daily activities to address a child's individual needs. While the curriculum is organized according to a developmental sequence, it is not expected that a child will simply progress through the objectives in sequence. The programming is designed to ensure that a child uses functional skills that are generalized and maintained. The IGS carefully blends assessment and intervention with an accompanying computerized format that adds to the systematization and to successful linkage with the individualized educational plan and monitoring processes.

Much of the research on ABA practices has been done in center-based programs and has resulted in the refinement of ABA techniques. For example, the work of McGee at Walden as to the use of incidental teaching in included settings (McGee, Krantz, Mason, & McClannahan, 1983) has contributed to efforts to increase the application of learned skills by children with autism in more natural environments. Incidental teaching strategies can meet the needs of both children with autism and typical children by blending with normalized classroom activities (McGee et al., 2001). The teacher maintains a high level of enthusiasm, makes a series of rapid and complex teaching judgments, continually tracks the interests of the students, and capitalizes on appropriate moments for instruction. In addition, attention

is given to the selection and delivery of reinforcing events and materials. This systematic environmental engineering is a critical feature of incidental teaching for maintaining high levels of engagement by the children.

Fostering the independence of children with autism is another focus of educational research, and the work of McClannahan, Krantz, and their staff at PCDI on the effective use of activity schedules has greatly influenced this effort (McClannahan & Krantz, 1999). Photographic or written activity schedules can provide a framework for children to make choices and to manage changes in daily routines and can promote generalization across settings such as school and home (Krantz, MacDuff, & McClannahan, 1993). Activity schedules can also be a vehicle for teaching social interaction by the use of scripts and script-fading procedures, which aim to promote spontaneous conversations (McClannahan & Krantz, 1999).

The effectiveness of ABA instruction depends on comprehensive, ongoing staff training. A hallmark of the Alpine model is a competency-based staff training program that contains preservice, in-service, and technical assistance components (Meyer et al., 2001). Didactic and hands-on practice is followed by ongoing training, and supervision occurs throughout the year with classroom observations and staff meetings. In addition, regularly scheduled in-service sessions and research meetings ensure that the staff remains current in innovative practices. A comprehensive annual staff evaluation based on performance indicators serves as a measure of staff competency, as well as the effectiveness of the overall staff training program.

Including children with autism or preparing children with autism to be included with typically developing peers has become a standard for center-based programs (Harris & Handleman, 1997). Strain and his colleagues were among the first to systematically blend children with autism into a more typical preschool setting at the LEAP program (Strain, Hoyson, & Jamieson, 1985). Since its inception, the LEAP preschool has operated a full inclusion program based on the premises that children with autism can: (1) benefit from integrated educational environments; (2) benefit when early intervention is conducted across school, home, and community settings; (3) make the greatest progress when professionals and parents collaborate; (4) learn many important skills from typical same-age peers; (5) benefit when early intervention efforts are systematic and individualized; and (6) benefit together with their typical peers from developmentally appropriate activities (Strain & Cordisco, 1994).

Inclusion for children with autism has also become an important outcome measure for center-based programs. While the six center-based programs that have been described in this chapter may vary as to the relative importance or definition of inclusion, many report data in this area (Handleman & Harris, 2001; Harris & Handleman, 1994). Interpreting the outcome data about inclusion, however, can be complicated because of the interchangeable use of terms such as *mainstreaming, inclusion,* and *integration* (Harris & Handleman, 1997), and caution is recommended when reviewing the data.

When discussing outcome, each of the six programs emphasizes the importance of defining progress that is relevant to an individual child's strengths and challenges. Using this criterion, on the whole, children with autism tend to benefit from enrollment in center-based programs. Considering outcome with relation to the degree of inclusion that is necessary for successful achievement in public school programs, the data available seem to be distributed along the dimensions of full-time inclusion, part-time inclusion, and full-time special program placement, and vary according to program (Handleman & Harris, 2001). For example, Romanczyk and his colleagues (2001) found that over the years, approximately 15% of children who graduated from the *Children's Unit* entered typical classroom, 60% entered special education classes, 22% entered center-based special settings, and 3% entered residential programs. McClannahan and Krantz (2001) factored in age of admission in their outcome findings and reported that 42% to 67% of the students who entered PCDI before age 5 made successful transitions to public school classrooms. Both age and IQ were considered in a 4- to 6-year follow-up study conducted by Harris and Handleman (2000). They found that of 27 preschool-age children who were enrolled at the DDDC, those who started treatment before age 4 tended to have a better placement outcome

(i.e., included settings with limited supports). In addition, their results indicated that children with higher IQs upon being admitted to the program made a 26-point increase in IQ and generally transitioned to regular public school classrooms. Although children with lower IQs or those that began the program after age 4 most often entered special education settings upon graduation, their progress was confirmed with a 13-point increase in IQ. While the data may not be conclusive, most programs stress the importance of conducting well-designed and replicated studies. Reports of the beneficial effects of early intensive intervention for promoting successful participation in an inclusive setting are growing (Harris & Handleman, 2000).

HOME-BASED PROGRAMS

The pioneering research of Lovaas (1987) on early intensive intervention for young children with autism employed a home-based model. The common feature of home-based programs is that the initial work with the child with autism is done in the home. Beyond that core feature, there are many variations in service delivery, such as the intensity of the demand on parents to provide direct instruction to their child as opposed to having trained staff come into the home to work with the child. Some families, especially those living in isolated rural areas with access to few resources, may provide essentially all of their child's instruction, while other families may rely almost exclusively on professional staff to provide services. Even among those families who count on others to do most of the teaching, there is still a demand on the family to coordinate services. Most home-based programs operate in an ABA framework, although within this framework there is considerable variation among the programs in the details of their services.

Young Autism Project at the University of California at Los Angeles (UCLA)

Lovaas's program at UCLA is the prototype for a number of other organizations that have attempted a full or partial replication of his original project. Our description of his services is based on Lovaas's (1987) report of the research in which he demonstrated significant benefits from home-based instruction. The children in his ABA intensive treatment group received an average of 40 hours a week of instruction for 2 years or more. Trained undergraduate students who worked in the child's home did much of this teaching. Parents were also trained in ABA technology so that the child received intensive teaching around the clock and across the year. Lovaas notes that his approach relied heavily on the ABA principles of discrimination learning. He provides some detail about that initial curriculum in *Teaching Developmentally Disabled children: The Me Book* (Lovaas, 1981). During the first year of treatment, there was an emphasis on bringing maladaptive behaviors such as self-stimulation and aggression under control, teaching the child to comply with instructions, to imitate what others do, and the basic elements of toy play. The second year focused on increasing verbal language and play with the child's peers. Instruction also moved beyond the home into the community where children learned how to behave in a preschool class. In the third year, the children learned about expression of emotion and about learning by watching what other children did (observation learning), and they mastered preacademic tasks. Lovaas (1987) made considerable effort to ensure that children were placed in typical classrooms rather than special education classes for their first school placement.

In the research, children who received this intensive programming were compared to two other groups of youngsters, including one group that received 10 hours or less of one-to-one treatment a week and another group who did not receive ABA treatment although they might be enrolled in other special education services in the community. The most striking finding was that 47% of the children who had intensive ABA treatment, beginning with a home-based component, achieved normal intellectual and educational functioning while only 2% of the control children achieved this level of performance. This dramatic finding was greeted with enthusiasm by many families and professionals and sparked controversy (e.g., Lovaas, Smith, & McEachin, 1989; Schopler, Short, & Mesibov, 1989). A follow-up of the 19 intensively treated children when they were 13 years old

showed that they remained superior in educational and intellectual functioning compared to the control group children; 8 of these 19 children were regarded as indistinguishable from their peers (McEachin, Smith, & Lovaas, 1993).

Smith, Groen, and Wynn (2000) did a partial replication of Lovaas's work. This study was significant because Lovaas trained the authors in the treatment methods and the study was carried out at UCLA, but Lovaas had little direct involvement in the research, and this was in large part an independent replication. A major difference between Smith et al.'s study and Lovaas's (1987) work was that the children in the intensive treatment group had 25 hours a week of intensive treatment for 2 to 3 years, as opposed to the 40 hours or more reported by Lovaas. Smith and his colleagues note that they used Lovaas's (1981) book as their guide to curriculum. Unlike the Lovaas study where many parents were asked to take a year off from their outside employment to work with their child, Smith's group expected each caretaker to spend only 5 hours a week doing treatment. The Smith et al. research also used contingent aversive techniques less often than did Lovaas. The comparison group in the Smith et al. study was a group of children whose parents participated in two parent training sessions in ABA a week for between 3 and 9 months.

Although the children who received intensive training made greater progress than those whose parents underwent parent training alone (Smith et al., 2000), the progress of the intensive treatment group was not as great as that made by the children in Lovaas's original study. Only 27% of the Smith et al. sample went to a regular class as compared to 47% in the Lovaas study. Smith et al. note that in spite of the limitations of their study, it does add support for the benefits of intensive treatment as compared to minimal treatment (Lovaas, 1987) or parent training (Smith et al., 2000). It is difficult to know exactly why Smith and his colleagues obtained less impressive outcomes for their children than did Lovaas. One hypothesis is that the children in the Smith et al. study had lower initial IQs than did Lovaas's sample (1981). Smith et al. note that the mean IQ at intake of their children was 50 while for Lovaas (1981) it was 63. We have elsewhere reported on the impact of IQ on outcome for children at the DDDC (Harris & Handleman, 2000), and our data lend some support to Smith et al.'s hypothesis that IQ at intake is an important factor in outcome. Another hypothesis to consider is that 25 hours a week with limited parent involvement may be less effective than at least 40 hours a week with considerable parent involvement.

Pivotal Response Training at the University of California at Santa Barbara (UCSB)

The research of Lovaas (1987) inspired other researchers and practitioners to offer home-based services. Although none of these have as extensive a database documenting their benefits as does the work by Lovaas, some have at least limited outcome data or a strong empirical basis for specific treatment methods. For example, Lynn and Robert Koegel have spent a number of years developing the pivotal response model at UCSB. They focus on teaching parents how to use this framework that emphasizes a naturalistic approach to educating young children with autism. The fundamental assumption underlying the parent training (and child treatment) is that some behaviors are especially key to effective functioning in childhood (Koegel, Koegel, Harrower, & Carter, 1999). These skills are taught to parents and used in closely linked school settings. For example, they teach children to respond to more than one cue, to be motivated to respond, to manage their own behavior, and to initiate behavior rather than waiting for cues from others. Parents are taught the techniques for supporting these skills in their children and are then expected to provide instruction at home. The techniques for teaching these behaviors have been developed through a series of lab-based studies (e.g., Koegel, Camarata, Valdez-Menchaca, & Koegel, 1998). Research on pivotal response training suggests that children who learn these self-initiation responses have better longer term outcome than do children who are not given this training (Koegel, Koegel, Shoshan, & McNerney, 1999).

SCHOOL-BASED PROGRAMS

In contrast to home-based programs, the common feature of school-based programs is that students receive their educational services in classrooms in regular public schools, although the type of classrooms varies from self-contained classrooms to regular classrooms with inclusion. This model also contrasts with center-based programs in which the classrooms are in specialized schools for students with autism. The two school-based programs described next, the TEACCH program at the University of North Carolina and Rogers's program in Denver, are unique in that both programs have established treatment methodologies and demonstration classrooms at their respective universities, but they also disseminate this methodology through their consultative services to the public schools in their surrounding areas to increase the number of children and families to receive their services.

Treatment and Education of Autistic and Related Communication Handicapped Children (TEACCH) at the University of North Carolina

The TEACCH program was founded in 1972 by Schopler at the University of North Carolina Department of Psychiatry and is a statewide program mandated by state law to provide a variety of services to individuals with autism and their families in North Carolina. TEACCH has regional centers across North Carolina that have contracts with public school systems to set up and consult in specialized classrooms based on the TEACCH principles. There are hundreds of public school classrooms in North Carolina receiving this service, and they are typically set up as self-contained classes for students with autism.

The primary aspects of the TEACCH philosophy are understanding and respecting the characteristics of autism, a reliance on the parent-professional collaboration, and lifelong community-based service (Schopler, 1997). The educational approach and a core feature of the TEACCH program is the use of structured teaching in the education of individuals with autism (Schopler et al., 1995). Structured teaching evolved from the findings that individuals with autism learn better in structured environments than unstructured environments (Schopler, 1971, as cited in Schopler et al.,

1995) and is a specialized approach for autism, as it is based on the characteristics and learning profiles of this population. The primary goals in the education of children with autism through structured teaching are to improve their level of skills, often relying on their special interests, and to modify the environment to accommodate the autism deficits (Schopler et al., 1995). While there is a definite emphasis on the gaining of skills, the philosophy of TEACCH differs from many other programs in its belief of respecting and supporting the individual's functioning in society rather than working to eliminate behaviors that make the individual appear different (Mesibov & Shea, 2004). Thus, the structured teaching approach attempts to make the rules of the environment more understandable and predictable, set up expectations, and make tasks meaningful to the individual by taking into account the neuropsychological profiles of individuals with autism. This is done with the use of different types of visual supports, such as schedules, the physical structure of the environment, and the visual structure of the work task. Another main focus of the TEACCH curriculum is an emphasis on communication. The approach to communication is built on behavioral theory and emphasizes generalization, functionality, incidental teaching, as well as alternative communication techniques (Mesibov, 1997).

The structured teaching approach has demonstrated efficacy in a few studies examining these principles as applied in home-based programs. For example, Ozonoff and Cathcart (1998) found that students who received home-based structured teaching significantly improved on developmental and cognitive tasks in the areas of imitation, fine-motor skills, gross-motor skills, and nonverbal cognitive skills compared to students who did not receive this type of intervention at home. In addition, the experimental group exceeded the control group on other developmental measures by two to three times and gained 9.6 months after 4 months of treatment. In another study, Short (1984) compared behaviors of children during the waiting period for treatment and then after their parents had received training in structured teaching and implemented these methods at home. These children showed significant

increases in appropriate play, work, communication, and social interactions compared to their behavior during the waiting period. Although both of these studies evaluated the use of the methodology at home, they also lend support to the effectiveness of structured teaching as an educational approach for children with autism. However, we found no studies examining the effectiveness of structured teaching in the classroom.

Denver Model at the University of Colorado

The Denver Model at the University of Colorado Health Sciences Center was started in 1981 by Sally Rogers with a grant from the U. S. Department of Education. The treatment approach is based on a developmental model of autism first theorized by Rogers and Pennington (1991), which describes the main deficits of autism as involving key skills such as imitation, emotion sharing, theory of mind, and social perception. The resulting intervention approach is designed to address these deficits directly and involves the use of play, interpersonal relationships, and activities to foster symbolic thought and teach the power of communication (Rogers & Lewis, 1989; Rogers et al., 2001). By focusing on these primary areas of deficit at an early age, a main goal of the program is to alter the social experiences of the child to prevent or remediate other secondary deficits (Rogers et al., 2001).

As a key part of the service delivery model, the Denver Model provides educational consultation to local school districts that are responsible for educating preschool-age children with autism in an inclusive setting. Although the model's overall intervention approach is based on a developmental model, it uses state-of-the-art empirically supported treatment techniques, including behavioral teaching techniques and structured teaching, to fulfill its curriculum goals.

The Denver Model has demonstrated and replicated treatment efficacy for its approach to educating children with autism. In one study (Rogers & Lewis, 1989), children with both autism and pervasive developmental disorder showed significant developmental changes in cognitive, social-emotional, perceptual-motor,

motor activities, symbolic play, and social relatedness beyond what would be expected for the passage of time after about 7 months of treatment. The treatment gains were maintained after 12 months. Additionally, the mean autism rating score, as measured by the Childhood Autism Rating Scale (CARS), decreased from moderately autistic to not autistic after 7 months of treatment. These findings were replicated in other studies (e.g., Rogers & DiLalla, 1991) and at other independent sites (Rogers, Lewis, & Reis, 1987).

STRENGTHS AND LIMITATIONS OF THE MODELS

Each of the three models we have described has advantages and limits. We are not aware of any research that directly compares one of the models with another, so our look at models must focus on our experience and clinical impressions rather than on data.

Home-Based Treatment

There are many advantages to the home-based model of treatment. For many preschool-age children, home is the focus of their days, and parents expect to spend many hours a day in childcare. For some families, the home-based approach meshes well with their expectations of how they wish to raise their child. Nonetheless, in many contemporary Western cultures, it is common for both parents to be employed full time outside the home. In some cases, this reflects parental preference, and in others, economic necessity. As we noted earlier, Lovaas (1987) often expected one parent to quit his or her job and be at home full time during the early intensive phase of home-based treatment. This home-based model appears to work best for intact families where one parent's income is sufficient to allow the other parent to be at home full time. It would not be feasible for single parent families or for families whose income is not sufficient for this level of demand.

Home-based treatment allows parents to become skillful in the use of the treatment methods. As a result, they can infuse every moment of their child's day with consistent demands, expectations, and incentives for performance—a significant advantage for a child with autism

who requires intensive and highly consistent intervention for optimal benefits. However, that consistency comes at a cost because other children in the family and/or the marital relationship may be stressed by the relative deprivation that occurs if one or both parents are devoting their full attention to the child with autism.

Similarly, parents using a home-based program enjoy the benefits of full control over their child's treatment. They select the treatment team, determine the course of treatment in discussion with their consultant, and oversee the activities on a day-to-day basis. They are familiar with the nuances of their child's programs and progress. Given their intimate knowledge of their child as a person, this added technical expertise gives them a knowledge that is rarely achieved by others, including professionals. However, this role also casts the parents in a position of unrelenting demand. They must schedule their day around the needs of their child with autism and set aside other activities for themselves and their family.

An advantage of this model for the child is that there is little idle time. The children do not have to take a bus to school, participate in fire drills, wait their turn in line for the toilet, eat lunch on a group schedule, and so forth. Naps, toileting, and other essentials can be built around the needs of the individual child. This maximizes the amount of instructional time available for the child and is a clear plus for this approach.

Center-Based Models

A major advantage of the center-based model of treatment for children with autism is that the entire staff is focused on the treatment of autism, and most of the treatment resources needed—including special educators, classroom support staff, psychologists, speech therapists, and other professionals—are typically available on site. There is no need to travel from one place to another to get specialized services for a child. If one staff member leaves, there are usually others to fill in. That stands in contrast to a school-based model where there may be a single classroom for children with autism in a larger regular education facility, and the loss of the classroom teacher may pose a grave challenge to meeting the needs of those students. It also contrasts with the home-based model where parents or other staff members have to recruit and train replacement staff.

Because center-based programs are designed to meet the special needs of children with autism and are staffed by autism experts, the pressure on parents to ensure that their child's needs are being met is considerably reduced in contrast to a home-based program. However, the center-based program requires that parents work collaboratively with staff and that they forgo the day-to-day control and involvement that parents experience in a home-based program. Developing an effective collaboration can sometimes be challenging for parents and staff alike. The implicit and explicit demands to conform to staff expectations can be stressful for parents just as the expectations of parents for faster progress can be stressful for staff.

A center-based program may or may not include typically developing peers in some or all of its classrooms. If there are no typical peers, it is necessary to transport the child with autism to other places for this essential contact. For example, at our facility, the DDDC, we have an integrated preschool classroom where children with autism and their age-mates learn along with one another. In addition, when our preschool children are ready, we transport them on a regular basis to the school where they will begin kindergarten. Because center-based programs by definition are not in regular schools, this places a demand on staff and parents to ensure that appropriate integration experiences are available to the child.

Children who attend center-based programs have to follow a schedule. They are brought to the center either by a school bus or by their parents. There are lunch schedules and classroom routines that have to be followed; this can be time consuming and may reduce the number of instructional minutes in the day. In addition, there is less opportunity to respect the rhythm of the individual child's schedule and more demand to conform to a classroom schedule than in a home-based program.

School-Based Programs

A major advantage of a school-based program is that it allows the child to enjoy the benefits of a mainstreamed educational experience to the fullest extent possible. All of the resources of a typical school are available, including opportunities for social interaction on the playground, in the lunchroom, and in physical education classes. However, such opportunities are meaningful only if there are trained staff members who have the skills to facilitate the social interactions. Although some public schools seek the resources to support that kind of systematic development by the child with autism, others have a more laissez-faire attitude toward the child's needs.

Children in school-based classrooms have the opportunity to learn the routines of a typical classroom, including the morning pledge to the flag, raising their hands to use the toilet, getting hall passes, sitting quietly at their desks, lining up to go to recess, and so forth. Some variation of these routines is integral to a school experience in most Western cultures, and they are essential skills for the child with autism if he or she is to function in a typical setting.

As we noted in the discussion of center-based programs, if there is a single teacher with an expertise in autism and he or she leaves, there may be no depth of staffing talent to replace that teacher in the classroom. Other supports such as parent training and home consultation about behavior management concerns may or may not be available in a typical school setting and may or may not be provided by professionals who understand autism. These kinds of services are integral to the home-based and center-based programs.

CONCLUSION

There are no high-quality studies that have directly compared the home-based, center-based, and/or school-based models with one another. Nor is there any quality work that has compared different approaches within a model. For example, we have no study comparing the developmental approach of Rogers with the structured teaching of TEACCH nor the benefits of two center-based programs such as Walden and Alpine. In the absence of such data, the consumer must examine the available data for each program and make a decision based on best judgment about the quality of the work and the best judgment about differential benefits.

Each of the three models we have described has advantages and disadvantages. Choice of program must be based on the needs of the individual child and the resources of the family. What works well for an intact, affluent family may be quite different from what would be effective for a home where there is a single parent and a modest income. Similarly, a placement that would be superb for a child with Asperger disorder might be dreadful for a youngster with childhood disintegrative disorder. In addition, a program that was a fine match for a child early in treatment often needs to be supplanted by a very different program as the child grows older and his or her needs change. One size does not fit all.

Cross-References

The development of school-age children is discussed in Chapter 9, aspects of intervention are described in Chapters 33 to 44, and Chapter 45 addresses personnel preparation.

REFERENCES

Handleman, J. S., & Harris, S. L. (2001). *Preschool education programs for children with autism* (2nd ed.). Austin, TX: ProEd.

Harris, S. L., & Handleman, J. S. (1994). *Preschool education programs for children with autism.* Austin, TX: ProEd.

Harris, S. L., & Handleman, J. S. (1997). Helping children enter the mainstream. In D. J. Cohen & F. R. Volkmar (Eds.), *Handbook of autism and pervasive developmental disorders* (2nd ed., pp. 665–675). New York: Wiley.

Harris, S. L., & Handleman, J. S. (2000). Age and IQ at intake as predictors of placement for young children with autism: A four- to six-year follow-up. *Journal of Autism and Developmental Disorders, 30,* 137–142.

Harris, S. L., Handleman, J. S., Arnold, M. S., & Gordon, R. F. (2001). The Douglass Developmental Disabilities Center. In J. S. Handleman & S. L. Harris (Eds.), *Preschool education programs for children with autism* (2nd ed., pp. 233–260). Austin, TX: ProEd.

Koegel, L. K., Camarata, S. M., Valdez-Menchaca, M., & Koegel, R. L. (1998). Setting generalization of question asking by children with autism. *American Journal on Mental Retardation, 102,* 346–357.

Koegel, L. K., Koegel, R. L., Harrower, J. K., & Carter, C. M. (1999). Pivotal response intervention: I. Overview of approach. *Journal of the Association for Persons with Severe Handicaps, 24,* 174–185.

Koegel, L. K., Koegel, R. L., Shoshan, Y., & McNerney, E. (1999). Pivotal response intervention: II. Preliminary long-term outcome data. *Journal of the Association for Persons with Severe Handicaps, 24,* 186–198.

Krantz, P. J., MacDuff, M. T., & McClannahan, L. E. (1993). Programming participation in family activities for children with autism: Parents' use of photographic activity schedules. *Journal of Applied Behavior Analysis, 26,* 137–139.

Lovaas, O. I. (1981). *Teaching developmentally disabled children: The me book.* Baltimore: University Park Press.

Lovaas, O. I. (1987). Behavioral treatment and normal educational and intellectual functioning in young autistic children. *Journal of Consulting and Clinical Psychology, 55,* 3–9.

Lovaas, O. I., Smith, T., & McEachin, J. (1989). Clarifying comments on the young autism study: Reply to Schopler, Short, and Mesibov. *Journal of Consulting and Clinical Psychology, 57,* 165–167.

McClannahan, L. E., & Krantz, P. J. (1999). *Activity schedules for children with autism: Teaching independent behavior.* Bethesda, MD: Woodbine House.

McClannahan, L. E., & Krantz, P. J. (2001). Behavior analysis and intervention for preschoolers at the Princeton Child Development Institute. In J. S. Handleman & S. L. Harris (Eds.), *Preschool education programs for children with autism* (2nd ed., pp. 191–214). Austin, TX: ProEd.

McEachin, J. J., Smith, T., & Lovaas, O. I. (1993). Long-term outcome for children with autism who received early intensive behavioral treatment. *American Journal on Mental Retardation, 4,* 359–372.

McGee, G. G., Krantz, P. J., Mason, D., & McClannahan, L. E. (1983). A modified incidental teaching procedure for autistic youth: Acquisition and generalization of receptive object labels. *Journal of Applied Behavior Analysis, 16,* 329–338.

McGee, G. G., Morrier, M. J., & Daly, T. (2001). The Walden Early Childhood Programs. In J. S. Handleman & S. L. Harris (Eds.), *Preschool education programs for children with autism* (2nd ed., pp. 157–190). Austin, TX: ProEd.

Mesibov, G. B. (1997). Formal and informal measure of the effectiveness of the TEACCH programme. *Autism: International Journal of Research and Practice, 1,* 25–35.

Mesibov, G. B., & Shea, V. (2004). The culture of autism: From theoretical understanding to educational practice. *Structured teaching: The TEACCH approach to working with autism.* New York: Plenum Press.

Meyer, L. S., Taylor, B. A., Levin, L., & Fisher, J. R. (2001). Alpine Learning Group. In J. S. Handleman & S. L. Harris (Eds.), *Preschool education programs for children with autism* (2nd ed., pp. 135–156). Austin, TX: ProEd.

National Research Council. (2001). *Educating children with autism* (Committee on Educational Interventions for Children with Autism. Division of Behavioral and Social Sciences and Education). Washington, DC: National Academy Press.

Ozonoff, S., & Cathcart, K. (1998). Effectiveness of a home program intervention for young children with autism. *Journal of Autism and Developmental Disorders, 28,* 25–32.

Rogers, S. J., & DiLalla, D. L. (1991). A comparative study of the effects of a developmentally based instructional model on young children with autism and young children with other disorders of behavior and development. *Topics in Early Childhood Special Education, 11,* 29–47.

Rogers, S. J., Hall, T., Osaki, D., Reaven, J., & Herbison, J. (2001). The Denver Model: A comprehensive, integrated educational approach to young children with autism and their families. In J. S. Handleman & S. L. Harris (Eds.), *Preschool education programs for children with autism* (2nd ed., pp. 95–134). Austin, TX: ProEd.

Rogers, S. J., & Lewis, H. C. (1989). An effective day treatment model for young children with pervasive developmental disorders. *Journal of the American Academy of Child and Adolescent Psychiatry, 28,* 207–214.

Rogers, S. J., Lewis, H. C., & Reis, K. (1987). An effective procedure for training early special education teams to implement a model program. *Journal of the Division of Early Childhood, 11*(2), 180–188.

Rogers, S. J., & Pennington, B. F. (1991). A theoretical approach to the deficits in infantile autism. *Development and Psychopathology, 3,* 137–162.

Romanczyk, R. G., & Lockshin, S. B. (1982). *The IGS curriculum.* Vestal, NY: CBTA.

Romanczyk, R. G., Lockshin, S. B., & Matey, L. (2001). The Children Unit for treatment and evaluation. In J. S. Handleman & S. L. Harris (Eds.), *Preschool education programs for children with autism* (2nd ed., pp. 49–94). Austin, TX: ProEd.

Schopler, E. (1997). Implementation of the TEACCH Philosophy. In D. J. Cohen & F. R. Volkmar (Eds.), *Handbook of autism and pervasive developmental disorders* (2nd ed., pp. 767–795). New York: Wiley.

Schopler, E., Mesibov, G. B., & Hearsey, K. (1995). Structured teaching in the TEACCH system. In E. Schopler & G. B. Mesibov (Eds.), *Learning and cognition in autism* (pp. 243–268). New York: Plenum Press.

Schopler, E., Short, A., & Mesibov, G. B. (1989). Relation of behavioral treatment to "normal functioning": Comment on Lovaas. *Journal of Consulting and Clinical Psychology, 57,* 162–164.

Short, A. B. (1984). Short term treatment outcome using parents as cotherapists for their own autistic children. *Journal of Child Psychiatry and Allied Disciplines, 25,* 443–458.

Smith, T., Donahoe, P. A., & Davis, B. J. (2001). The UCLA Young Autism Project. In J. S. Handleman & S. L. Harris (Eds.), *Preschool education programs for children with autism* (2nd ed., pp. 29–48). Austin, TX: ProEd.

Smith, T., Groen, A. D., & Wynn, J. W. (2000). Randomized trial of intensive early intervention for children with pervasive developmental disorder. *American Journal on Mental Retardation, 105,* 269–285.

Strain, P. S., & Cordisco, L. K. (1994). LEAP Preschool. In S. L. Harris & J. S. Handleman (Eds.), *Preschool education programs for children with autism* (pp. 225–244). Austin, TX: ProEd.

Strain, P. S., Hoyson, M., & Jamieson, B. (1985, Spring). Normally developing preschoolers as intervention agents for autistic-like children: Effects on class deportment and social interaction. *Journal of the Division for Early Childhood,* 105–115.

CHAPTER 42

Working with Families

LEE M. MARCUS, LINDA J. KUNCE, AND ERIC SCHOPLER

Approaches to working with parents of individuals with autism have undergone significant changes over the past 3 decades. Increasingly, autism has been recognized as a biologically based neurodevelopmental disorder with diverse etiologies rather than as an emotional disturbance (Coleman & Gillberg, 1985; Dykens & Volkmar, 1997; Schopler & Mesibov, 1987). Parallel to this, parents, once viewed as the cause of their child's problems, have been recognized as able to play a key role in the effective treatment of their child (Harris, 1994b; Howlin, 1989; Kozloff, 1984; Lovaas, 1987; Marcus & Schopler, 1989; Schopler, Mesibov, Shigley, & Bashford, 1984; Schopler & Reichler, 1971; Schreibman, Koegel, Mills, & Burke, 1984; Volkmar, Cook, & Pomeroy, 1999). By the beginning of the twenty-first century, the pragmatic and philosophical stance that parents can and should collaborate in the design and implementation of intervention services for their children with autism had achieved international acceptance (Schopler & Mesibov, 2000).

In this chapter, we discuss basic concepts and strategies for supporting families of individuals with autism spectrum disorders (ASDs). To achieve this, we draw from the research and clinical literature as well as from the 35-year experience of Division TEACCH (Treatment and Education of Autistic and Related Communication Handicapped CHildren) in the Department of Psychiatry at the University of North Carolina School of Medicine and its predecessor, the Child Research Project (Reichler & Schopler, 1976; Schopler, 1997). To provide a framework for understanding the specialized approaches needed to help these families, we

begin by describing the unique pattern of stressors that these families confront. We then place work with families of children with autism into (1) the broader context of the professional literature on parent training and family support and (2) the focused context of the basic concepts and support strategies of the TEACCH program. We conclude the chapter with an extended description of family experiences and related intervention issues as they develop across the life span of the child and the family.

STRESSORS CONFRONTING FAMILIES OF INDIVIDUALS WITH AUTISM

Parents and siblings describe many benefits of living with a person with autism. For example, family members report experiencing delight in the person's accomplishments, finding greater meaning in their own lives, and feeling enhanced empathy for others. Despite these positive experiences, substantial research evidence indicates that parents of children with autism, especially mothers, report greater amounts of stress and depression than do parents of children who are typically developing or who have other developmental disorders (Hastings & Johnson, 2001; Olsson & Hwang, 2002; Seltzer, Krauss, Orsmond, & Vestal, 2001; Tobing & Glenwick, 2002). Thus, although family members of children with developmental, behavioral, or health-related problems may share many common concerns, the parents and siblings of children with autism must cope with a unique and more intense pattern of stressors. Ten of the most stressful factors, any of which may influence needs for family support, are described next.

Diagnostic Confusion

Despite evidence that professionals are identifying and diagnosing children with autism at younger ages (Howlin & Moore, 1997; Marcus & Stone, 1993; B. Smith, Chung, & Vostanis, 1994), the assessment and diagnostic process continues to be highly stressful for many parents. First, although parents may feel relief at finding answers to their questions and concerns about their child's development, most also experience anxiety, anger, and sadness during the process of learning or confirming that their child has a serious developmental disorder (Randall & Parker, 1999; Siegel, 1997). Complicating these responses, the diagnostic process is frequently uncertain, complex, and drawn out for families of children with autism. On average, parents of children with autism report having their first concerns about their child's development when their child is 18 months old (Howlin & Moore, 1997; B. Smith et al., 1994). It may be months or years, however, before the child receives an autism diagnosis. A sizable proportion of parents, perhaps one-third to one-half, are told that there is no cause for concern or immediate action while others are referred to other professionals who may offer contradictory opinions or bury the autism diagnosis in terms such as "developmental delays in social and language areas," "autistic tendencies," and similarly nonspecific labels (De Giacomo & Fombonne, 1998; Howlin & Moore, 1997; B. Smith et al., 1994). Even when the autism diagnosis is given, all too often parents leave with a label but not with a clear and informative description of their child's problems and intervention needs.

Professional failure to clearly establish or communicate a diagnosis of autism adds to parents' stress of coping with the difficult behaviors and learning problems of their child. For example, parent surveys indicate that parents are less satisfied and more frustrated when delays are longer and the diagnosis less clear (Howlin & Moore, 1997). Given that the diagnostic process tends to be even more drawn out for children later diagnosed with Asperger disorder (Howlin & Asgharian,

1999), parents of these children may experience even greater frustration. Regardless of child functioning level, when diagnostic confusion prevents the child from obtaining appropriate services, not only is there obvious potential harm to the child, but also parents may experience intensified anger, guilt, or sadness when contemplating missed opportunities for earlier intervention.

Uneven and Unusual Course of Development

Autism is a disorder marked by both delay and deviance in development across multiple areas of functioning. First, the course of development can vary from apparently early normal development followed by plateauing or regression, to generally slow development with the gradual unfolding of the autism characteristics (American Psychiatric Association, 2000; De-Myer, 1979). Second, unevenness across skill areas is common, although no single pattern is characteristic of all children with ASDs. Children with autistic disorder, for example, typically exhibit relatively intact visual spatial and motor skills alongside deficient language, social, and problem-solving abilities; however, this pattern is not reliably seen in children with high-functioning autism (HFA) or Asperger syndrome (AS; Miller & Ozonoff, 2000; Wing, 1989).

Variability across skills and time is confusing to parents, whose natural inclination is to expect normal development. When their child's development seems to be slowing, parents may consider such a process to be temporary and assume that their child will soon catch up. For example, when they see their child solve a complex puzzle or remember a route to a fast-food restaurant, they may view these as evidence of healthy development and, understandably, overlook receptive language delays or weak imitation skills. Further, the child's uneven profile makes gauging appropriate expectations difficult and predicting future development challenging (Schuntermann, 2002). For example, a child may be able to operate a computer but be unable to follow simple verbal directions. Basing expectations on the strong mechanical skills can result in considerable parental frustration when their child appears to be acting obstinately.

The "Can't versus Won't" Dilemma

Related to the confusion generated by the child's uneven developmental pattern is the stress that occurs when the child with autism fails to carry through with expected actions, such as responding to requests, getting dressed, or completing homework. Frequently, it is unclear whether the child is unable to carry out the action (i.e., "can't") or if he or she is able but refusing to do so (i.e., "won't"). Children with autism frequently are inconsistent in their responses across settings, people, and time. For example, a child might respond to a request to come to the table at dinnertime for one parent, but not the other. Naturally, the child's parents might assume that the child is unmotivated or is being stubborn, and this interpretation would be strengthened by the child's occasional impression of understanding what is being asked. An alternative explanation, however, is that the child is responding to contextual cues rather than language (e.g., food being placed on the table as parent says "time to eat") and thus appears to have a greater understanding of language than is the case. If parents assume that their child is being oppositional, their discipline techniques tend to be confrontational and result in negatively charged situations (Dix, 1993). Appropriate intervention can help parents recognize which behaviors are the result of lack of understanding or ability and which are oppositional. In the absence of such guidance, parents experience considerable stress.

Atypical Social Communication

The core deficits in social communication characteristic of ASD can be particularly stressful for family members. In survey and interview studies, parents have indicated that their earliest and most significant worries concerned their child's language development and social abnormalities (De Giacomo & Fombonne, 1998; Howlin & Moore, 1997; B. Smith et al., 1994). Even among families of children with HFA, who typically have intact basic language skills, disruptions in emotional relations among family members appear to be a central challenge in the parents' struggle to attain a "normal" family life (Gray, 1997). Although many children with autism exhibit attachment behaviors similar to those of nonautistic children in

function and style (Dissanayake & Crossley, 1997; Rogers, Ozonoff, & Maslin-Cole, 1993), impairments in emotional and social reciprocity may mean that family members do not receive expected verbal or social feedback from the child. For example, parents usually use spoken language, along with emotional expression, to communicate with their children; however, their child with autism is unlikely to initiate or respond adequately to either form of communication, thereby heightening the parents' anxiety and confusion. More broadly, Tobing and Glenwick (2002) found that mothers of children with autism who viewed their child as less reinforcing and who described themselves as less accepting of the child simultaneously reported greater child-related stress.

Social communication deficits may also have an impact on sibling relationships. It is important that siblings of children with autism report similar levels of acceptance and closeness and lower levels of quarreling and conflict in their sibling relationships than do siblings of typically developing children (Kaminsky & Dewey, 2001; McHale, Sloan, & Simeonsson, 1986; Roeyers & Mycke, 1995). Additional research data, however, indicate that the overall rates of sibling interaction are lower when one sibling has autism and that typical siblings report experiencing less intimacy with and nurturing from their sibling with autism (Dellve, Cernerud, & Hallberg, 2000; Kaminsky & Dewey, 2001; Knott, Lewis, & Williams, 1995; Strain & Danko, 1995). Of concern, then, is the degree to which these interaction patterns create stress for siblings and parents.

Typical Physical Appearance

Because most children with autism appear normal and, from the strictly physical standpoint, do not stand out from their peers, parents experience additional frustration and stress when their child acts unusual or seems to mimic a much younger child. Unlike obvious impairments such as blindness or cerebral palsy, autism is almost invisible; it creates expectations of average social and communicative behavior that are rarely met. The discrepancy between these expectations and the reality of the disability increases the burden on the family as they seek to understand the child's condition and learn how to deal with it.

Behavior in Public

Two of the most frequently described sources of stress for family members are (1) the potentially disruptive or embarrassing behavior of the child with autism in public places and (2) the corresponding restrictions this behavior places on family activities, outings, and spontaneity (Gray, 1997, 2002; R. L. Koegel et al., 1992; Roeyers & Mycke, 1995). When the child has a major tantrum, disrupts a church service, approaches strangers indiscriminately, or is loud or intrusive, the day-to-day stress on families intensifies. In addition, simply completing daily chores, such as shopping, can be a monumental task, so family life is further disrupted. Anxiety can be highest in family members whose child has not been diagnosed or who have not yet developed the "thick skin" necessary to cope with the myriad predictable and unpredictable situations that develop in public settings. Parents understandably may worry that others judge them as being unable to control what appears to be a physically normal child, while siblings may worry that peers may tease either their sibling or themselves. Thus, it is not surprising that some family members report feeling rejected or isolated (Avdi, Griffin, & Brough, 2000; Gray, 2002; Sharpley, Bitsika, & Ephrimidis, 1997).

Broader Autism Phenotype

Some researchers studying the genetic basis of autism have concluded that autism and autism-like conditions occur more frequently in biological relatives of persons with autism (MacLean, Szatmari, & Jones, 1999; Piven, 1999; Yirmiya, Shaked, & Erel, 2001). For example, the recurrence rate of autistic disorder in siblings is 3% to 7%, or an estimated 50 to 100 times the general population rate (Yirmiya et al., 2001). Further, family members appear to be at elevated risk for exhibiting a lesser variant of autism, referred to as the *broader autism phenotype,* which is characterized by similar, yet milder, impairments in social, communication, and cognitive functions (MacLean et al., 1999; Piven, 1999). Despite mounting evidence for this phenotype, not all researchers have found measurable differences between family members of persons with autism and those of persons with typical development or other

disorders (Yirmiya et al., 2001). Further, even in studies reporting significant differences, these difficulties are far from universal. In summary, this means that some parents and siblings experience the stress of coping with autism or autistic-like characteristics not only in the identified child but also in other family members, including themselves. In addition, it means that family members may be judged unfairly if professionals mistakenly attribute natural and justifiable parental and sibling concerns, anger, or confusion to impairments associated with the phenotype.

Professional Relationships

Given the complexity of autism and its impact on multiple aspects of development, it is not surprising that effective intervention programs typically involve input from numerous professionals. The resulting need to manage relationships with these professionals creates multiple stressors for the families of children with autism. First, the sheer number of professionals can be overwhelming. T. Smith and Antolovich (2000) surveyed parents of children involved in an intensive behavior analytic program and found that children were engaged in an average of seven supplemental interventions. More concretely, in the context of their child's services, a given parent might be collaborating with a psychologist, physical therapist, occupational therapist, autism consultant, speech and language pathologist, vocational rehabilitation counselor, physician, and multiple classroom teachers.

Second, professionals from various disciplines typically promote treatment goals and strategies that reflect their particular perspectives. Unfortunately, varying perspectives can conflict, leaving parents struggling for clarification and support that may or may not be available. Too often, parents are forced to choose between intervention strategies and approaches, not because of sound reasoning but because professionals are committed to their methods and "turf."

Finally, given their child's extensive intervention needs, many parents move into a professional role themselves with respect to their child. Parents often serve as their children's therapists, teachers, case coordinators, and job coaches. Over time, therefore, parents may develop greater expertise in autism than many of the professionals working with their child, many of whom may not have had any specialized training in autism (Helps, Newsom-Davis, & Callias, 1999). Although parental expertise is acquired for the child's benefit, the resulting intensive and complex role demands create inevitable stress, especially for mothers who continue to be more likely to give up pursuit of their own careers to focus on their child's intervention needs (Gray, 2002; Seltzer et al., 2001).

Fads and Unproven Therapies

Like other chronic or incurable disorders, autism has been the target for quick-fix practitioners whose techniques end up victimizing families desperate for easy answers to difficult questions. For example, Volkmar and colleagues (1999) identified several treatments, such as facilitated communication and patterning, that generated substantial enthusiasm but failed to show reliable results when rigorously tested. In seeking out as much information as possible, especially in an era of indiscriminate and rapid electronic communication, parents become susceptible to the promotions of specific therapies that usually have little to offer other than hope.

Schopler (1995) discussed several factors that these techniques have in common:

- The technique appears to be a good idea at first impression or helpful for a certain condition and is now assumed to be generalizable to autistic individuals,
- Reports of effectiveness are anecdotal, and one or two cases of a "cure" are sufficient to capture the attention of news-hungry media and vulnerable families, and
- The techniques may have negative and costly side effects such as the unfounded accusations of sexual abuse following the indiscriminate use of facilitated communication or the loss of truly individualized educational placements in the midst of the excitement over universal inclusion.

Parents' efforts to sort through the claims of the widely touted therapies add to their stress. Further, they are diverted from dealing with the fundamental needs of their child and focusing energies in useful teaching and behavioral approaches.

Empirically Supported Therapies: The Demand for Proof

Paradoxically, the move toward identifying and demanding empirically supported therapies has placed parents under additional stress. The publication of practice parameters and other state-of-the-art intervention documents in the autism field (e.g., National Research Council, 2001; New York State Department of Health Early Intervention Program, 1999; Volkmar et al., 1999) can be understood as part of the general trend in mental health and education. This trend, which became widely influential during the 1990s, has been characterized by calls for empirically validated or empirically supported treatments (EVTs, ESTs), identification of specific criteria for identifying empirical validity, and descriptions of ESTs for specific conditions (e.g., Chambless & Ollendick, 2000; Christophersen & Mortweet, 2001; Stoiber & Kratochwill, 2000). The publication of high-quality reviews and best practices documents in the autism field has somewhat reduced stress for parents and practitioners alike by providing clear accounts of the large, although often contradictory, research literature on autism intervention.

On the other hand, the level of demand for "proven" therapies far surpasses the current research base. For example, there are no large-scale, rigorously designed, replicated intervention studies that compare the major autism intervention approaches. Thus, parents of children with autism are placed in an inherently stressful position: They are encouraged to select and even demand empirically validated therapies without the necessary data to do so. Further, an incomplete understanding of the complexities of research design leaves parents vulnerable to simplified claims such as, "This is the only *proven* therapy," or "*Our* study *proves* this treatment *works*."

FAMILY SUPPORT AND INTERVENTION: AN OVERVIEW

Given the intensity and unique pattern of stressors faced by families of children with autism, the need for parent-professional collaboration in autism intervention is paramount. Direct parent involvement has become accepted as a sound and often necessary component of a total autism intervention program (Dunlap, 1999; Harris, 1998; Kozloff, 1984; Lovaas, 1987; Marcus & Schopler, 1989; Schopler et al., 1984; Volkmar et al., 1999). That is, although intervention models may vary substantially in methodology and content, there is no longer any dispute that the earlier psychodynamically oriented approaches (e.g., DesLauriers & Carlson, 1969) have been superseded by strategies that give parents control over the teaching and therapy of their child. It is helpful to view this shift in the context of a broader movement toward parent-professional collaboration that occurred in mental health and education during the latter half of the twentieth century. In both fields, professionals increasingly have emphasized active parent involvement in treatment, respect for family decisions, and greater equality in parent-professional relationships (C. E. Cunningham, 1989; Seligman & Darling, 1997; Singer & Powers, 1993).

The philosophical and societal movement toward empowerment of parents and families has been supported by research and clinical evidence indicating that when parents serve as active change agents in their child's treatment, positive effects extend beyond improvement in the child's condition. For example, actively involved parents have reported greater feelings of competence and self-efficacy, treatment gains have been maintained longer, and non-treated child behaviors or other children in the family have shown collateral positive changes (e.g., Dadds, Sanders, & James, 1987; Eyberg, Edwards, Boggs, & Foote, 1998; Humphreys, Forehand, McMahon, & Roberts, 1978; R. L. Koegel, Bimbela, & Schreibman, 1996).

To date, parents have been directly involved in the treatment of child conditions as diverse as enuresis, oppositional defiant disorder, motor tics, childhood depression, and autism (e.g., Briesmeister & Schaefer, 1998; Graziano & Diament, 1992; Schopler, 2001; Webster-Stratton, Reid, & Hammond, 2001). This general literature on parent training, parent education, and other approaches to working with and supporting families is relevant to work with families of children with autism. In the following sections, we discuss commonalities among family-based intervention programs and their relevance for the autism field. We address, in the following order, goals, principles, approaches, modalities, and techniques.

Goals

The basic goals of parent training and other family-based approaches include decreasing inappropriate and increasing appropriate child behavior, improving the quality of family relationships, increasing adaptive family functioning, and enlisting family members in the change process. Clearly, these fundamental goals are applicable when working with parents and siblings of children with autism; nevertheless, caution is warranted when identifying specific intervention goals and objectives. Graziano and Diament (1992), in a review of parent training for mental retardation, concluded that the parents do *not* benefit from "general behavioral training" but that they *do* profit from practically oriented training specific to their unique situation. Similarly, although the preceding basic goals are relevant for parents of children with autism, identification of more specific goals and objectives relies on an understanding of autism, appreciation for the common stressors facing family members, and individualized assessment of each family's challenges and resources.

Principles

Scholars from a variety of disciplines have sought to identify principles shared by intervention programs that emphasize work with families (Seligman & Darling, 1997; Singer & Powers, 1993). Although a complete discussion of this topic is beyond the scope of this chapter, three general principles highly applicable for work with families of children with autism are noted. First, for both ethical and pragmatic reasons, family-based programs place high value on genuinely collaborative parent-professional relationships in which family views are sought and respected (Fine & Gardner, 1994; Seligman & Darling, 1997). Second, family-focused programs tend to explain parent-child relationships in terms of transactional models, describing patterns of parent and child behavior as becoming established and maintained over time, through a cycle of mutual influences—regardless of any original "cause" (Bell & Harper, 1977; Greenspan & Weider, 1998; Patterson, 1982). This type of model helps parents and professionals lay aside blame and counteract helplessness by focusing attention on ways parents can develop more satisfying patterns of interaction with their children. Finally, individualization to the child and family's specific needs and desires is considered essential. This means that assessment is needed not only of (1) the target child's behaviors and (2) relevant situational factors, but also of (3) parent and sibling concerns, beliefs, and problem-solving skills, and (4) any factors that may affect family participation (e.g., siblings' need for care, employment responsibilities, financial hardship, parental psychopathology; Assemany & McIntosh, 2002; Barkley, 1987; Webster-Stratton & Herbert, 1993).

General Approaches and Targeted Outcomes

Despite shared goals and principles, parent training and other family-focused intervention programs vary widely in the types of general approaches and outcomes they emphasize. Eight general approaches that are most relevant to working with families of children with autism are listed in Table 42.1: education, parents as (co)therapists, behavioral approach, relationship enhancement, cognitive approach, emotional support, instrumental support, and advocacy training. For each approach, Table 42.1 includes a brief definition, representative general citation(s), and illustrative list of desired outcomes. The reader is cautioned that the division between the eight general approaches is heuristic rather than absolute, and most intervention programs incorporate multiple approaches in order to reach a broad range of desired outcomes.

Examples of all eight general approaches can be found in the clinical and research autism literature. The *education* approach, for example, is considered especially important during early childhood, when family members need a basic understanding of the autism label and its implications (Shea, 1993; Whitaker, 2002). A specific example is Schuntermann's

(2002) interview developed to help parents of children better understand and predict the developmental progress of their child with autism.

Many researchers and clinicians have used a "parents as (co)therapists" model (also referred to as *parent training*), arguing that parents can implement interventions such as photographic activity schedules, natural language strategies, structured teaching, and general behavioral change strategies (Harris, 1986; Krantz, MacDuff, & McClannahan, 1993; Laski, Charlop, & Schreibman, 1988; Marcus & Schopler, 1989; Ozonoff & Cathcart, 1998; Tonge, Brereton, & King, 2004). In autism intervention, most programs using a "parents as (co)therapists" approach simultaneously utilize a *behavioral* approach. While sharing roots in the behavioral tradition, however, these programs vary widely in the overall strength of their behavioral emphasis as well as in their inclusion of specific learning principles, change strategies, and outcome behaviors (e.g., Harris, 1986; R. L. Koegel, Koegel, & Schreibman, 1991; Lovaas et al., 1987; Schopler, 1997). In some behaviorally oriented programs, especially home-based applied behavior analysis models, autism experts train parents to "manage" rather than directly deliver their child's intervention (e.g., Bibby, Eikeseth, Martin, Mudford, & Reeves, 2001). In other behaviorally oriented interventions, siblings have been trained successfully to use behavior modification strategies or social initiation techniques when interacting with the child with autism (e.g., Schreibman, O'Neill, & Koegel, 1983; Strain & Danko, 1995).

Many intervention programs—such as the TEACCH program (described in detail later) and pivotal response training (R. L. Koegel et al., 1991)—blend the education, "parents as (co)therapist," and behavioral approaches. These programs, however, also have reported collateral gains in family relationship quality and parent functioning, even when those additional outcomes were not targeted directly (Bristol, Gallagher, & Holt, 1993; R. L. Koegel et al., 1996). Other professionals, as described next, have taken a more direct approach to relationship enhancement, social-emotional support, and cognitive restructuring.

Greenspan (Greenspan & Weider, 1998), for example, has written extensively about *relationship enhancement* methods, especially

TABLE 42.1 General Intervention Approaches Relevant to Work with Families of Children with Autism: Definitions, Citations, and Illustrative Outcomes

General Approach	Definition and Representative Citations	Illustrative Outcomes
Education	Provide family members with information from the professional literature in an organized and accessible format (e.g., C. Smith, Perou, & Lesesne, 2002).	Family members develop understanding of: –Child's disorder, condition, or problems –General child development –Learning principles –Transactional model of relationships
Parents as (co)therapists	Train parents to implement instructional techniques or behavior management strategies (e.g., Briesmeister & Shafer, 1998; Kazdin, 1997).	Family members learn and implement skills such as: –Goal identification & monitoring –Speech and language therapy techniques –Medication or life style management –Structured teaching
Behavioral approach	Help family members apply principles of learning to child education and management (e.g., Barkley, 1987; McMahon & Wells, 1998; Webster-Stratton, Reid, & Hammond, 2001).	Family members learn to use strategies such as: –Shaping techniques –Extinction/Ignoring –Positive reinforcement –Relaxation procedures
Relationship enhancement	Work with family members to increase the positive valence and decrease the negative aspects of parent-child relationships (e.g., Eyberg, Edwards, Boggs, & Foote, 1998; Toth, Maughan, Manly, Spagnola, & Cicchetti, 2002).	Family members develop skills such as: –Attending ("play therapist") skills –Use of a child-directed play time –Delivery of effective commands –Use of therapeutic games and books
Cognitive approach	Train family members in cognitive techniques in order to modify emotional and behavioral responses (e.g., Sanders & McFarland, 2000).	Family members develop skills such as: –Problem solving –Cognitive restructuring –Self-monitoring –Setting realistic expectations
Emotional support	Provide family member with empathy, a listening ear, and basic problem solving support either through individual sessions or group work (e.g., Ireys, Chernoff, Stein, DeVet, & Silver, 2001).	Family members experience: –Understanding and acceptance –Emotional Release –Opportunity to identify priorities –Reflection on family coping strategies

Instrumental support	Assist family member in obtaining access to resources, services, and basic necessities (e.g., Cowen, 2001; Singer & Powers, 1993).	Family members gain access (as needed) to: –Basic living necessities –Financial assistance –Appropriate educational and special services –Connections to families in similar situations
Advocacy training and support	Assist family member in advocating for the identified child's needs across the lifetime (e.g., P. B. Cunningham, Henggeler, Brondino, & Pickrel, 1999; Sheridan, 1997).	Family members develop skills and receive support in: –Interacting with professionals & service systems –Obtaining needed services and supplies –Making child needs known in the community –Influencing the legislative process

Note: The citations provided in column two refer the reader to representative reports in the broader literature (e.g., not specific to autism). The desired outcomes listed in column three are meant to be illustrative rather than exhaustive.

in improving the quality of parent-child interactions. Other researchers have focused on enhancing the sibling interactions, either by training the nonautistic sibling (e.g., Strain & Danko, 1995) or by modifying the behavior of the siblings with autism (e.g., L. K. Koegel, Stiebel, & Koegel, 1998; Taylor, Levin, & Jasper, 1999). Bitsika and Sharpley (1999, 2000) emphasized the *emotional support* approach, reporting that parents positively evaluated both a general support group and one designed to teach them specific stress management techniques. Similarly, sibling support groups typically emphasize sharing and exploring emotions (e.g., Lobato & Kao, 2002).

The *cognitive approach* underlies the research and theoretical work explaining stress in parents of children with autism from a stress-and-coping, or cognitive appraisal, perspective (e.g., Bristol, 1984; Tunali & Power, 2002). In contrast, cognitive approaches have seldom been used alone or studied explicitly in clinical interventions with families of children with autism. Nevertheless, descriptions of cognitive techniques appear occasionally in the autism literature: Bitsika and Sharpley (2000) taught parents how to dispute irrational beliefs as a stress reduction strategy; Sofronoff and Farbotko (2002) attempted to improve the self-efficacy of parents of children with AS; and, Clark, Cunningham, and Cunningham (1989) trained siblings to apply a general problem-solving strategy to cope with difficult sibling interactions.

As to the last two approaches listed in Table 42.1, families of children with autism share many common needs for *instrumental support* and *advocacy training and support.* At various points in the family life cycle, for example, parents may need assistance obtaining services, including but not limited to educational programming, language therapy, practical help at home, respite care, vocational services, residential care, and connections with other parents (e.g., Howlin & Moore, 1997). In addition, siblings, who typically have the longest lasting relationship with the child with autism, may need help understanding autism, connecting with other siblings, and learning how to manage services for their sibling in adulthood. Instrumental and advocacy support may be provided directly or in the context of ongoing services. The TEACCH program, for example, has worked with a mothers' support group for years (Marcus, Wertheimer, Clement, & Kuhr, 1995). Over a decade, this group evolved from a small group of about 10 mothers into a large network of parents who have ongoing contact with one another, take retreat trips together, and have produced a useful resource guide for parents of newly diagnosed children. The regular meeting times of the group with TEACCH professionals provide a structured format for both emotional and instrumental support, but the informal networking and advocacy work that occur outside the group setting are equally important.

Modalities

Work with families of children may occur in a clinic setting or the home environment, either individually or in groups, the latter of which may be educationally oriented, therapeutic, or emphasize parent-to-parent support (Seligman & Darling, 1997). Professionals working with families of children with autism typically use one or more of the following four modalities: (1) clinic-based (e.g., Ozonoff & Cathcart, 1998; Schopler et al., 1984; Sheinkopf & Siegel, 1998), (2) home-based (e.g., Bibby et al., 2001; Howlin, 1989), (3) school-based, and (4) group-based.

The clinic method involves the use of a training center, where techniques are demonstrated and parents are coached to develop effective ways of teaching and managing their child. Parents are then expected to carry out these methods at home. Home visits by clinic staff supplement the center teaching, but the evaluation of effectiveness derives primarily from parental report of progress at home and observation of parent skills in the clinic setting. In contrast, the home-based approach brings trainers into the natural daily environment, where demonstration and instruction take place. The advantages and disadvantages of these two basic approaches are reciprocal. The clinic-based, but not the home-based, model makes full and efficient use of the clinic resources and provides an atmosphere relatively free of distractions and cues that can interfere with training. In contrast, the home-based, but not the clinic-based, model occurs in the family's natural environment, increasing potential for immediate generalization of training and improving ease with which professionals can adapt their methods to the individual family. In the absence of conclusive evidence of the superiority of one model over the other, a logical intermediate strategy would include elements of both and would permit flexibility in approach, depending on family needs and circumstances.

Two alternate approaches to working with families are the school-based and group models. The school-based model can be considered a variation of the clinic-based approach in which the school classroom, rather than the clinic, is used as a setting to demonstrate teaching methods and activities to parents; therefore, its advantages are similar to those mentioned earlier for the clinic-based approach. In addition, however, the school-based model has the advantage of clarifying communication and expectations among family members, school professionals, and autism consultants. However, it has the corresponding disadvantages inherent in organizing greater numbers of individuals to meet and work together.

The fourth approach involves working with parents of children with autism in groups (e.g., Kozloff, 1984). Groups may be educative and practical in nature, typically combining lectures and discussions with homework assignments to provide information a family can utilize in raising their child with autism (Micheli, 1999; Sofronoff & Farbotko, 2001; Tonge et al., 2004). Groups for parents (e.g., Bitsika & Sharpley, 1999, 2000; Marcus et al., 1995) and those for siblings (e.g., Lobato & Kao, 2002) also tend to include a focus on sharing experiences, practical information, and emotional support. The advantages of group approaches include their economy, efficiency, and use of informal support systems. Disadvantages include the loss of individualization and the high cost to families who miss sessions. A group approach can be integrated with the individualized methods described earlier. Most families need opportunities to share experiences and feelings with other families in a comparable situation. Often, ingenious solutions to problems can be suggested by other parents (Schopler, 1995). In other circumstances, simply realizing that a family is not alone can be a source of relief for both parents and siblings.

Techniques

In additional to traditional counseling strategies such as empathic listening and talking through problems, a wide variety of specific techniques are used to help family members develop their knowledge and skills (cf. Briesmeister & Schaefer, 1998). For example, reading materials, videos, and discussions are frequently used to educate family members about child development and disorders. Parents and siblings are helped to master skills through the use of modeling, role playing, in-session and real-life practice, coaching, feedback, and homework assignments. Further, to monitor change and provide additional motivation for using learned skills, parents are often encouraged to gather data on the targeted child's behavior, their own behaviors, and the child's responses to intervention attempts. Most, if not all, of the techniques used in parent training and other family-focused programs can be useful when working with families of children with autism.

Summary and Implications

In summary, any and all of the general goals, principles, approaches, modalities, and techniques for working with families can be appropriate when the target child is diagnosed with ASD. Work with family members, however, is apt to be ineffective, and perhaps even harmful, if goals are targeted and approaches selected without careful consideration of the special demands, needs, and stressors associated with autism. For example, if a parent of a child with autism is trained in behavior modification and relationship enhancement approaches according to a prepackaged general child management program, without simultaneous education on the unique characteristics associated with autism, difficulties will arise. In this situation, the parent might be trained to use timeout procedures to punish self-stimulatory behavior and to rely on social praise to encourage child communication. Rather than respond as expected, the child may experience isolation as a form of reward and social praise as a foreign language.

Once again, parents of children with autism face a number of special stressors, not the least of which is the failure of some of the most "tried and true" parenting techniques, such as timeout and social praise, to work for their child. Therefore, intervention goals, approaches, and techniques need to be selected not only in light of family priorities, child needs, and professional capabilities, but also with respect to the unique characteristics of autism. Some of the ways in which the TEACCH program attempts to meet this complex set of challenges are described in the following sections.

PRINCIPLES OF THE TEACCH APPROACH TO WORKING WITH FAMILIES

Collaborative work with families has been integral to the TEACCH program since its inception: Rather than placing blame on parents for their child's autism, emphasis consistently has been placed on educating parents about autism, training parents to work directly with their children, and engaging in coadvocacy with families for persons with autism (Schopler, 1997, 2002; Schopler & Reichler, 1971). Currently, TEACCH is best understood not as a single intervention approach, but as a statewide network of autism services for individuals with autism and their families, a university-based research and professional resource center, and as a base for international outreach and training. Direct work with parents of children and adults with autism forms a substantial component of the clinical intervention work carried out at Division TEACCH.

To help parents handle the special stressors that confront them and to support them in their efforts to effectively deal with their child's problems, the TEACCH program has evolved a number of principles and concepts that guide our treatment efforts and philosophy (Marcus & Schopler, 1989; Schopler & Mesibov, 2000), outlined next.

Understanding Autism as a Developmental Disorder

Perhaps the single most important concept for parents and other professionals to grasp is that autism is a disorder of development and not a psychiatric disturbance caused by inadequate parenting. The nature of the disorder is such that the cognitive, communicative, and social learning processes are impaired at least to a mild degree and often more seriously. We teach parents that understanding autism as a developmental disorder has three primary implications:

1. The atypical behaviors manifested by individuals with autism are best understood as the result of inadequate coping and maladaptive response patterns, rather than as signs of an obstinate nature. That is, behavior problems can be reframed productively as the child's frustration at, or attempts to cope with, an environment that he or she does not fully understand. Professionals can help parents understand that by modifying the child's environment, they can improve their child's understanding and decrease his or her maladaptive behaviors.
2. Autism is a chronic disorder, which can be adapted to without being totally removed. Therefore, parents need to expect to deal with their child's developmental problems to some extent over the child's lifetime. In collaboration with parents, professionals need to be sensitive to the long-term nature of the condition and to the realities that the parents face over an indefinite period of years.
3. Autism is pervasive; that is, it occurs across all settings and needs to be treated accordingly. A total program requires implementation in various community settings as well as in the home.

Individualization and Flexibility

Autism is a highly heterogeneous condition (Szatmari, 2000; Wing, 1976). Although it is defined by a core set of characteristics, the wide range of manifestations of these features, within and across individuals, reduces the likelihood that any two individuals with autism will be very similar. For example, individuals with autism vary widely in (1) intelligence level, ranging from profound mental retardation to above-average abilities; (2) associated medical conditions, such as seizure disorders or sensory impairments (e.g., blindness); (3) activity level, including hyperactivity, hypoactivity, and fluctuation between the two; and (4) level of family resources, whether financial, psychological, or social. Therefore, in helping families, it is necessary to recognize these individual and family differences. A highly individualized and flexible approach requires an in-depth understanding of the child and his or her family as a point of departure during the assessment process. Further, this type of approach implies that ideological positions and packaged training methods may interfere with the helping process by deemphasizing the uniqueness of each situation.

Importance of Structure

A central teaching concept in the TEACCH program involves the use of structure (Mesibov, Schopler, & Hearsey, 1995; Schopler, Brehm, Kinsbourne, & Reichler, 1971). Structured teaching includes the consistent use of a predictable work routine, physical placement and arrangement of materials, and demonstration of the action requested or physically helping the child through the activity. Structure is used to compensate for an autistic child's difficulties in organizing and understanding his or her world. Individuals with autism tend to get fixed into routines, probably as a means of establishing predictability for themselves. The maladaptive form of that tendency is an obsessive preoccupation with maintaining sameness or a strong reaction to change. By establishing positive routines through structured teaching, parents can capitalize on this need in their child and help develop competencies and improved learning patterns. The implication of this concept for parent training is that a clinician working with parents should use methods that effectively demonstrate the structured teaching process.

Parent–Professional Collaboration

The overriding principle of the TEACCH approach to family work involves adherence to the goal of building a collaborative relationship between parents and professionals (Marcus, 2003; Marcus & Schopler, 1989; Schopler, 1997; Schopler & Mesibov, 2000). Professionals respect parental priorities and carefully consider parental perspectives on child behavior and proposed intervention methods. The

belief in a partnership based on mutual respect, trust, and shared expertise is paramount. To this partnership, the professional brings experience with a wide range of clinical issues and a breadth of knowledge of what has been effective or ineffective. The parents, however, have a deep and unique perspective on their own child's development, idiosyncrasies, likes, and dislikes. The sensitive merging of these two sources of information strengthens the parent-professional relationship.

Over the years, four types of parent-professional role relationships have been identified:

1. Parents may relate to professionals as trainees, with an emphasis on home teaching programs, behavior management, and related activities.
2. Parents often serve as trainers of professionals with emphasis on sharing information with staff and broadening the professionals' understanding of autism and how families cope.
3. Parents and professionals provide mutual emotional support, utilizing techniques such as ongoing discussions, parent counseling, and support groups.
4. Parents and professionals work together to develop advocacy skills as a means of promoting improved services and addressing other social action issues.

No set formula can be applied to every case, and TEACCH staff therapists and parents usually shift among these different roles in attempting to strengthen the parent-child relationship and to help families cope effectively with this chronic disorder.

Competencies and Coping

The focus of intervention should be on the development and building of potential survival skills and competencies in the child and the family. The emphasis should be on pragmatic, problem-solving approaches that fit within the family's lifestyle. This necessitates collaborative, action-oriented approaches rather than strictly verbal or prescriptive interactions. In this philosophical and pragmatic stance, TEACCH work with families is similar to other family support and empowerment programs (e.g., Singer & Powers, 1993) and dissimilar from models that emphasize psychopathology and professional control.

Consideration of Total Family Needs

There is a need for awareness of other pressures and demands on the family that are unrelated to the child with autism. It is easy to neglect other facets of a parent's identity and life circumstances, such as economic, social, and emotional pressures. There is also a need to understand the child and family beyond the clinic or classroom; that is, the clinician should be alert to and concerned about the impact of the child on normal siblings (Fisman, Wolf, Ellison, & Freeman, 2000; McHale et al., 1986) as well as the child's potential effects on the parents' marital, social, and work situations. In addition, the personal or psychological implications of coping with a child with autism (Bristol, 1984) should be considered.

The Developmental Continuum

It is not only important for the professional to understand autism from a developmental perspective (Burack, Charman, Yirmiya, & Zelazo, 2001) but also helpful to consider developmental stages in the life cycle of a family with an autistic child and the role the professional can play at different points. During early childhood, primacy is placed on early diagnosis, emotional support during the grief process, and parent training and counseling. In middle childhood, the emphasis is home-teacher relationships, learning problems, and adaptive behavior. The adolescent and adult periods are a time for focusing on maximizing independence and obtaining relevant residential and work opportunities. The problems faced by families across time and related solutions or strategies form the basis for the remainder of the chapter.

AUTISM AND THE FAMILY LIFE CYCLE

Families, like the individuals of which they are composed, are not static over time. In developing empirical and theoretical frameworks for understanding families, professionals have described multiple ways in which family structures, functions, and interactional patterns change over time (e.g., McGoldrick & Carter, 2003). Developmental disabilities professionals, including those that work in the autism field, have found it especially useful to conceptualize family functioning within the context of age-related phases characterized by specific developmental tasks and stressors (Bristol & Schopler, 1984; DeMyer, 1979; Gray, 2002; Seligman & Darling, 1997). In this section, we describe family experiences and related intervention issues as they occur during the early childhood, middle childhood, adolescence, and adulthood of the individual with autism.

Early Childhood

During this period, parents often are dealing with a number of stressful circumstances: the ambiguity of the handicap, fatigue caused by the child's irregular sleep patterns and high activity level, lack of an effective communication system, the child's engagement in dangerous activities due to a lack of understanding or fear, peculiar food habits, and a lack of adequate and willing babysitters or respite care (Bristol & Schopler, 1984; Schopler, 1995). Increased understanding of autism and its manifestations during the early years (ages 2 to 4) has helped professionals be of greater assistance to families (Marcus & Stone, 1993). Of special importance during this period are issues related to diagnosis, early intervention, and supplemental community-based services.

Diagnosis

Early diagnosis and assessment is the crucial first step in helping parents develop awareness of what they face as parents of a child with autism. Although clinicians might not be certain whether the problems should be called autism or another pervasive developmental disorder, they are able to convey to parents the need for appropriate intervention and to enable them to begin the process of obtaining services and learning more about autism. The manner in which information is shared is important; however, it is likely that the weight of the news of having a child with a significant developmental disorder cannot be mitigated fully by any particular approach. Still, that initial conference should be structured in a way that presents the data clearly, descriptively, and sensitively, without underplaying the seriousness of the situation (Morgan, 1984; Shea, 1993). The age of the child, the severity of the autism, and the level of intellectual and adaptive impairment control prognostic implications to some extent, but autism should be explained as a spectrum disorder with regard to both severity of autistic symptomatology and degree of associated intellectual impairment. For example, the spectrum includes individuals with severe mental impairment as well as those with special talents in the arts, computer technology, or science. Examples of high-functioning individuals, such as Temple Grandin, who sees her autism as a personality trait rather than as a disease, may be used to encourage parents as well as to help them view autism through lenses other than those that idealize "normal" development.

During this session, parents should be told that even though a precise cause may not be known, their child's disorder did not result from improper parenting or related environmental circumstances. Even if parents do not express a sense of guilt, they may live with daily self-recriminations. They may feel that they should have provided more stimulation, identified the problem sooner, or sought help more aggressively. Extended family may add to this self-imposed pressure by hinting that the parents could be using more effective child-rearing strategies or by suggesting that the parents are "spoiling" the child by giving in to the child's demands. Sharpley, Bitsika, and Ephrimidis (1997) found that parents who believed that extended family members did not understand the needs and challenges of autism also described themselves as experiencing greater stress. The professional communicating diagnostic findings must be sensitive to these background factors and to the possible need for correcting parental misconceptions about the autism symptoms and etiology.

Along with grasping the long-range implications of autism, parents typically need help understanding the unique learning patterns of their child with autism. Parents of children with classic autism are often confused by the child's atypical pattern of higher skills in motor development and visual memory combined with deficits in language and abstract problem solving (DeMyer, 1979; Marcus, Flagler, & Robinson, 2001; Wing, 1989). Parents of high-functioning children often struggle with understanding why the child behaves in difficult or socially inappropriate ways when other indicators suggest that their child is developing well (e.g., excellent vocabulary, passion for certain interests). Like professionals, parents may assume that the child's relative proficiencies suggest normal development and that difficulties in other areas are caused by temporary phenomena, a lack of motivation, or an emotional disturbance.

Parents must understand the implications of the uneven developmental profile, in particular, that average or above-average abilities in one area should not be interpreted as potential for typical cognitive, social, and communicative development. One of the first steps in helping parents deal effectively with their child is to establish appropriate expectations (Schuntermann, 2002), which in turn lead to more effective and satisfying interactions with the child. For example, by simplifying language demands and individualizing their teaching approach based on a realistic appraisal of developmental functioning, parents can initiate a process that will facilitate improved behavior as well as basic competencies (Schopler et al., 1984).

Although many questions are raised at interpretative conferences and detailed explanations should be provided, parents vary in their understanding of, and receptivity to, the facts and opinions presented. The emotional impact of discovering that their child has a chronic disorder that may involve mental retardation as well as autism should not be underestimated (Akerley, 1975; Siegel, 1997). Although some families respond with remarkable calm or great relief at having an explanation for their concerns, it is natural also to react with worry, anger, or a form of denial. In the clinic, such feelings may not be manifested, but they are likely to emerge over time. Similarly, because the assessment and diagnostic process is so intensely focused on the child with autism, parents may not fully share information about additional family stressors that may affect intervention needs, such as financial resources, difficulties with extended family, or sibling concerns. Thus, the clinician must be available for follow-up, to continue to discuss the findings and the family response, to help the family learn more about autism, and to plan an intervention program consistent with family needs and resources.

In summary, in addition to listening carefully to parent concerns and delivering information in a sensitive manner, the clinician begins what will be an ongoing educative process, helping parents better understand autism as a developmental disability and the child's unique developmental profile. As important, the diagnostic process can be considered incomplete if it does not lead directly to identification and implementation of an effective intervention plan (discussed in the following section). Throughout the process, the clinician should be careful not to destroy the hope and optimism parents need to work with their child. There is a thin line between making a "realistic prognosis" and undermining hope, and the clinician should be guided by a simple principle: Do not disturb parental expectations except when they interfere with appropriate current management.

Intervention

Working in collaboration, the professional and the family should develop a systematic plan of action (Marcus & Schopler, 1989). Although parents may feel overwhelmed and helpless at the point of diagnosis, they require involvement in decision making and in intervention strategies. At the outset, the momentum may be provided by the professional, but parents should be supported in taking as much responsibility as they realistically can at this stage. At a minimum, parents should be informed about, and their feelings and opinions solicited about, any additional diagnostic or intervention procedures. For example, a series of medical procedures might be recommended; but if the family is apprehensive, this plan should be postponed unless considered essential. If a preschool classroom is being considered, the parents should be encouraged to visit, ask questions of the director, and freely discuss concerns and hopes with the clinician. If a parent training, education, or counseling program is recommended, the family's schedule, other demands, and priorities that affect their time and willingness to participate should be reviewed.

During this first stage, most families are eager for maximum participation, unless other circumstances greatly prohibit their engagement. Parents of young children with autism are themselves usually young, have more energy, and are more hopeful than parents of older children with autism. It is typical of parents to be actively involved in teaching their preschool child and in carefully scrutinizing available support services. When parents have just received a diagnosis, it is important to capitalize on their normal reactions to possibly reverse the course of the disorder, to gain control over the situation, and to help their child fully develop his or her potential. Although not every family is capable of learning specialized teaching and management skills or of becoming an articulate advocate, with appropriate support most are able to make a valuable contribution to their child's habilitation. Further, although parental involvement has the potential for increasing parents' stress, several researchers have found that such involvement tends to decrease, or have no impact on, parental stress levels (Birnbrauer & Leach, 1993; Bristol et al., 1993; Hastings & Johnson, 2001).

The TEACCH approach to working with families of children with autism during the preschool period, therefore, emphasizes a practical, action-focused, and yet emotionally supportive approach. The core model, developed and refined over 3 decades, involves training parents as cotherapists for their young children, with a focus on helping parents better understand autism, control distressing behavior, and implement effective instructional strategies. We typically deliver these services in clinic-based settings, although in-home training is provided in some instances, based on availability of services and family needs. In addition to basic education on autism and their child's unique characteristics, we focus on teaching parents how to implement structured teaching strategies with their child, both in instructional situations and daily routines. Based on the child's needs and parents' goals, we also help parents learn and implement a variety of empirically based strategies, including, but not limited to, natural language, activity schedules, and behavior modification techniques. As the incidence of diagnosed cases of autism has risen dramatically (e.g., Yeargin-Allsopp et al.,

2003) and waiting lists for services have grown unwieldy, the TEACCH program has experimented with workshop-based models for educating family members about autism and basic intervention strategies. Although this model results in less individualization in the delivery of information, it has allowed us to reach parents more quickly as they wait for individualized services during this critical period.

The need for emotional support varies across families and covers the age spectrum; however, we find that emotional support is extremely important in the early years, as the family slowly comes to grips with the impact of having a child with autism. Such support is provided not only in the context of the parent education and training but also through encouraging families to form connections with other families in similar situations. Parents, for example, may join clinic-based support groups, form informal groups on their own, or join formally structured family support and advocacy groups. At TEACCH, we have developed a parent mentor program, which involves the matching of experienced and trained volunteer parents with parents of newly identified or diagnosed children with autism (Palmer & Marcus, 1998). The purpose of the mentor assignment is for the parents of newly diagnosed children to have an immediate source of support and information. In the past 5 years, approximately 300 families have been matched with one of the 47 parent mentors. For some families, the mentoring may involve one or two phone conversations; for others, an ongoing relationship may occur. The role of the parent mentor is to provide support to families of children with autism by listening and understanding, providing information about resources in the community, and providing information about autism and related topics.

Sibling intervention needs in this period have not been well studied. Siblings, at this time, are likely to be in the early childhood age range themselves; therefore, "intervention" for these children typically involves helping parents provide developmentally appropriate support. Clinical literature suggests that such support involves (1) providing the sibling with developmentally appropriate explanations, (2) ensuring that the sibling is safe, especially if the child with autism engages in aggressive behavior, (3) having some special one-to-one child and parent time, and (4) helping the sibling interact successfully with the child with autism (e.g., Gibbs, 1996; Harris, 1994a). In addition, given the elevated rates of autism and the broader autism phenotype in siblings, professionals should listen carefully and respond proactively to any concerns parents have about sibling development.

Community Services

The need for a wide range of community-based services is somewhat less during the early years than during adolescence and adulthood. Nevertheless, parents need instrumental and advocacy support as they begin to deal with day care programs, specialized medical services, and early childhood public school programs. It is too common, for example, for a child with autism not to have had a complete medical examination because of the child's lack of cooperation. Ongoing pediatric or dental care requires, for many children with autism, sensitive health professionals who are willing to listen to parents and to become familiar with autism. The professional working with the parents should be available both to provide names of physicians and dentists experienced with children who have special needs and to discuss with these professionals relevant aspects of the child's condition.

Similarly, parents usually require support in searching for and placing the child in an appropriate preschool setting (Marcus, Schopler, & Lord, 2000). The decision to try a typical preschool program versus a specialized one is complicated, and the pros and cons of each alternative need discussion. A preschool for typical children provides a natural environment with normal peers; however, teachers usually are not trained or prepared to work with a preschooler with autism. An autism-specific or other specialized preschool provides structure and a tailored curriculum but may not provide the social opportunities found with normally developing peers. For many parents, entrusting the child's early education to an "outside" agency can arouse anxiety, and the emotional support of the professional can facilitate this process. As with health providers, the autism professional should work with the preschool program, not just to consult around issues concerning the child but to ensure that the parental views and concerns are being considered. Parents of children with autism will have many years of coordinating their efforts with the educational establishment; the initial school experience can set the tone for developing sound practices in the teacher-parent dialogue.

The early years for families are thus characterized by the emotional stress of discovering that they have a child with a serious developmental disorder, working through the initial period of grief while assuming the challenge of helping the child at home, finding community services, and anticipating what the future might bring. The helping professional needs to be a part of this process, guiding and supporting the family through this difficult stage.

Middle Childhood

For many families, the elementary school years are relatively less stressful than the preschool years, particularly if an adequate school program is available (Bebko, Konstantareas, & Springer, 1987; DeMyer, 1979). As the child develops cognitively and socially, behavioral difficulties often diminish in intensity and frequency. In addition, many parents have begun to redefine expectations and develop individualized standards of "success" for their families and child with autism (Randall & Parker, 1999). When early diagnosis and intervention occur, parents learn basic management and coping skills, and the child is prepared better for adjusting to the public school environment. When early services have not been provided, families continue in a state of limbo and pressures mount. Fortunately, in the past decade, improved early diagnosis and intervention services have reduced the likelihood of a complete absence of services for families of children with autism. Three major issues in working with families in this phase involve collaboration with the school system, the child's adaptive behavior, and sibling concerns.

School System

The transition to the public school system is not necessarily a uniformly positive experience. Although parents are satisfied that their child is a part of a community system, they sometimes welcome their child's placement in a special class or a special school. In addition to the normal anxieties parents face when their child goes to school for the first time, parents of the child with autism have to deal with the recognition that theirs is an atypical child who may not be integrated into the mainstream. Parents whose children are fully included in a typical classroom setting also have a number of experiences that emphasize their child's atypical development. For many parents, these events may reawaken the worries associated with the first awareness of having a disabled child and remind them that the future course of development will continue to be challenging.

The public school system is more impersonal than the typical preschool environment, and parents are less likely to have the built-in support network they have previously experienced. Many parents who have had their child served in a developmental day care program or public school preschool program with additional family support services have appreciated the informal, caring atmosphere of a small program, often staffed with a social worker or parent coordinator. Because the main business of public schools is education, ancillary personnel are in shorter supply and are spread thinly across large numbers of children, whether normal or handicapped.

Parents need to be prepared for this change, and the helping professional again should be available for advice and guidance. As in the selection of a preschool program, the clinician should be knowledgeable about the variety of early elementary programs that are appropriate and should explore these possibilities with the parents and school system personnel. Again, parents should be central to the decision-making process, although reality usually results in fewer options than desirable, many of which may be unacceptable or at least far from ideal. The active intervention of the professional during this transition can (1) ease the concerns of parents justifiably worried about their child's adaptation to public school, (2) indicate to the school system that the family and child have an outside advocate on whose support they can draw, and (3) establish a foundation for a satisfactory relationship between home and school.

When a solid groundwork is laid, the supportive professional can facilitate the development of a smooth relationship between the family and the classroom teacher over time. Sometimes the child's elementary school classroom does not change, and if a teacher remains with a program, the child may have the same teacher for as many as 5 to 7 years. This arrangement may have the advantages of continuity and consistency, but, from the standpoint of parent-teacher relationships, there will be a natural tendency for conflicts to occur and possible competitive feelings to arise. At the opposite extreme, children who are placed in more mainstream or inclusive settings may change teachers on a yearly basis. In these situations, especially likely to occur for higher functioning children, transition issues arise yearly and each new teacher may have only a minimal understanding of autism and effective instructional strategies, again increasing home-school tensions.

The professional should be alert to such tensions and be ready to serve as a mediator or troubleshooter, making certain that the teacher and the family understand the other's perspective. If the child and family are no longer seen regularly by the professional, it may be useful to conduct an annual evaluation involving the current (and future) educational professionals to provide an objective forum for reviewing concerns.

Many school systems advocate full inclusion of all special education students (Kauffman & Hallahan, 1995; Mesibov & Shea, 1996), including those with autism. Inclusion typically is defined as full-time placement in regular education with whatever supports are necessary. Parents whose children are fully included may have mixed feelings about this arrangement: On the one hand, they are excited and hopeful about the opportunity for their child to be educated alongside typically developing peers; on the other hand, they are worried about whether their child will get the individualized attention he or she needs and about how successful the integrated experience will be. The professional engaged with the family whose child is included needs to be alert to parental emotions about the situation as well as available to help educators handle the variety of problems that will inevitably occur. In the long run, helping the parents and the schools work out an individualized solution, rather than simply a fully inclusive or totally contained program, is most constructive and can lead to reduced parental stress.

In summary, TEACCH professionals work with families in an educative, instrumental, advocating, and emotionally supportive manner to develop effective working relationships with school professionals. This involves activities such as conducting school-based observations and teacher training, supporting parents at individualized education program (IEP) and teacher-parent meetings, as well as making specific educational recommendations.

Adaptive Behavior

In addition to promoting a strong home-school relationship, the professional should be available to help the family with the child's at-home and community functioning. As the primary responsibility for education shifts from home to school, the focus of home-based intervention correspondingly shifts from teaching cognitive skills to activities that facilitate the child's continued adaptation to home and community. Although some parents remain active in basic academic and cognitive skills training, either to supplement the school program or to feel integral to their child's developmental progress, middle childhood is an auspicious time to build daily living and functional communication skills for many reasons.

First, our clinical experience is that parents often recognize that work on home routines and adaptive behaviors, through structured teaching and other methods, enhances their personal interactions with their child (Davis & Marcus, 1980). Second, parents have come to realize the importance of these areas for their child's future adaptation. Third, many parents, after being frustrated in their efforts to teach complex cognitive skills, are gratified at the relative ease with which their child learns household routines and tasks. Fourth, the child's ability to learn behaviors in the context of routine and his or her possible predilection toward orderliness can be recognized by the family as pleasant qualities that fit in with everyday chores. The professional can help in this area by encouraging parents to work on functional skills and by suggesting task analysis and other teaching techniques.

On a related note, as the child with autism is included in more public settings, the need for specific work on adaptive *social* behaviors becomes more apparent. Parents may become frustrated with school professionals who often lack expertise in designing and implementing effective social interventions. Further, parents often feel distressed about the failure of others to invite the child to parties or to welcome the child to sports teams, scouting groups, religious schools, and the like. Professionals can assist parents in working on social skills at home, in advocating for an appropriate social communication curriculum at school, and in connecting with other families. We have found that parent-to-parent support is especially effective at helping parents create new and appropriate social interaction opportunities.

Siblings

Although not confined to this phase, issues involving siblings often take on increased significance during the autistic child's elementary school years. As the child with autism grows older, the developmental delays and atypical behavior become more obvious, especially in social relationships. Depending on their age, siblings may become increasingly sensitive to having a brother or sister who behaves oddly, demands considerable time from their parents, and is not a typical playmate. Siblings, like their parents, have common worries and concerns that need recognition (Harris, 1994a; Lobato & Kao, 2002; Powell & Ogle, 1985). These include concerns about the reason(s) for their disabled sibling's problems, whether they might also have similar problems, what the future holds regarding a long-term responsibility for care, how to cope with embarrassment or teasing, and how they should behave toward their sibling with autism. Although the typical sibling's ability to understand autism matures over time, it tends to lag behind the understanding of comparison groups of children who have siblings with medical or physical conditions (Bagenholm & Gillberg, 1991; Glasburg, 2000; Lobato & Kao, 2002). Further, parents tend to overestimate the degree to which siblings understand the implications of autism (Glasburg, 2000). Parents, who are struggling with their own reactions and stress, have the additional burden of making sure their nonaffected children are having their personal and developmental needs met.

Not all siblings respond in the same way to the stresses of living with a child who has autism (McHale et al., 1986), and sibling responses may be mediated by family and parent factors (e.g., family cohesion), disorder variables (e.g., prognosis), and child variables (e.g., age; Williams, 1997). In a recent survey of 250 families of children with developmental disabilities and other chronic conditions, Williams and colleagues (2002) identified three main predictors of sibling adjustment problems: family financial difficulties, lower family cohesion, and less sibling knowledge about the illness or disorder. Research specific to families of children with autism has failed to confirm the importance of family cohesion in sibling adjustment (Fisman et al., 1996) but has pointed to buffering effects of social support (Kaminsky & Dewey, 2002; Wolf, Fisman, Ellison, & Freeman, 1998) as well as open communication about and sibling understanding of autism (e.g., Bagenholm & Gillberg, 1991; Dellve et al., 2000; Gold, 1993; Lobato & Kao, 2002; Roeyers & Mycke, 1995).

Important goals for working with siblings in the middle childhood age range include increasing open communication about autism, providing siblings with social support, improving sibling knowledge about autism, and enhancing sibling interactions. The professional can help by offering parent education on strategies for reaching these goals, training both the child with autism and the typical sibling in social interaction skills (e.g., Strain & Danko, 1995; Taylor et al., 1999) and, when needed, offering individualized counseling for siblings. Sibling groups, in particular, offer siblings an opportunity to learn important information and skills while sharing emotional experiences and connecting with others in similar situations (e.g., Meyer & Vadasy, 1994). Although the research on sibling support groups is plagued by multiple design problems and inconsistent outcomes about effects on sibling adjustment, such groups generally have been evaluated positively by participating parents and siblings (e.g., Dyson, 1998; Lobato & Kao, 2002; Williams 1997). Bristol and Schopler (1989) note that, based on the research literature, it may *not* be necessary in many, if not most, cases to provide for specialized services for siblings but that it is appropriate for counseling or training to be an optional part of a comprehensive program for children with autism.

Adolescence

During the 1980s and 1990s, there was a dramatic increase in the awareness of autism in adolescences and a proliferation of writing on this topic (e.g., Schopler & Mesibov, 1983). This surge of interest was stimulated, in large part, by the openly expressed needs of parents whose younger autistic children were now growing older and continuing to show the major problems of autism. That is, the same groups of parents who previously helped build public awareness and program support for younger children with autism now approached the professional community for methods and services to help with the issues of managing their adolescent and young adult children (Mesibov, Schopler, & Sloan, 1983).

Findings from the resulting surge of clinical and research work indicated that the adolescent period produces additional stress for families of individuals with autism (Bristol & Schopler, 1983; DeMyer & Goldberg, 1983; Seltzer et al., 2001). Recently, in a 10-year longitudinal study of 28 families of children with autism (ages 13 to 27 at follow-up), Gray (2002) found *improvements* over time in (1) parents' psychological well-being, (2) relationships with extended family, (3) the child's public behavior, and (4) parents' ability to cope with stigmatizing experiences. In contrast to these encouraging results and consistent with earlier reports of high stress during adolescence, more than half of the parents in Gray's sample reported significant anxiety and depression, with family members of aggressive or severely obsessive children at special risk. Further, replicating earlier findings (Bristol & Schopler, 1983; Fong, Wilgosh, & Sobsey, 1993), parents' anxiety about their child's future was especially high during adolescence. The need for ongoing parental support, therefore, remains high during this phase, especially as the parents' energy level decreases and their potential for burnout increases (Marcus, 1984). Major efforts in working with families during this phase

involve behavioral concerns and interventions, the child's educational program, and residential placement.

Behavioral Concerns and Interventions

General problems and concerns raised by families during the adolescent period reflect the continuation of earlier issues such as the need for specialized services, dealing with the community, and the realization that the disorder is lifelong. Added to these are complications brought by the physical changes in adolescence, the onset of seizures for some adolescents, the stress of many years of raising a child with autism, and an increased awareness of the parents' own mortality. Specific behavioral matters that are likely to emerge include increased sexuality and inappropriate ways of expressing it (Van Bourgondien, Reichle, & Palmer, 1997), aggressiveness and openly expressed defiance, and the emerging sense of independence in someone who lacks many of the prerequisites for self-direction (Fong et al., 1993; Mesibov, 1983). The core issues are common to typical adolescence, but the individual hampered by dysfunctions in communication, social understanding, and cognitive facility cannot cope as readily with the profound biological changes this stage brings.

The direct help that can be provided by the professional at this point includes discussion (with parents) of the implications of adolescence for a person with autism; suggestions on behavior management geared to the practical realities of the home situation; sex management and counseling; relaxation training; cognitive-behavioral therapy; medication management, which often becomes more necessary during this period; information about respite care, including after-school, weekend, and summer programs; and work toward obtaining a future residential placement.

As with parents of younger children, support groups for the parents of adolescents remain crucial because these parents continue to seek quality services and solutions for daily problems (Marcus et al., 1995). Maturing siblings, who may be exhibiting fewer problems with regard to the child with autism during this phase (Gray, 2002), are also able to think more abstractly about the sibling's future (Glasberg,

2000) and are likely to have a number of concerns about that future as well as their role in it (Damiani, 1999; Dellve et al., 2000). Professionals can talk with parents about strategies for improving family communication, offer sibling support groups, or work directly with siblings to develop coping strategies.

Educational Program

Another area in which parents often require support involves the changing educational needs of the adolescent with autism. Parents who have worked tirelessly to obtain adequate early school programs often have to follow the same route to continue their child's education into secondary school. If the school system has not planned ahead, the adolescent may be left adrift or kept in the elementary school setting despite the chronological age discrepancy. In addition, with increased age the type of curriculum must shift, in most cases, away from academics and toward vocational and career preparation (Fredericks, Buckley, Baldwin, Moore, & Stremel-Campbell, 1983). Parents, and the educational professionals they work with, may require assistance in recognizing and addressing the adolescent's need for functional, job-related skill development as early as possible in this period. Thus, during this phase, professionals can support parents in channeling their elevated and natural anxiety about their child's future into productive efforts to obtain a suitable educational setting and curriculum as well as multiple real-life opportunities for job-relevant skill practice.

Residential Placement

Individuals with autism who exhibit aggressive or severe maladaptive behaviors are among those most likely to be placed in residential treatment (Perry & Black, 1997). Consideration of residential placement, however, often comes as a jolt to families who, during the preadolescent years, rarely thought that their child could not remain at home indefinitely. The combination of their own decreasing control of the situation, other family needs and priorities, and the visible daily reminder that their child is becoming a young adult has an unexpected impact that few families fully anticipate.

For many families, there is a need to develop a plan of action regarding residential placement that takes into account both logistical and emotional considerations. From the practical standpoint, appropriate group homes or other residential options may not be available, and parents need to work with community agencies to develop such programs (LaVigna, 1983; Mesibov et al., 1983; Van Bourgondien & Reichle, 2001). The professional has to collaborate with the parent in this effort. From an emotional perspective, parents need to know that placement outside the home is a natural and logical next step in the move toward independence of the child and is not the result of the family's failure to provide a good home. Unfortunately, emergencies often allow little opportunity for adequate preparation, and placement can occur in an abrupt and somewhat traumatic manner. The professional needs to be sensitive to the emotional pain experienced by parents in these circumstances and should thoughtfully counsel them through the crisis.

Finally, in the absence of full-time residential care, the professional should help locate adequate respite and emergency relief services, after-school and recreational programs, and summer programs. These services are required to some extent at all stages of development, but they become particularly critical as the child grows older.

In summary, from the standpoint of the role of the professional over time, although the scope of activities broadens during the adolescent phase, the need to remain engaged in a partnership remains constant. Overall, there is less emphasis on direct treatment of the child, heightened alertness to crisis situations, and an expansion of instrumental and advocacy support activities, especially concerning community services and resources.

Adulthood

Compared to early childhood, substantially less has been written about autism in adulthood. Beyond clinical experience, information is available from outcome studies (Lotter, 1978; Piven, Harper, Palmer, & Arndt, 1996; Venter, Lord, & Schopler, 1992), parental narratives (e.g., Park, 1982, 2001), professional publications on treatment and care (Holmes & Carr, 1991; Schopler & Mesibov, 1983), and autobiographies of higher functioning individuals (e.g., Grandin & Scariano, 1986). The major issues confronted by families during this phase both parallel and extend beyond those of earlier periods. Of special importance are issues related to behavioral concerns, residential placement, education and employment, and long-term advocacy and planning.

Behavioral Concerns and Interventions

The majority of outcome studies support descriptions of autism as a lifelong condition in which development occurs but in which deficits, including those in cognition and social adaptation, persist (Piven et al., 1996; Venter et al., 1992). There is a dearth of research on autism family experiences in this phase; however, two small sample studies obtained similar results (Holmes & Carr, 1991; Seltzer et al., 2001). In these studies, parents of adults with autism reported greater behavioral problems in their adult child, such as self-harm and social withdrawal, than did parents of adults with Down syndrome. It appears that these challenges continue to affect family functioning as parents of adults with autism described themselves as more vigilant, as more likely to give into the adult's demands, and as feeling less close to the individual. Similarly, consistent with sibling research in childhood (Kaminsky & Dewey, 2001; Knott et al., 1995), Seltzer et al. found that siblings of adults with autism were engaged in fewer social activities with, and felt less close to, their sibling than did adult siblings of persons with Down syndrome.

The assistance that families require during adulthood is consistent in many ways with the help required during the adolescent period, especially with regard to intervention strategies for managing difficult behavior and promoting adaptive functioning. Direct services that are especially helpful include individual counseling with higher functioning adults (Mesibov, 1992), social skills training and related social activities experiences (Mesibov, 1984), and parent support groups (Harris, 1994b). Over time, however, the ability of most families to continue to take the initiative in procuring services is compromised by their declining strength. Further, there is substantial agreement that, for all but a minority,

long-range residential and employment support are necessary.

Residential Placement

Historically, by adulthood most individuals with autism were institutionalized (DeMyer & Goldberg, 1983); however, the deinstitutionalization movement has all but eliminated that option, and the responsibility of the home and community to arrange for residential care and vocational opportunities has and will become more prevalent. Thus, there is an urgency for the professional to explore these options with families and, more so than ever before, to take a leadership role in creating opportunities and advocating for a wide range of supported living situations in the community. By their early adulthood years, persons with autism should have the opportunity to live independently, whether in a group home, an apartment complex with supervision, or a comparable facility.

Seltzer et al. (2001) reported data from Mental Retardation/Developmental Disabilities (MR/DD) agencies in New York on the living situations in 1998 of almost 8,000 persons with autism. Of these individuals, 54% of the 20- to 29-year-olds and 34% of 30- to 39-year-olds still lived with their parents. The percentage of adults living at home, then, did decline over time, but a substantial proportion were still living with their parents. Parents of adults with autism should be able to have the same expectations as parents of normal individuals: to see their adult offspring live his or her life away from home. It is clear, however, that many parents actually increase the level of support they provide to their child during the adult years.

Education and Employment

Upon leaving school, parents need assistance ensuring that the individual with autism does not languish at home but, instead, is involved in vocational training, supported or direct employment, college education, or other productive options. In too many situations, the adult with autism lacks a structured program, increasing the possibility of behavioral problems and placing a substantial burden on the parents. The professional must anticipate this situation *before* the conclusion of the school years and work toward an appropriate day program and, it is hoped, meaningful employment (M. Smith, Belcher, & Johrs, 1997) or continued education.

Parents of high-functioning individuals who pursue a college education have few, if any, empirically supported guidelines to follow. Too often, the assumption is that the college education, alone, is sufficient for launching the individual successfully. The professional can work in collaboration with the parent *and* the individual with autism to develop a plan for supports needed in college (e.g., organizational supports, social supports for dormitory living, and learning implicit social rules on campus; Ozonoff, Dawson, & McPartland, 2002). Research and clinical evidence suggests that higher functioning individuals, due to deficits in job-related skills and behaviors, end up unemployed or underemployed, even despite postsecondary education (Howlin, 2000). The professional can help parents as well as the high-functioning individual identify and obtain needed supports for maximizing the chances of a successful college-to-work transition.

Advocacy and Planning Efforts

Needs for advocacy and instrumental support exist for the long-term future of the individual with autism. Parents, and sometimes siblings, must become involved in estate and guardianship planning (Frolile, 1983; Turnbull, Turnbull, Bronicki, Summers, & Roeder-Gordon, 1989). In addition, the importance of self-determination for individuals with developmental disabilities has been increasingly recognized (Ward & Meyer, 1999), and many adults with autism are taking a stronger role in advocating for their own needs and for those of others in the autism community. Again, the professional can provide emotional, problem-solving, and instrumental support to family members as they address these issues. For example, professionals may talk concerns over with parents, make referrals to knowledgeable legal counsel, and work jointly or individually with the parent and adult with autism to maximize self-determination.

In summary, if the adult with autism has received adequate educational services and parents have been actively involved in their child's programs and received good support for themselves, then the shift into adulthood can be smooth and rewarding. Even in the smoothest transitions, however, the professional-family partnership remains an important component of effective intervention during the adulthood period. As the first generation of clearly diagnosed individuals with autism progresses into middle and older adulthood, accumulating clinical and research evidence will assist professionals in working more effectively with families during these years.

CONCLUSION

In this chapter, we reviewed the sources of stress and needs of families across the developmental spectrum as well as the roles and strategies that can be adopted by the helping professional. The importance of working as partners cannot be emphasized enough, nor can the necessity of maintaining a flexible attitude, a willingness to avoid building barriers, and individualized understanding of family stressors, characteristics, and intervention goals. In working with family members of children with autism, professionals should be knowledgeable about the range and variety of approaches that may be needed.

The fundamental approach for addressing early and ongoing needs is an *education* approach in which family members are helped to better understand autism, the unique needs of the child, and effective coping strategies. Substantial clinical and research evidence supports the use of a *parents as (co)therapists* approach, both in training parents in structured teaching strategies and *behavioral* techniques and strategies. Further, families of children have needs, throughout the family life cycle, for *emotional, instrumental, and advocacy support*. Finally, *cognitive approaches* have been used less frequently and explicitly, but strategies such as self-monitoring, reframing, and problem solving are used frequently when working with families of children with autism. Professionals also need to be prepared to deal with families whose problems extend beyond the stresses of having a child with autism, such as marital discord, financial hardship, or entrenched maladaptive perceptions (e.g., believing the family members have no control over life events).

The developmental perspective presented in this chapter provides a practical framework for working with families: In *early childhood,* the emphasis is on early diagnosis, emotional support during the grief process, as well as parent training, counseling, and networking; in *middle childhood,* the focus is on enhancing home-school relationships, collaboration in the design of educational programs, enhancing the development of adaptive and functional skills, and awareness of sibling issues; and the *adolescent and adult periods* require focus on maximizing independence and obtaining relevant vocational opportunities.

As families continue to contend with reckless promoters of faddish therapies and the pressure to find a cure, both of which reinforce the natural tendency to doubt or deny the chronicity of the disorder, professionals must remain sensitive to the vulnerable situation in which parents are placed, their need for support, and the importance of identifying sound, empirically based interventions. As our knowledge of the condition of autism continues to grow and effective interventions for those affected by it are documented and replicated, professionals will still need to be available for families throughout the life span of the person with autism. Professionals knowledgeable about and sensitive to the needs of these families will be major contributors to successful outcomes.

Cross-References

Issues of diagnosis and classification are reviewed in Section I (Chapters 1 through 6), developmental aspects of autism and related conditions are addressed in Chapters 8 through 10, interventions are discussed in Chapters 33 through 44, and personal perspectives in autism are presented in Section IX (Chapters 49 through 53).

REFERENCES

Akerley, M. S. (1975). The invulnerable parent. *Journal of Autism and Childhood Schizophrenia, 5,* 275–281.

American Psychiatric Association. (2000). *Diagnostic and statistical manual of mental disorders* (4th ed., text rev.). Washington, DC: Author.

Assemany, A. E., & McIntosh, D. E. (2002). Negative treatment outcomes of behavioral parent training programs. *Psychology in the Schools, 39,* 209–219.

Avdi, E., Griffin, C., & Brough, S. (2000). Parents' constructions of professional knowledge, expertise and authority during assessment and diagnosis of their child for an autistic spectrum disorder. *British Journal of Medical Psychology, 73,* 327–338.

Bagenholm, A., & Gillberg, C. (1991). Psychosocial effects on siblings of children with autism and mental retardation: A population-based study. *Journal of Mental Deficiency Research, 35,* 291–307.

Barkley, R. A. (1987). *Defiant children: A clinician's manual for parent training.* New York: Guilford Press.

Bebko, J. M., Konstantareas, M. M., & Springer, J. (1987). Parent and professional evaluations of family stress associated with characteristics of autism. *Journal of Autism and Developmental Disorders, 17,* 565–576.

Bell, R. Q., & Harper, L. V. (1977). *Child effects on adults.* Hillsdale, NJ: Erlbaum.

Bibby, P., Eikeseth, S., Martin, N. T., Mudford, O. C., & Reeves, D. (2001). Progress and outcomes for children with autism receiving parent-managed intensive interventions. *Research in Developmental Disabilities, 22,* 425–447.

Birnbrauer, J. S., & Leach, D. J. (1993). The Murdoch early intervention program after 2 years. *Behaviour Change, 10,* 63–74.

Bitsika, V., & Sharpley, C. (1999). An explanatory examination of the effects of support groups on the well-being of parents of children with autism: I. General counselling. *Journal of Applied Health Behaviour, 1,* 16–22.

Bitsika, V., & Sharpley, C. (2000). Development and testing of the effects of support groups on the well-being of parents of children with autism: II. Specific stress management techniques. *Journal of Applied Health Behaviour, 2,* 8–15.

Briesmeister, J. M., & Schaefer, C. E. (Eds.). (1998). *Handbook of parent training: Parents as co-therapists for children's behavior problems* (2nd ed.). New York: Wiley.

Bristol, M. M. (1984). Family resources and successful adaptation to autistic children. In E. Schopler & G. B. Mesibov (Eds.), *The effects of autism on the family* (pp. 289–310). New York: Plenum Press.

Bristol, M. M., Gallagher, J. J., & Holt, K. D. (1993). Maternal depressive symptoms in autism: Response to psychoeducational intervention. *Rehabilitation Psychology, 38,* 3–10.

Bristol, M. M., & Schopler, E. (1983). Family resources and successful adaptation in autistic children. In E. Schopler & G. B. Mesibov (Eds.), *Autism in adolescents and adults* (pp. 251–279). New York: Plenum Press.

Bristol, M. M., & Schopler, E. (1984). Developmental perspective on stress and coping in families of autistic children. In J. Blacher (Ed.), *Families of severely handicapped children: Review of research* (pp. 91–134). New York: Academic Press.

Bristol, M. M., & Schopler, E. (1989). The family in the treatment of autism. In American Psychiatric Association (Ed.), *Treatment of psychiatric disorders: A task force report of the American Psychiatric Association* (pp. 249–266). Washington, DC: American Psychiatric Association.

Burack, J. A., Charman, T., Yirmiya, N., & Zelazo, P. R. (Eds.). (2001). *The development of autism: Perspectives from theory and research.* Mahwah, NJ: Erlbaum.

Chambless, D. L., & Ollendick, T. H. (2000). Empirically supported psychological interventions: Controversies and evidence. *Annual Review of Psychology, 52,* 685–716.

Christophersen, E. R., & Mortweet, S. L. (2001). *Treatments that work with children: Empirically supported strategies for managing childhood problems.* Washington, DC: American Psychological Association.

Clark, M. L., Cunningham, L. J., & Cunningham, C. E. (1989). Improving the social behavior of siblings of autistic children using a group problem solving approach. *Child and Family Behavior Therapy, 11,* 19–33.

Coleman, M., & Gillberg, C. (1985). *The biology of the autistic syndromes.* New York: Praeger.

Cowen, P. S. (2001). Crisis child care: Implications from family interventions. *Journal of the American Psychiatric Nurses Association, 7,* 196–203.

Cunningham, C. E. (1989). A family-systems-oriented training program for parents of language-delayed children with behavior problems. In C. E. Schaefer & J. M. Briesmeister (Eds.), *Handbook of parent training: Parents as co-therapists for children's behavior problems* (pp. 133–176). New York: Wiley.

Cunningham, P. B., Henggeler, S. W., Brondino, M. J., & Pickrel, S. G. (1999). Testing underlying assumptions of the family empowerment perspective. *Journal of Child and Family Studies, 8,* 437–449.

Dadds, M. R., Sanders, M. R., & James, J. E. (1987). The generalization of treatment effects in parent training with multidistressed parents. *Behavioural Psychotherapy, 15,* 289–313.

Damiani, V. B. (1999). Responsibility and adjustment in siblings of children with disabilities: Update and review. *Families in Society, 80,* 34–40.

Davis, S., & Marcus, L. M. (1980). Involving parents in the treatment of severely communication-disordered children. *Journal of Pediatric Psychology, 5,* 189–197.

De Giacomo, A., & Fombonne, E. (1998). Parental recognition of developmental abnormalities in autism. *European Child and Adolescent Psychiatry, 7,* 131–136.

Dellve, L., Cernerud, L., & Hallberg, L. R. M. (2000). Harmonizing dilemmas: Siblings of children with DAMP and Asperger syndrome's experiences of coping with their life situations. *Scandanavian Journal of Caring Science, 14,* 172–178.

DeMyer, M. K. (1979). *Parents and children in autism.* New York: Wiley.

DeMyer, M. K., & Goldberg, P. (1983). Family needs of the autistic adolescent. In E. Schopler & G. B. Mesibov (Eds.), *Autism in adolescents and adults* (pp. 225–250). New York: Plenum Press.

DesLauriers, A. M., & Carlson, C. F. (1969). *Your child is asleep: Early infantile autism.* Homewood, IL: Dorsey.

Dissanayake, C., & Crossley, S. A. (1997). Autistic children's responses to separation and reunion with their mothers. *Journal of Autism and Developmental Disorders, 27,* 295–312.

Dix, T. (1993). Attributing disposition to children: An interactional analysis of attribution and socialization. *Personality and Social Psychology Bulletin, 19,* 633–643.

Dunlap, G. (1999). Consensus, engagement, and family involvement for young children with autism. *Journal of the Association for Persons with Severe Handicaps, 24,* 222–225.

Dykens, E. M., & Volkmar, F. R. (1997). Medical conditions associated with autism. In D. J. Cohen & F. R. Volkmar (Eds.), *Handbook of autism and pervasive developmental disorders* (2nd ed., pp. 388–407). New York: Wiley.

Dyson, L. L. (1998). A support program for siblings of children with disabilities: What siblings learn and what they like. *Psychology in the Schools, 35,* 57–63.

Eyberg, S. M., Edwards, D., Boggs, S. R., & Foote, R. (1998). Maintaining the treatment effects of parent training: The role of booster sessions and other maintenance strategies. *Clinical Psychology, 5,* 544–554.

Fine, M. J., & Gardner, A. (1994). Collaborative consultation with families of children with special needs: Why bother? *Journal of Educational and Psychological Consultation, 5,* 283–308.

Fisman, S., Wolf, L., Ellison, D., & Freeman, T. (2000). A longitudinal study of siblings of children with chronic disabilities. *Canadian Journal of Psychiatry, 45,* 369–375.

Fisman, S., Wolf, L., Ellison, D., Gillis, B., Freeman, T., & Szatmari, P. (1996). Risk and protective factors affecting the adjustment of siblings of children with chronic disabilities. *Journal of the American Academy of Child and Adolescent Psychiatry, 35,* 1532–1541.

Fong, L., Wilgosh, L., & Sobsey, D. (1993). The experience of parenting an adolescent with autism. *International Journal of Disability, Development and Education, 40,* 105–113.

Fredericks, H. D., Buckley, J., Baldwin, V. L., Moore, W., & Stremel-Campbell, K. (1983). In E. Schopler & G. B. Mesibov (Eds.), *Autism in adolescents and adults* (pp. 79–109). New York: Plenum Press.

Frolile, L. A. (1983). Legal needs. In E. Schopler & G. B. Mesibov (Eds.), *Autism in adolescents and adults* (pp. 319–334). New York: Plenum Press.

Gibbs, B. (1996). Providing support to sisters and brothers of children with disabilities. In G. H. S. Singer & L. E. Powers (Eds.), *Families, disability, and empowerment: Active coping skills and strategies for family interventions* (pp. 343–363). Baltimore: Paul H. Brookes.

Glasberg, B. A. (2000). The development of siblings' understanding of autism spectrum disorders. *Journal of Autism and Developmental Disorders, 30,* 143–156.

Gold, N. (1993). Depression and social adjustment in siblings of boys with autism. *Journal of Autism and Developmental Disorder, 23,* 147–163.

Grandin, T., & Scariano, M. M. (1986). *Emergence: Labeled autistic.* Novato, CA: Arena.

Gray, D. E. (1997). High functioning autistic children and the construction of "normal family life." *Social Science and Medicine, 44*(8), 1097–1106.

Gray, D. E. (2002). Ten years on: A longitudinal study of families of children with autism. *Journal of Intellectual and Developmental Disability, 27,* 215–222.

Graziano, A. M., & Diament, D. M. (1992). Parent behavioral training: An examination of the paradigm. *Behavior Modification, 16,* 3–38.

Greenspan, S. I., & Weider, S. (1998). *The child with special needs: Intellectual and emotional growth.* Reading, MA: Addison-Wesley.

Harris, S. L. (1986). Parents as teachers: A four to seven year follow up of parents of children with autism. *Child and Family Behavior Therapy, 8,* 39–47.

Harris, S. L. (1994a). *Siblings of children with autism: A guide for families.* Rockville, MD: Woodbine House.

Harris, S. L. (1994b). Treatment of family problems in autism. In E. Schopler & G. B. Mesibov (Eds.), *Behavioral issues in autism* (pp. 161–175). New York: Plenum Press.

Harris, S. L. (1998). Behavioral and educational approaches to the PDD's. In F. R. Volkmar (Ed.), *Autism and pervasive developmental disorders* (pp. 195–208). Cambridge, England: Cambridge University Press.

Hastings, R. P., & Johnson, E. (2001). Stress in UK families conducting home-based behavioral intervention for their young child with autism. *Journal of Autism and Developmental Disorders, 31,* 327–336.

Helps, S., Newsom-Davis, I. C., & Callias, M. (1999). Autism: The teacher's view. *Autism: Journal of Research and Practice, 3,* 287–298.

Holmes, N., & Carr, J. (1991). The pattern of care in families of adults with a mental handicap: A comparison between families of autistic adults and Down syndrome adults. *Journal of Autism and Developmental Disorders, 21,* 187–196.

Howlin, P. (1989). Help for the family. In C. Gillberg (Ed.), *Diagnosis and treatment of autism* (pp. 185–202). New York: Plenum Press.

Howlin, P. (2000). Outcome in adult life for more able individuals with autism or Asperger syndrome. *Autism: Journal of Research and Practice, 4,* 63–83.

Howlin, P., & Asgharian, A. (1999). The diagnosis of autism and Asperger syndrome: Findings from a survey of 770 families. *Developmental Medicine and Child Neurology, 41,* 834–839.

Howlin, P., & Moore, A. (1997). Diagnosis in autism: A survey of over 1200 patients in the UK. *Autism: Journal of Research and Practice, 1,* 135–162.

Humphreys, L., Forehand, R., McMahon, R., & Roberts, M. (1978). Parent behavioral training to modify child noncompliance: Effects on untreated siblings. *Journal of Behavior Therapy and Experimental Psychiatry, 9,* 235–238.

Ireys, H. T., Chernoff, R., Stein, R. E. K., DeVet, K. A., & Silver, E. J. (2001). Outcomes of community-based family-to-family support: Lessons learned from a decade of randomized trials. *Children's Services: Social Policy, Research, and Practice, 4,* 203–216.

Kaminsky, L., & Dewey, D. (2001). Sibling relationships of children with autism. *Journal of Autism and Developmental Disorders, 31,* 399–410.

Kaminsky, L., & Dewey, D. (2002). Psychosocial adjustment in siblings of children with autism. *Journal of Child Psychology and Psychiatry and Allied Disciplines, 43,* 225–232.

Kauffman, J. M., & Hallahan, D. P. (1995). *The illusion of full inclusion.* Austin, TX: ProEd.

Kazdin, A. E. (1997). Parent management training: Evidence, outcomes, and issues. *Journal of the American Academy of Child and Adolescent Psychiatry, 36,* 1349–1356.

Knott, F., Lewis, C., & Williams, T. (1995). Sibling interaction of children with learning disabilities: A comparison of autism and Down's syndrome. *Journal of Child Psychology and Psychiatry, 6,* 965–976.

Koegel, L. K., Stiebel, D., & Koegel, R. L. (1998). Reducing aggression in children with autism toward infant or toddler siblings. *Journal of the Association for Persons with Severe Handicaps, 23,* 111–118.

Koegel, R. L., Bimbela, A., & Schreibman, L. (1996). Collateral effects of parent training on family interactions. *Journal of Autism and Developmental Disorders, 26,* 347–359.

Koegel, R. L., Koegel, L. K., & Schreibman, L. (1991). Assessing and training parents in teaching pivotal behaviors. *Advances in Behavioral Assessment of Children and Families, 5,* 65–82.

Koegel, R. L., Schreibman, L., Loos, L. M., Dirlich-Wilhelm, H., Dunlap, G., Robbins, F. R., et al. (1992). Consistent stress profiles in mothers of children with autism. *Journal of Autism and Developmental Disorders, 22,* 205–216.

Kozloff, M. A. (1984). A training program for families of children with autism: Responding to family needs. In E. Schopler & G. B. Mesibov (Eds.), *The effects of autism on the family* (pp. 163–186). New York: Plenum Press.

Krantz, P. J., MacDuff, M. T., & McClannahan, L. E. (1993). Program participation in family activities for children with autism: Parents' use of photographic activity schedules. *Journal of Applied Behavior Analysis, 26,* 137–138.

Laski, K. E., Charlop, M. H., & Schreibman, L. (1988). Training parents to use the natural language paradigm to increase their autistic children's speech. *Journal of Applied Behavior Analysis, 21,* 391–400.

LaVigna, G. W. (1983). The Jay Nolan Center: A community-based program. In E. Schopler & G. B. Mesibov (Eds.), *Autism in adolescents and adults* (pp. 381–410). New York: Plenum Press.

Lobato, D. J., & Kao, B. T. (2002). Integrated sibling-parent group intervention to improve sibling knowledge and adjustment to chronic illness and disability. *Journal of Pediatric Psychology, 27,* 711–716.

Lotter, V. (1978). Follow-up studies. In M. Rutter & E. Schopler (Eds.), *Autism: A reappraisal of concepts and treatment* (pp. 475–495). New York: Plenum Press.

Lovaas, O. I. (1987). Behavioral treatment and normal education and intellectual functioning in young autistic children. *Journal of Consulting and Clinical Psychology, 55,* 3–9.

MacLean, J. E., Szatmari, P., & Jones, M. B. (1999). Familial factors influence level of functioning in pervasive developmental disorder. *Journal of the American Academy of Child and Adolescent Psychiatry, 38,* 746–753.

Marcus, L. M. (1984). Coping with burnout. In E. Schopler & G. B. Mesibov (Eds.), *The effects of autism on the family* (pp. 311–326). New York: Plenum Press.

Marcus, L. M. (2003, April). *The role of parent support in the TEACCH program.* Paper presented at the International Institute for Educational Therapy, Tokyo, Japan.

Marcus, L. M., Flagler, S., & Robinson, S. (2001). Assessment of children with autism. In R. J. Simeonsson & S. L. Rosenthal (Eds.), *Psychological and developmental assessment* (pp. 267–291). New York: Guilford Press.

Marcus, L. M., & Schopler, E. (1989). Parents as co-therapists with autistic children. In C. E. Schaefer & J. M. Briesmeister (Eds.), *Handbook of parent training: Parents as co-therapists for children's behavior problems* (pp. 337–360). New York: Wiley.

Marcus, L. M., Schopler, E., & Lord, C. (2000). TEACCH services for preschool children. In J. S. Handleman & S. L. Harris (Eds.), *Preschool education programs for children with autism* (2nd ed., pp. 215–232). Austin, TX: ProEd.

Marcus, L. M., & Stone, W. L. (1993). Assessment of the young autistic child. In E. Schopler, M. E. Van Bourgondien & M. M. Bristol (Eds.), *Preschool issues in autism* (pp. 149–173). New York: Plenum Press.

Marcus, L. M., Wertheimer, A., Clement, S., & Kuhr, R. (1995, July). *Support groups for parents of autistic children from preschool to adulthood.* Paper presented at the annual meeting of the Autism Society of America, Greensboro, NC.

McGoldrick, M., & Carter, B. (2003). The family life cycle. In F. Walsh (Ed.), *Normal family processes: Growing diversity and complexity* (3rd ed., pp. 375–398). New York: Guilford Press.

McHale, S. M., Sloan, J., & Simeonsson, R. J. (1986). Sibling relationships of children with autistic, mentally retarded, and nonhandicapped brothers and sisters. *Journal of Autism and Developmental Disorders, 16,* 399–413.

McMahon, R. J., & Wells, K. C. (1998). Conduct problems. In E. J. Mash & R. A. Barkley (Eds.), *Treatment of childhood disorders* (pp. 73–134). New York: Guilford Press.

Mesibov, G. B. (1983). Current perspectives and issues in autism and adolescence. In E. Schopler

& G. B. Mesibov (Eds.), *Autism in adolescents and adults* (pp. 37–53). New York: Plenum Press.

Mesibov, G. B. (1984). Social skills training with verbal autistic adolescents and adults: A program model. *Journal of Autism and Developmental Disorders, 14,* 395–404.

Mesibov, G. B. (1992). Treatment issues with high-functioning adolescents and adults with autism. In E. Schopler & G. B. Mesibov (Eds.), *High-functioning individuals with autism* (pp. 143–155). New York: Plenum Press.

Mesibov, G. B., Schopler, E., & Hearsey, K. (1994). Structured teaching. In E Schopler & G. B. Mesibov (Eds.), *Behavioral issues in autism* (pp. 195–207). New York: Plenum Press.

Mesibov, G. B., Schopler, E., & Sloan, J. L. (1983). Service development for adolescents and adults in North Carolina's TEACCH Program. In E. Schopler & G. B. Mesibov (Eds.), *Autism in adolescents and adults* (pp. 411–432). New York: Plenum Press.

Mesibov, G. B., & Shea, V. (1996). Full inclusion and students with autism. *Journal of Autism and Developmental Disorders, 26,* 337–346.

Meyer, D. J., & Vadasy, P. F. (1994). *Sibshops: Workshops for siblings of children with special needs.* Baltimore: Paul H. Brookes.

Micheli, E. (1999). A training group for parents of autistic children. *International Journal of Mental Health, 28,* 100–105.

Miller, J. N., & Ozonoff, S. (2000). The external validity of Asperger Disorder: Lack of evidence from the domain of neuropsychology. *Journal of Abnormal Psychology, 109,* 227–238.

Morgan, S. B. (1984). Helping parents understand the diagnosis of autism. *Developmental and Behavioral Pediatrics, 5,* 78–85.

National Research Council. (2001). *Educating children with autism* (Committee on Educational Interventions for Children with Autism, Commission on Behavioral and Social Sciences and Education). Washington, DC: National Academy Press.

New York State Department of Health Early Intervention Program. (1999). *Clinical practice guideline: Report of the recommendations. Autism/pervasive developmental disorders, assessment and intervention for young children (Age 0–3 years).* Retrieved August 2, 2003, from http://www.health.state.ny.us/nysdoh/eip/menu.htm.

Olsson, M. B., & Hwang, C. P. (2002). Sense of coherence in parents of children with different developmental disabilities. *Journal of Intellectual Disability Research, 46,* 548–559.

Ozonoff, S., & Cathcart, K. (1998). Effectiveness of a home program intervention for young children with autism. *Journal of Autism and Developmental Disorders, 28,* 25–32.

Ozonoff, S., Dawson, G., & McPartland, J. (2002). *A parent's guide to Asperger syndrome and high-functioning autism: How to meet the challenges and help your child thrive.* New York: Guilford Press.

Palmer, A., & Marcus, L. M. (1998, December). *Developing a parent mentoring program for families with children with autism.* Paper presented at the 10th annual Leo M. Croghan Conference, Raleigh, NC.

Park, C. (1982). *The siege.* Boston: Little, Brown.

Park, C. (2001). *Exiting Nirvana: A daughter's life with autism.* Boston: Little, Brown.

Patterson, G. (1982). *Coercive family process.* Eugene, OR: Castalia.

Perry, A., & Black, A. (1997). A prospective study of out-of-home placement tendency in families of children with autism. *Journal on Developmental Disabilities, 5,* 1–23.

Piven, J. (1999). Genetic liability for autism: The behavioural expression in relatives. *International Review of Psychiatry, 11,* 299–308.

Piven, J., Harper, J., Palmer, P., & Arndt, S. (1996). Course of behavioral change in autism: A retrospective study of high-IQ adolescents and adults. *Journal of the American Academy of Child and Adolescent Psychiatry, 35,* 523–529.

Powell, T. H., & Ogle, P. A. (1985). *Brothers and sisters: A special part of exceptional families.* Baltimore: Paul H. Brookes.

Randall, P., & Parker, J. (1999). *Supporting the families of children with autism.* Chichester, England: Wiley.

Reichler, R. J., & Schopler, E. (1976). Developmental therapy: A program model for providing individual services in the community. In E. Schopler & R. J. Reichler (Eds.), *Psychopathology and child development: Research and treatment* (pp. 347–372). New York: Plenum Press.

Roeyers, H., & Mycke, K. (1995). Siblings of a child with autism, with mental retardation and with a normal development. *Child: Care, Health and Development, 21,* 305–319.

Rogers, S. J., Ozonoff, S., & Maslin-Cole, C. (1993). Developmental aspects of attachment behavior in young children with pervasive developmental disorders. *Journal of the American Academy of Child and Adolescent Psychiatry, 32,* 1274–1282.

Sanders, M. R., & McFarland, M. (2000). Treatment of depressed mothers with disruptive children: A controlled evaluation of cognitive behavioral family intervention. *Behavior Therapy, 31,* 89–112.

Schopler, E. (1995). *Parent survival manual: A guide to crisis resolution in autism and related developmental disorders.* New York: Plenum Press.

Schopler, E. (1997). Implementation of TEACCH philosophy. In D. J. Cohen & F. R. Volkmar (Eds.), *Handbook of autism and pervasive developmental disorders* (2nd ed., pp. 767–795). New York: Wiley.

Schopler, E. (2001). Treatment for autism: From science to pseudo-science or anti-science. In E. Schopler, N. Yirmiya, C. Shulman, & L. M. Marcus (Eds.), *The research basis for autism intervention* (pp. 9–24). New York: Kluwer Academic/Plenum Press.

Schopler, E. (2002, September). *Forming the blueprint for TEACCH.* Proceedings of autism conference, Tokyo, Japan.

Schopler, E., Brehm, S., Kinsbourne, M., & Reichler, R. J. (1971). Effect of treatment structure on development in autistic children. *Archives of General Psychiatry, 24,* 415–421.

Schopler, E., & Mesibov, G. B. (1983). *Autism in adolescents and adult.* New York: Plenum Press.

Schopler, E., & Mesibov, G. B. (Eds.). (1987). *Neurobiological issues in autism.* New York: Plenum Press.

Schopler, E., & Mesibov, G. B. (2000). Crosscultural priorities in developing autism services. *International Journal of Mental Health, 29,* 3–21.

Schopler, E., Mesibov, G. B., & Hearsey, K. (1995). Structured teaching in the TEACCH system. In E. Schopler & G. B. Mesibov (Eds.), *Learning and cognition in autism* (pp. 243–268). New York: Plenum Press.

Schopler, E., Mesibov, G. B., Shigley, R. H., & Bashford, A. (1984). Helping autistic children through their parents: The TEACCH model. In E. Schopler & G. B. Mesibov (Eds.), *The effects of autism on the family* (pp. 65–81). New York: Plenum Press.

Schopler, E., & Reichler, R. J. (1971). Parents-as-cotherapists in the treatment of autistic children. In S. Chess & A. Thomas (Eds.), *Annual progress in child psychiatry and child development* (pp. 679–697). New York: Brunner/Mazel.

Schreibman, L., Koegel, R. L., Mills, D. L., & Burke, J. C. (1984). Training parent-child interactions. In E. Schopler & G. B. Mesibov (Eds.), *The effects of autism on the family* (pp. 187–205). New York: Plenum Press.

Schreibman, L., O'Neill, R. E., & Koegel, R. L. (1983). Behavioral training for siblings of autistic children. *Journal of Applied Behavior Analysis, 16,* 129–138.

Schuntermann, P. (2002). Pervasive developmental disorder and parental adaptation: Previewing and reviewing atypical development with parents in child psychiatric consultation. *Harvard Review of Psychiatry, 10,* 16–27.

Seligman, M., & Darling, R. B. (1997). *Ordinary families, special children: A systems approach to childhood disability.* New York: Guilford Press.

Seltzer, M. M., Krauss, M. W., Orsmond, G. I., & Vestal, C. (2001). Families of adolescents and adults with autism: Uncharted Territory. *International Review of Research in Mental Retardation, 23,* 267–294.

Sharpley, C. F., Bitsika, V., & Ephrimidis, B. (1997). Influence of gender, parental health, and perceived expertise of assistance upon stress, anxiety, and depression among parents of children with autism. *Journal of Intellectual and Developmental Disability, 22,* 19–28.

Shea, V. (1993). Interpreting results to parents of preschoolers. In E. Schopler, M. E. Van Bourgondien, & M. M. Bristol (Eds.), *Preschool issues in autism* (pp. 185–198). New York: Plenum Press.

Sheinkopf, S. J., & Siegel, A. (1998). Home-based behavioral treatment of young children with autism. *Journal of Autism and Developmental Disorders, 28,* 15–23.

Sheridan, S. M. (1997). Conceptual and empirical bases of conjoint behavioral consultation. *School Psychology Quarterly, 12,* 119–133.

Siegel, B. (1997). Coping with the diagnosis of autism. In D. J. Cohen & F. R. Volkmar (Eds.), *Handbook of autism and pervasive developmental disorders* (2nd ed., pp. 745–766). New York: Wiley.

Singer, G. H. S., & Powers, L. E. (1993). Contributing to resilience in families: An overview. In G. H. S. Singer & L. E. Powers (Eds.), *Families, disability, and empowerment: Active coping skills and strategies for family interventions* (pp. 1–25). Baltimore: Paul H. Brookes.

Smith, B., Chung, M. C., & Vostanis, P. (1994). The path to care in autism: Is it better now? *Journal of Autism and Developmental Disorders, 24,* 551–563.

Smith, C., Perou, R., & Lesesne, C. (2002). Parent Education. In M. H. Bornstein (Ed.), *Handbook of parenting: Vol. 4. Social conditions and applied parenting* (2nd ed., pp. 389–410). Mahwah, NJ: Erlbaum.

Smith, M., Belcher, R., & Johrs, P. (1997). *A guide to successful employment for individuals with autism.* Baltimore: Paul H. Brookes.

Smith, T., & Antolovich, M. (2000). Parental perceptions of supplemental interventions received by young children with autism in intensive behavior analytic treatment. *Behavioral Interventions, 15,* 83–97.

Sofronoff, K., & Farbotko, M. (2002). The effectiveness of parent management training to increase self-efficacy in parents of children with Asperger syndrome. *Autism: Journal of Research and Practice, 6,* 271–286.

Stoiber, K. C., & Kratochwill, T. R. (2000). Empirically supported interventions and school psychology: Rationale and methodological issues—Part I. *School Psychology Quarterly, 15,* 75–105.

Strain, P. S., & Danko, C. D. (1995). Caregivers' encouragement of positive interaction between preschoolers with autism and their siblings. *Journal of Emotional and Behavioral Disorders, 3,* 2–12.

Szatmari, P. (2000). The classification of autism, Asperger's syndrome, and pervasive developmental disorder. *Canadian Journal of Psychiatry, 45,* 731–738.

Taylor, B. A., Levin, L., & Jasper, S. (1999). Increasing play-related statements in children with autism toward their siblings: Effects of video modeling. *Journal of Developmental and Physical Disabilities, 11,* 253–265.

Tobing, L. E., & Glenwick, D. S. (2002). Relation of the Childhood Autism Rating Scale-Parent version to diagnosis, stress, and age. *Research in Developmental Disabilities, 23,* 211–223.

Tonge, B., Brereton, A., & King, N. (2004, March). *A parent education and skills training early intervention for children with autism.* Paper presented at the Gatlinburg Conference on Research and Theory in Intellectual and Developmental Disabilities, San Diego, CA.

Toth, S. L., Maughan, A., Manly, J. T., Spagnola, M., & Cicchetti, D. (2002). The relative efficacy of two interventions in altering maltreated preschool children's representational models: Implications for attachment theory. *Development and Psychopathology, 14,* 877–908.

Tunali, B., & Power, R. (2002). Coping by redefinition: Cognitive appraisals in mothers of children with autism and children without autism. *Journal of Autism and Developmental Disorders, 32,* 25–34.

Turnbull, H. R., Turnbull, A. P., Bronicki, G. J., Summers, J. A., & Roeder-Gordon, C. (1989). *Disability and the family: A guide to decisions for adulthood.* Baltimore: Paul H. Brookes.

Van Bourgondien, M. E., & Reichle, N. C. (2001). Evaluating treatment effects for adolescents and adults with autism in residential settings. In E. Schopler, N. Yirmiya, C. Shulman, & L. M. Marcus (Eds.), *The research basis for autism intervention* (pp. 187–198). New York: Kluwer Academic/Plenum Press.

Van Bourgondien, M. E., Reichle, N. C., & Palmer, A. (1997). Sexual behavior in adults with autism. *Journal of Autism and Developmental Disorders, 27,* 113–125.

Venter, A., Lord, C., & Schopler, E. (1992). A follow-up study of high-functioning autistic children. *Journal of Child Psychology and Psychiatry, 33,* 489–507.

Volkmar, F. R., Cook, E. H., Jr., & Pomeroy, J. (1999). Practice parameters for the assessment and treatment of children, adolescents, and adults with autism and other pervasive developmental disorders. *Journal of the American Academy of Child and Adolescent Psychiatry, 38,* 32S–54S.

Ward, M. J., & Meyer, R. N. (1999). Self-determination for people with developmental disabilities and autism: Two self-advocates' perspectives. *Focus on Autism and Other Developmental Disabilities, 14,* 133–139.

Webster-Stratton, C., & Herbert, M. (1993). What really happens in parent training? *Behavior Modification, 17,* 407–456.

Webster-Stratton, C., Reid, M. J., & Hammond, M. (2001). Preventing conduct problems, promoting social competence: A parent and teacher training partnership in Head Start. *Journal of Clinical Child Psychology, 30,* 283–302.

Whitaker, P. (2002). Supporting families of preschool children with autism: What parents want and what helps. *Autism: Journal of Research and Practice, 6,* 411–426.

Williams, P. D. (1997). Siblings and pediatric chronic illness: A review of the literature. *International Journal of Nursing Studies, 34,* 312–323.

Williams, P. D., Williams, A. R., Graff, J. C., Hanson, S., Stanton, A., Hafeman, C., et al. (2002). Interrelationships among variables affecting well siblings and mothers in families of children with a chronic illness or disability. *Journal of Behavioral Medicine, 25,* 411–424.

Wing, L. (1976). Diagnosis, clinical description, and prognosis. In L. Wing (Ed.), *Early child autism* (2nd ed., pp. 15–64). New York: Pergamon Press.

Wing, L. (1989). The continuum of autistic characteristics. In E. Schopler & G. B. Mesibov (Eds.), *Diagnosis and assessment in autism* (pp. 91–110). New York: Plenum Press.

Wolf, L., Fisman, S., Ellison, D., & Freeman, T. (1998). Effect of sibling perception of differential parental treatment in sibling dyads with one disabled child. *Journal of the American Academy of Child and Adolescent Psychiatry, 37,* 1317–1325.

Yeargin-Allsopp, M., Rice, C., Karapurkar, T., Doernberg, N., Boyle, C., & Murphy, C. (2003). Prevalence of autism in a US metropolitan area. *Journal of the American Medical Association, 289,* 49–55.

Yirmiya, N., Shaked, M., & Erel, O. (2001). Comparison of siblings of individuals with autism and siblings of individuals with other diagnoses: An empirical summary. In E. Schopler, N. Yirmiya, C. Shulman, & L. M. Marcus (Eds.), *The research basis for autism intervention* (pp. 59–73). New York: Kluwer Academic/Plenum Press.

CHAPTER 43

Employment: Options and Issues for Adolescents and Adults with Autism Spectrum Disorders

PETER F. GERHARDT AND DAVID L. HOLMES

I first met Max, a young adult with autism spectrum disorder (ASD), about 10 years ago at a meeting regarding developing services for him. "So tell me, Max," I said after the introductions were completed, "what type of job do you think you would like?" He thought for a moment and then proceeded to describe what he envisioned as the perfect job. "First," he said, "I don't want to get up early. Second, I don't want to sweat." He thought a minute longer, then added, "Oh yeah, and I want to make a lot of money." Fine, I thought, he wants the same job as I do.

It should come as no surprise that children with ASD grow up to become adults with ASD. However, only recently have we begun to actually consider the myriad issues that may either contribute to or challenge what constitutes the process of adulthood for learners with ASD.

Adulthood, as discussed in this chapter, needs to be understood as more than just a chronological state. Adulthood represents a time in an individual's life where there are increased levels of independence, choice, and personal control. Further, adulthood is generally recognized as a period of increased responsibility, commitment, and, more often than not, delayed gratification. It is during this time of life that we generally experience our greatest successes as well as some of our greatest difficulties. Adulthood, despite some popular perceptions, is a time of continued growth and learning and not a period of

stagnation and is, in many ways, the defining period of a person's life. We may look back fondly on our childhood, but it is our accomplishments as adults for which we are generally most proud. Adulthood for the adult with ASD should be viewed as no different.

Until recently, the focus of intervention with adults with ASD has been on developing, shaping, or increasing socially valid skills while decreasing socially challenging or problematic behaviors. However, as put to the primary author at a meeting of a support group for high-functioning adults with ASD: "If you neurotypicals (NTs) have all the skills, why don't you adapt for a while?" The not-so-subtle implication is that reasonable targets for intervention exist beyond the persons themselves, if increasing levels of societal inclusion are indeed the goal.

As part of this discussion, the tendency to focus intervention strategies solely on intervening with the person with ASD was placed in contrast to how no one, generally, spends a significant amount of time trying to teach a person who is blind to read a page of printed text. Instead, the focus is on the modification of the task (i.e., braille or electronic readers), direct instruction in the modified task, and community education (obtaining an electronic reader for use on the job, providing coworking information, etc.) to the benefit of all concerned. By expanding the sphere of intervention beyond the individual, it was explained, more effective and, importantly, efficient interventions can be developed in support of both the individual with ASD and those with whom they may interact.

Consider the difference between a disability and a handicap. A disability can be understood as permanent reduction in the function of a particular body part or structure. A handicap, on the other hand, is defined by the challenges that the disability presents to the individual's participation in desired, life-relevant activities. Any system of intervention or support needs, first, to identify those individual, environmental, instructional, and community conditions under which ASD may present an individual learner with challenges that result in a "handicap." Then, as a function of this assessment, the adult with ASD becomes one target of intervention among a variety of targets (e.g., coworkers, cashiers, modifications to job requirements or the physical environment, the provision of community training and support) designed to support increasingly greater levels of personal independence and social and vocational competence.

A word of caution: This perspective on supporting adults is sometimes misinterpreted as supporting a system of services or supports that provide little in the way of active instruction to the adult learner with ASD. Nothing can be further from the truth. What it does mean is that as individuals age out of the educational system, many targets for instruction and support emerge in addition to the learners themselves. For example, while it is a simple matter to teach a waiter to accept a written (or graphic) order from a nonverbal diner, teaching the same waiter to casually accept this same person eating with his or her hands would be both extremely difficult and situationally inappropriate. Independent of who we are or what we do, there exist certain culturally determined standards of acceptable behavior that we are expected to meet if we are to be accepted into the community at large. For that reason, and independent of other interventions, attention to skill development never stops.

THE ISSUE OF EMPLOYMENT

In the United States, participation in employment and the resulting job-related social status and increased financial independence are generally seen as integral components of an individual's postschool life (Grandin & Duffy, 2004; Inge, Banks, Wehman, Hill, & Shafer, 1988; Kiernan & Stark, 1986a; Levy, 1983). For better or worse, what we do for a living is one way in which we define ourselves and attempt to define others. For example, within minutes of meeting someone new, most of us will ask, "What do you do for a living?" (unless the person responsible for the introduction has already told us that "John is a teacher" or "Susan is an accountant" or "Bill is a bartender"). The importance we place on whether an individual is employed and, if so, at what, cannot be underestimated.

Unfortunately, for most adults with disabilities, employment remains elusive. According to a recent poll conducted by Lewis Harris and Associates (2002):

- Up to 75% of all people with disabilities are unemployed.
- 79% of all people with disabilities who are unemployed wish to be employed.
- Approximately 50% of working-age people with disabilities who are unemployed believe employers are not sensitive to the need of workers with disabilities.

These results reflect a diverse mix of people with varying disabilities and may, unfortunately, be somewhat optimistic as to the level of employment for persons with ASD. The significant social, communicative, behavioral, and learning challenges associated with ASD present the individual, the family, the employer, and support personnel with any number of complex challenges (e.g., Burt, Fuller, & Lewis, 1991). Peraino (1992) and, more recently, Howlin, Goode, Hutton, and Rutter (2004) note that despite increased attention to post-21 employment outcomes (e.g., Kemp & Carr, 1995; Rogan, Banks, & Howard, 2000; Shields-Wolfe & Gallagher, 1992; Unger, 1999), poor employment achievement continues to be the norm, rather than the exception, for adult learners with ASD.

This does not mean that persons with ASD cannot and should not have greater access, support, and success in the employment arena. What it does mean, however, is that there is a "disconnect" between what research indicates is possible in terms of employment support for adult learners with ASD and the services currently being provided. Further, there appears to be a critical need to revisit the way in which such learners are prepared for life beyond the classroom, in the community, and on the job. Some considerations toward that end are presented later in this chapter.

HISTORICAL OVERVIEW

During the latter part of the nineteenth and earlier part of the twentieth centuries, the public perception of individuals with disabilities as generally nonproductive and best suited for custodial care resulted in the growth of institutions as the primary service system for persons with mental retardation and other disabilities (Janicki, Castellani, & Norris, 1983). Individuals with ASD, with their myriad behavior, learning, and social idiosyncrasies, were among the many who were routinely placed in such custodial settings (Holmes, 1990; Sullivan, 1981) with little or no voice in the matter or opportunity for proactive programming once placed.

By the late 1960s, the deinstitutionalization movement was gaining professional and popular acceptance, and the movement from the institution to the community had begun (Mesibov, 1990). However, while an understanding of the needs of individuals with mental retardation may have entered a new era, the needs of persons with ASD remained unaddressed (Schopler & Hennick, 1990). The bulk of literature available at that time focused primarily on theoretical perspectives of etiology and classification of ASD (Celiberti, Alessandri, Fong, & Gill, 1993). With the critical exception of the debate about psychodynamic models of intervention (Rimland, 1964) and the noteworthy early investigations into the efficacy of behavioral systems of learning (e.g., Ferster & DeMyer, 1962; Lovaas & Simmons, 1969), the treatment literature at this time was hard to come by and, in the case of psychodynamic interventions (Bettleheim, 1967), misdirected and, ultimately, harmful.

Celiberti et al. (1993), in their review of the behavioral treatment literature, note that it was not until the mid- to late-1970s that a more comprehensive body of literature specifically devoted to addressing the educational and behavioral needs of children with ASD came into being. From these early investigations (e.g., Carr, Binkoff, Kologinsky, & Eddy, 1978; Solnick, Rincover, & Peterson, 1977) came the basis for our understanding of many of the systems of education, training, and support currently in use today (e.g., the use of applied behavior analysis in the classroom).

As the cohort of children referenced in these early studies aged out of educational services, the attention of the families, interested professionals, and, most importantly, the individuals themselves turned to issues relevant to adulthood. Despite a tendency to view these "new adults" with ASD as larger versions of the children with whom there may have been a degree of comfort and familiarity, they obviously were not (Markowitz, Gerhardt, Christopher, Christopher, & McKean, 1994). Subsequently, service delivery entered a new phase: the recognition of differing needs of individuals with ASD across the life span (e.g., Holmes, 1998).

As part of this new attention to life span issues, the 1980s saw a national emphasis on the school-to-work transition process for all special needs learners (e.g., Lagomarcino & Rusch, 1987; Will, 1984). The recognition of the appropriateness and subsequent benefits of employment for many individuals with disabilities during this time prompted nationwide development of a variety of supported employment initiatives intended to provide individuals with severe disabilities access to the world of work. This process continues today.

Unfortunately, despite the growing recognition of the employment-related needs and abilities of adolescents and adults with ASD, the development of employment-related services for persons with ASD continues to lag far behind those currently available for persons with less severe disabilities (Kregel & Wehman, 1989; Mank, 1994; Wehman & Kregel, 1988). This disparity between what can be done and what is being done in terms of services for adults with ASD represents an ongoing challenge to the field.

LEGISLATION

It is lamentable that there are no federal laws or regulations designed to specifically address the needs and rights of adolescents and adults with ASD in the vocational and employment arena. These specific concerns are generally subsumed under the laws that provide personal and systemic protection for individuals with disabilities in general (Kaplan & Moore, 1989). Included in this cadre of relevant disability legislation are: (1) the Individuals with Disabilities Education Act (PL 105-17), (2) the Vocational Rehabilitation Act of 1973 (PL 93-112) and its subsequent amendments (1988, 1992), and (3) the Americans with Disabilities Act (PL 101-336). While other legislative initiatives exist (e.g., Perkins Vocational Education Act and the Job Training Partnership Act), their impact on services for individuals with ASD has proven to be somewhat less extensive than for these three legislative initiatives.

The Individuals with Disabilities Education Act

In 1975, congress passed the Education of all Handicapped Children Act (PL 94-142), which mandated that all children with disabilities are to be provided a free appropriate public education in the least restrictive environment. Later reauthorized in 1990 as the Individuals with Disabilities Education Act (IDEA; PL 101-476) and again in 1997 (PL 105-17), one of the law's primary purposes is to ensure that systems are in place to effectively prepare special needs learners for postgraduation employment and independent living.

To this end, IDEA includes wording requiring that the provision of transition planning and subsequent services be part of a student's individualized education program (IEP) beginning as early as an individual's 14th, and no later than his or her 16th, birthday. Section 300.29 of IDEA defines *transition services* as a "coordinated set of activities for a student with a disability that is designed within an outcome-oriented process that promotes movement from school to postschool activities including postsecondary education, vocational training, integrated employment (including supported employment), continuing and adult education, adult services, independent living, or community participation." Further, transition planning is to be based on an individual student's needs, taking into account the student's preferences and interests, and includes the development of employment and other

postschool adult living objectives and, if appropriate, acquisition of daily living skills and functional vocational evaluation.

As to future employment, of primary importance is that IDEA requires transition planning to be an "outcome-oriented process," based on the anticipated demands of the postschool environment. Previously, secondary special education tended to rely more on the continued provision of skill training in activities that may have been of more use in the classroom than in the adult life (e.g., Brown, Nietupski, & Hamre-Nietupski, 1976). While potentially producing successful students, successful graduates often failed to materialize. Outcome-oriented transition planning incorporates the needs of the learner and the demands of the next environment so that more effective transition planning may be undertaken and employment an increasingly realistic outcome.

IDEA is the legislative architect of school-based responsibility for the provision of transition planning. In addition, IDEA has served to highlight the need for transition services to be developed and provided in a comprehensive, thoughtful, and consumer-based manner and has stimulated greater public and professional awareness of the issues surrounding transition planning. The practical impact of functional transition planning as mandated by IDEA will continue to be seen in the coming years, as greater numbers of learners with ASD graduate from a system mandated by law to more effectively meet their postschool needs.

The Vocational Rehabilitation Act of 1973

The Vocational Rehabilitation Act of 1973 provided access for individuals with disabilities to any program, service, or activity receiving federal funds. One component in particular, Section 504 of the Vocational Rehabilitation Act, is known as the "Bill of Rights" for individuals with disabilities as a result of its strong, antidiscrimination language. In 1986, Congress authorized a set of amendments (PL 99-506) to the Rehabilitation Act, which, by including language on the importance of transition and transition services, "offered a major avenue of transition opportunity for young adults" (Wehman, 1992, p. 10). In particular, Title I of PL 99-506 specifically allowed states to fund supported employment services from the basic state grant program. More recently, the Rehabilitation Act Amendments of 1992 (PL 102-569) codified the assumption of employability regardless of the severity of the disability and removed time limits on supports provided under the legislation's state grant program (Smith, Belcher, & Juhrs, 1995).

The Americans with Disabilities Act

The Americans with Disabilities Act (ADA; PL 101-336) has been called the "capstone" to a public policy promoting access and participation by people with disabilities within their community (Ward, 1992). Under ADA, individuals with disabilities cannot be discriminated against in the areas of employment, transportation, public accommodations, public services, and telecommunications. According to the employment provisions, employers are unable to discriminate, on the basis of a disability, against potentially qualified employees. In addition, employers are required by law to provide "reasonable accommodations" to workers who are able, with such accommodations, to perform the essential functions of the job.

The impact of ADA on the employment of individuals with ASD remains to be seen. Far greater public attention has been paid to issues associated with the access and accommodation of persons with physical disabilities than those with more neurological or behavioral disabilities such as ASD. While physical accessibility standards exist and are enforced, questions as to what may constitute a reasonable accommodation for a person with ASD (e.g., flex time, more/less frequent breaks, modified production standards) remain unanswered (and can, in actuality, be answered only on a case-by-case basis). While ADA represents a great move forward in the protection of persons with disabilities from discriminatory practices, the extent to which this protection has benefited persons with ASD remains undocumented.

Summary

Federal legislation in the form of IDEA mandates the provision of school-to-work transition services for all individuals with ASD beginning as early as age 14. Beyond that, however, both the Vocational Rehabilitation Act and ADA mandate only equal access and not the provision of necessary services and supports once access is obtained. Equal access, then, should be viewed as only half the battle. What would appear to be essential is some form of employment services legislation, whereby funding is made available so that individuals with ASD and other disabilities may take full advantage of the access granted them as citizens by ADA and the Vocational Rehabilitation Act.

THE SCHOOL-TO-WORK TRANSITION PROCESS

IDEA, as discussed earlier, provides for functional transition planning to support the movement of the individual learner from school-age services and supports to the postschool world of work, living, and adult services and supports. At issue, then, is what constitutes functional transition planning for individuals with ASD. Berkell (1992) cites several potential challenges relevant to the provision of transition services to individuals with ASD. Among these are high anticipated costs due to anticipated lower teacher to student ratios; societal misperceptions about the nature and needs of individuals with ASD; the need for, in many cases, intensive social/communication skills and behavior management training; and concerns about personnel preparation.

In terms of shared needs, several authors (e.g., Rusch, DeStefano, Chadsey-Rusch, Phelps, & Szymanski, 1992; Steere, Wood, Pancsofar, & Rucker, 1993; Wehman, Kregel, & Barcus, 1985) have written on the overall importance of the transition process in obtaining desired postsecondary outcomes. Wehman et al., in discussing the essential components of a functional transition, emphasize the importance of developing a formal, comprehensive transition plan that incorporates input from both the individual and his or her family and delineates the steps necessary for effective interagency cooperation. Comprehensive planning, the authors contend, is so important that failure to develop a comprehensive plan functionally negates the potential significance of all other aspects of transition services.

Stowitschek (1992), in his review of the literature on transition planning, presents a consensus list of best practices in transition planning. Practices noted can generally be grouped together along the lines of relating to: (1) transition planning, (2) transition implementation, or (3) transition evaluation. Included in transition planning are the development of appropriate long-term goals and short-term objectives, the development of a plan to ensure eligibility for posttransition services, the provision of case management services, and the development of a time line for transition activities. Implementation items cited by Stowitschek include the provision of appropriate vocational, leisure, and residential options; transportation training; money management training; and vocationally relevant social skills training. Long-term support and follow-up of the transition process and specific outcome evaluations (as appropriate to each transition program) comprise the evaluatory component of the transition process.

Planning and Coordination

Referring again to the issue of comprehensive planning and interagency coordination (e.g., DeStefano & Wermuth, 1992; Foley, Butterworth, & Heller, 2000; Snauwaert, 1992; Wehman et al., 1985), a practical dilemma presents itself: To what is the learner with ASD transitioning? As noted by Lagomarcino and Rusch (1987), even the best school-based employment development programs will not benefit students if they do not coordinate their activities beyond the school years. Although some states have recognized the importance of the adult services component of transition planning (Wehman, 1991), issues relating to the availability of post-21 (i.e., post-IDEA) funds, the length of service(s) available, and the degree of individualization and appropriateness of available services remain unresolved. In many states, waiting lists for postgraduation services act as barriers to the continuation of transition programming to its desired employment outcome (Moore, 1994; Thomas & Halloran, 1987). The best planning cannot overcome the prospect of nothing on the other side of transition.

Recognizing the concerns generated by the lack of a post-21 mandate for services, Bates, Bronkema, Ames, and Hess (1992) state that the "focus [of transition] must be on assisting agencies to work more efficiently in coordination with one another" (p. 128). The authors note that, as a general rule, state agencies tend to act as isolated entities and not as cooperative units. As a result, the complexities of transition, especially for those with more complex needs, are not fully addressed, and strategies that are developed may be destined for failure.

The authors cite several steps as integral to the resolution of this challenge. The development of a state interagency transition committee, composed of representatives from all concerned agencies, with the mission of identifying and resolving areas of concern and/or competition between agencies, is discussed as a first but important step. As a product of this committee, formal, written agreements outlining interagency responsibilities in the transition process need to be developed and enforced by member agencies. Last, Bates et al. (1992) contend that comprehensive statewide assessments of transition needs and resources need to be completed with special attention to the degree to which individual needs may or may not be met by existing specialized and generic services. Thus, generally scarce resources may be directed to those areas of most critical need, and the duplication of existing services is avoided. By enacting such steps, the question, "To what are learners with ASD transitioning?" may be more readily answered.

The Role of the Family

Several authors have written on the important role of the family in effective educational programming (Iovannone, Dunlap, Huber, & Kincaid, 2003) and the transition-to-work process (Brotherson et al., 1988; Hosack & Malkmus, 1992; Irvin, Thorin, & Singer, 1993; Turnbull & Turnbull, 1988). Fully acknowledging the importance of parental involvement, Wehman (1991) asserted that while parents are not excluded, neither have they, in many cases, come "fully on board" (p. 7) with the transition process. Restricted parental involvement, whether due to limited access, restrictions placed on the family by the school or school district, competing demands for parental time, or fear of "rocking the boat," presents a significant challenge to comprehensive transition planning. Beyond their personal knowledge of and relationship with their son or daughter, many parents of learners with ASD are well versed in the current state of ASD research, services, and supports through their attendance at conferences, subscription to journals, and reading of relevant texts (Gerhardt, Mannion, Weidenbaum, Andretta, & Wallace, 2003). As a result, any reduction in parent involvement denies the transition team access to valuable information about the individual learner in question and, in many cases, an educated colleague. As such, steps need to be taken to encourage a family's active participation in, and support of, the transition-to-work process for their son or daughter (Sowers & Powers, 1991).

Perhaps the most important role, among many, that parents and family members can play in the transition-to-work process is their continuing role as the advocate for their child (Freidlander, 1989). It can be argued that in the advocacy process, the voice of one insistent parent is louder and often more effective than that of 10 professionals. Despite a multitude of new stressors that may appear as their child enters the transition years (e.g., an unfamiliarity with the adult system of services and supports; the potential inability of this system to meet the needs of their, now, nearly adult child; and the stress associated with life cycle transitions in general [Brotherson et al., 1988] and uncertainty about the future [Fong, Wilgosh, & Sobsey, 1993]), the need for parents to forcefully advocate on behalf of their son or daughter does not, in most instances, diminish with age. In point of fact, given the systemic challenges that they and their child with ASD will face in the transition process, the need for parental advocacy may be even more critical than it had previously been. From ensuring the provision of job sampling services to the development, to the extent possible, of interagency cooperative planning, the role that parent support, input, and advocacy plays is critical.

Summary

While there has been a good degree of attention to the transition needs and process of and for special needs learners in general (Snauwaert, 1992), much still needs to be done. Comprehensive planning needs to include the learner with ASD, parents, teachers,

and representatives from all concerned agencies. Given the often complex and long-term needs of many individuals with ASD, of particular importance is the development and maintenance of systems of interagency cooperation to best provide for a continuity of services on the other side of transition. Practical considerations for the transitioning learner with ASD include the provision of structured community experience, community-referenced behavior management and social skills training (Berkell, 1992), and the incorporation of individual choice in the job development process (Winking, O'Reilly, & Moon, 1993).

Unfortunately, despite the best efforts and intentions of many schools to provide transition programming, the process, in many cases, remains incomplete with employment remaining a clearly defined but functionally unobtainable goal. As such, if the transition planning requirement of IDEA is to be consistently and effectively implemented, the discrepancy between legislative intent and systemic practice needs to be fully resolved so that the necessary resources and services are more readily available on the terminal side of transition.

CURRENT SERVICE MODELS

While employment is generally the goal of all models of adult services, an argument can be made (e.g., Holmes, 1989) that no single model of service delivery would be adequate to meet the needs of all individuals with ASD. Current program options include supported employment, entrepreneurial supports, secure employment training, and sheltered workshops.

Supported Employment

Supported employment can generally be defined as "an employment option that recognizes the capacity of the adult with developmental disabilities while acknowledging his or her need for ongoing support" (Kiernan & Stark, 1986b, p. 109). Over the past decade, increasing numbers of individuals with developmental disabilities, including ASD (e.g., Burt, Fuller, & Lewis, 1991; Kregel, 1999; Smith et al., 1995, Wehman & Kregel, 1988), have obtained employment within the general workforce through supported employment initiatives (Revell, Wehman, Kregel, West, & Rayfield, 1994). Among the reasons most often cited for this increase are changing societal perceptions of the employability of individuals with disabilities (Hopkins, 1992), improved employment assessment processes (Menchetti & Flynn, 1990), the noted emphasis on school-to-work transitions (Lagomarcino & Rusch, 1987), the development of increasingly sophisticated employment strategies (Buckley, Mank, & Sandow, 1990), a heightened awareness of the role that social competence plays in the maintenance of employment (Herbert & Ishikawa, 1991), and the reported cost efficiency of supported employment as a service option (Tines, Rusch, Mc-Caughrin, & Conley, 1990).

Models of Supported Employment

Rusch and Hughes (1990) describe four models of supported employment placement that are applicable to individuals with ASD. They are the (1) individual placement model, (2) clustered placement or enclave model, (3) mobile crew, and (4) entrepreneurial model, which is discussed separately. In the individual placement model, a job coach works to develop a job for an individual with a disability within a private sector enterprise. Intensive on-site training and support provided by the job coach in a one-to-one setting are subsequently faded as job competencies increase, freeing up the job coach to "job-develop" for another individual. In general, social integration is high in the individual placement model as is the degree of individuality. Troublesome, however, is the desire to fade support over a relatively brief time period. This would, in effect, eliminate all but the most able individuals from participation in the individualized placement model. A modification of the model to provide the long-term individualized supports often required by persons with ASD would present a much more functional application.

The clustered or enclave model requires that, instead of one individual, the job coach now works to support a small group of individuals (usually two to six) with disabilities at a private sector location. Job coach support is generally provided for the length of employment, although more intensive supervision may

be faded over time. Social integration may be high, but limitations associated with the physical setup of a clustered placement may restrict more normalized interactions. For this reason, the clustered model has been criticized as being a "private sector sheltered workshop" and perhaps less ideal than the individual placement model for some individuals.

Similar to clustered placements, mobile crews generally consist of a small number of individuals who provide an agreed-on level of contracted services (e.g., office cleaning) throughout a specific geographical area. Due to the nature of many of the services offered by mobile crews and the fact that many of these jobs are generally accomplished during times when few people may be working, the level of social integration tends to be somewhat limited under this model.

Entrepreneurial Supports

Entrepreneurial supports involve the development and promotion of a business entity, sometimes referred to as a self-directed support corporation (Center for Self-Determination, 2004) around a very limited number of individuals. In this model, the skills and interests of the individual[s] are used as the basis to form a for-profit corporation, the intent of which is to generate sufficient income to pay the salary of not only the individual but also the individual's support staff. Entrepreneurial models generally require the development of a governing microboard (a small, functional board formed to support an individual learner), consisting of family members, support personnel, community members, and, ideally, at least one member with experience running a for-profit business. As with any small business, start-up costs may be high, but future earned income is generally expected to offset these early expenses. Along with potentially high start-up costs, a challenge to the expanded use of the entrepreneurial model is that, as with any business venture, there is no guarantee of short- or long-term profitability. As such, investments may not be recouped, and the necessary supports for the adult with ASD may not materialize. While the entrepreneurial model was initially discussed as an option for those individuals with "the most severe disabilities who require intensive, continuous supervision" (Rusch, 1990, p. 10), this would appear to be dependent on the nature and needs of the developed business.

Secure Employment

Holmes (1989, 1998), proposes an approach to employment-related services, which he refers to as "secure employment" (Holmes, 1989, p. 263). Tenets of this system include a commitment to (1) individualized assessments, planning, and services; (2) increasingly less restrictive environments and increasingly more normalized life experiences; (3) the provision of a personally compatible physical environment; (4) the provision of remedial programming to the extent necessary; (5) supporting appropriate behavior across environments; and (6) a lifetime of continually evolving services designed to meet changing needs.

Holmes (1998) describes the hallmark of secure employment as being its ecobehavioral approach to employment-related services for individuals with ASD. Individuals are able to participate in a variety of employment (subcontracted, supported, and competitive) and/or employment development and training activities (e.g., from personal hygiene training to the development of appropriate interviewing skills [Holmes et al., 1994]) within a system designed to meet their particular needs at their particular point in life. Further, the author argues for a commitment to life span services and a continuum of services to provide a "safety net" (Holmes, 1989, p. 261) by which concerns such as job loss or the challenges associated with aggressive behavior do not result in a loss of services.

The secure employment paradigm, with its multiple options including supported and competitive employment and individualized approach to employment development and support, appears to be a viable option for those individuals with ASD and their families who value the employment security and life span commitment that this model offers.

Sheltered Workshops

Levy (1983), in discussing the appropriateness of the sheltered workshop or activity center-based

program for individuals with ASD, argues that concerns about the lack of functional work tasks and employment training, little if any attention to training beyond the skills for minimal production, and insufficient levels of staff training and expertise may result in the sheltered workshop being a less than desirable option for many individuals with ASD. Others (Bellamy, Rhodes, Bourbeau, & Mank, 1986; Gold, 1975) claim that, in addition, sheltered workshops tend to function more as final placements for individuals with disabilities rather than as the transitional service (to a less restrictive employment placement) that they were meant to be. Perhaps more importantly, critics such as Moore (1994) and Gerhardt and Markowitz (1993) argue that the sheltered workshop system appears to be a system geared more toward the fostering of dependence within a tightly supervised, nontherapeutic environment rather than toward encouraging independence in the less supervised community at large.

Although still common, the appropriateness of the sheltered workshop for many people with ASD is in question. Concerns with sheltered workshops are apparently twofold. First, the apparent lack of training and supports prevents sheltered employees from moving beyond the physical and social confines of the workshop. Second, the basic design of the sheltered workshop—large numbers of persons with disabilities, isolated from more normalized daily events and interactions, working on repetitive tasks with limited reinforcement or supervision—simply does not appear to offer an optimal program model for individuals with ASD if the prospect of continued personal growth and the development of real employment opportunities are the accepted goals of adult services for persons with ASD (Gerhardt & Markowitz, 1993).

Summary

A number of viable services models designed to offer employment training and support to adults with ASD are noted in the literature. However, adult learners with ASD continued to be unemployed and/or underemployed at levels far greater than should be possible or desirable. Limited access to appropriate services continues to represent a significant challenge to correcting the noted disconnect, the potential for desirable employment outcomes, and the achievement of the same. In addition, the assumption of some adult learners as inherently more employable (perhaps as a function of IQ or the absence of challenging behavior) than others may unnecessarily restrict access to employment for a large number of potential successful employees.

RECOMMENDATIONS TOWARD GREATER EMPLOYABILITY

The following recommendations are intended to help promote a broader, professional definition of employability and, thereby, promote more positive occupational outcomes.

Consider All Adults to Be Employable

If we consider all adult learners to be employable, the concept of *work readiness* needs to be redefined. Historically, work readiness has been used to describe a cohort of skills that were considered prerequisites for employment success. These might include extended time on task, the absence of challenging behavior, some degree of social competence, conversational skills, and so on. Unfortunately, this arbitrary standard of competence has inadvertently excluded far more people with ASD from the workforce than it has helped gain access. For example, if we acknowledge that, in the United States, many of the basic skills necessary to have and keep a job are best learned while on the job (hence the phrase "on-the-job training"), the previous definition of work readiness places many individuals with ASD in a Catch 22 type of situation. In brief, it seems you can't get a job because you don't have the skills, and you can't learn the skills because you can't get a job, but you can't get a job because you don't . . . and so on.

Therefore, a redefining of the concept of work readiness to acknowledge all persons with ASD as being potentially viable candidates for employment is in order. Once acknowledged, a more appropriate and functional transition plan consisting, in part, of community-based instruction and experience, job sampling, social coaching, transportation training, functional communication, and

instruction in self-management strategies can be implemented for all learners, not just for some whose learning curve may be shorter or behavioral challenges may be fewer.

View First Jobs as Learning Experiences and Not Final Placements

For very few adults, their first job turns out to be their dream job. Most adults go through a series of jobs—some bad, some good—on the way to finding something that more closely meets their definition of a good job. The same process should prove of value for learners with ASD. First jobs are simply first jobs and, more often than not, they are not ideal jobs. First jobs are important, though, because they are where adult learners with ASD can begin to: (1) develop the skills necessary to keep and hold a job, (2) develop a sense of which types of jobs and job conditions are best for them, and (3) increase their level of community involvement and standing.

Thus, even a first job that fails to last longer than a day can be a valuable experience. This is particularly true if we are subsequently able to determine what it was about the job that did not meet the learner's needs, abilities, interests, and idiosyncrasies. Was the job too noisy? Were the production demands too high? Was there too much general activity and confusion? Was there not enough for him or her to do? This meeting of individual preferences and job characteristics is at times referred to as the "job match" (e.g., Ochocka, Roth, & Lord, 1994) or goodness of fit (e.g., Shalock & Jensen, 1986).

A high degree of job match means that the production, social, and environmental components of a job are viewed as favorable by the employee. A low degree indicates an unfavorable view of these conditions. For many learners with ASD for whom pay may not be a primary motivating factor, the degree of job match can be *the* critical variable between employee and employer satisfaction and a return to unemployment.

Promote Creativity in Job Development

The job market in the United States is both highly technical and generally complex, with most employees required to handle multiple components of a given job. This can play to the advantage of adult learners with ASD through a process referred to as *job carving* (Nietupski & Hamre-Nietupski, 2000). Job carving is a specialized job development process that recognizes and takes advantage of this complexity by "carving" separate tasks from more complex jobs and combining these tasks into a new job that meets both the needs of the adult learner and the potential employer. If the needs of both parties are not met, no job can be carved. Effective job carving requires direct knowledge of a potential employee's abilities, interests, and limitations along with observational and negotiating skills.

Provide Coworker Training and Support

Despite professional recognition of the diversity of expression associated with ASD, the community at large has generally come to understand the disorder through the character of Raymond Babbit in the movie *Rainman*. A potentially safe assumption is that, for the most part, employers and coworkers will have a limited understanding of ASD in general and almost no understanding as to the expression of the disorder in the life of a potential employee/coworker. As such, employers, supervisors, and coworkers may need to be provided with some degree of individual specific training if increasingly greater levels of independence and social inclusion on the job are to be realized. Potential training areas may include:

- A brief, jargon-free introduction to ASD
- Strategies helpful in communicating with their new colleague/employee
- The role of on-site support personnel (e.g., the job coach)
- Social support on the job
- Information on how they might most effectively provide performance-related feedback to their new colleague/employee
- Basic information about the display and function of any idiosyncratic or unusual behavior

Develop Active Ties with the Local Business Community

Most organizations working to support adult learners with ASD are incorporated as nonprofit corporations and, as such, may be organized and administered differently than a for-profit corporation of similar size. Differences in mission, organization, and finances may result in something of a "culture clash" between the goals of the nonprofit organization (i.e., helping persons with ASD obtain employment) and those of the for-profit corporation (e.g., promoting an efficient workforce to maximize investors' profits). At these times, the development of an active business advisory council (BAC) may help the employees of the nonprofit better understand the needs, language, and culture of the for-profit business.

The overall goal of the BAC is to increase employment opportunities for individuals with disabilities through actively engaging members of the business community with the nonprofit organization. BAC members are generally solicited from the local business community, many of whom may already have ties to the nonprofit. For examples, BAC members may be solicited from companies with which the nonprofit organization does business (e.g., their primary bank) or through board and family contacts. The BAC can promote greater access to employment by:

- Identifying areas of potential job development and local hiring trends
- Providing training to the agency on how to more effectively interact with potential employers in securing employment for adults with ASD
- Providing direct access to potential employers
- Assistance in the development of employer-friendly informational materials
- Networking with potential employers through their membership in local business or professional associations
- Promoting fund-raisers to the local business community

For the nonprofit whose mission it is to promote employment for adult learners with ASD, the development of an active and involved BAC should be considered a worthwhile, if not essential, tool toward translating the goals of the organization into terms that potential employers can readily understand and, thereby, access a relatively untouched resource in the form of competent employees with ASD.

CONCLUSION

In the United States, adults with ASD continue to exist outside the employment mainstream in numbers far greater than is appropriate. Among the many reasons for this continued underemployment are the disconnect between the potential of adult learners with ASD and the resources of the systems designed to provide programmatic support, the absence of a legislative entitlement to services as an adult, inadequate or inappropriate transition planning, and, to some extent, limited interest in supporting adult learners in general and, in particular, those with greater cognitive or behavioral challenges. While these challenges are significant, they are not insurmountable.

Across the country, there are a number of excellent programs (e.g., Eden WERCs in New Jersey, Community Services for Autistic Adults and Children in Maryland, and Division TEACCH in North Carolina) that are successfully supporting adults of divergent ability levels to become employed, participating, and contributing members of their community and the local economy. We know what is possible: It is possible for adults with ASD to be employed and to live a life of quality where they actively participate in decisions that affect their lives (e.g., Bannerman, Sheldon, Sherman, & Harchik, 1990). The task ahead is to make this limited possibility into a near-certain probability and, in so doing, demonstrate to the community at large that persons with ASD, despite their disability, do not always have to be understood as having a handicap.

Cross-References

Features of autism and related conditions in adolescents and adults are addressed in Chapter 10, assessment issues are discussed in Section V (Chapters 27 to 32), and Chapter 51 provides a personal perspective on autism.

REFERENCES

Bannerman, D. J., Sheldon, J. B., Sherman, J. A., & Harchik, A. E. (1990). Balancing the right to habilitation with the right to personal liberties: The rights of people with developmental disabilities to eat too many doughnuts and take a nap. *Journal of Applied Behavior Analysis, 23,* 79–89.

Bates, P. E., Bronkema, J., Ames, T., & Hess, C. (1992). State-level interagency planning models. In F. R. Rusch, L. DeStefano, J. Chadsey-Rusch, L. A. Phelps, & E. Szymanski (Eds.), *Transition from school to adult life: Models, linkages, and policy* (pp. 115–129). Sycamore, IL: Sycamore Press.

Bellamy, G. T., Rhodes, L. E., Bourbeau, P. E., & Mank, D. M. (1986). Mental retardation services in sheltered and day activity programs: Consumer benefits and policy alternatives. In F. R. Rusch (Ed.), *Competitive employment issues and strategies.* Baltimore: Paul H. Brookes.

Berkell, D. E. (1992). Transition issues for secondary school students with ASD and developmental disabilities. In F. R. Rusch, L. DeStefano, J. Chadsey-Rusch, L. A. Phelps, & E. Szymanski (Eds.), *Transition from school to adult life: Models, linkages, and policy* (pp. 460–472). Sycamore, IL: Sycamore Press.

Bettleheim, B. (1967). *The empty fortress.* New York: Free Press.

Brotherson, M. J., Turnbull, A. P., Bronicki, G. J., Houghton, J., Roeder-Gordon, C., Summers, S. A., et al. (1988). Transition into adulthood: Parental planning for sons and daughters with disabilities. *Education and Training in Mental Retardation, 23,* 165–174.

Brown, L., Nietupski, J., & Hamre-Nietupski, R. (1976). The criterion of ultimate functioning. In M. A. Thomas (Ed.), *Hey, don't forget about me!* (pp. 2–15). Reston, VA: Council for Exceptional Children.

Buckley, J., Mank, D., & Sandow, D. (1990). Developing and implementing support strategies. In F. R. Rusch (Ed.), *Supported employment: Methods, models and issues* (pp. 131–144). Sycamore, IL: Sycamore Press.

Burt, D. B., Fuller, S. P., & Lewis, K. R. (1991). Functional utilization of splinter skills for the employment of a young adult with autism. *Focus on Autistic Behavior, 7,* 1–16.

Carr, E. G., Binkoff, J. A., Kologinsky, E., & Eddy, M. (1978). Acquisition of sign language by autistic children: I. Expressive labeling. *Journal of Applied Behavior Analysis, 11,* 489–501.

Kemp, D. C., & Carr, E. G. (1995). Reduction of severe problem behavior in community employment using a hypothesis driven, multicomponent intervention approach. *Journal of the Association for Persons with Severe Handicaps, 20,* 229–247.

Celiberti, D. A., Alessandri, M. O., Fong, P. L., & Gill, M. J. (1993). Past, current, and future trends in the behavioral treatment of ASD. *Behavior Therapist, 16,* 127–132.

Center for Self-Determination. (2004). *Self directed support corporations* (Microboards). Available from http://www.self-determination.com/publications/microboard.htm.

DeStefano, L., & Wermuth, T. R. (1992). IDEA (PL 101-476): Defining a second generation of transition services. In F. R. Rusch, L. DeStefano, J. Chadsey-Rusch, L. A. Phelps, & E. Szymanski (Eds.), *Transition from school to adult life: Models, linkages, and policy* (pp. 537–549). Sycamore, IL: Sycamore Press.

Ferster, C. B., & DeMyer, M. K. (1962). A method for the experimental analysis of the behavior of autistic children. *American Journal of Orthopsychiatry, 32,* 89–98.

Foley, S. M., Butterworth, J., & Heller, A. (2000). Vocational rehabilitation interagency activity improving supported employment for people with severe disabilities. *Focus on Autism and Other Developmental Disabilities, 15,* 37–42.

Fong, L., Wilgosh, L., & Sobsey, D. (1993). The experience of parenting an adolescent with ASD. *International Journal of Disability, Development and Education, 40,* 105–113.

Freidlander, B. (1989). Becoming an advocate. In M. Powers (Ed.), *Children with ASD: A parent's guide* (pp. 231–252). Bethesda, MD: Woodbine House.

Gerhardt, P. F., Mannion, K., Weidenbaum, M., Andretta, M., & Wallace, B. (2003, May 25). *Knowledge of ASD and ABA: A comparison between parents of children with ASD and direct care staff.* Poster presented to Association for Behavior Analysis, San Francisco.

Gerhardt, P. F., & Markowitz, J. (1993). Employment programming and the adult with ASD: Options, issues and challenges. *1993 International Conference Proceedings: ASD—A world of options* (pp. 93–97). Arlington, TX: Future Education.

Gold, M. W. (1975). Vocational training. In J. Wortis (Ed.), *Mental retardation and developmental disabilities: An annual review* (pp. 254–264). New York: Brunner/Mazel.

Grandin, T., & Duffy, K. (2004). *Developing talents: Careers for individuals with Asperger syndrome and high functioning autism.* Shawnee Mission, KS: Autism Asperger.

Herbert, J. T., & Ishikawa, T. (1991). Employment related interpersonal competence among workers with mental retardation. *Vocational Evaluation and Work Adjustment Bulletin, 24,* 87–94.

Holmes, D. L. (1989). The years ahead: Adults with ASD. In M. D. Powers (Ed.), *Children with ASD: A parents' guide* (pp. 253–273). Bethesda, MD: Woodbine.

Holmes, D. L. (1990). Community-based services for children and adults with ASD: The Eden family of programs. *Journal of Autism and Developmental Disorder, 20,* 339–351.

Holmes, D. L. (1998). *Autism through the lifespan: The Eden model.* Bethesda, MD: Woodbine House.

Holmes, D. L., Storm, K., Milton, R., Gerhardt, P., Holmes, A. S., Cohen, M., et al. (1994). *The Eden Services Employment Curriculum.* Princeton, NJ: Eden Press.

Hopkins, K. R. (1992). *Willing to act: A summary of the 1991 Harris Survey on public attitudes towards people with disabilities.* (Available from the National Organization on Disability, 910 Sixteenth St. NW, Washington, DC, 20006)

Hosack, K., & Malkmus, D. (1992). Vocational rehabilitation of persons with disabilities: Family inclusion. *Journal of Vocational Rehabilitation, 2,* 11–17.

Howlin, P., Goode, S., Hutton, S., & Rutter, M. (2004). Adult outcome for children with autism. *Journal of Child Psychology and Psychiatry, 45,* 212–229.

Inge, K. J., Banks, P. D., Wehman, P., Hill, J. W., & Shafer, M. S. (1988). Quality of life for individuals who are labeled mentally retarded: Evaluating competitive employment versus sheltered employment. *Education and Training in Mental Retardation, 23,* 97–104.

Iovannone, R., Dunlap, G., Huber, H., & Kincaid, D. (2003). Effective educational practices for students with autism spectrum disorders. *Focus on Autism and Other Developmental Disorders, 18,* 150–165.

Irvin, L. K., Thorin, E., & Singer, G. H. S. (1993). Family-related roles and considerations: Transition to adulthood by youth with developmental disabilities. *Journal of Vocational Rehabilitation, 3,* 38–46.

Janicki, M. P., Castellani, P. J., & Norris, R. G. (1983). Organization and administration of service delivery systems. In J. Matson & J. Mulick (Eds.), *Handbook of mental retardation* (pp. 3–23). New York: Pergamon Press.

Kaplan, J. E., & Moore, R. J. (1989). Legal rights and hurdles. In M. D. Powers (Ed.), *Children with ASD: A parents' guide* (pp. 203–228). Bethesda, MD: Woodbine.

Kemp, D. C., & Carr, E. G. (1995). Reduction of severe problem behavior in community employment using a hypothesis-driven multicomponent intervention approach. *Journal of the Association for Persons with Severe Handicaps, 20,* 229–247.

Kiernan, W. E., & Stark, J. A. (1986a). Comprehensive design for the future. In W. Kiernan & J. Stark (Eds.), *Pathways to employment for adults with developmental disabilities.* Baltimore: Paul H. Brookes.

Kiernan, W. E., & Stark, J. A. (1986b). Demographic characteristics. In W. Kiernan & J. Stark (Eds.), *Pathways to employment for adults with developmental disabilities.* Baltimore: Paul H. Brookes.

Kregel, J. (1999). Why it pays to hire workers with developmental disabilities. *Focus on Autism and Other Developmental Disabilities, 14,* 130–132.

Kregel, J., & Wehman, P. (1989). Supported employment: Promises deferred for persons with severe disabilities. *Journal of the Association of Persons with Severe Handicaps, 14,* 293–303.

Lagomarcino, T., & Rusch, F. R. (1987). Supported employment: Transition from school to work. *American Rehabilitation, 13,* 4–5, 26–27.

Levy, S. M. (1983). School doesn't last forever; Then what? Some vocational alternatives. In E. Schopler & G. B. Mesibov (Eds.), *Autism in adolescents and adults* (pp. 133–148). New York: Plenum Press.

Lewis Harris and Associates. (2002). *The National Organization on Disability/Harris survey program on participation and attitudes: Survey of Americans with disabilities.* New York: Author.

Lovaas, O. I., & Simmons, J. Q. (1969). Manipulation of self-destruction in three retarded children. *Journal of Applied Behavior Analysis, 2,* 143–157.

Mank, D. (1994). The underachievement of supported employment: A call for reinvestment. *Journal of Disability Policy Studies, 5,* 24.

Markowitz, J., Gerhardt, P. F., Christopher, W., Christopher, B., & McKean. T. (1994). Quality of life issues for adults with autism. *1994 Autism Society of America Conference Proceedings: A new dawn of awakening* (pp. 89–90). Arlington, TX: Future Education.

Menchetti, B. M., & Flynn, B. M. (1990). Vocational evaluation. In F. R. Rusch (Ed.), *Supported employment: Methods, models and issues* (pp. 111–130). Sycamore, IL: Sycamore Press.

Mesibov, G. B. (1990). Normalization and its relevance today. *Journal of Autism and Developmental Disorders, 20,* 379–390.

Moore, S. C. (1994). Adult services: Opportunities to demonstrate competence. In L. J. Hayes, G. J. Hayes, S. C. Moore, & P. M. Ghezzi (Eds.), *Ethical issues in developmental disabilities* (pp. 135–136). Reno, NV: Context Press.

Nietupski, J. A., & Hamre-Nietupski, S. (2000). *Journal of Developmental and Physical Disabilities, A systematic process for carving supported employment positions for people with severe disabilities, 12,* 103–119.

Ochocka, J., Roth, D., & Lord, J. (1994). Workplaces that work: Successful employment for people with disabilities. *Journal of Developmental Disabilities, 3,* 29–50.

Peraino, J. M. (1992). Post-21 follow-up studies: How do special education graduates fare? In P. Wehman (Ed.), *Life beyond the classroom: Transition strategies for young people with disabilities* (pp. 21–70). Baltimore: Paul H. Brookes.

PL 93-112. (1973). The Rehabilitation Act of 1973, Sec. 504.

PL 94-142. (1975). Education of All Handicapped Children Act.

PL 101-336. (1990). Americans with Disabilities Act of 1990 (ADA).

PL 105-17. (1997). Individuals with Disabilities Education Act Ammendments (IDEA).

Revell, W. G., Wehman, P., Kregel, J., West, M., & Rayfield, R. (1994). Supported employment for persons with severe disabilities: Positive trends in wages, models and funding. *Education and Training in Mental Retardation and Developmental Disabilities, 29,* 256–264.

Rimland, B. (1964). *Infantile autism: The syndrome and its implications for a neural theory of behavior.* New York: Appleton-Century-Crofts.

Rogan, P., Banks, B., & Howard, M. (2000). Workplace supports in practice: As little as possible, as much as necessary. *Focus on Autism and Developmental Disabilities, 15,* 37–42.

Rusch, F. R. (Ed.). (1990). *Supported employment: Methods, models and issues.* Sycamore, IL: Sycamore Press.

Rusch, F. R., DeStefano, L., Chadsey-Rusch, J., Phelps, L. A., & Szymanski, E. (1992). *Transition from school to adult life: Models, linkages, and policy.* Sycamore, IL: Sycamore Press.

Rusch, F. R., & Hughes, C. (1990). Historical overview of supported employment. In F. R. Rusch (Ed.), *Supported employment: Methods, models and issues* (pp. 5–14). Sycamore, IL: Sycamore Press.

Schopler, E., & Hennick, J. M. (1990). Past and present trends in residential treatment. *Journal of Autism and Developmental Disorders, 20,* 291–298.

Shalock, R. L., & Jensen, C. M. (1986). Assessing the goodness-of-fit between persons and their environment. *Journal of the Association for Persons with Severe Handicaps, 11,* 103–109.

Shields-Wolfe, J., & Gallagher, P. A. (1992). Functional utilization of splinter skills for the employment of a young man with autism. *Focus on Autistic Behavior, 7,* 1–6.

Smith, M. D., Belcher, R. G., & Juhrs, P. D. (1995). *A guide to successful employment for individuals with autism.* Baltimore: Paul H. Brookes.

Snauwaert, D. T. (1992). Transition policy. In F. R. Rusch, L. DeStefano, J. Chadsey-Rusch, L. A. Phelps, & E. Szymanski (Eds.), *Transition from school to adult life: Models, linkages, and policy* (pp. 509–517). Sycamore, IL: Sycamore Press.

Solnick, J. V., Rincover, A., & Peterson, C. R. (1977). Some determinants of the reinforcing and punishing effects of timeout. *Journal of Applied Behavior Analysis, 10,* 415–424.

Sowers, J., & Powers, L. (1991). *Vocational preparation and employment of students with physical and multiple disabilities.* Baltimore: Paul H. Brookes.

Steere, D. E., Wood, R., Pancsofar, E. L., & Rucker, R. E. (1993). Vocational training for secondary-level students with severe disabilities. *Teaching Exceptional Children, 27,* 7–11.

Stowitschek, J. J. (1992). Policy and planning in transition programs at the state agency level. In F. R. Rusch, L. DeStefano, J. Chadsey-Rusch, L. A. Phelps, & E. Szymanski (Eds.), *Transition from school to adult life: Models, linkages, and policy* (pp. 519–536). Sycamore, IL: Sycamore Press.

Sullivan, R. C. (1981). What does institutionalization mean for our children? *Journal of Autism and Developmental Disabilities, 11,* 347–356.

Thomas, M. A., & Halloran, W. (1987). Facts and attitudes about adult services for people with severe disabilities. *American Rehabilitation, 13,* 20–25.

Tines, J., Rusch, F. R., McCaughrin, W., & Conley, R. W. (1990). Benefit-cost analysis of supported employment is ILL: A statewide evaluation. *American Journal on Mental Retardation, 95,* 44–54.

Turnbull, A. P., & Turnbull, H. R. (1988). Toward great expectations for vocational opportunities: Family professional partnerships. *Mental Retardation, 26,* 337–342.

Unger, D. D. (1999). Workplace supports: A view from employers who have hired supported employees. *Focus on Autism and other Developmental Disabilities, 14,* 167–191.

Ward, M. J. (1992). Introduction to secondary special education and transition issues. In F. R. Rusch, L. DeStefano, J. Chadsey-Rusch, L. A. Phelps, & E. Szymanski (Eds.), *Transition from school to adult life: Models, linkages, and policy* (pp. 387–389). Sycamore, IL: Sycamore Press.

Wehman, P. (1991). Transition: What lies ahead in the 1990's. *Journal of Vocational Rehabilitation, 1,* 7–8.

Wehman, P. (1992). *Live beyond the classroom: Transition strategies for young people with disabilities.* Baltimore: Paul H. Brookes.

Wehman, P., & Kregel, J. (1988). Supported competitive employment for individuals with autism and severe retardation: Two case studies. *Focus on Autistic Behavior, 3,* 1–11.

Wehman, P., Kregel, J., & Barcus, M. J. (1985). From school to work: A vocational transition model for handicapped students. *Exceptional Children, 52,* 25–37.

Will, M. (1984). *OSERS programming for the transition youth with disabilities: Bridges from school to working life.* Washington, DC: U.S. Department of Education.

Winking, D. L., O'Reilly, B., & Moon, M. S. (1993). Preference: The missing link in the job match process for individuals without functional communication skills. *Journal of Vocational Rehabilitation, 3,* 27–42.

CHAPTER 44

Psychopharmacology

LAWRENCE SCAHILL AND ANDRÉS MARTIN

Although psychopharmacological treatment of children and adults with autism appears to be common in clinical practice (Aman, Collier-Crespin, & Lindsay, 2000; Martin, Scahill, Klin, & Volkmar, 1999), empirical support is limited, especially in children. With notable exceptions, clinical trials in this population have tended to be in small, inadequately characterized samples, impeding replication of findings, and offering minimal guidance to clinicians. Nonetheless, a wide range of compounds has been considered for the treatment of both core and associated target symptoms of the disorder. This chapter provides a critical overview of the major drug categories that are commonly used in the treatment of children and adults with autism and related conditions. The chapter contains four parts according to the drug category: (1) atypical antipsychotics, (2) serotonin reuptake inhibitors, and (3) stimulants. The fourth and final section reviews data from a miscellaneous set of chemically unrelated compounds, including mood stabilizers, alpha agonists, opiate antagonists, and secretin. Each section includes a brief background on the class of compound, the empirical support for use in patients with developmental disorders, and clinical applications specifically relevant to autism.

ATYPICAL ANTIPSYCHOTICS

Atypical antipsychotics (AAPs), including clozapine, risperidone, olanzapine, quetiapine, ziprasidone, and aripiprazole have garnered considerable interest in the treatment of children and adults with pervasive developmental disorders (PDDs). These compounds are frequently used for treating severe maladaptive behaviors and symptoms associated with autism and other PDDs (McDougle et al., 2000) and have largely replaced traditional antipsychotics (neuroleptics) such as haloperidol in this population. The target symptoms for pharmacotherapy with AAPs typically include aggression, self-injury, property destruction, or severe tantrums. Support for the claim that these agents may be useful in PDD derives from the line of research with haloperidol done by Campbell and colleagues (Anderson et al., 1989; Campbell et al., 1997). The AAPs, however, offer distinct advantages over the typical antipsychotics exemplified by haloperidol. Importantly, the AAPs have a lower risk of extrapyramidal symptoms (EPS) and, presumably, of long-term tardive dyskinesia as well. In addition, because these newer compounds may also improve negative

This work was supported in part by the following federal grants: Program Project MH-49351; Children's Clinical Research Center grant (M01-RR06022), the Mental Health Research Center grant (MH-30929), RUPP-MH70009-04 and RUPP-PI MH 66762-02, and STAART Grant U54 MH66494.

The authors acknowledge the advice and collaboration of Michael Aman, PhD; Christopher J. McDougle, MD; James T. McCracken, MD; Elaine Tierney, MD; Ben Vitiello, MD; and L. Eugene Arnold, MD, MED. Thanks also to Erin Kustan for assistance in preparing this manuscript.

symptoms in adults with schizophrenia, researchers have shown interest in the possibility that they may also improve core symptoms of autism such as social withdrawal and lack of spontaneous interaction. The AAPs are also as effective in the treatment of tics (Bruggeman et al., 2001; Scahill, Leckman, Schultz, Katsovich, & Peterson, 2003), as the high potency traditional antipsychotics. This suggests that the AAPs may reduce stereotypic behaviors associated with PDDs as well.

The reduced occurrence of dyskinesias and the purported improvement in negative symptoms of schizophrenia may be related to the dual action of serotonin (5-HT) and dopamine (DA) receptor blockade (Meltzer, 1999). Alternatively, it has been suggested that the AAPs do not bind as tightly to postsynaptic dopamine receptors, permitting them to be displaced by endogenous dopamine in striatum (Kapur & Seeman, 2001). To date, clinical investigators have examined clozapine, risperidone, olanzapine, quetiapine, or ziprasidone in the treatment of autism and other PDDs. Recent data suggest that risperidone is emerging as the *standard treatment* for aggression, tantrums, and self-injury in children, adolescents, and adults with PDDs.

Clozapine

Clozapine was the first atypical antipsychotic to be introduced in the United States (Baldessarini & Frankenburg, 1991). The drug's ability to block 5-HT_{2A}, 5-HT_{2C}, 5-HT_{3} and DA $D_{1}\text{-}D_{4}$ receptors has been proposed as its mechanism of action. Two reports have described the use of clozapine in autism. In the first study, three children who displayed marked hyperactivity, fidgetiness, or aggression were treated for up to 8 months with doses ranging from 200 to 450 mg per day (Zuddas, Ledda, Fratta, Muglia, & Cianchetti, 1996). Two of the 3 children showed sustained improvement, though the third had a return of symptoms to baseline levels after an initial response. More recently, Chen, Bedair, McKay, Bowers, and Mazure (2001) reported the case of a 17-year-old male with autism and severe mental retardation who showed a significant reduction in signs of overt tension, hyperactivity, and repetitive motions in response to clozapine, 275 mg per day, during a 15-day hospitalization. The low use of clozapine in autism probably reflects concern about the risk of agranulocytosis and seizures that are associated with the drug. Additionally, the requirement for frequent blood draws can be challenging to obtain in children with autism.

Risperidone

Risperidone has high affinities for DA D_{2}, D_{4}, 5-HT_{1D}, 5-HT_{2A}, 5-HT_{2C} receptors (Leysen et al., 1988). Multiple open-label reports and case series, as well as double-blind, placebo-controlled trials in children and adolescents and adults, have described the beneficial effects of risperidone in individuals with autism and other PDDs (for a detailed review, see McDougle et al., 2000).

The Research Units on Pediatric Psychopharmacology (RUPP) Autism Network recently completed a multisite trial to evaluate the short- and long-term safety and efficacy of risperidone in children and adolescents with autism accompanied by severe tantrums, aggression, or self-injurious behavior (RUPP Autism Network, 2002). The *first phase* of the study was an 8-week, randomized, double-blind trial of risperidone versus placebo. The primary outcome measures were the *Irritability* subscale of the Aberrant Behavior Checklist (ABC) and the Improvement item of the Clinical Global Impression scale (CGI-I). One hundred one (101) children were recruited into the study (82 boys and 19 girls, mean age 8.8 years). Of these, 49 were randomized to risperidone and 52 to placebo. Eight weeks of risperidone treatment (mean dose, 2.0 mg per day in divided doses) resulted in a 57% reduction on the ABC Irritability score, compared to a 14% decrease for the placebo group ($t = 6.4$, $p < .0001$ effect size = 1.2; see Table 44.1). Based on an a priori definition of response (at least a 25% reduction on the Irritability score and a score of *Much Improved* or *Very Much Improved* on the CGI-I), the improvement rate was 69.4% (34 of 49) on risperidone and 11.5% (6 of 52) on placebo (Chi square = 32.9; $p < .0001$).

Risperidone was associated with an average weight gain of 2.7 kg after 8 weeks, compared to 0.8 kg for placebo ($t = 3.7$; $p = .0004$). Increased appetite, fatigue, drowsiness, tremor, and drooling were all more common in the

TABLE 44.1   Baseline and Endpoint Scores on Aberrant Behavior Checklist by Treatment Group

ABC Effect Subscale	Risperidone (N = 49)		Placebo (N = 52)		F^a	p^b	Size[c]
	Baseline Mean (SD)	Endpoint Mean (SD)	Baseline Mean (SD)	Endpoint Mean (SD)			
Irritability	26.2 (7.9)	11.3 (7.4)	25.5 (6.6)	21.9 (9.5)	27.57	< .0001	1.2
Social withdrawal	16.4 (8.2)	8.9 (6.4)	16.1 (8.7)	12.0 (8.3)	4.89	.03	0.4
Stereotypy	10.6 (4.9)	5.8 (4.6)	9.0 (4.4)	7.3 (4.8)	11.32	< .0001	0.8
Hyperactivity	31.8 (9.6)	17.0 (9.7)	32.3 (8.5)	27.6 (10.6)	25.56	< .0001	1.0
Inappropriate speech	4.8 (4.1)	3.0 (3.1)	6.5 (3.6)	5.9 (3.8)	6.68	.03	0.3

[a] Degrees of freedom = 1,262
[b] Derived from random regression analysis using data from baseline, weeks 2, 4, 6, and 8
[c] Calculated with baseline and endpoint scores only: difference in active minus difference in placebo, divided by pooled standard deviation.

Source: From "Risperidone in Children with Autism and Serious Behavioral Problems," by Research Units on Pediatric Psychopharmacology Autism Network, 2002, *New England Journal of Medicine, 347,* pp. 314–321. Used with permission.

risperidone group compared to placebo (p < .06 for each). These adverse effects were typically mild to moderate, and most were transient. The results of this large-scale clinical trial in children with autism provide convincing evidence that risperidone is safe and effective for the short-term treatment of severe behavioral problems in autism (RUPP Autism Network, 2002).

The *second phase* of the study included 63 subjects in a 4-month open-label extension, all of whom showed a positive response during the 8-week trial (nonresponders to placebo were treated openly and joined the extension phase, after evidence of positive response). The positive effects of risperidone were remarkably stable, and it was not necessary to raise the dose above the average 1.8 mg per day established at the start of the extension phase. The open-label extension was followed by a third phase in which subjects were randomly assigned to continue active medication at the same maintenance dose, or to a gradual withdrawal to placebo over a 3-week period. The rate of medication withdrawal was roughly 25% per week. The maximum observation period in this final phase of the study was 8 weeks, but relapse marked the end of the study for any given subject. Relapse was defined as a 25% or greater increase on the Irritability subscale of the Aberrant Behavior Checklist and two consecutive ratings of "Much Worse" or "Very Much Worse" on the CGI-I. The investigators also

developed a stopping rule for this phase of the study. A planned interim analysis after 32 subjects (16 per group) showed that the relapse rate was significantly greater in the placebo group compared to the group that continued on risperidone, leading to study termination (see Scahill et al., 2001, for a detailed description of the design). Two of 16 (12.5%) subjects in the risperidone maintenance group relapsed compared to 10 of 16 (62.5%) in the placebo-discontinuation group (Chi square = 6.53; p = .01; RUPP Autism Network, in press). Although the difference in the relapse rate was significant, the fact that 6 of 16 subjects who withdrew to placebo did not relapse suggests that some children may be safely withdrawn from the medication after 6 months.

The large magnitude of treatment effect (43% difference in the mean change from baseline between risperidone and placebo on the ABC Irritability scale) is striking. By contrast, past studies of haloperidol in autism showed differences in the 15% to 20% range, depending on the behavioral measure used (Anderson et al., 1989). Another important contrast is the rate and severity of adverse effects. Haloperidol was associated with sedation in 31 of 40 subjects (77.5%), compared with generally mild sedation in about half of the subjects in the risperidone group. Acute dystonic reactions occurred in 25% of haloperidol-treated patients, compared to none in this risperidone trial.

An important limitation of this study is that, by design, it focused on the target behaviors of tantrums, aggression, or self-injury rather than the core symptoms of autism. Although there was significant improvement in hyperactivity and stereotypy, there was little evidence of benefit in adaptive functioning (socialization, communication, or daily living skills), even for subjects who completed 6 months of treatment. The focus on severe behavior problems leaves an open question about possible additive effects of medication and behavior therapy. For example, the improvement in serious behavior problems associated with risperidone may enable a child to make better use of psychoeducational interventions directed at improving daily living skills. The addition of behavior therapy might also permit the successful discontinuation of risperidone without relapse.

Olanzapine

Olanzapine has high affinity for DA D_1, D_2, and D_4 receptors, for 5-HT$_{2A}$, 5-HT$_{2C}$, and 5-HT$_3$ receptors (Bymaster et al., 1996). To date, it has not been studied in a randomized, placebo-controlled study in children or adults with PDD. Rubin (1997) described a 17-year-old male with autistic disorder who demonstrated decreased agitation on olanzapine, 30 mg per day. A 10-year-old boy with autism, mental retardation, and bipolar disorder, not otherwise specified, showed reduced aggression following the addition of olanzapine, 20 mg per day, to ongoing treatment with lithium (Horrigan, Barnhill, & Courvoisie, 1997). Heimann (1999) treated a hospitalized 14-year-old boy with autism accompanied by psychotic symptoms. Following an ineffective trial with risperidone, olanzapine up to 40 mg per day resulted in substantial improvement and the child's return to school. In a recently published study employing a randomized, parallel groups design, 12 children with autism (mean age, 7.8 ± 2.1 years) were randomized to either 6 weeks of open-label treatment with olanzapine or haloperidol (Malone, Cater, Sheikh, Choudhury, & Delaney, 2001). Mean final dosages were 7.9 ± 2.5 mg per day for olanzapine and 1.4 ± 0.7 mg per day for haloperidol. Both groups showed symptom reduction. Five of six subjects in the olanzapine group and three of six in the haloperidol group were rated as responders based on the CGI-I. Weight gain from baseline to the end of treatment was significantly higher in the olanzapine group (mean, 9.0 ± 3.5 lbs) than in the haloperidol group (mean, 3.2 ± 4.9 lbs). One subject in the haloperidol group demonstrated mild rigidity, but no subjects in the olanzapine group showed extra pyramidal symptoms (EPS). Results from an open-label trial olanzapine monotherapy in children, adolescents, and adults with PDDs ($N = 7$) were generally positive, though significant weight gain did occur (Potenza, Holmes, Kanes, & McDougle, 1999). Recent reports of drug-induced diabetes in adults treated with olanzapine may promote reluctance on the part of clinicians to use this drug in autism.

Quetiapine

Quetiapine has a relatively low to moderate affinity for D_1 and D_2 receptors, moderate affinity for 5HT$_{2A}$ receptors, and higher affinity for alpha$_1$-adrenergic, H$_1$-histaminic receptors (Hirsch, Link, Goldstein, & Arvanitis, 1996). In the only published report of its use in PDD, 6 males with autism and mental retardation, ages 6 to 15 years (mean, 10.9 $\pm$ 3.3) entered a 16-week open-label study (mean daily dose, 225 ± 108 mg; range, 100 to 350 mg). Two subjects were considered responders, but there was no statistically significant improvement for the group on various rating scales. The other four subjects dropped out due to lack of response and sedation ($n = 3$), and a possible drug-induced seizure during the fourth week of treatment ($n = 1$). Other side effects included behavioral activation, increased appetite, and weight gain (range, 2 to 18 lbs). The authors concluded that quetiapine was poorly tolerated and ineffective in their sample, with the caveat that the sample size was small (Martin, Koenig, Scahill, & Bregman, 1999).

Ziprasidone

Ziprasidone is potent antagonist of 5HT$_{2A}$ and D_2 receptors, though it has relatively greater affinity for 5HT$_{2A}$ receptors. In contrast to quetiapine, it has low affinity for adrenergic and histaminergic receptors (Seeger et al., 1995). In the one published report of ziprasidone use in the PDDs, McDougle, Kem, and Posey (2002) conducted a preliminary evaluation of its safety and effectiveness in children, adolescents, and young adults with autism. Twelve patients (mean age = 11.6 ± 4.38 years; range, 8 to 20 years) with autism ($n = 9$) or pervasive developmental disorder not otherwise specified ($n = 3$) received open-label treatment with ziprasidone (mean daily dose, 59.2 ± 34.76 mg; range, 20 to 120 mg). Treatment ranged from 6 to 30 weeks (mean = 14.1 ± 8.29). Six (50%) of the 12 patients were considered responders based on a CGI-I rating of *Much Improved* or *Very Much Improved*. Transient sedation was the most common side effect. No cardiovascular side effects, including chest pain, tachycardia, palpitations, dizziness, or syncope, were observed or reported. The mean change in body weight for the group was −5.8 ± 12.52 lbs (range, −35 to +6 lbs). Scahill, Martin, Koenig, Katsovich, and Kustan (submitted) conducted an open-label pilot study of ziprasidone in 7 children with PDDs. Entry into the study required that subjects had failed two previous drug trials. After 12 weeks of treatment, 3 of 7 cases were rated as Very Much Improved; 3 subjects were rated as Much Worse; and 1 subject showed no change. The dose range in this study was 5 to 40 mg per day, far less than the daily doses used in the McDougle et al. (2002). Based on these pilot studies, ziprasidone appears to be a potentially useful treatment in PDD. Double-blind, placebo-controlled studies are needed to substantiate these preliminary findings.

Aripiprazole

Aripirazole is the most recent addition to the list of available AAPs. It is reported to have a novel mechanism of action and is classified as a partial dopamine agonist (Tamminga, 2002). This term refers to the fact that aripiprazole has the capacity to bind (affinity) with presynaptic dopamine receptors, but has lower biological effect than dopamine itself. Thus, it is presumed to have an overall antidopamine or antagonist effect. In addition, aripiprazole has serotonin blocking properties at the 5-HT$_2$ site. As with the other AAPs, studies in adults with schizophrenia have shown that aripiprazole is an effective antipsychotic medication with a low risk of neurological side effects (rigidity, dystonia, and dyskinesia; Kane et al., 2002). There was no difference in weight gain across active treatment and placebo groups. This profile of action suggests that aripiprazole has features in common with other AAPs, but may also be fundamentally different. To date, there are no published studies with aripiprazole in PDD, though pilot studies are underway at several centers.

SEROTONIN REUPTAKE INHIBITORS (SRIS)

Serotonin reuptake inhibitors (SRIs) such as clomipramine, fluoxetine, fluvoxamine, sertraline, paroxetine, citalopram, and escitalopram are a group of chemically unrelated compounds that potently inhibit the reuptake of serotonin (5-hydroxytryptamine, 5-HT) at the presynaptic transporter site. Clomipramine is a tricyclic antidepressant (TCA) that inhibits the reuptake of both norepinephrine and serotonin. The other compounds are more selective for serotonin reuptake and are collectively termed *selective* serotonin reuptake inhibitors (SSRI). Although commonly used in clinical practice (Martin, Scahill, et al., 1999) the SRIs have not been well studied in the PDDs.

Clomipramine

In a pair of studies, Gordon and colleagues first compared clomipramine to desipramine in seven subjects with autism in a crossover design (Gordon, Rapoport, Hamburger, State, & Mannheim, 1992). In that study, clomipramine was superior to desipramine in reducing repetitive behaviors and stereotypies. The second study was a double-blind crossover study that compared clomipramine to desipramine and to placebo (Gordon, State, Nelson, Hamburger, & Rapoport, 1993). Twenty four subjects with a mean age of 9.7 years (range, 6 to 18 years) were included in the study. Of these, 12 were randomly assigned to clomipramine and desipramine in a crossover design, and the other 12 to clomipramine and placebo in a crossover design. Clomipramine was superior to both desipramine and placebo in reducing autistic symptoms (as measured by the 14-item Children's Psychiatric Rating Scale), as well as repetitive, obsessive compulsive disorder-like symptoms (as measured by a global measure of OCD). One subject treated with clomipramine had a seizure; other adverse effects of clomipramine included a prolonged QT interval on electrocardiogram, in one subject and tachycardia in another.

Four open-label studies of clomipramine, which included both children and adults, reported beneficial effects in mixed populations of PDD patients (Brasic et al., 1994; Brodkin, McDougle, Naylor, Cohen, & Price, 1997; Garber, McGonigle, Slomka, & Monteverde, 1992; McDougle et al., 1992). However, a fifth study, composed solely of prepubertal subjects ($n = 8$, 3.5 to 8.7 years old) showed a generally poor response to clomipramine (Sanchez et al., 1996). Indeed, only one subject showed even moderate improvement. Adverse effects, including urinary retention, drowsiness, aggressive behavior, and mood instability were common. Concerns about lowered seizure threshold in this seizure-prone population, the need for electrocardiographic and blood level monitoring, against the inconsistent results to date, have made many clinicians reluctant to use clomipramine in children with PDDs.

Fluoxetine

An early open-label study of fluoxetine in 23 patients with autism, ranging in age from 7 to 28 years of age showed promising effects on repetitive behaviors. At doses ranging from 10 to 80 mg per day, 15 of 23 subjects were classified as responders on a global measure of severity (Cook, Rowlett, Jaselskis, & Leventhal, 1992). Although the primary outcome measure was crude, the study provided hints of age-related effects on therapeutic response. In the younger age group (subjects less than 15 years of age), 6 of 11 were classified as responders. By contrast, 9 of 12 subjects older than 15 years were classified as responders. Cook and colleagues also observed symptoms of activation, including hyperactivity, restlessness, agitation, elation, irritability, and insomnia in 6 of 23 subjects. Whether these symptoms of

behavioral activation were more common in the younger age group was not reported.

In a retrospective study of fluoxetine in 37 young children with autism, not selected for any specific set of target symptoms, DeLong and colleagues (DeLong, Teague, & McSwain-Kamran, 1998) reported that 22 of 37 subjects improved in core symptoms of autism. The children ranged in age from 2 to 7 years of age (mean, 4.5 years). The dose of fluoxetine was not reported. In addition, the characteristics of the sample were not provided. Among nonresponders, a high (though unspecified) percentage of children showed signs of activation as evidenced by hyperactivity, insomnia, agitation, and, occasionally, aggression. Thus, the results of this trial may be useful for hypothesis generation, but offer little guidance to clinicians regarding the use of fluoxetine in children with autism.

Fluvoxamine

A double-blind, placebo-controlled trial of fluvoxamine in adults with autism showed that 8 of 15 were judged *Much Improved* or *Very Much Improved* on the Improvement scale of the Clinical Global Impression scale, as compared to 0 of 15 in the placebo group (McDougle et al., 1996). Improvements included reduced compulsive behavior and aggression, and increased prosocial behavior. Based on these encouraging results, McDougle and colleagues conducted a placebo-controlled study in 34 children and adolescents (age range 5 to 18 years) with PDD. In stark contrast to the positive findings in the adult study, only 1 of 16 patients showed a positive response to fluvoxamine (C. McDougle, personal communication, 2002). Behavioral activation characterized by hyperactivity, disinhibition, insomnia, and aggression occurred in 12 of 16 subjects, resulting in discontinuation of the trial. The dose of fluvoxamine ranged from 2.5 to 3.0 mg per kg, which is lower than the average fluvoxamine dose of 4.4 mg per kg used in a recent multisite study of typically developing children with anxiety disorders (RUPP Anxiety Group, 2001). At this higher dose level, the RUPP investigators did observe behavioral activation in 27% of those on fluvoxamine, compared to 12% on placebo. Taken together, these findings suggest that younger children may be at higher risk for SSRI-induced behavioral activation and that children with PDD may be at greater risk than typically developing children.

In a follow-up of the two studies by McDougle et al. and Martin, Koenig, Anderson, and Scahill (2003) conducted a pilot study of fluvoxamine in 18 children and adolescents with PDD and anxiety symptoms. The aim of the study was to examine the apparent age-related differences in response to fluvoxamine suggested by the two prior studies. In order to reduce the risk of behavioral activation in youngsters with PDD, the investigators used even lower doses of fluvoxamine (1.5 mg per kg per day) than in the McDougle et al. study. The subjects had a mean age of 11.3 ± 3.6 years (range, 8 to 16 years). Fluvoxamine was started at either 12.5 or 25 mg daily (for subjects weighing less or more than 40 kg, respectively). In the absence of significant side effects, medication was adjusted weekly in increments of 12.5 or 25 mg until the maximum dosage was reached (1.5 mg per kg per day—rounded to the nearest 12.5 mg dose), given on a bid schedule. This dose showed clear evidence of effective serotonin reuptake inhibition as measured by blockade at the platelet membrane level (see Epperson et al., 2001). Fourteen children (78%) completed the 10-week study, and only 3 subjects had to leave the study prematurely due to behavioral activation. This observation suggests that SSRI-activation is indeed related to starting dose and the pace of dose escalation. Although there were no significant benefits for the group as a whole, eight subjects (including all four females) showed a positive response (Martin et al., 2003). The lack of efficacy for the whole group was likely related to the heterogeneity of the sample, as the study included children with obsessive-compulsive symptoms or anxiety symptoms.

Sertraline

No controlled studies of sertraline in subjects with autistic disorder or other PDDs have been published, although a number of open-label reports have appeared. In a 28-day trial of sertraline (at doses of 25 mg to 150 mg daily) in nine adults with mental retardation (five of whom had autistic disorder), significant decreases in aggression and self-injurious behavior occurred in eight as rated on the CGI severity scale (Hellings, Kelley, Gabrielli, Kilgore, & Shah, 1996). In a case series of nine autistic children (ages 6 to 12 years) treated with sertraline (25 mg to 50 mg daily), 8 showed significant improvement in anxiety, irritability, and ability to manage transitions (Steingard, Zimnitzky, DeMaso, Bauman, & Bucci, 1997). Two children exhibited agitation when the dose was raised to 75 mg daily.

A 12-week, open-label, prospective study of 42 adults with PDDs (including patients with autistic disorder, Asperger disorder, and pervasive developmental disorder not otherwise specified [PDD NOS]) reported that sertraline (mean dose, 122 mg per day) was effective for improving aggression and repetitive behavior (McDougle et al., 1998). As determined by the Improvement item of the CGI, 15 of 22 subjects with autistic disorder, none of 6 with Asperger disorder, and 9 of 14 with PDD NOS were categorized as responders. Three of the 42 subjects dropped out of the study as a result of intolerable agitation and anxiety.

Paroxetine

Only a few reports, none of them placebo-controlled, have appeared on the use of paroxetine in autistic disorder. Paroxetine, 20 mg per day, decreased self-injurious behavior in a 15-year-old boy with high-functioning autistic disorder (Snead, Boon, & Presberg, 1994). In another report, paroxetine was effective for a broader range of symptoms, including irritability, temper tantrums, and preoccupations in a 7-year-old boy with autistic disorder (Posey, Litwiller, Koburn, & McDougle, 1999). The optimal dose of paroxetine was 10 mg daily; an increase of paroxetine to 15 mg per day was associated with agitation and insomnia. A retrospective case analysis found paroxetine to be effective in approximately 25% of adults with PDD NOS (Branford, Bhaumik, & Naik, 1998).

In a 4-month, open-label study of 15 adults with severe and profound mental retardation (7 with PDD), paroxetine at doses of 20 mg to 50 mg daily was effective for symptoms of aggression at 1 month, but not at 4-month follow-up (Davanzo, Belin, Widawski, & King, 1998).

Citalopram and Escitalopram

To date, there have been no published reports on the effects of these two agents, newer SSRIs recently introduced to the United States, among patients with autistic disorder or other PDDs. A multisite study of citalopram in children with PDD targeting repetitive behavior is currently being conducted by the federally funded STAART centers.

Mirtazapine

The atypical antidepressant mirtazapine (an agent with both serotonergic and noradrenergic properties) has been studied for the treatment of children with autism or other PDDs (Posey, Guenin, Kohn, Swiezy, & McDougle, 2001). In that report, 26 subjects (mean age 10.1 ± 4.8 years) with PDDs were treated with open-label mirtazapine (dose range, 7.5 to 45 mg daily; mean 30.3 ± 12.6 mg daily). Nine subjects were medication-free at baseline, and 17 were taking concomitant psychotropic medications. Twenty-five of 26 subjects completed at least 4 weeks of treatment (mean 150 ± 103 days). Nine of the 26 (34.6%) were judged responders (*Much Improved* or *Very Much Improved* on the CGI) based on improvement in a variety of symptoms including aggression, self-injury, irritability, hyperactivity, anxiety, depression, and insomnia. Mirtazapine did not improve core symptoms of social or communication impairment. Adverse effects were minimal and included increased appetite, irritability, and transient sedation. In summary, mirtazapine was well tolerated in that preliminary report, but showed only modest efficacy for treating the associated symptoms of autistic disorder and other PDDs. Mirtazapine deserves more study to determine whether it is useful for the treatment of anxiety-related symptoms in youngsters with PDDs.

In summary, available evidence provides only limited support for the use of SSRIs in children with PDD. To date, studies of the SSRIs in this population have been conducted in small samples with poorly described target symptoms. Support for the use of these drugs in adults with PDD for repetitive behavior is stronger, but still relies on relatively few randomized, placebo-controlled studies. Despite the meager evidence, the SSRIs are commonly used in children and adolescents with PDD. Although generally safe in short-term trials, the SSRIs can cause behavioral activation, which appears to be more common in younger children. Given the poor empirical support and the apparently widespread clinical use of the SSRIs, large-scale, placebo-controlled studies aimed at clearly defined target symptoms are warranted.

STIMULANTS

The stimulants, methylphenidate, d-amphetamine, and d,l-amphetamine are standard medications for the treatment of Attention Deficit Hyperactivity Disorder (ADHD) in typically developing children. Recent reviews (Spencer, Biederman, Wilens, & Greene, 2003) and the results of the National Institute of Mental Health sponsored Multimodal Treatment of ADHD (MTA, 1999) provide strong evidence that the stimulants are effective for the treatment of ADHD. Newer formulations offer additional options for once-a-day administration and the potential for more even behavioral control across the day (Greenhill, Findling, Swanson, & ADHD Study Group, 2002; Swanson et al., 2002; Wolraich et al., 2001). The efficacy and safety of stimulants in the PDDs, however, have been less well studied. Although the *DSM-IV* precludes the diagnosis of ADHD in children with PDDs, the symptoms of motor restlessness, overactivity, distractibility, and disruptive behavior are common clinical complaints for children with developmental disabilities (Expert Consensus Guideline Series, 2000). Indeed, community and clinic-based surveys indicate that the stimulants are commonly used in children with PDD (Aman et al., 2000; Martin, Scahill, et al., 1999). Despite their common use in clinical practice, the rate of positive response appears to be lower, and the frequency of side effects may be higher, in developmentally disabled populations (see Aman, Buican, & Arnold, 2003, for a review). Of particular concern in this population is the apparently higher rate of adverse effects such as stereotypies, tics, social withdrawal, and stimulant-induced psychosis. In order to provide insight on the use of stimulant medications in children with PDD, this review will include studies in developmental disabled (DD) populations more generally.

Stimulant Treatment Studies of ADHD in Developmentally Disabled Populations

Table 44.2 presents controlled studies of methylphenidate in DD populations (Aman, Kern, McGhee, & Arnold, 1993; Aman, Marks, Turbott, Wilsher, & Merry, 1991; Aman et al., 1997; Hagerman, Murphy, & Wittenberger, 1988; Handen, Breaux, Gosling, Ploof, & Feldman, 1990; Handen, Feldman, Gosling, Lurier, & Murray, 1999; Handen, Johnson, & Lubetsky, 2000; Pearson et al., 2003; Quintana et al., 1995; Varley & Trupin, 1982). Aman and colleagues (1991) compared the efficacy of methylphenidate (MPH) with that of thioridazine in a sample of 30 children and adolescents with mental retardation and comorbid disruptive behavior disorders. In this double-blind, cross-over trial, methylphenidate (MPH) (but not thioridazine) significantly reduced ADHD symptoms on standard teacher rating scales and significantly improved performance on a continuous performance task (CPT). Parents, however, did not report much improvement with either medication. Clinical benefit from methylphenidate was observed in subjects with IQ scores above 45. In two other double-blind, cross-over studies, these same investigators confirmed the efficacy of MPH (as well as fenfluramine) in improving inattention, hyperactivity, and noncompliance among 28 mentally retarded children with ADHD (Aman et al., 1993, 1997). Laboratory measures also improved, including reaction time and impulsive responding on CPT. Hagerman and colleagues (1988) evaluated methylphenidate and d-amphetamine in their placebo-controlled crossover study of 15 children with ADHD symptoms and fragile X syndrome.

In a series of double-blind, cross-over investigations, Handen and colleagues (Handen et al., 1990, 1999, 2000) showed that MPH was successful in reducing hyperactivity, irritability, inattention, and off-task behavior among two-thirds to three-quarters of subjects with

TABLE 44.2   Placebo-Controlled Studies of Methylphenidate in Developmentally Disabled Populations

Study	N	Age	Population	Design	Dose	Measure (%) Teacher	Measure (%) Parent
Varley et al., 1982	10	4–15	ADHD+ MR	X-Over	5–60 mg/day 15–120 mg/day	13[b] 19[b]	14[c] 20[c]
Hagerman et al., 1988	15	4–12	ADHD+ Fra-X	X-over (d-amphetamine)[d]	0.3 mg/kg/dose	21[b]	11[b]
Handen et al., 1990	12	6–9	ADHD+ MR	X-Over	0.3mg/kg/dose 0.6mg/kg/dose	44[b] 58[b]	— —
Aman et al., 1991	30	4–16	ADHD+ MR	X-Over (thioridazine)[d]	0.4 mg/kg/dose	18[b]	—
Aman et al., 1993	28	5–13	ADHD+ MR	X-Over (fenfluramine)[d]	0.4 mg/kg/dose	35[a]	20[a]
Aman et al., 1997	30	5–14	ADHD+ MR	X-Over (fenfluramine)[d]	0.4 mg/kg/dose	23[a]	21[a]
Quintana et al., 1995	10	7–11	Autism	X-Over	10–20mg bid	11[b]	31[a]
Handen et al., 1999	10	4–6	ADHD+ MR	X-Over	0.3mg/kg/dose 0.6mg/kg/dose	32[b] 47[b]	— —
Handen et al., 2000	13	5–11	ADHD+ PDD	X-Over	0.3 mg/kg/dose 0.6 mg/kg/dose	43[b] 56[b]	— —
Pearson et al., 2003	24	10.9 (mean)	ADHD+ MR	X-Over	0.15 mg/kg/dose 0.3 mg/kg/dose 0.6 mg/kg/dose	13[b] 27[b] 58[b]	7[c] 12[c] 16[c]

[a] ABC Hyperactivity; [b] Conners Teacher Hyperactivity Index; [c] Conners Parent Hyperactivity Index from *Conners' Rating Scales Manual,* by C. K. Conners, 1989, North Tonowanda, NY: Multi-Health Systems; [d] Drug in parenthesis was an additional treatment condition.

Note: Percent change = Change in active treatment − Change in placebo/Baseline or Placebo endpoint − Active endpoint/Placebo

ADHD and mild to moderate mental retardation. One of these trials included subjects with autism (Handen et al., 2000). A dosage of 0.6 mg per kg was more effective than a dosage of 0.3 mg per kg on some measures, but increased frequency of irritability, social withdrawal, and tics was associated with the higher dose (Handen, Feldman, Gosling, Breaux, & McAuliffe, 1991; Handen et al., 2000). Similar observations were reported by Pearson and colleagues (2003) in a sample of 24 children with mental retardation and ADHD treated with 0.15, 0.3, 0.6 mg per kg per dose and placebo in a crossover design. Taken together, data from these studies suggest that children with mentally retarded with ADHD are at higher risk for adverse effects from the stimulants than typically developing children with ADHD. Table 44.2 summarizes findings from controlled studies that used either the Aberrant Behavior Checklist or the Conners Hyperactivity Index. As shown in the table, the level of improvement with methylphenidate was modest to large in this population with clear evidence of dose response. As expected, adverse effects are also dose related. Parents generally report less benefit than teachers.

Collectively, these data suggest that stimulant medication can be effective in children with developmental disabilities and ADHD symptoms. The rate of responders and the mean percentage of improvement are somewhat lower than those observed in typically developing children with ADHD, and large-scale studies are warranted to determine whether side-effect profiles and response rates are indeed different in this population. The RUPP Autism Network has recently completed such a study in children with PDD accompanied by hyperactivity, impulsiveness, and distractibility. When the results are analyzed, this randomized clinical trial should provide useful guidance to clinicians and families.

MISCELLANEOUS COMPOUNDS

Although many other agents have been tried in the treatment of children with PDD including buspirone (Buitelaar, van der Gaag, & van der Hoeven, 1998), clonidine (Frankhauser, Karumanchi, German, Yates, & Karumanchi, 1992), and amantadine (King et al., 2001), this review

will focus primarily on secretin and the opiate antagonist, naltrexone. Each of these compounds was introduced with great expectations about efficacy in PDD, but neither drug has accumulated persuasive clinical evidence. As newer pharmacological alternatives emerge for the treatment of autism (e.g., congeners of oxytocin, which may be involved in the neurobiology of affiliative behaviors; Insel, 1997; Leckman et al., 1994), the secretin and naltrexone trials may guide research efforts.

Mood Stabilizers

Anticonvulsant medications are commonly used among individuals with PDDs (Aman et al., 2000), in part given the high rates of seizure disorders associated with the PDDs (Volkmar & Nelson, 1990). In addition to their anti-seizure properties, this class of compounds has been evaluated in few case series and small open-label trials for the treatment of aggression and behavioral dyscontrol associated with autism. Single cases have been reported on the use of lithium carbonate (Kerbeshian, Burd, & Fisher, 1987; Steingard & Biederman, 1987) in the treatment of refractory aggression in adults with autism. More recently, a retrospective case series of divalproex sodium use among children and adults with autism (ages 5 to 40; mean dose = 768 mg per day) reported favorable changes in affective instability, repetitive behaviors, and aggression (Hollander, Dolgoff-Kaspar, Cartwright, Rawitt, & Novotny, 2001). A study of lamotrigine in 28 children with autism (Belsito, Law, Kirk, Landa, & Zimmerman, 2001) showed no separation between active drug and placebo on any of the outcome measures used. Higher rates of adverse skin reactions in children compared to adults (including exfoliative dermatolysis and Stevens Johnson syndrome) provide further caution on the use of this agent in the treatment of children with autism (Messenheimer, 1998).

Naltrexone

Naloxone and naltrexone are the opiate antagonists that have been evaluated in autism. Given that naloxone is short-acting and has to be administered parenterally, its clinical applications are limited. By contrast, the plasma half-life of orally administered naltrexone is between 4 and 10 hours. The use of these agents in autism is based on the putative role of endogenous opioids such as beta-endorphin and encephalins in the regulation of social behavior (Benton & Brain, 1988). Results from animal studies suggest that opioids may play a role in maternal-infant attachment by influencing feelings of social comfort and reducing separation distress reactions (Panksepp, Herman, Connor, Bishop, & Scott, 1978).

Initial reports of open-label studies with naltrexone in autism seemed promising (Campbell et al., 1989; Panksepp & Lensing, 1991), but results of subsequent placebo-controlled studies were disappointing. For example, in a 3-week, placebo-controlled parallel trial of 41 children with autism, ages 2 to 7 years, Campbell and colleagues (1993) showed modest improvements in hyperactivity, but no other beneficial effects. Feldman, Kolmen, and colleagues conducted a crossover study with naltrexone in 24 children with autism who ranged in age from 3 to 8 years. Again, modest benefits were observed in hyperactivity (Kolmen, Feldman, Handen, & Janosky, 1997), but no positive effects were observed in language function communication (Feldman, Kolmen, & Gonzaga, 1999). The dose level in these three studies was 1.0 mg per kg per day. At this dose level, the drug was well tolerated, with sedation and decreased appetite being common adverse effects. One small study of four children with autism compared three dose levels of naltrexone (0.5 mg per kg, 1.0 mg per kg and 2.0 mg per kg) to placebo in a cross-over design (Leboyer et al., 1992). Although the sample was small, visual inspection of the data suggests an unusual dose-response. For example, self-injurious behavior appeared to improve on the lowest and the highest dose, but worsen on the medium dose (1.0 mg per kg). These intriguing, but somewhat perplexing, results provide insufficient direction for clinicians. Finally, the modest effects on hyperactivity suggest that the usefulness of naltrexone in the treatment of autism and related conditions is limited.

Secretin

The excitement concerning the use of the gastrointestinal peptide secretin in the treatment of three children with autism (Horvath et al., 1998) was followed by a series of randomized, double-blind, placebo-controlled trials of intravenous infusion of the agent. The results of these studies are remarkably consistent, showing no evidence of efficacy for secretin in autism. The first controlled study showed that a single dose of synthetic human secretin was no better than placebo for the treatment for 60 youngsters with autism or pervasive developmental disorder (Sandler et al., 1999). Since then, several randomized clinical trials of secretin, involving some 500 children with autism or PDD, have been conducted. Indeed, secretin is the best studied drug for the treatment of autism. For example, a 3-week, parallel study by Dunn-Geier and colleagues (2000) in 95 children with autism compared secretin to placebo. There was no change on a standardized language measure, on parent-rated or clinician-rated core symptoms of autism in either treatment group. Yet another study of 60 children showed that a single dose of intravenous secretin was no better than placebo on parent-rated symptoms of autism or language skills 6 weeks after injection (Coniglio et al., 2001). Four additional studies were conducted through 2002; two of them (Carey et al., 2002; Corbett et al., 2001) at single sites and with modest sample sizes (12 or 8, respectively), and two larger ones the result of multisite collaborations (Owley et al., 2001, $N = 56$; Unis et al., 2002, $N = 85$). These studies too showed little or no beneficial effects. Thus, although it is the best-studied treatment in autism, secretin is not effective.

CONCLUSION

Advances have been modest in the pharmacological treatment of autistic disorder and other PDDs since the 1950s, when biological research in this area began. To date, only a limited number of informative randomized, placebo-controlled studies have been published. Recent action by the NIMH to fund the RUPP Autism Network has resulted in completion of the largest controlled drug treatment study in autistic disorder to date. Continued support by the federal government and voluntary organizations will be necessary to guide clinical care of children with autism and related conditions. Although the results are disappointing, the recent series of studies with secretin shows improved capacity in the field to carry out rigorous clinical trials to determine safety and efficacy. Future research should include additional controlled trials of atypical antipsychotics in individuals with autistic disorder and other subtypes of PDD. In particular, assessment of longitudinal efficacy and safety is needed with all of these agents. Larger controlled studies of stimulants and definitive studies of SSRIs are underway and will likely provide important information to guide clinical practice. Novel treatment approaches, including agents affecting glutamatergic function should also be pursued. Finally, trials looking at the combination and sequencing of pharmacological and behavioral treatments are needed to promote optimal development in this population.

Cross-References

Neurochemical aspects of autism are discussed in Chapter 17; other aspects of intervention are addressed in Chapters 34 to 43.

REFERENCES

Aman, M. G., Buican, B., & Arnold, L. E. (2003). Methylphenidate treatment in children with borderline IQ and mental retardation: Analysis of three aggregated studies. *Journal of Child and Adolescent Psychopharmacology, 13,* 29–40.

Aman, M. G., Collier-Crespin, A., & Lindsay, R. L. (2000). Pharmacotherapy of disorders in mental retardation. *European Child and Adolescent Psychiatry, 9,* 98–107.

Aman, M. G., Kern, R. A., McGhee, D. E., & Arnold, L. E. (1993). Fenfluramine and methylphenidate in children with mental retardation and ADHD: Clinical and side effects. *Journal of the American Academy of Child and Adolescent Psychiatry, 32,* 851–859.

Aman, M. G., Kern, R. A., Osborne, P., Tumuluru, R., Rojahn, J., & del Medico, V. (1997). Fenfluramine and methylphenidate in children with mental retardation and borderline IQ: Clinical effects. *American Journal of Mental Retardation 101,* 521–534.

Aman, M. G., Marks, R. E., Turbott, S. H., Wilsher, C. P., & Merry, S. N. (1991). Methylphenidate and thioridazine in the treatment of intellectually subaverage children: Effects on cognitive-motor performance. *Journal of the American Academy of Child and Adolescent Psychiatry, 30,* 816–824.

Anderson, L. T., Campbell, M., Adams, P., Small, A. M., Perry, R., & Shell, J. (1989). The effects of haloperidol on discrimination learning and behavioral symptoms in autistic children. *Journal of Autism and Developmental Disorders, 19,* 227–239.

Baldessarini, R. J., & Frankenburg, F. R. (1991). Clozapine. A novel antipsychotic agent. *New England Journal of Medicine, 324,* 746–754.

Belsito, K. M., Law, P. A., Kirk, K. S., Landa, R. J., & Zimmerman, A. W. (2001). Lamotrigine therapy for autistic disorder: A randomized, double-blind, placebo-controlled trial. *Journal of Autism and Developmental Disorders, 31,* 175–181.

Benton, D., & Brain, P. F. (1988). The role of opioid mechanisms in social interaction and attachment. In R. J. Rodgers & S. J. Cooper (Eds.), *Endorphins, opiates and behavioural processes* (pp. 215–235). New York: Wiley.

Branford, D., Bhaumik, S., & Naik, B. (1998). Selective serotonin re-uptake inhibitors for the treatment of perseverative and maladaptive behaviours of people with intellectual disability. *Journal of Intellectual Disability Research, 42,* 301–306.

Brasic, J. R., Barnett, J. Y., Kaplan, D., Sheitman, B. B., Aisemberg, P., Lafargue, R. T., et al. (1994). Clomipramine ameliorates adventitious movements and compulsions in prepubertal boys with autistic disorder and severe mental retardation. *Neurology, 44,* 1309–1312.

Brodkin, E. S., McDougle, C. J., Naylor, S. T., Cohen, D. J., & Price, L. H. (1997). Clomipramine in adults with pervasive developmental disorders: A prospective open-label investigation. *Journal of Child and Adolescent Psychopharmacology, 7,* 109–121.

Bruggeman, R., van der Linden, C., Buitelaar, J. K., Gericke, G. S., Hawkridge, S. M., & Temlett, J. A. (2001). Risperidone versus pimozide in Tourette's disorder: A comparative double-blind parallel-group study. *Journal of Clinical Psychiatry, 62,* 50–56.

Buitelaar, J. K., van der Gaag, R. J., & van der Hoeven, J. (1998). Buspirone in the management of anxiety and irritability in children with pervasive developmental disorders: Results of an open-label study. *Journal of Clinical Psychiatry, 59,* 56–59.

Bymaster, F. P., Calligaro, D. O., Falcone, J. F., Marsh, R. D., Moore, N. A., Tye, N. C., et al. (1996). Radioreceptor binding profile of the atypical antipsychotic olanzapine. *Neuropsy-chopharmacology, 14,* 87–96.

Campbell, M., Anderson, L. T., Small, A. M., Adams, P., Gonzalez, N. M., & Ernst, M. (1993). Naltrexone in autistic children: Behavioral symptoms and attentional learning. *Journal of the American Academy of Child and Adolescent Psychiatry, 32,* 1283–1291.

Campbell, M., Armenteros, J. L., Malone, R. P., Adams, P. B., Eisenberg, Z. W., & Overall, J. E. (1997). Neuroleptic-related dyskinesias in autistic children: A prospective, longitudinal study. *Journal of the American Academy of Child and Adolescent Psychiatry, 36,* 835–843.

Campbell, M., Overall, J. E., Small, A. M., Sokol, M. S., Spencer, E. S., Adams, P., et al. (1989). Naltrexone in autistic children: An acute open dose range tolerance trial. *Journal of the American Academy of Child and Adolescent Psychiatry, 28,* 200–206.

Carey, T., Ratliff-Schaub, K., Funk, J., Weinle, C., Myers, M., & Jenks, J. (2002). Double-blind placebo-controlled trial of secretin: Effects on aberrant behavior in children with autism. *Journal of Autism and Developmental Disorders, 32,* 161–167.

Chen, N. C., Bedair, H. S., McKay, B., Bowers, M. B., Jr., & Mazure, C. (2001). Clozapine in the treatment of aggression in an adolescent with autistic disorder. *Journal of Clinical Psychiatry, 62,* 479–480.

Coniglio, S. J., Lewis, J. D., Lang, C., Burns, T. G., Subhani-Siddique, R., Weintraub, A., et al. (2001). A randomized, double-blind, placebo-controlled trial of single-dose intravenous secretin as treatment for children with autism. *Journal of Pediatrics, 138,* 649–655.

Cook, E. H., Jr., Rowlett, R., Jaselskis, C., & Leventhal, B. L. (1992). Fluoxetine treatment of children and adults with autistic disorder and mental retardation. *Journal of the American Academy of Child and Adolescent Psychiatry, 31,* 739–745.

Corbett, B., Khan, K., Czapansky-Beilman, D., Brady, N., Dropik, P., Goldman, D. Z., et al. (2001). A double-blind, placebo-controlled crossover study investigating the effect of porcine secretin in children with autism. *Clinical Pediatrics, 40,* 327–331.

Davanzo, P. A., Belin, T. R., Widawski, M. H., & King, B. H. (1998). Paroxetine treatment of aggression and self-injury in persons with mental retardation. *American Journal of Mental Retardation, 102,* 427–437.

DeLong, G. R., Teague, L. A., & McSwain-Kamran, M. (1998). Effects of fluoxetine treatment in young children with idiopathic autism. *Developmental Medicine and Child Neurology, 40,* 551–562.

Dunn-Geier, J., Ho, H. H., Auersperg, E., Doyle, D., Eaves, L., Matsuba, C., et al. (2000). Effect of secretin on children with autism: A randomized controlled trial. *Developmental Medicine and Child Neurology, 42,* 796–802.

Epperson, N., Czarkowski, K. A., Ward-O'Brien, D., Weiss, E., Gueorguieva, R., Jatlow, P., et al. (2001). Maternal sertraline treatment and serotonin transport in breast-feeding mother-infant pairs. *American Journal of Psychiatry, 158,* 1631–1637.

Expert Consensus Guideline Series. (2000). Expert Consensus Guideline Series: Treatment of psychiatric and behavioral problems in mental retardation. *American Journal of Mental Retardation, 105,* 159–226.

Feldman, H. M., Kolmen, B. K., & Gonzaga, A. M. (1999). Naltrexone and communication skills in young children with autism. *Journal of the American Academy of Child and Adolescent Psychiatry, 38,* 587–593.

Frankhauser, M., Karumanchi, V., German, M., Yates, A., & Karumanchi, S. (1992). A double-blind, placebo-controlled study of the efficacy of transdermal clonidine in autism. *Journal of Clinical Psychiatry, 53,* 77–82.

Garber, H. J., McGonigle, J. J., Slomka, G. T., & Monteverde, E. (1992). Clomipramine treatment of stereotypic behaviors and self-injury in patients with developmental disabilities. *Journal of the American Academy of Child and Adolescent Psychiatry, 31,* 1157–1160.

Gordon, C. T., Rapoport, J. L., Hamburger, S. D., State, R. C., & Mannheim, G. B. (1992). Differential response of seven subjects with autistic disorder to clomipramine and desipramine. *American Journal of Psychiatry, 149,* 363–366.

Gordon, C. T., State, R. C., Nelson, J. E., Hamburger, S. D., & Rapoport, J. L. (1993). A double-blind comparison of clomipramine, desipramine, and placebo in the treatment of autistic disorder. *Archives of General Psychiatry, 50,* 441–447.

Greenhill, L. L., Findling, R. L., Swanson, J. M., & ADHD Study Group. (2002). A double-blind, placebo-controlled study of modified-release methylphenidate in children with attention-deficit/hyperactivity disorder. *Pediatrics, 109,* E39.

Hagerman, R. J., Murphy, M. A., & Wittenberger, M. D. (1988). A controlled trial of stimulant medication in children with the fragile X syndrome. *American Journal of Medical Genetics, 30,* 377–392.

Handen, B. L., Breaux, A. M., Gosling, A., Ploof, D. L., & Feldman, H. M. (1990). Efficacy of methylphenidate among mentally retarded children with attention deficit hyperactivity disorder. *Pediatrics, 86,* 922–930.

Handen, B. L., Feldman, H. M., Gosling, A., Breaux, A. M., & McAuliffe, S. (1991). Adverse side effects of methylphenidate among mentally retarded children with ADHD. *Journal of the American Academy of Child and Adolescent Psychiatry, 30,* 241–245.

Handen, B. L., Feldman, H. M., Lurier, A., & Murray, P. J. (1999). Efficacy of methylphenidate among preschool children with developmental disabilities and ADHD. *Journal of the American Academy of Child and Adolescent Psychiatry, 38,* 805–812.

Handen, B. L., Johnson, C. R., & Lubetsky, M. (2000). Efficacy of methylphenidate among children with autism and symptoms of attention-deficit hyperactivity disorder. *Journal of Autism and Developmental Disorders, 30,* 245–255.

Heimann, S. W. (1999). High-dose olanzapine in an adolescent. *Journal of the American Academy of Child and Adolescent Psychiatry, 38,* 496–498.

Hellings, J. A., Kelley, L. A., Gabrielli, W. F., Kilgore, E., & Shah, P. (1996). Sertraline response in adults with mental retardation and autistic disorder. *Journal of Clinical Psychiatry, 57,* 333–336.

Hirsch, S. R., Link, C. G., Goldstein, J. M., & Arvanitis, L. A. (1996). ICI 204, 636: A new atypical antipsychotic drug. *British Journal of Psychiatry, 29*(Suppl.), 45–56.

Hollander, E., Dolgoff-Kaspar, R., Cartwright, C., Rawitt, R., & Novotny, S. (2001). An open trial of divalproex sodium in autism spectrum disorders. *Journal of Clinical Psychiatry, 62,* 530–534.

Horrigan, J. P., Barnhill, L. J., & Courvoisie, H. E. (1997). Olanzapine in PDD. *Journal of the American Academy of Child and Adolescent Psychiatry, 36,* 1166–1167.

Horvath, K., Stefanatos, G., Sokolski, K. N., Wachtel, R., Nabors, L., & Tildon, J. T. (1998). Improved social and language skills after secretin administration in patients with autistic spectrum disorders. *Journal of the Association for Academic Minority Physicians, 9,* 9–15.

Insel, T. R. (1997). A neurobiological basis of social attachment. *American Journal of Psychiatry, 154,* 726–735.

Kane, J. M., Carson, W. H., Saha, A. R., McQuade, R. D., Ingenito, G. G., Zimbroff, D. L., et al. (2002). Efficacy and safety of aripiprazole and haloperidol versus placebo in patients with schizophrenia and schizoaffective disorder. *Journal of Clinical Psychiatry, 63,* 763–771.

Kapur, S., & Seeman, P. (2001). Does fast dissociation from the dopamine d(2) receptor explain the action of atypical antipsychotics?: A new hypothesis. *American Journal of Psychiatry, 158,* 360–369.

Kerbeshian, J., Burd, L., & Fisher, W. (1987). Lithium carbonate in the treatment of two patients with infantile autism and atypical bipolar symptomatology. *Journal of Clinical Psychopharmacology, 7,* 401–405.

King, B. H., Wright, D. M., Handen, B. L., Sikich, L., Zimmerman, A. W., McMahon, W., et al. (2001). Double-blind, placebo-controlled study of amantadine hydrochloride in the treatment of children with autistic disorder. *Journal of the American Academy of Child and Adolescent Psychiatry, 40,* 658–665.

Kolmen, B. K., Feldman, H. M., Handen, B. L., & Janosky, J. E. (1997). Naltrexone in young autistic children: Replication study and learning measures. *Journal of the American Academy of Child and Adolescent Psychiatry, 36,* 1570–1578.

Leboyer, M., Bouvard, M. P., Launay, J., Tabuteau, F., Waller, D., Dugas, M., et al. (1992). Brief report: A double-blind study of naltrexone in infantile autism. *Journal of Autism and Developmental Disorders, 22,* 309–319.

Leckman, J. F., Goodman, W. K., North, W. G., Chappell, P. B., Price, L. H., Pauls, D. L., et al. (1994). The role of central oxytocin in obsessive compulsive disorder and related normal behavior. *Psychoneuroendocrinology, 19,* 723–749.

Leysen, J. E., Gommeren, W., Eens, A., de Chaffoy de Courecelles, D., Stoof, J. C., & Janssen, P. A. (1988). Biochemical profile of risperidone, a new antipsychotic. *Journal of Pharmacology and Experimental Therapeutics, 247,* 661–670.

Malone, R. P., Cater, J., Sheikh, R. M., Choudhury, M. S., & Delaney, M. A. (2001). Olanzapine versus haloperidol in children with autistic disorder: An open pilot study. *Journal of the American Academy of Child and Adolescent Psychiatry, 40,* 887–894.

Martin, A., Koenig, K., Anderson, G. M., & Scahill, L. (2003). Low-dose fluvoxamine treatment of children and adolescents with pervasive developmental disorders: A prospective, open-label study. *Journal of Autism and Developmental Disorders, 33,* 77–85.

Martin, A., Koenig, K., Scahill, L., & Bregman, J. (1999). Open-label quetiapine in the treatment of children and adolescents with autistic disorder. *Journal of Child and Adolescent Psychopharmacology, 9,* 99–107.

Martin, A., Scahill, L., Klin, A., & Volkmar, F. R. (1999). Higher-functioning pervasive developmental disorders: Rates and patterns of psychotropic drug use. *Journal of the American Academy of Child and Adolescent Psychiatry, 38,* 923–931.

McDougle, C. J., Brodkin, E. S., Naylor, S. T., Carlson, D. C., Cohen, D. J., & Price, L. H. (1998). Sertraline in adults with pervasive developmental disorders: A prospective open-label investigation. *Journal of Clinical Psychopharmacology, 18,* 62–66.

McDougle, C. J., Kem, D. L., & Posey, D. J. (2002). Case series: Use of ziprasidone for maladaptive symptoms in youths with autism. *Journal of the American Academy of Child and Adolescent Psychiatry, 41,* 921–927.

McDougle, C. J., Naylor, S. T., Cohen, D. J., Volkmar, F. R., Heninger, G. R., & Price, L. H. (1996). A double-blind, placebo-controlled study of fluvoxamine in adults with autistic disorder. *Archives of General Psychiatry, 53,* 1001–1008.

McDougle, C. J., Price, L. H., Volkmar, F. R., Goodman, W. K., Ward-O'Brien, D., Nielsen, J., et al. (1992). Clomipramine in autism: Preliminary evidence of efficacy. *Journal of the American Academy of Child and Adolescent Psychiatry, 31,* 746–750.

McDougle, C. J., Scahill, L., McCracken, J. T., Aman, M. G., Tierney, E., Arnold, L. E., et al. (2000). Research Units on Pediatric Psychopharmacology (RUPP) Autism Network: Background and rationale for an initial controlled study of risperidone. *Child and Adolescent Psychiatric Clinics of North America, 9,* 201–224.

Meltzer, H. Y. (1999). The role of serotonin in antipsychotic drug action. *Nueropsychopharmacology, 21,* 106S–115S.

Messenheimer, J. A. (1998). Rash in adult and pediatric patients treated with lamotrigine. *Canadian Journal of Neurological Sciences, 25,* S14–S18.

Multimodal Treatment of ADHD. (1999). A 14-month randomized clinical trial of treatment strategies for attention-deficit/hyperactivity disorder (MTA Cooperative Group; Multimodal Treatment Study of Children with ADHD). *Archives of General Psychiatry, 56,* 1073–1086.

Owley, T., McMahon, W., Cook, E. H., Laulhere, T., South, M., Mays, L. Z., et al. (2001). Multi-site, double-blind, placebo-controlled trial of porcine secretin in autism. *Journal of the American Academy of Child and Adolescent Psychiatry, 40,* 1293–1299.

Panksepp, J., Herman, B., Connor, R., Bishop, P., & Scott, J. P. (1978). The biology of social attachments: Opiates alleviate separation distress. *Biological Psychiatry, 13,* 607–618.

Panksepp, J., & Lensing, P. (1991). Brief report: A synopsis of an open-trial of naltrexone treatment of autism with four children. *Journal of Autism and Developmental Disorders, 21,* 243–249.

Pearson, D. A., Santos, C. W., Roache, J. D., Casat, C. D., Loveland, K. A., Lachar, D., et al. (2003). Treatment effects of methylphenidate on behavioral adjustment in children with mental retardation and ADHD. *Journal of the American Academy of Child and Adolescent Psychiatry, 42,* 209–216.

Posey, D. J., Guenin, K. D., Kohn, A. E., Swiezy, N. B., & McDougle, C. J. (2001). A naturalistic open-label study of mirtazapine in autistic and other pervasive developmental disorders. *Journal of Child and Adolescent Psychopharmacology, 11,* 267–277.

Posey, D. J., Litwiller, M., Koburn, A., & McDougle, C. J. (1999). Paroxetine in autism. *Journal of the American Academy of Child and Adolescent Psychiatry, 38,* 111–112.

Potenza, M. N., Holmes, J. P., Kanes, S. J., & McDougle, C. J. (1999). Olanzapine treatment of children, adolescents, and adults with pervasive developmental disorders: An open-label pilot study. *Journal of Clinical Psychopharmacology, 19,* 37–44.

Quintana, H., Birmaher, B., Stedge, D., Lennon, S., Freed, J., Bridge, J., et al. (1995). Use of methylphenidate in the treatment of children with autistic disorder. *Journal of Autism and Developmental Disorders, 25,* 283–294.

Rubin, M. (1997). Use of atypical antipsychotics in children with mental retardation, autism, and other developmental disabilities. *Psychiatric Annals, 27,* 219–221.

Research Units on Pediatric Psychopharmacology Anxiety Group. (2001). Fluvoxamine for the treatment of anxiety disorders in children and adolescents (The Research Unit on Pediatric Psychopharmacology Anxiety Study Group). *New England Journal of Medicine, 344,* 1279–1285.

Research Units on Pediatric Psychopharmacology Autism Network. (2002). Risperidone in children with autism and serious behavioral problems. *New England Journal of Medicine, 347,* 314–321.

RUPP Autism Network. (in press). Risperidone treatment of autistic disorder: Longer term benefits and blinded discontinuation after six months. *American Journal of Psychiatry.*

Sanchez, L. E., Campbell, M., Small, A. M., Cueva, J. E., Armenteros, J. L., & Adams, P. B. (1996). A pilot study of clomipramine in young autistic children. *Journal of the American Academy of Child and Adolescent Psychiatry, 35,* 537–544.

Sandler, A. D., Sutton, K. A., DeWeese, J., Girardi, M. A., Sheppard, V., & Bodfish, J. W. (1999). Lack of benefit of a single dose of synthetic human secretin in the treatment of autism and pervasive developmental disorder. *New England Journal of Medicine, 341,* 1801–1806.

Scahill, L., Leckman, J. F., Schultz, R. T., Katsovich, L., & Peterson, B. S. (2003). A placebo-controlled trial of risperidone in Tourette syndrome. *Neurology, 60,* 1130–1135.

Scahill, L., Martin, A., Koenig, K., Katsovich, L., & Kustan, E. (submitted). *Ziprasidone in children and adolescents with refractory psychiatric conditions.*

Scahill, L., McCracken, J. T., McDougle, C. J., Aman, M., Arnold, L. E., Tierney, E., et al. (2001). Methodological issues in designing a multisite trial of risperidone in children and adolescents with autism. *Journal of Child and Adolescent Psychopharmacology, 11,* 377–388.

Seeger, T. F., Seymour, P. A., Schmidt, A. W., Zorn, S. H., Schulz, D. W., Lebel, L. A., et al. (1995). Ziprasidone (CP-88, 059): A new antipsychotic with combined dopamine and serotonin receptor antagonist activity. *Journal of Pharmacology and Experimental Therapeutics, 275,* 101–113.

Snead, R. W., Boon, F., & Presberg, J. (1994). Paroxetine for self-injurious behavior. *Journal of the American Academy of Child and Adolescent Psychiatry, 33,* 909–910.

Spencer, T., Biederman, J., Wilens, T., & Greene, R. (2003). Attention-deficit hyperactivity disorder. In A. Martin, L. Scahill, D. S. Charney, & J. F. Leckman (Eds.), *Pediatric psychopharmacology, principles and practice* (pp. 447–465). New York: Oxford University Press.

Steingard, R. J., & Biederman, J. (1987). Lithium responsive manic-like symptoms in two individuals with autism and mental retardation. *Journal of the American Academy of Child and Adolescent Psychiatry, 26,* 932–935.

Steingard, R. J., Zimnitzky, B., DeMaso, D. R., Bauman, M. L., & Bucci, J. P. (1997). Sertraline treatment of transition-associated anxiety and agitation in children with autistic disorder. *Journal of Child and Adolescent Psychopharmacology, 7,* 9–15.

Swanson, J. M., Lerner, M., Wigal, T., Steinhoff, K., Greenhill, L., Posner, K., et al. (2002). The use of a laboratory school protocol to evaluate concepts about efficacy and side effects of new formulations of stimulant medications. *Journal of Attention Disorders, 6,* S73–S88.

Tamminga, C. A. (2002). Partial dopamine agonists in the treatment of psychosis. *Journal Neural Transmission, 109,* 411–420.

Unis, A. S., Munson, J. A., Rogers, S. J., Goldson, E., Osterling, J., & Gabriels, R. (2002). A randomized, double-blind, placebo-controlled trial of porcine versus synthetic secretin for reducing symptoms of autism. *Journal of the American Academy of Child and Adolescent Psychiatry, 41,* 1315–1321.

Varley, C. K., & Trupin, E. W. (1982). Double-blind administration of methylphenidate to mentally retarded children with attention deficit disorder; a preliminary study. *American Journal of Mental Deficiency, 86,* 560–566.

Volkmar, F. R., & Nelson, D. S. (1990). Seizure disorders in autism. *Journal of the American Academy of Child and Adolescent Psychiatry, 29,* 127–129.

Wolraich, M. L., Greenhill, L. L., Pelham, W., Swanson, J., Wilens, T., Palumbo, D., et al. (2001). Randomized, controlled trial of oros methylphenidate once a day in children with attention-deficit/hyperactivity disorder. *Pediatrics, 108,* 883–892.

Zuddas, A., Ledda, M. G., Fratta, A., Muglia, P., & Cianchetti, C. (1996). Clinical effects of clozapine on autistic disorder. American Journal of Psychiatry, 153, 738.

SECTION VII

PUBLIC POLICY PERSPECTIVES

Public policy defines a society's beliefs, values, and practices. In relation to individuals with developmental disabilities, such as autism and pervasive developmental disorders, public policy also reflects emerging knowledge about causes, course, and outcome. Policy is shaped by various forces—a society's ethical and value-based commitments, its legal and judicial traditions, competition and balancing among interest groups for setting priorities and allocating resources, and the processes of political action. Policy reflects the success of advocates—parents, professionals, and organizations—in having their own views become established in law, practice, and budgets. A major force in shaping public policy has been the recognition that particular types of interventions are able to facilitate the development of individuals with autism, mental retardation, and other developmental disorders. These interventions emphasize the potential of individuals with disabilities to learn, to have pleasures and successes in the mainstream of society, to cope with challenges and failures, to achieve vocational skills, and to work toward and take pride in personal independence. There are differences in degree among individuals with autism and pervasive disorders in the extent to which these potentials are actualized. For the most severely retarded and behaviorally disordered individuals, life opportunities remain severely limited and high levels of both familial and societal support are needed throughout the lifespan. For individuals at the other end of the autistic spectrum, such as those with Asperger's syndrome, the milder

variants of pervasive developmental disorder, and higher functioning autism, life in the mainstream of society, including holding jobs and competing with normal individuals, is more often achieved.

Twenty or 30 years ago, public policy that foresaw only very sheltered lives in public institutions for individuals with retardation led to public and family expectations and actions that almost assured lower levels of adaptation. Placed in large institutions, individuals with retardation tended to loose personal motivation and to comply with stagnant routines; they were not expected to assert themselves as individuals; and they often did not achieve the level of personal adaptation of which they might otherwise have been capable. Public policy recognized the dangers of low, self-fulfilling expectations for individuals with disabilities and the consequent isolation that followed. This recognition has shaped policy and the concept of self-fulfilling expectations has altered the course of disability law. Living at home or in their own apartments, individuals with autism and retardation are more likely to be able to function in the broader community context, to act like others and respond to the natural contingencies of life—to be able to shop, ride public transportation, try new things, decide when and what to eat, deal with disappointments and hurt feelings, and use their successes as well as errors and mistakes to help alter their behavior. There has been virtually universal acceptance of the goal of inclusion or mainstreaming as the target for public policy in relation to individuals with disabilities. Such a model makes important demands on services, organizations, and professionals, as well as parents. Between an ideology and a successful system there are many intervening steps, often costly in terms of time, energy, and money, as well as in terms of creativity, dedication, and determination. Simply placing children in a classroom with typical normal children or adults in a single-room occupancy hotel will not assure inclusion or promote competence. Rather, supports are needed to develop prosthetic, supportive environments that will help lead to success. Just as physically disabled children cannot be integrated without the elimination of physical boundaries, using devices like ramps, those with severe behavioral problems require accommodations, such as personal aides to make inclusion possible.

Similarly, education and interventions with "normal" peers are needed to help them include the individual with disabilities and accept special provisions that may be needed in the classroom. To engineer successful integration, there is a also a need for change in the educational environmental itself, so that awareness and acceptance differences among children is fostered and valued as an important aspect of education that promotes a more tolerant and less divisive society. This process also includes a shift in the common belief that rather than "sacrificing" for the common good, the role typical children play in the integration of disabled peers can actually benefit their own growth and promote a better educational environment to all involved.

While inclusion is embodied in law and regulations, there are situations in which specialized programs and services are preferable or needed. Just as with children with distinctive medical needs, treatment in more restrictive environments occasionally may be required for individuals with developmental disabilities. When the "standard model" is for inclusion, as it is today, the use of a more restrictive environment needs to be justified and accepted by everyone involved with the individual, including the family and the individual himself or herself. In a society that has dealt adequately with the needs of individuals with disabilities, there should be a spectrum of services from least to more restrictive, from fully inclusive to more specialized. A long-standing debate

has tended to pit advocates of two poles—full inclusion versus segregated services—against each other. Today, the inclusion viewpoint is the paradigm; families, professionals, and advocates generally recognize the value of an available spectrum of educational, living, and rehabilitation services to meet individual needs and, especially, when these are in the service of ultimate integration, to the degree possible.

Much of the tension in this debate is defused if the discussion focuses on individual children rather than general ideological stance, so that practical decisions are made first and foremost on the basis of the child's individual profile of strengths and deficits, and his or her realistic capacities to benefit from the various aspects of this continuum of services. Research in relation to the development of individuals with mental retardation showed the value of thinking about retarded individuals as whole people (Zigler & Hodapp, 1986). This ideology captured an important set of empirical findings about the role of motivation and personality in shaping behavior of individuals with retardation. It was found that an individual's intelligence is only one factor in determining adaptation and ultimate level of functioning. In addition, motivational factors and phenomena such as self-direction, effectance, esteem, modeling normal behavior, and history of success made enormous differences in functioning. Indeed, within a broad range of IQ scores, the level of adaptive functioning has less to do with intelligence than with these psychological characteristics and the presence of maladaptive behavior. The developmental approach to understanding individuals with intellectual disabilities also emphasizes the importance of enhancing the experiences and the environments of individuals with disabilities. An extension of the research and policy concerning individuals with intellectual disabilities has been seeing the "autistic child as a whole person." This now is a cornerstone of public policy and underlies the most innovative programs, as described in this Section.

Ethical considerations have profound affects on personal, social, and professional activities. Usually, ethics are implicit in daily life and most social relations. However, in the study, care, and treatment of individuals with disabilities, ethics need to be made explicit. Through the discussion of ethical issues, professionals and families are able to articulate their personal values and define a shared perspective. This is particularly relevant to complex issues where there are more shades of gray than clearly right versus wrong answers, for example, in the use of new and unproven therapies and in decisions about participation of children and those with intellectual and behavioral disabilities in research (Klin & Cohen, 1997). Ethical discussion highlights issues and possibilities, but cannot be expected to provide an authoritative conclusion. Rather, ethical discourse is an important process of societal and personal self-reflection. In relation to autism and others with severe developmental disorders, ethical discussions emphasize the importance of appreciating the humanity of those who are most different from normal while working to improve their future.

Contemporary legal understanding of the rights of individuals with disabilities, including those with autism and pervasive developmental disorders, is the result of a process of politics, advocacy, and scientific and educational advancements. Current law reflects many convergent forces, including the legal analysis of the dangers of previous special educational and institutional practices, the extension of civil rights to the disabled, the success of advocates and, increasingly, self advocates, in shaping legislation. The available legislative mandates and legal remedies are a powerful force for influencing the services and programs delivered to individuals with disabilities and their rights for inclusion and participation. However, there are enormous gaps between rights and practice, between what might be hoped for and what actually exists. Even in the most affluent and programmatically advanced nations, educational and therapeutic services for children and adolescents with disabilities are often limited and far from what the law may mandate. Almost everywhere, the special educational, vocational, social, therapeutic, and living opportunities for adults are far more limited than for children and adolescents.

Public policy is expressed in laws, regulations, budgets, and programs; it also defines shared, public goals and aspirations. Public policy has changed over the past years and will continue to reflect new knowledge and changing values and priorities. The study of the history of public policy and differences in policies among communities and nations can help shape the future directions of public attitudes and guide informed public policy.

REFERENCES

Klin, A., & Cohen, D. J. (1997). Ethical issues in research and treatment. In D. J. Cohen & F. R. Volkmar (Eds.), *Handbook of autism and pervasive developmental disorders* (2nd ed., pp. 828–841). New York: Wiley.

Zigler, E., & Hodapp, R. (1986). *Understanding mental retardation.* Cambridge, England: Cambridge University Press.

CHAPTER 45

Preparation of Autism Specialists

GAIL G. MCGEE AND MICHAEL J. MORRIER

To ensure the optimal progress of individuals with autism, the professional personnel who serve them need specialized training that prepares them to address the unique characteristics associated with autism. In addition to having a foundation in their discipline and area of practice, along with familiarity with developmental disabilities, autism specialists also need knowledge and skills specific to autism (Simpson, 2004). For example, teachers who educate children with autism in inclusive settings need a foundation in both general education and special education, along with information and specialty skills that are specific to children with autism. This chapter examines relevant research findings on personnel preparation and uses this information to outline an empirically based strategy for developing a comprehensive training plan that meets the multifaceted needs of children and adults with autism.

There are pressing needs to prepare professionals from various disciplines to serve individuals with autism and their families. The irregular developmental patterns displayed by children with autism require that diagnosticians have specialized skills in assessment and differential diagnosis of developmental disorders, and both assessment specialists and interventionists need training in how to conduct progress evaluations. All providers who serve young children who potentially have autism need familiarity with a number of symptoms that occur almost exclusively in children and adults with autism, such as: (1) a strong preference for being alone, (2) active avoidance of other children, (3) a lack of interest in social

reinforcement, (4) a pervasive lack of interest in the environment, (5) intense distress over interruption of nonfunctional routines, and (6) a fascination with (or aversion to) irrelevant details of an object.

Part of the challenge of preparing autism specialists is due to the number and severity of impairments that individuals with autism may present (American Psychiatric Association, 2000). The heterogeneity of the population, along with the scatter of skills that is common within the developmental pattern of an individual with autism, makes it necessary for autism specialty training to cover how to assess and intervene across wide-ranging developmental abilities. In addition, children with autism, including some who have normal or above-average cognitive ability, often present with severe deficits in generalization, symbolic play, and abstract reasoning. As a result, although typical children can readily tolerate many flaws in their education, children with autism require precise implementation of complex teaching procedures to learn at an optimal pace.

Further broadening the training agenda for autism specialists are numerous special needs that are not specific to autism, but nevertheless can be diagnostic indicators when occurring in tandem with severe social and communication impairments (e.g., obsessive-compulsive behaviors, self-stimulatory behaviors, and language delays). Frequent comorbidity of autism and disorders such as mental retardation, seizures, hyperactivity, and attention deficits also expand the range of knowledge and skills that autism specialists must acquire. Even though associated features such as self-injury and aggression are relatively rare, the risk of harm presented by such severe behavioral challenges dictates the need for autism interventionists to develop a strong foundation in functional behavioral analysis. Finally, autism specialists must become proficient in addressing a host of routine early childhood difficulties, such as sleep and eating disorders, temper tantrums, and misbehavior in public places.

Without question, however, the biggest training challenge is due to the inevitable social deficits and irregularities presented by every child and adult with autism. Preparing autism specialists to assess and intervene effectively with the social difficulties that define autism is a daunting task. Not only have social deficits proven relatively impermeable to traditional interventions, but there is also virtually no discipline that has provided affiliated professionals with an adequate foundation of knowledge and skills in the area of regular and irregular social development.

GROWING DEMAND FOR QUALIFIED PERSONNEL

The unique skills in which autism specialists must be prepared correspond closely to the extensive and unique needs of individuals with autism. Considering the enormity of the training challenge from the perspective of both trainer and trainee, it comes as no surprise that the shortages of fully qualified autism specialists are even greater than the shortages that exist for special educators in general (National Research Council [NRC], 2001). Unfortunately, all indications are that the supply-demand gap in the number of professionals available and prepared to serve individuals with autism will continue to expand in the foreseeable future, because increased numbers of young children are being identified (Yeargin-Allsopp et al., 2003). Among the factors contributing to increased autism prevalence are: (1) more sensitive diagnostic instruments (Lord, Rutter, DiLavore, & Risi, 2002; Lord, Rutter, & Le Couteur, 1994; Lord et al., 2000; Rutter, Le Couteur, & Lord, 2003); (2) expanded child-find initiatives in early intervention legislation; and more recently, (3) the establishment of practice parameters that are informing neurologists, psychiatrists, and pediatricians on the

importance of identifying the "red flags" associated with autism (Filipek et al., 2000; Volkmar, Cook, Pomeroy, Realmuto, & Tanguay, 1999). If improvements in early identification of autism are the primary cause of dramatic increases in estimated numbers of children with autism, the size and variability in the population should stabilize in the near future. However, even if the most optimistic forecasts materialize, the strain on already undercapacity service delivery systems will likely worsen before it gets better.

Impact of the Individuals with Disabilities Education Act (IDEA)

Another pressure to step up efforts to recruit and train autism specialists derives from stipulations in the IDEA reauthorization legislation (1997), which created a specific autism eligibility category under which children may qualify for special education services (Turnbull, Wilcox, & Stowe, 2002). Both the IDEA and a National Academy of Science report on the education of young children with autism (NRC, 2001) specify that the social needs of children with autism are best met in the context of inclusive educational placements.

Personnel preparation needs also result from the 1997 IDEA provisions that specifically mandate the use of functional behavior assessment (FBA) and positive behavioral intervention (PBI), which are procedures developed to reduce or prevent severe behavioral challenges. Although FBA and PBI have long been familiar to autism intervention researchers, and effective "training the trainer" initiatives are already underway in more than 20 states (Anderson, Russo, Dunlap, & Albin, 1996), there is a long way to go before every school will have someone on staff who has been trained to competency in use of these assessment/intervention procedures.

Impetus and Impact of Parent-Initiated Litigation

The lack of adequate numbers of educational personnel who are fully qualified to meet the needs of students with autism can become a self-perpetuating problem in which the costs of not providing training can rapidly exceed the costs that would have been required to provide training. When a school fails to offer sufficiently trained personnel, it has become increasingly likely that parents of children with autism will seek compensation from their public school system to pay the costs of private tuitions (Dussault, 1996). If the school refuses, litigation often ensues along with heated debate over preferred intervention methodologies (Mandlawitz, 2002). Court rulings nearly always favor parents when inadequate education has been offered, with the result that legal costs are added to tuition costs and the school system has even less funds to allocate for staff training.

EMPIRICAL EVOLUTION OF BEST PRACTICE PROVIDER PREPARATION

In his later years, Professor B. F. Skinner shared the wisdom of his experience by reflecting, "The word training should never be applied to people. I learned the hard way that some people find the concept of training people to be terribly offensive. You train dogs. You train dolphins. You *teach* people" (personal communication, September 12, 1987). To some extent, his invention of a teaching machine bypassed the issue of human training altogether (Skinner, 1954, 1958).

Early Educational Applications of Operant Conditioning Procedures

The goal of the teaching machine was to convey knowledge using an errorless learning paradigm, which had been developed in basic research that demonstrated that pigeons learned most efficiently when the initial instruction minimized opportunities for mistakes (Holland, 1960; Markle, 1962).

In the 1960s and 1970s, a fervent optimism developed concerning the use of programmed instruction, which became a popular format in which principles of errorless learning were incorporated into the preparation of college course textbooks or supplementary workbooks (Malott, Hartlep, & Hartlep, 1974). Programmed instruction involved breaking the information to be taught into small bits of easily remembered facts, which were subsequently presented in incremental steps (Markle, 1962,

1969). Each bit of information was interspersed by an opportunity to respond to a brief question, along with immediate feedback on response accuracy (i.e., a question might be inserted after a small passage of text, and the answer to the question was immediately available by looking at the back of the page or under a flap of paper). With occasional exceptions, the boon of interest in programmed instruction gradually subsided because the preparation of teaching materials was time-consuming and required sophisticated behavior analytic skills (McGee & McCoy, 1981).

Applications of Behavior Analysis to Problems of Children with Autism

Children with autism were participants in some of the earliest applications of operant conditioning techniques to human problems, in a field that came to be known as applied behavior analysis (ABA). Initial applications were often aimed at changing the behavior of an individual by changing the behavior of parents, teachers, or institutional staff (Ayllon & Azrin, 1968; Ayllon & Michael, 1959; Hall, Lund, & Jackson, 1968; Martin, 1972; Zeilberger, Sampen, & Sloane, 1968). However, relatively little information was provided on how that adult preparation was accomplished.

In one of the first case studies describing behavioral intervention for a 3-year-old boy with autism, direct care attendants in a state institution were prepared and supervised in the use of contingency management procedures to reduce severe tantrums and bedtime problems (Wolf, Risley, & Mees, 1964). However, even more importantly, "Little Dickey" was at risk of losing his eyesight unless he could be taught to wear special eyeglasses. Unfortunately, the assigned attendant was unable to implement the required shaping procedure with the precision necessary to be effective. After 5 weeks of unsuccessful effort, the experimenter eventually had to take on the role of clinician and spend a day doing the shaping himself. The experimenter succeeded in less than a day, during which Dickey first learned to wear his glasses at mealtime. Direct care attendants were next trained to take Dickey for walks in the hallway if he wore his glasses, and he gradually wore them throughout the day.

Direct care attendants were later trained to use behavioral interventions to stop Dickey from throwing (and breaking) his glasses and to resolve eating problems.

Perhaps the earlier difficulties in using complex shaping procedures encouraged a more systematic approach to training Dickey's mother how to shape meaningful verbal language (Risley & Wolf, 1966). First, an expert shaped the boy's echolalia into meaningful verbal language in a research clinic setting. His mother was then invited into the clinic and coached in how to use praise and food snacks to teach Dickey to play with puzzles. The next step was to teach the mother how to promote further language growth in the clinic, and eventually she was assisted in using her new teaching skills at home.

Behavior Modification Training Manuals

Written training guides were among the first attempts at widespread dissemination of information on applications of behavior analysis. Books and manuals were prepared for a wide variety of audiences, including parents (Becker, 1971), teachers (Buckley & Walker, 1970; Givner & Graubard, 1974; Hall, 1971), college students (Malott, 1972; Malott et al., 1974), nurses (Loomis & Horsley, 1974), institutional direct care attendants (Foxx & Azrin, 1973), and even probation officers (Thorne, Tharp, & Wetzel, 1967). One of the first manuals on behavior modification for children with autism was written for administrators, teachers, parents, and nurses (Watson, 1973).

Research and Development Aimed at Enhanced Job Performance

Research in ABA gradually began to focus more directly on how to teach adult caregivers the skills needed to serve individuals with disabilities (cf. Gardner, 1973, for a detailed review). Although many of the early staff training studies provided only scant descriptions of the clinical population to be served by the trainees, behaviors targeted by the interventions that direct care providers were being trained to implement suggested the possibility that at least some subjects had autism. For example, in a study of institutionalized children with severe mental retardation, ages 9 to 14 years, their challenging behaviors included knocking others down by storming into them, refusing to wear shoes, butting heads into other people, smearing feces on head and walls, and putting left thumb in mouth and jumping up and down (Horner, 1980).

Specification of Job Duties

Results of clarifying job expectations through detailed written instructions have been mixed. Some studies found performance improvements as the result of a specific delineation of job responsibilities or "duty cards" (Sneed & Bible, 1979). Other studies showed some benefit when staff were told what they should be doing with clients, at least when written job specifications were components of a comprehensive training plan (Ivancic, Reid, Iwata, Faw, & Page, 1981; Iwata, Bailey, Brown, Foshee, & Alpern, 1976). However, written job descriptions have not been consistently effective in changing job performance (Greene, Willis, Levy, & Bailey, 1978).

Workshops and Lectures

Job performances (or simulated job performance) improved following participation in workshops that conveyed detailed descriptions of relatively straightforward skills, such as how to manage a seizure or how to document administration of medication (Neef, Parrish, Egel, & Sloan, 1986; Panyan, Boozer, & Morris, 1970). A comparison of training via reading assignments versus workshop participation revealed that both approaches were equally effective, but written materials had the cost-efficiency advantage (Neef et al., 1986).

However, numerous studies have provided repeated documentation of the failure of traditional training workshops to develop new skills, particularly when outcomes of workshop training were compared to "hands on" training (Greene et al., 1978; Iwata et al., 1976; Montegar, Reid, Madsen, & Ewell, 1977; Reid & Whitman, 1983). Most likely, these differences are due to the increasing complexity of interventions for children with autism. Workshop participants put it succinctly, "I now know what to do but not how to do it" (Deibert & Golden, 1973).

Despite the preponderance of research evidence that workshops will not develop the complex intervention skills needed to teach children with autism, didactic instruction continues to be the primary form of training provided to teachers of children with autism. For example, during the 1990s, a growing recognition of the potential of early autism intervention, along with rapidly increasing demand for services, inspired state-sponsored early intervention programs across the country to launch large-scale autism training initiatives. Although these served a purpose in educating professionals and parents about autism spectrum disorders and various intervention approaches, much of this funding was expended in a manner that did very little to increase the nation's capacity to provide intensive early intervention to children with autism.

Feedback on Work Performances

Three approaches to changing the work behavior of institutional staff were compared in terms of the impact on client behavior (Quilitch, 1975), including: (1) a traditional instructional memo from the administration to the staff, (2) workshop training, and (3) performance feedback to staff based on the behavior of residents under their care. The memo was altogether ineffective and, despite high consumer satisfaction ratings, workshops also yielded little impact on the skills of trainees. Consistent with findings from other research, feedback was the only method that changed both staff and resident behavior.

Other studies suggested that feedback alone is not always a sufficient condition in which to develop new skills. For example, when specific performance feedback was provided to direct care providers in an institutional setting, there were benefits in terms of a decrease in the amount of time that the staff engaged in non-work behavior, and the staff showed improved organization of their existing skills (Brown, Willis, & Reid, 1981). However, feedback alone produced no demonstrable impact on the trainees' acquisition of new skills.

Behavior-Specific Praise

By far, the most common consequence used in the staff training research and in practice in leading autism intervention programs has been a combination of specific performance feedback and praise (Brown et al., 1981). Numerous studies have documented that behavior-specific praise was more effective than just feedback alone (Kreitner, Reif, & Morris, 1977; Montegar et al., 1977).

A court order to move adolescents with autism out of a state institution and into community-based group homes created a unique opportunity to assess a combination of setting and training effects on quality of care (McClannahan, McGee, MacDuff, & Krantz, 1990). *Quality of care* was defined as the presence of various permanent product indicators (i.e., "Are fingernails clean?," "Are clothes without tears?," or "Has hair been brushed today?"). Results showed that the quality of care for youth with autism improved immediately upon transition to community-based group homes. When the group homes' live-in "teaching parents" were provided with detailed behavior-specific praise for the care indices scored positively for their home's youth, along with graphic displays of their group home ratings in comparison to the ratings of other group homes, the quality of care improved even further to levels similar to those of children who lived at home with their natural parents.

Privileges as Positive Reinforcement

In research that explored the effects of various motivational systems on the work performances of direct care providers, cash bonuses awarded contingent on improved work performances were predictably more effective than individual performance feedback alone (Patterson, Griffin, & Panyan, 1976; Pomerleau, Bobrove, & Smith, 1973; Pommer & Streedbeck, 1974). A wide variety of work-related privileges (i.e., free lunch, opportunity to change work assignments, relief from lunch duty with clients, opportunity to accompany clients on special activities, preferred scheduling of work shifts, and first choice for vacation/holiday leave, weekend schedules, and days off) are among the consequences that have functioned as positive reinforcers for work improvements (Iwata et al., 1976; Reid, Schuh-Wear, & Brannon, 1978; Seys & Duker, 1978). For example, when provided with access to menus of positive and negative consequences contingent on their weekly work attendance, 73% of participating staff members who had histories of chronic absenteeism showed improvements in attendance (Shoemaker & Reid, 1980).

Public Posting: Individual and Group Contingencies

There is a sizeable body of research documenting the efficacy of a procedure known as public posting, which involves posting the results of individual performance appraisals in a public place so that each staff member can view and compare his or her own performance to those of other staff members (Page, Iwata, & Reid, 1982; Panyan et al., 1970; Quilitch, 1975). In this application, work attendance was improved by posting individual attendance records in a place accessible by other staff members (Hutchison, Jarman, & Bailey, 1980). Absenteeism has also been responsive to group contingencies. Thus, when a designated reward became available to the entire group depending on the group's average attendance record, peer pressure encouraged improvement in chronically absent staff members. (Reid et al., 1978).

Public posting of data on client performance has also been used in evaluations of staff performance. In one study, all staff members who worked day or night shift in a given residence formed a team, which competed against staff member teams from other residences on the same residential program campus (Greene et al., 1978). Each team was evaluated on the consistency of its clients' participation in toilet training and physical therapy. Data on client participation were posted by residence to permit each team to compare its outcomes with those of other teams, and results proved successful.

In sum, public posting is one of the most empirically robust training procedures. With the exception of occasional anecdotal reports that high performers can be at risk of teasing by other staff, direct care providers have generally given high satisfaction ratings to public posting systems (Reid & Whitman, 1983).

Self-Monitoring

With or without public posting, providers have also shown improvements when they evaluated

and/or reinforced their own work performances (Burg, Reid, & Lattimore, 1979; Kissel, Whitman, & Reid, 1983). In a study that examined the effects of training staff to use self-monitoring techniques, improvements were demonstrated in staff adherence to intervention schedules and in clients' on-task behavior. However, outcomes were even more favorable when each staff member was provided with supervisory feedback on his or her self-monitoring (Richmond, Riordan, Reiss, Pyles, & Bailey, 1988).

Application of Organizational Behavior Management to Autism Intervention

The accumulating body of research on staff training gradually came under the rubric of organizational behavior management (OBM), which is essentially the application of principles of ABA to effect changes in job performances. The May Institute provides a comprehensive example of the ways in which OBM can impact a program that serves individuals with autism (Christian, 1981a, 1983a). The May Institute began as a private, nonprofit program in Chatham, Massachusetts, which was originally opened as a more traditional residential program for children with autism. In 1978, administration of the program was assumed by behavior analysts, who pulled together and further contributed to a body of research aimed at effective organization of a human service agency (Christian & Hannah, 1983; Hannah, Christian, & Clark, 1981). Among the numerous management strategies developed and evaluated at the May Institute were: (1) a format for summarizing program evaluation data in a biannual report (Christian, 1981b); (2) a model for administrative work performance standards (Christian, 1981c, 1982); (3) a system for protection of privacy, confidentiality, and informed consent (Christian, 1983b; Hannah et al., 1981); and (4) a supervision system (Dyer, Schwartz, & Luce, 1984). In sum, an empirically grounded approach to program development yielded a multidimensional program that has been able to expand in types of services, geographic distribution of programs, and populations of individuals with disabilities that may be served, while maintaining a reputation for high-quality service delivery.

SPECIALIZED TRAINING TO ADDRESS CURRENT INTERVENTION TRENDS

Current intervention trends pose a need to develop corresponding professional training sequences. Thus, nearly all providers for individuals with autism have a need to establish productive working relationships with the families of individuals with autism, yet there is relatively little information available for direct provider trainees. The disability advocacy movement, the IDEA reauthorization, and growing consensus on the benefits of inclusion (NRC, 2001) have cumulatively resulted in increasing numbers of parents calling for supported inclusion for their children. Finally, naturalistic teaching approaches rely heavily on the interface between setting or environmental events and teaching conditions, and there is accumulating data on long-term successes in providing inclusive education for children with autism. In sum, relationship building, inclusion, and environmental arrangements are all areas in which specialized skills will be needed by autism specialists.

Parent–Professional Relationships

There is a sizeable literature on approaches to preparing parents to provide instruction and other intervention to their children with autism (Koegel, Schreibman, et al., 1992; Laski, Charlop, & Schreibman, 1988; McGee, Jacobs, & Regnier, 1993). Methods of preparing staff to work with parents of children with autism have also been detailed (McClannahan, Krantz, & McGee, 1982).

However, far less attention has been devoted to strategies for professionals to use to develop productive and supportive relationships with parents. A recent qualitative study organized parents of children with severe behavior problems (including autism) into focus groups, who were queried on the professional attributes they viewed as most important (Park & Turnbull, 2002). There was a consensus that parents value professionals who: (1) treat children with respect, (2) demonstrate competency in intervention skills, and (3) show commitment. For example, parents feel that their child is treated with respect when professionals appreciate unique things about the child, believe in the child's ability to learn, and demonstrate a willingness to continue their own learning. Professional behaviors viewed as disrespectful include a focus on the child's negative behaviors, use of overly restrictive punishments, assignment of demeaning tasks (e.g., cleaning toilets), talking about a child in front of the child as if he or she could not hear.

Inclusion Providers

The professional competencies that parents deemed essential to supporting a child's school inclusion were: (1) the ability to facilitate interactions between children with and without disabilities, (2) the ability to adapt academic activities and tasks to ensure a child's success, and (3) the ability to advocate for a child's continuing inclusion (Park & Turnbull, 2002). Parents voiced concerns about the common practice of assigning 1:1 paraprofessional "shadows" to children with behavior problems, especially when the paraprofessionals were untrained and inexperienced.

Although the earliest staff training literature had been focused primarily on direct care staff in institutional settings, and the focus of personnel preparation efforts gradually shifted toward special education teachers (Koegel, Russo, & Rincover, 1977), the most recent educational trend has been to educate children with autism in general education classrooms. The growing demand for inclusion has created a need to expand training and technical assistance to general education teachers, school administrators, and special service personnel such as school psychologists (Simpson, 2004). In fact, experienced trainers of inclusion providers often go further and extend training to school support staff such as the librarian, cafeteria worker, bus driver, and even the custodian. In short, everyone in a school who has the potential to make or break the success of an autism inclusion program should be targeted for specialized autism training.

Guidelines have also been suggested for training teachers to promote peer interactions among children with and without autism in inclusive preschool classrooms, which is a very different sequence from that recommended for initial language training (Strain, McGee, &

Kohler, 2001). Thus, incidental teachers of language are trained to interact enthusiastically and to vigorously seize as many opportunities as possible for language training. In contrast, effective social intervention changes the teacher's role to one of a background facilitator, who at firsts trains the peers to interact with the child with autism, who in turn cooperates because the toys provided have been specially selected to attract him or her. But as soon as the peer can do incidental teaching independently, the teacher gradually fades into a support and then observer role (McGee, Almeida, Sulzer-Azaroff, & Feldman, 1992). The point is that if a teacher gets down to where children are interacting, the children's interaction will be disrupted and all eyes will be on the teacher. Another training strategy found useful in inclusive classrooms is to provide assistance from behind, rather than beside or in front of, the child. In this way, the child remains focused on the classroom teacher, which is the goal, and not on the more artificial crutch of a 1:1 paraprofessional.

"How to" manuals now offer regular educators a wide array of practical strategies for encouraging acts of kindness among all students in an elementary school classroom that includes one or more children with autism (Wagner, 1999). Materials are also available to highlight the social promotion activities that blend easily into regular middle school classrooms, and which apply to students with autism, students with Asperger disorder, and even typical peers (Wagner, 2002). However, texts such as these are intended as supplements, not substitutes, for direct skill training.

Natural Environments: Interface of Environmental Arrangements and Staff Performance

A few years ago, early intervention programs in Georgia, Texas, and other states enacted policies requiring that all reimbursed services be delivered in "natural environments" or at least restrictive environments. This situation created immediate needs to retrain the majority of therapists who were accustomed to providing services in clinic settings.

Additional environmental variables of relevance include the interface of setting and the schedule of intervention activities, along with the interface of environment and teacher behaviors. For example, a program's staff training agenda should take into account the interaction between staffing pattern and intervention setting. Multiple studies have shown that environmental enrichment (i.e., by adding toys or other entertaining materials) will produce little or no effect on the behavior of children or adults unless providers have been trained to demonstrate and encourage sampling and use of the newly-offered leisure items (Flavell, 1973; Hart, Reynolds, Baer, Brawley, & Harris, 1968; Horner, 1980; McClannahan & Risley, 1975). In other words, environmental enrichment works best when staff have been trained to "market" new toys or hobbies.

Another study compared two childcare staffing patterns, including "man-on-man" teacher assignments and "zone-based" teacher assignments (LeLaurin & Risley, 1972). Man-on-man assignments were based on the common practice of assigning one or more children to the care of a specific teacher. The concept of teaching zones encompassed all aspects of a curriculum component, including the educational goal, environmental arrangements, and teaching routine. Man-on-man assignments required children to move as a group across activities, while teachers in zone-based classrooms were assigned to a specific area in which they offered the associated zone curriculum to all children who elected to enter and participate. Zone-based staffing patterns yielded higher levels of naturalistic teaching opportunities because the waiting time that is inherent to large group transitions was decreased.

BEST TRAINING PRACTICES IN AUTISM INTERVENTION MODELS

The research reviewed on staff training has yielded generally consistent findings, which have been applied to training practices in virtually all model demonstration programs for individuals with autism. Table 45.1 highlights common features of training plans that are currently in place in several of the well-known autism intervention programs, including: (1) the Children's Unit for Treatment and Evaluation (State University of New York at Binghamton; Romanczyk, Lockshin, & Matey,

TABLE 45.1 Comprehensive Training Systems at Model Early Intervention Programs

	Children's Unit	Douglass Developmental Center[a]	Princeton Child Developmental Institute	TEAACH	Walden	UCLA Young Autism Project
Ages served	1–21 years	2–adult	2–adult	2–adult	1–6	2–6
Setting	School	School	School	School	School	Home
Inclusion?	Readiness	Readiness	Readiness	Readiness	Inclusion	Readiness
Priority goals	1. Cognitive 2. Decrease atypical behavior	1. Cognitive 2. Decrease atypical behavior	1. Verbal language 2. Decrease atypical behavior	1. Cognitive 2. Self-help	1. Social 2. Verbal language	1. Cognitive 2. Decrease atypical behavior
Teaching methodology	Discrete trial	Discrete trial	Discrete trial	Structured teaching	Incidental teaching	Discrete trial
Preservice orientation	5-day workshop	Fall workshop	5-day workshop	5-day summer workshop	1-day workshop	College course
"Hands on" training	Apprenticeship Supervisory observation in-vivo and video	Sequences match class content	Apprenticeship Checklists for assigned procedures	Support by therapist or director	Apprenticeship Checklists for assigned zones and procedures	Supervisory observation in 2-hour clinic (every 2–4 weeks)
Ongoing supervision	Weekly meeting(s) Observation and feedback	Monthly meetings, new teacher meetings	Ongoing checklist appraisals with feedback	Consultation with trainer for 6–12 months	Monthly checklists with feedback (prn)	Observation (9 months) with Sr. therapist (>2 years experience)
Inservice didactic	Weekly seminars	Annual conferences	Biannual workshops	Biannual workshops Annual conference	Monthly seminars (optional)	Varies
Initial evaluation	Pre/post videos Written exam	Oral/written feedback	Oral/written feedback Formal evaluation at 6–8 months	Interview assignment with child and parent plus report	Mastery on checklists, objectively-scored video	Course grade, objectively-scored video
Performance reviews	Biannual specific objectives, annual global	Monthly classroom observation and feedback	Annual formal review based on 4–5 hour observation	Informal supervisory review, consumer evaluation	Weekly program evaluations, annual caregiver	Video samples of 1:1 sessions, recommendation from trainer, experience hours

[a] Douglass Developmental Center has several level programs, and space permitted presentation of only traditional program.

2001); (2) the Douglass Developmental Disabilities Center (State University of New Jersey at Rutgers University; Harris, Handleman, Arnold, & Gordon, 2001); (3) Princeton Child Development Institute (affiliation with University of Kansas at Lawrence; McClannahan & Krantz, 2001); (4) TEACCH Services for Preschool Children (University of North Carolina at Chapel Hill; Marcus, Schopler, & Lord, 2001); (5) the UCLA Young Autism Project (University of California at Los Angeles; Lovaas, 1987; Smith, Donahoe, & Davis, 2001); and (6) the Walden Early Childhood Program (Emory University School of Medicine in Atlanta; McGee, Morrier, & Daly, 1999, 2001).

The programs represented in Table 45.1 were selected according to criteria similar to those outlined in the National Academy of Sciences report on autism education (NRC, 2001), with an added stipulation that the model had to be currently operational in a demonstration classroom under the administrative control of the program developer(s). In addition, certain qualifying programs that elected not to participate in the National Academy of Science review process were either added to the table or highlighted elsewhere in the literature review.

Ironically, the systematic training plans common to well-known demonstration programs are rarely replicated in most autism classrooms. In other words, the developers of state-of-the-art early intervention programs, who presumably have more autism expertise than is present in most intervention settings, are cognizant of the high priority that must be placed on training. If most children with autism are in programs in which effective staff training is not a priority, then it should not be expected that their outcomes will be comparable to those of the model demonstration programs.

Limitations of Staff Training Research

The field of autism intervention has mushroomed in the volume of service demands, in the sophistication of intervention procedures, and in the variety of participating professions, yet widespread attention to staff training appears to be on the decline. Review of the literature on preparation of professionals to serve individuals with autism revealed primarily program evaluation studies, which were rarely aimed directly at the unique needs of individuals with autism. Much of the research on staff training methods is dated, although not necessarily outdated, because it seems reasonable to assume that several replicated findings continue to be applicable. Specifically, numerous studies have highlighted the limitations of didactic training approaches. There have also been multiple demonstrations that task-analyzed job responsibilities, combined with a systematic reinforcement plan, provide a reliable means for improving work performances.

Unfortunately, implementation of empirical findings on effective staff training methods has been limited largely to use in the well-known "model" autism intervention programs. In short, there is a need to put into action what is already known about staff training, while continuing to develop updated training systems. Though budgetary constraints have made it increasingly difficult to implement systematic personnel preparation plans in publicly funded programs, there is a need for a comprehensive provider curriculum in virtually every educational and health care setting that serves children and adults with autism. Toward that end, specific data-based recommendations are offered on how such training packages might be assembled.

DEVELOPING A COMPREHENSIVE AGENDA FOR PROVIDER PREPARATION

A little bit of treatment for autism, or a little bit of preparation for personnel who will provide the treatment, is probably a waste of resources. Moreover, as concluded in the National Academy of Science report on educating children with autism, a program's intensity cannot be defined solely by the number of hours that children are enrolled (NRC, 2001). Rather, an intervention program's true intensity is best evaluated by measuring the program's success in securing the sustained engagement of participants.

Unfortunately, the task of maintaining high levels of engagement by individuals with autism is often easier said than done (McGee, Daly, Izeman, Mann, & Risley, 1991). Virtually all young children with an autism spectrum disorder enter treatment with a need to increase the quantity and/or improve the quality of their engagement. Careful monitoring of the ways that school-age children and adolescents with autism spend their time remains important throughout the school years. However, the need for ongoing intervention to improve engagement should gradually lessen over time, if there has been reasonably effective earlier intervention.

Adults with autism have the right to choose how they spend their time, assuming that they contribute to their own support to the best of their ability and given the absence of severe behavioral challenges or learning deficits that interfere with daily living. In fact, when challenging behaviors are present in individuals with autism at all ages, the positive behavior support plan must invariably address ways to support more independent engagement. Under ideal circumstances, even the highest functioning adults with autism are likely to benefit from at least some guidance on ways to improve the quality, enjoyment, and range of options in how they invest their time and attention.

The only way to keep children with autism, and others who require intensive intervention, actively participating in productive activity across the majority of their waking hours is to prepare their providers with a comprehensive array of knowledge and skills. At the least, the skills of all of their providers must cumulatively combine to create the capacity for a full range of intervention options. In addition, someone within the system must know how to pull together an effective intervention package, and trainers must be available who have the skills needed to prepare and supervise the direct intervention providers.

An individualized educational or behavior support plan must specify the goals and objectives for an individual, as well as the methods that will be used to achieve those goals. Similarly, a comprehensive training plan should specify a program's goals, as well as the personnel preparation strategies that will be used to obtain program goals. The process of developing a comprehensive training package requires answers to a number of essential questions (Campbell, 1990), as outlined next.

Primary Group That the Provider Preparation Is Designed to Benefit

The overall project aim should be the major force that drives plans for a provider preparation curriculum. Specific characteristics of the group to be served exert a primary influence on plans for project impact.

Impact of Age on a Provider Preparation Curriculum

Conventional wisdom might assume that the complexity of preparing staff to provide intervention for individuals with autism might increase as children grow into adulthood. To the contrary, the preparation of early intervention personnel is often a more challenging endeavor than the training of staff to work with adults with autism (assuming the absence of severely challenging behaviors). The goal for early autism intervention is fundamental change in the natural course of development that is usually associated with autism. To dramatically alter the developmental trajectory of a young child with autism or to at least ensure each child's optimal progress usually requires that a series of highly systematic interventions be implemented with precision.

On the other hand, the current state-of-the-art intervention for an adult with autism now tends to be focused on arranging an improved quality of life (Risley, 1996). The goal is no longer the impossible task of "fixing" every unusual behavior, nor one of teaching to every skill deficit. Rather, the goal is to enhance the individual's ability to function as independently as possible in the community activities of his or her choice and to increase the individual's overall enjoyment of life. Quality of life improvements are usually achieved by common sense planning of ways to use natural community supports, in combination with any crucially needed therapeutic supports.

In short, quality of life improvements for adults with autism tend to require low-tech interventions, while early interventions tend to be high-tech (Risley, 1996). These distinctions have obvious implications for the degree and kind of preparation needed by the people who will serve as direct providers.

Impact of Heterogeneity on a Provider Preparation Curriculum

The diversity of needs presented by the group targeted for benefit will directly influence the complexity of the training task. Although most individuals with autism share a similar pattern of developmental irregularities, which consist of deficits in social and communication domains that are not necessarily in line with their development in other domains, an individual with autism may also present wide-ranging strengths and weaknesses within a given developmental domain. Further complicating the task of personnel preparation, there is enormous variability in the specific abilities and disabilities presented by different individuals with autism.

A variety of demographic variables also impact the heterogeneity of a group of targeted beneficiaries, such as the range of ages, the type and number of intervention settings, and the specificity and size of diagnostic subgroups or levels of functioning that characterize eligible participants. For example, toddlers with autism are a more homogeneous group because all tend to share certain needs (e.g., toilet training, learning to talk). On the other hand, prekindergarten-age children are a more diverse group if they have received intensive early intervention, because extended intervention contributes to a wide range of treatment responses.

When individuals with autism present with diverse ages and needs, it is likely to be a challenge to train a special education teacher to serve as the inclusion specialist for an entire school system. Far less training would be needed to prepare a high school guidance counselor to serve a small and homogeneous subset of the population, such as 12th-grade students with Asperger disorder who attend a given school.

In sum, the ages and heterogeneity of the subgroup of individuals with autism who are intended to be the primary beneficiaries of a given training project will directly influence the complexity of the training curricula. The more detail available on the age, size, and range of developmental levels of the target population, the more focused the provider preparation plan can be.

Quality of Life Improvements Needed by the Targeted Group

The extensiveness of training that will be needed also varies according to how the lives of the target beneficiaries are expected to be improved. Specifically, training plans will be influenced by the complexity of the competencies required to achieve the desired impact. Temporal dimensions of the desired impact are also pertinent. The primary goal of a provider preparation program is to benefit individuals with autism, but the time frame during which that benefit must occur will vary according to both the trainees' stage of training and the needs of the individuals with autism.

Impact of Number of Competencies Needed to Achieve Desired Life Improvements

The complexity of the training curriculum is directly influenced by whether the desired impact on the lives of individuals with autism will be very narrow (i.e., toilet training) or whether the scope of impact will be broad (i.e., medical management of symptoms associated with autism that interfere with daily functioning).

In the case of toilet training, there is a well-tested intervention available, which has been demonstrated as effective for both young typical children (Azrin & Foxx, 1974) and for institutionalized adults with severe mental retardation (Azrin & Foxx, 1971). Because this curriculum is packaged, in terms of logistical and environmental arrangements, instructions and rewards, and specific guidelines for how to implement several phases of a bladder-control conditioning procedure, the task of training providers to do toilet training is relatively simple.

In contrast, to prepare psychiatry residents to successfully manage autism symptoms requires a multifaceted training agenda that corresponds to practice standards established by the American Academy of Psychiatry (Volkmar et al., 1999). Psychiatry residents will also need hands-on mentoring in how to prescribe medication for a wide range of problems that are frequently associated with autism (i.e., sleep difficulty, fears, hyperactivity, eating challenges), and they must be prepared to address the needs of patients of virtually all ages and levels of functioning. Ideally, residents will become proficient in conducting clinical trials for purposes of research and practice. In addition, they require training in how to assess whether adjunctive behavioral intervention is indicated; if so, residents will need knowledge and skills that enable them to either: (1) provide the intervention, (2) advise the parents or other providers in how to conduct the intervention, or (3) refer the patient for additional treatment.

They will need to be knowledgeable about the comorbidity of autism with other psychiatric and medical disorders (anxiety, depression, seizure disorders) and in the discrimination of symptoms of physical illness that require referral or follow-up. Psychiatry residents will need information on a full range of issues specific to autism in order to effectively counsel parents, including: (1) an understanding of the enormous pressures that are unique to parenting a child with autism, (2) answers to questions about the genetics and neurobiology of autism, and (3) best practice educational and placement recommendations. Additional skills needed by psychiatry residents who plan to become autism specialists include: how to establish rapport with both patients with autism and their families, how to offer supportive counseling and stress management, how to provide crisis intervention and coordinate emergency care, and how to consult with other health care and educational providers.

Although the preceding competencies represent only a subset of knowledge and skills that a psychiatry resident must learn (e.g., they do not address the need for competency in diagnostic evaluations, research), it is apparent that a considerable amount of training time will be required to thoroughly prepare residents to provide medical management of autism symptoms. Unfortunately, to some extent, preparation of autism specialists in any field will by definition require training that is broad in scope and, therefore, costly in training time and resources.

Impact of the Immediacy of Need for Trainees to Contribute to Desired Life Improvements

Training plans are also influenced by the urgency with which intervention benefits must be achieved. When children with autism have challenging behaviors of such severity that there is a substantial risk of harm to self or others (e.g., a child with pica eats rocks on the playground), staff training must be vigorously aimed at producing immediate benefit. In the long run, a chronic problem such as obesity may prove to be even more dangerous than eating rocks, yet it is unlikely that harm will result if provider training in nutrition and weight reduction cannot take place until several weeks after training for management of pica.

Influence of Desired Durability of Life Improvements

A related consideration that may affect staff training plans pertains to whether the desired life improvement is for short-term versus long-term gains. When the project aim is to show lasting improvements, a provider(s) will often need additional preparation in how to maintain new behavior changes. Similarly, if lifelong medication compliance is the goal for an adult with Asperger disorder, the intervention of choice may be to: (1) prepare the individual with Asperger in self-management skills, (2) prepare the individual's parent in skills needed to monitor his or her self-management accuracy, and (3) prepare the provider who will provide the training and follow-up assistance to both patient and parent. In contrast, very little training may be needed to prepare a student intern to teach a musically inclined child with autism a song for the school's holiday pageant because it won't matter if the song is remembered the day after the event.

Influence of Planned or Projected Future Impact

In-service training is usually aimed at having an immediate impact, while the time frame for expected impact of preservice training is more variable. When all new staff are provided with initial preservice training, the intended impact is usually similar to that of in-service training (i.e., relatively immediate). However, when a program provides preservice training for undergraduate or graduate-level college students, the trainee may not be expected to independently produce an impact until years later after completing his or her studies. In such situations, it is important to prepare trainees with information and skills that are unlikely to become obsolete. For example, it may be unnecessary for student trainees to memorize the content of standardized instruments that will be updated and changed in newer editions.

If the goal is for either student trainees or in-service trainees to benefit as many individuals with autism as possible, then it will be important to document the number of individuals with autism who are served immediately after training and the number who are served by staff and student trainees in the future. When long-term impact is the desired goal, the training plan (and trainee selection strategy) must take special precautions to guard against attrition. Thus, professional training opportunities may be viewed as a long-term investment in each staff member. To the extent that legal guidelines permit (i.e., you can't ask whether there are plans to have children), it is important to screen for trainees with long-term career commitments and enthusiasm for working with individuals with autism.

Summary

The number of information and skill competencies that the trainee will need to deliver the desired life improvement and the urgency with which the desired life improvement must be accomplished will directly influence the complexity and duration of the training curriculum. Similarly, whether the goal is to achieve short-term or long-term life improvements and whether the emphasis is on improving fewer lives immediately or on improving more lives in the future will influence the content of the training curriculum and determine whether training plans can accommodate student trainees as well as current providers.

Identifying the Trainees Who Will Be Prepared to Provide Instruction, Care, or Support

Although training programs should be built around the needs of individuals with autism,

the trainees themselves are clearly secondary beneficiaries of well-designed training programs. Autism specialty training is increasingly an interdisciplinary endeavor, partially due to the multifaceted needs that characterize autism. Health care providers who routinely serve children with autism include their pediatricians, child psychiatrists, pediatric neurologists, psychologists, audiologists, and speech-language pathologists, many of whom have gained familiarity with autism through trial-and-error experience. The advent of managed care is putting nurses and nurse practitioners in the position of first contact for increasing numbers of children with autism, creating the need for nursing schools to add early identification of autism to their curricula. Occupational therapists have become routine providers for children with autism almost by default, in the sense that occupational therapy is sometimes assigned as the primary intervention for children who have no motor impairments, due to an absence of other personnel who are experienced and interested in working with students with autism.

Also needing preparation are the paraprofessionals who serve in a variety of nontraditional roles. Job coaches are well suited to capitalizing on the strengths of adults with autism, while accommodating periodic needs for increased support. At the other end of the age span, early intervention programs often recruit energetic daycare providers, who must then be trained to implement precise treatment protocols.

Training needs for support staff vary with the nature of a program. For example, a private practice group of developmental pediatricians may identify the need to retool their existing secretarial staff, so that they may become better able to listen to and communicate more effectively with parents of children with autism. Imaging researchers may need to train research assistants in shaping skills and use of conditioned reinforcers, so that they will become able to get children to lie still in the scanner. A statewide autism center may be charged with training a variety of groups, such as the intake coordinators in mental health centers, emergency room staff in an inner-city hospital, police officers, and early intervention special instructors and child-find team members.

In short, almost anyone who comes into contact with individuals with autism becomes a potential candidate for specialized autism training. However, those who will become "autism specialists" are the front-line trainees who will be charged with identification, diagnosis, intervention, and research that will yield substantial benefit to current and/or future individuals with autism and their families.

Current intervention trends create the need to focus training on the areas in which the personnel shortages are most acute, including professionals and paraprofessionals who will serve as adult care providers. In addition, consideration of trainee needs could not be complete without acknowledgment of the role played by college students in filling the critical manpower gap and the inherent obligation that university-sponsored autism programs have to train them.

Consultants on Adult Care

In coming years, there will be an expanding population of identified adults with autism spectrum disorders, which will further strain already overburdened human service systems. There are currently long wait lists in most states for services that may be helpful to adults with autism. However, the majority of existing services being waited for are not directed at the needs of individuals with autism, but rather, community mental health services have usually been designed to serve adults with mental retardation or emotional/thought disorders. Perhaps the most acute personnel shortage is for both professional and paraprofessional personnel with expertise in severe challenging behaviors. Problems in retaining experienced paraprofessionals are often exacerbated by the fact that they seldom receive adequate supervisory support, and their salaries are often the same low pay as that of personnel with much lower risk jobs.

The medication needs of adult patients with autism often continue under the jurisdiction of child psychiatry or pediatric neurology; however, some of these providers are uncomfortable with their lack of experience with adults, especially when there are medical complications such as diabetes or hypertension. Adults with autism are not a profitable

clientele because they present complex and time-consuming problems, they may be high risk for emergencies, their waiting room behavior is sometimes less than exemplary, and their services are usually poorly reimbursed. The higher functioning adults with autism or Asperger disorder may be less challenging from a medical perspective, but the vast majority of these individuals are unemployed and uninsured, and they bring with them a host of social work issues that many (if not most) physicians are ill-equipped to manage. Many of these patients need medication they cannot afford. For these reasons and because of self-perceived lack of competence in autism, physicians who refer adults with autism spectrum disorders for specialty care are often reluctant to take them back. Given the paucity of physicians who are confident of their ability to provide medical care to adults with autism, the best option may be to equip physicians who are autism specialists with the skills they will need to set up and operate consult and liaison service models.

College Student Trainees/Providers

Implementation of current intensive early intervention models aimed at the needs of children with autism require high levels of physical energy by staff, who must simultaneously recall multiple overlapping and often complex procedures. As a result, early intervention and private preschool programs, including home-based programs, have developed widespread reliance on college students as direct care providers. Despite short-term savings that accrue from staffing with low- or no-cost students, turnover is usually a predetermined outcome that sooner or later adds back in the costs of training new replacements. Further, when a substantial proportion of a program's staff are students, training plans must be developed that will ensure intervention consistency in the face of part-time and changing schedules.

Despite the challenges, when autism programs are staffed with undergraduate students (or any students up to postdoctoral fellows), the program fulfills one of the sponsoring university's primary missions while simultaneously addressing the field's long-term personnel needs. Ideally, the sponsoring university may contribute to the endeavor in the form of training resources. This scenario is available to the Children's Program at the State University of New York in Binghamton (Romanczyk et al., 2001), which provides an outstanding agenda for preservice orientation. The multi-component training package includes a weekend "immersion" retreat, which is primarily didactic, as well as opportunities to observe, model, and receive hands-on training by experienced teachers. Each student receives several layers of ongoing supervision and mentoring. Feedback is based on evaluation data, including tests on information content, review of videotaped work performances, structured assessments of on-the-job performance, and qualitative performance reviews.

In the absence of university support, feasibility often dictates that skill-based training takes precedence over more comprehensive training aimed at establishing a foundation of knowledge about autism. In these situations, it is important that students be informed of the extent and limits of their preparation and of the importance of accurately representing their training background. In short, students must be aware and make parents aware of their lack of preparation to function as independent providers in the absence of clinical supervision.

Preparing Specialized Autism Consultants

Several comprehensive training packages have been developed to prepare specific provider groups in skills that will enhance their capacity to serve individuals with autism and related disabilities. For example, detailed training plans have been packaged and evaluated for training foster care providers (Chock & Glahn, 1984), foster grandparents (Fabry & Reid, 1978), and respite workers (Neef et al., 1986).

Summary of Trainee Considerations

The wide-ranging needs of individuals with autism, in combination with the severe shortage of personnel who are specialized in autism, have created a need to recruit and train willing professionals from virtually any and all disciplines. However, the complexity of a training plan will often increase in proportion to the variety of backgrounds and experience that trainees bring to training. When

it becomes necessary to select among potential trainees due to limits on training capacity, priority candidates should be those applicants who are predicted to have the best potential for longevity.

Knowledge and Skills Essential to the Trainees' Success

When selecting among the many knowledge and behavioral competencies that may be of potential use to a provider for individuals with autism, the most realistic strategy is to target as few competencies as possible, but as many as necessary. There must be a sufficient number of training objectives to ensure that direct care staff will be able to implement the intervention with a reasonable degree of fidelity. However, it is wise to be conservative when choosing the number of competencies to be addressed in training, because mastery of a few skills will yield greater impact than a little information about a lot of topics.

Behavioral competencies are the skills needed to achieve impact on clients with autism. Knowledge of the theoretical principles and background information for a given intervention will help the trainee offer rationales to parents and colleagues and knowledge may contribute to clinical decision-making abilities. When resources do not permit the luxury of training both knowledge and skills simultaneously, and when the goal is to achieve immediate positive impact on the lives of individuals with autism, the emphasis of the training curriculum should be on skill development.

Knowledge Competencies

Certain information is universally required at the beginning of training and employment. Table 45.2 outlines a minimal knowledge base, or orientation content, for new staff in a program that provides service or conducts research with individuals with autism and their families. In an era of increased attention to issues of confidentiality and other aspects of the Health Insurance Portability and Accountability Act (HIPPA), it is advisable to provide at least basic training in ethics. In addition, given the probability that all personnel will encounter parents enduring stressful situations, positive communication skills will be needed

TABLE 45.2   Examples of "Need to Know" Orientation Competencies

Goal Area	Knowledge Competencies
Safety	1. State location of: (a) first aid kit, (b) emergency procedures postings, and (c) parent phone list. 2. Answer random first aid question while working with children. 3. Describe: (a) environmental safety checklist and (b) child abuse prevention.
Ethics	1. State location of program library on Ethical Codes, Patient Rights, HIPPA. 2. Know extent and limits of confidentiality and informed consent. 3. Explain principles of avoiding dual relationships and accurate representation of credentials.
Organizational citizenship	1. Explain what to do if going to miss work due to final exam. 2. Know facility guidelines or who to ask if want desk from office down the hall. 3. Register car for parking.
Professionalism	1. Role-play what to do during challenging parent interactions. 2. Explain why certain clothing and jewelry cannot be worn on the job. 3. Explain personal and program accountability.
Big picture	1. Describe what is the desired impact of the project to which assigned. 2. Explain how the project's big picture will interact with personal career plans. 3. Provide an overview of the program's research, clinical, and training missions.
Dissemination	1. Explain what is autism, to a parent, to a teacher, to your neighbor. 2. Answer the question, "What causes autism?" 3. Do children with autism spectrum disorders also have mental retardation?
Distinctive features	1. Why do you have typical peers in the classroom, and what is the effect on them? 2. What is incidental teaching? 3. What is a teaching zone?

by virtually all personnel, including employees, trainees, volunteers, and secretarial staff. Moreover, all personnel need at least a basic understanding of the defining characteristics of autism spectrum disorders to serve as effective ambassadors of information to the larger community.

Other information must be conveyed in tandem with training of associated skills in order to permit action on that knowledge. For example, it is likely that medical residents specializing in child psychiatry, pediatrics, and pediatric neurology will most efficiently develop skills in making differential diagnoses when provided a foundation of the knowledge represented in their field's practice parameters (Filipek et al., 2000; Volkmar et al., 1999). Front-line providers such as early intervention caseworkers and nurses need knowledge of rationales for early intervention, as well as skills in presenting that information in a family-friendly manner when referring a child for evaluation of possible autism.

The Medical College of New Jersey offered medical residents an innovative program for developing empathy with the hardships and joys faced by parents of children with disabilities (R. MacDonald, personal communication, April 4, 1995). Each resident was invited to dine in the home of a particular family who had a child with a disability over the course of a 1-year period, providing the opportunity to observe firsthand the hardships and joys that these families routinely encounter. The premise was that the stresses faced by parents of a child with a disability may not be readily apparent from the vantage point of a clinic visit, but the longitudinal experience may shed light on issues such as why medication compliance problems arise or what can be said to calm the concerns of an irate or acutely distressed parent. Similarly, parents of children with autism have volunteered time to explain to Emory's pediatric residents the hurtful and helpful things that professionals said to them at the time of their child's diagnosis.

Behavioral Competencies

The specific skills that providers must be prepared in vary substantially according to the provider group and goals for project impact. However, the core deficits and irregularities associated with autism define some common goal areas in which nearly all individuals with autism will need specific treatment objectives. It follows that a curriculum for training autism intervention specialists must address certain global intervention skills (e.g., language development), as well as more specific skills that are needed to address frequently targeted individualized treatment objectives (e.g., pronoun reversals, topic maintenance).

Common Intervention Goals for Children with Autism

There is general consensus among professionals who developed and oversee the well-known early autism intervention programs on the common goal areas that a comprehensive intervention should address (NRC, 2001). Thus, the intervention goals for young children with autism usually fall into the following domains: productive engagement, play skills, social interactions, communication, independent daily living skills, cognitive/academic abilities, and (reduction of) atypical behaviors. It is obvious that all these domains (except the last area of excess atypical behaviors) represent areas of potential skill deficits, the remediation of which usually requires highly specialized instructional programs.

There are conceptual differences among well-known early intervention models with respect to the intervention emphases placed on motor skills. For example, the concept of irregularities in motor development is central to Greenspan's developmental intervention model (Greenspan & Wieder, 1999), but the Walden incidental teaching approach makes a simple assumption that motor weaknesses often resolve when a child is kept regularly engaged in normal early childhood activities (McGee, Daly, & Jacobs, 1994).

Training Objectives

Personnel preparation objectives or competencies should correspond directly to the children's intervention curriculum. Thus, staff training objectives should vary according to the desired project impact or according to how the lives of the targeted subgroup of individuals with autism will be improved. For example, if the desired life improvement, or the reason training is being provided, is to advance participants' abilities to live more independently, then it may be important to focus on correction of a client's relevant deficits in daily living skills. The translation to the training curriculum might be to prepare the trainee to mastery in use of faded guidance procedures.

Behavioral competencies that must be included in a provider preparation curricula will also vary according to the ages of the children or adults served, according to the type of educational placement or intervention setting in which services are delivered, and especially, according to the intervention procedures that will be used to help the individual achieve the desired goal. For example, early intervention providers must be trained in how to teach play skills to young children, while fourth-grade teachers need training in how to improve reading comprehension. Similarly, safety competencies need to be addressed in the preparation of all personnel who work with dependent populations, but safety training may need to be highlighted in the training of preschool teachers who must escort children from the classroom facility to a nonadjoining playground (especially given nearby traffic). Finally, environmental arrangements are relatively straightforward for discrete-trial therapists, while incidental teachers must be trained in how to display and dispense reinforcers in a manner that elicits frequent child initiations.

Individualized client needs should exert the primary influence on training objectives. Individualized objectives that are frequently targeted in education and treatment plans for a given subgroup of individuals with autism will suggest the behavioral competencies that the training curriculum must accommodate. The most complex objectives (e.g., shaping initial contingent vocalizations in a preschool-age child) may sometimes be easier to address by assigning only experienced staff members to those intervention responsibilities, while student trainees are assigned to more robust and easily replicable tasks.

Training Objectives Prioritized and Sequenced

Despite agreement among autism interventionists on the general goals of intervention, there is considerable variability in the priority and order in which various intervention models address these goals. These differences among intervention models directly impact both the intervention objectives that compose an individualized treatment plan, as well as the provider competencies that compose a training curriculum.

Prioritize According to Immediate Need

When budgetary and time constraints preclude the feasibility of preparing all staff to do everything, the general rule of thumb should be to prioritize those skills needed most immediately by a given trainee (Favell, Favell, Riddle, & Risley, 1984). A program's training burden is greatly reduced when initial training of practicum students, part-time staff, and community volunteers is limited to the interventions to which trainees will first be assigned. This approach has implications for how new trainees and staff members should be scheduled because new behavioral competencies will be mastered most quickly when there are consistent opportunities to practice implementation of the same interventions, with the same children, at the same time of day, across at least 3 days per week.

Level the Order in Which Objectives Are Sequenced

Sequencing dilemmas arise when planning the preparation of full-time professional staff members, who must eventually be trained to mastery in the complete provider curriculum. A practical strategy for sequencing a comprehensive set of competencies is to level the provider curriculum (Chock & Glahn, 1984).

There are several advantages to staggering the introduction of components of an extensive training agenda. The bulk of autism intervention is provided by young professionals who are employed in jobs that are high in demands and low in pay (Zaharia & Baumeister, 1978). Rapid staff turnover is commonplace in virtually all kinds of human service delivery programs, and turnover is especially problematic in autism programs because skilled work

performances are essential to client progress. Staff attrition is likely the worst when new staff members are overloaded by the pressure to simultaneously learn many new skills and by expectations that they will almost immediately be able to implement each and every intervention with precision. In short, attempts to front-load intensive staff training run a significant risk of wasting a costly training investment, when the trainee leaves exhausted after a few weeks or months.

The well-known UCLA Young Autism Project (Lovaas, 1987; Smith et al., 2001) has a detailed training curriculum that has been leveled in terms of qualifying experience, and objective criteria have been formalized for obtaining certification at each level. Training requirements advance across levels from positions of student "therapists" through advanced roles of providing supervision of the supervisors. Leveled training systems clarify training expectations and underline the availability of a career ladder within the program, which may both attract and motivate developing professionals.

In summary, the most efficient means of preparing trainees is to sequence training of knowledge and behavioral competencies in the order that they will be needed. Thus, preservice training must convey the knowledge that a trainee needs before assuming the responsibility of working toward the desired project impact. The duration and number of training phases will vary according to the trainee's experience and schedule of availability, as well as with the extensiveness and difficulty of the training agenda.

Most Effective Training Methods in Preparing Personnel with Targeted Knowledge and Behavioral Competencies

Competencies should be matched with a compatible training method. Knowledge competencies can be conveyed through a variety of formats, while behavioral competencies are most efficiently taught using an apprenticeship model.

Didactic Training of Knowledge Competencies

Didactic training is a common and relatively efficient means for garnering enthusiasm for the job to be accomplished, for transmitting information, and for explaining basic principles or best practice standards (e.g., ABA or developmentally appropriate practices). Another appropriate goal of didactic training may be to provide the trainees with rationales for various intervention procedures (e.g., "Why can't Bill rest under the table when he needs time to just be autistic?"). A major advantage of didactic instruction exists in the capacity for training large groups with minimal use of the trainer's time. It is, perhaps, this economy feature that has accounted for an overwhelming reliance on didactic training, irrespective of repeated research findings that lectures and workshops are not effective means by which to teach new skills.

Technological Innovations

Rapidly advancing technology is revolutionizing the interest value of presentations and accompanying training materials, which may remedy the age-old challenge of preventing didactic instruction from being boring. Thus, colorful and dynamic visual aids are provided far more easily with PowerPoint than with the traditional chalkboard, flip charts, and overhead transparencies (although duplicate mediums may still be advisable). Increasingly sophisticated slides and digital films can now be produced inexpensively and easily modified.

When staff development resources are plentiful, trainers may opt to use one of the new interactive training devices. For example, equipment is now available that permits a trainer to ask multiple-choice questions during the course of a presentation; audience participants enter their answers into remote control data collection devices, which transmit responses back to a central computer for rapid data analysis. The trainer can almost instantly present a slide that summarizes trainee input in an attractive graphic display.

There are a growing number of autism-related college courses offered via Web TV, and at least one specialty degree in autism can now be obtained by partial completion of requirements on the Internet (e.g., a professional in West Virginia can earn an advanced degree from a university in Florida, with a minimal amount of time away from family and job). Distance-learning formats have also had a sig-

nificant impact on the access of autism providers and college students to didactic training by autism experts.

Moreover, a variety of inexpensive and easily transportable low-tech telemedicine equipment have become available within recent years. Administrators of Georgia's early intervention program collaborated with autism specialists at Medical College of Georgia and Emory University School of Medicine in a project that distributed to every regional office a lunch-box-size case, which contained audio and visual transmission equipment that can be hooked into regular telephone lines. In-home case consultations are now easily arranged between a university-based autism clinic and the home of a child with autism who resides in a geographically distant location. Computer surveillance cameras can also be used to improve supervisory capabilities (e.g., a college student can be sent to the home of a child with autism to assist the parents with toilet training their child, while an autism specialist supervises from the university).

Finally, the topics of autism and technology cannot be raised together without reference to the Internet, which provides seemingly endless information and misinformation to parents and providers who serve and care for children with autism. The Internet is extremely vulnerable to use in widespread transmission of information on unproven "treatments" (e.g., Secretin), and professionals must be prepared in ways to tactfully address the questions that inevitably arise. However, at best, the Internet can be an invaluable (and free) source of information about autism (e.g., the National Academy of Science report on education of children with autism is available online at http://www.nas.edu).

Dissemination of Written Knowledge about Autism

Written materials, in the form of journal articles, books, and lecture handouts, are probably the most common mechanism for transmitting knowledge about autism. The growing numbers of books and journals that specifically address the needs of children with autism reflect the growth of the market. The fact that the UCLA Young Autism Project (Lovaas et al., 1981) is one of few comprehensive autism interventions that have been detailed in published training manuals may account for the widespread dissemination of this model.

A variety of useful texts offer specific recommendations and clearly worded how-to instructions on empirically validated intervention procedures, which can expedite the development of individualized clinical interventions for children with autism. Thus, there is no need for an autism specialist to waste valuable time in task-analyzing routine daily living skills, because numerous books and journal articles offer step-by-step breakdowns of skills ranging from toothbrushing (Horner & Keilitz, 1975), to shopping (Haring, Kennedy, Adams, & Pitts-Conway, 1987), to eating in restaurants (Van den Pol et al., 1981).

Several studies have assessed the readability of manuals, under the logical assumption that training materials that match the reading level of the audience are more likely to be read (Andrasik, Klare, & Murphy, 1976; Andrasik & Murphy, 1977). Now that computers instantly calculate the grade level at which training materials have been prepared, it is important that trainers remember to check the fit between audience and written training materials. .

Although reading materials are a low-cost training medium, the caveat can be in getting trainees to actually read what has been assigned. One way to probe whether reading assignments are being completed is to embed an out-of-context direction near the end of the reading material ("If you have read this far, report to your supervisor to claim early dismissal on Friday"; cf. McGee, Krantz, & McClannahan, 1981). Recall of essential information (e.g., first aid or emergency procedures) can be probed, one fact at a time, while the staff member is conducting a teaching routine in which that information may be needed (O'Brien, Porterfield, Herbert-Jackson, & Risley, 1979). Knowledge of important information can also be probed during a brief portion of staff meeting that is allocated for presenting questions and answers in the format of a game show such as Wheel of Fortune (T. Daly, personal communication, April 2, 1994).

Cost Effectiveness of Didactic Training Formats

The relatively low costs of providing training through reading materials and lectures, and

the exciting training potential created by new technology, will likely perpetuate almost exclusive use of these methods for preparing autism providers. However, it is important to keep sight of the fact that savings will not accrue if the goal is to develop behavioral competencies or skills through didactic training, because effectiveness requires an accurate match of training content and training method.

Hands-On Training of Behavioral Competencies

The goal of hands-on training is to provide the mentoring needed for trainees to perfect, at a minimum, the skills needed to independently fulfill their immediate responsibilities. In the historical apprenticeship model used to prepare a shoemaker or a blacksmith, the trainee usually shadowed the mentor over a period of years until he had learned all the skills needed to do his job. Even today, apprenticeship training continues to be provided to some skilled laborers, such as plumbers or carpenters, especially when there is a family-owned business that values quality control. In the professional world, some degree of mentoring has been built into the system of training for physicians, psychologists, and teachers. Residencies, internships, and practicum experiences have been standardized according to varied accreditation requirements, yet there is still considerable variability across placements and supervisors in terms of how much time the trainee works side by side with a mentor.

Although less structured, the hands-on mentoring received by many autism researchers more closely approximates the original apprenticeship (e.g., it is not uncommon for a researcher to train several years or more in the lab of a mentor). Similarly, perhaps due to the complexities of training clinical judgment, mentoring has been built into the process established for certification of evaluators who are being trained for research use of the gold standard instruments for diagnosing autism (Lord et al., 2002; Rutter et al., 2003).

Unfortunately, immediate personnel needs are so extensive that time is not available to prepare autism providers with the same degree of care that used to be allotted to the preparation of horseshoe providers. Although virtually all of the well-known autism early intervention programs provide some degree of hands-on training (Handleman & Harris, 2001; Harris & Handleman, 1994; NRC, 2001), comprehensive training plans are not yet available to the vast majority of providers who serve children with an autism spectrum disorder. The hope must be that research has isolated the correct "active ingredients" of effective mentoring, as follows:

• *Operational definitions of behavioral competencies:* The first ingredient of an efficient mentoring process is a concrete description of every skill that the trainee must be prepared to do, in terms that are easily observed and measured. The goal is to ensure that each targeted skill can be performed at a consistent level of competence, which meets at least minimum standards (Favell et al., 1984).

One strategy for developing an operational description of a complex teaching skill is to closely observe the performance of a highly skilled teacher. The next step is to isolate the components of the modeled performance that appear to be essential to the child's learning. This was the approach taken in pilot work for the first incidental teaching studies, which were conducted with typical children from disadvantaged backgrounds (Hart & Risley, 1968). Teachers were sought out, from Montessori programs, Head Start, and a university child care center, who had reputations as "naturally born super teachers." However, the goal was to discover the precise conditions in which children best learn how to use language, rather than to discover what conditions are essential for children to learn to talk. When the goal is efficient staff preparation, the performance of interest is not the "ideal" performance, but rather the performance that is adequate to get the job done.

• *Performance appraisal checklists:* The most efficient way to teach a new skill is to use a performance appraisal checklist to focus the trainee on the essential steps of a given teaching routine. A performance appraisal checklist is basically a task analysis of a given skill or an expansion of the operational definition of the behavioral competency. Every element that is viewed as an essential component of the skill to be acquired is presented as a discrete step, and steps are sequenced according to the order in which each component should occur.

Performance appraisal checklists may also include important safety or logistical steps.

The larger purpose of a performance appraisal checklist is to focus both trainer and trainee on the most salient features of a targeted skill. Checklists could be used to train a research skill (such as how to videotape experimental sessions), or checklists can be used to specify an administrative task (such as depositing tuition checks). Incidental teaching checklists are used to prepare preschool teachers at the Walden Early Childhood Program, where complex skills are needed to do incidental teaching with an inclusive group of children with and without autism. A new trainee is first prepared with the checklist shown in Figure 45.1 to do incidental teaching in the easiest case scenario, which is a 1 : 1 session.

At the same time, the trainee may be prepared to conduct a specific teaching routine, which blends incidental teaching into a regular childhood activity. A slightly different performance appraisal checklist (illustrated in Figure 45.2) is used to prepare teachers to conduct teaching routines, each of which provides the foundation for a specific component of the Walden curriculum. For example, Special Art Activity is a teaching routine in which incidental teaching is used to teach descriptive adjectives (e.g., colors, shapes) at a small group tabletop activity (e.g., painting, collages). The trainee can initially learn the logistics, pacing, and topography of a teaching routine. When the trainee has mastered incidental teaching in the 1 : 1 session, he can next learn how to blend the incidental teaching procedure into the Special Art Activity routine.

In other words, the checklist for incidental teaching specifies the steps of a procedure that is blended into each of the Walden teaching routines. Checklists for teaching routines ensure that every teacher who conducts an instructional activity, no matter what their personal style, will be able to cover the key bases. For this reason, performance appraisal checklists are especially helpful when there is high staff turnover, such as the situation that arises when college student labor makes up a sizeable portion of a program's labor force. Thus, performance appraisal checklists make it possible to maintain the consistency that is important

WALDEN Incidental Teaching Checklist

Teacher Name: _____   Child's Init. _____   Trainer Name: _____

Date: _____/_____/04   Circle Day: M T W T F   Time of Day: _____ AM/PM

Training Phase: Initial Maintenance   # I.T. Cklists: _____   Activity: 1:1 FP TT Meal OS

Did the teacher:	1st episode	2nd episode
1. ARRANGE the environment to attract children? _____		
a. Do children want the teaching toys/activity?	a. Y N NA	a. Y N NA
b. Does teacher "market" toys/activity as fun?	b. Y N NA	b. Y N NA
c. Does teacher get alternative toys if needed?	c. Y N NA	c. Y N NA
2. WAIT for or elicit child initiation (5 sec)? _____		
a. Look/pause at child's eye level?	a. Y N NA	a. Y N NA
b. Talk-up or comment on child's play?	b. Y N NA	b. Y N NA
c. Control access if needed	c. Y N NA	c. Y N NA
3. PROMPT by blending into child's interest Objective? _____		
a. At teachable moment (< 5 sec of initiation?)	a. Y N NA	a. Y N NA
b. Teach to designated objective	b. Y N NA	b. Y N NA
c. Backup to easier prompt as needed (< 4 ×)	c. Y N NA	c. Y N NA
4. GIVE CONTINGENT ACCESS to desired toy/activity? _____		
a. Give behavior-specific praise immediately?	a. Y N NA	a. Y N NA
b. Follow praise with delivery of desired reward?	b. Y N NA	b. Y N NA
c. Reinforce only desired behaviors? (record + for correct episode/0 for other episodes)	c. Y N NA _____	c. Y N NA _____

MASTERY? 1×   2×   Improved?   Y N NA

Teacher's Init. If Rec'd Feedback _____

Comments:

Figure 45.1   Procedural Performance Appraisal Checklist.

WALDEN Special Art Activities (SA) Checklist

Teacher: _____   Trainer: _____

children present? T/CWA _____/_____   Activity: _____ Goal(s) _____

Training Phase: Initial Maintenance   Indiv. Obj. posted? Y N NA

Enter Date: Did the teacher? Score each item + or 0					
1. Get activity ready and announce zone open to Lead Teacher (LT)?					
2. Conduct FUN Activity?					
3. Keep children engaged?					
4. Teach to the goal designated for zone?					
5. Distribute attention across all children present?					
6. Teach to individualized level/objective for children with autism?					
7. Challenge typical peers to expand vocabulary?					
8. Reinforce correct responses with powerful rewards (avoid accidental pairing with challenging behavior)?					
9. Keep zone inclusive by alternating seating & notifying LT when ratio is imbalanced?					
10. Encourage children to share materials ?					
11. Permit children to leave on request?					
Observe 5 min. and tally # teaching opportunities + = child responded correctly 0 = opportunity with no or incorrect response					
Trainee initials after receiving formal feedback					

Figure 45.2   Teaching Routine Performance Appraisal Checklist.

for children with autism, despite the patchwork and part-time schedules that students commonly present.

Training to a Mastery Criterion

When years of apprenticeship training were available, it was unnecessary and probably not to the mentor's advantage to define a precise moment when it would be possible to put the trainee on the job. But in current conditions that require training efficiency, there must be measurable indicators of when a job performance may be considered to be at mastery. Because well-constructed performance appraisals are composed of objective descriptions of the components of an adequate performance, the ability to complete every step without prompting is an important achievement. However, the criterion for a mastery-level performance is set by deciding how many times the trainee needs to perform the skill perfectly to be reasonably sure that the performance can be replicated consistently in the absence of the trainer. At a minimum, two consecutive perfect performances may be necessary to ensure that the trainee's first demonstration of a skill was not a fluke (e.g., only well-behaved girls were attending school on the day that a teacher was evaluated for implementing a behavior problem prevention plan). On the other hand, it is difficult for anyone to do everything perfectly all the time, so it may be unrealistic (and prolong training unnecessarily) to require 10 or more perfect performances.

The implication of establishing a mastery criterion at the level of an adequate performance is that trainees should not be assigned to work independently while their job performances are inadequate. However, there is usually pressure to fill open staff positions as soon as possible, and trainers are highly motivated to reduce their own time commitment. However, if a trainee is put on the job before being fully prepared, he or she may be unfairly placed in a position of responsibility before becoming able to protect children's safety. It is also likely that children's progress will be compromised if their teachers' instruction was lacking essential components. Trainers sometimes justify their decision to "slow down" training based on the hope that the trainee will benefit from opportunities to practice the new skill(s) between performance appraisals. Unfortunately, when initial training is distributed thinly across an extended period of time, acquisition of new skills is most likely to be impeded because the trainee will have been allowed to practice uncorrected errors. The longer trainees are permitted to practice mistakes, the more difficult it will be for them to achieve mastery of a behavioral competency.

Alternatively, when a policy is strictly enforced that requires skill mastery prior to placing a trainee on independent assignment, trainers and supervisors are more likely to train almost continually until their job is completed. Initial training proceeds most quickly when it begins with massed practice and coaching of one or two skills. When a trainee quickly masters the first behavioral competencies, he or she can be placed on assignments that require skills that have been mastered, and a couple of new skills can be introduced into training.

After trainees have mastered a skill at an adequate level of competency, the assumption is that their performance will continue to be refined through a process of on-the-job experience and ongoing supervision and feedback. When performance appraisal checklists provide an outline of essential job components, trainees may also enhance the fluency of their own performances through periodic self-monitoring. In sum, a combination of experience, self-monitoring, and coaching throughout a maintenance period will usually advance a mastery-level performance to a fluent (or ideal) performance over time.

The process of hands-on training every needed skill to mastery is a streamlined version of the apprenticeships of old. A clinical advantage of hands-on training, relative to more traditional workshop training, is that it minimizes the amount of time that trainers and trainees must be away from the children or adults with autism. The downside is that the trainer's time investment can seem overwhelming, because hands-on training is by definition a one-on-one and, therefore, a costly activity. A practical advantage of performance appraisals is that different trainers can alternate training responsibilities because the checklists standardize training feedback. In the end, the time investment required to provide hands-on training to mastery is offset by the time that program supervisors (who are often the trainers) would otherwise have to invest in discovering why some children are not progressing, assessing why other children are developing serious behavioral challenges, and responding to parents' complaints over playground injuries. Fully prepared teachers are also likely to be more confident and less stressed. If hands-on training reduces staff turnover, the trainer ultimately saves the time it would have taken to recruit and train a new staff member from the beginning. The bottom line is that it is not an option to staff a program with inadequately prepared personnel if there is a commitment to achieving improved lives for children (or adults) with autism.

Rewarding Trainees and Staff Members for Exceptional Performances

Despite research findings that tangible rewards can empower a training system, even the most comprehensive training systems often fail to specify positive contingencies other than praise. In fact, the most common so-called "rewards" are often either implicit or explicit threats of punishment (i.e., "in order to keep your job, you better. . . ."), which the animal learning literature suggests will increase stress. In a study that directly compared the effectiveness of using threats to fire staff for poor performances versus salary increases for good performances, threats were found to be ineffectual in altering the performances of aides working in an urban recreation center (Pierce & Risley, 1974). However, salary bonuses greatly improved their work output.

Many argue that intrinsic motivation and a paycheck (or course credit) should be sufficient motivation for professionals to do their best. In fact, the dean of a medical school made exactly such an argument at a faculty meeting, in response to several professors' complaints that inadequate research space was a disincentive to applying for new grants. The faculty's response to the dean's proposition that intrinsic motivation should suffice was a collective, "You've got to be kidding" laughter.

The program directors of autism programs enjoy various positive consequences as a result of their contributions, including paid speaking engagements, international studies travel, positive attention from colleagues, and the gratitude of parents. Yet there is a common failure to consider why poorly paid young professionals and busy college students may need more than an occasional pat on the back and the knowledge they are doing good in an evil world to consistently give their best performances of physically demanding teaching routines. Unfortunately, in many if not all autism intervention programs, the direct care personnel who are expected to work the hardest are given the fewest rewards. Human behavior is responsive to reward contingencies, so if direct care providers (and their trainers) are expected to implement complex procedures with precision and enthusiasm, the costs of an enriched schedule of rewards will be money well invested.

Salary Rewards

A logical starting point is staff salary, raises, and bonuses (Pierce & Risley, 1974; Pomerleau et al., 1973), but these are invariably smaller than they should be (i.e., a 3% increase in a salary of $10 per hour is not much of a bonus). Intensive autism interventions are expensive to run because they require a sizeable staff, and when parents are paying there is added pressure to keep tuition costs as low as possible. These challenges are often solved by paying teachers below their worth.

If possible, there should be at least a token salary increase when trainees achieve full mastery of all routines to which they are assigned, because trainees will then prompt their supervisors to keep training going as fast as possible. However, depending on the bureaucracy and labor laws where the program is located, bonuses or nonannual increases are not always under the direct control of even the program director. Administrators have an obligation to work within their systems to improve compensation, but alternative rewards are usually needed in the interim.

Personal Privileges

One strategy for ensuring that rewards actually serve as reinforcers, which increase the probability of recurrence of the behavior that they follow, is to offer the trainee a rewards menu. Consequences that are related to supply/demand imbalances often function as reinforcers (e.g., access to a nearby parking place, assignment to a corner office, or early dismissal on Friday afternoon are tried and true rewards).

Group Contingencies

As shown in personnel preparation research, group contingencies can also be effective reward options. For example, a pizza luncheon could be offered to the entire staff after all of the trainees meet boot camp requirements, because it is likely that most or all classroom staff will have contributed to the training of the new trainees. In a public school system that sponsored a network of toddler programs for children with autism, a clever special education administrator offered $1,000 for the purchase of new classroom toys as a reward to each classroom in which every staff member (including special support staff such as the speech pathologist) demonstrated mastery of competencies in reinforcer assessment and environmental design (S. Brown, personal communication, October 5, 1998; Johnson, Wagner, & Goudy, 2000). When using group contingencies, however, individual staff performances should be kept confidential to prevent either the highest or lowest performers from being ridiculed.

Professional Reinforcers

Numerous professional reinforcers can be made contingently available for autism specialists, including job advancement, training opportunities, letters of recommendation, and special assignments. Leveled training systems, which provide clearly specified criteria for advancement across levels, have rewards built into the system in the form of contingent promotion. An advantage of delineating reward contingencies in advance is that staff members develop a shared perception of fairness (i.e., anyone who does the time and completes the training can advance). When advancement across training levels cannot be paired with a substantive pay increase, accomplishments can be highlighted with a change in status. For example, when a trainee advances from boot camp to an intermediate level of training, he or she could be rewarded with a change in status from trainee to teacher, or from temporary to permanent employee. Similarly, when a teacher meets criteria for mastery of all instructional competencies, it could qualify him or her for promotion (and training) as a trainer. When a teacher moves into advanced training status, there could be an array of options that are compatible with long-term career plans (i.e., a teacher planning to apply to graduate school in a year or so may want to enrich her experience by moving to the research team, while a postdoctoral fellow who is planning to open a similar program of his own may elect to move into a supervisory role).

Progress across training levels can also be tied to external professional growth opportunities, ranging from paid attendance at a local conference or workshop to attendance at national or international meetings. If the program can fund long-distance travel, it is reasonable to require that even major achievers submit and be accepted for presentation of research or program evaluation data. It is also important to

remember that although travel may be a powerful reinforcer for some, alternatives may need to be available for staff who are inordinately inconvenienced by travel (e.g., certain individuals may appreciate books for their office library more than a trip they did not want to take).

For students and other upwardly mobile staff members, credentials are extremely powerful rewards. Letters of recommendation, signed by the program director, may be reserved for staff members who successfully complete one or more years of training. Those staff or students who give an exemplary performance for at least 6 to 12 months may be provided with a less elaborate checklist format recommendation, signed by their immediate supervisor, and all others can be referred to the organization's personnel office that releases only basic employment data. College students who qualify for a written recommendation can be encouraged to file a copy in the university's career placement office to prevent the burden of frequently reissuing the same letter. Long-term personnel who make substantial contributions to the program will request and deserve letters throughout their careers, so that either staff archives must be maintained or the staff members themselves can be made accountable for keeping and sending both hard and disk copies of their recommendation along with requests for new letters.

Documentation of training and job placements of former staff and trainees can provide an impressive set of training curriculum outcome data. One way to track future placements is to set up a system in which requests for letters of recommendation require completion of an update form (including number of individuals with autism served since last contact). Whatever the policy on recommendations, trainees should be provided with written guidelines at the beginning of training.

A less expensive array of rewards is available in privileges for a change or expanded variety of assignments, project ownership, or other special assignments. The point is to make privileges available contingent on specific achievements. For example, if a couple of staff members complain that the recess curriculum is boring, their next stellar performances can be rewarded by assigning them a few hours each week to redesign and evaluate new outdoor games, to write up the new procedures, and to conduct the staff training needed to implement what could ulti-mately become a new curriculum component. Similarly, a teacher who is especially enthusias-tic about holiday decorations could be awarded a role as a seasonal events planner contingent on some outstanding achievement; this new role may require allocation of two paid hours per week for planning, making decorations, setting up thematic activities, and soliciting parent participation.

Distribution of Rewards

There are advantages of delivering planned and preadvertised rewards, and other advan-tages of surprising staff with unanticipated rewards. The advantage of planned rewards is that trainees know exactly what is expected of them, and they may have added motivation to progress through training as quickly as possi-ble. The advantage of spontaneous rewards is that intermittent reinforcement is more con-ducive to maintenance of good performances. If distributed fairly and contingent on excep-tional performances or when rewards are given for acts of "going the extra mile" (e.g., volunteering to work over a holiday break), the effect can be to boost staff morale in ad-dition to reinforcing specific behaviors. How-ever, if the perception is that individual rewards are distributed unfairly, mutiny may transpire. One protection is to let staff have some involvement in either selecting the re-cipient or in structuring rules about how many times in a row the same recipient can win (i.e., if one staff member is far more ex-perienced than the rest of the group, he or she may take permanent possession of a coveted parking place unless some reasonable rules have been established).

The best arguments against staff rewards are that autism specialists usually work pretty hard without using external rewards as motiva-tors and that autism programs cannot afford the costs of time and money to operate a lavish reward system for nondisabled adults. It is true that autism specialists work very hard, but it is also true that supervisors and parents often want them to work even harder and smarter. As for the costs of rewards, many of the re-wards outlined earlier cost only a bit of extra supervisory time to deliver, and this time

should be quickly recouped when the training system meets desired objectives.

In fact, any materials or equipment that are typically purchased for the good of the program (i.e., a laptop computer, a new printer, or a lam-inating machine) can be transformed into rein-forcers by making the purchases contingent on an excellent performance by one or more de-serving staff members. This strategy will both increase appreciation of the new equipment and reinforce stellar performances. In other words, in many cases, the problem is not that autism programs cannot afford any rewards, but that goods tend to be distributed indiscriminately. However, keep in mind that contingent delivery of program goods is not the same as withholding a fundamental privilege, such as health insur-ance, for use as a future reward.

Providing the Training

An interesting perspective on trainers was of-fered by a highly successful executive, who built and managed internationally famous ho-tels. In fact, one of his hotels had won the Mal-colm Baldrige Award (i.e., the "Academy Award" for excellence in business manage-ment). His philosophy on who is ultimately re-sponsible for training was summed up as follows: "I can do every job in my hotels, from changing the sheets to working the front desk to cooking the creme brulée. I know all the members of my hotels' staff, and they know me, because I personally attend the initial ori-entation for every staff member hired, and I pop in at random times to work alongside them." He went on to explain that the benefits of his personal involvement are that all staff members know that their job is valued, they know that the highest standards are achiev-able, and they know that the boss knows that top-quality performance is achievable. In sum, by taking the time to participate in the training of each employee, this accomplished executive earns credibility and loyalty from his staff, he provides a model for personal accountability, and he creates a culture in which civility is routine. This kind of training and work climate would no doubt be greatly appreciated by autism specialists, as well as by the families whom they serve.

Trainer Selection

Practical considerations in trainer selection boil down to: (1) Who has the expertise to demonstrate the job? (2) Who has been prepared as a trainer? and (3) Who is available? In a pyramidal training system, every staff member is responsible not only for training the staff who are their direct reports, but also for ensuring that those supervisees are implementing the training system with the people who report to them (Favell et al., 1984). For training to be a program priority, the person in every position throughout an organization must have explicit responsibilities for active participation as both a trainer and a trainee. Program directors may seek the counsel of their mentors, and even children may participate as peer tutors for one another (and as trainers of their teachers). A "training the trainer" strategy makes optimal use of the time invested by a program's top-level experts, who can broaden their impact by mentoring the key staff members who hold primary responsibility for training the direct care providers.

Part of the beauty of an objective performance appraisal system is that anyone can be trained to do the same job. Approximately 6 months after the initial training, an undergraduate student teacher may be proficient in only one-quarter of the program's routines or procedures, but in these areas his or her expertise is likely to be comparable to that of a postdoctoral fellow who has been training for the same amount of time. In other words, the ability to execute an objectively specified behavioral routine is often credential-free. As a result, most "teachers" will be potential trainers by the time they are fluent in a targeted teaching procedure. A program's training capacity can be enhanced with relative ease by providing intermediate-level staff with basic skills in how to provide training to other staff. By spreading training responsibility throughout the system, there is the additional benefit that accrues when teaching automatically enhances the teacher's knowledge.

In sum, an effective training system should create a climate in which training is an expected and appreciated mechanism for improving the quality of care for individuals with autism and their families. Assumption of the role of a trainer should be regarded as both a serious responsibility and an honor.

Preparation of Trainers

Proficiency in the skill to be trained is a necessary but insufficient qualification for becoming a trainer. Effective trainers must learn skills in how to give positive and corrective feedback to other adults. More specifically, trainers must become comfortable in using performance appraisal checklists to structure their feedback to trainees. Checklist-based training may sound and feel threatening to a new trainee, but if the trainer is sensitive to the need to emphasize the positive and to gradually fade in corrective feedback, then what may have initially been a source of anxiety can quickly be transformed into a rewarding experience in which the trainee feels appreciated for the details of his or her performance. On the other hand, an effective trainer will not err on the side of being reluctant to bring out the checklist, because checklists speed up the process and prevent the frustration that ensues when training drags on for longer than necessary. When positive and corrective feedback have been correctly balanced, staff will complain when their hard-earned performances are not regularly checklisted.

In addition to standardizing the job descriptions of what providers are expected to do, well-formulated performance appraisals standardize what trainers should do. When the content of trainer feedback has been standardized, different trainers can rotate training responsibility without the risk of burdening a trainee with differing or conflicting opinions on how a task should be performed. Consistency across multiple trainers is further ensured by standardizing the rules for using the performance appraisals. Therefore, trainers should be prepared with a performance appraisal checklist for training skills. For example, evaluation of a trainer's performance in conducting a checklist-based performance appraisal should include feedback to the trainer on whether the content of the feedback to the trainee was focused on the key features of the targeted teaching routine as outlined in the routine's checklist.

The precise steps for conducting a performance appraisal checklist are outlined in Table 45.3. With minor adjustments, this task analysis can itself be formatted as a performance appraisal checklist for training the trainer.

Maintaining the Trainees' New Skills

In organizations with high staff turnover, which qualifies the majority of programs that serve children and adults with autism, there are times when the demand to train a sizeable number of new staff members at the same time can create a burden of such proportions that the training system is ultimately dismantled. This is an ideal time for top-level management to pitch in direct assistance in conducting checklist-based performance appraisals. Management's involvement at times of critical need provides modeling for trainers and supervisors, underlines the premiere importance of preserving the integrity of the training system, and "rallies the troops" by showing interest in individual trainees.

Ongoing Supervision

Following initial training, an effective supervisory system is needed to maintain and refine providers' skills through a process of ongoing monitoring, periodic performance appraisals, and technical assistance when complications arise. The effectiveness of supervision is directly related to the amount of time the supervisor is present and dispensing abundant levels of both formal and informal cheerleading to online staff.

Informal positive feedback should occur whenever the supervisor notices an outstanding teaching interaction, exceptional child performances, creative marketing of toys and play materials, or an unusually clean and attractive classroom appearance. In other words, an incidental teaching approach to supervision occurs when naturally occurring opportunities are seized to reinforce stellar performances.

However, formal performance appraisal checklists are needed periodically to ensure fair distribution of both positive and corrective feedback. As in initial training, the primary function of checklist-based performance appraisals is to prompt supervisors to notice and comment on relevant details of the trainee's positive accomplishments. When checklists are not used in busy settings, the tendency is for supervisors to comment primarily on errors.

Formal performance appraisals should be scheduled to occur on a regular basis. For example, after a trainee has mastered a training checklist(s), his or her performance of the newly mastered routine might be checked at least weekly during the first month, then monthly during the second and third months following mastery. After a 3-month follow-up, the supervisor may opt to use a more generic maintenance checklist on a monthly basis, which would be designed to monitor elements of good teaching that are needed in all teaching routines (e.g., "Did the teacher ad-

TABLE 45.3   How to Conduct Checklist-Based Performance Appraisals

Training Steps	How To
Talk	trainee through key components of performance appraisal checklist.
Narrate	in-vivo demonstration of mastery-level performance of routine/procedure.
Observe	with trainee who scores performance of mastery-level teacher on checklist.
Coach	trainee's first attempts to perform the new skill, with praise only.
Introduce checklist	by scoring as trainee practices routine/procedure, giving ongoing positive feedback and suggestions to practice two of the easiest missing components.
Rehearse	trainee with behavior-specific praise at end of 5 minute observation.
Formal feedback	when > half of steps are correct, score 5-minute performances by trainee and then show and review checklist for positive and corrective feedback.
Continue	formal checklist more than 1 time per day, at least 3 days per week.
Celebrate	first perfect performance, and give abundant behavior-specific praise.
Proclaim mastery	when two consecutive checklists have been completed perfectly.

dress the goals designated for the activity?). When a staff member's performance shows slippage on the maintenance checklist, the supervisor should drop back to specific routine or procedural checklists until mastery has been restored.

Without performance appraisals, the most common supervisory feedback is delivered in the form of haphazard comments (i.e., "Looks great"), which are often focused on an isolated incident rather than in the context of the staff member's overall job performance. Corrective feedback should generally be reserved for formal training, because it is unnecessary to risk demoralizing a staff member who is supposed to be interacting with children. The only exception to this rule is in the case of safety lapses, because corrective feedback must obviously be immediate when a supervisor identifies a potentially dangerous situation. Child safety trumps concern for staff morale, but little else should.

Managing the Training System

Ongoing operation of a comprehensive system for training and supervision is preventive of problems. Unfortunately, supervisors tend to gradually drop the supervisory system over time, unless it is required and regularly checked by the supervisor's supervisor. The primary complaint about requirements to implement a highly structured training system is that the supervisors and trainers may view it as time-consuming and unnatural. Another problem is that busy supervisors, who may also be the primary trainer and lead teacher in a classroom, often fail to appreciate why their own performances should be checked. When each layer of the training system is checked more and more infrequently, the entire system eventually folds and training is relegated to a role of occasional crisis management. The problem when the prevention system is dismantled is that the crises needing management occur with increasing frequency.

The solution to keeping training and supervisory systems operational is to develop a monitoring system, and the documentation involved must be as simple and time efficient to complete as possible. There are at least three layers in a permanent product tracking apparatus, including: (1) individualized training plans,

which document the knowledge and behavioral competencies targeted for each trainee; (2) a master training plan that summarizes, by trainee, what competencies are currently in active training, planned for active training, and maintenance; and (3) a weekly training plan, which schedules who has to be provided with which performance appraisal in a given week to keep the system up-to-date. The trainer should prepare in advance by putting copies of all the checklists that should be conducted in the coming week on a clipboard, which is topped by the weekly training plan. The weekly training plan provides for easy monitoring of the training system by the trainer, the supervisor, and the program evaluator.

Evaluating a Comprehensive Training Curriculum

The purpose of a program evaluation is to monitor quality indicators, which will vary according to specifics of the targeted individuals with autism, the desired life improvements for those individuals, and the intervention approach (or assessment procedures or research questions). Quality control of training systems is essential for intervention programs in which research is conducted, because it is becoming increasingly common for reviewers to expect objective measures of fidelity of implementation of the independent variable. In other words, is there objective evidence that the intervention was delivered exactly as specified in the research protocol?

Ideally, to achieve a project's desired outcome, this same level of quality control should be in place with or without concurrent research obligations. It is impossible to fully evaluate a child's response to intervention unless there is evidence that the child actually received the intervention as specified. In turn, it is unlikely that interventions will be implemented as specified unless the training system is fully operational. A program evaluation provides the mechanism for evaluating these questions, not just once a year, but on an ongoing basis.

The best way to ensure the integrity of the program evaluation or to guarantee that objective and unbiased answers are obtained from a program evaluation is to appoint an external evaluator. Ideally, the program evaluator may be considered external when he or she does not have daily contact with the program being evaluated. The problem with internal evaluators is that they can be overly sympathetic with the problems that contribute to poor implementation of intervention or training systems. Everyday problems impose limitations on optimum program operation, but with large numbers of staff and children, everyday problems occur every day. If individuals with autism are to benefit, there must be contingency plans to ensure that "the show must go on."

Performance monitoring may be accomplished via direct observations, videotaped observations, and a review of records. A comprehensive program evaluation examines, at least: (1) Is the training system in place? (2) Are all interventions scheduled for a given time taking place as scheduled? (3) Is the environment a safe place for children to be? and (4) Are the individuals with autism benefiting from their association with the program? It goes without saying that a comprehensive training system must be fully operational in order to ensure procedural integrity, safety, and realization of benefit.

Evaluating Implementation of a Training Curriculum

The most efficient method of checking whether the training system is being fully implemented is to inspect the weekly training log and accompanying checklists. If the weekly plan doesn't change from one week to another, it will be necessary for the evaluator to delve deeper into the master training plan and/or individual training plans to detect the problem.

The next question relevant to operation of the training system pertains to whether the trainee can actually do what the training system says he or she can do. Checklist-based training permits independent certification of staff performance. More specifically, the program evaluator should be able to get the same answer as the trainer when conducting a routine performance appraisal checklist on a randomly selected trainee who recently achieved mastery.

Although performance appraisals provide the best objective gauge of skill development, there are additional more subjective dimensions of caregiving that are relevant to

periodically evaluate. A supervisor might complete a rating form biannually to provide the staff member with feedback about the warmth, fun, enthusiasm, gentleness, happiness, and so on that he or she brings to the job. The program evaluator might occasionally check individual training plans for evidence of such feedback, or the evaluator could directly observe teacher affect and energy levels, as well as make a global assessment of individual children's apparent happiness at the time of the evaluation.

The trainees' acquisition of knowledge competencies is most efficiently evaluated with permanent product records. These records may include a review of accident and injury reports, on-the-spot queries to teachers on emergency procedures (emergency queries must require a very brief answer such as, "Where is the first aid kit kept?"). An environmental safety survey, designed specifically for the space being evaluated, should be conducted at least monthly by the program evaluator, and teachers may be required to conduct safety surveys at the end of each day or at least weekly (e.g., Any broken toys need to be removed from the toy shelves).

Evaluating the Effectiveness of a Training Curriculum

The bottom line of quality control is how much progress is made by children with autism, or how much better the quality of life is for adults with autism. Records review may examine whether data are being collected as planned and whether data indicate change in the desired direction. When there is a lack of progress, there should be corresponding adjustments in intervention plans. The most sensitive indicator of staff performance and program quality is obtained via assessment of the engagement of participants, which can usually be obtained in less than 10 minutes of direct observation using a pla-chek observational system (Doke & Risley, 1972). Ideally, program evaluation and engagement probes will be conducted on differing days of the week, at varying times of day.

Evaluating a Training Curriculum's Scope of Impact

The estimated size of a training project's impact may also be relevant, depending on the initial goal. The fundamental question is:

"How many people have benefited directly or indirectly as a result of the training program." Because long-term impact is increasingly difficult to track objectively, future data must initially be estimated based on career plans of individual trainees.

CONCLUSION

The demands for effective autism intervention, and the shortages in numbers of autism specialists, have not been met with corresponding increases in the resources allocated for training. Further, at a time when there are more and more questions about how to best meet the needs of individuals with autism, there are fewer and fewer new answers about how to prepare the providers that will be assigned to meet those needs.

The title of one of Professor B. F. Skinner's papers on human training has turned out to be somewhat prophetic: "The Science of Learning and the Art of Teaching" (Skinner, 1954). There is a critical need to revive interest in the area of specialty training for professionals who serve individuals with autism, and to resume research and development activities aimed at discovering more efficient ways to provide better training. But it's no wonder nobody wants to do staff training research anymore or comprehensive staff training, for that matter. The immediate consequence of a firm commitment to effective training is a tremendous amount of hard work.

One unspecified attribute shared by all successful autism providers, or they wouldn't have lasted, is perspective. The progress of children with autism is sometimes too slow to detect on a day-by-day basis, especially when providers are focused on the gaps that must be closed and the problems that must be eliminated. Parents of children with autism experience chronic stress, sometimes made worse by the demands of intervention, and remembering to praise the staff working with their children is seldom a top priority. For these reasons, it is especially important that trainees being prepared for careers in autism be taught how to keep sight of the big picture.

During Walden's early years, the students (back then, everyone was a student) took hot-dog picnics to the top of a mountain, from which the big picture was reviewed with great reverence. The program is older and relocated now, and retreats are more organized and held in more luxurious quarters. Yet there was a perspective from the mountaintop that is not easily recouped. Fantastic dreams were shared about the program, the children, and plans for individual careers. Amazing ideas were hatched, some of which turned into spectacular flops and some that worked out surprisingly well. Big dreams are big reinforcers. But trainees must be taught how to have them and provided with an opportunity to share them.

Big dreams may be the key to suffering through the drudgery of implementing rigorous and comprehensive training programs for the teachers, physicians, researchers, and all other providers who are in a position to impact the lives of individuals with autism. The long-term payoff for consistent implementation of the highest quality training program possible is likely to be significant developmental progress by children with autism. Sadly, the alternative to effective preparation of specialists to serve children with autism is the all-too-familiar outcome of adult lives spent doing basically nothing. Staff training is neither sexy nor exciting, and the area holds little promise for a career that will culminate in winning the Nobel prize. But when attempting to positively improve the lives of individuals with autism, nothing works very well without it.

Cross-References

Behavioral interventions are discussed in Chapters 35 and other aspects of program development and implementation are addressed in Chapters 33 and Chapters 38 to 43.

REFERENCES

American Psychiatric Association. (2000). *Diagnostic and statistical manual of mental disorders* (4th ed., text rev.). Washington, DC: Author.

Anderson, J. L., Russo, A., Dunlap, G., & Albin, R. W. (1996). A team training model for building the capacity to provide positive behavioral supports in inclusive settings. In L. K. Koegel, R. L. Koegel, & G. Dunlap (Eds.), *Positive behavioral support: Including people with difficult behavior in the community* (pp. 467–490). Baltimore: Paul H. Brookes.

Andrasik, F., Klare, G. R., & Murphy, W. D. (1976). Readability and behavior modification texts: Cross-comparisons and comments. *Behavior Therapy, 7,* 539–543.

Andrasik, F., & Murphy, W. D. (1977). Assessing the readability of thirty-nine behavior-modification training manuals and primers. *Journal of Applied Behavior Analysis, 10,* 341–344.

Ayllon, T., & Azrin, N. H. (1968). *The token economy: A motivational system for therapy and rehabilitation.* New York: Appleton-Century-Crofts.

Ayllon, T., & Michael, J. (1959). The psychiatric nurse as a behavioral engineer. *Journal of the Experimental Analysis of Behavior, 2,* 323–334.

Azrin, N. H., & Foxx, R. M. (1971). A rapid method of toilet training the institutionalized retarded. *Journal of Applied Behavior Analysis, 2,* 89–99.

Azrin, N. H., & Foxx, R. M. (1974). *Toilet training in less than a day.* Champaign, IL: Research Press.

Becker, W. C. (1971). *Parents are teachers: A child management program.* Champaign, IL: Research Press.

Brown, K. M., Willis, B. S., & Reid, D. H. (1981). Differential effects of supervisor verbal feedback and feedback plus approval on institutional staff performance. *Journal of Organizational Behavior Management, 3,* 57–68.

Buckley, N. K., & Walker, H. M. (1970). *Modifying classroom behavior: A manual of procedure for classroom teachers.* Champaign, IL: Research Press.

Burg, M. M., Reid, D. H., & Lattimore, J. (1979). Use of a self-recording and supervision program to change institutional staff behavior. *Journal of Applied Behavior Analysis, 12,* 363–375.

Campbell, P. (1987). Meeting personnel needs in early intervention. In A. Kaiser & C. McWhorter (Eds.), *Preparing personnel to work with persons with severe disabilities* (pp. 111–134). Baltimore: Paul H. Brookes.

Chock, P., & Glahn, T. J. (1984). Care provider and respite care services. In W. P. Christian, G. T. Hannah, & T. J. Glahn (Eds.), *Programming effective human services: Strategies for institutional change and client transition* (pp. 357–382). New York: Plenum Press.

Christian, W. P. (1981a). Behavioral administration of the residential treatment program. *Behavior Therapist, 4*(1), 3–6.

Christian, W. P. (1981b). The biannual report: A model for structuring human service program evaluation and dissemination. *Journal of Rehabilitation Administration, 5*(3), 108–114.

Christian, W. P. (1981c). Programming quality assurance in the residential rehabilitation setting: A model for administrative work performance standards. *Journal of Rehabilitation Administration, 5*(1), 26–33.

Christian, W. P. (1982). Work performance contracting: An essential feature of accountable human service administration. *Journal of Mental Health Administration, 9*(2), 39–42.

Christian, W. P. (1983a). A case study in the programming and maintenance of institutional change. *Journal of Organizational Behavior Management, 5,* 99–153.

Christian, W. P. (1983b). Legal issues relevant to child development and behavior. In M. D. Levine, W. B. Carey, A. C. Crocker, & R. T. Gross (Eds.), *Developmental-behavioral pediatrics* (pp. 1175–1190). Philadelphia: W. B. Saunders.

Christian, W. P., & Hannah, G. T. (Eds.). (1983). *Effective management in human services.* Englewood Cliffs, NJ: Prentice-Hall.

Deibert, A. N., & Golden, F. (1973). Behavior modification workshops with juvenile officers: Brief report. *Behavior Therapy, 4,* 586–588.

Doke, L. A., & Risley, T. R. (1972). The organization of day care environments: Required vs. optional activities. *Journal of Applied Behavior Analysis, 5,* 405–420.

Dussault, W. L. E. (1996). Avoiding due process hearings: Developing an open relationship between parents and school districts. In L. K. Koegel, R. L. Koegel, & G. Dunlap (Eds.), *Positive behavioral support: Including people with difficult behavior in the community* (pp. 265–278). Baltimore: Paul H. Brookes.

Dyer, K., Schwartz, L. S., & Luce, S. C. (1984). A supervision program for increasing functional activities for severely handicapped students in a residential setting. *Journal of Applied Behavior Analysis, 17,* 249–259.

Fabry, P. L., & Reid, D. H. (1978). Teaching foster grandparents to train severely handicapped persons. *Journal of Applied Behavior Analysis, 11,* 111–123.

Favell, J. E. (1973). Reduction of stereotypies by reinforcement of toy play. *Journal of Applied Behavior Analysis, 11,* 21–23.

Favell, J. E., Favell, J. E., Riddle, J. I., & Risley, T. R. (1984). Promoting change in mental retardation facilities: Getting services from the paper to the people. In W. P. Christian, G. T. Hannah, & T. J. Glahn (Eds.), *Programming effective human services: Strategies for institutional change and client transition* (pp. 15–37). New York: Plenum Press.

Filipek, P. A., Accardo, P. J., Ashwal, S., Baranek, G. T., Cook, E. H., Jr., & Dawson, G. (2000). Practice parameter: Screening and diagnosis of autism. *Neurology, 55,* 468–479.

Foxx, R. M., & Azrin, N. H. (1973). *Toilet training the retarded: A rapid program for day and nighttime independent toileting.* Champaign, IL: Research Press.

Gardner, J. M. (1973). Training the trainer: A review of research on teaching behavior modification. In R. D. Rubin, J. P. Brady, & J. D. Henderson (Eds.), *Advances in behavior therapy* (pp. 37–54). New York: Academic Press.

Givner, A., & Graubard, P. S. (1974). *A handbook of behavior modification for the classroom.* New York: Holt, Rinehart and Winston.

Greene, B. F., Willis, B. S., Levy, R., & Bailey, J. S. (1978). Measuring client gains from staff-implemented programs. *Journal of Applied Behavior Analysis, 11,* 395–412.

Greenspan, S. I., & Wieder, S. (1999). A functional developmental approach to autism spectrum disorders. *Journal of the Association for Persons with Severe Handicaps, 24,* 147–161.

Hall, R. V. (1971). *Behavior modification: Applications in school and home.* Lawrence, KS: H & H Enterprises.

Hall, R. V., Lund, D., & Jackson, D. (1968). Effects of teacher attention on study behavior. *Journal of Applied Behavior Analysis, 1,* 1–12.

Handleman, J. S., & Harris, S. L. (Eds.). (2001). *Preschool education programs for children with autism* (2nd ed.). Austin, TX: ProEd.

Hannah, G. T., Christian, W. P., & Clark, H. B. (1981). *Preservation of client rights: A handbook for practitioners providing therapeutic, educational, and rehabilitative services.* New York: Free Press.

Haring, T. G., Kennedy, C. H., Adams, M. J., & Pitts-Conway, V. (1987). Teaching generalization of purchasing skills across community settings to autistic youth using videotape modeling. *Journal of Applied Behavior Analysis, 20,* 89–96.

Harris, S. L., & Handleman, J. S. (Eds.). (1994). *Preschool education programs for children with autism.* Austin, TX: ProEd.

Harris, S. L., Handleman, J. S., Arnold, M. S., & Gordon, R. F. (2001). The Douglass Developmental Disabilities Center: Two models of service delivery. In J. S. Handleman & S. L. Harris (Eds.), *Preschool education programs for children with autism* (2nd ed., pp. 233–260). Austin, TX: ProEd.

Hart, B. M., Reynolds, N. J., Baer, D. M., Brawley, E. R., & Harris, F. R. (1968). Effect of contingent and non-contingent social reinforcement on the cooperative play of a preschool child. *Journal of Applied Behavior Analysis, 1,* 73–76.

Hart, B. M., & Risley, T. R. (1968). Establishing the use of descriptive adjectives in the spontaneous speech of disadvantaged children. *Journal of Applied Behavior Analysis, 1,* 109–120.

Holland, J. G. (1960). Teaching machines: An application of principles from the laboratory. *Journal of the Experimental Analysis of Behavior, 3,* 275–287.

Horner, R. D. (1980). The effects of an environmental "enrichment" program on the behavior of institutionalized profoundly retarded children. *Journal of Applied Behavior Analysis, 13,* 473–491.

Horner, R. D., & Keilitz, L. (1975). Training mentally retarded adolescents to brush their teeth. *Journal of Applied Behavior Analysis, 8,* 301–309.

Hutchinson, J. M., Jarman, P. H., & Bailey, J. S. (1980). Public posting with a habilitation team: Effects on attendance and performance. *Behavior Modification, 4,* 57–70.

Individuals with Disabilities Education Act of 1997, 20 U.S.C. § 1400 et. seq. (1997).

Ivancic, M. T., Reid, D. H., Iwata, B. A., Faw, G. D., & Page, T. J. (1981). Evaluating a supervision program for developing and maintaining therapeutic staff-resident interactions during institutional care routines. *Journal of Applied Behavior Analysis, 14,* 95–107.

Iwata, B. A., Bailey, J. S., Brown, K. M., Foshee, T. J., & Alpern, M. (1976). A performance-based lottery to improve residential care and training by institutional staff. *Journal of Applied Behavioral Analysis, 9,* 417–431.

Johnson, C., Wagner, S. J., & Goudy, K. (2000, April). Social skills for young children with autism: What to teach, how to teach. In G. G. McGee & P. S. Strain (Chairs), *Educating young children with autism: What are the goals?* Presented at the annual convention of the Council for Exceptional Children, Vancouver, British Columbia, Canada.

Kissel, R. C., Whitman, T. L., & Reid, D. H. (1983). An institutional staff training and self-management program for developing multiple self-care skills in severely/profoundly retarded individuals. *Journal of Applied Behavior Analysis, 16,* 395–415.

Koegel, R. L., Russo, D. C., & Rincover, A. (1977). Assessing and training teachers in the generalized use of behavior modification with autistic children. *Journal of Applied Behavior Analysis, 10,* 197–205.

Koegel, R. L., Schreibman, L., Loos, L. M., Dirlich-Wilhelm, H., Dunlap, G., Robbins, F. R., et al.

(1992). Stress profiles for mothers and fathers of children with autism. *Journal of Autism and Developmental Disorders, 22,* 205–216.

Kreitner, R., Reif, W. E., & Morris, M. (1977). Measuring the impact of feedback on the performance of mental health technicians. *Journal of Organizational Behavior Management, 1,* 105–109.

Laski, K. E., Charlop, M. H., & Schreibman, L. (1988). Training parents to use the natural language paradigm to increase their autistic children's speech. *Journal of Applied Behavior Analysis, 21,* 391–400.

LeLaurin, K., & Risley, T. R. (1972). The organization of day-care environments: "Zone" versus "man-to-man" staff assignments. *Journal of Applied Behavior Analysis, 5,* 225–232.

Loomis, M. E., & Horsley, J. A. (1974). *Interpersonal change: A behavioral approach to nursing practice.* New York: McGraw-Hill.

Lord, C., Risi, S., Lamabrecht, L., Cook, E. H., Jr., Leventhal, B. L., DiLavore, P. C., et al. (2000). The autism diagnostic observation schedule-generic: A standard measure of social and communication deficits associated with the spectrum of autism. *Journal of Autism and Developmental Disorders, 30*(3), 205–233.

Lord, C., Rutter, M. L., DiLavore, P. C., & Risi, S. (2002). *Autism Diagnostic Observation Schedule (ADOS) manual.* Los Angeles: Western Psychological Services.

Lord, C., Rutter, M. L., & Le Couteur, A. (1994). Autism Diagnostic Interview-Revised: A revised version of a diagnostic interview for caregivers of individuals with possible pervasive developmental disorders. *Journal of Autism and Developmental Disorders, 24*(5), 659–685.

Lovaas, O. I. (1987). Behavioral treatment and normal educational and intellectual functioning in young autistic children. *Journal of Consulting and Clinical Psychology, 55,* 3–9.

Lovaas, O. I., Ackerman, A. B., Alexander, D., Firestone, P., Perkins, J., & Young, D. (1981). *Teaching developmentally disabled children: The ME book.* Austin, TX: ProEd.

Malott, R. W. (1972). *Contingency management.* Kalamazoo, MI: Behaviordelia.

Malott, R. W., Hartlep, P., & Hartlep, S. (1974). Contingency management in education and other equally exciting places or I've got blisters on my soul and other equally exciting places. In R. Ulrich, T. Stachnik, & J. Mabry (Eds.), *Control of human behavior* (Vol. 3, pp. 161–168). Glenview, Illinois: Scott, Foresman, & Co.

Mandlawitz, M. R. (2002). The impact of the legal system on educational programming for young children with autism spectrum disorder. *Journal of Autism and Developmental Disorders, 32,* 495–508.

Marcus, L., Schopler, E., & Lord, C. (2001). TEACCH services for preschool children. In J. S. Handleman & S. L. Harris (Eds.), *Preschool education programs for children with autism* (2nd ed., pp. 215–232). Austin, TX: ProEd.

Markle, S. M. (1962). Teaching machines versus programmers. *Audiovisual Communication Review, 10,* 4.

Markle, S. M. (1969). *Good frames and bad* (2nd ed.). New York: Wiley.

Martin, G. L. (1972). Teaching operant technology to psychiatric nurses, aides, and attendants. In F. W. Clark, D. R. Evans, & L. A. Hamerlynk (Eds.), *Implementing behavioral programs for schools and clinics* (pp. 63–87). Champaign, IL: Research Press.

McClannahan, L. E., & Krantz, P. J. (2001). Behavior analysis and intervention for preschoolers at the Princeton Child Development Institute. In J. S. Handleman & S. L. Harris (Eds.), *Preschool education programs for children with autism* (2nd ed., pp. 191–213). Austin, TX: ProEd.

McClannahan, L. E., Krantz, P. J., & McGee, G. G. (1982). Parents as therapists for autistic children: A model for effective parent training. *Analysis and Intervention in Developmental Disabilities, 2,* 223–252.

McClannahan, L. E., McGee, G. G., MacDuff, G. S., & Krantz, P. J. (1990). Assessing and improving child care: A personal appearance index for children with autism. *Journal of Applied Behavior Analysis, 23,* 469–482.

McClannahan, L. E., & Risley, T. R. (1975). Design of living environments for nursing home residents: Increasing participation in recreation activities. *Journal of Applied Behavior Analysis, 8,* 261–268.

McGee, G. G., Almeida, M. C., Sulzer-Azaroff, B., & Feldman, R. S. (1992). Promoting reciprocal interactions via peer incidental teaching. *Journal of Applied Behavior Analysis, 25,* 117–126.

McGee, G. G., Daly, T., Izeman, S. G., Mann, L. H., & Risley, T. R. (1991). Use of classroom materials to promote preschool engagement. *Teaching Exceptional Children, 23,* 44–47.

McGee, G. G., Daly, T., & Jacobs, H. A. (1994). The Walden Preschool. In S. L. Harris & J. S. Handleman (Eds.), *Preschool education programs for children with autism* (pp. 127–162). Austin, TX: ProEd.

McGee, G. G., Jacobs, H. A., & Regnier, M. C. (1993). Preparation of families for incidental teaching and advocacy for their children with autism. *OSERS News in Print, 5,* 9–13.

McGee, G. G., Krantz, P. J., & McClannahan, L. E. (1981). *The Princeton Child Development Institute specialized preservice manual: Extension of the Teaching-Family Model to autistic children and youth* (Achievement Place Project Phase IV, University of Kansas). Unpublished manuscript.

McGee, G. G., & McCoy, J. F. (1981). Training procedures for acquisition and retention of reading in retarded youth. *Applied Research in Mental Retardation, 2,* 263–276.

McGee, G. G., Morrier, M. J., & Daly, T. (1999). An incidental teaching approach to early intervention for toddlers with autism. *Journal of the Association for Persons with Severe Handicaps, 24,* 133–146.

McGee, G. G., Morrier, M. J., & Daly, T. (2001). The Walden Early Childhood Programs. In J. S. Handleman & S. L. Harris (Eds.), *Preschool education programs for children with autism* (2nd ed., pp. 157–190). Austin, TX: ProEd.

Montegar, C. A., Reid, D. H., Madsen, C. H., & Ewell, M. D. (1977). Increasing institutional staff-to-resident interactions through inservice training and supervision approval. *Behavior Therapy, 8,* 533–540.

National Research Council. (2001). *Educating children with autism* (Committee on Educational Interventions for Children with Autism, Commission on Behavioral and Social Sciences and Education). Washington, DC: National Academy Press.

Neef, N. A., Parrish, J. M., Egel, A. L., & Sloan, M. E. (1986). Training respite care providers for families with handicapped children: Experimental analysis and validation of an instructional package. *Journal of Applied Behavior Analysis, 19,* 1–20.

O'Brien, M., Porterfield, P. J., Herbert-Jackson, E., & Risley, T. R. (1979). *The Toddler Center manual: A practical guide to day care for one- and two-year olds.* Baltimore: University Park Press.

Page, T. J., Iwata, B. A., & Reid, D. H. (1982). Pyramidal training: A large-scale application with institutional staff. *Journal of Applied Behavior Analysis 15,* 335–351.

Panyan, M., Boozer, H., & Morris, N. (1970). Feedback to attendants as a reinforcer for applying operant techniques. *Journal of Applied Behavior Analysis, 3,* 1–4.

Park, J., & Turnbull, A. P. (2002). Quality indicators of professionals who work with children with problem behavior. *Journal of Positive Behavior Interventions, 4,* 118–122.

Patterson, E. T., Griffin, J. C., & Panyan, M. C. (1976). Incentive maintenance of self-help skill training programs for non-professional personnel. *Journal of Behavior Therapy and Experimental Psychiatry, 7,* 249–253.

Pierce, C., & Risley, T. R. (1974). Improving job performance of neighborhood youth corps aides in an urban recreation program. *Journal of Applied Behavior Analysis, 7,* 207–215.

Pomerleau, O., Bobrove, P., & Smith, R. (1973). Rewarding psychiatric aides for the behavioral improvement of assigned patients. *Journal of Applied Behavior Analysis, 6,* 383–390.

Pommer, D. A., & Streedback, D. (1974). Motivating staff performance in an operant learning program for children. *Journal of Applied Behavior Analysis, 7,* 217–221.

Quilitch, H. R. (1975). A comparison of three staff management procedures. *Journal of Applied Behavior Analysis, 8,* 59–66.

Reid, D. H., Schuh-Wear, C. L., & Brannon, M. E. (1978). Use of a group contingency to decrease staff absenteeism in a state institution. *Behavior Modification, 2,* 251–266.

Reid, D. H., & Whitman, T. L. (1983). Behavioral staff management in institutions: A critical review of effectiveness and acceptability. *Analysis and Intervention in Developmental Disabilities, 3,* 131–149.

Richman, G. S., Riordan, M. R., Reiss, M. L., Pyles, D. A. M., & Bailey, J. S. (1988). The effects of self-monitoring and supervisor feedback on staff performance in a residential setting. *Journal of Applied Behavior Analysis, 21,* 401–409.

Risley, T. R. (1996). Get a life! Positive behavioral intervention for challenging behavior through life arrangement and life coaching. In L. K. Koegel, R. L. Koegel, & G. Dunlap (Eds.), *Positive behavioral support: Including people with difficult behavior in the community* (pp. 425–437). Baltimore: Paul H. Brookes.

Risley, T. R., & Wolf, M. M. (1966). Experimental manipulation of autistic behaviors and generalization into the home. In R. Ulrich, T. Stachnik, & J. Mabry (Eds.), *Control of human behavior* (Vol. 1, pp. 193–198). Glenview, Illinois: Scott, Foresman, & Co.

Romanczyk, R. G., Lockshin, S. B., & Matey, L. (2001). The Children's Unit for treatment and evaluation. In J. S. Handleman & S. L. Harris (Eds.), *Preschool education programs for children with autism* (2nd ed., pp. 49–94). Austin, TX: ProEd.

Rutter, M. L., Le Couteur, A., & Lord, C. (2003). *Autism Diagnostic Interview—Revised (ADI-R) manual.* Los Angeles: Western Psychological Services.

Schreibman, L., Koegel, R. L., Mills, J. I., & Burke, J. C. (1984). Training parent-child interactions. In E. Schopler & G. B. Mesibov (Eds.), *The effects of autism on the family* (pp. 187–205). New York: Plenum.

Seys, D. M., & Duker, P. C. (1978). Improving residential care for the retarded by differential reinforcement of high rates of ward-staff behaviour. *Behavioural Analysis and Modification, 2,* 203–210.

Shoemaker, J., & Reid, D. H. (1980). Decreasing chronic absenteeism among institutional staff: Effects of a low-cost attendance program. *Journal of Organizational Behavior Management, 2,* 317–328.

Simpson, R. L. (2004). Finding effective intervention and personnel preparation practices for students with autism spectrum disorders. *Exceptional Children, 70,* 135–144.

Skinner, B. F. (1954). The science of learning and the art of teaching. *Harvard Educational Review, 29,* 86–97.

Skinner, B. F. (1958). Teaching machines. *Science, 128,* 969–977.

Smith, T., Donahoe, P. A., & Davis, B. J. (2001). The UCLA Young Autism Project. In J. S. Handleman & S. L. Harris (Eds.), *Preschool education programs for children with autism* (2nd ed., pp. 29–48). Austin, TX: ProEd.

Sneed, T. J., & Bible, G. H. (1979). An administrative procedure for improving staff performance in an institutional setting for retarded persons. *Mental Retardation, 2,* 92–94.

Strain, P. S., McGee, G. G., & Kohler, F. W. (2001). Inclusion of children with autism in early intervention environments: An examination of rationale, myths, and procedures. In M. J. Guralnick (Ed.), *Early childhood inclusion: Focus on change* (pp. 337–363). Baltimore: Paul H. Brookes.

Thorne, G. L., Tharp, R. G., & Wetzel, R. J. (1967). Behavior modification techniques: New tools for probation officers. *Federal Probation, 231,* 21–26.

Turnbull, H. R., Wilcox, B. L., & Stowe, M. J. (2002). A brief overview of special education law with focus on autism. *Journal of Autism and Developmental Disorders, 32,* 479–493.

Van den Pol, R. A., Iwata, B. A., Ivancic, M. T., Page, T. J., Neef, N. A., & Whitley, F. P. (1981). Teaching the handicapped to eat in public places: Acquisition, generalization, and maintenance of restaurant skills. *Journal of Applied Behavior Analysis, 14,* 6–-69.

Volkmar, F. R., Cook, E. H., Jr., Pomeroy, J., Realmuto, G. M., & Tanguay, P. (1999). Practice parameters for the assessment and treatment of children, adolescents, and adults with autism and other pervasive developmental disorders. *Journal of the American Academy of Child and Adolescent Psychiatry, 38*(12), 32S–54S.

Wagner, S. (1999). *Inclusive programming for elementary students with autism.* Arlington, TX: Future Horizons.

Wagner, S. (2002). *Inclusive programming for middle school students with autism/Asperger's syndrome.* Arlington, TX: Future Horizons.

Watson, L. S. (1973). *Child behavior modification: A manual for teachers, nurses, and parents.* New York: Pergamon Press.

Wolf, M. M., Risley, T. R., & Mees, H. (1964). Application of operant conditioning procedures to the behavior problems of an autistic child. *Behaviour Research and Therapy, 1,* 305–312.

Yeargin-Allsopp, M., Rice, C., Karapurkar, T., Doernberg, N., Boyle, C., & Murphy, C. (2003). Prevalence of autism in a U. S. metropolitan area. *Journal of the American Medical Association, 289,* 49–55.

Zaharia, E. S., & Baumeister, A. A. (1978). Technician turnover and absenteeism in public residential facilities. *American Journal of Mental Deficiency, 82,* 580–593.

Zeilberger, J., Sampen, S., & Sloane, H. N. (1968). Modification of a child's problem behaviors in the home with the mother as therapist. *Journal of Applied Behavior Analysis, 1,* 47–53.

CHAPTER 46

Educating Children with Autism:
Current Legal Issues

MYRNA R. MANDLAWITZ

The Individuals with Disabilities Education Act (IDEA), enacted originally as the Education for All Handicapped Act (EHA) in 1975 and amended most recently in 1997, entitles eligible children and youth with disabilities ages birth through 21 to receive special education and related services. The essence of the Act is "to ensure that all children with disabilities have available to them a free appropriate public education . . . designed to meet their unique needs and prepare them for employment and independent living" (Sec. 601(d)(1)(A), IDEA, 1997).

This chapter is based on the author's extensive experience in reviewing the administrative rulings and court cases pertaining to the education of children with autism spectrum disorder. In addition to delivering presentations at national law conferences and providing training for state departments of education, the author was also invited to present a commissioned paper before the National Academy of Sciences Committee on Interventions for Children with Autism (*The Impact of the Legal System on Educational Programming for Young Children with Autism Spectrum Disorder,* 1999).

The U.S. Department of Education has defined the six main principles of the IDEA as the provision of a free appropriate public education, completion of an appropriate evaluation, development and implementation of an individualized education program (IEP), placement in the least restrictive learning environment, parent and student participation in decision-making, and provision and enforcement of procedural safeguards (*Annual Report to Congress,* 1998). Some or all of these six principles figure prominently in legal decisions regarding educational services for children with autism.

The IDEA is unique in its inclusion of families in the decision-making process. The law assumes that parents of children with disabilities understand their child's strengths and problems, and can advocate for an educational plan that will meet the child's needs. In fact, strong advocacy may depend on the parents' educational background and understanding of their rights, and may be impacted by socioeconomic and cultural impediments, such as language difficulties or the inability to obtain childcare or release time from work to attend meetings. Parents may also have difficulty facing up to the child's problems or feel they are not knowledgeable enough to engage school personnel, even when they are dissatisfied with the school program. Because of the sometimes uneven playing field, the law allows parents a series of procedural safeguards (see below) to ensure that children make appropriate educational progress.

The procedural safeguards were originally included in the law to ensure access to education at a time when many students with disabilities were excluded from public schools.

This chapter is derived, in part, from work sponsored by the U.S. government, National Academy of Science, Committee on Educational Interventions for Children with Autism, 1999.

Advocates for people with disabilities viewed the EHA and now the IDEA as legislation to redress the denial of the basic civil right to a public education. If families believe that school districts are not providing appropriate services or have violated procedural requirements of the law, the procedural safeguards allow a mechanism to redress their grievances through administrative hearings and judicial processes.

This chapter addresses the legal issues peculiar to the provision of special education and related services to children with autism spectrum disorders. For those children, early identification and early provision of services can be critical to continued development. Prior to 1990, the majority of states and local school districts had not adopted policies specific to the education of children with autism. Since 1990, educational programming for children with autism has emerged as an issue of critical concern for school districts, as a result of several factors. Among these factors are the increased identification of children with autism, including reclassification of children previously deemed eligible under other disability categories; publicity about specific educational methodologies; parent advocacy for those methodologies; the cost of providing intensive services; and shortages of qualified personnel. As a result of these and other factors, the policies and practices of state and local educational agencies (SEA, LEA) have evolved to meet changing educational needs and parental concerns.

To understand the effects of these changes on educational programming, it is necessary to understand more fully the six key principles of the IDEA and to examine the substantive and procedural issues presented in legal proceedings and the legal standards used by administrative hearing officers and judges.

IDENTIFICATION AND EVALUATION OF CHILDREN WITH DISABILITIES

States are required to identify, locate, and evaluate all children with disabilities who may possibly need special education and related services. Children may be identified and referred for evaluation by their parents or other family members, or by a healthcare or childcare provider. Parents may have concerns about their children, but lack the knowledge or confidence

to broach these concerns with a doctor or other professional.

Therefore, it is important that healthcare or childcare providers be aware of available services and support parents in seeking assistance.

In 1997, the "child find" requirement was extended to include children with disabilities in private schools, highly mobile children, for example, migrant and homeless, and children who are suspected of meeting the eligibility criteria, even though they are progressing from grade to grade (20 U.S.C. § 1412(3)(A); 34 C.F.R. § 300.125(a)). States are also obligated to identify children ages birth through two and provide services if those children meet the eligibility criteria for the IDEA-Part C program for infants and toddlers with disabilities.

Once a child has been identified, the LEA must conduct an initial evaluation, assessing the child in all areas of suspected disability, to ascertain if the child is eligible to receive services under the IDEA. Parents must provide informed consent before an initial evaluation can be made. However, if the parent withholds consent, the LEA may use the due process mechanism to pursue an evaluation (20 U.S.C. § 1414(a)(1)).

The evaluation must be sufficiently comprehensive to identify all of the child's special education and related service needs. Therefore, evaluators must determine any needs the child may have that are not commonly associated with the child's primary disability (34 C.F.R. § 300.532, *Analysis of Comments,* IDEA Final Regulations, 1999). This is of particular importance for children with autism spectrum disorders, where there may be involvement in a number of areas of functioning.

If parents have had their child independently evaluated before the formal LEA evaluation process has occurred, the results of the independent evaluation must be part of the equation in determining the child's eligibility for services (20 U.S.C. § 1414(b)(2)(A)). If parents disagree with the results of the LEA's evaluation, they may request an independent educational evaluation at the district's expense (20 U.S.C. § 1415(b)(1)). Districts are not obligated to pay for such evaluations unless parents first register their disagreement with the district evaluation. If that criterion is met, the LEA must either provide the requested evaluation or use the due process procedures to defend its own evaluation. If the district prevails in the due process proceeding, parents may be obligated to pay the costs of the independent evaluation (34 C.F.R. § 300.502). This issue arises frequently in cases related to children with autism, because concerned parents may seek outside assistance prior to a determination of eligibility by the LEA (*Amanda J. v. Clark County Sch. Dist.*, 2001; *CM v. Board of Pub. Educ. of Henderson County*, 2002; *DiBuo v. Board of Educ. of Worcester County*, 2002). Prior to the 1997 IDEA amendments, LEAs were required to conduct a triennial reevaluation of each eligible child. Parents and LEAs often felt a comprehensive reevaluation, similar in scope to the initial evaluation, was unnecessary to establish the child's continuing eligibility for services. Therefore, in 1997 the law was amended to require a reevaluation at least every 3 years, through which a team of qualified professionals and the parents would decide what, if any, tests and evaluative materials would be necessary to establish the continued need for services (20 U.S.C. § 1414(c)). The results of the reevaluation help the LEA determine not only continued eligibility, but also whether any changes are needed in the child's program or placement in order to meet annual goals and objectives.

PROVIDING A FREE APPROPRIATE PUBLIC EDUCATION

The foundation of the IDEA is the provision of a free appropriate public education (FAPE) to all children with disabilities who meet the eligibility requirements of the law (20 U.S.C. § 1401(8)). Special education advocates consider provision of a FAPE a civil right to which all eligible children with disabilities are entitled.

Eligibility for Services

In order to receive a FAPE under the IDEA, a child must meet the definition of a "child with a disability" and, as a result of that disability, require special education and related services. A child must qualify in 1 of 12 enumerated disability categories, including autism (20 U.S.C. § 1401(3)(A)). In 1997, states were given the prerogative to add a "developmental delay" category for children within the age range of three through nine (20 U.S.C. § 1401(3)(B)). This allows LEAs to provide services to young children experiencing developmental delays without the requirement of a disability label.

Autism is defined in the IDEA regulations as a "developmental disability significantly affecting verbal and nonverbal communication and social interaction, generally evident before age 3, that adversely affects a child's educational performance" (34 C.F.R. § 300.7(c)(1)(i)). The definition also lists a number of characteristics often associated with the disorder. Some LEAs and courts interpreted the definition to bar provision of services based on a diagnosis of autism made after the child passed age three. In 1997, a provision was added to clarify that children who did not receive a diagnosis of autism until after age three cannot be denied services if they meet the rest of the autism definition (34 C.F.R. § 300.7(c)(1)(ii)).

Children with autism spectrum disorders may also qualify for IDEA services under other eligibility categories, such as mental retardation or speech/language impairment. However, under the IDEA, the category may not dictate what services the child receives. In other words, the LEA may not have a prescribed list of services for children with autism or any other disability. Rather, the team must examine the unique needs of that individual child and provide the appropriate services, regardless of whether those services are typically required by a child in that disability category.

Eligible children will receive, based on their Individualized Education Program (IEP) (see below), special education, or "specially designed instruction . . . to meet the unique needs of a child with a disability" (20 U.S.C. § 1401(25)), and related services (20 U.S.C. § 1401(22)). Related services may include "such developmental, corrective, and other supportive services . . . as may be required to assist a child with a disability to benefit from special education" (20 U.S.C. § 1401(22)). The list of services includes among others speech-language pathology and audiology services, psychological services, occupational and physical therapy, counseling and social work services, and parent counseling and training. The list is not exhaustive and may include such other services as the IEP team determines necessary (34 C.F.R. § 300.24,

Analysis of Comments, Final IDEA Regulations, 1999). This is critically important for children with autism who may require music or art therapy, for example, as a means to develop and enhance communication and social skills.

Provision of a FAPE may not be confined to the bounds of the normal school day or school year. The decision to provide extended day or year services is made by a team of professionals and the parents and is based on considerations such as possible regression during periods away from school or assessment of the rate of educational progress.

The Educational Benefit Standard

The United States Supreme Court interpreted the IDEA and set the standard for judging provision of a FAPE in *Board of Education of the Hendrick Hudson Cent. Sch. Dist. v. Rowley* (1982):

"Implicit in the Congressional purpose of providing access to a 'free appropriate public education' is the requirement that the education to which access is provided be sufficient to confer some education benefit upon the handicapped child. . . . We therefore concluded that the 'basic floor of opportunity' provided by the Act [IDEA] consists of access to specialized instruction and related services which are individually designed to provide educational benefit." (pp. 200–201)

Hearing officers and judges must determine if the school district's program is "reasonably calculated to provide some educational benefit" (*Rowley,* 1982). It is accepted in special education law and practice that the provision of services must be more than the minimum (*Faulders v. Henrico County Sch. Bd.,* 2002; *M.A. v. Voorhees Township Bd. of Educ.,* 2002; *MM v. Sch. Dist. of Greenville County,* 2002; *Polk v. Susquehanna Interm. Unit 16,* 1988). However, courts also do not require the LEA to provide "optimal" services (*Rowley,* 1982).

Meeting the FAPE Requirement

The *Rowley* decision included a two-pronged inquiry to guide district courts in determining whether the LEA has complied with the FAPE requirement:

First, has the state complied with the procedures set forth in the Act? And second, is the individualized education program developed through the Act's procedures reasonably calculated to enable the child to receive educational benefits?

The Supreme Court's questions address both the procedural and substantive aspects of the law and reiterate that, although the Cadillac version of special education is not required, neither will the jalopy version be acceptable. Children are entitled to a basic level of services that provide the opportunity for educational growth.

INDIVIDUALIZED EDUCATION PROGRAM

An Individualized Education Program (IEP), or for infants and toddlers an Individualized Family Service Plan (IFSP; see below), must be developed for each eligible child (20 U.S.C. §§ 1412(a)(4) 636). The IEP is the formula for the child's education, describing the child's current performance level and detailing goals and objectives that will allow the child to progress in the general education curriculum. The written document also includes the specific special education and related services, with supplementary aids and services, that the child must receive. Those services must enable the child to "advance appropriately toward attaining annual goals, to be involved and progress in the general curriculum and participate in extracurricular and other nonacademic activities, and to be educated and participate with other children with disabilities and nondisabled children" (20 U.S.C. § 1414(d)(1)(A)). The IEP includes any accommodations necessary for the child to benefit from the educational program, including accommodations for participation in district and statewide standardized assessments. The plan also must address transition needs, with a particular emphasis on what courses and services are necessary for the student to achieve his or her post-high school goals.

In 1997, the IDEA was amended to include several special factors that must be considered in developing an IEP, including factors relating to behavior and communication (20 U.S.C. § 1414(d)(3)(B)). The first requires the IEP team to consider strategies and supports to address behaviors "in the case of a child whose behavior impedes his or her learning or that of others." The second requires consideration of the child's communication needs.

The IEP must be based on the unique educational needs of the individual child as determined by a multidisciplinary evaluation, rather than make the child fit a predetermined general program (*Livermore Valley Joint Unified Sch. Dist.*, 1994; *T.H. v. Bd. of Educ. of Palatine Community Consol. Sch. Dist. 15*, 1998). The team making service and placement decisions includes the parents; a regular education teacher, if the child is or may be participating in the general education environment; a special education teacher or service provider; an individual qualified to interpret the evaluation results; and other knowledgeable individuals who may be invited by either the parents or the LEA (20 U.S.C. § 1414(d)(1)(B)). Decisions are made by consensus, rather than by formal vote.

One of the issues that arises in cases related to children with autism is the assertion that parents are not fully included in educational decision making (*Amanda*, 2001; *Burilovich v. Bd. of Educ. of the Lincoln Consol. Schs.*, 2000; *DiBuo*, 2002; *Letter to Anonymous*, 2000). LEAs are not required to include parents in informal meetings and discussions about day-to-day programming. However, formal meetings are required to make any decisions related to identification, evaluation, educational placement, and provision of FAPE. Parents must receive notice of these meetings and be afforded an opportunity for meaningful participation (34 C.F.R. § 300.501).

LEAST RESTRICTIVE ENVIRONMENT

Another key tenet of the IDEA is known as "least restrictive environment" (LRE). To comply with the IDEA, states must ensure that "to the maximum extent appropriate, children with disabilities . . . are educated with children who are not disabled, and special classes, separate schooling, or other removal of children with disabilities from the regular educational environment occurs only when the nature or severity of the disability of the child is such that education in regular classes with the use of supplementary aids and services

cannot be achieved satisfactorily" (20 U.S.C. § 1312(a)(5)).

This principle requires that children with disabilities be included to the maximum extent possible in the general education classroom. Removal from that setting is allowed only when, even with "supplementary aids and services," the student cannot benefit from that educational environment. The team, including the parents, must review a continuum of placement options to determine where the student can be most appropriately educated. Those placement options must include the regular classroom, special classes, special schools, home instruction, and institutional settings (34 C.F.R. § 300.551). The team must also consider inclusion in nonacademic activities such as recess and lunch, and classes such as music, art, and physical education. Placement decisions are reviewed at least annually, must be based on the child's IEP, and must be as close as possible to the child's home. The LEA must also consider any potentially harmful effects of the placement on the child or on the quality of services needed (34 C.F.R. § 300.552).

Richmond Community Sch. Corp. (1999), provides a good examination of LRE. In *Richmond*, the Appeals Panel cited the four-prong test adopted by several federal circuits to evaluate the appropriateness of a placement in the LRE (*D.F. v. Western Sch. Corp.*, 1996; *Oberti v. Clemson Sch. Dist.*, 1993; *Sacramento City Unified Sch. Dist. v. Holland*, 1994):

1. What are the educational benefits to the student in the general education classroom, with supplementary aids and services, as compared to the educational benefits of a special education classroom?
2. What will be the nonacademic or personal benefits to the student in interactions with peers who do not have disabilities?
3. What would be the effect of the presence of the student on the teacher and other students in the general education classroom?
4. What would be the relative costs for providing necessary supplementary aids and services to the student in the general education classroom?

Although this test generally has been applied to school-aged children, the Appeals Panel in *Richmond* noted that the test is also applicable to preschoolers in determining whether inclusion in an integrated preschool is the least restrictive environment.

Because LRE is specific to the individual child's circumstances and needs, this is an area that may be controversial. Parents and educators may disagree about the best placement for the child. Some parents support full inclusion, regardless of the severity of the disability, while others prefer to have the child in a setting where the child can receive more intensive supports. Educators' opinions may also differ widely on this issue. Courts, in deciding LRE issues, may consider the benefits of inclusion for children with disabilities and the concomitant benefits to the nondisabled children, projected success in meeting the child's needs in a less restrictive environment, and what accommodations may be required to keep the child in a regular classroom (*Beth B. v. Van Clay,* 2001; *Deptford Township Sch. Dist. v. H.B.,* 2002; *L.B. and J.B. v. Nebo Sch. Dist.,* 2002; *Letter to Anonymous,* 2000; *M.A. v. Voorhees Township Bd. of Educ.,* 2002).

In cases regarding young children with autism, courts often must decide the appropriateness of home instruction, particularly regarding applied behavioral analysis or discrete trial programs. Home-based instruction is considered the most restrictive placement for school-aged children, since it does not allow interaction with other children. However, for infants and toddlers, the home may be the most natural environment in which to provide services (34 C.F.R. § 300.551, *Analysis of Comments,* IDEA Final Regulations, 1999). Hearing officers and courts are increasingly less disposed to endorse programs that totally segregate a child from typically developing peers, even for those youngsters who require a very structured environment and intensive individual instruction (*Voorhees,* 2002; *T.R. v. Kingwood Township Bd. of Educ.,* 2000).

PROCEDURAL SAFEGUARDS

The IDEA guarantees parents certain procedural rights to encourage full and meaningful participation in their child's education. The Act ensures that parents are apprised of their child's progress on a regular basis and are provided notice of when the school intends to make changes in the child's program or placement. Further, the law outlines a process by which parents may receive redress if they feel the LEA has not complied with the procedural and substantive parts of the law. These rights are coupled with responsibilities, most particularly the addition to the Act in 1997 of parents as full members of the team that determines program and placement.

Notice Requirements

The LEA must provide prior written notice to parents, in their native language to the extent feasible, whenever it proposes to change or refuses to change the child's identification, evaluation, or educational placement, or the provision of FAPE. Parents must be given official notice of their right to participate in any official meetings about their child and of the opportunity to present complaints through mediation or due process procedures (20 U.S.C. § 1415(b), (c), (d)).

Parental Consent

Parents must give informed consent before the LEA conducts an initial evaluation or a reevaluation and before special education and related services may be provided (34 C.F.R. § 505). If the parents do not consent to the initial evaluation, the LEA may conduct the evaluation pursuant to a due process hearing or mediation. If parents do not provide consent for reevaluation and the LEA has made a good faith attempt to engage them in the process, the LEA may conduct the reevaluation without parental consent.

Mediation

Another major change occurred through the 1997 IDEA amendments. States were required to establish and implement procedures making mediation available to parents and LEAs whenever a due process hearing is requested. This provision gives families and school districts a less adversarial means of resolving disagreements, while continuing to provide the more formal due process procedures whenever either party wishes to use them (20 U.S.C. § 1415(e)).

Due Process

Parents or the LEA may initiate a due process hearing on any matters relating to identification, evaluation, educational placement, or provision of FAPE. The LEA is obligated, when this process is started, to inform parents of the mediation option and to advise them of available low-cost legal services (34 C.F.R. § 300.507(a)). This is particularly important for families who cannot afford to hire private attorneys and may not be aware of free or low-cost legal programs. Without an attorney or an advocate working on their behalf, families may find the process overwhelming and unfair.

The law allows parties to a hearing the right to be advised by counsel or other individuals knowledgeable about children with disabilities, to present evidence, and to cross-examine and compel the attendance of witnesses (20 U.S.C. § 1415(h)). Parties also have the right to appeal an unfavorable decision (20 U.S.C. § 1415(i)). In some states, the LEA conducts the administrative hearing, and appeal is made to a state review board. Further appeals may be made in state or federal district court. In other instances, the initial hearing is at the state level, and appeal is made directly to state or federal court.

Stay Put Requirement

The IDEA provides that, during the pendency of an administrative or court proceeding, children remain in their current educational placement (20 U.S.C. § 1415(j)) (*Johnson v. Special Educ. Hearing Office, State of Calif.,* 2002; *Sanford Sch. Comm. v. Mr. and Mrs. L.,* 2001; *Wagner v. Bd. of Educ. of Montgomery County, Md.,* 2002). In other words, if the child is in an integrated preschool program before the due process proceeding begins, the child remains in that placement until a decision has been reached. This provision is commonly known as "stay put."

If the parents and the school agree that the child would be more appropriately placed in a different setting during the proceeding, that change may be made. However, the LEA may not unilaterally change the child's placement during legal proceedings. Parents may opt to unilaterally remove their child, but this action is taken at the family's own risk and expense (300 C.F.R. § 300.514, *Analysis of Comments,* IDEA Final Regulations, 1999).

The 1997 IDEA amendments addressed stay put for children with disabilities who are suspended or expelled (20 U.S.C. § 1415(k)(7)). For infractions related to weapons or drugs or in cases where there is a danger to the student or others, the child may be removed to an interim alternative educational setting for up to 45 days. During that period, the IEP team must determine if the behavior is a manifestation of the child's disability and what if any changes must be made to the IEP and placement. If parents challenge the interim alternative educational setting, the child remains in the interim setting pending the outcome of the appeal or until the expiration of the 45-day period, whichever comes first. If a decision has not been reached at the end of the 45-day period and school officials believe there is a threat to the child or others, another 45-day period may be ordered.

SERVICES FOR INFANTS AND TODDLERS WITH DISABILITIES

The IDEA covers not only preschool and school-aged children, but also provides a program of early intervention services for children with disabilities, ages birth through two (20 U.S.C. §§ 1431 et seq., also known as Part C). The purposes of the program are to "enhance the development of infants and toddlers with disabilities and to minimize their potential for developmental delay" and to "enhance the capacity of families to meet the special needs of their infants and toddlers with disabilities" (20 U.S.C. § 1431(a)).

Part C was designed as a comprehensive, interagency service delivery system for infants and toddlers with disabilities with delays in physical, cognitive, communication, social or emotional, or adaptive development (20 U.S.C. § 1432(5)). Services are also provided to infants and toddlers with disabilities who have a "diagnosed physical or mental condition which has a high probability of resulting in developmental delay" and, at the state's discretion, to at-risk children under three who would experience substantial developmental delays without early intervention services (20 U.S.C. § 1432(1), (5)).

Unlike the program for school-aged children, Part C services are provided on a voluntary basis. Payment for Part C services is made through a combination of federal, state, and local funds, as well as private and public insurance. Family may be responsible for payment for certain services, based on a sliding fee scale; however, families may not be denied services if they are unable to pay (34 C.F.R. § 520(b)(3)(ii)).

Identification and Assessment

Part C requires that states develop a system to identify, locate, and evaluate all infants and toddlers eligible for services (20 U.S.C. § 1435(a)(5)). This system must be coordinated across all state agencies responsible for providing education, health, and social services programs. Evaluation and assessment activities must be completed and an Individualized Family Service Plan (IFSP) meeting (see below) held within 45 days after a referral is received.

The evaluation and assessment of the child includes a review of health records and medical history, determination of the child's level of functioning in all developmental domains, an assessment of the unique needs of the child in each of the developmental areas, and identification of services to meet those needs (34 C.F.R. § 303.322(c)). Another part of the process is a voluntary family assessment, designed to determine the resources, priorities, and concerns of the family and what services they need to address the child's developmental problems (34 C.F.R. § 303.322(d)).

Individualized Family Service Plan

Services are delivered to eligible children based on an Individualized Family Service Plan (IFSP), a document equivalent to the IEP. The IFSP is developed, with the family, after a multidisciplinary assessment of the child's strengths and weaknesses and an assessment of supports and services necessary to enable the family to meet the child's developmental needs (20 U.S.C. § 1436(a)). Informed parental consent must be given prior to provision of early intervention services, and only those services are provided for which consent has been obtained (20 U.S.C. § 1436(e)).

The IFSP includes statements of the child's present levels of development in all domains, the family's priorities and concerns related to enhancing the child's development, the major outcomes expected, and the criteria to be used to measure progress. The document also includes a listing of the specific services and the "natural environments" in which those services will be provided (20 U.S.C. § 1436(d)). The 1997 IDEA amendments added the notion of "natural environment," consistent with the LRE concept for school-aged children. States must ensure that, to the maximum extent appropriate, early intervention services to infants and toddlers are provided in natural environments, such as the home and community settings in which children without disabilities participate. Services may be provided in other settings only if early intervention cannot be achieved in a natural environment (34 C.F.R. § 303.167(c)).

The IFSP also designates a service coordinator responsible for the plan's implementation. As noted earlier, transition is a critical issue as children move from Part C to preschool. Therefore, the document also includes steps necessary to transition the child from one service delivery system to the other (20 U.S.C. § 1436(d)).

Transition

A number of cases related to children with autism arise as the child is transitioning from Part C services to the preschool program. The early intervention program is a family-centered system, and services are often provided in the home. Tensions may arise when the family is faced with moving from the nurturing environment of Part C to the bureaucratic complexities of a school district. In fact, the preschool staff is usually, if not always, as child- and family-focused as the early intervention providers. Rather, it is the often complicated procedure, much of which is mandated in the IDEA, that can be overwhelming. This is particularly so for families for whom this is the first interaction with the school district.

Procedural Safeguards

The procedural safeguards under Part C include the same requirements as for families of school-aged children. Parents must receive prior written notice before the agency may initiate or refuse to make changes in identification, evaluation, placement, or provision of early intervention services. In turn, parents must provide consent before services are provided (34 C.F.R. § 403, 404). Parties are also afforded the right to mediation and due process proceedings. States may opt to adopt the system already in use for school-aged children (34 C.F.R. § 419, 420).

LEGAL ISSUES RELATED TO THE EDUCATION OF CHILDREN WITH AUTISM

Both substantive and procedural issues arise in cases related to children with autism. The basic issue in most special education cases is the alleged failure by the LEA to provide a FAPE. This allegation may be based on procedural errors on the part of the LEA, rather than on differences of opinion on substantive educational issues regarding programs, services, or placements (*Amanda*, 2001; *DiBuo*, 2002; *Gadsby v. Grasmick*, 1997; *Wagner*, 2002). Procedural violations may be fairly inconsequential, such as missing a deadline by a few days. However, violations may be more egregious, for example, failure to evaluate in all areas of suspected disability, specifically autism; or making eligibility and placement decisions based on a prescribed program, rather than on the child's individual needs (*Blackmon v. Springfield R-XII Sch. Dist.*, 1998; *Portland Early Intervention/Early Childhood Special Educ. Prog.*, 1999; *Windsor C-1 Sch. Dist.*, 1998).

Substantive issues addressed in these cases focus on methodology; services, such as various therapies or extended year services; and, placement. Parents most often prevail on substantive questions when the court determines the LEA's program insufficient to meet the child's needs. LEAs will prevail on substantive questions when there are only minor or no procedural errors and a FAPE has been provided.

Before examining some of these issues, one observation is critical. Winning a case involving provision of services for children with autism often turns on the use of qualified experts to support or refute the LEA's program. These experts will offer the perspectives of the party they represent, sometimes with the

imprimatur of having examined and become familiar with the child and, at other times, giving voice to a particular educational philosophy with little knowledge of the unique needs of the specific child in question (*Beth B.*, 2001; *Faulders*, 2002; *Board of Educ. of the County of Kanawha v. Michael M.*, 2000; *Winthrop Pub. Schs.*, 1998).

Hearing officers and judges may determine the credibility of expert testimony based on a variety of factors: the professional credentials of the witness, direct knowledge over time of the child, experience in using a number of methodologies with children with autism, and professional bias toward one specific methodology over others. Expert testimony can be the decisive factor for the hearing officer or judge, especially if the expert witnesses for the opposing party do not have direct knowledge of the child.

Cost

The concept of a FAPE dictates that services must be provided, regardless of cost (*Irving Indep. Sch. Dist. v. Tatro*, 1984). However, the *Rowley* (1982) standard, that is, that the optimal level of services need not be provided, does not preclude school districts from reasonable consideration of budget constraints. As the cost of educational services for all students continues to escalate and school districts experience rising enrollments, allocation of resources has become a significant issue. In serving children with autism, school districts may be faced with serious cost consequences in providing certain therapies. The IDEA does not demand that a school district provide every possible service, nor does it specify particular services.

School districts exercise broad discretion in deciding services and placement for children with autism. If two programs are presented, both of which will adequately meet the child's needs, the school district may legally opt for the less costly of the two. If families proceed to a due process hearing to request a different and more costly program, hearing officers and judges will weigh the appropriateness of the district's program and whether the child is showing educational progress. If the child is making progress, more likely than not the arbiter will decide in favor of the district.

Determining Educational Methodology

Rowley clearly addresses the choice of educational methodology, a central issue in cases focusing on programs for children with autism. The Supreme Court stated that the goal of the IDEA is to provide "appropriate, not optimal, special education, and to that end courts may not substitute their notions of sound education policy for those of the school authorities" (*Rowley,* 1982). Administrative hearing officers and judges have interpreted this statement to confer serious weight on the educational judgments of school personnel (*Burilovich,* 2000; *MM v. School Dist. of Greenville County.,* 2002; *T.S. v. Lee's Summit R-7 Sch. Dist.,* 2000; *Tucker v. Calloway County Bd. of Educ.,* 1998; *Tyler v. Northwest Indep. Sch. Dist.,* 2002; *Union Sch. Dist. v. Smith,* 1994).

Although hearing officers and judges decide substantive educational issues, they generally do not prescribe a particular methodology. They may hold that the methodology in use at the time of the proceeding is providing educational benefit and therefore should be continued. Going a step further, the arbiter may support one-on-one instruction, a particular level of intensity, or in-home rather than school instruction. However, the arbiter will not state, for example, that the Lovaas method is preferable to TEACCH or other methodologies (*Michael M.,* 2000; *Board of Educ. of the North Rose-Wolcott Cent. Sch. Dist.,* 1997; *Delaware County Intermediate Unit #25 v. Martin K.,* 1993; *L.B. and J.B. v. Nebo Sch. Dist.,* 2002).

Fairfax County Pub. Schs. (1995), a case that has been cited extensively, represented the first decision in which a court stated that the LEA was not responsible for providing the program preferred by the parents, if the district can offer appropriate services:

The mother's sincere respect for the Lovaas program . . . is neither disbelieved nor disregarded. The sincerity of the . . . school witnesses also is not doubted. . . . The hard simple truth, however, is that the LEA is not charged with providing the program of the parents' choice.

The court stated, "If personalized instruction is being provided with sufficient supportive services to permit the child to benefit from the instruction, and the other items on the definitional checklist are satisfied, the child is receiving a 'free appropriate public education' as defined by law."

Reimbursement for Private Services

If the family believes the services and program delineated on the IEP or IFSP are not being provided or are not appropriate, they may opt to remove the child and provide home-based or private therapies at their own expense. If such cases go to a hearing, parents may request that the school district reimburse them for those costs.

In deciding the merits of a request for reimbursement of expenses, arbiters use as their guide *Burlington Sch. Comm. of the Town of Burlington v. Dept. of Educ.* (1985). In *Burlington,* the Supreme Court held that parents of a child with disabilities may be reimbursed for money spent on educational programs or services, provided that the district's IEP is found to be inappropriate and the programs delivered at the parent's expense conferred educational benefit. Appropriateness is defined in *Burlington* using the *Rowley* (1982) "educational benefit" standard.

In 1993, the Supreme Court reinforced its decision in *Burlington* and added a new dimension. In *Florence County Sch. Dist. 4 v. Carter,* the Court held that parents may be reimbursed for expenses, even if they have enrolled their child in a private, non-state-approved program conducted by uncertified personnel. The determination still rests on whether the LEA's program is appropriate, and, if it is determined to be inappropriate, whether the private placement provides educational benefit. This ruling may be particularly significant for cases related to autism services, because some home-based service providers for therapies such as Lovaas are college students or individuals who do not possess state teacher certification. *Carter* has cleared the way for attorneys to argue that state certification of personnel or programs is not necessary for parents to claim and receive reimbursement for costs incurred in providing private therapies for children with autism (*Capistrano Unified Sch. Dist.,* 1995; *Malkentzos ex rel. MM v. DeBuono,* 1996).

Intensity of Services

This issue focuses on the core IDEA principle of individualized instruction, that is, what intensity level is necessary for this particular child to receive educational benefit. Intensity of services remains a key issue in cases dealing with methodologies such as Lovaas (*Nebo Sch. Dist.,* 2002). Parents may request that the LEA fund 30 to 40 hours a week of therapy, while the LEA counters with fewer hours of home-based therapy and a more intensive school component. The average amount of therapy ordered in these cases ranges from 10 to 40 hours per week. If fewer hours of home-based therapy are ordered, that therapy is usually a part of an integrated program. An order for 30 to 40 hours a week of individual home instruction most likely will be an exclusively home-based program.

Placement

It is the LEA's responsibility to ensure that parents are aware of the range of placement options available to meet the needs of their child. Although some districts may have established programs and classrooms designated specifically for children with autism, these classrooms may not be the right fit for every child. Options representing a continuum of possible placements must be presented, and the placement decision must turn on the child's unique educational needs. These options may range from a fully inclusive setting to private residential programs and should include a wide array of choices between the two extremes.

As in all decisions regarding the education of children with disabilities, a team of professionals and the child's parents make an informed decision about appropriate placement based on evaluative and observational data. The initial assumption in placement decisions, based on the principle of least restrictive environment, is provision of services within the public school system. If public school placements are not appropriate, the placement team must examine alternatives in private or, on occasion, residential settings.

In some cases when parents and the LEA are not able to agree on an appropriate program, parents opt to remove the child from the public placement to a private school. In such instances, the parents may then seek reimbursement for the private placement (see previous discussion; *Central Bucks Sch. Dist.,* 2003; *Gwinnett County Sch. Sys.,* 1999).

In other instances where educational needs cannot be met in either the public schools or a private day school, residential treatment may be suggested. Again, the test of appropriateness hinges on whether or not the child will receive educational benefit in a more restrictive setting (*Bensalem Township Sch. Dist.,* 2003; *S.C. v. Deptford Township Bd. of Educ.,* 2003).

Conflicts surrounding placement may also arise when parents request that a methodology requiring home-based services be provided. The LEA may argue that an integrated setting with typically developing peers will be of more benefit to the child. Therefore, in only the most severe cases, that is, children who are not developmentally ready or able to benefit from peer interactions, will a hearing officer or judge order a program with only home-based services (*Redlands Unified Sch. Dist.,* 1998).

Extended School Year

The IEP may include extended school year services for children with autism, if there is documentation of regression during prolonged periods away from school (*DiBuo,* 2002; *Faulders,* 2002; *MM v. School Dist. of Greenville County,* 2002). In determining the need for extended year services, the team may also consider the educational progress made during the regular school year and the need for consistency to maintain that level of progress.

CONCLUSION

As more children are identified with autism spectrum disorders, school districts are faced with reexamining their service models and balancing budgetary and legal considerations. In approaching these issues, state and local policymakers must become more knowledgeable and sensitive about the educational and emotional supports necessary for children with autism and their families. Parents must understand that school districts do not have unlimited resources and must provide appropriate services for all children with and without disabilities. Further, the mistrust that sometimes exists between families and schools must be addressed. Without a basic level of trust, the legal battles will rage on.

It is a fact that provision of special education and related services can be quite costly. Again, a basic level of understanding is essential between parents and schools about an acceptable level of service and an acceptable level of expenditure. Parents should expect their children to receive a quality education, and school districts must be prepared to deliver the same. Parental expectations are unrealistic if they assume that school districts can or must deliver every service or institute any program they desire. There is no such legal requirement. On the other hand, attempts by school districts to circumvent their legal responsibility to provide an adequate level of services is also unacceptable. In short, parents and school districts together must make a genuine effort to understand the child's real needs and to address them in the proper manner.

School districts and parents should be cognizant of the legal standards as programs are proposed and designed for children with autism. The cookie-cutter approach to special education will not, and should not, be acceptable. Any programs proposed must fit the child's unique educational needs. The program must be reasonably calculated to provide some educational benefit through a broad range of program options. Most important, to ensure that the child makes appropriate progress, communication between parents and schools must be open and honest, with the use of the due process system as the last resort.

On a final note, the process of reauthorizing the IDEA began in 2001. Reauthorization is the process whereby Congress, on a periodic basis, reexamines current law to determine if any changes are necessary to improve implementation. At the writing of this chapter, the House of Representatives had completed action on its reauthorization bill. The Senate Committee on Health, Education, Labor and Pensions had sent a bill to the full Senate; however, debate on the Senate floor was still pending.

Proposed amendments to the law include, among many others, elimination of short-term objectives on the IEP and elimination of functional behavioral assessments and behavioral

intervention plans (House). Both House and Senate also propose instituting optional multiyear IEPs and the use of general education intervention strategies before moving to referral for special education services. Finally, both bills also include several amendments to address dispute resolution, including voluntary binding arbitration (House) and resolution sessions allowing the LEA an opportunity to cure any complaints brought by parents before moving to a due process hearing.

Cross-References

Development during the school years is discussed in Chapter 9; autism in adolescents and adults in Chapter 10; and interventions in Chapters 33 through 44.

REFERENCES

Amanda J. v. Clark County Sch. Dist., 260 F.3d 1106 (9th Cir. 2001).

Analysis of Comments and Changes, Assistance to States for the Education of Children with Disabilities, 64 Fed. Reg. 12405 (1999).

Assistance to States for the Education of Children with Disabilities, 34 C.F.R. Part 300 (1999).

Beth B. v. Van Clay, 35 IDELR 150 (N.D. Ill., 2001).

Blackmon v. Springfield R-XII Sch. Dist., 29 IDELR 855 (W.D. Mo., 1998).

Board of Educ. of the County of Kanawha v. Michael, M., 96 F. Supp. 2d 600 (S.D. W.Va., 2000).

Board of Educ. of Henrick Hudson Cent. Sch. Dist. v. Rowley, 458 U.S. 176 (1982).

Board of Educ. of the North Rose-Wolcott Cent. Sch. Dist., 26 IDELR 325 (SEA NY 1997).

Burilovich v. Board of Educ. of the Lincoln Consol. Schs., 208 F.3d 560 (6th Cir. 2000).

Burlington Sch. Comm. of the Town of Burlington v. Department of Educ., 471 U.S. 359 (1985).

CM v. Board of Pub. Educ. of Henderson County, 184 F. Supp. 2d 466 (W.D. N.C., 2002).

Capistrano Unified Sch. Dist., 2 ECLPR ¶ 187 (SEA CA 1995).

Delaware County Interm. Unit #25 v. Martin, K., 20 IDELR 363 (E.D. Pa., 1993).

Deptford Township Sch. Dist. v. H. B., 36 IDELR 94 (D. N.J., 2002).

D. F. v. Western Sch. Corp., 921 F. Supp. 559 (S.D. Ind., 1996).

DiBuo v. Board of Educ. of Worcester County, 37 IDELR 271 (4th Cir. 2002).

Early Intervention Program for Infants and Toddlers with Disabilities, 34 C.F.R. Part 303 (1998).

Fairfax County Pub. Sch., 22 IDELR 80 (SEA VA 1995).

Faulders v. Henrico County Sch. Bd., 190 F. Supp. 2d 849 (E.D. Va., 2002).

Florence County Sch. Dist. Four v. Carter, 510 U.S. 7 (1993).

Gadsby v. Grasmick, 109 F.3d 940 (4th Cir. 1997).

Gwinnett County Sch. Sys., 4 ECLPR ¶ 98 (SEA GA 1999).

Individuals with Disabilities Education Act, 20 U.S.C. § 1400 et seq. (1997).

Irving Indep. Sch. Dist. v. Tatro, 468 U.S. 883 (1984).

Johnson v. Special Educ. Hearing Office, State of Calif., 36 IDELR 207 (9th Cir. 2002).

L. B. and J. B. v. Nebo Sch. Dist., 37 IDELR 123 (D. Utah, 2002).

Letter to Anonymous, Office of Special Education Programs, U.S. Department of Education (July 25, 2000).

Livermore Valley Joint Unified Sch. Dist., 2 ECLPR ¶ 65 (SEA VA 1994).

M. A. v. Voorhees Township Bd. of Educ., 202 F. Supp. 2d 345 (D. N.J., 2002).

Malkentzos ex rel. MM v. DeBuono, 923 F. Supp. 505 (S.D. N.Y., 1996).

Mandlawitz, M. R. (1999). "The Impact of the Legal System on Educational Programming for Young Children with Autism." National Academy of Science, Committee on Educational Interventions for children with Autism.

MM v. School Dist. of Greenville County, 303 F.3d 523 (4th Cir. 2002).

Oberti v. Clemson Sch. Dist., 995 F.2d 1204 (3d Cir. 1993).

Polk v. Susquehanna Interm. Unit 16, 853 F.2d 171 (3d Cir. 1988).

Portland Early Intervention/Early Childhood Special Educ. Prog., 4 ECLPR ¶ 86 (SEA OR 1999).

Redlands Unified Sch. Dist., 3 ECLPR ¶ 236 (SEA CA 1998).

Richmond Community Sch. Corp., 30 IDELR 208 (SEA IN 1999).

Sacramento City Unified Sch. Dist. v. Holland, 14 F.3d 1308 (9th Cir. 1994).

Sanford Sch. Comm. v. Mr. and Mrs. L., 34 IDELR 262 (D. Me., 2001).

S.C.V. Deptford Township Bd. of Educ., 258 F. Supp. 2d 368 (D.N.J. 2003).

T. H. v. Board of Educ. of Palatine Community Consol. Sch. Dist. 15, 29 IDELR 471 (N.D. Ill., 1998).

T. R. v. Kingwood Township Bd. of Educ., 205 F.3d 572 (3d Cir. 2000).

T. S. v. Lee's Summit R-7 Sch. Dist., 32 IDELR 237 (W.D. Mo., 2000).

Tucker v. Calloway Cty. Bd. of Educ., 27 IDELR 599 (6th Cir. 1998).

Tyler v. Northwest Indep. Sch. Dist., 36 IDELR 236 (N.D. Tex., 2002).

Union Sch. Dist. v. Smith, 20 IDELR 987 (9th Cir. 1994).

United States Department of Education, *20th Annual Report to Congress on the Implementation of the Individuals with Disabilities Education Act* (1998).

Wagner v. Board of Educ. of Montgomery County, Md., 36 IDELR 232 (D. Md., 2002).

Windsor C-1 Sch. Dist., 29 IDELR 170 (SEA MO 1998).

Winthrop Pub Schs., 29 IDELR 558 (SEA MA 1998).

CHAPTER 47

Cross-Cultural Program Priorities and Reclassification of Outcome Research Methods

ERIC SCHOPLER

In the last edition of this *Handbook,* I reviewed North Carolina's statewide program for the Treatment and Education of Autistic and Related Communication-Handicapped Children (Division TEACCH). It is the first University based statewide program mandated by law to provide service, research, and multidisciplinary training on behalf of autism and related developmental disorders. The relationship between organizational structures, population served, and program philosophy were reviewed, as were several dimensions in both the formal and informal forms of program evaluation. Since that time, some significant changes have occurred in the field, some signify important progress in the understanding and treatment of the autism spectrum, while the effects of others are not yet fully understood. These changes have not taken place in a specific time period but they have become increasingly noticeable in the past 10 years.

Changes that appear to have an increasingly national and international impact include:

1. The unifying effects of worldwide Internet communication have made it possible to share a larger body of information.
2. Internet access has also increased the potential for unqualified individuals to introduce research and treatment claims without peer review, and generally to increase the proliferation of possible treatment techniques. One recent example has been the claim that vaccination causes autism. When insufficient supporting evidence was found to jeopardize the vaccination program, the claim was reformulated and reexamined for the simultaneous administration of three shots. This was further refined to a claim that unsafe levels of mercury used in the vaccine preservative compound cause the developmental disability. This claim is still being studied and debated. The concern has threatened the vaccination program around the world, posing new threats of unleashing new epidemics previously controlled by vaccination programs.
3. Greater funding priorities have been established for studying the genetics of autism. The open-ended potential of genetic engineering has also diminished public funding for long-term care.
4. Over the past 2 decades, a growing body of research has been focused on Asperger's syndrome, its unique characteristics, and whether it is a distinct clinical entity clearly differentiated from high-functioning autism. The controversy has been resolved for all practical purposes. Not only is it ratified by *DSM-IV,* but the diagnostic category has permeated most services dealing with children around the globe. One publisher deals only with Asperger syndrome publications (Autism Asperger Publishing Co., P.O. Box 2373, Shawnee Mission, Kansas 66283).
5. The acceptance of Asperger's syndrome has muted the question of whether high-functioning autism is different. It has, however, broadened the definition of autism. This may play a role in the striking increase

in the prevalence rates from 4 to 5 per 10,000 (Wing, 1979) to 27.5 per 10,000. Fombonne (2003) and others have projected an increasing rate of more than 40 per 10,000 by the year 2050. This increase has been noted internationally in all countries recognizing autism, though the recognition is usually based on increasing referrals.

6. The increasing public recognition and prevalence rate of autism also appears to correlate with greater numbers of professionals and students across multiple disciplines becoming concerned and involved with autism.

This chapter focuses on two aspects of these changes: (1) As the numbers of programs both state supported and privately funded have increased, both nationally and internationally, a frequently voiced concern about what should be the main elements in a comprehensive and coordinated statewide program; and (2) given the progressive aspiration toward evidence-based treatment in medical, psychological, social, and educational services, what evidence is relevant for decisions of replication, implementation, and funding?

CROSS-CULTURAL PRIORITIES FOR AUTISM SERVICES

The editorial staff of the *International Journal of Mental Health,* accepted the challenge of identifying the major program components to be recommended to the ministries of Health and Education of any country planning a comprehensive and coordinated service program for this population. The North Carolina TEACCH Program is not the only program offering statewide services. Moreover, there are many programs serving this population with different goals and priorities. A survey of such programs can be found in Chapter 41 of this volume. However, as the only university-based statewide program mandated by law (Senate Bill 383) to provide service, research, and multidisciplinary training focused on the autism spectrum, it seemed that our program priorities would be of interest to other programs. During our more than 35 years in existence, we also had extensive experience internationally in applying the TEACCH Program.

We asked countries in which we had an active exchange of students or in which we had repeated training and follow-up consultation experience to send us a report reviewing their country's programs and their application of our TEACCH components. Identifying the program priorities most useful for each country presented some complicating factors. Reports published in the *International Journal of Mental Health,* Spring and Summer of 2000, originated mainly from economically developed countries in Europe and Asia.

Many developing countries, struggling under great economic handicaps, have become active in developing services for the autism spectrum. Although we have had continuing contacts with such countries, we were unable to obtain formal reports because of insurmountable barriers to communication, including language difference, inadequate access to telephones, e-mail, and postal service.

Our training, consultation, and demonstrations involved a multifaceted approach to the understanding and treatment of autism. Some programs components had more appeal and relevance in one country than in another. The degree of intervention implementation was not always comparable between countries, nor was multidisciplinary help equally available in all countries. However, these cross-cultural variations and different program component priorities in each country enabled us to gain a clearer sense of the significance of service needs.

The first section of this chapter reviews the eight major program components emphasized in our training, consultation, and publications, and then assesses which program components were preferred in both reporting and nonreporting countries. The second section of this chapter reviews the difficulties in using a rigid research methodology for evaluating effectiveness of treatment outcome, making recommendations for more effective outcome research design.

Over its 35-year existence, eight primary components have been developed for the TEACCH program. These are briefly summarized next, not necessarily in the order of their importance:

1. *Service-research interaction:* The program began with an emphasis on service and

education and an intent to correct the misunderstanding of autism based on inappropriate use of Freudian theories (Schopler, 1971). These had implicated parental child rearing practices for the disorder, and separate residential treatment as the preferred treatment (Schopler, 1998). While these issues no longer dominate the field, problems of diagnosis, appropriate treatment, and community attitudes continue to pose unresolved problems. These can best be studied and implemented when the program has a strong service—research connection (Schopler, 1986).

2. *Parent professional collaboration:* This has been the cornerstone of the TEACCH system from the very beginning, when mental health views held parents responsible for their child's autism (Schopler, 1971). From the outset, parents were seen as collaborators in treatment rather than causal agents of their child's disorder (Schopler & Reichler, 1971). One-way observation rooms were established at all relevant facilities so that parents could observe and later use constructive developmental and educational interactions (Schopler & Reichler, 1972). However, parent-professional collaboration was soon extended to include collaboration with related agencies including medical, educational, vocational rehabilitation, and with any agency participating in an individual's treatment.

3. *Administrative organization:* When TEACCH was first supported by the North Carolina General Assembly, our immediate effort was to decentralize and form satellite centers throughout the state, rather than build a medical super-clinic at our Chapel Hill Medical School. Instead of having to travel long distances, families would be able to obtain help through their local center and in their local school. In North Carolina, this has evolved into nine regional centers and more than 300 TEACCH-affiliated public school classrooms (Schopler & Olley, 1980, 1982). Moreover, the stimulating effect of university involvement through training in relevant disciplines has contributed to the collaborative efforts with related government agencies. The use of an administrative component is reflected in work reported by Masami Sasaki (2000) in Japan, Cory Shulman (2000) in Israel, and others in

developing countries such as Venezuela and the Philippines.

4. *Regional centers* were established in response to family needs for diagnostic understanding of their child and how best to respond to each child's requirements. This function plays an especially important role when the child is very young and parents are still new to the challenge of developmental disabilities. In North Carolina, the nine TEACCH centers are located in cities that also have branches of our state university. The center staff establishes a direct relationship with each family, conducts diagnostic evaluations, formulates individualized educational programs (IEPs) and demonstrates them to the parents, trains teachers and others in related disciplines, and consults with teachers and schools in implementing the IEPs. They also offer consultation to our supportive employment program; parent support groups; and counseling for parents, social skill groups, and training on TEACCH procedures and assessment instruments.

The diagnostic instruments developed at TEACCH have been translated into many foreign languages and are used in countries that have adopted the TEACCH Program. These instruments are currently undergoing revision to reflect current program priorities. The PEP-R (Schopler et al., 1990) has been revised to include a large national comparison group comprised of over 400 children with autism and a typical group without autism (PEP-3, Schopler, Lansing, Reichler, & Marcus, in press). It includes the more current emphasis on social reciprocity and imaginative play, with a Caretaker Form including home observations and informal assessments. The AAPEP (Mesibov, Schopler, Schaffer, & Landrus, 1988) now revised as the TEACCH Transition Assessment Profile (TTAP; Mesibov, Thomas, Chapman, Denzler, & Schopler, in press), includes detailed transitional education information from community/vocational placements from middle school to adolescence and adulthood. The CARS (Schopler, Reichler, & Renner, 1988) is also being revised. In addition to their diagnostic work, the North Carolina TEACCH centers engage in family counseling and consultation. They provide staff for training activities and play a vital role in community advocacy and parent training. This type of center structure has been used in Belgium, England, France, Ireland, Israel, Italy, Scotland, Spain, and Venezuela (Peeters, 2000).

5. *Structured classrooms:* Adaptations of educational services for the entire autism spectrum have been used in every country utilizing the TEACCH Program. The concept that autistic children with autism were better educated in a school system than in a psychiatric facility had gradually been gaining international acceptance. Moreover, there was increasing research evidence that autistic children learned better under structured conditions (Schopler, Brehm, Kinsbourne, & Reichler, 1971) than in the unstructured program advocated by Freudian prescriptions and used with children diagnosed as emotionally disturbed.

Both our research and our experience soon caused us to refine the use of structure to capitalize on the autistic child's tendency to be stronger is the use of visual rather than auditory modality, which is generally emphasized in verbal interaction. We developed visual cues and supports in the layout of the classroom, the understanding of time, and changes in activities. We also developed visual learning systems and visual organization of work materials (Mesibov, Schopler, & Hearsey, 1994; Schopler, Mesibov, & Hearsey, 1995).

6. *Continuum of services:* A continuum of services has evolved in North Carolina primarily because of the close parent-professional collaboration. Parents demanded early school attendance of preschool children (Marcus, Schopler, & Lord, 2000) and most persons with autism need special help throughout childhood and into adult life. For example, adults need help in both their living arrangements and their work situation (Mesibov, 1996) and Chapter 10 of this text.

In most countries, when the treatment and education of persons with autism have become part of public policy, programs have usually first focused on preschool and younger children. A notable exception can be found in the report by Durnik et al. (2000) concerning Sweden where the emphasis is placed on work with adults.

7. *Multidisciplinary training:* The importance of disseminating information to correct

the misunderstanding of autism was obvious from the inception of TEACCH. Such unnecessary misinterpretation frequently demoralized and confused parents, increased behavior problems, and ignored intriguing skill potential among persons with autism. Such negative factors are reported in all the different countries in our sample.

Training has been offered to students and others at the preservice level and to interested professionals and parents at the in-service level. This training is important because even where professionals and staff are available, their training may not have covered the understanding and treatment approaches currently available.

The most condensed and effective TEACCH training is an intensive, 1-week course. The specialized information available on autism is taught with a generalist orientation. Didactic lectures covering the major topics described next, are thoughtfully combined with hands-on experience with preschool and elementary school pupils and adolescents and adults.

This intensive training was first offered to North Carolina teachers and other professionals with a special interest in the autism spectrum. Over the years, a growing number of professionals from many countries have taken this training. Some have continued on with a special TEACCH internship lasting up to 1 year. Current training information is available on the TEACCH web site: TEACCH.com.

Some states and countries have given the establishment of such training opportunities in their country their highest priority. This is reflected in the reports of Belgium (Margerotte, 2000; Peeters, 2000), Japan (Sasaki, 2000), and England (Preece, Lovett, Lovett, & Burke, 2000).

8. *TEACCH philosophy and principles:* In some countries, the TEACCH philosophy was considered the most important program component. This has been especially true when parents or professionals in a particular location have had access to our TEACCH publications in lieu of more direct experience. This component is more elusive than the others discussed above. TEACCH principles are sometimes combined with existing programs designed for other diagnostic groups, such as

the "emotionally disturbed" programs that are not always compatible with TEACCH principles. The nine principles guiding TEACCH philosophy are spelled out elsewhere (Mesibov, 1994, 1996; Schopler, 1989, 1997), but are summarized next:

1. *Understanding the characteristics of autism:* Without resort to the indirect inference of Freudian theory, but recognizing the clear, cognitive, and behavioral characteristics first identified in Kanner's (1943) description and indirectly carried forward from empirical research in the criteria specified in *DSM-IV* (American Psychiatric Association, 1994).

2. *Parent-professional collaboration:* From 1940 to 1960, parents' relationship to their children's autism was misinterpreted by the mental health establishment not only in the United States but also 'in France and other European countries. To challenge and change widely held misconceptions, parent-professional collaboration was required. This collaboration has continued for the past 2 decades and has contributed to the advances in services for autistic people in North Carolina and elsewhere (Schopler, Mesibov, Shigley, & Bashford, 1984). This principle is also considered a program component because it has been given high priority in most regions.

3. *Improved adaptation:* As the biologic basis of autism became more widely established (Schopler & Mesibov, 1987), it became evident that a meaningful treatment program for most persons with autism would need to be long term. Accordingly, rather than promising a cure, multifaceted programs like TEACCH aim for optimum adaptation and improved quality of life, which would also be any parent's goal for a child. Optimum adaptation can be achieved by teaching new skills. When skill acquisition is blocked by developmental delay, the environment can be modified to accommodate the deficit. Both new skills and environmental accommodation produce optimum adaptation.

4. *Assessment for individualization:* The problem of when to stress skill acquisition and when to stress environmental accommodation can best be resolved by both formal and informal assessment procedures. Formal TEACCH assessment instruments have been described. Informal assessment techniques are taught in TEACCH training.

5. *Structured teaching:* From formal and informal assessment, we can identify priorities in teaching the individual new skills for communication, social interaction, and daily living. We can also determine some of the autism-related deficits, including difficulty with organization, auditory processing, attention, and memory. These can be minimized by using the strength in visual processing, rote memory, and special interests commonly observed in people with autism. Visual structures for organizing physical space, schedules, work-learning systems, and task organization have been useful and applicable across the life-span continuum (Grandin, 1995; Mesibov et al., 1994; Schopler et al., 1995).

6. *Cognitive and behavioral theories:* These are important for guiding both intervention and empirical research. Both are accountable to the rules of evidence. In recent years, behavioral and cognitive theories have become more integrated with each other. These are emphasized by Micheli (2000) and Shulman (2000) in their reports.

7. *Skill enhancement and deficit acceptance:* The most effective educational treatment approach is to give priority to recognition of the person's skills and to acknowledge and accept his or her deficits. This important principle parallels an important finding from behavioral treatment: The most effective results are achieved from frequent use of positive reinforcement and rewards. This concept holds true not only for children's skill acquisition but also for parents' and teachers' use of consultation and for professional staff development.

8. *Holistic orientation:* TEACCH-based programs are often begun in reaction to professionals' misunderstanding of autism. This was most noticeable when parents' unconscious wishes and attitudes were seen as the primary cause of the symptoms of autism. However, parental complaints that their child was misunderstood frequently referred also to professionals from various disciplines who viewed the child narrowly within

the focus of their specialized discipline. Overreacting to their specialized training, professionals would be interested in a behavior problem, a speech deficit, a perceptual motor impairment, or a new medical syndrome. They were unable to see the whole child within the context of a unique family.

Our holistic orientation has encountered less resistance in developing countries, places where people have not been exposed to specialists, than in places with universities offering training in many specialized disciplines.

9. *Lifelong, community-based service:* Autism still has lifelong effects. In the early years of TEACCH, both parents and staff soon recognized that most autistic persons and their families would require some special help from cradle to grave (Mesibov, 1983). Such continuing services are most cost effective when coordinated with consistency in teaching strategy and support systems, as needed, throughout the life cycle.

Having summarized the major program components, the primary components from the 11 countries whose reports were published will now be discussed (Schopler, 2000). Our evaluation was based not only on the material discussed in the reports, but also on our observations during training and consultation. These were conducted by various TEACCH faculty who also identified each site's program priorities. We recognized that different community autism programs might have selected different program components, but we believed that most of our components had generic applications. In addition, our extensive experience in different cultures and nations would make our observations more applicable than either arm-chair speculation or estimates based on less experienced programs.

Of the 11 reporting programs, two represented France (Paris and the southern region). The remainder represented northern Italy, Sweden, Israel, Japan, United Kingdom, Kuwait, Flemish Belgium, French Belgium, and Spain. There are more than 25 regions represented who were not able to file a report because of economic and technological difficulties, or because they were still in beginning phases of program development. These included Taiwan, Okinawa, Portugal, Australia, Greece, New Zealand, India, Hong Kong, Mainland China, Nigeria, Morocco, Philippines, Mexico, Argentina, Brazil, Venezuela, Ireland, Saudi Arabia, Netherlands, Germany, Czech Republic, Poland, four regions in Denmark, Norway, and Sweden. More details about this review are available in Schopler and Mesibov's article (2000). Some regions had programs developed by local individuals trained in TEACCH, and they were developing their own training programs, therefore, they could not be surveyed.

Findings

To summarize our cross-cultural experience, we have tabulated for both reporting and nonreporting countries, the TEACCH Program components identified as most useful. The reporting countries identified almost twice as many useful components as did the nonreporting countries, indicating that they usually were the most developed countries with greater availability of resources and longer periods of service development.

Of the eight components cited, three have been adopted most frequently in both reporting and nonreporting countries. They were: (1) Parent-professional collaboration, an emphasis maintained even within a great range of "collaboration." In some western countries, this meant that parents has a sense of entitlement, enabling them to lead the direction of the collaboration, while in others parents deferred to professional expertise for leadership and direction (see also Chapter 36 of this volume). (2) The TEACCH Philosophy that included the operational concepts and procedures cited earlier. (3) The structured classrooms, usually employing visual structures. On the other hand, administrative organization and regional centers have been established in 10 reporting countries, but in only one nonreporting country. The multidisciplinary training component was used in more than three times as many reporting as nonreporting countries. The discrepancy is probably due to the greater availability of professional specialists in the reporting countries and the more highly developed economic base in comparison with the nonreporting countries. More details on this survey are available in the spring and summer Issue of the *International Journal of Mental Health* (2000).

So far I have discussed some of the major changes in the field of autism in recent times, including the increase of autism programs accompanying the increasing prevalence rates and the increasing multidisciplinary professionals concerned with developmental disorders and the autism spectrum. These are accompanied in many developed countries by a greater emphasis on evidence-based treatment. For the remainder of this chapter, I review some of the obstacles that are created when evidence for effectiveness is applied in rigid or inappropriate research design, resulting in a gap between basic research and clinical application. I review the historic roots in the field of psychology and its application to treatment outcome evaluation, for a spectrum disorder like autism, ranging over a spectrum of severity, engaging a spectrum of professionals, followed by a spectrum of intervention techniques. I then identify the direction in which the research application gap can be reduced, and evidence for effectiveness can be more clearly established.

Historical Background

At the turn of the twentieth century, scientific interest in the physical sciences and the natural sciences, based primarily on the experimental deductive methods increased while psychology and so-called social sciences were based more on inductive reasoning. At universities in the United States, psychology was studied as a branch of philosophy. However, with the advent of World War II and the need for more advanced military technology, Defense Department contracts were farmed out to major U.S. universities to develop the more effective military destruction and defense technology. Their development depended on the methods of the physical science for isolating variables in a controlled laboratory situation. As this scientific technology won the war, a more broadly funded federal research program evolved. The celebrated scientific methods were applied to the social sciences devoted to the study of complex cultural and social interactions, defined and mediated by political and human aspirations and behavior. The result was frequently flawed

research with findings that were either self-evident or irrelevant outside the experimental laboratory. The gap between the "hard" and the "soft" science has been carried forward in many research pursuits, including psychology. Pavlov and Watson had established the rather robust relationship between stimulus and response. Rewards tended to increase the frequency and intensity of contingent behavior while punishment had the reverse effect. Because such relationships were readily tested by experimental methods, they were employed by behaviorists such as Lovaas, Koegel, Simmons, and Long (1973) to the treatment of autism. They played an important role in rescuing autism first defined by Kanner (1943) from the untested assumptions of psychodynamic theories. These had produced wide-spread assumptions of autism as social withdrawal from emotionally cold parents (Schopler, 1971; Schopler & Loftin, 1969). At the same time, the practice of operant conditioning and discrete trial teaching did not eliminate concerns of losing the child in behavior reductionism. The methods producing such "laws of human behavior" were soon over-extended to many related questions with rat running experiments, repetition of nonsense syllables, and measurement of galvanic skin response, to name only a few. This research did build a body of experimental knowledge replicated in other laboratories but was too frequently unable to predict complex human behavior outside the controlled laboratory. With human subjects, there were individual variations. What was rewarding or punishing for one individual was quite different for another. These differences were affected by diverse factors such as age, developmental level, experience, sensory thresholds, and so on.

This led to the rise of a theoretical orientation less bound to specific behavioral responses, sometimes called the "cognitive revolution" (Gardner, 1985), bringing renewed interest in the "mind" including the work of psycholinguists, brain modelers, and computer scientists. For this group of researchers, primary interest in stimulus strength and response patterns was replaced by mental actions such as thinking, attending, comprehension, imagining, remembering, feeling, knowing the minds of others, and executive functioning. The relevance of these broader concepts to social intervention and special education is perhaps self-evident, but the demonstration of effectiveness of resulting intervention still relied primarily on methods derived from experimental methodology.

The parallel research trends in behaviorism, information processing, and neurobiologic specificity have also been lined with risks of reductionisms, prompting Bruner (1996) to promote a new direction, "cultural psychology" as composed of selected information and shared values, conveyed by oral history. In the context of these important historical trends, it is not surprising that attempts at prioritizing therapies according to supporting research evidence has not helped to reduce controversy over the most effective intervention for developmental disorders such as autism.

Defining the Gap between Research Design and Application

An APA Task Force (1995) was convened to develop guidelines for the selection of therapies for mental disorders and psychosocial aspects of physical disorders. The Task Force tried to bridge the aforementioned research gap by making a fine distinction between treatment *efficacy* and *effectiveness*. The latter term was applied to treatments supported by the methods based on the physical sciences, while the term *efficacious* was confined to clinical application with variable interventions and comorbidity of diagnosis. The similarity in sound between efficacy and effectiveness did not disguise the fact that clinical trial research did not provide guidance for actual clinical practice (Goldfried & Wolfe, 1996). The criteria for "good science" research are quite different from the criteria for a good clinical or service program. Scientific demonstration of treatment effectiveness are expected to be tested according to criteria derived from experimental methods. The shorthand for this design rigidity is randomized control trials (RCTs). These include random assignment of subjects to the experimental group and to a matched control group. Both inclusion and exclusion criteria are to be specified. These may include age group, gender, language level, and intelligence test scores—in other words, variables appropriate to the intervention and its outcome claims. The

length and frequency of the intervention must be specified, as treatment dosage is likely to affect outcome. If the intervention is designed for a particular disorder, such as autism, it is important that all subjects meet the same diagnostic criteria and that these are not confounded by dual diagnoses. When these criteria are met in a treatment outcome study, compelling evidence for effectiveness is shown. Unfortunately, this rarely happens, and has not yet occurred in the case of autism (Rogers, 1998).

On the other hand, clinical or public service programs cannot readily meet such research criteria. They may come into existence by special legislative or service mandate, for a broad diagnostic category such as developmental disorders, with parent involvement and diagnostic assessment for individualized treatment and educational structures fitting the individual child. These complex variables are not easily controlled for, especially in the past in what has been considered a low-incidence disorder. In such a program, random assignment of subjects to a treated and an untreated control group may not be legal or feasible. A fixed length of intervention is not consistent with individualized treatment requirements, and the exclusion of dual diagnoses can violate the right to an appropriate intervention. Superimposing artificial research criteria on such programs may not result in the most useful measurement of treatment effectiveness. In short, such programs have valid differences in the selection, treatment, and study of their populations. Recognizing this state of affairs, the chairs of the APA Task Force, and Lonigan, Elbert, and Johnson (1998) acknowledged that "treatments are never fully validated, and validation of any sort would imply that the mechanisms for the effectiveness of the intervention were a known condition that exists for only few interventions."

Although the Task Force chair had published the suggestion that most treatments have not been fully validated, a member of the Task Force representing services for children stated that it is the responsibility of professionals to be knowledgeable about validated treatment effectiveness and to provide families with such information.

Reviewing the Lovaas Early Intervention Project (1987), Rogers recognized that he had not yet met the Task Force criteria for treatment effectiveness. Yet she made the difficult-to-interpret assertion that his Early Intervention Project used "the strongest scientific design" (Rogers, 1998, p. 169). Perhaps she did not have access to all the published shortcomings of his research methods and procedures (Feinberg & Beyer, 1997; Gresham & MacMillan, 1998; Schopler, Short, & Mesibov, 1989). Possibly she merely confused the term scientific with empirical evidence. She then selected seven additional programs approximating the same kind of experimental research criteria as being "probably efficacious," criteria not designed to fit clinical service programs. There is no reason to doubt that these programs are probably efficacious, but not because they almost met inapplicable experimental laboratory criteria. There are significant differences between treatment programs that claim or expect major improvement from a single factor intervention emphasis, like a drug therapy or a behavior therapy, anticipating recovery, return to normal, and so on, and a multifaceted intervention program that aims for optimum adaptation, or for improvement in the quality of life. These two types of intervention require appropriate differences in research design. With the autism spectrum, another therapeutic effect exists when special interests and talents result in social validation for the individual. A related problem was identified by Detweiler (2000) when he reviewed that most recent compendium of effective treatments for both pharmacological and psychosocial therapies. He noted that reports of effectiveness varied greatly according to whether they addressed researchers, clinicians, educators, or consumers. These groups have different goals and expectations depending on the interventions selected. Differences in their claims of effectiveness may also be reduced when more flexible and appropriate research designs are used for demonstrations of effectiveness.

Autism as a Spectrum of Diagnoses, Professionals, and Interventions

In recent years, increasing numbers of professionals refer to autism as a *spectrum disorder* (Wing, 1997). This comes from a growing understanding that autism is not a single condition. It involves a range of disabling behaviors, both in intensity and frequency. Moreover, it is increasingly recognized that these behavior problems vary and change with development (Burack et al., 2001). Autism is defined as a spectrum of social impairments, ranging from lack of awareness when autism and mental retardation coexist, to the high functioning autism or Asperger syndrome end of the continuum, in which a computer specialist has no interest in social interaction outside his computer screen. A similar spectrum can be found in the area of communication ranging from muteness and limited language skills to normal-sounding speech. Autism also involves restricted interest—from repetitive body motions and interests in parts of toys to special interest in plane schedules, higher mathematics, and computer technology.

For research purposes, autism is frequently considered a unitary category, especially if the study hopes to identify a specific chromosome location or a neurological locus. However, it is unlikely that anyone having seen individuals of varying ages and developmental functions with the diagnosis of autism would not also consider it a spectrum disorder.

SPECTRUM OF SOCIAL ROLES

Parents newly initiated to the challenges of autism soon learn that autism is usually a lifelong disorder, with no known cure. On the other hand, a great many treatment techniques are disseminated on the Internet. In addition, pilot research, often attended by anecdotal reports of dramatic improvement, receives premature publicity. Many such pilot studies are disseminated in the television news or published in a convincing account of recovery written by an enthusiastic parent. The resulting confusion is often resolved in different directions. Some parents regard their child's autism like an unacceptable disease that they seek to remove or cure. Such parents are frequently attracted to experimental interventions that may have been reported anecdotally as miracle cures. They may be attracted to such therapies as certain diets, doses of megavitamins, fenflouramine, certain drugs, or single factor therapies for which effectiveness has not been established or even tested. Other parents accept a lifelong involvement for their child and look to maximize their child's potential through education and behavioral interventions that will enable their child to develop the best adaptive skills for the most satisfying and independent adult existence. A third group of parents with children at the higher functioning end of the autism spectrum, including also Asperger's syndrome, may accept their child's diagnosis, think of it as a personality trait, with both peculiar and productive manifestations. Many individuals with autism see themselves in this light.

Spectrum of Professionals

As the prevalence and public awareness of autism has increased, a growing spectrum of professionals have committed their studies and interest to this developmental disorder. Those with the longest special training in medicine or research are frequently attracted to the search for a specific causal mechanism or intervention. This may include the search for genetic sites with the potential for genetic engineering, biochemical causes leading to specific psychopharmacologic intervention. Other professionals have a primary aspiration to help, teach, or otherwise improve lives of their clients. They function as allied health professionals or public teachers and will tend to be involved with services offering habilitation and improvements. The third group of professionals, dealing with the AS end of the spectrum, could include job coaches, university counselors, and others.

INTERVENTION SPECTRUM

The single mechanism intervention involves an emphasis on the etiology, or underlying causal mechanism, for autism. Like the disease model, it carries an assumption of a causal mechanism as has been demonstrated for many diseases, and is carried over to a syndrome such as autism. Even when the investigator recognized that the condition is a multiple-determined syndrome, the research strategy tends to focus on a specific mechanism, related treatment techniques with treatment outcomes often identified as cure or recovery, that is, made "normal." Interventions in this category usually include various biochemical agents such as

fenflouramine, secretin, and a variety of drugs. However, this category also includes behavioral cognitive techniques such as intensive early intervention.

Such treatments may share with single factor interventions the expectation of identifying an explicit treatment technique for a specific disorder or disease, derived from a demonstrated causal mechanism, with an outcome expectation of cure or recovery. This most-valued aspiration has not been achieved to date for the autism spectrum, although breakthroughs in genetic engineering, alluded to in Chapter 16 of this book, hold such potential. The RCS methodology has been shown effective for a variety of specific behavioral interventions. For example, aerobic exercise has been shown to reduce aggression (Gabler-Halle, Halle, & Chung, 1993), disruptive behavior (McGimsey & Favell, 1988), and stereotyped and self-injurious behavior (Baumeister & MacLean, 1984; Morressy, Franzini, & Kosen, 1992), it also improved attention span and on-task behavior (Powers, Thibadeau, & Rose, 1992) and a score of other behaviors (Koegel & Koegel, 1995). Such specific behavioral changes are useful, and their achievement has been demonstrated with methods adopted from laboratory science. However, these behavioral changes are a far cry from treatment claims of "cure," "recovery," or "return to normal functioning" for the individuals whose specific behavior has been modified. When such global treatment claims are made, they should be supported by the same kind of evidence used for demonstrating any behavioral change. This is especially important when such treatment is to be converted into social policy through judicial or legislative action. It is the treatment developers' desire to produce the political pressure needed for converting personal access to a specific treatment technique into social policy that increases the tendency to drift into pseudo-science. Specific examples such as fenflouramine and ABA intervention are detailed elsewhere (Schopler, 2001).

Habilitation Programs

In this category, interventions are based on the recognition that autism is not a disease or mental illness, but a lifelong process in which negative effects can be improved and even re-versed into socially useful activities performed by individuals living a positive quality lifestyle. Both research and intervention are in the realm of education, using the most appropriate indi-vidualized techniques derived from cognitive, behavioral, and special education theory. These intervention techniques are applied in multifac-eted forms like TEACCH, described earlier, and programs described in Chapter 35. Many of these programs combine the techniques of the new generation of behaviorists who attempt to bridge the distinction between theories of be-havior, cognition, and development by working with pivotal commonalities such as motivation and learning style within each child.

The primary purpose of these interventions is not so much directed at connecting cause and cure as it is to help each individual to achieve optimum adaptation. This is achieved by im-proving the skill level of each individual. Where there is an autism-related obstacle or delay in specific skill acquisition, environmental ac-commodations to the deficit can be made. Both skill acquisition and environmental accommo-dation are essential components for optimum adaptation. The successful outcome of habilita-tion interventions may be quite different, de-pending on the individual's placement in the autism spectrum. Optimum adaptation may be in the form of successful attendance in gradu-ate school, living independently with supported employment, or effectively participating in a sheltered workshop. Outcome can be appropri-ately measured with methods different from the experimental paradigm applied in the single mechanism approach. Skills acquisition can be measured according to the realization of the In-dividualized Educational Program (IEP). Ques-tions about the effectiveness of environmental accommodation can be assessed by observa-tional methods and peer review.

INTERVENTIONS OF CULTURE

With this orientation, autism is seen as a cul-tural phenomenon. Mesibov and Shea (in press) have discussed the commonly defining features of autism as producing a culture parallel to the culture of the deaf. Consistent with this per-spective, there are elements in the mainstream

that match the autism culture and produce a connecting link for the individuals involved. An example is introduction of visual structure into the classroom to promote learning and indepen-dent functioning for a student with autism. In addition, some individuals use their autistic characteristics to develop important products for the mainstream community. These may be in the form of art, animal science, or computer technology. Individuals who promote improve-ment through cultural changes do not always have special educational preparation and may include artists, computer specialists, and scien-tists like Temple Grandin, who elect to identify themselves publicly with the autism diagnosis because they recognize it as a part of their own identity, an integral part of their special talent, providing unique and valued contributions to society.

Temple Grandin is a talented individual with a PhD in animal science and a diagnosis of autism. Grandin thought that her autism de-veloped from insufficient tactile experience during her infancy. Possibly she has a low threshold for touch, or adults refrained from such touching. From her subjective under-standing of this experience, she resolved that the anxiety she experienced from tactile de-privation might be remediated by a squeeze machine in which she could control the amount of tactile contact she desired. After extensive use, she claimed it made her feel better. She did not claim it would cure autism or even make all users feel better. She allowed interested buyers to try it out. If it made them feel better, she would sell them a copy of her machine. Without outcome claims, no scien-tific outcome study seemed warranted. In-stead, the squeeze machine may be regarded as a kind of furniture of potential interest to individuals in the autism culture.

Grandin's subjective experience of autism also led her to produce changes in the main-stream culture. She applied her subjective autism-tactile experience to the design of the chute through which cattle move for process-ing (Grandin, 1992a, 1992b). She designed the sideboards of the chutes of a width and height that touched the animals on both sides so they could feel more secure while passing through and avoid frightening visual distractions. This design has been exported and used in many other countries. She also has been very effective in explaining autism to professionals and the larger community (Grandin, 1992b), and she has been a popular lecturer. The changes made by Grandin's contributions have helped other individuals with autism by making better connections for them with the mainstream through improved popular acceptance and understanding of autism.

Another example is Jessy Park, whose autism is brilliantly observed and described by her mother (Park, 1992, 2001). Jessy has a fine sense of color, which she uses for expressing her artistic talents and special interest in astronomy shown in many paintings of the façade of houses against a starry night sky. These paintings have been purchased with increasing interest by professionals working with autism. By converting her autistic preoccupation with stars into paintings, Jessy Park has achieved sufficient popularity to have one-person shows in New York City for an audience well beyond the autism community.

Other cultural interventions involve a process by which an individual with autism is brought into the mainstream culture. For example, pony therapy brings the individual into a mainstream of activity with horseback riding, and dolphin therapy enjoins a cultural interest in wildlife. An interesting example of positive cultural effect is reported for Facilitated Communication.

Although Facilitated Communication (FC) has been shown ineffective in most replicated outcome research, it can also be reviewed for its cultural effects. Although virtually no research evidence supported the sophisticated level of communication claimed by FC advocates, and even though FC was used for specious lawsuits alleging sexual abuse, Bilu and Goodman (2001) showed this technique to have some positive cultural effects in the ultra-orthodox Jewish community. Using interview methods appropriate to cultural anthropology, they learned that FC offered the children's families a new, highly positive perception of autism, while at the same time reaffirming the validity of core values of their ultra-orthodox community in Israel. The community celebrated this positive cultural effect, while being aware that this technique did not change the children as claimed by FC advocates. Clearly, then, FC can be a failure by the research criteria of habilitation intervention categories and still have positive cultural effects for an extreme subculture. But these unique effects can be understood only with research methods appropriate to cultural anthropology.

IMPLICATIONS FOR TREATMENT OUTCOME RESEARCH DESIGN

What should the differences between different intervention categories involve? For individuals, parents, and professionals who see autism principally as a disease, and a condition too devastating to be tolerated with symptoms to be extinguished or suppressed, the single factor emphasis may be of greatest interest. This group may sponsor or participate in the testing of new experimental methods using randomized control trials. RCTs are applicable, even when used with adjustment for the uses of a particular technique.

The habilitation category is most important to families and professionals who have accepted autism as a chronic developmental disorder that, with appropriate education and community acceptance, can lead to a satisfying life. At this time, the majority of individuals in the autism spectrum probably belong to this group, or have the potential for belonging to the next higher functioning category. Intervention programs, using multifaceted educational and behavioral programs cannot appropriately be measured by a RCT design for the reasons cited earlier. They should be measured by standardized criteria that can be used for evaluating both an individual's educational progress as well as the effectiveness of environmental accommodations.

At the highest level of functioning in the autism spectrum are the artists and scientists; making social contributions with their special interest or gifts is their most affirming and satisfying outcome. It should be evaluated by market values and other criteria of social desirability. Likewise cultural treatment methods like pony therapy, squeeze machine, and FC can be measured by standards appropriate to their claims.

CONCLUSION

This chapter reviewed some of the major causes of a persistent gap between formal experimental research methods and the application of these findings in the clinical situation. These factors include the historic, post-World War II trend for the U.S. National Institute of Health to implement experimental research methods, misapplied to other fields such as psychology, psychiatry, and social science. The resulting gap between scientific research and clinical application has presented problems for evidence-based outcome research and has made it easier to market pseudo-scientific research results (Schopler, 2001).

To reduce this gap, three different intervention categories have been defined:

1. Consumers and professionals who see autism primarily as a condition too devastating to be tolerated, with symptoms to be suppressed or eliminated, will sponsor or participate in the testing of many new experimental techniques, even when they are aware that the intervention is untested and is likely to mean high costs and potential unknown or negative side effects.

2. The habilitation category is more important to families and professionals who have accepted autism as a lifelong developmental disorder that, with appropriate education and community acceptance, can lead to a satisfying life. At this time, the majority of individuals and their families probably belong to this group. They seek for their children the best adaptation possible and the best quality of life, regardless of existing handicap. This is very much like the goal they have for their typical children. Even though it is difficult to measure effectiveness by research methods derived from experimental science. Instead the evaluation must examine evidence for improved adaptation, including changes both in the individual and his environment: and such difficult-to-define outcomes as improvement in the quality of life. Evidence for such complex changes is more reliably obtained by methods derived from an external review protocol than from experimental methods.

3. Interventions produced by cultural factors emphasize accepting autism traits and matching aspects of the main culture with certain autism characteristics. It can involve training and employment that matches special interest of autism and related activities. Interests in routines can be matched with sorting and cleaning tasks: interests in numbers (instead of people) can be channeled into a wide range of accounting and computer tasks. This kind of cultural matching can be beneficial to both autistic and typical groups.

While the interventions from different treatment categories cannot be shown effective by the same research criteria, the differences in their research methodologies maintain the empiricism of systematic knowledge. Single-factor research emphasizes cause and cure. The habilitation effort seeks to develop optimum adaptation and the cultural end of the spectrum makes special contributions by changing the environment. Although this group is perhaps the smallest in number, it holds a most important promise both to the remaining individuals in the autism spectrum and to the general society. The few with the most talent serve to remind the others that it is possible to move along the autism spectrum to improvement and better adaptation. For the general public, these individuals with autism serve as an especially important reminder that they can make a special contribution to social change. Because they are unfettered by preoccupations of social reciprocity and competing interests, it is easier for them to engage in divergent thinking then it is for more typical individuals. They may be able to join the talented few who throughout history produced social-cultural change through new technology, art, and science. The acceptance of individuals in the autism spectrum is important not only to members of the spectrum, but also to the remainder who are beneficiaries of divergent thinking.

Professionals engaged in turf struggles about scientific validity of knowledge from different disciplines need to develop more compassion for each other's access to the true nature of autism. We might remember that the extent to which any of our methods have enabled us to glimpse better knowledge of course, treatment, and outcome, what we have seen is based on images floating upside down on each of our retinas, an image less precise than the constructs of our models and our quantifications of behavior.

REFERENCES

American Psychiatric Association. (1994). *Diagnostic and statistical manual of mental disorders* (4th ed.). Washington, DC: Author.

American Psychological Association, Task Force on Psychological Intervention Guidelines. (1995). *Template for developing guidelines: Interventions for mental disorders and psychosocial aspects of physical disorders.* Washington, DC: Author.

Baumeister, A., & MacLean, W. E., Jr. (1984). Deceleration of self injurious and stereotypic responding by exercise. *Applied Research in Mental Retardation, 5,* 385–393.

Bilu, Y., & Goodman, Y. (2001). The other worldly gifts of autism: Mystical implementation of facilitated communication in the ultra-orthodox community in Israel. In E. Schopler, N. Yirmiya, C. Shulman, & L. M. Marcus (Eds.), *The research basis for autism intervention* (pp. 43–55). New York: Kluwer Academic/ Plenum Press.

Bruner, J. (1996). *The culture of education.* Cambridge, MA: Harvard University Press.

Burack, J. A., Pasto, L., Porparino, M., Iarocci, G., Mottron, L., & Bowler, D. (2001). Applying developmental principles to the study of persons with autism. In E. Schopler, N. Yirmiya, C. Shulman, & L. M. Marcus (Eds.), *The research basis for autism interventions* (pp. 25–38). New York: Kluwer Academic/Plenum Press.

Detweiler, J. B. (2000). A guide to treatment that works. *APA Review of Books, 45*(2), 148–151.

Durnik, M., Dougherty, J. M., Anderson, T., Persson, B., Bjorevall, G. B., & Emilsson, B. (2000, Spring). Influence of the TEACCH Program in Sweden. *International Journal of Mental Health, 29*(1), 51–72.

Feinberg, E., & Beyer, J. (1997). Creating public policy in a climate of clinical indeterminancy: Lovaas as the case example du jour. *Infants and Young Children, 10*(3), 54–66.

Fombonne, E. (2003). Epidemiological surveys of autism and other pervasive developmental disorders: An update. *Journal of Autism and Developmental Disorders, 33*(4), 365–382.

Gabler-Halle, D., Halle, J. W., & Chung, Y. B. (1993). The effects of aerobic exercise on psychological and behavioral variables of individuals with developmental disabilities: A

critical review. *Research in Developmental Disabilities, 14*(5), 359–386.

Gardner, H. (1985). *The mind's new science: A history of the cognitive revolution.* New York: Basic Books.

Goldfried, M. R., & Wolfe, B. E. (1996). Psychotherapy practice and research: Repairing a strained relationship. *American Psychologist, 5*(10), 1007–1016.

Grandin, T. (1992a). Calming effects of deep touch pressure in patients with autistic disorders: College students and animals. *Journal of Child and Adolescent Psychopharmacology, 2,* 63–72.

Grandin, T. (1992b). An inside view of autism. In E. Schopler & G. B. Mesibov (Eds.), *High functioning individuals with autism* (pp. 105–124). New York: Plenum Press.

Grandin, T. (1995). How people with autism think. In E. Schopler & G. B. Mesibov (Eds.), *Learning and cognition in autism* (pp. 137–156). New York: Plenum Press.

Gresham, F. M., & MacMillan, D. L. (1998). Early intervention project: Can its claims be substantiated and its effect replicated? *Journal of Autism and Developmental Disorders, 28,* 5–13.

Kanner, L. (1943). Autistic disturbances of affective contact. *Nervous Child, 2,* 217–250.

Koegel, R. L., & Koegel, L. K. (Eds.). (1995). *Teaching children with autism.* Baltimore: Paul H. Brookes.

Lonigan, C. J., Elbert, J. C., & Johnson, S. B. V. (1998). Empirically supported psychosocial interventions for children: An overview. *Journal of Clinical Psychology, 27*(2), 138–145.

Lovaas, O. I. (1987). Behavioral treatment and normal educational and intellectual functioning in young autistic children. *Journal of Consulting and Clinical Psychology, 55,* 3–9.

Lovaas, O. I., Koegel, B. L., Simmons, J. O., & Long, S. J. (1973). Some generalization follow-up measures on autistic children in behavior therapy. *Journal of Applied Behavior Analysis, 6,* 131–166.

Marcus, L., Schopler, E., & Lord, C. (2000). TEACCH services for preschool children. In J. S. Handleman & S. L. Harris (Eds.), *Preschool education programs for children with autism* (2nd. ed., pp. 215–232). Austin, TX: ProEd.

Margerotte, G. (2000, Summer). From quality of services to quality of life of persons with autism. *International Journal of Mental Health, 29*(2), 60–77.

McGimsey, J. F., & Favell, J. E. (1988). The effects of increased physical exercise on disruptive behavior in retarded persons. *Journal of Autism and Developmental Disorders, 18,* 162–179.

Mesibov, G. B. (1983). Service development for adolescents and adults in North Carolina's TEACCH program. In E. Schopler & G. B. Mesibov (Eds.), *Autism in adolescents and adults* (pp. 37–53). New York: Plenum Press.

Mesibov, G. B. (1994). A comprehensive program for serving people with autism and their families: The TEACCH model. In J. L. Matson (Ed.), *Autism in children and adults: Etiology, assessment, and intervention* (pp. 85–97). Pacific Grove, CA: Brooks/Cole.

Mesibov, G. B. (1996). Division TEACCH: A program model for working with autistic people and their families. In M. C. Roberts (Ed.), *Model practices in service delivery in child and family mental health.* Hillsdale, NJ: Erlbaum.

Mesibov, G. B., Schopler, E., & Hearsey, K. (1994). Structured teaching. In E. Schopler & G. B. Mesibov (Eds.), *Behavioral issues in autism* (pp. 195–208). New York: Plenum Press.

Mesibov, G. B., Schopler, E., Schaffer, B., & Landrus, R. (1988). *Individualized assessment and treatment for autistic and developmentally disables children: Adolescent and Adult Psychoeducational Profile* (AAPEP). Austin, TX: ProEd.

Mesibov, G. B., & Shea, V. (in press). The culture of autism. In G. B. Mesibov & E. Schopler (Eds.), *The TEACCH approach to autism* (pp. 215–230). New York: Plenum Press.

Mesibov, G. B., Thomas, J., Chapman, M., Denzler, B., & Schopler, E. (in press). *Adolescent and Adult Psychoeducational Profile* (AAPEP) *TEACCH Transition Assessment Profile* (TTAP). Austin, TX: ProEd.

Micheli, E. (2000, Spring). Dealing with the reality of autism: A psychoeducational program in Milan, Italy. *International Journal of Mental Health, 29*(1), 50–71.

Morressy, P. A., Franzini, L. R., & Kosen, R. L. (1992). The salutary effect of light calisthenics and relaxation training on self-stimulation in the developmentally disabled. *Behavioral Residential Treatment, 7,* 373–386.

Park, C. (1992). Autism and art: A handicap transfigured. In E. Schopler & G. B. Mesibov (Eds.), *High functioning individuals with autism* (pp. 250–259). New York: Plenum Press.

Park, C. (2001). *Exiting Nirvana.* Boston: Little, Brown.

Peeters, T. (2000, Summer). The role of training in developing services for persons with autism and their families. *International Journal of Mental Health, 29*(2), 44–59.

Powers, S., Thibadeau, S., & Rose, K. (1992). Antecedent exercise and its effects on self-stimulation. *Behavioral Residential Treatment, 7,* 15–22.

Preece, D., Lovett, K., Lovett, P., & Burke, C. (2000, Summer). The adoption of TEACCH in Northhamptonshire, UK. *International Journal of Mental Health, 29*(2), 19–31.

Rogers, S. J. (1998). Empirically supported comprehensive treatments for young children with autism. *Journal of Clinical Child Psychology, 27*(2), 168–179.

Sasaki, M. (2000, Summer). Aspects of autism in Japan before and after the Introduction of TEACCH. *International Journal of Mental Health, 29*(2), 3–18.

Schopler, E. (1971). Parents of psychotic children as scapegoats. *Journal of Contemporary Psychotherapy, 4,* 17–22.

Schopler, E. (1986). Relationship between university research and social policy: Division TEACCH. *Popular Government, 51*(4), 23–32.

Schopler, E. (1989). Principles for directing both educational treatment and research. In C. Gillberg (Ed.), *Diagnosis and treatment of autism* (pp. 167–183). New York: Plenum Press.

Schopler, E. (1997). Implementation of TEACCH philosophy. In D. J. Cohen & F. R. Volkmar (Eds.), *Handbook of autism and developmental disorders* (2nd ed., pp. 767–798). New York: Wiley.

Schopler, E. (1998). Misleading metaphors of Bruno Bettelheim. *Contemporary Psychology, 43*(1), 19–21.

Schopler, E. (2000, Spring). International priorities for developing autism services. *International Journal of Mental Health, 29*(1), 3–21.

Schopler, E. (2001). Treatment for autism: From science to pseudo-science or anti science. In E. Schopler, N. Yirmiya, C. Shulman, & L. M. Marcus (Eds.), *The research basis for autism intervention* (pp. 9–24). New York: Kluwer Academic/Plenum Press.

Schopler, E., Brehm, S. S., Kinsbourne, M., & Reichler, R. J. (1971). Effect of treatment structure on development in autistic children. *Archives of General Psychiatry, 24,* 415.

Schopler, E., Lansing, M., & Marcus, L. (in press). *Psychoeducational profile* (3rd revision, PEP-3). Austin, TX: ProEd.

Schopler, E., & Loftin, J. (1969). Thought disorders in parents of psychotic children: A function of test anxiety. *Archives of General Psychiatry, 20,* 174–181.

Schopler, E., & Mesibov, G. B. (Eds.). (1987). *Neurobiological issues in autism.* New York: Plenum Press.

Schopler, E., & Mesibov, G. B. (2000). Cross-cultural priorities in developing autism services. *International Journal of Mental Health, 29*(1), 3–21.

Schopler, E., Mesibov, G. B., & Hearsey, K. (1995). Structured teaching in the TEACCH system. In E. Schopler & G. B. Mesibov (Eds.), *Learning and cognition in autism* (pp. 243–268). New York: Plenum Press.

Schopler, E., Mesibov, G. B., Shigley, R. H., & Bashford, A. (1984). Helping autistic children through their parents: The TEACCH model. In E. Schopler & G. B. Mesibov (Eds.), *The effects of autism on the family* (pp. 129–142). New York: Plenum Press.

Schopler, E., & Olley, J. G. (1980). Public school programming for autistic children. *Exceptional Children, 46,* 461.

Schopler, E., & Olley, J. G. (1982). Comprehensive educational services for autistic children: TEACCH model. In C. R. Reynolds & T. R. Gutkin (Eds.), *Handbook of school psychology* (pp. 629–643). New York: Wiley.

Schopler, E., & Reichler, R. J. (1971). Parents as co-therapists in the treatment of psychotic children. *Journal of Autism and Childhood Schizophrenia, 1,* 1–87.

Schopler, E., & Reichler, R. J. (1972). How well do parents understand their own psychotic child? *Journal of Autism and Childhood Schizophrenia, 2,* 387.

Schopler, E., Reichler, R. J., Bashford, A., Lansing, M., & Marcus, L. (1990). *Individualized assessment and treatment for autistic and developmentally disabled children: 1. Psychoeducational profile* (PEP-R). Austin, TX: ProEd.

Schopler, E., Reichler, R. J., & Renner, B. R. (1988). *The Childhood Autism Rating Scale (CARS).* Los Angeles, CA: Western Psychological Services.

Schopler, E., Short, A., & Mesibov, G. (1989). Relation of behavioral treatment to "normal functioning": Comment on Lovaas Study. *Journal of Consulting and Clinical Psychology, 57*(1), 162–164.

Shulman, C. (2000, Spring). Services for persons with autism in Israel. *International Journal of Mental Health, 29*(1), 88–98.

Wing, L. (1997). The autistic spectrum. *Lancet, 350*(9093), 1761–1766.

Wing, L., & Gould, J. (1979). Severe impairments of social interaction and associated abnormalities in children: Epidemiology and classification. *Journal of Autism and Childhood Schizophrenia, 9,* 11–29.

INTERNATIONAL PERSPECTIVES

CHAPTER 48

International Perspectives

FRED R. VOLKMAR

From the time of its description 60 years ago by Leo Kanner, autism has been recognized throughout the world. To a remarkable degree, the essential features and natural history of individuals with autism are consistent wherever they have been studied over these 5 decades. With surprising similarity, professional disciplines and nations also have gone through similar processes of development in recognizing and responding to the needs of autistic individuals and their families. And, again with remarkable consistency in nation after nation, parents have organized themselves as the most effective advocates for their children and have taken the lead in shaping national policies and creating programs.

A comparative, cross-national analysis of the history and current status of knowledge, programs, and theories concerning autism reveals not only broadly shared features but also areas of individuality related to differing resources, theories, and other cultural and historical differences. The study of autism thus offers a special and, in some ways, unique lens on the spread and sharing of clinical knowledge about serious clinical problems as well as on the shaping of ideas and practice by national traditions and cultural differences. It is gratifying to note that the earlier edition of this *Handbook* provided one of the first international perspectives on autism. Subsequently, a handful of articles and chapters have appeared, and the study of cultural, ethnic, and national perspectives on autism has just begun to emerge as an important topic in its own right (Brown & Rogers, 2003).

The comparative study of autism also benefits immeasurably by broadly shared conceptions of diagnosis. Diagnostic schema developed during the past 15 years have enhanced communication and are unifying the world's literature. The introduction of the *Diagnostic and Statistical Manual of Mental Disorders (DSM)* of the American Psychiatric Association in 1980 and its revisions in *DSM-III-R* (1987) and, most recently, *DSM-IV* (1994) have led the way in the operational definition of autism and in the creation of the concept of pervasive developmental disorder (PDD). The *International Classification of Diseases (ICD),* most recently revised as *ICD-10* (World Health Organization [WHO], 1992), has similarly provided an approach to diagnosis of autism within the broader medical nosology. Fortunately, in their most recent versions, the diagnosis of autism in these two dominant systems of nosology has converged. This is a major achievement of the international scientific community. The criteria are largely based on a unique, multinational field trial conducted for *DSM-IV.* The international collaboration also demonstrated that clinicians everywhere are able to achieve good reliability in the diagnosis of autism. The *DSM* and *ICD* systems are also supplemented by regional approaches, most particularly in France, with their own emphases.

There is no other childhood developmental or psychiatric disorder (or, perhaps, any other psychiatric disorder) for which such well-grounded and internationally accepted diagnostic criteria exist. The availability of these diagnostic standards allows for important comparisons in epidemiology, natural history, treatment methods and systems, and research findings, and for international sharing of knowledge.

In the following chapters, we provide a broad survey of the state of the field of autism around the world. We have invited prominent clinicians and leaders in the field of autism from various countries to discuss a series of topics about the history of autism in their country or region, current status of diagnosis and treatment services, research, theory, parents' organizations, and publications in the field. We encouraged the authors to respond to the topic in a way that was suitable for conveying their own national situation. The results of this first, comparative study are intriguing.

The authors of the various chapters responded in manners that are also reflective of their national orientations and personal perspectives and interests. The similarities across nations, noted earlier, are apparent in the nearly universal acceptance of the diagnostic conventions of *DSM* and *ICD* and general approaches to diagnosis and treatment. There are interesting differences, however, in theoretical and treatment emphasis. For example, the contributions from several nations (in Latin America and France) emphasize the contributions of psychoanalytic theory to understanding the inner experience of autistic individuals and psychological pathogenesis; the contributions from other nations are relatively silent on these matters and emphasize a pragmatic or more empirical approach. Other areas of national difference relate to differing emphases on education *and* treatment and the role of parents. A major difference across nations concerns the availability of resources *and* access and the inclusion of individuals with autism in a full, national medical and mental health system.

The following national reports do not include accounts from the United States or Africa. The latter omission reflects the limitations in resources in most of Africa, as well as in professional contacts, which we hope to remedy. A history of autism in the United States, on the other hand, deserves a scholarly study beyond the scope of a short chapter. The outlines of this history emerge from the contributions of all the chapters in this *Handbook*. We present a very condensed, selective review

only as an outline, particularly for those who have not lived this history directly.

AUTISM IN THE UNITED STATES

As in many areas of clinical medicine, the brilliant observations of one pioneer marks the starting point of the history of autism—Leo Kanner's intuitive application of the emerging field of developmental research, including the charting of social behavior by Arnold Gesell (Kanner, 1943). In his first reports, Kanner was struck by a particular pattern of social disabilities in forming relationships and areas of unexpected competence (e.g., rote memory and duplication of patterns). He highlighted the inborn nature of the children's social disturbance and selected the term *autism* from the field of schizophrenia as the hallmark of the new syndrome. Kanner also recognized the unusual nature of family interactions and, initially, wrongly attributed the disorder to environmental and, particularly, parental influences. He later revised his opinion as he appreciated how the child's abnormality influenced the home and family environment and parental behavior. More recent research, reviewed in this *Handbook,* has returned attention to the contributions of genetically transmitted vulnerabilities and to shared difficulties in emotional engagement within families, particularly evident in Asperger syndrome. Kanner also noted the complex relations between autism and mental retardation, initially distinguishing these conditions sharply and later appreciating that most autistic individuals are, and remain, cognitively retarded and that intellectual level is a major determinant of later functioning.

Kanner's first papers attracted wide attention, and within a few years many clinicians and clinical centers were replicating his observations. Throughout the 1950s, the major emphasis in the field was work with young, preschool children, and the full, lifetime course of the disorder was not yet apparent. Also, the major theoretical approach was drawn from the broader field of child psychoanalytic theory, and clinicians and investigators attempted to understand pathogenesis and provide intervention within a psychodynamic framework. At times and in certain places, this was associated with a causal theory that led to attributing a child's disorder to particular, often subtle, patterns of parental interaction.

This "blaming" of parents continues, now decades later, to be remembered and resurrected in criticisms of child mental health professionals and therapeutic approaches. A major force underlying the parental blaming was the publications by Bettelheim (1967) about his work with autistic children. His papers and books achieved great popularity in the United States and abroad because of their literary power and therapeutic claims. It is now recognized that his reports of therapeutic success with autistic children removed from what he considered pathogenic families are grossly inaccurate and, perhaps, intentionally deceptive. Yet, they remain cited outside the United States and are a source of continuing misunderstanding. Their fame is a black mark on the history of autism in the United States.

By the 1960s, limitations were apparent in available theories and treatments. The landmark book on autism by Bernard Rimland, a parent and advocate, heralded a new era in research and treatment. Rimland (1964) argued for a biological base, postulated a specific pathogenesis, and advocated for a more rational, empirical treatment approach. The new era was also facilitated by the observation in 1961 by Daniel X. Freedman, a biological psychiatrist and pharmacologist, of elevated whole blood serotonin among autistic individuals (Schain & Freedman, 1961); this finding remains the single, consistently replicated biological finding internationally.

Within a few years, the field of autism was enriched by a growing cadre of biologically and psychologically sophisticated researchers and clinicians. Research programs were increasingly broad gauged, used methods from associated fields of neurobiological and behavioral research, and focused on the range of developmental deviations among autistic children. New approaches to studying brain development (including assessment of neurotransmitters and metabolites) and language and other psychological processes were applied to individuals with autism.

Concurrently, during the 1960s, parent groups began to be organized with the support of professionals. The National Society for Autistic Children (NSAC) and, in Great Britain, the National Autism Society, emerged as major voices of parent advocacy and support. (In the U.S., NSAC has evolved over the years into the Autism Society of America.) Parents created new educational programs; influenced local, state, and national policy; challenged legislation and policies that excluded autistic individuals from services; and encouraged researchers. During the 1970s, access to services dramatically increased. In large part, the nature of these services was influenced heavily by emerging theories and methods from operant conditioning and applied behavioral analysis.

By the mid-1970s, research focusing on autism was in the mainstream of child psychiatric and special educational programs, and large numbers of psychologists, educators, and child and adolescent psychiatrists devoted their attention to research and intervention. The large number of publications concerning autism, always remarkable from the earliest years of the field, now found a special home in a journal devoted to this work as well as in other, general publications. Numerous books were devoted to research, clinical descriptions, and, increasingly, parental accounts.

During the past decades, the field of research on autism has continued to expand along with new knowledge about brain development, new techniques for studying neurobiology of brain functioning, theories of cognitive and social development, innovative methods for intervention that emphasize adaptive functioning and normalizing life experiences, genetic methods that can be applied to complex disorders, pharmacological approaches to symptom reduction, and other advances in the behavioral and medical world. An important development has been the interest of parents and others in supporting and facilitating work. Groups such as the National Alliance for Autism Research (NAAR) and Cure Autism Now (CAN) have been active at local, state, and federal levels. These groups, along with parents, have helped increase the awareness of members of Congress, state legislatures, schools, and the news media about autism. Partly as a result of this interest, funding for research has increased and the pace of research over the past decade has increased dramatically. Two noteworthy examples include the visionary initial funding of the Collaborative Program of Excellence in Autism (CPEA) by the National Institute of Child Health and Human Development and the more recent funding of the Studies to Advance Autism Research and Treatment (STAART) by the National Institute of Health; both programs have dramatically increased the level and quality of research on autism in the United States.

Today, clinicians and educators take a lifetime perspective on autistic individuals and recognize the multiple influences on outcome. The range of services and programs for individuals with autism has expanded enormously over the past decade. Judicial and legislative mandates ensure, at least in theory, that all autistic individuals will have the right to education within the least restrictive environments. For many, these rights do in fact lead to optimally delivered services. For many autistic individuals, programs are also available into adulthood, although for too many these are still quite limited. Throughout the United States, there are exemplary educational programs and varied models of longer term, supported living. There are also numerous examples of autistic individuals who are now able to function as productive members of society in fully mainstreamed life situations. While noting these achievements, it must also be recognized that large numbers of autistic adults are in inadequate situations and that for autistic children and adults with the most severe behavioral problems (e.g., self-abuse) and with the lowest levels of functioning, opportunities and outlook remain bleak.

Along with advances, there have been various controversies. Virtually every theory of human development that has emerged during the past decades has been applied to autism and has attracted, at least for a while, adherents. Similarly, numerous therapeutic enthusiasms have been imported from other branches of medicine or have taken root in the field of autism, often without firm empirical support but with the passionate commitment that is heated by distress and hope. Often, parents and their advocates have been caught in a maelstrom of different and opposing viewpoints: Mainstreaming has competed with spe-cialized services; parents hear of wonder cures achieved in intensive, short-term programs while, at the same time, reading about the lifelong nature of their child's problems; young parents must decide whether to pursue dietary treatments, allergic treatments, hugging and holding, use or nonuse of aversive methods, the dangers or benefits of medications, and a host of different other modalities, including ones that claim (in a return to some of the most extreme claims of the 1950s) that autistic individuals are always really brilliant people who are held captive by their autism and who can, if given the right chance, express profound truths about their inner life.

At this moment, the power of modern molecular biology and other scientific methods offers new opportunities to study the basis for developmental disorders such as autism; the field of autism will no doubt benefit greatly from scientific advances. At the same time, in the United States and indeed around the world, there are heated controversies among well-intentioned advocates and professionals. Why has autism had such a history, and what accounts for its current status?

In large part, the controversies reflect the fact that where there is no cure, there are a hundred treatments. In spite of major advances in understanding the history and psychological features of autism, effective behavioral and pharmacological remediation is somewhat limited and there is no simple cure. Behavioral and other approaches provide amelioration and habilitation, sometimes to a remarkable degree, but we are not yet able to fundamentally address the cause of the disorder. The wish to be helpful by clinicians and other professionals fuels the development of new ideas, new approaches, and unfounded and overenthusiastic claims. The only antidote, and the source of greatest hope, is empirical, rigorous, scientific investigation by well-trained multidisciplinary teams; the translation of scientific knowledge into clinical intervention; and full, honest sharing of knowledge and continuing ignorance among professionals, parents, and advocates. Indeed, one of the major challenges for the next decade of work on autism will be in disseminating knowledge that has emerged from research into actual clinical practice and educational interventions.

COMPARATIVE STUDIES OF AUTISM

In the remainder of this chapter, leading clinicians and researchers from throughout the world reflect on specific domains of interest—epidemiology, diagnosis, treatment, and theory. The appreciation of shared interests and knowledge, as well as differences in emphasis and view, should encourage further international exchanges, as well as a tolerance for differences. The international pooling of concepts and knowledge should also increase the rate of change in the field of autism and help disseminate knowledge to clinicians, educators, and parents across national and language boundaries. For 50 years, autism has been a shared focus of attention for clinicians and researchers throughout the world. We hope that the enhanced communication within the field across nations will also serve as a model of international collaboration in relation to other psychiatric problems and concerns.

AUSTRALIA

Bruce J. Tonge and Avril V. Brereton

Australia covers an area almost the size of mainland United States, with much of the land comprising semiarid and arid bush and grasslands or desert. The population is around 17 million, of which the great majority live in the cities of Brisbane, Sydney, Melbourne, and Adelaide on the eastern and southern seaboard and Perth in the southwest. The society is multicultural with progressive immigration from many parts of the world including Great Britain, Ireland, Europe, the Middle East, Southeast Asia, the Indian subcontinent, and South America, as well as an indigenous population of Australian Aborigines.

Government and the administration of society are based on a federation of states (New South Wales, Queensland, South Australia, Tasmania, Victoria and Western Australia, and the Australian Capital Territory) with a national parliament and parliaments in each of the states and territories. The delivery of the predominantly free health, education, and welfare services is administered by each state government, but the Commonwealth government provides a range of social service benefits and pensions as well as reimbursement through its Medicare organization for part of the costs of private medical and pharmaceutical services. This system in general delivers a high standard of education, health, and welfare services throughout the nation, but variations in services provided, for example, to persons with autism and their families, do occur between states because of different service delivery policies and among urban, rural, and far outback areas because of access to services.

Prevalence and Epidemiology

There is some evidence that the prevalence of PDD (autism) in Australia is somewhat higher than the 0.04% reported by Wing (1981a) in Great Britain but more consistent with a level of around 0.07% reported by Gillberg (1984) in Sweden. To determine the prevalence of autism in the Australian population, the authors used the Developmental Behavior Checklist (DBC; Einfeld & Tonge, 1991, 1994, 1995). The DBC is a reliable and valid 96-item checklist completed by parents or caregivers, designed to assess a broad range of behavioral and emotional disturbances in children and adolescents with intellectual disabilities.

The capacity of the DBC to act as a screening instrument for autism has been investigated. The subjects comprised 97 children and adolescents who met the *DSM-III-R* (1987) criteria for PDD (autism; PDD autism) based on a combination of observation of the child, interview with the parents or caregivers, and information from others such as teachers. This sample was matched for age, gender, and IQ range with nonautistic children who were part of an epidemiological representative sample of Australian children with intellectual disability. The mean age of the autistic and control subjects was 9.3 years, and 81% were males. DBC items were included as predictor variables in a discriminant function analysis if there was a statistically significant univariate difference between the autistic and control subject scores on that item. This provided a list of canonical loadings for 48 items, sorted by magnitude of their discriminating power. The discriminant function was highly significant, and the analysis correctly classified 92% of the autistic and the control subjects, which indicates that the DBC can be used to differentiate autistic children from intellectually disabled nonautistic children with a high degree of precision.

DBC data were available from an epidemiological sample of 514 intellectually disabled children ages 4 to 18 years (Einfeld & Tonge, 1994). The authors were confident about virtually complete ascertainment of children with moderate intellectual disability (IQ less than 52), but as with any population survey of intellectually disabled children, the completeness of ascertainment of children with mild-borderline intellectual disability is less certain. These children lived in a selection of census areas in New South Wales, which when taken together represented a cross-section of social class and urban and rural distribution reflecting the Australian community and comprised a total population of 172,914 children and adolescents (4 to 18 years). Using the results from the linear discriminant function analysis, 116 (23%) of the epidemiological sample of 514 children were identified as autistic on the basis of their DBC profile. This is equivalent to a prevalence for PDD (autism) of 6.7 per 10,000 Australian children. Further, this figure is likely to be an underestimate of the prevalence of autism in the Australian population because it was confined to a survey of intellectually disabled children. Estimates of the proportion of children with autism who have normal intellectual ability are 20% to 30% (DeMyer, Hington, & Jackson, 1981). Taking this into account, the prevalence of autism in Australian children, across the full spectrum of intellectual abilities, might be around 9.5 to 10 per 10,000 children.

Assessment and Diagnosis

Although each state and territory has its own approach to assessment, there is much in common in the philosophy and standards applied that enables a general picture of the Australian approach to assessment to be described. This situation is influenced by the existence of a national umbrella organization of nongovernment autism associations in each state. These state associations bring together active groups of parents and professionals involved in the assessment, management, and education of children, adolescents, and adults with autism. These associations either provide, on the basis of government grants, their own assessment services often associated with early intervention, education, employment, and social skills programs, or are active participants in the government health, education, and welfare management advisory committees that run a range of publicly funded services for persons with disabilities including autism. The aim is to provide a comprehensive assessment of children suspected of having autism as early as possible in order to organize an early intervention program and family support. Prior to assessment, most families have sought help from a range of early childhood community services; therefore, referrals for assessment usually come from maternal and child health nurses, preschool teachers, speech therapists, general medical practitioners, and pediatricians.

Early detection depends on professionals who work in early childhood services having some knowledge of autism. Therefore, the state autism associations are all active in providing various autism awareness programs. For example, the autism associations in Victoria and South Australia have both produced quality videotapes and educational material for use in undergraduate and continuing professional education. Seminars on autism are also a component in the curriculum of all Australian medical schools and professional training programs for pediatricians, psychiatrists, and clinical psychologists.

The majority of children with autism in Australia are now detected and assessed during the preschool years before entry into primary school (5 to 6 years). Some children are still not diagnosed until later in primary school or even in adolescence. This delay is usually due to the child having a normal level of intellectual ability with better language development or having Asperger syndrome, or the child may live in a relatively isolated rural setting, or the child might be a member of a recently arrived immigrant or refugee family from a country with more limited services for children.

In most cases, the assessment is multidisciplinary, recognizing that apart from a diagnosis, assessment of the child's language, social, and cognitive skills as well as his or her health and medical status is necessary in order to plan the most effective and comprehensive management program. These assessments may be undertaken by a multidisciplinary team funded specifically for that purpose or undertaken by a variety of professionals in both public and private practice but whose assessments are brought together and coordinated by professionals working for the state autism association or by staff working for a state regional child and adolescent mental health service. In general, an assessment comprises the following components (Tonge, Dissanayake, & Brereton, 1994):

- *Pediatric medical assessment:* Full physical assessment, laboratory investigations, and chromosome analysis, including search for fragile X chromosome, screens for known causes of intellectual disability. When indicated on clinical grounds, further more complex investigations such as EEG and MRI scans are done. In most instances, an audiological assessment is also done.
- *Cognitive assessment:* The cognitive ability and profile of the child is assessed by a psychologist or a special educator using psychological tests appropriate to the child's developmental level and behavior, such as the Psychoeducational Profile (Schopler) or the Wechsler Intelligence Scale for Children-Revised (WISC-R, fourth edition).
- *Communication assessment:* An assessment of communication skills and language development undertaken by a speech pathologist often forms part of the assessment.
- *Sensory integrative and motor assessment:* Some centers have occupational therapists or physiotherapists available to undertake these assessments, which can provide information of further use in the development of a comprehensive treatment program.
- *Diagnostic consultation:* This is usually conducted by a child psychiatrist or a pediatrician or clinical psychologist with expertise in the assessment of children with autism. Information on direct behavioral observations of the child in the preschool and home setting is available together with the results of the other assessments. The diagnostic consultation includes an interview with the parents or caregivers to obtain a

developmental history and assess the psychosocial context as well as direct behavioral and mental status examination of the child. Rating scales are also used to provide a comprehensive description of the child's behavior. In particular, the DBC (Einfeld & Tonge, 1994), completed by the parents or caregivers, the Autistic Behavior Checklist (ABC; Krug, Arick, & Almond, 1980), and the Childhood Autism Rating Scale (CARS; Schopler, Reichler, & Renner, 1988), completed by the clinician, are used.

Following this assessment procedure, it is common for the clinician responsible for the diagnostic consultation or the coordinator of the autism assessment clinic to call together a multidisciplinary case conference in which the diagnosis is discussed, management and therapy program planned, and consultation with other agencies and support for the family are arranged. A clinician is identified who will be responsible for providing the parents with feedback and the opportunity to discuss the diagnosis and management plan and who will then often remain available to provide further advice and support for the parents if necessary. In the capital cities such as Melbourne, there are specialized multidisciplinary teams that provide this full and comprehensive assessment and diagnostic service. These teams usually undertake the assessment together using a one-way observation screen so that all members of the team can observe the various components of the assessment. This can also be used as a training exercise for students and professionals coming from less specialized settings. It is not always possible for a comprehensive assessment to be undertaken in more isolated rural areas. In these situations, either children and their families will travel to the capital city, such as Sydney, for an assessment, or a specialist, such as a child psychiatrist, may travel to a country center on a regular basis to consult with local health, education, and welfare professionals and contribute to the local assessment of children with developmental problems.

Although the approach to information gathering and the professional backgrounds of the clinicians may vary from team to team, in general throughout Australia, the diagnosis of autism and allied disorders is based on *DSM-IV* (1994) criteria and the *ICD* (10th edition; WHO, 1992).

Approaches to Management

Early intervention and the provision of appropriate education form the centerpiece of the management of children with autism in Australia. Early intervention usually is centered on part-time attendance at a preschool with the provision of a teacher's aide, who provides one-to-one help and support for the child. In the capital cities and the larger country centers, some preschools provide special programs for young children with developmental disabilities. A range of ancillary therapy such as speech therapy and motor skills programs are provided when appropriate to supplement the preschool program. Advice on behavioral management, the provision of family support, home help, and respite care are further services provided to the families to enable them to effectively care for their autistic child.

The delivery of school-based educational programs can vary among states, but essentially it is determined by the cognitive and communication ability of the child. For children with moderate and greater levels of intellectual impairment, educational programs are available either in a normal class setting with the one-to-one assistance of an integration teacher's aide, in a special small class within a normal school, or in a special school setting. In both Melbourne and Sydney, some special schools are dedicated exclusively to children with autism but have the aim of preparing the child for integration into a more normal setting as soon as possible. Educational and treatment programs, including several residential schools, have been available in Australia since the 1960s. This long experience of service delivery informs current practice and has facilitated the development of new services and research.

All schools are able to receive advice and consultation on educational programs and behavioral management from psychologists and special educators and, to some extent, speech therapists. Services for the management of more severe behavioral problems and psychopathology are more patchy and less well distributed. Each of the capital cities has a well-developed network of child and adolescent psychiatric clinics, many of which provide secondary consultation services to country areas.

The government service for intellectually disabled persons in each state also employs psychologists and other professionals to provide advice on behavioral management. Child psychiatrists and pediatricians with an interest in behavioral pediatrics, supported by general medical practitioners, are available in the capital cities and major population centers to provide behavioral advice and pharmacotherapy. In most parts of rural Australia, medical services are predominantly provided by general medical practitioners, but telephone consultation with city-based specialists, who also provide secondary consultation visits to country areas, is available to support the general practitioner. Overall, although more resources could be available, the great majority of children with autism and their families in Australia have access to a good range of essentially free education, welfare, and health services further supported by a vigorous system of private medical and psychology services.

An innovative augmentative communication system was developed in Australia in 1982 using computerized picture graphs, in the form of stylized single line drawings, which symbolically represent a range of concrete objects, emotions, actions, and social interchanges. This system is referred to as *compic* and forms the basis of an effective alternative channel of communication for autistic children with delayed and disordered language and communication skills (COMPIC, 1992).

In line with international experience, various unsubstantiated and expensive treatment fads are present in Australia, but there is also an Australian tradition of wariness toward cure-alls and exaggerated claims for improvement. Active research is being conducted in Australia on auditory training (Bettison, 1996), facilitated communication (Hudson, 1995), and vitamin B group therapy. The autism associations remain well informed of the international literature and provide summaries to parents in regular newsletters and seminars.

Research

Australian academics have made a contribution to the international literature on autism.

Autism research in Australia is most diverse covering a broad range of biopsychosocial fields and education. Although it would not be appropriate in the confines of this chapter to mention all those academics working in Australia who have published in the field, it is necessary to mention several landmark researchers. Bartak, who has an academic appointment at Monash University, undertook landmark studies in the education of children with autism and continues to foster a range of educational and psychological studies (Bartak & Rutter, 1973). Prior (e.g., 1987; Prior & Tonge, 1990) first at Latrobe and now at the University of Melbourne, has led a number of important neurobiological and psychological research projects on autism and allied conditions.

Conclusion

The services provided to persons with autism in Australia are based on a comprehensive assessment using internationally recognized criteria for diagnosis and an understanding that education and the acquisition of social skills and communication ability is central to management. Strong parent associations, together with professionals, are active in lobbying, developing, and coordinating a range of services, community and professional education, and family support. These programs are generally supported by a range of research and academic programs based predominantly in the universities. The need for a wider range of services for adults is becoming apparent as our identified autistic population ages. As in a number of other countries, the refinement of diagnostic classification, such as the introduction of criteria for Asperger syndrome, and the recognition of comorbidity are raising new assessment and service delivery challenges.

CANADA

Peter Szatmari

The care of children with autism in Canada has been influenced by both the advance of scientific knowledge and government policy. The first clinic to take a special interest in the diagnosis and treatment of children with autism was established at the West End Creche in Toronto by Dr. Milada Havelkova, who immigrated to Canada from Czechoslovakia after World War II. She was given an appointment in the Department of Psychiatry at the University of Toronto and did her clinical work at the West End Creche (perhaps the oldest mental health center for preschool children in Canada). Dr. Havelkova developed a keen and abiding interest in children with developmental problems and worked at the Creche for more than 30 years. She was the first child psychiatrist in Canada to initiate studies into the etiology and natural history of children with infantile autism, and these studies resulted in several important early publications.

The first major influence that profoundly transformed the care of children with autism was the introduction of universal health care to Canada during the 1950s. This was a single-tier system that aimed to provide comprehensive, accessible, and universally available medical services to all citizens regardless of income. Although private health insurance was still available, it became increasingly irrelevant. The impact of this financing arrangement was that every family with an autistic child could receive both diagnostic and treatment services regardless of level of income.

The second major influence on the development of services for children with autism was that treatment programming generally developed in community mental health clinics rather than in general psychiatric hospitals. Diagnostic and assessment services were often carried out in children's hospitals in large metropolitan centers by pediatricians and child psychiatrists, but treatment programs often took place in community settings or schools. There were very few hospital-based treatment centers that provided either residential or day programming for children with autism and other forms of developmental disabilities. Instead, several large institutions that serviced developmentally disabled children and adults were established in rural settings. Many of the residents of these facilities qualified for a diagnosis of autism although a review of records often revealed a diagnosis of mental retardation or mental handicap instead. However, with recent changes in funding and the move to "least restrictive environments," many of these large institutions have either closed or else care for a much smaller number of severely disabled adults who cannot be cared for in community settings. There are now very few community resources available for adults with autism.

This separation between diagnostic and treatment services has, however, had the unfortunate consequence of not promoting the training of physicians with expertise in developmental handicap, in general, and autism, in particular. Compared to the United Kingdom, for example, there are few pediatricians or child psychiatrists in Canada with specialized expertise in the diagnosis and assessment of children with autism. Very little instruction is provided in medical school, and subspecialty training programs in both psychiatry and pediatrics have tended to emphasize acute illnesses rather than chronic developmental disabilities.

The third major influence on the delivery of services for children with autism in Canada has been the emphasis on integration of disabled children within community settings. This emphasis has arisen from a number of sources including advocacy movements for integration in the United States, the lack of hospital-based residential services, and the pioneering work on integration done by several school boards in Ontario. In most parts of Canada, schools are administered by two separate, publicly funded systems generally divided along religious lines. A public school board is open to children of all religious affiliation, while children in Catholic families are usually served by Catholic school boards. Many of these boards have taken a forceful role in integrating children with developmental handicaps into the regular school system. For example, the Hamilton-Wentworth Roman Cathologic Separate School Board has been integrating children with severe mental and physical disabilities into community classrooms since the early 1970s. Specialized support services were available for these children, and the schools have learned to accommodate the child's special needs in a creative way. Although the move away from segregated classrooms of autistic children in several school regions has been slow, the integration of children with autism into regular classrooms has been accomplished now in many parts of Canada. Unfortunately, due to the nature of the disability, many children with autism continue to languish in segregated settings without the kind of treatment programming that is needed for these types of disabilities. In addition, resources available to support the integration of children with autism appear to be diminishing in some jurisdictions.

The fourth important influence on the delivery of services was the introduction of the *DSM* (third edition) of the American Psychiatric Association in 1980. Prior to *DSM-III,* there was considerable confusion and lack of clarity in Canada and elsewhere about the diagnostic criteria for autism. Different diagnostic labels such as *childhood psychosis, brain dysfunction, childhood schizophrenia,* and *infantile autism* were used in a haphazard way. Moreover, the use of diagnostic categories often divided along professional lines. For example, pediatricians tended to use the term *infantile autism* infrequently but used instead labels such as *autistic tendencies* or *autistic features* to identify large numbers of developmentally handicapped children. Similarly, child psychiatrists preferred to use *childhood schizophrenia* or *childhood psychosis* rather than *autism* and interpreted the disorder along psychodynamic lines. With *DSM-III,* however, specific diagnostic criteria for autism became available and could be relatively easily applied. In addition, the introduction of the term *pervasive developmental disorder* in *DSM-III* to identify a spectrum of conditions that shared features of the "autistic continuum" gained wide acceptance. As a result, the number of children given a diagnosis of autism increased, and there was further interest in the characterization of children with other forms of PDD. Indeed, in Canada, the term *PDD* has gained considerable popularity, and no distinction is made between autism and PDD in terms of access to services or school programs. With the broadening of the criteria for autism in *DSM-III-R* in 1987, the number of children who received a diagnosis of autism increased substantially as did the number of children who received a diagnosis of PDD-not otherwise specified (NOS). However, these children were generally given a diagnosis of PDD instead, and as a result, autism and PDD were often seen as mutually exclusive terms by both the lay and professional communities. This confusion persists to this day but may have improved with the publication of *DSM-IV.* The end result of these changes in classification is that the number of children with autism and other forms of PDD has grown substantially. There is now much greater recognition of the disorder among those who provide services for preschool children, and considerable interest exists in programming for these children in community preschools and day care centers. The current demand for services for children with PDD has grown substantially, and the available treatment centers and services are finding it difficult to cope with this increasing demand.

An important role has been played throughout these developments by parent organizations. The Autism Society of Ontario was founded in 1973, and a national organization was started in 1976. Currently, there are autism parent societies in all 10 provinces as well as a national organization that receives funding from both the private sector and the federal government. These organizations have provided an extremely important forum for education, a means of disseminating information, and parental support. On many occasions, these organizations have also provided direct treatment such as summer camps and other recreational activities. As government funding for hospital-based and community-based services decreases, it is anticipated that these voluntary organizations will become even more important in the delivery of services to children with autism.

CHINA

Kuo-Tai Tao and Xiao-Ling Yang

Infantile and early childhood autism as a PDD were unknown to most people and even medical professionals in China until the past decade. The programs of clinical studies, treatment, and rehabilitation training have now been started but are just at an early developmental stage.

Diagnostic Concept

Kanner in 1943 described a group of 11 children with a previously unrecognized disorder and noted a number of characteristic features in these children to which he first gave the diagnosis of early infantile autism. This diagnostic concept was introduced into China as late as 1982 by one of the authors (Tao) in an article

titled "Issues of Diagnosis and Classification of Infantile Autism." In this article, Tao described four cases and emphasized the qualitative change in behaviors for the purpose of differentiation from other developmental and mental disorders in childhood. In a later article, Tao (1987) provided a brief report titled "Infantile Autism in China" in which 15 cases were described. It was news to the rest of the world that infantile autism definitely existed and was being diagnosed in mainland China. Following this report, Yang (1990) reported on an additional 30 cases of children with autism. From this time onward, other reports have appeared in journals for special education teachers, and articles about autism have appeared in magazines and newspapers. Most people, except those illiterate, now have some idea of autism.

Epidemiology of Autism in China

In China, people usually cannot imagine that a disorder such as autism can even occur in infancy and early childhood. This impression has also influenced the thinking of many pediatricians and psychiatrists. Because child psychiatry developed recently in China, most professionals working with children have no child psychiatry training. The few child psychiatrists in China have worked in several large cities. Both of us had the opportunity for training in the United States. Many autistic children were referred to us from different parts of China. These children have been diagnosed with mental retardation, hyperactive syndrome, childhood schizophrenia, and even sporadic encephalitis and other conditions.

In China, children usually are sent to the clinic for evaluation and treatment by their parents. Thus, the first step of professional recognition of this disorder is largely dependent on whether the parents consider the behavior of their children somewhat wrong and seek help from medical professionals. In fact, a few of the parents in our series have shown this ability for several reasons:

- Most parents do not have scientific knowledge about developmental milestones of the first 2 years of their children, so they cannot recognize problems that might raise the suspicion of a disorder, unless their children do not speak at 3 or 4 years of age. Usually, delayed speech leads to otolaryngological examination of hearing and, when hearing is found to be normal, to psychiatric help.

- Knowing that there are different speeds of normal development of children, some parents think that their children's maturational lag would be made up in the future. So they wait.

- Perhaps in line with the Chinese biological medical model, parents pay more attention to physical symptoms of illness than to behavioral symptoms. Also, the stigma attached to mental disorder still exists, especially in undeveloped areas. Young parents feel guilty or ashamed and try to hide their children's behavioral problems from the outside world.

These factors may influence the early recognition and diagnosis of autism and may be the reason both of us (working in Nanjing and Beijing) have found that autistic children come to clinics an average of 3 years after parents have noticed abnormal behavior in their children.

The difficulties in early recognition and evaluation have given the impression that autism is very rare in China. Also, it does seem likely that autism is less common in China. Tao reported 15 cases, and only 2 came from Nanjing, a city with a population over 5 million; similarly, the population of Beijing was 11 million in 1990 and Yang reported 30 cases, only 10 coming from Beijing. The rarity of autism in China needs to be studied in further detail.

Classification and Diagnostic Criteria

The first draft of a Chinese classification of mental disorders was proposed in 1958. It classified mental disorders exclusively in relation to mental retardation. The first official classification was published in 1981 as the Chinese Classification of Mental Disorders (CCMD-1) and included other childhood mental disorders besides mental retardation. In 1989, CCMD-2 was published, and the diagnostic category of childhood autism (PDD) first appeared, with diagnostic criteria essentially adopted from *ICD-9.* In 1995, CCMD-2-R was prepared.

One of the most important features is its provision of more detailed diagnostic criteria than CCMD-2. To improve the reliability of diagnostic judgment, the clinician has two tasks: to determine the presence or absence of specific clinical features and then to use the criteria provided as guidelines for making the diagnosis. The term *childhood autism* is adopted from *ICD-10,* the diagnostic criteria are close to *ICD-10,* and *DSM-III-R* is used as a major reference.

Diagnostic Procedures

The diagnostic procedures of our clinics are essentially the same as those in the United States. The importance of histories of development and present illness and psychiatric examination (unstructured and structured) is emphasized. This is usually supplemented by physical examination and laboratory tests. Formal psychological tests include the Denver Developmental Screening Test (DDST), the Bayley, Wechsler Preschool and Primary Scale of Intelligence (WPPSI), and the Japanese S-M Social Adaptive Ability Test (Chinese version). The children with autism we have examined mostly belong to lower or moderate functional levels and cannot cooperate with psychological testing. We also use rating scales and other methods, including the ABC, CARS, and Clancy Behavior Scale. As indicated, we perform biological tests, including chromosome and fragile-X testing, EEG, CT, MRI, and other tests.

Treatment and Care Services

China is a vast and most populous country with a population of 1.8 billion, and 80% of the people live in rural areas and in less developed bordering provinces. Services are just beginning to be developed:

- *Early identification:* We believe that the first step in ensuring professional help at an early age is public education, and we are emphasizing this in our work.

- *Counseling services:* In the mental hospitals in Nanjing and Beijing, we receive many letters asking for our help from parents of sick children from different parts of China.

We have developed parent counseling services for those who seek help. We send parents a questionnaire including family history, parents' education level and economic status and their relationship with the child, developmental and present illness, and so on. If we consider the child possibly to be autistic, we ask for more information, including developmental history and a rating scale (Clancy Behavior Scale for Autism). If the patient is autistic, we invite the families to one of our special services. If the parents cannot come, we send complete and written materials about autism, about care and training, and ask parents to seek help from local rehabilitation centers for handicapped children or other facilities. We believe that this situation will change by developing a national rehabilitation training program that will also include mental retardation.

- *Outpatient clinic:* In addition to Nanjing and Beijing, a few child health clinics, pediatric neurological clinics, and mental hospitals have set up programs for children with behavioral disorders. These clinics usually are able to make a provisional diagnosis of autism, PDD, or other severe disorders and to refer the children to Nanjing or Beijing for a final diagnosis and management planning.

In our clinic, the child psychiatrist takes a brief medical and developmental history and performs a physical and psychiatric examination, including a direct interview and observation of the child. If the child can cooperate, we refer the patient to a psychologist for behavioral and developmental assessment. We also obtain an EEG, neuroradiological examination, chromosome analysis, and other indicated studies.

Following this assessment, the child psychiatrist may make the diagnosis of autism or invite the child, accompanied by parents, to remain at the hospital for a short period or return to the outpatient clinic for further observation. If the parents cannot remain in Beijing or Nanjing, the physician usually provides a prescription for medication to control overactivity, aggressive self-injurious, and stereotyped behaviors. Medication includes mostly high potency vitamin supplements, minerals, antianxiety drugs, antidepressants, and psychotropic drugs—for example, haloperidol, sulpiride, thioridazine—as indicated. Antiepileptic medication is prescribed, if necessary. The physician also maintains correspondence with the family for counseling.

- *Day treatment:* In Nanjing and Beijing, we can provide autistic children with day treatment. Generally, the children come to the outpatient clinic at 8:30 A.M. and remain until 4 P.M. We believe that day treatment, combined with medication and special training, is the major part of the treatment program. Special teachers and psychiatrists work together on assessment and setting goals, and behavior modification methods are used.

- *Residential treatment:* Residential care is limited to those autistic children with severe behavioral disorders who come from other parts of China. Children are accompanied by their parents and are cared for 24 hours a day by nurses. During residential treatment, detailed clinical studies are performed. The drug and behavioral treatments are similar to those in the day treatment program. In the period of hospitalization or residential care, the psychiatrists and psychologists help the parents to improve their ability to give more love, patience, time, and knowledge to their child.

- *Kindergarten and special programs:* Kindergartens and special educational care centers may accept autistic children into special education groups. Also, there are a few special programs in Beijing for special education of autistic children.

The limitation of available studies on behavioral intervention leaves a number of questions unanswered about the most effective intervention. We emphasize the involvement of parents in treatment and helping parents to understand and cope with the autistic child and the practical and emotional problems faced by families.

Education and Employment of the Handicapped

The education law in China provides obligatory education for 9 years. In the past decade, special education has developed very rapidly in big cities. There are schools for blind, deaf, handicapped, and mentally retarded children. For diverse reasons, autistic children are not included in the national special education project. From 1994, however, the Ministry of Education of China has begun a research program to investigate how to educate and train autistic children. This will lead to a new national autistic education program. In Beijing, there are several schools and kindergartens accepting autistic children. These autistic children receive treatments and training in these programs, but the number of positions is limited. Some autistic children with more serious syndromes cannot enter schools and are cared for by their families.

Employment is very difficult for autistic adolescents, even after special education for several years. Their social protection is not yet established, and their families must take care of them.

Parents' Association

The preparation and foundation of a parents' association began in 1991. One of the authors has organized a group of parents in Beijing to form an association for autistic children. By organizing meetings, video shows, and discussions, the parents and medical specialists have improved understanding of autism and what can be done for autistic children by exchange of information between parents and doctors. The parents receive not only knowledge, experience, and confidence about medical treatments, education, and training but also become friends and are released from their feelings of helplessness, isolation, and depression, which helps support the parents in their difficult situation and improve their psychological health.

Parents recognized that for the autistic children's health care, education, and other rights, they should unite and work together and that an official association was necessary. In December 1993, the Beijing Rehabilitation Association for Autistic Children was officially inscribed and funded. Currently, the association has more than 100 members (about half from other cities and provinces). The purpose of this association is to improve the material and social environments for autistic children, ensure their equality in social life, and create rehabilitation, education, and medical care conditions that will help them achieve their highest level of living abilities.

The tasks of the association are (1) to investigate the social situation of the autistic children; (2) to present wishes and requests of autistic children to local and central governments; (3) to exchange information and to give consultative services of rehabilitation, education, and social care of autistic children; (4) to promote coordination between members and promote governmental projects concerning autistic children; (5) to promote international scientific exchange; and (6) to support research on autism.

Law for Protection of the Disabled

The Chinese government has attached great importance to the welfare of the disabled. This policy has been implemented in various laws, including the laws of 1991. A full plan was developed between 1988 and 1992, including national work programs for the disabled involving rehabilitation, education, and employment. Compulsory education will be ensured to most children and teenagers with various disabilities, including autistic disorder. The major problem has been the recognition of individuals with autism and the creation of sufficient services.

FRANCE

Pierre Ferrari

Psychotic disorders of early childhood have long been ignored in France as well as in the rest of the world. During the past century, intellectual deficiency was the banner under which all child mental pathology was grouped, and clinical studies were limited to the description of different forms of mental retardation. In 1888, the French alienist Moreau de Tours, in his famous treatise, "La Folie chez l'enfant" ("Madness in the Child"), deemed inconceivable that anyone could refer to the possible existence of psychosis in the child. In his view, psychotic manifestations could only be exceptionally observed and only in children close to puberty.

Later, during the first half of the twentieth century, French clinicians recognized the existence of and described a schizophrenia in the child similar to that of the adult, but with a childhood onset. This led G. Heuyer to describe forms of schizophrenia beginning around the age of 10. Around the 1950s and 1960s, at the same time as Kanner was involved in his research in the United States, French child psychiatrists, such as Diakine, Lebovici, Lang, and Mises, who often had a psychoanalytic orientation, became interested in psychotic manifestations of very early childhood and created a nosographic frame for early childhood psychoses. Their research has led to the construction of a French classification of child and adolescent mental disorders (Mises amd Quemada, 1993). This classification, comprising two axes (axis I devoted to basic clinical categories and axis II in which possibly etiological associated factors are taken into account), regroups child psychoses and separates them into five categories:

1. Autism
2. Atypical forms of autism
3. Psychoses with mental deficiency
4. Dysharmonic psychoses
5. Child schizophrenia

This classification differs somewhat from the classifications suggested by the *DSM-III-R* and the *ICD-10*.

The form of autism that was described by Leo Kanner maintains a central place in the French nosology. The criteria that have been retained for this diagnosis are: onset during the first year of life, with organization of a full picture before the age of 3; and presence of all the characteristic features, including major autistic withdrawal, immutability, stereotypies, absence of language or specific language disorders, and cognitive development dysharmony.

In addition to autism, other forms of early psychoses have been characterized—early psychosis and dysharmonies. In the *early psychoses with mental deficiency,* aspects and mechanisms of psychoses are implicated from the onset, with severe disorders in the organization of cognitive and instrumental functions. These forms are characterized by association with two patterns: (1) a syndrome involving severe mental retardation (marked by intellectual deficiency and severe instrumental deficits) or (2) symptoms suggesting the presence of a psychotic nucleus.

Symptoms associated with a psychotic nucleus include withdrawal attitudes, denoting important communication difficulties; presence of major anxieties that increase the withdrawal attitudes, the regressive behaviors, the impulsive behaviors, and mainly the self-aggressive ones; and presence of certain language disorders evocative of a psychotic dimension of language (mutism, soliloquy, verbal stereotypies).

The characterization of the *psychotic dysharmonies* as forms of child psychosis (similar in some respects to "other pervasive developmental disorders" of *DSM-IV*) is one of the original features of the French classification. French authors have considered that these forms differ from autism as well as other developmental disorders because of the following characteristics:

• Their later onset, around the age of 3 to 4, often after a seemingly normal period of early development
• Their frequency: two to three times greater than that of autism
• The variety of symptomatic manifestations: major psychomotor instability or, conversely, important psychomotor inhibition; severe pseudoneurotic manifestations (with overwhelming phobia or severe obsessive symptoms), severe language disorders characteristic of psychotic language, intolerance to frustration accompanied by violent fits of anger, important mood changes, failure of the first attempts at schooling

Behind this varying series of symptoms, the diagnosis is based on a close psychopathological examination that makes it possible to reveal, beyond the symptoms, the presence of psychotic mechanisms:

—Contact with reality and capacities of adaptation to reality are always fragile; relatively maintained at certain moments, contact with reality is severely

disorganized at others by the invasion of psychotic processes.
—Relation with others, apparently possible at certain moments, seems at other moments completely disrupted. In general, relation with others, when it is possible, takes place in a poorly differentiated dual way.
—Anxieties are always important but they are of a variety of natures (annihilation anxiety, depressive anxieties of object loss, separation anxieties).
—Thought processes are invaded and overwhelmed by very crude and intense affects, fantasies, and representations (often marked by the importance of aggressive and destructive instincts).

The main feature of this French classification is that it maintains the term *early psychosis,* rather than that of *pervasive developmental disorder* used by the *DSM-III-R* and *DSM-IV.* The term *psychosis* was preferred to better indicate that the specificity of the disorder is related to the presence of a psychotic process underlying the developmental disorders and delays and to emphasize the unity of the group of early psychoses, marked by the existence of a continuum and of forms of passage between autism and psychotic dysharmony. Therefore, the aim of the French classification is not to mark the boundaries of entities that strictly exclude each other and are stable over time, but rather to enable the identification of different psychopathological modes of organization that can essentially evolve and change into each other under the effect of therapy.

Research

The investigations of French child psychiatrists have been oriented during past decades in several directions: toward biology, clinical practice, and therapeutics. These investigations are based on a multifactorial conceptualization of the origin of child psychosis and emphasize the close interdependence of factors originating in the field of social relations as well as factors originating in the field of biology during the first period of the infant's mental life. Inside the interactive melting pot

where the beginning of the child's psyche becomes organized, two aspects become interactively engaged: the newborn's competence and his or her possible failures, whether the latter are biological or of another nature, on the one hand, and the components of the relational field, with their possible failures, wherever they originate, on the other.

In the field of biological research, several research teams are interested in the study of visual auditory evoked potentials in the cortex and the cerebral stem (Lelord & Sauvage, 1990). Others have centered their research on the study of genetic factors involved in child psychosis (e.g., Herault et al., 1994). Finally, other studies have focused on alterations in the systems of neurotransmitters (serotonin, epinephrine and norepinephrine, endorphins) and the correlations of these findings with clinical data (Bursztejn, 1983; Ferrari, 1993) as well as a possible dysfunction of the hypothalamic-pituitary-adrenal axis (Tordjman et al., 1997).

In the clinical field, French clinicians have emphasized the necessity to carry out a very early diagnosis during the first 2 years of the child's life. The precocity of the diagnosis allows for early therapeutic care that will itself condition—at least in part—the quality of the natural history of the disorder. According to this point of view, different authors have applied themselves to specific, very early symptoms of autistic evolution, through a careful observation of child-parent interactions during the first 18 months of life. These symptoms are:

- In the realm of psychomotricity, the absence of anticipatory attitudes and of postural adaptation
- In the realm of perceptive communication, abnormalities concerning the gaze and the reactions to sounds and to the human voice
- Spitz's organizers (e.g., separation distress) do not appear
- Absence of interest in objects and the surrounding world
- Massive and poorly organized phobias
- Lack of expression and of understanding of emotions
- Gesture stereotypies and visual and auditory self-stimulations

- Lack of development of transitional and play activities

Despite the multiplicity of these symptoms, French researchers have stressed the difficulty in making a very early diagnosis, because symptoms vary, are inconspicuous, or sometimes lack specificity. Thus, investigators suggest that, rather than speaking of early signs of autism, it might be preferable to speak of "early interactive dysfunctions with a risk of autistic evolution." Autism would then appear less as an independent disease—strictly speaking—than as one path of pathological evolution, among others, of certain severe and early interactive disturbances.

In the realm of psychopathology, French clinical researchers have applied themselves to understand, with the help of psychoanalytic concepts, the psychopathological mechanisms of autistic and psychotic states. They emphasize the importance of this understanding for good treatment planning. This understanding notably calls on the concepts of the Kleinian and post-Kleinian theories of Tustin and Meltzer. This viewpoint has developed in France under the influence of the ideas of D. Anzieu, D. Houzel, G. Haag, among others.

This perspective on psychopathology has recognized the value of some concepts for the understanding of autistic states as, for example, adhesive identification, self-sensoriality, the feeling of bodily discontinuity (black hole), and a self with no envelope and no interior. Concerning psychotic disharmonies, these authors have stressed the importance of mechanisms such as splitting, projective identification, the depressive position, and "instinctual disintrication."

Diagnosis

The diagnosis of early psychosis in France is formulated by the child psychiatrist on the basis of a diagnostic process, which involves the following steps:

1. An anamnestic inquiry to specify the child and his or her family's past record.
2. A search for early signs of autism previous to the consultation.
3. A psychiatric clinical examination, in search of clinical signs and relational modalities that could support the diagnosis. This clinical examination is completed by an assessment of the psychopathological mechanisms underlying the symptoms.
4. An organic clinical examination in search of an associated organic disease (encephalopathy, sensorial deficiencies, malformations, other biological abnormalities, etc.).
5. Psychological evaluation, with a range of important aims, including:
   - Projective tests for specifying the characteristics of the child's personality and the nature of the psychopathological mechanisms that are operating.
   - Cognitive assessment to evaluate the child's intellectual level and cognitive capacities, using standardized psychological tests such as the Brunet-Lezine, EDEI, WISC, WIPPSI, or Kaufman Assessment Battery for Children (K-ABC).
   - Assessment of psychomotor behavior.
   - Language assessment (including the psycholinguistic assessment set of Chevry-Muller).
   - Other assessment methods are also used, including rating scales for autistic symptoms (CARS), structured interviewing and observational methods (Autism Diagnostic Interview [ADI]), and measures of adaptive functioning (Vineland scales).
6. Organic tests, as indicated by the clinical picture, including:
   - Search for genetic abnormalities.
   - EEG, as well as studies of evoked potentials in the cortex and the brain stem.
   - Neuroimaging (CAT-Scan or MRI).
   - Neurochemical studies (neurotransmitter metabolism).

Treatment

The goals of treatment are quite broad and include:

- Enabling the child to recognize himself or herself as a subject and to give the child the means to reach a genuine communication with others. For this, the child must be recognized as a subject with his or her unique personal history and endowed with a specific psychic life that organizes his or her relationship modalities with his or her environment. The psychoanalytic theory is an important tool for the understanding of this psychological functioning.

- Offering the child the educative measures necessary to help him or her become autonomous.
- Offering the child the pedagogic and academic measures necessary for his or her academic, professional, and social insertion.

Although the broader, therapeutic goal remains essential, the contribution of educative measures should not be neglected. These educative measures are part of an exchange that takes into account the nature of the child's relation with his or her environment to enable the child to integrate these educative measures. The pedagogic and academic approaches are considered essential to help the child reach autonomy and become integrated into society. They are offered to the child according to his or her own learning abilities.

The presence of a multidisciplinary mental health team is a guarantee that the child will be approached as a whole person. A heterogeneity of points of view within the same team, in which educators, nurses, teachers, psychiatrists, psychologists, and occupational therapists come into contact with one another, helps ensure a nonrestrictive, more global vision of the child.

There are varied *treatment settings* and methods of delivering care, including:

- *The day hospital (*hopital de jour*):* This is the most flexible approach and offers the greatest chance of maintaining the child in his or her family. It is thus the most favored solution whenever possible.
- *The therapeutic living-in facility (*internat therapeutique*):* The separation of the child from his or her family environment and admission to a therapeutic, living-in facility is justified in some cases (e.g., extreme severity of the pathology, absent or deeply pathogenic family).
- *Part-time therapeutic "welcoming" centers (*Centres d'Accueil Therapeutique a Temps Partiel*):* These are less intensive care facilities that deliver part-time care and, at the same time, enable the continuation of the child's academic integration into a normal environment.
- *Therapeutic family placement ("welcoming"; accueil familial therapeutique):* This setting may be indicated for the very young child when the family conditions do not make it possible to maintain the child in his or her natural environment and when the child's very young age does not allow admission to a living-in facility. The maternal workers (*assistantes maternelles*), paid by the hospital, receive supervision and support from the sector's psychiatric team. (Since 1972, public regional sectors, *secteurs,* of child psychiatry cover the totality of France and form the pillar of child mental health.)
- Finally, when early mother-baby interactive dysfunctions, with a "psychotic potential," have been discovered, early mother-baby therapy by specially trained psychotherapists may be implemented, possibly in the child's home.

Specific aims of institutional treatment for autistic individuals include:

- *The institution as a meeting space.* The aim of the treatment is to put into place new modes of mental functioning that are correlative of the establishment of new exchange modalities with others.
- *The institution as a stimulus barrier.* The institution is a protecting and protected frame that sets a sort of nondistorting but attenuating filter between the child and the outside world. It aims at protecting the child against the return of experiences the traumatic character of which could not be mastered by his or her psyche.
- *The institution as a containing function.* This function implies on the part of the mental health workers a true capacity to welcome, contain, and live the nonorganized emotions and affects felt by the child, to verbalize them, and give them meaning in order to return them to the child in a form that he or she can assimilate. This enables children to build their own psychic space and to organize their emotional life.

- *The institution as a mothering function.* This function implies an exchange and communication through bodily care that enables children to affect a libidinal cathexis of their own body and to help them take possession of their own body.
- *The institution as a transitional space.* The institution should enable children to practice their primary creativity while confronting them with the perception of the reality of objects in the world.

The performance and the stability of health workers are basic conditions if the therapeutic processes in the institution are to succeed. Children should be able to recover, through their everyday relations with the team members, stable reference figures that will give them a feeling of security.

The *schooling of the psychotic child* may take place in two different settings:

1. *Inside the day hospital or the therapeutic living-in facility.* In this case, pedagogic help is brought by teachers who depend on the Ministry of National Education and who work in close collaboration with all the team members.
2. *The integration of a psychotic child into a normal schooling system.* The success of such an integration depends, among other things, on the quality of the exchanges and the cooperation that have been established between the team members and the teachers who welcome the child.

Along with the care of the child, parents also require intervention. These include:

- Parental guidance measures that aim at supporting the parents in their educative task with their children are implemented
- Specific therapeutic measures are offered to the parents and aim at:
  —enabling them to recover their capacity for anticipatory illusion toward their child; to perceive, understand, and accept the fluctuations in their child's evolution
  —restoring their self-esteem (narcissism) that has been so deeply wounded by the arrival of a psychotic child

The care offered to psychotic children in the different public mental health institutions is free, the expenditures being totally paid by the social security agencies as long as necessary. Also, a special pension for education may be allocated, in certain conditions, to parents of psychotic children.

In France, medication is little used, only during limited periods, and only to lessen certain symptoms that are particularly bothersome for the child. Medications that are used include sedative neuroleptic medication, antianxiety medication, and antidepressants.

Evolution and Results

The evolution of psychotic disharmonies is favorable. Almost half of these children may, when leaving mental health institutions, integrate within a normal academic or professional environment. Part of the other children are professionally integrated into a protected environment. The evolution of autistic children and those with psychoses with mental retardation is more severe.

A small number of autistic children evolve little, if at all, and when they do, it is toward a picture of retardation (50%). When they become adults, these patients are referred either to "life settings" (*lieux de vie*) or to psychiatric hospitals. The other half succeeds in acquiring language, and their lives will be enriched with relations with others. When they are adults, these patients may become integrated into a protective environment.

Parents' Associations

The first psychotic children's parents' association was created in 1963 under the name *Association su Service des Enfants Inadaptes ayant des Troubles de la Personnalite* (ASITP; Association at the Service of Maladjusted Children with Personality Disorders). The parents who founded ASITP wanted to end their isolation and to promote institutions adapted to their children's specific problems. It is on these parents' initiative that one of the first day hospitals in Paris was established.

At the beginning of the 1980s, different controversies pertaining to the importance that should be given to education in the treatment of psychotic children led to a schism inside ASITP, which has led to two parents' associations in France:

1. *Autisme-France* tends to promote the establishment of integrated school classes in which the main recommended educative approach, inspired by the Treatment and Education of Autistic and Related Communication-Handicapped CHildren (TEACCH) method, aims at giving children an "educative prosthesis" to improve their socialization and understanding of the world.
2. *Sesame Autisme* (Federation Francaise Autisme et Psychose Infantile) comprises 24 regional associations. This federation publishes a quarterly journal, *Sesame,* with which many child psychiatrists collaborate. Today, 1,200 families, regrouped in regional associations, belong to the federation Sesame Autisme. In 1985, its national committee adopted the charter of a national movement on autism and child psychoses with goals:
   - To improve the well-being of persons handicapped because of autistic disorders and child psychoses and help them reach the best accomplishments possible
   - To improve them socially as much as possible
   - To place at the children and their families' disposal a large range of therapeutic means that may satisfy their needs while offering adequate guarantees

Sesame Autisme encourages close cooperation between parents and professionals and an approach that respects the child's educative needs as the necessity to help him or her progress in the relational realm and in the domain of psychic functioning.

GERMANY AND AUSTRIA

Martin Schmidt

Through the relations of the Marburg child and adolescent psychiatrist Hermann Stutte with the Dutch child and adolescent psychiatrist Van Krevelen, the diagnostic concept of autism was introduced in Germany very soon after World War II. From 1947 onward, Doris Weber (1985) from Marburg studied the diagnosis of "autistic

children"; she delimited this classification from the traditional diagnosis of dementia infantilis of Heller (1908) (childhood disintegrative disorder) that was given to autistic children frequently at that time. In the 1950s, Bosch, in Frankfurt, started to work on the differentiation of Kanner's autism and schizophrenia. In the 1960s, Nissen originally described the distinction between Kanner's infantile autism and Asperger syndrome and between somatogenic and psychogenic autism. Until the mid-1980s, nosological considerations in Germany followed the concepts of the *ICD-9* in which autism was seen as the earliest and most extensive form of infantile psychosis. But since the 1980s, Kanner's autism has increasingly been regarded as a developmental disorder. Recently, specialists have started to focus on other PDDs, but little research has yet been done.

The concept of Asperger syndrome was not used in Germany until the early 1960s. Autistic psychopathy described by Hans Asperger in 1944 is amazingly similar to the present diagnostic criteria, although more attention has focused on the B-criteria listed in *DSM-IV* than on the A-criteria, which are more characteristic for the diagnosis in childhood. Until the introduction of *ICD-10,* this disorder was mostly treated as equivalent to an infantile form of schizoid personality disorder. In Germany today, Asperger syndrome in adults is generally regarded as a variant of schizoid personality disorder.

Within Germany, there is broad acceptance of the view that autism may reflect a common final pathway of various underlying disorders and dispositions (as suggested by Nissen and more recently by Gillberg & Coleman [2000]).

History of Care of Individuals with Autism and Related Disorders

Originally, autistic children were diagnosed and treated in university hospitals, but soon institutions for long-term residential care were established. These followed the example of the pioneering Swiss institution created by Lutz in the 1950s. Also, many autistic children were placed in institutions for the mentally retarded, but it became more acceptable for many parents to have a child diagnosed as autistic rather than as mentally retarded. In the 1960s, a parent association for mentally retarded children opened the Kerstin-Haus in Marburg, an institution caring for both mentally retarded and autistic children. There, Weber (1985) carried out a great part of her follow-up studies on autistic children. For a long time, there was no apparent need for special preschool programs, since autism was not generally diagnosed until school age or differentiated from mental retardation. In some regions, day care centers for autistic schoolchildren were set up combining school and therapeutic interventions. Also in the 1960s, medical treatments were tried in some of these centers, with varying success. Starting in the late 1960s, the Max-Planck Institute for Psychiatry was the first institution to utilize behavior therapy methods with autistic children, using American concepts of this approach. The first main focus of therapy was the reduction of stereotyped behavior and rituals; later, methods were aimed at improving the child's development and modeling behavioral patterns. This change in therapy paralleled the change in concept of the disorder from infantile psychosis to developmental disorder.

Unlike France, where children with Kanner's autism were treated by psychoanalysis, in Germany, there were no special psychoanalytic institutions for the treatment of autism. Currently in Germany, the treatment of an autistic child only on the basis of psychoanalysis is, as a rule, due to misdiagnosis.

Current Status of Treatment Services

In Germany, treatment services for autistic individuals can be separated into four types:

1. Most treatment services were organized by the Parent Society of Autistic Children. Special outpatient clinics and mobile support services of the Parent Society are in charge of many autistic individuals of preschool age. Only a minority of these younger children are cared for by early health promotion services and social-pediatric centers.
2. Autistic individuals of school age occasionally are treated within child guidance clinics; more frequently, their care is within child psychiatric outpatient or inpatient clinics.
3. Special school classes provide day care.
4. Long-term residential care is the fourth pillar of treatment services. Many residential programs for psychiatrically ill or behaviorally disordered children also have special units for autistic children, mainly taking care of higher functioning autistic children who do not fit into the local schools for mentally retarded or behaviorally disturbed children.

Appropriate care for high-functioning autistic children remains a great problem for treatment services. Extra domestic placement is required in most cases. Lately, attempts to integrate such high-functioning autistic children into normal schools are on the increase. But most such attempts work well only by use of specially trained additional staff.

When and by Whom Is the Condition Diagnosed?

In most cases, autism is diagnosed by child psychiatrists or clinical psychologists working in special outpatient clinics of the Parent Society of Autistic Children, but only seldom by early health promotion services of social pedagogical centers or pediatric clinics. In spite of educational efforts, very early diagnosis of autism is unusual. Autism is diagnosed mostly at 5 or 6 years of age. In 3-year-olds, autism is hardly ever suspected; in 4-year-olds, it can be diagnosed if autistic behavior is accompanied by mental retardation. Asperger syndrome is diagnosed mostly at age 7 or 8 years if special restricted interests are the predominating symptom and interfere with school to a great extent, and at age 9 to 11 years or later if the social deficits predominate.

Specific National and Theoretical Issues

Changes in therapeutic concepts for autism have mirrored changing trends and ideologies. Two particular examples are worth mentioning. First, the integration of high-functioning autistic children has been pushed along with the implementation of the ideology of integrating other handicapped children into normal schools. This procedure requires additional staff and sometimes leads to the misinterpretation that all autistic children ought to be integrated into normal schools. Second, the policy of the parent organizations correctly insists that autism is a multiple and not only a mental handicap. The intended effect of this policy is to counteract the ideology of psychogenic causation (still proposed by educators, in contrast with psychologists and medical doctors). Also, the parents' emphasis helps to guarantee a multilevel approach of care and continued services after school age.

Services over the Life Span and Barriers to Services

The transition from adolescence to adulthood is the highest barrier for treatment services of autistic individuals. They lack housing possibilities, especially in the absence of mental retardation, as well as sheltered workplaces. Therefore, most live in institutions run by the Parent Society for Mentally Retarded People. Only a few autistic adults receive proper treatment, often limited to psychopharmacology. Different institutions for autistic adults without mental retardation have been established chiefly by the Parent Society. Their aim is not therapy and "normalization" but providing a suitable life residence for autistic adults. Currently, a bottleneck in the system of care is services required for crisis intervention in case of autoaggressive or violent behavior. Many psychiatrists lack knowledge of autistic disorders, comparable to the similarly difficult situation in the treatment of adults with hyperkinetic disorder.

Parents' Association

In 1970, parents of autistic children founded the Parent Society noted earlier. At present, the Society counts 3,200 members and 35 regional agencies spread all over Germany. Initially, the main task was to educate doctors, psychologists, and pedagogues about the importance of early diagnosis of autistic disorders. The second focus was promoting social integration and nonacademic opportunities. The Parent Society cooperated with health insurances and other state agencies bearing financial responsibility for handicapped people. But only little has been achieved for full school integration. The third main task of the Parent

Society was the establishment of regional outpatient clinics, and the fourth goal was setting up services for autistic adults. At present, the central concerns are the relationship of autistic individuals with their families and their lifelong care. Furthermore, the national Parent Society is in constant contact with the European International Parent Society. Its scientific committee processes specialist literature about Kanner and Asperger syndrome and passes on important information to concerned groups. Scientific investigations on autistic individuals—for example, studies on the genetics of autistic disorders—are also supported by the Parent Society. Moreover, the Society tries to move legislation toward accepting autistic individuals as generally multiply handicapped people. The Parent Society does not include the concerns of children with Rett's syndrome, for whom there is a separate parent organization, nor does it deal with other PDDs.

History and Status of Treatment Services in Austria

In Austria, a special concept of treatment services established in 1975, the *Wiener Modell* (Vienna model), uses the same standardized concept from early childhood to adulthood. Apart from client-centered therapeutic and family therapeutic approaches, the main elements of this concept are involvement therapy and learning by model. The Vienna model can be divided into four phases. In 1975, it started with an orthopedagogic, outpatient clinic that provided special consultation services for autistic preschool children. As the children grew older, further services were required. Therefore, a day care center for autistic preschool and school children was opened in 1983. The third section, a special school for autistic children, was set up in 1986. At present, it has seven classes with eight pupils and two teachers per class. The latest section, established in 1993, is Rainman's Home, an institution for vocational and social integration of autistic adolescents and adults initiated by the parent society of the same name.

National Parent Society

In the early 1990s, the parent society Rainman's Home was founded in Austria. The parents of autistic adolescents took this urgent step motivated by the massive problems of autistic adolescents at the threshold of working life. The main task of the parent society is to enable autistic adolescents and adults to live a positive and meaningful life.

GREECE

Vaya Papageorgiou

Interest in autistic disorders in Greece began in the early 1960s (Anastasopoulos, Ierodiakonou, & Routsoni, 1964). However, autism as a diagnosis in children and adolescents has been used for many years infrequently and interchangeably with childhood schizophrenia, mental retardation, or mental handicap (Karantanos, 1984). The majority of adults with autism and learning disabilities were considered as psychotic and a proportion as mentally retarded. Some of the more able individuals have been labeled as depressed, bipolar, schizoid, or schizophrenic. For many years, psychoanalytic concepts concerning psychopathology and treatment approaches were dominant.

The recognition of autistic spectrum disorders as complex developmental lifelong conditions has been influenced by the introduction of *DSM-III* classification of diseases (American Psychiatric Association, 1980). Knowledge regarding diagnosis and care provision for people with autism has increased considerably in recent years as a result of the internationally accepted diagnostic criteria and the similarities between the two major diagnostic and classification systems, *DSM-IV* (American Psychiatric Association, 1994) and *ICD-10* (WHO, 1992). This knowledge has been reinforced by the evolution of child psychiatry as a separate discipline from general psychiatry in this country in the early 1980s. Furthermore, the increased dissemination of information on the condition was affected by the European Community Charter of Recognition of the Fundamental Social Rights of the Disabled, the related legislation of the European Community for people with special needs, and the foundation of the parents' Greek Autism Society for the Protection of Autistic People.

Greek studies using clinical samples show that the complexity of the current situation in this country cannot be estimated. Systematic epidemiological data do not exist. On the basis of conservative estimates from other countries, there should be about 15,000 to 20,000 people with autism in Greece, while the number of children with autism up to 14 years of age is 4,000 to 5,000. On this estimate, a number of 200 to 250 children with autism born in this country every year should be added.

Diagnosis

For many years, people with autism in Greece have been served by mental health and welfare services. However, knowledge among professionals regarding diagnosis and intervention was basic, and specialized services able to provide assessment and treatment for this population have been almost nonexistent. At present, mental health services are limited to the big cities. Access to the services for people from distant areas is complicated (Alexiou, 1995).

Currently, all children are regularly assessed by pediatricians, and those suspected of developmental disorders are usually referred for further assessment to child development clinics. The majority of children suspected of having autism are more often than not referred at some point to child psychiatric services.

Sharing of information among professionals from different countries has influenced the diagnostic and intervention process for autism in some child psychiatric services in Greece, enabling the development of expertise in them over time. Presently, the focus of dealing with children with autism is on a comprehensive multidisciplinary assessment of functioning and on an individualized intervention program. Different professionals such as child psychiatrists, psychologists, speech therapists, occupational therapists, psychiatric nurses, and health visitors are involved in the assessment and treatment process. Physical assessment is conducted by the child's pediatrician at the local hospital or in private practice, and the results are communicated to the physician involved with the case. Assessment is based on an interview with the parents and the child. Cognitive abilities as well as communication and social skills are assessed. Diagnostic accuracy is enhanced by the use of specialized instruments such as the ADI-R (Lord, Rutter, & Le Couteur, 1994) and the Diagnostic Interview for Social and Communication Disorders (Wing, 1999), the Autism Diagnostic Observation Schedule-Generic (Lord, Rutter, & DiLavore, 1998), the Psychoeducational Profile-Revised (Schopler, Reichler, Bashford, & Marcus, 1990), and the Adolescent and Adult Psychoeducational Profile (Mesibov, Schopler, Schaffer, & Landrus, 1988).

Data from a National Health Service clinic for children and adolescents in northern Greece (Papageorgiou, Vogindroukas, & Vostanis, 2002) show an increasing rate of referrals of children with autism during the past 5 years. Most are 6- to 10-year-old boys followed by those under 5 years. Referral is usually initiated by the parents, with serious delays in most of the cases as a result of the parents not knowing of the existence of relevant services. Children are often assessed by a number of professionals of different disciplines and receive up to six different diagnoses. Autism is diagnosed at first assessment in one-third of the cases, while a considerable number of cases with Asperger syndrome do not receive any diagnosis. The number of referrals from pediatricians is lower than expected, considering that they are the first line of health professionals involved with the child's care in this country. A small number of cases are referred by teachers. A proportion of those seen in the clinic are cases with Asperger syndrome or autism and mild learning disabilities referred by adult psychiatrists for differential diagnosis and intervention. This suggests there is a need for greater expertise and training in the diagnosis and management of autistic spectrum disorders within adult psychiatry services.

Case Management and Educational Provision

The most common therapeutic intervention for young children with autism in Greece is a combination of speech and occupational therapy, predominantly carried out in private practice, replacing the psychoanalytically oriented practices of the past. At present, an increasing number of therapists are focusing on communication and social skills training. Support and intervention at home is minimal, while a considerable number of the cases do not receive any therapeutic intervention at all. Adolescents are more likely to receive drug treatment without any other help (Papageorgiou et al., 2002).

The evolving practice in some child psychiatric clinics is to base their case management on needs assessment. Support and advice to the family is of primary importance. The most needy families of young children are offered 8 to 12 weekly sessions, focusing on communication and social skills. Parents have the opportunity to observe the clinician working with the child and are encouraged to work under the clinician's supervision, supporting them in communicating and relating more effectively with their child and generalizing improvement at home. Follow-up sessions are offered as required. Work with high-functioning adolescents is focused on self-awareness and support to the family. Close collaboration with voluntary organizations manpowered by university students has been proven valuable in promoting the young person's development of skills toward understanding of social environment. Volunteers are supported by the specialist to act as mentors to the young person. Adolescents are thus offered the opportunity to experience a relationship in a safe and supportive way, while their social skills and social awareness are promoted. Close collaboration with mainstream and special schools as well as with preschool nurseries and special classes in the area has also been shown to be valuable. Individual consultation to teachers and other health professionals working at distant areas is provided by some services in northern Greece through the use of videotaped sessions of their work.

Children and adolescents with autistic spectrum disorders can be found at all levels of education, that is, kindergarten, mainstream and special schools, and special classes for children with learning disabilities, according to the severity of their condition. Most of the children ages 6 to 10 years are likely to attend mainstream or special schools, while there isn't any specialized educational provision for those 0 to 5 years old and those in late adolescence. From the mid-1970s to 1992–1993, a total of 200 special schools were established all over Greece. These included kindergartens, primary and secondary schools, vocational training centers, and 602 special classes in mainstream schools for 14,136 students. Among these schools, there has not been a single one for children with autism (Alexiou, 1995). The number of special schools and vocational centers for disabled children was further increased over the following years. Only recently, children with autism have been included in the legislation concerning special education (Greek Government Bulletin, 2000), and three schools for students with autism have been established in the country. A study on Greek teachers' perceptions of autism showed that very few teachers have any knowledge of and experience with the special educational needs of this population. All teachers in special needs or mainstream education required training on their perceptions and understanding of autism, as well as on the principles of educational strategies for the sufferers of autism (Mavropoulou & Padeliadou, 2000). Teaching children with autism is based mainly on general special educational principles, while remedial teaching is provided to a small number of cases.

Placement at children's homes or institutional care for people with autism in Greece increases with age (Papageorgiou et al., 2002). In 1989, there were 41 day care centers and nine residence units for disabled children and adolescents with an unknown number of cases of autism. Additionally, there were some five day care units in the big cities for a small number of children and adolescents with autism, which were mainly developed by parents of sufferers. Of all these units, very few have the necessary means for teaching and learning or sufficient, specially trained staff. Neither do they have curricula adjusted to the needs and abilities of each category of people with special needs. The most severe cases with autism are still treated in psychiatric hospitals while a considerable number do not receive any kind of intervention and stay home (Alexiou, 1995). There is usually no introduction for the transition to an adult environment such as a sheltered autistic community because there are none in Greece.

In response to this situation, the parents' Society for the Protection of People with Autism was established in 1992. It works closely with professionals interested in autism in Greece and elsewhere, as well as with international parents' societies, particularly Autism Europe. The primary aim of the Society is the promotion of the rights of people with autism for appropriate educational provision and social care. The efforts of the Society led to the recognition of autism as a condition in its own right, for which specialized services are needed (Greek Government Bulletin, 1998, 1999, 2000). A training program of 600 hours for 120 teachers and other specialists from all over the country has been organized in collaboration with the Ministry of Education and the European Community. This training program has produced a number of classes in special schools for a number of students with autism all over the country based on the TEACCH philosophy and structured teaching. Additionally, two learning and living centers in northwestern and central Greece for 12 adolescents and young adults have been established. They are both financially supported by the Ministry of Health and Welfare and run by the Autism Society.

Conclusion

Mental health professionals, educators, and policy makers in Greece are facing new challenges regarding diagnosis, assessment of needs, and care provision of people with autism. The creation of a continuum of specialized services able to diagnose and meet the needs of the individual and the family across the life span is mandatory for the Ministry of Health and Welfare and Education.

At present planning of services should be focused on an integrative model based on the experience other countries have, taking into account cultural differences and structure of the Greek Education and National Health System (Papageorgiou et al., 2002). Creation of specialized services able to diagnose autism at all ages with relative accuracy is of primary importance, with emphasis on early diagnosis and intervention as well as educational placements at an early stage along with support to the family. Development of strong links, clear referral pathways and collaborative protocols with primary care, pediatric and education services is a priority, as well as research focused on adults with autism in order to plan appropriate services for this population such as residencies and sheltered communities. Emphasis should be given on ongoing training on autism spectrum disorders among mental health professionals, pediatricians, and teachers not only in detection but particularly in the management of autistic spectrum disorders. Collaboration with European bodies, Autism Europe and, predominantly, relevant organizations under the hospice of the European Communities is paramount in developing policies, service specifications and targets, training programs, and cross cultural research.

ISRAEL

Tamar Moses and Sam Tyano

Psychiatric wards for children were established in Israel in the mid-1950s. A legal ruling separated the administrative responsibility for the care of retarded children from that of psychotic children. The care of retarded children was placed in the hands of the Ministry of Welfare, and that given to the "mentally ill" remained under the responsibility of the Ministry of Health. The distinction between the two groups of patients was based on making the diagnosis of "mental illness" according to the "Bleulerian" approach and that of retardation by testing cognitive function (Rahav, Cohen, & Porat, 1981).

In the early 1960s, autistic children began to be identified and diagnosed according to the description of Kanner. In that period, the number of diagnosed children was small, and they were treated primarily in combined psychiatric-educational settings. Later, the diagnostic approach broadened, and "autism" was used to refer to isolation from the environment in disproportion to the child's mental ability.

Three main groups of children were identified: (1) a "Kannerian" group, (2) aphasic children who exhibit a tendency to introversion and behave "autistically" but who still have some motivation to develop and "get out" from this syndrome, and (3) retarded children with some brain damage, where the socialization level is in disproportion to the level of retardation. Different treatment approaches were developed in accordance with these categories. These approaches included both the educational and psychiatric aspects of care. The overall approach was not to separate the treatment of autistic children from that of children who suffer from other syndromes, but to give treatment in accordance with the functional level (Rahav et al., 1981).

In 1974, the National Organization for Autistic Children (ALUT) was established by parents and advocates. This organization opposed the conception that autism is part of a spectrum of mental illness. ALUT viewed autism as a developmental disorder, for which the recommended treatments are educational as well as rehabilitative in nature. ALUT's main targets were to establish educational and rehabilitation centers for autistic children, to prepare professionals to work in the field, and to provide help to the families.

In 1974, the first school for autistic children, Yachdav, was established with the help of the Ministry of Education and the Tel Aviv Municipality. With time, more schools, special classes, and kindergartens were opened throughout the country. The basic approach of these programs has been educational and rehabilitative, along with an effort to build for each child a program that meets his or her individual needs. As the students in the schools grew older, the system developed boarding houses, hostels, day care centers, and employment facilities for autistic adults.

In 1990, counseling centers for autism (MILA) were established by the Ministry of Education, in cooperation with the parents' organization, ALUT. MILA's goals are both professional and educational. The organization organizes professional seminars and plans and develops databases and formulates new concepts. It also distributes up-to-date information to professionals as well as the lay communities. In cooperation with ALUT, MILA offers counseling and deals with issues related to the care of the different age groups of autistic individuals.

In 1991, another parent organization, Foundation for Children at Risk, was established with similar goals, especially for promotion and development of services for preschool children. In the beginning, treatment was diagnostically limited to children suffering from the autistic syndrome as diagnosed by Kannerian criteria; with time, services were also extended to individuals with the diagnosis of PDDs.

Controversies continue among the medical psychiatric establishment, the educational system, and parents' organizations concerning diagnosis and treatment.

Organization of Services

Three government authorities share responsibility for the care of autistic children. In 1992, a joint committee was set up by the director of the Ministry of Health. This committee included representatives from the ministries of Education, Health, and Welfare. The main indications for the establishment of this committee were the following:

1. Traditionally, the care of autistic patients was the responsibility of the Ministry of Health's Mental Health Services. Although this service generally provided the psychiatric and other mental health needs of the patients, it did not cover important needs in the areas of welfare, education, and housing.
2. Various community services were missing, and no special resources were allocated for this population.
3. The spheres of responsibility of the various governmental ministries were unclear, due to the complexity of the demands imposed by the complexity of the autistic syndrome.

The committee agreed that autism represents a clinical syndrome, resulting in complex behavioral and dysfunctional manifestations. There was also agreement that optimal treatment of this multidimensional and complex disorder requires a coordinated and multidisciplinary team approach. The committee reached the conclusion that in this approach, the autistic population should be divided according to age groups and in accordance with the developmental-functional level. In terms of areas of responsibility, the Ministry of Health will be responsible for the developmental and mental health domain, the Ministry of Education for educational needs, and the Ministry of Welfare for rehabilitation.

Parents' Organizations

The parents' organizations and the counseling service for the autistic population (MILA) work hand in hand with the government offices. They advocate for the opening of new programs for different age groups and distrib-

ute information within the organization. They also support seminars for professionals from Israel and abroad as well as the development of professional educational materials and their distribution.

Epidemiology

In 1993, a survey studied all the existing known programs for autism in Israel, and 378 individuals with the clinical diagnosis of autism were identified (Cohen & Levinson, 1993). The age group distribution was as follows:

Ages in Years	Number of Cases
0–3	64
4–6	62
7–21	158
22+	94

This survey does not deal with the complexity in the definition of autism, as the diagnosis was made in different programs. Currently, 10 to 12 autistic children are born every year in Israel (Cohen & Levinson, 1993).

Frameworks for Treatment of Autism

Programs for treatment are based on a two-dimensional approach: age groups and clinical condition. There is a wide spectrum of programs. At one end are special kindergartens and psychiatric day care centers, which combine ambulatory therapy and participation in the activities of the local kindergarten. There are also classes in the regular schools, specially designed for autistic children, as well as day care and employment centers for the adolescents and adults. On the other end of the spectrum are those programs with full hospitalization, day hospitalization, and lifetime care centers.

The framework for the adult autistic population is also varied and includes:

- Sheltered day workshops for those who are able to remain in the family home.
- Hostels, which provide a protected live-in community, where residents work in local sheltered workshops.
- A village (Kfar Ofarim) for 75 young adults who require a more protected environment

but are capable of some self-care management and some occupational training.

- A lifetime care center for those autistic adults who require a total protected environment.

There are possibilities for combining various programs, that is, full hospitalization with attending special schools or rehabilitation centers. This enables the system to tailor the treatment to the individual's needs. The survey data indicate that prior to the development of ambulatory wards and special kindergartens, most autistic patients were institutionalized or hospitalized for life. Presently, the low number (10 children) of autistic children hospitalized in psychiatric wards gives testimony to the efficiency of community intervention and care and reflects the community's preparedness to make an appropriate investment in the care and rehabilitation of this group of vulnerable individuals.

Identification

A network of well-baby clinics provides medical and developmental follow-up for most of the pediatric population of Israel until 3 years of age. When a developmental disorder is detected, the child is referred to one of the 25 existing, widely dispersed child development centers that offer neurologic and psychiatric evaluation and counseling. If need arises, the child is referred to a local psychiatric clinic. If the disorder is in the autistic spectrum but no psychiatric treatment is needed, the child is referred to the appropriate educational institution.

Diagnosis

The *ICD* system provides the official criteria for psychiatric disorders, as dictated by the Ministry of Health. In the light of other diagnostic criteria and the desire to reach a common language, the use of the concept of PDD was introduced as defined in the *DSM-III-R* and later in *DSM-IV*. Social diagnoses are based on functional criteria with emphasis on the nature of the illness as a social disturbance. In autism, the emphasis is on the developmental disturbance of socialization skills relative to that which are expected at a given mental

age. Treatment and rehabilitation programs are linked with the diagnostic assessments.

Treatments

A range of treatments are offered in Israel to autistic children. At the core of all methods, there is a basic educational cognitive treatment that relies heavily on behavioral and developmental approaches, coupled with an openness to existing approaches worldwide. There is a willingness to consider less conventional approaches. In cases of psychiatric treatment, pharmacological treatment is included in accordance with symptomatology. Each institution tends to offer a broad spectrum of therapeutic options to suit the individual patient's needs.

Research

Research plays an important role in enhancing the treatment of autism. Over the past several years, relevant studies concerning the biological and behavioral aspects of this disorder have been conducted in Israel.

A series of studies on the psychobiology of autism, the presence of autoantibodies to basic myelin protein, was demonstrated in some autistic patients (A. Weizman, Weizman, Szekely, Wijsenbeek, & Livni, 1982), and reduced plasma levels of endogenous opioids were detected in autistic children, as compared to normal controls and nonautistic children (R. Weizman et al., 1984, 1988). Despite the responsiveness of obsessive-compulsive disorder symptoms in autistic children to serotonin reuptake inhibitors, no alteration was found in the expression of the platelet serotonin transporter (A. Weizman, Gonen, Tyano, Szekely, & Laron, 1987).

Studies on cyclical birth rate in patients with autistic disorder born in Israel during the period of 1964 to 1986 demonstrated a significant increase for autistic children born in March and August (Barak, Ring, Sulkes, Gabbay, & Elizur, 1995). The studies found an annual periodicity of 17.6 years, 3.2 years, and 4.1 years.

Finally, Israel was a site for the international collaborative research project on the criteria for *DSM-IV*. Through this collaboration, investigators in Israel are able to utilize the current nosology with a high level of expertise (Volkmar et al., 1994).

ITALY

Gabriel Levi and Paola Bernabei

Between 1905 and 1910, De Sanctis described 22 cases of children ages 4 to 10 years who exhibited features that were different from those exhibited by children with mental retardation. De Sanctis stressed that these children's behavioral disorders and emotional and cognitive problems were linked to an early psychotic disturbance.

One of De Sanctis's students, Maria Montessori, became interested (between 1899 and 1907) in the educational problems of mentally retarded children after she graduated from medical school; she developed her theories and educational methods with the aim to promote a great project on mental health for all children from 2 to 6 years of age. The diffusion of kindergartens in which her methods were applied made it easier to identify atypical children.

At the end of the 1940s and during the 1950s, an interesting debate on Kanner's and especially on Asperger's work took place among Italian clinicians. There was broad agreement on childhood psychosis as a nosographic entity that could be diagnosed before 4 years of age. Many clinicians thought that a psychotic breakdown (with autism, delusions, and hallucinations as cardinal signs) marked the beginning of autistic disorder while some maintained that the disorder depended on a psychotic development.

In the late 1960s, Professor G. Bollea pointed out that, on the basis of a peculiar vulnerability occurring during the first year of life, some children could develop a cognitive disturbance and others a psychotic disturbance, depending on the type of perceptual integration and affective interactions.

Levi (1973) studied 30 autistic children, ages 3 to 7 at diagnosis, and with a 4-year follow-up. He found that there are different degrees of severity in the autistic disorder and that autistic children develop cognitive and emotional skills according to a sequence of recognizable evolutionary phases. The degree of severity and the type of prognosis is correlated with the interval that separates the atypical phases, with each phase of the psychotic development characterized by learning strategies and sense of identity that are in some ways coherent.

In the 1980s, two viewpoints emerged in Italy. The majority of Italian neuropsychiatrists, following Tustin's and Meltzer's theories, considered that childhood psychoses were linked to an emotional catastrophe occurring during the first year of life and that the treatment of choice, even for low-functioning cases, was psychoanalytic psychotherapy (often for both mother and child). A minority position related the autistic disorder to an atypical development of communicative and symbolic skills and to a noninteractive development of verbal comprehension (Levi, Bernabei, Fabrizi, & Zollinger, 1984).

During the past few years, Italian researchers have been involved in the worldwide debates on *ICD* and *DSM* that have brought about interesting discussions on subtypes and on diagnostic criteria.

Treatment Approaches

Until 1977, autistic children attended special schools and special institutions, as any other handicapped child in Italy. The main therapeutic models were based on special pedagogy (strongly affected by Montessori's methods) and on psychoanalytic psychotherapy.

Legislation introduced in 1977 required that all handicapped children attend normal schools and classes. Autistic children today are supposed to be in classrooms with no more than 15 children, instead of the standard 25. A remedial teacher is provided for at least 2 hours a day; this teacher tries to link the autistic child's work to other children's work to improve learning and socialization potentialities. Concurrent with this integration, the idea spread that behavioral conditioning techniques may provide some therapeutic success, but it is felt that they tend to implement imitative, echopraxic, and echolalic behavior and prevent identification processes.

In spite of much improvisation and enthusiasm not always supported by practical technique, the wide diffusion of kindergartens and the integration of handicapped children have brought advantages. More than a half of the autistic children are now recognized as atypical between 2.6 and 3 years of age, before they enter kindergarten, and nearly all autistic children start a treatment program between 5.6 and 6 years of age, before they enter elementary school. By that age, most high-functioning autistic children are known to schools and community centers. Autistic children start elementary school 1 or 2 years later to allow a greater development of their communicative and symbolic skills.

There is a lively discussion on treatment strategies for low-functioning children and a tendency toward a drastic reduction of psychoanalytical psychotherapies. The following criteria prevail in choosing the type and time of intervention: (1) correlation among mental age, symbolic and communicative development, and chronological age; (2) development of verbal comprehension; and (3) cognitive skills and interaction and identification mechanisms in the peer group (Levi, 1993). Early treatment in small groups is gaining in acceptance, and great emphasis is put on the integration of nonverbal and verbal communication. The central roles of communication and symbolization dysfunctions in the autistic disorder make interactions during play and in imitation and identification processes in small groups important. Behaviorally based teaching methods (e.g., TEACCH) are frequently used and are in many cases integrated with active pedagogical methodologies such as Montessori's, methods based on group work, and psychodynamic models that do not use verbal interpretation but focus on the verbalization of affects and the awareness of the self.

Diagnosis

Autism is diagnosed by child neuropsychiatrists who usually see the child and the parents; a clinical psychologist and a therapist specialized in communication disorders also see the child. Children are in most cases referred by schools or pediatricians, but often parents come to the service on their own. Sometimes, usually in private practice, diagnoses are made by psychotherapists. In Italy, there are nearly 150 community centers and about 40 child neuropsychiatry units in hospitals and universities. There are approximately 900 to 1,000 neuropsychiatrists in community centers (the ratio being between 1:5,000 and 1:12,000 children, depending on the area). There are more than 4,000 clinical psychologists and therapists working in teams with child neuropsychiatrists and more than 50,000 remedial teachers in state schools.

Specialized centers for autistic children are available only at universities and about 20 community centers. In the other centers, great attention is nevertheless paid to the problem of autism.

The 1977 law for the integration of handicapped children has allowed an earlier diagnosis and treatment for autistic children. Between 1975 and 1988, the prevalence of autism was, however, grossly overestimated because children with mental retardation and emotional disorders were frequently diagnosed as autistic, as were children with behavioral disorders and environmental isolation. Increased attention to standard diagnostic criteria (ICD and DSM) has contributed to progressive refinement of diagnostic assessment, and recent epidemiological research has shown that the prevalence of autism in Italy tallies with international data.

Communication disorders and specific language disorders tend to be referred early in Italy because of particular sensitivity in the general population. This attitude helps identify a group of children in the age range of 18 to 30 months with features of language disorder, PDD, and mild or moderate mental retardation.

Parents' Association

A parents' association for autistic children was created in Italy as a reaction against the dominant psychoanalytical approach to autism. The association supports the parents of autistic children through a self-help strategy and educational plans based on short- and medium-term goals. Parent associations for different kinds of handicaps also exist, and they are usually prepared to recognize and treat the possible comorbidity with autism in their centers.

Laws that regulate the assistance provided to autistic children and adults are the same as for other kinds of handicaps. Individuals with autism may get a monthly allowance, and their integration into working settings is promoted by law. Legislation passed in 1992 formalized the relationships between schools and community centers, stressed the right to education for handicapped people, and defined the role of remedial teachers within this process. In addition, one parent is entitled to stay at home during the first 3 years of life of the handicapped child, without losing his or her job, and can have 3 paid days off a month.

Conclusion

From the point of view of services, in Italy, autistic children generally receive an early diagnosis and an early start on treatment. The policy of promoting integration of all handicapped children permits autistic children to have an intensive and prolonged educational treatment that is focused on social skills. Such an approach is giving interesting results with low- and medium-functioning autistic children. During the past 10 years, there has been an excessive investment in individual psychotherapies. At the moment, group therapy based on interactions with peers, intentional exchanges, and mutual identifications is also available.

From a diagnostic point of view, the use of *DSM* criteria is progressively gaining acceptance. There is a strong trend to add to a *DSM* diagnosis a cognitive and neuropsychological evaluation and an emotional assessment. Clinical groups that evaluate and treat very young children tend to look for possible symbolization and communication disorder (between 8 and 20 months) from which an autistic or other disorder might develop.

From the research point of view, recent debates have focused on three problems:

1. Autism is a multiphase disorder, with developmental phases that may be reconstructed and may be anticipated; this model emphasizes the importance of understanding natural history.
2. Autistic children with communication problems (preverbal, extraverbal, or an integration of nonverbal and verbal) and supposed left hemisphere involvement should be distinguished from autistic children who exhibit early dyspractic problems and supposed right hemisphere involvement (Bernabei, Levi, Mazzoncini, & Penge, 1994); treatment of the dyspractic core may lessen the severity of the autistic component.
3. Low- and high-functioning autistic children should be diagnostically separated; it is debated whether among low-functioning children it is possible to distinguish children with an early cognitive impairment from children who, because of mental retardation, are more vulnerable to an autistic disorder.

JAPAN

Yoshihiko Hoshino and Shin-chi Niwa

Autism is one of the major research objectives in child psychiatry in Japan and, in fact, it is no exaggeration to state that there is no child psychiatrist in Japan who is not interested in autism. Among the studies of this clinical entity, the subjects of particular concern include the early signs in infancy and early childhood, developmental regression, psychopathology, problems of social adaptation among youths, biological research, and investigation of pharmacological treatments.

Early Symptoms

Studies on the early symptoms of autism are considered important to discover children with this clinical entity and initiate appropriate therapy at an early stage. Yamazaki (1992) conducted a retrospective study of the early symptoms of autism by analyzing home videos that had been recorded by family members. They reported that in contrast to normal children or those with other types of developmental disorders, autistic children more frequently exhibit early symptoms such as "a lack of response when called by their names," "absence of interest in a game of peek-a-boo," "uncooperative response when an adult approaches to pick him up," "a lack of eye-to-eye contact," "a loss of meaningful taste expressions that were acquired by the age of 1 to 2 years," and "sudden outbursts of laughter or crying without any obvious reasons." Shirataki, Taira, and Kashiwagi (1984) employed the strange situation procedure (SSP) that was designed by Ainsworth, Blehar, Waters, & Wall (1978) and evaluated the mother-child bonding pattern involving children around the age of 2 years with a high risk for infantile autism. They found that, in contrast to the control group, those children with a high risk for infantile autism lack emotional expression at scenes of separation from their mothers or strangers and subsequent encounters with them. Specifically, they stated, "they failed to smile when they meet their mothers after a brief separation," "they frequently approach strangers," and "they were indifferent to the presence of their mothers."

Hoshino et al. (1982) also investigated early symptoms of autistic children up to 2 years and recognized that apart from normal or mentally retarded children, they frequently exhibited behavior such as "refusal to make eye contact," "absence of pointing behavior," "a lack of body imitation behavior," "refusal to be held by their parents," "indifference to their parent's presence," "no fear of strangers," "short and irregular sleeping times," "insensitive to being left alone," "a limited smiling response," and "a loss of the spoken words that have already been acquired."

Studies on the early symptoms of autism are useful in the discovery and treatment of young children as well as in delineating pathophysiology.

Setback Course and Developmental Regression

Studies have been actively conducted in Japan on setback courses and developmental regression associated with autism from the 1970s to the present. The pioneering activities are represented by Ishii (1987), who reported that 25% to 30% of autistic children undergo a "setback course" by the age of 2 years, in which language that they have already acquired becomes extinct. These children, in comparison with other autistic infants, suffer from lower developmental or intelligence levels and their long-term prognosis is rather poor. Later, Kobayashi (1993b) and Hoshino et al. (1987) reported similar research results. Specifically, they recognized that autism with a setback course is frequently associated with the development of epilepsy as well as perinatal abnormalities, suggesting a strong possibil-

ity that an organic brain disorder is implicated. Kurita (1985), on the other hand, compared the *percentage development* of setback courses among 164 autistic children, 114 with other pervasive developmental disorders (OPDDs), 16 with disintegrative psychoses, and 62 with mental retardation without association of PDD. They reported that the occurrence of a setback course is much higher in autism (24.4%) in comparison with mental retardation (1.6%), not significantly different from OPDD (21.7%) but significantly lower than disintegrative psychoses (100%). In view of these results, Kurita concluded that the setback course is not specific to autism but is commonly recognized in disintegrative psychoses and OPDDs.

Psychopathology

It is difficult to conduct a detailed psychopathological study on autism with individuals who have a low language development level. In Japan, however, several psychopathological studies have been conducted on autistic children with high intellectual levels. Sugiyama (1994) pointed out that some autistic children or youths suddenly remember an event that occurred in the past (sometimes these events occurred several years ago) and consider them as if they had taken place only recently. These investigators assigned a term, "time slip phenomenon," to this psychopathological event. According to them, the phenomenon represents a disorder of the memory function associated with autism. The so-called delayed echolalia and sudden panic attack are also most likely caused by this phenomenon. Kobayashi (1993a) cited the "phenomenon of sensory distortion" for sensory abnormalities that are unique to autism. These abnormalities include a "distorted visual perception phenomenon," by which the patient gazes at or examines an object from an oblique angle as if he or she had never seen it before; a "distorted auditory perception phenomenon," by which the patient expresses extreme pain when exposed to a certain voice or sound or exhibits sensitivity when he or she becomes the topic of conversation; and a "distorted situational phenomenon," an exaggerated confusion at a situation that leads to a pathological state suggestive of a delusion of persecution. Kobayashi states that these perception-distorting phenomena suggest the mode of perception by autistic children, where they perceive the environment differently from what had been discerned earlier.

Nagai (1983) and Hoshino, Komatsu, and Kumashiro (1992) investigated the psychopathology of autistic children by observing their patterns of food preference or abnormal eating behavior. In their surveys, the following abnormal behavior patterns were recognized: "persistence on certain food," "insistence on sniffing food before eating," "refusing drinks except for a selected few types of beverages," "disregarding the appearance of food (contrary to the expected behavior of normal children)," "liberal use of certain condiments," and "refusal to eat food unless it is flavored in a certain manner." These behavior patterns suggest the obsessive desire for the maintenance of sameness, as well as perceptual immaturity, by which the child relies more heavily on the proximal perceptions (e.g., gustatory and olfactory perceptions), rather than distal perception (e.g., visual and auditory perceptions).

Problems of Social Adaptation during Early Adulthood

It has been noted in Japan that autistic individuals who have reached adolescence and early adulthood experience various psychiatric problems and exhibit social maladaptation. These problems occur more frequently among highly intelligent autistic individuals who attend regular elementary, middle, and high schools. They constitute a serious obstacle to their social adaptation.

Kamio et al. (1993) noted conditions such as obsessive-compulsive disorder, mood disorder, conversion disorder, Tourette's disorder, and schizophrenia-like reactions in autistic individuals who had reached early adulthood. Yokota, Sakaguchi, & Nagai (1989) report that these individuals in adolescence or early adulthood exhibit exaggerated aggressive or self-mutilative behavior when their obsessive-compulsive acts are restrained. Kusunoki (1988) and Hoshino and Kumashilo (1989) also state that autistic individuals with high intellectual capacities

are unable to adapt to the school environment or interpersonal relations and often develop neurosis-like reactions during adolescence or early adulthood.

Kobayashi, Oshima, and Kaneko (1992) describe a female autistic patient who developed anorexia nervosa at 23 years of age. They noted a negative emotion in this patient toward her mother, which suggested the presence of a personality disorder or delusional behavior. Yashima, Hoshino, and Murata (1991) also reports on an autistic child who became obsessed with the concept of death following the sudden demise of a family member and subsequently suffered from a demented or panic state.

Biological Studies

Biological studies of autism are scarce in Japan because of a high degree of consideration of ethical problems. However, a few neuroendocrinological studies and those using Magnetoencephalography (MEG) have recently been published.

The early studies in this area are represented by Hoshino, Kaneko, Kumashiro, et al. (1987), who determined circadian rhythms in the salivary cortisol contents and the response to the dexamethasone suppression test in high- and low-functioning groups of autistic individuals, those with mental retardation, and normal controls, to investigate their hypothalamo-hypophyseal-adrenocortical function. They found that those in the low-functioning autistic group exhibited abnormal circadian rhythms in the salivary cortisol level and aberrations in the response to the dexamethasone suppression test. In contrast, the high-functioning autistic group and the group with mental retardation showed normal circadian rhythms in the salivary cortisol levels and reacted normally to the dexamethasone suppression test. These findings suggest the presence of abnormalities in the hypothalamo-hypophyseal-adrenocortical functions in the low-functioning autistic individuals.

Kawasaki et al. (1994) followed up 158 autistic children to the age of 15 years and investigated their electroencephalographic abnormalities. They detected "paroxysm at F" (paroxysm at the frontal lobe) in 75 patients, which coincided with the development of epileptic seizures. However, they added that some exhibited this "paroxysm at F" without epileptic complications. In addition, Kawasaki and his colleagues conducted a magnetoencephalographic study on four autistic patients and found that in all subjects, the focus of the "paroxysm at F" was either at the cingulate gyrus or at the superior frontal gyrus. According to these investigators, these findings indicate that autistic lesions are located in the frontal area, especially the fronto-limbic system.

Pharmacology

In Japan, as in the United States, major tranquilizers such as haloperidol and pimozide are used as the first choice in the treatment of autism. When complicated by epilepsy, diphenylhydantoin, carbamazepine, and sodium valproate are also employed.

Recently, the so-called coenzyme therapy of autism has been attempted, which produced a marked efficacy in certain cases in Japan. Naruse, Hayashi, Takesada, Nakane, & Yamazaki (1989) first analyzed the in vivo metabolic turnover using an aromatic amine that had been labeled with a stable isotope (deuterium,[13]C). They recognized reductions in cerebral catecholamine and serotonin metabolism in some of the autistic children. Based on this finding, they administered R-tetrahydrodiopterin, a coenzyme for three dehydrogenases of phenylalanine, tyrosine, and tryptophan and closely related to cerebral catecholamine and serotonin synthesis, and compared the result in a double-blind study using a placebo. They proved a significant efficacy for this agent in the treatment of autism, especially in those under the age of 5 years. In a subsequent follow-up employing a double-blind multicenter study, however, the result was not favorable. The reason for this therapeutic failure is unknown, but the inadequacy of the survey table for abnormal behavior of children used to rate the symptoms in assessing autistic symptoms and subtle changes in language functions and variability in the diagnostic concept of autism in each facility (thus resulting in a lack of homogeneity in the patient group) may explain the discrepancy. We hope that another double-blind test will be conducted in the future that takes these factors into consideration.

Conclusion

Studies on autism have been conducted from various angles in Japan. Researchers are actively engaged in psychopathological and phenomenological studies in this country, but biological research and investigations on the chemotherapy for the disease are still scarce. It is hoped that more energetic research activities will also be directed toward this end.

KOREA

Soo Churl Cho

In Korea, the diagnostic concept for autism was introduced in 1979, when Dr. Michael Hong returned to Korea from the United States, where he completed his training and was on the faculty of a leading medical school. In Korea, he established an academic clinical and training program for children with psychiatric disorders. In 1981, the first care unit for autism was founded at Seoul National University Hospital. Previously, autistic children were diagnosed by social workers or teachers in special schools; many children were classified as "emotionally disturbed," or "mentally retarded."

History of the Care of Individuals with Autism and Related Disorders

In the 1970s, there were no special educational programs for autistic children and other PDDs. Autism and related developmental disorders were often undiagnosed. The autistic children were often admitted to a treatment center for mentally retarded children, and their condition was considered to be a variant of mental retardation. In the 1980s, five to six centers for autistic children were founded, and the number of treatment centers for autism started to increase in that decade. In the 1990s, a primary and junior high school for special education of autistic children was built in Kyounggi Province around Seoul City. More schools for autistic children will be built on more sites in Korea. For kindergarten-age children, an integrative education program (education of autistic children with normal children at the same time) has become popular since the 1990s.

Current Status of Treatment Services

There are not accurate data on treatment centers in Korea. We assume that about 1,000 treatment centers for autistic children and other PDDs may exist. Three universities have treatment service programs for autism, and these programs are considered to be fairly intensive. There are about as many private treatment centers all over the country. About 60% to 70% of these centers are in or near Seoul City. The other centers are located in rural areas. Although the number of autistic children who are cared for by these centers differs, the average capacity is about 10 autistic children. Thus, nationwide, about 10,000 autistic and similar children receive special treatment. One group home, founded by parents of autistic children, is located near Seoul City.

Treatment Program Day Care Center of Seoul National University Hospital

The Seoul National University Hospital is Korea's leading academic center for child and adolescent psychiatry. In the treatment program for autistic children, there are two classes; each serves about six to eight children with autism and a wide range of developmental disorders, including Rett's disorder, childhood disintegrative disorder, and reactive attachment disorder. They range in age from 24 to 72 months. The ratio of staff to patients remains at 1:2 to 1:3. The program provides 3 hours of service daily.

The program is headed by a medical director from the faculty of the Division of Child Psychiatry, who has overall medical responsibility for all patients in the day care center. The director develops and administers the educational treatment program, teaching, and research, and is responsible for the daily functioning of the day care center, as well as long-term planning and treatment.

A fellow in training in child psychiatry is the primary physician for up to three children and acts as team leader for these patients. The fellow writes all orders for his or her patients, including admission and discharge orders.

Special educators and nurses who have had special training in the management of autistic children and other PDDs are directly involved in the treatment of the children and the education and guidance of parents. They meet weekly with the medical director or child psychiatry fellow for supervision.

Before being admitted to the day care center, the children receive a thorough diagnostic assessment as prescribed by the child psychiatrists. The diagnosis system used is *DSM-IV* or *ICD-10*. After admission, the special educator or the nurse specialist who is responsible for the child administers Krug's ABC, Schopler's CARS, or the Psychoeducational Profile (PEP) to evaluate the child. Psychologists evaluate intelligence, using WISC-R, WPPSI, and Peabody Picture Vocabulary Test (PPVT). The Social Maturation Scale (SMS) is also administered to assess social functioning.

Many types of individualized programs are used; most are based on a developmental approach. The programs provide training in behavior control and in various skills, including communication, social, motor, and academic skill. Various nonaversive behavioral techniques are also frequently used; positive or negative reinforcement, stimulus control, and shaping are most commonly applied. Sometimes, low doses of major tranquilizers (mainly haloperidol) are prescribed when behavioral problems of the children are so severe that they cannot be controlled effectively with behavioral methods.

A parent education program aims at instructing parents, both intellectually and behaviorally, and providing them with specific training for postdischarge management. Child psychiatrists, individual therapists, social workers, and nurses are involved in this program, which provides education in normal development as well as language, social, motor, self-care, and cognitive development. Parents are helped to understand the concept of autistic disorder and related PDDs, the principles of behavior modification, and how to interact with a problem child.

Diagnostic Issues

Usually, child psychiatrists are responsible for making diagnoses. Twenty-three universities from all over the country have child psychiatrists, and about 120 to 130 child psychiatrists are practicing in local clinics. When children suspected of having autism or other PDDs are brought to the treatment centers, they are referred to these child psychiatrists for a specific diagnosis.

Specific National Issues

Since 2000, the Korean government (the Ministry of Health and Welfare) has included autistic and other PDDs in the law for welfare of the disabled. Many autistic children can receive diverse benefits from this law, especially education service. One national treatment center for autistic children was founded at the National Institute of Mental Health. About 40 to 50 autistic children are treated at this treatment center.

National Parent Society

In Korea, the National Parent Society has about 600 families as members. The main purposes of this society are (1) helping each other emotionally, (2) educating the parent members, (3) exchanging information, (d) promoting early detection and treatment, and (4) raising research funds.

LATIN AMERICA

Miguel Cherro Aguerre and Natalia Trenchi

This discussion is based on information provided by institutions in Latin America and in the region, computer search of the literature, and our personal experience in the field.

Background and History of the Concept

N. Mills Costa (1989) from Brazil offers a good synthesis about autism in Latin America. She explicates three important aspects of the history and current situation:

1. The decisive influence of the North American and European ideas on Latin American concepts about autism.
2. The relatively recent consideration of the entity in Latin America, together with a lack of institutional resources.
3. The general lack of specific legislation that would permit fully adequate care of autistic individuals.

The diagnostic concept of autism was introduced to Uruguay by Prof. Luis E. Prego Silva in 1951 when he returned from a psychiatric fellowship at the Harriet Lane Clinic of Johns Hopkins Medical School in Baltimore, Maryland. A multidisciplinary team was created in the Child Psychiatric Clinic of the Dr. Pedro Visca Hospital with the purpose of doing research and treating autistic children on an outpatient basis. Since then, other public and private groups have worked in the field. In 1989, a parents' association was created (Asociación Uruguaya de Padres de Personas con Autismo Infantil or [AUPPAI]), which has worked hard and effectively for autistic individuals.

In Uruguay, there are health systems with programs and projects launched by the Department of Public Health as well as laws that protect the handicapped. However, the coverage in both cases is partial and insufficient and should be restructured in order to care adequately for the complex needs of autistic individuals. Similarly, the intentions for institutional resources are good, but the resources are not really suitable. It is our impression that the situation in the rest of Latin America is not very different from that in Uruguay.

Assessment

An older tendency of talking about autism in a general fashion is now being abandoned. Instead, diagnosis within Latin America is mainly based on the *DSM* or *ICD* criteria. In their discussion of *DSM* criteria for autism, Tallis and Soprano (1991) of Argentina wonder about the value of not including autism in the ambiguous field of psychoses, but among the PDDs. Is the latter a less ambiguous field? In their opinion, this approach implies that in autism there is a deficit of cognitive competence and that autism is related to some kind of biological dysfunction. These ideas exclude the concept that autism can be found in a biologically intact organism.

We believe that pediatricians and teachers and the multidisciplinary team working in the mental health services should be properly trained to recognize any feature suggesting autism at an early stage. A child psychiatrist should provide the formal diagnostic assessment.

Etiology and Psychopathology

Prego Silva (1980), influenced in his work by Winnicott, distinguishes between "psychosis" and "the psychotic." He conceptualizes "the psychotic" as a way of reacting when looking for solutions and when faced by the consequences of very difficult environmental conditions. Mendilaharsu and de Mendilaharsu (1987), inspired by some of the ideas of Bion, hypothesize an "amalgamatic nucleus" that constitutes the destructive part of the personality. This nucleus, generally disorganizing and destructive, is related to the ego in various ways. The massive introjection of the "amalgamatic nucleus" stops the normal construction of the psychological system. As long as the malignant introjections remain "encapsulated," they permit the development of the mental apparatus, until the destructive element invades and disorganizes it.

In another psychoanalytic conception, Garbarino (1990) maintains that the psychological apparatus as conceived by S. Freud accounts for mental disorders in subjects that retain their psychological coherence as individuals; this model of the mind, he contends, is not always useful to understand some other types of patients. According to Freud, he contends, an individual is born with an id, and the ego appears after a "new psychological action" configures it. Freud's id is delimited so that it can get into the psychological apparatus. For Garbarino, an individual is born with an unlimited id, which is perceived by the newly born and favored by the narcissistic imbalance provoked by birth. He calls this original narcissism, narcissism of the Being (Ser), which is not endowed with an individual's own image but with a sense of the universe in an unlimited centrifugal movement. That internal perception of the unlimited id originates in an instance called Being. The Being constitutes a presentiment of presence, for at birth there is not yet an ego capable of perceiving feelings. The inner perception of sensations of the id would originate in this dark presentiment of presence before the psychological apparatus is formed. In autism, where the interaction of the dyad mother-child fails, the first interhuman identification cannot be made. Then the incipient psychological ego relates more to the cosmic order than to the interhuman order.

In Argentina, Bleger (1972), in an article written shortly before his death, says that in autism there is a lack of discrimination between the outer and the inner worlds, between the ego and the objects. He also says that in the autistic individual there is not a loss of the sense of reality, but a construction of his or her own sense of reality. As a whole, he calls the phenomenon "syncretism," which might seem confusing for the observer but not for the patient. He thinks that autism has a syncretic structure.

Dio Bleichmar (1987) recognizes that we have not arrived at the ultimate foundation of the genesis of the dysfunction that leads to the psychotic process in childhood. However, she assigns prime relevance to the intersubjective failure in the distortion or absence of psychological representations of the child's own body, the mother's body as a separate being, and reality. The symbolic function that permits the location of self and the other is disturbed in such a way that the child seems submerged in a world of sensorial and physical stimuli without categorization.

Oelsner (1989), influenced by the concepts of Winnicott, Bion, and Tustin, states that the psychological birth implies the notion of separation, that is, being "one" separated from the "mother," in the Winnicottian sense; that is, the baby experiences the loss of the object that ensured the illusion of omnipotence, of being one that had everything. Normally, the mother's mind serves as a substitute uterine matrix and contains the baby, allowing the baby to maintain the idea of being one until it is mature enough to tolerate the separation and to then accept that they are two persons. If this uterine relationship is prematurely interrupted, either for inner or outer causes, the continuity of the being is threatened; in response, the ego that is in the process of blossoming might capitulate and develop a protection against itself that becomes the autistic capsule. The essential problem is that the child would come to separation at a stage still dominated by its self-generated sensuality. The premature and abrupt disillusionment hinders the development of transitional activities and the creation of transitional objects as the child's first, nonego possessions. The hard reality, the hard nonego compared to the pleasant and soft sensuality, opens a gap in the primitive bodily ego and creates unthinkable anxieties. Its extreme vulnerability has forced the child to wrap itself into a hard nonego formed by a capsular cover or a fusion and interpenetration with soft objects. In both cases, the result is inaccessibility to the outside world, the interruption of the psychological development, and alienation.

Jarast (1990), following the ideas of Bick and Anzieu, contrasts the ego skin with the second muscular skin. Normally, the first skin, through the bond with the mother, has a constraining and cohesive function that allows the baby to acquire a notion of its inner self and approach the separation of self and object, each contained in its own skin. However, if the constraining motherly functions are not properly accomplished, there is a permanent pathologic identification that creates a confusion of identity. States of nonintegration persist, with a consequent desperate search by the baby for an object (light, voice, smell) that maintains a unifying attention on the parts of his or her body. The inadequate performance of the first skin drives the baby to form a second, muscular skin that replaces the dependency on the constraining object by a pseudodependency.

Tallis and Soprano (1991) divide the etiologic theories of autism into major subtypes. They consider two different types of primary pathways into autism: problems of the psychological surroundings of the child (genetic or environmental factors) and organic problems specifically linked with genetic problems. Another major pathway includes the group of psychological and psychophysiological dysfunctions that create cognitive deficits affecting both language and symbolic abilities. These cognitive dysfunctions result in a limited capacity to establish relations between new and previously experienced stimuli and a weak capacity to establish relations between the basic mechanisms of communication and verbal language. The cognitive deficits are hypothesized to result from a biological dysfunction of the central nervous system, from a different organization of the brain, and/or clear organic disorders related to different pathologies and heterogeneous groups of biological disorders. These biological factors are also influenced by psychosocial factors.

In Perú, Gomberoff, Noemi, and de Gomberoff (1991) make use of Tustin's conceptualizations of the autistic object. They differentiate the autistic object from other objects, such as the auto-sensorial, the transitional, and the fetishistic, and they use the concept of autistic object to explain resistances as well as transference and countertransference reactions that are found in some kinds of patients. The autosensorial stage is a very early stage of normal human development in which the baby perceives objects as sensation objects. For example, the nipple-breast of the mother, like the pacifier, is an autosensorial object joined to the tongue-mouth of the baby. The origin of the autistic object is found in the substitution of the loss of a part of the feeding mother that is felt as a loss of a part of the child's own body and that produces in the child a sense of desolate anguish. The autistic object produces a massive mental restriction with lack of motivation and basic confidence. Like a crust, the autistic object blocks the intolerable injury provoked by the physical separation from the mother that is experienced as a violent tear. That same crust or scar obstructs the healing relationship between parent and child. The autistic object helps the child avoid the pain produced by the consciousness of the nonego, felt as a tear of the self; it is used as a permanent replacement instead of as a transitory substitute for the parental functions. The transitional object, on the other hand, is used to regulate and handle the tension produced by the awareness of normal separation. The fetishistic object, as pathological as the autistic one, is experienced as an external object by the child, foreign to the self; it represents or substitutes for the absent mother or part of her. This type of object allows the child to satisfy sexual impulses that are prohibited with the real mother.

In Brazil, Pinto (1982) uses neuroscience and embryological research to revive Kanner's old hypothesis about the high intellectual level of autistic parents. He thinks that the autistic syndrome may be present in children with a brain not only mature but also ready for socialization that did not receive adequate stimulation during intrauterine life. In this hypothesis, the child develops behaviors similar to those of animals that do not establish imprinting during a critical period. Pinto, citing the work of Lorenz, suggests that the disorder arises from a situation as if the child developed imprinting on his or her own hands (mannerisms, rhythmic games, a search for sameness).

In Mexico, Marcin (1991) suggests that autism is a primary cognitive disorder that involves the perceptual processes and communication systems. He lists findings that originate in the neuroscience and points out that it is not possible to draw definite conclusions yet. The goal of assessment is to take into account the multiple therapeutic strategies required by each child, with his or her own special rhythm and need for therapeutic timing. Also in Mexico, Guisa Cruz (1991) have studied a sample of 20 subjects defined as autistic according to the *DSM-III-R* criteria. They verified alterations in brain-evoked potentials and brain stem conduction. They also found EEG evidence for possible structural damage, as well as signs of epileptic activity.

In Colombia, Villareal and Gaviria (1987) analyzed the characteristics of the learning process in autistic children that accompany their idiosyncratic way of interacting with the environment. They describe the processes of stimulus control and motivation, paying special attention to the factors that should be taken into account to achieve efficiency in treatment strategies. Villareal and Gaviria consider learning as a process of stimulus control that can be affected by different factors, including:

1. *Overselectivity of stimuli; that is, autistic individuals respond to one feature or component of the stimulus array while ignoring the others.* This leads to adaptive disadvantage since the majority of environmental stimuli have a complex configuration. Learning is interfered with because the autistic child does not respond functionally to the different signals or because his or her behavior remains under the control of irrelevant incidental stimuli.

2. *Perseveration of inaccurate response strategies, in which the child repeatedly emits a response or responds repeatedly to a determined stimulus, independently of the reinforcement.* Autistic children choose a determined response instead of exploring other possibilities. This is presumed to lead to a limited behavioral repertoire and constitutes an important handicap for learning and socialization.

3. *Abnormalities of motivation basic for learning.* The motivational structure of autistic individuals is characterized by an orientation to one kind of behavior, self-stimulating, with a sequence that alternates between different types of behavior in the same behavioral line with periods of rest without any activity. The reinforcement of the self-stimulating behaviors reduces the power of diverse potential sources of reinforcement.

Treatment

In Latin America, there has been a gradual transition from uni- to multidisciplinary types of treatment. Together with the spread of multidisciplinary approaches and the organization of teams, a need for institutional frameworks has emerged at both public and private levels.

The organization of teams proved to be effective because it allows for sharing knowledge and coordinating efforts. However, the team approach has also brought difficulties, such as contradictions and confrontations among team members. These can be resolved as long as a true team spirit, with real respect for each of the disciplines and orientations, can be created.

There are publications that exemplify different types of approaches: psychoanalytic, behavioral, cognitive-behavioral, linguistic, psychomotor, musical therapy, and so on. In Uruguay, the psychoanalytical approach has been the most widely accepted, so we consider it relevant to examine a synthesis offered by Marcin (1991) from Mexico. Marcin offers a view of psychotherapy and associated controversies. He affirms the importance of carefully evaluating the child's situation holistically; psychotherapy is most beneficial for those patients with a high level of functioning, whose cognitive and verbal capacities are adequate for understanding and expressing thoughts and emotions. In psychotherapy, a very special bond is created, and there is work that requires symbolic capacities, work with fantasy, and with the past; in a sense, psychotherapy is a cryptic game that represents the bonds between the self and its objects. In the treatment of an autistic child, there are two stages. The first aims at establishing a significant relationship focused on the organization of the presence of an object that talks, listens, and helps differentiate the ego from the nonego. The therapist encloses and holds. The therapist's thoughts mediate between the child and the outside world providing protection and techniques for experiencing security that the child can incorporate through routine. These techniques are support and withdrawal mechanisms that help the child deal with his or her impulses and help set the child free from aberrant behaviors. In the second stage, after the concrete and archaic modes of functioning have been established, the therapist works with the incipient identification processes, the omnipotent primitive mechanisms, the analysis of unusual stages in the formation of symbols, the fear of physical disintegration, unifying relationships, the progressive creation of the imaginary world, and the emergence of the self as a unique entity that is ideally integrated for the establishment of genuine relationships. In short, the later stages are an attempt to find the path that leads to the psychological development.

Marcin insists on the relevance of an accurate evaluation before initiating treatment. He also mentions that it is necessary to recognize other therapeutic options with autistic individuals. With a view that we share, he describes the aims of the work carried out at the Mexican Clinic of Autism (CLIMA); he points out that the connotation of the acronym in Spanish—it means climate—suggests an environmental purpose of the institution. The therapeutic models they use are related to the severity of each case. They involve structured therapies, sensory integration, the "forced embrace" therapy and psychotherapy, individual and family. He highlights that therapists must be open to all contributions that prove effective for the different levels and types of autism. The treatment is not chosen by theoretical favoritism but by thoughtful analysis of the pathology of the child, the needs of the family, and a deep respect for individuality.

Also in Mexico, de Plá (1991) considers the autistic individual as a willing being; she argues for the role of the unconscious dimension. Nonetheless, she postulates a multidisciplinary approach and describes the general conditions under which the personalized teaching of an autistic child should be carried out. She also points out that the personalization of the bond, the openness to learning and to change, implies conflict—psychological pain that the child, his or her parents, and those who care for him or her must be ready to assume.

In Argentina, Wernicke (1991) proposes a holistic therapeutic approach aimed at solving diverse psychopathologic conditions including autism. It consists of a multimodal approach that includes neurologic and pharmacologic treatments, orientation to parents, rehabilitation, and the technique after which the approach has been named, the "forced" or "fastening embrace." This technique uses the embrace of the mother in a process with several steps: confrontation, rejection, and reconciliation. Through this process, there is an intention of a "flooding of security."

In Chile, Donovan and Olivari (1989) propose a treatment model in which professional procedures are minimized and the work is contextualized in the family and the immediate social world of the child. Parents and significant others are integrated in the therapy. The model encourages that the changes in the interaction introduced by the treatment be kept in the family world through the "live" learning of the parents, using a unidirectional mirror. The therapy aims at helping the child establish meaning in acts and things. It first encourages the parents to discover abilities in the child, so they would not become hopeless from the very beginning. At the proper moment, a "labeling procedure" is started, so that the parents' expectations meet the real possibilities of the child.

In Ecuador, a directory has been published (FEPAPDEM, 1992–1993) that contains a list of institutions that take care of mentally handicapped persons. The list mentions 78 institutions spread throughout the country; five include autism as a condition treated.

It is generally recognized in Latin America that the treatment should respond to both the child and his or her environment. Parents and teachers should be trained properly. In Panama, Audero (1980) proposes a model of workshop-seminar to train personnel that will work with parents and teachers. It is based on the behavioral conceptualization of autism and mainly uses the operant conditioning paradigm.

In Colombia, Villareal and Gaviria (1987) propose an approach to treatment based on their analysis of the learning process of autistic children. From their concept of problems in stimulus control and overselectivity of stimuli, they advise a careful use of support procedures when guiding the responses during the first stages of the programs. They warn that the autistic child might respond to the supports instead of the specific stimuli of the task. They suggest the use of supports inserted in the stimulus for the task, fading progressively in such a way that the response is finally controlled by the relevant characteristics of the stimulus. Likewise, they warn of not presupposing that a child has learned a behavior until knowing which stimuli control the behavior. The other feature that has therapeutic implications is the perseveration of responses. In this respect, they underline the need for structuring objectives to help the child learn key strategies of exploration and response. Another prime objective is the amplification of the motivational structure. Finally, to facilitate learning therapeutic activities, they advise the creation of a situation that limits potential competition—a clear separation between work and free activities and strategies that maximize the reinforcement used by the therapist.

Our own therapeutic work (Cherro Aguerre, 1990) is influenced by the theory of attachment. Our therapeutic team includes child psychiatrists and psychologists with different theoretical orientations: psychoanalytic and cognitive-behavioral. We emphasize work with the child and parents through various techniques. For example, we videotape sequences of daily life interactions between the child and parents (free play, bathing, feeding) and then view and discuss the film with parents. This allows parents to examine their own behavior and to think about their relationships with the child. The aim is to establish as much as possible a facilitating child-parent relationship.

Conclusion

The current status of research and clinical work in Latin America emphasizes the importance of consistency in classification to allow for accurate exchange of information. The availability of *DSM-IV* and *ICD-10* will assist in achieving this goal. Second, we need further epidemiological research to guide the creation of national policies. Within therapeutic centers, there should be multidisciplinary teams created on the basis of a respect for the contributions of each discipline.

Finally, the active participation of parents and resources of the community are important elements when trying to implement optimal health policies. This will undoubtedly require passing laws and transforming services so that they meet the real needs of the autistic child, his or her family, and the community.

THE NETHERLANDS

Herman van Engeland

Insofar as it can be established, the term *autism* was used in the paedological institute in Nijmegen, Holland, as early as 1937 to 1940 to indicate certain forms of child behavior. This term was used to describe children who were excessively self-absorbed and who had markedly stereotyped behavior, excessive anxiety, impaired social interaction with their environment, and retarded development of communicative abilities, and whose form perception and form control were remarkably better developed than other functions.

And yet, it was not until 1952 that Van Krevelen published the first case study of a 4-year-old boy who fulfilled all the criteria of infantile autism as published by Kanner in 1943. Van Krevelen noted that, in his opinion, this was not an early case of schizophrenia as there were no signs of dementia and in some areas there was developmental progress.

In 1953, Kamp showed that some autistic children are not characterized by massive aloofness but demonstrate "symbiotic empty clinging" in their contact with their primary caregiver. Kamp suggested the term *autistic continuum*. This continuum was supposed to have two extremes: on the one hand, the children as described by Kanner and, on the other hand, Rank's atypical children and the symbiotic psychotic children as described by Margaret Mahler. He suggested this continuum to be indicated by the term *developmental psychosis,* and with Van Krevelen, he was convinced that this was not dementia or regression of functions as in schizophrenia, but rather a developmental disorder.

Since then, the autistic syndrome has been the subject of numerous studies: More than 10 PhD dissertations have been published focusing on pedagogic, psychophysiological, neurochemical, pharmacological, psychometric, and cognitive psychological aspects. Autism can be regarded as the syndrome that has been examined most extensively in Dutch child and adolescent psychiatry.

The term developmental psychosis proposed by Kamp was used until the early 1980s; since then, the *DSM-III* (and since 1994, *DSM-IV*) terminology and diagnostic criteria have been used.

Not only have the diagnostic criteria changed over the years, but the treatment of the autistic disorder has also altered. Until the early 1980s, psychotherapy (often on psychoanalytical lines) was used particularly for autistic children functioning at a higher level, while their parents received intensive parental guidance. The idea behind this approach was that the autistic disorder could be seen as a form of fixation or regression to what was considered to be an autistic stage of the child's development; that is, autism was conceptualized as a "developmental arrest," which could be treated by intensive psychotherapy. By the mid-1980s, this view had been relegated to obscurity. Currently, autism is regarded as a congenital developmental disorder in which behavior therapy and "home training" combined with specialized day care are used to optimize the child's cognitive development as much as possible, to improve his or her communicative skills, and to restrict bizarre, unmanageable, and unacceptable behavior. Tools used in this treatment approach are the TEACCH programs developed by Schopler and pharmacotherapy as an adjunct, when necessary.

History of Care

In the early 1970s, the parents of autistic children founded support groups in various places in the Netherlands, usually supported by child psychiatrists and psychologists. These "foundations for autism" had a strong regional character. They were geared to increasing awareness of the autistic disorder and the possibilities for diagnosis and treatment, as well as to stimulate research.

In 1974, the foundation Hulp aan Autistische Kinderen en Adolescenten (Help for Autistic Children and Adolescents) was licensed to establish a psychiatric clinic for autistic adolescents: The "Dr Leo Kannerhuis" in Oosterbeek. In this clinic, adolescents from the age of 16 with a performance intelligence within the normal range can receive intensive treatment with the hope that they ultimately will be able to live and work independently. Treatment mainly consists of remedial teaching and behavior therapy, with an emphasis on rehabilitation, job training, and training in social skills. In the 1980s, a *work home* was created as an extension of the treatment program. This extension was due to the fact that the treatment started with so much enthusiasm, and effort in the Leo Kannerhuis unfortunately did not lead to complete independent and autonomous functioning for adult autistics. It was realized that as adults these individuals with autism also required continuous support and protection, a goal of the work home. Currently, a number of autistic people live in such work homes under the guidance of group leaders. They work on the land (e.g., their own gardens), keep cattle, and do simple handicrafts. They try to sell the products. The work homes are subsidized by the government. Several work homes have been or are in the process of being established throughout the Netherlands (usually affiliated with a psychiatric hospital).

In the early 1980s, the National Parents' Association for Autism (NVA) was established. This association works in close cooperation with autism experts, and an estimated 80% of parents of autistic children are members. The association organizes regional support groups in which parents are informed about the possibilities of home treatment options, weekend and holiday care, and new treatments.

Because of intensive contact with experts in the field of autism, the possibility of referrals for parents who are having problems with their child have improved considerably. The parents' association publishes a professional-looking magazine in which parents are kept up-to-date about the latest developments in diagnosis and treatment and where parents write about their experiences and autistic people sometimes contribute first-person accounts or publish their artistic products (drawings, paintings, and poems). The NVA has made a considerable contribution to improving the care given to the autistic human being.

Treatment Services

The NVA's political lobby influenced the Dutch government to publish an "Autism Memorandum" in 1984. This memorandum regulates that each regional institution for outpatient mental health care (RIAGG) must make facilities available for diagnosis of and assistance of autistic people. The Netherlands has a population of 15 million, and there are 60 RIAGGs throughout the country. In most cases, three or four RIAGG juvenile care teams have combined to form regional autism teams. These teams consist of a child psychiatrist, a child psychologist, a remedial teacher, and a social worker, who usually work in close cooperation with university centers for child and adolescent psychiatry. The autism teams focus on diagnosis, treatment, and guidance of autistic people and their parents. Diagnosis is usually made in a university center for child and adolescent psychiatry so that the medical aspects of the diagnosis are fully integrated. Treatment and guidance consist mainly of home-training projects, organizing day care, placing the children in special educational centers, and assistance in organizing admission to mental institutions in the case of poorly functioning autists. By now, all of the Netherlands is covered by these regional autism teams, which are easily accessible to parents and which provide assistance free of charge. (They receive funding through the Exceptional Medical Expenses Act [AWBZ].) Unfortunately, the teams' capacity is rather restricted, which causes waiting lists varying from 2 to 6 months.

The "Autism Memorandum" also generated a special subsidy regulation for schools that have autistic children as pupils. Special "autism schools" have not been established in the Netherlands. However, the subsidy regulation mentioned has the effect of some schools becoming more or less specialized in dealing with autistic children: These are mainly special education schools (schools for children with speech/language disorders and with learning and educational problems). Some of these schools have even created special classes for autistic children. However, autism classes or autism groups are not limited to schools. Special autism groups have been created in some medical kindergarten day care centers, day care centers for the mentally handicapped, and institutions for the mentally deficient.

Departments of Child and Adolescent Psychiatry generally offer the possibility of extensive diagnosis and special treatment (pharmacotherapy) for those children with complicated problems whose treatment requires a special approach. Usually, admission to child psychiatry centers is relatively brief, and treatment is then continued by the outpatient autism teams.

Help for the autistic child or adolescent is currently well organized in the Netherlands and is actively stimulated by the government. Nevertheless, a number of bottlenecks remain in the organization of providing assistance. In particular, help and backup systems for autistic adolescents and adults are much in need of improvement. Although the number of work homes is being increased, accessibility to sheltered workplaces and social workplaces could be improved.

Another problem is the care for children with disorders closely related to autism (PDD-NOS). The subsidy regulations implemented by the "Autism Memorandum" apply only to children who have been diagnosed autistic. Children with an autism-related disorder (PDD-NOS) fall outside the subsidy terms; their special education is not compensated and a special teacher cannot be appointed. Unfortunately, in these days of fiscal cutbacks, it does not seem likely that these bottlenecks in the service system will be resolved in the foreseeable future.

SPAIN

Joaquin Fuentes

Modern interest in Autism as an identifiable disorder to be studied empirically originated in Spain soon after a national meeting held in Madrid in 1978. Prior to this date, sporadic papers were published in the Spanish psychiatric journals in 1955, 1965, and 1974, but the disorder was considered extremely rare and not deserving of a great deal on interest. In fact, it has been pointed out (Cobo, 1981) that, in

Spain, interest in Autism arose not from the field of psychiatry but from psychology.

Three elements coincided in the Madrid Conference that were to influence the future unfolding of the situation in Spain. First, many international experts were present, mainly from the Anglo-Saxon scientific community, which led to the establishment of professional bonds. Second, the conference served as the initial melting pot for many psychologists, teachers, and psychiatrists interested in Autism, who later founded, under the leadership of the late Prof. Angel Rivière, the Spanish Society of Professionals in Autism (AETAPI). Third, the meeting gave birth to many parents' associations which have played a very significant role. This triple configuration of new scientific data, interested professionals and determined parents needs to be considered within the framework of the historical events of that time. Spain, after many years of dictatorship, underwent a profound political change. Democracy led to decentralization of state services, and the nation was organized according to a quasi-federal model. The new political leaders, influenced by the fast growing economic bonanza and the spirit of renaissance, were sensitive to consumers' initiatives. The whole country was involved in a modernization effort, related to full participation in the European arena, and the changes that occurred in the education, health and social programs were very relevant to the field of Autism.

Decentralization, nevertheless, generated very diverse conditions, depending on the geographical area under consideration. Parents' and professionals' local initiatives had varying impacts and were met with different degrees of support by respective authorities. Because of this, it is erroneous to speak of Spain as a homogeneous country. Similar to other countries, highly developed and qualified services in some communities coexist with severe deficiencies in others locations.

Services

The current model of Autism as a PDD familial to other handicaps such as mental retardation, which is best managed within an educational framework, was accepted, in contrast to other neighboring countries, with little controversy. Very few families had to suffer the interpretative abuse of psychoanalysis and, in general, the vast majority had to cope more with sheer ignorance on the part of professionals, rather than a skewed and guilt-provoking view of the problem.

It may be interesting to understand the reason behind this lack of rejection of the modern view of autism. First, official psychiatry in the old regime could be hardly described as innovative. The predominant model was biologically oriented and public psychiatric assistance was limited to institutionalization in state hospitals. Psychoanalysis, which had an incipient influence during the Spanish Republic, did not really develop later (in part, because many of its leaders had to flee the country during the Civil War). Only in some big cities, such as Barcelona and Madrid, did psychoanalysis have some influence, though restricted to private practice and without real presence in the academic world. Psychiatric assistance was not really considered a health matter and was linked to the regional departments of social welfare. The national health system of that time did not even consider psychiatry as a separate specialty. It was linked to neurology in a medical specialty called neuropsychiatry. The neuropsychiatrists of the national health system outpatient clinics had to deal with a vast number of patients, and basically the only treatment available was psychopharmacology, with little time to individualize the needs of the patients.

The beginning of the 1980s coincided with the progressive acceptance of a community psychiatry model. Credit for this has to be given to different mental health professionals (many trained abroad), who initiated what was known as the "psychiatry reform." Originating in Galicia and Asturias, this effort contested the old predominant model, much in the same way that other European radical psychiatry alternatives were developing at the same time.

In a simplistic manner it can be said that the community psychiatry movement proposed ideas such as decentralization of resources, coordination with other community services, de-institutionalization and so forth. In a parallel way, other means of intervention besides psychopharmacology were promoted. The steps taken have been slow and although many significant advances have been made, much remains to be achieved in the area of public psychiatry in Spain.

The lack of community psychiatry resources coincided with the limited educational services available for students with severe learning difficulties, such as autism. The majority of these students were excluded from the first special schools that opened for children with mental retardation in the 1970s and were sent, if sent anywhere, to residential centers, dependent on social services, characterized by their almost nonexistent educational interest.

Given these antecedents it can be understood that, after the Madrid Conference, focus was centered on the development of the first schools for students with autism, which were established in major Spanish cities in the 1980s. The model frequently entailed the initial organization of a parents' association, which then hired professionals to manage services largely covered by public funds. This alternative has both advantages and risks, but it has proven to be an effective way to initiate programs in under-served areas.

The new national Law on Social Services passed by the democratic Parliament introduced many innovative concepts and led the way to an integrative approach to handicaps, giving credit to the role played by consumers and assigning planning and funding responsibilities to local authorities.

The first years of the Centers for Persons with Autism in Spain were characterized by their adherence to the predominant approach utilized in many Anglo-Saxon countries at that time. Thus, behavior modification techniques were used to teach self-help skills and language. A very small number of schools, mainly in the Catalonia area, followed a psychoanalytic orientation, but, in general, the few programs that were created sustained a behavioral-linguistic approach.

Later, the mid-1980s were associated with a strong movement in favor of school integration. The educational authorities accepted, little by little, and in agreement with the guidelines by the European Union, the principle of nonexclusion in catering to the needs of all students. A new language emerged, not clinical but educational and many initiatives to provide schooling in a minimally restrictive environment were developed. Students with autism and other PDDs were recognized as deserving of a high teacher-to-student ratio but were excluded from the integration effort by many local authorities, as they felt that these students posed too many difficulties and would be better served in special schools.

A particular region of Spain, the Basque Country, did consider all students, including those with autism, in its integrative approach. For example, by the end of the 1980s, the small Basque province of Gipuzkoa had a network of special classes, run by the GAUTENA Autism Society, located in ordinary schools, as well as availability for individual integration with different degrees of support in many schools. In conjunction with this network, inspired on the TEACCH program, families had access to other services such as home programs, respite care, adult services, group homes and leisure opportunities. GAUTENA has been the first European program for autism to be granted an ISO (International Standards Organization) quality registration—an achievement later followed by other programs in Spain. Also, equivalent comprehensive networks have been developed in other areas such as Burgos, Galicia, Cadiz, Madrid or Palma de Mallorca.

In recent years the British concept of "special educational needs" has had an enormous impact in Spain, both in special education at large and in the domain of autism in particular. The initial move of the 1980s from a clinical perspective to a more socioeducational approach has become stabilized. For many, although not all involved, this is a positive and irreversible achievement. Educational authorities have recognized autism and have opened sections on autism in their special education resource centers. Many people feel that, at this point, problems are related more to resource limitations and lack of well-trained staff with proper institutional support rather than to confusion about the model to follow.

In a parallel way, many changes have occurred in the conceptualization of autism. Initial emphasis on language and cognitive skills has been substituted with aspects such as socioemotional deficits, theory of mind, visually supported learning, alternative communication means, normal peer tutoring, adaptation to national curriculum, functionality, inclusion with support, incidental teaching and so on. Advances in the field find quick application in the majority of available programs and the rigid behaviorism of 20 years ago has disappeared.

AETAPI remains the key influential channel for the dissemination of innovative research and service models. The society has almost 200 members from all related professions and held in 2004 its Twelfth Congress. Also, in 1994 two national federations of parents' associations, AUTISM SPAIN and FESPAU, were constituted to coordinate local efforts and influence national policy. These societies are present in almost 90% of the autonomous communities that constitute Spain today. Recently, a small new association on Asperger Disorder has been established in Spain; an initiative met with excitement by those who feel that traditional associations were not responding to their particular needs, but also with criticism by others who are concerned about competition among societies in the spectrum and will rather support creating special interest groups inside the current associations.

With the new millennium, a greater interest in autism can be observed in Spain. Issues related to the field are present in the media and better awareness among professionals is favoring earlier diagnosis. Families, persons with autism, and professionals are readily accessing the Internet and sharing information. Universities are becoming more involved, such as the University of Salamanca and the Autonomous University of Madrid, and there are 17 published doctoral thesis on autism. Literature review shows that 80 autism papers, originated in Spain, have been incorporated in Medline and PsycINFO. Many groups are working in innovative trans-European projects, and the current main areas of interest are services for adults and quality of life. The ADI-R and the ADOS-G in Spanish have been incorporated in the country, and this will assure future international comparability of research samples.

In 2002, the Spanish National Institute of Health Carlos III—the agency that funds medical research in the country—established his Study Group on autism. In its first 2 years, this task force has analyzed the reasons for the diagnostic delay experienced by many families and has produced guideline materials for early detection, diagnosis and research programs in autism. Its work is available at http://iier.isciii.es/autism, along with many useful resources and national and international links.

Conclusion

Autism in Spain enjoys the active participation of many involved parents and professionals. Despite the fact that areas still remain in the country that are underserved, there are elements that would allow us to anticipate a brighter future. Autism is recognized and diagnosed following internationally accepted criteria (*DSM-IV-TR* and *ICD-10*), there are structured organizations both for parents and professionals and the general attitude of authorities and laypersons toward autism is a positive one. The challenge now is to extend throughout the country the model programs currently providing services in certain areas. In a time of economical uncertainty and social welfare restrictions, joint lobbying by parents and professionals as well as fluent international communication, will still be needed, much in the same way they proved essential in the past.

SWEDEN AND OTHER NORDIC NATIONS

Per-Anders Rydelius

The history of child and adolescent psychiatry and theories used to explain psychiatric disorders in the Nordic countries (Sweden, Finland, Norway, Denmark, and Iceland) provides an important context for understanding the treatment of autistic and PDDs.

Although the Nordic countries have had much in common, including religious, ethnic, cultural, and social aspects and closely related languages (except Finnish), there are important differences. While child and adolescent psychiatry in the five countries has been an independent medical discipline since the beginning of the 1950s, the situation in Finland and Sweden is different from Norway, Denmark, and Iceland (Hannesdóttir, 1993; Piha & Almqvist, 1994; Rydelius, 1993; Smedegaard,

Hansen, & Isager, 1993; Vandvik & Spurkland, 1993).

Child and adolescent psychiatry is closer to general psychiatry in Norway, Denmark, and Iceland, as in Great Britain and the United States; in Sweden and Finland, child and adolescent psychiatry for a long time has been far closer to pediatrics. While it could be said that the main influence on Swedish and Finnish child and adolescent psychiatry originated from Central Europe, a situation that is partly relevant also for Denmark, the British and American influence has been stronger on the establishment of child and adolescent psychiatry in Norway and Iceland.

In Sweden, child and adolescent psychiatry was established as a medical discipline in 1951. The initiatives for the establishment of a "new" discipline originated from pediatrics, school mental health work, child social welfare, and general psychiatry, in that order, starting with Ellen Key's book (1909) introducing the twentieth century as "The Century of the Child." As shown by the pamphlet *Broken Minds,* the strongest influence came from pediatrics and not from general psychiatry. In 1915, Jundell (chairman of the Department of Pediatrics at the Karolinska Institute) presented his arguments based on a pediatric developmental perspective for a new discipline in order to understand childhood mental health problems (Jundell, 1915). The history of child and adolescent psychiatry has been very much influenced by the corresponding histories of the discipline's development in Austria, France, Germany, and Switzerland.

From *Heilpedagogie* (Curative Education) to a Psychodynamic Approach to Understand and Treat Child Psychiatric Disorders

Over the past 100 years, several historical periods can be delineated in relation to the theories and ideas used in Central Europe, the Nordic countries, and Sweden to explain and treat child psychiatric disorders.

At the beginning of the twentieth century, the ideas of *Heilpedagogie,* curative education, had a major influence on the development of child and adolescent psychiatry. In Sweden, the "phase of curative education" later influ-

enced by the mental health movement originating in the United States was succeeded in the 1930s by a "genetic phase" and theories based on genetic explanations for child psychiatric disorders. In turn, this period was followed by a "neuropsychiatric phase" in the 1940s and the 1950s.

A Shift of the Use of the Scientific Language in the Nordic Countries after World War II

Until World War II, German was the main scientific language in all five Nordic countries. Thus, there are historical similarities between these nations and Central Europe. During the 1950s, new ideas were introduced for explaining child psychiatric problems. Clinicians began to use a psychoanalytically oriented frame of reference. There was also a shift of the main scientific language as British and American scientific literature became most important. Swedish child psychiatrists were influenced by Kanner's *Textbook in Child Psychiatry,* second edition (Kanner, 1948), which successively replaced the German textbooks, *Lehrbuch der Psychopathologie des Kindesalters* (Benjamin, Hanselmann, Isserlin, Lutz, & Ronald, 1938) and *Lehrbuch der allgemeinen Kinderpsychiatrie* (Tramer, 1942). The shift in the use of scientific language also meant that child psychiatrists in their clinical work became more dependent on the American and British child psychiatry and the close connections to general psychiatry in those countries.

The Concept of Childhood Psychosis

In the Nordic countries, until the introduction of infantile autism by Kanner in the United States and *Autistische Psychopathie* by Asperger in Austria, psychotic disorders in childhood were mainly categorized either as dementia infantilis (described by Heller in 1908), dementia praecox (suggested by Kraepelin), or as dementia praecocissima (as suggested by Sante De Sanctis). These disorders were distinguished clinically. In the psychosis of Heller, the child had normal development for the first 3 to 4 years of life and then deteriorated, lost speech, developed an autistic status, and successively showed "dementia." The disorder most often showed itself in children who had a degenerative brain disorder. Dementia praecox and dementia praecocissima (although in some cases organic brain disorder was included) were descriptions of what later was called childhood schizophrenia.

Later, the Danish psychiatrist Strömgren suggested the following categorization of childhood psychotic disorders: psychosis of psychogenic origin; psychosis of physiogenic— "organic"—origin (including Heller's disorder); and psychosis of cryptogenic origin (including schizophrenia, manic-depressive disorders, and early infantile autism-Kanner syndrome). The diagnosis of a childhood psychosis required that the symptoms appear before the age of 10 to 11 years (Annell, 1958).

Children with these psychotic disorders were looked on as mentally ill and not as mentally handicapped. This was still the case when two new Parliament acts were passed In the 1960s, giving special services and support to the mentally retarded and transferring the responsibility for psychiatric hospitals and psychiatric care in Sweden from the government to the county councils. Also, according to the *ICD-7* and *ICD-8,* children with childhood psychosis were still looked on as mentally ill. In 1986, a new law was passed to support the mentally retarded, and children with childhood psychosis were considered mentally handicapped.

The *ICD* system of classification has been used in all Nordic countries. However, from 1980, the American *DSM-III/DSM-III-R* systems were also increasingly taken into consideration in daily clinical work. The multiaxial system for child psychiatric diagnoses proposed by Rutter, Shaffer, and Shepherd (1975) was also translated to Swedish and used simultaneously with *DSM*. In 1987, after a study of the *ICD* and *DSM* systems, the Swedish Association of Child and Adolescent Psychiatry adopted the *DSM* approach to diagnostic considerations. Thus, the concept of PDDs was introduced, followed by the change from infantile autism in the *DSM-III* to autistic disorders in the *DSM-III-R*.

The most important treatment program for autistic children in Sweden since the 1930s has been curative education, *Heilpedagogie* (in its anthroposophical form). This treatment approach continues to link Sweden with child psychiatry in Central Europe and with European concepts of nosology. In the second edition of the German textbook *Lehrbuch der speziellen Kinder- und Jugendpsychiatrie* (Harbauer, Lempp, Nissen, & Strunk, 1974), Nissen makes the following clinically helpful suggestions about differentiation of autistic disorders. He suggests that autistic factors can be manifested in a spectrum ranging from psychogenic autism (autistic reaction) at one pole, through Asperger syndrome, Kanner syndrome, somatic autism, infantile autism, and pseudoautism.

Nissen hypothesized that the autistic syndromes depend on an autistic hereditary factor that shows itself with different degrees of penetration. This factor results in an autistic psychogenic reaction if psychosocial environmental factors are severe or through an Asperger syndrome or a Kanner syndrome. In children with brain disorders, the same autistic factor could give a somatic form of brain-organic autism. He uses the term *pseudoautism* for an autistic state without the influence of a hereditary autistic factor, in which autism is found together with other severe handicaps such as mental retardation, deafness, or blindness.

Treatment of Childhood Psychosis

During the first decades of this century, no specific treatment was given to children with childhood psychosis. Until the 1930s, these patients were mainly cared for in mental hospitals or in special homes for the mentally retarded. Curative education has been the major approach to children with childhood psychosis from the 1930s until today. Also, during the past 2 to 3 decades, as a consequence of the orientation toward theories originating from psychoanalysis, psychodynamic approaches also have had a major influence on the treatment of child psychiatric disorders, including the treatment of childhood psychosis and autistic disorders, in all Nordic countries.

Heilpedagogie—Curative Education

In Central Europe, curative education (Hanselmann, 1933) has been used to treat and take care of children with handicaps for a long time. Heller and Asperger in Vienna (Harbauer et al., 1974; Remschmidth & Schmidt, 1988) suggested *Heilpedagogie* to treat children with childhood psychosis. The concept of curative education was also used by Steiner ("Antroposofisk läkepedagogik och socialterapi i Norden," 1991) combining *Heilpedagogie* with his anthroposophical philosophy. His anthroposophical variant of curative education remains the most important form of treatment of children with autistic disorders, especially in Sweden.

From 1935, treatment homes based on anthroposophical curative education were established in all Nordic countries. Today there are more than 50 such treatment homes. In Sweden, there is a center south of Stockholm, with almost 20 independent treatment homes arranged in villages. For the first 15 years of their existence, the main goal of the activities was to support mentally handicapped children and youth, but from the 1950s mentally handicapped adults were also included because children coming to these homes tended to stay for their lifetime. Since the 1980s, these anthroposophical "villages" in Järna have become national centers for the treatment of autistic children. Since 1967, Stockholm County Council has had a special agreement with five of these treatment homes to offer autistic children from the Stockholm area treatment and care.

In a research report by Rydelius (1986), the patients attending the programs in four of the treatment homes and their treatment were described from a child psychiatric point of view. At that time, 136 children, youth, and adults stayed in these four homes; 101 male and 35 female patients ages 4 to 62 years were investigated, and two-thirds were ages 4 to 19 years. Among the youngest up to the age of 16 years, 15 of 39 boys and 6 of 23 girls met the criteria for the *DSM-III* diagnosis infantile autism. Two boys and one girl had infantile autism, residual state; another four boys and one girl fulfilled the criteria for childhood onset pervasive disorder, while the remaining patients suffered from other disorders and handicaps.

The treatment program in these villages is based on individual plans for each patient. The programs are evaluated on a regular basis and follow the anthroposophical view that children develop in three 7-year periods, from birth until adulthood, with different support needed during each period. In the treatment, it is necessary that the staff adjust to each patient in a similar way based on the patient's own capacity. School, occupational therapy, eurytmi (a kind of training to support attention, concentration, and motoric control), and other group activities are added to the individual supporting program. By the daily care given on an individual basis, the children seem to function on a maximum personal level. The majority of the patients in the villages were admitted because of severe behavior symptoms, with hyperactive/restless/aggressive behavior, sleeping and eating problems, symptoms that diminished or disappeared soon after their arrival. If necessary, the patients were treated with anthroposophical pharmacology and/or "ordinary" drugs. As the staff had a very long experience with autistic children (some had lived and worked with autistic children for their lifetime), it was interesting to find out that they had learned to predict prognosis in a similar way compared to the *DSM*-system. They said that an early onset of language and a short period of an "autistic echo-speech" indicated a capacity for development.

The majority of the patients in these programs have had lifelong handicaps and are in need of a 24-hour supportive program. However, some have developed rather well and need only day care as adults. A very few can handle their life situation as adults with only limited support.

The programs of these treatment homes resemble programs in different child psychiatric centers in Europe and in the United States, from psychiatric, psychological, pedagogical, and social points of view. The main differences are the Nordic emphasis on anthroposophical treatment. In Sweden, there have been recent critical remarks concerning the fact that the children staying in these villages are segregated from and will not have influences from normal society. Another critical concern is the absence of supportive programs for families.

Two Unusual Autistic Patients

Members of one village staff were responsible in the 1950s for the care of a 4-year-old girl with an autistic state. She had been carefully investigated both by pediatricians and child psychiatrists at the Crown Princess Lovisas' Hospital in Stockholm (the university department for child and adolescent psychiatry at that time) and was given the diagnosis of early infantile autism, Kanner syndrome. Expressive aphasia also had been discussed as a possible differential diagnosis, but the clinical picture was better captured by Kanner syndrome. The girl started to speak at the age of 6 years. She successively improved and could attend normal school. In her teenage years, she had individual psychotherapy. When the research report was done, she was married and working but had no children. A retrospective review of her file (done by me in 1984) revealed that the clinical picture in the 1950s fulfilled the *DSM-III* criteria for infantile autism. So far, no other child coming to these treatment homes has had such a good development.

The oldest known individual in Sweden with an autistic disorder lives at one of the treatment homes. In the middle of the 1930s at the age of 12 years, he was admitted to the Mikaelgården, the oldest of the Swedish anthroposophical treatment homes. As he grew older, he became the first patient who needed a program for autistic adults, and he has stayed in this program for his whole life. He is still living there but now is considered "retired." This individual was born in 1923 in a very wealthy and capable family. He had a late development of language, developed "echospeech" when he was around 3 years of age, and could, at the age of 4, say words but could not communicate. As a preschooler (in Sweden until 7 years of age), he had temper outbursts, stereotyped behavior, was impulsive, and played monotonously and alone even if other children were there. He was placed in a Montessori kindergarten but had to be taken out of the group. Although he could not communicate through language, he learned poems by heart and could read before the age of 7. In 1929, at the age of 6 and after an examination at the pediatric university department in Stockholm, he was given the diagnosis of dementia praecox. After this, he was admitted to a hospital for the mentally retarded and then to Beckomberga, a newly built mental hospital in Stockholm, for 1 year before he came to the treatment home. For his whole life, he has had stereotyped behavior, rituals, and severely disturbed language without communicative skills. As a child, he walked on tiptoe. During his 20s, he showed strong emotional affection for one staff member, but after some time he again lost interest in other persons. He has had a tendency for anxiety paroxysms all his life and is especially afraid of certain noises. On the other hand, he has always been interested in music and as a child, he could listen in a very concentrated fashion and "be absorbed" by classical music. Over the years, he also showed mood changes, with periods of very passive behavior and periods of aggressive outbursts with impulsive behavior and self-damaging incidents. As an adult, his behavior has raised suspicions of hallucinations, and he has been treated with phenothiazines and lithium. His neurological status is normal, without epileptic seizures, and his cognitive level in the 1970s was severe mental retardation.

From a clinical point of view, he fulfills the criteria for infantile autism as a child and childhood onset PDD later according to *DSM-III*. Today, he presents a "schizophrenic autistic" impression. His behavior has been slightly improved by medication. In retrospect, it is difficult to say whether this has been the life history of a child with a severe form of an autistic disorder or an early form of schizophrenia and that the diagnosis of dementia praecox in 1929 when he was 6 was correct. However, the information given by the now-deceased head of the treatment home where he has spent his life and who knew him from the 1930s favors the diagnosis of infantile autism.

This patient, now age 72, lives at the same treatment home where he was admitted in the beginning of the 1940s. When he became 67, the age of retirement in Sweden, he, too, became aware of his "new status" and adjusted himself and his habits to more gentle activities.

Treatment Programs Based on a Psychodynamic Approach

In the 1960s, when the shift toward a psychodynamic view on child psychiatric problems had been firmly established in clinical practice in the Nordic countries, the treatment of childhood psychosis was also influenced by these views. Although the emphasis was on habilitation and not on cure, strong influences came from Bettelheim's view on infantile autism and from Mahler's theory of separation-individuation (Bettelheim, 1967; Mahler, 1952, 1955). In Stockholm, there was a psychoanalytically based treatment program offered at the Ericastiftelsen (a private foundation instituted in 1934 for *Heilpedagogie* and child and adolescent psychiatric treatment, today also a training institute for psychotherapy) between 1976 and 1981. As a part of this program, there was a scientifically based evaluation of Mahler's model of development, presented as a PhD thesis in psychology. A comparison of normal preschool children and children with severely disturbed development including autistic disorders could not confirm Mahler's model of development. However, Mahler's theory, used in a dimensional model, was found to be of interest when studying and assessing children's development during psychotherapy (Elwin, 1994).

Current Treatment

From the 1980s, alternatives to curative education and to the psychodynamic approaches have been successively developed. From studies in different parts of Sweden (Bohman, Bohman, & Sjöholm-Lif, 1988; Gillberg, 1994; Magnusson, Rydell, & Dahlin, 1975) and in the other Nordic countries (Sommerschild & Grøholt, 1989), habilitation programs are based on early diagnosis, support for the families, pedagogically based day care programs for the children, and education in special classes. The treatment programs today are similar to those given in other countries and are influenced by the current British and American views on autistic disorders. In a way, they are similar to those programs given at the anthroposophical curative education treatment homes, especially concerning the pedagogical aspects. The major differences are that the children are more integrated into the normal society and that the support to the parents and families is emphasized. National parent societies are established (in Sweden since 1973) and have been very important in the development of better services for autistic children and their parents.

THE UNITED KINGDOM

Richard Mills and Lorna Wing

In the 1940s and 1950s, interest in autism in the United Kingdom was limited, and autism was generally considered to be a manifestation of early-onset schizophrenia (Cameron, 1955). Changes in the diagnostic concept and acceleration in the growth of interest can be dated from the beginning of the 1960s when two separate influential events occurred. First, Creak (1961, 1964) chaired a working party of professionals in the field of child psychiatry, the ostensible aim of which was to clarify the use of the term *psychosis* in childhood. The members chose the term *schizophrenic syndrome of childhood.* The diagnostic criteria they produced, known as the "Nine Points," listed the major features of what are now known as autistic spectrum conditions. Despite this confusion over terminology, the "Nine Points" represented the first attempt to introduce operational criteria for autistic disorders.

Second, a group of parents with children with autism decided in 1962 to form an association. The group has evolved into the British National Autistic Society, with both parent and professional members, and is concerned with adults as well as children. The structure now comprises the National Society and a large number of local autistic societies, almost all of which are associated with the national body.

In the 1960s, the events described earlier took place against a backdrop of the struggle between those professionals who accepted and those who rejected the diagnostic concept of autism. There was a belief common among professionals at that time that autism was a middle-class euphemism for mental retardation. The newly formed society had to battle against this prejudice.

The concept of autism began to acquire scientific respectability with the publication of well-designed research in the field. One of these studies in the United Kingdom was the epidemiological work of Lotter (1966, 1967), which identified children with typical autism. Wing and Gould (1979) carried out another epidemiological study and introduced the concept of the wider autistic spectrum of disorders having in common a triad of impairments of social interaction, communication and imagination, and a repetitive pattern of activities. Twelve years later, Wing (1981b) published an account of the syndrome originally described by and named after Asperger (1944; translated by Frith, 1991). This expanded even wider the concept of an autistic spectrum. Ehlers and Gillberg (1993) carried out the first epidemiological study of this syndrome. Another aspect of research was the clarification of the clinical picture of typical childhood autism and a follow-up into adolescence and early adult life (Rutter, 1968, 1970, 1978).

Despite the growing volume of publications in the field from the 1960s to the present, the level of awareness within the general professional community remains low. An evaluation of community care services (Baldwin & Hattersley, 1991) contains no reference to autism.

Care of Individuals with Autistic Disorders

Before the 1960s, there were no services specifically for people with autism. Probably the single most commonly used residential placements were the long-stay institutions for the mentally retarded. The "treatments" varied from psychoanalysis to electroconvulsive therapy (ECT), depending on the belief systems of the therapists involved. However, the only two methods that have been subject to controlled investigation are structured education (Bartak & Rutter, 1973; Rutter & Bartak, 1973) and behavior management based on behavioral techniques (Howlin et al., 1987).

Well before the Bartak and Rutter studies of education, some teachers had found— through intuition, trial, and error—methods that were helpful with children with autistic disorders. The members of the parents' association were more impressed by the results of education than of any other approaches. From the outset, they had decided to use all their resources for setting up specialized schools. In 1964, the Society started the first school for children with autistic disorders. One of the major problems in the early years was that children with severe learning disabilities or disruptive behavior could be excluded from education. It was a struggle for parents to persuade the education authorities that their children should be funded to attend a special

school. In 1970, in England and Wales an act of Parliament established the right of all children to education in schools. Scotland and Northern Ireland had similar acts later. More schools, with day and/or residential places, and some special classes were set up following the success of the first school, most run by the national or local autistic societies but some by other voluntary or private bodies and some by local education authorities.

In the early 1970s, a team of workers at the Institute of Psychiatry began to develop a program in which parents were helped, through advice and guidance in their own homes, to improve their management strategies using behavioral methods in a flexible way (Howlin et al., 1973). This started as a research project but is now carried on as a clinical service within the National Health Service (Howlin & Rutter, 1987). The service is much appreciated by parents but has been copied in very few other areas of the country.

After some years, it became apparent that many children with autistic disorders would never become independent, so efforts began to be made to develop services for adults. The first adult residential community was started in 1974. Other specialized residential and day services have followed, almost all set up and run by the national or local autistic societies.

Current Status of Treatment Services

Currently in the United Kingdom, the only treatments dedicated to autistic disorders are the specialized schools and adult centers, the home-based service described earlier, a very few therapeutic groups run for more able adolescents or adults, and a newly begun National Society scheme to organize supported employment for those able to benefit. There are no schemes for early intervention, apart from some preschool units for children with all kinds of language problems. The national and local autistic societies arrange parent support groups, meetings and weekend courses for parents and professional workers, and various other social or educational activities. Overall, despite the success of the specialized service, they provide for only a tiny proportion of children and adults with autistic disorders. Most are catered for within the generic education, health, or social services. Such places have a hard struggle to provide a suitable environment for those with autistic disorders even if their special needs are recognized. The generic psychiatric services in hospitals or outpatient clinics provide most of the advice on behavior management and medication. Only a minority of the professionals involved have any knowledge of or interest in autistic disorders. There are no specialized services for the adolescents or adults who develop superimposed psychiatric illnesses that can occur in adolescence or adult life. The generic adult psychiatric hospitals and clinics have to be used and are often not equipped to cope.

The first residential centers for adults were for groups of 20 or more residents in large houses with large grounds. Currently, the national and local autistic societies are working in conjunction with housing associations to develop small group homes or individual apartments with staff supervision. These have proved beneficial for more able individuals with autistic disorders, including Asperger syndrome. However, the larger homes on their own grounds are still needed for many adults with more marked levels of disability and behavior disturbance. There is, therefore, a need to provide a range of community services catering for a spectrum of need (Landesman-Dwyer, 1981).

While there are some advantages to the emphasis on community-based approaches for some people, one unfortunate result has been to place relatives in the front line of care for individuals with highly complex needs, many of whom require intensive specialist resources that are rarely provided. The development of community-based services for individuals with severe behavior disorders has posed a particular challenge. Evaluation of some of these services, notably by the Special Development Team at the University of Kent, has demonstrated the high cost and scarcity of such provision (Emerson, McGill, & Mansell, 1994). There has been growing awareness of autistic disorders in the forensic field. Offenders with such conditions were specifically mentioned for the first time in a major policy review of services by Reed (1994). The National Autistic Society has recently collaborated with the Special Hospital's Authority, the government

agency responsible for secure provision for mentally disordered offenders, in running a conference to raise awareness among the staff of the special hospitals. The National Society is soon to open a unit for adults with autistic disorders who need a secure placement and is working closely with the authorities involved in this field.

As already mentioned, those who started the original parents' association were firm in their belief that structured education was the most important way of helping their children. In recent years, as it has become clear that autistic disorders have lifelong effects, a number of different approaches that have promised either cures or remarkable improvements have appealed to some parents who want to pursue any line that offers hope. These include holding therapy, facilitated communication, auditory integration training, the options method, and treatment with various medications. None of the claims made have been validated by properly controlled research. So far, the British, with their typical caution, have tended to show less uncritical enthusiasm for these treatments than has been seen in some other countries.

Over the past 3 years, in addition to the long-recognized emphasis on structure, consistency, reduction of disturbing stimuli, and a high degree of organization, the approach in the National Autistic Society schools and adult centers has concentrated on specific programs to overcome or reduce the effects of the impairments of imagination, communication, and social skills that underlie autistic behavior (Wing & Gould, 1979). This has proved helpful because it provides a clear framework for the staff working with children and adults.

Problems of Diagnosis

In 1962, when the parents' association was formed, few people had heard of autism. Now, as a result of the efforts of the national and local autistic societies and the popularity of the film *Rain Man,* almost everyone has. Despite this change, parents still often have major difficulties in obtaining a diagnosis, and many children and adults remain undiagnosed, especially those with Asperger syndrome or variants other than typical autism. Many different pathways are followed by children with autistic disorders, depending on the type and severity of their condition and the degree of mental retardation. They may be referred at any age to pediatric, psychiatric, educational, or social service professionals. Recognition of the autistic disorder depends on the depth of interest and experience in the field of the professional concerned. Many parents have years of struggle and distress at being made to feel that they have caused their child's behavior before they learn the truth. There is some evidence of a positive reluctance in some quarters to recognize autism as a clinical condition requiring a specialized approach possibly because of the financial implications for the services concerned.

In the early 1990s, in response to the parents' problems in obtaining diagnoses, the Society set up the Centre for Social and Communication Disorders in Bromley, the function of which is to make detailed diagnostic assessments and give advice on service needs. Individuals of all ages are seen. There are three other centers specializing in the diagnosis of autistic disorders—in Radlett, Southampton, and Nottingham—that see children but not adults. A few child psychiatric clinics, such as that at the Maudsley Hospital, have a special interest in autism but see other childhood psychiatric conditions as well.

National Policies

Changes in recent years in government policies on health, education, social, and economic policies have had some positive and many negative effects on services for people with autistic disorders. The importance of early assessment and diagnosis and provision of education appropriate for the needs of children with disabilities has been emphasized in legislation, but cuts in local government funding have militated against the implementation of these ideals. This is especially true for children with autistic disorders who have expensive needs.

A further complication has been government support for integrating children with disabilities into mainstream schools. This works for some children with autistic disorders but has been detrimental for many more. One piece of evidence for this is the growing number of referrals to the specialist schools of children who have failed in mainstream, including more able children with Asperger syndrome whose social difficulties set them apart from their peers.

Similar pressures have affected the services for adults. The normalization philosophy (Wolfensberger, 1972; Wolfensberger & Thomas, 1983), coupled with rising costs, resulted in government agendas to close institutions. Community-based services for more able individuals who were the first to be moved out of the institutions worked well and were economical in cost. However, this policy has resulted in major problems in the case of people with autistic disorders and disturbed behavior. The change in the environment and the lack of a structured routine were more than they could cope with (Wing, 1989). The eventual costs were much higher than anticipated.

On the positive side, the Department of Health has supported initiatives in the field of autistic disorders, including an evaluation of the effects of legislation on services for children and adults with these conditions. The Department has also helped finance the accreditation process piloted by the National Autistic Society to develop, demonstrate, and disseminate models of good practice within specialist and other services catering for individuals with autistic disorders.

Services over the Life Span

From this account, it can be seen that all types of services for individuals with autistic disorders from diagnosis onward are patchily distributed. They vary widely throughout the country, being excellent in a few places and virtually nonexistent in many. There is a statutory right to education from 5 to 19 years in the case of children with special needs but no legal right to preschool or adult services.

The crisis points for parents are, first, when their child approaches school age. They usually have to battle to obtain the type of education they believe is needed, and they may not succeed. Some parents have moved to an area where there is a specialist school. The second crisis is at school-leaving age when the battle for appropriate services, day or residential, begins all over again. Even for the most able group, there are many difficulties on entering adult life. The National Autistic Society and its affiliated network of local autism societies continue to expand and develop specialist provision. Despite their efforts, the great majority of individuals are not given specialist help but are fitted into whatever services are available in their local area that will accept and keep them. People with autistic disorders are to be found in schools, hostels, hospitals, day centers, lodging houses for the homeless, or even living on the streets. The precise numbers in these different settings are unknown. Even so, children and adults with autistic disorders are more likely to find some kind of help in a country such as the United Kingdom that still preserves some aspect of the welfare state than in countries with no such provision. How the situation will evolve in the uncertain future is impossible to predict.

Cross-References

Issues of diagnosis are discussed in Section I (Chapters 1 to 7); interventions are addressed in Section VI (Chapters 33 to 44); public policy perspectives on autism are provided in Chapters 45 to 47.

REFERENCES

Ainsworth, M. D. S., Blehar, M. C., Waters, E., & Wall, S. I. (1978). *Patterns of attachment: A psychological study of the stranger situation.* Hillsdale, NJ: Erlbaum.

Alexiou, C. (1995). Hope at last: Adults with autism in Greece. *Autism Europe, Link, 17*(3), 4–6.

American Psychiatric Association. (1980). *Diagnostic and statistical manual of mental disorders* (3rd ed.). Washington, DC: Author.

American Psychiatric Association. (1987). *Diagnostic and statistical manual of mental disorders* (3rd ed., rev.). Washington, DC: Author.

American Psychiatric Association. (1994). *Diagnostic and statistical manual of mental disorders* (4th ed.). Washington, DC: Author.

Anastasopoulos, G., Ierodiakonou, C., & Routsoni, C. (1964). *Childhood schizophrenia with temporal epilepsy.* Paper presented at the 1st Panhellenic Conference of Neurology, Athens, Greece.

Annell, A.-L. (1958). *Elementär barnpsykiatri.* Stockholm: Norstedts.

Antroposofisk läkepedagogik och socialterapi i Norden. (1991). Telleby bokförlag, Södertälje.

Asperger, H. (1944). Die autistischen psychopathen im kindersalter. *Archives fur psychiatrie und Nervenkrankheiten, 117,* 76–136.

Audero, M. A. (1980). Seminario taller de tratamiento conductual a niños y adolescentes autistas. *Edes Revista Educación Especial, 2,* 131–164.

Baldwin, S., & Hattersley, J. (Eds.). (1991). *Mental handicap: Social science perspectives.* London: Tavistock.

Barak, Y., Ring, A., Sulkes, J., Gabbay, U., & Elizur, A. (1995). Season of birth and autistic disorder in the Middle-East. *American Journal of Psychiatry, 152*(5), 798–800.

Bartak, L., & Rutter, M. L. (1973). Special educational treatment of autistic children. *Journal of Child Psychology and Psychiatry, 14,* 161–179.

Benjamin, E., Hanselmann, H., Isserlin, M., Lutz, J., & Ronald, A. (1938). *Lehrbuch der psychopathologie des kindesalters far rzte und erzieher.* Rotapfel-Verlag, Erlenbach-Zurich und Leipzig.

Bernabei, P., Levi, G., Mazzoncini, B., & Penge, R. (1994). Un nucleo disprattico nei disturbi generalizzati dello sviluppo [The core dyspractic disturbance in pervasive developmental disorders]. *Psichiatria dell'Infanzia e dell'Adolescenza, 61,* 337–346.

Bettelheim, B. (1967). *The empty fortress—Infantile autism and the birth of the self.* New York: Free Press.

Bettison, S. (1996). The long-term effects of auditory training on children with autism. *Journal of Autism and Developmental Disorders, 26,* 361–374.

Bleger, J. (1972). Esquizofrenia,autismo y psicosis; enfoque psicoanal_tico. *Acta Psiquiátrica psicoanalitco, 18*(4), 227–231.

Bohman, M., Bohman, I.-L., & Sjöholm-Lif, E. (1988). *Barndomspsykos—Att känna igen, förstå och behandla.* Stockholm: Almqvist & Wiksell.

Brown, J. R., & Rogers, S. J. (2003). Cultural issues in autism. In R. L. Hendren, S. Ozonoff, & S. Rogers (Eds.), *Autism spectrum disorders* (pp. 209–226). Washington, DC: American Psychiatric Press.

Bursztejn, C. (1983). Biochemical research in early psychoses. *Neuropsychiatrie de l Enfance et de l Adolescence, 31,* 241–244.

Cameron, K. (1955, September). Psychosis in infancy and early childhood. *Medical Press,* 280–283.

Cherro Aguerre, M. (1990). *Therapeutic approach of an autistic syndrome.* Unpublished presentation to the 12th International Congress of the International Association of Child and Adolescent Psychiatry and Allied Professions, Kyoto, Japan.

Cobo, C. (1981, September 27–30). Ser hoy nino autista en Espana. *Profesion Medica, 21*–27.

Cohen, Y., & Levinson, D. (1993). *Planning programs for autistic population for the year 2000.* Jerusalem: Israel Ministry of Health.

COMPIC. (1992). *Your guide to COMPIC.* Melbourne, Australia: Spastic Society of Victoria.

Creak, E. M. (Chairman). (1961, April). Schizophrenic syndrome in childhood: Progress report of a working party. *Cerebral Palsy Bulletin, 3,* 501–504.

Creak, E. M. (1964). Schizophrenic syndrome in childhood: Further progress report of a working party (April 1961). *Developmental Medicine and Child Neurology, 6,* 530–535.

DeMyer, M. K., Hington, J. N., & Jackson, R. K. (1981). Infantile autism reviewed: A decade of research. *Schizophrenia Bulletin, 7,* 388–451.

de Plá, E. P. (1991). El niño Psicótico y la Escuela: Un enfoque Psicoanalítico. *Psicosis y Retardo Mental, Amerpi, 3,* 1–47.

De Sanctis, S. (1906). Sopra alcune varieta della demenza precoce. Rivista Sperimentale De Feniatria E. Di Medicina Legale, 32, 141–165.

Dio Bleichmar, E. (1987). Psicosis y Autismo. In N. Fejerman & E. Fernandez Alvarez (Eds.), *Fronteras entre Neuropediatría y Psicología* (pp. 193–213). Buenos Aires, Argentina: Edic. Nueva Visión.

Donovan, L., & Olivari, C. (1989). Autismo Infantil. Un proceso co-terapéutico a dos voces. *Revista Terapia Psicológica, 8*(12), 44–49.

Ehlers, S., & Gillberg, C. (1993). The epidemiology of Asperger syndrome. A total population study. *Journal of Child Psychology and Psychiatry, 34,* 1327–1350.

Einfeld, S. L., & Tonge, B. J. (1991). Psychometric and clinical assessment of psychopathology in developmentally disabled children. *Australian and New Zealand Journal of Developmental Disability, 17*(2), 147–154.

Einfeld, S. L., & Tonge, B. J. (1994). *Manual for the Developmental Behavior Checklist.* Department of Child and Adolescent Psychiatry, School of Psychiatry, University of New South Wales and Centre for Developmental Psychiatry, Monash University.

Einfeld, S. L., & Tonge, B. J. (1995). The Developmental Behavior Checklist: The development and validation of an instrument to assess behavioral and emotional disturbance in children and adolescents with mental retardation. *Journal of Autism and Developmental Disabilities, 25*(2), 81–104.

Elwin, B. (1994). *Separation-individuation according to Mahler: Empirical studies of normal and pathological development in early childhood.* Unpublished master's thesis, Stockholm University, Department of Psychology.

Emerson, E., McGill, P., & Mansell, J. (Eds.). (1994). *Severe learning disabilities and challenging behaviours: Designing high quality services.* London: Chapman & Hall.

Ferrari, P. (1993). Psychoses infantiles. In P. Ferrari & C. Epelbaum (Eds.), *Psychiatrie de l'Enfant et de l'Adolescent.* Paris: Medicine-Science-Flammarion, 116–136.

Frith, U. (1991). Asperger and his syndrome. In U. Frith (Ed.), *Autism and Asperger syndrome.* Cambridge, England: Cambridge University Press.

Garbarino, H. (1990). *El Ser en Psicoanálisis.* Montivideo, Uruguay: EPPAL.

Gillberg, C. (1984). Infantile autism and other childhood psychosis in a Swedish urban region: Epidemiological aspects. *Journal of Child Psychology and Psychiatry, 25,* 35–43.

Gillberg, C. (1994). *Autism och autismliknande tillst_nd hos barn, ungdomar och vuxna* (2nd ed.). Stockholm: Natur & Kultur.

Gillberg, C., & Coleman, M. (2000). *The biology of autistic syndromes, 3rd ed.* London: Mac Keith Press.

Gomberoff, M., Noemi, C., & de Gomberoff, L. P. (1991). Detección del objeto autista en el análisis de una niña psicótica. *Transiciones, 2,* 36–52.

Greek Government Bulletin. (1998). Development of a national system of social security [Athens]. *Law, 2646*(1), 236.

Greek Government Bulletin. (1999). Development of mental health services [Athens]. *Law, 2716*(1), 96.

Greek Government Bulletin. (2000). Education of people with special needs [Athens]. *Law, 281*(1), 78.

Guisa Cruz, V. M. (1991). Potenciales evocados auditivos y electroencéfalograma en el niño autista. *Amerpi, 3,* 47–64.

Hannesdóttir, H. (1993). Child and adolescent psychiatry in Iceland—The state of the art, past, present, and future. *Nordic Journal of Psychiatry, 47*(1), 9–13.

Hanselmann, H. (1933). *Einführung in die heilpädagogik.* Rotapfel-Verlag, Erlenbach-Zürich und Leipzig.

Harbauer, H., Lempp, R., Nissen, G., & Strunk, P. (1974). *Lehrbuch der speciellen Kinder- und Jugend-psychiatrie.* Heidelberg, Germany: Springer-Verlag.

Heller, T. (1908). Dementia Infantilis. *Zeitschrift fur die Erforschung und Behandlung des Jugenlichen Schwachsinns, 2,* 141–165.

Herault, J., Martineau, J., Petit, E., Perrot, A., Sauvage, D., Barthelemy, C., et al. (1994). Genetic markers in autism: Association study on short arm of chromosome 11. *Journal of Autism and Developmental Disorders, 24,* 233–236.

Hoshino, Y., Kaneko, M., Yashima, Y., Kumashiro, H., Volkmar, F. R., & Cohen, D. J. (1987). Clinical features of autistic children with setback course in their infancy. *Japanese Journal of Psychiatric Neurology, 41,* 237–246.

Hoshino, Y., Komatsu, F., & Kumashiro, H. (1992). The investigation on unbalanced diet and abnormal dietary behavior in autistic children. *Psychiatric Neurologic Pediatry of Japan, 32,* 59–67.

Hoshino, Y., & Kumashilo, H. (1989). *Clinica of infantile autism.* Tokyo: Shinko-Igaku-Shuppan Sha.

Hoshino, Y., Kumashiro, H., Yashima, Y., Tachibana, R., Watanabe, M., & Furukawa, H. (1982). The early symptoms of autistic children and its diagnostic significance. *Folia Psychiatrica et Neurologica Japonica, 36,* 367–374.

Hoshino, Y., Yokoyama, F., Watanabe, M., Murata, S., & Kaneko, M. (1987). The diurnal variation and the response to dexamethasone suppression test of saliva cortisol level in autistic children. *Folia Psychiatrica Japonica, 41,* 227.

Howlin, P., Marchant, R., Rutter, M., Berger, M., Hersov, L., & Yule, W. (1973). A home based approach to the treatment of autistic children. *Journal of Autism and Childhood Schizophrenia, 4,* 308–336.

Howlin, P., Rutter, M., Berger, M., Hemsley, R., Hersov, L., & Yule, E. (1987). *Treatment of autistic children.* Chichester, England: Wiley.

Hudson, A. (1995). Disability and facilitated communication: A critique. In T. H. Ollendick & R. J. Prinz (Eds.), *Advances in clinical child psychology* (Vol. 17, pp. 197–232). New York: Plenum Press.

Ishii, T. (1987). Long-term prognosis of infantile autism. *Japanese Journal of Clinical Psychiatry, 7,* 907.

Jarast, R. (1990). Yo-piel psicótico infantil. *Diarios Clínicos, Revista de Psicoanálisis con niños y adolescentes,* 107–113.

Jundell, I. (1915). *Broken minds.* Stockholm: Barnens Dagblad.

Kamio, Y., Ishizaka, Y., Koshimoto, T., et al. (1993). The mental disorders of autistic children in their adolescence. *Proceedings of Japanese Child and Adolescent Psychiatry meetings,* 72.

Kamp, L. N. J. (1953). Les psychoses chex l'enfant. *Acxtal Neurol. Et Psychiatr. Bel, 53,* 309–330.

Kanner, L. (1943). Autistic disturbances of affective contact. *Nervous Child, 2,* 217–250.

Kanner, L. (1948). *Textbook in child psychiatry* (2nd ed.). Springfield, IL: Charles C Thomas.

Karantanos, G. (1984). *Infantile autism: Facts, current classifications and study of neurochemical factors.* Doctoral dissertation, University of Athens School of Medicine, Athens, Greece.

Kawasaki, Y., Shinomiya, M., Niwa, S., et al. (1994). Regions of EEG paroxysms in autism-evidence for possible frontal lobe involvement in the pathogenesis of autism. *Proceedings of 13th International Association for Child and Adolescent Psychiatry and Allied Professions, 19.*

Key, E. (1909). *The century of the child.* London: G. P. Putnam Sons.

Kobayashi, R. (1993a). Phenomenological study on the perception, metamorphosis phenomena in autism. *Japanese Journal of Clinical Psychiatry, 35,* 804–811.

Kobayashi, R. (1993b). Set-back phenomena in and the long term prognoses for autistic children. *Japanese Journal of Child Adolescent Psychiatry, 34,* 239–248.

Kobayashi, R., Oshima, M., & Kaneko, S. (1992). Developmental psychopathology as related to the eating disorder of an autistic adult. *Japanese Journal of Child Adolescent Psychiatry, 33,* 311–320.

Krug, D. A., Arick, J., & Almond, P. (1980). Behavior checklist for identifying severely handicapped individuals with high levels of autistic behavior. *Journal of Child Psychology and Psychiatry, 21,* 221–229.

Kurita, H. (1985). Infantile autism with speech loss before the age of thirty months. *Journal of American Academic and Child Psychiatry, 24,* 191–196.

Kusunoki, T. (1988). Neurotic maladaption state in group setting of adolescent autism. *Proceedings of 29th Association of Japanese Child and Adolescent Psychiatry, 57.*

Landesman-Dwyer, S. (1981). Living in the community. *American Journal of Mental Deficiency, 86*(3), 223–234.

Lelord, G., & Sauvage, D. (1990). *L'autisme de l'enfant.* Paris: Masson.

Levi, G. (1973). Sviluppo psicotico e sviluppo cognitivo [Psychotic development and cognitive development]. *Neuropsichiatria Infantile, 147,* 661–677.

Levi, G. (1993). Psicosi infantili precoci [Early childhood psychosis]. In *Enciclopedia Medica Italiana* (Vol. 4, pp. 6208–6220). Florence, Italy. USES Edizioni Scientifiche Firenze.

Levi, G., Bernabei, P., Fabrizi, A., & Zollinger, B. (1984). Disturbi precoci di simbolizzazione: Un nucleo patogenetico comune per i disturbi di sviluppo e le disarmonie evolutive [Early symbolisation's disorders: A common pathogenetic core for developmental disorders]. *Psichiatria dell'Infanzia e dell'Adolescenza, 51,* 179–187.

Lord, C., Rutter, M. L., & DiLavore, P. C. (1998). *Autism Diagnostic Observation Schedule-Generic.* San Antonio, TX: Psychological Corporation.

Lord, C., Rutter, M. L., & Le Couteur, A. (1994). Autism Diagnostic Interview-Revised: A revised version of a diagnostic interview for caregivers of individuals with possible pervasive developmental disorders. *Journal of Autism and Developmental Disorders, 24,* 659–685.

Lotter, V. (1966). Epidemiology of autistic conditions in young children: I. Prevalence. *Social Psychiatry, 1,* 124–137.

Lotter, V. (1967). Epidemiology of autistic conditions in young children: II. Some characteristics of the parents and children. *Social Psychiatry, 1,* 163–173.

Magnusson, K., Rydell, A.-M., & Dahlin, G. (1975). *Autism hos barn. Teorier, vård och behandling.* Stockholm: Natur & Kultur.

Mahler, M. (1952). On child psychosis and schizophrenia: Autistic and symbiotic infantile psychosis. In *The psychoanalytic study of the child* (Vol. 7, pp. 286–305). New York: International Universities Press.

Mahler, M. (1955). On the symbiotic child psychosis: Genetic, dynamic and restitutive aspects. *Psychoanalytical Study of the Child, 10,* 195–211.

Marcin, C. (1991). Modelos de intervención terapéutica en el autismo. *Amerpi, 3,* 65–85.

Mavropoulou, S., & Padeliadou, S. (2000). Greek teachers' perceptions of autism and implications for educational practice. *Autism, 4,* 173–183.

Mendilaharsu, C., & de Mendilaharsu, S. A. (1987). Reflexiones sobre el Psicoanálisis de la Psicosis. *Rev. Uruguaya de Psicoanálisis, 66,* 9–37.

Mesibov, G., Schopler, E., Schaffer, B., & Landrus, R. (1988). *Individualized assessment and treatment for autistic and developmentally disordered children: Vol. IV. Adolescent and adult psychoeducational profile (AAPEP).* Austin, TX: ProEd.

Mills Costa, N. (1989). Educacao especial e tratamento da crianca autista *Integracao, 2*(4), 7–8.

Mises, R., & Quemada, N. (1993). Classification Francaise des Troubles Mentaux de l'Enfant et de l'Adolescent. Classification Internationale des Troubles Mentaux et du Comportement. (ch. V de la CIM 10-O. M. S.), Paris: C. T. N. E. R. H. I., Paris.

Nagai, Y. (1983). The characteristics and mechanism of food preference in infantile autism. *Japanese Journal of Child and Adolescent Psychiatry, 24,* 260–278.

Naruse, H., Hayashi, T., Takesada, M., Nakane, A., & Yamazaki, K. (1989). Metabolic changes of aromatic amino acids and monoamines in infantile autism and development of new treatment related to the finding. *Japanese Journal of Child Neurology, 21,* 181–189.

Oelsner, R. R. (1989). Vulnerabilidad y fenómenos autistas. *Psicoanalysis, 11*(1), 177–190.

Papageorgiou, V., Vogindroukas, I., & Vostanis, P. (2002). Characteristics of referral, diagnosis and management for autism spectrum disorders in Greece. *Good Autism Practice, 3*(2), 75–88.

Piha, J., & Almqvist, F. (1994). Child psychiatry as an academic and clinical discipline in Finland. *Nordic Journal of Psychiatry, 48*(1), 3–8.

Pinto, M. C. B. (1982). O autismo infantil. Análise de uma hipótese etiopatogenética. Consideracoes sobre a neurobiologia da senso-percepcao. *Journal bras Psiq, 31*(2), 79–85.

Prego Silva, L. E. (1980). Qué es lo posicótico del punto de vista clínico? *Rev. APPIA, 7*(1–2), 83–90.

Prior, M. (1987). Biological and neurophysiological approaches to childhood autism. *British Journal of Psychiatry, 150,* 8–17.

Prior, M., & Tonge, B. J. (1990). Pervasive developmental disorders. In B. Tonge, B. J. Burrows, & G. D. Werry (Eds.), *Handbook of studies in child psychiatry* (pp. 193–208). Amsterdam: Elsevier.

Rahav, M., Cohen, Y., & Porat, S. (1981). *Autism in Israel.* Jerusalem: Israel Ministry of Health.

Reed, J. (Chairman). (1994). People with learning disabilities (mental handicap) or with autism. In *Review of health and social services for mentally disordered attendees and others requiring similar services* (Vol. 17). London: Her Majesty's Stationery Office.

Remschmidt, H., & Schmidt, M. (1988). *Kinder- und Jugendpsychiatrie in Klinik und Praxis. In drei Bänden.* New York: Georg Thieme Verlag Stuttgart, Germany.

Rimland, B. (1964). *Infantile autism.* New York: Appleton-Century-Crofts.

Rutter, M. L. (1968). Concepts of autism: A review of research. *Journal of Psychology and Psychiatry, 9,* 1–25.

Rutter, M. L. (1970). Autistic children: Infancy to adulthood. *Seminars in Psychiatry, 2,* 435–450.

Rutter, M. L. (1978). Diagnosis and definition. In M. Rutter & E. Schopler (Eds.), *Autism: A reappraisal of concepts and treatment* (pp. 1–26). New York: Plenum Press.

Rutter, M. L., & Bartak, L. (1973). Special educational treatment of autistic children: A comparative study: II. Follow-up findings and implications for services. *Journal of Child Psychology and Psychiatry, 14,* 241–270.

Rutter, M., Shaffer, D., & Shepherd, M. (1975). *A multiaxial classification of child psychiatric disorders.* Geneva, World Health Organization.

Rydelius, P.-A. (1986). *Barn, ungdomar och vuxna vid fyra lkepedagogiska behandlingshem i Jrna.* Stockholm, Sweden: Karolinska Institutet, Institutionen f.r barn och ungdomspsykiatri, Forskningsrapport Nr: 5, ISSN 1103–0887.

Rydelius, P.-A. (1993). Child and adolescent psychiatry in Sweden—from yesterday until today. *Nordic Journal of Psychiatry, 47*(6), 395–404.

Schain, R., & Freedman, D. X. (1961). Studies on 5-hydroxyindole metabolism in autistic and other mentally retarded children. *Journal of Pediatrics, 58,* 315–320.

Schopler, E., Reichler, R. J., Bashford, A., & Marcus, L. M. (1990). *Psychoeducational Profile Revised (PEP-R).* Austin, TX: ProEd.

Schopler, E., Reichler, R. J., & Renner, B. R. (1988). *The Childhood Autism Rating Scale (CARS).* Los Angeles: Western Psychological Services.

Shirataki, S., Taira, R., & Kashiwagi, H. (1984). Abnormal attachment relationship as an early sign of autistic disorders. *Proceedings of 13th International Association for Child and Adolescent Psychiatry and Allied Professions, 53.*

Smedegaard, N., Hansen, N., & Isager, T. (1993). Danish child psychiatry—Past, present, future. *Nordic Journal of Psychiatry, 47*(2), 75–79.

Sommerschild, H., & Grøholt, B. (1989). *Laëewbok I barnepsychiatri.* Tano, Norway.

Sugiyama, T. (1994). A strange recollection phenomenon seen in autistic patients; the time slip phenomenon in autism. *Proceedings of 13th In-*

ternational Association for Child and Adolescent Psychiatry and Allied Professions, 21.

Tallis, J., & Soprano, A. M. (1991). *Neuropediatria, Neuropsicología y aprendizaje.* Buenos Aires, Argentina: Edic. Nueva Visión.

Tao, Kuo-Tai. (1982). Issues of diagnosis and classification of infantile autism. *Chinese Neuropsychiatric Journal, 2,* 104.

Tao, Kuo-Tai. (1987). Infantile autism in China. *Journal of Autism and Developmental Disorders, 2,* 289.

Tonge, B. J., Dissanayake, C., & Brereton, A. V. (1994). Autism: Fifty years on from Kanner. *Journal of Paediatrics and Child Health, 30,* 102–107.

Tordjman, S., Anderson, G. M., McBride, P. A., Hertzig, M. E., Snow, M. E., Hall, L. M., et al. (1997). Plasma B-endorphin, adrenocorticotropin hormone, and cortisol in autism. *Journal of Child Psychology and Psychiatry, 38,* 705–715.

Tramer, M. (1942). *Lehrbuch der allgemeinen Kinderpsychiatrie—einschliesslich /der allgemeinen Psychiatrie der Pubertät und Adoleszenz.* Basel, Switzerland: Benno Schwabe & Co Verlag.

Vandvik, I. H., & Spurkland, I. (1993). Child and adolescent psychiatry in Norway—Today and tomorrow. *Nordic Journal of Psychiatry, 47*(3), 155–160.

van Krevelen, D. (1952). Een geval van [Early infantile autism]. *Nederlands Tijdschrift voor Geneeskunde, 96,* 202–206.

Villareal, L., & Gaviria, P. (1987). Características del aprendizaje en los niños autistas: sus implicaciones para las estrategias de tratamiento [Colombia]. *Encuentro Nacional de Educación Especial, 35–63.*

Volkmar, F. R., Klin, A., Siegel, B., Szatmari, P., Lord, C., Campbell, M., et al. (1994). Field trial for autistic disorder in *DSM-IV. American Journal of Psychiatry, 151,* 1361–1367.

Weber, D. (1985). Autistische Syndrome [Autistic syndrome]. In *Kinder und Jugenpsychiatry in Klinik und Praxis. Band II: Entwicklungsstrungen, organisch bedingte St. rungen, Psychosen, Begutashtung.* Stuttgart, Germany: Georg Thieme Verlag.

Weizman, A., Gonen, N., Tyano, S., Szekely, G. A., & Laron Z. I. (1987). Platelet (H3) imipramine binding in autistic and schizophrenic children. *Psychopharmacology, 91,* 101–103.

Weizman, A., Weizman, R., Szekely, G. A., Wijsenbeek, H., & Livni, E. (1982). Abnormal immune response to brain tissue antigen in syndrome of autism. *American Journal of Psychiatry, 139,* 1462–1465.

Weizman, R., Gil-Ad, I., Dick, J., Tyano, S., Szekely, G. A., & Laron, Z. (1988). Low plasma immunoreactive B-endorphin levels in autism. *Journal of the American Academy of Child and Adolescent Psychiatry, 27,* 430–433.

Weizman, R., Weizman, A., Tyano, S., Szekely, G., Weissman, B. A., & Sarne, Y. (1984). Humoral endorphin blood levels in autistic, schizophrenic and healthy subjects. *Psychopharmacology, 82,* 368–370.

Wernicke, C. (1991). El autismo y la terapia de contención. In G. Fernandez (Ed.), *Autismo, un síntoma?* (pp. 149–157). Buenos Aires, Argentina: Ed. Gabas.

Wing, L. (1981a). Language, social, and cognitive impairments in autism and severe mental retardation. *Journal of Autism and Developmental Disorders, 11,* 31–44.

Wing, L. (1981b). Asperger's syndrome: a clinical account. *Psychological Medicine, 11,* 115–129.

Wing, L. (1989). *Hospital closure and the effects on the residents.* Aldershot, England: Avebury.

Wing, L. (1999). *Diagnostic Interview for Social and Communication Disorders (DISCO)* (10th ed.). London: Autistic Society.

Wing, L., & Gould, J. (1979). Severe impairments of social interaction and associated abnormalities in children: Epidemiology and classification. *Journal of Autism and Childhood Schizophrenia, 9,* 11–29.

Wolfensberger, W. (1972). *The principle of normalization in human services.* Toronto, Ontario, Canada: National Institute on Mental Retardation.

Wolfensberger, W., & Thomas, S. (1983). *Programme analysis of service systems implementation of normalization goals.* Toronto, Ontario, Canada: National Institute on Mental Retardation.

World Health Organization. (1992). *International classification of diseases* (ICD-10). Geneva, Switzerland: Author.

Yamazaki, K. (1992). Early signs of infantile autism. In H. Naruse & E. M. Ornitz (Eds.), *Neurobiology of infantile autism: Proceedings of the International Symposium on Neurobiology of Infantile Autism, Tokyo, 10–11 November 1990* (pp. 165–175). Amsterdam: Excerpta Medica.

Yang, X.-L. (1990). Clinical analysis of 30 cases of childhood autism. *Chinese Journal of Mental Health, 6,* 250.

Yashima, Y., Hoshino, Y., & Murata, S. (1991). The various problems of the death of autistic children. *Proceedings of the 32nd Association of Japanese Child and Adolescent Psychiatry, 16.*

Yokota, K., Sakaguchi, M., & Nagai, Y. (1989). The aggressive behavior of autistic adolescence. *Proceedings of the 30th Association of Japanese Child and Adolescent Psychiatry, 20.*

PERSONAL PERSPECTIVES

Clinicians and researchers have a great deal to contribute to understanding and caring for individuals with autism. Yet, the authentic voice of individuals who have lived with autism has an unmistakable authority. The descriptions provided by individuals with autism, their families, and their teachers convey the full meaning of the disorder as a way of being in the world and the impact of the disorder on all who care about and live with a person with autism. These descriptions are also the source of rich understanding of how the various domains and dimensions of the disorder come together in a full person.

The individual with autism is cut off from others, even those who are closest, in a fundamental way. Fortunately, there are individuals with autism with the capacity to express their sense of being different from others, their unique modes of experiencing sounds and sights, how they navigate through the social world, and their attempts to communicate their thoughts and worries to others. From these descriptions, we can cautiously try to extrapolate to the dilemmas of those who are less able to communicate—who remain far more detached from ordinary social intercourse.

Being the parent of a child with any disability can be experienced by parents as a crushing burden; it is the kind of pain that extended families and clinicians can only partially share. On the other hand, parents, family members, and professionals have, over the past decade, made great strides in working together to improve the lives of individuals with autism and related conditions. This is the culmination of a process that began during the 1960s and gained pace in subsequent decades. Originally, advocacy efforts understandably centered on supporting intervention and treatment programs. As time went on, this effort included advocacy for expanded services and new legislation and regulations to protect individual rights and encourage community inclusion. Early efforts to support and facilitate research have expanded in recent years as national and international research networks have been organized. These efforts have led to a tremendous expansion of knowledge; they have also had the very important effect of bringing a generation of new investigators into the field. The efforts of parents, family members, teachers, and professionals have been critical in this process.

This section captures the voices of a cross-section of those who have lived with autism—individuals with autism themselves, who are now speaking out; parents and siblings, teachers, and professionals.

CHAPTER 49

Community-Integrated Residential Services for Adults with Autism: A Working Model (Based on a Mother's Odyssey)

RUTH CHRIST SULLIVAN

Autism Services Center (ASC) in Huntington, West Virginia, came into existence in March 1979. My son Joseph, then 19 and a classic case of autism, would have no services after he graduated from high school in 1981. He was 15 years old in 1975 when the Individuals with Disabilities Education Act (IDEA; then named Education for All Handicapped Act, Public Law 94-142) gave him a federally mandated right to receive a free and appropriate education. Though he had been in a public school since he was 6, it had been only because of my advocacy and a few creative administrators and teachers who helped make it possible. Before 1975, no special funds or mandates were available for a child like mine. In fact, some states (e.g., California) specifically excluded children with a diagnosis of autism.

I knew that when Joseph aged-out of school at age 21, there would be no more mandatory services in place to address his special needs and that services he *might* get (e.g., vocational rehabilitation) were short term and not specific for someone with autism. At that time, I had already spent more than 15 years working on legislation, regulations, and appropriations (at local, state, and federal levels) for individuals with autism, and there was still no entitlement for adult services. I knew that if I did not develop these services myself, they would be a long time coming—and maybe too late for Joseph. So with a small loan from my family

and using my dining room as an office, I started ASC in 1979. It is a private, nonprofit, 501(c)3 organization providing comprehensive services to individuals with developmental disabilities (DD) of all ages, in a community-integrated setting. Our specialty is autism. Today, with a staff of 420, we serve approximately 375 clients, of whom 120 have a diagnosis of autism. We operate 11 group homes, for 32 clients, most of whom have autism. Our goal is to serve individuals in such a way that they can make significant progress toward independence in a caring and supported learning environment that enhances positive outcomes. We want to provide services that earn parents' trust that we will appropriately care for their loved ones.

INTRODUCTION TO COMMUNITY-INTEGRATED RESIDENTIAL SERVICES FOR ADULTS WITH AUTISM

Most individuals with autism will be adults for decades longer than they are children. This major portion of their lives has not been seriously addressed by our society. As parents get older, they worry—with good reason—about what will happen to their loved ones when they can no longer care for them.

In the United States, there are only about 25 agencies that voluntarily provide services specifically designed to serve adults with autism in community intergrated residential settings. An informal survey from their new national association, the National Association of Residential Providers for Adults with Autism (NARPAA, founded February 2002 by Ruth Christ Sullivan) reports that they collectively serve approximately 1,500 individuals. According to the 2000 U.S. Census Bureau report (Census 2000 Summary, File 1), there are approximately 193 million adults ages 22 and over.

Since the Centers for Disease Control (CDC) states (CDC web site, 11/30/04, p. 1) that they have inadequate data on prevalence for adults with autism, at this time we can only project prevalence from the child counts.

In 1996, CDC reported 3.4 of every 1,000 (1 per 300) children with autism. Using that rate to project the number of individuals with autism who are 22 and over, the numbers would come out to 643,333 (193 million divided by 300). CEC also reports, "Studies done in Europe and Asia since 1985 have found that as many as 6 of every 1,000 children have [autism]." Those rates project 1 per 166, or 1,171,250 (193 million divided by 166) adults with autism.

A study reported by the California Department of Developmental Studies (May 2003) reports a prevalence in that state of 1 per 320, which projects to 603,125 adults nationwide.

Whether one uses 1 per 166, or 1 per 300, or 1 per 320, it is clear that these numbers show a staggering disconnect between client needs and available, appropriate services. The situation is so severe that the Autism Society of America (ASA) calls it a national crisis (See ASA Position Paper, 2001).

Adults with autism are not easy to serve. Most non-autism-specific residential agencies are "normed" on people with mental retardation, whose social skills, behavior problems, and learning deficits tend to be noticeably milder. A study (Van Bourgondien & Reichle, 1997) conducted by the TEACCH program at the University of North Carolina at Chapel Hill reported that, compared with nonautistic mentally retarded people, adults with autism were far more likely to have problem behaviors, including rituals, obsession with sameness, easily provoked agitation, and self-isolation. Serving them in residential settings takes intensive staffing, institutional will, and know-how. The costs are high. But the benefit is great: We now know that an adult with autism can become a relatively calm, functioning member of society if given the proper supports.

Because there are currently so few residential services specifically for adults with autism, few parents or professionals are familiar with a working model. In the literature about autism, there is much discussion about the importance of providing appropriate services and of ensuring dignity and respect for clients. The principle is also found in legislation, regulations, accreditation guidelines, and so on, but very little has been written anywhere about how to make it happen—with real clients and real staff, 24 hours a day, on a long-term basis.

The ASC in Huntington, West Virginia, is one of the 25 agencies in NARPAA. This chapter discusses ASC's programs, philosophy, and design, as well as how our staff are trained, monitored, supervised, and supported. We have seen that, with an appropriate program, adults with autism can live a busy, fruitful, and progressively improving life.

HISTORICAL PERSPECTIVE

Fifteen to 25 years ago, families in most parts of the country who were looking for government assistance for their adult relative with autism had mainly one choice: a state institution. Though there were a few private day and residential programs, the costs were beyond what most families could pay. Even state "hospitals" or "schools"—euphemisms for large institutions housing hundreds, even thousands, of patients with minimal staff— might charge fees. The facility was often a long way from home.

When the family visited the state institution, they were often appalled at what they saw and made a solemn pledge that their loved one would never go there. One family told me after such a visit, "If he has to live in a cage, we'll build one in our kitchen. At least he can be with us, and every day we can reach out and tell him we love him."

In those days, admission might be denied to an individual who was diagnosed with autism, or there might be a quota for people with that label. Sometimes the family had to legally relinquish the custody of their relative to the state in order to receive services for him or her. Some parents had to agree to therapy or counseling for themselves and participate in their child's program—for instance, half a day per week for a year. When parents came to visit, they were sometimes not allowed to see the parts of the building where their child slept or ate (Sullivan, 1977).

It was generally assumed that care would be custodial only. Institutionalization was usually a lifetime sentence. Parents could only hope that their loved ones with autism would be safe. That they might be happy, might improve, or eventually return to the family in better condition than they left was not typically on the list of possibilities. It is not difficult to imagine the pain of placing a son or daughter in such a place. The instinct for psychological survival could, in some cases, cause a complete separation from the placed relative. It was still too common in those days for parents to be told, "Put him away and forget he was ever born."

By the late 1960s and through the 1970s, there was a swell of national advocacy for community-integrated services, including several high-profile and successful class-action court cases against institutions. This resulted in Congressional legislation in 1981, amending the federal Social Security Act, adding Title XIX to the Medicaid Act. The new law made funds available to community-integrated services, not only state institutions as before. The program, now familiar to families whose developmentally disabled children (of any age) are receiving these services, is called the Home and Community-Based Waiver (HCBW, sometimes referred to as "Waiver"). This program allows state dollars to match federal dollars, according to a state's economic health. This new funding source allowed states to reimburse qualified private community providers who started up programs for individuals with DD. Soon there began a large exodus from state institutions, allowing residents to move back into their communities, closer to their families.

At first, Waiver funds were available only to individuals coming out of institutions. For families of children with autism, that policy seemed blatantly unfair, since their children had often been denied admission to the institutions because of the autism diagnosis. By the late 1980s, however, most individuals with a DD diagnosis—not just those coming out of institutions—were allowed to apply if they met the criteria for Waiver eligibility.

However, meeting the criteria for Waiver eligibility is not, at this time, an entitlement to funding and Waiver services. This is the dilemma. Unlike eligibility for special education in our state education systems, where there is an entitlement to services, a special education student who turns 22 and ages out of school *loses* entitlement.

Although Waiver funding has greatly contributed to a well-established system of services for adults with mental retardation—especially those *without* behavior problems—individuals with a diagnosis of autism have had great difficulties in having access to appropriate services based on *their* diagnosis. Their problematic behavior and need for intensive staffing, training, and support mean costs are significantly higher for this group, and providers are generally not eager to admit many into their programs. It is not difficult to understand why there are so few agencies offering autism-specific residential services.

FOUR MAJOR COMPONENTS OF A SUCCESSFUL RESIDENTIAL PROGRAM FOR INDIVIDUALS WITH AUTISM

First Component: There Must Be a Sound, Firmly Held Mind-Set/Philosophy on How Clients Are to Be Treated

Our agency was founded on the belief that all people with autism and other developmental disorders, though having a wide range of disabilities, have the capacity for growth and development. Even clients with the most challenging behaviors respond to gentle, humane treatment in a structured program. ASC aims at the use of best clinical practices and at positive, measurable outcomes for the client.

Without this mind-set, there cannot be a good, consistent, long-term program. Progress will be slow or nonexistent, or worse, the client will regress.

The Client Must Be Treated with Dignity and Respect

If you were to walk into any agency serving individuals with autism or other DD and ask to see its mission statement, it is highly likely you would see words such as *dignity* and *respect*. But what does that mean? How do you train caretakers to understand? Following are some concrete examples, based on real stories.

Thoughtful, Sensitive Communication Skills Are Essential

Caretakers must be respectful in their manner of speaking. They must not talk in front of clients as though they are not there. Let's say you meet Mary (throughout the chapter, all names are changed), age 30, a mostly nonverbal client you know well. You are visiting a group home, put up your hand, palm out, inviting a "high five," as you have done many times before. It is clear immediately that Mary is in no mood to visit, so you do not press for an interaction. As you turn away, the client's direct care staff (DCS) quickly volunteers, "Mary has had a bad morning. She wet her bed last night, has taken a long time to get dressed, refuses to comb her hair, and hasn't made her bed yet. She's in a bad mood. I don't know what's wrong with her. That's just the way she is." Since Mary cannot verbally express herself well, it is likely her mood just got even worse.

A better way for the staff to respond would have been to say nothing about Mary's lack of response while the visitor was present, but to address the issue with her later, in a quiet manner, helping her to understand the social rule: When spoken to, react in a friendly manner. When the client is calmer, perhaps later in the day when they are alone, the staff could go over the episode again and show what the correct response should have been, then practice it, with role playing, giving praise for Mary's correct performance. If moodiness is a consistent problem, perhaps more practice is necessary. The reasonably based expectation is that the natural reinforcer—someone smiling back—will even-

tually have meaning for the client and become routine behavior.

We expect our staff to be like teachers, asking themselves daily, "What did my client learn from me today that he didn't know when I came on duty?" Also, "What did I learn about my client today that I didn't know?"

Caretakers Must Be Careful with Terminology in Referring to the Clients

ASC uses the word *client,* meaning "a person who engages the professional advice or service of another." Our clients are, in a real sense, our employers. It is their funds—whether public or private—that pay for the service we provide. They are adults and are not to be called "boys," "girls," or "kids"—or for that matter, "sweetie," "dearie," "honey," "baby doll," and so on. They are to be called by their names. Those who live in our group homes or apartments are referred to as "residents."

Staff Must Treat Clients' Families as Valued Partners

Families are invited to, and are essential members of, all meetings of their child's Individual Program Plan committee and his or her Interdisciplinary Team. A majority of our Human Rights Committee are parents of clients we serve. Also, parents are free to call or visit their child's residence at their convenience. We do not require appointments. In our experience, parents rarely misuse this privilege. They also have access to all their child's ASC records. Families are invited to Christmas, Valentine's Day, Halloween, and other parties. There is always a good turnout.

Staff, Families, Friends, Neighbors, and the General Public Need to See These Clients as People Whose Dignity and Worth Are Highly Valued by Their Caretakers

Caretakers must meet society's norms by making sure clients are well groomed, appropriately dressed, and have good physical hygiene. This includes simple and basic things such as well-brushed teeth, clean and trimmed fingernails, a good haircut, and clean, well-combed hair. It means attractive clothes that fit and that are neat, clean, and well ironed. Also, clothes are to be modest—no short shorts or short skirts. For female clients, no tight, clinging tops or bottoms or low-cut blouses are allowed.

Not only must our *clients* look nice, but we expect our *staff* to project a good image as they take our clients out into the community each day. We have very explicit requirements for staff dress, codified in our personnel policies. In this era of casual wear and with our young DCS, this can be a troublesome issue. We give copies of our staff dress code and behavior code to applicants at their first interview, just to make sure they understand and are not surprised after they are hired. We are serious about how our staff represent our clients and ASC in our community.

Once they reach adulthood, individuals with autism can no longer pass as just eccentrics. Their behavior often attracts unwanted attention: talking or laughing too loudly, flipping a string, brushing leg hairs or eyebrows with a brush, placing a paper towel in the palm before shaking hands, not responding when spoken to, or asking inappropriate questions, such as, "Why doesn't that man have any hair on his head?" within hearing distance of the man.

However, if our clients and their staff are well dressed and the staff is seen as helping the client through anxious moments when aberrant behavior is most likely to occur, the public is more likely to understand that staff are in control of the situation and that they care for and respect the client.

Over the years, I've heard parents say that one of the most difficult things for them when visiting their loved ones in large congregate living facilities is to see them poorly dressed: pants too long or too short, no belts, wrinkled clothes, buttons missing, zippers broken, shirts buttoned wrong, unattractive clothes, dirty or worn-out shoes, no socks, and so on. Clothes are among the first things people see when meeting another person. Whether in an institution or a small community group home, a bad appearance shouts a lack of caring by the caregivers and the institution that employs them. When clients are shabbily dressed and go out into the community looking so unattractive, it is easy for society to assume it would be best to keep them far out in the country, out of sight. Being nicely dressed helps to give dignity and respect to the client

and the staff and increases the goodwill of the community.

Clients' Living Quarters Must Be in Homes and Neighborhoods That Society Accepts as Good Locations, Well Constructed, Attractive, and Well-Kept (Especially When No Longer Living with Their Families)

Feeling the heavy responsibility of being pioneers in placing autistic adults in typical homes on a typical block, we at ASC make a point of being good neighbors. Our lawns are nicely kept, our walks are swept, lawns mowed, leaves raked, garbage cans neat, and our houses kept in excellent repair. We have had no long-term trouble with *any* of our neighbors. However, several times when we moved into a new house, some neighbors were upset and sometimes rude when we introduced ourselves that first day. One man told me, "I don't want those retarded people on the sidewalk on my block. Lady, you've just told me my property values have fallen drastically." He closed his door abruptly, obviously quite unhappy.

On one street, initially, a few neighbors contacted their city councilmen and went to city hall to see the mayor. The mayor (who knew our programs well) not only let them know about the Fair Housing Act of 1988, which forbids discrimination against group homes such as ours, but also assured them that their fears of falling property values for their homes were unfounded. Indeed, our houses often *enhance* the value of surrounding homes. (Copies of the Fair Housing Act are available from any Housing and Urban Development [HUD] office or its counterpart of a county or city. It is critical that families, their advocates, and agencies providing residential services know about this law.)

About a year later, a lady who lives close by and was originally one of those who went to city hall saw our staff and client at a McDonald's and came over to say how much she enjoyed having us as neighbors. Later, when one of our staff at the house died, the nearest, and originally most upset neighbor, the one who had shut the door on me, came over for a little memorial service to which we had invited him and his wife. He was among the last to leave, obviously pleased to be, himself, a good neighbor.

A successful group home is also a source of pride for the community. Our work is different from that done by more traditional agencies such as the Red Cross, Heart or Cancer Associations, Easter Seals, and so on. We are new. It is only in the past 10 to 15 years that people with autism are seen with any regularity in public places. Though there is much more heightened awareness of autism—thanks to media events such as Dustin Hoffman's *Rain Man*[1]—this condition is still a poorly understood disability. When the community sees our clients doing well in their group homes, it makes the jobs of our staff less stressful and helps to enhance the lives of those we serve.

Home Decor and Furnishings Need to Be Attractive and Must Be Kept Neat, Clean, Sanitary, Safe, and in Good Repair

This is a challenge, especially when we first open a home. Many of our clients have come to us from institutions and arrive with severely disruptive behaviors. We have never denied admission, nor discharged a client, based on behavior. In those first few weeks and months, we experience things such as broken windows, holes in walls, smashed TV sets, torn clothes, doors ripped off their hinges, broken chairs—and the worst of worst, feces smearing. Sometimes staff are injured.

Our policy is to replace and restore quickly—if possible, the same day. We do not want our clients *or* our staff to get used to living in a house where things are broken, unsightly, and/or not working. We often replace glass in windows with plexiglass while such behavior is a problem. If punching holes in the walls is a persistent issue in a house, we replace ordinary drywall structures with 3-quarter-inch

plywood, which is then covered with ordinary drywall, looking like the original walls, contributing to the normalization and dignity of the clients' living space. The thicker, more rigid plywood does not "give"; therefore, it does not provide the feedback (satisfaction?) of causing destruction. Also, making holes with fists or heads becomes a painful activity for the client. Hole punching immediately stops.

We have a codified housekeeping manual for each house, with detailed instructions for chores such as making beds. Beds are made daily before clients leave their rooms in the morning. "Sanitary" was left out of this manual when it was first written, until I saw a staff wiping the kitchen floor with a dishcloth!

Good, Informal Records of the Clients' Personal History Must Be Maintained

Staff and families must be conscious that they probably will not be around in a few years. Therefore, staff keep careful informal records of clients' lives—well-organized, up-to-date photograph albums, videotape footage of the clients (done monthly at ASC), and an anecdote book that highlights the clients' significant happy and sad times. We encourage families to send pictures for the clients' albums; and for their rooms. It must be recognized that preserving the clients' personal history is important. In a fire, the first thing most people want to save is the family photo album. This history is available to clients' next caregivers and to their families.

When a 75-year-old man, who had been in an institution since he was 5 (circa 1916), came to live in one of our group homes, the record sent with him from the institution was not even one inch thick—70 years of his life. Not one picture was in it. That was when we started the policy of carefully keeping photo albums and other records. We have learned

---

[1] My son Joseph was one of the two major autism models Dustin Hoffman studied to create the character "Raymond" in *Rain Man*. The other was Peter Guthrie of New Jersey. The "Raymond" in Barry Morrow's original manuscript was based on Kim Peek of Salt Lake City, Utah, who is a prodigious savant but does not have a diagnosis of autism. In later iterations of the script, the character's disability was changed to autism. A "prescreening benefit performance" was held in Huntington, West Virginia, on December 11, 1988, as a benefit for Autism Services Center. The beautiful, old Keith-Albee Theater was filled to capacity—1,800 people. Dustin Hoffman, his wife Lisa, as well as Barry Levinson, director, and Mark Johnson, producer, and their wives were present at the gala celebration. The film's official premiere occurred the next night in New York City. It won four Oscars in April of 1989.

how important these personal records are to the clients and their families. When one of our near-mute clients was told his mother died, he immediately went down to the living room (where he had chosen to keep his album) and began to look at pictures of his mother. It dignifies and confirms the value of an individual's life to have a record of his or her existence.

Yes, there must be a firmly held mindset/philosophy about how clients are treated. These principles must permeate the agency *at all levels.* If only top staff believe the philosophy, there will be "leakage." If only DCS believe the philosophy, there will be burnout, which can be a breeding ground for abuse. Staff will find little support for their intensive and difficult work and will leave—probably sooner than later. At ASC, *all* our staff—direct care, managers, administration, department heads, nurses, secretaries, maintenance, records clerks, human resources personnel, finance, and service coordinators—must go through the initial training we give to DCS—and occasionally family members. These initial classes stress the importance of relationships between staff and client. Even during a client's extremely aggressive, out-of-control incidents, our crisis procedure mandates a respectful intervention.

The principles of dignity and respect must be implemented and incorporated into all the details of the daily program and practice. Because this first component is the most important, and critical, it has taken the most space. The next three discuss what else needs to be in place to help ensure long-term progress for these often-most-difficult-to-serve clients.

Second Component: Supervisors and Senior Management Staff Must Be Experienced, Knowledgeable, and Committed to Positive Programming

Managers must believe all clients can make significant progress, regardless of the severity of their handicap.

They Must Carefully Train, Supervise, Monitor, and Support Direct Care/Hands-On Staff and Be Able to Motivate Them to See the Full Potential of Each Individual in Their Charge

Training DCS at ASC starts with a week-long, formal, classroom-type training, with lectures, films, and CPR/first aid. The new employee is then assigned to a specific client at one of our 11 group homes[2] or to a "community" client—one who lives with his or her family. The new staff receives client-specific training and "shadows" the current staff until management feels the new staff and his or her assigned client are ready to "solo." This happens only after a careful transition, when a house or community manager, in consultation with the client, "old" staff and new staff, all agree the next step (fading out old staff) is appropriate for that client. If the client is fairly new to ASC's residential services and if the client's family is interested in checking out the new staff at the beginning of the transition, we arrange a meeting.

Training Must Be Ongoing

All our group homes have a house manager for that house, with an office in the house. We have no live-in staff, and we have three shifts per day. Every two houses have a coordinator (almost always they have been managers) who supervises the two managers. The coordinator knows the clients well and can assist the two managers when, for instance, there is a client crisis (e.g., two staff need to accompany a client to an ER) or there is a sudden staff shortage (e.g., someone calls in sick), and the coordinator can be relief when the manager has to leave for any reason. House managers are available during most of the clients' awake hours at the residence. They and their coordinators wear pagers or cell phones. The night shift is awake staff, with managers occasionally—and unannounced—starting their shifts at, say, 3:00 A.M. This serves the purpose of not only monitoring but also supporting staff on this shift.

---

[2] There are generally only three residents in each of our 11 group homes. Of the 375 individuals we serve, only 33 live in our group homes (which, with the exception of one case, serve adults). Others are served in their own apartments or in their family homes. Also, of the 375 clients, about 120 have a diagnosis of autism. Most clients in our residences are individuals with autism. We have a staff of 420.

There are periodic and mandatory house staff meetings where extra training occurs, especially for client-specific issues. When a client has a problem behavior, staff are encouraged to get support from their manager. An eyes-on, physically present manager is more likely to see problems developing and be able to monitor and do timely retraining of the DCS.

Additionally, a large part of a manager's responsibilities is support and encouragement. Almost always, the manager has risen from the DCS ranks, knows the signs of burnout, and can often offer assistance to DCS immediately. Managers also usually know the clients well, so that is an important support for new or anxious staff. The managers also know firsthand the progress—whether slow or dramatic—that has been made by our clients. Knowing that history, managers can encourage and motivate the new staff in adopting the belief that every client can and does indeed improve.

Third Component: Direct Care Staff Must Accept the Mind-Set Philosophy

The DCS must be well trained, supervised, monitored, and supported. They must be taught how to interact with clients in a way the clients approve and accept, so that, ultimately, the clients learn self-control.

Eleven-year-old Katrina (Katrina's mother has given permission to use her name in this chapter) came to us from a private psychiatric hospital where she had been placed in the locked juvenile ward, in a locked room because of violent behavior. After a careful 6-week transition back into her community and after many dramatic ups and downs, one day several months into the program, Katrina was upset with her two favorite staff. They had just come back from a pleasant outing, but Katrina wanted, and was perseverating on, having a Coke, even though the staff had carefully prepared her not to expect one when they got home. She suddenly lunged at the neck of one of the staff, but when her hands were within a fraction of an inch of the young woman's throat, she pulled back and threw herself to the ground. Within those few months, Katrina had learned self-restraint. She had kept herself

from harming someone she truly liked. The two are still friends 19 years later. Today Katrina lives in an ASC group home with two other residents. Though she still needs 1:1 staffing, her outbursts are rare, the last one occurring 2 years ago. After years of slowly reducing the high doses of Haldol, she recently went off the drug completely—for the first time in her adult life. She has been off obsessive-compulsive drugs for more than 2 years and now works—with a job coach—as a volunteer at a women's shelter.

Our job is to keep anxiety down by, for example, understanding antecedents that might cause anxiety. However, when that fails, the staff must know which procedures to use to reestablish calm, including *staff* remaining calm—no small task when a 6-foot, 175-pound man is screaming obscenities in your face.

In other clients, the clue to overload might be certain bizarre and idiosyncratic head or hand movements, verbalizations, picking scabs, peeling skin off knuckles, or pulling out hair, which if not recognized and properly dealt with can escalate into banging fists against the head or head into the wall, physically assaulting staff, or throwing heavy items. As our staff get to know the clients better and the clients come to *trust* and like their staff, this list of behaviors typically gets shorter, begins to be milder, or disappears.

There Must Be an Appropriate Staff-to-Client Ratio for an Intensive, Individualized Program

The goals are self-control, increased learning, and, eventually, reduced staff-client ratio and independence.

Jack, age 17, with no speech, weighing over 300 pounds, is one of our most recent admissions. He arrived from an institution with four staff, after a 7-hour drive. He was tired, anxious, scared, and angry. We assigned two male staff to him, 24 hours a day for the first 2 weeks. Even so, he threw a microwave oven, turned over the refrigerator, punched holes in the wall with his fists, broke windows, wet the bed, and tore a door off its hinges—among other destructive acts. This had become his method of communicating.

At this point, it is useful to find out what clients like and make that an important element in their initial program. Our staff soon learned that Jack enjoyed walking, so a large part of his day was spent doing just that. He lost weight and enjoyed being outdoors. One day, while the staff were playing the word game "Hangman," Jack blurted out letters that spelled the winning word—to the amazement of the staff. No one knew he could read or speak! He had been with us 3 weeks. Subsequently, they often played "Hangman" with him. Jack won most of the time. They introduced "Boggle," another spelling game, and gradually began to increase his responsibilities for activities of daily living—such as setting the table, taking out the garbage, making his bed, doing his own laundry, washing dishes, cooking, vacuuming, and grocery shopping. Within 6 weeks, he needed only one staff. Now that staff can be female, we no longer assign him only strong male staff. He now visits his single mother on some weekends, alone, with no staff—to her delight.

Because Jack came to trust and like his teachers (staff) and they can more easily introduce new activities, he has improved dramatically. Today Jack is mild-mannered and pleasant. He has had no dangerous behavior in the past 3 years. He has two part-time paid jobs. He has a job coach, who is also his residential staff, so they know each other well. Recently, a new client moved into Jack's house—a man with mental retardation who came from an institution. The two immediately became friends. Although there is not much verbal communication, it is apparent to anyone who sees them together that there is a genuine feeling of friendship.

Without individualized programs and one-on-one specially trained and supported staffing, this kind of dramatic progress for people with autism is unlikely to occur.

Fourth Component: Staff Must Be Around Long Enough to Get to Know the Clients Well

Frequent turnover of staff is one of our greatest challenges. It works against clients, families, the provider/agency, and society. Frequent turnover is not cost effective—whether measured in cost to clients' lives or providers' resources of money, energy, and time.

There is a national crisis in funding for adequate DCS for individuals in programs—especially residential—that serve adults with DDs, *especially those with autism.* The problem is beginning to be discussed at the highest level of state and federal legislative bodies and government agencies. The American Network of Community Options and Resources (ANCOR, 2003) newsletter, *Links,* reported in March 2003:

[Individual] states' . . . reports showed that fiscal pressures states faced last year have increased in recent months—leading to deterioration in services and supports to individuals and gravely undermining provider stability. (p. 11)

The turnover in DCS staff is as high as 80% in some areas of the United States. For a client population that is as upset at change as adults with autism, the constant change in staff can be devastating. The Autism Society of America's position paper (Sullivan, 2001) calls for a strong national effort to address the egregious deficits in appropriate services to adults with autism.

Knowing Clients Well Helps Staff to Be More Effective

The better the staff know their clients and come to understand their autism-based behaviors (e.g., learning what kind of events "set them off" and how to plan so that those things are appropriately dealt with), the more sympathy the staff will have. The more staff respect their clients' severely handicapping deficits, the more they can successfully teach.

How long it takes parents and professionals to be open to and understand such behavior! Yet we expect a mostly college-student staff of late teenagers and those in their early 20s, with no experience except our training, to work daily with and make progress with some of society's most difficult-to-serve clients. Additionally, they work for minimum or near-minimum wage, because reimbursement rates from Medicaid for this service is so poor. That we as providers can keep DCS at all is a testimony to many things, including the fact that there are many good young people in our communities who feel invigorated by the daily challenges of working with these interesting, enigmatic, fey, lovable human beings we call clients.

CONCLUSION

This chapter described a successful working model of a community-integrated residential program, designed specifically for adults with autism. At its center is a discussion of what I believe, based on 20 years' experience as a provider, are the four major components of a program of this kind. Specific, detailed situations were presented to demonstrate a solution that not only bestows dignity and respect on the clients but also sets the stage for an ongoing trustful relationship between staff and client, which enhances learning on both sides. Although the great majority of our residents are not likely to become independent as we "normals" know it, we have seen that with the right support, their progress can continue over a lifetime. It is not a perfect solution, but it works.

Cross-References

Autism in adolescents and adults with autism is discussed in Chapter 10, behavioral assessment and intervention are addressed in Chapters 34 and 35, vocational supports are described in Chapter 43, and personnel preparation in Chapter 45. Chapters 50 to 53 provide other personal perspectives on autism and related disorders.

REFERENCES

American Network of Community Options and Resources. *Links.* (March 2003). Alexandria, VA: ANCOR.

California Department of Developmental Services. (2003, May 30). Available from www.dds.ca .gov/autism, p. 8.

CDC.gov/ncbddd/dd/aic/about/default.htm.

Census Summary File 1. (2000). U.S. Census Bureau, Economics and Statistics Administration, Washington, DC 20402.

Sullivan, R. C. (1977). *U.S. facilities and programs for children with severe mental illnesses: A directory* (DHEW Publication No. ADM 74-47). Rockville, MD: National Institute of Mental Health.

Sullivan, R. C. (2001). *Autism Society of America's position paper on The National Crisis in Adult Services for Individuals With Autism.* Bethesda, MD.

Van Bourgondien, M. E., & Reichle, N. C. (1997). Residential treatment for individuals with autism. In D. J. Cohen & F. R. Volkmar (Eds.), *Handbook of autism and developmental disorders* (2nd ed., p. 692). New York: Wiley.

CHAPTER 50

A Sibling's Perspective on Autism

JASON B. KONIDARIS

When I was 2 years old, I had bite marks on my back. At the time, we had no dog or other household pets. My parents were alarmed and took me to the pediatrician. The pediatrician attributed the situation to severe sibling rivalry. It was my brother who had been doing the biting. My brother was diagnosed as autistic in 1974 at the Developmental Evaluation Clinic of the Aid for the Retarded in Stamford, Connecticut. Sent by his pediatrician due to questionable hyperactivity and emotional overlay, he was first seen by a team consisting of a neurologist, speech pathologist, psychologist, social worker, and a family relations counselor. He was reevaluated by Dr. Donald Cohen's team at the Yale University Child Study Center and diagnosed as a "classic case" of childhood autism. He was 3½ years old, I was a year younger.

RESPONSIBILITY

"Who left the front door open? How long was it open? Where is he? He's gone! Jason, did you leave the front door open? He's lost now!" The hysteria that ensued remains a vivid picture within my mind. I had left the front door unlocked, allowing my brother to run away one rainy afternoon. Less than 4 years old, I called out to the 5-year-old runaway from our front porch. He was volatile, nonverbal, barefoot, and gone. Slowly, a sickening feeling washed over me. My brother was lost forever and it was my fault. It was the first yet only time I resented my parents and their means of handling the relationship between their two children. I

was clearly blamed for my brother's disappearance. It is common in sibling relationships for the "normal" child to bear the burden of the autistic child's actions.

A far-off neighbor brought my brother back to us after hours of searching. The incident was an isolated one but sent my life in an entirely new direction. From that early age, I was consumed by a self-imposed sense of responsibility for my brother's safety and well-being. It was not a demand placed on me by my parents, nor a common attitude that a younger sibling would care for an older one. It took a place as a focus and priority within my life—a given.

I began trying to figure my brother out. I was wrought with questions. What does he want? What does he feel? Why does he not seem to love me? My brother had a complete inability to understand social conventions, matched by my inability to understand him. Day by day I kept a mental journal of my brother's peculiar habits—those we have now come to know as typical characteristics of autism. I was 5, he was 6. He refused to make eye contact with me or anyone else for that matter. I learned to not take offense at it. He was echolalic and would repeat TV commercials he had heard for hours on end. I learned to appreciate his precision and even laughed at times. He broke anything and everything he could get his hands on. I learned to take better care in putting my things away. He had pica and ate Play-Doh, among other things. I learned to work with clay. He ate staples. I learned to berate him without guilt because I drew the line at his health and well-being. By the age of 8, he still refused to use the toilet. I learned to clean up after him. He feared strange surroundings. I learned to comfort and talk him through new experiences. I learned to challenge but also respect his little world. I did not realize it then, but my brother emerged as one of my greatest teachers—through whom I learned responsibility, accountability, patience, stamina, self-discipline, and unconditional love.

EARLY SCHOOLING

My brother lived at home and attended a day school. From the beginning, my parents had made a conscious decision to keep him with the family during a time when the norm was to gravitate toward institutionalization. It was a decision that I was not a part of. I was too young. This decision proved to be the single most significant force affecting my upbringing—one with long-lasting implications. I have always agreed with the decision for as long as I recall.

I remember my brother's first preschool. It had a large back yard, easels out on the playground, bicycles, tricycles, and an enormous sandbox all within a country setting—a child's utopia. I enjoyed visiting and had a hard time leaving. The teachers were patient, gentle souls and spent a lot of "quality" time with me as well. My playful youth, however, always gave way to a sense of concern and responsibility uncharacteristic of a child my age. I always observed my brother's school surroundings with a critical eye—constantly trying to ascertain if this was the right place for my brother. I was 5 years old.

LANGUAGE ACQUISITION

By the age of 3, my brother had lost what few communications skills he had. He began speaking earlier than most children, but soon fell very far behind. His phrases degenerated from, "I want water please" to "wa." "Open the door" became a pointing fit and tantrum in front of the door to convey his message. He wanted out but could no longer say it for some reason. His singing and recitation of poems remained intact, even in two languages. When it came to speaking clearly, though, his mind failed him. Pronouns were reversed, vocabulary forgotten,

words omitted from sentences. He was categorized as nonverbal during his evaluations.

It was very easy for me to see my brother's shortcomings when it came to verbal expression. The weaknesses were blaring and needed a great deal of work. It was not my place to solve the enigma of his language disappearance. My task was to get around his obstacles in order to communicate with him. His physical prompts, short utterances, and fragmented sentences began to mean a great deal to me. I reached the point where I could decipher most of his meanings and needs. The second half of the puzzle was even trickier. I learned to speak to him in a language that he could understand, using similar fragments, changing my intonations, order of words, and adding physical gestures to pronouns and prepositions. While accomplishing my goal of being able to communicate with my brother, I also fell into "the trap." It is a common trap that many siblings, parents, and educators fall into—sacrificing any improvement in the child's communications skills in favor of being able to understand and "get by." When my brother said "shoe" as we were leaving the house in a hurry, it was much easier to acknowledge and help him tie his shoe, rather than coach his language or lack of it. In actuality, I was harming my brother severely by catering to his inadequacies. It took an independent speech therapist to blow the whistle on me and my family. This is usually the case because the therapist looks with an objective eye, listens with an objective ear, and truly has the child's best interest in mind.

We had new demands placed on us. We were to no longer accept my brother's perceived inability to communicate clearly. I say "perceived" because, in retrospect, it is striking to see how much improvement can be drawn from an autistic child when that child is truly challenged. Inability and laziness are two very different forces, but can be easily confused at times. At home our job was to turn on my brother. The plan was to stop reacting to or acknowledging his one-word prompts, in the hope of coaxing more speech from him. "Water" became "want water please" as I made him give me more complete sentences. Soon we began to tackle one of his weakest points: pronouns and the reversal of "I" and "you." This problem is not rare and has been cited by Kanner (1946) as one of the most reliably observed behavioral features of autism. We aimed to rid my brother of this behavior. If he wanted a cookie and said, "You want cookie," I would eat it. This happened often. He angered more often. I was jeopardizing the easy-going relationship and the rare understanding of each other that we had—until the day I heard his learning process come full circle. He passed through the stages of confusion and anger to finally reach the goal stage—understanding. "*I* want cookie" yielded the result my brother was looking for. There was no reason to make the same mistake a second time. The success was obvious to him. I again state that self-interest stirs the mind and breeds creativity.

My brother started receiving professional speech therapy on a consistent basis at the age of 12. The difficulty of invading my brother's routine faded, and he began accepting his speech sessions once a week. There, he worked on completing thoughts and sentences, matching appropriate phrases with pictures, and starting the reading process from scratch. His speech therapist carried the aura of an authority figure. This was critical in penetrating my brother's mind and undoing many mental processes that he had grown used to over time. In the years that have passed, my brother has had numerous therapists and many teaching philosophies as a result. In the process, his language has improved tremendously, he understands commands better, and he reads out loud at a first-grade level. Language acquisition has been one of the few areas where I have been able to note tangible and significant progress in my brother's development. He has learned to work with language instead of against it.

TOILET TRAINING

Toilet training was one of the most challenging issues our family had to deal with. My brother showed absolutely no interest in our games to win him over to our idea that "pee-pee and BM" belonged in the toilet. Our father would take him into the bathroom and demonstrate how "men" urinated. I joined them in the game of "let's make an X" or "X marks the spot" to no avail. My mother even thought up songs coaxing my brother to go.

Professionals from the Yale Child Study Center encouraged us to buy a lock box and keep it in the bathroom. We were to place a favorite food item in that box that would serve as my brother's tangible reward the instant he used the toilet. He made no connection between the box and the toilet. It was comforting to learn that even the doctors were at a loss on occasion.

One day my mother heard of a grandmother who used a child's suppository on her grandson, also autistic, when she saw him straining behind the drapes in the living room. She marched him into the bathroom and sat him down. He went instantly and she praised him instantly. This was repeated for several days until her grandson got the message. He was bowel trained in 4 days.

We were torn between what could work, the psychological ramifications, the response from professionals if we were to tell them, and our exasperation of having to clean up the messes over and over again. (It had already gone on for 12 years.) My mother felt strongly about the suppository idea and went for it. It took much longer than 4 days. She used the suppositories only when my brother indicated by facial expression or bodily movement when he needed to go. He finally reacted while sitting on the toilet and, *voila,* toilet training was accomplished. Ultimately, my brother was ready for his big step when he chose to be—it was definitely a control issue. A few months later, we stripped our family room carpet and replaced it with a plush beige-colored one. How great it looked without stains or odors. We were beginning to resemble a normal family.

SELF-ABUSE

In the early 1970s, I witnessed autistic self-abuse in my brother's special education classes. I was exposed to head banging, biting, and hair pulling. Later, I recall a slide show at an autism conference in Rhode Island highlighting students with hands tied behind their backs to prevent them from hitting themselves, children forced to wear helmets to protect from cranial damage, and a porcelain bathroom sink that an autistic boy had cracked open with his bare forehead. It was not a slide show that a typical preteen would be privy to or view with understanding.

My brother's self-abuse took the form of wrist biting. A loud and prolonged squeal would accompany his bite. It was a piercing squeal, one that would trigger a sense of fright and anguish within me. Aside from dealing with my brother's tantrum, I was also compelled to deal with curious onlookers and even police who thought they had spotted some type of abuse. Hearing the squeal, you would think that his "bark" was worse than his "bite." A look at his wrist told a different story. The bite was always severe and would usually break the skin. The self-abuse was so concentrated and destructive that a solid callus eventually formed over the majority of his right wrist. It was nature's way of protecting my brother from his most powerful enemy—himself.

I do not recall the first time I saw my brother bite himself. I do recall the first time my mother explained his actions to me. I was 4 years old. I learned that my brother's autism precluded him from communicating effectively. This left him with no conventional outlet to express his anger and frustration. King (1990) states, "The consequences of an inability to organize sensory input are devastating to normal function." Wrist biting was his outlet. I can truly say that by the age of 7 my brother's biting hurt me as much as it hurt him. My anxiety would turn to despair as I could find no means of stopping him. As a normal child, I had always been taught to go to the root of a conflict to resolve it. However, I also learned that theory and logic do not always play a role in rearing an autistic individual. Although the occasional obvious loud noise or uncomfortable situation would set my brother off, finding what made my brother fly off the handle was one of life's great mysteries a majority of the time. As a child, I cared less about the cause and more about the effect. My brother was hurting himself right in front of me and I wanted to stop it. On one occasion, I decided to bite his other arm as he bit himself. He seemed oblivious. The intensity of his biting fits reminded me of seizures. He did not give me a moment's notice. On a separate occasion, I imitated his actions, biting myself. He stopped his biting and looked at me with a startled stare, but only for a moment. He then continued his tantrum. For a brief moment, I thought I had broken through to him. I was naive.

I was still intent on making my brother stop one day. I wanted to startle him out of his rage with something equally as powerful and intense. The day finally came when I addressed him with sheer impulse rather than calculated thought. On this particular day, my brother was headed toward permanent physical damage with an extremely aggressive biting fit. My father and I pulled on his arm with all our might to save my brother from his own powerful jaws. In a rare moment, we got his arm free. Knowing that the biting would start again at any moment, I instinctively shot my own wrist into my brother's mouth. Part of me would rather have my brother hurt me than himself. Another part wanted to learn if he had enough irrational rage to inflict that kind of damage on another person. He never bit again that day! The sweat and redness left his face; his breathing slowed to normal. He maintained eye contact with me the entire time—a rarity. I had done the unthinkable. I had penetrated his defenses and his irrationality with my own irrationality. In his eyes, I saw a newfound unspoken trust between us.

SOCIALIZATION

Very early on, my family realized that it was crucial for my brother and for us to come into contact with neighbors, friends, and relatives. In retrospect, I feel that social immersion was the best tack ever taken in my brother's upbringing; it outpaced education, training, and speech in terms of his overall development. I credit my parents with its early success. I urge it to all parents, having seen this success not only in my family but also in many of those equally as brave within our special education "circle." Avoid social "shock" but gently test the bounds of the child's tolerance for social interaction.

It took a lot of ingenuity and planning on our part to accomplish this task. It did not take long before we realized who tolerated and even accepted my brother in their homes and who were more concerned with their knickknacks and furnishings and reluctant to have us over more than once. We felt much more at ease entertaining within our home and having people meet my brother in his own familiar surroundings. It turns out that he enjoyed these gatherings immensely and always anticipated the meals and dessert, which were the highlights of his evening. His curiosity and hunger outweighed his reclusiveness.

If we did visit friends, we made sure that one of us was always "on duty." On duty involved checking the TV room to make sure that my brother was still in that room watching a show. We made sure that he did not venture into the bathroom where, if given the opportunity, he would empty shampoo bottles and any other lotions down the sink. A favorite pastime in someone else's home was to open and close the refrigerator every few minutes in the hope of finding food that normally was not available at home such as cheesecake, cold cuts, and soda. He was and still is a junk-food fanatic, common with many autistic individuals that I have come to know. Food often serves as one of the few pure satisfactions that these individuals receive, hence its common use in rewarding good behavior.

NEW SITUATIONS

A preview of new environments often helped my brother adjust. If we knew we were going to a restaurant on Saturday evening, we would drive by during the day. Selection of an eating establishment would be and still is based on its noise level because my brother is hypersensitive to many sounds. Other considerations included how formal the establishment was and what type of food it offered.

Attending church services meant sitting in the back of the church in the last pew. This allowed my brother the flexibility of sitting when he felt like it and even standing up when he chose without sticking out like a sore thumb. After several years of this, the back pew was informally reserved for our family. I do not recall ever being embarrassed in church by my brother's actions. I was simply happy to be participating in an event as an entire family.

Going to the movies was more an adventure in eating than an experience in cinematography. Popcorn was definitely more important than the movie—but we graduated to the point where we could sit through an entire movie and all have a good time. There were moments where his demands for a drink would be heard over the dialogue, but I grew used to it without undue embarrassment.

Shopping was still is a headache. If we went to a mall, my brother had to straighten out every hanger askew and rehang clothes that had fallen down. His compulsive behavior always came to the forefront when we went shopping. My brother also tended to wander. He would spot a water fountain instantly and take off without regard for leaving my presence. Grocery shopping is still a challenge. I will tell him prior to entering the store, "No cookies today." Once in the store, he will carefully push the carriage around, picking out items from a list and then, like lightning, run off—not to the cookie aisle as he has been told "no," but rather to the potato chips. He has figured out that if he tears open the bag, I will be compelled to purchase it. Self-interest tends to provoke creativity within the mind—a very active and underestimated mind.

For some mysterious reason, visits to doctors' and dentists' offices posed no problem. In this respect, my brother differed greatly from most "normal" children. He enjoyed the attention he was given, not to mention the magical rising chairs. He even requested that his blood pressure be taken! When my brother was younger, we would try to arrange for dental appointments early in the day when he was fresh and relaxed and so was the pediodontist. My parents clued in early that professionals who were familiar with autism were also caring individuals for the most part.

My brother's eventual attendance at my high school soccer and basketball games gave me the greatest pleasure of all. I may have gotten as much if not more out of it than he did. What better way to involve, entertain, and teach my brother while also educating my friends as to who he was and what he was all about. I always tried to spot my brother in the bleachers before a game. Even while playing, I worried about how he behaved and if he was enjoying himself. He soon got over the noise level at games and even learned to clap at the appropriate time. He was my number one fan.

VACATIONS

Family trips were a vacation from the everyday life at home, but never from the responsibility surrounding the care of my brother. He was a full-time job. At 9 years old, I was at an age where I could handle my brother mentally, but not physically. He was still bigger than me and two steps faster. Although he had curtailed most of his running-away episodes, keeping up with him was still a chore. I will always remember an incident where after a 10-hour flight to Europe, my mother asked me to sit on a suitcase and keep my brother close as she ran to the restroom for a moment. She was a perennial presence in his life, but some things were unavoidable. Fear washed over me as she left. What if my brother decided to make a run for a snack bar? What about the luggage? How would Mom find us? It was the type of unrelenting worry usually felt after being dropped off on the first day of kindergarten. After what seemed like an eternity to me, the knot in my stomach loosened as my mother approached.

I went to the restroom not to use the toilet, but to look in the mirror for wrinkles on my forehead. I had asked my father once why people get wrinkles. He told me it was from worrying. I was convinced I would find wrinkles after a worrying episode like the one I had just gone through. I was still young.

Disney World was exciting but not fun to me. I remember constantly looking over my shoulder to make sure my brother was following. My concern bordered on obsession at times. I had heard stories of autistic children getting lost in crowds and recovered by police who had no inkling of sense in communicating with them. I definitely believed in being better safe than sorry. My saddest moments revolved around my brother's disinterest in most activities and the rest of the family's lack of involvement as a result. My brother would keep walking on if he was not willing to participate or wait in line. We did a lot of walking that vacation. My happiest times were when we found a ride that my brother would enjoy—a ride that we could get on together. Any time we approached "normal" sibling situations, it brought me great pride. Such minor rewards were signs that my brother had

promise. It brought my parents great joy as well.

Hotel rooms and rented vacation homes were fun. They afforded good close family ties. In smaller living quarters, my brother had no choice but to spend time with us or at least in our presence. Many times we were joined by close relatives who offered respite and companionship to us all. My brother could not run off to his room to be alone and rock back and forth as he could at home. I cannot theorize for all autistic children, but a smaller home than the one we had may have been beneficial to my brother's overall development.

RECREATION

My brother loved parks, swings, and climbing equipment when he was young. We did our rounds of all the city parks and discovered out-of-the-way country parks and arboretums. He eventually outgrew these outings, and it became a challenge finding activities that would provide enjoyment.

Our church had a sports center with an Olympic-size pool. We would have family swim times when the pool was not crowded. Mom would dress him at home, and I would be responsible for getting him ready in the locker room and dress myself. Mom could no longer take him into the ladies' locker rooms so he became my responsibility. I was 8.

We tried basketball over the years. My brother learned to shoot baskets quite well but always wanted to stop after making the first shot. He reasoned that his task was complete; his job was done—a product of his rigid and confined thinking.

Attempts were made to go bowling. His school took him on outings of this kind, and we thought it was our responsibility to do the same. The truth is that bowling was not something our family did normally. It was an activity we were imposing on my brother. Most of the recreational activities were activities that we imposed on my brother, not something he truly enjoyed. I have used the term "guardian's guilt" to describe the sibling's or parent's need to make the autistic child get involved in an activity. It is human nature to try to counter another person's isolation, perceived boredom, or introversion—typical by-products of autism. For all I know, he may have enjoyed simply sitting in front of the television. Regardless, I felt the need to force my brother to be more active.

We washed the cars together and had fun doing this. The radio blared "our" music, the sun burned our backs, and the soapsuds covered the windows in well-defined circles, which my brother would repeat over and over again.

PLAY

Like many autistics, my brother had trouble with interactive play. When he was younger, he focused on puzzles. He focused on ball bouncing, as well as anything else tactile—Slinkies were the toys of choice. He also enjoyed playing on the computer, again with the focus of being alone. He mastered educational games while becoming more and more comfortable with the nuances of the computer and the mouse. He was self-taught for the most part. As was the case in the past, his abilities were coaxed by self-interest. This spread to most of the activities that he enjoyed such as using the stereo, VCR, and TV. He gathered knowledge and skill through observation of others instead of asking others. Often he would surprise me with his minor independent successes. It was obvious that he was watching me all along. Ultimately, he was alone, though. He was always true to his disorder.

Although it was difficult to teach my brother how to play with others, it would have been easier for parents or educators to teach me instead. In nursery school, I learned the basics of playing with other children. I did not learn how to play with an autistic child, though. No one taught me. It is something that I regret because my trial and error approach at a young age met with limited success. The times that we did find success were momentous and remain in my mind today as some of the best experiences I have had with my brother over the years. He never objected to kicking a ball around the yard with me. I placed few demands on him at the time in the hope of avoiding discouragement and keeping him playing as long as possible. In the spring of 1987, I was told about a modified Special Olympics event called the ball kick. Without changing our routine too much, I began "training" my brother

for the event. We did our stretches together as he counted to 10. We used the same ball minus some air to make it harder to kick. I also placed my new athlete toward the bottom of a hill so he would always be kicking uphill. He smiled appropriately as I clapped at his successful kicks. He was getting more out of the game than he realized. I was ecstatic. The event finally came—a kick for distance on a flat surface with a much lighter ball. We came home with a gold medal that day. It was a perfect day for two brothers to have in an otherwise imperfect relationship.

ABSTRACT EMOTION

Rarely would my brother show any proper and outright emotion when he was younger. Like many autistic individuals, he would giggle and laugh at irrelevant or inappropriate moments. His angry moments were generally excessive in light of the usually minor catalyst. He showed signs of agitation and discomfort in settings that most would find pleasant and soothing. This brought out one of the biggest problems I have had with my brother's autism. I tended to take on his moods. His sour day would become my sour day as my mood was gauged by his. Other times, he would smile and giggle for half the day. It brought about my own happiness. Outsiders would wonder why I was the only one in the group who seemed agitated on a particular day. If they had looked in the periphery, they would have seen my brother's mood and its mirror reflection on me. Few understood enough to make the connection.

SEPARATION

Eventually, I left for college. Siblings who do plan to leave home to pursue higher learning generally fall into one of two schools of thought. Many attend relatively close to home for the obvious purpose of being near the family and the subsequent ability to continue helping the autistic sibling. Often, an emotional attachment to the autistic sibling can play a role in choosing a geographic location for school. The second mind-set takes an opposite approach. In some cases, families consider the opportunity for the "normal" sibling to alleviate some responsibility and gain a greater sense of freedom by attending school far away. Both are valid and realistic.

I chose the first option. During my college search, I focused on getting into the best school possible within a relatively close distance to home. We made our home in Connecticut, and I was fortunate enough to gain admission to Yale University for the fall of 1989. Our plans for maintaining the direct connection with my brother were changed dramatically when my family was transferred halfway across the country that August, due to my father's work. My parents were superior providers and caregivers for my brother. My presence was not a necessity in those respects. The need to stay near my brother was a personal one. I felt a very strong emotional tie to him and wanted the luxury of continuing to participate in his development.

Our one valid concern was how my brother would adjust to the major change within my home. By nature, autistic children do not adjust well to changes within their environment. No major figure had ever left the mosaic that made up my brother's limited world. During his mid-teen years, he had become more independently minded and extremely rebellious. Much like a child in his "terrible twos," he refused to listen to my parents' directions. By his own choice, as most things were, he listened to me almost exclusively. When he refused to dress, I dressed him. When no one could get him to join us for a meal or event, I brought him. When no one could curtail his noises, a small prompt from me would put an end to it. I never knew why. My actions were not very different from those of other authority figures surrounding my brother. I was powerful. I was flattered. My brother, an autistic child, showed an undeniable affinity for me. It was a feat in and of itself. I can never confirm it but I felt that we had an unspoken understanding—irrespective of any disciplinary action I may have taken, I was always on *his* side. I believe he felt this wholeheartedly because he never rebelled against me. How would he react to complete and prolonged separation from his brother? For that matter, how would I react?

My family's move away from Connecticut and my departure to school developed surprisingly well. My brother chose a critical time in his life to shine. He was forced to deal with a new home, a new school, unfamiliar faces, a

different climate, and not having his brother around for the first time in his 18 years. His initial reaction was a frustrated and confused one. He showed no anger, though. I am told that during the first two months, he displayed signs of sadness. Unfortunately, our "experiment" was not a controlled one. There was little way of knowing which new factor affected him most adversely. However, a couple of months passed and my brother settled into a routine—his routine—the routine that brought equilibrium back into his life. He surprised his family as well as the experts around him. He exhibited tangible progress.

Back on the East Coast, I missed my brother tremendously. At the same time, though, I realized something that I had never felt before. I no longer looked over my shoulder after several months when out shopping or walking through large crowds. I was able to walk freely without the pressing fear of losing my brother. I also seemed to have much more time on my hands. There was no pressing feeling of need to occupy my brother with learning or activities. I never mentioned this to any of my friends at school. I assumed that they would not have understood. I was probably right.

My parents would give me news of how my brother was getting along. Speaking with him on the telephone was not an option because he refused to hold the receiver close to his ear for more than a few seconds. I began to feel the direct effects of his limited communication skills. Even though he could never carry on a conversation at home, I could still gauge his thinking and ask appropriate questions that he would answer. Without having my brother in front of me, I was at a loss in terms of communicating with him. I sent occasional photographs and postcards home, which my mother would read to him explaining where I was and what I was doing. When I flew home on breaks, I would find the pictures in small frames by his bed. He enjoyed them.

Going home for Thanksgiving break worried me. I was not sure how or even if my brother would welcome me. Worse, if he did, how would he feel about my leaving again? It seemed like a possible no-win scenario. He came to the airport to greet me with my father, armed with a small bag of potato chips and a big grin. I like to think that the grin was due to my presence and not the chips. We spent a lot of time together that week. I probably got more out of it than he did; I had missed having him around. When it was time for me to leave, we explained to my brother that I was going back to the place that he called "campus" and would be back for Christmas. It seemed to have little effect on him. It is difficult to know what he internalized versus what he never really felt at all.

CHANGING OF THE GUARD

My stay in the Northeast extended past college as I began working in New York after earning my undergraduate degree. My reason for staying was twofold. Initially, it was understood that after my father took retirement, the family would move back to Connecticut where they could be closer to friends and relatives and I could be within better proximity to my brother once again. Even deeper thought went into my New York stay. As I contemplated career decisions years before, I always viewed them within the context of my brother's future. How would I be able to help him best in the years to come? This is a question that strikes many similar siblings. It rings of logic. It also rings of burden. Many see it as an inescapable future— becoming the eventual guardian of the autistic sibling. I had been fortunate enough to not view it this way while growing up. Whether a product of my upbringing, moral fiber, or simply my affinity for my brother, I did not view a future with him as a negative.

In answer to the question of helping my brother, I considered a wide range of interests including special education. After a lot of thought, my family and I concluded that I had already committed my life to special education in certain respects. My greatest contribution would come in the form of future promise and stability. A successful career in something I was interested in would afford me the ability to care for my brother later on in every respect—personally, financially, and otherwise. I began a career on Wall Street in 1993.

DEALING WITH TRAGEDY

My brother had two strong, capable guardians in my parents and one in the making. If only life were so simple. Within 2 years my father was diagnosed with terminal cancer.

My mother curtailed her work. I remained on leave of absence from my firm in New York. We banded together with a focused effort that rivaled even our assault on autism. My brother's world was truly turned upside down as he tagged along to clinics and hospitals around the country. He paid notice to the degeneration of a once mentally and physically strong being he knew as his father, but reacted very little. If asked, he would comment, "Daddy's sick." Siegel (1985) cites the difficulty autistic individuals have expressing appropriate emotion. Once the event is internalized, opinions differ as to how those events are dealt with. My brother never cried during Dad's illness. He observed the peculiar setting of many people crying around him. I have yet to see a tangible reaction. It may come tomorrow. It may come years from now.

My brother and I lost our father after a 7-month fight with cancer. As the medical staff carried our father's body from the house, my brother observed quietly, then finally spoke. "Bye Daddy" was all he said. It was as if he were saying goodbye to someone leaving the house for an afternoon of shopping. Years ago, I was worried about my brother's reaction to my temporary absence during school. It was a minor concern in light of the more permanent change taking place in my brother's life. As far as I know, my brother has never understood the concept or finality of death. How do you teach such an individual that someone central to his life is never coming back?

My mother and I sat, as true equals, mapping out the benefits and consequences of exposing my brother to the entire situation. To others in similar situations, I would argue that such an issue can only be dealt with on a case-by-case basis. There is no *one* right answer for siblings or parents. I can only offer the decisions that we came to. We felt that sharing the entire experience would be better for my brother, rather than allowing him to see only fragments. The assumption was that the powers of the imagination are far stronger and more destructive than reality. We also took solace in having him with us. My mother explained, "Daddy is in heaven now." Would he understand the meaning of "heaven," or was this another geographic place like California or Washington or Chicago? These were places he was accustomed to hearing over the years as

Dad took off for his various business trips. There had to be clarification: "Daddy is in heaven with Jesus." That would make his departure and his absence permanent. Our family has found comfort in our religion, and my brother over the years learned to recite certain prayers of our faith. We turned to these prayers as a means of having him share in the mourning and grieving. He was a part of this family, and he was given the opportunity to be just like us. In looking back, I am amazed that even during the days prior to the burial, we continued to plan ahead so that my brother would be somewhat at ease in an environment he was unfamiliar with. We never quit our full-time job of preplanning and mind reading, trying to clear away any emotional stumbling blocks that could get in my brother's way. We took him to the funeral home before visitation hours. He was given the opportunity to find his comfortable chair, to look out into the garden, and to see his peaceful father long before the crowds would arrive. We had a familiar person accompany him that afternoon so that he would not be our total responsibility. We had a right to mourn and not look over our shoulders. Regardless, my brother was very well behaved. My father would have been proud of how much his older son had learned. I do not wish many more of these harsh lessons upon my brother. Overload tends to breed regression.

The loss of a parent is a devastating event in the life of any young adult. Toward the end of my father's illness, I was faced with the task of parenting my parent. It was a very different role, one that I grew into as circumstances changed. I was assuming a role that I had already fallen into with my autistic brother. I could no longer be my father's child. He could no longer be my mentor. I had to assume the role of being my brother's guardian and my mother's advisor. Surely this must get in the way of the grieving process; it is something that we must deal with. With this loss in my life, I have now come to realize completely what my parents have given us in love and support and how much they sacrificed to achieve these goals. We will never be able to re-create what we had as a family of four, but we will strive to create an environment where my brother will continue to grow. My mother and I will always be a part of his life yet encourage as much independence as possible. The course we will take may be in a different direction from our family's original plans for his future, but not drastically different. My family always had plans for the future, which never quite fit the typical scenario of a group home in the suburbs. We have seen some of these group homes and give a lot of credit to the dedicated parents and community organizations that have undertaken the commitment of maintaining and staffing these residences. Often the concept is good in theory, but inadequate staffing, poor compensation, and high staff turnover result in subpar conditions for clients who need stability in their lives. I feel that we can offer my brother far more stability.

I have been fortunate to know that neither one of my parents ever assumed that I would be completely responsible for my brother's well-being. That in itself removes an otherwise immense pressure. It has been *my* unspoken desire to oversee my brother's future. Why would I not do that as an adult, when I had already assumed that responsibility as a child of 4 years old?

CONCLUSION

I am 24; my brother, a year older. Together, we have worked toward a stronger understanding of each other for the better part of two decades. I have been labeled as, "The Sibling of an Autistic Individual." With this label come the highs and lows of a dozen lifetimes. As such a sibling, I work with little to no feedback from the target of my eternal efforts—my brother. I speak for a majority of siblings when I say that we are self-motivating. We expect little in return for our work. When minor successes do emerge, they take their place as trophies on a shelf—highlights of our lives. We battle to maintain a normal lifestyle for ourselves, all the while bearing a responsibility that few "normal" siblings could comprehend. We are not martyrs. I am not a martyr. I have gained infinitely from the relationship I have with my brother. To him I owe my character. I am a better person, a more complete person, one that achieves the daunting balance between compassion, discipline, and understanding. Although I have always felt extra pressure to live up to the combined expectations for two sons, I have also raised my own expectations of myself in the process. I carry this benefit, which my brother has fostered within me, to all other aspects of my life. My infinite patience is matched only by my ubiquitous cynicism. Solving the enigma of autism has proven elusive to the medical field. Autism is clearly a problem with no solution at present. As siblings, however divergent our means are in managing the disorder, our ends are exactly the same—we wish for a cure.

Cross-References

Changes in the expression of autism with development are discussed in Chapters 8 to 11, work with families in Chapter 42.

REFERENCES

Kanner, L. (1946). Irrelevant and metaphorical language in early infantile autism. *American Journal of Psychiatry, 103,* 242–246.

King, L. (1990). *Methods for reducing hypersensitivity to sensory stimulation in autistic individuals.* Conference: Arizona.

Siegel, L. (1985). *Cognitive development in atypical children.* New York: Springer-Verlog.

CHAPTER 51

A Personal Perspective of Autism

TEMPLE GRANDIN

Many people ask me, "What was the big breakthrough that enabled you to lead a successful life?" There was no single breakthrough. My development was a gradual evolution that had many small but important steps. If I had fallen off any of these steps, I would have ended up in a school for the retarded or at a job that would have been below my abilities. Today, at the age of 55, I am an associate professor of animal science at Colorado State University. I have designed equipment and stockyards for most of the major U.S. meat companies and have published two books on livestock handling (Grandin, 1998, 2000). During the past 5 years, I have continued to develop and mature. Being autistic is like having a very long childhood. I did not feel like an adult until I was 30 years old.

There were 10 major steps in my development, and a good education accounted for 5 of them. My education steps were:

1. I was enrolled, by age 30 months, in a structured nursery school program run by a talented speech therapist. I stayed in the nursery school for 2 years. Five or six other children were in the nursery school class, which lasted for about 3 hours each day. I had about 2 hours of structured group activities and a half-hour of one-to-one speech therapy three times a week. The therapist held my chin, forced eye contact, and made me say different words. She stretched out hard consonant sounds to help me hear them. I returned home in the middle of the day and then spent another 3 hours each afternoon playing games with my governess. The games forced me to interact so I would not withdraw into the world of self-stimulation, where I shut off my ears. The governess participated with me during sledding, swinging on the swings, making snowmen, jumping rope, swimming, and catching a ball. I was constantly encouraged to interact with her.

2. I mainstreamed in a normal kindergarten at a school that had small classes (only 12 to 14 students) taught by experienced teachers. I remained in this school through sixth grade. Mother and the teachers worked closely with each other. The rules of behavior were the same at home and school.

3. My mother taught me how to read when I was in third grade.

4. At the age of 14, I was enrolled in a small country boarding school after I had been expelled from a large junior high school for fighting with a girl who had teased me. My problems in junior high started at puberty.

5. Two teachers at the boarding school developed my interest in science and used it to motivate me to study. One of the teachers continued to serve as an important mentor after I enrolled at a small liberal arts college near the boarding school. He was an important source of encouragement and support during the first 2 years in college, which were very difficult.

My educational program was not a heroic magical cure. Steps 1 through 3 could have easily been achieved in a well-run public education program. I owe my success to my mother, who defied the professionals who told her that I belonged in a school for the retarded.

Fortunately, my parents had the financial resources to send me to the boarding school. I speculate, with dread, what would have happened to me as a teenager if my parents had not had the money to send me to the boarding school. I would have been in big trouble. However, many of the problems in junior high could have been avoided if the mentor teachers I found at the boarding school had been available. Good mentors would have kept me out of trouble and stimulated my interest in science.

The sixth step was Aunt Ann at her ranch in Arizona. I visited her during the summers in the years I was in high school and college. She tolerated my endless fixations and helped me to understand myself. Other people, and professionals, wanted to normalize my behavior. Ann strove to understand it and direct it toward constructive goals.

High-functioning autistic students in high school and college also need mentors to prepare them for the world of work. At autism conferences, I have met many talented people with autism who have successfully graduated from high school or college and then have been unable to find jobs. Their problem is that they lack the social skills needed to get through the job interviews. The traditional job interview process has to be short circuited; people with autism must be able to demonstrate their abilities to the people they will actually work for.

The seventh important step was finding mentors in the business community who recognized my abilities and were willing to work with me. Through a freelance writing job for a farm magazine, I found two important mentors who helped me to learn about the meat industry and feedlot construction. Tom Rohrer managed the Swift Meat Packing Plant, and Emil Winnisky worked at a feedlot construction company. Both of these men tolerated my eccentricities and helped to develop my abilities. Emil hired me, and his secretaries gave me lessons in grooming and social niceties. Educators who work with autistic children need to seek out helpful businesspeople who are willing to employ and work with people with autism.

EMPLOYMENT AND INTERESTS

Before going on to the eighth step, I outline ways in which people with autism can be helped to gain employment. First, they need a gradual transition from the structured environment of school to the less structured workplace. Autistic students in high school should start working at least one afternoon a week before they graduate. (Sudden transitions were very stressful for me.) Second, people with autism should go into jobs that use their skills and interests. They often become fixated on a favorite subject. Educators should use fixations to motivate schoolwork, instead of trying to stamp them out. My interest in election posters could have been broadened into a way of teaching me arithmetic. My teachers could have had me calculate electoral votes. If an autistic child likes trains, a good teacher can use trains in teaching reading or math. A narrow fixation, with assistance, can be broadened out into a career (Grandin & Scariano, 1986). Leo Kanner (1971) recognized the value of directing fixations into careers and useful activities.

Many high-functioning people with autism have skills in art, computers, mathematics, or mechanics. Talent often shows up early in autistic children. When I was a child, I was encouraged to use my artistic abilities. Young autistic children sometimes draw in three-dimensional perspective. Teachers should work on developing the children's talents. Talents can be turned into a career. The educational system places too much emphasis on children's deficits and not enough emphasis on developing their talents. Among the good jobs for college graduates or high school-educated, high-functioning autistic people are computer programming, architectural drawing, computer graphics, auto repair, and electronic equipment repair. These jobs fully utilize the individuals' abilities and shield them from complicated social interactions where they are likely to get into trouble. A person with autism can work at these jobs and have almost no contact with customers. I have heard two sad stories involving an autistic laboratory technician and a draftsman who lost their jobs after having social problems. One was fired after he was promoted to a job with customer contact, and the other was fired after he went drinking with his friends. Employers need to recognize the social limitations of people with autism and protect them from situations that are beyond their capacity. An autistic person may be most productive and happy working in an assigned cubicle—fixing cars, drawing, or programming computers. As rewards, these people should be given pay raises or a better computer instead of being promoted into social situations that they are unable to handle. In my own case, I work for many clients, designing livestock systems on a freelance basis. I go to a client's meat plant, design the system, and leave before I get too involved. My life is my work. At the university, I teach my classes and do my research. I carefully avoid university politics. I always stay at an arm's length from conflicts and fights between faculty members. Even today, my social interactions are limited to work-related activities. I spend most Friday and Saturday nights designing equipment and writing papers. I am happiest when I have my nose to the grindstone doing useful and satisfying work that contributes something of value to society.

To get a good job, people with autism need to develop a portfolio of their work to impress potential employers. I always used to carry photos and drawings of major projects I had done, and I would show them to potential clients. Even though they may have thought I was weird, they were impressed with my work. Many people found it hard to believe that I could create such beautiful drawings. People respect talent. Individuals with autism must demonstrate their talents to get hired.

My advice for other high-functioning people with autism is that they should develop a skill in which they can really excel. After the skill is developed, they should make a portfolio of their work. The portfolio can consist of computer disks and printouts of programs, drawings, photographs, or graphic art samples. People with autism who are good at fixing things can often start by repairing computers, automobiles, or small engines for no charge. A person who is really competent at repairs will quickly develop a good reputation. Freelance work is often a good way to get started because it helps to avoid social problems. The worker leaves when the job is finished and avoids social interactions that could cause trouble. Technical writing is another field in which some autistic persons do well. A person can start out doing a column for a local computer magazine. The Internet is another useful avenue for making contacts. Written communication is often easier than face-to-face contacts, and it allows social awkwardness to be concealed. For people with autism who have poor social skills, jobs such as tuning pianos and reshelving books at a library make use of inborn talents of memory for numbers and absolute pitch. Both of these jobs can be done in a closely supervised work situation. More information on employment is in Grandin and Duffy (2004).

VISUALIZATION OF THOUGHTS

Teachers who work with autistic children need to understand visual thinking. I could never handle long strings of verbal directions; I simply could not remember them. Written directions are best. All my thinking is in pictures. When somebody speaks to me, I have to translate the words into a video movie on my imagination's screen. When I search my memory for a piece of information, my brain works like a CD-ROM playing back in a computer. I have to find the right spot on the disk and then play the video in my imagination. Visual thinking is somewhat slower than verbal thought. I have to play an entire videotape segment before I can recall it.

Visual thinking is a great asset for an equipment designer (Grandin, 1992b, 1995). When I design equipment, I can test-run the entire system or a video movie in my imagination. My ability to run the equipment in my imagination far exceeds the best virtual reality computer systems available. If I were 14 years old today, I would be fascinated by virtual reality computer systems that allow organic chemists to walk around inside complex molecules and feel the strength of chemical bonds through a data glove. Virtual reality computer systems would make maximum use of my visualization capabilities and bypass my inability to do algebra. The mathematics of organic chemistry is in the computer program. With these systems, my ability to visualize—which makes designing steel and concrete structures easy for me—could be used to build new organic molecules. Manipulating computer images of organic molecules would make organic chemistry totally concrete and avoid the abstract mathematics that I cannot do. Designing new molecules would be as easy for me as designing a chute system for a meat packing plant.

Algebra is impossible for me because equations cannot be translated into pictures. For me to understand them, abstract concepts have to be represented by pictures. For example, the word *liberty* is represented in my mind by a picture of the Statue of Liberty, the Declaration of Independence, and images from various movies of people escaping from prisons. The word *over* is represented in my memory as a video of a dog I used to play with as a child. The dog liked to jump over the neighbor's fence.

Basic principles and concepts in my memory are formed from specific examples that are stored as pictures in my imagination. For example, when somebody says the word *boat,* the first memories that are triggered are of specific boats I went on as a child, such as the ferryboat that took the family to our summer house. It was not a general boat that took the family to our summer house. There is no general boat concept in my memory. My concept of what a boat is comes from images of specific boats I have seen. All my thinking starts with specific examples that are used to form basic principles. During the past few years, I have learned, through interviews, that most people have a generalized concept of boat in their memory.

To learn social skills, I had to use the same specific-to-general pattern of thinking. When I had only a few previous experiences in my memory, I often made horrible social blunders. My concept of how to act improved as my knowledge base increased. Asperger (1944) reported that people with autism have to learn social skills through their intellect. I totally agree with Dr. Asperger's assessment. My concepts about many things greatly improved as I was able to fill my memory with more specific examples. If the only boat I had ever seen had been a ferry, I would have had a very limited boat concept. After I had seen many types of specific boats, my boat concept became much broader. However, none of my specific boat images merges into a single generic boat concept. When I think of the concept of boats in general, I see a wall chart or a series of TV screens or Internet web pages displaying specific boats I am familiar with, such as the ferry boat, my father's boat, the neighbor's boat, and so on. Childhood memories or very recent memories appear first. All

the boats are very specific and identifiable. Like Internet web pages, my boat images also have associative links. The image of my father's boat is linked to memories of fishing and picnics, but the image of a ferry boat with a horn that hurt my ears is linked to other memories of loud noises that hurt my ears. All of these associations are in the form of video pictures. My memory system works just like searching the Internet with a web browser. When I find the first memory web page, I then look at the other pages that it is linked to. Readers who spend time surfing the Internet will have a good understanding of how the autistic mind functions.

When I was a child, my ability to do art showed up early, but I had to learn to link the video pictures in my imagination with the symbolic lines on architectural blueprints. One summer, while I was building a house on my aunt's ranch, I struggled with relating the symbolic squares on the house plans to the square concrete foundation columns. When I finally made the connection between the drawing and the real thing, understanding drawings suddenly became really easy. Now I look at an engineering drawing, and I almost instantly see the finished piece of equipment in my imagination.

I learned what a blueprint drawing symbolized by taking a drawing of a completed building or piece of equipment and walking around the structure, comparing the drawing to the finished building. A drawing that is an abstract symbol is useless to me. I have to make the blueprint become a real building when I look at it. In college, I learned to read electronic schematics by wiring actual circuits, using a kit I bought from Radio Shack. The kit contained about 20 electronic gadgets that could be assembled on a board with spring clip connectors. I covered up the step-by-step instructions and practiced wiring the board while looking only at the schematics. By studying my mistakes, I was able to decipher the abstract symbols on the electrical diagrams. After doing this for several weeks, I experienced a sudden integration of my knowledge. When I looked at the schematic, I saw the actual wired circuit. When I learned drafting at the cattle feedlot construction company, I studied many drawings until the gates, fences, and feed troughs instantly appeared in my imagination when I looked at drawings of them. Learning drafting was more like turning on a computer plotter than step-by-step learning. The company had a talented draftsman named David. I studied his drawings for hours. When David left the company, I had to do all my own finished drawings. I just bought the same pencils and tools that David used and started drawing. One day, I sat down and said to myself, "Draw like David," and I did. I had input sufficient data into my brain computer that I could do it. My earlier attempts to do architectural drawings had been very crude because I had insufficient images in my memory. My drawings also improved when I slowed down and carefully used a ruler to trace the image in my imagination.

My mind works and solves problems as though I were putting together a mosaic or a jigsaw puzzle. If only a few pieces of the puzzle are in place, I cannot tell what the picture or the puzzle will be. When half or more of the pieces are assembled, I suddenly see what the picture on the puzzle is. I input data into my memory and read constantly. This is the method I used to learn drafting and circuit wiring. I keep adding data. Suddenly, an entire picture forms and I am able to draw blueprints or wire electronic circuits. My thinking process does not work in a step-by-step linear manner. It jumps around, taking a piece of data here and another piece of data there until enough pieces are assembled for me to see the picture on the puzzle. This method of thinking is very useful when I have to troubleshoot problems in equipment. When a problem arises, I scan my memory and replay previous experiences where similar problems occurred.

Using visual thinking to understand steps in my life is more difficult. When I was in high school, I had very little information in my library of experiences, so I had to use actual objects to provide concrete symbols of life's stages. My first book (Grandin & Scariano, 1986) contains much discussion about the use of doors to symbolize significant changes in my life, such as graduating from high school and graduating from college. Just thinking about graduation was not enough. I had to actually walk through a door to make the abstract idea of graduation seem real. Graduation was symbolized by a door that led to the roof of the dormitory. Most of the doors that symbolized

progress in my life led to high places on campus. Later on in life, after I put much more information into my CD-ROM video memory, I was finally able to discard the door symbols. This process was similar to making the lines on the blueprints turn into real buildings in my imagination. My memory finally held enough facts, information, and knowledge that I no longer needed to physically walk through a door, just as I no longer had to walk through a building to understand a blueprint drawing of that building.

SENSORY PROBLEMS

This next section will cover problems I had with over sensitivity to sound and touch. Good autism programs should make accommodations for sensory over sensitivity.

Touch Sensitivity

I now return to the remaining steps that enabled me to succeed. The eighth step was dealing with horrible oversensitivity to sound and touch. Unfortunately, these problems were not handled well when I was a child because nobody knew I had them. When people touched me, I experienced an overwhelming, drowning wave of overstimulation (Grandin, 1984, 1992a, 1992b; Grandin & Scariano, 1986). Wearing scratchy wool hats and party dresses was torture. Scratchy clothes were a major cause of tantrums in church, when I had to wear my Sunday best. They felt like sandpaper on exposed nerve endings. I used to think everybody else was stronger and better than I was because they were able to tolerate the clothes I hated. I did not realize that my senses were different until I started talking to other people with autism and to Lorna King, an occupational therapist in Arizona. Reading about touch sensitivity problems in a book by Jean Ayres (1979) was also very helpful. I was relieved to learn that other people were not better or stronger than I was. One big problem was changing from one type of clothing to another. Switching from pants to a dress or vice versa is difficult because it takes me up to 2 weeks to fully adapt to the feeling of pants against my legs or the absence of pants against my legs. Today, I have solved the clothing problem by wearing soft cotton underwear against my skin. My work clothes and my dress clothes now feel the same.

When people hugged me, I stiffened up and pulled away. It was an approach-avoid situation. I wanted to feel the nice feeling of being hugged, but the sensation was too intense. As a child, I craved deep pressure and often crawled under sofa cushions to attempt to satisfy this craving. Many parents of autistic children report that their autistic child will often pull away when hugged, but he or she will seek pressure by getting under mattresses, rugs, or large pillows. Touch was easier to tolerate if I initiated the touching.

When I was 18, I built a pressure machine that I could use to apply pressure to my body (Grandin, 1984, 1992a, 1992b, 1995; Grandin & Scariano, 1986). Using this machine helped me to relax and learn how to tolerate touch. It also helped me to learn empathy. Volkmar and Cohen (1985) and Bemporad (1979) report that people with autism often lack empathy. I think this gap may be partially related to the absence of comforting touching. The pressure machine consists of foam-padded panels that press against the sides of the body. The user of the machine can completely control the amount and duration of the pressure by pulling a control lever. I get into the machine in a hands-and-knees position between two padded sides and I place my head through a padded neck opening. When I first started using the machine, I flinched and pulled away, but gradually I relaxed and gave in to the soothing pressure. When I fully relax in the machine, I feel waves of soothing comfort.

I find that using the machine once a week keeps bad thoughts out of my mind and helps me to be a kinder and gentler person. I think that people have to feel the comfort of being held in order to have kind feelings. As a child, my hypernervous system would not allow me to be touched by people. Some autistic children, including me, squeeze pets too hard because they have seldom been able to experience comforting touching. After I built the squeeze machine, I learned to pet our cat more gently, and then he stayed with me. I had to experience a feeling of comfort myself before I could give comfort to the cat.

I became fixated on the squeeze machine. Mr. Carlock, my high school science teacher,

wisely used the fixation to motivate me in science and schoolwork. Because many of the other professionals I was in contact with thought the machine was weird, I was highly motivated to search the scientific literature and find evidence that pressure has calming effects on both people and animals (Ayres, 1979; Kumazawa, 1963; Takagi & Kobagasi, 1956). I wanted to prove that pressure's relaxing effect was due to physiological mechanisms. I wanted to show people that the machine was not just a product of my weird psychological fixation. Since then, I have written scientific papers and done research on the calming effects of pressure on people and animals (Grandin, 1992a, 1993; Grandin, Dodman, & Shuster, 1989).

My fixation to figure out how the squeeze machine worked was a key to the beginning of my career in livestock equipment design. I got the idea for the squeeze machine from a cattle squeeze chute that is used to hold cattle for veterinary work. When I was in graduate school at Arizona State University, I visited many cattle feedlots to study the effect of the squeeze chute on animals. Fixations are great motivators; teachers should help students with autism to channel them into motivations for a career.

Sound Sensitivity

Certain noises affected me like a dentist's drill hitting a nerve. I hated balloons. I often became anxious when balloons were present because I was afraid they would pop. Other noises that hurt my ears were the school bell's ringing and hum of the big industrial vacuum cleaner that was used to clean the elementary school classrooms. Many people with autism have sound sensitivity problems (McKean, 1994; Stehli, 1991; White & White, 1987). I know one autistic woman whose sound sensitivity is so severe that she cannot tolerate a baby's crying, even when she is wearing earplugs and earmuffs. Autistic children need to be protected from noisy, confusing environments. I often misbehaved in the loud school cafeteria, where noise echoed off the tile floor.

Even today, I have problems with screening out background noise. When I am using a telephone in a noisy airport, I am unable to screen out the background sounds. If I screen out the background noise, I am unable to hear the telephone. Auditory processing tests in my 40s indicated that I have below-normal ability in a listening task where I hear a man's voice in one ear and a woman's voice in the other. It is difficult for me to screen out one voice and listen to the other. I do not hear auditory details. Most people can differentiate between two sounds separated by a half-second gap. I hear the two sounds as one sound. A magnetic resonance imaging scan of my brain indicated that my cerebellum is 20% smaller than normal. I also have balance problems, and I am unable to tandem walk along a line. During the past several years, I have noticed increasing problems with accurate hand movements under certain conditions. When I am alert, I never poke my eyes when I want to scratch my eyebrow. If I become distracted while reaching to scratch my eyebrow, however, I almost poke my eye. I have always had a mild version of these problems, but they are worsening with age.

Cerebellar and brain-stem abnormalities could be involved in the sensory problem in autism. Research by Bauman (1994) and Courchesne, Hesselink, Jernigan, Press, and Yeung-Courchesne (1988) indicates that cerebellar abnormalities accompany autism. Animal research indicated that the cerebellum may be involved in modulating sensory input (Chambers, 1947; Crispino & Bullock, 1984). Bauman's (1994) work on autopsied brains has shown that, in autistic individuals, both the cerebellum and the limbic system have immature development.

ANXIETY AT PUBERTY

The ninth step was finding medication to control panic and anxiety attacks. If I had not been able to take antidepressants in my early 30s, I would have crashed. Stress-related health problems such as colitis and headaches were ripping me apart. These problems worsened as I approached age 30. At puberty, the horrible anxiety attacks started. I was in a constant state of stress. I felt as if a lion would attack me at any second. My sympathetic nervous system was in full fight-or-flight mode all the time. My brain was running at 150 miles per hour. The anxiety attacks, triggered by hormones at puberty, were one reason my

behavior got worse. I was finally expelled from high school.

For 20 years, I tried in vain to psychoanalyze myself. I found that using the squeeze machine provided some relief from the nervous anxiety, but as the attacks worsened, the squeeze machine had less and less effect. I desperately tried to find the deep dark secrets of my mind that would make the anxiety go away.

Then I discovered Tofranil® (imipramine). Fifty milligrams at bedtime made the nervous reaction disappear. I learned about Tofranil® from an article in *Psychology Today* and searching the *Index Medicus* in the library. I found a paper that explained how antidepressants could control anxiety (Sheehan, Beh, Ballenger, & Jacobsen, 1980). It was a revelation to discover that biochemistry could solve my anxiety problem whereas years of probing my inner psyche had been futile. After being on Tofranil® for 4 years, I switched to Norpramin (desipramine) because it had fewer side effects.

For the past 21 years, I have been on the same 50 mg dose of Norpramin. I plan to never stop taking it. After I had been on Tofranil® for 3 months, I had another anxiety attack. I resisted the urge to take more Tofranil®, and the attack subsided in a few weeks. I have found that my nerve attacks have cycles. I have stayed on the same dose of medication, and the nerve attack relapses have subsided on their own. Today, more effective drugs are available for autism. Research at Yale University has indicated that Anafranil (clomipramine) significantly improves the behavior of adults with autism (McDougle et al., 1992). I know many high-functioning people with autism who have been helped with Prozac or other similar drugs. After age 50, I have had some worsening anxiety. Taking progesterone and daily vigorous exercise has helped to control it.

Discussions with other people with autism who take antidepressant medications indicate that care must be taken to avoid overdosing. Doses that are effective for autistic people are often lower than the usual doses for treating depression (J. Ratey, personal communication, 1993). Too high a dose may result in insomnia, agitation, or aggression. I have talked to high-functioning people with autism who are doing well on Prozac (fluoxetine), Anafranil, and

Zoloft. One person who takes two 20 mg Prozac pills per week is doing very well. Several people with autism told me they felt like they were going to jump out of their skin when the dose was too high. When antidepressants are used in autism, the clinician must find the lowest effective dose and then avoid raising it. The correct dose will vary from person to person. A dose that is too high can result in serious side effects, such as aggression and agitation (J. Ratey, personal communication, 1993). More information on Prozac and other SSRI's can be found in Couzin, 2004, Edwards and Anderson, 1999, and Whittington et al., 2004.

GRADUAL CHANGE AND MY EMOTIONAL LIFE

The 10th step has been more like a ramp—a continuous, gradual improvement in my ability to get along with people. Many people have told me that, during the past 5 years, my ability to lecture keeps steadily improving. I am often not aware of these positive changes until people tell me about them. My learning is continuous. Each day, I collect more data to place in my library of experience. When I encounter a new social situation, I have to search my memory for a similar experience that I can use as a model for my next action. As I fill my database with more and more information, I become better and better at handling different social situations. I have to rehearse how to deal with a person before I interact with him or her. I have a very difficult time when I am confronted with unexpected social surprises. For common social interactions with clients, I use programmed, prerehearsed responses. Everything is done with logic.

In my business, I have learned how to deal with clients under different conditions. Logic has taught me how to detect a plant engineer's jealousy, when he thinks I am invading his turf. Jealous engineers can ruin a project; I have learned how to detect them and stroke their egos. I use logic, not emotions. In my library of experience, I have videolike memories of previous encounters with jealous engineers. I can spot one a mile away, and I have an arsenal of effective responses.

Dr. Oliver Sacks really figured out my mind in his book chapter about me (Sacks,

1995). I did not realize how my emotions differed from those of nonautistic people. My emotions are simplified. Anger, fear, and sadness are my primary emotions; if I feel cornered or threatened, anger or fear is triggered. I am like a scared animal when I get into a situation to which I do not know how to respond. I also have a kind of gleeful joy when I figure out how to solve a design problem. Emotionally, I am a small child.

It is important to me that I do work that is of value to society. I want to be appreciated for the work I do. I am happiest when I am doing something for fun, such as designing an engineering project, or something that makes a contribution to society. I can understand only tangible results, such as those that come from writing a paper, designing a livestock facility, or stopping abuse of animals.

I have no complex emotions, and my emotions pass by quickly. When I become angry, I get over it quickly and I do not hold a grudge. I have replaced emotional intensity with intellectual intensity. The medication removed the emotional intensity driven by anxiety. Now I spend hours and hours trying intellectually to understand the meaning of life. Intellectual intensity provides me with a motivation to work hard at my job. I want my life to make a difference, just in case there is no afterlife when I die.

Many people with autism become disillusioned and upset because they do not fit in socially and they do not have a girlfriend or boyfriend. I have just accepted that such a relationship will not be part of my life. Learning the complex social interactions that would be expected is too complicated. Recently, I sat on a plane next to a couple who were flirting. I felt like the anthropologist from Mars whom Oliver Sacks wrote about. The natives are very strange. I think I will stick to writing and equipment design.

DIFFERENCES IN AUTISM

My discussions with other high-functioning people with autism and reading of first-person accounts have indicated to me that the slightly intrusive type of education program that worked for me as a young child may be confusing and painful to a person who has more severe sensory processing problems. My speech therapist forced me to look at her. Doing so jerked me out of my autistic world. I needed to be pulled back into the real world. Intrusive programs that force interaction with a therapist are often very effective in young children ages 18 months to 4 years. The program developed by Lovaas (1987) is effective in about half of very young children. Intrusive programs that are effective in young children, however, may cause sensory overload in older children and adults.

Donna Williams explained to me that if she had been forced to make eye contact, her mind would have shut down. Her sensory processing problems are more severe than mine. She can attend to only one sensory modality at a time. If Donna is listening to somebody speak, she has difficulty processing visual information. In *Somebody Somewhere,* she describes how she confused the intonation of speech with the words. If she listened to the intonation, she was unable to hear the words being spoken (Williams, 1994). Cesaroni and Garber (1991) interviewed a man with autism who described mixing of sensory channels. Sometimes he confused sound with color or experienced a sensation of sound if he was touched. I have touch and sound sensitivity, but my sensory modalities never get mixed up. My vision is normal.

Donna Williams and Therese Joliffe both describe body boundary problems (Joliffe, Lakesdown, & Robinson, 1992; Williams, 1994). Both women have difficulty determining where their body boundaries are. The tapping behavior of many nonverbal persons with autism may be an attempt to determine boundaries in the environment. Therese reports that touch was her most reliable sense and that she could learn most easily through touch. Therese learned to put her shoes on the correct feet after someone guided her hand down her leg and then allowed her to touch both her foot and the correct shoe (Joliffe et al., 1992).

A classroom full of bright colors made learning fun for me, but it could totally confuse a child with visual processing problems. Some children need a quiet environment and a teacher speaking softly to avoid overloading a defective sensory system.

I was attracted to visually stimulating things such as kites and automatic sliding doors. Parents of children with more severe sensory problems have told me that their children run and scream when they see automatic doors. Fluorescent lights cause problems for some people with autism because they see the 60-cycle flicker. These lights caused problems for Donna Williams (1994). Other people with autism have reported that a laptop computer is easier to use than a TV type monitor because TV type screens flicker. A sound or sight that is pleasant to one autistic child may terrify another. I loved the sound of splashing water, but another autistic child may be fearful of it (Stehli, 1991). Teachers must be observant because each child is different. I was never echolalic. My speech was stressed, and I said "bah" for ball. My problem was getting my words out. I could understand what was being said to me; however, conversations between two adults sounded like gibberish. When I was 2 years old, my mother told me, I appeared to be deaf. Other autistic children can talk easily and often repeat what has been said.

Donna Williams (1994), Jim Sinclair (1992), and Therese Joliffe (Joliffe et al., 1992), all have sensory processing problems that are more severe than mine. Jim and Therese had difficulty figuring out that speech was used for communication. They were both echolalic. They had to repeat words in order to figure out what was being said. Therese reports that she often missed the first few words of a sentence. Teachers working with children similar to Donna, Therese, or Jim need to speak slowly and give the children time to respond. When Donna and Jim finally learned to talk, they became very articulate.

I learned how to read with old-fashioned phonics. Because I understood speech before I knew how to read, learning with phonics was easier for me than other methods might have been. Whole words were too abstract to remember. However, children who have difficulty understanding speech may learn to read before they can speak. Jim Sinclair (1992) learned to read at age 3 but did not speak until he was 12. These children can often be helped with flashcards that have words and pictures on them. It is often helpful to teach the child to ask questions. Teaching verbs along with nouns is useful. For example, a shovel is used to dig. Use toys to act out verbs such as making a doll walk or a plane fly. My teachers played lots of turn-taking games.

Foreign languages have always been diffi-cult for me. When I go to a non-English-speaking country, the native language sounds like gibberish. I would have to learn a foreign language by reading. When I was in Mexico, I gradually figured out what a few words meant by looking at billboards and TV commercials. Maybe this is how a nonverbal child learns to read. Because speech sounds like gibberish, the child may be able to learn printed words by relating them to pictures in magazines and books. A lady with autism explained to me that she did not know that words were used for communication. She learned to speak when her teacher used flashcards that had a printed word and the picture of an object on them. The teacher spoke the word while showing her the flashcard. When she spoke a word, she was immediately given the object such as a cup. This enabled her to learn that words had meaning and that they could be used for communication.

CONCLUSION

A successful adaptation to autism is a slow, steady progression. In my early life, a good ed-ucation and intervention by age $2\frac{1}{2}$ were cru-cial. My mother was dedicated to my learning. She located the best schools for me. There was no single, dramatic breakthrough. My parents had the financial resources to provide me with top-notch schooling, but I did not experience a heroic or miraculous cure. The methods used on me worked when sensible amounts of effort were applied. They could easily be implemented in any well-run public school system. Success was made possible for me through the patient efforts of the dedicated people who worked with me. Medication was an essential part of my treatment. If I had not discovered antide-pressants 20 years ago, I don't think I would have been successful. I talked to several very talented people with autism who quit good jobs in computers or graphic arts due to anxiety. Anxiety worsened in my late 20s but medica-tion controlled it.

Cross-References

Developmental and behavioral aspects of autism are discussed in Chapters 8 through 15, vocational and integration issues are dealt with in Chapters 40 and 43, and psychophar-macology is the topic in Chapter 44.

REFERENCES

Asperger, H. (1944). Autistic psychopathy in child-hood. In U. Frith (Ed. & Trans.), *Autism and Asperger syndrome* (pp. 37–92). Cambridge, England: Cambridge University Press.

Ayres, J. A. (1979). *Sensory integration and the child*. Los Angeles: Western Psychological Service.

Bauman, M. L. (1994). Neuroanatomic observa-tions of the brain in autism. In M. L. Bauman (Ed.), *Neurobiology of autism* (pp. 119–145). Baltimore: Johns Hopkins University Press.

Bemporad, M. L. (1979). Adult recollections of a formerly autistic child. *Journal of Autism and Developmental Disorders, 9,* 179–197.

Cesaroni, L., & Garber, M. (1991). Exploring the experience of autism through first person ac-counts. *Journal of Autism and Developmental Disorders, 21,* 303–312.

Chambers, W. W. (1947). Electrical stimulation of the interior cerebellum of the cat. *American Journal of Anatomy, 80,* 55–93.

Courchesne, E., Hesselink, J. R., Jernigan, T. L., Press, G. A., & Yeung-Courchesne, R. (1988). Hypoplasia of cerebellar vermule lobules VI and VII in autism. *New England Journal of Medicine, 318,* 1349–1354.

Couzin, J. (2004). Volatile chemistry: Children and antidepressants. *Science, 305,* 468–470.

Crispino, L., & Bullock, T. M. (1984). Cerebellum mediates modality specific modulation of sen-sory responses of midbrain and forebrain of rats. *Proceedings National Academy of Sciences, USA, 81,* 2917–2929.

Edwards, J. G., & Anderson, I. (1999). Systematic review and guide to selection of selective sero-tonin reuptake inhibitors. *Drugs, 57,* 507–533.

Grandin, T. (1984). My experiences as an autistic child and review of related literature. *Journal of Orthomolecular Psychiatry, 13,* 144–174.

Grandin, T. (1992a). Calming effects of deep touch pressure in patients with autistic disorder: Col-lege students and animals. *Journal of Child and Adolescent Psychopharmacology, 2,* 63–72.

Grandin, T. (1992b). An inside view of autism. In E. Schopler & G. B. Mesibov (Eds.), *High func-tioning individuals with autism* (pp. 105–126). New York: Plenum Press.

Grandin, T. (1995). *Thinking in pictures*. New York: Doubleday.

Grandin, T. (1998). *Genetics and the behavior of domestic animals*. San Diego, CA: Academic Press.

Grandin, T. (2nd ed.). (2000). Editor. *Livestock handling and transport.* Wallingford, Oxon, England CAB International.

Grandin, T., Dodman, T. N., & Shuster, L. (1989). Effect of naltrexone on relaxation induced by lateral flank pressure in pigs. *Pharmacology and Biochemistry of Behavior, 33,* 839–842.

Grandin, T., & Duffy, K. (2004). *Developing talents.* Shawnee Mission, KA: Autism Asperger Publishing Co.

Grandin, T., & Scariano, M. M. (1986). *Emergence labeled autistic.* Novato, CA: Arena Press.

Joliffe, T., Lakesdown, R., & Robinson, C. (1992). Autism: A personal account. *Communication, 3*(26), 12–19.

Kanner, L. (1971). Follow-up study of eleven autistic children originally reported in 1943. *Journal of Autism and Childhood Schizophrenia, 1,* 119–145.

Kumazawa, T. (1963). Deactivation of the rabbit's brain by pressure application to the rabbit's skin. *Electroencephalography and Clinical Neurophysiology, 15,* 660–671.

Lovaas, O. I. (1987). Behavioral treatment and normal educational and intellectual functioning in young autistic children. *Journal of Consulting and Clinical Psychology, 55,* 3–9.

McDougle, C. J., Price, L. H., Volkmar, F. R., Goodman, W. K., O'Brien, D. W., Nielson, J., et al. (1992). Clomipramine in autism: Preliminary evidence of efficacy. *Journal of the American Academy of Child and Adolescent Psychiatry, 31,* 746–750.

McKean, T. (1994). *Soon will come the light.* Arlington, TX: Future Horizons.

Sacks, O. (1995). *An anthropologist on Mars* (pp. 245–296). New York: Alfred A. Knopf.

Sheehan, D. V., Beh, M. B., Ballenger, J., & Jacobsen, G. (1980). Treatment of endogenous anxiety with phobic, hysterical and hypochondriacal symptoms. *Archives of General Psychiatry, 37,* 51–59.

Sinclair, J. (1992). Bridging the gaps: An inside view of autism (or, do you know what I don't know?). In E. Schopler & G. B. Mesibov (Eds.), *High-functioning individuals with autism* (pp. 294–302). New York: Plenum Press.

Stehli, A. (1991). *The sound of a miracle.* New York: Doubleday.

Takagi, K., & Kobagasi, S. (1956). Skin pressure reflex. *Acta Medica et Biologica, 4,* 31–37.

Volkmar, F. R., & Cohen, D. J. (1985). The experience of infantile autism: A first-person account by Tony, W., *Journal of Autism and Developmental Disorders, 15,* 47–54.

White, G. B., & White, M. S. (1987). Autism from the inside. *Medical Hypothesis, 24,* 223–229.

Whittington, C. J., Kendall, T., Fonagy, P., Cottrel, D., Cotgrove, A., & Boddington, E. (2004). Selective seratonin reuptake inhibitors in childhood depression: Systematic review of published versus unpublished data. *Lancet, 363,* 1341–1345.

Williams, D. (1994). *Somebody somewhere.* New York: Times Books.

CHAPTER 52

A Teacher's Perspective: Adult Outcomes

VIRGINIA WALKER SPERRY

From 1966 to 1972, the years that I was director of the Elizabeth Ives School for Special Children in New Haven, Connecticut, I often saw the painful frustration on the faces of parents as they endured the confusion and emotional turmoil that went with trying to cope with a child with autism.

Soon after my retirement in 1972, I ran into an 11-year-old former Ives pupil and his mother at a local supermarket. I had last seen the child when he was 7 or 8. Sandy-haired, freckle-faced, and rangy in build, he beamed as he recognized me. Compared with the hyperactive, constantly chattering boy I had known, he seemed focused and in control. His mother told me proudly that her son was managing well in the special education program of his public school system. The change in him was remarkable. She thanked me for the attention he had received at Ives, without which, she felt, he never would have come so far. In a flash of conviction and inspiration, it occurred to me that it could be beneficial to share with others, especially the parents of such children, some of the hard-won knowledge we at Ives had gained from working with autism.

I began to collect data on the careers of 11 children I knew with clear autism. I have included here eight stories of those whose original diagnoses were "autistic" or "autistic-like."

The parents gave me permission to obtain information from the various institutions and programs that had treated their children. The Yale University Child Study Center in New Haven, Connecticut, which originally tested and diagnosed the eight children, provided facts on their early toddlerhood, doctors' and social workers' analyses, accounts, interviews, test scores, and final diagnoses. (Doctors at the Center's Child Development Unit, specifically Dr. Sally Provence, Dr. Martha Leonard, and Dr. Mary McGarry, referred their most puzzling younger children to the Ives School from the school's inception. These three particular doctors also became consultants for the school.) Other information came from records at nursery schools, public school special education programs, state-funded programs, and private special schools.

I compiled a full set of testing results for each child, from the earliest examinations through scores and grade-level achievements when each of the eight turned 21 and "graduated" from high school. To help complete the profiles, seven of the eight children were retested as adults at the Yale Child Study Center.

I interviewed the children's teachers, social workers, and parents, and as they grew older I went to their graduations, their workshops, group homes, and places of work. I took many of the eight out to lunch several times and kept on interviewing them and their parents through 1989. At the time my original research was complete, the children's ages ranged from 23 to approximately 30. My plan

This chapter is adapted from *Fragile Success: Ten Autistic Children Childhood to Adulthood*, by Virginia Walker Sperry, second edition, 2001, Baltimore: Paul H. Brookes.

to find out how they would develop as young adults had been accomplished. Nevertheless, I continued to keep in touch with them and to update the stories of their lives to the year 2002.

It is now nearly 40 years since these children, now adults, attended Ives School, and the study and treatment of autism have broadened and developed so that the process they experienced as virtual pioneers—the programs for special children and the availability of special schools—is largely taken for granted. The description of these early years is a history of those who were among the first children to receive such special treatment. But the children of these eight stories are not history. Although they are now adults and many have learned how to cope with their disability, their needs and characteristics have not changed. Nor has the problem of diagnosis been solved: There are still many children all over this country whose behavior, whether diagnosed autistic or atypical or even undiagnosed, confounds and disturbs their parents, doctors, and teachers. Such children present a challenge very similar to the challenge faced by those involved in the lives of the children I have taught and followed.

As my research grew, I questioned who would be the principal audience for my observations. There were the pediatricians, who, in the early years of Ives, seemed largely unaware of childhood autism; parents today are still dissatisfied with the ability of some pediatricians to recognize the syndrome. Then there were the parents, fumbling, often despairing, and totally bewildered, constantly asking for guidance and reassurance or at least some predictions as to the future. Other medical specialists and social workers, too, were baffled by these strange children. I wanted to address all of these groups.

During the 1960s and 1970s, we teachers of youngsters with autism were in a no-man's land, where information, resources, and guidance were largely unavailable and where intuition and innovation were required daily tools of the trade. I wanted to record what we learned in an accessible manner so others, whether doctors, teachers, or parents, could benefit from it. I hoped to broaden the understanding of autism for various audiences, including employers and those in the community who deal with the autistic on a day-to-day basis.

The subjects of my study are the young adults themselves from infancy to the present, their parents' experience of raising a developmentally disabled person, and the effect this had on the lives of parents and siblings. These individuals are dramatic examples of the wide range of autistic behaviors, and their stories demonstrate the kinds of parental interventions and the medical, educational, vocational, and recreational services that played an important part in their growing up.

Early diagnosis and medical and educational intervention saved each of these children. Without the unceasing dedication of parents, doctors, teachers, and other professionals, many, as adults, would be vegetating at home or in an institution. Instead, all have achieved a comparatively successful adulthood. Like all youngsters, each of these children had talents that might well have been lost, totally blocked by their various handicaps. The effectiveness of our work at the Ives School was due largely to our firm belief that each child has his or her strengths and that only by the discovery and use of the child's own individual talents could he or she become strong and accomplish a limited or, in at least one case, total independence.

To obscure the identities of the children (and families) discussed, names and birth dates have been changed, and permission has been obtained for all material herein. The children, mothers, fathers, and siblings here stand as archetypes of developmentally handicapped children and their families across the country. The problems and solutions touched on are universal.

BILL

Bill is the most independent and the least typical of even the highest functioning children with autism. His outcome is probably representative of no more than a few within the population of high-functioning children. For instance, very few young adults with autism can go to college, write a book and a collection of poetry, marry and have a family, and live totally independently, all of which Bill has done. While Bill is not representative, his case is included to illustrate a very positive outcome for a child with autism who is of average intelligence.

Blond, blue-eyed, and handsome, Bill looked like a typical 5-year-old. But he was in trouble from his first day in public school kindergarten. Although he had fluent speech, he frequently babbled nonsense and had severe confusion about what was real and what was fantasy. He came to us with the diagnosis of "atypical personality disorder with autistic features." But he was cooperative, enjoyed being taught on a one-on-one basis, and learned, showing some writing ability.

While at Ives, Bill loved to write "plays." After 3 years with us, he returned to regular classes in his public school. He went to college and did well, majoring in journalism. He has written a history of his family and published a book of poetry. After graduation, he decided that newspaper work was not for him and went to a culinary institute.

Bill is the only one of all the children whom I followed originally who is completely independent. For 5 or 6 years, he worked in a restaurant at Disney World. He had his own apartment and drove his own car, something many high-functioning adults with autism cannot do. He joined a church and became totally involved in all church-related activities.

Although Bill trained as a chef, he could not stand the pace of a big kitchen, so he asked his boss to let him do the ordering of restaurant supplies. Thereafter, he had his own office where, with his computer, he managed the ordering of supplies. He later worked in Disney World's very large gift shop, in charge of the computerized ordering. But, wonder of wonders, several days a week, dressed in his best clothes, he acted as a greeter to the would-be customers.

In his adult testing, Bill's full-scale IQ score was 95, the average range of intellectual functioning. His verbal score of 103 was significantly higher than his performance score of 95 and much stronger in verbal expression and comprehension than in nonverbal spatial tasks. On the Vineland, Bill's score of 90 places him in the average range of his peers. He is stronger in daily living skills than in socialization, which shows today in a certain shyness and diffidence of manner. Yet, he had a job as floor manager in a big gift shop, an extraordinary job for someone once diagnosed as autistic.

He and his wife, who is legally blind, now have two children, both planned. The boy is a healthy, outgoing toddler. The younger child, a girl, up to now seems "fine," according to Bill's wife.

Because of his wife's impaired vision, they moved a year ago to another town to be near her family. Bill's commute to work was more than an hour each way, with Bill coming home to help with the children and household chores. It was an exhausting schedule, added to which he worked for Habitat for Humanity, so that eventually they could have their own home. Whether all this pressure was a factor in the sudden development of performance problems at work is unclear. For whatever reason, he lost his job.

He worked briefly for an electronics firm, supervising repairs, but lost that job in the cutbacks after September 11, 2001. He then returned to restaurant work. He and his family have moved into their own Habitat for Humanity house. To get such a house for himself, Bill put in 500 hours in helping to build other houses.

I visited Bill and his family in their new home in early 2002. He and his wife are obviously very proud of their new home, and they should be. It represents determination, independence, and hard work. Their son, Jim, $4\frac{1}{2}$ years old, and daughter, Sara, 3 years old, are slim and blonde, somewhat more fragile-looking than their sturdier father was at their age. Bill's wife said that Sara was receiving occupational therapy through the public school system. Jim had difficult-to-describe subtle characteristics that reminded me of his father as a child. He had an air of tentativeness, not exactly shyness, more as if he were "trying out" the situation. Naturally, I watched him with great interest. I was curious to see whether there was any trace of characteristics similar to Bill's when he came to Ives School. Bill's wife talked about how necessary she felt diagnosis both of Bill and of the children to be. She seemed to me too outspoken about Bill's occasional difficulties with social situations. The children have some signs of problems—speech for Sara, for which she is receiving therapy at school, but nothing specific was mentioned for Jim.

Bill protested his wife's characterization of some of his problems; he clearly felt that she exaggerated. And I must say he has overcome most of the symptoms of autism that he presented as a 5- to 6-year-old. To those who recall the Bill of kindergarten years, he has made dramatic progress. He seemed to be in wonderful shape. He greeted us with a happy smile, hugged me, and seemed clearly delighted to see me—very different from the typical concept of autism. There was, however, an almost stuttering hesitation in his discussion with me when we ordered lunch. This reminded me vividly of the Bill of 10 years ago, at our previous meeting.

Because both Bill and his wife are eager for further diagnosis of his case as well as for investigation of any problems the children may have, he and his family made plans to come to the Yale Child Study Center the following summer.

I should emphasize that Bill's quite happy outcome—a college graduate, living independently with a wife and children—is a rare exception among individuals with autism. That he is of normal intelligence is surely a factor. Aspects of his case are highly suggestive of Asperger syndrome.

DAVID

At age 3, David could say only, "Mama." A year later he scored at a 2-year, 11-month level. He said, "ball," "cookie," "key," "car," and "water." The doctor remarked that his language was more delayed than his other performance scores indicated and, for this reason, David was referred to a specialist in aphasia. The pediatrician concluded her summary by saying that both she and the specialist believed that he was not aphasic since he understood language, but the cause of his developmental slowness was unclear. Therefore, his placement at our preschool was to be therapeutic and diagnostic.

David started speech therapy in his second year at Ives to help him overcome his lack of spontaneous speech. The therapist used a dollhouse, small dolls, and play furniture, and soon David could name all of them. He responded to his name by echoing it. He wanted desperately to learn how to write his name, and he worked on that daily with the therapist.

By the time he was 6 years old, he was talking so that he could be understood. He no longer whispered or covered his eyes. He played with other children, although it was still more of a side-by-side play than a true give-and-take.

After 2 years at Ives preschool, David was ready to go on to the newly established public school program for children with developmental disabilities. There, he went into the communication disorders program, where he learned sign language. He blossomed and began to make fantastic strides. He quickly progressed from signing to talking, at first hesitantly and then fluently. The teacher also said he loved to read aloud.

At age 21, David graduated from the communication disorders program of the special education high school. "He is this school's proudest achievement!" exclaimed his supervisor. She glowed with pride as she described his fluency, warm friendliness, sense of responsibility, and popularity with other students. David talked with give-and-take fluency. He was often humorous. Academically, he was at a fourth-grade level in reading and math. Socially, he was limited and tentative, as though looking for signposts to guide his behavior.

Now in his late 30s, David has always lived at home at the insistence of his parents. Dr. Volkmar felt that David's highly protective family might have limited their son when they discouraged him from living in a group home where his socialization skills would have been given a better chance to develop.

Over the past 15 years, David has held many different jobs. For example, he has worked at the telephone company and at a discount store. David worked in the "back room" where he unloaded and distributed items to their proper storage space. But the store cut back on employees, so David is now back working in the community house. His father wishes he could get a paying job. His father and I talked about the necessity of educating employers about autism. He agreed with me that this is an urgent need. It is worth noting that David's father has a severe speech impediment, as does David's sister.

On my most recent visit in 2000 to David's home, I observed that he seemed fully grown up. He stands about 5 feet, 6 inches tall, still a stocky figure, and he now appears as a handsome, self-confident, and very dignified young man. Yet, as I observed him, he still had that impervious quality. His shining eyes and broad smile lacked spontaneity, as his teachers had described him years ago.

In recent years, once a month, David has gone with friends to a camp where they hike, dance, and keep busy with many other activities. David smiles as he talks about the camp, and I sense that he really has a good time on these outings. On other weekends, a department of mental retardation (DMR) counselor takes David and other friends bowling. His sister and other family members take him out to eat or to the movies so that, all and all, I feel that David's life has fallen into a satisfactory pattern.

When asked whether he remembered a former schoolmate, he replied, "Yes," and then added, "And what about Eric? How's he doing?" He was pleased, obviously, to learn that Eric was doing so well. It had been at least 14 years since David had last seen Eric at their special education high school, and his memory of Eric seemed amazing to me. When it was time for good-byes at the end of the visit, David's mother wished me a "Merry Christmas!" Without prompting, David shook my hand, smiled, and said, "Have a good holiday!"

KAREN

When Karen entered our preschool at age 4, she was a delicate, anxious child who had many fears, particularly of balloons and lightbulb shapes. She was diagnosed as possibly autistic and functionally retarded. She spoke only four words: "Mom," "Daddy," "balloon," and "light." By the end of 3 years, she attempted to interact with her classmates and talked in two- or three-word sentences.

Subsequently, her education included four other schools, two day and two boarding, all for emotionally disturbed and developmentally disabled children and adolescents. At 21, she graduated from her "special" boarding school, classified as "educable mentally retarded" with an academic level of seven years, 2 months. The school's psychological examiner described her as profoundly handicapped in visual, motor, and sensory areas, in his opinion, probably of an organic nature. Low self-esteem and a high anxiety level impeded her performance. Yet, Karen had blossomed socially. From little or no language, she had be-

come a nonstop talker, had friends at school, and a boyfriend. After graduation, she lived in an apartment-type group home but now lives in her own apartment in a house in a small seaside town by the water.

At one of my early visits to Karen's home, I saw that the apartment was small and strewn with clothes. The living room was more organized, with a bookcase full of bird and flower books. A fish tank stood in one corner and a birdcage with a parakeet (named Samantha) was perched on a footstool. On the floor in front of the sofa were neat piles of bird and flower books, a plastic freezer bag full of necklaces, and a thick J.C. Penney catalogue. On the walls hung two of her paintings—brilliant, incisive pictures of flowers conveying a style and integrity all their own, but in the style of a talented second grader. This visual statement of Karen's interests since early childhood—birds, flowers, fishing, pretty clothing, and art—fascinated me.

Karen, 5 feet, 6 inches tall, has lost the original dark good looks of her 20s. The flashing dark blue eyes and fine dark eyebrows remain, but the aquiline nose, finely drawn mouth, and chin have become blurred with too much flesh. It is this appearance, along with her chunky figure, that produces the effect of "something wrong." I did most of the talking at that visit. Karen, at first, did not talk; but then, suddenly, out of her smiling silence, came brief, crisp, clearly enunciated sentences.

Karen has worked at various jobs over the years. Initially, she worked in the bakery run by her former school, crimping the piecrusts, a task that took her several months to master. Later she worked at a Home Depot, putting price labels on tiles, and at a seafood factory, she stuffed and packed clams. She later worked in a discount store similar to Price Club where she was thrilled to be making more than $7 an hour. Her boss said that Karen was worth every cent because she was so dependable and pleasant.

At 37 years of age, Karen now lives alone in her own apartment, close to the shore. The summers she spent with her family on an island developed in her an intense love of the seashore and the natural world. Her main interest from childhood has been birds and flowers. With an incredible memory, she is able to paint flowers and birds in exact detail, to describe types of nests, and to recognize the songs of birds.

Karen's original diagnosis was "atypical development with autistic behavior." She had little speech and seemed surrounded by an invisible, impenetrable wall. Yet, through this, I felt that she wanted to relate, despite overwhelming anxiety. Karen was in an autism clinic research group. She was put on Luvox®, and her social awareness and ability to focus much improved. Although when she came to Ives she had little speech, she responded to patient, one-on-one teaching. Her remarkable memory certainly played a part in her acquisition of speech. Her adult speech is comparatively fluent, now flowing smoothly and easily. Usually, she answers questions in three or four words. Even so, her enunciation is clear and less stressed. When I mentioned having a bad knee, Karen asked, "Will your knee get better? My mother had knee surgery!"

Two episodes from a follow-up visit in 1998 illustrate the complexity of her thinking. When asked whether she knew the restaurant where she and her family went often for lunch, she responded that she could show the way. But after two false tries, it was clear that she couldn't give the directions, nor could she recall the name of the restaurant, despite her remarkable memory. It seemed likely that her intense anxiety blocked her ability to put directions into words.

In contrast, a short ride down to the shore after lunch showed Karen's ability in another light. Looking out across the bay, she changed totally as she stood and watched the bird life on the water. A gull flew up and Karen said, "That's a herring gull." "There goes a white heron," as she pointed to a white flash with extended legs settling on the water. Entranced by the presence of the birds, she lost her anxiety. No more spasmodic covering her face with her hands. Her intense interest in the birds gave her focus, wiping out her confusions and anxiety. She was transformed into the Karen that might have been, without the handicap of autism.

One day a week, Karen volunteers at a park run by the Audubon Society, "picking up trash." She still goes frequently to the library where she invariably chooses books about nature, flowers, birds, snakes, and forest animals. This information was elicited by questions, to which Karen gave brief answers, but always with a smile and a subtle air of self-confidence. She showed her visitors these books at her apartment, and clearly she had read some of the text. This amazed me, as I recalled the little girl who spoke only four words when I first taught her more than 30 years ago.

She seemed settled and self-confident in a way that would have been impossible to imagine even a year before. Her jobs were going well. Although she still covers her face with her hands and occasionally is shaken by an almost imperceptible tremor, her intense anxiety has lessened greatly. The fact that she now goes to the library and picks out books following her interest in nature is another sign of her improved self-image.

Karen's successful continuing development is a tribute to the intense one-on-one teaching, the unceasing intelligent care of her parents, particularly her mother, and the highly professional supervision of doctors, social workers, job coaches, and case managers. She now works very successfully full time in the kitchen of a retirement home where she makes salads and helps serve meals. She's very happy. Her family says: "Karen is a joy to herself and gives happiness to all of us."

JIMMY

Jimmy, between the ages of 3 and 4, attended a small preschool. This period was unsuccessful, as shown on the school's report, which stated, "The only way in which Jimmy can be present at group activities was by the teacher holding him on her lap." When he did participate in play activities, he had to be watched closely.

During the time he attended this school, Jimmy was evaluated by several clinics at Yale-New Haven Hospital and by the local state-run rehabilitation center. Each evaluation gave a similar diagnosis: organic brain damage and mental retardation. His parents were confused by this diagnosis because Jimmy appeared intelligent and was responsible for caring for himself at home. The pediatric specialist explained that although in all probability Jimmy had some brain impairment, he was, above all, disabled by his emotional disturbance, which left him afraid, angry, very upset, and puzzled. With no ability to talk out his problems, the physician said, Jimmy would behave as if he had mental retardation and would have the same needs as such a child.

Jimmy was a wild man when he came to us at Ives School! Completely nonverbal, his frustration found outlet in biting, kicking, and hitting. He was diagnosed as having autistic symptoms accompanied by severe emotional disturbance. During the fall, he sat in the sand pile and poured sand on his head or ate it. On outings to the park, he insisted on walking buttoned up inside his teacher's coat. By spring, he had improved, smiling and looking at people. On walks, he ran ahead with the other children. Through patient one-on-one teaching, he improved during the first year at Ives and then regressed the second year. He became more and more belligerent and often had to go back to the one-room, one-teacher routine. His Yale Child Study Center specialist recommended a residential school.

After 5 years, Jimmy returned to enter the Communication Disorders Program at Area Cooperative Education Services (ACES), a state-run school program for disabled individuals in the New Haven area. There, Jimmy became the star of his particular group. He made rapid progress in sign language, for he was determined to do well.

In his junior year, I took Jimmy to be tested at the Communication Disorders Program at Southern Connecticut State University. The result of the thorough testing was a recommendation that Jimmy start studying sign language in a program at Southern. He was intelligent and had excellent fine motor skills. The program staff felt he would never talk but that he was so motivated he could master sign language easily. Unfortunately, both his parents worked. There was no way to get him to the school for further training at that time. He graduated from the ACES high school program and transitioned into a supervised workshop.

Now, as an adult, he lives at home, through the choice of his mother. Throughout these years, he has worked in a sheltered workshop. His boss had respect and admiration for Jimmy's determination and ability. There was a period when he worked at a shipping company, his one experience at being out in the community. But Jimmy was unhappy in this job and went back to the workshop. A couple of

years ago, Jimmy was put on medication because his behavior had become uncharacteristically aggressive. His mother, Jimmy's social worker, and the head of the workshop were delighted at his improvement. Jimmy has come a long way, but his improvement is still a work in progress.

Jimmy is blessed with that intangible quality of charm. From his first day at school, he charmed all of us. This quality, along with his sense of humor, awareness of people, and quickness to learn (as shown by his rapid and eager acquisition of sign language) have certainly determined what he is today—an attractive, rather dignified young man of 36. Thanks to his mother's determined efforts, Jimmy is now under effective and committed supervision by a local provider organization. He has been trained as a gardener and, his mother says, he enjoys his work. He also delivers Meals on Wheels, again an astonishing development. At home, he helps with chores such as housecleaning, cooking, and laundry. He has both a bird and a dog for pets, and he is totally responsible for their care. Three evenings a week, he works as a deacon at his mother's church. He sets up chairs for the service and tidies up afterwards, all on his own initiative.

One touching incident occurred during my most recent visit to Jimmy's home. The phone rang and Jimmy picked it up. His mother prompted, "Say, 'Hello,' Jimmy. . . ." By his inflection and the tone of his unintelligible sounds, I could sense how hard he was trying, unsuccessfully, to produce that single word. How tragic to have this frustrating neurological handicap, combined with intelligence, and yet no ability to verbalize it.

Increasingly, Jimmy is using sign language, even teaching and correcting his mother. You could conjecture that with his new, caring instructors, signing may become a form of outlet for this charming, determined young man.

JOHN

At age 3, John was diagnosed as "a brain-impaired child of normal intellectual ability" and referred to the Ives preschool. He was a handsome, sturdy, little boy with a round face, blue eyes, and a thatch of brown hair; his smile was beguiling. My first impression was of total normalcy. A casual observer might have asked, "Why is this child in a 'special' nursery school?" During his first week in school, John was agreeable and anxiously conforming. His nonstop, apparently friendly, chatter captivated the teachers. But this persuasive charm was deceptive. He disintegrated rapidly into hyperactive, angry, often hysterical behavior. With constant teacher attention and praise, he could play with one toy for 1 or 2 minutes.

John stayed at nursery school for 3 years. He was almost 7 and still distractible and anxious. John was reading at mid-first-grade level, but he could stick with an activity only briefly. He refused to paint or play with trucks or blocks. His printing was illegible. He could not build a block structure after a model or place three-dimensional shapes on a paper pattern. He could sing on tune and accurately reproduce a simple, tapped-out pattern.

John attended a private elementary and high school for handicapped children and adolescents. After 8 years, he transferred to a residential school for emotionally disturbed adolescents and then to a new special education program in his hometown.

John began vocational training, first working part time as a kitchen aide in a fast-food restaurant. His verbal ability and superficial ability to relate to people as well as his cooperativeness ensured that, given a sympathetic employer, John would do well. In his senior year in high school, he began getting an hourly wage, but the job ended the summer after graduation. His work history has been spotty: Jobs were lost because the pressure of the work produced high anxiety and hysterical tears. One job was in a business cafeteria where he fell apart under the amount of dishes to be washed, and as the work piled up, his anxiety increased proportionately. He found the need to be an efficient part of a chain of workers "too much pressure." John's subsequent jobs have been volunteer.

Throughout John's academic career, his strengths and weaknesses remained the same. He had a persuasive, highly verbal charm, with an ability to master subjects such as reading, English, and social studies comparatively well. At graduation, he read on an eight-grade level, and he was a star speller. He had a fine singing voice and sang in his church choir. But he con-

tinued to be emotionally unpredictable, with sudden, angry flare-ups and unexpected tears. In group therapy, he could interpret his classmates' feelings, but not his own.

After graduation, John lived in a supervised apartment group home until he moved to a condominium, which he shares with another young man from the group home. He has lived at the same rental condo now for nearly 15 years.

John and his family have accepted this situation. His good looks and apparent normalcy have always been his worst enemy. But, with his family's acceptance of his disability and consequent placement under the supervision of the DMR, he has been able to achieve a stable life. In essence, John is completely independent, although his parents and a DMR caseworker check in with him regularly.

John's superficial charm and good nature have always made him well liked. However, his emotional instability became such a clear hazard that he himself recently took matters in hand. While he has taken courses in stress management, he has been adamant that he would not see a psychologist. He has worked out at a gym to lose weight.

On his own initiative, he got an application for a volunteer job at a local hospital, filled it out, sent it in, had several interviews, and eventually started working in the dietetics department, where he is now. In describing this job-seeking process, he repeated proudly, "Yep. I did that all on my own. No-sir-ee, nobody helped me!" His work at the hospital consists of setting up trays for patients and helping with the dishwasher. He leaves home at 7:00 A.M., is through by noon, and gets home, via two buses, by 1:00 P.M.

He is touching in his description of his attacks of hysteria. When he feels an explosion coming on, he tries to isolate himself. "When I do that, when I start to cry, I say to myself, 'Why?' But I'm better now. I try to get by myself until I'm quiet again."

He is also taking a computer course and a course in ceramics. He produced two life-size statues of cats, which were very lifelike, with alert expressions. He was delighted by the comment that he had real talent in art. On the computer, he uses e-mail and surfs the Internet. (Individuals with autism are often notably good with computers.) When reminded how well he had done at his special high school—the top reader and speller—John recalled how surprised he was to be asked to graduate with his regular high school class. "I was nervous in the inside. But I did all right!" He was obviously very proud of graduating with his regular high school.

John's parents have never agreed that he has any autistic characteristics. But, again, his case is an illustration of the vast differences that exist within the syndrome of autism. John looks at people directly in the eye; he has a surface ease in social situations. But, in fact, even going back to early childhood schooling, his contacts and understandings have been described as lacking in depth.

One other instance of the conundrum of this disease: John's father had a heart attack several years ago. John winced, shutting his eyes as he talked about this. "Don't even talk about! My mother called me and told me. Oh, it was awful! Things were going through my mind that you wouldn't believe." Although his father is fine now, when he recalled this painful experience, John expressed such true depth of emotion, shock, and horror—and so verbally, which is most unautistic.

In considering John's current situation, his family declare themselves "content." John has independence, with some minimal supervision. A caseworker comes in once a week to make sure his checkbook is balanced and that all is well. John, incidentally, is proud of "never being overdrawn. My checkbook is always balanced!" He has enough self-knowledge to try, mostly successfully, to control his bouts of hysteria.

POLLY

At age 5, Polly came to Ives School with the diagnosis of "personality disturbance with autistic tendencies." We learned, however, as we taught her, that she was perceptually handicapped to a severe degree. In addition, she was her own worst enemy. She was determined to succeed, and frustration sent her into wild tantrums. Despite two tall teachers holding her, she would attempt to (and nearly succeed) turn over a large nursery school table. Her behavior at home nearly destroyed her family because she was so violent, at one point even attempting

to kill herself. At this time, her psychiatrist described her as a brain-damaged perfectionist.

After just 1 year at Ives and with the help of medication, Polly improved enough to go into her public school's special education class. She graduated from the special education section of her high school and was trained to be a waitress. She worked for a time in a restaurant where, because of her inclination to take command, she became the manager's "right hand," as he put it to me. Her other jobs have consisted of working in an eyeglass factory and being a salesperson at T.J. Maxx. She is currently working at a biomedical factory. To all of these jobs, she has taken the public bus—a thing her family thought she would never do.

For many years, Polly lived at home, but she was finally able to move into a supervised condominium, which she shares with another handicapped woman. Polly says matter-of-factly, "She has Down syndrome."

I had lunch with Polly in March 1999, and she told me how much she loves being independent. Incidentally, Polly has always called herself "mentally retarded."

Polly had changed markedly in several ways in 2 years. She still had the exquisitely pretty face, chiseled features, china-white complexion, blue eyes, and blonde hair. The change for the worse was her weight. She had put on almost 20 pounds and verged on being overweight.

Polly immediately announced that she had something very exciting to tell. She was going on vacation to Wisconsin with her parents to visit her brother. She would see her nephew. She had never gone away on a vacation with her family before as an adult, so this was a big event for her. Polly once competed in track for Special Olympics, winning a prize. However, she said she had stopped that many years ago. She swims often at the Y and planned to swim at her brother's place in Wisconsin.

Her excitement at going on this trip with her family was pathetically out of proportion. It brought to mind how unpredictable she had been growing up, too difficult perhaps to take on trips. So, for Polly, traveling with her family was a new and exciting experience.

Dr. Sally Provence of Yale Child Study Center, who edited all of my original case studies, added this comment at the end of Polly's: "Polly had such potential that had she had the advantage of current-day medical knowledge and current treatment technology, she would today be realizing more fully her abilities."

When Polly came to us at age 5, she had the vocabulary of a normal 5-year-old, unlike the majority of our students. She also (on the surface) behaved with social appropriateness. She learned the kindergarten and first-grade academics fairly easily and was determined to succeed. But, her acute perceptual handicaps (particularly lack of depth perception) certainly added to her emotional unpredictability.

Her full-scale IQ score of 61 indicates moderate mental retardation. The communication score on the Vineland of 36 indicates that mysterious autistic inability to pick up general social cues. Her high daily living score of 85, thus, is all the more surprising; but here test scores can sometimes reflect personality. Driven to succeed, Polly has always wanted to be "in charge" or to be "the best." The Autism Behavior Checklist (ABC) score may add some understanding: Dr. Volkmar rated her score of 55 as more atypical, probably not autistic. Putting all the scores together explains her ability to travel on buses independently, to work as a salesperson (surely a socialized skill astonishing in a person described in early years as having autistic tendencies), and now to work happily, she says, and successfully in a biomedical factory.

Now age 40, Polly continues to work at the biomedical factory and is still living in the same condo, with the same condo-mate. She has also gained in maturity and has an air of having "settled something." At the same time, she has a reserve in her attitude, which did not exist before. It is as if, motivated to succeed as she has always been, the realization of her limitations bitterly discourages her. On the other hand, she told me that she went to a psychiatrist at the Yale Child Study Center and perhaps from this comes her more acute sense of her handicaps. She told me that she had a caseworker named Susie, who helps with grocery shopping, keeping house, and so on. Polly said, with a decisive shake of her head, "I told Susie that I must take my medication myself and I must balance my checkbook by myself!" She seemed determined to take complete responsibility for herself.

During the last visit, I noticed another element in Polly's changed attitude that recalled to me Dr. Provence's comment about her potential. What I noticed in Polly's changed attitude was pride.

When we said good-bye after lunch, Polly observed: "I look at my life . . . and I think I have accomplished a lot. I say to myself, 'I have a job, and I go there on my own. I have a nice place to live. I have staff to help me do things. I have friends. I go places with my family and my friends. . . . ' I have accomplished a lot."

TOM

Tom came to Ives School with a diagnosis of slow development with an indication of "atypical personality disorder," one of several broad terms used in the 1960s to define autism. He was a pale blonde child, tall, and thin. He whispered three or four words, was echolalic, and always avoided eye contact. He was remote and very stubborn.

The stubbornness made him a teaching challenge but also made him determined to succeed. Tom left Ives School after 3 years and went into his public school system's special education department. In high school, he had vocational training as a dishwasher and started working in a local restaurant. He is still there today. During his years at work at minimum wage, Tom accumulated a healthy savings account. With this, and through the research and help of his father, Tom bought and moved into his own condo.

Tom was described by the specialist who referred him to Ives School as "bland, slow in all developmental landmarks." This is still true of Tom at 39. However, blandness developed into an advantage. It was perceived in his high school years as amiability and is, in fact, just that today. His stubbornness translated into determination.

Through a research group at a local mental health center, Tom was diagnosed with "fragile X," a variation sometimes found in the syndrome of autism. He was put on Luvox®, and his social awareness and ability to focus much improved. At lunch with Tom in 1997, he shook my hand and said, "I liked your book." Then he told the waitress proudly, "She wrote a book about *me*,"—a far cry from the bland, difficult-to-reach little boy who came to Ives School some 30 years before.

Tom has been working at the same restaurant for 20 years and is a valued and popular employee. He is a dishwasher, but he also now is in charge of food storage, putting away orders, and bringing down from the stockroom what is needed for the day. When it was suggested to the restaurant owner that Tom was lucky to have found such support and understanding at his place of work, the owner retorted, "It's quite the reverse. *We* are lucky to have found Tom!"

Tom's scores, in tests at 27 years of age, placed him in the mild range of mental retardation. But his daily living and socialization scores of 80 and 83 are astonishing in view of the general picture presented by the IQ and communication scores and the fact that he has a pervasive development disorder. Testing, no matter how accurate, cannot define that intangible called "personality." In Tom's case, his stubborn determination and availability to teaching meant that he was open to and took advantage of every educational and other experience. He has now been able to live with comparative independence in his own condominium for more than 5 years. (*Comparative independence* means 3 to 4 hours daily of staff support and hands-on parental oversight.) Although he is driven by a caseworker to various appointments, he rides his bike to work, as he has done for years. Although he does not mention it himself, it has been reported to his parents that he is seen riding his bike around the seaside community where he lives, apparently content to move around the area and find his own way back home.

Tom now lives alone by choice. His two-bedroom condo is in a pleasant area about 2 miles from his parents' home. But finding someone to share it presented problems. In mid-1999, his caseworkers introduced him to a possible roommate. They tried to get Tom to say whether he liked this young man. Did he really want a condo-mate? The effort to get him to express his wishes was to no avail. He would *not* tell them. Finally, his mother asked Tom to write her a note saying whether he wanted a person to share the condo. Wonder of wonders, Tom wrote his mother saying emphatically that he did *not* want a roommate. He wanted to live alone.

So that issue has been settled. But his ability to express himself in writing illustrates the autistic trait of difficulty with social relationships. He could write his opinions, but he could not express his feelings during direct social contact.

Tom's social life today consists of different activities planned by the local Association for Retarded Citizens (ARC), and Tom signs up for those that interest him—usually swing dancing or going to a ballgame or movie. He also joins his family for a summer vacation in the West where, at their cabin by a lake, he enjoys fishing.

In the summer of 1999, Tom's mother and I met for lunch on the open upper deck of the restaurant where Tom works. On his lunch break, Tom brought up his plate of pasta and salad. In many ways, he resembles the little 5-year-old boy who came to Ives School. He looks away, usually to the left, and, in answer to a question such as, "What did you do on vacation, Tom?" he says, "Yes, I did fish . . . fish . . . did fish. . . ."

Maturity had changed Tom's appearance. At 6 feet, 3 inches in height, he is heavier, and, as he walked into the restaurant dining room, he seemed to tower over the other occupants. The lean lantern-jawed look has filled out. He wears glasses now, a new development. Behind the glasses, his eyes show more awareness, even though he turns his glance away immediately, to the left. Despite his abbreviated speech, the mutterings, and the evasive glances, Tom appears today to be a mature, quietly self-confident human being.

Tom's parents say that they are "content" with his situation as it is today. There is no doubt that Tom constitutes something of a triumph over the disabilities of autism in that he has achieved comparative independence. He is grounded enough in reality to take pride in doing a job well, and he has a well-developed sense of responsibility.

ERIC

Eric came to the preschool at Ives in September 1969. He was referred because of lack of speech with the diagnosis of "congenital autism." Characteristic behavior was self-absorption, compulsive walking in circles with his head cocked to one side, smiling at everyone, and yet smiling at nothing. Dr. Fred Volkmar called him, "the young adult most typically autistic," of the children I have followed to adulthood.

When he was 3½ years old, he tested at a 21-month level. When he was 12, he scored in the mentally defective range and was described by the psychological examiner as a child who had at least a moderate central nervous system impairment, and, as such, he functioned within the trainable retarded range. His specialist emphasized his air of imperviousness. Of all the children I followed to adulthood, he was the most remote, impervious to any kind of social contact, although he would sit at the nursery school table and do simple puzzles. He most often was seen walking around the schoolyard, his head cocked to one side, smiling up at the sky but, in truth, smiling at nothing we could define.

Yet, there was an area of ability unimpaired in Eric. He had demonstrated good coordination in fine motor skills as a young child. Later, in high school vocational class, he became skilled at woodworking and simple carpentry. He had unusually good fine motor skills, but his neurological impairment was so severe that it prohibited the development of this skill.

At age 12, Eric's test report said that he was so neurologically impaired that he could not hear words as words, only as meaningless sounds.

Eric went into the lowest level at his special school, but he became so violent, nearly killing his teacher once, that he was always accompanied by a male aide. After graduation, Eric went into a sheltered workshop run by a school for children with severe autism. He lived at home, cared for by a devoted extended family.

In 1999, Eric was put on the medication risperidone. His mother and his social worker reported a dramatic change. He has been far less aggressive and, most of the time, seems amiable and even cooperative. When we took his picture (at his home), he seemed to recognize me, smiling and shaking my hand.

At age 22, Eric was working in a sheltered workshop run by a school for young adults with autism. He did well in all jobs requiring fine motor skills. However, he still suffered from a tautly controlled violence, which interfered with his ability to focus and stay on task. His family had wanted him to be placed in a group home but feared that his bursts of aggression would make this impossible.

But by the time Eric had reached his early 30s, happily, his situation had much improved. He has now been in a group home for more than 5 years and is doing very well there. He comes home every other weekend. However, whereas he originally spent the whole weekend at home, he now returns to the group home every night. His mother reported that Eric tore up the beds and pillows in his room and "made such a mess" that she requested that he return to the group home for stronger supervision at night.

Eric now works in a local sheltered workshop. He rides in their delivery van, responsibly delivering products. No one thought this would ever be possible in view of his bouts of aggressiveness. When I saw him several years ago at his mother's apartment, he was a well-dressed, nice-looking 32-year-old man. He shook my hand with a smiling gibberish greeting ("Hello," perhaps) and then went into the kitchen, took the laundry basket, and went downstairs to his sister's laundry room to do the laundry. This indicates a socialized purposeful behavior, which 10 years earlier would have been impossible.

As an adult, Eric tested with a full-scale IQ score of 46, in the moderately mentally retarded range. His mother could not be present for the Vineland, hence no scores. But he was diagnosed as congenitally autistic, and his ABC score of 101 was rated by Dr. Volkmar as probably autistic.

Like Tom, Eric has become focused. His whole attitude, in his stance and directness of gaze, now seems to be in touch with reality. He is now able to say words, although parroting them, but he understands what is said, a miraculous development in view of his testing at age 12 that had reported that he heard sounds only and not words as such.

In the summer of 1999, I visited Eric in his group home, and I was astonished. We discussed what he did on each day of the week: Monday? Tuesday? and so on. "Work," he would respond. Or, for afternoons, "Play ball" or "walk." And on one day, "Music!" Then, to my exclamation, "Music!" Eric started to sing, "Old MacDonald had a farm." And he was on tune!

The final question, "Sunday?" brought forth, "See Mama . . . eat lunch . . . barbecued chicken . . . string beans . . . APPLE PIE!"

For his former teacher, who remembered the 4-year-old wandering aimlessly about the schoolyard, to see and hear this was truly inspiring. Eric's life at the moment is happy and for all who knew him over many years, a surprising success. Understandably, his mother is delighted. To a teacher, parent, caseworker, or whoever works with children like Eric, the message is clear: Miracles do happen!

WHERE DOES THIS LEAVE PARENTS, TEACHERS, AND CHILDREN?

The original purpose of my study was to present case studies of children with varying autistic behaviors whom I taught and followed to adulthood. As of the year 2002, the eight surviving children vary in age from 35 to 42. These stories lead to some bittersweet conclusions. The eight are fairly representative of the general population of people with autism, neither as severely impaired as the most disabled nor as brilliant in astonishing ways as some autistic savants. If this chapter and the stories in it represented the status quo, the inference to be drawn about the future of adults with autism would be at once encouraging—intensive education and one-on-one care of the child with autism through to adulthood does ameliorate and adjust autistic behaviors—and equally discouraging, for no matter what the improvement, the young adult remains basically the same, handicapped by problems in relating to the world.

Fortunately, my follow-up does not present the status quo. There are continuing advances in medical research and various new methods of treatment for individuals with autism, and, although there is no cure, the outlook now is brighter than it ever has been. In fact, there are so many promising new treatments available that some experts suggest families explore any new therapy they think might have an effect. Ruth Sullivan, director of the Autism Services Center in Huntington, West Virginia, and mother of Joseph Sullivan, one of the models for the character of Raymond in the movie *Rain Man,* feels encouraged. She has said, "Some very exciting things have been happening—

we've never seen progress to this extent." So, where do we stand now? In what way is the current situation better for teachers, for parents, and for children with autism now grown to adulthood?

Teachers

A great deal has been learned about autism and childhood developmental disorders since the 1960s. No longer is the teaching of developmentally disabled children nebulous or a matter of guesswork. The special education field has become better delineated, and its goals have been clarified. Teaching materials and techniques are constantly improving and expanding. Years of clinical and teaching experience and numerous longitudinal studies have led to the acceptance of the concept of an underlying organic, though still enigmatic, etiology of autism. The variety and degree of the abnormalities of behavior and impairments of function found are considerable (see Chapter 1). The great variation in the syndromes of autism and atypical development underscore the importance of precision in diagnosis. Progress in the diagnosis and definition of autism and its related syndromes has been an important factor in the growth and implementation of theories on teaching, as the specificity of diagnosis directly affects the choice of teaching techniques and materials available to the present-day teacher.

In the 1960s, teachers, however well educated, had to teach with intuition and often with handmade materials. The teachers at Ives used innovative paper cutouts of red, blue, green, and yellow squares, triangles, and circles; block pattern designs; and so on. None had used such materials before, and all had to learn, from scratch, how, when, and why to use them and other novel techniques. Teachers now have special textbooks and workbooks as well as other teaching aids such as computers, cassettes, television, videocassette recorders, and copying machines. A generation of teachers has developed and refined teaching approaches such as behavior modification, signing, mainstreaming, prevocational and vocational training, special physical education, music, art, and recreation. Special educators have been joined by occupational therapists, physical therapists, speech and language specialists, music and dance therapists, and specialists in other disciplines in addressing the difficult tasks of communicating with and enhancing the general learning potential and otherwise solving or alleviating developmental problems. Even with transdisciplinary, multiple, coordinated teaching methods and improved teaching materials and strategies, however, there remains a constant need for teachers and their colleagues to be able to individualize their materials and approaches to a particular child. Resourcefulness, flexibility, knowing a child well, and having the courage to modify and question existing methods remain crucial for the most effective education and therapy.

Teachers now have some idea of what to expect. Since the passage of the Education of the Handicapped Act in 1970, the courses in child development at teachers' colleges have paid progressively more attention to the educational problems of handicapped children. There is also now an educated stratum of sophisticated and well-trained professionals, from the directors of these programs, who are often themselves specialists, to social workers who back up the teachers through liaison with parents, and psychologists who perform and score developmental testing. In addition, physicians at child development and mental health clinics and in private practice are now able to identify specific developmental problems that were poorly understood a generation ago.

Many teachers today also have the advantage of a state-regulated, federally funded plan, developed in the 1980s, to educate handicapped children as well as older preschool and school-age children in "Birth to Three" programs. The thrust of this program is early intervention, and its intention is to give everyone—child, teacher, and parents—a head start. The earlier the intervention, the better the chance for improving the child's modification of his or her disabilities, for effective teaching, and for parents' informed coping with autistic behaviors.

College students who today contemplate teaching children with autism have a good chance of making a realistic decision. They have the opportunity to observe a variety of classes and programs: private schools (nursery school to high school), public school special education programs, state-sponsored service centers, and early intervention programs. From these, potential future teachers can assess whether they have the capabilities and personality traits needed to be successful teachers. But all the progress made in the past 25 years still has not made it an easy job. Anyone starting off on a career of teaching developmentally handicapped children often feels lost, not knowing which way to turn, where to go, or what to do. Physical endurance, emotional stability, flexibility, ability and willingness to improvise, and a respect for the value of one's own intuition are all needed. This kind of teaching is not everyone's cup of tea.

As noted in other chapters in this volume, various methods of research, intervention, and treatment are becoming available. These methods will, ultimately, have an impact on teachers and teaching methods. Even now, they are raising questions and beginning to cause change. The basic necessary approach to teaching, however, has not changed: Each child's strengths must be analyzed and used.

The Parents

The central purpose of this chapter is to show a group of children and the problems faced by their families. After years of enduring bitter struggle, minor hopes, major disappointments, and some victories and of dealing with pressures that can lead to quarrels, disagreement, resentment, and sometimes divorce, parents are facing a comparatively improved situation, but only comparatively. These families long ago accepted the fact of their daughters' and sons' multiple impairments. But in their hearts, they hoped for a release from their children's disabilities. Now in their late 30s to early 40s, the young people themselves are for the most part only marginally independent, and all but Bill and John continue to rely on their parents and families in ways that unimpaired people do not.

It is astonishing, in light of how these children began life, that not one of them is institutionalized. All are living, most with financial support, in the community. Two are living at home, through the choice of their parents.

Although none of the families had the good fortune to be supported by a coordinated treatment approach over the period of many years when it was needed, these families illustrate—

effectively in some instances, less so in others—the practical day-to-day progress and setbacks experienced in learning to cope with a child with autism.

The parents' stories illustrate their common problems, the limited answers, and the qualified future possibilities for all of their children. Each of the families—mother, father, siblings—experienced the pain, embarrassment, and hopelessness of having a child with autism in the family. The following concerns emerge in all of the accounts:

- The shock of realizing that an infant or toddler is different from other babies.
- The search for diagnosis and the realization that there is no treatment other than education and, in some cases, medication and that there is no cure.
- The search for guidance on management of the child's behavior once the diagnosis is given.
- The necessity of locating a school appropriate for the child's needs.
- The day-to-day stress of living with puzzling, difficult, and often violent behavior.
- The social isolation caused by lack of understanding of a handicapped child. There is inability and unwillingness to entertain at home, either because of family feelings or because the handicapped child cannot tolerate strangers. Siblings are unable to invite friends home.
- The certainty that the mother is trapped. As Karen's mother said, "The buck stops here."
- The need for competent babysitters. Once found, they must be trained to care for a developmentally disabled, perplexing child.
- How to manage vacation time, even a long weekend. One family (not in this group of eight) is taking their first vacation in 22 years because their 22-year-old son is now in a group home.
- Constant pressure to guard the interests of the child. Families must cope with bureaucratic red tape to get financing, proper educational placement, and necessities such as medical insurance. They must read the fine print of all relevant state and federal regulations to figure out where they can find programs that might benefit the child. As the child gets older, parents must master the rapidly changing field of prevocational and vocational training.

- Costs of clinics, doctors, therapists, medicine, and home care. Parents must work out how they can finance these staggering costs. There is need for counseling for all the family, including siblings.
- For the over 21 developmentally disabled adult, appropriate living arrangements. The choice is between group homes and more independent situations or keeping the young adult at home.
- The social life of the child. How do parents handle the isolation of the child who usually cannot play with his or her peers and who when older is left out of normal teenage social activities?
- Dealing with a sexually maturing disabled adult.
- The ever-present worry about how to make sure that the semi-independent adult with autism is cared for appropriately when the parents can no longer do so. Guardianship? Stand-by guardianship? Proper estate planning and wills? What is the answer?

The dilemma of acceptance is acute. Most developmentally disabled children are deceptively normal in appearance and often handsome as infants and toddlers, as were all eight children in this group. The superficial normality can hinder parents' acceptance of their child as he or she truly is and affect their ability to handle pragmatic day-to-day living with autism. Everyone with a developmentally disabled child feels bitterness, disbelief, and bewilderment at first. The disabilities often are contradictory, with the autistic component being the most difficult to understand. It is normal to feel lost and not to know where to turn for a solution. Parents experience love mixed with hate, black despair, rebellion, and anger that they should be saddled with such a hopeless problem. And there is guilt—guilt over their feelings that they might be responsible for the child's condition and guilt over the common conscious wish that the problem, or the child, would disappear or die. Acceptance of the child and his or her handicap, no matter how agonizing, slow, and hesitant at first, sets a parent free to act as a fighter and advocate for the child.

The Children Grown Up

The stories presented here demonstrate that persons with autism can accommodate their behavior sufficiently so that many of them can become comparatively self-sufficient adults. Bill is completely independent. All developmentally handicapped people have talents and abilities that, when encouraged, can help them grow from emotionally distant young children to adults who work in workshops or jobs in the community. As is apparent from the stories I have presented, adults with autism can fill a variety of jobs: They work as janitors and clerks (collating and filing), do simple assembly work, and work in fast-food or other restaurants as dishwashers (Tom) and simple cooks. Polly has a responsible job in a biomedical factory. They can be aides in hospitals or nursing homes, as John is, or kitchen workers, like Karen, or gardeners in landscaping services, or baggers in grocery stores. Others work in more complicated jobs. Bill supervised repairs in an electronics company and is now a chef in a large hotel.

It is a measure of victory over their disability that many individuals with autism can earn salaries, work with coworkers, live away from home in groups, and have some social life in the community.

But although there has been improvement in services and a growing emphasis on helping people with autism live and work in the community, the ideal is not always the reality. Each of the young adults I have known has had serious difficulties along the way, even when the appropriate services were in place. Jimmy was excluded from his bus for unacceptable behavior (masturbation) and had to go by special car for four-hour stints at his workshop, instead of the usual eight; his mother had nowhere else to turn for help. In 1992, however, this changed. Jimmy has learned to appreciate what is unacceptable behavior in public and is now back in his eight-hour program and on the bus. John came close to failing his tests in fast-food services and being dropped by the Department of Vocational Rehabilitation. Thanks to his mother's fighting an entire government bureaucracy for him, he was given a second chance.

Even with the best services that can be offered generally, society must still deal with these people as individuals. Some manage well enough that they do not appear markedly different from others in their age group, even when some problems of social functioning and intimacy remain. Nevertheless, after all their schooling, these adults often read and do math on only a second- to fourth-grade level. And each one who can verbalize his or her feelings is conscious of being different. John once said that he hated his explosions, losing his control, and wondered why it happened to him. Polly describes herself matter-of-factly as mentally retarded, but she cries about it. Karen denies feeling different from other people, yet her actions betray her awareness.

None of the handicaps of the people in this book will go away. Jimmy will probably never talk, and he will have to express himself through sign language and confused attempts at words. Eric, of whom it was said that he would never talk, now talks. His speech is not fluent, but he clearly understands what is said and can respond appropriately. John is still puzzled by his outbursts of crying, his tantrums, and his intense anxiety in dealing with people but feels now that he has more control. Tom is inarticulate and shy and still needs some supervision in the work environment.

All of these people have a high anxiety level that may come partially from their perceptual disabilities, which apparently distort their picture of the environment and interfere with their ability to organize and understand their experiences. Karen's lack of depth perception and visual-motor control showed up in her clumsy attempts to use a push-button telephone. David had to be trained to find his way to his workshop and home again by taking note of landmarks.

The most difficult thing for these adults to manage is not their lack of ability to be with or to talk with other people but their difficulty in using speech for communication. Many of them find it impossible to understand the feelings of the people around them, so they often say or do inappropriate things. This can cause bewilderment and sometimes amusement or fear in other people, which sometimes leads to rejection. Like a pebble thrown into the water, creating ever-widening circles, the behavior of people with autism increases their oddness and isolation and perhaps their loneliness as well.

CONCLUSION

I offer a plea for understanding of autism. We have white canes, seeing-eye dogs, and braille for the visually handicapped; we have adjusted jobs so that they may work out in the community. Deaf people have sign language, special captions on television programs, enhanced-hearing telephones, and hearing aids. They, too, find jobs that have been adjusted to their handicap. Most of the general public are handicapped by their lack of knowledge of autism. Isn't it time we made a determined effort to educate the public so that people with autism are not ruled out of jobs on the presumption that they "won't fit" when in fact they may be quite capable? If we could better understand their thought processes and establish better communication, perhaps we would no longer find them "odd," even sometimes "crazy"? Rather, we could welcome the strength of this hitherto unused human potential to our world.

The fact that autistic and atypical disorders comprise a heterogeneous group rather than define a unitary disease makes generalizations difficult, even hazardous. Their behavior as young children, especially the problems in establishing relationships and social communication and the problems of anxiety and cognitive confusion, has justified the terms *autism* or *autistic syndrome* in providing a terminological distinction between them and other developmental disabilities and neuropsychiatric disorders. Variations in the severity of the symptoms have been documented repeatedly. Only continued efforts to understand and clarify, through basic and clinical research, are likely to yield information that defines clearly the underlying, and probably multiple, causes of this spectrum of disorders.

Meanwhile, those who live and work with children like the people represented here may find some comfort in the knowledge that appropriate services, rendered early and sustained over many years, can make a difference in the lives of children with autism and their families.

Cross-References

Outcome in autism and related disorders is discussed in Chapter 7, developmental changes in the expression of autism and related disorders are discussed in Chapters 8 to 10, working with families is addressed in Chapter 42, and vocational supports are discussed in Chapter 43.

CHAPTER 53

Autism: Where We Have Been, Where We Are Going

ISABELLE RAPIN

The mission of this final chapter of the *Handbook* is to take stock: Where did we come from, and where are we going (or should we go)? The term *autism* came from Eugene Bleuler, a psychiatrist from Zürich who coined it around 1916 to describe the negative symptoms of schizophrenia, its flat affect, and social withdrawal. It is probably no accident that in 1943 Leo Kanner, a child psychiatrist in Baltimore (Kanner, 1943), and in 1944 Hans Asperger, a pediatrician in Vienna (Asperger, 1991), independently used this term to describe children with what we now call autism (short for the autistic spectrum or, since 1980 in official parlance, pervasive developmental disorder [PDD]). Both men were Viennese and were no doubt intimately familiar with Bleuler, arguably the leading European hospital psychiatrist of the time. Although their original descriptions do not come down strongly in favor of organic causation, neither did Kanner nor Asperger vehemently espouse a psychogenic causation, although Kanner in particular had more to say about the influence of the parents of the children he evaluated. The psychogenic hypothesis, with its implied or explicit blame of parental ineptitude for the autism of their children, rapidly spread because the tenor of the time was strongly influenced by the other leading psychiatrist of the time, Sigmund Freud, until well into the 1970s. The influence of Freud on the psychogenic hypothesis for autism is paradoxical because he started his career as a neurologist and neurobiologist who studied childhood aphasia and the neuropathology of cerebral palsy, and he originally anticipated that the neurologic foundation for his psychodynamic theories would become evident.

The psychogenic hypothesis was bolstered by the observations of Rene Spitz, who, in 1945, described the dire consequences for infants' personalities of the profound social deprivation many endured in orphanages, an experience repeated in our time by many infants in Romanian and Chinese orphanages and elsewhere. The experiments of Harry Harlow in the late 1950s on infant monkeys brought up on wire mothers (Harlow & Harlow, 1962) seemed to add further legitimacy to the environmental hypothesis of maternal deprivation as causation of autism. The consequence was that mothers were psychoanalyzed rather than the children treated because it was assumed that the children were inherently normal if only they could be brought out of their shell.

Autism was considered a psychosis at the time, and well up to the 1970s many publications lumped autism with childhood schizophrenia. Evidence contrary to the maternal deprivation theory was contributed by Marion DeMyer (DeMyer et al., 1972), who pointed out that the mothers of children with autism were no more inept than other mothers; her detailed longitudinal behavioral observations did much to emphasize the reality of the social and intellectual deficits of children with autism. Although 1970 can be considered the watershed between the neurologic and psychogenic theories of autism, it took at least a decade for the demise of the psychogenic hypothesis, which remains alive in some parts of the world.

One of the lethal blows to the psychogenic theory was the publication of papers reporting markedly increased risk for *epilepsy* in autism (Deykin & MacMahon, 1979). Subsequent studies showed that the risk is greatest when autism is associated with severe mental retardation or a motor deficit, in other words, with a more abnormal brain (Olsson, Steffenburg, & Gillberg, 1988; Tuchman, Rapin, & Shinnar, 1991b). More unexpected was that the probability of epilepsy was also linked to children's type of language disorder in both autism and developmental language disorder without autism in those with verbal auditory agnosia (VAA; a severe deficit in the ability to decode phonology) at highest risk for epilepsy, whether VAA was associated with autism or not (Tuchman et al., 1991b).

ANATOMIC STUDIES

The 1970s saw the start of an exponential growth in research on the biologic basis of autism, as well as on its behavioral manifestations. The search for its anatomic basis was on. A primitive *neuroimaging* study in 1975 in 18 children with autism had drawn attention to suggestive dysgenesis of the temporal lobes (Hauser, DeLong, & Rosman, 1975). The first autopsy report on the brains of four severely retarded individuals, which dates to 1980 (Williams, Hauser, Purpura, DeLong, & Swisher, 1980), described neuronal maldevelopment in the cerebellum and cerebral cortex. The cerebellar findings were ignored until Bauman and Kemper's 1985 publication, soon followed by several others, of blind comparisons of the brains of affected individuals with those of unaffected controls (Bauman & Kemper, 1985, 1994; Kemper & Bauman, 1998). The initial Bauman and Kemper report prompted a series of MRI morphometric studies that described average differences in the size of the cerebellum (Courchesne, Yeung-Courchesne, Press, Hesselink, & Jernigan, 1988), with the majority of individuals, most of whom were retarded, tending to have smaller cerebella, and the less numerous high-functioning individuals, larger cerebella (Courchesne, Townsend, & Saitoh, 1994). A spinoff of the discovery that the cerebellum is implicated in autism renewed interest in its role in complex abilities such as focused attention, language, and cognition (Schmahmann, 1997).

The *neuropathologic studies* of Bauman and Kemper also disclosed subtle cellular changes in diencephalic and limbic structures, which was hardly surprising, but, counterintuitively, none in the neocortex. Yet a number of imaging studies documented subtle volumetric differences in cerebral as well as cerebellar structures (Abell et al., 1999; Brambilla et al., 2003; Levitt et al., 2003). It was not until 2002 that Casanova and colleagues (Casanova, Buxhoeveden, Switala, & Roy, 2002), using computerized methods, presented preliminary evidence of smallness of neocortical neurons and narrower cortical minicolumns, which suggests an impoverished neuropil, subtle changes that paralleled those described in the hippocampus, diencephalon, and cerebellar system by Bauman and Kemper. Paradoxically, the brain as a whole, at least in individuals who are not retarded, tends to be large rather than small in autism (Bailey et al., 1993) with the increased volume involving the white matter rather than the gray (Herbert et al., 2003, 2004). As yet unexplained is the observation that, in autism, the velocity of brain growth accelerates excessively in the first years of extrauterine life and decelerates thereafter (Courchesne, Carper, & Akshoomoff, 2003).

Although there are still a number of conflicting reports, the consensus from these morphologic studies is that the autism phenotype typically reflects very early alterations in brain development and is seldom the consequence of later acquired damage. A word of caution must be injected here: The number of brains studied histologically is still ridiculously small and is counted in the dozens, not the hundreds or thousands, placing severe restraints on the generality of the findings (Courchesne et al., 2003).

BEHAVIORAL STUDIES

By 1980, a consensus was reached that the three domains of behavior regularly affected in autism were sociability and empathy, language and imagination, and cognitive and behavioral flexibility (Wing & Gould, 1979). Early studies focused on classic autism, named *autistic disorder* in the *Diagnostic and Statistical Manual of Mental Disorders (DSM)* of 1980. But more and more clinical and research studies revealed that there were many less severely affected persons with deficits in some or all of these domains and that there were more than a few gifted individuals among them, so the criteria for the spectrum of autism were broadened in the 1987 *DSM-III-R*. Ute Frith's translation into English of Asperger's original 1944 paper (Asperger, 1991) introduced Asperger to the English-speaking public. By 1994, and the *DSM-IV*, the term *Asperger syndrome* was to be used for nonretarded individuals whose language had developed at the expected age, although Lorna Wing's comparison of Kanner's and Asperger's descriptions (Wing, 1991) revealed few differences between them as both had described some nonretarded children. This was the start of the conceptualization of autism as a continuum with a spectrum of severities rather than as a specific disease.

Cognition had never been considered a defining symptom of autism. Studies that focused on children with classic autism determined that some 70% had IQs below 70, the majority between 50 and 70, with about a quarter below 50 (G. Allen & Courchesne, 2001; Sandberg, Nyden, Gillberg, & Hjelmquist, 1993). With the widening of the criteria for autistic spectrum disorders, which now include Asperger disorder where by definition the IQ is above 70, it has become clear that the proportion of individuals on the spectrum with normal or near normal IQ is considerably higher than 30% and, in fact, that the spectrum includes some very bright or gifted persons. Although a normal or high IQ alone does not guarantee independent living in adulthood, it is clear that the IQ is arguably the best predictor of a favorable outcome at school age (Stevens et al., 2000). Neuropsychologic investigations show that the subtest profile of even nonretarded individuals is uneven, which is evidence for the selective dysfunction of some but not other neural networks (Minshew, Goldstein, & Siegel, 1997). Impairment of executive skills and attentional deficits suggests involvement of circuitry that implicates prefrontal cortex, limbic, striatal, brainstem, and cerebellar relays (G. Allen & Courchesne, 2001; Mundy, 2003); relative ineffectiveness

of conventional behavioral reinforcers point to dysfunction of networks that include the amygdala and dopaminergic pathways (Amaral et al., 2003; Rosenkranz & Grace, 2002; Tucker, 2001).

It became clear that studying autism in individuals without the confound of mental retardation or brain damage was more likely to shed light on its pathophysiology than focusing on the more obvious, severely impaired individuals with one of the many single gene defects, cytogenetic abnormalities, and brain malformations that account for a minority, probably no more than 10% to 15%, of individuals on the spectrum (Barton & Volkmar, 1998). What will count for explaining the phenotype is the identification of the defective circuitry, not the cause of its malfunction. Electrophysiology, functional imaging, and sophisticated behavioral methods are only now moving from investigations of high-functioning adults during the performance of particular tasks to young children who can be studied noninvasively, passively, or even asleep (Steinschneider & Dunn, 2002).

Impaired *sociability* and empathy are among the most salient, lifelong deficits in persons on the autistic spectrum, and many investigators consider them its core deficit (Fein, Pennington, Markowitz, Braverman, & Waterhouse, 1986; Wing & Gould, 1979). Factors that may contribute, such as defective facial scanning and recognition (Pierce, Muller, Ambrose, Allen, & Courchesne, 2001), insensitivity to the nuances of prosody (McCann & Peppe, 2003), and impaired joint attention, have attracted a great deal of research scrutiny (Mundy & Crowson, 1997). The hypothesis that inability to read others' minds has become a dominant theme of some behavioral research in autism (Stone, Baron-Cohen, & Knight, 1998) and has been linked to putative frontal lobe dysfunction. Oxytocin deficiency has been implicated in the pathophysiology of impaired sociability in autism (Insel, O'Brien, & Leckman, 1999).

A number of researchers have investigated the *language* deficits of autism. Psychologists and language specialists described in detail the characteristics of verbal children on the autistic spectrum (Baltaxe & Simmons, 1975; Bartak, Rutter, & Cox, 1975; Tager-Flusberg, 2003). Their consensus was that once the children started to speak they usually spoke fluently, with adequate phonology and syntax, but with inadequate conversational skills, stilted prosody, odd word choices, and difficulty answering questions. The optic of clinical investigators who had the opportunity to study the language of all comers differed as they observed that preschool children on the autistic spectrum suffered from several distinct types of language disorders, which, except for universally defective pragmatics, paralleled those of preschoolers with developmental language disorders (D. A. Allen & Rapin, 1992; Tuchman, Rapin, & Shinnar, 1991a). In addition to the fluent verbal children, with their distorted semantics and severe comprehension problems at the level of discourse, there were children with inadequate phonology and syntax, the most severely affected among them having great difficulty or being unable to comprehend language through the auditory channel, which severely jeopardized or precluded their ability to develop speech (Rapin & Dunn, 2003). These investigators considered it unlikely that mental retardation or the severity of the autistic disorder provided an adequate explanation for lack of speech in all the individuals who remained essentially nonverbal into adulthood and proposed profound inability to process language through the auditory channel as an alternate explanation. Genetics has recently supported the concept of more than one language disorder in autism because only individuals with phonologic deficits in themselves and their immediate family members show linkage to chromosome 7q31-33, a locus which contains a gene identified in a nonautistic family with a severe dominantly inherited language disorder that involves phonology (Lai et al., 2000; Wassink et al., 2001).

Deficient imaginative *play* was found to be a useful marker for autism in preschoolers (Jarrold, Boucher, & Smith, 1993; Wainwright & Fein, 1996) and is an early surrogate for the persistent lack of imagination in autism. Lack of pretend play presents so early and is so ubiquitous that it is included in a brief screening questionnaire for detecting autistic tendencies as early as age 18 months (Baird et al., 2000).

Rigidity and especially *stereotypies and perseveration* figure prominently among the symptoms parents and educators view as troublesome, yet they have received less research attention than other behavioral symptoms. In both preschoolers and school-age children, neurologists found that stereotypies, although not limited to those with autism, were considerably more frequent than in controls in both those with and without mental retardation, albeit mental retardation increased its prevalence in both children with autism and nonautistic controls (Mandelbaum et al., in preparation; Rapin, 1996). Stereotypies may be but one of the subtle motor deficits of many children on the autistic spectrum and may implicate fronto-striatal networks, whereas behavioral rigidity might reflect defective executive skills dependent on the integrity of lateral prefrontal circuitry. The sensorimotor deficits of children on the spectrum such as low muscle tone/increased joint laxity, toe walking, motor apraxia, hyper-and hyporeactivity to sensory stimuli in every sensory modality, not to mention distressing self-injury—all too well known to clinicians and therapists and troublesome to the affected individuals and their families—have hardly been investigated to date.

Inability to focus *attention* on a target introduced by someone else is very prominent and has already been mentioned as detectable in infancy. But more generalized attention deficits are so prominent in some nonretarded children (Smalley et al., 2002) as to suggest an erroneous diagnosis of attention deficit disorder with or without hyperactivity rather than autism with attention deficit. Disorders of *sleep*, especially frequent nocturnal awakenings, are a major source of difficulty for some families, yet sleep studies in autism are just starting to appear (Elia et al., 2000).

CLASSIFICATION ISSUES: AUTISM AS A SPECTRUM WITH FUZZY BORDERS AND OVERLAPS

Autism, like dementia, schizophrenia, dyslexia, mental retardation, and most disorders of complex human abilities, is defined behaviorally, not biologically. Diagnosis of most of these and many other behaviorally defined disorders of the brain is based on dimensional, not categorical, criteria (Kraemer, 1992). This does not make them any less organic than height, weight, blood pressure, and blood calcium, which are also defined dimensionally; at the extremes of their distributions, there is 100% consensus about dwarfism, obesity, arterial hypertension, or tetany as pathologic, even though none of them has a crisp margin that separates it from normality. Like dimensionally defined phenotypes arising from brain disorders, dimensionally defined medical conditions have a number of etiologies, which include several single gene defects and, more often, the interaction of several complex, largely undefined metabolic predispositions strongly influenced by environmental effects.

Autism is dimensionally defined and has an extremely broad range of severity. The change of focus from classic autistic disorder to less severely affected individuals has brought with it the realization that there is no sharp cut between mild autism and the borders of normalcy. Baron-Cohen (Baron-Cohen & Hammer, 1997) asks whether autism is the extreme of the neuropsychologic profile of maleness and whether autism without mental retardation/Asperger syndrome is necessarily a disability (Baron-Cohen, 2000). Where do we make the cut between the rigidity and stereotypies of autism and those of obsessive-compulsive disorder, especially in those families with members who manifest one or another of these disorders (Bradshaw & Sheppard, 2000) and especially in view of the likelihood that they share some cortico-subcortical anatomic substrates (Tucker, 2001)? Genetic studies in families with individuals with distinct but overlapping disorders indicate that most of these disorders, including autism, are polygenic and that the variety of phenotypes within families reflects the diversity of inherited traits.

It is largely to this broadening of the autism phenotype that the recently perceived so-called "autism epidemic" can be ascribed and almost certainly not to environmental toxins, vaccines, and other nongenetic influences (Fombonne, 2003). This is not to say that the environment has no influence on brain development: It is abundantly clear that the genetic programs that determine maturation of the developing brain and its phenotypic expression are strongly influenced by outside factors such as education and practice, as well as by accidental nefarious insults (Blake, Byl, & Merzenich, 2002; Temple et al., 2003).

Broadening of the autistic spectrum and the use of multiple labels by professionals from different fields have created a great deal of confusion in the public. Because of its genuinely fuzzy margins, it is easy to apply to children the label that will fulfill their parents' educational wishes. The autistic label has thus morphed from a feared diagnosis to be choked down and hidden at all costs to the magic key that opens the coffers of the educational or medical establishment. Autism has become a more acceptable diagnosis than mental retardation, although with less cachet than Asperger syndrome. This perception is not entirely unjustified as it seems that early intensive intervention, which is undoubtedly effective in autism (National Research Council, 2001), may be less effective in mental retardation, although this has not been rigorously demonstrated in IQ-matched children.

PARENT ADVOCACY

An escalating phenomenon of the past decade is the discovery of the power of parent advocacy on both government and scientists. Parents who perceived the lack of knowledge and effective interventions for autism banded together to put pressure on the government to increase research funding by earmarking National Institutes of Health (NIH) dollars for the investigation of their children's particular disorders. There are now a large number of parent groups lobbying for many of the rare neurologic (and other) diseases of children and adults. The Autism Society of America (www.autism-society.org) is the largest public organization concerned with autism; two more recent grassroots organizations created by parents, the Cure Autism Now Foundation (CAN; www.canfoundation.org) and the National Alliance for Autism Research (NAAR; www.naar.org), have been particularly effective. These two foundations have not limited their efforts to lobbying; they have gone national and between them have succeeded in raising sufficient monies to fund several dozen modest but innovative research projects per year. These projects have had a strong influence on the direction taken by the field of autism research and, indirectly, on the NIH. CAN and NAAR have also encouraged families to enroll in genetic studies and have publicized the tremendous need for tissue donation to advance understanding of the biologic basis of autism. Like other foundations devoted to particular diseases, they have recruited prominent investigators to their boards, and they organize a yearly high-caliber meeting that provides the opportunity for investigators to present their research and, equally beneficial, for parents to meet one another and listen and speak to the investigators they support and to other professionals in the field.

One result of the legislative push on the NIH has been the creation of a countrywide network of NIH-funded centers of excellence in autism research, which has brought together clinicians and researchers from many disciplines to pursue interinstitutional collaborative research. Autism has gained enormously in visibility so that it is now commonplace to have pieces in prestigious journals and newspapers that bring the public and researchers up-to-date with the latest in autism research. Autism is following in the footsteps of what happened some 30 years ago to dementia of the aging and Alzheimer's disease. Pressure by families brought both dementia and autism out of the closet with, as a result, dramatic enhancement of public awareness, better diagnostic criteria, and more than tenfold increase in monies being spent on research and intervention.

The press, TV, and the Internet now play an extremely important role in educating the public. Parents often diagnose autism in their children earlier and more accurately than many professionals; mildly affected adolescents and adults not infrequently diagnose themselves. The downside of this flood of information is that there is a great deal of misinformation among the valuable and now widely available reliable data. Well-meaning but uncritical or frankly opportunistic individuals have an accessible podium from which to tout all manner of tests and interventions of unproven—or even disproven—efficacy that waste public and private resources and raise unrealistic hopes.

PROGRESS IN GENETICS

Studies in multiplex families and genome-wide searches for candidate genes, together with increasing awareness that many rare single gene defects, cytogenetic abnormalities, brain malformations, and acquired brain pathologies may have autism as one of their manifestations, have revolutionized thinking about the causation of autism (Muhle, Trentacoste, & Rapin, 2004). It is now well established that complex polygenic influences are the major causes of autism and many other developmental disorders. It has also become clear that genetically driven brain development is to a greater degree than previously imagined influenced in its details throughout childhood and even later by chance environmental influences. As progress is made in identifying abnormal gene products, it will become possible to begin to understand how these molecules subvert the sequential unfolding of normal brain development. Whether biological methods can be developed to bypass errors in embryonic brain maturation remains to be seen. No one would argue against the desirability of being able to prevent the birth of severely affected retarded children with autism. It is quite another matter—and will no doubt raise thorny ethical and philosophical debate if it comes to pass—to prevent less severe aberrations such as those responsible for some of the clearly affected yet gifted individuals with Asperger-like phenotypes, some of whom contribute uniquely and desirably to human diversity.

What is not widely understood is that it is not the specific cause, be it genetic or acquired, of the altered brain structure and function that determines the autism phenotype. It is what aberrant brain networks and what aberrant neurotransmitters within these networks that determine individual symptoms. Progress in neuroscience, especially in imaging and electrophysiology, is starting to supplement and channel the torrent of genetic and biochemical information. It not only has become possible to image the brain with ever finer resolution and to measure in real time alterations in the timing and distribution of electrophysiologic activity, but also advances are already providing the capability of imaging some specific molecules of interest in the living functioning brain. Functional imaging can be yoked with recordings of eye movements; of reaction times marking decisions whether to react to and discriminate specific sensory, language, or emotional stimuli; and even of thoughts during tasks that do not require any overt response. The future is bright, but the complexities of all these new research developments are daunting, and much more water will flow under the bridge before they find an application in the clinic.

INTERVENTION

Education as intervention for children with autism started slowly in the 1970s as the psychogenic theory of its causation withered and early, intensive education of the child supplanted psychiatric treatment of the parents, spearheaded by a number of investigators who described favorable outcomes. Lovaas, undoubtedly the most influential, published his approach in a book in 1981 (Lovaas, 1981) and reported in a 1987 paper (Lovaas, 1987) that systematic and intensive application of operant conditioning methods achieved impressive and sustained progress in language and behavior in close to 50% of a small sample of children. His applied behavioral analysis (ABA) approach is arguably the one most widely applied today, especially with toddlers and preschoolers, with many variations in the details and intensity of its implementation (Schreibman, 1997). It is clear that it is the less severely affected children who benefit the most and that the method fails with those with substantial mental retardation. Interventions have been developed that are less burdensome, expensive, and, frankly, unrealistic for the majority than the 40 hours per week one adult to one child advocated by Lovaas. Eric Schopler (Schopler & Olley, 1982) and D. A. Allen (D. A. Allen & Mendelson, 2000) have focused on supporting the parents and entire family and teaching them techniques to deal more effectively with troublesome behaviors and to foster learning in a more naturalistic manner. Greenspan has emphasized the need to enter into activities generated by the children to entice them out of their preference for solitary pursuits (Greenspan et al., 1997). Under the aegis of the Education Act of All Handicapped Children (Public Law 94-142) and the Individual with Disabilities Education Act of 1986, states established early intervention programs, which mandate education and other therapies for any infant or toddler suspected or diagnosed with an autistic spectrum disorder. New York State published guidelines in 1999 (New York State Department of Health: Early Intervention Program, 1999) that make available to children 0 to 3 years more intensive

intervention for autism than for any other developmental disorder is an indicator of the public's perception that autism is the one most likely to benefit. This is a far cry from previous views that autism was hopeless, but we need to keep in mind that this optimism is in part a function of practice parameters that have resulted in earlier diagnosis of many less severely affected children (American Academy of Child and Adolescent Psychiatry, 1998; American Academy of Pediatrics: Committee on Children with Disabilities, 2001; Filipek et al., 2000). Innumerable preschools of varying quality have sprung up, and public schools have had to struggle to develop special classes for the more severely affected children and to integrate others into regular classrooms, often with a paraprofessional aide to help one or several of them cope, and with varying amounts of extra help provided by specially trained teachers, psychologists, and speech pathologists (National Research Council, 2001). What is still less well developed are adequate programs to help teenagers and young adults transition into the world of work and function outside the support of their families. Group homes have largely replaced warehousing of the most seriously handicapped in large institutions for the retarded or psychiatric hospitals.

Psychopharmacologic intervention for autism has followed in the footsteps of progress in drug development for adults with psychiatric illnesses, which is largely based on research on neurotransmitters and their receptors. The first large double-blind study of an atypical neuroleptic was the 2002 risperidone study carried out in 101 children over an 8-week period (McCracken et al., 2002). Lack of guidelines for children and very imperfect understanding of the neurochemical basis of the many troublesome manifestations of autism such as unprovoked aggression, self-injury, sleep disorders, and agitation means that most of the drugs used in the clinic, be they serotonin uptake inhibitors, stimulants, anticonvulsants, or a host of other neuropharmacologic agents, are being prescribed in a trial-and-error fashion, often without full awareness of their potential harmful side effects. Clearly, this is an area of great need for research.

The public has not yet digested the hard reality that there is no cure for autism, be it with medication or education. What the much more effective interventions available today can do is mitigate some of autism's symptoms. Mildly affected children can be taught social and communication skills that will allow them to meet the challenges of society, skills that the average child with adequate parents and teachers will pick up without explicit and intensive training (Dunn, 2004). This statement does not gainsay the remarkable progress in understanding and intervention of the past century but is meant to point out how much is not known and that breakthroughs are few and far between and cannot be counted on.

WHERE WE NEED TO GO

So much remains to be done, but I limit discussion in this section to a few very specific issues that have been particular thorns in my flesh, although they may not be the most crucial in the long run. Of course, we need progress in genetics, in psychopharmacology, in understanding neurologic pathophysiology, in more effective treatments, and in other fronts. No doubt other clinicians would chose other priorities. Here are some I see as urgent:

1. *Enhanced public education about autism:* Autism has made it into the media. The movie *Rain Man* (1988)*;* Mark Haddon's recent amusing but informative novel/murder mystery, *The Curious Incident of the Dog in the Night-Time* (2003), which made it onto the best seller list; the autobiographical book by Temple Grandin, a gifted professional on the autistic spectrum, *Thinking in Pictures and Other Reports from My Life with Autism* (1995); Clara C. Park's two books about her artist/mail sorter daughter Jessy (2001a, 2001b); and a host of other first-person and family accounts have raised the public's awareness of autism. There are now a number of web sites concerned with autism on the Internet. Professionals have been educated by a growing torrent of scientific books, papers, and research meetings concerned with autism. So why do I cite public education as my first priority?

There is still a tremendous amount of misinformation, both in the public and even among professionals unfamiliar with up-to-date views of autism. As a consequence, many

unnecessary, uninformative, and expensive tests are being performed; parents spend fortunes on unproven and largely ineffective treatments; and the psychogenic theory of autism has not been buried once and for all. Besides well-meaning professionals genuinely bent on helping families, there are predators who take the opportunity to make a buck on the backs of desperate and naive parents. The word needs to get out more effectively about appropriate and timely investigations and interventions.

Physicians and other professionals, including educators, need to be better informed about early symptoms so that parents are not falsely reassured and those who are convinced something is amiss do not get the runaround and waste time and resources. Information about the relatively low but significant recurrence risk within sibships has to become more widely disseminated so young parents can make informed decisions about the size of their family.

The news that there are intelligent and successful persons with autism needs to be more widely publicized. The diagnosis of an autistic spectrum disorder is no longer the kiss of death, but there also has to be awareness that a great deal of ongoing work, on social skills especially, will have to be carried out to help the majority of persons on the spectrum reach their potential and lead more comfortable lives. A large proportion, but not all, will require help lifelong, and the quality of life of all affected persons will improve with better coping skills.

2. *Understanding of autistic/language regression and disintegrative disorder:* At present, we have no satisfactory explanation, but a lot of speculation, about what is responsible for the regression of language and sociability that some third of parents report. Its very existence was doubted at first, even though it was reported by Japanese (Kurita, 1985) and American (Tuchman et al., 1991a) investigators. The advent of home videos has documented that it is all too real (Osterling, Dawson, & Munson, 2002). Subclinical epilepsy has come under suspicion by analogy with acquired epileptic aphasia, in which language regression without autism is associated with either clinical seizures or an epileptiform EEG, although definitive evidence remains elusive (Tuchman & Rapin, 1997). Some parents report that language

regression was ushered in by a nondescript ill-ness, a change in the family, or other emotional stress (Kurita, 1985; Shinnar et al., 2001). Such reports bring up the possibility of some geneti-cally inherited immune factor making predis-posed children vulnerable to some usually trivial infectious or toxic insult (Korvatska, Van de Water, Anders, & Gershwin, 2002), to routine immunizations (Halsey & Hyman, 2001), or to a genetic difference in level of a neurotransmitter or modulator or their recep-tors enhancing carrier children's vulnerability to stresses other children withstand without long-lasting effects (Kurita, Kita, & Miyake, 1992). The course of the regression-decline—plateau, then improvement but rarely full recov-ery—clearly differs from that of a degenerative disease of the brain. There is lack of pathologic evidence and because the regression, which is usually insidious and likely to be overlooked at first, is only exceptionally investigated soon after its inception, very little electro-physiologic or other data are available to clarify its cause(s). There is also lack of con-sensus on its influence on long-term prognosis (Davidovitch, Glick, Holtzman, Tirosh, & Safir, 2000; Kobayashi & Murata, 1998).

Another vexing question is the relationship between language/autistic regression and the fortunately much rarer disintegrative disorder (Catalano, 1998; Hendry, 2000). Is the latter a distinct disorder or but a later and more pro-found and irreversible regression? Is the re-gression of girls with Rett syndrome a model for either autistic regression or disintegrative disorder (Zoghbi, 2003)?

Most frustrating for clinicians is lack of di-rectives on how to treat children with a history of regression or in whom subclinical epilepti-form activity in the EEG is discovered. Guided by physicians' and parents' beliefs about the pathophysiology of the regression, treatments as disparate as infusion of immunoglobulin G, antiepileptic drugs, and even subpial transsec-tion for those with regression in the context of intractable epilepsy are widely offered, with-out the guidance of systematic scientifically conducted trials.

3. *Much more systematic investigation of in-terventions provided to children with autism:* Few medical or other treatments provided to children with autism, paid for either by the

public or the parents, have undergone rigorous evaluation of their effectiveness. Some recent exceptions are assisted communication, se-cretin, and most recently, risperidone. But what about the vitamins, diets, antifungal agents, and the myriad pharmacologic medications and other so-called natural supplements children with autism are made to swallow (Levy, Mandell, Merhar, Ittenbach, & Pinto-Martin, 2003)? Despite a dearth of systematic studies of speech and language, social, and educational interventions, these interventions do address core deficits of autism (National Research Council, 2001). But how many of the children with and without motor impairment require physical and occupational therapies routinely offered to many of them? Even in the realm of education, there is lack of systematic data on the specificity of conditioning approaches ver-sus others and on the appropriateness of each one for the vastly different needs of children on the spectrum. How and how intensively a tod-dler or preschooler is treated varies a great deal depending on the state in which the family happens to live and on the beliefs of the profes-sionals who evaluate the child. It is not surpris-ing that indigent socially deprived children are likely to receive less intensive and lower qual-ity interventions than the children of better educated and more affluent parents. This state of affairs, added to all the other unknowns in the field, is unacceptable from many stand-points and needs to be addressed promptly and vigorously.

4. *Better services for older children and adults:* A lot of progress in education for chil-dren on the autistic spectrum has taken place over the past 2 decades. There are now in place in every state various levels of services for infants and preschoolers. Grade schools have been charged with providing educational ser-vices for all children with handicaps, including those with autism. High schools have set up vo-cational programs to assist students in finding a type of work they are capable of performing and, it is hoped, one that provides them with enough gratification so they will stick with it. Group homes exist instead of warehouses for older adolescents and adults whose families can no longer care for them. The federal government provides Supplementary Social Se-curity Income for those unable to support

themselves so that none will be entirely destitute. What is still missing?

More important than their level of intelligence, it is the adequacy of their social skills that enables persons with autism to get along in the world. Unless social skills appropriate to each age are taught and practiced systematically, children will be bullied in school, which may understandably lead to anger with often explosive retaliation and, under the worse scenario, expulsion from the school and placement into often inappropriately harsh psychiatric or legal custody and, almost certainly, to the administration of neuroleptic drugs of limited utility with the potential for undesirable side effects.

Adults will not last long, even in protected employment, unless they understand the rules: comply with supervisors' directives, be at work every day and arrive on time, be adequately groomed, do not explode if criticized or if teased, know whom and when to ask for help when it is needed, and have a buddy who can act as an ombudsman.

The need for sexual education is rarely met adequately, nor is it clear whose responsibility it is to provide this service. Many schools and social workers have difficulty presenting it in a manner that is intelligible and meaningful to adolescents with autism, including specific guidance on how to behave with the opposite sex and how to satisfy sexual urges in private. Pediatricians may overlook the need of girls for long-lasting contraceptive protection as soon as they approach puberty and the need to give both girls and boys clear directives on acceptable and unacceptable behaviors. It is important to educate parents because many do not even consider the possibility of rape or arrest for sexual misconduct.

It is a lot to ask of schools and the inadequate number of social agencies in the community to provide so many complex services, many of which fall far outside the primary mission of education to provide academic skills and, in special education settings, some degree of vocational training and counseling. Awareness of the importance of social skills training in grade school and of effective programs to implement it is new (Dunn, 2004). Like other offerings to persons with autism mentioned earlier, the utility of which is questionable, the effectiveness of social skills training programs will need to be investigated rigorously lest they, too, consume resources that might be better spent on other priorities.

CONCLUSION

This third edition of the *Handbook of Autism and Allied Disorders* showcases the great strides made over the past 20 years in understanding autism's clinical manifestations, its genetics, its brain basis, and its management. This progress, which is a reason for optimism, has been accomplished by the heightened interest, concern, and hard work of scientists and other professionals, but merit goes to the parents who lobbied for their children and set the field in motion. If what has happened with dementia and Alzheimer's disease is any example, as information continues to mushroom it will reveal unexpected complexities, not simple solutions, but also this information will open the perspective for novel and more effective interventions. The autistic spectrum is not a single disease, so it would be naive to anticipate fix-it interventions appropriate for all affected persons. It is hoped that a better educated public and professionals will be prepared for the complexities to come and for the illuminating findings and new ideas dependent on dazzling technological advances and rigorous research on all aspects of autism and its management.

Cross-References

Issues of diagnosis are discussed in Section I and Chapter 22. Genetic issues, neurological processes, and associated medical conditions are addressed in Chapters 16, 18, and 20, respectively. Interventions are described in Section V (Chapters 33 through 43).

REFERENCES

Abell, F., Krams, M., Ashburner, J., Passingham, R., Friston, K., Frackowiak, R., et al. (1999). The neuroanatomy of autism: A voxel-based whole brain analysis of structural scans. *Neuroreport, 10,* 1647–1651.

Allen, D. A., & Mendelson, L. (2000). Parent, child, and professional: Meeting the needs of young autistic children and their families in a multidisciplinary therapeutic nursery model. In S. Epstein (Ed.), *Autistic spectrum disorders and psychoanalytic ideas: Reassessing the fit* (pp. 704–731). Hillsdale, NJ: Analytic Press.

Allen, D. A., & Rapin, I. (1992). Autistic children are also dysphasic. In H. Naruse & E. Ornitz (Eds.), *Neurobiology of infantile autism* (pp. 73–80). Amsterdam: Excerpta Medica.

Allen, G., & Courchesne, E. (2001). Attention function and dysfunction in autism. *Frontiers in Bioscience, 6,* D105–D119.

Amaral, D. G., Bauman, M. D., Capitanio, J. P., Lavenex, P., Mason, W. A., Mauldin-Jourdain, M. L., et al. (2003). The amygdala: Is it an essential component of the neural network for social cognition? *Neuropsychologia, 41,* 517–522.

American Academy of Child and Adolescent Psychiatry. (1998). Practice parameters for the assessment and treatment of children and adolescents with language and learning disorders. *Journal of the American Academy of Child and Adolescent Psychiatry, 37,* 46S–62S.

American Academy of Pediatrics: Committee on Children with Disabilities. (2001). The pediatrician's role in the diagnosis and management of autistic spectrum disorder in children. *Pediatrics, 107,* 1221–1226.

Asperger, H. (1991). Autistic psychopathy in childhood. In U. Frith (Ed. & Trans.), *Autism and Asperger syndrome* (pp. 37–92). Cambridge, England: Cambridge University Press. (Original work published 1944)

Bailey, A., Luthert, P., Bolton, P., Le Couteur, A., Rutter, M. L., & Harding, B. (1993). Autism and megalencephaly. *Lancet, 341,* 1225–1226.

Baird, G., Charman, T., Baron-Cohen, S., Cox, A., Swettenham, J., Wheelwright, S., et al. (2000). A screening instrument for autism at 18 months of age: A 6-year follow-up study. *Journal of the American Academy of Child and Adolescent Psychiatry, 39,* 694–702.

Baltaxe, C., & Simmons, J. Q. (1975). Language in childhood psychosis: A review. *Journal of Speech and Hearing Disorders, 40,* 439–458.

Baron-Cohen, S. (2000). Is Asperger syndrome/high-functioning autism necessarily a disability? *Developmental Psychopathology, 12,* 489–500.

Baron-Cohen, S., & Hammer, J. (1997). Is autism an extreme form of the male brain? *Advances in Infancy Research, 11,* 193–217.

Bartak, L., Rutter, M. L., & Cox, A. (1975). A comparative study of infantile autism and specific developmental receptive language disorder: I. The children. *British Journal of Psychiatry, 126,* 127–145.

Barton, M., & Volkmar, F. R. (1998). How commonly are known medical conditions associated with autism? *Journal of Autism and Developmental Disorders, 28,* 273–278.

Bauman, M. L., & Kemper, T. L. (1985). Histoanatomic observations of the brain in early infantile autism. *Neurology, 35,* 866–874.

Bauman, M. L., & Kemper, T. L. (1994). Neuroanatomic observations of the brain in autism. In M. L. Bauman & T. L. Kemper (Eds.), *The neurobiology of autism* (pp. 119–145). Baltimore: Johns Hopkins University Press.

Blake, D. T., Byl, N. N., & Merzenich, M. M. (2002). Representation of the hand in the cerebral cortex. *Behavioural Brain Research, 135,* 179–184.

Bradshaw, J. L., & Sheppard, D. M. (2000). The neurodevelopmental frontostriatal disorders: Evolutionary adaptiveness and anomalous lateralization. *Brain and Language, 73,* 297–320.

Brambilla, P., Hardan, A., di Nemi, S. U., Perez, J., Soares, J. C., & Barale, F. (2003). Brain anatomy and development in autism: Review of structural MRI studies. *Brain Research Bulletin, 61,* 557–569.

Casanova, M. F., Buxhoeveden, D. P., Switala, A. E., & Roy, E. (2002). Minicolumnar pathology in autism. *Neurology, 58,* 428–432.

Catalano, R. A. (1998). *When autism strikes: Families cope with childhood disintegrative disorder.* New York: Plenum Press.

Courchesne, E., Carper, R., & Akshoomoff, N. (2003). Evidence of brain overgrowth in the first year of life in autism. *Journal of the American Medical Association, 290,* 337–344.

Courchesne, E., Townsend, J., & Saitoh, O. (1994). The brain in infantile autism: Posterior fossa structures are abnormal. *Neurology, 44,* 214–223.

Courchesne, E., Yeung-Courchesne, R., Press, G. A., Hesselink, J. R., & Jernigan, T. L. (1988). Hypoplasia of cerebellar vermal lobules VI and VII in autism. *New England Journal of Medicine, 318,* 1349–1354.

Davidovitch, M., Glick, L., Holtzman, G., Tirosh, E., & Safir, M. P. (2000). Developmental regression in autism: Maternal perception. *Journal of Autism and Developmental Disorders, 30,* 113–119.

DeMyer, M. K., Pontius, W., Norton, J. A., Barton, S., Allen, J., & Steele, R. (1972). Parental practices and innate activity in normal, autistic, and brain-damaged infants. *Journal of Autism and Childhood Schizophrenia, 2,* 49–66.

Deykin, E. Y., & MacMahon, B. (1979). The incidence of seizures among children with autistic symptoms. *American Journal of Psychiatry, 136,* 1310–1312.

Dunn, M. (2004). *S.O.S: Social Skills in our Schools* (A social skills program for children with Pervasive Developmental Disorders and their typical peers). Shawnee Mission, KS: Autism Asperger.

Elia, M., Ferri, R., Musumeci, S. A., Del Gracco, S., Bottitta, M., Scuderi, C., et al. (2000). Sleep in subjects with autistic disorder: A neurophysiological and psychological study. *Brain and Development, 22,* 88–92.

Fein, D., Pennington, B. F., Markowitz, P., Braverman, M., & Waterhouse, L. (1986). Toward a neuropsychological model of infantile autism: Are the social deficits primary? *Journal of the American Academy of Child Psychiatry, 25,* 198–212.

Filipek, P. A., Accardo, P. J., Ashwal, S., Baranek, G. T., Cook, E. H., Jr., Dawson, G., et al. (2000). Practice parameter: Screening and diagnosis of autism: Report of the Quality Standards Subcommittee of the American Academy of Neurology and the Child Neurology Society. *Neurology, 55,* 468–479.

Fombonne, E. (2003). Epidemiological surveys of autism and other pervasive developmental disorders: An update. *Journal of Autism and Developmental Disorders, 33,* 365–382.

Grandin, T. (1995). *Thinking in pictures and other reports from my life with autism.* New York: Doubleday.

Greenspan, S. I., Kalmanson, B., Shahmoon-Shanok, R., Wieder, S., Gordon-Williamson, G., & Anzalone, M. (1997). *Assessing and treating infants and young children with severe difficulties in relating and communicating.* Washington, DC: National Training Institute of Zero to Three.

Haddon, M. (2003). *The curious incident of the dog in the night-time.* New York: Doubleday.

Halsey, N. A., & Hyman, S. L. (2001). Measles-mumps-rubella vaccine and autistic spectrum disorder (Report from the New Challenges in Childhood Immunizations Conference convened in Oak Brook, IL, June 12–13, 2000). *Pediatrics, 107,* e84–e1226.

Harlow, H. F., & Harlow, M. (1962). Social deprivation in monkeys. *Scientific American, 207,* 136–146.

Hauser, S. L., DeLong, G. R., & Rosman, N. P. (1975). Pneumographic finding in the infantile autism syndrome: A correlation with temporal lobe disease. *Brain, 98,* 667–688.

Hendry, C. N. (2000). Childhood disintegrative disorder: Should it be considered a distinct diagnosis? *Clinical Psychology Reviews, 20,* 77–90.

Herbert, M. R., Ziegler, D. A., Deutsch, C. K., O'Brien, L. M., Lange, N., Bakardjiev, A., et al. (2003). Dissociations of cerebral cortex, subcortical and cerebral white matter volumes in autistic boys. *Brain, 126,* 1182–1192.

Herbert, M. R., Ziegler, D. A., Makris, N., Filipek, P. A., Kemper, T. L., Normandin, J. J., et al. (2004). Localization of white matter volume increase in autism and developmental language disorder. *Annals of Neurology, 55,* 530–540.

Insel, T. R., O'Brien, D. J., & Leckman, J. F. (1999). Oxytocin, vasopressin, and autism: Is there a connection? *Biological Psychiatry, 45,* 145–157.

Jarrold, C., Boucher, J., & Smith, P. (1993). Symbolic play in autism: A review. *Journal of Autism and Developmental Disorders, 23,* 281–307.

Kanner, L. (1943). Autistic disturbances of affective contact. *Nervous Child, 2,* 217–250.

Kemper, T. L., & Bauman, M. (1998). Neuropathology of infantile autism. *Journal of Neuropathology and Experimental Neurology, 57,* 645–652.

Kobayashi, R., & Murata, T. (1998). Setback phenomenon in autism and long-term prognosis. *Acta Psychiatrica Scandinavica, 98,* 296–303.

Korvatska, E., Van de Water, J., Anders, T. F., & Gershwin, M. E. (2002). Genetic and immunologic considerations in autism. *Neurobiology of Disease, 9,* 107–125.

Kraemer, H. C. (1992). Measurement of reliability for categorical data in medical research. *Statistical Methods in Medical Research, 1,* 183–199.

Kurita, H. (1985). Infantile autism with speech loss before the age of thirty months. *Journal of the American Academy of Child and Adolescent Psychiatry, 24,* 191–196.

Kurita, H., Kita, M., & Miyake, Y. (1992). A comparative study of development and symptoms among disintegrative psychosis and infantile autism with and without speech loss. *Journal of Autism and Developmental Disorders, 22,* 175–188.

Lai, C. S., Fisher, S. E., Hurst, J. A., Levy, E. R., Hodgson, S., Fox, M., et al. (2000). The SPCH1 region on human 7q31: Genomic characterization of the critical interval and localization of translocations associated with speech and language disorder. *American Journal of Human Genetics, 67,* 357–368.

Levitt, J. G., Blanton, R. E., Smalley, S., Thompson, P. M., Guthrie, D., McCracken, J. T., et al. (2003). Cortical sulcal maps in autism. *Cerebral Cortex, 13,* 728–735.

Levy, S. E., Mandell, D. S., Merhar, S., Ittenbach, R. F., & Pinto-Martin, J. A. (2003). Use of complementary and alternative medicine among children recently diagnosed with autistic spectrum disorder. *Journal of Developmental and Behavioral Pediatrics, 24,* 418–423.

Lovaas, O. I. (1981). *Teaching developmentally disabled children: The "me" book.* Austin, TX: ProEd.

Lovaas, O. I. (1987). Behavioral treatment and normal educational and intellectual functioning in young autistic children. *Journal of Consulting and Clinical Psychology, 55,* 3–9.

Mandelbaum, D. E., Stevens, M., Rosenberg, E., Wiznitzer, M., Steinschneider, M., Filipek, P., et al. (submitted for publication, 2004). Comparison of sensorimotor performance in school-age children with autism, developmental language disorder or low IQ.

McCann, J., & Peppe, S. (2003). Prosody in autism spectrum disorders: A critical review. *International Journal of Language and Communication Disorders, 38,* 325–350.

McCracken, J. T., McGough, J., Shah, B., Cronin, P., Hong, D., Aman, M. G., et al. (2002). Risperidone in children with autism and serious behavioral problems. *New England Journal of Medicine, 347,* 314–321.

Minshew, N. J., Goldstein, G., & Siegel, D. J. (1997). Neuropsychologic functioning in autism: Profile of a complex information processing disorder. *Journal of the International Neuropsychological Society, 3,* 303–316.

Muhle, R., Trentacoste, S. V., & Rapin, I. (2004). The genetics of autism. *Pediatrics, 113:e472-e486.*

Mundy, P. (2003). Annotation: The neural basis of social impairments in autism: The role of the dorsal medial-frontal cortex and anterior cingulate system. *Journal of Child Psychology and Psychiatry and Allied Disciplines, 44,* 793–809.

Mundy, P., & Crowson, M. (1997). Joint attention and early social communication: Implications for research on intervention with autism. *Journal of Autism and Developmental Disorders, 27,* 653–676.

National Research Council. (2001). *Educating children with autism* (Committee on Educational Interventions for Children with Autism, Division of Behavioral and Social Sciences and Education). Washington, DC: National Academy Press.

New York State Department of Health: Early Intervention Program. (1999). *Clinical practice guideline for autism/pervasive developmental disorders: Assessment and intervention for young children (age 0–3 years).* Albany: New York Department of Health.

Olsson, I., Steffenburg, S., & Gillberg, C. (1988). Epilepsy in autism and autisticlike conditions: A population-based study. *Archives of Neurology, 45,* 666–668.

Osterling, J. A., Dawson, G., & Munson, J. A. (2002). Early recognition of 1-year-old infants with autism spectrum disorder versus mental retardation. *Developmental Psychopathology, 14,* 239–251.

Park, C. (2001a). *Exiting Nirvana: A daughter's life with autism.* Boston: Little, Brown.

Park, C. (2001b). *The siege: A family's journey into the world of an autistic child* (2nd ed.). Boston: Little, Brown.

Pierce, K., Muller, R. A., Ambrose, J., Allen, G., & Courchesne, E. (2001). Face processing occurs outside the fusiform "face area" in autism: Evidence from functional MRI. *Brain, 124,* 2059–2073.

Rapin, I. (1996). Neurological examination. In I. Rapin (Ed.), *Preschool children with inadequate communication: Developmental language disorder, autism, low IQ* (pp. 98–122). London: Mac Keith Press.

Rapin, I., & Dunn, M. (2003). Update on the language disorders of individuals on the autistic spectrum. *Brain and Development, 25,* 166–172.

Rosenkranz, J. A., & Grace, A. A. (2002). Cellular mechanisms of infra limbic and prelimbic prefrontal cortical inhibition and dopaminergic modulation of basolateral amygdala neurons in vivo. *Journal of Neuroscience, 22,* 324–337.

Sandberg, A. D., Nyden, A., Gillberg, C., & Hjelmquist, E. (1993). The cognitive profile in infantile autism: A study of 70 children and adolescents using the Griffiths Mental Development Scale. *British Journal of Psychology, 84,* 365–373.

Schmahmann, J. D. (1997). *The cerebellum and cognition.* New York: Academic Press.

Schopler, E., & Olley, J. G. (1982). Comprehensive educational services for autistic children: The TEACCH model. In C. R. Reynolds & T. R. Gutkin (Eds.), *The handbook of school psychology* (pp. 629–643). New York: Wiley.

Schreibman, L. (1997). Theoretical perspectives on behavioral intervention for individuals with autism. In D. J. Cohen & F. R. Volkmar (Eds.), *Handbook of autism and pervasive developmental disorders* (2nd ed., pp. 920–933). New York: Wiley.

Shinnar, S., Rapin, I., Arnold, S., Tuchman, R. F., Shulman, L., Ballaban-Gil, K., et al. (2001). Language regression in childhood. *Pediatric Neurology, 24,* 185–191.

Smalley, S. L., Kustanovich, V., Minassian, S. L., Stone, J. L., Ogdie, M. N., McGough, J. J., et al. (2002). Genetic linkage of attention-deficit/hyperactivity disorder on chromosome 16p13, in a region implicated in autism. *American Journal of Human Genetics, 71,* 959–963.

Spitz, R. A. (1945). Hospitalism: An inquiry into the genesis of psychiatric conditions in early childhood. *Psychoanalytic Study of the Child, 1,* 53–74.

Steinschneider, M., & Dunn, M. (2002). Electrophysiology in developmental neuropsychology. In S. Segalowitz & I. Rapin (Eds.), *Handbook of neuropsychology: Child neuropsychology* (2nd ed., Vol. 8, pp. 91–146). Amsterdam: Elsevier.

Stevens, M. C., Fein, D. A., Dunn, M., Allen, D., Waterhouse, L. H., Feinstein, C., et al. (2000). Subgroups of children with autism by cluster analysis: A longitudinal examination. *Journal of the American Academy of Child and Adolescent Psychiatry, 39,* 346–352.

Stone, V. E., Baron-Cohen, S., & Knight, R. T. (1998). Frontal lobe contributions to theory of mind. *Journal of Cognitive Neuroscience, 10,* 640–656.

Tager-Flusberg, H. (2003). Language impairments in children with complex neurodevelopmental disorders: The case of autism. In Y. Levy & J. Schaeffer (Eds.), *Language competence across populations: Toward a definition of specific language impairment* (pp. 297–321). Mahwah, NJ: Erlbaum.

Temple, E., Deutsch, G. K., Poldrack, R. A., Miller, S. L., Tallal, P., Merzenich, M. M., et al. (2003). Neural deficits in children with dyslexia ameliorated by behavioral remediation: Evidence from functional MRI. *Proceedings of the National Academy of Sciences of the USA, 100,* 2860–2865.

Tuchman, R. F., & Rapin, I. (1997). Regression in pervasive developmental disorders: Seizures and epileptiform EEG correlates. *Pediatrics, 99,* 560–566.

Tuchman, R. F., Rapin, I., & Shinnar, S. (1991a). Autistic and dysphasic children: I. Clinical characteristics. *Pediatrics, 88,* 1211–1218.

Tuchman, R. F., Rapin, I., & Shinnar, S. (1991b). Autistic and dysphasic children: II. Epilepsy. *Pediatrics, 88,* 1219–1225.

Tucker, R. M. (2001). Motivated anatomy: A core-and-shell model of corticolimbic architecture. In G. Gainotti (Ed.), *Handbook of neuropsychology: Emotional behavior and its disorders* (2 ed., Vol. 5., pp. 125–160). Amsterdam: Elsevier.

Wainwright, L., & Fein, D. (1996). Play. In I. Rapin (Ed.), *Preschool children with inadequate communication: Developmental language disorder, autism, low IQ* (pp. 173–189). London: Mac Keith Press.

Wassink, T. H., Piven, J., Vieland, V. J., Huang, J., Swiderski, R. E., Pietila, J., et al. (2001). Evidence supporting WNT2 as an autism susceptibility gene. *American Journal of Medical Genetics: Part B (Neuropsychiatric Genetics), 105,* 406–413.

Williams, R. S., Hauser, S. L., Purpura, D. P., DeLong, G. R., & Swisher, C. W. (1980). Autism and mental retardation: Neuropathologic studies performed in four retarded persons with autistic behavior. *Archives of Neurology, 37,* 749–753.

Wing, L. (1991). The relationship between Asperger's syndrome and Kanner's autism. In U. Frith (Ed.), *Autism and Asperger syndrome* (pp. 93–121). Cambridge, England: Cambridge University Press.

Wing, L., & Gould, J. (1979). Severe impairments of social interaction and associated abnormalities in children: Epidemiology and classification. *Journal of Autism and Developmental Disorders, 9,* 11–29.

Zoghbi, H. Y. (2003). Postnatal neurodevelopmental disorders: Meeting at the synapse? *Science, 302,* 826–830.

Author Index

Subject Index